A-Z SURR

GW00580019

CONTENTS

REFERENCE

Motorway	M3	**Built Up Area**	HIGH STREET
A Road	A246	**Local Authority Boundary**	— · — · —
Under Construction		**Posttown Boundary**	
Proposed		**Postcode Boundary** Within Posttown	
B Road	B3430	**Map Continuation**	80
Dual Carriageway			
One Way Street Traffic flow on A Roads is indicated by a heavy line on the driver's left	→	**Car Park** Selected	P
		Church or Chapel	†
Junction Name	APEX CORNER	**Fire Station**	■
Pedestrianized Road		**Hospital**	H
Restricted Access		**House Numbers** A & B Roads only	51 19 22 48
Track and Footpath		**Information Centre**	i
Residential Walkway		**National Grid Reference**	35
Railway	Tunnel Station Level Crossing	**Police Station**	▲
		Post Office	★
Underground Station	●	**Toilet**	▽
Croydon Tramlink (Est. Open 2000) The Boarding of Tramlink trains at stations may be limited to a single direction, indicated by the arrow.	Tunnel Station	**Toilet with Disabled Facilities**	♿
		Viewpoint	☀

SCALE approx. 3 Inches to 1 Mile

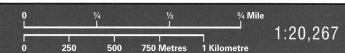

1:20,267

Copyright of Geographers' A-Z Map Company Limited

Head Office : Fairfield Road, Borough Green, Sevenoaks, Kent TN15 8PP   Telephone 01732 781000
Showrooms : 44 Gray's Inn Road, London WC1X 8HX   Telephone 0171 242 9246

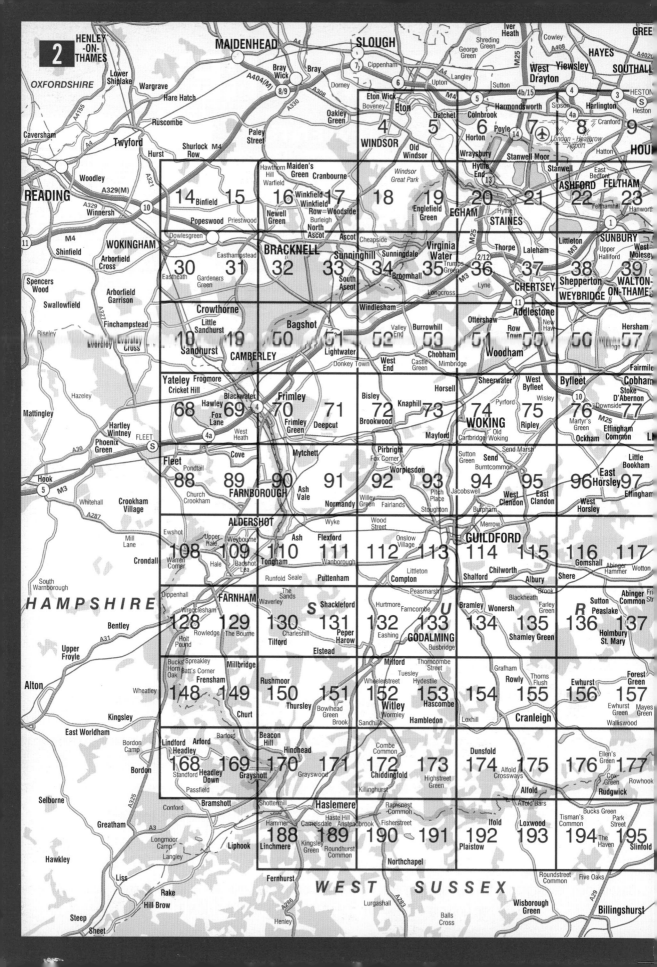

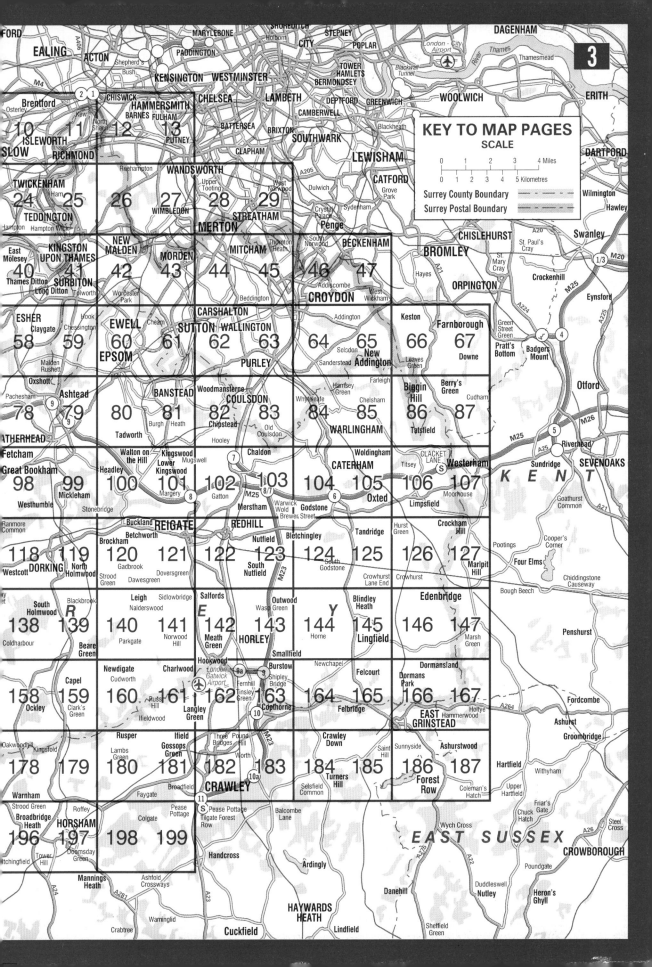

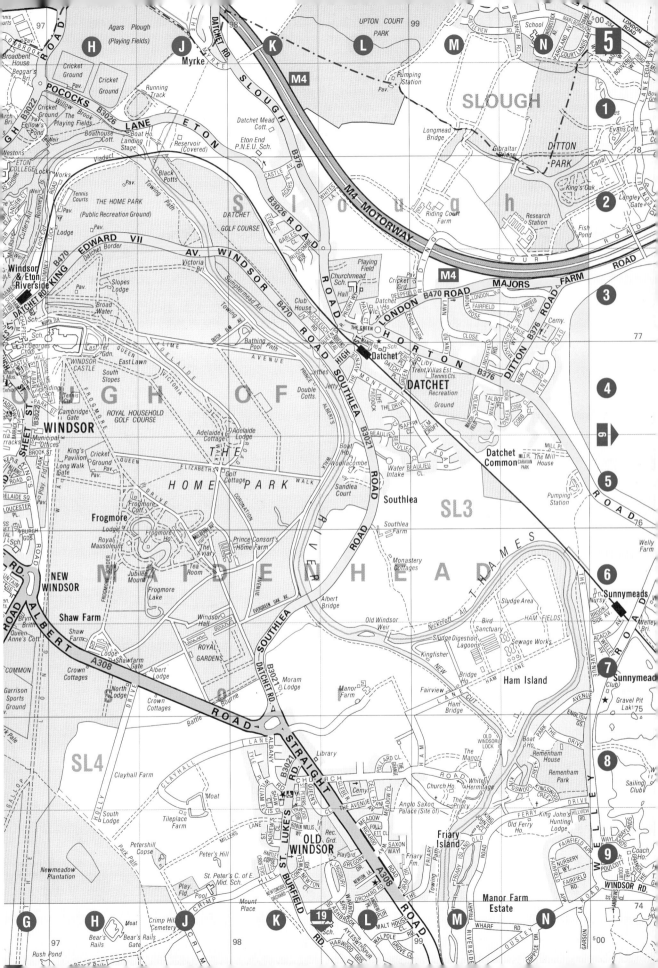

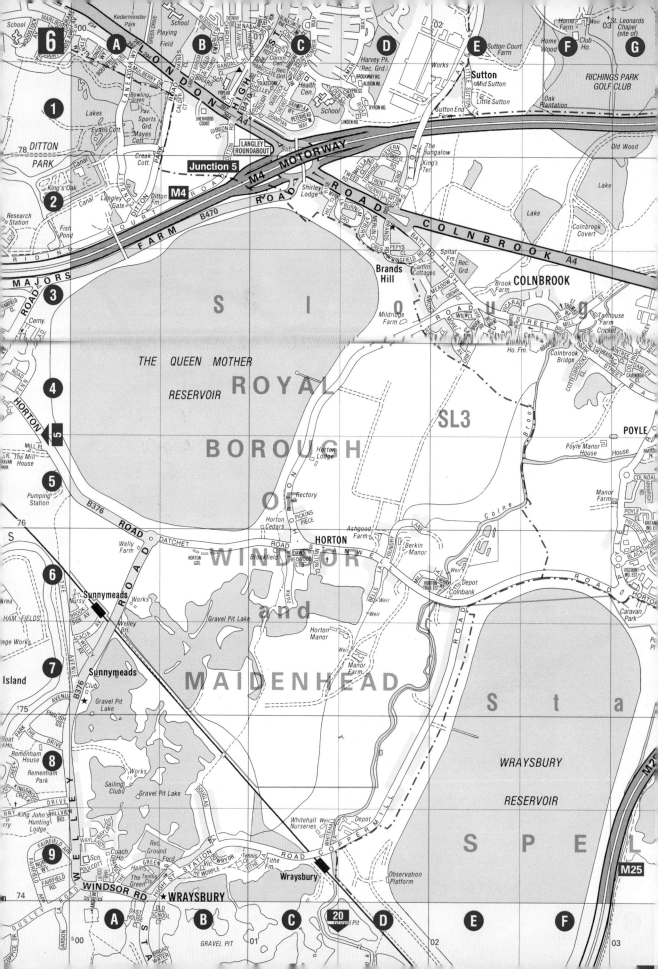

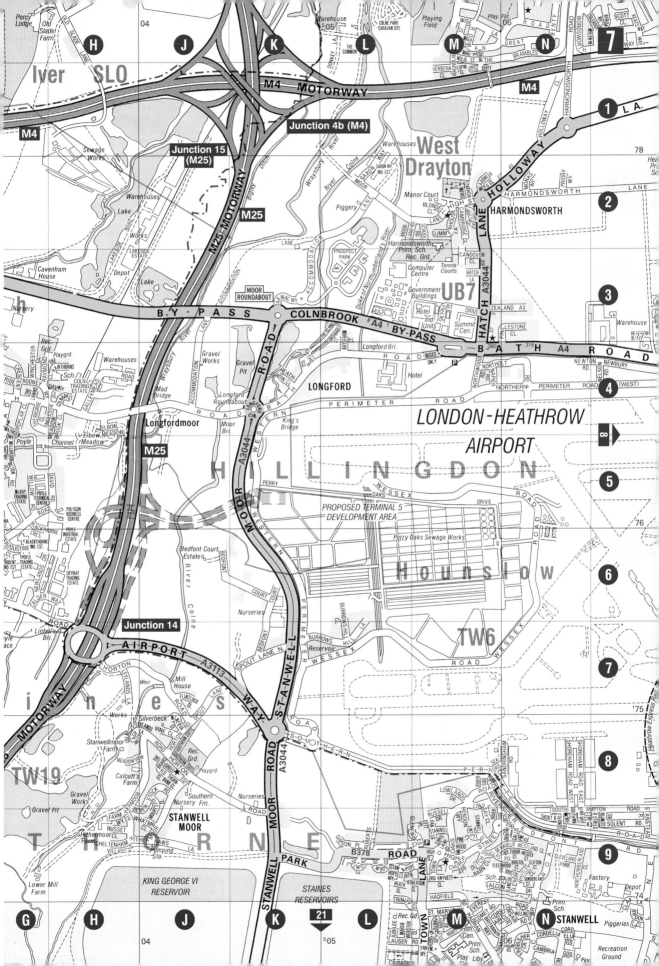

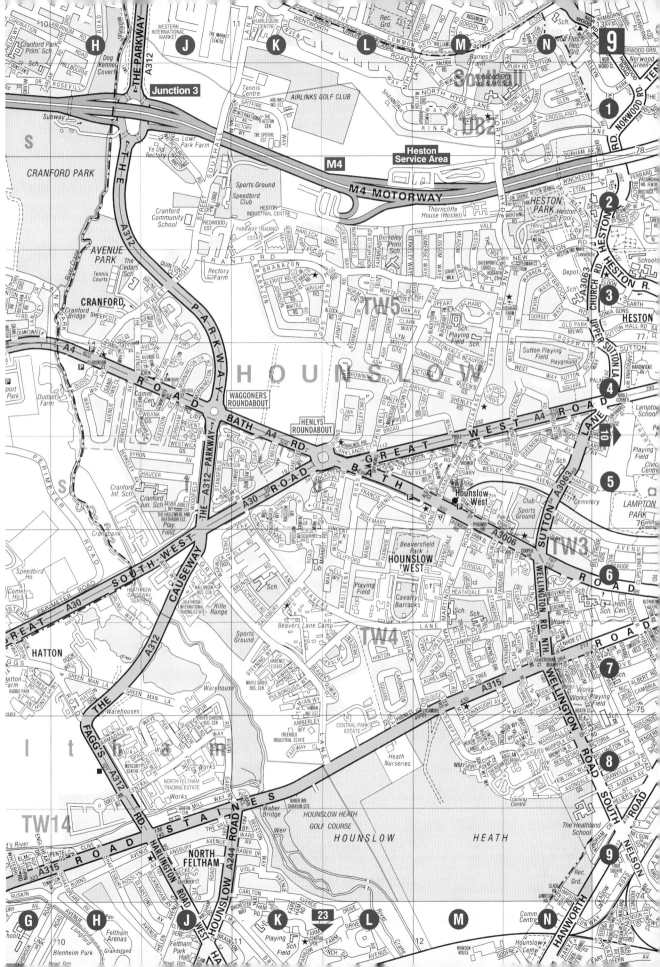

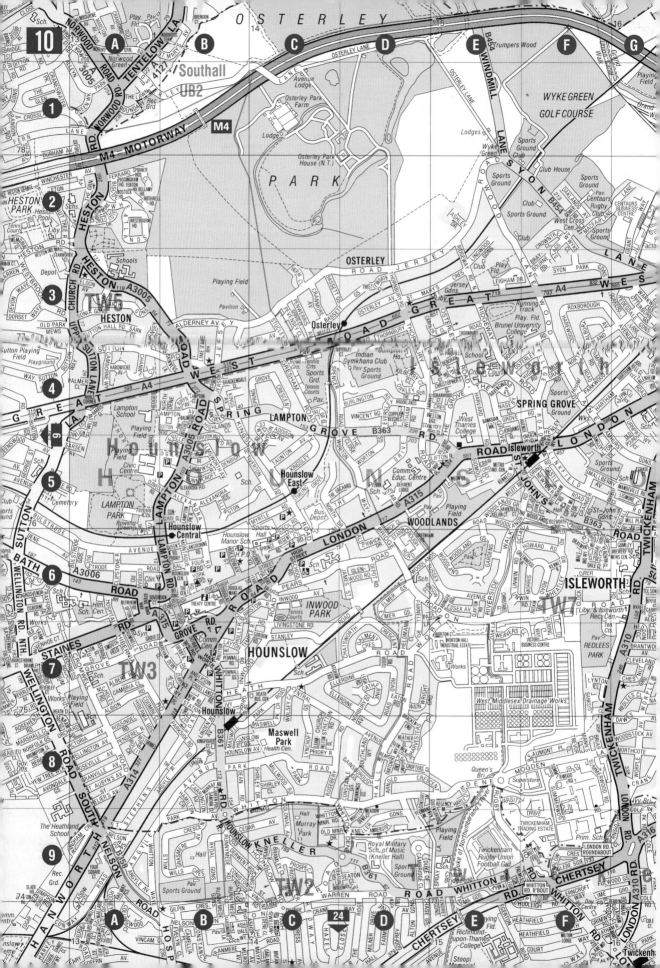

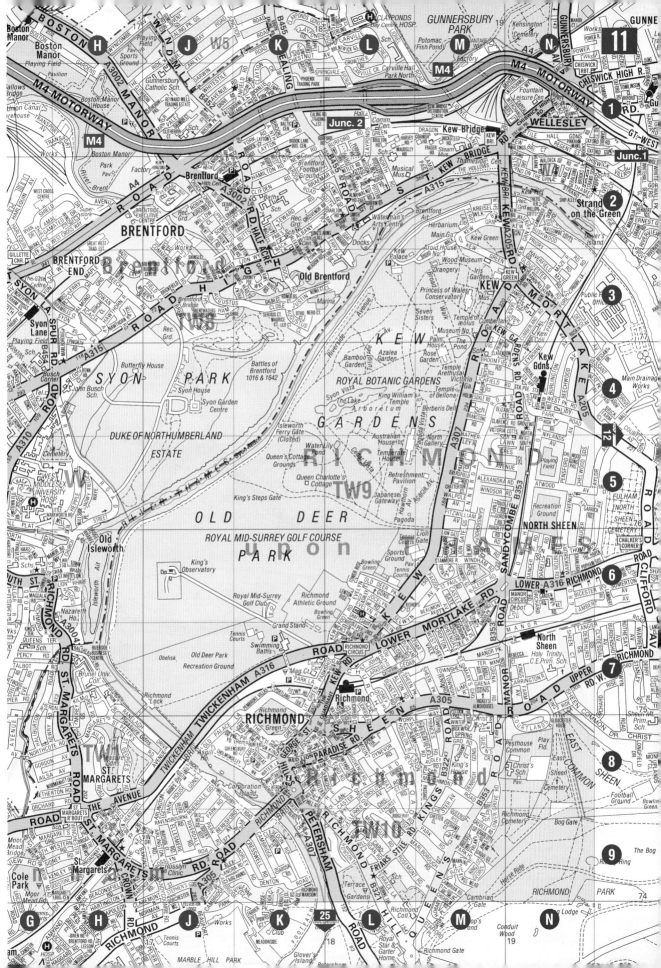

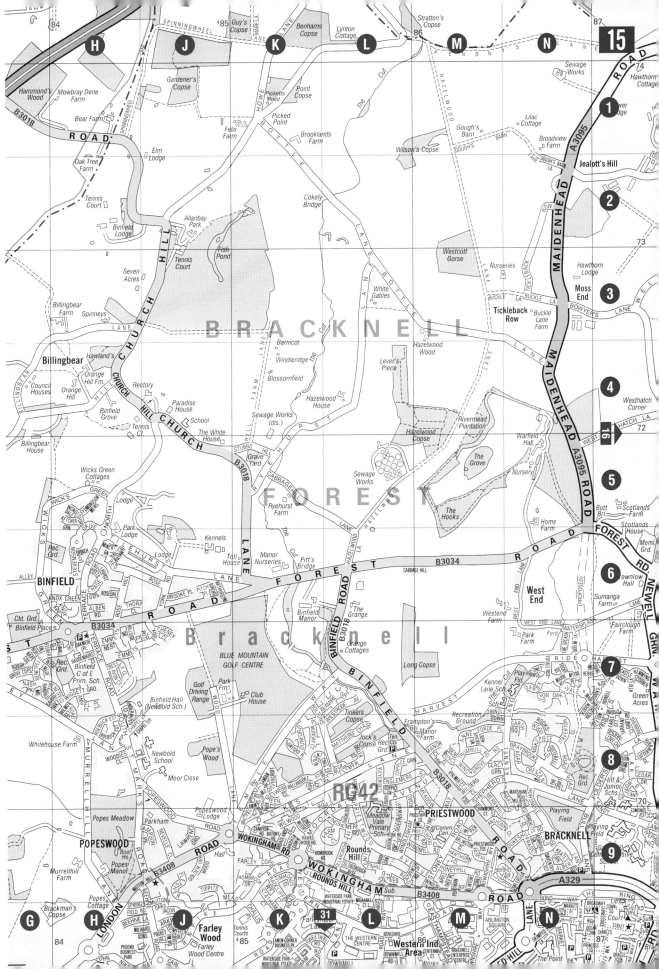

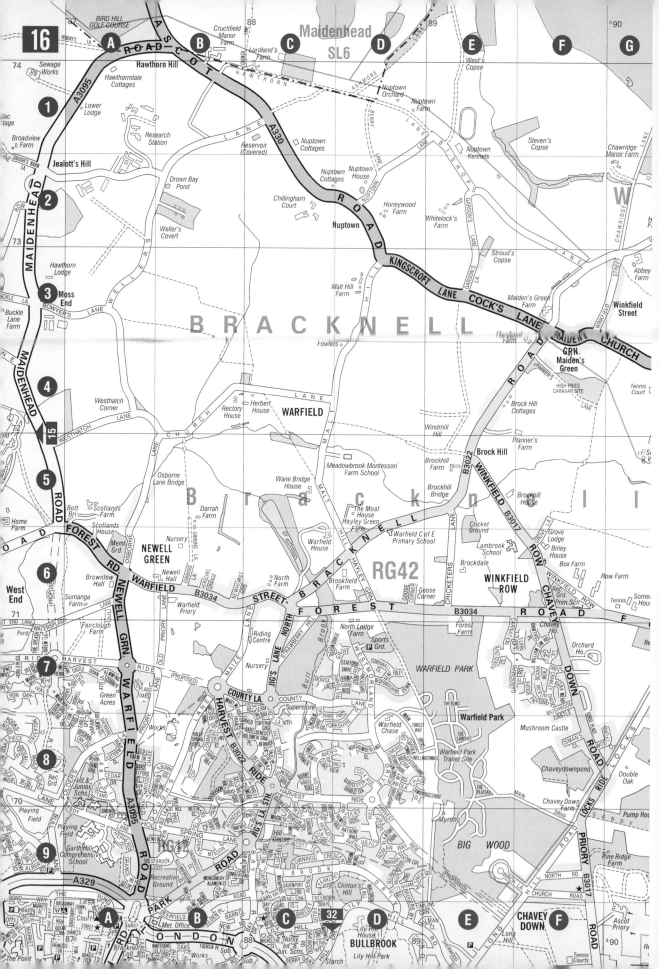

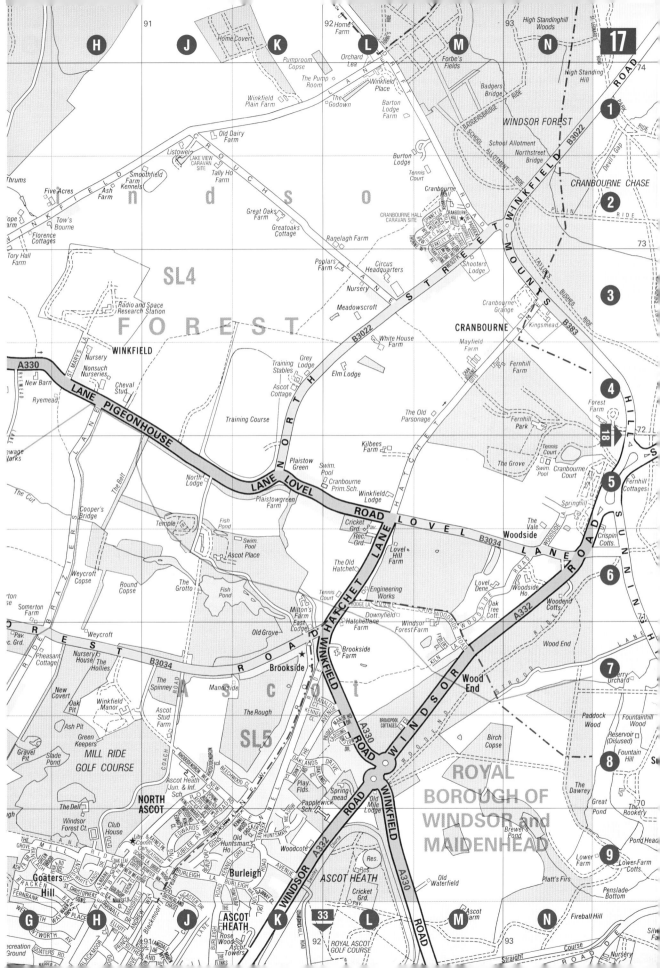

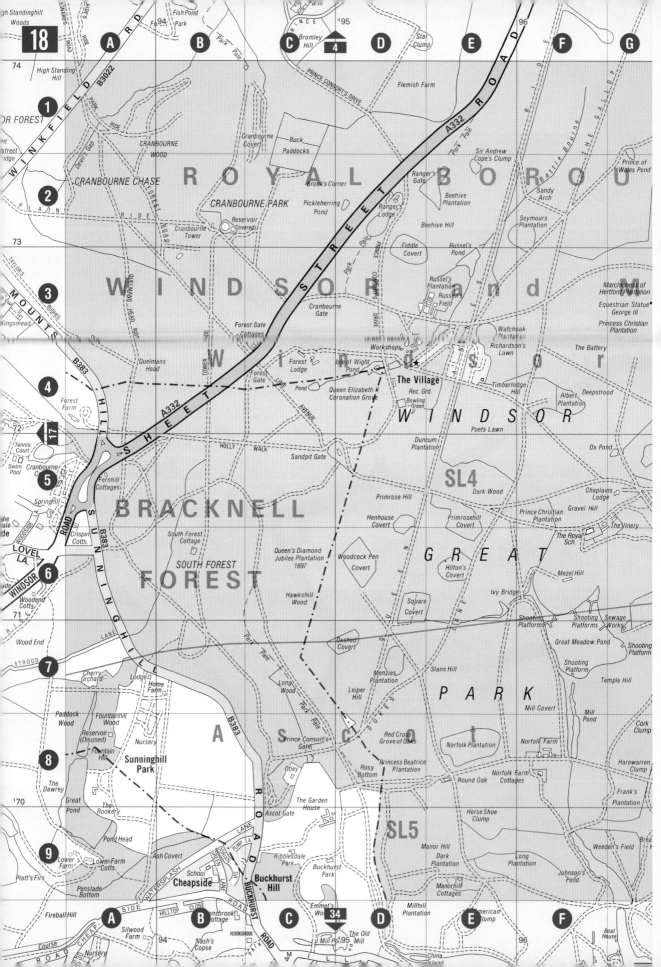

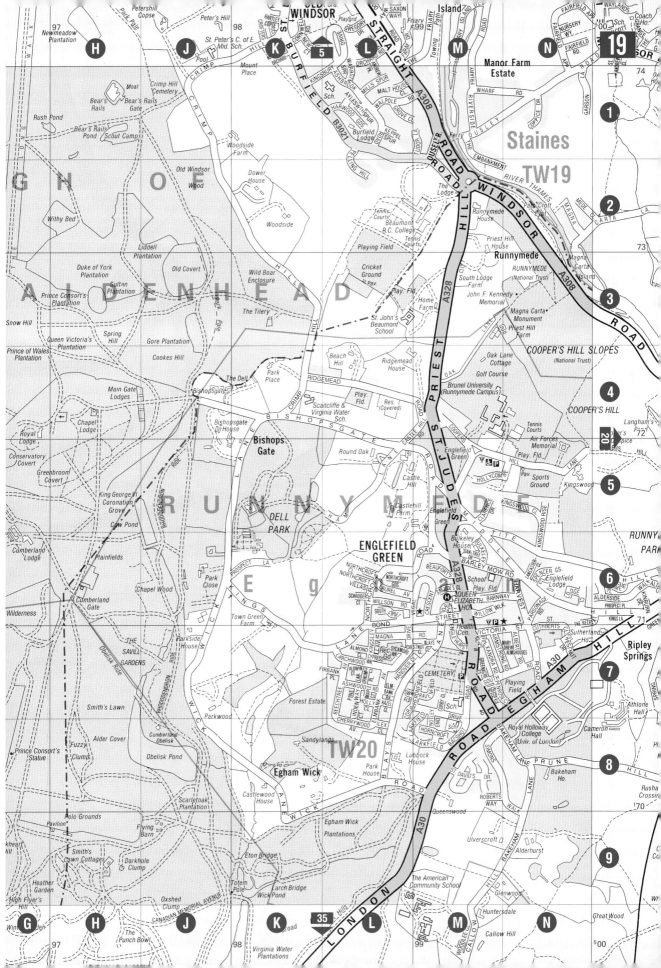

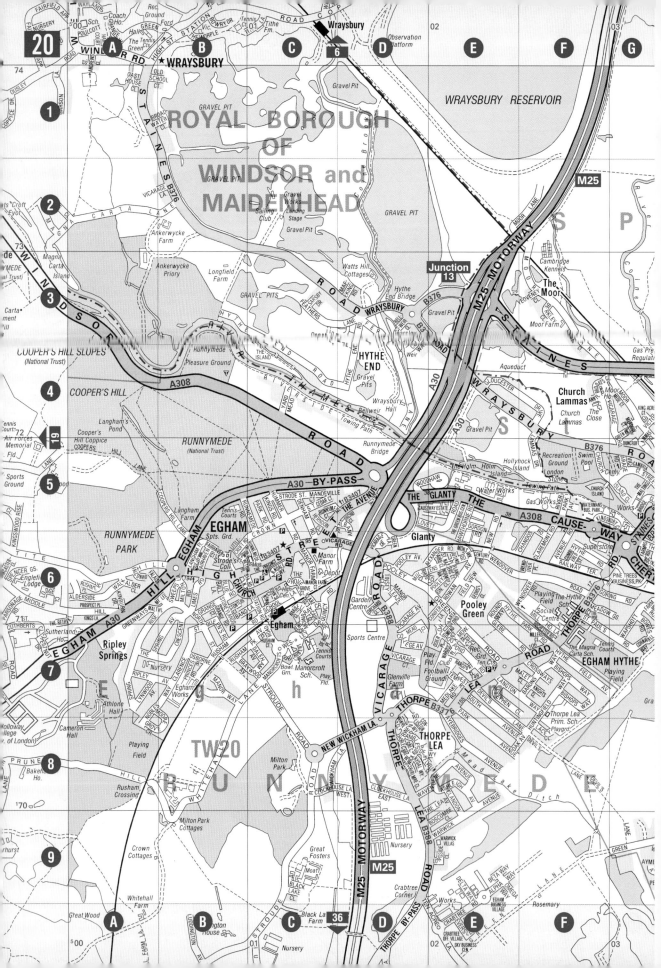

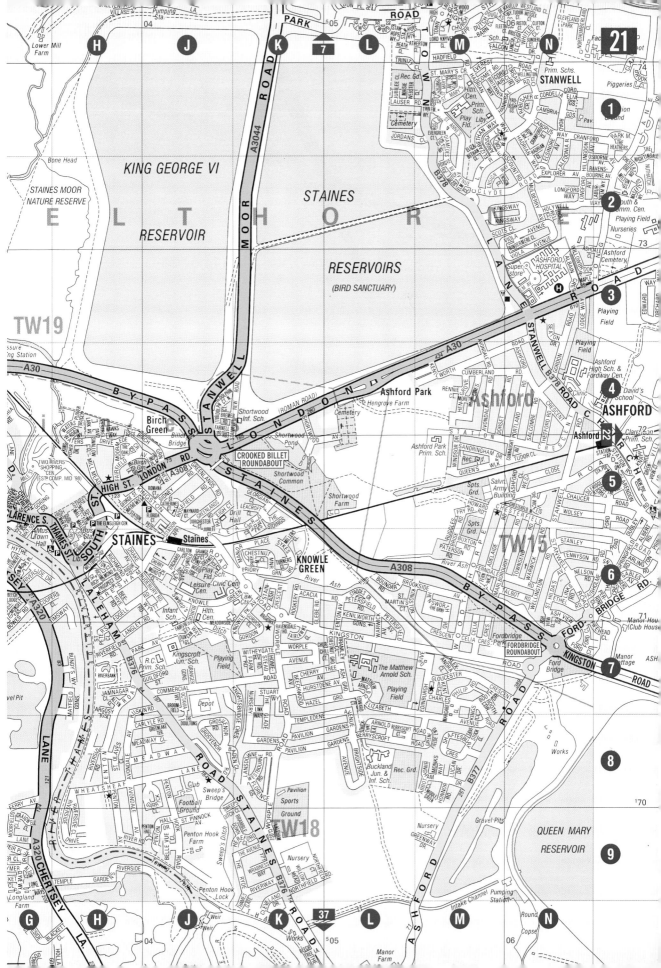

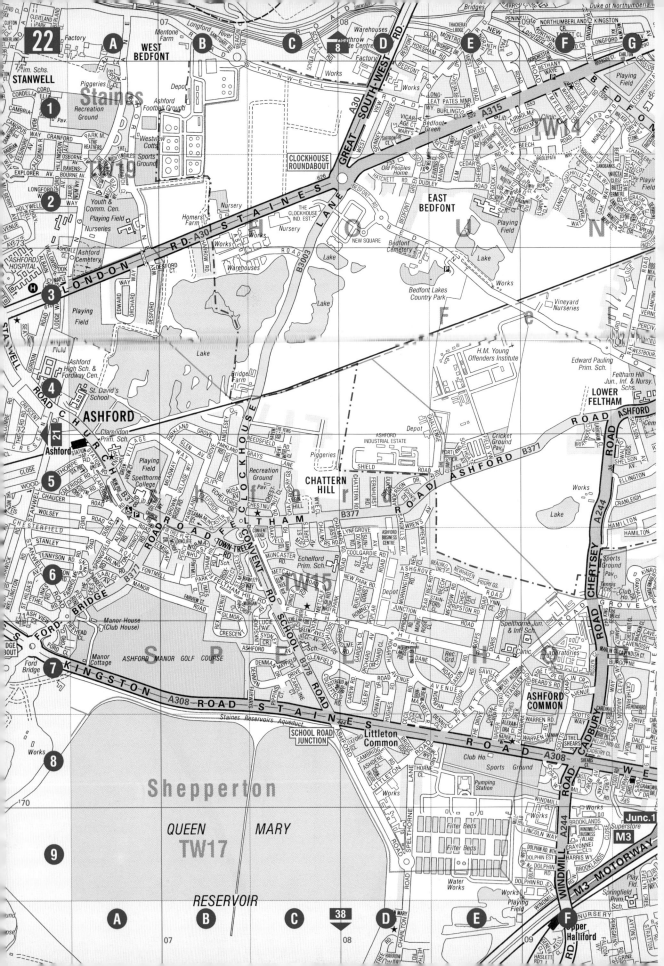

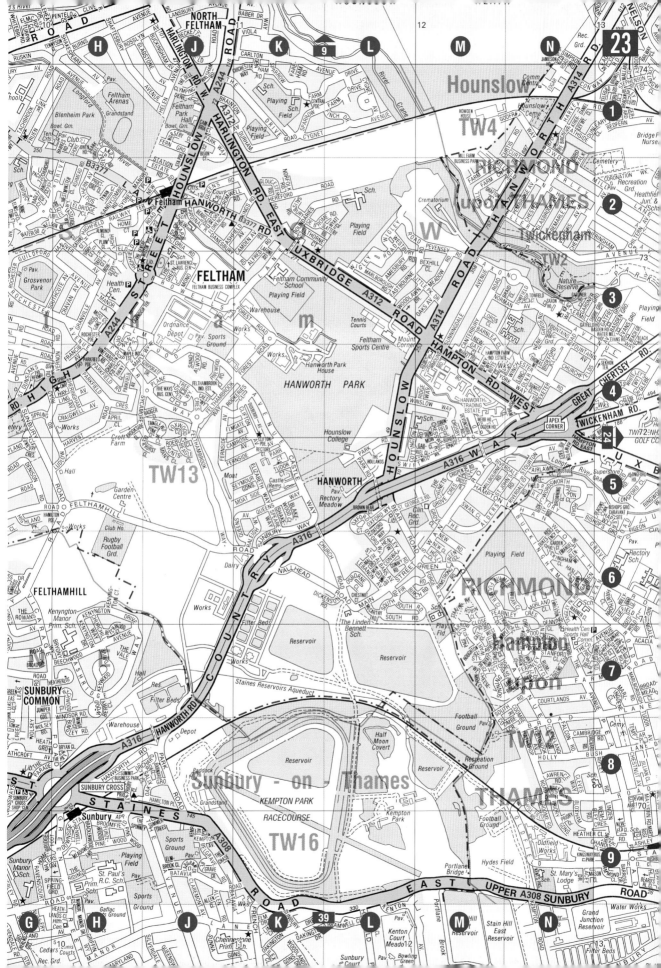

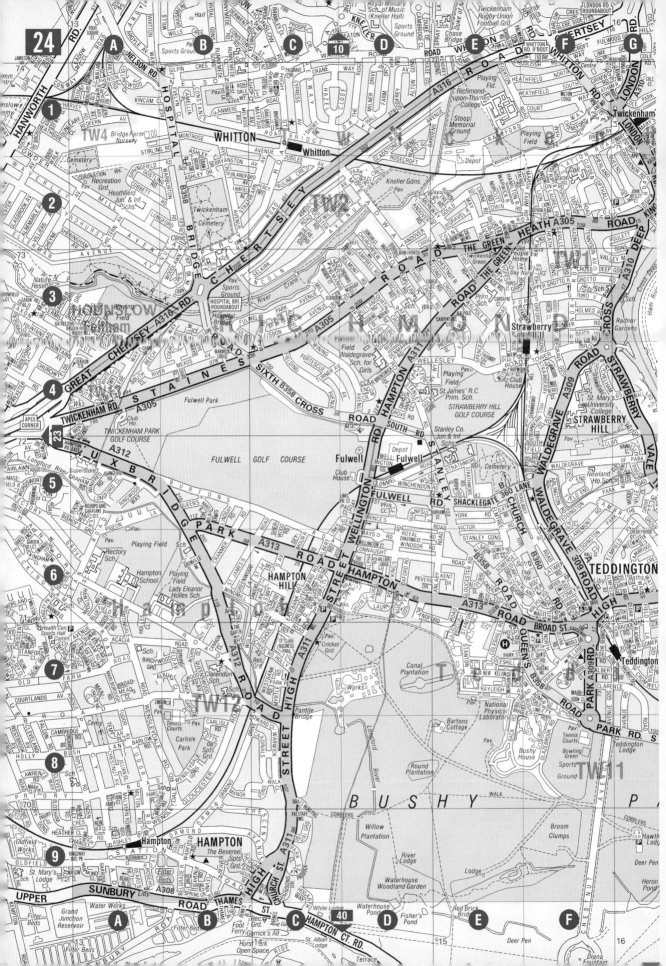

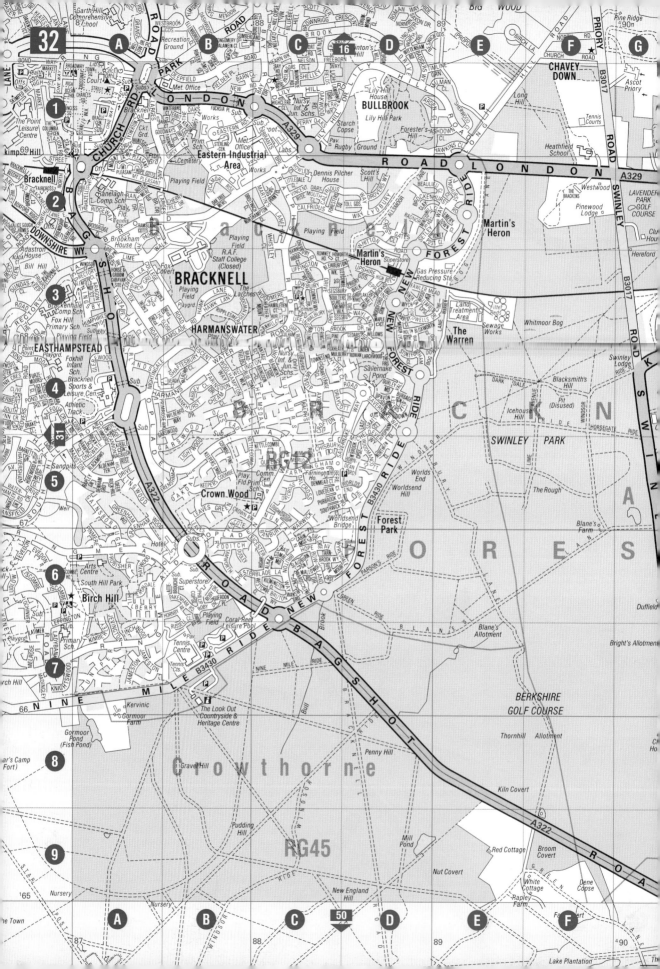

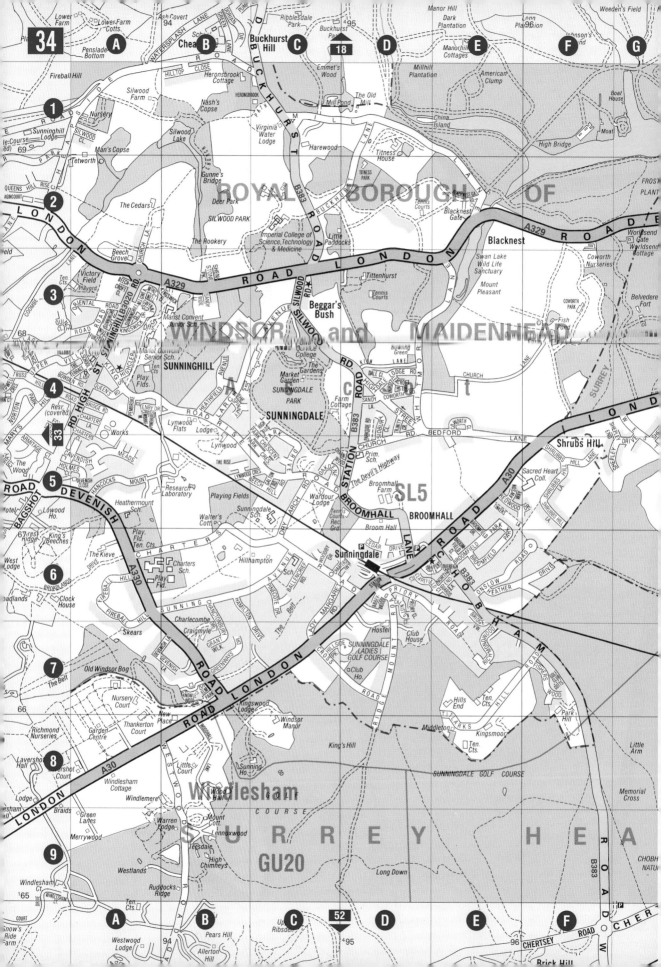

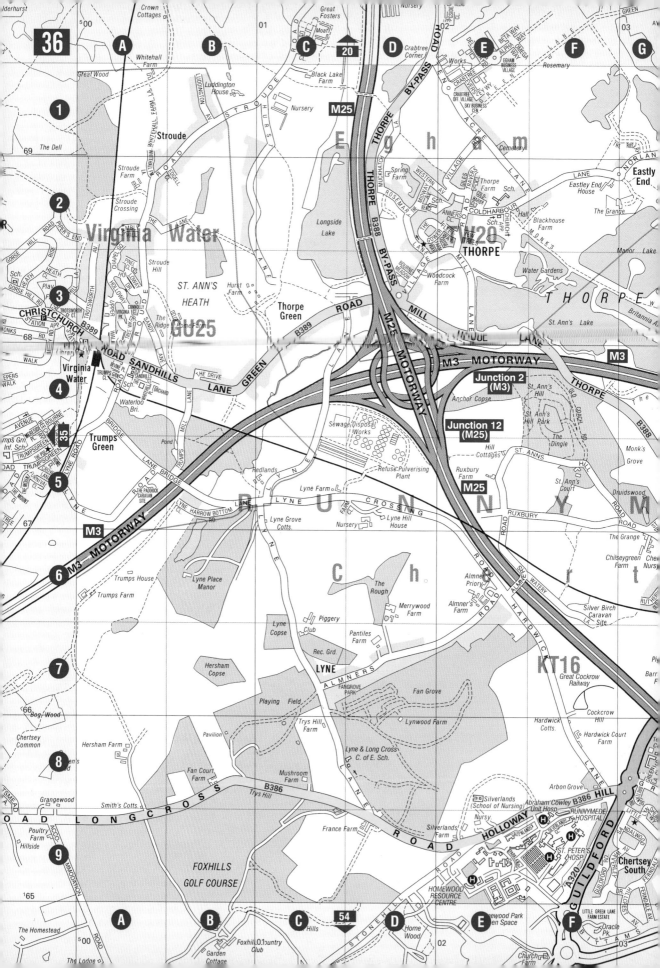

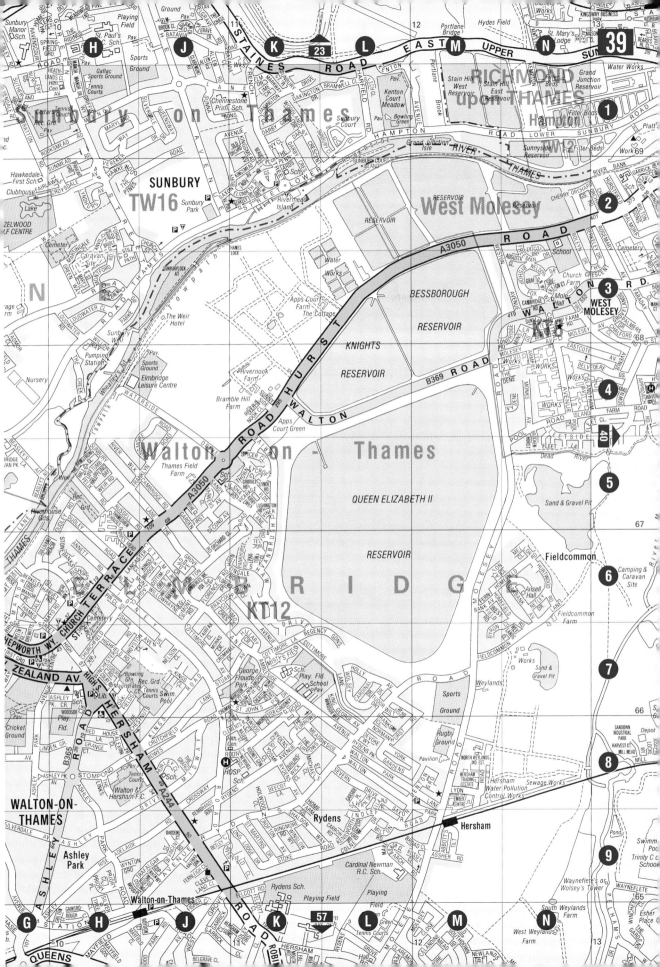

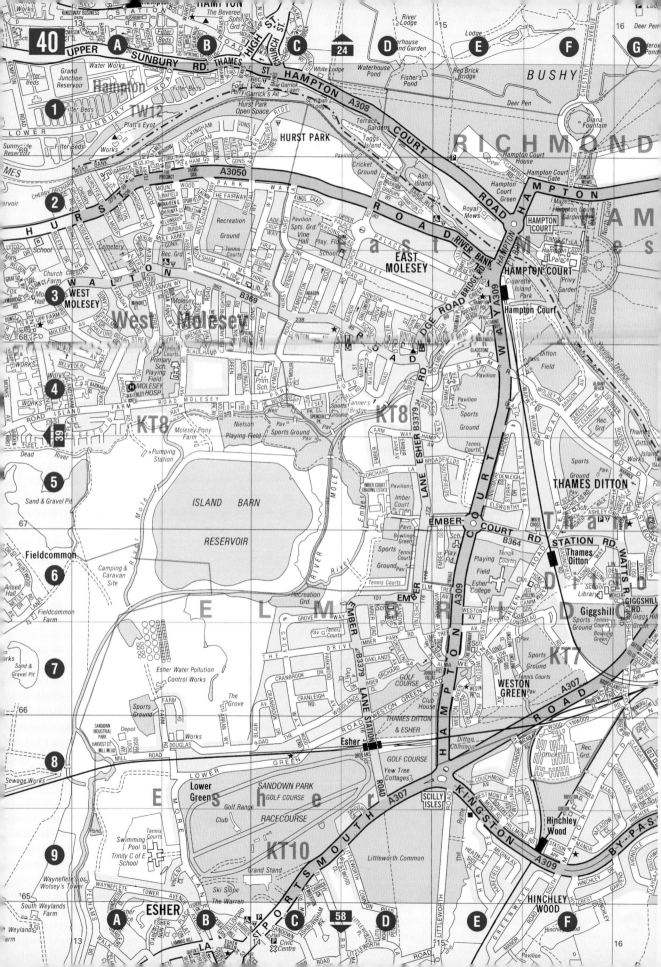

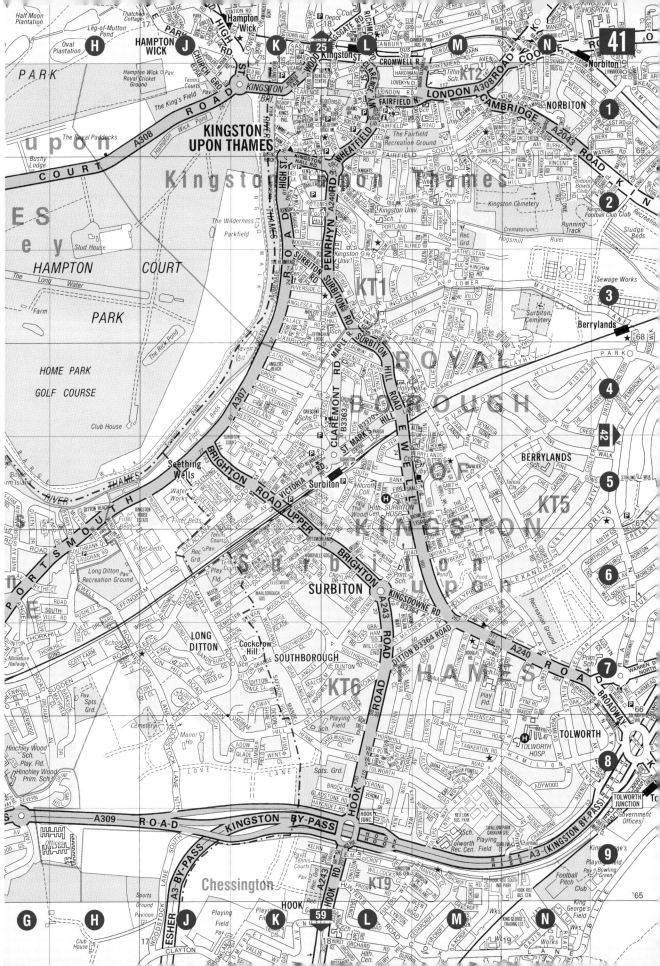

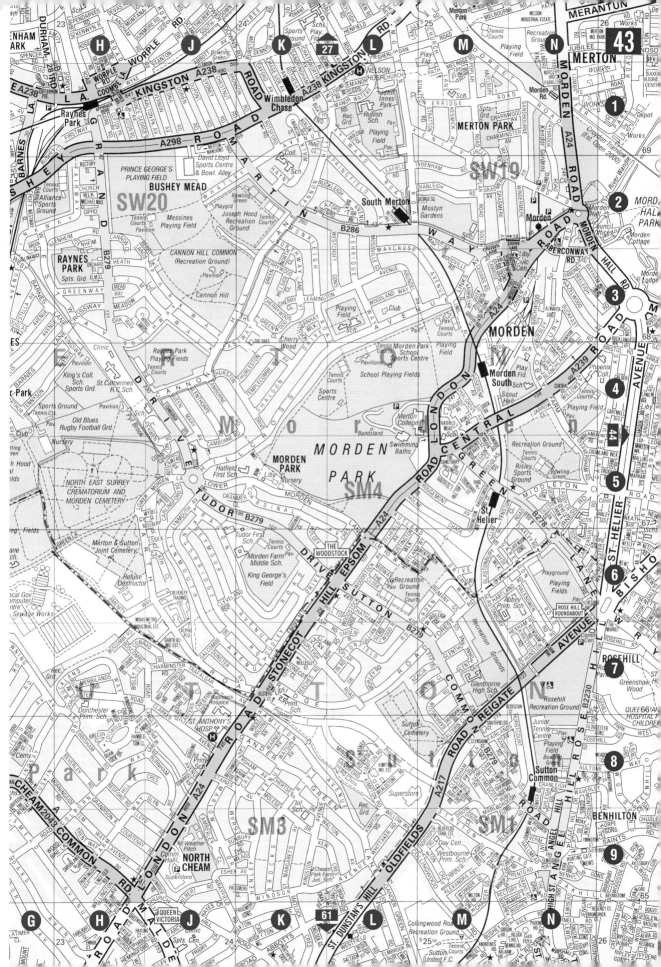

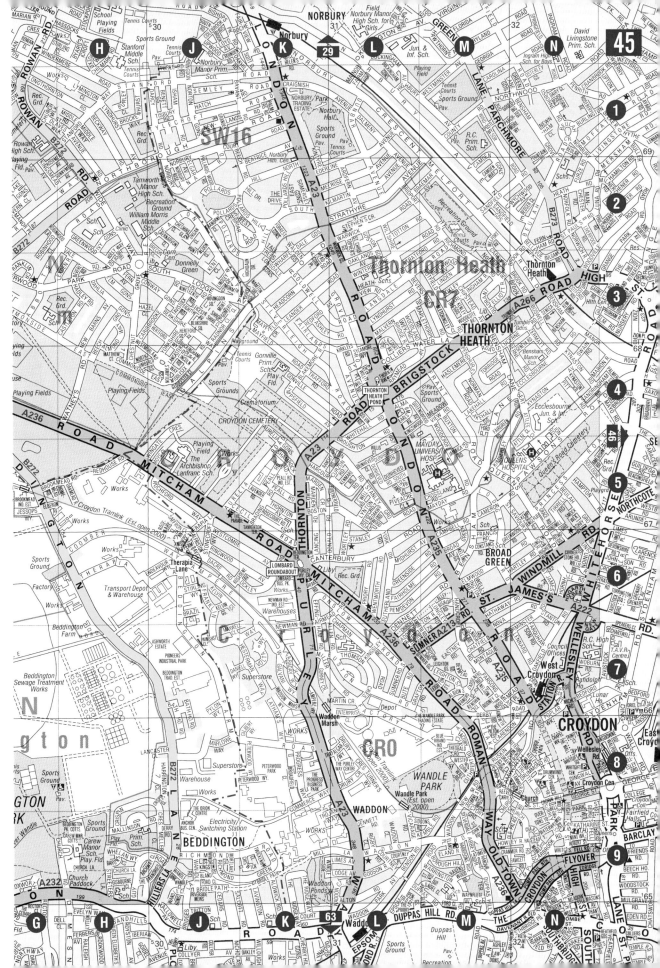

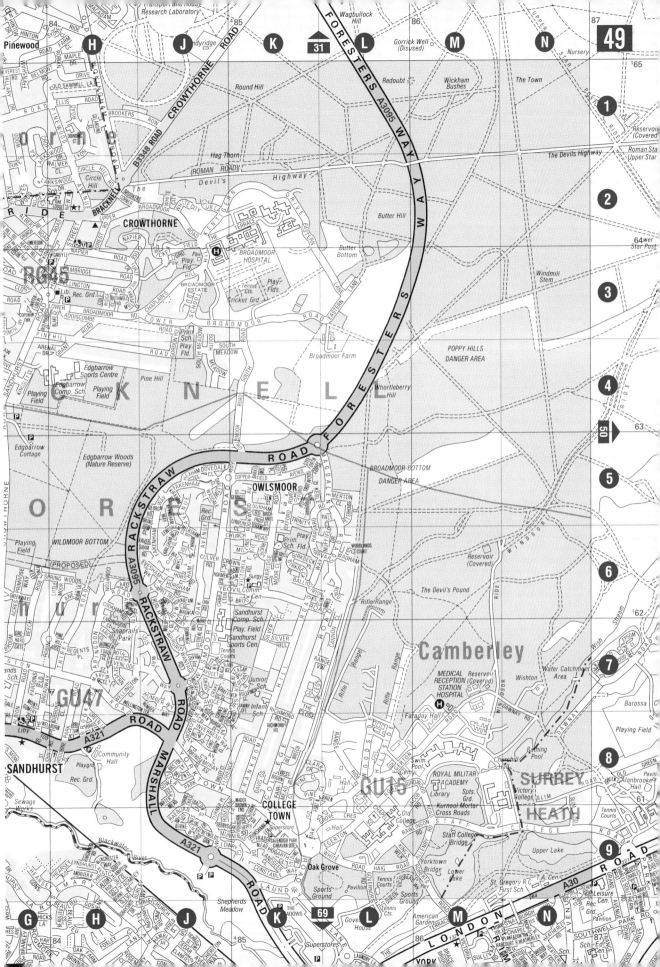

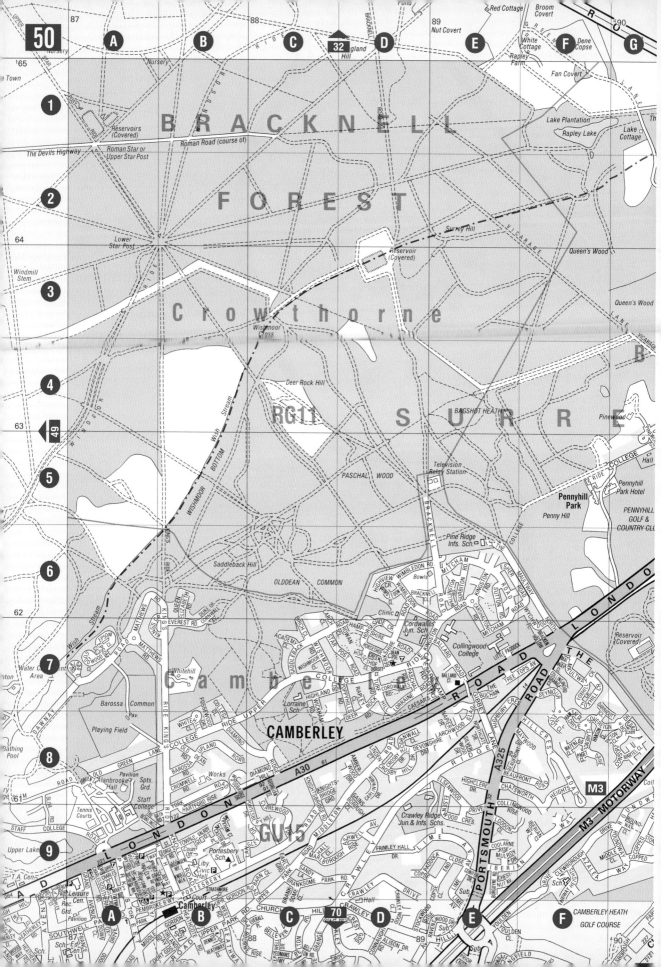

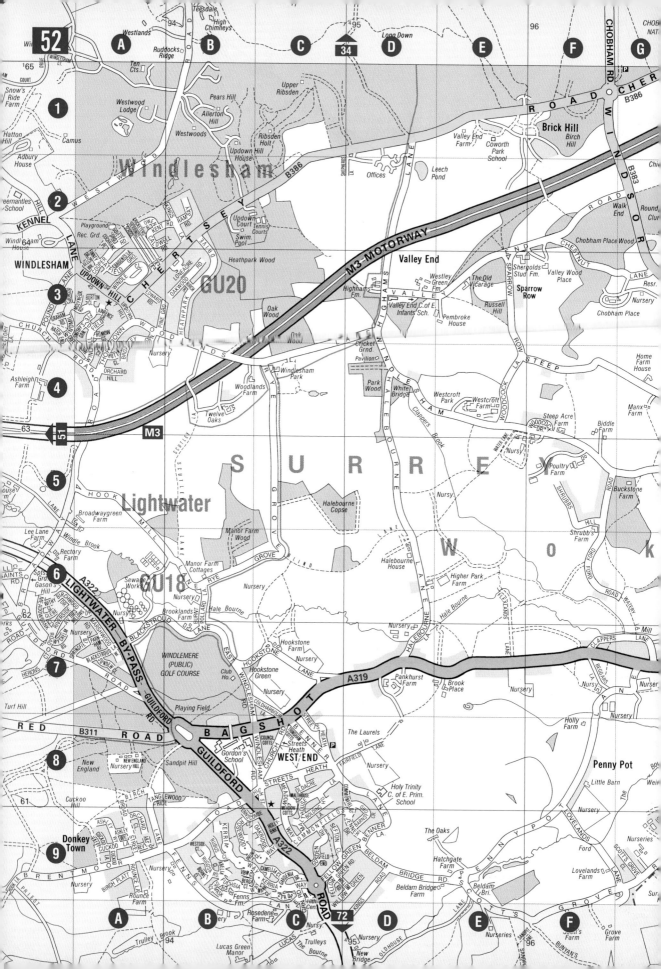

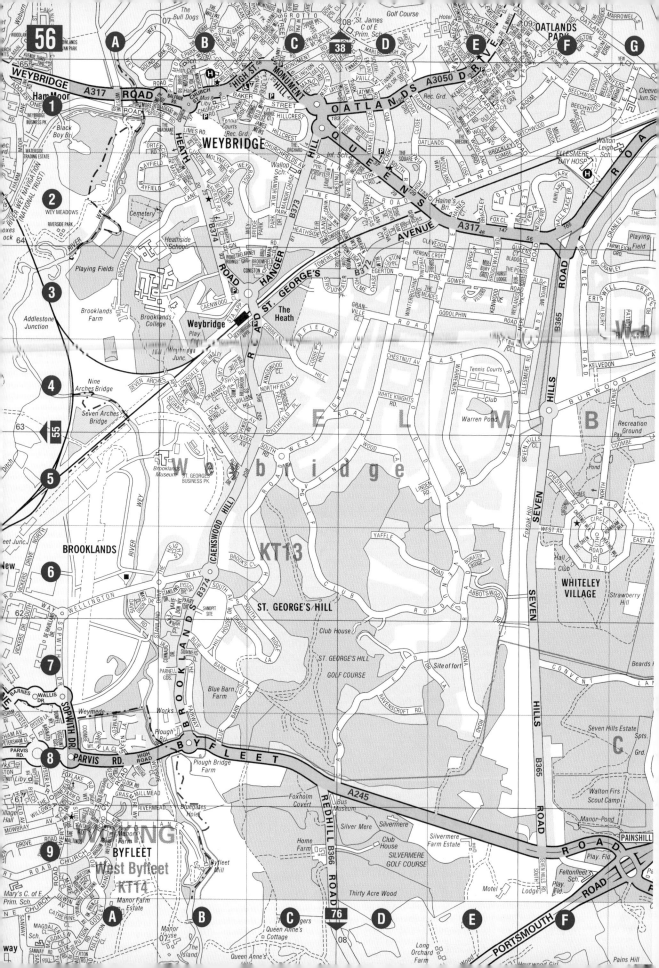

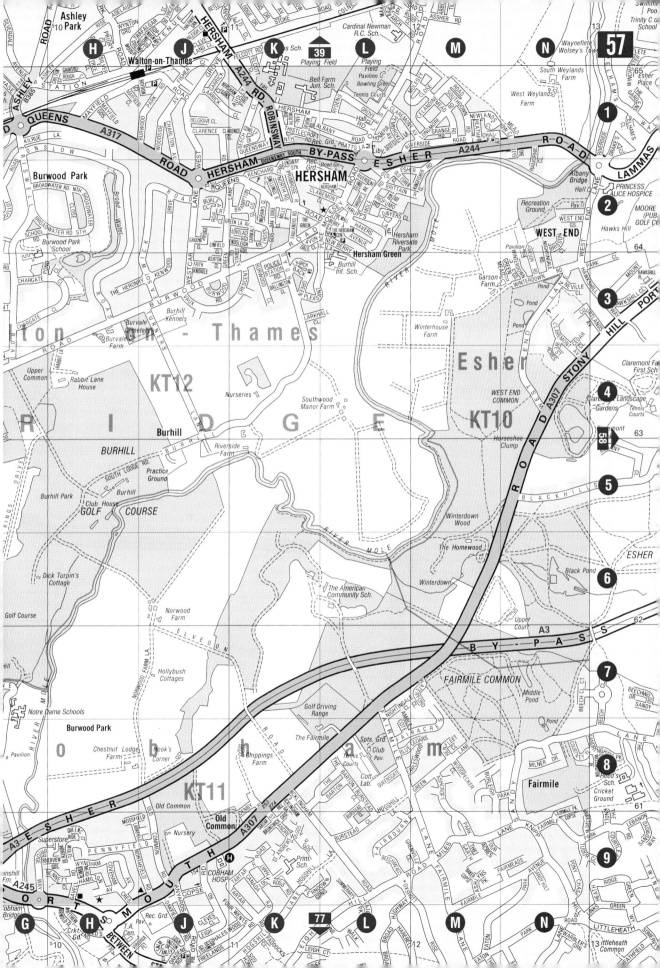

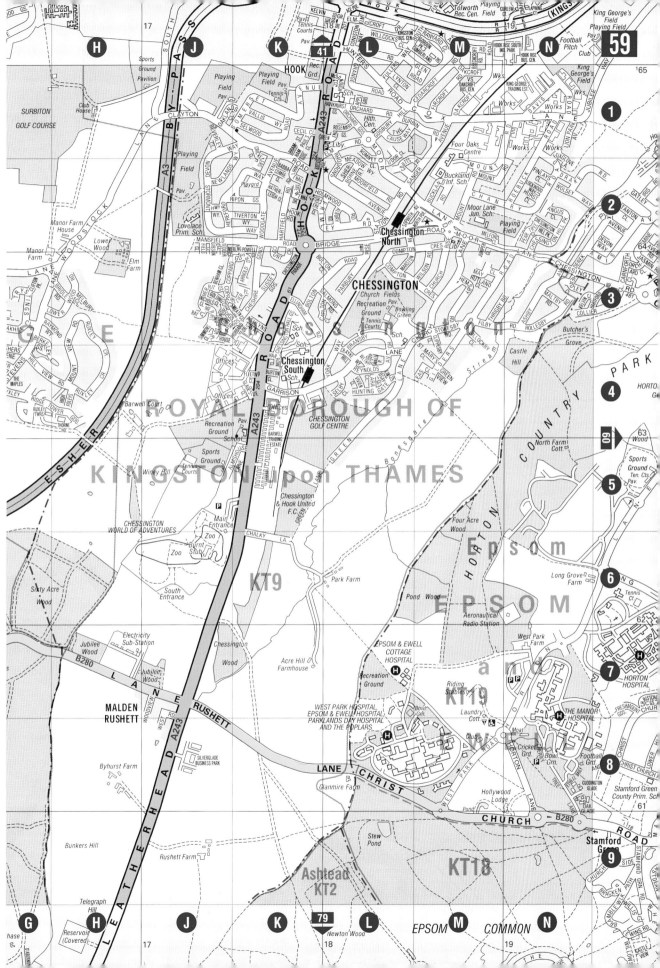

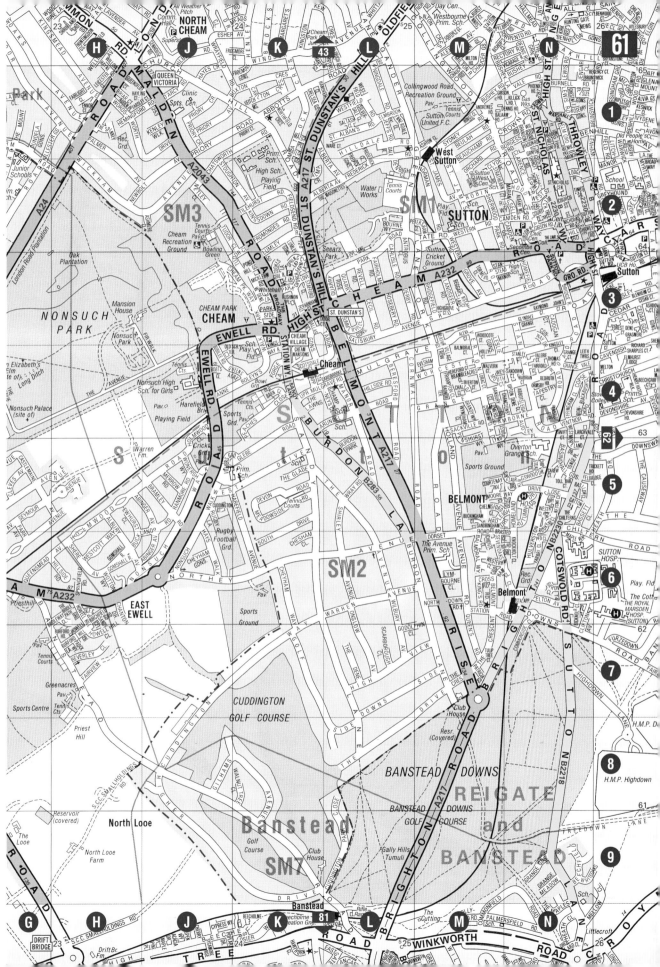

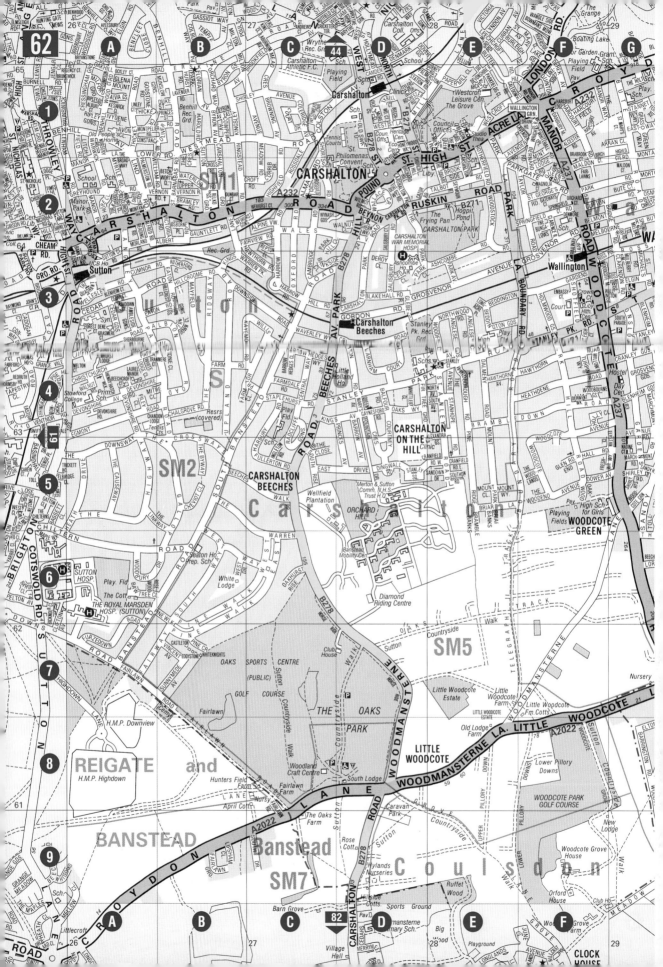

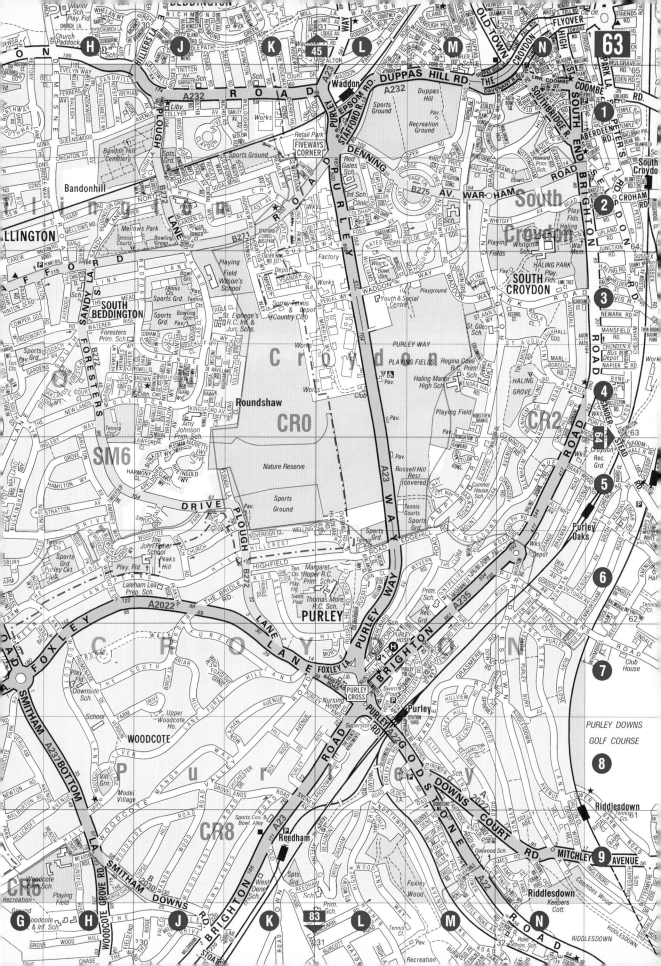

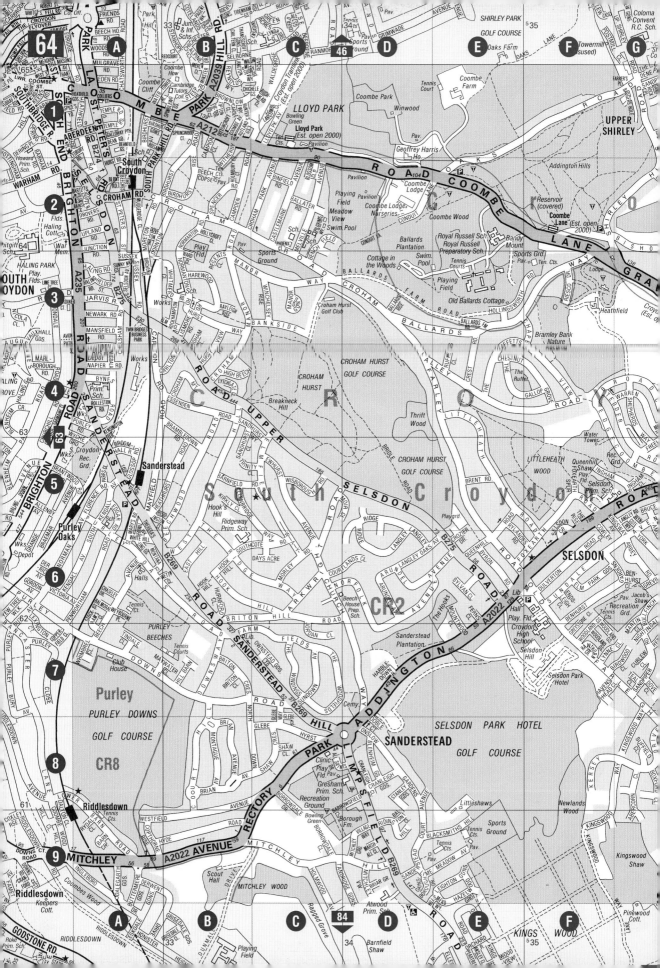

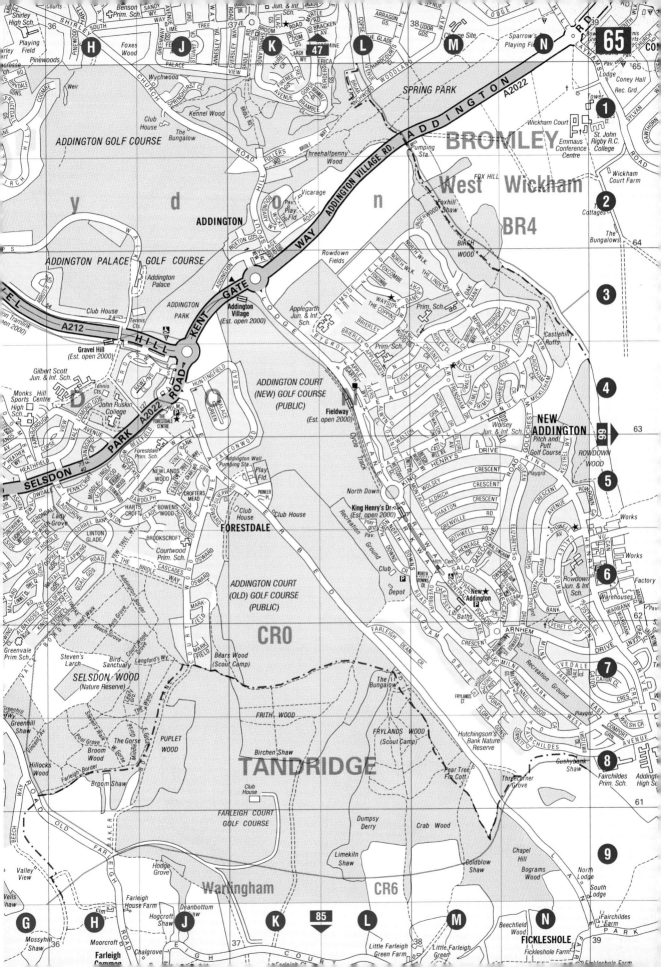

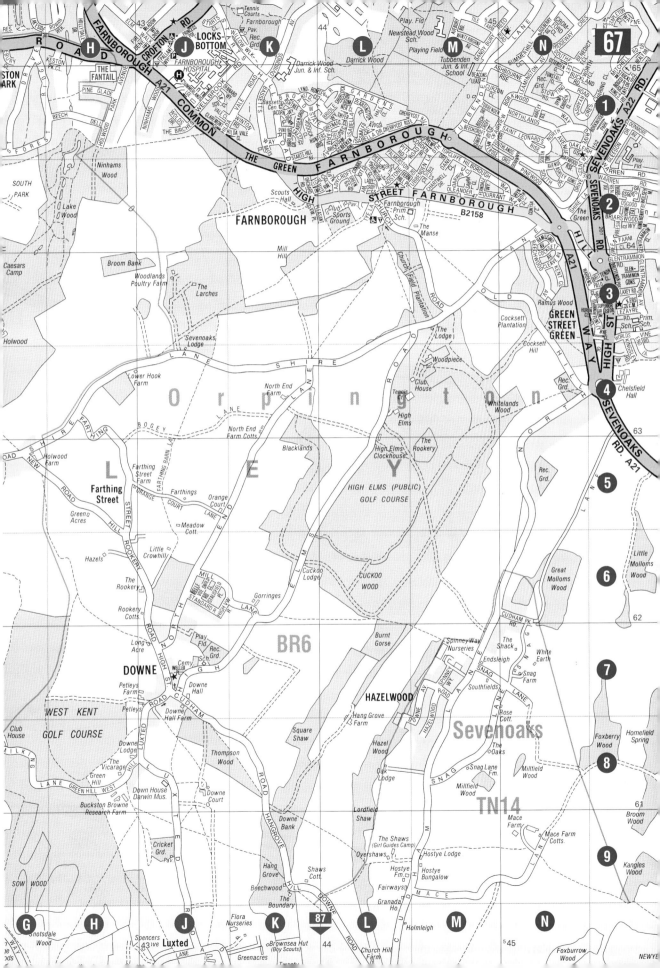

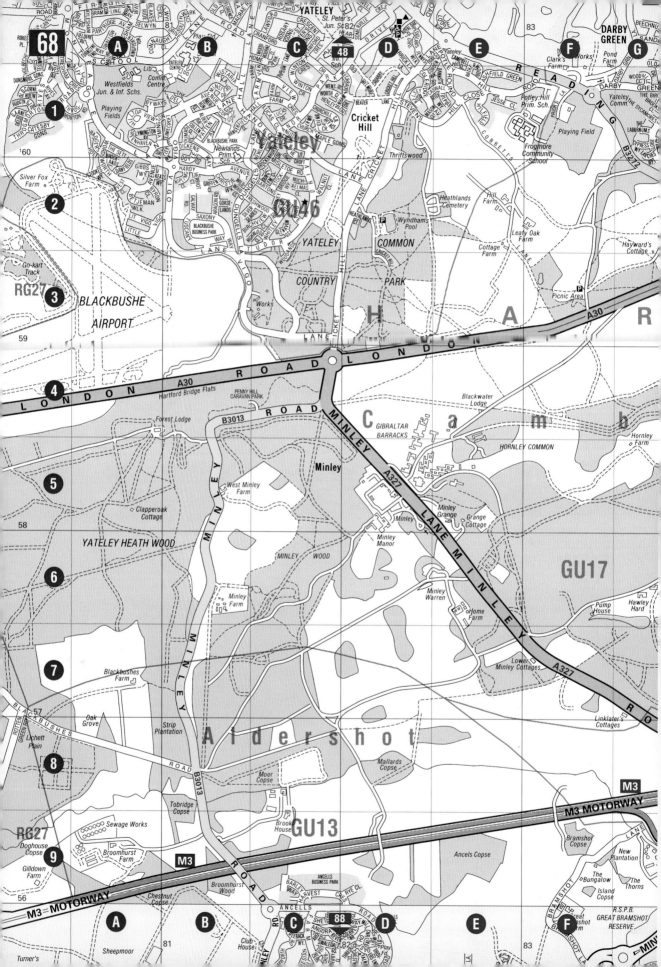

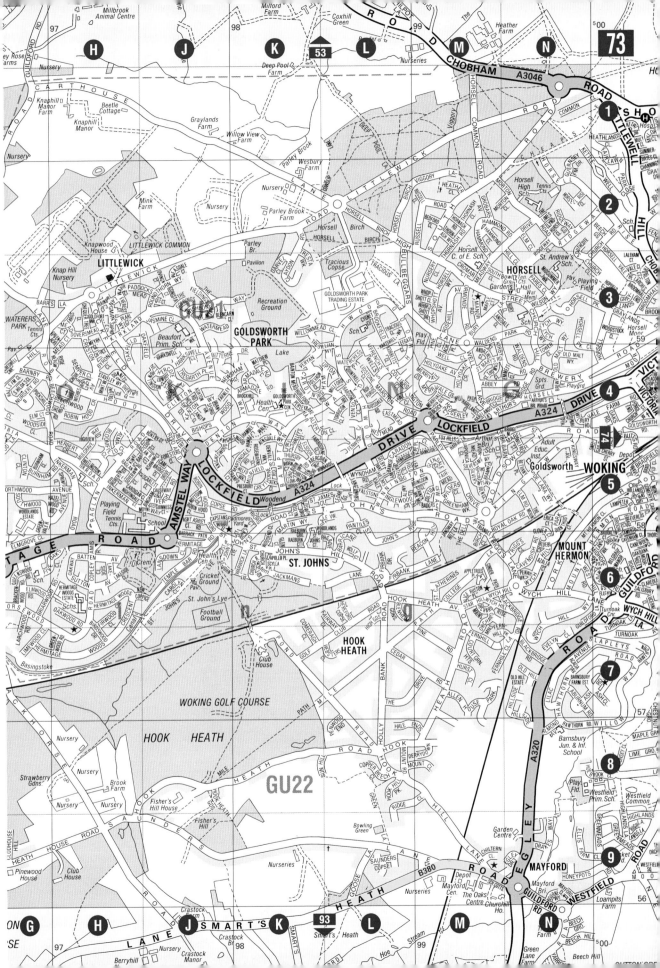

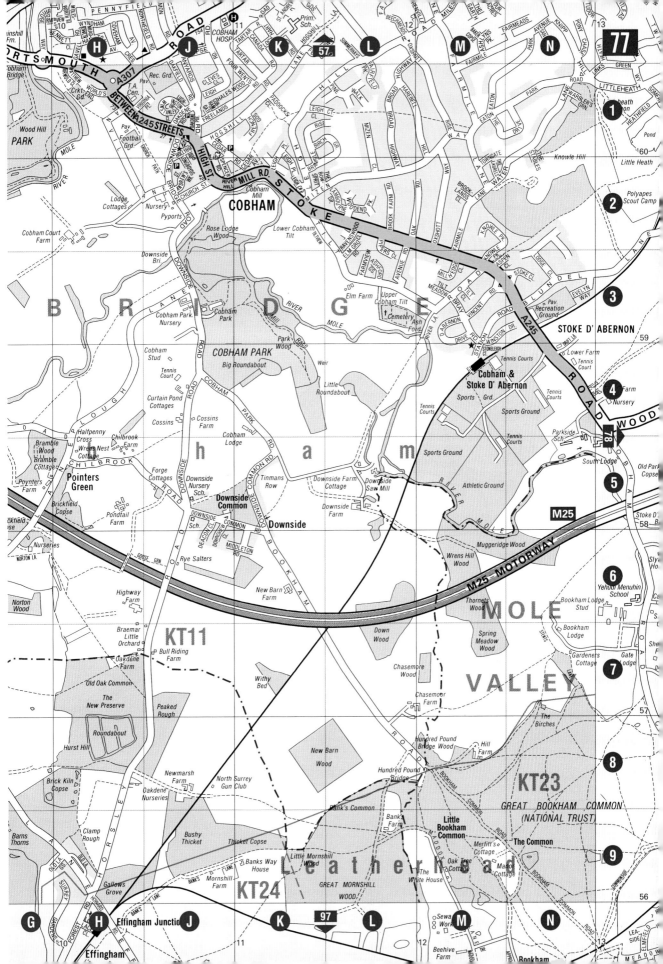

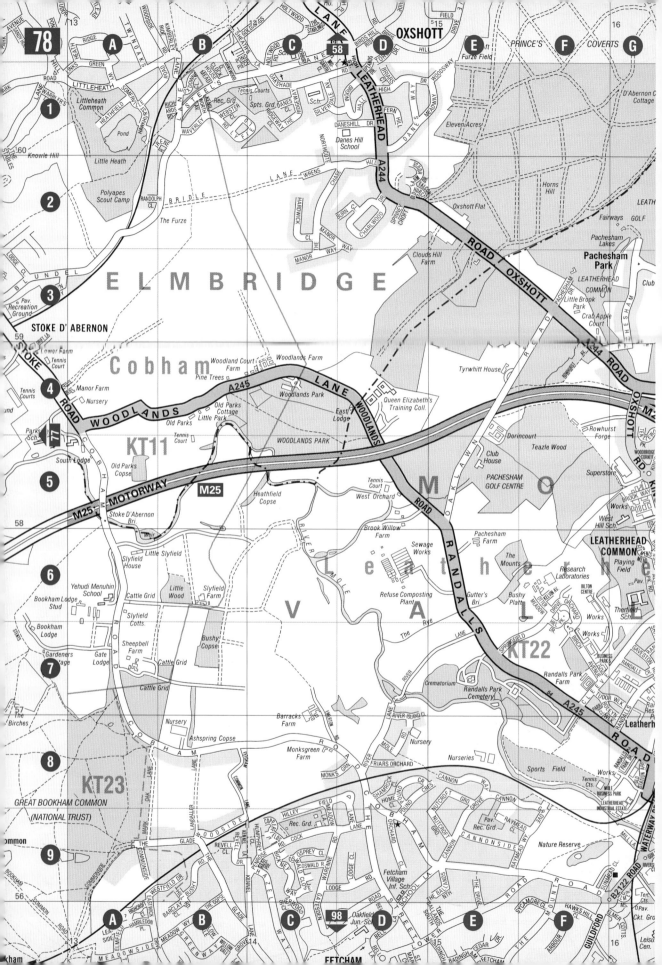

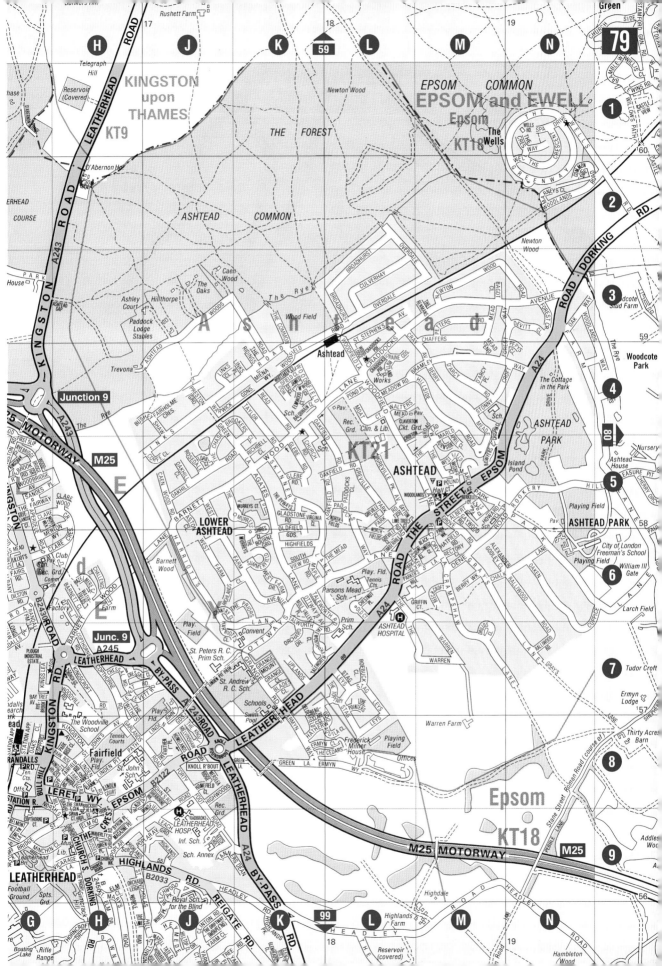

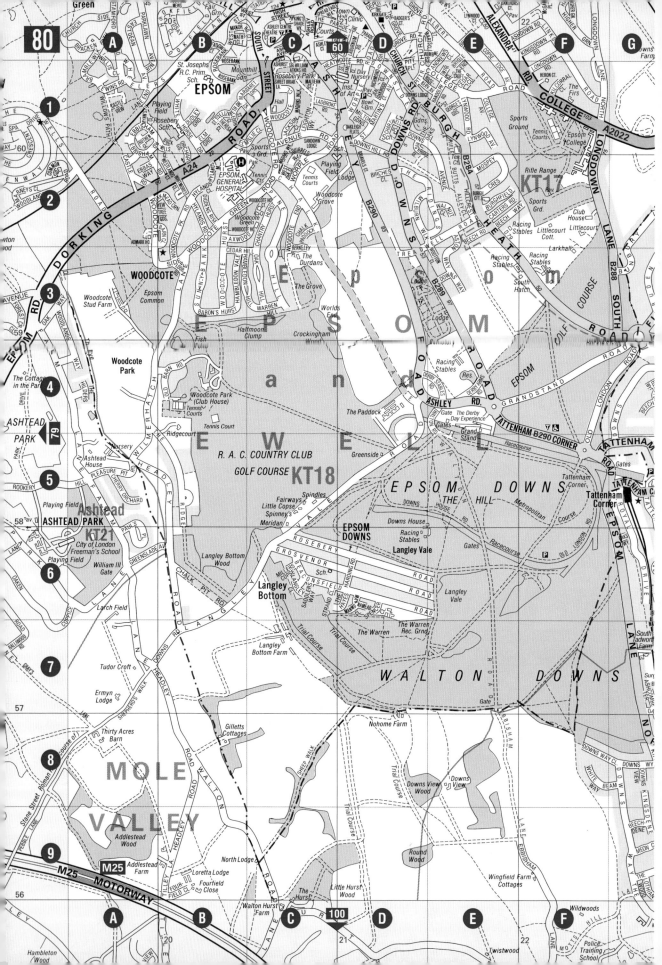

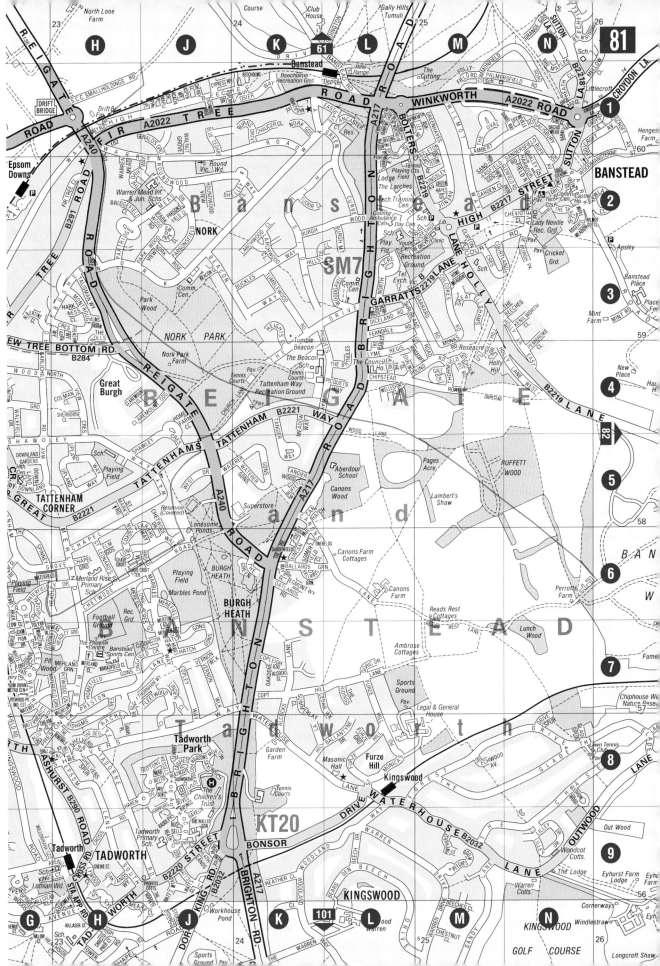

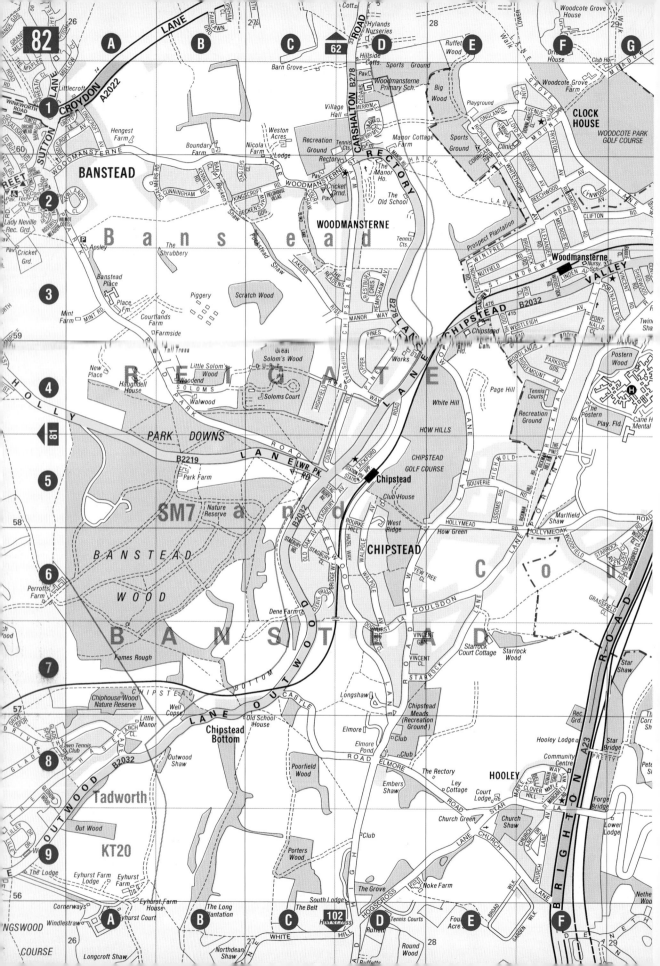

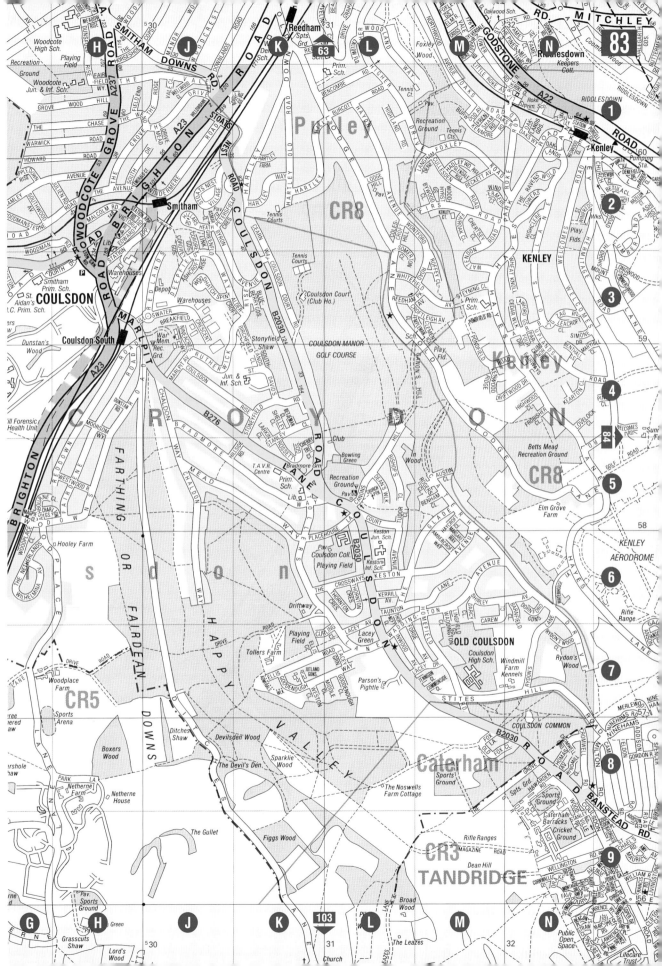

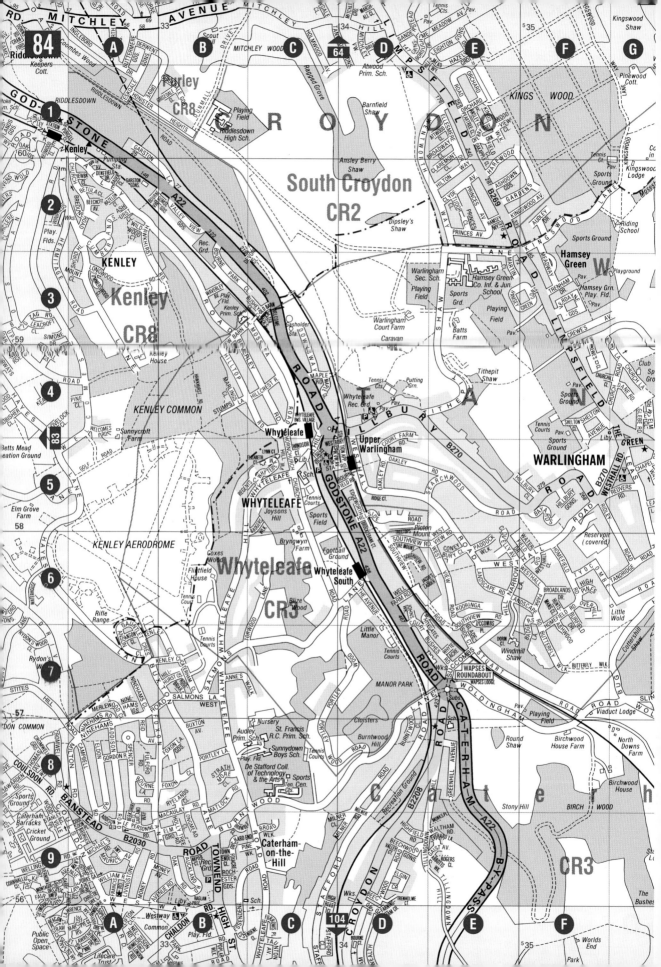

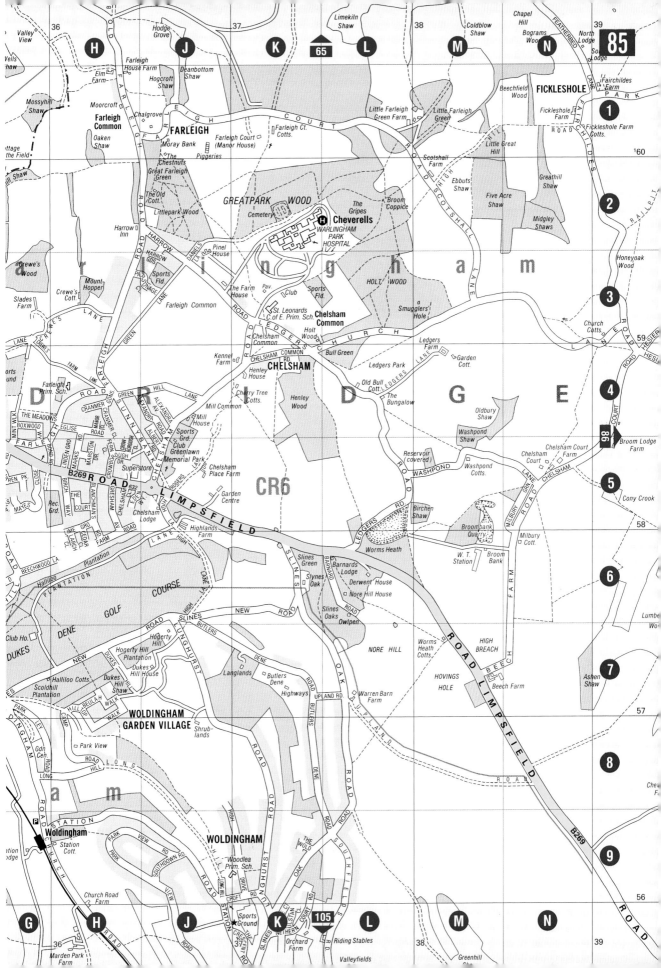

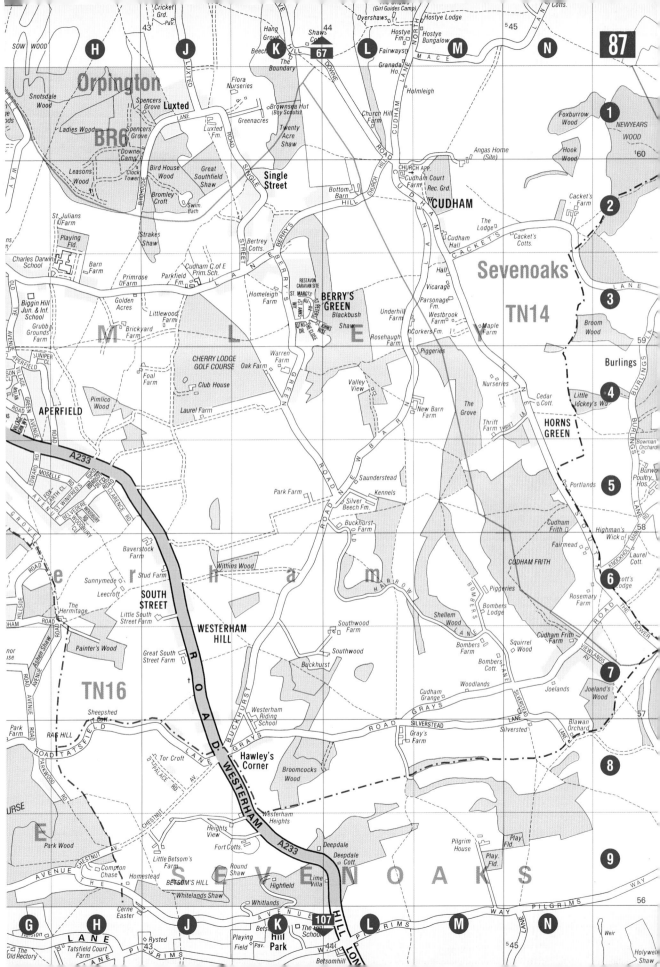

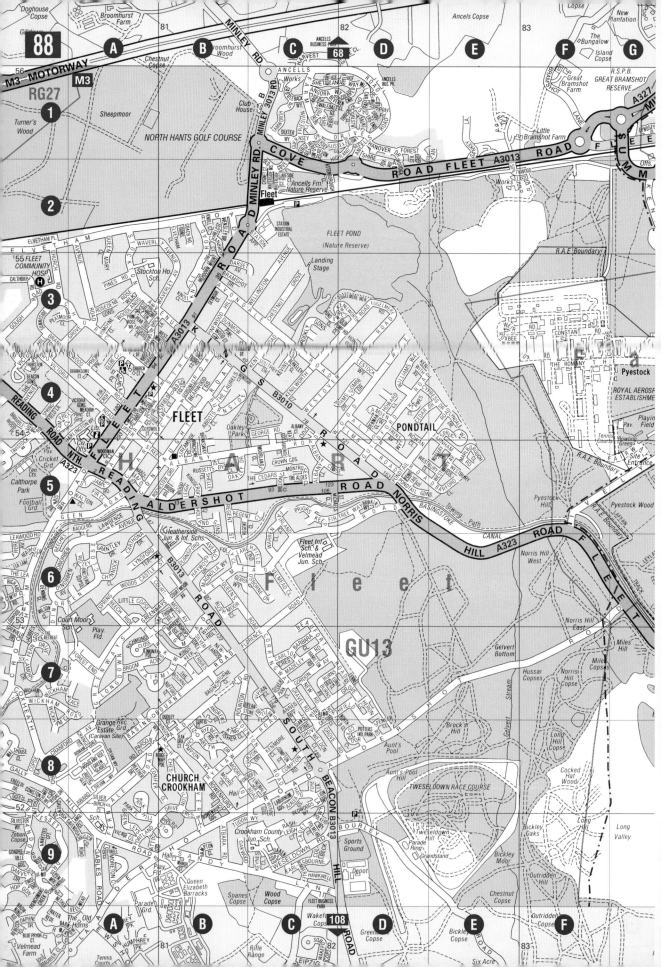

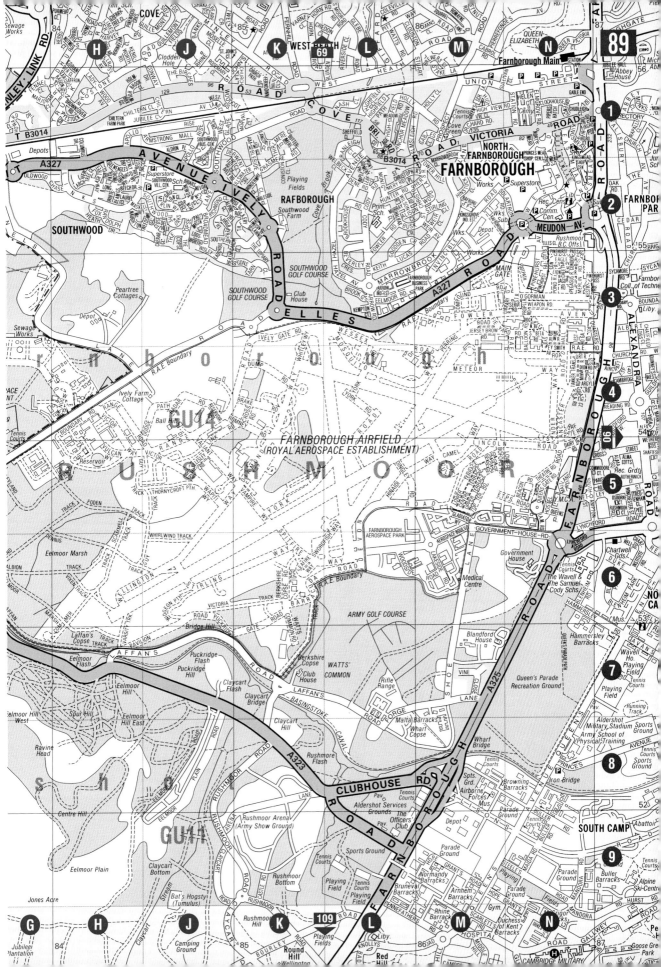

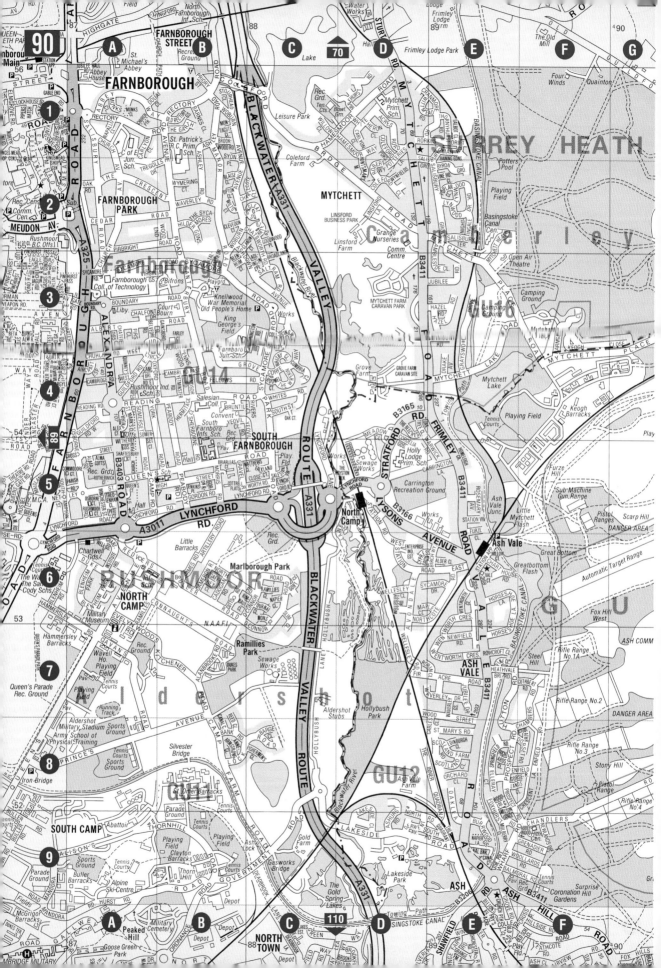

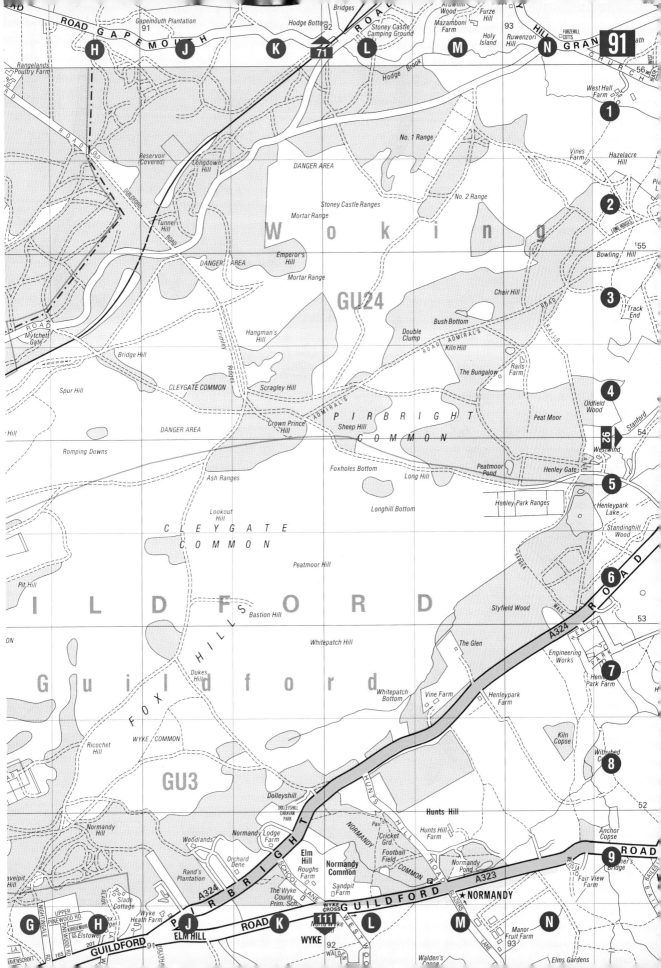

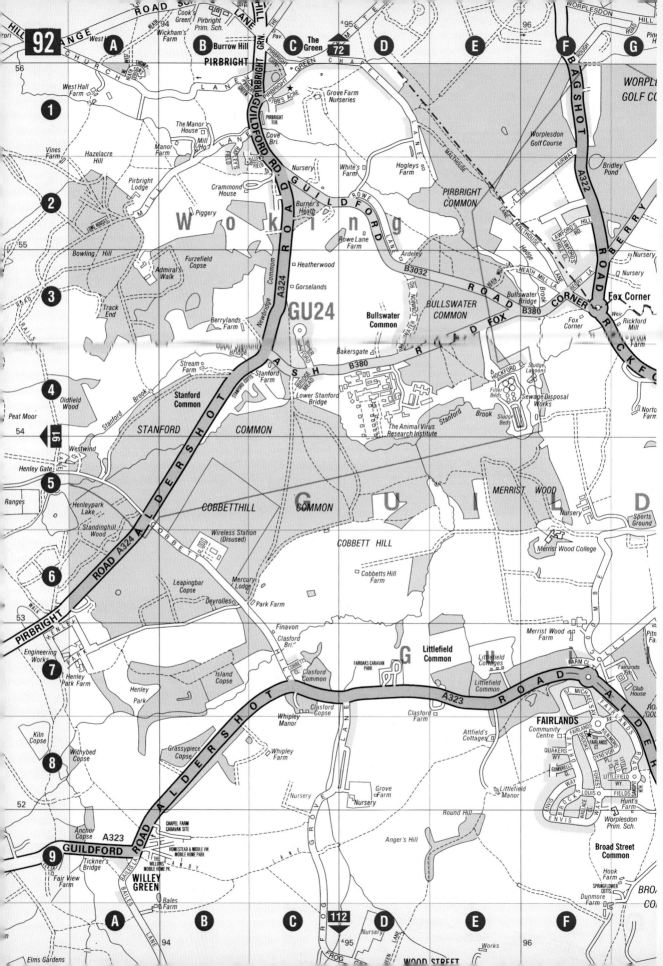

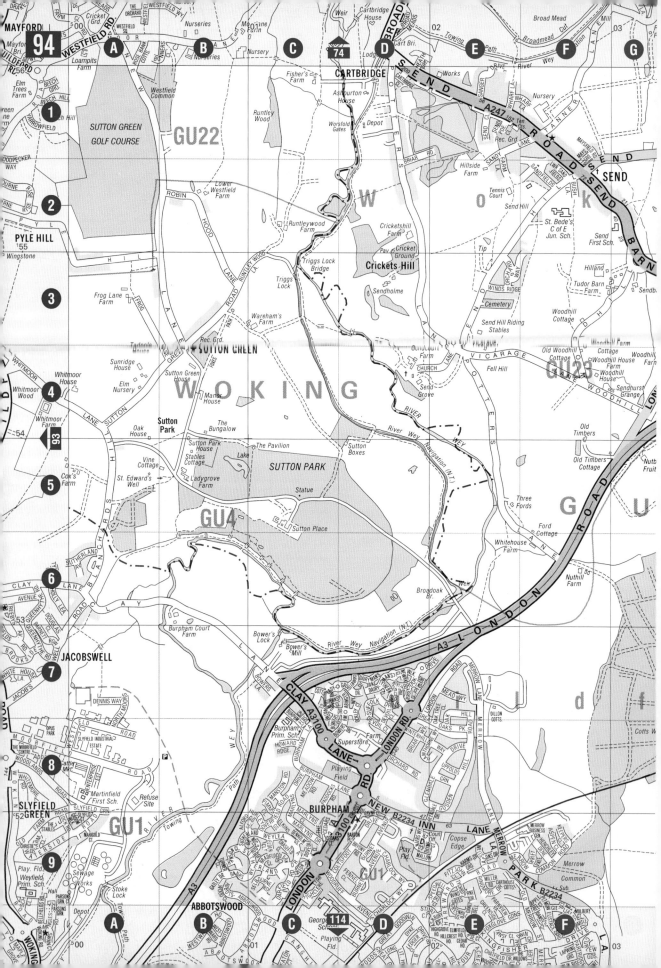

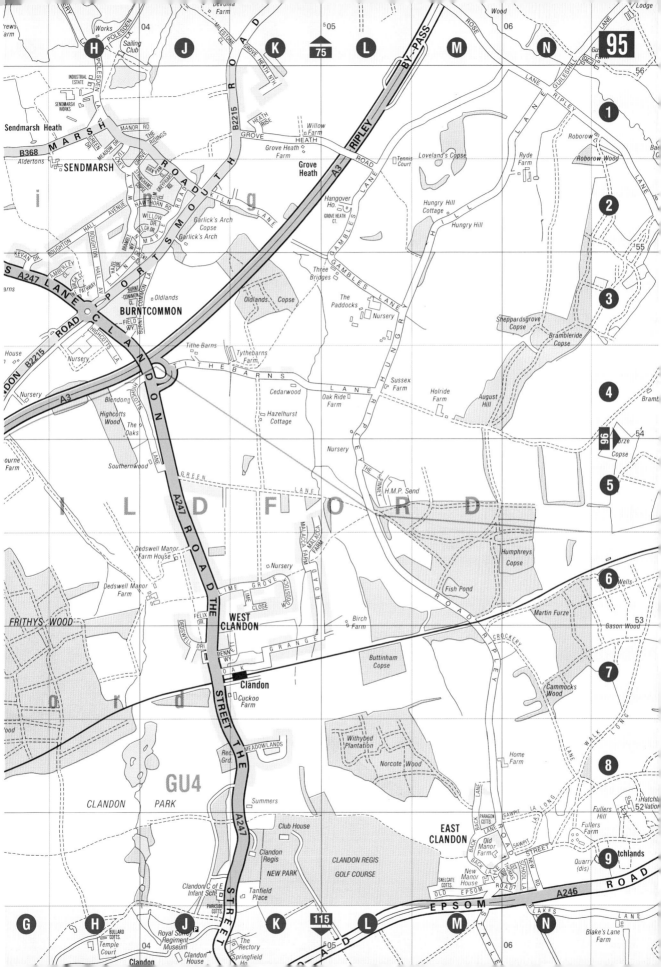

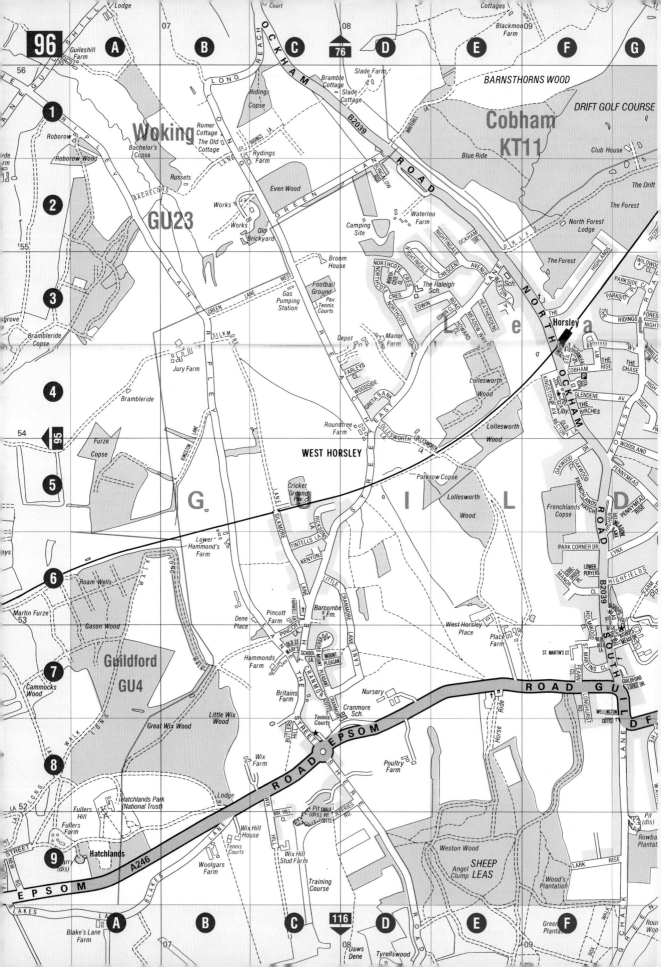

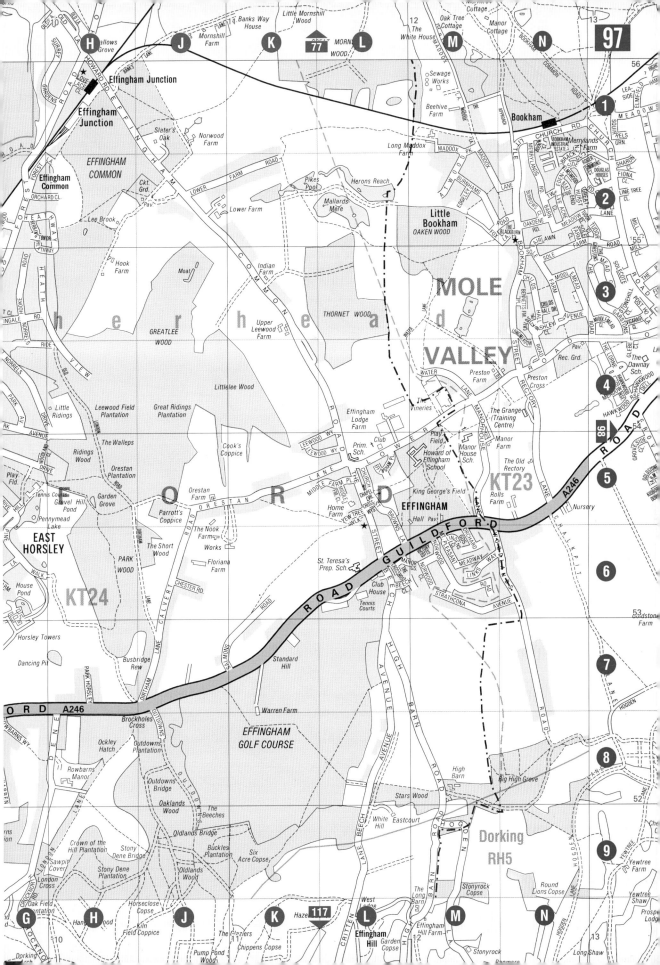

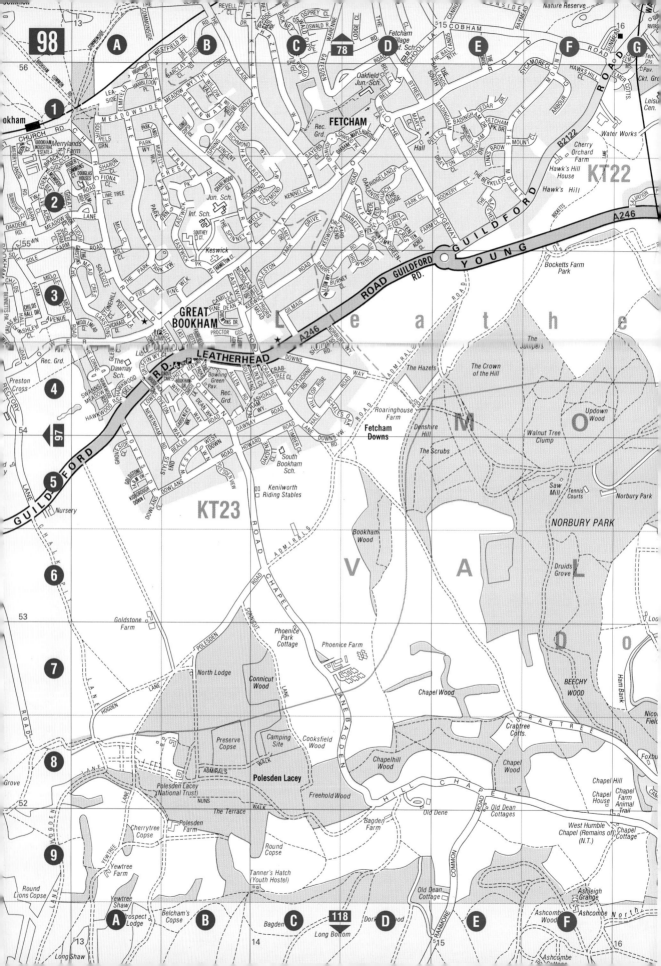

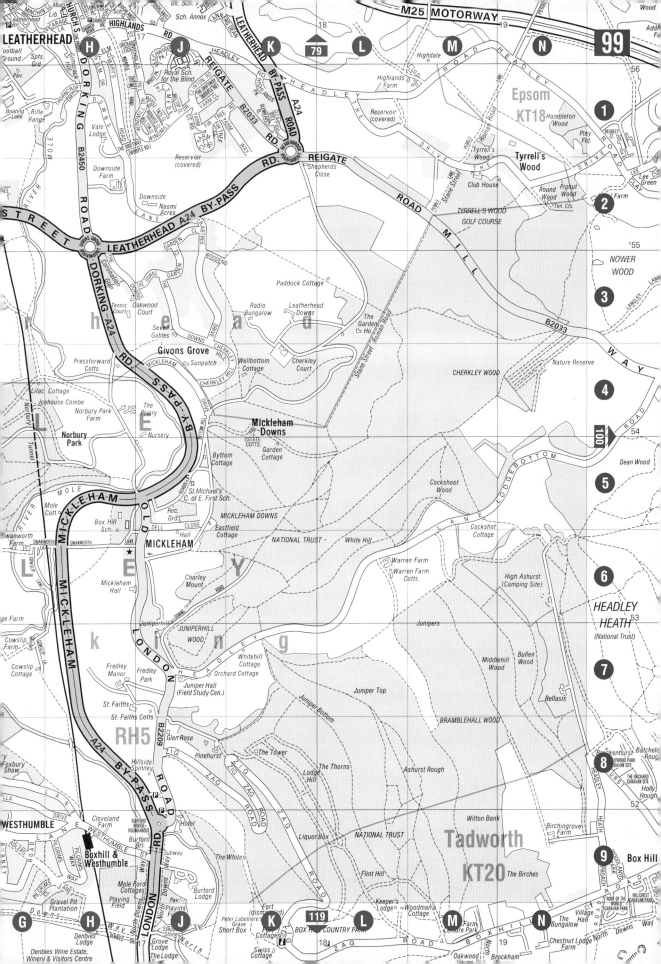

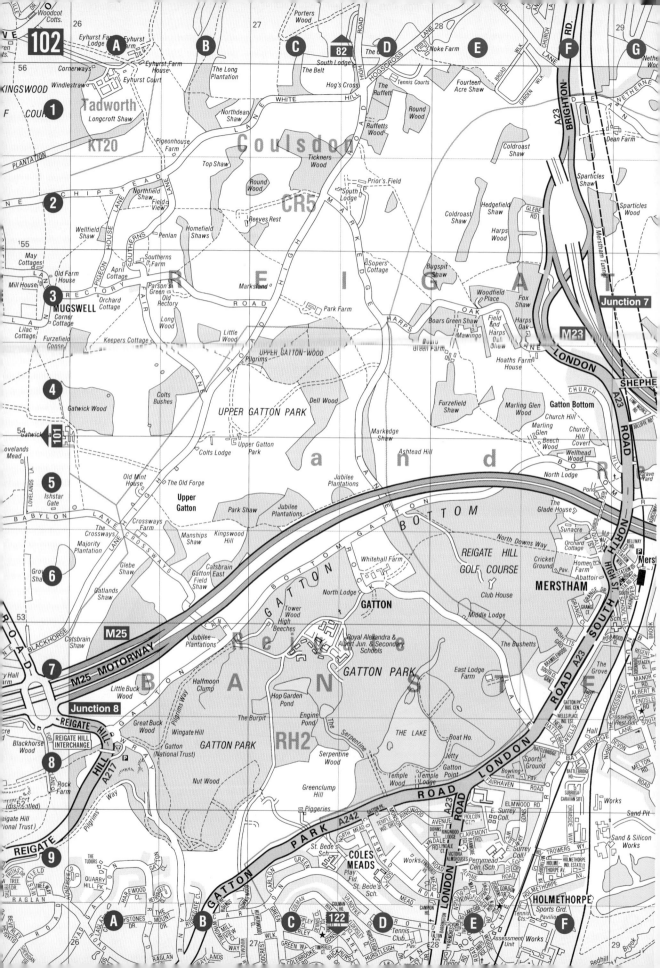

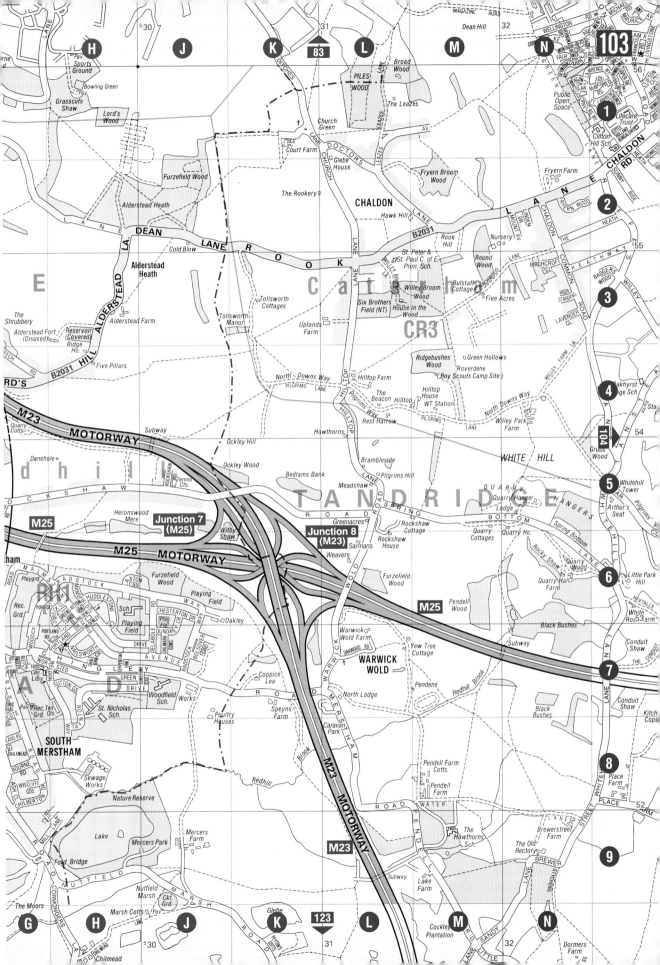

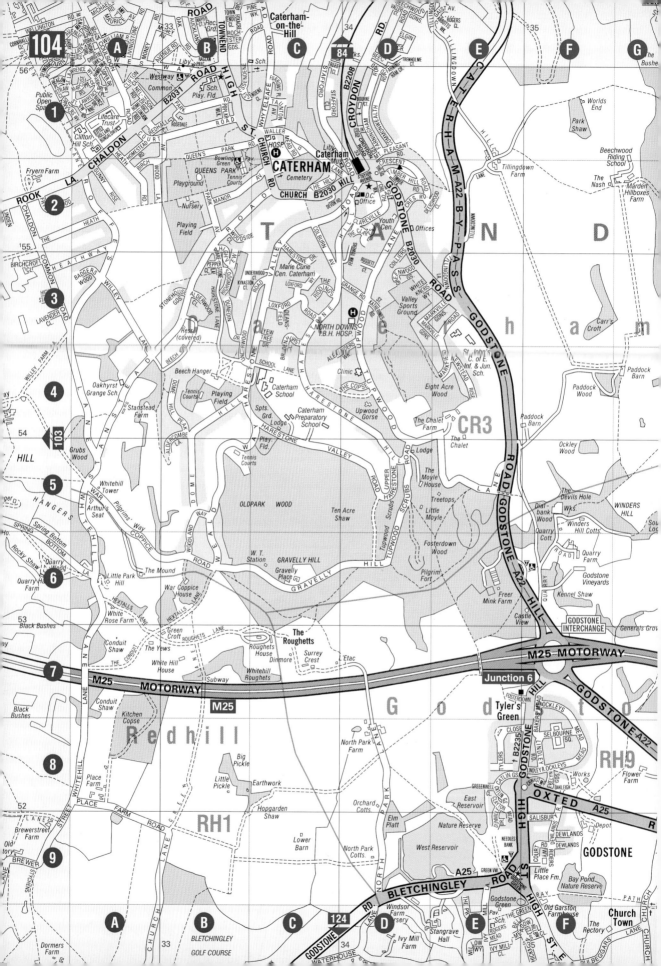

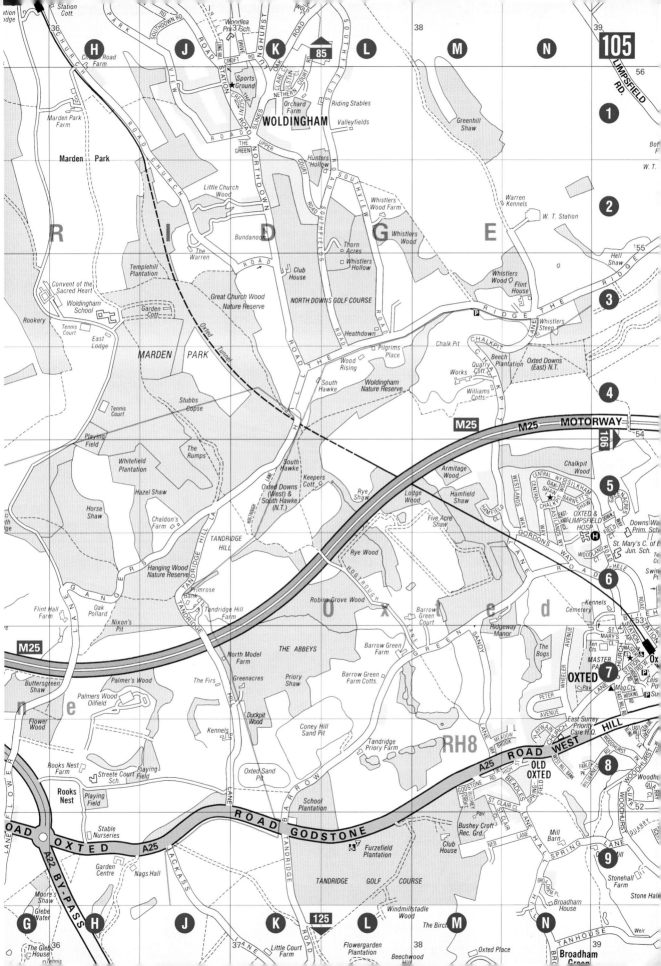

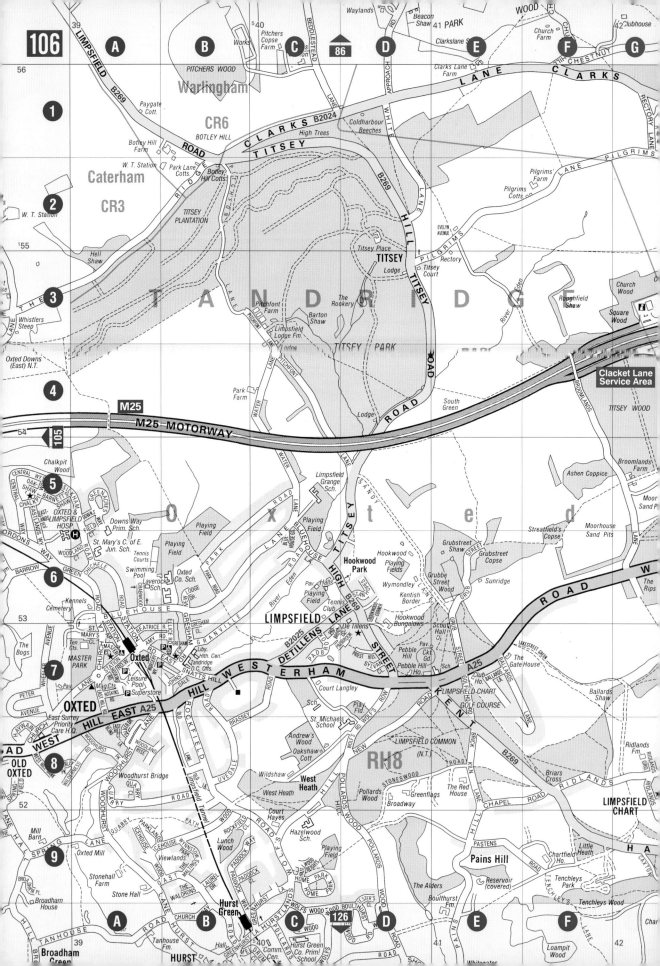

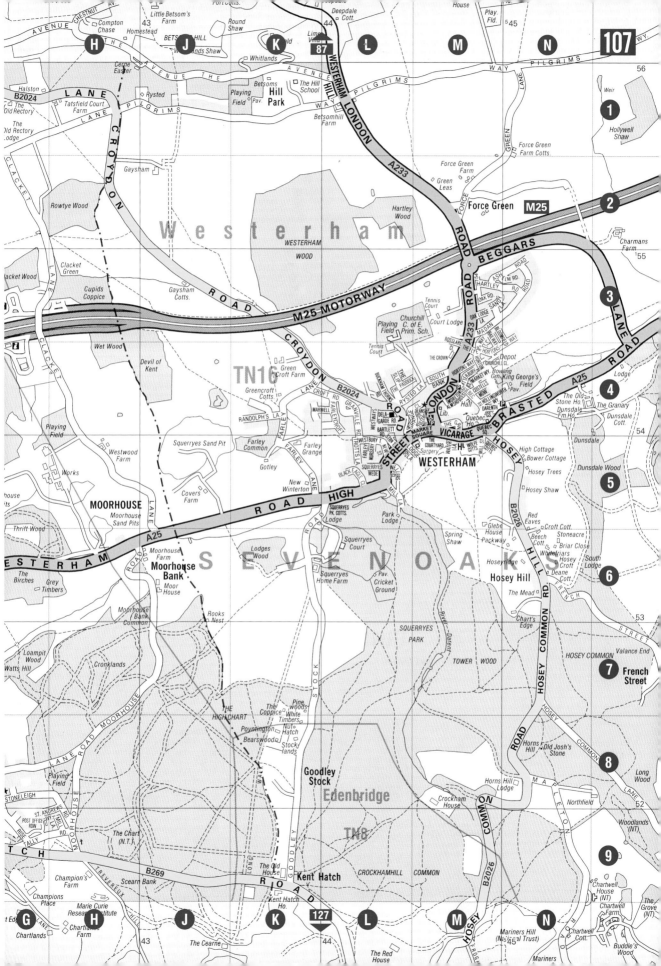

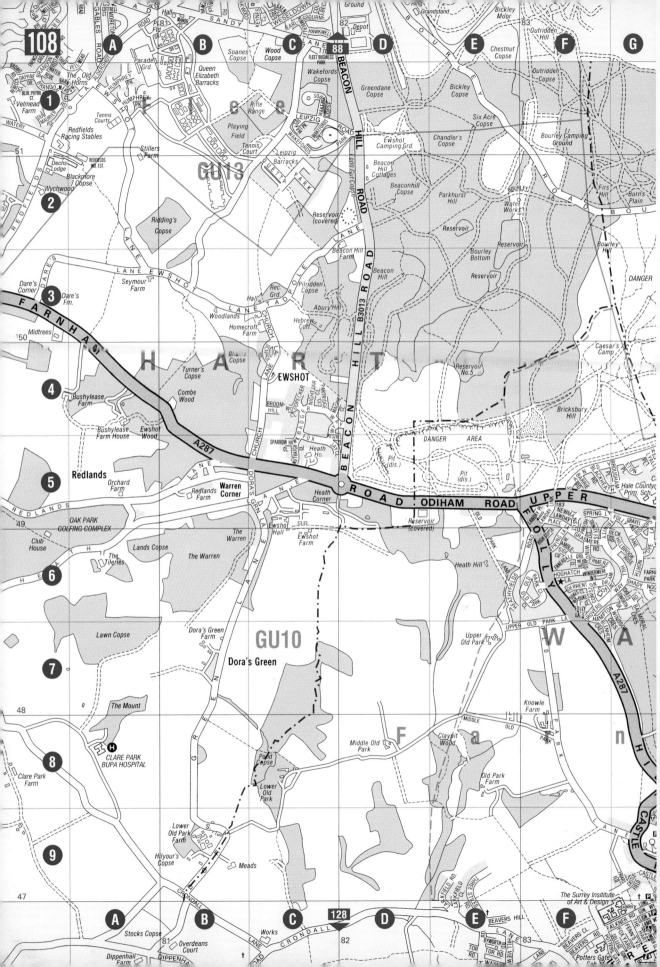

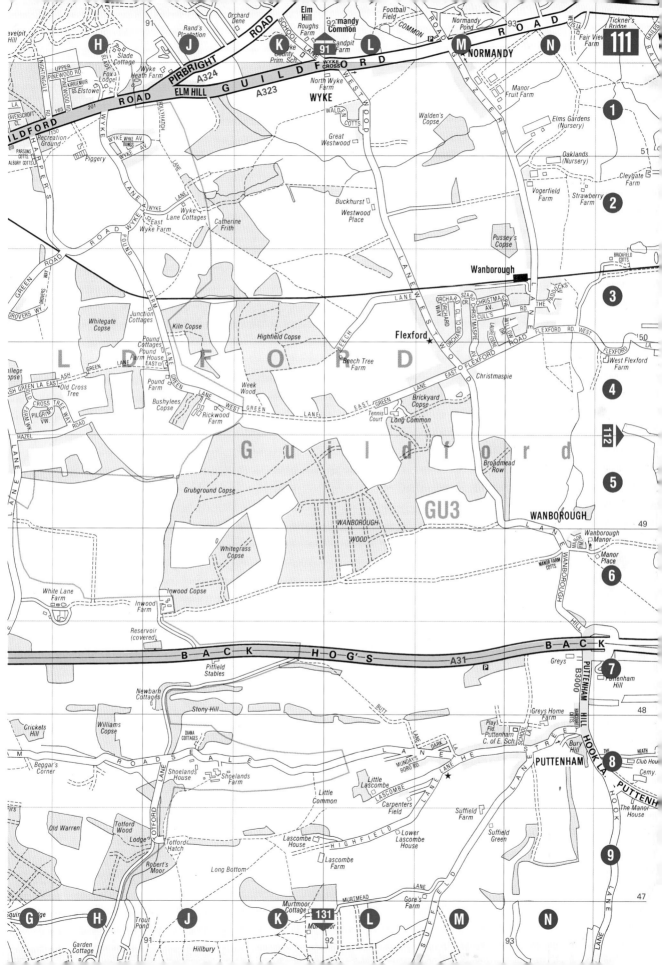

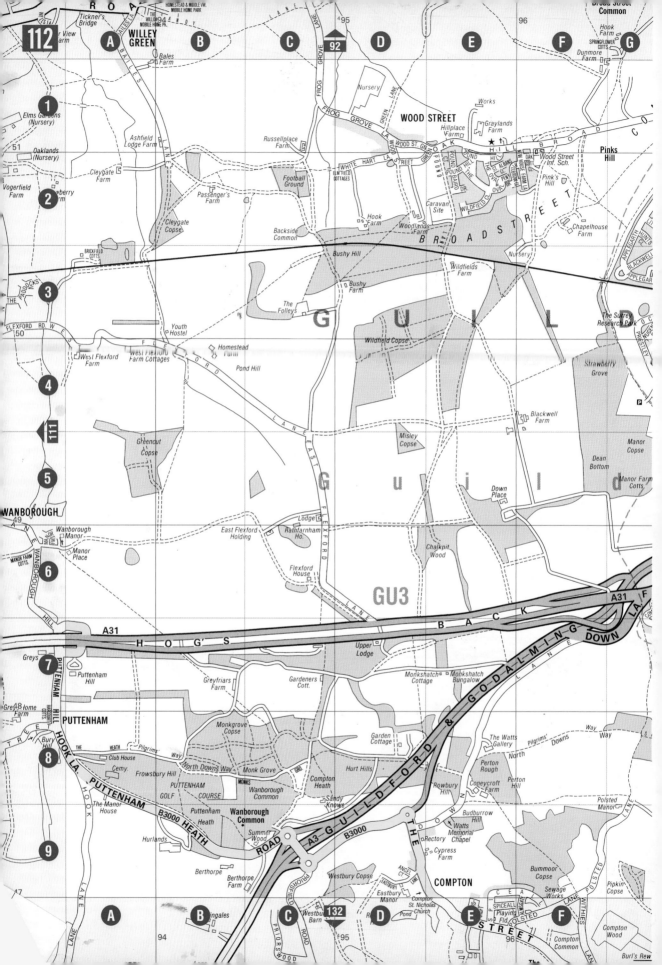

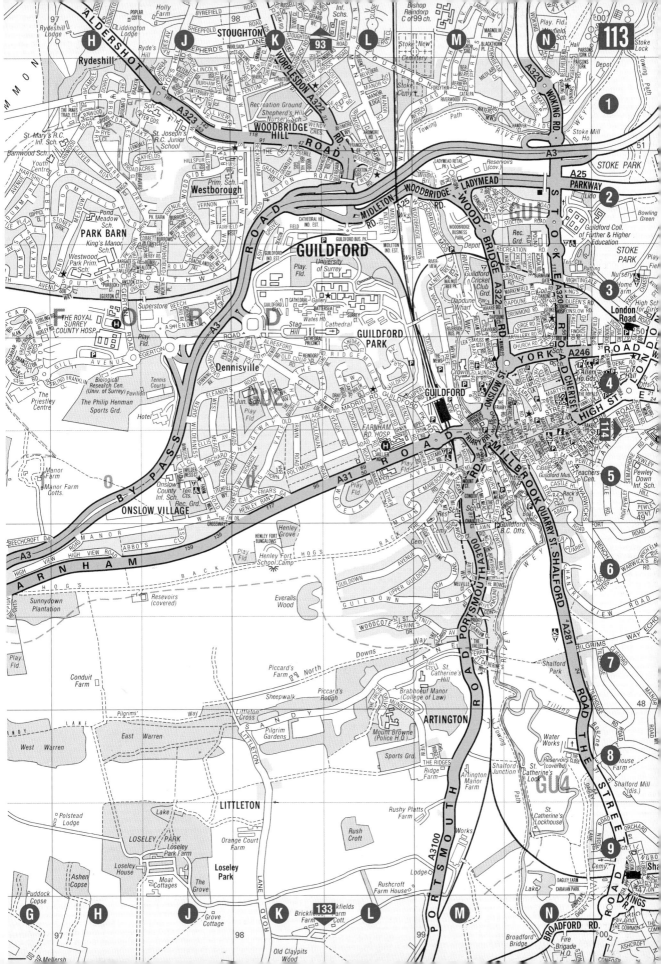

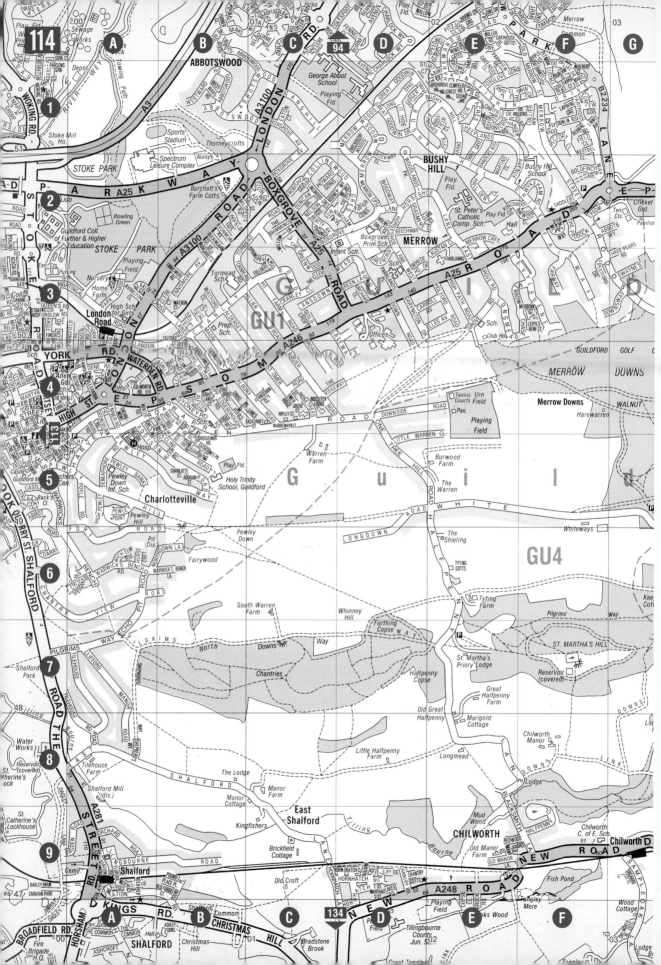

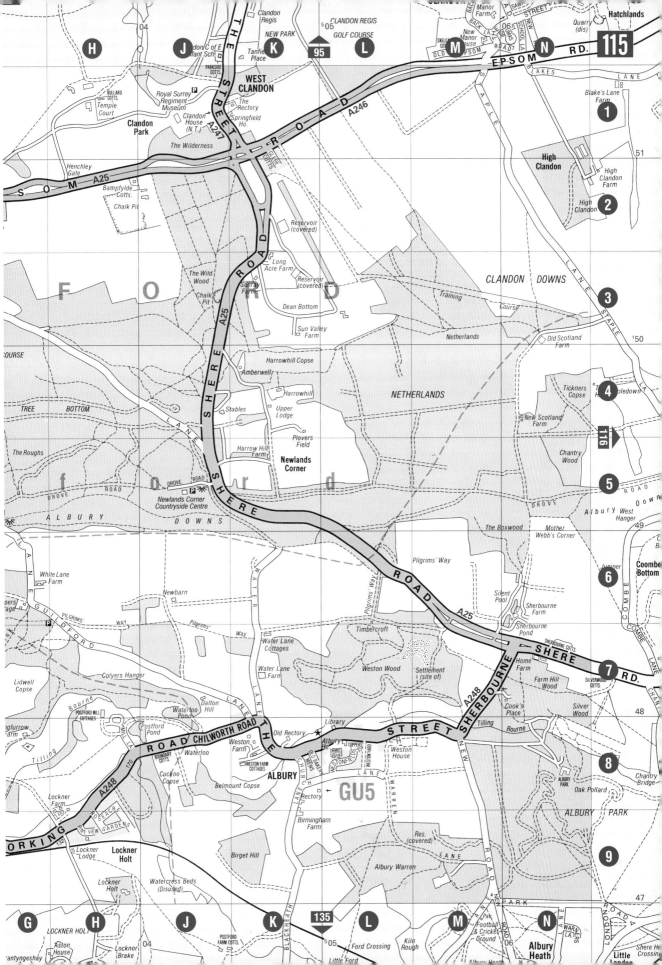

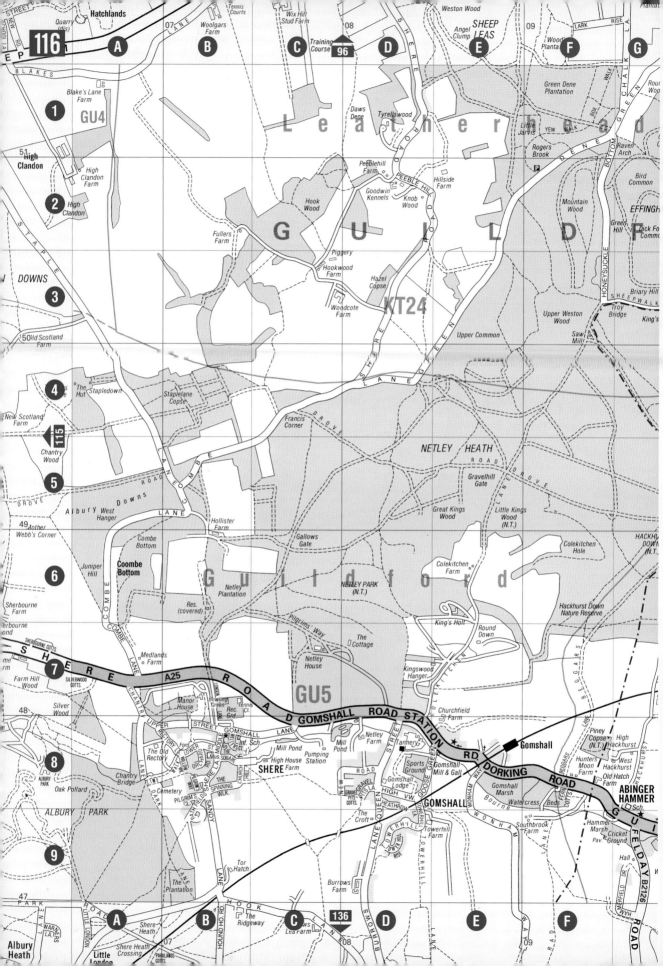

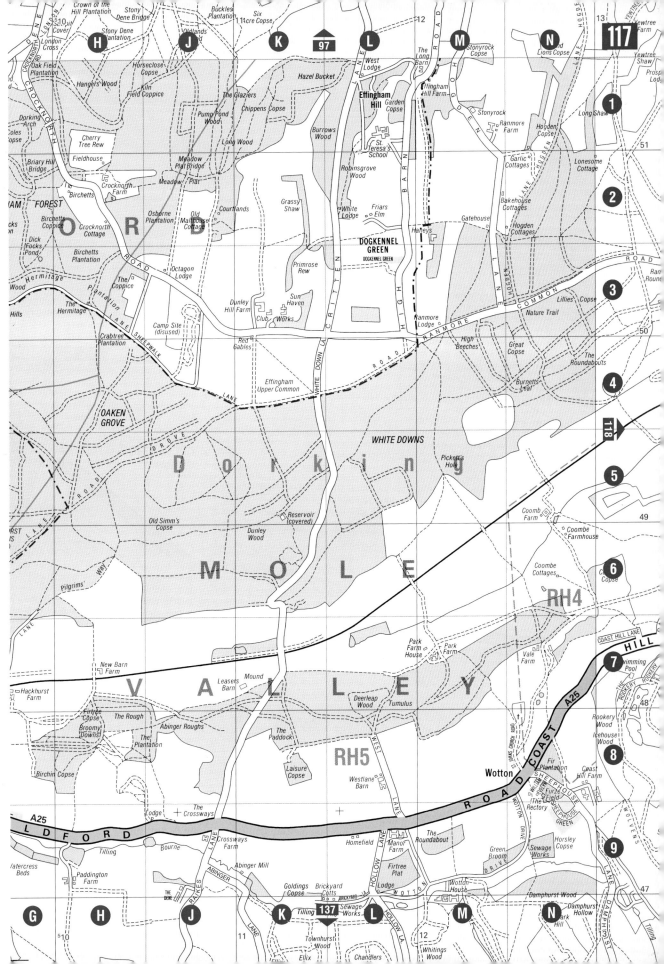

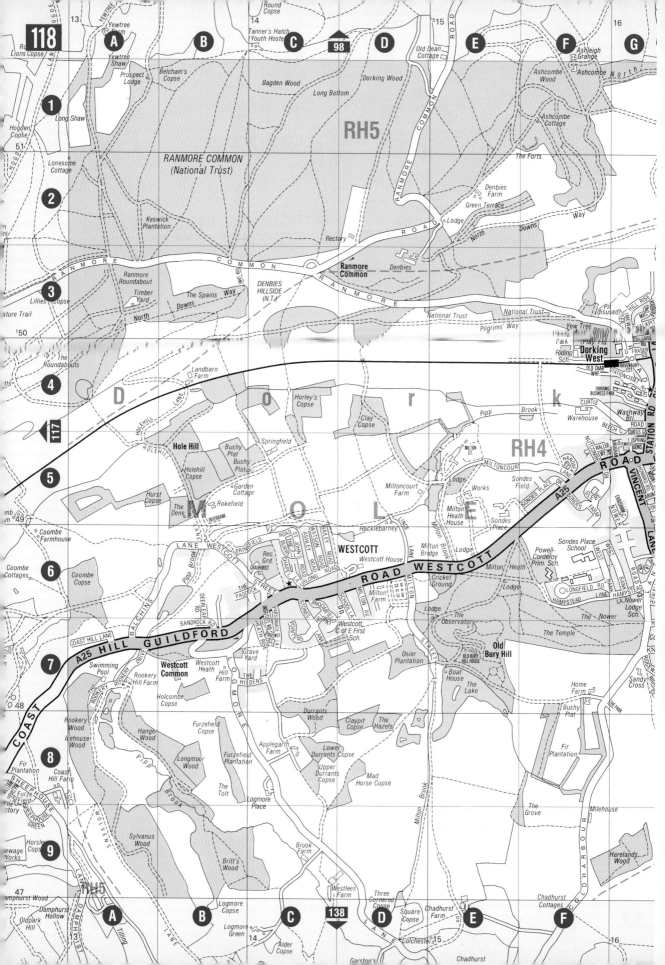

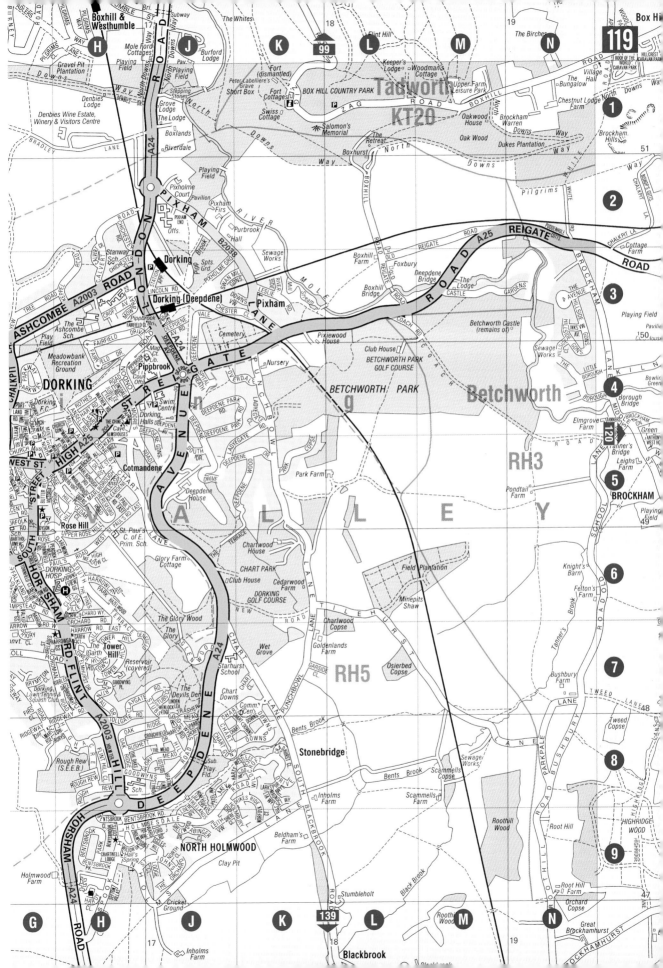

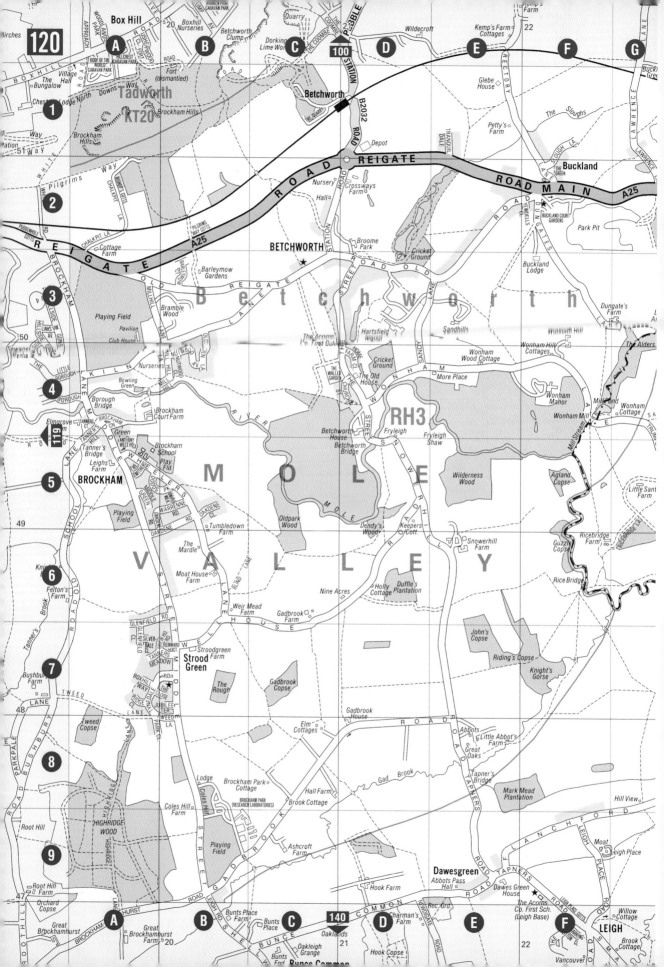

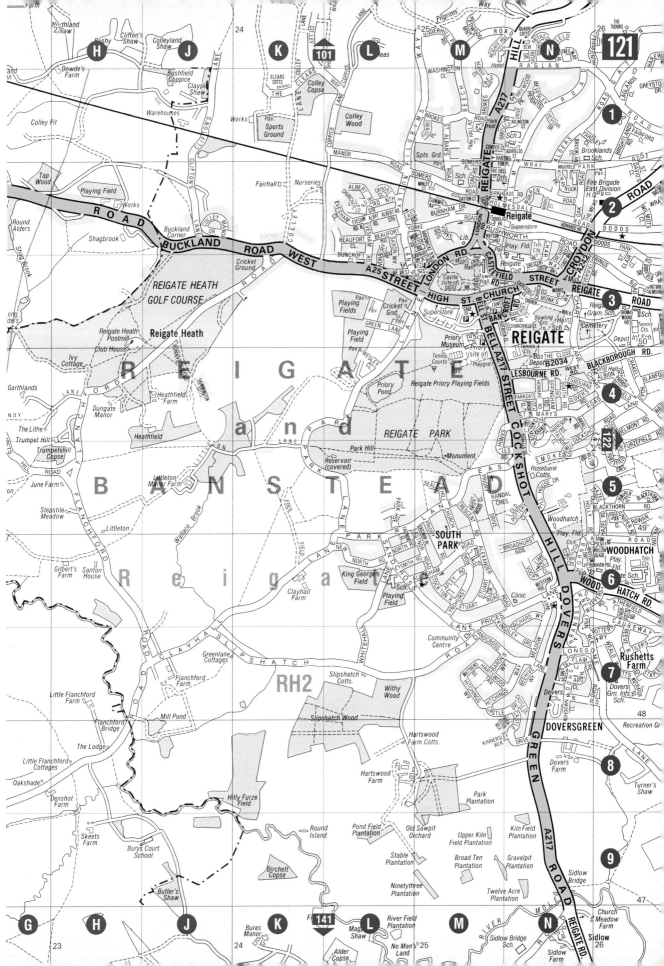

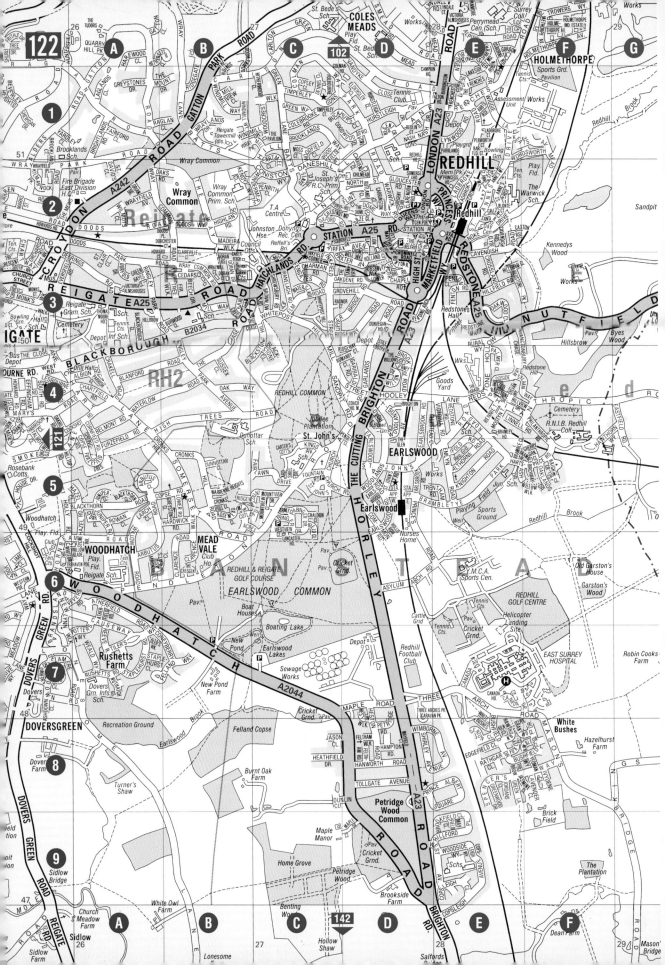

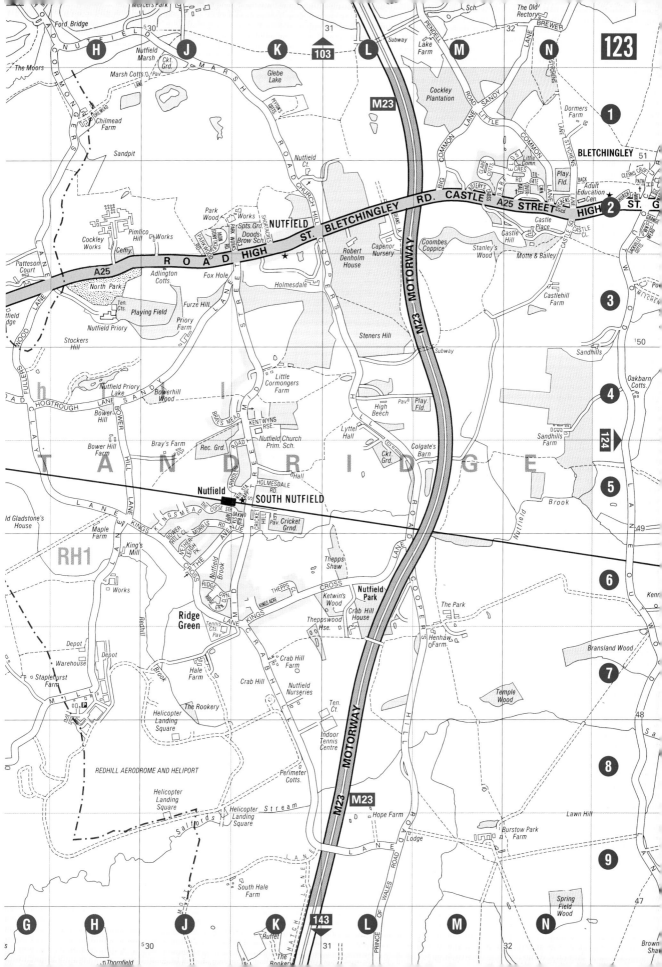

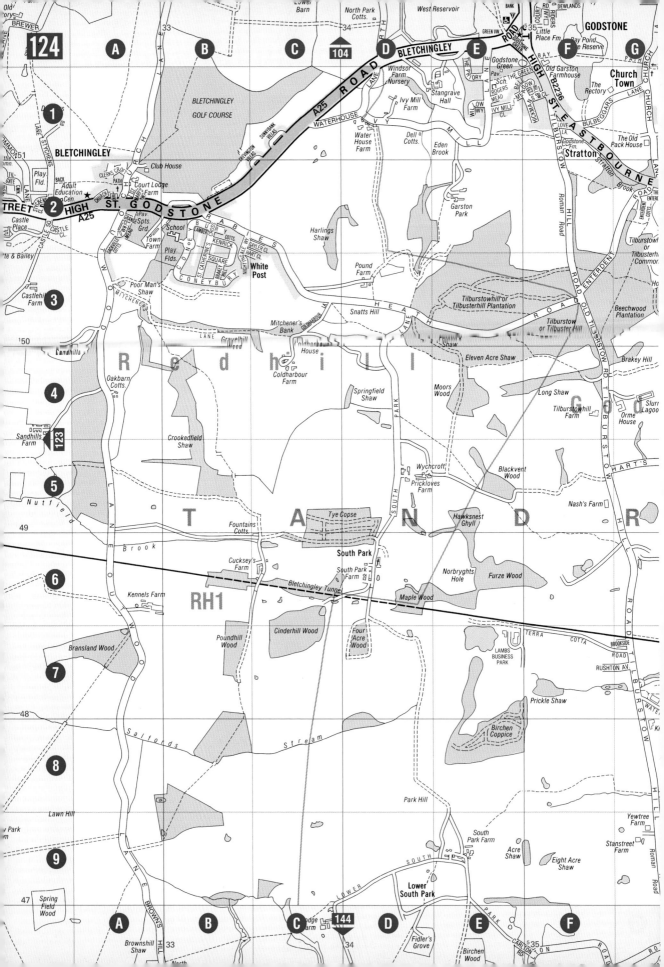

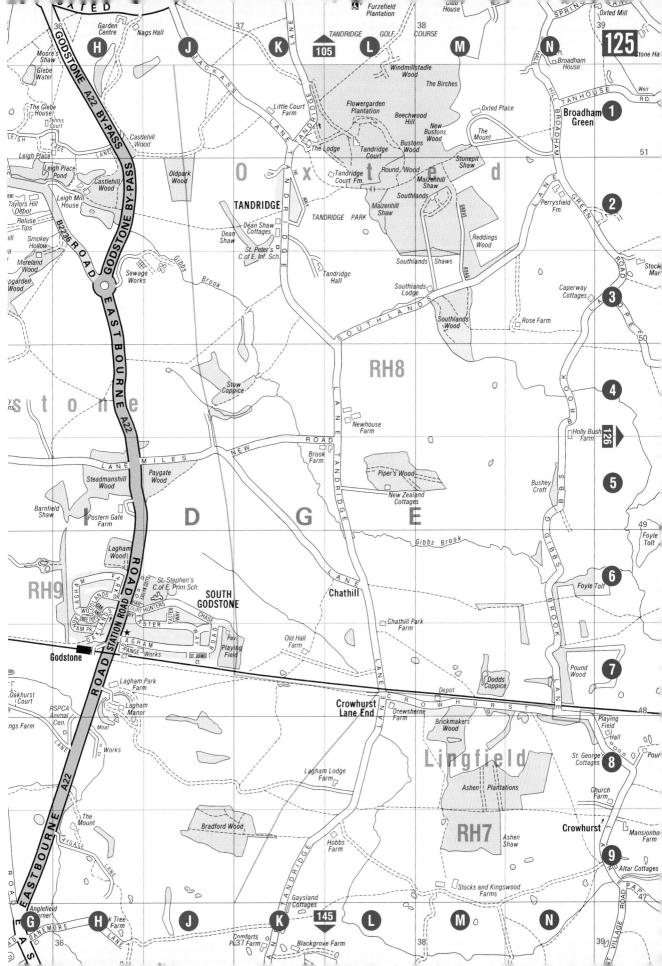

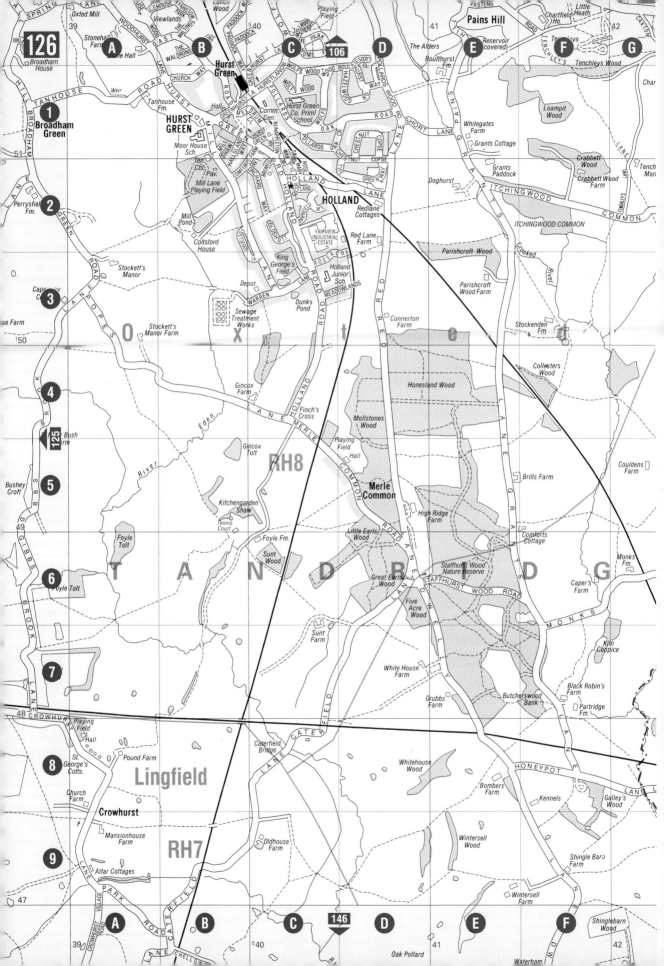

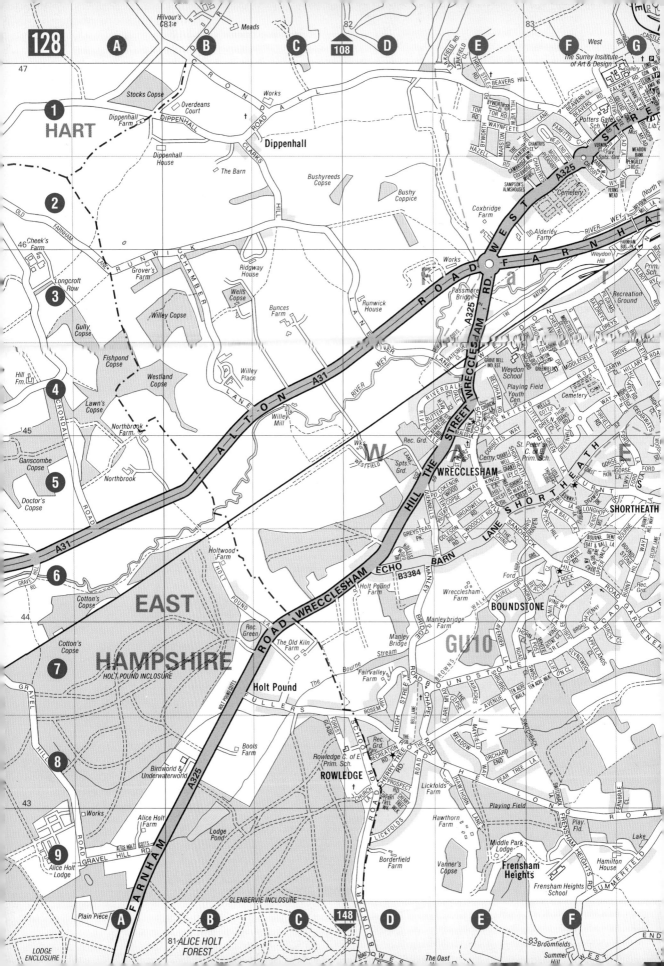

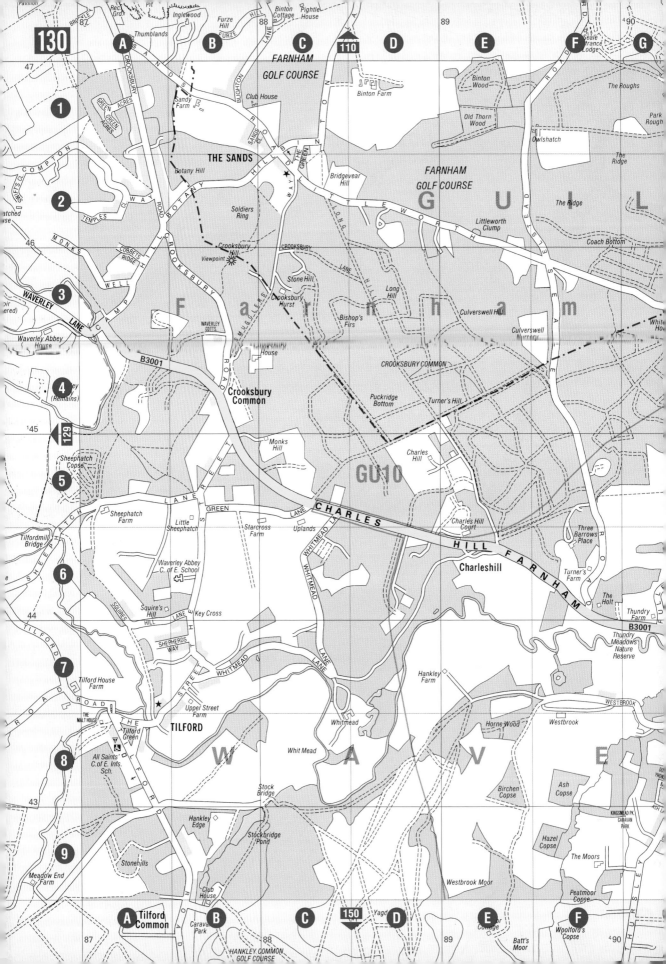

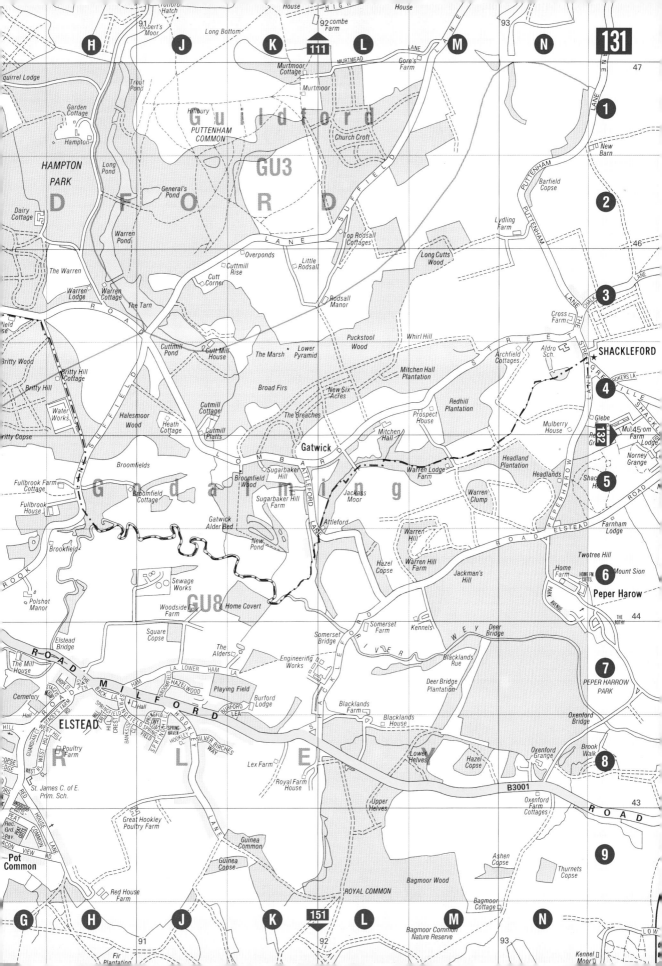

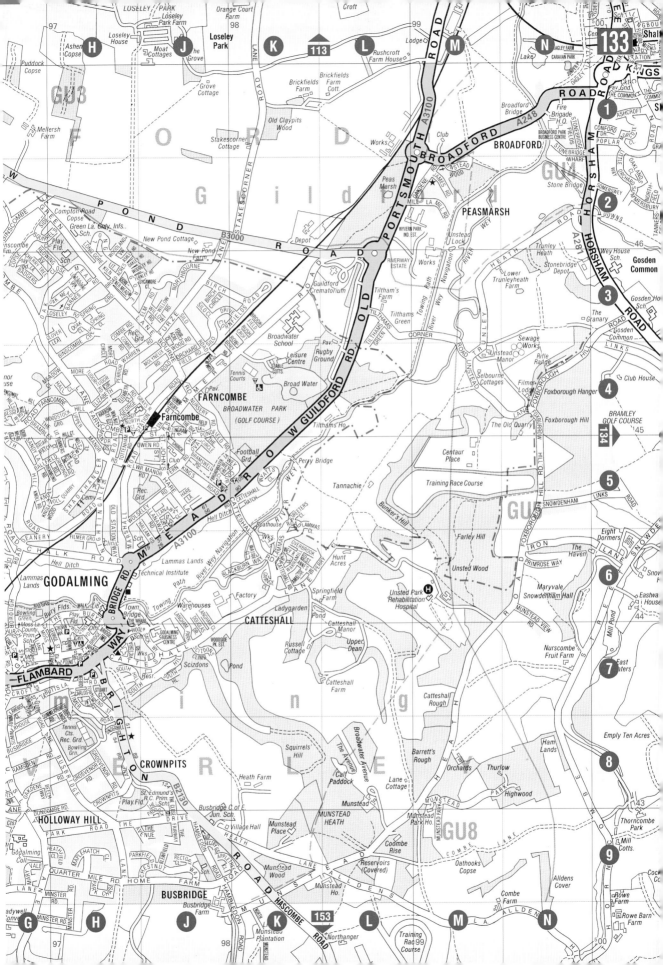

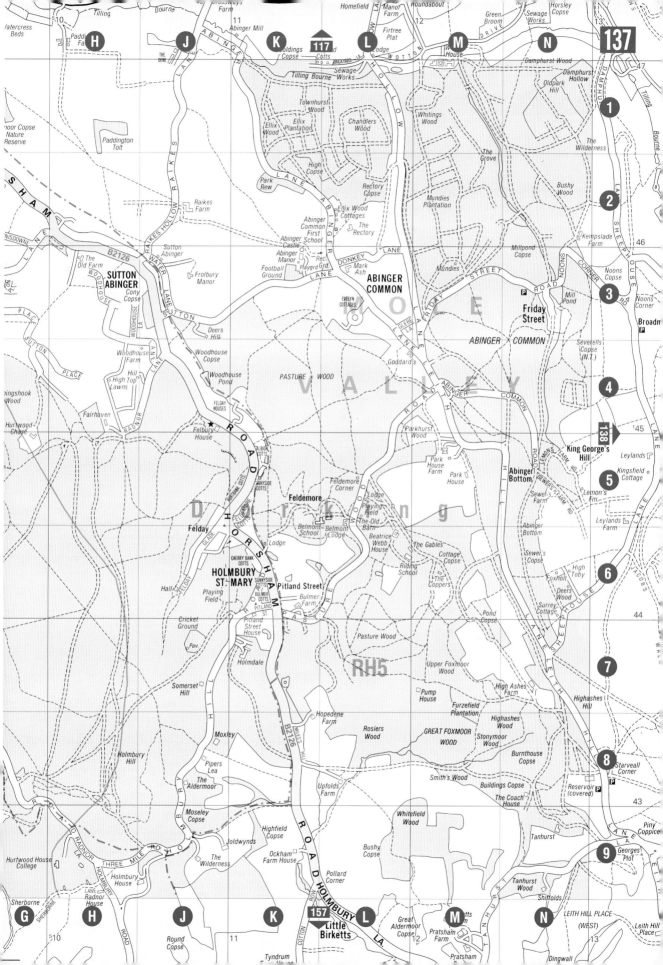

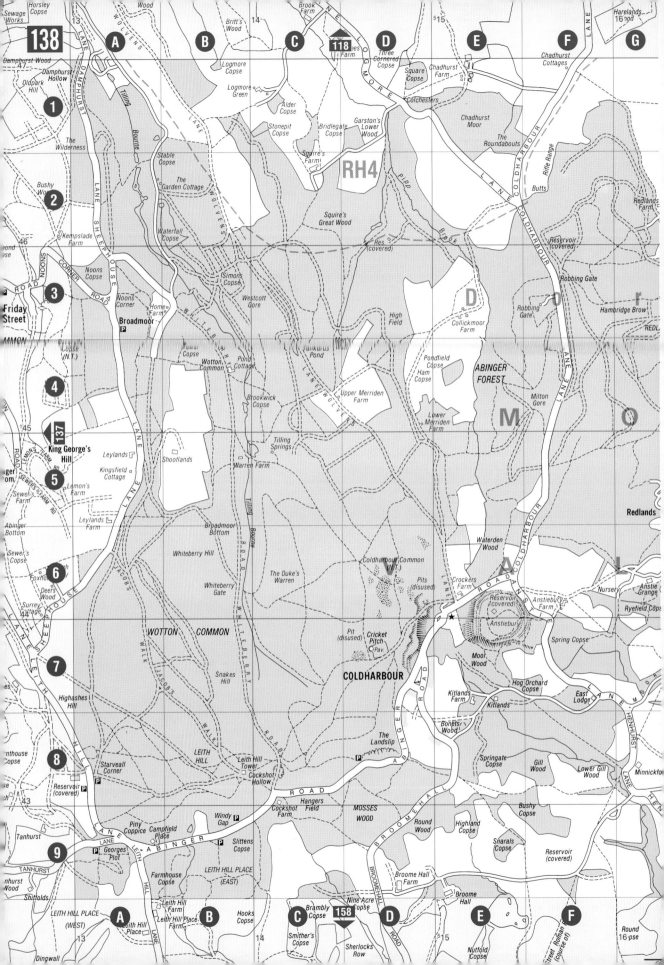

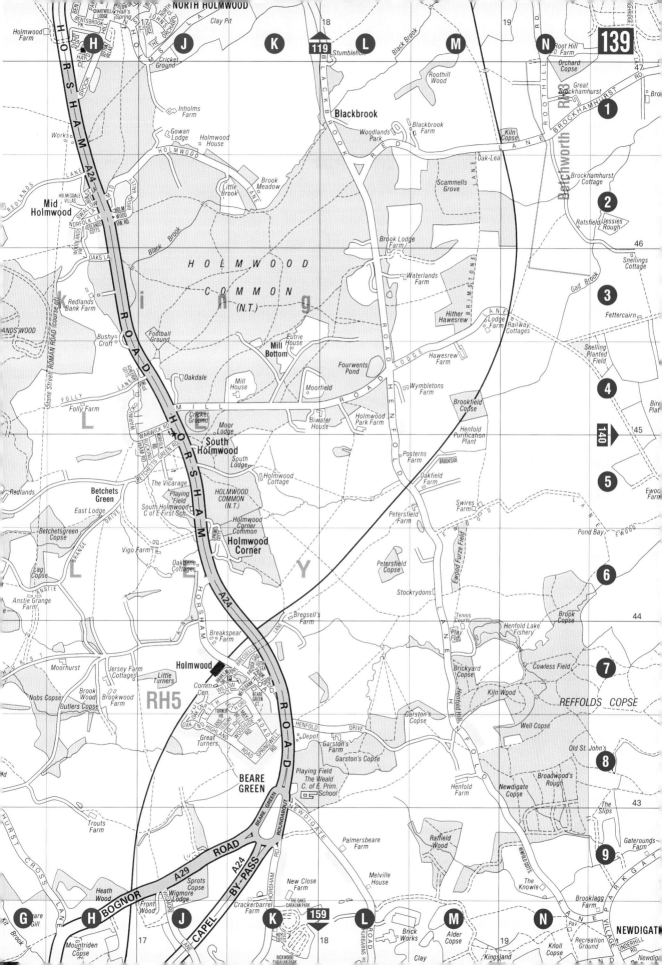

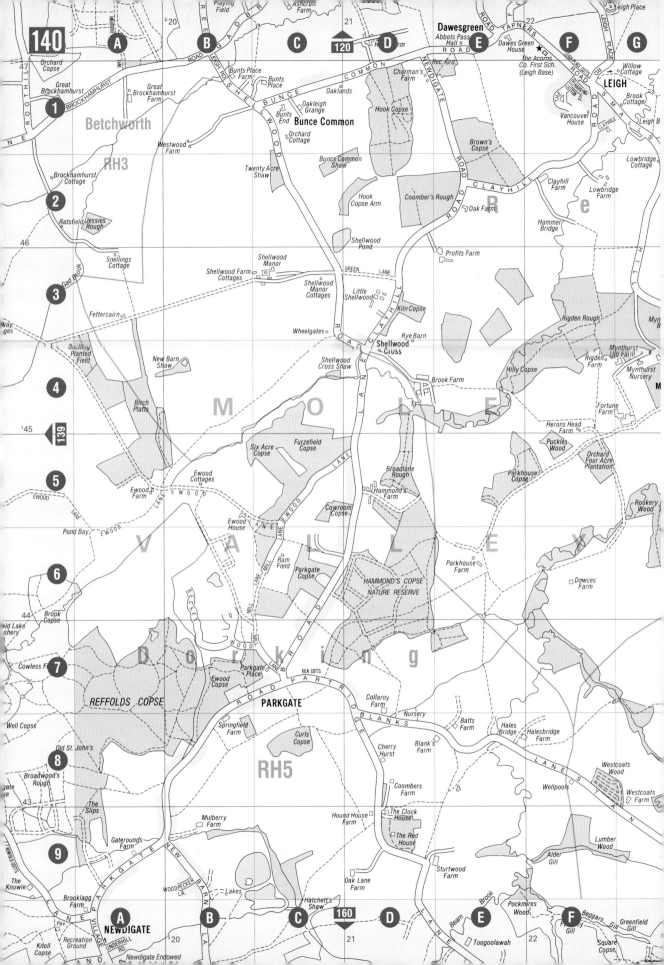

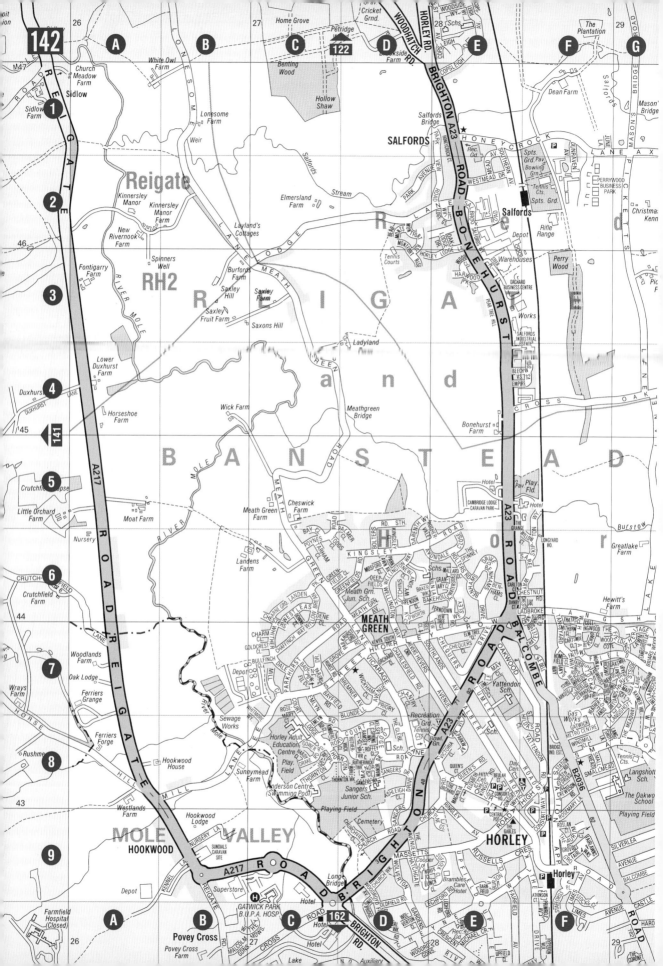

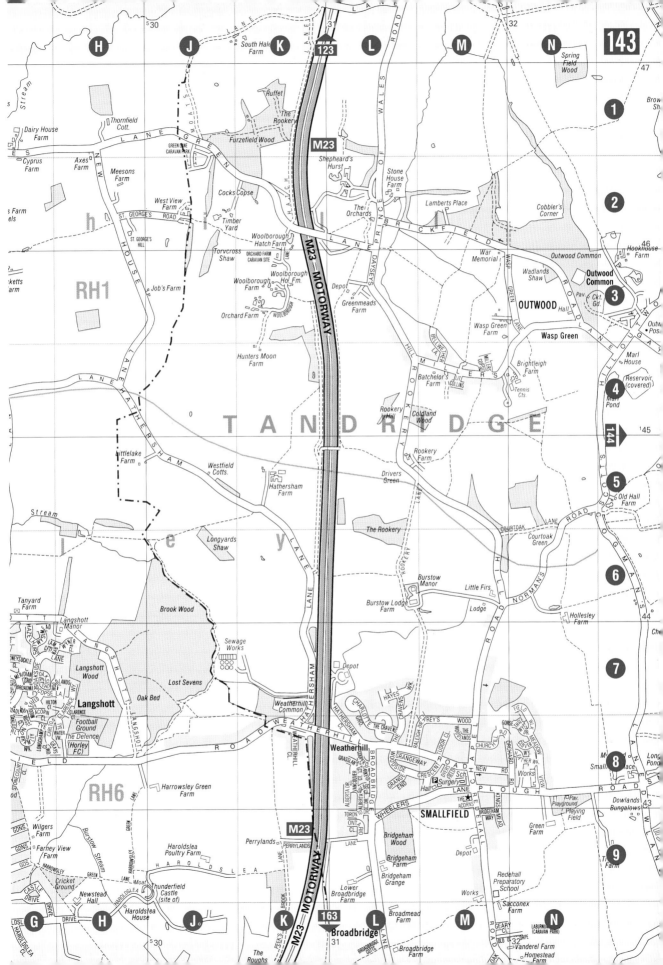

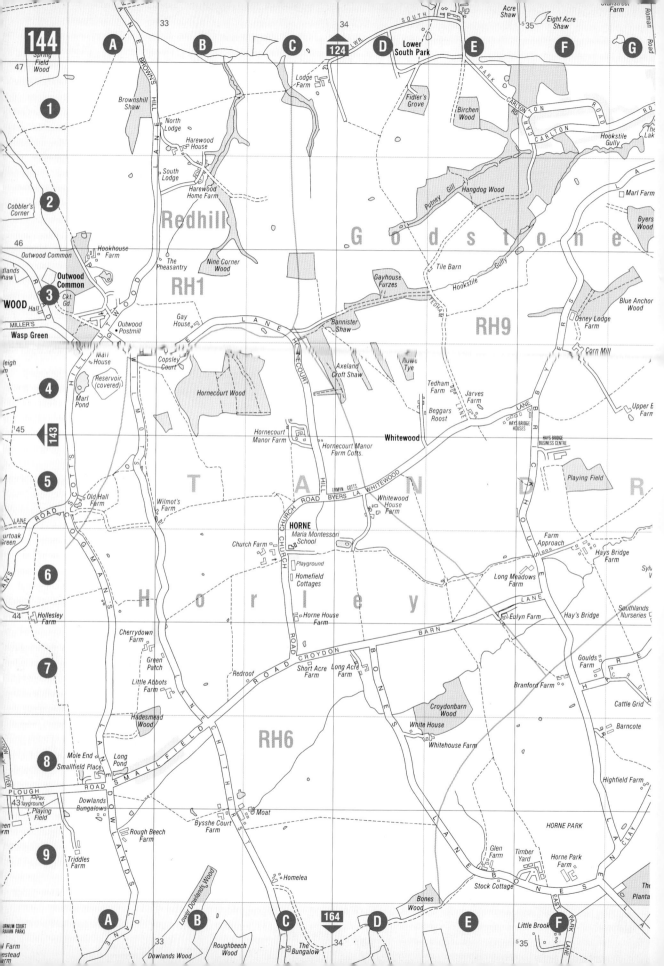

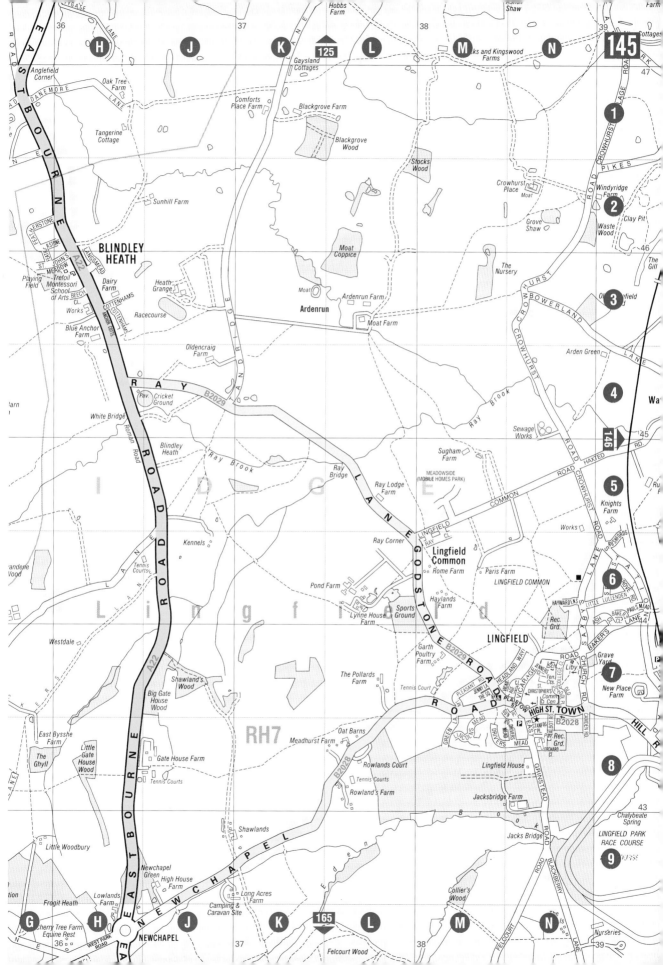

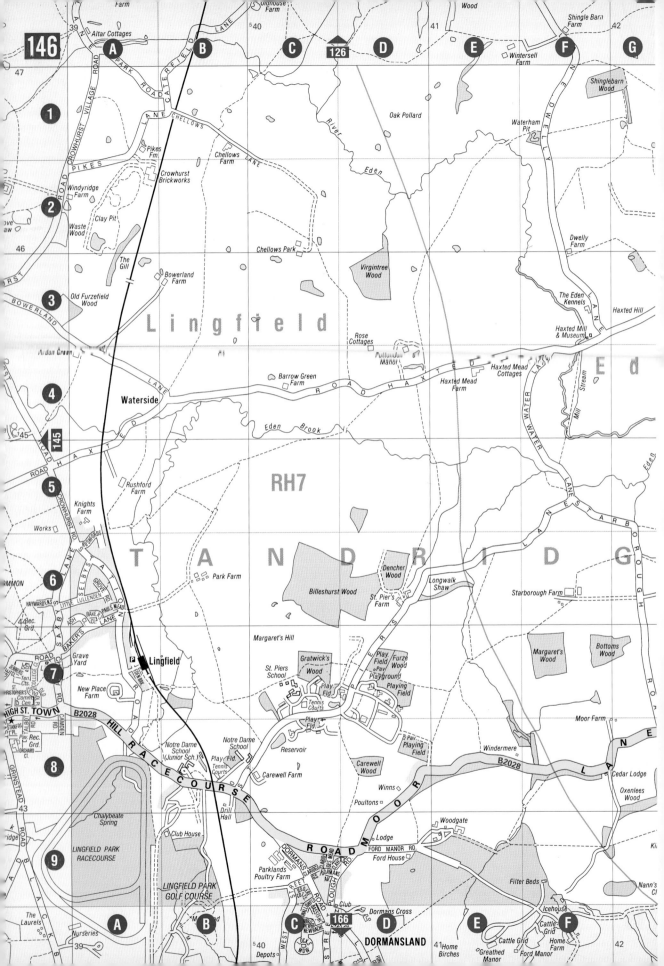

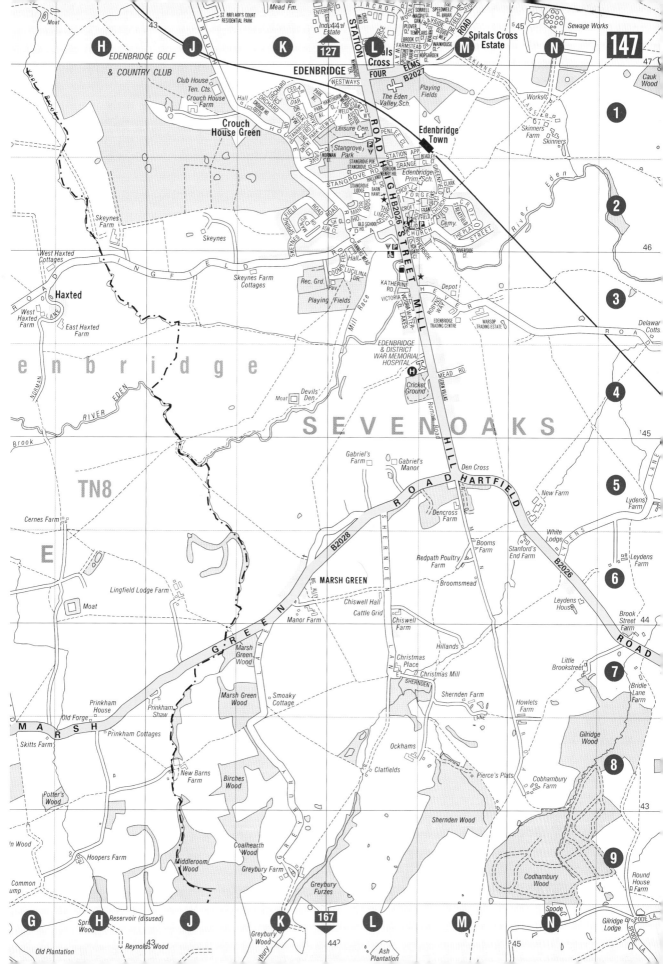

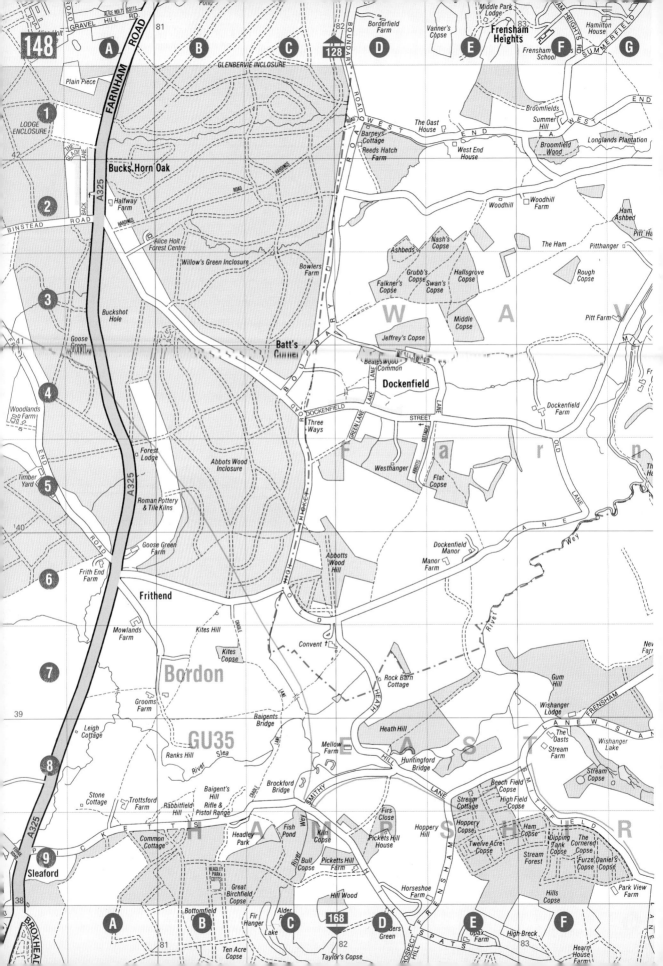

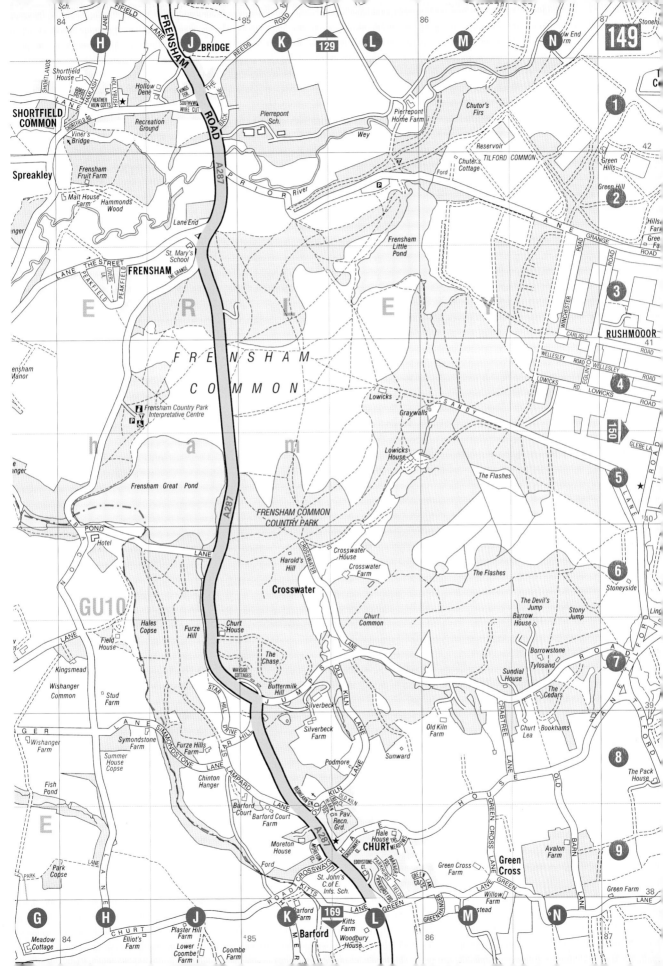

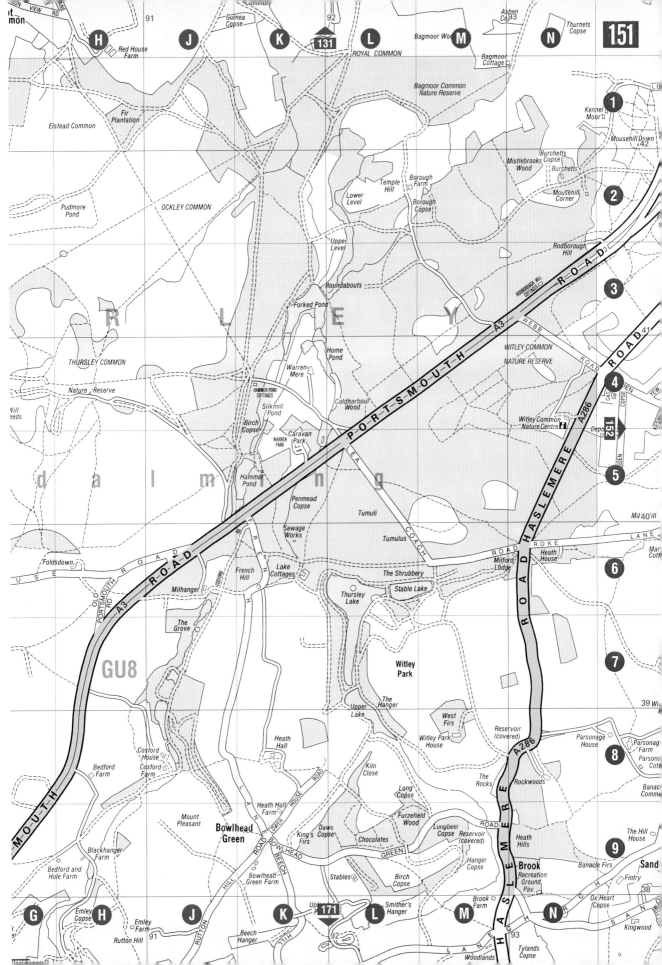

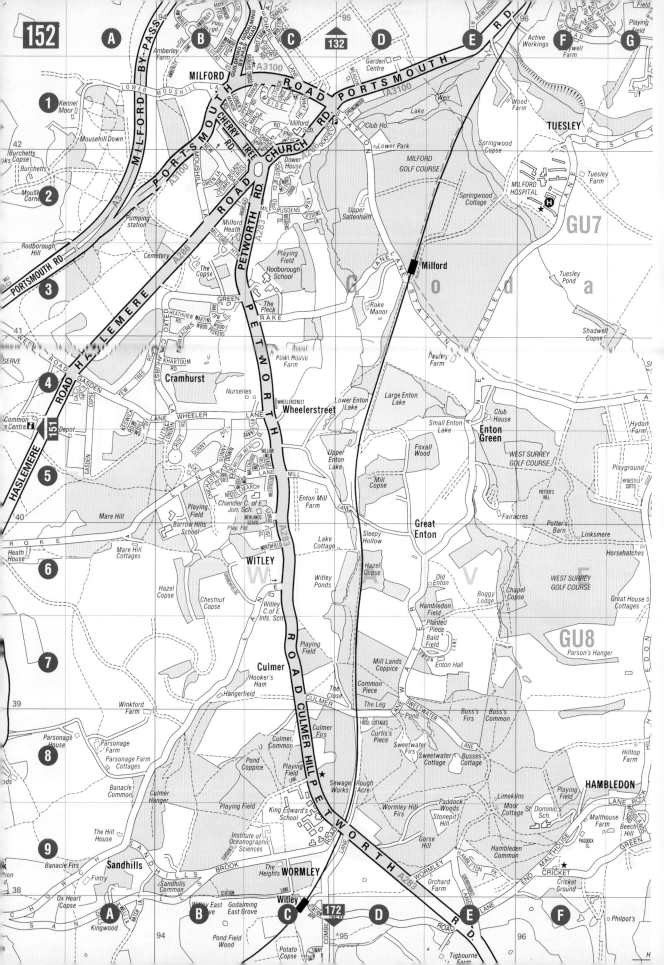

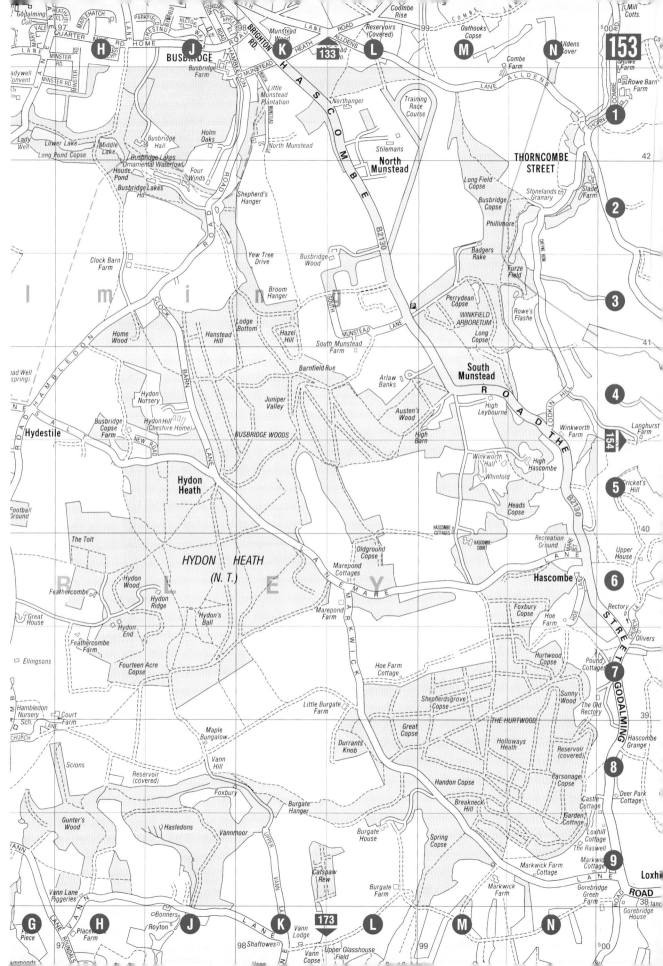

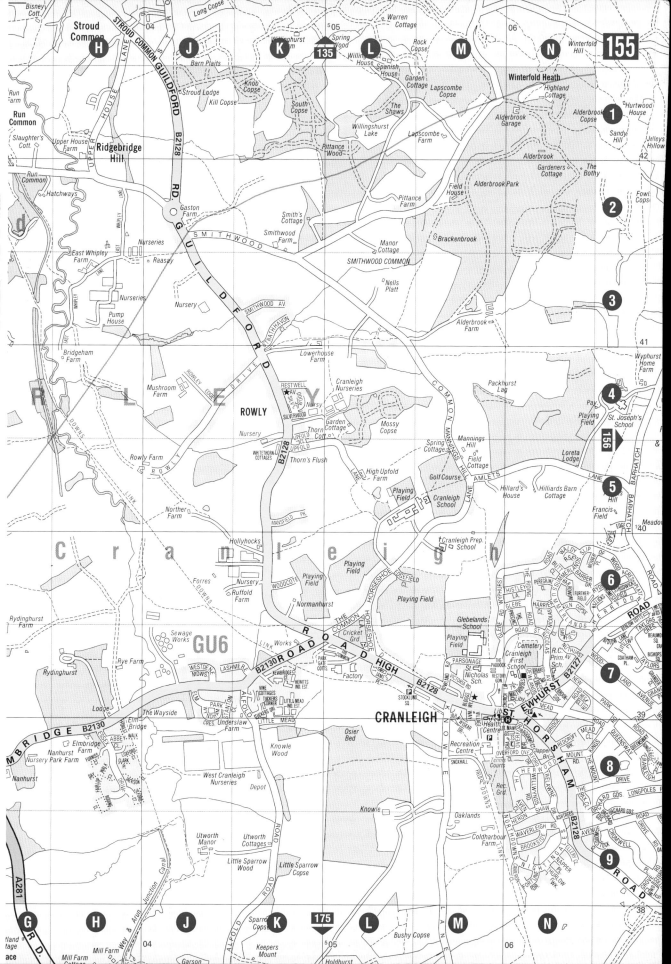

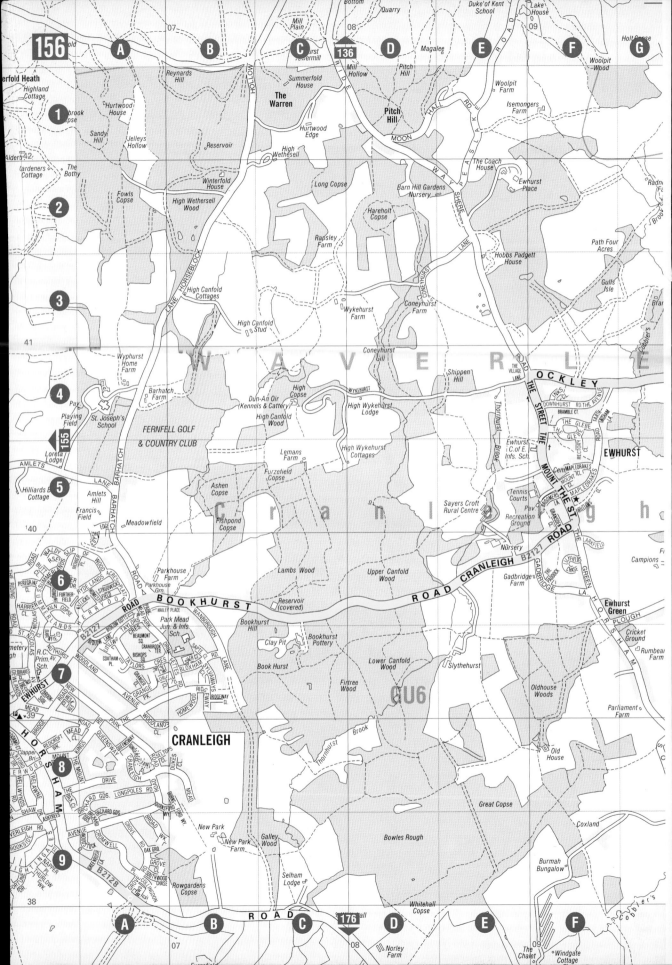

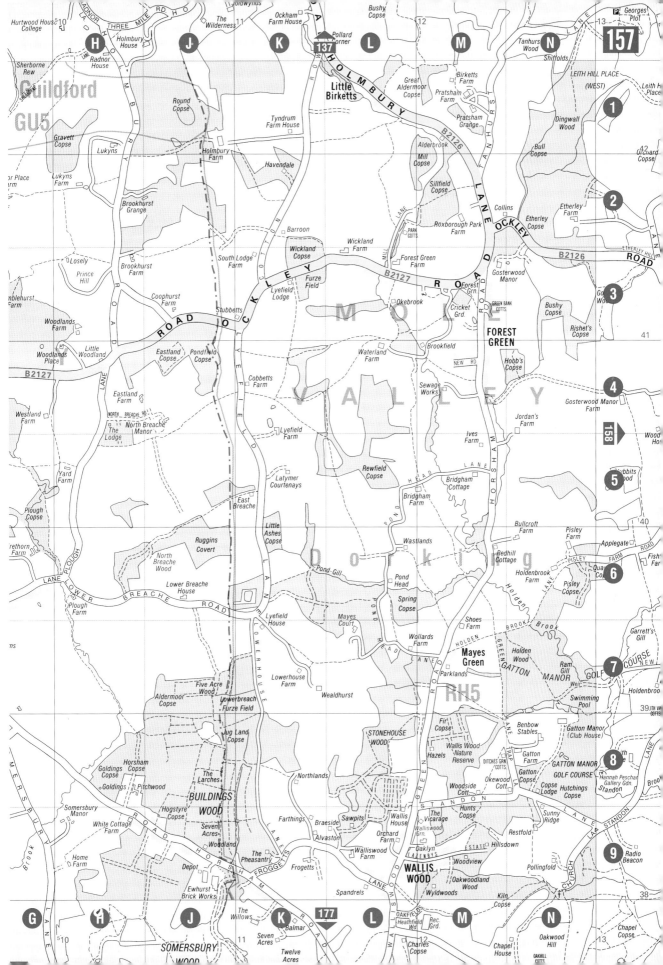

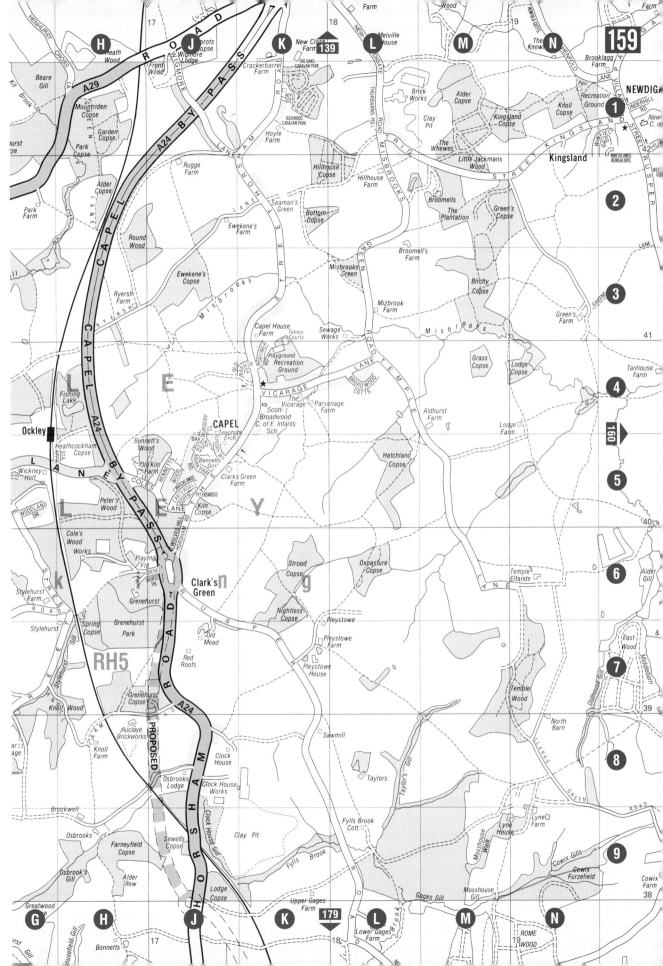

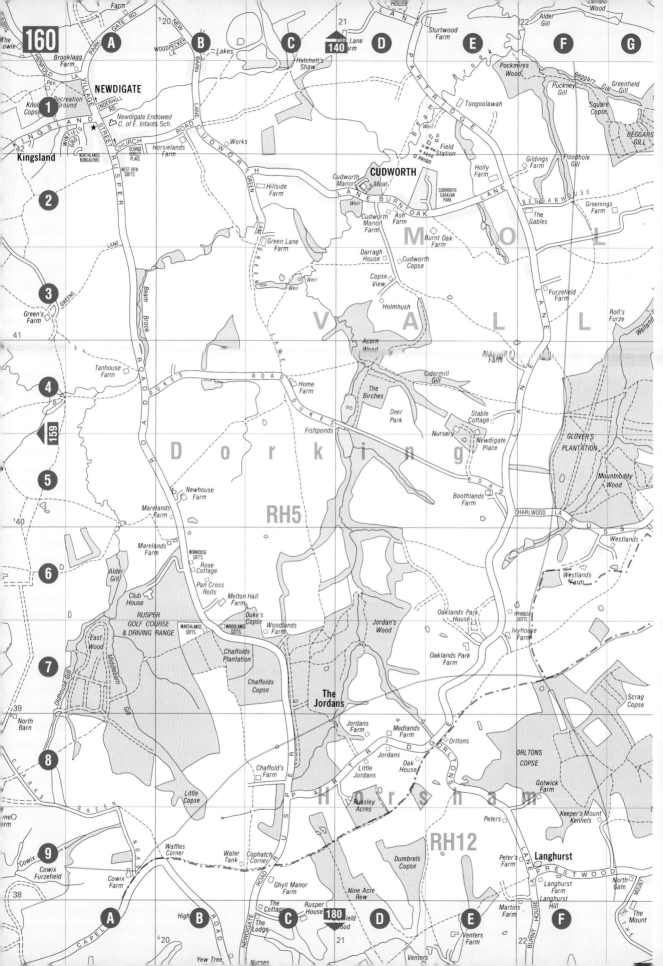

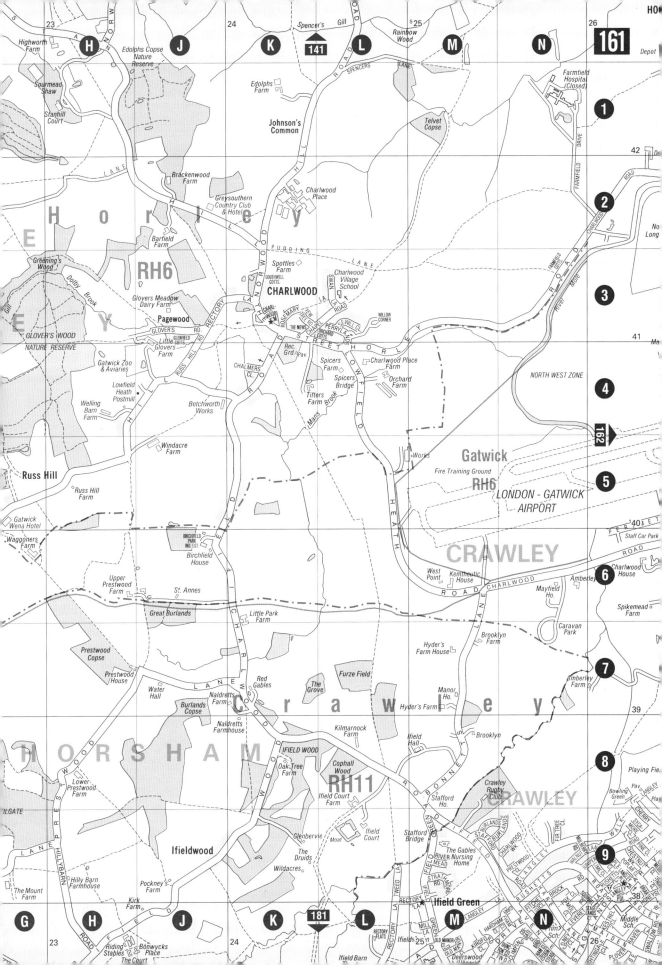

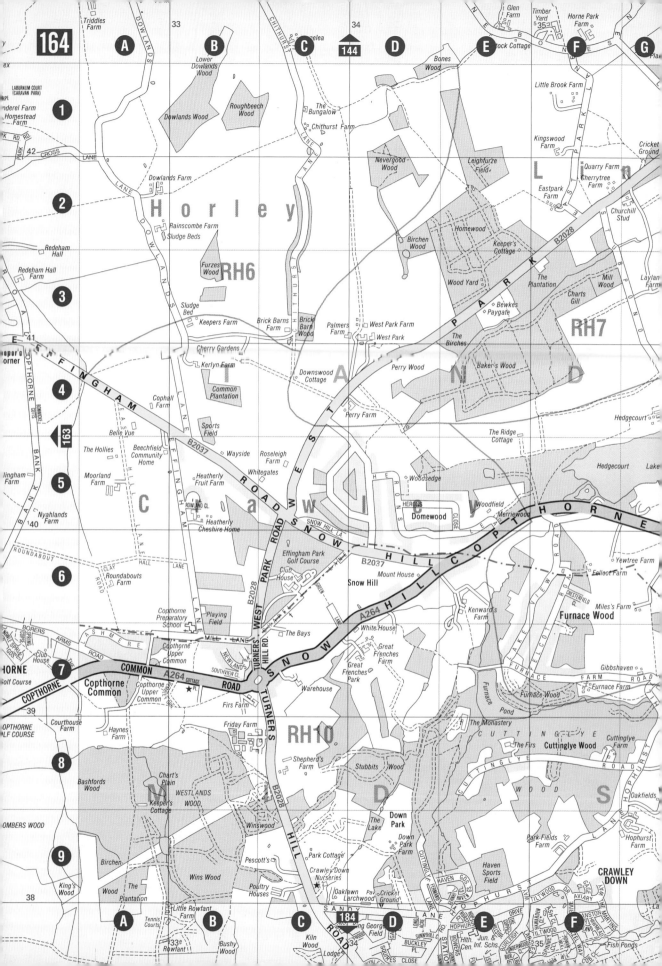

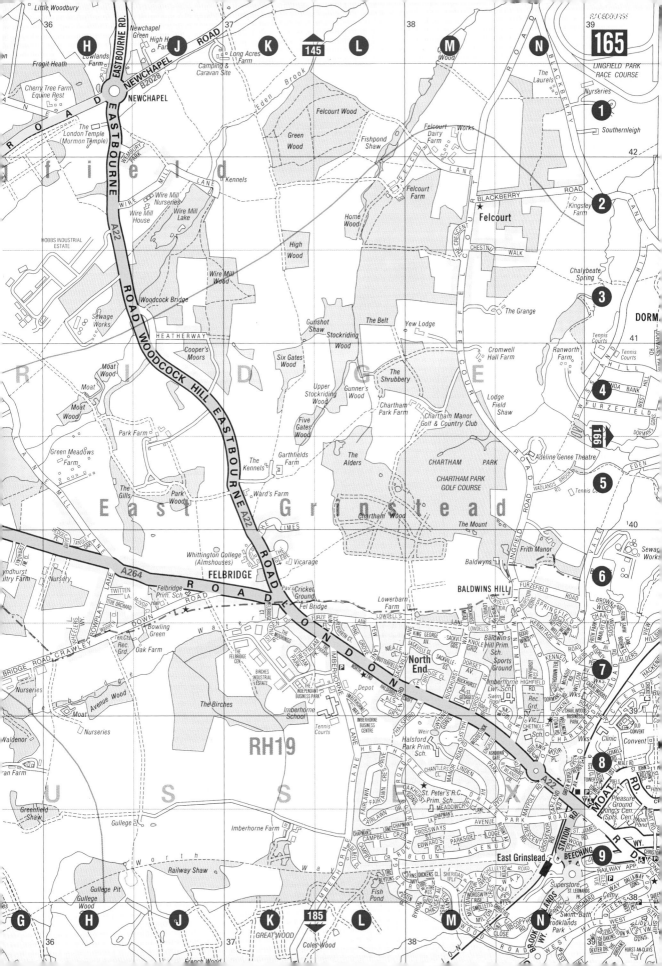

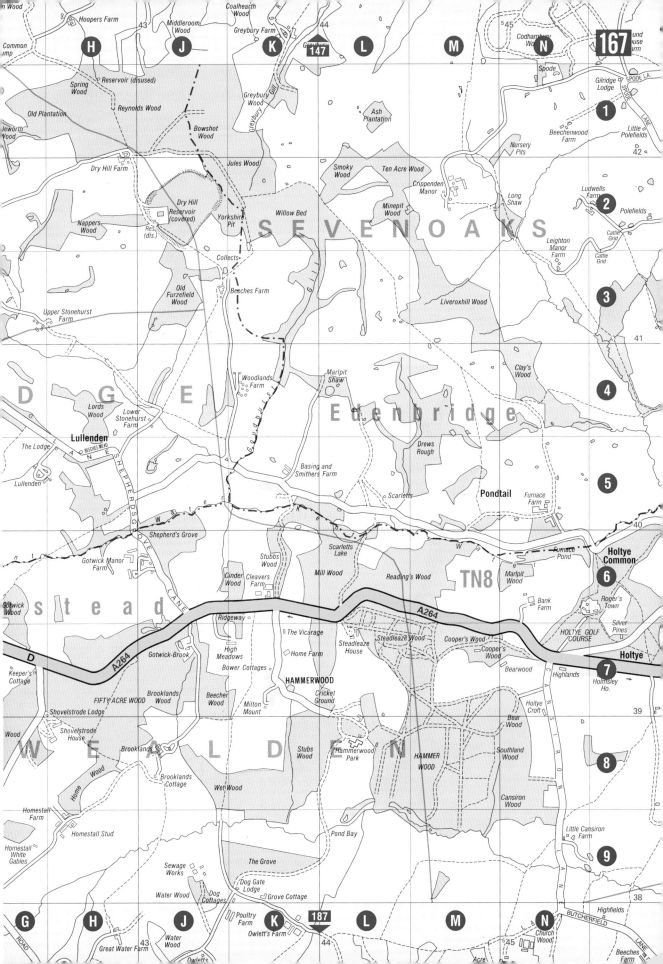

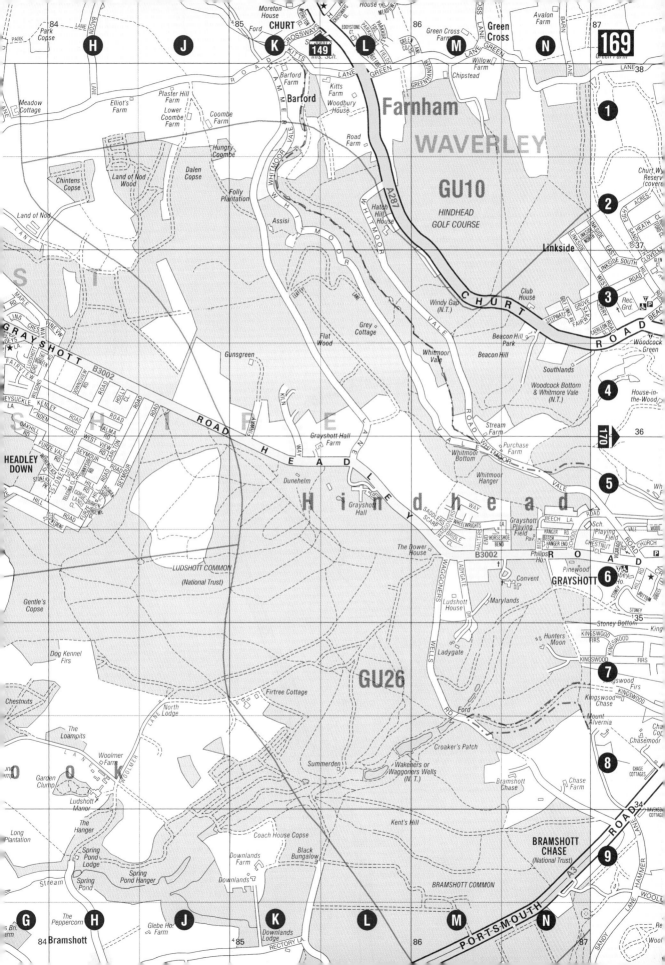

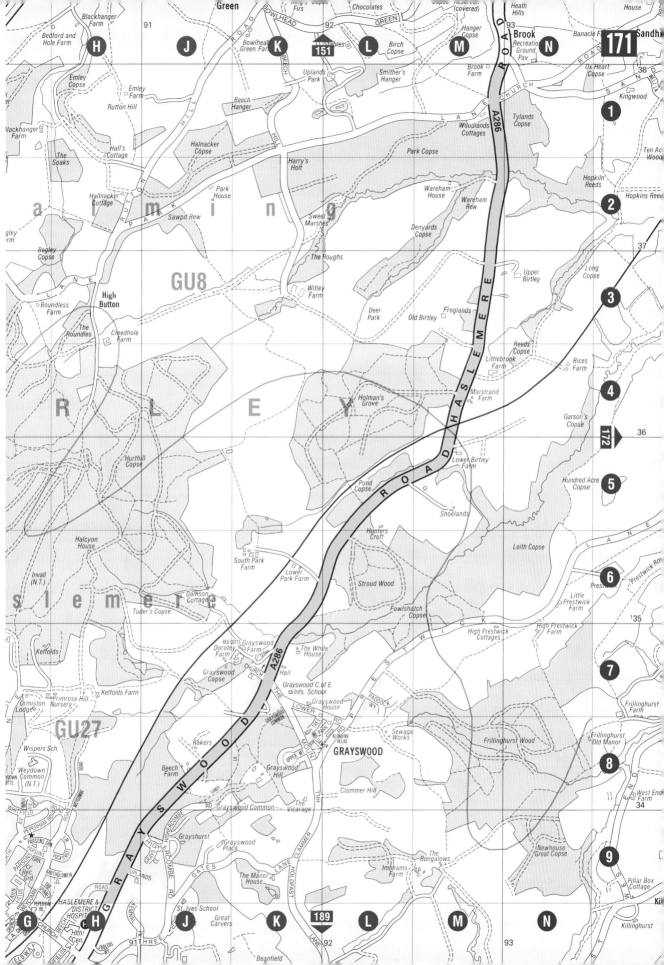

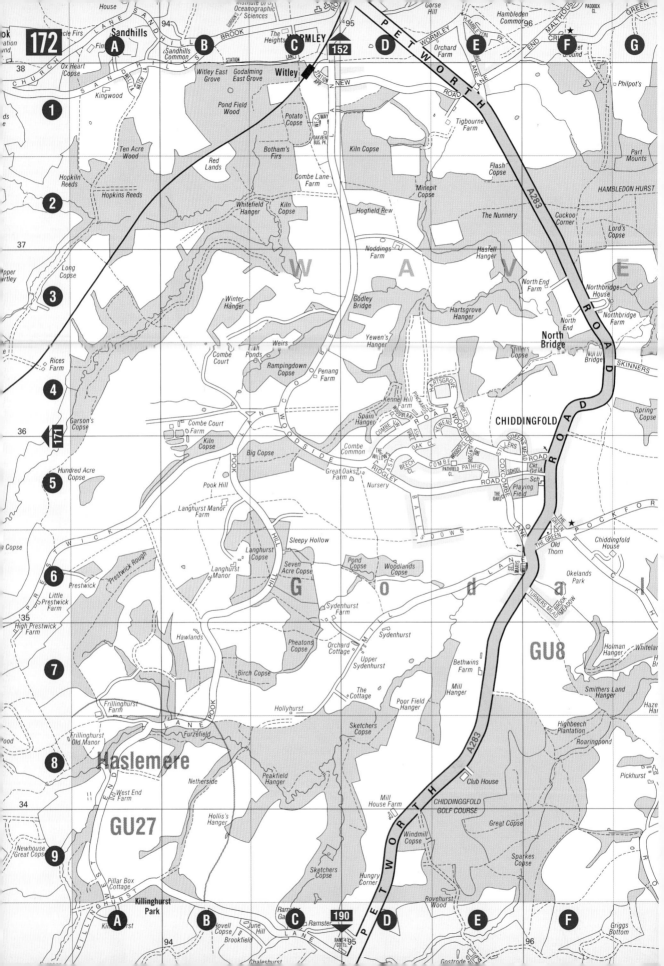

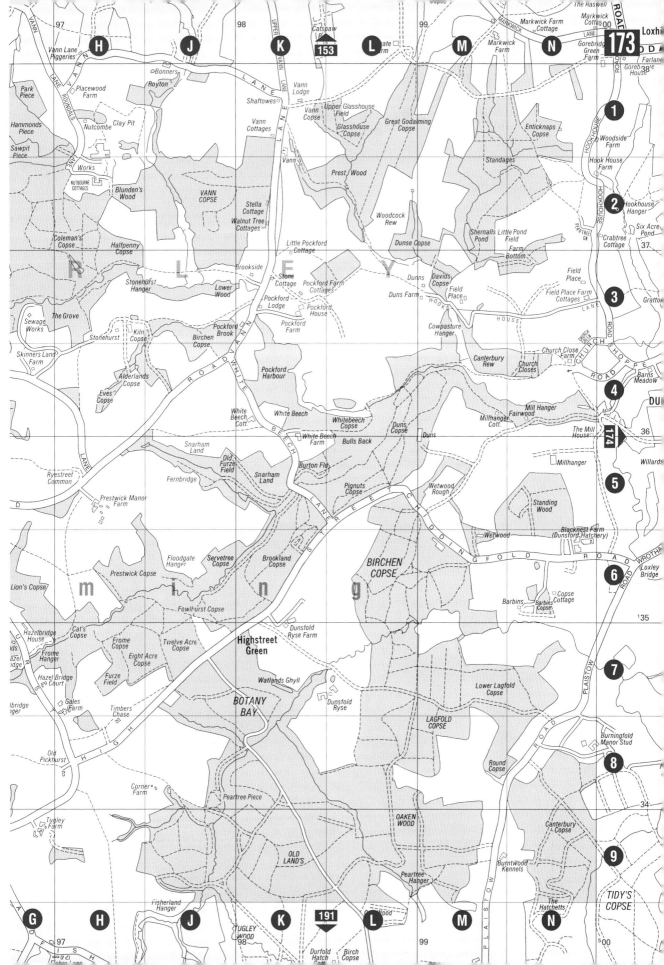

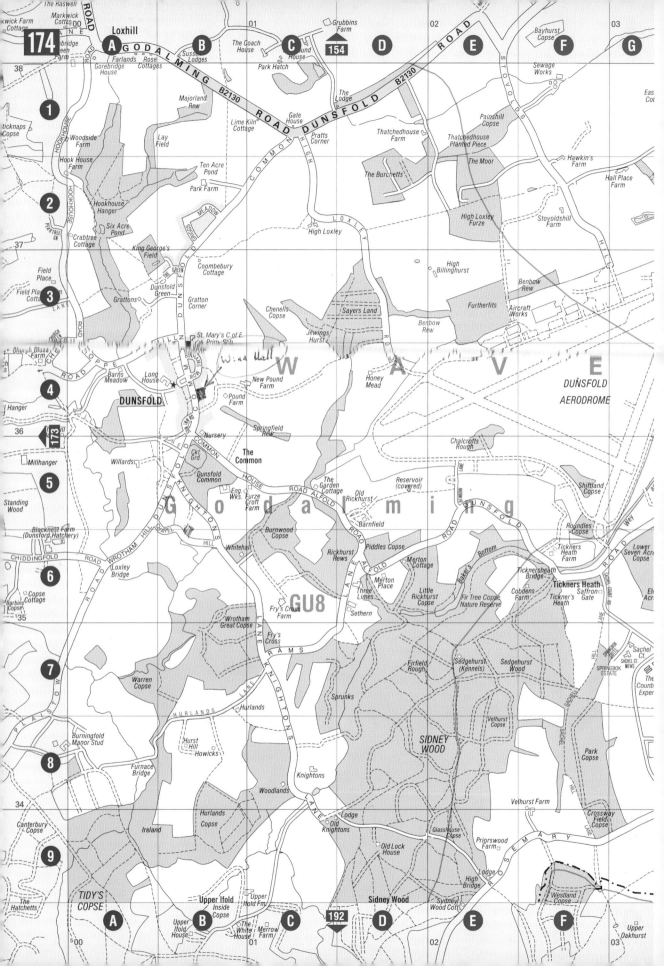

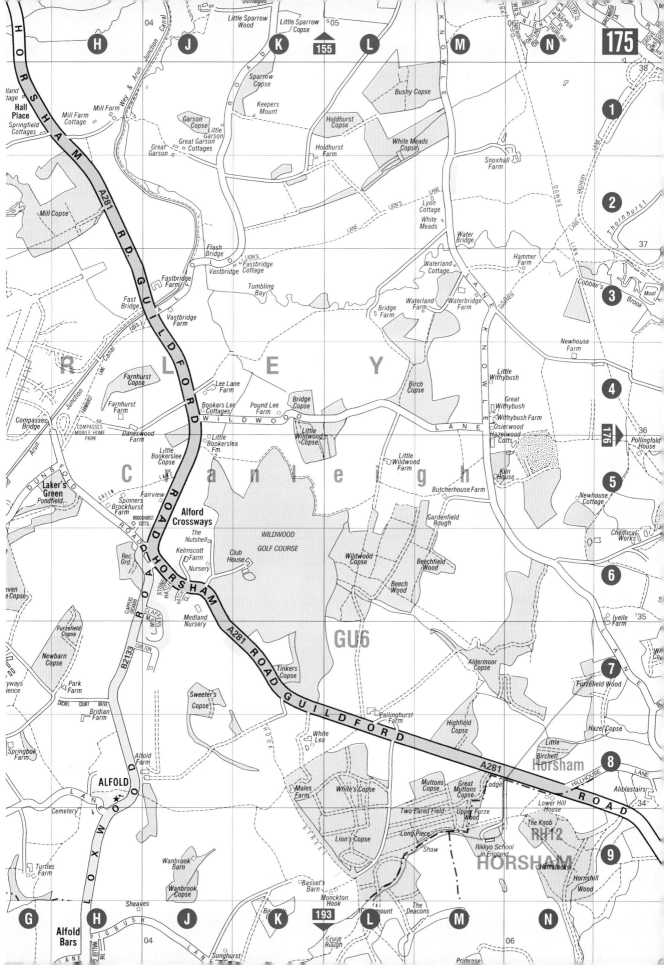

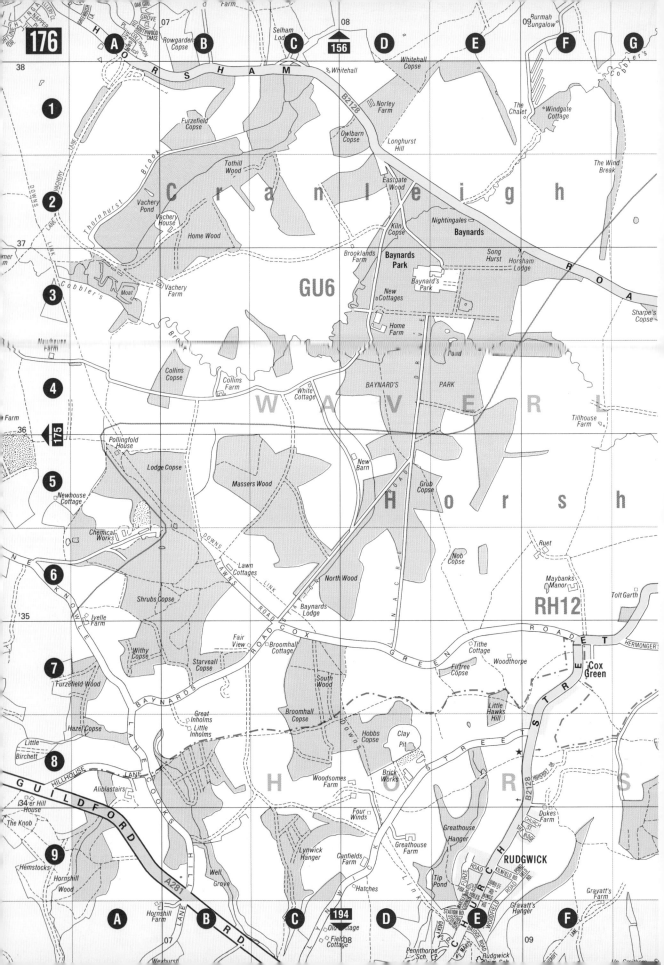

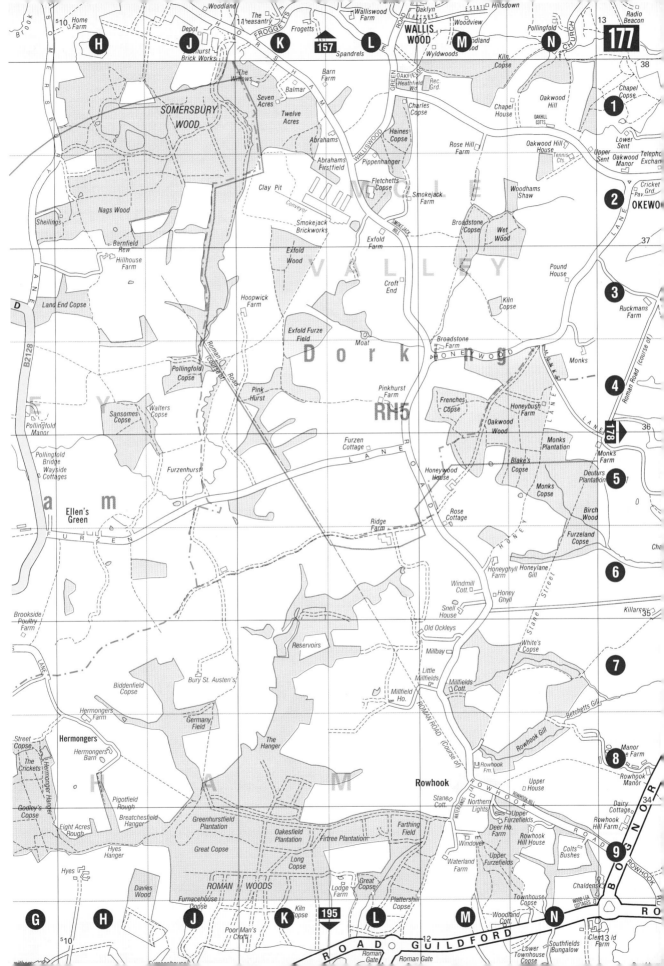

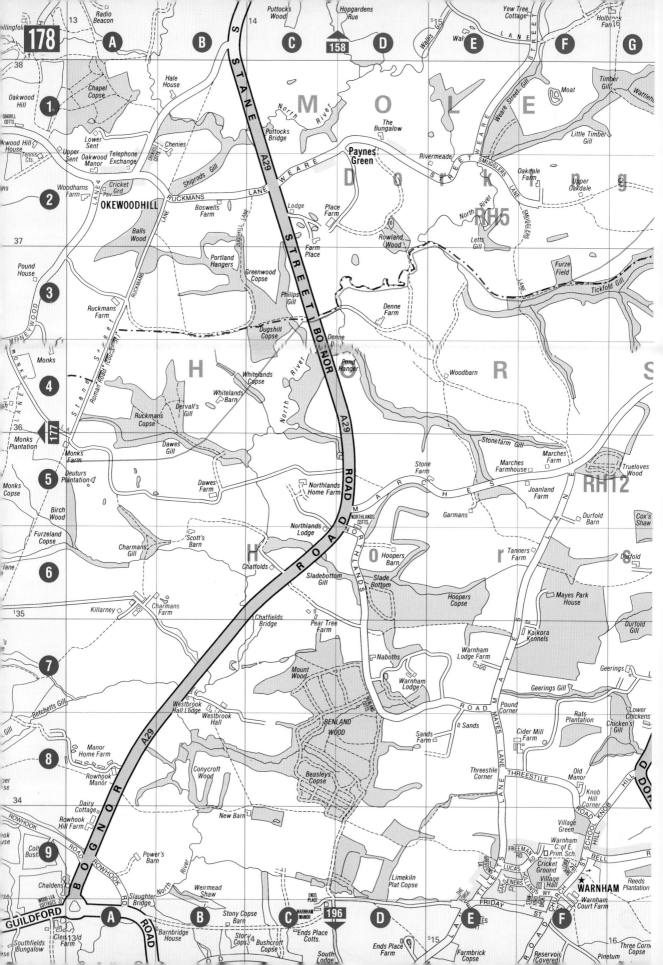

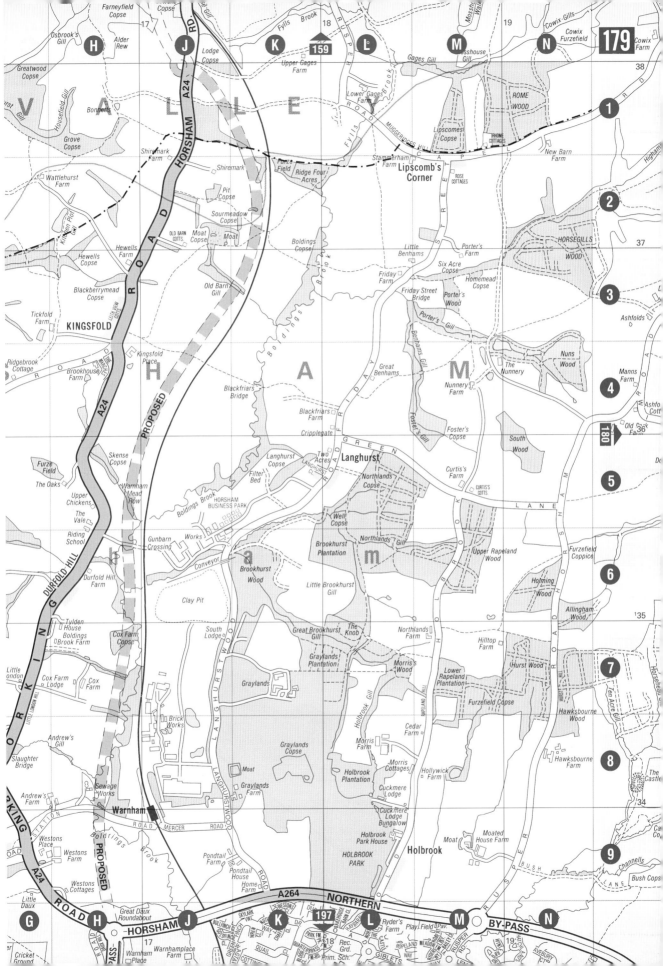

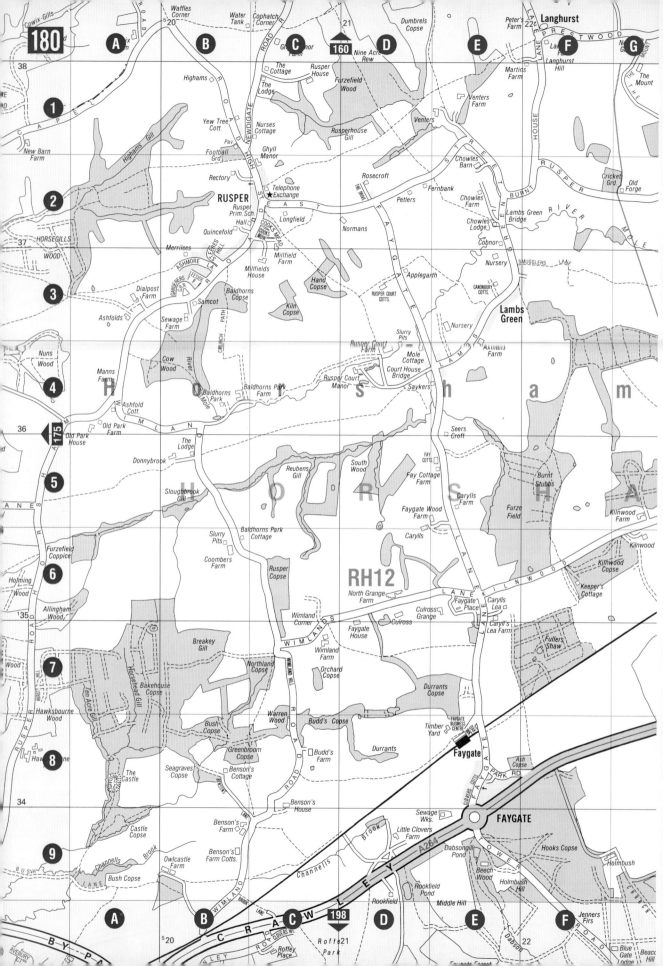

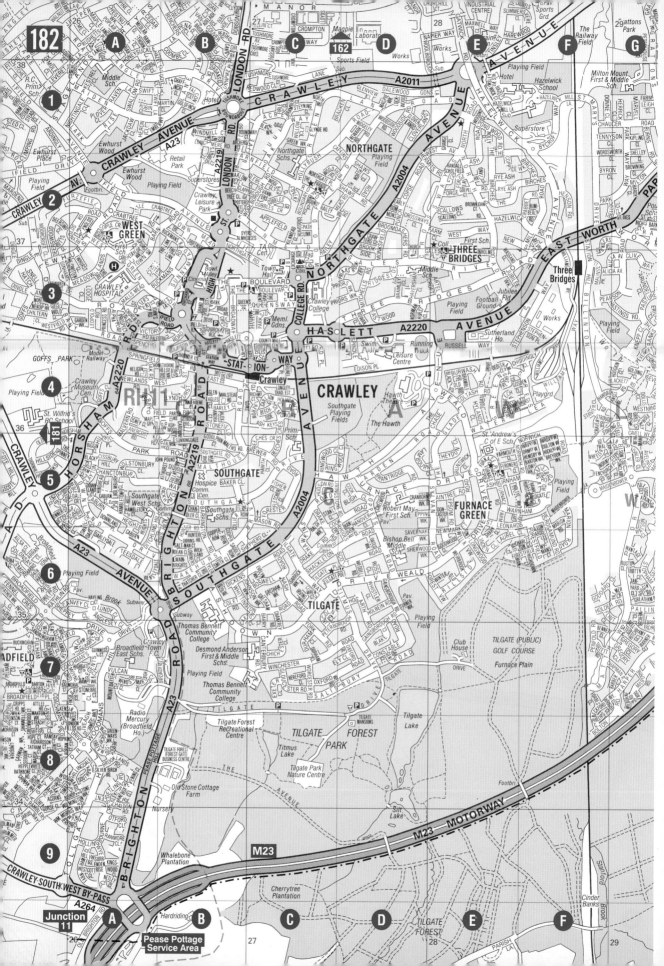

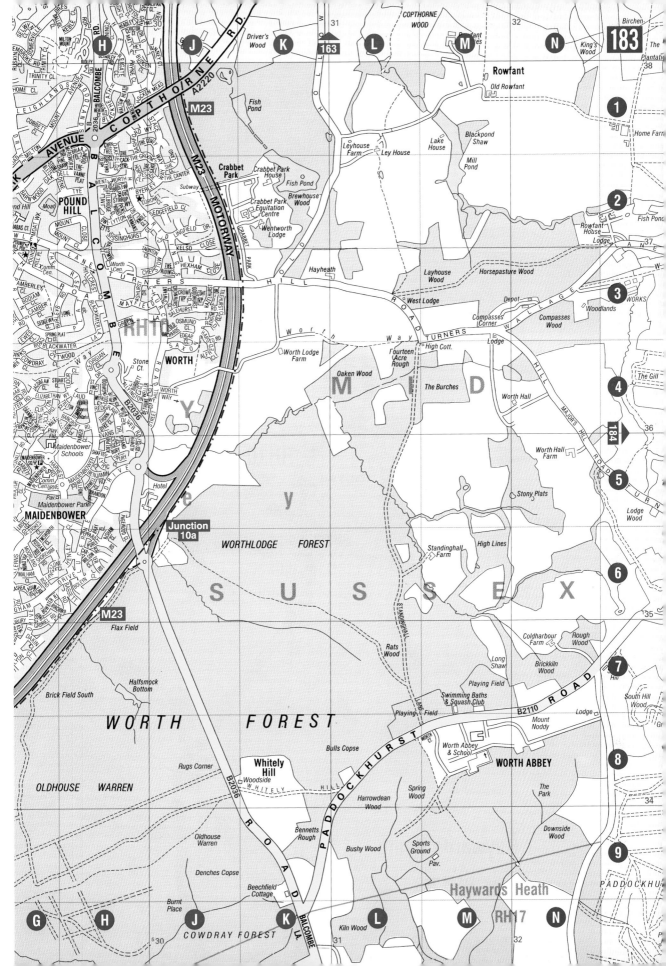

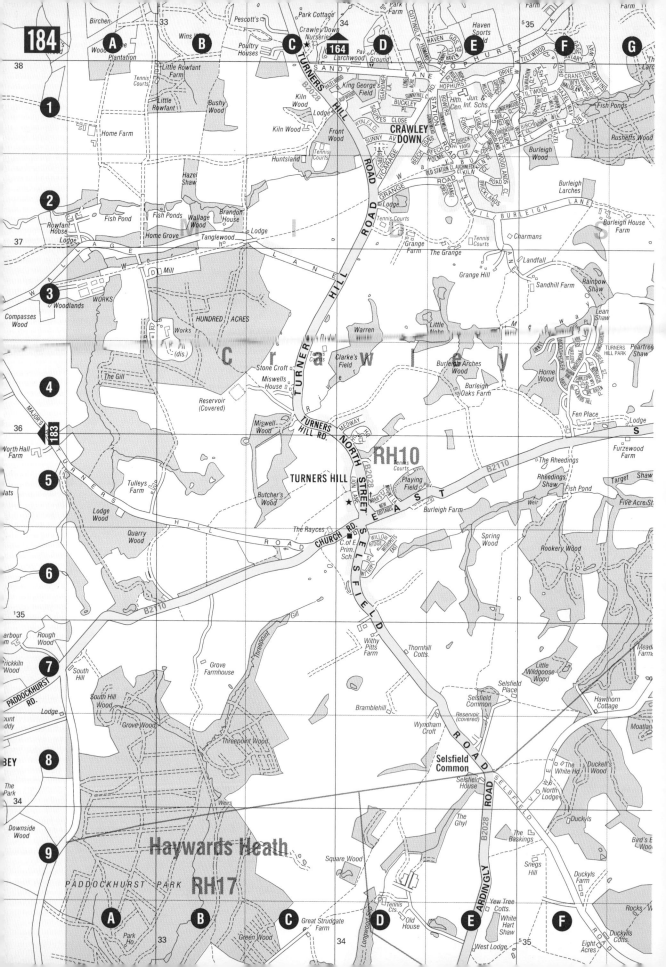

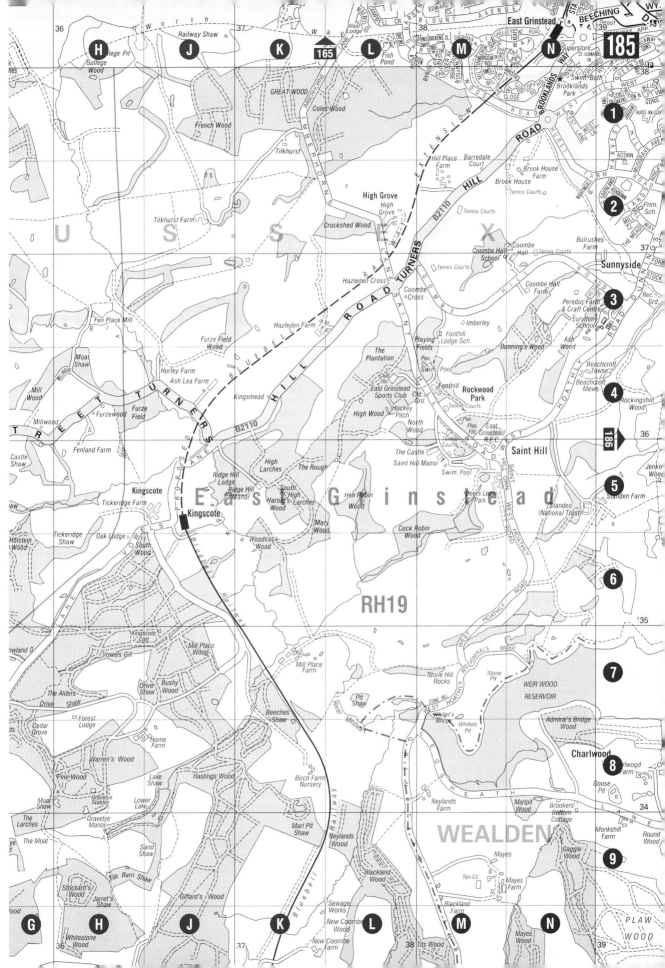

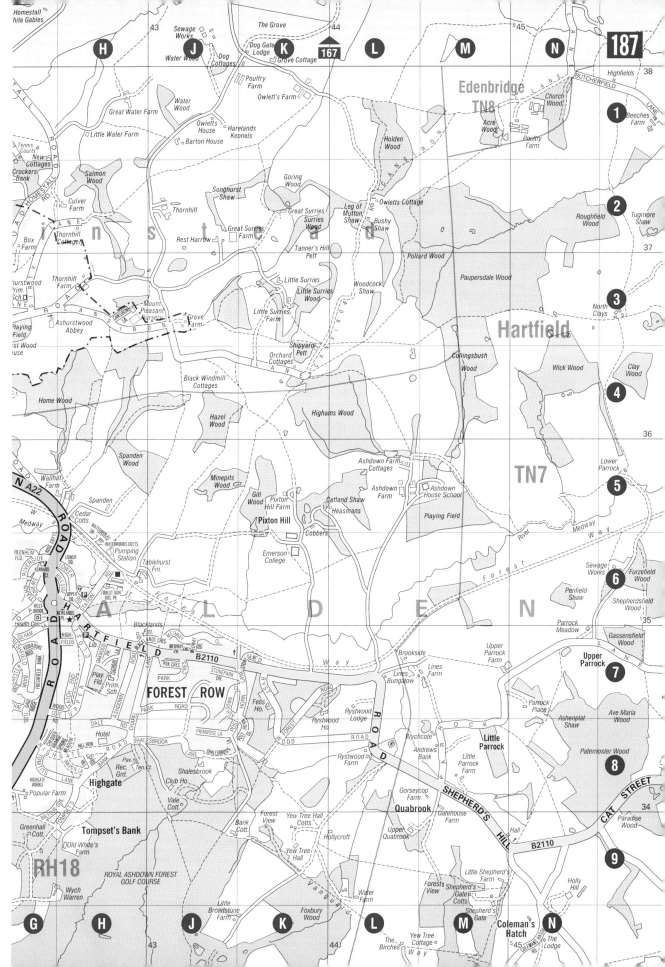

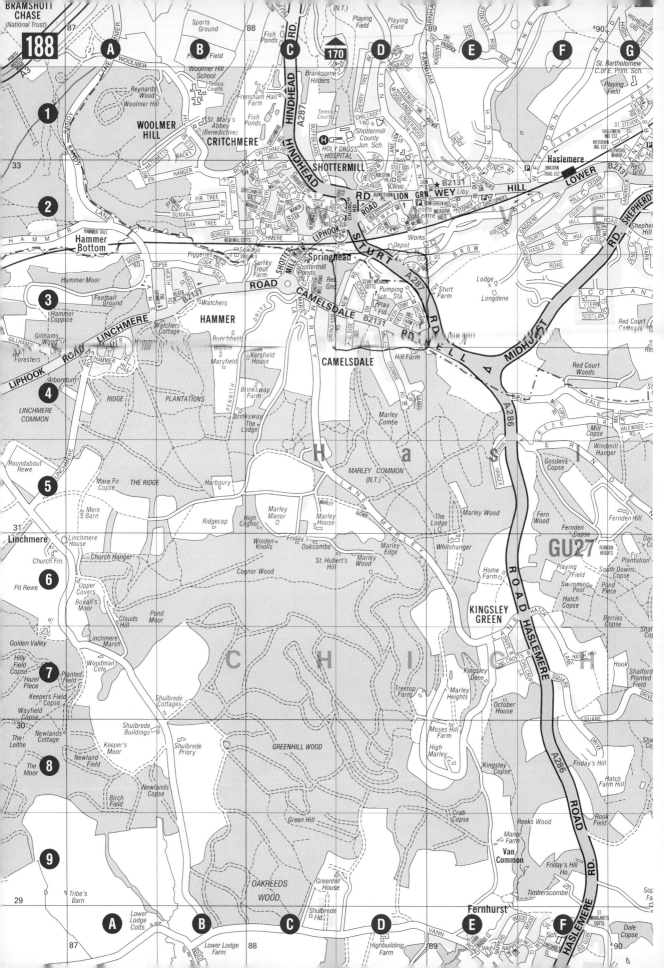

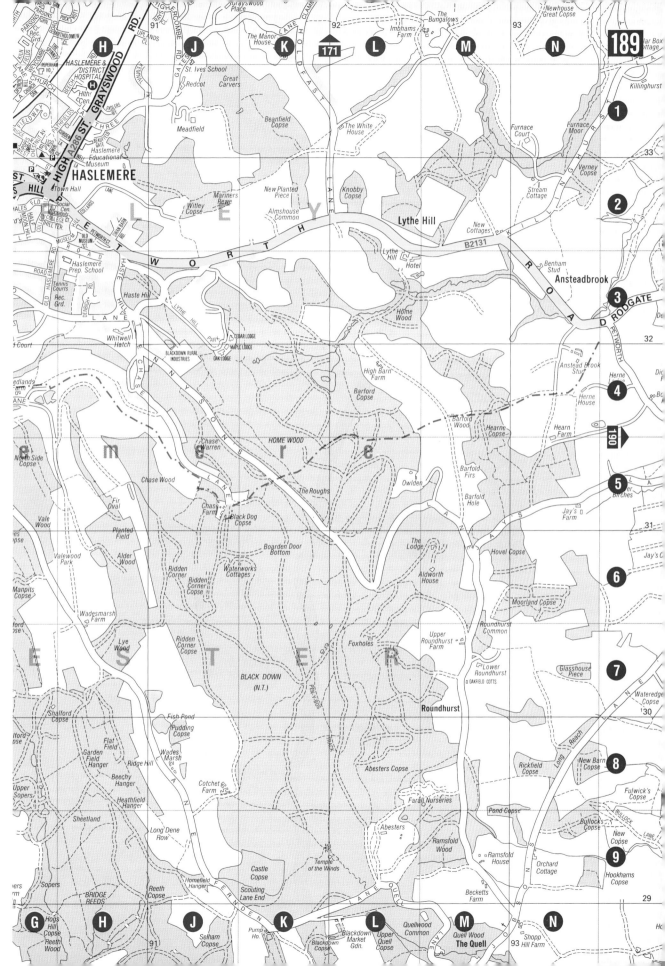

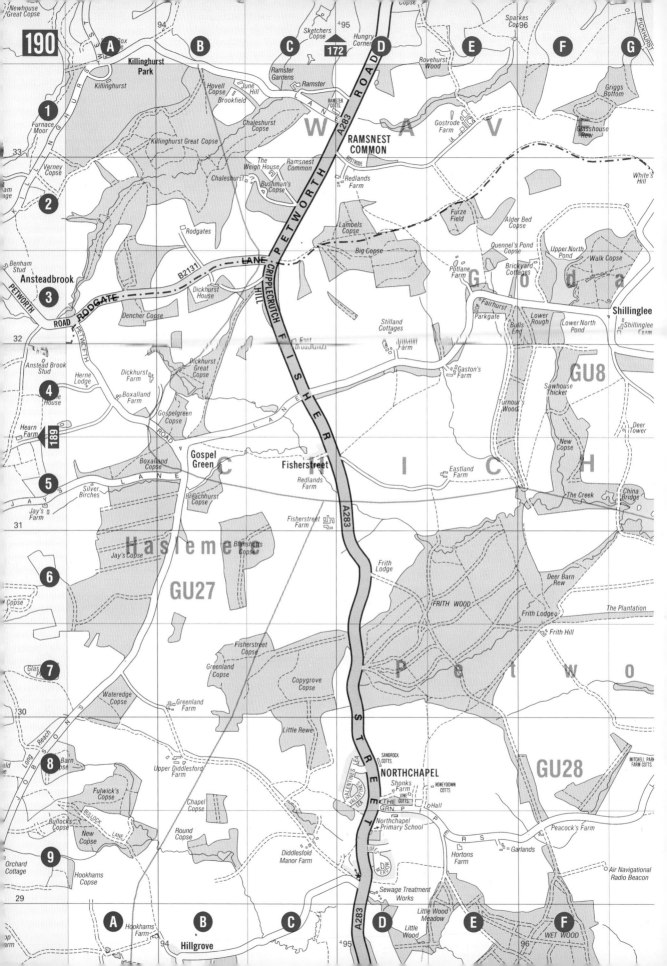

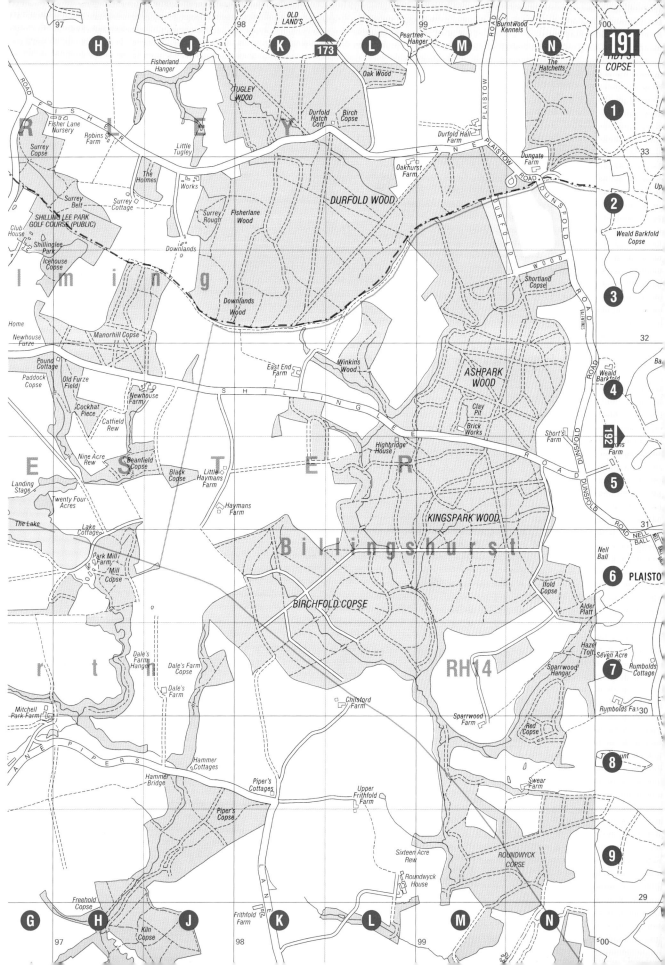

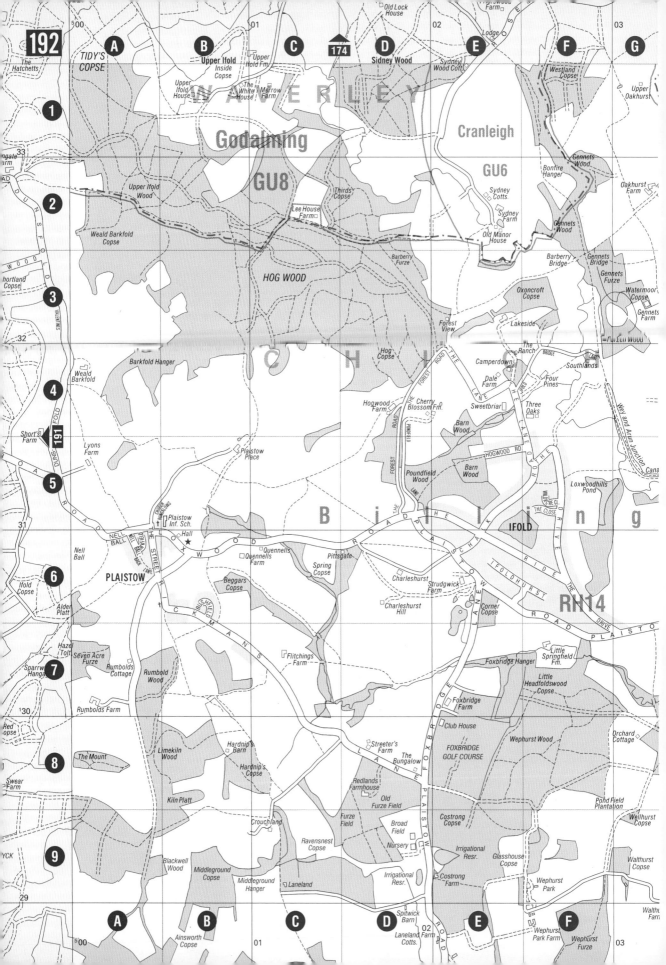

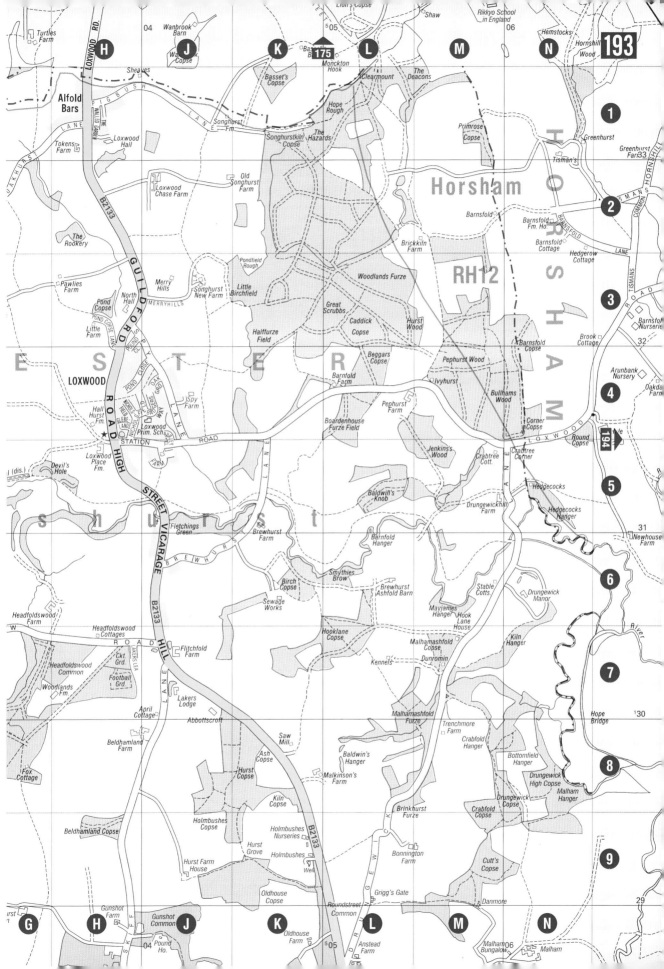

A   B   C   D   E   F   G

1   2   3   4   5   6   7   8   9

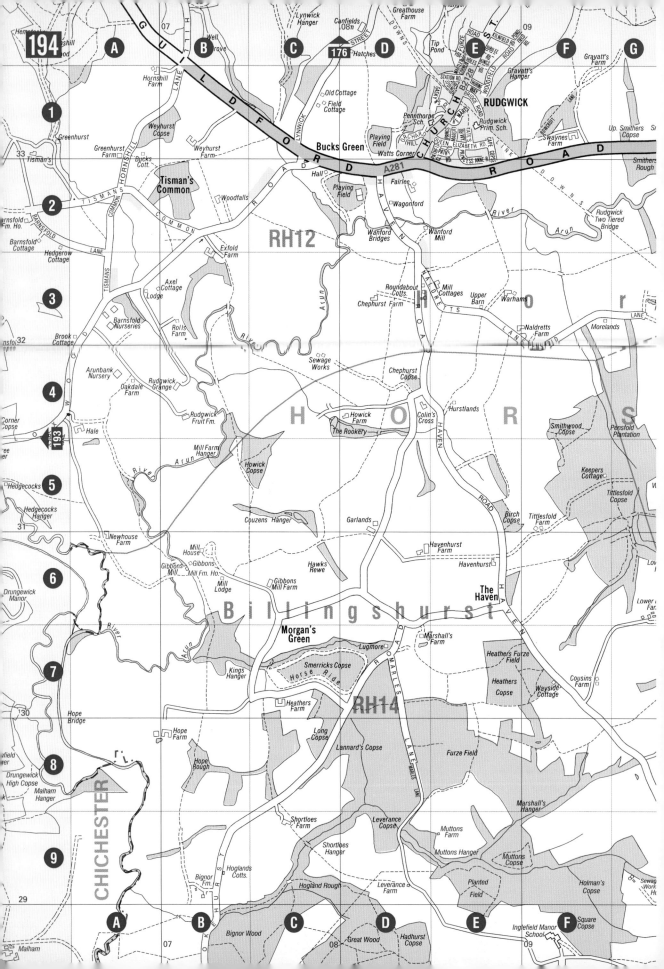

Hemstede
Hornshill Road
Hornshill Farm
Greenhurst
Tisman's
33
Greenhurst Farm
Bucks Cott.
Weyhurst Copse
Weyhurst Farm
Well Grove
Lynwick Hanger
Canfields
176
Hatches
STREET
Greathouse Farm
Tip Pond
Gravatt's Hanger
FURZE
KILNHILL FIELD RD
JUBILEE
KINGS
09
KNIGHTS HOLES
FOX
STATION RD.
Gravatt's Farm
RUDGWICK
Pennthorpe Sch.
Rudgwick Prim. Sch.
Swaynes Farm
Up. Smithers Copse
ST.
CHURCH
ROAD
B2128
BRIDGE
ORCHARD
QUEEN ELIZABETH RD
PRINCESS ANNE R.
LINK

Tisman's Common
Bucks Green
Hall
A281
Fairlee
Playing Field
Watts Corner
Woodfalls
Woodfalls
Playing Field
Wagonford
Wanford Bridges
Wanford Mill
River
Arun
Rudgwick Two Tiered Bridge
Smithers Rough

RH 12
Barnsfold Fm. Ho.
Barnsfold Cottage
Hedgerow Cottage
Exfold Farm
Axel Cottage
Lodge
Roundabout Cotts.
Chephurst Farm
Mill Cottages
Upper Barn
Warhams
Naldretts Farm
Morelands
HO
NALDRETTS ROAD
LANE
R

Barnsfold Nurseries
Rolls Farm
Brook Cottage
Arunbank Nursery
Oakdale Farm
Rudgwick Grange
Rudgwick Fruit Fm.
Sewage Works
Chephurst Copse
HO
TISMANS
COMMON
HORNSHILL LANE
GUILDFORD ROAD
LYNWICK ROAD
HAVEN ROAD

193
Hale
Mill Farm Hanger
Howick Farm
The Rookery
Colin's Cross
Hurstlands
Smithwood Copse
Pensfold Plantation
Keepers Cottage
Tittlesfold Copse

Hedgecocks
Hedgecocks Hanger
31
Howick Copse
Couzens Hanger
Garlands
Birch Copse
Tittlesfold Farm

Drungewick Manor
Newhouse Farm
Mill House
Gibbons Mill
Mill Fm. Ho.
Gibbons
Mill Lodge
Gibbons Mill Farm
Hawks Rewe
Havenhurst Farm
Havenhurst
ROAD
HAVEN

Billingshurst
Morgan's Green
Kings Hanger
Smerricks Copse
Horse Ride
Lugmore
Marshall's Farm
The Haven
Heathers Furze Field
Heathers Copse
Wayside Cottage
Cousins Farm

30
Hope Bridge
Heathers Farm
RH 14
MARLES LANE
ROAD

Drungewick High Copse
Malham Hanger
Hope Farm
Hope Rough
Long Copse
Lannard's Copse
Furze Field
Marshall's Hanger

CHICHESTER
29
Shortloes Farm
Shortloes Hanger
Leverance Copse
Muttons Farm
Muttons Hanger
Muttons Copse

Bignor Fm.
Hoglands Cotts.
Hogland Rough
Leverance Farm
Planted Field
Holman's Copse
Sewage Works

Malham
07
A   B   Bignor Wood   C   08   Great Wood   D   Hadhurst Copse   E   Inglefield Manor School   F   Square Copse   09

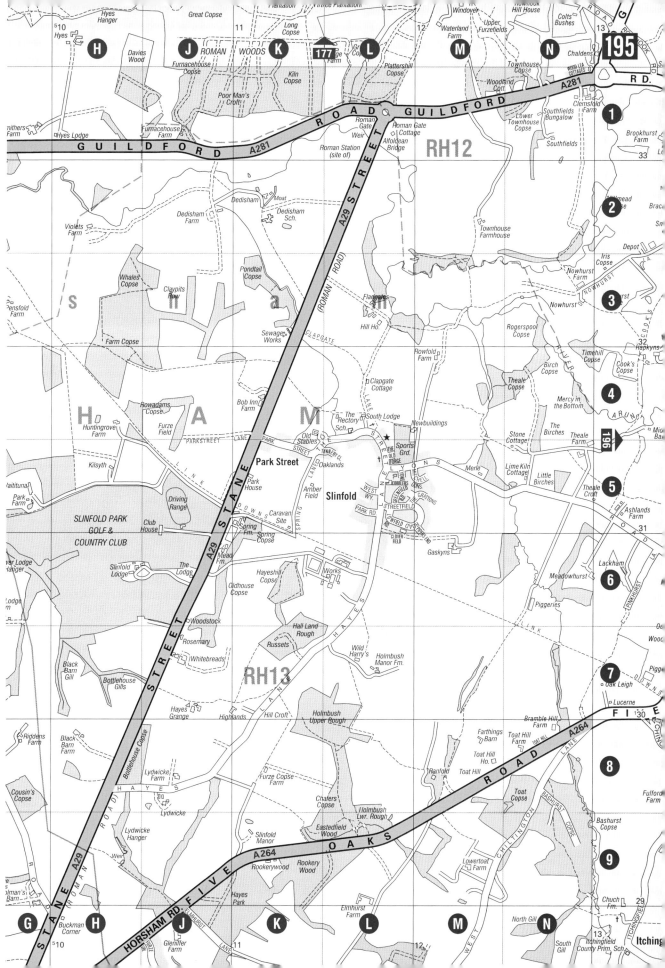

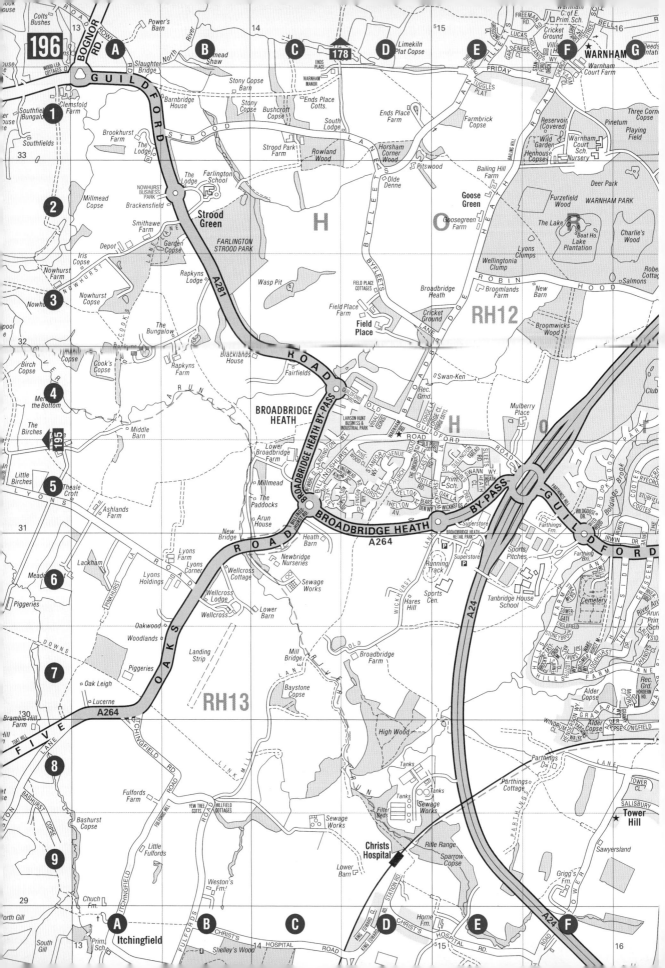

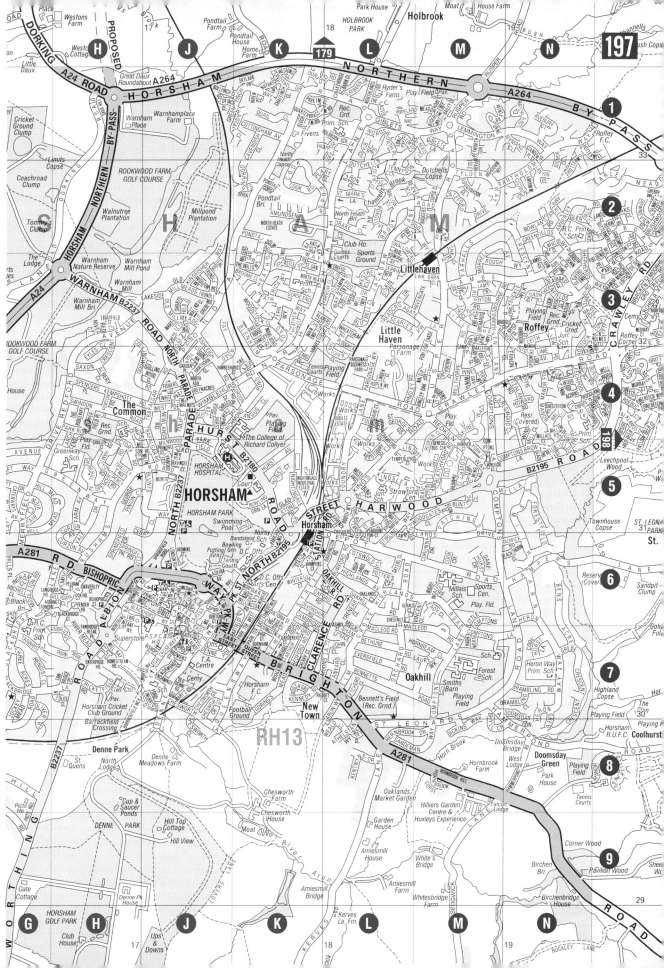

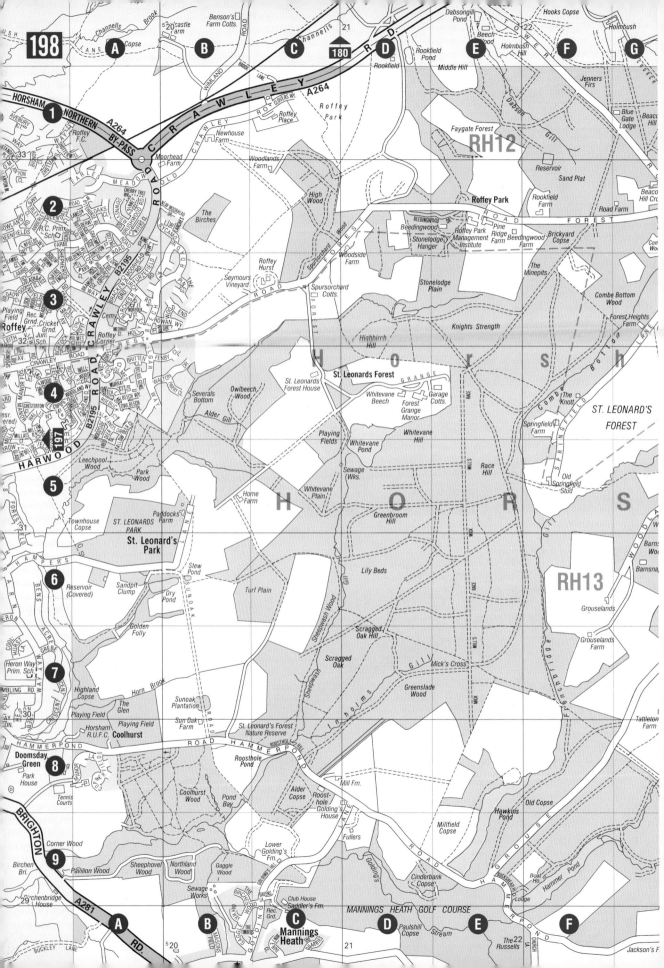

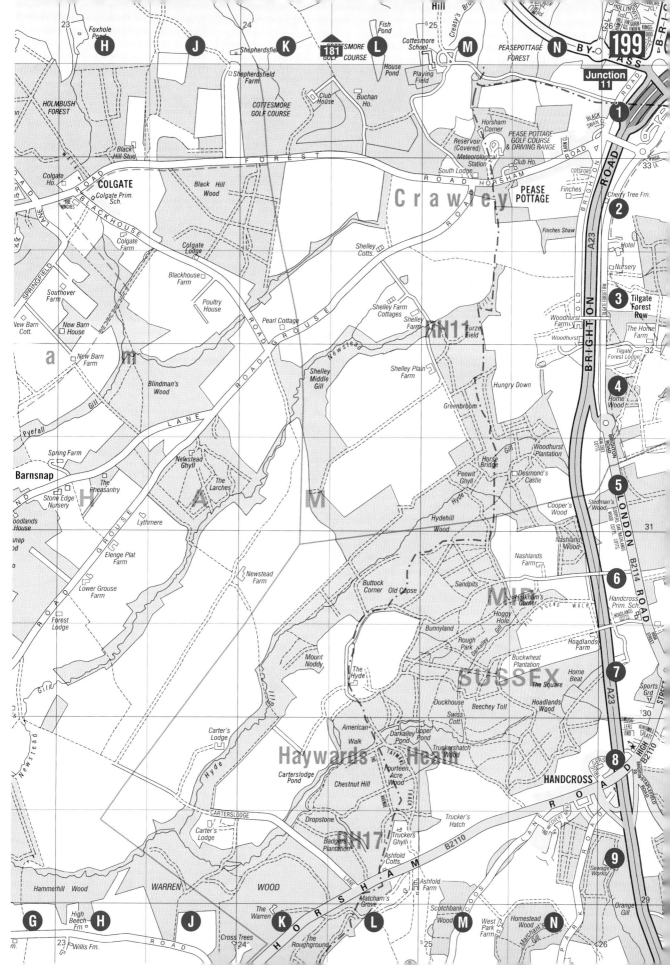

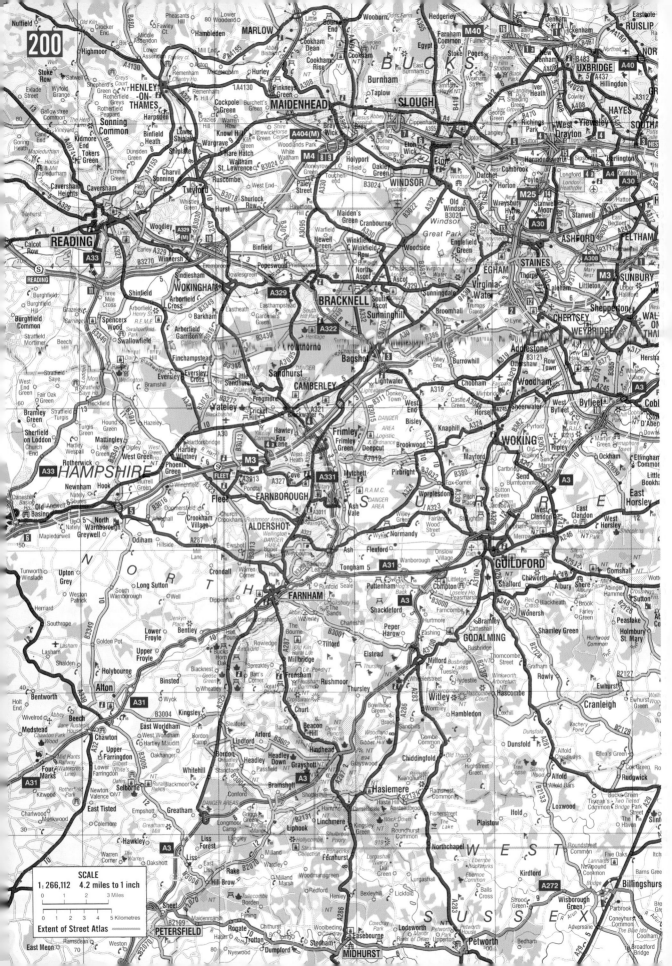

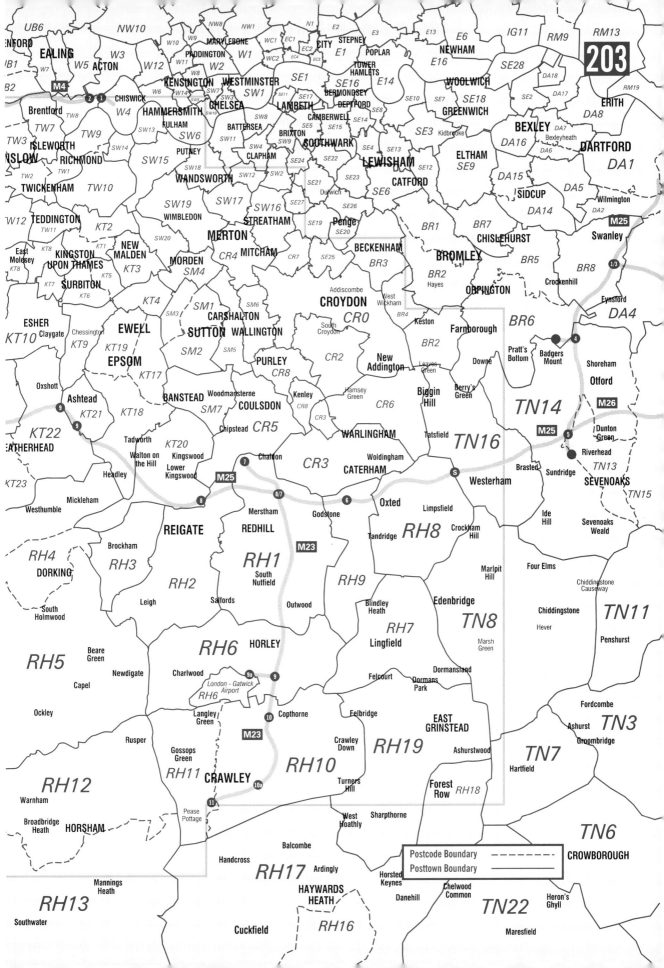

AREAS COVERED BY THIS ATLAS

with their map square reference

Names in this index shown in CAPITAL LETTERS, followed by their Postcode area are Postal addresses (Postal Districts in London)

Areas covered by this atlas

INDEX TO STREETS

Including Industrial Estates, Junction Names and a selection of Subsidiary Addresses

HOW TO USE THIS INDEX

1. Each street name is followed by its Postal District (or, if outside the London Postal Districts, by its Posttown or Postal Locality), and then by its map reference; e.g. Abbey Dri. *Stai* —3L **37** is in the Staines Posttown and is found in square 3L on page **37**. The page number being shown in bold type.
A strict alphabetical order is followed in which Av., Rd., St. etc. (though abbreviated) are read in full and as part of the street name; e.g. Abbots La. appears after Abbotsford Clo. but before Abbotsleigh Clo.

2. Streets and a selection of Subsidiary names not shown on the Maps, appear in this index in *Italics* with the thoroughfare to which it is connected shown in brackets; e.g. *Abbey Pde. SW19 —8A* ***28*** *(off Merton High St.)*

3. With the now general usage of Postcodes for addressing mail, it is not recommended that this index be used for such a purpose.

GENERAL ABBREVIATIONS

All : Alley
App : Approach
Arc : Arcade
Av : Avenue
Bk : Back
Boulevd : Boulevard
Bri : Bridge
B'way : Broadway
Bldgs : Buildings
Bus : Business
Cvn : Caravan
Cen : Centre
Chu : Church
Chyd : Churchyard
Circ : Circle
Cir : Circus
Clo : Close
Comn : Common
Cotts : Cottages
Ct : Court
Cres : Crescent
Dri : Drive
E : East
Embkmt : Embankment
Est : Estate
Gdns : Gardens
Ga : Gate
Gt : Great
Grn : Green
Gro : Grove
Ho : House
Ind : Industrial
Junct : Junction
La : Lane
Lit : Little
Lwr : Lower
Mnr : Manor
Mans : Mansions
Mkt : Market
M : Mews
Mt : Mount
N : North
Pal : Palace
Pde : Parade
Pk : Park
Pas : Passage
Pl : Place
Quad : Quadrant
Rd : Road
Shop : Shopping
S : South
Sq : Square
Sta : Station
St : Street
Ter : Terrace
Trad : Trading
Up : Upper
Vs : Villas
Wlk : Walk
W : West
Yd : Yard

POSTTOWN AND POSTAL LOCALITY ABBREVIATIONS

Ab C : Abinger Common
Ab H : Abinger Hammer
Add : Addlestone
Alb : Albury
Ald : Aldbury
Alder : Aldershot
Alf : Alfold
Adgly : Ardingly
Asc : Ascot
Ash : Ash
Ashf : Ashford
Asht : Ashtead
Ash V : Ash Vale
Ash W : Ashurst Wood
Bad L : Badshot Lea
Bag : Bagshot
Bans : Banstead
B'ham : Barkham
Bar G : Barns Green
B'bear : Billingbear
Bear G : Beare Green
Beck : Beckenham
Bedd : Beddington
Bedf : Bedfont
Belm : Belmont
Berr G : Berrys Green
Bet : Betchworth
Bew : Bewbush
Big H : Biggin Hill
Big A : Biggin Hill Airport
Bil : Billingshurst
Binf : Binfield
Bisl : Bisley
B'hth : Blackheath
B'water : Blackwater
Blet : Bletchingley
Blind H : Blindley Heath
Bookh : Bookham
Bord : Bordon
Bourne : Bourne, The
Brack : Bracknell
Brmly : Bramley
Bram : Bramshott
Bram C : Bramshott Chase
Bras : Brasted
Bren : Brentford
Broad H : Broadbridge Heath
Broadf : Broadfield
Brock : Brockham
Brom : Bromley
Brook : Brook
Brook E : Brooklands Ind. Est.
Brook P : Brooklands Ind. Pk.
Brkwd : Brookwood
Buck : Buckland
Bur H : Burgh Heath
Burp : Burpham
Burs : Burstow
Busb : Busbridge
Byfl : Byfleet
Camb : Camberley
Capel : Capel
Cars : Carshalton
Cat : Caterham
Charl : Charlwood
Chav D : Chavey Down
Cheam : Cheam
Chels : Chelsfield
Cher : Chertsey
Chess : Chessington
Chev : Chevening
C'fold : Chiddingfold
Chil : Chilworth
Chips : Chipstead
Chob : Chobham
C Hosp : Christs Hospital
C Crook : Church Crookham
Churt : Churt
Clar P : Claremont Park
Clay : Claygate
Cobh : Cobham
Cold : Coldharbour
Cole H : Colemans Hatch
Colg : Colgate
Col T : College Town
Col H : Colney Heath
Coln : Colnbrook
Comp : Compton
Copt : Copthorne
Cotm : Cotmandene
Coul : Coulsdon
Coul N : Coulsdon North
Cowd : Cowden
Cowf : Cowfold
Cran : Cranford
Cranl : Cranleigh
Craw : Crawley
Craw D : Crawley Down
Crook C : Crockham Hill
Cron : Crondall
Crock H : Crookham Common
Crow : Crowhurst
Crowt : Crowthorne
Croy : Croydon
Cud : Cudham
Dat : Datchet
Deep : Deepcut
Dit H : Ditton Hill
Dock : Dockenfield
Dork : Dorking
D'land : Dormansland
Dor P : Dormans Park
Dor : Dorney
Dow : Downe
D'side : Downside
Duns : Dunsfold
Earl : Earlswood
E Clan : East Clandon
E Grin : East Grinstead
E Hor : East Horsley
E Mol : East Molesey
Eden : Edenbridge
Eff : Effingham
Eff J : Effingham Junction
Egh : Egham
Elst : Elstead
Eng : Englefield
Ent : Enton
Eps : Epsom
Esh : Esher
Eton : Eton
Eton C : Eton College
Eton W : Eton Wick
Eve : Eversley
Ewe : Ewell
Ewh : Ewhurst
Ews : Ewshot
F'boro : Farnborough (Hants)
Farn : Farnborough (Kent)
Farnc : Farncombe
Farnh : Farnham
Fay : Faygate
Felb : Felbridge
Felc : Felcourt
Felt : Feltham
Fern : Fernhurst
Fet : Fetcham
Finch : Finchampstead
Five O : Five Oaks
Fleet : Fleet
F Grn : Forest Green
F Row : Forest Row
Fren : Frensham
Frim : Frimley
Frim G : Frimley Green
Frogm : Frogmore
Gat : Gatwick
G'ming : Godalming
God : Godstone
Gom : Gomshall
Gray : Grayshott
G'wood : Grayswood
Grn St : Green Street Green
Guild : Guildford
Hack : Hackbridge
Ham : Ham
Hamb : Hambledon
Hamm : Hammerwood
Hamp : Hampton
Hamp H : Hampton Hill
Hamp W : Hampton Wick
Hand : Handcross
Hanw : Hanworth
Harm : Harmondsworth
Hartf : Hartfield
Hasc : Hascombe
Hasl : Haslemere
Hawl : Hawley
Hay : Hayes (Kent)
Hayes : Hayes (Middlesex)
Head : Headley (Hants)
H'ley : Headley (Surrey)
H'row : Heathrow
Hers : Hersham
Hever : Hever
Hin W : Hinchley Wood
Hind : Hindhead
Holm M : Holmbury St Mary
Holmw : Holmwood
Holt P : Holt Pound
Hkwd : Hookwood
Hool : Hooley
Horl : Horley
Horne : Horne
Hors : Horsell
H'ham : Horsham
Hort : Horton
Houn : Hounslow
Hurst : Hurst
Hurt : Hurtmore
Hyde : Hydestile
If'd : Ifield
Ifold : Ifold
Iswth : Isleworth
Itch : Itchingfield
Jac : Jacob's Well
Kenl : Kenley
Kes : Keston
Kew : Kew
Kingf : Kingfield
K'fold : Kingsfold
King G : Kingsley Green
King T : Kingston upon Thames
Kgswd : Kingswood
Kird : Kirdford
Knap : Knaphill
Knock : Knockholt
Lale : Laleham
Langl : Langley
Lav P : Lavington Park
Lea : Leatherhead
Leigh : Leigh
Light : Lightwater
Limp : Limpsfield
Lind : Lindford
Ling : Lingfield
Gat A : London Gatwick Airport
H'row A : London Heathrow Airport
Longc : Longcross
Lwr Bo : Lower Bourne
Lwr K : Lower Kingswood
Low H : Lowfield Heath
Loxh : Loxhill
Loxw : Loxwood
Lyne : Lyne
M'bowr : Maidenbower
Maid G : Maidens Green
Man H : Mannings Heath
M Grn : Marsh Green
Mayf : Mayford
Mers : Merstham
Mick : Mickleham
Mid H : Mid Holmwood
Milf : Milford
Mitc : Mitcham
Mit J : Mitcham Junction
Mord : Morden
Myt : Mytchett
New Ad : New Addington
Newc : Newchapel
Newd : Newdigate
New H : New Haw
N Mald : New Malden
Norm : Normandy
N Asc : North Ascot
N'chap : Northchapel
N Holm : North Holmwood
Nup : Nuptown
Nutf : Nutfield
Ock : Ockham
Ockl : Ockley
Oke H : Okewood Hill
Old Win : Old Windsor
Old Wok : Old Woking
Onsl : Onslow Village
Orp : Orpington
Ott : Ottershaw
Out : Outwood
Owl : Owlsmoor
Oxs : Oxshott
Oxt : Oxted
Pass : Passfield
Peas P : Pease Pottage
Peasl : Peaslake
Peas : Peasmarsh
Pep H : Peper Harow
Pirb : Pirbright
Plais : Plaistow
P Hill : Pound Hill
Purl : Purley
Putt : Puttenham
Pyr : Pyrford
Ran C : Ranmore Common
Read : Reading
Red : Redhill
Reig : Reigate
Rich : Richmond
Rip : Ripley
Rowh : Rowhook
Rowl : Rowledge
Rud : Rudgwick
Runf : Runfold
Rusp : Rusper
St G : St Georges Hill
St J : St Johns
Salf : Salfords
Sand : Sandhurst
Seale : Seale
Send : Send
Shack : Shackleford
Shalf : Shalford
Sham G : Shamley Green
Sheer : Sheerwater
Shep : Shepperton
Shere : Shere
Ship B : Shipley Bridge
Short : Shortlands
Shot : Shottermill
Shur R : Shurlock Row
Slin : Slinfold
Slou : Slough
Sly I : Slyfield Ind. Est.
Small : Smallfield
S'hall : Southall
S Asc : South Ascot
S Croy : South Croydon
S God : South Godstone
S Nut : South Nutfield
S Pk : South Park
Stai : Staines
Stand : Standford
Stanw : Stanwell
Stoke D : Stoke D'abernon
S'leigh : Stoneleigh
Str G : Strood Green
Sun : Sunbury-on-Thames
S'dale : Sunningdale
S'hill : Sunninghill
Surb : Surbiton
Sur R : Surrey Research Park
Sutt : Sutton
Sut G : Sutton Green
Swan : Swanley
Tad : Tadworth
Tand : Tandridge
Tap : Taplow
Tats : Tatsfield
Tedd : Teddington
Th Dit : Thames Ditton
T Hth : Thornton Heath
Thorpe : Thorpe
Thur : Thursley
Tilf : Tilford
Tin G : Tinsley Green
T'sey : Titsey
Tong : Tongham
Turn H : Turners Hill
Twic : Twickenham
Up Hal : Upper Hale
Up Har : Upper Hartfield
Vir W : Virginia Water
Wall : Wallington
Wal W : Wallis Wood
Wanb : Wanborough
Warf : Warfield
Warf P : Warfield Park
Warl : Warlingham
W On T : Walton-on-Thames
Warn : Warnham
Wel C : Wellington College
W Byf : West Byfleet
W Cla : West Clandon
Westc : Westcott
W Dray : West Drayton
W End : West End
W'ham : Westerham
W Ewe : West Ewell
W Hor : West Horsley
Westh : Westhumble
W Mol : West Molesey
W Wick : West Wickham
Wey : Weybridge
W'hill : Whitehill
W Vill : Whiteley Village
Whit : Whitton
Whyt : Whyteleafe
W'sham : Windlesham
Wind : Windsor
Wind C : Windsor Castle
Wink : Winkfield
Wink R : Winkfield Row
Wis G : Wisborough Green
Wis : Wisley
Witl : Witley
Wok : Woking
Wokgm : Wokingham
Wold : Woldingham
Won : Wonersh
Wdhm : Woodham
Wood S : Wood Street Village
Wor Pk : Worcester Park
Worm : Wormley
Worp : Worplesdon
Worth : Worth
Wott : Wotton
Wray : Wraysbury
Wrec : Wrecclesham
Yat : Yateley

INDEX TO STREETS

Aaron's Hill. *G'ming* —7E **132**
Abbess Clo. *SW2* —2M **29**
Abbetts La. *Camb* —3N **69**
Abbey Chase. *Cher* —6K **37**
Abbey Clo. *Brack* —4B **32**
Abbey Clo. *Cranl* —8H **155**
Abbey Clo. *Wok* —3G **75**
Abbey Clo. *Wokgm* —1B **30**
Abbey Ct. *Camb* —1B **70**
Abbey Ct. *Cher* —6K **37**
Abbey Ct. *Farnh* —1H **129**
Abbey Ct. *Hamp* —8A **24**
Abbey Dri. *SW17* —6E **28**
Abbey Dri. *Stai* —3L **37**
Abbey Gdns. *W6* —2K **13**
Abbey Gdns. *Cher* —5J **37**
Abbey Grn. *Cher* —5J **37**
Abbey Pde. SW19 —8A ***28***
(off Merton High St.)
Abbey Pl. *Cher* —2J **37**
Abbey Rd. *SW19* —8A **28**
Abbey Rd. *Cher* —6K **37**
Abbey Rd. *Croy* —9M **45**
Abbey Rd. *Shep* —7B **38**
Abbey Rd. *S Croy* —6G **64**
Abbey Rd. *Vir W* —4N **35**
Abbey Rd. *Wok* —4M **73**
Abbey St. *Farnh* —1H **129**
Abbey Wlk. *W Mol* —2B **40**
Abbey Way. *F'boro* —1A **90**
Abbeywood. *Ash V* —9F **90**
Abbey Wood. *S'dale* —6D **34**
Abbot Clo. *Byfl* —6M **55**
Abbot Clo. *Stai* —8M **21**
Abbot Rd. *Guild* —5N **113**
Abbotsbury. *Brack* —4L **31**
Abbotsbury Ct. *H'ham* —5L **197**
Abbotsbury Rd. *Mord* —4N **43**
Abbots Clo. *Fleet* —4B **88**
Abbot's Clo. *Guild* —6H **113**
Abbots Dri. *Vir W* —4L **35**
Abbotsfield Rd. *If'd* —5J **181**
Abbotsford Clo. *Wok* —4C **74**
Abbots La. *Kenl* —3N **83**
Abbotsleigh Clo. *Sutt* —4N **61**
Abbotsleigh Rd. *SW16* —5G **28**
Abbots Pk. *SW2* —2L **29**
Abbot's Ride. *Farnh* —3K **129**
Abbots Rise. *Red* —1E **122**
Abbotstone Rd. *SW15* —6H **13**
Abbots Wlk. *Wind* —5B **4**
Abbots Way. *Beck* —4H **47**
Abbots Way. *Guild* —2F **114**
Abbotswood. *Guild* —1B **114**
Abbotswood Clo. *Guild* —9B **94**
Abbotswood Dri. *Wey* —6E **56**
Abbotswood Rd. *SW16* —4H **29**
Abbott Av. *SW20* —9J **27**
Abbott Clo. *Hamp* —7M **23**
Abbotts Cotts. *Dock* —5D **148**
Abbott's Grn. *Croy* —3G **65**
Abbottsmede Clo. *Twic* —3F **24**
Abbotts Rd. *Mitc* —3G **45**
Abbotts Rd. *Sutt* —1K **61**
Abbott's Tilt. *W On T* —9M **39**
Abbotts Wlk. *Cat* —9E **84**
Abelia Clo. *W End* —9B **52**
Abercairn Rd. *SW16* —8G **28**
Aberconway Rd. *Mord* —3N **43**
Abercorn Clo. *S Croy* —9G **64**
Abercorn Ho. *Hawl* —5K **69**
Abercorn Way. *Wok* —5K **73**
Aberdare Clo. *W Wick* —8M **47**
Aberdeen Rd. *Croy* —1A **64**
Aberfoyle Rd. *SW16* —8H **29**
Abingdon Clo. *SW19* —7A **28**
Abingdon Clo. *Brack* —4C **32**
Abingdon Clo. *Wok* —5M **73**
Abingdon Rd. *SW16* —1J **45**
Abingdon Rd. *Sand* —7H **49**
Abinger Av. *Sutt* —5H **61**
Abinger Clo. *N Holm* —9J **119**
Abinger Clo. *Wall* —2J **63**

A-Z Surrey 207

Abinger Comn. Rd.—Amberwood Rise

Abinger Comn. Rd. *Dork* —4M **137**
Abinger Ct. *Wall* —2J **63**
Abinger Dri. *Red* —5C **122**
Abinger Gdns. *Iswth* —6E **10**
Abinger Keep. Horl —7G 142
(off Langshott La.)
Abinger La. *Dork* —9J **117**
Abinger Rd. *Dork* —9A **138**
Abinger Way. *Guild* —7D **94**
Aboyne Dri. *SW20* —1F **42**
Aboyne Rd. *SW17* —4B **28**
Abrahams Rd. *Craw* —8M **181**
Abury La. *Brack* —5E **32**
Acacia Av. *Bren* —3H **11**
Acacia Av. *Owl* —6J **49**
Acacia Av. *Rich* —5M **11**
Acacia Av. *Shep* —4B **38**
Acacia Av. *Wok* —7N **73**
Acacia Av. *Wray* —7A **6**
Acacia Clo. *SE20* —1D **46**
Acacia Clo. *Wdhm* —6H **55**
Acacia Ct. *Brack* —3N **31**
Acacia Dri. *Bans* —1J **81**
Acacia Dri. *Sutt* —7M **43**
Acacia Dri. *Wdhm* —6H **55**
Acacia Gdns. *W Wick* —8M **47**
Acacia Gro. *SE21* —3N **29**
Acacia Gro. *N Mald* —2C **42**
Acacia M. *W Dray* —2M **7**
Acacia Rd. *SW16* —9K **29**
Acacia Rd. *Beck* —2J **47**
Acacia Rd. *Guild* —3N **113**
Acacia Rd. *Hamp* —7A **24**
Acacia Rd. *Mitc* —1E **44**
Acacia Rd. *Stai* —6K **21**
Academy Clo. *Camb* —7C **50**
Academy Gdns. *Croy* —7C **46**
Accommodation La. *W Dray*
(in three parts) —4J **7**
Accommodation Rd. *Longc* —9N **35**
Accommodation Rd. *Wor Pk* —2F **60**
A.C. Court. *Th Dit* —5G **40**
Ace Pde. *Chess* —9L **41**
Acer Dri. *W End* —9C **52**
Acer Rd. *Big H* —3F **86**
Acfold Rd. *SW6* —4N **13**
Acheulian Clo. *Farnh* —4H **129**
Achilles Pl. *Wok* —4M **73**
Ackmar Rd. *SW6* —4M **13**
Ackrells Mead. *Sand* —6E **48**
Acorn Clo. *E Grin* —1A **186**
Acorn Clo. *Hamp* —7B **24**
Acorn Clo. *Horl* —7G **143**
Acorn Dri. *Wokgm* —1B **30**
Acorn Gdns. *SE19* —1C **46**
Acorn Gro. *Hayes* —3G **9**
Acorn Gro. *Tad* —2K **101**
Acorn Gro. *Wok* —8A **74**
Acorn M. *F'boro* —7M **69**
Acorn Rd. *B'water* —1G **69**
Acorns. *H'ham* —4N **197**
Acorns, The. *Craw* —8N **181**
Acorns, The. *Small* —8M **143**
Acorns Way. *Esh* —2C **58**
Acorn Way. *Orp* —1K **67**
Acre La. *Cars & Wall* —1E **62**
Acre Pas. *Wind* —4G **4**
Acre Rd. *SW19* —7B **28**
Acre Rd. *King T* —9L **25**
Acres Gdns. *Tad* —6J **81**
Acres Platt. *Cranl* —6A **156**
Acris St. *SW18* —8N **13**
Acton La. *W4 & W3* —1B **12**
(in three parts)
Acuba Rd. *SW18* —3N **27**
Adair Clo. *SE25* —2E **46**
Adair Wlk. *Pirb* —8M **71**
Adam Ct. SW7 —1N 13
(off Gloucester Rd.)
Adams Clo. *Surb* —5M **41**
Adams Croft. *Brkwd* —7N **71**
Adams Dri. *Fleet* —4D **88**
Adamson Ct. *Craw* —8N **181**
Adams Pk. Rd. *Farnh* —8J **109**
Adams Rd. *Beck* —4H **47**
Adams Wlk. *King T* —1L **41**
Adams Way. *SE25* —5C **46**
Adams Way. *Croy* —5C **46**
Adam Wlk. SW6 —3H 13
(off Crabtree La.)
Adare Wlk. *SW16* —4K **29**
Addington Clo. *Wind* —6D **4**
Addington Ct. *SW14* —6C **12**
Addington Heights. *New Ad* —7M **65**
Addington Rd. *Croy* —7L **45**
Addington Rd. *S Croy* —8D **64**
Addington Rd. *W Wick* —1M **65**
Addington Village Rd. *Croy*
(in two parts) —3J **65**
Addiscombe Av. *Croy* —7D **46**
Addiscombe Ct. Rd. *Croy* —7B **46**
Addiscombe Gro. *Croy* —8B **46**
Addiscombe Rd. *Crowt* —3H **49**
Addiscombe Rd. *Croy* —8B **46**
Addison Av. *Houn* —4C **10**
Addison Clo. *Cat* —9A **84**
Addison Ct. *Guild* —5B **114**
Addison Gdns. *Surb* —3M **41**
Addison Pl. *SE25* —3D **46**
Addison Rd. *SE25* —3D **46**
Addison Rd. *Cat* —8A **84**
Addison Rd. *Frim* —6C **70**
Addison Rd. *Guild* —5A **114**
Addison Rd. *Tedd* —7H **25**
Addison Rd. *Wok* —4B **74**
Addisons Clo. *Croy* —8J **47**
Addison Ter. W4 —1B 12
(off Chiswick Rd.)
Addlestone Moor. *Add* —8L **37**
Addlestone Pk. *Add* —2K **55**
Addlestone Rd. *Add & Wey* —1N **55**
Adecroft Way. *W Mol* —2C **40**
Adela Av. *N Mald* —4G **42**
Adelaide Ct. *Craw* —9B **162**
Adelaide Clo. *H'ham* —4M **197**
Adelaide Pl. *Wey* —1E **56**
Adelaide Rd. *SW18* —8M **13**
Adelaide Rd. *Ashf* —6M **21**
Adelaide Rd. *Houn* —4M **9**
Adelaide Rd. *Rich* —7M **11**
Adelaide Rd. *Surb* —4L **41**
Adelaide Rd. *Tedd* —7F **24**
Adelaide Rd. *W On T* —9H **39**
Adelaide Rd. *Wind* —4J **5**
Adelaide Sq. *Wind* —5G **5**
Adelaide Ter. *Bren* —1K **11**
Adelina M. *SW12* —2H **29**
Adelphi Clo. *M'bowr* —5H **183**
Adelphi Ct. *W4* —2C **12**
Adelphi Rd. *Eps* —9C **60**
Adeney Clo. *W6* —2J **13**
Adlers La. *Westh* —9G **99**
Adlington Pl. *F'boro* —3C **90**
Admark Ho. *Eps* —[illegible] **60**
Admiral Ct. *Cars* —7C **44**
Admiral Ho. *Tedd* —5G **25**
Admiral Kepple Ct. *Asc* —8J **17**
Admiral Rd. *Craw* —6M **181**
Admiral's Bri. La. *E Grin* —7M **185**
Admirals Ct. *Guild* —2D **114**
Admirals Rd. *Bookh & Lea* —6C **98**
Admiral's Rd. *Pirb* —4L **91**
Admirals Wlk. *Coul* —7K **83**
Admiral's Wlk. *Ran C* —8B **98**
Admiralty Rd. *Tedd* —7F **24**
Admiralty Way. *Camb* —2L **69**
Adrian Ct. *Craw* —8N **181**
Adrian M. *SW10* —2N **13**
Advance Rd. *SE27* —5N **29**
Aerodrome Way. *Houn* —2K **9**
Aerospace Boulevd. *F'boro* —6M **89**
Agar Clo. *Surb* —8M **41**
Agar Cres. *Brack* —8N **15**
Agars Pl. *Dat* —2K **5**
Agate La. *H'ham* —3L **197**
Agates La. *Asht* —5K **79**
Agincourt. *Asc* —2N **33**
Agnes Scott Ct. Wey —9C 38
(off Palace Dri.)
Agraria Rd. *Guild* —4L **113**
Ailsa Av. *Twic* —8G **11**
Ailsa Clo. *Craw* —6N **181**
Ailsa Rd. *Twic* —8H **11**
Ainger Clo. *Alder* —1B **110**
Ainsdale Way. *Wok* —5K **73**
Ainslie Wlk. *SW12* —1F **28**
Ainsworth Rd. *Croy* —8M **45**
Aintree Clo. *Coln* —4G **6**
Aintree Est. SW6 —3K 13
(off Aintree St.)
Aintree Rd. *Craw* —5E **182**
Aintree St. *SW6* —3K **13**
Airbourne Ho. Wall —1G 62
(off Maldon Rd.)
Aircraft Esplanade. *F'boro* —4A **90**
Airedale Av. *W4* —1E **12**
Airedale Av. S. *W4* —1E **12**
Airedale Rd. *SW12* —1D **28**
Airlinks Ind. Est. *Houn* —1K **9**
Airport Ind. Est. *Big H* —2F **86**
Airport Way. *Horl* —2E **162**
Airport Way. *Stai* —7J **7**
Aisgill Av. *W14* —1L **13**
(in two parts)
Aisne Rd. *Deep* —5J **71**
Aiten Pl. *W6* —1F **12**
Aitken Clo. *Mitc* —6D **44**
Akabusi Clo. *Croy* —5D **46**
Akehurst Clo. *Copt* —7L **163**
Akehurst St. *SW15* —9F **12**
Akerman Rd. *Surb* —5J **41**
Alamein Rd. *Alder* —2N **109**
Alanbrooke Clo. *Knap* —5F **72**
Alanbrooke Rd. *Alder* —7B **90**
Alan Hilton Ct. Ott —3F 54
(off Cheshire Clo.)
Alan Rd. *SW19* —6K **27**
Alan Turing Rd. *Sur R* —3G **113**
Albain Cres. *Ashf* —3N **21**
Albany Clo. *SW14* —7A **12**
Albany Clo. *Esh* —5A **58**
Albany Clo. *Fleet* —5C **88**
Albany Clo. *Reig* —9M **101**
Albany Ct. *Fleet* —4C **88**
Albany Cres. *Clay* —3E **58**
Albany M. *King T* —7K **25**
Albany M. *Sutt* —2N **61**
Albany Pde. *Bren* —2L **11**
Albany Pk. *Camb* —5A **70**
Albany Pk. *Coln* —3F **6**
Albany Pk. Rd. *King T* —7K **25**
Albany Pk. Rd. *Lea* —6G **79**
Albany Pas. *Rich* —8L **11**
Albany Pl. *Bren* —2K **11**
Albany Pl. *Egh* —5D **20**
Albany Reach. *Th Dit* —4F **40**
Albany Rd. *SW19* —6N **27**
Albany Rd. *Bren* —2K **11**
Albany Rd. *Craw* —3N **181**
Albany Rd. *Fleet* —5B **88**
Albany Rd. *N Mald* —3C **42**
Albany Rd. *Old Win* —8K **5**
Albany Rd. *Rich* —8M **11**
Albany Rd. *W On T* —1L **57**
Albany Rd. *Wind* —5G **4**
Albany Ter. Rich —8M 11
(off Albany Pas.)
Albatross Gdns. *S Croy* —7G **65**
Albemarle. *SW19* —3J **27**
Albemarle Av. *Twic* —2N **23**
Albemarle Gdns. *N Mald* —3C **42**
Albemarle Pk. *Beck* —1L **47**
Albemarle Rd. *Beck* —1L **47**
Alben Rd. *Binf* —6H **15**
Alberta Av. *Sutt* —1K **61**
Alberta Dri. *Small* —8L **143**
Albert Av. *Cher* —2J **37**
Albert Carr Gdns. *SW16* —6J **29**
Albert Crane Ct. *Craw* —1M **181**
Albert Dri. *SW19* —3K **27**
Albert Dri. *Wok* —2E **74**
Albert Gro. *SW20* —9J **27**
Albertine Clo. *Eps* —3G **81**
Albert Pl. *Eton W* —1D **4**
Albert Rd. *SE25* —3D **46**
Albert Rd. *Add* —1M **55**
Albert Rd. *Alder* —2N **109**
Albert Rd. *Ashf* —6A **22**
Albert Rd. *Asht* —5M **79**
Albert Rd. *Bag* —6J **51**
Albert Rd. *Brack* —9N **15**
Albert Rd. *Crowt* —2G **49**
Albert Rd. *Egh* —7N **19**
Albert Rd. *Eps* —9E **60**
Albert Rd. *F'boro* —3A **90**
Albert Rd. *Hamp* —6C **24**
Albert Rd. *Horl* —8E **142**
Albert Rd. *Houn* —7A **10**
Albert Rd. *King T* —1M **41**
Albert Rd. *Mitc* —2D **44**
Albert Rd. *N Mald* —3E **42**
Albert Rd. *Old Win* —6G **5**
Albert Rd. *Red* —7G **102**
Albert Rd. *Rich* —8L **11**
Albert Rd. *Sutt* —2B **62**
Albert Rd. *Tedd* —7F **24**
Albert Rd. *Twic* —2F **24**
Albert Rd. *Warl* —5J **85**
Albert Rd. *Wokgm* —2A **30**
Albert Rd. N. *Reig* —2L **121**
Albert Rd. S. *Reig* —2L **121**
Albert St. *Fleet* —5A **88**
Albert St. *Wind* —4E **4**
Albery Clo. *H'ham* —4H **197**
Albion Clo. *Craw* —4H **183**
Albion Cotts. *Dork* —5K **137**
Albion Ho. *Langl* —1D **6**
Albion M. *W6* —1G **13**
Albion Pl. *SE25* —2D **46**
Albion Pl. *W6* —1G **13**
Albion Rd. *Houn* —7A **10**
Albion Rd. *King T* —9B **26**
Albion Rd. *Reig* —4A **122**
Albion Rd. *Sand* —7G **49**
Albion Rd. *Sutt* —3B **62**
Albion Rd. *Twic* —2E **24**
Albion St. *Croy* —7M **45**
Albion Way. *Eden* —9K **127**
Albion Way. *H'ham* —7H **197**
Albury Av. *Iswth* —3F **10**
Albury Av. *Sutt* —5H **61**
Albury Clo. *Hamp* —7B **24**
Albury Clo. *Longc* —9K **35**
Albury Cotts. *Ash* —2G **111**
Albury Ct. *Sutt* —1A **62**
Albury Keep. Horl —8F 142
(off Langshott La.)
Albury Pk. *Abry* —8N **115**
Albury Pl. *Mers* —7G **103**
Albury Rd. *Chess* —2L **59**
Albury Rd. *Guild* —4B **114**
Albury Rd. *Red* —7G **102**
Albury Rd. *W On T* —3F **56**
Alcester Rd. *Wall* —1F **62**
Alcock Clo. *Wall* —4H **63**
Alcock Rd. *Houn* —3L **9**
Alcocks Clo. *Tad* —7K **81**
Alcocks La. *Kgswd* —8K **81**
Alcorn Clo. *Sutt* —8M **43**
Alcot Clo. *Crowt* —3G **48**
Alden Ct. *Croy* —9B **46**
Aldenham Ter. *Brack* —5A **32**
Aldenholme. *Wey* —3F **56**
Alden View. *Wind* —4A **4**
Alderbrook Clo. *Crowt* —3D **48**
Alderbrook Rd. *SW12* —1F **28**
Alderbury Rd. *SW13* —2F **12**
Alder Clo. *Ash V* —6E **90**
Alder Clo. *Craw D* —1E **184**
Alder Clo. *Egh* —6A **20**
Aldercombe La. *Cat* —5B **104**
Alder Copse. *H'ham* —8F **196**
Aldercroft. *Coul* —3K **83**
Alder Gro. *Yat* —1B **68**
Aldergrove Gdns. *Houn* —5M **9**
Alder Lodge. *SW6* —4J **13**
Alderman Judge Mall. *King T* —1L **41**
Alderman Willey Clo. *Wokgm* —2A **30**
Alderney Av. *Houn* —3B **10**
Alder Rd. *SW14* —6C **12**
Alder Rd. *Head* —3G **168**
Alders Av. *E Grin* —7N **165**
Aldersbrook Dri. *King T* —7M **25**
Aldersey Rd. *Guild* —3B **114**
Alders Gro. *E Mol* —4D **40**
Aldershot Lodge. *Alder* —4M **109**
Aldershot Rd. *Ash* —4C **110**
Aldershot Rd. *C Crook* —9A **88**
Aldershot Rd. *Fleet* —5B **88**
Aldershot Rd. *Guild* —8B **92**
Aldershot Rd. *Pirb* —5A **92**
Alderside Wlk. *Egh* —6A **20**
Aldersmead Av. *Croy* —5G **47**
Alders Rd. *Reig* —1N **121**
Alderstead La. *Red* —3H **103**
Alders, The. *SW16* —5G **29**
Alders, The. *Felt* —5M **23**
Alders, The. *Houn* —[illegible]
Alders, The. *W Wick* —8L **47**
Alders View Dri. *E Grin* —7A **166**
Alderton Rd. *Croy* —6C **46**
Alderville Rd. *SW6* —5L **13**
Alderwick Dri. *Houn* —6D **10**
Alderwood Clo. *Cat* —3B **104**
Aldingbourne Clo. *If'd* —2L **181**
Aldis M. *SW17* —6C **28**
Aldis St. *SW17* —6C **28**
Aldren Rd. *SW17* —4A **28**
Aldrich Cres. *New Ad* —5M **65**
Aldrich Gdns. *Sutt* —9L **43**
Aldrich Ter. *SW18* —3A **28**
Aldridge Pk. *Wink R* —7F **16**
Aldridge Rise. *N Mald* —6D **42**
Aldrington Rd. *SW16* —6G **29**
Aldrin Pl. *F'boro* —1J **89**
Aldwick Clo. *F'boro* —8M **69**
Aldwick Rd. *Croy* —9K **45**
Aldworth Clo. *Brack* —3M **31**
Aldworth Gdns. *Crowt* —2F **48**
Aldwych Clo. *M'bowr* —5H **183**
Aldwyn Ct. *Eng* —7L **19**
Alexa Ct. *Sutt* —3M **61**
Alexander Clo. *Twic* —3F **24**
Alexander Ct. *Beck* —1N **47**
Alexander Godley Clo. *Asht* —6M **79**
Alexander Rd. *Coul* —2F **82**
Alexander Rd. *Egh* —6E **20**
Alexander Rd. *Reig* —6M **121**
Alexanders Wlk. *Cat* —4C **104**
Alexander Wlk. *Brack* —4N **31**
Alexandra Av. *W4* —3C **12**
Alexandra Av. *Camb* —1M **69**
Alexandra Av. *Sutt* —9M **43**
Alexandra Av. *Warl* —4J **85**
Alexandra Clo. *Ashf* —8E **22**
Alexandra Clo. *Stai* —7M **21**
Alexandra Clo. *W On T* —8H **39**
Alexandra Ct. *Ashf* —7E **22**
Alexandra Ct. *Craw* —4B **182**
Alexandra Ct. *F'boro* —4A **90**
Alexandra Ct. *Houn* —5B **10**
Alexandra Ct. *Wokgm* —3B **30**
Alexandra Dri. *Surb* —6N **41**
Alexandra Gdns. *W4* —3D **12**
Alexandra Gdns. *Cars* —4E **62**
Alexandra Gdns. *Houn* —5B **10**
Alexandra Gdns. *Knap* —5F **72**
Alexandra M. *SW19* —7L **27**
Alexandra Pl. *SE25* —4A **46**
Alexandra Pl. *Croy* —7B **46**
Alexandra Pl. *Guild* —5B **114**
Alexandra Rd. *SW14* —6C **12**
Alexandra Rd. *SW19* —7L **27**
Alexandra Rd. *Add* —1M **55**
Alexandra Rd. *Alder* —2K **109**
(in two parts)
Alexandra Rd. *Ash* —3D **110**
Alexandra Rd. *Ashf* —8E **22**
Alexandra Rd. *Big H* —6D **86**
Alexandra Rd. *Bren* —2K **11**
Alexandra Rd. *Croy* —7B **46**
Alexandra Rd. *Egh* —7M **19**
Alexandra Rd. *Eps* —9E **60**
Alexandra Rd. *F'boro* —3A **90**
Alexandra Rd. *Houn* —5B **10**
Alexandra Rd. *King T* —8N **25**
Alexandra Rd. *Mitc* —8C **28**
Alexandra Rd. *Rich* —5M **11**
Alexandra Rd. *Th Dit* —4F **40**
Alexandra Rd. *Twic* —9J **11**
Alexandra Rd. *Warl* —4J **85**
Alexandra Rd. *Wind* —5G **4**
Alexandra Sq. *Mord* —4M **43**
Alexandra Ter. *Guild* —4A **114**
Alfold Rd. *Cranl* —7K **155**
Alfold Rd. *Duns* —5C **174**
Alfonso Clo. *Alder* —4A **110**
Alford Clo. *Guild* —9B **94**
Alford Grn. *New Ad* —3N **65**
Alfred Clo. *W4* —1C **12**
Alfred Clo. *Worth* —4J **183**
Alfred Rd. *SE25* —4D **46**
Alfred Rd. *Farnh* —2H **129**
Alfred Rd. *Felt* —3K **23**
Alfred Rd. *King T* —2L **41**
Alfred Rd. *Sutt* —2A **62**
Alfreton Clo. *SW19* —4J **27**
Alfriston. *Surb* —5M **41**
Alfriston Av. *Croy* —6J **45**
Alfriston Clo. *Surb* —4M **41**
Alfriston Rd. *Deep* —7G **71**
Algar Clo. *Iswth* —6G **10**
Algar Rd. *Iswth* —6G **11**
Algarve Rd. *SW18* —2N **27**
Alice Ct. *SW15* —7L **13**
Alice Gilliatt Ct. W14 —2L 13
(off Star Rd.)
Alice Gough Homes. *Brack* —2N **31**
Alice Holt Cotts. *Holt P* —9A **128**
Alice Holt Forest Cen. *Wrec* —2A **148**
Alice M. *Tedd* —6F **24**
Alice Rd. *Alder* —2N **109**
Alice Ruston Pl. *Wok* —6M **73**
Alice Way. *Houn* —7B **10**
Alicia Av. *Craw* —3F **182**
Alington Gro. *Wall* —[illegible]
Alison Clo. *Croy* —7G **46**
Alison Clo. *F'boro* —2L **89**
Alison Clo. *Wok* —2A **74**
Alison Dri. *Camb* —1D **70**
Alison's Rd. *Alder* —8M **89**
Alison Way. *Alder* —2L **109**
Alkerden Rd. *W4* —1D **12**
Allan Clo. *N Mald* —4C **42**
Allbrook Clo. *Tedd* —6E **24**
Allcard Clo. *H'ham* —4M **197**
Allcot Clo. *Craw* —6K **181**
Allcot Clo. *Felt* —2G **22**
Allden Av. *Alder* —5B **110**
Allden Gdns. *Alder* —5B **110**
Alldens Hill. *G'ming & Brmly* —1N **153**
Alldens La. *G'ming* —9L **133**
Allenby Av. *S Croy* —5N **63**
Allenby Rd. *Big H* —4G **86**
Allenby Rd. *Camb* —9M **49**
Allen Clo. *Mitc* —9G **28**
Allen Clo. *Sun* —9J **23**
Allendale Clo. *Sand* —5F **48**
Allenford Ho. SW15 —9D 12
(off Tunworth Cres.)
Allen Ho. Pk. *Wok* —7M **73**
Allen Rd. *Beck* —1G **46**
Allen Rd. *Bookh* —4B **98**
Allen Rd. *Croy* —7L **45**
Allen Rd. *Sun* —9J **23**
Allen's Clo. *Ash W* —3F **186**
Allestree Rd. *SW6* —3K **13**
Alleyn Pk. *S'hall* —1A **10**
Allfarthing La. *SW18* —9N **13**
Allgood Clo. *Mord* —5J **43**
Allingham Ct. *G'ming* —4J **133**
Allingham Gdns. *H'ham* —3A **198**
Allingham Rd. *Reig* —6M **121**
Allington Av. *Shep* —2F **38**
Allington Clo. *SW19* —6J **27**
Allkins Ct. *Wind* —5G **5**
Alloway Clo. *Wok* —5L **73**
All Saints Clo. *Wokgm* —1B **30**
All Saints Ct. Houn —4L 9
(off Springwell Rd.)
All Saints Cres. *F'boro* —5K **69**
All Saints Dri. *S Croy* —8C **64**
All Saints Pas. *SW18* —8M **13**
All Saints Rise. *Warf* —7B **16**
All Saints Rd. *SW19* —8A **28**
All Saints Rd. *Light* —6N **51**
All Saints Rd. *Sutt* —9N **43**
Allsmoor La. *Brack* —2D **32**
All Soul's Rd. *Asc* —3L **33**
Allum Gro. *Tad* —8G **81**
Allyington Way. *Worth* —4H **183**
Allyn Clo. *Stai* —7H **21**
Alma Clo. *Alder* —2B **110**
Alma Clo. *Knap* —4H **73**
Alma Cotts. *F'boro* —5A **90**
Alma Ct. Cat —8N 83
(off Coulsdon Rd.)
Alma Cres. *Sutt* —2K **61**
Alma Gdns. *Deep* —6H **71**
Alma Ho. *Bren* —2L **11**
Alma La. *Farnh* —5G **109**
Alma Pl. *T Hth* —4L **45**
Alma Rd. *SW18* —7N **13**
Alma Rd. *Bord* —6A **168**
Alma Rd. *Cars* —2C **62**
Alma Rd. *Esh* —7E **40**
Alma Rd. *Eton W* —1C **4**
Alma Rd. *Frim G* —6H **71**
Alma Rd. *Head* —4H **169**
Alma Rd. *Reig* —2N **121**
Alma Rd. *Wind* —5F **4**
Alma Sq. *F'boro* —5A **90**
Alma Ter. *SW18* —1B **28**
Alma Way. *Farnh* —5J **109**
Almer Rd. *SW20* —8F **26**
Almners Rd. *Lyne* —7C **36**
Almond Av. *Cars* —8D **44**
Almond Av. *Wok* —8N **73**
Almond Clo. *Craw* —4M **181**
Almond Clo. *Egh* —7L **19**
Almond Clo. *F'boro* —7M **69**
Almond Clo. *Felt* —2H **23**
Almond Clo. *Guild* —9N **93**
Almond Clo. *Shep* —1D **38**
Almond Clo. *Wind* —5E **4**
Almond Ct. *C Crook* —7C **88**
Almond Gro. *Bren* —3H **11**
Almond Rd. *Eps* —7C **60**
Almond Way. *Mitc* —4H **45**
Almorah Rd. *Houn* —4L **9**
Almsgate. *Comp* —1F **132**
Alms Heath. *Ock* —8C **76**
Almshouse La. *Chess* —5K **59**
Almshouses. *Cotm* —4H **119**
Alnwick Gro. *Mord* —3N **43**
Aloes, The. *Fleet* —5C **88**
Alphabet Gdns. *Cars* —5B **44**
Alpha Pl. *Mord* —7J **43**
Alpha Rd. *Chob* —6J **53**
Alpha Rd. *Craw* —3A **182**
Alpha Rd. *Croy* —7B **46**
Alpha Rd. *Surb* —5M **41**
Alpha Rd. *Tedd* —6D **24**
Alpha Rd. *Wok* —3D **74**
Alpha Way. *Egh* —[illegible]
Alphea Clo. *SW19* —8C **28**
Alphington Av. *Frim* —5C **70**
Alphington Grn. *Frim* —5D **70**
Alpine Av. *Surb* —8B **42**
Alpine Clo. *Croy* —9B **46**
Alpine Clo. *F'boro* —2J **89**
Alpine Rd. *Red* —9E **102**
Alpine Rd. *W On T* —6H **39**
Alpine View. *Sutt* —2C **62**
Alresford Rd. *Guild* —4K **113**
Alric Av. *N Mald* —2D **42**
Alsace Wlk. *Camb* —5N **69**
Alsford Clo. *Light* —8K **51**
Alsom Av. *Wor Pk* —1F **60**
Alston Clo. *Surb* —6H **41**
Alston Rd. *SW17* —5B **28**
Alterton Clo. *Wok* —4K **73**
Alt Gro. *SW19* —8L **27**
Althea St. *SW6* —5N **13**
Althorne Rd. *Red* —5E **122**
Althorp Rd. *SW17* —2D **28**
Alton Clo. *Iswth* —5F **10**
Alton Ct. *Stai* —9G **21**
Alton Gdns. *Twic* —1D **24**
Alton Ho. *Red* —1E **122**
Alton Ride. *B'water* —9H **49**
Alton Rd. *SW15* —2F **26**
Alton Rd. *Croy* —9L **45**
Alton Rd. *Farnh* —5B **128**
Alton Rd. *Fleet* —4D **88**
Alton Rd. *Rich* —7L **11**
Altyre Clo. *Beck* —4J **47**
Altyre Rd. *Croy* —8A **46**
Altyre Way. *Beck* —4J **47**
Alvernia Clo. *G'ming* —9F **132**
Alverstoke Gdns. *Alder* —3K **109**
Alverstone Av. *SW19* —3M **27**
Alverstone Rd. *N Mald* —3E **42**
Alverston Gdns. *SE25* —4B **46**
Alvia Gdns. *Sutt* —1A **62**
Alway Av. *Eps* —2C **60**
Alwyn Av. *W4* —1C **12**
Alwyn Clo. *New Ad* —4L **65**
Alwyne Ct. *Wok* —3A **74**
Alwyne Rd. *SW19* —7L **27**
Alwyns Clo. *Cher* —5J **37**
Alwyns La. *Cher* —5H **37**
Amalgamated Dri. *Bren* —2G **11**
Ambarrow Cres. *Sand* —6E **48**
Ambarrow La. *Sand* —5C **48**
Ambassador. *Brack* —4L **31**
Ambassador Clo. *Houn* —5M **9**
Amber Ct. *Alder* —2A **110**
Ambercroft Way. *Coul* —6M **83**
Amber Hill. *Camb* —2F **70**
Amberley Clo. *Craw* —3G **183**
Amberley Clo. *H'ham* —2N **197**
Amberley Clo. *Send* —3H **95**
Amberley Dri. *Wdhm* —7H **55**
(in two parts)
Amberley Gdns. *Eps* —1E **60**
Amberley Grange. *Alder* —4L **109**
Amberley Gro. *Croy* —6C **46**
Amberley La. *Milf* —1B **152**
Amberley Rd. *H'ham* —2N **197**
Amberley Rd. *Milf* —9B **132**
Amberley Way. *Houn* —8K **9**
Amberley Way. *Mord* —6L **43**
Amberside Clo. *Iswth* —9D **10**
Amberwood Dri. *Camb* —8D **50**
Amberwood Rise. *N Mald* —5D **42**

Amblecote—Ashurst Dri.

Amblecote. Cobh —8L 57
Ambleside. G'ming —6K 133
Ambleside Av. SW16 —5H 29
Ambleside Av. Beck —4H 47
Ambleside Av. W On T —7K 39
Ambleside Clo. F'boro —1K 89
Ambleside Clo. If'd —4J 181
Ambleside Clo. Myt —3E 90
Ambleside Clo. Red —8F 122
Ambleside Cres. Farnh —6F 108
Ambleside Dri. Felt —2G 22
Ambleside Gdns. SW16 —6H 29
Ambleside Gdns. S Croy —6G 64
Ambleside Gdns. Sutt —3A 62
Ambleside Rd. Light —7K 51
Ambleside Way. Egh —8D 20
Ambrey Way. Wall —5H 63
Ambrose Clo. Orp —1N 67
Amen Corner. SW17 —7E 28
Amen Corner Bus. Pk. Binf —1K 31
Amenity Way. Mord —6H 43
Amerland Rd. SW18 —8L 13
Amersham Rd. Croy —5N 45
Amesbury Av. SW2 —3J 29
Amesbury Clo. Wor Pk —7H 43
Amesbury Rd. Felt —3L 23
Amey Dri. Bookh —2C 98
Amhurst Gdns. Iswth —5F 10
Amis Av. Eps —3A 60
Amis Av. New H —6J 55
Amis Rd. Wok —6H 73
Amity Gro. SW20 —9G 27
Amity Way. Camb —1C 70
Amlets La. Cranl —5M 155
Ampere Way. Bedd —6J 45
(in two parts)
Amstel Way. Knap —5J 73
Amundsen Rd. H'ham —2K 197
Amyand Cotts. Twic —9H 11
Amyand La. Twic —1H 25
Amyand Pk. Gdns. Twic —1H 25
Amyand Pk. Rd. Twic —1G 25
Amy Rd. Oxt —7A 106
Ancaster Cres. N Mald —5F 42
Ancaster Dri. Asc —9J 17
Ancaster M. Beck —2G 47
Ancaster Rd. Beck —2G 46
Ancells Bus. Pk. Fleet —9C 68
Ancells Rd. Fleet —1C 88
Anchorage Clo. SW19 —6M 27
Anchor Bus. Cen. Croy —9J 45
Anchor Cotts. Ling —3H 145
Anchor Ct. H'ham —7J 197
Anchor Cres. Knap —4G 72
Anchor Hill. Knap —4G 72
Anchor Meadow. F'boro —1L 89
Anchor M. SW12 —1F 28
Ancill Clo. W6 —2J 13
Andermans. Wind —4A 4
Anderson Clo. Eps —8A 60
Anderson Dri. Ashf —5D 22
Anderson Pl. Bag —3J 51
Anderson Pl. Houn —7B 10
Anderson Rd. Wey —9E 38
Andover Clo. Eps —7C 60
Andover Clo. Felt —2G 23
Andover Rd. B'water —9H 49
Andover Rd. Twic —2D 24
Andover Way. Alder —5N 109
Andreck Ct. Beck —1L 47
Andrewartha Rd. F'boro —3C 90
Andrew Clo. Wokgm —3D 30
Andrewes Ho. Sutt —1M 61
Andrew Row. Wok —3G 74
Andrews Clo. C Crook —7B 88
Andrew's Clo. Eps —1E 80
Andrews Clo. Wor Pk —8J 43
Andrews Rd. E Grin —9M 165
Andrews Rd. F'boro —9K 69
Andromeda Clo. Bew —5K 181
Anerley Rd. SE20 —1E 20
Anfield Clo. SW12 —1G 29
Angas Ct. Wey —2D 56
Angel Ct. G'ming —7G 133
Angel Ct. Guild —9D 112
Angelfield. Houn —8B 10
Angel Ga. Guild —4N 113
Angel Hill. Sutt —9N 43
(in two parts)
Angel Hill Dri. Sutt —9N 43
Angelica Gdns. Croy —7G 46
Angelica Rd. Bisl —2D 72
Angelica Rd. Guild —8K 93
Angell Clo. M'bowr —4G 182
Angel Pl. Binf —7H 15
Angel Rd. Th Dit —6G 41
Angel Wlk. W6 —1H 13
Anglers Clo. Rich —5J 25
Anglers Reach. Surb —4K 41
Anglers, The. King T —2K 41
(off High St. Kingston upon Thames,)
Anglesea Rd. King T —3K 41
Anglesey Av. F'boro —7L 69
Anglesey Clo. Ashf —4B 22
Anglesey Clo. Craw —6A 182
Anglesey Ct. Rd. Cars —3E 62
Anglesey Gdns. Cars —3E 62
Anglesey Rd. Alder —3B 110
Angles Rd. SW16 —5J 29
Angora Way. Fleet —1C 88
Angus Clo. Chess —2N 59
Angus Clo. H'ham —4K 197
Angus Ho. SW2 —1H 29
Anlaby Rd. Tedd —6E 24
Annandale Dri. Lwr Bo —5J 129
Annandale Rd. W4 —1D 12
Annandale Rd. Croy —8D 46
Annandale Rd. Guild —5L 113
Anne Armstrong Clo. Alder —8B 90
Anne Boleyn's Wlk. King T —6L 25
Anne Boleyn's Wlk. Sutt —4J 61
Anne Case M. N Mald —2D 42
Anneforde Pl. Brack —8M 15
Anners Clo. Egh —2E 36
Annesley Dri. Croy —9J 47
Anne's Wlk. Cat —7B 84
Annes Way. C Crook —7C 88
Annett Clo. Shep —3F 38
Annettes Croft. C Crook —9A 88
Annett Rd. W On T —6H 39
Anne Way. W Mol —3B 40
Annie Brookes Clo. Stai —4F 20
Anningsley Pk. Ott —6D 54
Annisdowne. Dork —2G 137
Annsworthy Av. T Hth —2A 46
Annsworthy Cres. SE25 —1A 46
Ann Way. SE19 —8M 29
Ansell Gro. Cars —7E 44
Ansell Rd. SW17 —4C 28
Ansell Rd. Dork —4H 119
Ansell Rd. Frim —6C 70
Anselm Clo. Croy —9C 46
Anselm Rd. SW6 —2M 13
Ansley Clo. S Croy —1E 84
Anson Clo. Kenl —7A 84
Anstice Clo. W4 3D 12
Anstiebury Clo. Bear G —8J 139
Anstie Grange Dri. Dork —6G 139
Anstie La. Cold —6E 138
Anston Ct. Guild —3H 113
Anthony Rd. SE25 —5D 46
Anthony Wall. Warf —9D 16
Anthony W. Ho. Bet —5A 120
Antigua Wlk. SE19 —6N 29
Antlands La. Ship B —4J 163
Antlands La. E. Horl —4K 163
Antlands La. W. Horl —4J 163
Anton Cres. Sutt —9M 43
Antrobus Clo. Sutt —2L 61
Anvil Clo. SW16 —8G 28
Anvil La. Cobh —1H 77
Anvil Rd. Sun —2H 39
Anyards Rd. Cobh —9J 57
Anzio Clo. Alder —2M 109
Apeldoorn Dri. Wall —5J 63
Aperdele Rd. Lea —5G 79
Aperfield Rd. Big H —4G 87
Aperfields. W'ham —4G 86
Apers Av. Wok —8B 74
Apex Clo. Beck —1L 47
Apex Clo. Wey —9E 38
Apex Corner. (Junct.) —4N 23
Apex Dri. Frim —5B 70
Apley Rd. Reig —6M 121
Aplin Way. Iswth —4E 10
Aplin Way. Light —7L 51
Apollo Dri. Bord —7A 168
Apollo Pl. St J —6K 73
Apollo Rise. Swd P —1H 89
Apostle Way. T Hth —1M 45
Appleby Clo. Twic —3D 24
Appleby Gdns. Felt —2G 22
Appleby Ho. Eps —7C 60
Appledore. Brack —5L 31
Appledore Clo. SW17 —3D 28
Appledore M. F'boro —7M 69
Appledown Rise. Coul —2G 83
Applefield. Craw —2C 182
Apple Garth. Bren —1K 11
Applegarth. Clay —2F 58
Applegarth. G'ming —4F 132
Applegarth. New Ad —4L 65
(in two parts)
Applegarth Av. Guild —3G 112
Apple Gro. Chess —1L 59
Applelands Clo. Wrec —7F 128
Apple Mkt. King T —1K 41
Appleton Gdns. N Mald —5F 42
Appleton Sq. Mitc —9C 28
Appletree Clo. Brack —9M 15
Appletree Clo. G'ming —9J 133
Appletree Ct. Guild —9F 94
Appletree Pl. Brack —9M 15
Appletrees Pl. Wok —6M 73
Apple Tree Way. Owl —6J 49
Appley Ct. Camb —1N 69
Appley Dri. Camb —9N 49
Approach Rd. SW20 —1H 43
Approach Rd. Ashf —7D 22
Approach Rd. Farnh —2H 129
Approach Rd. Purl —8L 63
Approach Rd. Tats —1D 106
Approach Rd. W Mol —4A 40
Approach, The. Bookh —1N 97
Approach, The. Dor P —4C 166
April Clo. Asht —5M 79
April Clo. Camb —4A 70
April Clo. Felt —4H 23
April Clo. H'ham —4J 197
Aprilwood Clo. Wdhm —7H 55
Apsey Ct. Binf —8K 15
Apsley Ct. Craw —5L 181
Apsley Rd. SE25 —3E 46
Apsley Rd. N Mald —2B 42
Aquarius Ct. Craw —5K 181
Aquila Clo. Lea —8L 79
Arabella Dri. SW15 —7D 12
Aragon Av. Eps —6G 60
Aragon Av. Th Dit —4F 40
Aragon Clo. New Ad —6A 66
Aragon Clo. Sun —7G 22
Aragon Ct. Brack —3A 32
Aragon Ct. E Mol —3C 40
Aragon Rd. King T —6L 25
Aragon Rd. Mord —5J 43
Aragon Rd. Twic —1G 25
Aragon Rd. Yat —2B 68
Aragon Wlk. Byfl —9A 56
Aran Ct. Wey —8E 38
Arbor Clo. Beck —1L 47
Arborfield Clo. SW2 —2K 29
Arbour Clo. Fet —1F 98
Arbrook Chase. Esh —3C 58
Arbrook La. Esh —3C 58
Arbury Ct. SE20 —1E 46
Arbutus Clo. Red —5A 122
Arbutus Rd. Red —6A 122
Arcade Pde. Chess —2L 59
Arcade, The. Alder —2M 109
Arcade, The. Wokgm —2B 30
Arcadia Clo. Cars —1E 62
Archbishop's Pl. SW2 —1K 29
Archdale Pl. N Mald —2A 42
Archel Rd. W14 —2L 13
Archer Clo. King T —8L 25
Archer M. Hamp —7C 24
Archer Rd. SE25 —3E 46
Archers Ct. Craw —1B 182
Arches, The. Wind —4F 4
Arch Rd. W On T —9L 39
Archway Clo. SW19 —4N 27
Archway Clo. Wall —9J 45
Archway M. Dork —4G 119
Archway Pl. Dork —4G 119
Archway St. SW13 —6D 12
Arcturus Rd. Craw —6K 181
Arden Clo. Brack —1D 32
Arden Clo. Reig —7N 121
Arden Gro. Orp —1K 67
Arden Rd. Craw —5D 182
Ardent Clo. SE25 —2B 46
Ardesley Wood. Wey —1F 56
Ardfern Av. SW16 —2L 45
Ardingly. Brack —4M 31
Ardingly Clo. Craw —1N 181
Ardingly Clo. Croy —9G 47
Ardingly Rd. W Hoa —9E 184
Ardleigh Gdns. Sutt —6M 43
Ardlui Rd. SE27 —3N 29
Ardmay Gdns. Surb —4L 41
Ardmore Av. Guild —1L 113
Ardmore Ho. Guild —1L 113
Ardmore Way. Guild —1L 113
Ardrossan Av. Camb —2E 70
Ardrossan Gdns. Wor Pk —9F 42
Ardshiel Clo. SW15 —6J 13
Ardshiel Dri. Red —5C 122
Ardwell Clo. Crowt —2D 48
Ardwell Rd. SW2 —3J 29
Arena La. Alder —9J 89
Arenal Dri. Crowt —4G 49
Arethusa Way. Bisl —3C 72
Arford Comn. Head —3E 168
Arford Rd. Head —4E 168
Argent Clo. Egh —7E 20
Argente Clo. Fleet —1C 88
Argon M. SW6 —3M 13
Argosy Gdns. Stai —7H 21
Argosy La. Stai —1M 21
Argus Wlk. Craw —6M 181
Argyle Av. Houn —9A 10
Argyle Pl. W6 —1G 13
Argyle Rd. Houn —8B 10
Argyle St. Pirb —8L 71
Ariel Way. Houn —6J 9
Arkell Gro. SE19 —8M 29
Arklow M. Surb —8L 41
Arkwright Dri. Brack —1J 31
Arkwright Ho. SW2 —1J 29
(off Streatham Pl.)
Arkwright Rd. Coln —5G 6
Arkwright Rd. S Croy —6C 64
Arlesey Clo. SW15 —8K 13
Arlington Clo. Brack —9M 15
Arlington Clo. Sutt —8M 43
Arlington Clo. Twic —9J 11
Arlington Ct. Hayes —1F 8
Arlington Ct. Reig —1N 121
Arlington Dri. Cars —8D 44
Arlington Gdns. W4 —1B 12
Arlington Lodge. Wey —1C 56
Arlington M. Twic —9H 11
Arlington Pk. Mans. W4 —1B 12
(off Sutton La. N.)
Arlington Pas. Tedd —5F 24
Arlington Rd. Ashf —6A 22
Arlington Rd. Rich —3K 25
Arlington Rd. Surb —5K 41
Arlington Rd. Tedd —5F 24
Arlington Rd. Twic —9J 11
Arlington Sq. Brack —1M 31
Arlington Ter. Alder —2L 109
Armadale Rd. SW6 —2M 13
Armadale Rd. Felt —8H 9
Armadale Rd. Wok —4K 73
Armfield Clo. W Mol —4N 39
Armfield Cres. Mitc —1D 44
Armitage Ct. Asc —5N 33
Armitage Dri. Frim —5D 70
Armoury Way. SW18 —8M 13
Armstrong Clo. W On T —5H 39
Armstrong Mall. Swd P —1J 89
Armstrong Rd. Egh —7M 19
Armstrong Rd. Felt —6M 23
Armytage Rd. Houn —3L 9
Arnal Cres. SW18 —1K 27
Arncliffe. Brack —4M 31
Arndale Cen., The. SW18 —9N 13
Arndale Wlk. SW18 —8N 13
Arndale Way. Egh —6C 20
Arne Clo. Craw —6L 181
Arne Gro. Horl —6C 142
Arnewood Clo. SW15 —2F 26
Arnewood Clo. Oxs —1B 78
Arneys La. Mitc —5E 44
Arnfield Clo. If'd —4K 181
Arnhem Barracks. Alder —9M 89
Arnhem Clo. Alder —2N 109
Arnhem Dri. New Ad —7N 65
Arnison Rd. E Mol —3D 40
Arnold Cres. Iswth —8D 10
Arnold Dri. Chess —3K 59
Arnold Mans. W14 —2K 13
(off Queen's Club Gdns.)
Arnold Rd. SW17 —8D 28
Arnold Rd. Stai —8L 21
Arnold Rd. Wok —2D 74
Arnott Clo. W4 —1C 12
Arnulls Rd. SW16 —7M 29
Arodene Rd. SW2 —1K 29
Arosa Rd. Twic —9K 11
Arragon Gdns. SW16 —8J 29
Arragon Gdns. W Wick —9L 47
Arragon Rd. SW18 —2M 27
Arran Clo. Craw —6N 181
Arran Clo. Wall —1F 62
Arrancourt. H'ham —6H 197
Arran Way. Esh —8B 40
Arras Av. Mord —4A 44
Arreton Mead. Hors —1B 74
Arrol Rd. Beck —2F 46
Arrow Ct. SW5 —1M 13
(off W. Cromwell Rd.)
Arrow Ind. Est. F'boro —3L 89
Arrow Rd. F'boro —3L 89
Artel Croft. Craw —3E 182
Arterberry Rd. SW20 —8H 27
Arthur Clo. Bag —6J 51
Arthur Clo. Farnh —2G 129
Arthur Henderson Ho. SW6 —5L 13
(off Fulham Rd.)
Arthur Rd. SW19 —5M 27
Arthur Rd. Big H —2E 86
Arthur Rd. Farnh —2G 129
(in two parts)
Arthur Rd. H'ham —7K 197
Arthur Rd. If'd —3K 181
Arthur Rd. King T —8N 25
Arthur Rd. N Mald —4G 43
Arthur Rd. Wind —4F 4
Arthur's Bri. Rd. Wok —4N 73
Arthur's Bri. Wharf. Wok —4N 73
Arthurstone Birches. Binf —6J 15
Arthur St. Alder —3N 109
Artillery Rd. Alder —2N 109
(Aldershot)
Artillery Rd. Alder —6B 90
(North Camp)
Artillery Rd. Guild —3N 113
Artillery Ter. Guild —3N 113
Artington Clo. Orp —1L 67
Artington Wlk. Guild —6M 113
Arun Ct. SE25 —4D 46
Arundel Av. Eps —6G 60
Arundel Av. Mord —3L 43
Arundel Av. S Croy —6D 64
Arundel Clo. Craw —3G 182
Arundel Clo. Croy —9M 45
Arundel Clo. Fleet —5C 88
Arundel Clo. Hamp —6B 24
Arundel Clo. Pass —9C 168
Arundel Ct. Short —1N 47
Arundel Mans. SW6 —4L 13
(off Kelvedon Rd.)
Arundel Pl. Farnh —1G 128
Arundel Rd. Camb —2G 70
Arundel Rd. Croy —5A 46
Arundel Rd. Dork —5G 118
Arundel Rd. Houn —6K 9
Arundel Rd. King T —1A 42
Arundel Rd. Sutt —4L 61
Arundel Ter. SW13 —2G 13
Arunside. H'ham —7G 196
Arun Way. H'ham —7L 197
Aschurch Rd. Croy —6C 46
Ascot Ct. Alder —3M 109
Ascot M. Wall —5G 63
Ascot Rd. SW17 —7E 28
Ascot Rd. Felt —2B 22
Ascot Rd. M'head & Brack —1B 16
Ascot Wood Pl. Asc —2L 33
Ashbourne. Brack —5L 31
Ashbourne Clo. Ash —1G 110
Ashbourne Clo. Coul —5G 83
Ashbourne Ct. Ash —1G 110
Ashbourne Gro. W4 —1D 12
Ashbourne Rise. Orp —1N 67
Ashbourne Rd. Mitc —8E 28
Ashbourne Ter. SW19 —8M 27
Ash Bri. Cvn. Pk. Ash —4C 110
Ashbrook Rd. Old Win —1L 19
Ashburnham Ct. Beck —1M 47
Ashburnham Pk. Esh —1C 58
Ashburnham Rd. SW10 —3N 13
Ashburnham Rd. Craw —5E 182
Ashburnham Rd. Rich —4H 25
Ashburn Pl. SW7 —1N 13
Ashburton Av. Croy —7E 46
Ashburton Clo. Croy —7D 46
Ashburton Enterprise Cen. SW15 —9H 13
Ashburton Gdns. Croy —8D 46
Ashburton Memorial Homes. Croy —6E 46
Ashburton Rd. Croy —8D 46
Ashbury Cres. Guild —1E 114
Ashbury Dri. B'water —5M 69
Ashbury Pl. SW19 —7A 28
Ashby Av. Chess —3N 59
Ashby Ct. H'ham —6L 197
Ashby Wlk. Croy —5N 45
Ashby Way. W Dray —3B 8
Ash Chu. Rd. Ash —2F 110
Ash Clo. SE20 —1F 46
Ash Clo. Ash —1F 110
Ash Clo. B'water —1H 69
Ash Clo. Cars —8D 44
Ash Clo. Craw D —1F 184
Ash Clo. Eden —2K 147
Ash Clo. Ling —6A 146
Ash Clo. N Mald —1C 42
Ash Clo. Pyr —2J 75
Ash Clo. Red —8G 103
Ash Clo. Wok —7A 74
Ash Combe. C'fold —5D 172
Ashcombe Av. Surb —6K 41
Ashcombe Dri. Eden —8K 127
Ashcombe Rd. SW19 —6M 27
Ashcombe Rd. Cars —3E 62
Ashcombe Rd. Dork —3G 119
Ashcombe Rd. Red —5G 102
Ashcombe Sq. N Mald —2B 42
Ashcombe St. SW6 —5N 13
Ashcombe Ter. Tad —7G 80
Ash Ct. SW19 —8K 27
Ash Ct. Add —2K 55
Ash Ct. Eps —1B 60
Ash Ct. Wokgm —2B 30
Ashcroft. Shalf —1A 134
Ashcroft Pk. Cobh —8M 57
Ashcroft Rise. Coul —3J 83
Ashcroft Rd. Chess —9M 41
Ashcroft Sq. W6 —1H 13
Ashdale. Bookh —4C 98
Ashdale Clo. Stai —3N 21
Ashdale Clo. Twic —1C 24
Ashdale Pk. Finch —1B 48
Ashdale Way. Twic —1B 24
Ashdene Clo. Ashf —8D 22
Ashdene Cres. Ash —1E 110
Ashdene Rd. Ash —1E 110
Ashdown Av. F'boro —3B 90
Ashdown Clo. Beck —1L 47
Ashdown Clo. Brack —1E 32
Ashdown Clo. F Row —7J 187
Ashdown Clo. Reig —7N 121
Ashdown Ct. Sutt —3A 62
Ashdown Dri. Craw —6B 182
Ashdown Gdns. S Croy —2E 84
Ashdown Ga. E Grin —8N 165
Ashdown Rd. Eps —9E 60
Ashdown Rd. F Row —7H 187
Ashdown Rd. King T —1L 41
Ashdown Rd. Reig —7N 121
Ashdown View. E Grin —2A 186
Ashdown Way. SW17 —3E 28
Ash Dri. Red —5E 122
Ashenden Rd. Guild —3J 113
Ashen Gro. SW19 —4M 27
Ashen Vale. S Croy —5G 65
Asher Dri. Asc —9G 17
Ashfield Av. Felt —2J 23
Ashfield Clo. Rich —2L 25
Ashfield Grn. Yat —1E 68
Ashfields Ct. Reig —1N 121
Ashford Av. Ashf —7C 22
Ashford Bus. Complex. Ashf —5D 22
Ashford Clo. Ashf —5N 21
Ashford Cres. Ashf —4N 21
Ashford Gdns. Cobh —3L 77
Ashford Ind. Est. Ashf —5D 22
Ashford Rd. Ashf —8D 22
Ashford Rd. Felt —5E 22
Ashford Rd. Stai —1L 37
Ash Grn. La. E. Ash —4G 111
Ash Grn. La. W. Tong & Ash —4D 110
Ash Grn. Rd. Ash —3G 110
Ash Gro. SE20 —1F 46
Ash Gro. Felt —2F 22
Ash Gro. Guild —2K 113
Ash Gro. Houn —4L 9
Ash Gro. Stai —7L 21
Ash Gro. W Wick —8M 47
Ashgrove Rd. Ashf —6D 22
Ash Hill Rd. Ash —9E 90
Ashington Ct. H'ham —3K 197
(off Woodstock Clo.)
Ashington Rd. SW6 —5L 13
Ash Keys. Craw —4C 182
Ashlake Rd. SW16 —5J 29
Ash La. Elst —9G 130
Ash La. Wind —5A 4
Ashleigh Av. Egh —8E 20
Ashleigh Clo. Horl —8D 142
Ashleigh Cotts. Dork —4H 139
Ashleigh Gdns. Sutt —8N 43
Ashleigh Rd. SE20 —2E 46
Ashleigh Rd. SW14 —6D 12
Ashleigh Rd. H'ham —3J 197
Ashley Av. Eps —9C 60
Ashley Av. Mord —4M 43
Ashley Cen. Eps —9C 60
Ashley Clo. Bookh —3N 97
Ashley Clo. Frim G —8E 70
Ashley Clo. W On T —7G 38
Ashley Ct. Eps —9C 60
Ashley Ct. Wok —5J 73
Ashley Dri. Bans —1M 81
Ashley Dri. B'water —2H 69
Ashley Dri. Iswth —2E 10
Ashley Dri. Twic —1B 24
Ashley Dri. W On T —9H 39
Ashley Gdns. Orp —2N 67
Ashley Gdns. Rich —3K 25
Ashley Gdns. Shalf —1B 134
Ashley Ho. G'ming —3H 133
Ashley La. Croy —1M 63
Ashley Pk. Av. W On T —8G 39
Ashley Pk. Cres. W On T —7H 39
Ashley Pk. Rd. W On T —8H 39
Ashley Rise. W On T —1G 57
Ashley Rd. SW19 —7N 27
Ashley Rd. Eps —9C 60
Ashley Rd. F'boro —1B 90
Ashley Rd. Hamp —9A 24
Ashley Rd. Rich —6L 11
Ashley Rd. Th Dit —5F 40
Ashley Rd. T Hth —3K 45
Ashley Rd. W On T —1G 57
Ashley Rd. Westc —6C 118
Ashley Rd. Wok —5J 73
Ashley Sq. Eps —9C 60
(off Ashley Cen.)
Ashley Way. W End —9A 52
Ashling Rd. Croy —7D 46
Ash Lodge Clo. Ash —3E 110
Ash Lodge Dri. Ash —3D 110
Ashlone Rd. SW15 —6J 13
Ashlyns Pk. Cobh —9M 57
Ashlyns Way. Chess —3K 59
Ashmead Rd. Felt —2H 23
Ashmere Av. Beck —1N 47
Ashmere Clo. Sutt —2J 61
Ash M. Eps —9D 60
Ashmore Ct. Houn —2A 10
Ashmore Ho. Craw —9B 162
Ashmore La. Kes —7E 66
Ashmore La. Rusp —3B 180
Ashmore La. Wind —1D 16
Ashridge. F'boro —7L 69
Ashridge Grn. Brack —9N 15
Ashridge Rd. Wokgm —9C 14
Ashridge Way. Mord —3L 43
Ashridge Way. Sun —7H 23
Ash Rd. Alder —3A 110
Ash Rd. Craw —2E 182
Ash Rd. Croy —8K 47
Ash Rd. Pirb —4C 92
Ash Rd. Shep —3B 38
Ash Rd. Sutt —6K 43
Ash Rd. W'ham —3M 107
Ash Rd. Wok —7N 73
Ash St. Ash —3D 110
Ashtead Gap. Lea —3H 79
Ashtead La. G'ming —9F 132
Ashtead Woods Rd. Asht —4J 79
Ashton Clo. Sutt —1M 61
Ashton Clo. W On T —3J 57
Ashton Gdns. Houn —7N 9
Ashton Rd. Wok —4J 73
Ashtree Av. Mitc —1B 44
Ash Tree Clo. Croy —5H 47
Ash Tree Clo. F'boro —2H 89
Ash Tree Clo. G'wood —8K 171
Ashtree Clo. Orp —1K 67
Ash Tree Clo. Surb —8L 41
Ashtrees. Cranl —9N 155
Ash Tree Way. Croy —4G 47
Ashurst. Eps —1C 80
Ashurst Clo. SE20 —1E 46
Ashurst Clo. H'ham —3N 197
Ashurst Clo. Kenl —2A 84
Ashurst Dri. Craw —3H 183
Ashurst Dri. Shep —4N 37

Ashurst Dri.—Barn Elms Pk.

Ashurst Dri. Tad —8A 100
Ashurst Gdns. SW2 —2L 29
Ashurst Rd. Ash V —9D 90
Ashurst Rd. Tad —8G 81
Ashurst Wlk. Croy —8E 46
Ash Vale. C'fold —4D 172
Ashvale Rd. SW17 —6D 28
Ash View Clo. Ashf —7N 21
Ash View Gdns. Ashf —6N 21
Ashville Way. Wokgm —3A 30
Ashwell Av. Camb —9D 50
Ashwindham Ct. Wok —5J 73
Ashwood. Craw —4B 182
Ashwood. Warl —7F 84
Ashwood Gdns. Hayes —1G 8
Ashwood Gdns. New Ad —3L 65
Ashwood Pk. Fet —2C 98
Ashwood Pk. Wok —5C 74
Ashwood Rd. Egh —7L 19
Ashwood Rd. Wok —5B 74
Ashworth Est. Croy —7H 45
Ashworth Pl. Guild —3J 113
Asilone Rd. SW15 —6H 13
Askill Dri. SW15 —8K 13
Aslett St. SW18 —1N 27
Asmar Clo. Coul —2J 83
Aspen Clo. Guild —9F 94
Aspen Clo. Stai —4H 21
Aspen Clo. Stoke D —3M 77
Aspen Gdns. W6 —1G 13
Aspen Gdns. Mitc —4E 44
Aspenlea Rd. W6 —2J 13
Aspen Sq. Wey —9E 38
Aspen Way. Bans —1J 81
Aspen Way. Felt —4J 23
Aspen Way. H'ham —4L 197
Aspin Way. B'water —1G 68
Aspley Rd. SW18 —8N 13
Assembly Wlk. Cars —[illegible] 44
Assher Rd. W On T —9M 39
Astleham Rd. Shep —2N 37
Aston Clo. Asht —5J 79
Aston Ct. Craw —8N 181
Aston Grn. Houn —5K 9
Aston Mead. Wind —3B 4
Aston Rd. SW20 —1H 43
Aston Rd. Clay —2E 58
Astonville St. SW18 —2M 27
Aston Way. Eps —2E 80
Astor Clo. Add —1M 55
Astor Clo. King T —7A 26
Astoria Mans. SW16 —4J 29
Astra Bus. Cen. Red —4E 142
Astra Mead. Wink R —7F 16
Asylum Arch Rd. Red —6D 122
Atalanta Clo. Purl —6L 63
Atalanta St. SW6 —3J 13
Atbara Rd. C Crook —9B 88
Atbara Rd. Tedd —7H 25
Atcham Rd. Houn —7C 10
Atfield Gro. W'sham —3A 52
Atheldene Rd. SW18 —2N 27
Athelstan Clo. Worth —3J 183
Athelstan Rd. King T —3M 41
Athelstan Way. H'ham —8L 197
Athena Clo. King T —2M 41
Atherfield Rd. Reig —6A 122
Atherley Way. Houn —1N 23
Atherton Clo. Shalf —9A 114
Atherton Clo. Stai —9M 7
Atherton Ct. Wind —3G 4
Atherton Dri. SW19 —5J 27
Atherton Rd. SW13 —3F 12
Athlone. Clay —3E 58
Athlone Rd. SW2 —1K 29
Athlone Sq. Wind —4F 4
Atkins Clo. Wok —5K 73
Atkins Dri. W Wick —8N 47
Atkinson Ct. Horl —9F 142
Atkinson Rd. M'bowr —5G 182
Atkins Rd. SW12 —1G 28
Atney Rd. SW15 —7K 13
Atrebatti Rd. Sand —6H 49
Attebrouche Ct. Brack —6B 32
Atte La. Warf —7A 16
Attenborough Clo. Fleet —2C 88
Atterbury Clo. W'ham —4M 107
Attfield Clo. Ash —3D 110
Attlee Clo. Croy —5N 45
Attlee Gdns. C Crook —9A 88
Attlee Ho. Craw —7N 181
Attleford La. Shack —5K 131
Attwood Clo. S Croy —1E 84
Atwater Clo. SW2 —2L 29
Atwood. Bookh —2M 97
Atwood Av. Rich —5N 11
Atwoods All. Rich —4N 11
Aubyn Hill. SE27 —5N 29
Aubyn Sq. SW15 —8F 12
Auchinleck Ct. Craw D —2E 184
Auchinleck Way. Alder —2K 109
Auckland Clo. SE19 —1C 46
Auckland Clo. Craw —9B 162
Auckland Gdns. SE19 —1B 46
Auckland Hill. SE27 —5N 29
Auckland Rd. SE19 —1C 46
Auckland Rd. Cat —9B 84
Auckland Rd. King T —3M 41
Auden Pl. Cheam —1H 61
Audley Clo. Add —2K 55
Audley Ct. Twic —4D 24
Audley Dri. Warl —2F 84
Audley Firs. W On T —1K 57
Audley Ho. Add —2K 55
Audley Pl. Sutt —4N 61
Audley Rd. Rich —8M 11
Audley Way. Asc —2H 33
Audrey Clo. Beck —5L 47
Audric Clo. King T —9N 25
Augur Clo. Stai —6H 21
Augusta Clo. W Mol —3N 39
Augusta Rd. Twic —3C 24
Augustine Clo. Coln —6G 7
Augustine Wlk. Warf —8C 16
August La. Abry —4M 135
Augustus Clo. Bren —3J 11
Augustus Ct. SW16 —3H 29
Augustus Ct. Felt —5N 23
Augustus Gdns. Camb —1G 71
Augustus Rd. SW19 —2J 27
Aultone Way. Cars —9D 44
Aultone Way. Sutt —8N 43
Aurelia Gdns. Croy —4K 45
Aurelia Rd. Croy —5J 45
Auriol Clo. Wor Pk —9D 42
Auriol Pk. Rd. Wor Pk —9D 42
Auriol Rd. W14 —1K 13
Aurum Clo. Horl —9F 142
Austen Clo. E Grin —9L 165
Austen Rd. F'boro —8M 69
Austen Rd. Guild —4B 114
Austin Clo. Coul —5M 83
Austin Clo. Twic —8J 11
Australia Ter. Frim G —6H 71
(off Cyprus Rd.)
Austyn Gdns. Surb —7A 42
Autumn Clo. SW19 —7A 28
Autumn Dri. Sutt —5N 61
Avalon Clo. SW20 —1K 10
Avalon Rd. SW6 —4N 13
Avard Gdns. Orp —1L 67
Avarn Rd. SW17 —7D 28
Avebury. Brack —5M 31
Avebury Ct. H'ham —1N 197
Avebury Pk. Surb —6K 41
Avebury Rd. SW19 —9L 27
Avebury Rd. Orp —1M 67
Aveley Clo. Farnh —4H 129
Aveley La. Farnh —5G 129
Aveling Clo. M'bowr —5G 182
Aveling Clo. Purl —9K 63
Aven Clo. Cranl —8N 155
Avening Rd. SW18 —1M 27
Avening Ter. SW18 —1M 27
Avenue C. Add —9N 37
Avenue Clo. Houn —4J 9
Avenue Clo. Tad —9G 81
Avenue Ct. Tad —1G 101
Avenue Cres. Houn —4J 9
Avenue Elmers. Surb —4L 41
Avenue Gdns. SE25 —1D 46
Avenue Gdns. SW14 —6D 12
Avenue Gdns. Horl —9G 142
Avenue Gdns. Houn —3J 9
Avenue Gdns. Tedd —8F 24
Avenue One. Add —1N 55
Avenue Pde. Sun —2J 39
Avenue Pk. Rd. SE27 —3M 29
Avenue Rd. SE20 & Beck —1F 46
Avenue Rd. SE25 —1C 46
Avenue Rd. SW16 —1H 45
Avenue Rd. SW20 —1G 42
Avenue Rd. Bans —2N 81
Avenue Rd. Bren —1J 11
Avenue Rd. Cat —9A 84
Avenue Rd. Cobh —3L 77
Avenue Rd. Cranl —9N 155
Avenue Rd. Eps —1C 80
Avenue Rd. F'boro —1B 90
Avenue Rd. Felt —4G 23
Avenue Rd. Fleet —3A 88
Avenue Rd. Gray —6A 170
Avenue Rd. Hamp —9B 24
Avenue Rd. Iswth —4F 10
Avenue Rd. King T —2L 41
Avenue Rd. N Mald —3D 42
Avenue Rd. Stai —6F 20
Avenue Rd. Sutt —6M 61
Avenue Rd. Tats —7G 87
Avenue Rd. Tedd —8G 24
Avenue Rd. Wall —4G 62
Avenue S. Surb —6N 41
Avenue Sucy. Camb —2N 69
Avenue Ter. N Mald —2B 42
Avenue, The. SW18 —1C 28
Avenue, The. Alder —5B 110
Avenue, The. Asc —7L 17
Avenue, The. Brock —3N 119
Avenue, The. Camb —1N 69
Avenue, The. Cars —4E 62
Avenue, The. Chob —5J 53
Avenue, The. Clay —2E 58
Avenue, The. Coul —2H 83
Avenue, The. Cran —4H 9
Avenue, The. Craw —8C 182
Avenue, The. Crowt —2G 48
Avenue, The. Croy —9B 46
Avenue, The. Dat —4L 5
Avenue, The. E Grin —4D 166
Avenue, The. Egh —5D 20
Avenue, The. Eps & Sut —4G 60
Avenue, The. Ewh —4F 156
Avenue, The. Fleet —4A 88
Avenue, The. G'ming —9J 133
(Drive, The)
Avenue, The. G'ming —2G 132
(New Pond Rd.)
Avenue, The. Gray —6B 170
Avenue, The. Hamp —7N 23
Avenue, The. Hand —8L 199
Avenue, The. Hasl —1D 188
Avenue, The. Horl —9D 142
Avenue, The. Houn —8B 10
Avenue, The. Kes —1F 66
Avenue, The. Light —6L 51
Avenue, The. New H —6J 55
Avenue, The. Old Win —8L 5
Avenue, The. Oxs —7F 58
Avenue, The. Rich —5M 11
Avenue, The. Rowl —7E 128
Avenue, The. S Nut —6J 123
Avenue, The. Stai —9K 21
Avenue, The. Sun —1J 39
Avenue, The. Surb —6N 41
Avenue, The. Sutt —6L 61
Avenue, The. Tad —9G 80
Avenue, The. Twic —8H 11
Avenue, The. W'ham —9H 87
Avenue, The. W Wick —6N 47
Avenue, The. Whyt —6D 84
Avenue, The. Wokgm —7K 31
Avenue, The. Wor Pk —8D 42
Avenue, The. Worp —4H 93
Avenue, The. Wray —7A 6
Avenue Three. Add —9N 37
Avenue Two. Add —9N 37
Avenue Vs. Red —7G 103
Averil Gro. SW16 —7M 29
Averill St. W6 —2J 13
[illegible]
Avern Rd. W Mol —3B 40
Avery Ct. Alder —2N 109
(off Alice Rd.)
Aviary Rd. Wok —3J 75
Aviary Way. Craw D —9F 164
Aviemore Clo. Beck —4J 47
Aviemore Way. Beck —4H 47
Avington Clo. Guild —3A 114
Avoca Rd. SW17 —5E 28
Avocet Cres. Col T —7J 49
Avon Clo. Add —3J 55
Avon Clo. Ash —3D 110
Avon Clo. F'boro —7K 69
Avon Clo. Sutt —1A 62
Avon Clo. Wor Pk —8F 42
Avon Ct. Binf —7H 15
Avon Ct. Farnh —2H 129
Avondale. Ash V —6D 90
Avondale Av. Esh —9G 40
Avondale Av. Stai —8H 21
Avondale Av. Wor Pk —7E 42
Avondale Clo. Horl —6E 142
Avondale Clo. W On T —2K 57
Avondale Gdns. Houn —8N 9
Avondale Rd. SW14 —6D 12
Avondale Rd. SW19 —6N 27
Avondale Rd. Alder —4N 109
Avondale Rd. Ashf —4M 21
Avondale Rd. Fleet —3B 88
Avondale Rd. S Croy —3N 63
Avon Gro. Brack —8A 16
Avonmead. Wok —5M 73
Avonmore Av. Guild —2B 114
Avonmore Gdns. W14 —1L 13
Avonmore Pl. W14 —1L 13
(off Avonmore Rd.)
Avonmore Rd. W14 —1L 13
Avon Path. S Croy —3N 63
Avon Rd. Farnh —2H 129
Avon Rd. Sun —8G 22
Avon Wlk. Craw —4L 181
Avonwick Rd. Houn —5B 10
Avro Way. Wall —4J 63
Avro Way. Wey —6N 55
Award Rd. C Crook —8A 88
(in two parts)
Axbridge. Brack —4C 32
Axes La. Red —1G 142
Axwood. Eps —2B 80
Ayebridges Av. Egh —8E 20
Ayjay Clo. Alder —5N 109
Aylesbury Ct. Sutt —9A 44
Aylesford Av. Beck —4H 47
Aylesham Way. Yat —9A 48
Aylesworth Spur. Old Win —1L 19
Aylett Rd. SE25 —3E 46
Aylett Rd. Iswth —5E 10
Ayliffe Clo. King T —1N 41
Ayling Ct. Farnh —5L 109
Ayling Hill. Alder —3L 109
Ayling La. Alder —4L 109
Aylward Rd. SW20 —1L 43
Aymer Clo. Stai —9G 20
Aymer Dri. Stai —9G 21
Aynscombe Path. SW14 —5B 12
Ayrshire Gdns. Fleet —1C 88
Aysgarth. Brack —5L 31
Aysgarth Ct. Sutt —9N 43
Ayshe Ct. Dri. H'ham —5L 197
Azalea Av. Lind —4B 168
Azalea Ct. Wok —6N 73
Azalea Dri. Hasl —9D 170
Azalea Gdns. C Crook —8C 88
Azalea Way. Camb —9F 50

Babbacombe Clo. Chess —2K 59
Babbs Mead. Farnh —2F 128
Baber Bri. Cvn. Site. Felt —8K 9
Baber Dri. Felt —9K 9
Babington Rd. SW16 —6H 29
Babylon La. Tad —5M 101
Bachelors Acre. Wind —4G 5
Bachelors La. Ock —2A 96
Back All. Dork —5H 119
Back Grn. W On T —3K 57
Back La. Bren —2K 11
Back La. Bucks H —2A 148
Back La. E Clan —9M 95
Back La. Elst —7H 131
Back La. Fren —1J 149
Back La. Plais —6A 192
Back La. Rich —3J 25
(in two parts)
Backley Gdns. SE25 —5D 46
Bk. of High St. Chob —7H 53
Back Path. Red —2N 123
Back Rd. Tedd —8E 24
Bacon Clo. Col T —8J 49
Bacon La. Churt —6H 149
Badajos Rd. Alder —1L 109
Baden Clo. Stai —8J 21
Baden Dri. Horl —7C 142
Baden-Powell Clo. Surb —8M 41
Baden Rd. Guild —1K 113
Bader Clo. Kenl —2A 84
Bader Ct. F'boro —6L 69
Badger Clo. Felt —4J 23
[illegible]
Badger Clo. Houn —6K 9
Badger Dri. Light —6L 51
Badgersbridge Ride. Wind —1M 17
Badgers Clo. Ashf —6A 22
Badgers Clo. Fleet —5A 88
Badgers Clo. G'ming —3G 133
Badgers Clo. H'ham —2M 197
Badgers Clo. Wok —5M 73
Badgers Copse. Camb —3C 70
Badgers Copse. Wor Pk —8E 42
Badger's Ct. Eps —9D 60
Badgers Cross. Milf —1C 152
Badgers Hill. Vir W —4M 35
Badgers Hole. Croy —1G 64
Badgers Hollow. G'ming —5G 132
Badgers Holt. Yat —1A 68
Badgers La. Warl —7F 84
Badgers Sett. Crowt —2E 48
Badgers Wlk. N Mald —1D 42
Badgers Wlk. Purl —7G 63
Badgers Wlk. Whyt —5C 84
Badgers Way. Brack —9D 16
Badger's Way. E Grin —8B 166
Badgers Way. Loxw —4J 193
Badgers Wood. Cat —3A 104
Badgers Wood. Ott —3F 54
Badger Wlk. Guild —6N 91
Badger Way. Ews —4C 108
Badgerwood Dri. Frim —4B 70
Badingham Dri. Fet —1E 98
Badminton Rd. SW12 —1E 28
Badshot Farm La. Bad L —7M 109
Badshot Lea Rd. Bad L —7L 109
Badshot Pk. Bad L —6M 109
Bagden Hill. Westh —8D 98
Bagley's La. SW6 —4N 13
Bagot Clo. Asht —3M 79
Bagshot Grn. Bag —4J 51
Bagshot Rd. Asc —8M 33
Bagshot Rd. Brack & Crowt —2N 31
Bagshot Rd. Egh —8M 19
Bagshot Rd. Knap —5E 72
Bagshot Rd. W End —8B 52
Bahram Rd. Eps —6C 60
Baigents La. W'sham —3A 52
Bailes La. Norm —9A 92
Bailey Clo. Frim —6B 70
Bailey Clo. H'ham —1M 197
Bailey Clo. Wind —5D 4
Bailey Rd. Westc —6C 118
Baileys Clo. B'water —2H 69
Bailing Hill. H'ham —1E 196
Baillie Rd. Guild —4B 114
Bain Av. Camb —4N 69
Baines Clo. S Croy —2A 64
Bainton Mead. Wok —4K 73
(off Cardingham)
Baird Clo. Craw —9E 162
Baird Dri. Wood S —2E 112
Baird Rd. F'boro —8A 70
Bakeham La. Egh —8N 19
Bakehouse Barn Clo. H'ham —1L 197
Bakehouse Rd. Horl —6E 142
Baker Boy La. New Ad —9H 65
Baker Clo. Craw —5B 182
Baker La. Mitc —1E 44
Baker Pl. Dork —5H 119
Baker's Clo. Ling —6A 146
Bakers Ct. SE25 —2B 46
Bakers End. SW20 —1K 43
Bakers Gdns. Cars —8C 44
Bakers La. Ling —7A 146
Bakers Mead. God —8F 104
Bakers M. Grn St —3N 67
Baker St. Wey —1B 56
Bakers Way. Capel —5J 159
Baker's Yd. Guild —4N 113
Bakewell Way. N Mald —1D 42
Balaam Ho. Sutt —1M 61
Balaclava Rd. Surb —6J 41
Balchins La. Westc —7A 118
Balcombe Ct. Craw —2H 183
Balcombe Gdns. Horl —9G 142
Balcombe La. Adgly —9K 183
Balcombe Rd. Horl & Craw —7F 142
Baldreys. Farnh —3F 128
Baldry Gdns. SW16 —7J 29
Baldwin Clo. M'bowr —6G 183
Baldwin Cres. Guild —1E 114
Baldwin Ho. SW2 —2L 29
Baldwins Field. E Grin —6M 165
Baldwins Shore. Eton —2G 4
Balfern Gro. W4 —1D 12
Balfont Clo. S Croy —9D 64
Balfour Av. Wok —9A 74
Balfour Cres. Brack —4N 31
Balfour Gdns. F Row —9G 187
Balfour Pl. SW15 —7G 12
Balfour Rd. SE25 —3D 46
Balfour Rd. SW19 —8N 27
Balfour Rd. Cars —4D 62
Balfour Rd. Houn —6B 10
Balfour Rd. Wey —1B 56
Balgowan Clo. N Mald —4D 42
Balgowan Rd. Beck —1H 47
Balham Continental Mkt. SW12
(off Shipka Rd.) —2F 28
Balham Gro. SW12 —1E 28
Balham High Rd. SW17 & SW12 —4E 28
Balham Hill. SW12 —1F 28
Balham New Rd. SW12 —1F 28
Balham Pk. Rd. SW12 —2D 28
Balham Sta. Rd. SW12 —2F 28
Balintore Ct. Col T —7J 49
Ballands N., The. Fet —9E 78
Ballands S., The. Fet —1E 98
Ballantine St. SW18 —7N 13
Ballantyne Dri. Kgswd —8L 81
Ballantyne Rd. F'boro —8M 69
Ballard Clo. King T —8C 26
Ballard Ct. Camb —7E 50
Ballard Grn. Wind —3B 4
Ballard Rd. Camb —7E 50
Ballards Farm Rd. S Croy & Croy —3D 64
Ballards Grn. Tad —6K 81
Ballards La. Oxt —7E 106
Ballards Rise. S Croy —3D 64
Ballards Way. S Croy & Croy —3D 64
Ballater Rd. S Croy —2C 64
Ballencrief Rd. S'dale —6C 34
Ballfield Rd. G'ming —5G 133
Balliol Clo. Craw —9G 163
Balliol Way. Owl —6K 49
Ballsdown. C'fold —5D 172
Ball & Wicket La. Farnh —5H 109
Balmain Ct. Houn —4B 10
Balmoral. E Grin —1C 186
Balmoral Av. Beck —3H 47
Balmoral Clo. SW15 —9J 13
Balmoral Ct. SE27 —5N 29
Balmoral Ct. Beck —1M 47
Balmoral Ct. Craw —7A 182
Balmoral Ct. Sutt —4M 61
Balmoral Ct. Wor Pk —8G 42
Balmoral Cres. Farnh —6G 108
Balmoral Cres. W Mol —2A 40
Balmoral Dri. Frim —6C 70
Balmoral Dri. Wok —3E 74
Balmoral Gdns. S Croy —6A 64
Balmoral Gdns. Wind —6G 4
Balmoral Rd. Ash V —9E 90
Balmoral Rd. King T —3M 41
Balmoral Rd. Wor Pk —9G 42
Balmoral Way. Sutt —6M 61
Balmuir Gdns. SW15 —7H 13
Balquhain Clo. Asht —4K 79
Baltic Cen., The. Bren —1K 11
Baltic Clo. SW19 —8B 28
Balvernie Gro. SW18 —1L 27
Bampfylde Clo. Wall —9G 44
Bampton Way. St J —5K 73
Banbury. Brack —6C 32
Banbury Clo. Frim —7D 70
Banbury Ct. Sutt —4M 61
Bancroft Clo. Ashf —6B 22
Bancroft Ct. Reig —3N 121
Bancroft Rd. Craw —4H 183
Bancroft Rd. Reig —3M 121
Banders Rise. Guild —2E 114
Band La. Egh —6B 20
Bandon Rise. Wall —2H 63
Bangalore St. SW15 —6H 13
Bank Av. Mitc —1B 44
Bank La. SW15 —8D 12
Bank La. Craw —3B 182
Bank La. King T —8L 25
Bank M. Sutt —3A 62
Bank Rd. Alder —8B 90
Banksian Wlk. Iswth —4E 10
Bankside. Farnh —5L 109
Bankside. S Croy —3C 64
Bankside. Wok —5L 73
Bankside Clo. Big H —5E 86
Bankside Clo. Cars —3C 62
Bankside Clo. Elst —8H 131
Bankside Clo. Iswth —7F 10
Bankside Dri. Th Dit —7H 41
Banks La. Eff J —1H 97
Banks Rd. Craw —3G 182
Banks Way. Guild —9B 94
Bank Ter. Shere —8B 116
(off Gomshall La.)
Bannister Clo. SW2 —2L 29
Bannister Clo. Witl —5C 152
Bannister Gdns. Yat —1E 68
Bannister's Rd. Guild —5J 113
Banstead Rd. Cars —5B 62
Banstead Rd. Cat —8A 84
Banstead Rd. Eps & Bans —6G 61
Banstead Rd. Purl —7L 63
Banstead Rd. S. Sutt —7A 62
Banstead Way. Wall —2J 63
Barataria Cvn. Site. Rip —8H 75
Barbara Clo. C Crook —7C 88
Barbara Clo. Shep —4C 38
Barber Clo. M'bowr —7G 182
Barber Dri. Cranl —6N 155
Barberry Clo. Fleet —7B 88
Barberry Way. B'water —4L 69
Barbon Clo. Camb —[illegible] 71
Barchard St. SW18 —8N 13
Barclay Clo. SW6 —3M 13
Barclay Clo. Fet —1B 98
Barclay Rd. SW6 —3M 13
Barclay Rd. Croy —9A 46
Barcombe Av. SW2 —3J 29
Bardney Rd. Mord —3N 43
Bardolph Av. Croy —5H 65
Bardolph Rd. Rich —6M 11
Bardon Wlk. Wok —4L 73
Bardsley Clo. Croy —9C 46
Bardsley Dri. Farnh —3F 128
Barfield Ct. Red —1E 122
Barfields. Blet —2M 123
Barford Clo. Fleet —5E 88
Bargate Clo. N Mald —6F 42
Bargate Ct. Guild —3H 113
Bargate Rise. G'ming —7F 132
Barge Clo. Alder —8C 90
Barge Wlk. E Mol —2D 40
Barge Wlk. King T —9K 25
Barham Clo. Wey —1D 56
Barham Rd. SW20 —8F 26
Barham Rd. S Croy —2N 63
Barhatch La. Cranl —5A 156
Barhatch Rd. Cranl —5A 156
Baring Rd. Croy —7D 46
Barker Grn. Brack —4N 31
Barker Rd. Cher —6G 37
Barker St. SW10 —2N 13
Barker Wlk. SW16 —4H 29
Barkham Rd. Wokgm —3A 30
Barkhart Dri. Wokgm —1B 30
Barkhart Gdns. Wokgm —1B 30
Barkis Mead. Owl —5K 49
Barkston Gdns. SW5 —1N 13
Barley Clo. Craw —4B 182
Barleycorn Meadow. Horl —7F 142
Barleymead. Horl —7F 142
Barley Mead. Warf —8C 16
Barley Mow Clo. Knap —4G 72
Barleymow Ct. Bet —3B 120
Barley Mow Hill. Head —3E 168
Barley Mow La. Knap —3F 72
Barley Mow Pas. W4 —1C 12
Barley Mow Rd. Egh —6M 19
Barleymow Way. Shep —3B 38
Barley Way. Fleet —9C 68
Barlow Clo. Wall —3J 63
Barlow Rd. Craw —6K 181
Barlow Rd. Hamp —8A 24
Barmouth Rd. SW18 —9N 13
Barmouth Rd. Croy —8G 47
Barnard Clo. Frim —6D 70
Barnard Clo. Sun —8J 23
Barnard Clo. Wall —4H 63
Barnard Ct. Wok —5H 73
Barnard Gdns. N Mald —3F 42
Barnard Rd. Mitc —2E 44
Barnard Rd. Warl —6L 85
Barnards Pl. S Croy —5M 63
Barnato Clo. W Byf —8N 55
Barnby Rd. Knap —4G 73
Barn Clo. Ashf —6C 22
Barn Clo. Bans —2B 82
Barn Clo. Brack —1B 32
Barn Clo. Camb —9C 50
Barn Clo. Eps —2B 80
Barn Clo. Peas P —1N 199
Barn Cres. Purl —9A 64
Barncroft. Farnh —2H 129
(in two parts)
Barn Elms Pk. SW15 —6H 13

Barnes All.—Beldham Gdns.

Barnes All. Hamp —1C 40
Barnes Av. SW13 —3F 12
Barnes Av. S'hall —1N 9
Barnes Clo. F'boro —1B 90
Barnes End. N Mald —4F 42
Barnes High St. SW13 —5E 12
Barnes Rd. Frim —6C 70
Barnes Rd. G'ming —3H 133
Barnes Wallis Dri. Wey —7N 55
Barnett Clo. Lea —6H 79
Barnett Clo. Won —3E 134
Barnett Ct. Brack —1B 32
Barnett Grn. Brack —5N 31
Barnett La. Light —8K 51
Barnett La. Won —4D 134
Barnett Row. Guild —7N 93
Barnett's Shaw. Oxt —5N 105
Barnett Wood La. Lea & Asht —7H 79
Barnfield. Bans —1N 81
Barnfield. Cranl —7N 155
Barnfield. Horl —9E 142
Barnfield. N Mald —5D 42
Barn Field. Yat —1C 68
Barnfield Av. Croy —8F 46
Barnfield Av. King T —5K 25
Barnfield Av. Mitc —2F 44
Barnfield Clo. SW17 —4B 28
Barnfield Clo. Coul —6N 83
Barnfield Cotts. Ling —1C 166
Barnfield Gdns. King T —5L 25
Barnfield Rd. Craw —2B 182
Barnfield Rd. S Croy —5B 64
Barnfield Rd. Tats —7F 86
Barnfield Way. Oxt —2C 126
Barnfield Wood Clo. Beck —5N 47
Barnfield Wood Rd. Beck —5N 47
Barn Hawe. Eden —2L 147
Barnlea Clo. Felt —3M 23
Barnmead. Chob —6J 53
Barn Meadow Clo. C Crook —1A 108
Barn Meadow La. Bookh —2N 97
Barnmead Rd. Beck —1G 47
Barnsbury Clo. N Mald —3B 42
Barnsbury Cres. Surb —7B 42
Barnsbury Farm Est. Wok —7N 73
Barnsbury La. Surb —8A 42
Barnscroft. SW20 —2G 43
Barnsfold La. Rud —2N 193
Barnsford Cres. W End —9D 52
Barnsley Clo. Ash V —3F 90
Barnsnap Clo. H'ham —2K 197
Barnway. Egh —6M 19
Barnwood. Craw —2G 183
Barnwood Clo. Guild —1H 113
Barnwood Rd. Guild —2H 113
Barnyard, The. Tad —2F 100
Baron Clo. Sutt —6N 61
Baron Gro. Mitc —3C 44
Barons Ct. Wall —9H 45
Baron's Ct. Rd. W14 —1K 13
Baronsfield Rd. Twic —9H 11
Baron's Hurst. Eps —3B 80
Barons Keep. W14 —1K 13
Baronsmead Rd. SW13 —4F 12
Barons, The. Twic —9H 11
Baron's Wlk. Croy —5H 47
Barons Way. Egh —7F 20
Baron's Way. Reig —7M 121
Baron Wlk. Mitc —3C 44
Barony Ho. Brack —9K 15
Barossa Rd. Camb —8B 50
Barracane Dri. Crowt —2G 48
Barrackfield Wlk. H'ham —8H 197
Barrack La. Wind —4G 5
Barrack Path. Wok —5J 73
Barrack Rd. Alder —2M 109
Barrack Rd. Guild —1K 113
Barrack Rd. Houn —7L 9
Barracks, The. Add —9K 37
Barrens Brae. Wok —5C 74
Barrens Clo. Wok —5C 74
Barrens Pk. Wok —5C 74
Barrett Cres. Wokgm —2C 30
Barrett Rd. Fet —2D 98
Barrhill Rd. SW2 —3J 29
Barricane. Wok —6L 73
Barrie Clo. Coul —3G 82
Barrie Ho. Add —4J 55
Barrie Rd. Farnh —5F 108
Barrihurst La. Cranl —8F 154
Barringer Sq. SW17 —5E 28
Barrington Ct. Dork —6G 119
Barrington Ct. Red —1E 122
Barrington Lodge. Wey —2D 56
Barrington Rd. Craw —5B 182
Barrington Rd. Dork —6G 119
Barrington Rd. H'ham —6L 197
Barrington Rd. Purl —8G 62
Barrington Rd. Sutt —8M 43
Barrosa Dri. Hamp —9A 24
Barrow Av. Cars —4D 62
Barrowgate Rd. W4 —1B 12
Barrow Grn. Rd. Oxt —8K 105
Barrow Hedges Clo. Cars —4C 62
Barrow Hedges Way. Cars —4C 62
Barrowhill. Wor Pk —8D 42
Barrowhill Clo. Wor Pk —8D 42
Barrow Rd. SW16 —7H 29
Barrow Rd. Croy —2L 63
Barrowsfield. S Croy —8C 64
Barrow Wlk. Bren —2J 11
Barr's La. Knap —3G 72
Barry Av. Wind —3F 4
Barry Clo. Craw —6C 182
Barry Sq. Brack —6B 32
Bars, The. Guild —4N 113
Barston Rd. SE27 —4N 29
Barstow Cres. SW2 —2K 29
Bartholomew Clo. Hasl —9G 171
Bartholomew Ct. Dork —6G 119
Bartholomew Pl. Warf —8B 16
Bartholomew Way. H'ham —2N 197
Bartlett Rd. W'ham —4L 107
Bartlett St. S Croy —2A 64
Bartlett Ter. Croy —8H 47
Barton Clo. Add —3J 55
Barton Clo. Alder —3K 109
Barton Clo. Shep —5C 38
Barton Ct. W14 —1K 13
(off Barons Ct. Rd.)
Barton Cres. E Grin —1C 186
Barton Grn. N Mald —1C 42
Barton Ho. SW6 —6N 13
(off Wandsworth Bri. Rd.)
Barton Pl. Guild —9D 94
Barton Rd. W14 —1K 13
Barton Rd. Brmly —4C 134
Bartons Dri. Yat —2C 68
Bartons Way. F'boro —7H 69
Barton, The. Cobh —8L 57
Barton Wlk. Craw —5F 182
Barts Clo. Beck —4K 47
Barttelot Rd. H'ham —7K 197
Barwell Clo. Crowt —2E 48
Barwell Trad. Est. Chess —5K 59
Barwood Av. W Wick —7L 47
Basden Gro. Felt —3A 24
Basden Ho. Felt —3A 24
Basemoors. Brack —1C 32
Basford Way. Wind —6A 4
Bashford Way. Worth —1H 183
Bashurst Copse. Itch —8N 195
Basildene Rd. Houn —6L 9
Basildon Clo. Sutt —5N 61
Basildon Way. Bew —6K 181
Basil Gdns. SE27 —6N 29
Basil Gdns. Croy —7G 46
Basingbourne Clo. Fleet —7B 88
Basingbourne Rd. Fleet —8A 88
Basing Clo. Th Dit —6F 40
Basing Dri. Alder —5N 109
Basingfield Rd. Th Dit —6F 40
Basinghall Gdns. Sutt —5N 61
Basing Rd. Bans —1L 81
Basing Way. Th Dit —6F 40
Baskerville Rd. SW18 —1C 28
Basset Clo. Frim —6C 70
Basset Clo. Wdhm —6L 55
Bassett Clo. Sutt —5N 61
Bassett Gdns. Iswth —3C 10
Bassett Rd. M'bowr —6H 183
Bassett Rd. Wok —3E 74
Bassett's Clo. Orp —1K 67
Bassetts Hill. D'land —1C 166
Bassett's Way. Orp —1K 67
Bassingham Rd. SW18 —1A 28
Baston Mnr. Rd. Brom —1D 66
Baston Rd. Brom —1E 66
Basuto Rd. SW6 —4M 13
Batavia Clo. Sun —9J 23
Batavia Rd. Sun —9J 23
Bat & Ball La. Wrec —5F 128
(in two parts)
Batchelors Acre. Wind —4G 4
Batcombe Mead. Brack —6C 32
Bateman Ct. Craw —6E 182
Bateman Gro. Ash —4D 110
Bates Cres. SW16 —8G 29
Bates Cres. Croy —2L 63
Bateson Way. Wok —1E 74
Bates Wlk. Add —3L 55
Bathgate Rd. SW19 —4J 27
Bath Ho. Rd. Bedd —7J 45
Bath Pas. King T —1K 41
Bath Pl. W6 —1H 13
(off Fulham Pal. Rd.)
Bath Rd. Camb —9B 50
Bath Rd. Coln —2D 6
(Brands Hill)
Bath Rd. Coln —4G 6
(Poyle)
Bath Rd. Houn —4K 9
Bath Rd. Mitc —2B 44
Bath Rd. W Dray & Hay —4K 7
Baths App. SW6 —3L 13
Bathurst Av. SW19 —9N 27
Batley Clo. Mitc —6D 44
Batsworth Rd. Mitc —2B 44
Batten Av. Wok —6H 73
Battersea Ct. Guild —3K 113
Battlebridge Ho. Red —8F 102
Battlebridge La. Red —8F 102
Battle Clo. SW19 —7A 28
Batts Hill. Red —2C 122
Batts Hill. Reig —1B 122
Batty's Barn Clo. Wokgm —3C 30
Baulk, The. SW18 —1M 27
Bavant Rd. SW16 —1J 45
Bawtree Clo. Sutt —6A 62
Bax Clo. Cranl —8N 155
Baxter Av. Red —3D 122
Baxter Clo. M'bowr —5F 182
Bayards. Warl —5F 84
Bay Clo. Horl —6C 142
Bay Dri. Brack —1C 32
Bayeux. Tad —9J 81
Bayfield Av. Frim —4B 70
Bayfield Rd. Horl —7C 142
Bayford Clo. B'water —5M 69
Bayham Rd. Mord —3N 43
Bayhorne La. Horl —1G 162
Bay Ho. Brack —1C 32
Bayleaf Clo. Hamp H —6D 24
Baylin Rd. SW18 —9N 13
Bayliss Ct. Guild —4M 113
Baylis Wlk. Craw —8N 181
Baynards Rd. H'ham —7A 176
Bayonne Rd. W6 —2K 13
Bay Path. God —9F 104
Bay Rd. Brack —9C 16
Baysfarm Ct. W Dray —4L 7
Bay Tree Av. Lea —7G 79
Baywood Clo. F'boro —9H 69
Bazalgette Clo. N Mald —4C 42
Bazalgette Gdns. N Mald —4C 42
Beach Gro. Felt —3A 24
Beach Ho. Felt —3A 24
Beachy Rd. Craw —8M 181
Beacon Clo. Bans —3J 81
Beacon Clo. Wrec —6F 128
Beacon Gdns. Fleet —4A 88
Beacon Gro. Cars —1E 62
Beacon Hill. D'land —2D 166
Beacon Hill. Wok —6M 73
Beacon Hill Ct. Hind —3B 170
Beacon Hill Rd. C Crook & Ews —8C 88
Beacon Hill Rd. Hind —3A 170
Beacon Rd. H'row A —9B 8
Beaconsfield Clo. W4 —1B 12
Beaconsfield Pl. Eps —8D 60
Beaconsfield Rd. Clay —4E 58
Beaconsfield Rd. Croy —5A 46
Beaconsfield Rd. Eps —6C 80
Beaconsfield Rd. N Mald —1C 42
Beaconsfield Rd. Surb —6M 41
Beaconsfield Rd. Twic —9H 11
Beaconsfield Rd. Wok —7B 74
Beaconsfield Wlk. SW6 —4L 13
Beacon View Rd. Elst —9G 130
Beacon Way. Bans —3J 81
Beadles La. Oxt —8N 105
Beadlow Clo. Cars —5B 44
Beadman Pl. SE27 —5M 29
Beadman St. SE27 —5M 29
Beadon Rd. W6 —1H 13
Beaford Gro. SW20 —2K 43
Beagle Clo. Felt —5J 23
Beale Clo. Wokgm —1A 30
Beale Ct. Craw —6M 181
Beales La. Wey —9C 38
Beales La. Wrec —4E 128
Beales Rd. Bookh —5B 98
Bealeswood La. Dock —4D 148
Beam Hollow. Farnh —5H 109
Bean Oak Rd. Wokgm —2D 30
Beard Rd. King T —6M 25
Beard's Hill. Hamp —9A 24
Beard's Hill Clo. Hamp —9A 24
Beard's Rd. Ashf —7F 22
Beare Grn. Ct. Bear G —7K 139
Beare Grn. Roundabout. Dork —9K 139
Bearfield Rd. King T —8L 25
Bear La. Farnh —9G 109
Bear Rd. Felt —5L 23
Bears Den. Tad —9L 81
Bearsden Way. Broad H —5D 196
Bearwood Clo. Add —3J 55
Bearwood Gdns. Fleet —4B 88
Beasley's Ait. Sun —5G 39
Beasley's Ait La. Sun —5G 39
Beatrice Av. SW16 —2K 45
Beatrice Rd. Oxt —7A 106
Beatrice Rd. Rich —8M 11
Beattie Clo. Bookh —2N 97
Beattie Clo. Felt —2G 22
Beatty Av. Guild —2C 114
Beauchamp Rd. SE19 —9N 29
Beauchamp Rd. Sutt —1M 61
Beauchamp Rd. Twic —1G 25
Beauchamp Rd. W Mol —4B 40
Beauchamp Ter. SW15 —6G 13
Beauclare Clo. Lea —8K 79
Beauclerc Ct. Sun —1K 39
Beauclerk Clo. Felt —2J 23
Beauclerk Ho. SW16 —4J 29
Beaufield Ga. Hasl —1H 189
Beaufort Clo. SW15 —1G 27
Beaufort Clo. Reig —2L 121
Beaufort Clo. Wok —3E 74
Beaufort Ct. Rich —5J 25
Beaufort Gdns. SW16 —8K 29
Beaufort Gdns. Asc —9J 17
Beaufort Gdns. Houn —4M 9
Beaufort M. SW6 —2L 13
Beaufort Rd. C Crook —7C 88
Beaufort Rd. Farnh —9H 109
Beaufort Rd. King T —3L 41
Beaufort Rd. Reig —2L 121
Beaufort Rd. Rich —5J 25
Beaufort Rd. Twic —1J 25
Beaufort Rd. Wok —3E 74
Beauforts. Egh —6M 19
Beaufort Way. Eps —4F 60
Beaufoy Ho. SE27 —4M 29
Beaufront Clo. Camb —8E 50
Beaufront Rd. Camb —8E 50
Beaulieu Clo. Brack —2D 32
Beaulieu Clo. Dat —4L 5
Beaulieu Clo. Houn —8N 9
Beaulieu Clo. Mitc —9E 28
Beaulieu Clo. Twic —9K 11
Beaulieu Gdns. B'water —1H 69
Beaumaris Pde. Frim —6D 70
Beaumont Av. W14 —1L 13
Beaumont Av. Rich —6M 11
Beaumont Clo. If'd —4K 181
Beaumont Clo. King T —8N 25
Beaumont Ct. W4 —1B 12
Beaumont Cres. W14 —1L 13
Beaumont Dri. Ashf —6E 22
Beaumont Gdns. Brack —4C 32
Beaumont Gro. Alder —2K 109
Beaumont Pl. Iswth —8F 10
Beaumont Rd. SE19 —7N 29
Beaumont Rd. SW19 —1K 27
Beaumont Rd. Purl —9L 63
Beaumont Rd. Wind —5F 4
Beaumonts. Red —2D 142
Beaumont Sq. Cranl —7A 156
Beaverbrook Roundabout. Lea —1K 99
Beaver Clo. Hamp —9B 24
Beaver Clo. H'ham —2L 197
Beaver Clo. Wokgm —5A 30
Beaver La. Yat —1D 68
Beaver M. Bord —5A 168
Beavers Clo. Farnh —1F 128
Beavers Clo. Guild —2H 113
Beavers Cres. Houn —7K 9
Beavers Hill. Farnh —1E 128
Beavers La. Houn —5K 9
Beavers Rd. Farnh —1F 128
Beavor Gro. W6 —1F 12
(off Beavor La.)
Beavor La. W6 —1F 12
Beck Ct. Beck —2G 46
Beckenham Gro. Brom —1N 47
Beckenham Rd. Beck —1G 47
Beckenham Rd. W Wick —6M 47
Beckenshaw Gdns. Bans —2C 82
Becket Clo. SE25 —5D 46
Becket Clo. SW19 —9N 27
(off High Path)
Beckett Av. Kenl —2M 83
Beckett Clo. SW16 —3H 29
Beckett Clo. Wokgm —2D 30
Beckett La. Craw —9B 162
Becketts Clo. Felt —9J 9
Becketts Pl. Hamp W —9K 25
Beckett Way. E Grin —1B 186
Becket Wood. Newd —6B 140
Beckford Av. Brack —5N 31
Beckford Rd. Croy —5C 46
Beckford Way. M'bowr —7F 182
Beck Gdns. Farnh —6G 108
Beckingham Rd. Guild —2K 113
Beck La. Beck —2G 46
Beck River Pk. Beck —1K 47
Beck Way. Beck —2J 47
Beckway Rd. SW16 —1H 45
Beclands Rd. SW17 —7E 28
Becmead Av. SW16 —5H 29
Bective Pl. SW15 —7L 13
Bective Rd. SW15 —7L 13
Bedale Clo. Craw —5A 182
Beddington Farm Rd. Croy —6J 45
Beddington Gdns. Cars & Wall —3E 62
(in two parts)
Beddington Gro. Wall —2H 63
Beddington La. Croy —4G 44
Beddington Pk. Cotts. Wall —9H 45
Beddington Ter. Croy —6K 45
Beddington Trad. Est. Croy —7J 45
Beddlestead La. Warl —4B 86
Bedfont Clo. Felt —9D 8
Bedfont Clo. Mitc —1E 44
Bedfont Ct. Stai —6J 7
Bedfont Grn. Clo. Felt —2D 22
Bedfont La. Felt —1F 22
Bedfont Rd. Felt —2D 22
Bedfont Rd. Stai —9N 7
Bedford Av. Frim G —9D 70
Bedford Clo. Wok —2M 73
Bedford Cres. Frim G —8C 70
Bedford Hill. SW12 & SW16 —2F 28
Bedford La. Asc —4E 34
Bedford La. Frim G —8D 70
Bedford Pk. Croy —7N 45
Bedford Pas. SW6 —3K 13
(off Dawes Rd.)
Bedford Pl. Croy —7A 46
Bedford Rd. Guild —4M 113
Bedford Rd. H'ham —7K 197
Bedford Rd. Twic —4D 24
Bedford Rd. Wor Pk —8H 43
Bedfordshire Down. Warf —7D 16
Bedgebury Gdns. SW19 —3K 27
Bedlow Cotts. Cranl —6A 156
Bedlow La. Cranl —7A 156
Bedlow Way. Croy —1K 63
Bedser Clo. T Hth —2N 45
Bedser Clo. Wok —3C 74
Bedster Gdns. W Mol —1B 40
Bedwell Gdns. Hayes —1F 8
(in two parts)
Beech Av. Bren —3H 11
Beech Av. Camb —2B 70
Beech Av. Eff —6L 97
Beech Av. Lwr Bo —6H 129
Beech Av. S Croy —7A 64
Beech Av. Tats —6F 86
Beechbrook Av. Yat —1D 68
Beech Clo. SW15 —1F 26
Beech Clo. SW19 —7H 27
Beech Clo. Ashf —6E 22
Beech Clo. Blind H —3H 145
Beech Clo. Byfl —8N 55
Beech Clo. Cars —8D 44
Beech Clo. C'fold —5D 172
Beech Clo. Cobh —7A 58
Beech Clo. Dork —4F 118
Beech Clo. E Grin —8N 165
Beech Clo. Eff —6L 97
Beech Clo. Stai —1M 21
Beech Clo. Sun —1K 39
Beech Clo. W On T —1K 57
Beech Clo. Ct. Cobh —7N 57
Beech Copse. S Croy —2B 64
Beech Ct. Surb —6K 41
Beechcroft. Asht —6M 79
Beechcroft Av. Kenl —2A 84
Beechcroft Av. N Mald —9B 26
Beechcroft Clo. SW16 —6K 29
Beechcroft Clo. Asc —3A 34
Beechcroft Clo. Houn —3M 9
Beechcroft Clo. Orp —1M 67
Beechcroft Ct. Brack —2N 31
Beechcroft Dri. Guild —6G 113
Beechcroft Lodge. Sutt —4A 62
Beechcroft Mnr. Wey —9E 38
Beechcroft Rd. SW14 —6B 12
Beechcroft Rd. SW17 —3C 28
Beechcroft Rd. Chess —9M 41
Beechcroft Rd. Orp —1M 67
Beechdale Rd. SW2 —1K 29
Beech Dell. Kes —1H 67
Beechdene. Tad —9G 80
Beech Dri. B'water —2J 69
Beech Dri. Kgswd —9L 81
Beech Dri. Reig —3B 122
Beech Dri. Rip —2J 95
Beechen Cliff Way. Iswth —5F 10
Beechen La. Tad —3L 101
Beeches Av. Cars —4C 62
Beeches Clo. SE20 —1F 46
Beeches Clo. Tad —1M 101
Beeches Cres. Craw —5C 182
Beeches La. Ash W —3F 186
Beeches Mead. E Grin —5H 167
Beeches Rd. SW17 —4C 28
Beeches Rd. Sutt —7K 43
Beeches, The. Ash V —5D 90
Beeches, The. Bans —3N 81
Beeches, The. Brmly —5B 134
Beeches, The. Fet —2E 98
Beeches, The. Houn —4B 10
Beeches, The. S Croy —2A 64
Beeches Wlk. Cars —5B 62
Beeches Wood. Tad —9M 81
Beechey Clo. Copt —7M 163
Beechey Way. Copt —7M 163
Beech Farm La. Camb —2D 70
Beech Farm Rd. Warl —7M 85
Beechfield. Bans —9N 61
Beech Fields. E Grin —7B 166
Beech Gdns. Craw D —1D 184
Beech Gdns. Wok —2A 74
Beech Glen. Brack —3N 31
Beech Gro. Add —1K 55
Beech Gro. Brkwd —8N 71
Beech Gro. Cat —4B 104
Beech Gro. Eps —4G 80
Beech Gro. Guild —3J 113
Beech Gro. Mayf —1N 93
Beech Gro. Mitc —4H 45
Beech Gro. N Mald —2C 42
Beech Hall. Ott —4E 54
Beech Hanger End. Gray —6N 169
Beech Hanger Rd. Gray —6N 169
Beech Hill. Brook —9K 151
Beech Hill. Head —5F 168
Beech Hill. Wok —1N 93
Beech Hill Rd. Asc —5C 34
Beech Hill Rd. Head —3E 168
Beech Holme. Craw D —1E 184
Beech Holt. Lea —9J 79
Beech Ho. Rd. Croy —9A 46
Beeching Clo. Ash —1F 110
Beeching Way. E Grin —9N 165
Beech La. Gray —5N 169
Beech La. Guild —6M 113
Beech La. Norm —3L 111
Beechlawn. Guild —4B 114
Beechlee. Wall —6G 62
Beech Lodge. Stai —6G 21
Beechmeads. Cobh —9L 57
Beechmont Av. Vir W —4N 35
Beechmore Gdns. Sutt —8J 43
Beechnut Dri. B'water —9G 48
Beechnut Ind. Est. Alder —3N 109
Beechnut Rd. Alder —3N 109
Beecholme. Bans —1K 81
Beecholme Av. Mitc —9F 28
Beech Ride. Fleet —6A 88
Beech Ride. Sand —7G 49
Beech Rd. SW16 —1K 45
Beech Rd. Big H —6D 86
Beech Rd. Eps —2E 80
Beech Rd. F'boro —7M 69
Beech Rd. Felt —1F 22
Beech Rd. Frim G —8D 70
Beech Rd. Hasl —1H 189
Beech Rd. H'ham —3A 198
Beech Rd. Red —4G 103
Beech Rd. Reig —1M 121
Beech Rd. Wey —1E 56
Beech Row. Ham —5L 25
Beechside. Craw —4C 182
Beechtree Av. Egh —7L 19
Beech Tree Clo. Craw —2B 182
Beech Tree Dri. Bad L —7M 109
Beech Tree La. Stai —1K 37
Beech Tree Pl. Sutt —2M 61
Beechvale. Wok —5B 74
(off Fairview Av.)
Beech Wlk. Eps —7F 60
Beech Wlk. W'sham —3A 52
Beech Way. Eps —2E 80
Beech Way. G'ming —8G 133
Beechway. Guild —2D 114
Beech Way. S Croy —9G 65
Beech Way. Twic —4A 24
Beechwood Av. Coul —2F 82
Beechwood Av. Orp —3N 67
Beechwood Av. Rich —4N 11
Beechwood Av. Stai —7K 21
Beechwood Av. Sun —7H 23
Beechwood Av. Tad —8M 81
Beechwood Av. T Hth —3M 45
Beechwood Av. Wey —1F 56
Beechwood Cvn. Pk. Tad —9A 100
Beechwood Clo. Asc —8J 17
Beechwood Clo. Knap —4H 73
Beechwood Clo. Surb —6J 41
Beechwood Clo. Wey —1F 56
Beechwood Ct. W4 —2C 12
Beechwood Ct. Cars —1D 62
Beechwood Ct. Sun —7H 23
Beechwood Dri. Cobh —7A 58
Beechwood Dri. Kes —1F 66
Beechwood Gdns. Cat —9D 84
Beechwood Gro. Surb —6J 41
Beechwood La. Warl —6G 85
Beechwood Mnr. Wey —1F 56
Beechwood Pk. Lea —9J 79
Beechwood Rd. Cat —9D 84
Beechwood Rd. Knap —4H 73
Beechwood Rd. S Croy —6B 64
Beechwood Rd. Vir W —6K 35
Beechwood Vs. Red —4E 142
Beecot La. W On T —8K 39
Beeding Clo. H'ham —3N 197
Beedingwood Dri. Colg —2D 198
Beedon Dri. Brack —5J 31
Beehive La. Binf —1H 31
Beehive Ring Rd. Gat A —5F 162
Beehive Rd. Binf —1J 31
Beehive Rd. Stai —6H 21
Beehive Way. Reig —7N 121
Beeken Dene. Orp —1L 67
Beeleigh Rd. Mord —3N 43
Beemans Row. SW18 —3A 28
Beeston Way. Felt —9K 9
Beeton's Av. Ash —9E 90
Beggarhouse La. Dork & Horl —2F 160
Beggar's Hill. Eps —4E 60
Beggar's Hill. (Junct.) —3E 60
Beggars La. Ab H —8F 116
Beggars La. Chob —7F 52
Beggars La. W'ham —3M 107
Beggars Roost La. Sutt —3M 61
Begonia Pl. Hamp —7A 24
Behenna Clo. Bew —4K 181
Beira St. SW12 —1F 28
Belcombe Av. Wor Pk —7H 43
Beldam Bri. Rd. W End —9D 52
Beldham Gdns. W Mol —1B 40

Beldham Rd.—Blackcap Pl.

Beldham Rd. *Farnh* —4E **128**
Belfast Rd. *SE25* —3E **46**
Belfield Rd. *Eps* —5C **60**
Belfry Shop. Cen., The. *Red* —2D **122**
Belgrade Rd. *Hamp* —9B **24**
Belgrave Clo. *W On T* —1J **57**
Belgrave Ct. *W4* —1B **12**
Belgrave Ct. *B'water* —3J **69**
Belgrave Cres. *Sun* —9J **23**
Belgrave Mnr. *Wok* —6A **74**
Belgrave Rd. *SE25* —3C **46**
Belgrave Rd. *SW13* —3E **12**
Belgrave Rd. *Houn* —6N **9**
Belgrave Rd. *Mitc* —2B **44**
Belgrave Rd. *Sun* —9J **23**
Belgrave Wlk. *Mitc* —2B **44**
Belgravia Ct. Horl —8F 142
(off St Georges Clo.)
Belgravia M. *King T* —3K **41**
Bellamy Clo. *W14* —1L **13**
Bellamy Ho. *Houn* —2A **10**
Bellamy Rd. *M'bowr* —7G **182**
Bellamy St. *SW12* —1F **28**
Belland Dri. *Alder* —3K **109**
Bellasis Av. *SW2* —3J **29**
Bell Av. *W Dray* —1A **8**
Bell Bri. Rd. *Cher* —7H **37**
Bell Cen. *Craw* —8D **162**
Bell Clo. *F'boro* —8A **70**
Bell Cres. *Coul* —8F **82**
Bell Dri. *SW18* —1K **27**
Bellever Hill. *Camb* —1C **70**
Belle Vue Clo. *Alder* —2B **110**
Belle Vue Clo. *Stai* —9J **21**
Belle Vue Enterprise Cen. *Alder* —2C **110**
Bellevue Pk. *T Hth* —2N **45**
Bellevue Rd. [illegible]
Bellevue Rd. *SW17* —2C **28**
Belle Vue Rd. *Alder* —2B **110**
Bellevue Rd. *King T* —2L **41**
Belle Vue Rd. *Orp* —6J **67**
Bellew Rd. *Deep* —8F **70**
Bellew St. *SW17* —4A **28**
Bellfield. *Croy* —5H **65**
Bellfields Ct. *Guild* —8M **93**
Bellfields Rd. *Guild* —1N **113**
Bell Foundry La. *Wokgm* —8A **14**
Bell Hammer. *E Grin* —1A **186**
Bell Hill. *Croy* —8N **45**
Bell Ho. Gdns. *Wokgm* —2A **30**
Bellingham Clo. *Camb* —2G **71**
Bell Junct. *Houn* —6B **10**
Bell La. *B'water* —1H **69**
Bell La. *Eton W* —1C **4**
Bell La. *Fet* —1D **98**
Bell La. *Rowl* —8D **128**
Bell La. *Twic* —2G **25**
Bell La. Clo. *Fet* —1D **98**
Bellmarsh Rd. *Add* —1K **55**
Bell Meadow. *God* —1E **124**
Belloc Clo. *Craw* —2F **182**
Belloc Ct. *H'ham* —5N **197**
Bello Clo. *SE24* —2M **29**
Bell Pde. *Wind* —5C **4**
Bell Pl. *Bag* —4K **51**
Bell Rd. *E Mol* —4D **40**
Bell Rd. *Hasl* —4E **188**
Bell Rd. *Houn* —6B **10**
Bell Rd. *Warn* —9F **178**
Bells All. *SW6* —5M **13**
Bells La. *Hort* —6D **6**
Bell St. *Reig* —3M **121**
Belltrees Gro. *SW16* —6K **29**
Bell Vale La. *Hasl* —4F **188**
Bell View. *Wind* —6C **4**
Bell View Clo. *Wind* —5C **4**
Bellway Ho. *Mers* —6B **102**
Bellweir Clo. *Stai* —3D **20**
Bellwether La. *Out* —4M **143**
Belmont. *Wey* —3D **56**
Belmont Av. *Guild* —9J **93**
Belmont Av. *N Mald* —4F **42**
Belmont Clo. *F'boro* —7L **69**
Belmont Gro. *W4* —1C **12**
Belmont M. *Camb* —3A **70**
Belmont Rise. *Sutt* —3L **61**
Belmont Rd. *SE25* —4E **46**
Belmont Rd. *W4* —1C **12**
Belmont Rd. *Beck* —1J **47**
Belmont Rd. *Camb* —2A **70**
Belmont Rd. *Crowt* —1G **49**
Belmont Rd. *Lea* —9G **79**
Belmont Rd. *Reig* —4A **122**
Belmont Rd. *Sutt* —6M **61**
Belmont Rd. *Twic* —3D **24**
Belmont Rd. *Wall* —2F **62**
Belmont Ter. *W4* —1C **12**
Belmore Av. *Wok* —3F **74**
Beloe Clo. *SW15* —7F **12**
Belsize Gdns. *Sutt* —1N **61**
Belstone M. *F'boro* —7M **69**
Beltane Dri. *SW19* —4J **27**
Belthorn Cres. *SW12* —1G **29**
Belton Rd. *Camb* —1C **70**
Beltran Rd. *SW6* —5N **13**
Belvedere Av. *SW19* —6K **27**
Belvedere Clo. *Esh* —2B **58**
Belvedere Clo. *Guild* —1L **113**
Belvedere Clo. *Tedd* —6E **24**
Belvedere Clo. *Wey* —2B **56**
Belvedere Ct. *B'water* —3J **69**
Belvedere Ct. *Craw* —2F **182**
Belvedere Dri. *SW19* —6K **27**
Belvedere Gdns. *W Mol* —4N **39**
Belvedere Gro. *SW19* —6K **27**
Belvedere Rd. *Big H* —5H **87**
Belvedere Rd. *F'boro* —3A **90**
Belvedere Sq. *SW19* —6K **27**
Belvoir Clo. *Frim* —5D **70**
Bemish Rd. *SW15* —6J **13**
Benbow La. *Duns* —5E **174**
Benbricke Grn. *Brack* —8M **15**
Benbrick Rd. *Guild* —4K **113**
Bence, The. *Egh* —2D **36**
Bench Field. *S Croy* —2C **64**
Benchfield Clo. *E Grin* —1D **186**
Bench, The. *Rich* —4J **25**
Bencombe Rd. *Purl* —1L **83**
Bencroft Rd. *SW16* —8G **29**
Bencurtis Pk. *W Wick* —9N **47**
Bendemeer Rd. *SW15* —6J **13**
Bendon Valley. *SW18* —1N **27**
Benedict Clo. *Orp* —1N **67**
Benedict Dri. *Felt* —1E **22**
Benedict Grn. *Warf* —8C **16**
Benedict Rd. *Mitc* —2B **44**
Benedict Wharf. *Mitc* —2B **44**
Benen-Stock Rd. *Stai* —8J **7**
Benetfeld Rd. *Binf* —7G **15**
Benett Gdns. *SW16* —1J **45**
Benfleet Clo. *Cobh* —8M **57**
Benfleet Clo. *Sutt* —9A **44**
Benham Clo. *Chess* —3J **59**
Benham Clo. *Coul* —5M **83**
Benham Gdns. *Houn* —8N **9**
Benhams Clo. *Horl* —6E **142**
Benhams Dri. *Horl* —6E **142**
Benhill Av. *Sutt* —1N **61**
Benhill Rd. *Sutt* —9A **44**
Benhill Wood Rd. *Sutt* —9A **44**
Benhilton Gdns. *Sutt* —9N **43**
Benhurst Clo. *S Croy* —6G **64**
Benhurst Ct. *SW16* —6L **29**
Benhurst Gdns. *S Croy* —7F **64**
Benhurst La. *SW16* —6L **29**
Benjamin Rd. *M'bowr* —5H **183**
Benland Cotts. *H'ham* —7D **178**
Benner La. *W End* —8C **52**
Bennet Ct. *Camb* —1A **70**
Bennett Clo. *Cobh* —9H **57**
Bennett Clo. *Hamp W* —9J **25**
Bennett Clo. *M'bowr* —7F **182**
Bennetts Av. *Croy* —8H **47**
Bennetts Clo. *Mitc* —9F **28**
Bennetts Farm Pl. *Bookh* —3N **97**
Bennetts Rd. *H'ham* —7L **197**
Bennett St. *W4* —2D **12**
Bennetts Way. *Croy* —8H **47**
Bennetts Wood. *Capel* —5J **159**
Bennett Way. *W Cla* —7J **95**
Benning Clo. *Wind* —6A **4**
Bennings Clo. *Brack* —8M **15**
Benning Way. *Wokgm* —9B **14**
Benn's All. *Hamp* —1B **40**
Benns Wlk. *Rich* —7L **11**
Bens Acre. *H'ham* —6N **197**
Bensbury Clo. *SW15* —1G **27**
Bensham Clo. *T Hth* —3N **45**
Bensham Gro. *T Hth* —1N **45**
Bensham La. *T Hth & Croy* —4M **45**
Bensham Mnr. Rd. *T Hth* —3N **45**
Benson Clo. *Houn* —7A **10**
Benson Rd. *Crowt* —2E **48**
Benson Rd. *Croy* —9L **45**
Bensons La. *H'ham* —6B **180**
Bentall Cen., The. *King T* —9K **25**
Benthall Gdns. *Kenl* —4N **83**
Bentham Av. *Wok* —2E **74**
Bentley Copse. *Camb* —2F **70**
Bentley Dri. *Wey* —5B **56**
Bentons La. *SE27* —5N **29**
Bentons Rise. *SE27* —6N **29**
Bentsbrook Clo. *N Holm* —9H **119**
Bentsbrook Cotts. *Dork* —9H **119**
Bentsbrook Pk. *N Holm* —9H **119**
Bentsbrook Rd. *N Holm* —9H **119**
Benwell Ct. *Sun* —9H **23**
Benwell Rd. *Brkwd* —6C **72**
Benwood Ct. *Sutt* —9A **44**
Beomonds Row. *Cher* —6J **37**
Berberis Clo. *Guild* —1M **113**
(in two parts)
Bere Rd. *Brack* —5C **32**
Beresford Av. *Surb* —7A **42**
Beresford Av. *Twic* —9J **11**
Beresford Clo. *Frim G* —8D **70**
Beresford Gdns. *Houn* —8N **9**
Beresford M. *SW18* —9N **13**
Beresford Rd. *Dork* —5H **119**
Beresford Rd. *King T* —9M **25**
Beresford Rd. *N Mald* —3B **42**
Beresford Rd. *Sutt* —4L **61**
Berestede Rd. *W6* —1E **12**
Bergenia Ct. *W End* —9B **52**
Berger M. *Yat* —9A **48**
Berkeley Av. *Houn* —5H **9**
Berkeley Clo. *Bren* —2G **11**
Berkeley Clo. *Craw* —7J **181**
Berkeley Clo. *Fleet* —4C **88**
Berkeley Clo. *King T* —8L **25**
Berkeley Ct. *Asht* —5M **79**
Berkeley Ct. *Guild* —3A **114**
Berkeley Ct. *Surb* —6K **41**
Berkeley Ct. *Wall* —9G **44**
Berkeley Ct. *Wey* —8E **38**
Berkeley Cres. *Frim* —6E **70**
Berkeley Dri. *W Mol* —2N **39**
Berkeley Dri. *Wink* —2L **17**
Berkeley Gdns. *Clay* —3G **59**
Berkeley Gdns. *W On T* —6G **39**
Berkeley Gdns. *W Byf* —1H **75**
Berkeley Ho. Bren —2K 11
(off Albany Rd.)
Berkeley Pl. *SW19* —7J **27**
Berkeley Pl. *Eps* —3C **80**
Berkeley Rd. *SW13* —4F **12**
Berkeleys, The. *Fet* —2E **98**
Berkeley Waye. *Houn* —2L **9**
Berkely Clo. *Sun* —2K **39**
Berkley Clo. *Stai* —3F **20**
Berkley Clo. Twic —4E 24
(off Wellesley Rd.)
Berkshire Clo. *Cat* —9A **84**
Berkshire Ct. *Brack* —1L **31**
Berkshire Rd. *Camb* —7D **50**
Berkshire Sq. *Mitc* —3J **45**
Berkshire Way. *Mitc* —3J **45**
Berkshire Way. *Wokgm & Brack* —2G **31**
Bermuda Ter. Frim G —6H 71
(off Crimea Rd.)
Bernadine Clo. *Warl* —[illegible] **10**
Bernard Ct. *Camb* —2N **69**
Bernard Gdns. *SW19* —6L **27**
Bernard Rd. *Wall* —1F **62**
Bernel Dri. *Croy* —9J **47**
Berne Rd. *T Hth* —4N **45**
Bernersh Clo. *Sand* —6H **49**
Berney Ho. *Beck* —4H **47**
Berney Rd. *Croy* —6A **46**
Berrington Dri. *E Hor* —2G **97**
Berrybank. *Col T* —9K **49**
Berry Ct. *Houn* —8N **9**
Berrycroft. *Brack* —9B **16**
Berrylands. *SW20* —3H **43**
Berrylands. *Surb* —5M **41**
Berrylands Rd. *Surb* —5M **41**
Berry La. *Brack* —1D **16**
Berry La. *W On T* —2L **57**
Berry La. *Wok* —2G **92**
Berry La. *Worp & Wok* —3F **92**
(in two parts)
Berry Meade. *Asht* —4M **79**
Berrymeade Wlk. *If'd* —4K **181**
Berryscroft Ct. *Stai* —8L **21**
Berryscroft Rd. *Stai* —8L **21**
Berry's Grn. Rd. *Berr G* —3K **87**
Berry's Hill. *Berr G* —2K **87**
Berry's La. *Byfl* —7M **55**
Berry Wlk. *Asht* —6M **79**
Berstead Wlk. *Craw* —6L **181**
Bertal Rd. *SW17* —5B **28**
Bertram Cotts. *SW19* —8M **27**
Bertram Rd. *King T* —8N **25**
Bertrand Ho. SW16 —4J 29
(off Leigham Av.)
Bert Rd. *T Hth* —4N **45**
Berwyn Av. *Houn* —4B **10**
Berwyn Rd. *SE24* —2M **29**
Berwyn Rd. *Rich* —7A **12**
Beryl Rd. *W6* —1J **13**
Berystede. *King T* —8A **26**
Besley St. *SW16* —7G **29**
Bessant Dri. *Rich* —4N **11**
Bessborough Rd. *SW15* —2F **26**
Beswick Gdns. *Brack* —9D **16**
Beta Rd. *Chob* —6J **53**
Beta Rd. *F'boro* —9L **69**
Beta Rd. *Wok* —3D **74**
Beta Way. *Egh* —9E **20**
Betchetts Grn. Rd. *Holmw* —5J **139**
Betchley Clo. *E Grin* —7A **166**
Betchworth Clo. *Sutt* —2B **62**
Betchworth Way. *New Ad* —5M **65**
Bethany Pl. *Wok* —5N **73**
Bethany Waye. *Felt* —1F **22**
Bethel Clo. *Farnh* —6J **109**
Bethel La. *Farnh* —5H **109**
Bethune Clo. *Worth* —4H **183**
Bethune Rd. *H'ham* —7L **197**
Betjeman Clo. *Coul* —4K **83**
Betjeman Wlk. *Yat* —2A **68**
Betley Ct. *W On T* —9J **39**
Betony Clo. *Croy* —7G **47**
Bettridge Rd. *SW6* —5L **13**
Betts Clo. *Beck* —1H **47**
Betts Way. *SE20* —1E **46**
Betts Way. *Craw* —8B **162**
Betts Way. *Surb* —7H **41**
Betula Clo. *Kenl* —2A **84**
Between Streets. *Cobh* —1H **77**
Beulah Av. *T Hth* —1N **45**
Beulah Ct. *Horl* —8E **142**
Beulah Cres. *T Hth* —1N **45**
Beulah Gro. *Croy* —5N **45**
Beulah Hill. *SE19* —7M **29**
Beulah Rd. *SW19* —8L **27**
Beulah Rd. *Sutt* —1M **61**
Beulah Rd. *T Hth* —2N **45**
Beulah Wlk. *Wold* —7H **85**
Bevan Ct. *Craw* —8N **181**
Bevan Ct. *Croy* —2L **63**
Bevan Pk. *Eps* —6E **60**
Beveren Clo. *Fleet* —1C **88**
Beverley Av. *SW20* —9E **26**
Beverley Av. *Houn* —7N **9**
Beverley Clo. *SW13* —5F **12**
Beverley Clo. *Add* —2M **55**
Beverley Clo. *Ash* —3D **110**
Beverley Clo. *Camb* —9H **51**
Beverley Clo. *Chess* —1J **59**
Beverley Clo. *Eps* —7H **61**
Beverley Clo. *Wey* —8F **38**
Beverley Ct. *W4* —1B **12**
Beverley Ct. *Houn* —7N **9**
Beverley Cres. *F'boro* —3L **89**
Beverley Gdns. *SW13* —6E **12**
Beverley Gdns. *Wor Pk* —7F **42**
Beverley Heights. *Reig* —1N **121**
Beverley La. *SW15* —4E **26**
Beverley La. *King T* —8D **26**
Beverley Path. *SW13* —5E **12**
Beverley Rd. *SE20* —1E **46**
Beverley Rd. *SW13* —6E **12**
Beverley Rd. *W4* —1E **12**
Beverley Rd. *King T* —9J **25**
Beverley Rd. *Mitc* —3H **45**
Beverley Rd. *N Mald* —3F **42**
Beverley Rd. *Sun* —9G **22**
Beverley Rd. *Whyt* —[illegible]
Beverley Rd. *Wor Pk* —8H **43**
Beverley Trad. Est. *Mord* —6J **43**
Beverley Way. *N Mald & SW20* —9E **26**
Beverstone Rd. *T Hth* —3L **45**
Bevill Allen Clo. *SW17* —6D **28**
Bevill Clo. *SE25* —2D **46**
Bevington Rd. *Beck* —1L **47**
Bewbush Dri. *Craw* —6K **181**
Bewbush Pl. *Craw* —6L **181**
Bewlys Rd. *SE27* —6M **29**
Bexhill Clo. *Felt* —3M **23**
Bexhill Rd. *SW14* —6B **12**
Bexley St. *Wind* —4F **4**
Beynon Rd. *Cars* —2D **62**
Bicester Rd. *Rich* —6N **11**
Bickersteth Rd. *SW17* —7D **28**
Bickley Ct. *Craw* —6M **181**
Bickley St. *SW17* —6C **28**
Bicknell Rd. *Frim* —4C **70**
Bickney Way. *Fet* —9C **78**
Bicknoller Clo. *Sutt* —6N **61**
Biddulph Rd. *S Croy* —6N **63**
Bideford Clo. *F'boro* —7M **69**
Bideford Clo. *Felt* —4N **23**
Bidhams Cres. *Tad* —8H **81**
Bietigheim Way. *Camb* —9A **50**
Big All. *M Grn* —6K **147**
Big Barn Gro. *Warf* —8B **16**
Big Comn. La. *Blet* —2M **123**
Biggin Av. *Mitc* —9D **28**
Biggin Clo. *Craw* —5A **182**
Biggin Hill. *SE19* —8M **29**
Biggin Hill Bus. Pk. *Big H* —2F **86**
Biggin Hill Clo. *King T* —6J **25**
Biggin Way. *SE19* —8M **29**
Bigginwood Rd. *SW16* —8M **29**
Biggs Row. *SW15* —6J **13**
Bignor Clo. *H'ham* —1N **197**
Bilberry Clo. *Craw* —6N **181**
Bilbets. *H'ham* —5J **197**
Billet Rd. *Stai* —4J **21**
Billingbear Cvn. Pk. *Wokgm* —5E **14**
Billingbear La. *Binf* —4G **15**
Billing Pl. *SW10* —3N **13**
Billing Rd. *SW10* —3N **13**
Billingshurst Rd. *Broad H* —5C **196**
Billing St. *SW10* —3N **13**
Billinton Dri. *M'bowr* —3F **182**
Billockby Clo. *Chess* —3M **59**
Bilton Cen. *Lea* —6F **78**
Bilton Clo. *Coln* —5G **7**
Bilton Ind. Est. *Brack* —3K **31**
Bina Gdns. *SW5* —1N **13**
Bindon Grn. *Mord* —3N **43**
Binfield Rd. *Brack* —7L **15**
Binfield Rd. *Byfl* —8N **55**
Binfield Rd. *Shur R* —1F **14**
Binfield Rd. *S Croy* —2C **64**
Binfield Rd. *Wokgm* —7F **14**
Bingham Dri. *Stai* —8M **21**
Bingham Dri. *Wok* —5J **73**
Bingham Rd. *Croy* —7D **46**
Bingley Rd. *Sun* —8H **23**
Binhams Lea. *Duns* —4B **174**
Binhams Meadow. *Duns* —4B **174**
Binley Ho. *SW15* —9E **12**
Binney Ct. *Craw* —9J **163**
Binns Rd. *W4* —1D **12**
Binns Ter. *W4* —1D **12**
Binscombe. *G'ming* —3G **132**
Binscombe Cres. *G'ming* —4H **133**
Binscombe La. *G'ming* —2G **132**
(in two parts)
Binstead Clo. *Craw* —1N **181**
Binstead Copse. *Fleet* —6A **88**
Binstead Rd. *Bucks H* —2A **148**
Binsted Dri. *B'water* —1J **69**
Binton La. *Seale* —1C **130**
Birchanger. *G'ming* —7H **133**
Birchanger Rd. *SE25* —4D **46**
Birch Av. *Cat* —2A **104**
Birch Av. *Fleet* —3A **88**
Birch Av. *Lea* —7F **78**
Birch Circ. *G'ming* —3J **133**
Birch Clo. *Bren* —3H **11**
Birch Clo. *Camb* —7C **50**
Birch Clo. *Craw D* —1F **184**
Birch Clo. *Iswth* —6D **10**
Birch Clo. *New H* —5M **55**
Birch Clo. *Send* —3H **95**
Birch Clo. *Shep* —1F **38**
Birch Clo. *Tedd* —6G **25**
Birch Clo. *Wok* —6M **73**
Birch Clo. *Wrec* —7F **128**
Birch Ct. *Wall* —1F **62**
Birchcroft Clo. *Cat* —3N **103**
Birchdale Clo. *W Byf* —7L **55**
Birch Dri. *B'water* —3J **69**
Birchend Clo. *S Croy* —3A **64**
Birches Clo. *Eps* —2D **80**
Birches Clo. *Mitc* —2D **44**
Birches Ind. Est. *E Grin* —7K **165**
Birches Rd. *H'ham* —3A **198**
Birches, The. *B'water* —1G **68**
Birches, The. *Craw* —[illegible]
Birches, The. *E Hor* —4F **96**
Birches, The. *F'boro* —1J **89**
Birches, The. *Houn* —1N **23**
Birches, The. *Man H* —9B **198**
Birches, The. *Orp* —1J **67**
Birches, The. *Wok* —5B **74**
Birchett Rd. *Alder* —2M **109**
Birchett Rd. *F'boro* —9K **69**
Birchetts Clo. *Brack* —9N **15**
Birchfield Clo. *Add* —1K **55**
Birchfield Clo. *Coul* —3K **83**
Birchfield Gro. *Eps* —6H **61**
Birchfield Pk. Ind. Est. *Charl* —6J **161**
Birchfields. *Camb* —2A **70**
Birch Grn. *Stai* —5J **21**
Birch Gro. *Brack* —3A **32**
Birch Gro. *Cobh* —1K **77**
Birch Gro. *Guild* —9M **93**
Birch Gro. *Shep* —1F **38**
Birch Gro. *Tad* —2K **101**
Birch Gro. *Wind* —4A **4**
Birch Gro. *Wok* —2F **74**
Birch Hill. *Croy* —2G **65**
Birch Hill Rd. *Brack* —6N **31**
Birch Ho. SW2 —1L 29
(off Tulse Hill)
Birchington Rd. *Surb* —6M **41**
Birchington Rd. *Wind* —5D **4**
Birchlands Av. *SW12* —1D **28**
Birchlands Ct. *Sand* —5K **49**
Birch La. *Asc* —9E **16**
Birch La. *Purl* —7J **63**
Birch La. *W End* —8A **52**
Birch Lea. *Craw* —9E **162**
Birch Pde. *Fleet* —4A **88**
Birch Platt. *W End* —9A **52**
Birch Rd. *Felt* —6L **23**
Birch Rd. *G'ming* —3J **133**
Birch Rd. *Head* —3F **168**
Birch Rd. *W'sham* —3B **52**
Birch Side. *Crowt* —1E **48**
Birch Tree Av. *W Wick* —2B **66**
Birch Tree View. *Light* —6L **51**
Birch Tree Way. *Croy* —8E **46**
Birch Vale. *Cobh* —9A **58**
Birchview Clo. *Yat* —2B **68**
Birch Wlk. *Mitc* —9F **28**
Birch Wlk. *W Byf* —8J **55**
Birch Way. *Ash V* —6E **90**
Birchway. *Red* —5F **122**
Birch Way. *Warl* —5H **85**
Birchwood Av. *Beck* —3J **47**
Birchwood Av. *Wall* —9E **44**
Birchwood Clo. *Horl* —7F **142**
Birchwood Clo. *M'bowr* —6G **183**
Birchwood Clo. *Mord* —3N **43**
Birchwood Dri. *Light* —6N **51**
Birchwood Dri. *W Byf* —8J **55**
Birchwood Gro. *Hamp* —7A **24**
Birchwood La. *Cat* —3M **103**
Birchwood La. *Esh & Oxs* —5D **58**
Birchwood Rd. *SW17* —6F **28**
Birchwood Rd. *W Byf* —8J **55**
Birdham Clo. *Craw* —1N **181**
Birdhaven. *Wrec* —5F **128**
Birdhouse La. *Orp* —2H **87**
Birdhurst Av. *S Croy* —1A **64**
Birdhurst Gdns. *S Croy* —1A **64**
Birdhurst Rise. *S Croy* —2B **64**
Birdhurst Rd. *SW18* —8N **13**
Birdhurst Rd. *SW19* —7C **28**
Birdhurst Rd. *S Croy* —2B **64**
Bird M. *Wokgm* —2A **30**
Birdsgrove. *Knap* —5E **72**
Birds Hill Dri. *Oxs* —9D **58**
Birds Hill Rise. *Oxs* —9D **58**
Birds Hill Rd. *Oxs* —8D **58**
Birdswood Dri. *Wok* —6H **73**
Bird Wlk. *Twic* —2N **23**
Birdwood Clo. *S Croy* —7F **64**
Birdwood Clo. *Tedd* —5E **24**
Birdwood Rd. *Col T* —8L **49**
Birkbeck Hill. *SE21* —2M **29**
Birkbeck Pl. *SE21* —3N **29**
Birkbeck Pl. *Owl* —6K **49**
Birkbeck Rd. *SW19* —6N **27**
Birkbeck Rd. *Beck* —1F **46**
Birkdale. *Brack* —6K **31**
Birkdale Dri. *If'd* —4J **181**
Birkdale Gdns. *Croy* —1G **65**
Birkenhead Av. *King T* —1M **41**
Birkenholme Clo. *Head* —5H **169**
Birkheads Rd. *Reig* —2M **121**
Birkwood Clo. *SW12* —1H **29**
Birnham Clo. *Rip* —2J **95**
Birtley Rise. *Brmly* —6C **134**
Birtley Rd. *Brmly* —6C **134**
Biscay Rd. *W6* —1J **13**
Biscoe Clo. *Houn* —2A **10**
Bisenden Rd. *Croy* —8B **46**
Bisham Clo. *Cars* —7D **44**
Bisham Clo. *M'bowr* —6H **183**
Bishopdale. *Brack* —3M **31**
Bishop Duppas Pk. *Shep* —6F **38**
Bishop Fox Way. *W Mol* —3N **39**
Bishopric. *H'ham* —6H **197**
Bishopric Ct. *H'ham* —6H **197**
Bishop's Av. *SW6* —[illegible]
Bishops Clo. *W4* —1B **12**
Bishop's Clo. *Coul* —5L **83**
Bishops Clo. *Fleet* —7B **88**
Bishops Clo. *Rich* —4K **25**
Bishop's Clo. *Sutt* —9M **43**
Bishop's Cotts. *Bet* —2A **120**
Bishops Ct. *H'ham* —7J **197**
Bishops Ct. *Rich* —6L **11**
Bishop's Dri. *Felt* —9E **8**
Bishop's Dri. *Wokgm* —1B **30**
Bishopsford Rd. *Mord* —6A **44**
Bishopsgate Rd. *Egh* —4K **19**
Bishop's Gro. *Hamp* —5N **23**
Bishops Gro. *W'sham* —3N **51**
Bishops Gro. Cvn. Site. *Hamp* —5A **24**
Bishop's Hall. *King T* —1K **41**
Bishops Hill. *W On T* —6H **39**
Bishop's La. *Brack* —1E **16**
Bishop's Mans. *SW6* —5J **13**
(in two parts)
Bishops Mead. *Farnh* —1G **128**
Bishopsmead Clo. *E Hor* —6F **96**
Bishopsmead Dri. *E Hor* —7G **96**
Bishopsmead Pde. *E Hor* —7G **96**
Bishop's Pk. Rd. *SW6* —5J **13**
Bishops Pk. Rd. *SW16* —9J **29**
Bishops Rd. *SW6* —4K **13**
Bishop's Rd. *Croy* —6M **45**
Bishops Rd. *Farnh* —5G **108**
Bishops Sq. *Cranl* —7A **156**
Bishopstone Wlk. *Craw* —8A **182**
Bishop Sumner Dri. *Farnh* —6H **109**
Bishops Wlk. *Croy* —2G **64**
Bishops Way. *Egh* —7F **20**
Bishops Wood. *Wok* —4J **73**
Bisley Clo. *Wor Pk* —7H **43**
Bison Ct. *Felt* —1J **23**
Bissingen Way. *Camb* —9B **50**
Bitmead Clo. *If'd* —4K **181**
Bittams La. *Cher* —1F **54**
Bittern Clo. *Col T* —7J **49**
Bittern Clo. *If'd* —4J **181**
Bitterne Dri. *Wok* —4J **73**
Bittoms, The. *King T* —2K **41**
Blackberry Clo. *Guild* —9L **93**
Blackberry Clo. *Shep* —3F **38**
Blackberry Farm Clo. *Houn* —3M **9**
Blackberry La. *Ling* —9N **145**
Blackberry Rd. *Felc & Ling* —2M **165**
Blackbird Clo. *Col T* —7J **49**
Blackbird Hill. *Turn H* —4F **184**
Blackborough Clo. *Reig* —3A **122**
Blackborough Rd. *Reig* —4A **122**
Blackbridge Ct. *H'ham* —6H **197**
Blackbridge La. *H'ham* —7G **197**
Blackbridge Rd. *Wok* —7N **73**
Blackbrook Rd. *Dork* —9K **119**
Blackburn, The. *Bookh* —2N **97**
Blackburn Way. *G'ming* —6K **133**
Blackbush Clo. *Sutt* —4N **61**
Blackbushe Airport. *Yat* —3A **68**
Blackbushe Bus. Pk. *Yat* —2B **68**
Blackbushe Pk. *Yat* —1B **68**
Blackbushes Rd. *Fleet* —7A **68**
Blackcap Clo. *Craw* —5A **182**
Blackcap Pl. *Col T* —7K **49**

Black Dog Wlk.—Bradshaws Clo.

Black Dog Wlk. Craw —1C 182
Blackdown Av. Wok —2G 74
Blackdown Barracks. Frim G (in two parts) —6J 71
Blackdown Clo. Wok —3F 74
Blackdown Rd. Deep —7G 70
Blackdown Rural Industries. Hasl —4J 189
Black Eagle Clo. W'ham —5L 107
Blackett Clo. Stai —1G 37
Blackett Rd. M'bowr —4G 182
Blackett St. SW15 —6J 13
Blackfold Rd. Craw —4E 182
Blackford Clo. S Croy —5M 63
Blackford's Path. SW15 —1F 26
Blackheath. Craw —1H 183
Blackheath Gro. Won —3D 134
Blackheath La. Alb —1K 135
Blackheath La. Won & Chil —3D 134
Blackheath Rd. Farnh —5F 108
Blackhills. Esh —5N 57
Black Horse Clo. Wind —5A 4
Black Horse La. Croy —6D 46
Blackhorse La. Reig —7N 101
Blackhorse La. Tad —7N 101
Blackhorse Rd. Wok —7G 73
Blackhorse Way. H'ham —6H 197
Blackhouse Rd. Colg —2H 199
Black Lake Clo. Egh —9C 20
Blacklands Cres. F Row —7H 187
Blacklands Meadow. Nutf —2J 123
Black Lion La. W6 —1F 12
Black Lion M. W6 —1F 12
Blackman Gdns. Alder —4N 109
Blackman's La. Warl —1A 86
Blackmeadows. Brack —5A 32
Blackmoor Clo. Asc —1H 33
Blackmoor Wood. Asc —1H 33
Blackmore Cres. Wok —2E 74
Blackmore's Gro. Tedd —7G 24
Blackness La. Kes —4F 66
Blackness La. Wok —6A 74
Blacknest Ga. Rd. Asc —2E 34
Blacknest Rd. S'dale & Vir W —2G 35
Black Pond La. Lwr Bo —5H 129
Black Prince Clo. Byfl —1A 76
Blackshaw Rd. SW17 —5A 28
Blacksmith Clo. Asht —6M 79
Blacksmith La. Chil —8E 114
Blacksmith Row. Slou —1C 6
Blacksmiths Hill. S Croy —9D 64
Blacksmiths La. Cher —6J 37
Blacksmiths La. Stai —2L 37
Blacks Rd. W6 —1H 13
Blackstone Clo. F'boro —8J 69
Blackstone Clo. Red —4C 122
Blackstone Hill. Red —4C 122
Blackstroud La. E. Light —7A 52
Blackstroud La. W. Light —7A 52
Black Swan Clo. Peas P —1N 199
Blackthorn Clo. Craw —1A 182
Blackthorn Clo. H'ham —6N 197
Blackthorn Clo. Reig —5A 122
Blackthorn Ct. Houn —3M 9
Blackthorn Cres. F'boro —6L 69
Blackthorn Dri. Light —8M 51
Blackthorne Av. Croy —7F 46
Blackthorne Cres. Coln —5G 7
Blackthorne Ind. Est. Coln —6G 7
Blackthorne Rd. Bookh —4C 98
Blackthorne Rd. Coln —6G 6
Blackthorn Pl. Guild —9M 93
Blackthorn Rd. Big H —3F 86
Blackthorn Rd. Reig —5A 122
Blackwater Clo. Ash —3E 110
Blackwater Ind. Est. B'water —1K 69
Blackwater La. Craw —3H 183
Blackwater Trad. Est. Alder —4B 110
Blackwater Valley Relief Rd. Camb —2L 69
Blackwater Valley Route. Alder —6C 110
Blackwater Valley Route. F'boro —7B 70
Blackwater View. Finch —5A 48
Blackwater Way. Alder —4B 110
Blackwell Av. Guild —3G 112
Blackwell Farm Rd. E Grin —7B 166
Blackwell Hollow. E Grin —8B 166
Blackwell Ho. SW4 —1H 29
Blackwell Rd. E Grin —8B 166
Blackwood Clo. W Byf —8L 55
Blade M. SW15 —7L 13
Bladen Clo. Wey —3F 56
Blades Clo. Lea —7K 79
Blades Ct. SW15 —7L 13
Bladon Clo. Guild —2C 114
Bladon Ct. SW16 —7J 29
Blagdon Rd. N Mald —3E 42
Blagdon Wlk. Tedd —7J 25
Blair Av. Esh —8C 40
Blair Ct. Beck —1L 47
Blairderry Rd. SW2 —3J 29
Blaire Pk. Yat —7A 48
Blaise Clo. F'boro —2B 90
Blake Clo. Cars —7C 44
Blake Clo. Craw —7D 182
Blake Clo. Crowt —3H 49
Blake Clo. Wokgm —9D 14
Blakeden Dri. Clay —3F 58
Blake Gdns. SW6 —4N 13
Blakehall Rd. Cars —3D 62
Blakemore Rd. SW16 —4J 29
Blakemore Rd. T Hth —4K 45
Blakeney Clo. Eps —7C 60
Blakenham Rd. SW17 —5D 28
Blake Rd. Croy —8B 46
Blake Rd. Mitc —2C 44
Blakes Av. N Mald —4E 42
Blakes Ct. Cher —7J 37
Blake's Grn. W Wick —7M 47
Blake's La. E Clan & W Hors —1N 115
Blakes La. N Mald —4E 42
Blakesley Wlk. SW20 —1L 43
Blakes Ride. Yat —9A 48
Blakes Ter. N Mald —4F 42
Blakewood Clo. Felt —5K 23
Blamire Dri. Binf —7L 15
Blanchards Hill. Guild —6A 94
Blanchland Rd. Mord —4N 43
Blanchman's Rd. Warl —5H 85
Blandfield Rd. SW12 —1E 28
Blandford Av. Beck —1H 47
Blandford Av. Twic —2B 24
Blandford Clo. Croy —9J 45
Blandford Clo. Wok —4D 74
Blandford Rd. Beck —1F 46
Blandford Rd. S'hall —1A 10
Blandford Rd. Tedd —6D 24
Blane's La. Brack & Asc —7D 32
Blanford Rd. Reig —4A 122
Blanks La. Newd —8D 140
Blatchford Clo. H'ham —5M 197
Blatchford Rd. H'ham —5M 197
Blay's Clo. Egh —7M 19
Blay's La. Egh —8L 19
Blear Ho. Eps —7E 60
Blegborough Rd. SW16 —7G 29
Blencarn Clo. Wok —3J 73
Blenheim Clo. SW20 —2H 43
Blenheim Clo. Craw —9H 163
Blenheim Clo. E Grin —7C 166
Blenheim Clo. Tong —5C 110
Blenheim Clo. Wall —4G 63
Blenheim Clo. W Byf —9H 55
Blenheim Ct. F'boro —3B 90
Blenheim Ct. Sutt —3A 62
Blenheim Cres. Farnh —7F 108
Blenheim Cres. S Croy —4N 63
Blenheim Field. F Row —6G 187
Blenheim Gdns. King T —8A 26
Blenheim Gdns. S Croy —8D 64
Blenheim Gdns. Wall —3G 62
Blenheim Gdns. Wok —6L 73
Blenheim Ho. Houn —6A 10
Blenheim Pk. Alder —6A 90
Blenheim Pk. Rd. S Croy —5N 63
Blenheim Rd. SW20 —2H 43
Blenheim Rd. Alder —6N 89
Blenheim Rd. Eps —7C 60
Blenheim Rd. H'ham —3K 197
Blenheim Rd. Slou —1N 5
Blenheim Rd. Sutt —9M 43
Blenheim Way. Iswth —4G 11
Blenkarne Rd. SW11 —1D 28
Beriot Rd. Houn —3K 9
Bletchingley Clo. Red —7G 103
Bletchingley Clo. T Hth —3M 45
Bletchingley Rd. God —9D 104
Bletchingley Rd. Mers —7G 103
Bletchingley Rd. Nutf —2L 123
Bletchmore Clo. Hayes —1E 8
Blewburton Wlk. Brack —3C 32
Blewfield. G'ming —9J 133
Bligh Clo. Craw —5D 182
Blighton La. Farnh —9B 110
Blincoe Clo. SW19 —3J 27
Blind La. Bans —2C 82
Blind La. Bet —6B 120
Blind La. Oxt —8A 106
Blind La. W End —6C 52
Blindley Rd. Craw —9H 163
Bloggs Way. Cranl —7M 155
Blomfield Dale. Brack —1J 31
Blondell Clo. W Dray —2M 7
Bloomfield Clo. Knap —4H 73
Bloomfield Dri. Brack —8B 16
Bloomfield Rd. King T —2L 41
Bloomfield Ter. W'ham —3N 107
Bloom Gro. SE27 —4M 29
Bloomhall Rd. SE19 —6N 29
Bloom Pk. Rd. SW6 —3L 13
Bloomsbury Clo. Eps —6C 60
Bloomsbury Ct. Guild —5B 114 (off St Lukes Sq.)
Bloomsbury Ct. Houn —4J 9
Bloomsbury Pl. SW18 —8N 13
Bloomsbury Way. B'water —3H 69
Bloor Clo. H'ham —1L 197
Blossom Clo. S Croy —2C 64
Blossom Way. W Dray —1B 8
Blossom Waye. Houn —2M 9
Blount Av. E Grin —9M 165
Blount Cres. Binf —8K 15
Bloxham Cres. Hamp —8N 23
Bloxham Rd. Cranl —7B 156
Bloxworth Clo. Brack —3D 32
Bloxworth Clo. Wall —9G 45
Blue Anchor All. Rich —7L 11
Blue Ball La. Egh —6B 20
Blue Barn La. Wey —7B 56
Bluebell Clo. Craw —6N 181
Bluebell Clo. E Grin —9L 165
Bluebell Clo. H'ham —3L 197
Bluebell Clo. Wall —7F 44
Bluebell Ct. Wok —6N 73
Bluebell Hill. Brack —9C 16
Bluebell La. E Hor —7F 96
Bluebell Rise. Light —8M 51
Bluebell Rd. Lind —4B 168
Bluebell Wlk. Fleet —3A 88
Blueberry Gdns. Coul —3K 83
Blue Cedars. Bans —1J 81
Blue Cedars. Cobh —8L 57
Blue Coat Wlk. Brack —4B 32
Bluefield Clo. Hamp —6A 24
Bluegates. Ewe —4F 60
Bluehouse Gdns. Oxt —6C 106
Bluehouse La. Oxt —6A 106
Blue Pryor Ct. C Crook —1A 108
Blue Riband Ind. Est. Croy —8M 45
Bluethroat Clo. Col T —7K 49
Bluff Cove. Alder —1A 110
Blundel La. Stoke D —3N 77
Blundell Av. Horl —7D 142
Blunden Ct. Brmly —5C 134
Blunden Rd. F'boro —1L 89
Blunt Rd. S Croy —2A 64
Blunts Av. W Dray —3B 8
Blunts Way. H'ham —5J 197
Blyth Clo. Twic —9F 10
Blythewood La. Asc —2J 33
Blythwood Dri. Frim —4B 70
Blytons, The. E Grin —9L 165
Board School Rd. Wok —3B 74
Boars Head Yd. Bren —3K 11
Bocketts La. Fet —2F 98
Bockhampton Rd. King T —8M 25
Boddicott Clo. SW19 —3K 27
Boden's Ride. Asc —8H 33
Bodiam Clo. Craw —3G 183
Bodiam Rd. SW16 —8H 29
Bodley Clo. N Mald —4D 42
Bodley Mnr. Way. SW2 —1L 29
Bodley Rd. N Mald —5C 42
Bodmin Gro. Mord —4N 43
Bodmin St. SW18 —2M 27
Bodnant Gdns. SW20 —2F 42
Bogey La. Orp —4J 67
Bog La. Brack —4D 32
Bognor Rd. Dork —2F 158
Bognor Rd. H'ham —4C 178
Boileau Rd. SW13 —3F 12
Bois Hall Rd. Add —2M 55
Bolderwood Way. W Wick —8L 47
Bolding Ho. La. W End —9C 52
Boleyn Av. Eps —6F 60
Boleyn Clo. M'bowr —6H 183
Boleyn Clo. Stai —6G 20
Boleyn Ct. Red —2E 122 (off St Anne's Rise)
Boleyn Dri. W Mol —2N 39
Boleyn Gdns. W Wick —8L 47
Boleyn Gro. W Wick —8M 47
Boleyn Wlk. Lea —7F 78
Bolingbroke Gro. SW11 —1D 28
Bollo La. W3 & W4 —1B 12
Bolney Ct. Craw —6L 181
Bolney Way. Felt —4M 23
Bolsover Gro. Red —7J 103
Bolstead Rd. Mitc —9F 28
Bolters La. Bans —1L 81
Bolters Rd. Horl —6E 142
Bolters Rd. S. Horl —6D 142
Bolton Av. Wind —6G 4
Bolton Clo. SE20 —1D 46
Bolton Clo. Chess —3K 59
Bolton Cres. Wind —6F 4
Bolton Gdns. SW5 —1N 13
Bolton Gdns. Tedd —7G 24
Bolton Gdns. M. SW10 —1N 13
Bolton Pl. SW10 —1N 13
Bolton Rd. W4 —3B 12
Bolton Rd. Chess —3K 59
Bolton Rd. M'bowr —8F 182
Bolton Rd. Wind —6F 4
Boltons Clo. Wok —3J 75
Boltons La. Binf —7K 15
Bolton's La. Hayes —4D 8
Boltons La. Wok —3J 75
Boltons, The. SW10 —1N 13
Bombers La. W'ham —6M 87
Bomer Clo. W Dray —3B 8
Bonchurch Clo. Sutt —4N 61
Bond Gdns. Wall —1G 63
Bond Rd. Mitc —1C 44
Bond Rd. Surb —8M 41
Bond Rd. Warl —5G 85
Bond's La. Mid H —2H 139
Bond St. W4 —1C 12
Bond St. Egh —6L 19
Bond Way. Brack —9N 15
Bonehurst Rd. Salf & Horl —2E 142
Bones La. Horne & Ling —7D 144
Bonner Hill Rd. King T —1M 41
Bonners Clo. Wok —9B 74
Bonnetts La. If'd —8M 161
Bonneville Gdns. SW4 —1G 29
Bonnys Rd. Reig —4J 121
Bonser Rd. Twic —3F 24
Bonsey Clo. Wok —8A 74
Bonsey La. Wok —8A 74
Bonseys La. Chob —5B 54
Bonsor Dri. Tad —9K 81
Bonwicke Cotts. Craw —4N 163
Bookham Comn. Rd. Bookh —8M 77
Bookham Ct. Bookh —1N 97
Bookham Gro. Bookh —4B 98
Bookham Ind. Est. Bookh —1N 97
Bookham Rd. D'side —6K 77
Bookhurst Rd. Cranl —6B 156
Booth Dri. Stai —7M 21
Booth Rd. Craw —6K 181
Booth Rd. Croy —8M 45
Booth Way. H'ham —5L 197
Borage Clo. Craw —6M 181
Border Chase. Copt —8L 163
Border Gdns. Croy —1L 65
Bordergate. Mitc —9D 28
Border Rd. Hasl —2B 188
Borderside. Yat —9A 48
Bordesley Rd. Mord —3N 43
Bordon Wlk. SW15 —1F 26
Boreen, The. Head —4G 169
Borelli M. Farnh —1H 129
Borelli Yd. Farnh —1H 129
Borers Arms Rd. Copt —6M 163
Borkwood Pk. Orp —1N 67
Borkwood Way. Orp —1N 67
Borland Rd. Tedd —8H 25
Borneo St. SW15 —6H 13
Borough Hill. Croy —9M 45
Borough Rd. G'ming —6G 133
Borough Rd. Iswth —4E 10
Borough Rd. King T —9N 25
Borough Rd. Mitc —1C 44
Borough Rd. Tats —8F 86
Borough, The. Brock —4N 119
Borough, The. Farnh —1G 129
Borrodaile Rd. SW18 —9N 13
Borrowdale Clo. Craw —5N 181
Borrowdale Clo. Egh —8C 20
Borrowdale Clo. S Croy —9C 64
Borrowdale Dri. S Croy —8C 64
Borrowdale Gdns. Camb —1H 71
Bosco Clo. Orp —1N 67
Boscombe Clo. Egh —9E 20
Boscombe Gdns. SW16 —7J 29
Boscombe Rd. SW17 —7E 28
Boscombe Rd. SW19 —9M 27
Boscombe Rd. Wor Pk —7H 43
Bosham Rd. M'bowr —6G 183
Bosman Dri. W'sham —9M 33
Bostock Av. H'ham —3N 197
Bostock Ho. Houn —2A 10
Boston Gdns. W4 —2D 12
Boston Gdns. Bren —1G 11
Boston Mnr. Rd. Bren —1G 11
Boston Pde. W7 —1G 11
Boston Pk. Rd. Bren —1J 11
Boston Rd. Croy —5K 45
Boswell Path. Hayes —1G 8
Boswell Rd. Craw —6C 182
Boswell Rd. T Hth —3N 45
Botany Hill. Seale —2B 130
Botery's Cross. Blet —2M 123
Bothwell Rd. New Ad —6M 65
Bothwell St. W6 —2J 13
Bothy, The. Pep H —6A 132
Botsford Rd. SW20 —1K 43
Bottle La. Warf —1K 15
Boucher Clo. Tedd —6F 24
Boughton Hall Av. Send —2H 95
Bouldish Farm Rd. Asc —4K 33
Boulevard, The. SW17 —3E 28
Boulevard, The. Craw —3C 182 (in two parts)
Boulogne Rd. Croy —5N 45
Boulters Ho. Brack —3C 32
Boulter's Rd. Alder —2N 109
Boulthurst Way. Oxt —1D 126
Boulton Ho. Bren —1L 11
Boundaries Rd. SW12 —3D 28
Boundaries Rd. Felt —2K 23
Boundary Bus. Cen., The. Wok —2C 74
Boundary Clo. SE20 —1D 46
Boundary Clo. Craw —2C 182
Boundary Clo. King T —2A 42
Boundary Clo. S'hall —1A 10
Boundary Cotts. Chil —8J 115
Boundary Rd. SW19 —7B 28
Boundary Rd. Ashf —6L 21
Boundary Rd. Cars & Wall —3F 62
Boundary Rd. Craw —2C 182
Boundary Rd. Dock —4C 148
Boundary Rd. F'boro —3A 90
Boundary Rd. Gray —6B 170
Boundary Rd. Wok —3C 74
Boundary Vs. B'water —2K 69
Boundary Way. Croy —2K 65
Boundary Way. Wok —2C 74
Boundstone Clo. Wrec —6G 128
Boundstone Rd. Rowl —7E 128
Bourdon Rd. SE20 —1F 46
Bourg-de-Peage Av. E Grin —9C 166
Bourke Clo. SW4 —1J 29
Bourke Hill. Coul —5D 82
Bourley La. Ews —2E 108
Bourley Rd. C Crook & Ews —9D 88
Bourne Av. Cher —2J 37
Bourne Av. Wind —6F 4
Bourne Clo. Chil —9D 114
Bourne Clo. W Byf —9K 55
Bourne Ct. W4 —2B 12
Bourne Ct. Alder —4M 109
Bourne Ct. Cat —1D 104
Bourne Dene. Wrec —6F 128
Bourne Dri. Mitc —1B 44
Bournefield Rd. Whyt —5D 84
Bourne Firs. Lwr Bo —6J 129
Bourne Gro. Asht —6K 79
Bourne Gro. Lwr Bo —4K 129
Bourne Gro. Clo. Lwr Bo —4K 129
Bourne Gro. Dri. Lwr Bo —4K 129
Bourne La. Cat —8A 84
Bourne Meadow. Egh —3D 36
Bourne Mill Ind. Est. Farnh —9K 109
Bournemouth Rd. SW19 —9M 27
Bourne Pk. Clo. Kenl —3B 84
Bourne Pl. W4 —1C 12
Bourne Rd. G'ming —4J 133
Bourne Rd. Red —8G 103
Bourne Rd. Vir W —4N 35
Bourneside. Vir W —6K 35
Bourneside Rd. Add —1M 55
Bourne St. Croy —8M 45
Bourne, The. Fleet —7B 88
Bournevale Rd. SW16 —5J 29
Bourne View. Kenl —2A 84
Bourne Way. Add —2L 55
Bourne Way. Eps —1B 60
Bourne Way. Sutt —2L 61
Bourne Way. Wok —9N 73
Bourns Ct. H'ham —5L 197
Bousley Rise. Ott —3F 54
Bouverie Gdns. Purl —1J 83
Bouverie Rd. Coul —5E 82
Bouverie Way. Slou —1A 6
Boveney New Rd. Eton W —1B 4
Boveney Rd. Dor —1A 4
Bovingdon Rd. SW6 —4N 13
Bovingdon Sq. Mitc —3J 45
Bowater Ridge. St G —6E 56
Bowater Rd. M'bowr —6G 183
Bowcott Hill. Head —4E 168
Bowcroft La. H'ham —1F 194
Bowden Clo. Felt —2F 22
Bowden Rd. Asc —4N 33
Bowenhurst Gdns. C Crook —8B 88
Bowenhurst Rd. C Crook —8B 88
Bowens Wood. Croy —5J 65
Bower Ct. Wok —3D 74
Bower Cres. Wokgm —9B 14
Bowerdean St. SW6 —4N 13
Bower Hill Clo. S Nut —6J 123
Bower Hill La. S Nut —4H 123
Bowerland La. Ling —3N 145
Bower Rd. Wrec —6F 128
Bowers Clo. Guild —8C 94
Bowers Farm Dri. Guild —8D 94
Bowers La. Guild —7C 94
Bowers Pl. Craw D —1E 184
Bower, The. Craw —4G 182
Bowes-Lyon Clo. Wind —4F 4 (off Alma Rd.)
Bowes Rd. Stai —6G 20
Bowes Rd. W On T —8J 39
Bowfell Rd. W6 —2H 13
Bowie Clo. SW4 —1H 29
Bowland Dri. Brack —6C 32
Bow La. Mord —5K 43
Bowlhead Grn. Rd. Brook —9K 151
Bowling Grn. Clo. SW15 —1G 27
Bowling Grn. Ct. Frim G —7C 70
Bowling Grn. La. H'ham —5K 197
Bowling Grn. Rd. Chob —5H 53
Bowlings, The. Camb —9A 50
Bowman Ct. Craw —2B 182 (off London Rd.)
Bowman Ct. Wel C —3E 48
Bowman M. SW18 —2L 27
Bowmans Meadow. Wall —9F 44
Bowness Clo. If'd —4J 181
Bowness Cres. SW15 —6D 26
Bowness Dri. Houn —7M 9
Bowry Dri. Wray —9B 6
Bowsley Ct. Felt —3H 23
Bowsprit, The. Cobh —2K 77
Bowyer Cres. Wokgm —9B 14
Bowyers Clo. Asht —5M 79
Bowyer's La. Brack —3N 15
Bowyer Wlk. Asc —9J 17
Boxall's Gro. Alder —5M 109
Boxall's La. Alder —5M 109
Boxall Wlk. H'ham —7J 197
Box Clo. Craw —8A 182
Boxford Clo. S Croy —8G 64
Boxford Ridge. Brack —2N 31
Boxgrove Av. Guild —1C 114
Boxgrove La. Guild —2C 114
Boxgrove Rd. Guild —2C 114
Boxhill Rd. Dork —2L 119
Boxhill Rd. Tad —1M 119
Boxhill Way. Str G —7A 120
Box La. E Grin —3G 186
Boxley Rd. Mord —3A 44
Box Ridge Av. Purl —8K 63
Box Wlk. E Hor —1F 116
Boxwood Way. Warl —4G 85
Boyd Clo. King T —8N 25
Boyd Ct. Brack —9M 15
Boyd Rd. SW19 —7B 28
Boyle Farm Rd. Th Dit —5G 40
Brabazon Av. Wall —4J 63
Brabazon Rd. Houn —3K 9
Brabon Rd. F'boro —9L 69
Brabourne Rise. Beck —4M 47
Brabrook Ct. Wall —1F 62
Bracebridge. Camb —1M 69
Bracewood Gdns. Croy —9C 46
Bracken Av. SW12 —1E 28
Bracken Av. Croy —9L 47
Bracken Bank. Asc —9G 17
Bracken Clo. Bookh —2N 97
Bracken Clo. Copt —7M 163
Bracken Clo. Craw —1C 182
Bracken Clo. Sun —7G 22
Bracken Clo. Twic —1A 24
Bracken Clo. Wok —5B 74
Bracken Clo. Won —5C 134
Brackendale Clo. Camb —3C 70
Brackendale Clo. Houn —4B 10
Brackendale Rd. Camb —1B 70
Brackendene. Ash —1G 110
Brackendene Clo. Wok —2C 74
Bracken End. Iswth —8D 10
Bracken Gdns. SW13 —5F 12
Bracken Gro. H'ham —3A 198
Brackenhill. Cobh —8B 58
Bracken Hollow. Camb —7F 50
Bracken La. Yat —9A 48
Brackenlea. G'ming —4G 132
Bracken Path. Eps —9A 60
Brackenside. Horl —7F 142
Brackens, The. Asc —2F 32
Brackens, The. Crowt —9F 30
Bracken Way. Chob —6J 53
Bracken Way. Guild —1H 113
Brackenwood. Camb —1H 71
Brackenwood. Sun —9H 23
Brackenwood Rd. Wok —6G 73
Bracklesham Clo. F'boro —7M 69
Brackley. Wey —2E 56
Brackley Clo. Wall —4J 63
Brackley Rd. W4 —1D 12
Brackley Ter. W4 —1D 12
Bracknell Beeches. Brack —2N 31
Bracknell Clo. Camb —6D 50
Bracknell Enterprise Cen. Brack —1M 31
Bracknell Rd. Bag —1H 51
Bracknell Rd. Camb —5E 50
Bracknell Rd. Crowt —7D 32 (Bagshot Rd.)
Bracknell Rd. Crowt —2H 49 (Duke's Ride)
Bracknell Rd. Warf —6C 16
Bracknell Wlk. Bew —7K 181
Bracondale. Esh —2C 58
Bradbourne St. SW6 —5M 13
Bradbury Rd. M'bowr —6G 182
Braddock Clo. Iswth —5F 10
Braddon Rd. Rich —6M 11
Bradenhurst Clo. Cat —4C 104
Bradfield Clo. Guild —9C 94
Bradfield Clo. Wok —5A 74
Bradfields. Brack —4B 32
Bradford Dri. Eps —3E 60
Brading Rd. SW2 —1K 29
Brading Rd. Croy —5K 45
Bradley Dri. Wokgm —6A 30
Bradley La. Dork —1G 119
Bradley M. SW17 —2D 28
Bradley Rd. SE19 —7N 29
Bradmore Way. Coul —4J 83
Bradshaw Clo. SW19 —7M 27
Bradshaw Clo. Wind —4B 4
Bradshaws Clo. SE25 —2D 46

Bradstock Rd. Eps —2F 60
Bradstone Rd. Rich —4M 11
Braemar Av. SW19 —3M 27
Braemar Av. S Croy —6N 63
Braemar Av. T Hth —2M 45
Braemar Clo. Frim —6D 70
Braemar Clo. G'ming —8G 132
Braemar Gdns. W Wick —7M 47
Braemar Rd. Bren —2K 11
Braemar Rd. Wor Pk —9G 42
Braeside. New H —7K 55
Braeside Av. SW19 —9K 27
Braeside Clo. Hasl —9D 170
Braeside Rd. SW16 —8G 29
Braes Mead. S Nut —4J 123
Brafferton Rd. Croy —1N 63
Bragg Rd. Tedd —7E 24
Braid Clo. Felt —3N 23
Brailsford Clo. Mitc —8C 28
Brainton Av. Felt —1J 23
Brakey Hill. Blet —3B 124
Bramber Clo. Craw —1C 182
Bramber Clo. H'ham —3A 198
Bramber Ct. W5 —1L 11
Bramber Ct. Bren —1L 11
Bramber Rd. W14 —2L 13
Brambleacres Clo. Sutt —4M 61
Bramblebank. Frim G —8E 70
Bramble Banks. Cars —5E 62
Bramble Clo. Copt —7M 163
Bramble Clo. Croy —1K 65
Bramble Clo. Guild —1H 113
Bramble Clo. Red —5E 122
Bramble Clo. Shep —2E 38
Bramble Ct. Ewh —4F 156
Brambledene Clo. Wok —5M 73
Bramble Down. Stai —9K 21
Brambledown Rd. Cars & Wall —[illegible]
Brambledown Rd. S Croy —4B 64
Bramblegate. Crowt —1F 48
Bramble La. Hamp —7N 23
Bramble Rise. Cobh —2K 77
Brambles Clo. Ash —3F 110
Brambles Clo. Cat —9B 84
Brambles Clo. Iswth —3H 11
Brambles Pk. Brmly —5B 134
Brambles, The. SW19 —6L 27
(off Woodside)
Brambles, The. Crowt —1C 48
Brambles, The. G'ming —4G 133
Brambles, The. W Dray —1N 7
Brambleton Av. Farnh —3G 128
Bramble Twitten. E Grin —9C 166
Brambletye La. F Row —5F 186
Brambletye Pk. Rd. Red —5D 122
Brambletye Rd. Craw —4E 182
Bramble Wlk. Eps —1A 80
Bramble Wlk. Red —5E 122
Bramble Way. Rip —2H 95
Bramblewood. Red —7F 102
Bramblewood Clo. Cars —7C 44
Bramblewood Pl. Fleet —4A 88
Brambling Clo. H'ham —7N 197
Brambling Rd. H'ham —7N 197
Bramcote. Camb —1G 71
Bramcote Av. Mitc —3D 44
Bramcote Rd. SW15 —7G 13
Bramerton Rd. Beck —2J 47
Bramford Rd. SW18 —7N 13
Bramham Gdns. SW5 —1N 13
Bramham Gdns. Chess —1K 59
Bramley Av. Coul —2G 83
Bramley Av. Shep —2F 38
Bramley Clo. Cher —7K 37
Bramley Clo. Craw —3D 182
Bramley Clo. Red —5C 122
Bramley Clo. S Croy —2N 63
Bramley Clo. Stai —7L 21
Bramley Clo. Twic —9C 10
Bramley Ct. Crowt —3D 48
Bramley Gro. Crowt —2C 48
Bramley Hill. S Croy —2M 63
Bramley Ho. SW15 —9E 12
(off Tunworth Cres.)
Bramley Ho. Houn —7N 9
Bramley Ho. Red —4E 122
Bramley La. B'water —1G 69
Bramley Rd. Camb —4N 69
Bramley Rd. Cheam —5J 61
Bramley Rd. Sutt —2B 62
Bramley Wlk. Horl —8G 143
Bramley Way. Asht —4M 79
Bramley Way. Houn —8N 9
Bramley Way. W Wick —8L 47
Bramling Av. Yat —9A 48
Brampton Gdns. W On T —2K 57
Brampton Rd. Croy —5C 46
Bramshaw Rise. N Mald —5D 42
Bramshot Dri. Fleet —3B 88
Bramshot La. Fleet —1F 88
Bramston Rd. SW17 —4A 28
Bramswell Rd. G'ming —5J 133
Bramwell Clo. Sun —1L 39
Brancaster La. Purl —7N 63
Brancaster Rd. SW16 —4J 29
Brancker Clo. Wall —4J 63
Brandlehow Rd. SW15 —7L 13
Brandon Clo. Camb —2H 71
Brandon Clo. M'bowr —5H 183
Brandon Mans. W14 —2K 13
(off Queen's Club Gdns.)
Brandon Rd. C Crook —8A 88
Brandon Rd. S'hall —1N 9
Brandon Rd. Sutt —1N 61
Brandreth Rd. SW17 —3F 28
Brandries, The. Wall —9H 45
Brandsland. Reig —7N 121
Brands Rd. Slou —2D 6
Brandy Way. Sutt —4M 61
Brangwyn Cres. SW19 —9A 28
Branksea St. SW6 —3K 13
Branksome Clo. Camb —9C 50
Branksome Clo. W On T —8L 39
Branksome Ct. Fleet —4A 88
Branksome Hill Rd. Sand —8K 49
Branksome Pk. Rd. Camb —9C 50
Branksome Rd. SW19 —9M 27
Branksome Way. N Mald —9B 26
Branksomewood Rd. Fleet —3A 88
Bransby Rd. Chess —3L 59
Branson Rd. Bord —6A 168
Branstone Rd. Rich —4M 11
Brantridge Rd. Craw —5D 182
Brants Bri. Brack —1C 32
Brantwood Av. Iswth —7G 10
Brantwood Clo. W Byf —9J 55
Brantwood Ct. W Byf —9H 55
(off Brantwood Dri.)
Brantwood Dri. W Byf —9H 55
Brantwood Gdns. W Byf —9H 55
Brantwood Rd. S Croy —5N 63
Brassey Clo. [illegible]
Brassey Rd. Oxt —8B 106
Brasted Clo. Sutt —6M 61
Brasted Rd. W'ham —4N 107
Brathway Rd. SW18 —1N 27
Bratten Ct. Croy —5A 46
Bravington Clo. Shep —4A 38
Braxted Pk. SW16 —7K 29
Braybourne Dri. Iswth —3F 10
Braybrooke Rd. Brack —8N 15
Bray Clo. M'bowr —6H 183
Bray Ct. SW16 —6J 29
Braycourt Av. W On T —6J 39
Braye Clo. Sand —6H 49
Bray Gdns. Wok —3G 74
Bray Rd. Guild —4L 113
Bray Rd. Stoke D —3M 77
Braywood Av. Egh —7B 20
Braziers La. Wink R —6H 17
Brazil Clo. Bedd —6J 45
Breakfield. Coul —3J 83
Breamore Clo. SW15 —2F 26
Breamwater Gdns. Rich —4H 25
Breasley Clo. SW15 —7H 13
Brecon Clo. F'boro —7J 69
Brecon Clo. Mitc —2J 45
Brecon Clo. Wor Pk —8H 43
Brecon Rd. W6 —2K 13
Brecons, The. Wey —1E 56
Bredon Rd. Croy —6C 46
Bredune. Kenl —2A 84
Breech La. Tad —2F 100
Breech, The. Col T —8K 49
Breer St. SW6 —6N 13
Breezehurst Dri. Craw —6K 181
Bregsells La. Dork —7K 139
Bremer Rd. Stai —4J 21
Bremner Av. Horl —7D 142
Brenda Rd. SW17 —3D 28
Brende Gdns. W Mol —3B 40
Brendon Clo. Esh —3C 58
Brendon Clo. Hayes —3D 8
Brendon Ct. S'hall —1B 10
Brendon Dri. Esh —3C 58
Brendon Rd. F'boro —7J 69
Brenley Clo. Mitc —2E 44
Brentford Bus. Cen. Bren —3J 11
Brentford Ho. Twic —1H 25
Brent Lea. Bren —3J 11
Brentmoor Rd. W End —9N 51
Brent Rd. Bren —2J 11
Brent Rd. S Croy —5E 64
Brent Side. Bren —2J 11
Brentside Executive Cen. Bren —2J 11
Brentwaters Bus. Pk. Bren —3J 11
Brent Way. Bren —3K 11
Brentwick Gdns. Bren —1L 11
Brentwood Ct. Add —1K 55
Brethart Rd. Frim —5C 70
Bretlands Rd. Cher —8G 36
Brettgrave. Eps —6B 60
Brett Ho. Clo. SW15 —1J 27
Brettingham Clo. Craw —6K 181
Brewer Rd. Craw —5C 182
Brewers Clo. F'boro —9M 69
Brewers La. Rich —8K 11
Brewer St. Blet —9N 103
Brewery La. Byfl —9N 55
Brewery La. Twic —1F 24
Brewery M. Cen. Iswth —6G 10
Brewery Rd. Wok —4N 73
Brew Ho. Rd. Brock —7A 120
Brewhouse St. SW15 —6K 13
Brewhurst La. Loxw —6J 193
Breydon Wlk. Craw —5F 182
Brian Av. S Croy —8B 64
Briane Rd. Eps —6B 60
Briar Av. SW16 —8K 29
Briar Av. Light —9H 51
Briar Banks. Cars —5E 62
Briar Clo. Craw —9A 162
Briar Clo. Eden —9M 127
Briar Clo. Hamp —6N 23
Briar Clo. Iswth —8F 10
Briar Clo. W Byf —7L 55
Briar Ct. Sutt —1H 61
Briar Gro. S Croy —9D 64
Briar Hill. Purl —7J 63
Briar La. Cars —5E 62
Briar La. Croy —1L 65
Briarleas Ct. F'boro —5B 90
Briar Patch. G'ming —5G 133
Briar Rd. SW16 —2J 45
Briar Rd. Send —1D 94
Briar Rd. Shep —4A 38
Briar Rd. Twic —2E 24
Briars Clo. F'boro —2J 89
Briars Ct. Oxs —1D 78
Briars, The. Ash —3F 110
Briars, The. Slou —1B 6
Briars, The. Stai —9J 7
Briars Wood. Horl —7G 142
Briarswood Clo. Craw —1H 183
Briarswood Way. Orp —2N 67
Briar Wlk. SW15 —7G 13
Briar Wlk. W Byf —8J 55
Briar Way. Guild —8D 94
Briarwood Clo. Felt —4F 22
Briarwood Ct. Wor Pk —7F 42
(off Avenue, The)
Briarwood Rd. Eps —3F 60
Briarwood Rd. Wok —6G 73
Briary Lodge. Beck —1M 47
Briavels Ct. Eps —2D 80
Brickbat All. Lea —9H 79
Brick Farm Clo. Rich —4A 12
Brickfield Clo. Bren —3J 11
Brickfield Cotts. Crowt —4E 48
Brickfield Cotts. Guild —3A 112
Brickfield Farm Gdns. Orp —1L 67
Brickfield La. Hayes —2E 8
Brickfield Rd. SW19 —5N 27
Brickfield Rd. Out —2L 143
Brickfield Rd. T Hth —9M 29
Brickhouse La. S God & Newc —5F 144
Brick Kiln La. Oxt —8E 106
Bricklands. Craw D —2E 184
Brick La. Fleet —3A 88
Bricksbury Hill. Farnh —5H 109
Brickwood Rd. Croy —8B 46
Brickyard Copse. Ockl —6C 158
Brickyard La. Craw D —1E 184
Brickyard La. Wott —1L 137
Brideake Clo. Craw —6M 181
Bridge Av. W6 —1H 13
Bridge Barn La. Wok —5N 73
Bridge Clo. Byfl —8A 56
Bridge Clo. Stai —5G 20
Bridge Clo. Tedd —5F 24
Bridge Clo. W On T —6G 38
Bridge Clo. Wok —4M 73
Bridge Ct. Wey —1C 56
Bridge Ct. Wok —4N 73
Bridge End. Camb —2N 69
Bridgefield. Farnh —1J 129
Bridgefield Clo. Bans —2H 81
Bridgefield Rd. Sutt —3M 61
Bridgefoot. Sun —9G 23
Bridge Gdns. Ashf —8D 22
Bridge Gdns. E Mol —3D 40
Bridgeham Clo. Wey —2B 56
Bridgeham Way. Small —9M 143
Bridgehill Clo. Guild —2K 113
Bridge Ho. Sutt —3N 61
(off Bridge Rd.)
Bridge Ind. Est. Horl —8F 142
Bridgelands. Copt —7L 163
Bridge La. Vir W —4A 36
Bridgeman Dri. Wind —5D 4
Bridgeman Rd. Tedd —7G 24
Bridgemead. Frim —6A 70
Bridgemead. Pirb —4C 92
Bridge M. G'ming —7H 133
Bridge M. St J —4N 73
Bridge M. Tong —5D 110
Bridgend Rd. SW18 —7N 13
Bridgepark. SW18 —8M 13
Bridge Pl. Croy —7A 46
Bridge Rd. Alder —4M 109
Bridge Rd. Asc —4A 34
Bridge Rd. Bag —4J 51
Bridge Rd. Camb —3N 69
Bridge Rd. Cher —6K 37
Bridge Rd. Chess —2L 59
Bridge Rd. Cranl —8N 155
Bridge Rd. E Mol —3D 40
Bridge Rd. Eps —8E 60
Bridge Rd. F'boro —1L 89
Bridge Rd. G'ming —6H 133
Bridge Rd. Hasl —1G 189
Bridge Rd. Houn & Iswth —6D 10
Bridge Rd. Rud —1E 194
Bridge Rd. Sutt —3N 61
Bridge Rd. Twic —9H 11
Bridge Rd. Wall —2G 62
Bridge Rd. Wey —1A 56
Bridge Row. Croy —7A 46
Bridges Ct. H'ham —3N 197
Bridges La. Croy —1J 63
Bridges Pl. SW6 —4L 13
Bridge Sq. Farnh —1H 129
Bridges Rd. SW19 —7N 27
Bridges Rd. M. SW19 —7N 27
Bridge St. W4 —1C 12
Bridge St. Coln —3F 6
Bridge St. G'ming —7H 133
Bridge St. Guild —4M 113
Bridge St. Lea —9G 79
Bridge St. Rich —8K 11
Bridge St. Stai —5G 21
Bridge St. W On T —7F 38
Bridge View. W6 —1H 13
Bridge View. S'dale —6E 34
Bridge Wlk. Yat —8C 48
Bridgewater Ct. Slou —1C 6
Bridgewater Rd. Wey —3E 56
Bridgewater Ter. Wind —4G 4
Bridgewater Way. Wind —4G 4
Bridge Way. Cobh —9G 57
Bridge Way. Coul —6C 82
Bridge Way. Twic —1C 24
Bridge Wharf. Cher —6L 37
Bridge Wharfe Rd. Iswth —6H 11
Bridge Wharf Rd. Iswth —6H 11
Bridgewood Rd. SW16 —8H 29
Bridgewood Rd. Wor Pk —1F 60
Bridgford St. SW18 —4A 28
Bridle Clo. Eps —2C 60
Bridle Clo. Gray —6M 169
Bridle Clo. King T —3K 41
Bridle Clo. Sun —2H 39
Bridle Ct. Alder —2K 109
Bridle End. Eps —1E 80
Bridle La. Stoke D & Oxs —2B 78
Bridle La. Twic —9H 11
Bridle Path. Croy —9J 45
Bridle Path, The. Eps —6H 61
Bridlepath Way. Felt —2F 22
Bridle Rd. Clay —3H 59
Bridle Rd. Croy —9K 47
(in two parts)
Bridle Rd. Eps —9E 60
Bridle Rd. S Croy —5D 64
Bridle Rd., The. Purl —6J 63
Bridle Way. Craw —2H 183
Bridle Way. Croy —1K 65
Bridle Way. Orp —1L 67
Bridleway Clo. Eps —6H 61
Bridle Way, The. Croy —6H 65
Bridleway, The. Wall —2G 63
Bridlington Clo. Big H —6D 86
Bridport Rd. T Hth —2L 45
Brier Lea. Tad —4L 101
Brierley. New Ad —3L 65
(in two parts)
Brierley Clo. SE25 —3D 46
Brierley Rd. SW12 —3G 28
Brierly Clo. Guild —1K 113
Brier Rd. Tad —6G 81
Briggs Clo. Mitc —9F 28
Bright Hill. Guild —5A 114
Brightlands Rd. Reig —1A 122
Brightman Rd. SW18 —2B 28
Brighton Clo. Add —2L 55
Brighton Rd. Add —2L 55
Brighton Rd. Alder —4A 110
Brighton Rd. Coul & Purl —5G 83
Brighton Rd. G'ming —7H 133
Brighton Rd. Hand —8N 199
Brighton Rd. Hool & Coul —1F 102
Brighton Rd. Horl —9D 142
Brighton Rd. H'ham —7K 197
Brighton Rd. Peas P & Craw —5N 199
Brighton Rd. Red —4D 122
Brighton Rd. Salf —1E 142
Brighton Rd. S Croy —2N 63
Brighton Rd. Surb —5J 41
Brighton Rd. Sutt —7M 61
Brighton Rd. Tad & Bans —9K 81
Brighton Ter. Red —4D 122
Brightside Av. Stai —8L 21
Brightwell Clo. Croy —7L 45
Brightwell Cres. SW17 —6D 28
Brightwells Rd. Farnh —1H 129
Brigstock Rd. Coul —2F 82
Brigstock Rd. T Hth —4L 45
Brimshot La. Chob —5H 53
Brimstone La. Dork —3M 139
Brind Cotts. Chob —6J 53
Brindle Clo. Alder —5N 109
Brindles, The. Bans —4L 81
Brinkley Rd. Wor Pk —8G 42
Brinksway. Fleet —5B 88
Brinn's La. B'water —1H 69
Brinsworth Clo. Twic —3D 24
Brinsworth Ho. Twic —3D 24
Brisbane Av. SW19 —9N 27
Brisbane Clo. Craw —9B 162
Briscoe Rd. SW19 —7B 28
Brisson Clo. Esh —2N 57
Bristol Clo. Craw —9H 163
Bristol Clo. Stai —9N 7
Bristol Ct. Stanw —9N 7
Bristol Gdns. SW15 —1H 27
Bristol Rd. Mord —4A 44
Bristow Rd. Camb —3N 69
Bristow Rd. Croy —1J 63
Bristow Rd. Houn —6C 10
Britannia Clo. Bord —6A 168
Britannia Ind. Est. Coln —5G 6
Britannia La. Twic —1C 24
Britannia Rd. SW6 —3N 13
Britannia Rd. Surb —6M 41
Britannia Way. SW6 —3N 13
(off Britannia Rd.)
Britannia Way. Stai —1M 21
British Gro. W4 —1E 12
British Gro. Pas. W4 —1E 12
British Gro. S. W4 —1F 12
Briton Clo. S Croy —7B 64
Briton Cres. S Croy —7B 64
Briton Hill Rd. S Croy —6B 64
Brittain Ct. Sand —8H 49
Brittain Rd. W On T —2L 57
Britten Clo. Ash —2F 110
Britten Clo. Craw —6L 181
Britten Clo. H'ham —4A 198
Brittenden Clo. Orp —3N 67
Brittenden Pde. Grn St —3N 67
Brittens Clo. Guild —[illegible]
Brittleware Cotts. Horl —8L 141
Brixton Hill. SW2 —1J 29
Brixton Hill Pl. SW2 —1J 29
Broadacre. Stai —6J 21
Broad Acres. G'ming —3H 133
Broadacres. Guild —1H 113
Broadbridge Cotts. Horl —1L 163
Broadbridge Heath By-Pass. H'ham —5C 196
Broadbridge Heath Retail Pk. Broad H —6E 196
Broadbridge Heath Rd. H'ham —4D 196
Broadbridge Ind. Est. H'ham —4D 196
Broadbridge La. Small —8L 143
Broad Clo. W On T —9M 39
Broadcommon Rd. Hurst —1A 14
Broadcoombe. S Croy —4G 64
Broadfield Barton. Craw —7N 181
Broadfield Clo. Croy —8J 45
Broadfield Clo. Tad —7H 81
Broadfield Dri. Craw —6N 181
Broadfield Pk. Peas P —7B 182
Broadfield Pl. Craw —7N 181
Broadfield Rd. Peasl —2E 136
Broadfields. E Mol —5E 40
Broadford La. Chob —8H 53
Broadford Pk. Bus. Cen. Shalf —1N 133
Broadford Rd. Guild —1M 133
Broadgates Rd. SW18 —2B 28
Broad Grn. Av. Croy —6M 45
Broadham Grn. Rd. Oxt —1N 125
Broadham Pl. Oxt —9N 105
Broad Ha'penny. Wrec —7F 128
Broad Highway. Cobh —2L 77
Broadhurst. Asht —3L 79
Broadhurst. F'boro —1H 89
Broadhurst Clo. Rich —8M 11
Broadhurst Gdns. Reig —6N 121
Broadlands. F'boro —3C 90
Broadlands. Frim —6D 70
Broadlands. Horl —7G 143
Broadlands Av. SW16 —3J 29
Broadlands Av. Shep —5D 38
Broadlands Clo. SW16 —3J 29
Broadlands Ct. Brack —9K 15
Broadlands Ct. Rich —3N 11
(off Kew Gdns. Rd.)
Broadlands Dri. S Asc —6N 33
Broadlands Dri. Warl —6F 84
Broadlands, The. Felt —4A 24
Broadlands Way. N Mald —5E 42
Broad La. Brack —2A 32
Broad La. Hamp —8N 23
Broad La. Newd —7C 140
Broadley Grn. W'sham —4A 52
Broad Mead. Asht —5M 79
Broadmead. F'boro —2J 89
Broadmead. Horl —7G 143
Broadmead. Mers —6G 102
(off Station Rd.)
Broadmead Av. Wor Pk —6F 42
Broadmead Clo. Hamp —7A 24
Broadmead Rd. Send & Old Wok —9D 74
Broadmeads. Wok —9D 74
Broadmoor Est. Crowt —3J 49
Broadoak. Sun —7G 23
Broadoaks. Surb —8A 42
Broadoaks Cres. W Byf —9K 55
Broadpool Cotts. Asc —8L 17
Broadrick Heath. Warf —8B 16
Broad St. Guild —1F 112
Broad St. Tedd —7F 24
Broad St. W End —8A 52
Broad St. Wokgm —2B 30
Broad St. Wlk. Wokgm —2B 30
Broadview Rd. SW16 —8H 29
Broad Wlk. Cat —9C 84
Broad Wlk. Coul —1E 102
Broad Wlk. Cranl —9A 156
Broad Wlk. Craw —3B 182
Broad Wlk. Eps —6J 81
Broad Wlk. Frim —4C 70
Broad Wlk. Houn —4L 9
Broad Wlk. Rich —3M 11
Broad Wlk., The. E Mol —3F 40
Broadwater Clo. W On T —2H 57
Broadwater Clo. Wok —8F 54
Broadwater Clo. Wray —1A 20
Broadwater Gdns. Orp —1K 67
Broadwater La. G'ming —5J 133
Broadwater Pl. Wey —8F 38
Broadwater Rise. Guild —4C 114
Broadwater Rd. SW17 —5C 28
Broadwater Rd. N. W On T —2G 57
Broadwater Rd. S. W On T —2G 57
Broadway. Brack —1N 31
Broadway. Knap —5E 72
Broadway. Stai —6K 21
Broadway. Surb —7A 42
[illegible]
Broadway Arc. W6 —1H 13
(off Hammersmith B'way.)
Broadway Av. Croy —4A 46
Broadway Av. Twic —9H 11
Broadway Cen., The. W6 —1H 13
Broadway Clo. S Croy —1E 84
Broadway Ct. SW19 —7M 27
Broadway Ct. Beck —2M 47
Broadway Ct. Knap —4F 72
Broadway Gdns. Mitc —3C 44
Broadway Ho. Knap —5F 72
Broadway Mkt. SW17 —5D 28
Broadway Pl. SW19 —7L 27
Broadway Rd. Light & W'sham —6N 51
Broadway, The. SW13 —5D 12
Broadway, The. SW19 —7M 27
Broadway, The. Cheam —3K 61
Broadway, The. Craw —3B 182
Broadway, The. Croy —1J 63
Broadway, The. New H —6J 55
Broadway, The. Sand —7G 49
Broadway, The. Stai —2L 37
Broadway, The. Sutt —2A 62
Broadway, The. Th Dit —7E 40
Broadway, The. Wok —4B 74
Broadwell Ct. Houn —4L 9
(off Springwell Rd.)
Broadwell Rd. Wrec —5E 128
Broadwood Clo. H'ham —3N 197
Broadwood Cotts. Dork —4L 159
Broadwood Rise. Broadf —8M 181
Brocas St. Eton —3G 4
Brockbridge Ho. SW15 —9E 12
Brockdene Dri. Kes —1F 66
Brockenhurst. W Mol —5N 39
Brockenhurst Av. Wor Pk —7D 42
Brockenhurst Clo. Wok —1B 74
Brockenhurst Dri. Yat —2C 68
Brockenhurst Rd. Alder —4N 109
Brockenhurst Rd. Asc —3L 33
Brockenhurst Rd. Brack —2D 32
Brockenhurst Rd. Croy —6E 46
Brockenhurst Way. SW16 —1H 45
Brockham Clo. SW19 —6L 27
Brockham Cres. New Ad —4N 65
Brockham Dri. SW2 —1K 29
Brockham Grn. Brock —4A 120
Brockham Ho. SW2 —1K 29
(off Brockham Dri.)
Brockhamhurst Rd. Bet —1N 139
Brockham Keep. Horl —7G 142
(off Langshott La.)
Brockham La. Brock —3N 119
Brockham Pk. Bet —8B 120
Brockhill. Wok —4K 73
Brockhurst Clo. H'ham —7F 196
Brockhurst Cotts. Alf —5H 175
Brocklands. Yat —2A 68
Brocklebank Ct. Whyt —5D 84
Brocklebank Rd. SW18 —1A 28
Brocklesby Rd. SE25 —3E 46
Brockley Combe. Wey —1E 56
Brock Rd. Craw —9N 161
Brocks Clo. G'ming —6K 133
Brocks Dri. Guild —8F 92

Brocks Dri.—Burrow Wlk.

Brocks Dri. Sutt —9K 43
Brockshot Clo. Bren —1K 11
Brock Way. Vir W —4M 35
Brockway Clo. Guild —2D 114
Brockway Ho. Langl —1D 6
Brockwell Pk. Gdns. SE24 —1M 29
Broderick Gro. Bookh —4A 98
Brodie Rd. Guild —4A 114
Brodrick Rd. SW17 —3C 28
Brograve Gdns. Beck —1L 47
Broke Ct. Guild —9E 94
Broken Furlong. Eton —1E 4
Brokes Cres. Reig —1M 121
Brokes Rd. Reig —1M 121
Bromford Clo. Oxt —2C 126
Bromley Ct. Farnh —2J 129
Bromley Gro. Brom —1N 47
Bromley Rd. Beck & Short —1L 47
Brompton Clo. SE20 —1D 46
Brompton Clo. Houn —8N 9
Brompton Pk. Cres. SW6 —2N 13
Bronsart Rd. SW6 —3K 13
Bronson Rd. SW20 —1J 43
Bronte Ct. Red —2E 122 (off St Anne's Rise)
Bronte Ho. SW4 —1G 29
Brontes, The. E Grin —9N 165
Brook Av. Farnh —5L 109
Brook Clo. SW20 —2G 43
Brook Clo. Ash —1F 110
Brook Clo. Dork —3J 119
Brook Clo. E Grin —9D 166
Brook Clo. Eps —5D 60
Brook Clo. Fleet —5B 88
Brook Clo. Owl —6K 49
Brook Clo. Stanw —1A 22
Brook Cotts. Yat —9B 48
Brook Ct. Eden —9L 127
Brook Dri. Brack —3C 32
Brooke Ct. Frim G —8D 70
Brooke Forest. Guild —8F 92
Brooke Pl. Binf —6J 15
Brookers Clo. Asht —4K 79
Brookers Corner. Crowt —2H 49
Brookers Row. Crowt —1H 49
Brook Farm Rd. Cobh —2L 77
Brookfield. G'ming —3K 133
Brookfield. Wok —3L 73
Brookfield Av. Sutt —1C 62
Brookfield Clo. Ott —3F 54
Brookfield Clo. Red —9E 122
Brookfield Gdns. Clay —3F 58
Brookfield Rd. Alder —1D 110
Brookfields Av. Mitc —4C 44
Brook Gdns. SW13 —6E 12
Brook Gdns. F'boro —3L 89
Brook Gdns. King T —9B 26
Brook Grn. Brack —9L 15 (in two parts)
Brook Grn. Chob —6J 53 (off Chertsey Rd.)
Brook Hill. Alb —3M 135
Brook Hill. Oxt —8M 105
Brookhill Clo. Copt —7L 163
Brookhill Rd. Copt —8L 163
Brook Ho. Cranl —6A 156 (off Park Dri.)
Brook Ho. Farnh —6J 109 (off Fairview Gdns.)
Brookhouse Rd. F'boro —2L 89
Brookhurst Field. Rud —9E 176
Brookhurst Rd. Add —3K 55
Brookland Ct. Reig —1N 121
Brooklands. Alder —3K 109
Brooklands. Wey —6A 56
Brooklands Av. SW19 —3N 27
Brooklands Clo. Cobh —2M 77
Brooklands Clo. Farnh —5J 109
Brooklands Clo. Sun —9F 22
Brooklands Ct. Mitc —1B 44
Brooklands Ct. New H —6M 55
Brooklands Heliport. Wey —5A 56
Brooklands La. Wey —3A 56
Brooklands Rd. Craw —8A 182
Brooklands Rd. Farnh —5K 109
Brooklands Rd. Th Dit —7F 40
Brooklands Rd. Wey —7B 56
Brooklands, The. Iswth —4D 10
Brooklands Way. E Grin —1N 185
Brooklands Way. Farnh —5K 109
Brooklands Way. Red —1C 122
Brook La. Abry —2N 135
Brook La. Chob —7G 53
Brook La. Fay —9B 180
Brook La. Send —9G 74
Brook La. Bus. Cen. Bren —1K 11
Brook La. N. Bren —1K 11 (in two parts)
Brookley Clo. Farnh —9A 110
Brookleys. Chob —6J 53
Brookly Gdns. Fleet —3C 88
Brooklyn Av. SE25 —3E 46
Brooklyn Clo. Cars —8C 44
Brooklyn Clo. Wok —6A 74
Brooklyn Ct. Wok —6A 74
Brooklyn Gro. SE25 —3E 46
Brooklyn Rd. SE25 —3E 46
Brooklyn Rd. Wok —5A 74
Brook Mead. Eps —3D 60
Brookmead Ct. Cranl —8N 155
Brookmead Ct. Farnh —2G 128
Brookmead Ind. Est. Croy —5G 45
Brook Meadow. C'fold —6F 172
Brookmead Rd. Croy —5G 45
Brook Pas. SW6 —3M 13
Brook Rd. Bag —5J 51
Brook Rd. Camb —2N 69
Brook Rd. Chil —1E 134
Brook Rd. H'ham —2L 197
Brook Rd. Mers —7G 102
Brook Rd. Red —4D 122
Brook Rd. Surb —8L 41
Brook Rd. T Hth —3N 45
Brook Rd. Twic —9G 11
Brook Rd. Wmly —9B 152
Brook Rd. S. Bren —2K 11
Brooksby Clo. B'water —1G 68
Brooks Clo. Wey —6B 56
Brookscroft. Croy —6J 65
Brookside. Bear G —5M 139
Brookside. Cars —2E 62
Brookside. Cher —6G 37
Brookside. Coln —3E 6
Brookside. Copt —7L 163
Brookside. Cranl —7N 155 (Ewhurst Rd.)
Brookside. Cranl —9N 155 (Northdowns)
Brookside. Craw —2D 182
Brookside. Craw D —1E 184
Brookside. Farnh —6H 109
Brookside. Guild —7N 93
Brookside. Sand —8H 49
Brookside. S God —7G 124
Brookside Av. Ashf —6L 21
Brookside Av. Wray —6A 6
Brookside Clo. Felt —4H 23
Brookside Cres. Wor Pk —7F 42
Brookside Pk. F'boro —5M 69
Brookside Way. Croy —5G 46
Brooks La. W4 —2N 11
Brooks Rd. W4 —1N 11
Brook St. King T —1L 41
Brook St. Wind —5G 5
Brook Trad. Est., The. Alder —2C 110
Brook Valley. Mid H —2H 139
Brookview. Copt —7L 163
Brookview Rd. SW16 —6G 28
Brookville Rd. SW6 —3L 13
Brook Way. Lea —5G 78
Brookwell La. Brmly —1C 154
Brookwood. Horl —7F 142
Brookwood Av. SW13 —5E 12
Brookwood Lye Rd. Brkwd & Wok —7F 72
Brookwood Rd. SW18 —2L 27
Brookwood Rd. F'boro —1B 90
Brookwood Rd. Houn —5B 10
Broom Acres. Fleet —7A 88
Broom Acres. Sand —7G 49
Broom Clo. Esh —2B 58
Broom Clo. Tedd —8K 25
Broomcroft Clo. Wok —3F 74
Broomcroft Dri. Wok —2F 74
Broomdashers Rd. Craw —2D 182
Broome Clo. H'ley —4B 100
Broome Clo. H'ham —3K 197
Broome Clo. Yat —8B 48
Broome Ct. Brack —2N 31
Broome Ct. Tad —6K 81
Broomehall Rd. Cold —9D 138
Broome Rd. Hamp —8N 23
Broomers La. Ewh —5F 156
Broomfield. Elst —7J 131
Broomfield. Guild —2H 113
Broom Field. Light —8L 51
Broomfield. Stai —7J 21
Broomfield. Sun —9H 23
Broomfield Clo. Asc —6E 34
Broomfield Clo. Guild —1H 113
Broomfield Ct. Wey —3C 56
Broomfield Dri. Asc —5E 34
Broomfield Pk. Asc —6E 34
Broomfield Pk. Westc —6C 118
Broomfield Ride. Oxs —8D 58
Broomfield Rd. Beck —2J 47
Broomfield Rd. New H —7K 55
Broomfield Rd. Rich —4M 11
Broomfield Rd. Surb —7M 41
Broomfield Rd. Tedd —7J 25
Broomfields. Esh —2C 58
Broom Gdns. Croy —9K 47
Broom Hall. Oxs —1D 78
Broomhall End. Wok —3A 74
Broomhall La. Asc —5D 34
Broomhall La. Wok —3A 74
Broomhall Rd. S Croy —5A 64
Broomhall Rd. Wok —3A 74
Broomhill. Ews —4C 108
Broomhill Rd. SW18 —8M 13
Broomhill Rd. F'boro —9J 69
Broomhouse La. SW6 —5M 13
Broomhouse Rd. SW6 —5M 13
Broomhurst Ct. Dork —7H 119
Broomlands La. Oxt —4F 106
Broom La. Chob —5H 53
Broomleaf Corner. Farnh —1J 129
Broomleaf Rd. Farnh —1J 129
Broomloan La. Sutt —8M 43
Broom Lock. Tedd —7J 25
Broom Pk. Tedd —8K 25
Broom Rd. Croy —9K 47
Broom Rd. Tedd —6H 25
Broom Squires. Hind —5E 170
Broomsquires Rd. Bag —5K 51
Broom Water. Tedd —7J 25
Broom Water W. Tedd —6J 25
Broom Way. B'water —2K 69
Broom Way. Wey —1F 56
Broomwood Clo. Croy —4G 47
Broomwood Way. Lwr Bo —5H 129
Broster Gdns. SE25 —2C 46
Brougham Pl. Farnh —5G 108
Brough Clo. King T —6K 25
Broughton Av. Rich —4H 25
Broughton M. Frim —5D 70
Broughton Rd. SW6 —5N 13
Broughton Rd. T Hth —5L 45
Browell Ho. Guild —2F 114 (off Merrow St.)
Browells La. Felt —3J 23
Brown Bear Ct. Felt —5L 23
Brown Clo. Wall —4J 63
Browngraves Rd. Hayes —3D 8
Browning Av. Sutt —1C 62
Browning Av. Wor Pk —7G 42
Browning Barracks. Alder —8N 89
Browning Clo. Camb —2G 70
Browning Clo. Craw —2G 182
Browning Clo. Hamp —5N 23
Browning Rd. C Crook —1A 108
Browning Rd. Fet —3D 98
Brownings. Eden —8L 127
Brownings, The. E Grin —9M 165
Browning Way. Houn —4L 9
Brownjohn Ct. Craw —2E 182
Brownlow Dri. Brack —8A 16
Brownlow Rd. Croy —1B 64
Brownlow Rd. Red —3C 122
Brownrigg Cres. Brack —9C 16
Brownrigg Rd. Ashf —5B 22
Brown's Hill. Red —1A 144
Browns La. Eff —5L 97
Brownsover Rd. F'boro —1H 89
Brown's Rd. Surb —6M 41
Browns Wlk. Rowl —7E 128
Browns Wood. E Grin —6A 166
Brow, The. Red —8E 122
Broxhead Farm Rd. Lind —1A 168
Broxholme Ho. SW6 —4N 13 (off Harwood Rd.)
Broxholm Rd. SE27 —4L 29
Brox La. Ott —4E 54
Brox Rd. Ott —3E 54
Bruce Av. Shep —5D 38
Bruce Clo. Byfl —9N 55
Bruce Dri. S Croy —5G 64
Bruce Hall M. SW17 —5E 28
Bruce Rd. SE25 —3A 46
Bruce Rd. Mitc —8E 28
Bruce Wlk. Wind —5A 4
Brudenell. Wind —6C 4
Brudenell Rd. SW17 —4D 28
Brumana Clo. Wey —3C 56
Brumfield Rd. Eps —2B 60
Brunel Cen. Craw —8D 162
Brunel Clo. Houn —3J 9
Brunel Dri. Crowt —8H 31
Brunel Pl. Craw —4C 182
Brunel Wlk. Twic —1A 24
Bruneval Barracks. Alder —9L 89
Brunner Ct. Ott —2E 54
Brunswick. Brack —6M 31
Brunswick Clo. Craw —5E 182
Brunswick Clo. Th Dit —7F 40
Brunswick Clo. Twic —4D 24
Brunswick Clo. W On T —8K 39
Brunswick Ct. Craw —5E 182 (off Brunswick Clo.)
Brunswick Ct. Sutt —1N 61
Brunswick Dri. Brkwd —7A 72
Brunswick Gro. Cobh —9K 57
Brunswick M. SW16 —7H 29
Brunswick Rd. Deep & Pirb —8G 71
Brunswick Rd. King T —9N 25
Brunswick Rd. Sutt —1N 61
Bruntile Clo. F'boro —4B 90
Brushwood Rd. H'ham —2A 198
Bruton Rd. Mord —3A 44
Bruton Way. Brack —6C 32
Bryan Clo. Sun —8H 23
Bryanston Av. Twic —2B 24
Bryanstone Av. Guild —8J 93
Bryanstone Clo. C Crook —7C 88
Bryanstone Clo. Guild —9J 93
Bryanstone Ct. Sutt —1A 62
Bryanstone Gro. Guild —8J 93
Bryce Clo. H'ham —3N 197
Bryce Gdns. Alder —5A 110
Bryer Pl. Wind —6A 4
Brympton Clo. Dork —7G 119
Brynford Clo. Wok —2A 74
Bryn Rd. Wrec —4E 128
Bryony Ho. Brack —9K 15
Bryony Rd. Guild —9D 94
Bryony Way. Sun —7H 23
Buccleuch Rd. Dat —3K 5
Buchan Pk. Craw —7L 181
Buchans Lawn. Craw —7N 181
Buchan, The. Camb —7E 50
Bucharest Rd. SW18 —1A 28
Buckfast Rd. Mord —3N 43
Buckham Thorns Rd. W'ham —4L 107
Buckhold Rd. SW18 —9M 13
Buckhurst Av. Cars —7C 44
Buckhurst Clo. E Grin —7M 165
Buckhurst Clo. Red —1C 122
Buckhurst Gro. Wokgm —3E 30
Buckhurst Hill. Brack —3D 32
Buckhurst La. Asc —2C 34
Buckhurst Mead. E Grin —6M 165
Buckhurst Rd. Asc —1C 34
Buckhurst Rd. Frim G —8D 70
Buckhurst Rd. W'ham —8J 87
Buckhurst Way. E Grin —7M 165
Buckingham Av. Felt —9J 9
Buckingham Av. T Hth —9L 29
Buckingham Av. W Mol —1B 40
Buckingham Clo. Guild —2B 114
Buckingham Clo. Hamp —6N 23
Buckingham Ct. Craw —7N 181
Buckingham Ct. Sutt —5M 61
Buckingham Dri. E Grin —1C 186
Buckingham Gdns. T Hth —1L 45
Buckingham Gdns. W Mol —1B 40
Buckingham Ga. Gat A —3G 163
Buckingham Rd. Hamp —5N 23
Buckingham Rd. Holmw —5J 139
Buckingham Rd. King T —3M 41
Buckingham Rd. Mitc —4J 45
Buckingham Rd. Rich —3K 25
Buckingham Way. Frim —5D 70
Buckingham Way. Wall —5G 63
Buckland Clo. F'boro —7A 70
Buckland Ct. Gdns. Bet —2F 120
Buckland Cres. Wind —4C 4
Buckland La. Tad —6F 100
Buckland Rd. Chess —2M 59
Buckland Rd. Lwr K —7L 101
Buckland Rd. Orp —1N 67
Buckland Rd. Reig —2J 121
Buckland Rd. Sutt —6H 61
Bucklands Rd. Tedd —7J 25
Buckland's Wharf. King T —1K 41
Buckland Wlk. Mord —3A 44
Buckland Way. Wor Pk —7H 43
Bucklebury. Brack —6M 31
Buckleigh Av. SW20 —2K 43
Buckleigh Rd. SW16 —7H 29
Buckle La. Warf —3M 15 (in two parts)
Bucklers All. SW6 —2L 13
Buckler's Way. Cars —9D 44
Buckles Way. Bans —3K 81
Buckley La. H'ham —9N 197
Buckley Pl. Craw D —1D 184
Buckmans Rd. Craw —2B 182
Bucknills Clo. Eps —1B 80
Bucks Clo. W Byf —1K 75
Buckshead Hill. H'ham —9E 198
Buckswood Dri. Craw —5M 181
Buckthorn Clo. Wokgm —1D 30
Buckthorns. Brack —8K 15
Budd's All. Twic —8J 11
Budebury Rd. Stai —6J 21
Budge La. Mitc —6D 44
Budgen Clo. Craw —9H 163
Budgen Dri. Red —9E 102
Budge's Gdns. Wokgm —1C 30
Budge's Rd. Wokgm —1C 30
Budham Way Brack —5N 31
Buer Rd. SW6 —5K 13
Buff Av. Bans —1N 81
Buffbeards La. Hasl —1C 188
Bug Hill. Wold —7G 84
Bulbeggars La. God —1F 124
Bulganak Rd. T Hth —3N 45
Bulkeley Av. Wind —6E 4
Bulkeley Clo. Egh —6M 19
Bullard Cotts. Guild —1H 115
Bullard Rd. Tedd —7E 24
Bullbeggars La. Wok —3L 73
Bullbrook Dri. Brack —9C 16
Bullbrook Row. Brack —1C 32
Buller Barracks. Alder —9A 90
Buller Rd. Alder —9N 89
Buller Rd. T Hth —1A 46
Bullers Rd. Farnh —6K 109
Bullfinch Clo. Col T —7K 49
Bullfinch Clo. Horl —7C 142
Bullfinch Clo. H'ham —1J 197
Bullfinch Rd. S Croy —6G 64
Bull Hill. Lea —8G 79
Bull La. Brack —9N 15
Bullock La. Hasl —9A 190
Bullrush Clo. SE25 —5B 46
Bull's All. SW14 —5C 12
Bullswater Comn. Rd. Pirb —3D 92
Bulmer Cotts. Dork —6K 137
Bulow Est. SW6 —4N 13 (off Pearscroft Rd.)
Bulstrode Av. Houn —5N 9
Bulstrode Gdns. Houn —6A 10
Bulstrode Rd. Houn —6A 10
Bunbury Way. Eps —3G 80
Bunce Comn. Rd. Leigh —1C 140
Bunce Dri. Cat —1A 104
Bunce's Clo. Eton W —1E 4
Bunch La. Hasl —1E 188
Bunch Way. Hasl —2E 188
Bundy's Way. Stai —7H 21
Bungalow Rd. SE25 —3B 46
Bungalow Rd. Ock —2D 96
Bungalows, The. SW16 —8F 28
Bungalow, The. Guild —7J 93
Bunting Clo. H'ham —5M 197
Bunting Clo. Mitc —4D 44
Buntings, The. Farnh —3E 128
Bunyan Clo. Craw —6K 181
Bunyan's La. Knap —1F 72
Bunyard Dri. Wok —1E 74
Burbage Grn. Brack —4D 32
Burbage Rd. SE24 —1N 29
Burbeach Clo. Craw —6N 181
Burberry Clo. N Mald —1D 42
Burbidge Rd. Shep —3B 38
Burchets Hollow. Peasl —4E 136
Burchetts Way. Shep —5C 38
Burcote. Wey —3E 56
Burcote Rd. SW18 —1B 28
Burcott Gdns. Add —3L 55
Burcott Rd. Purl —1L 83
Burden Clo. Bren —1J 11
Burdenshott Av. Rich —7A 12
Burdenshott Hill. Worp —3K 93
Burdenshott Rd. Worp —3K 93
Burden Way. Guild —7L 93
Burdett Av. SW20 —9F 26
Burdett Clo. Worth —4H 183
Burdett Rd. Croy —5A 46
Burdett Rd. Rich —5M 11
Burdock Clo. Craw —7M 181
Burdock Clo. Croy —7G 47
Burdock Clo. Light —7M 51
Burdon La. Sutt —4K 61
Burdon Pk. Sutt —5L 61
Burfield Clo. SW17 —5B 28
Burfield Dri. Warl —6F 84
Burfield Rd. Old Win —9K 5
Burford Bri. Roundabout. Dork —9J 99
Burford Ct. Wokgm —3D 30
Burford Ho. Bren —1L 11
Burford Ho. Eps —7H 61
Burford La. Eps —7H 61
Burford Lea. Elst —7K 131
Burford Rd. Bren —1L 11
Burford Rd. Camb —2N 69
Burford Rd. H'ham —6L 197
Burford Rd. Sutt —8M 43
Burford Rd. Wor Pk —6E 42
Burford Wlk. SW6 —3N 13
Burford Way. New Ad —3M 65
Burges Gro. SW13 —3G 13
Burgess Clo. Felt —5M 23
Burgess Rd. Sutt —1N 61
Burges Way. Stai —7J 21
Burgh Clo. Craw —9H 163
Burgh Croft. Eps —2E 80
Burghead Clo. Col T —8J 49
Burghfield. Eps —2E 80
Burgh Heath Rd. Eps —1E 80
Burgh Hill Rd. Pass —9E 168
Burghley Av. N Mald —9C 26
Burghley Hall Clo. SW19 —2K 27
Burghley Pl. Mitc —4D 44
Burghley Rd. SW19 —5J 27
Burgh Mt. Bans —2L 81
Burgh Wood. Bans —2K 81
Burgos Clo. Croy —3L 63
Burgoyne Rd. SE25 —3C 46
Burgoyne Rd. Camb —9E 50
Burgoyne Rd. Sun —7G 22
Burhill Rd. W On T —5J 57
Burke Clo. SW15 —7D 12
Burket Clo. S'hall —1M 9
Burlands. Craw —9M 161
Burlea Clo. W On T —2J 57
Burleigh Av. Wall —9E 44
Burleigh Clo. Add —2K 55
Burleigh Clo. Craw D —1E 184
Burleigh Gdns. Ashf —6D 22
Burleigh Gdns. Wok —3B 74
Burleigh La. Asc —9J 17
Burleigh La. Craw D —2E 184
Burleigh Pk. Cobh —8M 57
Burleigh Pl. SW15 —8J 13
Burleigh Rd. Add —2K 55
Burleigh Rd. Asc —1J 33
Burleigh Rd. Frim —6B 70
Burleigh Rd. Sutt —7K 43
Burleigh Way. Craw D —1E 184
Burley Clo. SW16 —1H 45
Burley Clo. Loxw —4J 193
Burley Orchard. Cher —5J 37
Burleys Rd. Craw —3G 183
Burley Way. B'water —9H 49
Burlingham Clo. Guild —1F 114
Burlings La. Knock —4N 87
Burlings, The. Asc —9J 17
Burlington Av. Rich —4N 11
Burlington Clo. Felt —1E 22
Burlington Ct. Alder —3M 109
Burlington Ct. B'water —3J 69
Burlington Gdns. W4 —1B 12
Burlington La. W4 —3B 12
Burlington Pl. SW6 —5K 13
Burlington Rd. SW6 —5K 13
Burlington Rd. W4 —1B 12
Burlington Rd. Iswth —4D 10
Burlington Rd. N Mald —3E 42
Burlington Rd. T Hth —1N 45
Burlsdon Way. Brack —9C 16
Burma Rd. Chob —9J 35
Burmarsh Ct. SE20 —1F 46
Burmester Rd. SW17 —4A 28
Burnaby Cres. W4 —2B 12
Burnaby Gdns. W4 —2A 12
Burnaby St. SW10 —3N 13
Burnbury Rd. SW12 —2G 29
Burn Clo. Add —1M 55
Burn Clo. Oxs —2D 78
Burne-Jones Dri. Col T —9J 49
Burne Jones Ho. W14 —1K 13 (off N. End Rd.)
Burnell Av. Rich —6J 25
Burnell Rd. Sutt —1N 61
Burnet Av. Guild —9D 94
Burnet Clo. W End —9B 52
Burnet Gro. Eps —9B 60
Burnetts Rd. Wind —4B 4
Burney Av. Surb —4M 41
Burney Clo. Fet —3C 98
Burney Ct. Craw —6M 181
Burney Rd. Westh —9G 99
Burnfoot Av. SW6 —4K 13
Burnham Clo. Knap —5G 73
Burnham Clo. Wind —5A 4
Burnham Dri. Reig —2M 121
Burnham Dri. Wor Pk —8J 43
Burnham Gdns. Croy —6C 46
Burnham Gdns. Houn —4J 9
Burnham Ga. Guild —3N 113
Burnham Gro. Brack —8A 16
Burnham Pl. H'ham —7K 197
Burnham Rd. Knap —5G 73
Burnham Rd. Mord —3N 43
Burnhams Rd. Bookh —2M 97
Burnham St. King T —9N 25
Burnhill Rd. Beck —1K 47
Burnings La. Knock —4N 87
Burn Moor Chase. Brack —6C 32
Burnsall Clo. F'boro —8N 69
Burns Av. C Crook —7C 88
Burns Av. Felt —9H 9
Burns Clo. SW19 —7B 28
Burns Clo. F'boro —8L 69
Burns Clo. H'ham —1L 197
Burns Dri. Bans —1K 81
Burnside. Asht —5M 79
Burnside. Fleet —4B 88
Burnside Clo. Twic —9G 10
Burns Rd. Craw —1G 182
Burns Way. E Grin —9M 165
Burns Way. Fay —8H 181
Burns Way. Houn —5L 9
Burntcommon Clo. Rip —3H 95
Burntcommon La. Rip —3J 95
Burnt Hill Rd. Wrec —5F 128
Burnt Hill Way. Wrec —6G 128
Burnt Ho. Gdns. Warf —8C 16
Burnt Ho. La. Rusp —2E 180
Burnthouse Ride. Brack —3J 31
Burnthwaite Rd. SW6 —3L 13
Burntoak La. Newd —2D 160
Burnt Pollard La. Light —6B 52
Burntwood Clo. SW18 —2C 28
Burntwood Clo. Cat —8D 84
Burntwood Grange Rd. SW18 —2B 28
Burntwood La. SW17 —4A 28
Burntwood La. Cat —9B 84
Burpham La. Guild —8C 94
Burrell Clo. Croy —5H 47
Burrell Ct. Craw —5L 181
Burrell Rd. Frim —6A 70
Burrell Row. Beck —1K 47
Burrells, The. Cher —7K 37
Burrell, The. Westc —6C 118
Burr Hill La. Chob —5J 53
Burritt Rd. King T —1N 41
Burrow Hill Grn. Chob —5G 53
Burrows Clo. Bookh —2N 97
Burrows Clo. Guild —2J 113
Burrows Cross. Gom —1D 136
Burrows Hill Clo. H'row —6L 7
Burrows Hill La. H'row A —7K 7
Burrows La. Gom —1D 136
Burrow Wlk. SE21 —1N 29

Carrington La. Ash V —5E 90
Carrington Pl. Esh —1C 58
Carrington Rd. Rich —7N 11
Carroll Av. Guild —3D 114
Carroll Cres. Asc —4K 33
Carrow Rd. W On T —9L 39
Carshalton Gro. Sutt —1B 62
Carshalton Pk. Rd. Cars —2D 62
Carshalton Pl. Cars —2E 62
Carshalton Rd. Bans —1D 82
Carshalton Rd. Camb —6E 50
Carshalton Rd. Mitc —3E 44
Carshalton Rd. Sutt & Cars —2A 62
Carslake Rd. SW15 —9H 13
Carson Rd. SE21 —3N 29
Cartbridge Clo. Send —1D 94
Carter Clo. Wall —4H 63
Carter Clo. Wind —5D 4
Carterdale Cotts. Capel —5J 159
Carter Rd. SW19 —7B 28
Carter Rd. M'bowr —6H 183
Carters Clo. Wor Pk —7J 43
Carter's Cotts. Red —5C 122
Carter's Hill. B'bear —5F 14
Carters La. Wok —7E 74
Carterslodge La. Hand —9J 199
Cartersmeade Clo. Horl —7F 142
Carters Rd. Eps —2E 80
Carters Wlk. Farnh —4J 109
Carter's Yd. SW18 —8M 13
Carthona Dri. Fleet —6A 88
Carthouse Cotts. Guild —9E 94
Carthouse La. Wok —1H 73
Cartmel Clo. Reig —1C 122
Cartmell Gdns. Mord —4A 44
Cartwright Way. SW13 —3G 13
Carville Cres. Bren —1L 11
Cascades. Croy —6J 65
Caselden Clo. Add —2L 55
Casewick Rd. SE27 —6L 29
Casher Rd. M'bowr —6G 183
Cassidy Rd. SW6 —3M 13
Cassilis Rd. Twic —8H 11
Cassino Clo. Alder —2N 109
Cassiobury Av. Felt —1G 22
Cassland Rd. T Hth —3A 46
Cassocks Sq. Shep —6E 38
Castello Av. SW15 —8H 13
Castelnau. SW13 —4F 12
Castelnau Gdns. SW13 —2G 13
Castelnau Pl. SW13 —2G 12
Castelnau Row. SW13 —2G 12
Castle Av. Dat —2K 5
Castle Av. Eps —5F 60
Castle Clo. SW19 —4J 27
Castle Clo. Blet —2N 123
Castle Clo. Brom —2N 47
Castle Clo. Camb —2D 70
Castle Clo. Reig —7N 121
Castle Clo. Sun —8F 22
Castlecombe Dri. SW19 —1J 27
Castle Ct. Farnh —9G 108
Castlecraig Ct. Col T —8J 49
Castle Dri. Horl —9G 143
Castle Dri. Reig —7M 121
Castle Farm Cvn. Site. Wind —5A 4
(off White Horse Rd.)
Castle Field. Farnh —9G 108
Castlefield Ct. Reig —3N 121
Castlefield Rd. Reig —3M 121
Castle Gdns. Dork —3M 119
Castlegate. Rich —6M 11
Castle Grn. Wey —9F 38
Castle Gro. Rd. Chob —9G 53
Castle Hill. Farnh —9G 108
Castle Hill. Guild —5N 113
Castle Hill. Wind —4G 5
Castle Hill Av. New Ad —5L 65
Castle Hill Rd. Egh —4L 19
Castlemaine Av. Eps —5G 61
Castlemaine Av. S Croy —2C 64
Castle Pde. Eps —4F 60
Castle Pl. W4 —1D 12
Castle Rd. Alder —9K 89
Castle Rd. Broad H —5D 196
Castle Rd. Camb —2C 70
Castle Rd. Coul —7C 82
Castle Rd. Eps —2A 80
Castle Rd. Iswth —5F 10
Castle Rd. Wey —9F 38
Castle Rd. Wok —1B 74
Castle Row. W4 —1C 12
Castle Sq. Blet —2N 123
Castle Sq. Guild —5N 113
Castle St. Blet —2M 123
Castle St. Farnh —9G 109
Castle St. Fleet —6A 88
Castle St. Guild —5N 113
Castle St. King T —1L 41
Castle, The. H'ham —1L 197
Castleton. Cars —7B 62
Castleton Clo. Bans —2M 81
Castleton Clo. Croy —5H 47
Castleton Dri. Bans —1M 81
Castleton Rd. Mitc —3H 45
Castletown Rd. W14 —1K 13
Castle View. Eps —1A 80
Castleview Rd. Slou —1M 5
Castle View Rd. Wey —1C 56
Castle Wlk. Reig —3M 121
Castle Wlk. Sun —2K 39
Castle Way. SW19 —4J 27
Castle Way. Eps —6F 60
Castle Way. Felt —5K 23
Castle Yd. Rich —8K 11
Castor Ct. C Crook —8C 88
Castor Ct. Yat —8A 48
Caswall Clo. Binf —7H 15
Caswall Ride. Yat —1E 68
Caswell Clo. F'boro —8L 69
Catalpa Clo. Guild —1M 113
Catena Rise. Light —6L 51
Caterfield La. Crow & Oxt —1B 146
Cater Gdns. Guild —1J 113
Caterham By-Pass. Cat —8E 84
Caterham Clo. Cat —7B 84
Caterham Clo. Pirb —8B 72
Caterham Dri. Coul —5M 83
Caterways. H'ham —5G 197
Catesby Gdns. Yat —1A 68
Cathcart Rd. SW10 —2N 13
Cathedral Clo. Guild —4L 113
Cathedral Ct. Guild —3K 113
Cathedral Hill Ind. Est. Guild —2K 113
Cathedral Precinct. Guild —4K 113
Cathedral View. Guild —3J 113
Catherine Clo. Byfl —1N 75
Catherine Ct. SW19 —6L 27
Catherine Dri. Rich —7L 11
Catherine Dri. Sun —7G 22
Catherine Gdns. Houn —7D 10
Catherine Howard Ct. Wey —9C 38
(off Old Palace Rd.)
Catherine Rd. Surb —4K 41
Catherine Wheel Rd. Bren —3K 11
Cat Hill. Dork —7B 158
Cathill La. Ockl —7B 158
Cathles Rd. SW12 —1F 28
Catlin Cres. Shep —4E 38
Catlin Gdns. God —8E 104
Cator Clo. New Ad —7A 66
Cator Cres. New Ad —7A 66
Cator La. Beck —1J 47
Cator Rd. Cars —2D 62
Cato's Hill. Esh —1B 58
Cat St. Up Har —9N 187
Catteshall Hatch. G'ming —5K 133
Catteshall La. G'ming —7H 133
Catteshall Rd. G'ming —5K 133
(in two parts)
Catteshall Ter. G'ming —6K 133
(off Catteshall Rd.)
Causeway Cen. Houn —6J 9
Causeway Ct. Wok —5J 73
Causeway Est. Stai —5D 20
Causewayside. Hasl —2G 189
(off High St. Haslemere,)
Causeway, The. SW18 —8N 13
Causeway, The. SW19 —6H 27
Causeway, The. Cars —8E 44
Causeway, The. Chess —1L 59
Causeway, The. Clay —4F 58
Causeway, The. Felt & Houn —7J 9
Causeway, The. H'ham —7J 197
Causeway, The. Stai —5F 20
Causeway, The. Sutt —5A 62
Causeway, The. Tedd —7F 24
Cavalier Ct. Surb —5M 41
Cavalier Way. E Grin —2B 186
Cavalry Ct. Alder —2K 109
Cavalry Cres. Houn —7L 9
Cavalry Cres. Wind —6F 4
Cavalry Gdns. SW15 —8L 13
Cavan's Rd. Alder —7A 90
Cavell Ho. Ott —3F 54
Cavell Way. M'bowr —4G 182
Cavendish Av. N Mald —4G 42
Cavendish Clo. H'ham —1K 197
Cavendish Clo. Sun —7G 22
Cavendish Ct. B'water —3J 69
Cavendish Ct. Cher —7J 37
(off Victory Rd.)
Cavendish Ct. Coln —4G 6
Cavendish Ct. Sun —7G 22
Cavendish Dri. Clay —2E 58
Cavendish Gdns. SW4 —1G 29
Cavendish Gdns. C Crook —9A 88
Cavendish Gdns. Red —2E 122
Cavendish Meads. Asc —5A 34
Cavendish M. Alder —3M 109
Cavendish Pde. Houn —5M 9
Cavendish Pk. Cvn. Site. Sand —9K 49
Cavendish Rd. SW12 —1G 28
Cavendish Rd. SW19 —8B 28
Cavendish Rd. W4 —4B 12
Cavendish Rd. Alder —3M 109
Cavendish Rd. C Crook —9A 88
Cavendish Rd. Croy —7M 45
Cavendish Rd. N Mald —3E 42
Cavendish Rd. Red —2E 122
Cavendish Rd. Sun —7G 22
Cavendish Rd. Sutt —4A 62
Cavendish Rd. Wey —5C 56
Cavendish Rd. Wok —6N 73
Cavendish Ter. Felt —3H 23
Cavendish Way. W Wick —7L 47
Cavenham Clo. Wok —6A 74
Caverleigh Way. Wor Pk —7F 42
Cave Rd. Rich —5J 25
Caversham Av. Sutt —8K 43
Caversham Rd. King T —1M 41
Caves Farm Clo. Sand —7F 48
Cawcott Dri. Wind —4B 4
Cawdor Cres. W7 —1G 11
Cawsey Way. Wok —4A 74
Caxton Av. Add —3J 55
Caxton Clo. Craw —6B 182
Caxton Gdns. Guild —2L 113
Caxton La. Oxt —9G 106
Caxton M. Bren —2K 11
Caxton Rise. Red —2E 122
Caxton Rd. SW19 —6A 28
Cayley Clo. Wall —4J 63
Cearn Way. Coul —2K 83
Cecil Clo. Ashf —8D 22
Cecil Clo. Chess —1K 59
Cecil Pl. Mitc —4D 44
Cecil Rd. SW19 —8N 27
Cecil Rd. Ashf —8D 22
Cecil Rd. Croy —5K 45
Cecil Rd. Houn —5C 10
Cecil Rd. Sutt —3L 61
Cedar Av. B'water —1J 69
Cedar Av. Cobh —2K 77
Cedar Av. Twic —9B 10
Cedar Clo. SE21 —2N 29
Cedar Clo. SW15 —5C 26
Cedar Clo. Alder —4C 110
Cedar Clo. Bag —4J 51
Cedar Clo. Cars —3D 62
Cedar Clo. Craw —9A 162
Cedar Clo. Dork —5H 119
Cedar Clo. E Mol —3E 40
Cedar Clo. Eps —1E 80
Cedar Clo. Esh —3N 57
Cedar Clo. H'ham —5J 197
Cedar Clo. Reig —5A 122
Cedar Clo. Stai —2L 37
Cedar Clo. Warl —6H 85
Cedar Clo. Wokgm —2B 30
Cedar Ct. SW19 —4J 27
Cedar Ct. Bren —2K 11
(off Boston Mnr. Rd.)
Cedar Ct. Egh —5C 20
Cedar Ct. Hasl —2F 188
Cedar Ct. Sutt —3A 62
Cedar Ct. Wind —5D 4
Cedar Cres. Brom —1G 66
Cedarcroft Rd. Chess —1M 59
Cedar Dri. Asc —3G 35
(Blacknest Rd.)
Cedar Dri. Asc —6D 34
(Broomhall La.)
Cedar Dri. Brack —8A 16
Cedar Dri. Eden —1K 147
Cedar Dri. Fet —1E 98
Cedar Dri. Fleet —4D 88
Cedar Gdns. Sutt —3A 62
Cedar Gdns. Wok —5L 73
Cedar Gro. Bisl —2D 72
Cedar Gro. Wey —1D 56
Cedar Heights. Rich —2L 25
Cedar Hill. Eps —3B 80
Cedar Ho. Guild —1E 114
Cedarland Ter. SW20 —8G 27
Cedar La. Frim —6B 70
Cedar Lodge. Hasl —3K 189
Cedarne Rd. SW6 —3N 13
Cedar Rd. Cobh —1J 77
Cedar Rd. Croy —8B 46
Cedar Rd. E Mol —3E 40
Cedar Rd. F'boro —2A 90
Cedar Rd. Felt —2E 22
Cedar Rd. Houn —5K 9
Cedar Rd. Sutt —3A 62
Cedar Rd. Tedd —6G 24
Cedar Rd. Wey —1B 56
Cedar Rd. Wok —7L 73
Cedars. Bans —1D 82
Cedars. Brack —3D 32
Cedars Av. Mitc —3E 44
Cedars Clo. Sand —7E 48
Cedars Ct. Guild —9C 94
Cedars Rd. SW13 —5F 12
Cedars Rd. W4 —2B 12
Cedars Rd. Beck —1H 47
Cedars Rd. Croy —9J 45
Cedars Rd. Hamp W —9J 25
Cedars Rd. Mord —3M 43
Cedars, The. Byfl —8A 56
Cedars, The. Fleet —5C 88
Cedars, The. Guild —9C 94
Cedars, The. Lea —8K 79
Cedars, The. Milf —2B 152
Cedars, The. Pirb —9A 72
Cedars, The. Reig —3B 122
Cedars, The. Tedd —7F 24
Cedars, The. Wall —1G 63
Cedar Ter. Rich —7L 11
Cedar Tree Gro. SE27 —6M 29
Cedarville Gdns. SW16 —7K 29
Cedar Vista. Rich —5L 11
Cedar Wlk. Kenl —3N 83
Cedar Wlk. Tad —7K 81
Cedar Way. Guild —1M 113
Cedar Way. Slou —1A 6
Cedar Way. Sun —8F 22
Cedarways. Farnh —4G 128
Celandine Clo. Craw —6N 181
Celandine Clo. Crowt —1H 49
Celandine Ct. Yat —8A 48
Celandine Rd. W On T —1M 57
Celery La. Wrec —6G 128
Celia Cres. Ashf —7M 21
Cell Farm Av. Old Win —8L 5
Celtic Av. Brom —2N 47
Celtic Rd. Byfl —1N 75
Cemetery Pales. Brkwd —9D 72
Cemetery Rd. Fleet —6A 88
Centaurs Bus. Cen. Iswth —2G 10
Centennial Ct. Brack —1M 31
Central Av. Houn —7C 10
Central Av. Wall —2J 63
Central Av. W Mol —3N 39
Central Gdns. Mord —4N 43
Central Hill. SE19 —7N 29
Central La. Wink —2M 17
Central Pde. Felt —1K 23
Central Pde. Horl —9E 142
Central Pde. New Ad —6M 65
Central Pde. Red —2D 122
Central Pde. Surb —5L 41
Central Pk. Est. Houn —8L 9
Central Pl. SE25 —4D 46
Central Rd. Mord —5M 43
Central Rd. Wor Pk —7F 42
Central School Path. SW14 —6B 12
Central Ter. Beck —2G 47
Central Wlk. Wokgm —2B 30
Central Way. Cars —4C 62
Central Way. Felt —8H 9
Central Way. Oxt —5N 105
Central Way. Wink —2M 17
Centre Ct. SW19 —7L 27
Centre Ct. Shop. Cen. SW19 —7L 27
Centre Rd. Wind —3A 4
Centre, The. Felt —3H 23
Centre, The. Houn —6B 10
Centre, The. W On T —7G 39
Centurion Clo. Col T —7J 49
Centurion Ct. Hack —8F 44
Century Ho. SW15 —7J 13
Century Rd. Stai —6E 20
Century Way. Pirb —6A 72
Cerne Rd. Mord —5A 44
Cerotus Pl. Cher —6H 37
Ceylon Ter. Frim G —6H 71
(off Crimea Rd.)
Chadacre Rd. Eps —3G 60
Chadhurst Clo. N Holm —8K 119
Chadwick Av. SW19 —7M 27
Chadwick Clo. Craw —8N 181
Chadwick Clo. Tedd —7G 25
Chadworth Way. Clay —2D 58
Chaffers Mead. Asht —3M 79
Chaffinch Av. Croy —5G 46
Chaffinch Bus. Pk. Beck —3G 47
Chaffinch Clo. Col T —7J 49
Chaffinch Clo. Craw —1B 182
Chaffinch Clo. Croy —4G 46
Chaffinch Clo. H'ham —1K 197
Chaffinch Clo. Surb —9N 41
Chaffinch Rd. Beck —1H 47
Chaffinch Way. Horl —7C 142
Chailey Clo. Craw —6M 181
Chailey Clo. Houn —4L 9
Chailey Pl. W On T —1M 57
Chalcot Clo. Sutt —4M 61
Chalcot M. SW16 —4J 29
Chalcott Gdns. Surb —7J 41
Chaldon Clo. Red —5C 122
Chaldon Comn. Rd. Cat —2N 103
Chaldon Ct. SE19 —9N 29
Chaldon Rd. SW6 —3K 13
Chaldon Rd. Cat —2A 104
Chaldon Rd. Craw —8A 182
Chaldon Way. Coul —4J 83
Chale Rd. SW2 —1J 29
Chalet Hill. Bord —6A 168
Chale Wlk. Sutt —5N 61
Chalfont Dri. F'boro —3A 90
Chalfont Rd. SE25 —2C 46
Chalford Clo. W Mol —3A 40
Chalgrove Av. Mord —4M 43
Chalgrove Rd. Sutt —4B 62
Chalice Clo. Wall —3H 63
Chalker's Corner. (Junct.) —6A 12
Chalkhill Rd. W6 —1J 13
Chalk La. Asht —6M 79
Chalk La. E Hor —8G 96
Chalk La. Eps —2D 80
Chalk La. Shack —3A 132
Chalkley Clo. Mitc —1D 44
Chalkmead. Red —8G 103
Chalk Paddock. Eps —2C 80
Chalk Pit Cotts. W Hor —8C 96
Chalkpit La. Bet —2A 120
Chalkpit La. Bookh —6N 97
Chalkpit La. Dork —4G 119
Chalkpit La. Oxt —4M 105
Chalk Pit Rd. Bans —4M 81
Chalk Pit Rd. Eps —6B 80
Chalkpit Ter. Dork —3G 118
Chalk Pit Way. Sutt —3A 62
Chalkpit Wood. Oxt —5N 105
Chalk Rd. G'ming —6G 133
Chalk Rd. Ifold —6E 192
Chalky La. Chess —6K 59
Challen Ct. H'ham —5H 197
Challenge Ct. Lea —6H 79
Challenge Rd. Ashf —4E 22
Challice Way. SW2 —2K 29
Challis Pl. Brack —1K 31
Challis Rd. Bren —1K 11
Challock Clo. Big H —3E 86
Challoner Cres. W14 —1L 13
Challoners Clo. E Mol —3D 40
Challoner St. W14 —1L 13
Chalmers Clo. Charl —4K 161
Chalmers Rd. Ashf —6C 22
Chalmers Rd. Bans —2B 82
Chalmers Rd. E. Ashf —5C 22
Chalmers Way. Felt —8J 9
Chamberlain Cres. W Wick —7L 47
Chamberlain Wlk. Felt —5M 23
Chamberlain Way. Surb —6L 41
Chamber La. Farnh —3B 128
Chambers Rd. Ash V —8F 90
Chambers, The. SW10 —4N 13
(off Chelsea Harbour)
Chambon Pl. W6 —1F 12
Chamomile Gdns. F'boro —9H 69
Champion Way. C Crook —8B 88
Champness Clo. SE27 —5N 29
Champneys Clo. Sutt —4L 61
Chancellor Ct. Guild —4G 113
Chancellor Gdns. S Croy —5M 63
Chancellor Gro. SE21 —3N 29
Chancellor's Rd. W6 —1H 13
Chancellor's St. W6 —1H 13
Chancellors Wharf. W6 —1H 13
Chancel Mans. Warf —7A 16
Chancery La. Beck —1L 47
Chanctonbury Chase. Red —3E 122
Chanctonbury Dri. Asc —6B 34
Chanctonbury Gdns. Sutt —4N 61
Chanctonbury Way. Craw —5A 182
Chandler Clo. Craw —5B 182
Chandler Clo. Hamp —9A 24
Chandlers Clo. Felt —1G 22
Chandlers La. Yat —8B 48
Chandlers Rd. Ash V —9F 90
Chandlers Way. SW2 —1L 29
Chandon Lodge. Sutt —4A 62
Chandos Rd. Stai —6F 20
Channel Clo. Houn —4A 10
Channings. Hors —2A 74
Chantlers Clo. E Grin —8M 165
Chanton Dri. Sutt —6H 61
Chantree Grn. W4 —1B 12
Chantrey Rd. Craw —6C 182
Chantry Clo. Asht —6J 79
Chantry Clo. Horl —7D 142
Chantry Clo. Wind —4D 4
Chantry Cotts. Chil —9D 114
Chantry Ct. Frim —5B 70
(off Church Rd.)
Chantry Hurst. Eps —2C 80
Chantry La. Shere —7A 116
Chantry Rd. Bag —5H 51
Chantry Rd. Cher —6L 37
Chantry Rd. Chess —2M 59
Chantry Rd. Chil —9D 114
Chantrys Ct. Farnh —1F 128
(off Chantrys, The)
Chantrys, The. Farnh —1E 128
Chantry View Rd. Guild —6N 113
Chantry Way. Mitc —2B 44
Chapel Av. Add —1K 55
Chapel Clo. Milf —9C 132
Chapel Ct. Dork —4G 119
Chapel Farm Cvn. Site. Norm —9B 92
Chapel Fields. G'ming —4G 132
Chapel Gdns. Lind —4A 168
Chapel Gro. Add —1K 55
Chapel Gro. Eps —6H 81
Chapel Hill. Duns —6B 174
Chapel Hill. Eff —5L 97
Chapelhouse Clo. Guild —3H 113
Chapel La. Ash W —3F 186
Chapel La. Bag —5H 51
Chapel La. Binf —8H 15
Chapel La. Bookh —6C 98
Chapel La. Craw D —6C 164
Chapel La. F'boro & B'water —6L 69
Chapel La. Milf —9C 132
Chapel La. Pirb —9D 72
Chapel La. Westc —6C 118
Chapel La. Westh —8E 98
Chapel La. Ind. Est. Dork —6C 118
(off Chapel La.)
Chapel Pk. Rd. Add —1K 55
Chapel Rd. SE27 —5M 29
Chapel Rd. Camb —1N 69
Chapel Rd. Charl —3K 161
Chapel Rd. Houn —6B 10
Chapel Rd. Oxt —8E 106
Chapel Rd. Red —3D 122
Chapel Rd. Rowl —7D 128
Chapel Rd. Small —8M 143
Chapel Rd. Tad —1H 101
Chapel Rd. Twic —1H 25
Chapel Rd. Warl —5G 84
Chapel Sq. Vir W —3A 36
Chapel St. F'boro —8B 70
Chapel St. Guild —5N 113
Chapel St. Wok —4B 74
Chapel Ter. Binf —8H 15
Chapel View. S Croy —3F 64
Chapel Wlk. Croy —8N 45
Chapel Way. Eps —6H 81
Chapel Yd. SW18 —8M 13
(off Wandsworth High St.)
Chaplain's Hill. Crowt —3J 49
Chaplin Cres. Sun —7F 22
Chapman Rd. Croy —7L 45
Chapman Rd. M'bowr —7F 182
Chapman's La. E Grin —9L 165
Chapter M. Wind —3G 5
Chapter Way. Hamp —5A 24
Chara Pl. W4 —2C 12
Chardin Rd. W4 —1D 12
Chard Rd. H'row A —5C 8
Chargate Clo. W On T —3G 57
Charing Clo. Orp —1N 67
Charing Ct. Short —1N 47
Chariots Pl. Wind —4G 4
Charlbury Clo. Brack —3D 32
Charlecote Clo. F'boro —2C 90
Charlesfield Rd. Horl —7D 142
Charles Hill. Elst —5C 130
Charles Ho. Wind —4F 4
Charles Rd. SW19 —9M 27
Charles Rd. Stai —7M 21
Charles Sq. Brack —1A 32
Charles St. SW13 —5D 12
Charles St. Cher —7H 37
Charles St. Croy —9N 45
Charles St. Houn —5N 9
Charles St. Wind —4F 4
Charleston Clo. Felt —4H 23
Charleston Ct. Craw —6F 182
Charleville Mans. W14 —1K 13
(off Charleville Rd.)
Charleville Rd. W14 —1K 13
Charlmont Rd. SW17 —7C 28
Charlock Clo. Craw —7M 181
Charlock Way. Guild —9D 94
Charlotte Clo. Farnh —4J 109
Charlotte Ct. Craw —3A 182
(off Leopold Rd.)
Charlotte Ct. Guild —5B 114
Charlotte Gro. Small —7L 143
Charlotte M. W14 —1K 13
Charlotte M. Esh —1B 58
(off Heather Pl.)
Charlotte Rd. SW13 —4E 12
Charlotte Rd. Wall —3G 63
Charlotte Sq. Rich —9M 11
Charlow Clo. SW6 —5N 13
Charlton Av. W On T —1J 57
Charlton Ct. Owl —6J 49
Charlton Dri. Big H —4F 86
Charlton Gdns. Coul —5G 83
Charlton Ho. Bren —2L 11
Charlton Kings. Wey —9F 38
Charlton La. Shep —2D 38
Charlton Pl. Wind —5A 4
Charlton Rd. Shep —2D 38
Charlton Row. Wind —5A 4
Charlton Sq. Wind —5A 4
(off Guards Rd.)
Charlton Wlk. Wind —5A 4
Charlton Way. Wind —5A 4
Charlwood. Croy —5J 65
Charlwood Bus. Pk. E Grin —7N 165
Charlwood Clo. Bookh —2B 98
Charlwood Clo. Copt —6M 163
Charlwood Dri. Oxs —2D 78
Charlwood La. Dork & Horl —5F 160
Charlwood M. Horl —3K 161
Charlwood Rd. SW15 —7J 13
Charlwood Rd. Horl —2A 162
Charlwood Rd. If'd —7K 161
Charlwood Rd. Low H —6N 161
Charlwoods Av. E Grin —7A 166
Charlwoods Pl. E Grin —7A 166
Charlwood Sq. Mitc —2B 44
Charlwoods Rd. E Grin —8N 165
Charlwood Ter. SW15 —7J 13
Charlwood Wlk. Craw —9N 161
Charman Rd. Red —3C 122
Charmans Clo. H'ham —3A 198
Charm Clo. Horl —7C 142
Charminster Av. SW19 —1M 43
Charminster Ct. Surb —6K 41
Charminster Rd. Wor Pk —7J 43
Charmouth Ct. Rich —8M 11
Charnwood. Asc —5C 34
Charnwood Av. SW19 —1M 43

Charnwood Clo.—Christmas Hill

Charnwood Clo. *N Mald* —3D **42**
Charnwood Rd. *SE25* —4A **46**
Charrington Rd. *Croy* —8N **45**
Charrington Way. *Broad H* —5C **196**
Charta Rd. *Egh* —6E **20**
Chart Clo. *Brom* —1N **47**
Chart Clo. *Croy* —5F **46**
Chart Clo. *Dork* —7K **119**
Chart Downs. *Dork* —7J **119**
Charter Ct. *N Mald* —2D **42**
Charter Cres. *Houn* —7M **9**
Charterhouse. *G'ming* —5E **132**
Charterhouse Clo. *Brack* —4C **32**
Charterhouse Rd. *G'ming* —4G **132**
Charter Rd. *King T* —2A **42**
Charters Clo. *Asc* —4A **34**
Charters La. *Asc* —4A **34**
Charter Sq. *King T* —1A **42**
Charters Rd. *Asc* —6A **34**
Charters Way. *Asc* —6C **34**
Chartfield Av. *SW15* —8G **13**
Chartfield Rd. *Reig* —4A **122**
Chartfield Sq. *SW15* —8J **13**
Chart Gdns. *Dork* —8J **119**
Chartham Gro. *SE27* —4M **29**
Chartham Rd. *SE25* —2E **46**
Chart Ho. Rd. *Ash V* —6E **90**
Chart La. *Dork* —5H **119**
Chart La. *Reig* —3N **121**
Chart La. S. *Dork* —7K **119**
Charts Clo. *Cranl* —8N **155**
Chart Way. *H'ham* —6J **197**
Chartway. *Reig* —2N **121**
Chartwell. *Farnh* —5E **128**
Chartwell. *Frim G* —8D **70**
Chartwell Clo. *Croy* —7A **46**
Chartwell Dri. *Orp* —[illegible]
Chartwell Gdns. *Alder* —6A **90**
Chartwell Gdns. *Sutt* —1K **61**
Chartwell Lodge. *Dork* —9H **119**
Chartwell Pl. *Eps* —1D **80**
Chartwell Pl. *Sutt* —9L **43**
Chartwell Way. *SE20* —1E **46**
Char Wood. *SW16* —5L **29**
Charwood Rd. *Wokgm* —2D **30**
Chase Cotts. *Gray* —8A **170**
Chase Ct. *Iswth* —5G **10**
Chase End. *Eps* —8C **60**
Chasefield Clo. *Guild* —9C **94**
Chasefield Rd. *SW17* —5D **28**
Chase Gdns. *Binf* —6H **15**
Chase Gdns. *Twic* —1D **24**
Chase La. *Hasl* —4H **189**
Chaseley Dri. *W4* —1A **12**
Chaseley Dri. *S Croy* —6A **64**
Chasemore Clo. *Mitc* —6D **44**
Chasemore Gdns. *Croy* —2L **63**
Chase Rd. *Eps* —8C **60**
Chase Rd. *Lind* —5A **168**
Chaseside Av. *SW20* —1K **43**
Chaseside Gdns. *Cher* —6K **37**
Chase, The. *SW16* —8K **29**
Chase, The. *SW20* —9K **27**
Chase, The. *Asht* —5J **79**
Chase, The. *Coul* —1H **83**
Chase, The. *Craw* —4E **182**
Chase, The. *Crowt* —1F **48**
Chase, The. *E Hor* —4G **96**
Chase, The. *F'boro* —8B **70**
Chase, The. *Guild* —4K **113**
Chase, The. *Kgswd* —8A **82**
Chase, The. *Oxs* —2C **78**
Chase, The. *Reig* —3B **122**
Chase, The. *Sun* —9J **23**
Chase, The. *Wall* —2K **63**
Chasewater Ct. *Alder* —3M **109**
Chatelet Clo. *Horl* —7F **142**
Chatfield Clo. *F'boro* —3A **90**
Chatfield Ct. *Cat* —9A **84**
Chatfield Dri. *Guild* —1E **114**
Chatfield Rd. *Croy* —7M **45**
Chatfields. *Craw* —5N **181**
Chatham Clo. *Sutt* —6L **43**
Chatham Rd. *King T* —1N **41**
Chatsfield. *Eps* —6F **60**
Chatsworth Av. *SW20* —9K **27**
Chatsworth Av. *Hasl* —9G **170**
Chatsworth Clo. *W4* —2B **12**
Chatsworth Cres. *Houn* —7D **10**
Chatsworth Gdns. *N Mald* —4E **42**
Chatsworth Gro. *Farnh* —6G **108**
Chatsworth Heights. *Camb* —8E **50**
Chatsworth Lodge. W4 —1C 12
(off Bourne Pl.)
Chatsworth Pl. *Mitc* —2D **44**
Chatsworth Pl. *Oxs* —9D **58**
Chatsworth Pl. *Tedd* —5G **24**
Chatsworth Rd. *W4* —2B **12**
Chatsworth Rd. *Croy* —1A **64**
Chatsworth Rd. *F'boro* —2C **90**
Chatsworth Rd. *Sutt* —2J **61**
Chatsworth Way. *SE27* —4M **29**
Chattern Hill. *Ashf* —5C **22**
Chattern Rd. *Ashf* —5D **22**
Chatterton Ct. *Rich* —5M **11**
Chatton Row. *Bisl* —4D **72**
Chaucer Av. *E Grin* —9M **165**
Chaucer Av. *Houn* —5J **9**
Chaucer Av. *Rich* —6N **11**
Chaucer Av. *Wey* —4B **56**
Chaucer Clo. *Bans* —1K **81**
Chaucer Clo. *Wokgm* —2E **30**
Chaucer Ct. *Guild* —5M **113**
Chaucer Gdns. *Sutt* —9M **43**
Chaucer Grn. *Croy* —6E **46**
Chaucer Gro. *Camb* —1B **70**
Chaucer Ho. Sutt —9M 43
(off Chaucer Gdns.)
Chaucer Mans. W14 —2K 13
(off Queen's Club Gdns.)
Chaucer Rd. *Ashf* —5N **21**
Chaucer Rd. *Craw* —1F **182**
Chaucer Rd. *Crowt* —3G **48**
Chaucer Rd. *F'boro* —8L **69**
Chaucer Rd. *Sutt* —1M **61**
Chaucer Way. *SW19* —7B **28**
Chaucer Way. *Add* —3J **55**
Chave Croft. *Eps* —6H **81**
Chave Croft Ter. *Eps* —6H **81**
Chavey Down Rd. *Wink R* —6F **16**
Chaworth Clo. *Ott* —3E **54**
Chaworth Rd. *Ott* —3E **54**
Chawridge La. *Wink* —2G **16**
Cheam Clo. *Brack* —4B **32**
Cheam Clo. *Tad* —8G **81**
Cheam Comn. Rd. *Wor Pk* —8G **43**
Cheam Mans. *Sutt* —4K **61**
Cheam Pk. Way. *Sutt* —3K **61**
Cheam Rd. *Eps & Cheam* —6F **60**
Cheam Rd. *Sutt* —3L **61**
Cheam Village. (Junct.) —3K **61**
Cheapside. *Wok* —1N **73**
[illegible]
Cheddar Rd. *H'row A* —5C **8**
Cheeseman Clo. *Hamp* —7M **23**
Cheeseman Clo. *Wokgm* —1C **30**
Cheesemans Ter. *W14* —1L **13**
(in two parts)
Chellows La. *Crow* —1B **146**
Chelmsford Clo. *W6* —2J **13**
Chelmsford Clo. *Sutt* —5M **61**
Chelsea Clo. *Hamp* —6C **24**
Chelsea Clo. *Wor Pk* —6F **42**
Chelsea Gdns. *Sutt* —1K **61**
Chelsham Clo. *Warl* —5H **85**
Chelsham Comn. Rd. *Warl* —4K **85**
Chelsham Ct. Rd. *Warl* —5N **85**
Chelsham Rd. *S Croy* —4A **64**
Chelsham Rd. *Warl* —5J **85**
Cheltenham Av. *Twic* —1G **24**
Cheltenham Clo. *N Mald* —2B **42**
Cheltenham Vs. *Stai* —9H **7**
Chelverton Rd. *SW15* —7J **13**
Chelwood Clo. *Craw* —5D **182**
Chelwood Clo. *Eps* —8E **60**
Chelwood Dri. *Sand* —6E **48**
Chelwood Gdns. *Rich* —5N **11**
Chelwood Gdns. Pas. *Rich* —5N **11**
Cheney Clo. *Binf* —7J **15**
Chenies Cotts. *Dork* —2A **178**
Chenies Ho. W4 —2E 12
(off Corney Reach Way)
Cheniston Clo. *W Byf* —9J **55**
Cheniston Ct. *S'dale* —6D **34**
Chennells Way. *H'ham* —3K **197**
Chepstow Clo. *SW15* —8K **13**
Chepstow Clo. *Craw* —3J **183**
Chepstow Rise. *Croy* —9B **46**
Chepstow Rd. *Croy* —9B **46**
Chequer Grange. *F Row* —8G **187**
Chequer Rd. *E Grin* —9B **166**
Chequers Clo. *Horl* —7E **142**
Chequers Clo. *Tad* —3F **100**
Chequers Ct. *H'ham* —5L **197**
Chequers Dri. *Horl* —7E **142**
Chequers La. *Tad* —3F **100**
Chequers Pl. *Dork* —5H **119**
Chequers Yd. *Dork* —5H **119**
Chequer Tree Clo. *Knap* —3H **73**
Cherberry Clo. *Fleet* —1C **88**
Cherbury Clo. *Brack* —3C **32**
Cherimoya Gdns. *W Mol* —2B **40**
Cherington Way. *Asc* —1J **33**
Cheriton Ct. *W on T* —7K **39**
Cheriton Sq. *SW17* —3E **28**
Cheriton Way. *B'water* —1J **69**
Cherkley Hill. *Lea* —4J **99**
Cherrimans Orchard. *Hasl* —2D **188**
Cherry Bank Cotts. *Dork* —6K **137**
Cherry Clo. *SW2* —1L **29**
Cherry Clo. *Bans* —1J **81**
Cherry Clo. *Cars* —8D **44**
Cherry Clo. *Mord* —3K **43**
Cherrycot Hill. *Orp* —1M **67**
Cherrycot Rise. *Orp* —1L **67**
Cherry Cotts. *Tad* —2G **100**
Cherry Ct. *H'ham* —7K **197**
Cherry Cres. *Bren* —3H **11**
Cherrydale Rd. *Camb* —1H **71**
Cherry Garth. *Bren* —1K **11**
Cherry Grn. Clo. *Red* —5F **122**
Cherry Hill Gdns. *Croy* —1K **63**
Cherryhill Gro. *Alder* —3L **109**
Cherryhurst. *Hamb* —9E **152**
Cherry La. *Craw* —9A **162**
Cherry Laurel Wlk. *SW2* —1K **29**
Cherry Lodge. *Alder* —3N **109**
Cherry Orchard. *Asht* —5A **80**
Cherry Orchard. *Stai* —6J **21**
Cherry Orchard Gdns. *Croy* —7B **46**
Cherry Orchard Gdns. *W Mol* —2N **39**
Cherry Orchard Rd. *Croy* —8A **46**
Cherry Orchard Rd. *W Mol* —2A **40**
Cherry St. *Wok* —5A **74**
Cherry Tree Av. *Guild* —3J **113**
Cherry Tree Av. *Hasl* —1D **188**
Cherry Tree Av. *Stai* —7K **21**
Cherry Tree Clo. *F'boro* —9H **69**
Cherry Tree Clo. *Farnh* —9H **109**
Cherry Tree Clo. *Owl* —6J **49**
Cherry Tree Clo. *Worth* —1H **183**
Cherry Tree Ct. *Coul* —5K **83**
Cherrytree Dri. *SW16* —4J **29**
Cherry Tree Dri. *Brack* —2B **32**
Cherry Tree Grn. *S Croy* —1E **84**
Cherry Tree La. *Eps* —8N **59**
Cherry Tree La. *G'ming* —3G **133**
Cherry Tree Rd. *Milf* —1B **152**
Cherry Tree Rd. *Rowl* —8D **128**
Cherry Tree Wlk. *Beck* —2J **47**
Cherry Tree Wlk. *Big H* —3E **86**
Cherry Tree Wlk. *H'ham* —2A **198**
Cherry Tree Wlk. *Rowl* —8D **128**
(in two parts)
Cherry Tree Wlk. *W Wick* —1B **66**
Cherry Way. *Eps* —3C **60**
Cherry Way. *Hort* —6E **6**
Cherry Way. *Shep* —3E **38**
Cherrywood Av. *Egh* —8L **19**
Cherry Wood Clo. *King T* —8N **25**
Cherrywood Ct. *Tedd* —6G **24**
Cherrywood Dri. *SW15* —8J **13**
Cherrywood La. *Mord* —3K **43**
Cherrywood Rd. *F'boro* —7M **69**
Chertsey Bri. Rd. *Cher* —6M **37**
Chertsey Clo. *Kenl* —2M **83**
Chertsey Cres. *New Ad* —6M **65**
Chertsey Dri. *Sutt* —8K **43**
Chertsey La. *Stai* —6G **20**
Chertsey Rd. *Add* —8K **37**
Chertsey Rd. *Ashf & Sun* —8E **22**
Chertsey Rd. *Byfl* —7M **55**
Chertsey Rd. *Chob & Cher* —6J **53**
Chertsey Rd. *Shep* —6N **37**
Chertsey Rd. *Sun & Felt* —6F **22**
Chertsey Rd. *Twic* —3B **24**
Chertsey Rd. *W'sham & Chob* —3A **52**
Chertsey Rd. *Wok* —4B **74**
Chertsey St. *SW17* —6E **28**
Chertsey St. *Guild* —4N **113**
Chertsey Wlk. *Cher* —6J **37**
Chervil Clo. *Felt* —4H **23**
Cherwell Clo. *Slou* —2D **6**
Cherwell Ct. *Eps* —1B **60**
Cherwell Wlk. *Craw* —4L **181**
Cheryls Clo. *SW6* —4N **13**
Cheselden Rd. *Guild* —4A **114**
Chesfield Rd. *King T* —8L **25**
Chesham Clo. *Sutt* —6K **61**
Chesham Cres. *SE20* —1F **46**
Chesham M. *Guild* —4A **114**
Chesham Rd. *SE20* —1F **46**
Chesham Rd. *SW19* —6B **28**
Chesham Rd. *Guild* —4B **114**
Chesham Rd. *King T* —1N **41**
Cheshire Clo. *Cher* —3F **54**
Cheshire Clo. *Mitc* —2J **45**
Cheshire Gdns. *Chess* —3K **59**
Cheshire Ho. *Mord* —6N **43**
Cheshire Ho. Ott —3F 54
(off Cheshire Clo.)
Cheshire Pk. *Warf* —7C **16**
Chesholt Clo. *Fern* —9F **188**
Chesilton Cres. *C Crook* —8B **88**
Chesilton Rd. *SW6* —4L **13**
Chesney Cres. *New Ad* —4M **65**
Chessholme Rd. *Ashf* —7D **22**
Chessington Clo. *Eps* —3B **60**
Chessington Hall Gdns. *Chess* —3K **59**
Chessington Hill Pk. *Chess* —2N **59**
Chessington Ho. Eps —5E 60
(off Spring St.)
Chessington Pde. *Chess* —3K **59**
Chessington Rd. *Eps & Ewe* —3N **59**
Chessington Way. *W Wick* —8L **47**
Chesson Rd. *W14* —2L **13**
Chester Av. *Rich* —9M **11**
Chester Av. *Twic* —2N **23**
Chesterblade La. *Brack* —6B **32**
Chester Clo. *SW15* —6G **13**
Chester Clo. *Ash* —2F **110**
Chester Clo. *Ashf* —6E **22**
Chester Clo. *Dork* —3J **119**
Chester Clo. *Guild* —1J **113**
Chester Clo. *Rich* —9M **11**
Chester Clo. *Sutt* —8M **43**
Chesterfield Clo. *Felb* —6F **164**
Chesterfield Dri. *Esh* —8G **40**
Chesterfield M. *Ashf* —5N **21**
Chesterfield Rd. *W4* —2B **12**
Chesterfield Rd. *Ashf* —5N **21**
Chesterfield Rd. *Eps* —4C **60**
Chester Gdns. *Mord* —5A **44**
Chesterman Ct. W4 —3D 12
(off Corney Reach Way)
Chester Rd. *SW19* —7H **27**
Chester Rd. *Ash* —1F **110**
Chester Rd. *Eff* —6J **97**
Chester Rd. *Houn* —6J **9**
Chester Rd. *H'row A* —6B **8**
Chesters. *Horl* —6C **142**
Chesters Rd. *Camb* —1F **70**
Chesters, The. *N Mald* —9D **26**
Chesterton Clo. *SW18* —8M **13**
Chesterton Clo. *E Grin* —2B **186**
Chesterton Ct. *H'ham* —4N **197**
Chesterton Dri. *Red* —6J **103**
Chesterton Dri. *Stai* —2A **22**
Chesterton Sq. *W8* —1L **13**
Chesterton Ter. *King T* —1N **41**
[illegible]
Chestnut All. *SW6* —2L **13**
Chestnut Av. *SW14* —6C **12**
Chestnut Av. *Alder* —5C **110**
Chestnut Av. *Bren* —1K **11**
Chestnut Av. *Camb* —9E **50**
Chestnut Av. *E Mol & Tedd* —1F **40**
Chestnut Av. *Eps* —1D **60**
Chestnut Av. *Esh* —6D **40**
Chestnut Av. *Farnh* —3F **128**
Chestnut Av. *Guild* —7M **113**
Chestnut Av. *Hamp* —8A **24**
Chestnut Av. *Hasl* —1G **189**
Chestnut Av. *Vir W* —3J **35**
Chestnut Av. *W'ham* —9F **86**
Chestnut Av. *W Wick* —2A **66**
Chestnut Av. *Wey* —4D **56**
Chestnut Av. *W Vill* —5F **56**
Chestnut Clo. *SW16* —5L **29**
Chestnut Clo. *Add* —2M **55**
Chestnut Clo. *Asht* —5C **22**
Chestnut Clo. *B'water* —2K **69**
Chestnut Clo. *Cars* —7D **44**
Chestnut Clo. *E Grin* —9C **166**
Chestnut Clo. *Eden* —1K **147**
Chestnut Clo. *Egh* —7L **19**
Chestnut Clo. *Fleet* —1D **88**
Chestnut Clo. *Gray* —6A **170**
Chestnut Clo. *Red* —5F **122**
Chestnut Clo. *Rip* —3H **95**
Chestnut Clo. *Sun* —7G **22**
Chestnut Clo. *Tad* —1M **101**
Chestnut Clo. *W Dray* —3C **8**
Chestnut Copse. *Oxt* —1D **126**
Chestnut Ct. *SW6* —2L **13**
Chestnut Ct. *Alder* —2B **110**
Chestnut Ct. *Felt* —6L **23**
Chestnut Ct. *H'ham* —6L **197**
Chestnut Cres. *W Vill* —5F **56**
Chestnut Dri. *Egh* —7N **19**
Chestnut Dri. *Wind* —7B **4**
Chestnut End. *Head* —5F **168**
Chestnut Gdns. *H'ham* —3J **197**
Chestnut Gro. *SW12* —1E **28**
Chestnut Gro. *Fleet* —3C **88**
Chestnut Gro. *Iswth* —7G **10**
Chestnut Gro. *Mitc* —4H **45**
Chestnut Gro. *N Mald* —2C **42**
Chestnut Gro. *S Croy* —4E **64**
Chestnut Gro. *Stai* —7L **21**
Chestnut Gro. *Wok* —7A **74**
Chestnut La. *Chob* —2F **52**
Chestnut La. *Wey* —2C **56**
Chestnut Mnr. Clo. *Stai* —6K **21**
Chestnut Mead. *Red* —2C **122**
Chestnut Pl. *Asht* —6L **79**
Chestnut Rd. *SE27* —4M **29**
Chestnut Rd. *SW20* —1J **43**
Chestnut Rd. *Ashf* —5C **22**
Chestnut Rd. *F'boro* —9M **69**
Chestnut Rd. *Guild* —3N **113**
Chestnut Rd. *Horl* —6F **142**
Chestnut Rd. *King T* —8L **25**
Chestnut Rd. *Twic* —3E **24**
Chestnuts, The. *Horl* —6F **142**
Chestnuts, The. *W On T* —8H **39**
Chestnut Ter. *Sutt* —1N **61**
Chestnut Wlk. *Byfl* —8N **55**
Chestnut Wlk. *Craw* —9A **162**
Chestnut Wlk. *Felc* —2M **165**
Chestnut Wlk. *Shep* —3F **38**
Chestnut Wlk. *W Vill* —5F **56**
Chestnut Way. *Brmly* —7C **134**
Chestnut Way. *Felt* —4J **23**
Chestnut Way. *G'ming* —9J **133**
Cheston Av. *Croy* —8H **47**
Chesworth Clo. *H'ham* —8J **197**
Chesworth Cres. *H'ham* —7J **197**
Chesworth Gdns. *H'ham* —7J **197**
Chesworth La. *H'ham* —7J **197**
Chetnole. *E Grin* —8N **165**
Chetwode Clo. *Wokgm* —2D **30**
Chetwode Dri. *Eps* —5J **81**
Chetwode Pl. *Alder* —5A **110**
Chetwode Rd. *SW17* —4D **28**
Chetwode Rd. *Tad* —6H **81**
Chetwode Ter. *Alder* —3K **109**
Chetwood Rd. *Craw* —7J **181**
Chevening Clo. *Craw* —8A **182**
Chevening Rd. *SE19* —7N **29**
Chevington Vs. *Red* —1B **124**
Cheviot Clo. *Bans* —2N **81**
Cheviot Clo. *Camb* —2G **71**
Cheviot Clo. *F'boro* —7K **69**
Cheviot Clo. *Hayes* —3E **8**
Cheviot Clo. *Sutt* —5B **62**
Cheviot Ct. *S'hall* —1B **10**
Cheviot Dri. *Fleet* —1C **88**
Cheviot Gdns. *SE27* —5M **29**
Cheviot Rd. *SE27* —6L **29**
Cheviot Rd. *Sand* —5E **48**
Cheviot Rd. *Slou* —1C **6**
Cheviot Wlk. *Craw* —3N **181**
Chevremont. *Guild* —4A **114**
Chewter Clo. *Bag* —4K **51**
Chewter La. *W'sham* —1M **51**
Cheyham Gdns. *Sutt* —6J **61**
Cheyham Way. *Sutt* —6K **61**
Cheylesmore Dri. *Frim* —3H **71**
Cheyne Av. *Twic* —2N **23**
Cheyne Clo. *Brom* —1G **66**
Cheyne Ct. *Bans* —2N **81**
Cheyne Hill. *Surb* —3M **41**
Cheynell Wlk. *Craw* —5L **181**
Cheyne Rd. *Ashf* —8E **22**
Cheyne Row. *Brmly* —2N **153**
Cheyne Wlk. *Croy* —8D **46**
Cheyne Wlk. *Horl* —1D **162**
Cheyne Way. *F'boro* —7L **69**
Chichele Gdns. *Croy* —1B **64**
Chichele Rd. *Oxt* —6A **106**
Chichester Clo. *Craw* —7C **182**
Chichester Clo. *Dork* —3H **119**
Chichester Clo. *Hamp* —7N **23**
Chichester Clo. *Witl* —5B **152**
Chichester Ct. *Eps* —5E **60**
Chichester Dri. *Purl* —8K **63**
Chichester M. *SE27* —5L **29**
Chichester Rd. *Ash* —1E **110**
Chichester Rd. *Croy* —9B **46**
Chichester Rd. *Dork* —2H **119**
Chichester Rd. *H'ham* —6K **197**
Chichester Way. *Felt* —1K **23**
Chiddingfold Rd. *Duns* —5M **173**
Chiddingly Clo. *Craw* —4F **182**
Chiddingstone Clo. *Sutt* —6M **61**
Chiddingstone St. *SW6* —5M **13**
Chilberton Dri. *Red* —8G **103**
Chilbrook Rd. *D'side* —5H **77**
Chilcroft La. *Hasl* —7F **188**
Chilcroft Rd. *Hasl* —1D **188**
Chilcrofts Rd. *King G* —7E **188**
Child Clo. *Wokgm* —9C **14**
Childebert Rd. *SW17* —3F **28**
Childerley St. *SW6* —4K **13**
Childs Hall Clo. *Bookh* —3N **97**
Childs Hall Dri. *Bookh* —3N **97**
Childs Hall Rd. *Bookh* —3N **97**
Child's Pl. *SW5* —1M **13**
Child's St. *SW5* —1M **13**
Child's Wlk. *SW5* —1M **13**
Chilham Clo. *Frim* —6D **70**
Chillerton Rd. *SW17* —6E **28**
Chillingham Way. *Camb* —2A **70**
Chillingworth Gdns. *Twic* —4F **24**
Chilmans Dri. *Bookh* —3B **98**
Chilmark Gdns. *N Mald* —5F **42**
Chilmark Gdns. *Red* —7J **103**
Chilmark Rd. *SW16* —1H **45**
Chilmead. *Red* —2D **122**
Chilmead La. *Red* —1H **123**
Chilsey Grn. Rd. *Cher* —5G **37**
Chiltern Av. *F'boro* —1J **89**
Chiltern Av. *Twic* —2A **24**
Chiltern Clo. *C Crook* —7C **88**
Chiltern Clo. *Craw* —3N **181**
Chiltern Clo. *Croy* —9B **46**
Chiltern Clo. *F'boro* —1H **89**
Chiltern Clo. *Hasl* —3F **188**
Chiltern Clo. *Wok* —9M **73**
Chiltern Clo. *Wor Pk* —8H **43**
Chiltern Dri. *Surb* —5N **41**
Chiltern Farm Pk. *F'boro* —1H **89**
Chiltern Rd. *Sand* —6E **48**
Chiltern Rd. *Sutt* —5N **61**
Chilterns, The. *Sutt* —5N **61**
Chilton Clo. *Alf* —7H **175**
Chilton Ct. *W on T* —1H **57**
Chilton Rd. *Rich* —6N **11**
Chiltons Clo. *Bans* —2N **81**
Chilworth Ct. *SW19* —2J **27**
Chilworth Gdns. *Sutt* —9A **44**
Chilworth Hill Cotts. *Chil* —1G **134**
Chilworth Rd. *Abry* —8J **115**
Chinchilla Dri. *Houn* —5K **9**
Chine, The. *Dork* —4H **119**
Chine, The. *Wrec* —6E **128**
Chingford Av. *F'boro* —9B **70**
Chinnock Clo. *Fleet* —6A **88**
Chinthurst La. *Shalf & Brmly* —1A **134**
Chinthurst Pk. *Shalf* —2A **134**
Chippendale Clo. *B'water* —3K **69**
Chippendale Rd. *Craw* —8N **181**
Chipstead Av. *T Hth* —3M **45**
Chipstead Clo. *Coul* —3E **82**
Chipstead Clo. *Red* —4D **122**
Chipstead Clo. *Sutt* —5N **61**
Chipstead Ct. *Knap* —4H **73**
Chipstead La. *Tad & Coul* —3L **101**
Chipstead Rd. *Bans* —4L **81**
Chipstead Rd. *H'row A* —6B **8**
Chipstead St. *SW6* —4M **13**
Chipstead Valley Rd. *Coul* —3E **82**
Chipstead Way. *Bans* —3D **82**
Chirton Wlk. *Wok* —5K **73**
Chisbury Clo. *Brack* —5C **32**
Chisholm Rd. *Croy* —8B **46**
Chisholm Rd. *Rich* —9M **11**
Chislehurst Rd. *Rich* —8L **11**
Chiswick Bri. *SW14 & W4* —5B **12**
Chiswick Clo. *Croy* —[illegible]
Chiswick Comn. Rd. *W4* —1C **12**
Chiswick High Rd. *Bren & W4*
(in two parts) —1N **11**
Chiswick La. N. *W4* —1D **12**
Chiswick La. S. *W4* —2E **12**
Chiswick Mall. *W4 & W6* —2E **12**
Chiswick Plaza. *W4* —2B **12**
Chiswick Quay. *W4* —4B **12**
Chiswick Rd. *W4* —1B **12**
Chiswick Roundabout. (Junct.) —1N **11**
Chiswick Sq. *W4* —2D **12**
Chiswick Staithe. *W4* —3A **12**
Chiswick Ter. *W4* —1B **12**
Chiswick Village. *W4* —2N **11**
Chiswick Wharf. *W4* —2E **12**
Chithurst La. *Horne* —8B **144**
Chittenden Cotts. *Wis* —3N **75**
Chitterfield Ga. *W Dray* —3B **8**
Chittys Wlk. *Guild* —8J **93**
Chive Clo. *Croy* —7G **47**
Chive Ct. *F'boro* —1H **89**
Chivenor Gro. *King T* —6K **25**
Chives Pl. *Warf* —8B **16**
Chobham Clo. *Ott* —3D **54**
Chobham Gdns. *SW19* —3J **27**
Chobham La. *Chob* —9J **35**
Chobham Pk. La. *Chob* —6K **53**
Chobham Rd. *Asc & Wok* —6E **34**
Chobham Rd. *Frim* —4C **70**
Chobham Rd. *Knap* —5E **72**
Chobham Rd. *Ott* —4C **54**
Chobham Rd. *Wok* —9M **53**
Choir Grn. *Knap* —4H **73**
Cholmley Rd. *Th Dit* —5H **41**
Cholmondeley Wlk. *Rich* —8J **11**
Chrislaine Clo. *Stai* —9M **7**
Chrismas Av. *Alder* —3A **110**
Chrismas Pl. *Alder* —3A **110**
Christabel Clo. *Iswth* —6E **10**
Christchurch Av. *Tedd* —6G **24**
Christchurch Clo. *SW19* —8B **28**
Christchurch Clo. *C Crook* —9A **88**
Christchurch Dri. *B'water* —9H **49**
Christchurch Gdns. *Eps* —7A **60**
Christchurch Ho. SW2 —2K 29
(off Christchurch Rd.)
Christ Chu. Mt. *Eps* —8A **60**
Christchurch Pk. *Sutt* —4A **62**
Christchurch Pl. *Eps* —7A **60**
Christchurch Rd. *SW2* —2K **29**
Christ Chu. Rd. *SW14* —8A **12**
Christchurch Rd. *SW19* —8B **28**
Christ Chu. Rd. *Beck* —1K **47**
Christ Chu. Rd. *Eps* —8L **59**
Christchurch Rd. *H'row A* —6B **8**
Christchurch Rd. *Purl* —7M **63**
Christchurch Rd. *Surb* —5M **41**
Christchurch Rd. *Vir W* —2K **35**
Christchurch Way. *Wok* —4B **74**
Christian Fields. *SW16* —8L **29**
Christian Sq. *Wind* —4F **4**
Christie Clo. *Guild* —9N **93**
Christie Clo. *Light* —6N **51**
Christie Dri. *Croy* —4D **46**
Christies. *E Grin* —1N **185**
Christie Wlk. *Cat* —9A **84**
Christie Wlk. *Yat* —2B **68**
Christine Clo. *Ash* —3D **110**
Christmas Hill. *Shalf* —1B **134**

Christmaspie Av.—Clifton Way

Christmaspie Av. Norm —3M 111
Christopher Ct. Tad —1H 101
Christopher Rd. E Grin —9A 166
Christopher Rd. S'hall —1J 9
Christ's Hospital Rd. C Hosp (in two parts) —9B 196
Christy Est. Alder —2C 110
Christy Rd. Big H —2E 86
Chrystie La. Bookh —4B 98
Chucks La. Tad —2G 101
Chudleigh Ct. F'boro —1N 89
Chudleigh Gdns. Sutt —9A 44
Chudleigh Rd. Twic —9E 10
Chumleigh Wlk. Surb —3M 41
Church All. Croy —7L 45
Church App. Cud —2L 87
Church App. Egh —2E 36
Church App. Stanw —9M 7
Church Av. SW14 —6C 12
Church Av. Beck —1K 47
Church Av. F'boro —1A 90
Church Bungalows. Plais —5A 192
Church Circ. F'boro —3A 90
Church Clo. Add —1K 55
Church Clo. Brkwd —8C 72
Church Clo. Eton —2G 4
Church Clo. Fet —2D 98
Church Clo. G'wood —7K 171
Church Clo. Hors —3N 73
Church Clo. Houn —6N 9
Church Clo. Milf —1C 152
Church Clo. Stai —2L 37
Church Clo. Tad —5L 101
Church Cotts. Add —9N 37
Church Cotts. Craw —1L 181 (off Ilfield St.)
Church Ct. Fleet —4A 88 (off Branksomewood Rd.)
Church Ct. Fleet —4A 88 (off Church Rd.)
Church Ct. Reig —3N 121
Church Ct. Rich —8K 11
Churchcroft Clo. SW12 —1E 28
Church Dri. W Wick —1A 66
Church Farm La. Sutt —3K 61
Churchfield. Eden —2M 147
Churchfield Ct. Reig —3N 121
Churchfield Mans. SW6 —5L 13 (off New King's Rd.)
Churchfield Rd. Reig —2L 121
Churchfield Rd. W On T —7H 39
Churchfield Rd. Wey —1B 56
Churchfields. Guild —7C 94
Church Fields. Head —4C 168
Churchfields. Hors —3A 74
Churchfields. W Mol —2A 40
Churchfields. Witl —6B 152
Churchfields Av. Felt —4N 23
Churchfields Av. Wey —1C 56
Churchfields Rd. Beck —1G 47
Church Gdns. Dork —4H 119
Church Gdns. Lea —7H 79
Church Ga. SW6 —6K 13
Church Grn. Duns —3N 173
Church Grn. Hasl —1G 189
Church Grn. W On T —3K 57
Church Gro. Fleet —4A 88
Church Gro. King T —9J 25
Church Hill. SW19 —6L 27
Church Hill. Alder —4A 110
Church Hill. Brack —4H 15
Church Hill. Camb —1C 70
Church Hill. Cars —2D 62
Church Hill. Cat —2C 104
Church Hill. Cud —2L 87
Church Hill. Hasl —1G 189
Church Hill. Hors —3N 73
Church Hill. Mers —4F 102
Church Hill. Nutf —2K 123
Church Hill. Purl —6J 63
Church Hill. Pyr —4H 75
Church Hill. Sham G —7G 135
Church Hill. Shere —8B 116
Church Hill. Tats —9F 86
Churchill Rd. Slou —1B 6
Church Hill Rd. Surb —4L 41
Church Hill Rd. Sutt —9J 43
Churchill Av. Alder —4A 110
Churchill Av. H'ham —5H 197
Churchill Clo. F'boro —6N 69
Churchill Clo. Felt —2G 23
Churchill Clo. Fet —1E 98
Churchill Clo. Warl —4F 84
Churchill Clo. W'ham —4M 107
Churchill Ct. Craw —9E 162
Churchill Ct. Farn —2L 67
Churchill Ct. Stai —7K 21
Churchill Cres. F'boro —6N 69
Churchill Cres. Head —5E 168
Churchill Cres. Yat —1C 68
Churchill Dri. Wey —1D 56
Churchill Rd. Asc —1K 33
Churchill Rd. Guild —4A 114
Churchill Rd. Small —8M 143
Churchill Rd. S Croy —4N 63
Churchill Way. Big A —2F 86
Churchill Way. Sun —6H 23
Church Island. Stai —5F 20
Church La. SW17 —6D 28
Church La. SW19 —9M 27
Church La. Abry —8K 115
Church La. Asc —3A 34 (London Rd.)
Church La. Asc —4E 34 (Whitmore Rd.)
Church La. Ash —2F 110
Church La. Binf —6K 15
Church La. Bisl —2D 72
Church La. Blet —2A 124
Church La. Broad H —5D 196
Church La. Brook —1N 171
Church La. Burs —4J 163
Church La. Cat —2L 103
Church La. Chess —3M 59
Church La. Copt —8L 163
Church La. Coul —9E 82
Church La. Cranl —7M 155
Church La. Craw —2D 182
Church La. E Grin —9B 166
Church La. Eps —4J 81
Church La. Ews —3C 108
Church La. F'boro —1K 89
Church La. God —1G 124
Church La. Gray —6A 170
Church La. Hamb —8G 153
Church La. Hasc —7A 154
Church La. Hasl —1G 189
Church La. Head —3C 168
Church La. H'ley —2B 100
Church La. Man H —9C 198
Church La. Oke H —9N 157
Church La. Oxt —8N 105
Church La. Pirb —9N 71
Church La. Rich —2L 25
Church La. Rowl —8D 128
Church La. Send —4D 94
Church La. Tats —9F 86
Church La. Tedd —6F 24
Church La. Th Dit —5F 40
Church La. Twic —2G 25
Church La. Wall —9H 45
Church La. Warf —4B 16
Church La. Warl —3L 85 (Chelsham)
Church La. Warl —4G 84 (Warlingham)
Church La. Wind —4G 5
Church La. Wink —4G 16
Church La. Worp —5H 93
Church La. Wrec —4E 128
Church La. Av. Coul —9F 82
Church La. Dri. Coul —9F 82
Church La. E. Alder —3M 109
Church La. W. Alder —3L 109
Church Meadow. Surb —8J 41
Church M. Add —1L 55
Churchmore Rd. SW16 —9G 29
Church Pde. Ashf —5A 22
Church Pas. Farnh —1G 129
Church Pas. Surb —4L 41
Church Pas. Twic —2H 25
Church Path. SW14 —6C 12 (in two parts)
Church Path. SW19 —1L 43
Church Path. Ash V —9E 90
Church Path. Cobh —1J 77
Church Path. Coul —5L 83
Church Path. Croy —8N 45
Church Path. F'boro —1A 90 (Farnborough Park)
Church Path. F'boro —5A 90 (South Farnborough)
Church Path. F'boro —1K 89 (West Heath)
Church Path. H'ham —4B 180
Church Path. Mers —5F 102
Church Path. Mitc —2C 44
Church Path. S'hill —2B 34
Church Path. Wok —4B 74
Church Pl. Mitc —2C 44
Church Rise. Chess —3M 59
Church Rd. SE19 —1B 46
Church Rd. SW13 —5E 12
Church Rd. SW19 & Mitc (Merton) —9B 28
Church Rd. SW19 —6K 27 (Wimbledon)
Church Rd. Add —2J 55
Church Rd. Alder —5A 110
Church Rd. Asc —3L 33
Church Rd. Ashf —4A 22
Church Rd. Asht —5K 79
Church Rd. Bag —4H 51
Church Rd. Big H —4F 86
Church Rd. Bookh —1N 97
Church Rd. Brack —1A 32
Church Rd. Broad H —5D 196
Church Rd. Burs —3L 163
Church Rd. Byfl —1N 75
Church Rd. Cat —1C 104
Church Rd. Chav D —9F 16
Church Rd. Clay —3F 58
Church Rd. Copt —7M 163
Church Rd. Cran —1J 9
Church Rd. Croy —9N 45 (in two parts)
Church Rd. Duns —4N 173
Church Rd. E Mol —3D 40
Church Rd. Egh —6B 20
Church Rd. Eps —8D 60
Church Rd. Farn —2L 67
Church Rd. Felt —6L 23
Church Rd. Fleet —3A 88
Church Rd. Frim —5B 70
Church Rd. Guild —4N 113
Church Rd. Ham —5K 25
Church Rd. Hasl —1G 188
Church Rd. Horl —9D 142 (in two parts)
Church Rd. Horne —5C 144
Church Rd. Hors —2A 74
Church Rd. H'ham —3A 198
Church Rd. Houn —3A 10
Church Rd. Iswth —4D 10
Church Rd. Kenl —2A 84
Church Rd. Kes —4F 66
Church Rd. King T —1M 41
Church Rd. Lea —9H 79
Church Rd. Ling —7N 145
Church Rd. Low H —5C 162
Church Rd. Milf —2C 152
Church Rd. Newd —1A 160
Church Rd. Old Win —8K 5
Church Rd. Owl —6K 49
Church Rd. Purl —6J 63
Church Rd. Red —5C 122
Church Rd. Reig —5M 121
Church Rd. Rich —7L 11
Church Rd. Sand —6E 48
Church Rd. Shep —6C 38
Church Rd. Short —2N 47
Church Rd. Shot —2D 188
Church Rd. St J —6K 73
Church Rd. S'dale —5D 34
Church Rd. Surb —7J 41
Church Rd. Sutt —3K 61
Church Rd. Tedd —5E 24
Church Rd. Turn H —6C 184
Church Rd. Wall —9H 45
Church Rd. Warl —4G 84
Church Rd. W End —8C 52
Church Rd. W Ewe —4C 60
Church Rd. Whyt —5C 84
Church Rd. W'sham —3M 51
Church Rd. Wold —9H 85
Church Rd. Wor Pk —7D 42
Church Rd. Worth —3J 183
Church Rd. E. Crowt —2G 49
Church Rd. E. F'boro —4B 90
Church Rd. Ind. Est. Low H —5C 162
Church Rd. Trad. Est. Low H —5C 162
Church Rd. W. Crowt —3G 48
Church Rd. W. F'boro —4A 90
Church Side. Eps —9A 60
Churchside Clo. Big H —4E 86
Church Sq. Shep —6C 38
Church St. W4 —2E 12
Church St. Alder —2L 109
Church St. Bet —4D 120
Church St. Cobh —2J 77
Church St. Craw —3A 182
Church St. Crowt —2G 48
Church St. Croy —8M 45
Church St. Dork —5G 119
Church St. Eden —2L 147
Church St. Eff —5L 97
Church St. Eps —9D 60
Church St. Esh —1B 58
Church St. Ewe —5F 60
Church St. G'ming —7G 133
Church St. Hamp —9C 24
Church St. Iswth —6H 11
Church St. King T —1K 41
Church St. Lea —9H 79 (in two parts)
Church St. Old Wok —8E 74
Church St. Reig —3M 121
Church St. Rud —1D 194
Church St. Stai —5F 20
Church St. Sun —2J 39
Church St. Sutt —2N 61
Church St. Twic —2G 25
Church St. W On T —7H 39
Church St. Warn —1F 196
Church St. Wey —1B 56
Church St. Wind —4G 5
Church St. E. Wok —4B 74
Church St. W. Wok —4A 74
Church Stretton Rd. Houn —8C 10
Church Ter. Rich —8K 11
Church Ter. Wind —5B 4
Church View. Ash —2E 110
Church View. Rich —8L 11
Church View. Yat —8C 48
Churchview Clo. Horl —9D 142
Churchview Rd. Twic —2D 24
Church Wlk. SW13 —4F 12
Church Wlk. SW15 —8G 13
Church Wlk. SW16 —1G 45
Church Wlk. SW20 —2H 43
Church Wlk. Blet —2A 124
Church Wlk. Bren —2J 11 (in two parts)
Church Wlk. Cat —2D 104
Church Wlk. Cher —5J 37
Church Wlk. Craw —3B 182
Church Wlk. G'ming —5J 133
Church Wlk. Horl —9D 142
Church Wlk. H'ham —9G 180
Church Wlk. Lea —9H 79
Church Wlk. Reig —3N 121
Church Wlk. Rich —8K 11
Church Wlk. Th Dit —5F 40
Church Wlk. W On T —7H 39
Church Wlk. Wey —9B 38
Churchward Ho. W14 —1L 13 (off Ivatt Pl.)
Church Way. Oxt —1B 126
Church Way. S Croy —6C 64
Churston Clo. SW2 —2L 29
Churston Dri. Mord —4J 43
Churt Rd. Head & Churt —2F 168
Churt Rd. Hind —3M 169
Churt Wynde. Hind —2B 170
Chuters Clo. Byfl —8N 55
Chuters Gro. Eps —8E 60
Cicada Rd. SW18 —9N 13
Cinder Path. Wok —6M 73
Cinnamon Clo. Croy —6J 45
Cinnamon Gdns. Guild —7K 93
Circle Gdns. SW19 —1M 43
Circle Gdns. Byfl —9A 56
Circle Hill Rd. Crowt —2H 49
Circle Rd. W Vill —5F 56
Circle, The. G'ming —5J 133
Circuit Cen. Brook E —7N 55
Cissbury Clo. H'ham —2N 197
Cissbury Hill. Craw —5A 182
City Ho. Wall —7E 44 (off Corbet Clo.)
Clacket La. W'ham —2G 107
Clacy Grn. Brack —8M 15
Claireville Ct. Reig —2B 122
Clairvale Rd. Houn —4M 9
Clairview Rd. SW16 —6F 28
Clammer Hill Rd. G'wood —9K 171
Clancarty Rd. SW6 —5M 13
Clandon Av. Egh —8E 20
Clandon Clo. Eps —3E 60
Clandon Ct. F'boro —2B 90
Clandon Rd. Guild —4A 114
Clandon Rd. W Cla —3H 95
Clandon Ter. SW20 —9J 27
Clanfield Ride. B'water —1J 69
Clapgate La. Slin —3K 195
Clapham Pk. Est. SW4 —1H 29
Clappers Ga. Craw —2B 182
Clappers La. Chob —7F 52
Clappers Meadow. Alf —6J 175
Clappers Orchard. Alf —6H 175
Clare Av. Wokgm —1B 30
Clare Clo. Craw —9G 162
Clare Clo. W Byf —9J 55
Clare Cotts. Blet —2M 123
Clare Ct. Wold —1K 105
Clare Cres. Lea —5G 79
Claredale. Wok —6A 74
Clarefield Ct. Asc —6D 34
Clare Gdns. Egh —6C 20
Clare Hill. Esh —2B 58
Clare Lawn Av. SW14 —8C 12
Clare Mead. Rowl —7E 128
Clare M. SW6 —3N 13
Claremont. Shep —5C 38
Claremont Av. Camb —1D 70
Claremont Av. Esh —3N 57
Claremont Av. N Mald —4F 42
Claremont Av. Sun —9J 23
Claremont Av. W On T —1L 57
Claremont Av. Wok —6A 74
Claremont Clo. SW2 —2J 29
Claremont Clo. Orp —1J 67
Claremont Clo. S Croy —2E 84
Claremont Clo. W On T —2K 57
Claremont Ct. Dork —6H 119
Claremont Dri. Esh —3B 58
Claremont Dri. Wok —6A 74
Claremont End. Esh —3B 58
Claremont Gdns. Surb —4L 41
Claremont Gro. W4 —3D 12
Claremont La. Esh —2B 58
Claremont Pk. Rd. Esh —3B 58
Claremont Rd. Clay —4E 58
Claremont Rd. Croy —7D 46
Claremont Rd. Red —9E 102
Claremont Rd. Stai —6F 20
Claremont Rd. Surb —4L 41
Claremont Rd. Tedd —6F 24
Claremont Rd. Twic —1H 25
Claremont Rd. W Byf —8J 55
Claremont Rd. Wind —5F 4
Claremount Clo. Eps —4H 81
Claremount Gdns. Eps —4H 81
Clarence Av. SW4 —1H 29
Clarence Av. N Mald —1B 42
Clarence Clo. Alder —2A 110
Clarence Clo. W On T —1J 57
Clarence Ct. Horl —7H 143
Clarence Cres. SW4 —1H 29
Clarence Cres. Wind —4F 4
Clarence Dri. Camb —8F 50
Clarence Dri. E Grin —2B 186
Clarence Dri. Egh —5M 19
Clarence La. SW15 —9D 12
Clarence Rd. SW19 —7N 27
Clarence Rd. W4 —1N 11
Clarence Rd. Big H —5H 87
Clarence Rd. Croy —6A 46
Clarence Rd. Fleet —5A 88
Clarence Rd. H'ham —7K 197
Clarence Rd. Red —6B 122
Clarence Rd. Rich —4M 11
Clarence Rd. Sutt —2N 61
Clarence Rd. Tedd —7F 24
Clarence Rd. Wall —2F 62
Clarence Rd. W On T —1J 57
Clarence Rd. Wind —4D 4
Clarence St. Egh —7B 20
Clarence St. King T —1K 41
Clarence St. Rich —7L 11
Clarence St. Stai —5G 21
Clarence Ter. Houn —7B 10
Clarence Wlk. Red —6B 122
Clarence Way. Horl —7H 143
Clarendon Ct. Beck —1L 47 (off Albemarle Rd.)
Clarendon Ct. B'water —3J 69
Clarendon Ct. Fleet —4A 88
Clarendon Ct. Houn —4H 9
Clarendon Ct. Rich —4M 11
Clarendon Cres. Twic —4D 24
Clarendon Dri. SW15 —7H 13
Clarendon Ga. Ott —3F 54
Clarendon Gro. Mitc —2D 44
Clarendon Rd. SW19 —8C 28
Clarendon Rd. Ashf —5A 22
Clarendon Rd. Croy —8M 45
Clarendon Rd. Red —2D 122
Clarendon Rd. Wall —3G 62
Clare Pl. SW15 —1E 26
Clare Rd. Houn —6N 9
Clare Rd. Stai —2M 21
Clares, The. Cat —2D 104
Claret Gdns. SE25 —2B 46
Clareville Gro. SW7 —1N 13
Clareville Gro. M. SW7 —1N 13
Clareville Rd. Cat —2D 104
Clareville St. SW7 —1N 13
Clare Wood. Lea —5H 79
Clarewood Dri. Camb —9C 50
Clarice Way. Wall —5J 63
Claridge Ct. SW6 —5L 13
Claridge Gdns. D'land —9C 146
Claridges Mead. Ling —9C 146
Clarke Cres. Camb —8K 49
Clarkes Av. Wor Pk —7J 43
Clark La. Guild —2J 113
Clark Pl. Cranl —8H 155
Clark Rd. Craw —8M 181
Clark Rd. F'boro —9N 69
Clarks Grn. Rd. Capel —8N 159
Clarks Hill. Farnh —1B 128
Clarks La. Warl & Tats —1C 106
Clark Way. Houn —3L 9
Claudia Pl. SW19 —2K 27
Claverdale Rd. SW2 —1K 29
Claverdon. Brack —6M 31
Clavering Av. SW13 —2G 13
Clavering Clo. Twic —5G 24
Claverton. Asht —4L 79
Claxton Gro. W6 —1J 13
Clay Av. Mitc —1F 44
Claybrook Rd. W6 —2J 13
Claycart Rd. Alder —9J 89 (in two parts)
Clay Clo. Add —2K 55 (off Monks Cres.)
Clay Corner. Cher —7K 37
Claydon Dri. Croy —1J 63
Claydon Gdns. B'water —5M 69
Claydon Rd. Wok —3K 73
Clayford. D'land —9C 146
Claygate Cres. New Ad —3M 65
Claygate La. Esh —8G 40
Claygate La. Th Dit —7G 40
Claygate Lodge Clo. Clay —4E 58
Claygate Rd. Dork —7H 119
Clay Hall La. Copt —6A 164
Clayhall La. Old Win —8J 5
Clayhall La. Reig —7J 121
Clayhanger. Guild —1E 114
Clayhill. Surb —4N 41
Clayhill Clo. Brack —2D 32
Clayhill Clo. Leigh —1F 140
Clayhill Rd. Leigh —3D 140
Clay La. Guild —6N 93
Clay La. H'ley —2A 100
Clay La. Newc —9G 144
Clay La. S Nut —4G 123
Clay La. Stanw —1A 22
Clay La. Wokgm —2E 30
Claymore Clo. Mord —6M 43
Claypole Dri. Houn —4M 9
Clayponds Av. W5 & Bren —1L 11
Clayponds Gdns. W5 —1K 11
Clayponds La. Bren —1L 11
Clays Clo. E Grin —1A 186
Clayton Cres. Bren —1K 11
Clayton Dri. Guild —9J 93
Clayton Gro. Brack —9C 16
Clayton Hill. Craw —5A 182
Clayton Mead. God —8E 104
Clayton Rd. Chess —1J 59
Clayton Rd. Eps —8D 60
Clayton Rd. F'boro —5L 69
Clayton Rd. Iswth —6E 10
Cleardene. Dork —5H 119
Cleardown. Wok —5D 74
Clears Cotts. Reig —1K 121
Clearsprings. Light —6L 51
Clears, The. Reig —1K 121
Cleave Av. Hayes —1F 8
Cleave Av. Orp —3N 67
Cleaveland Rd. Surb —4K 41
Cleave Prior. Coul —6C 82
Cleaverholme Clo. SE25 —5E 46
Cleeve Ct. Felt —2F 22
Cleeve Rd. Lea —7F 78
Cleeves Ct. Red —2E 122 (off St Anne's Mt.)
Cleeve, The. Guild —3C 114
Clem Attlee Ct. SW6 —2L 13
Clem Attlee Est. SW6 —2L 13
Clem Attlee Pde. SW6 —2L 13 (off N. End Rd.)
Clement Clo. Purl —3M 83
Clement Gdns. Hayes —1F 8
Clement Rd. SW19 —6K 27
Clement Rd. Beck —1G 47
Clements Ct. Houn —7L 9
Clements Mead. Lea —6G 78
Clements Pl. Bren —1K 11
Clements Rd. W On T —8J 39
Clensham Ct. Sutt —8M 43
Clensham La. Sutt —8M 43
Cleopatra Pl. Warf —8C 16
Clerics Wlk. Shep —6E 38
Clerks Croft. Blet —2A 124
Clevedon. Wey —2E 56
Clevedon Ct. F'boro —2B 90
Clevedon Ct. Frim —6E 70
Clevedon Gdns. Houn —4J 9
Clevedon Rd. SE20 —1G 46
Clevedon Rd. King T —1N 41
Clevedon Rd. Twic —9K 11
Cleve Ho. Brack —3C 32
Cleveland Av. SW20 —1L 43
Cleveland Av. W4 —1E 12
Cleveland Av. Hamp —8N 23
Cleveland Clo. W On T —9J 39
Cleveland Dri. Stai —1K 37
Cleveland Gdns. SW13 —5E 12
Cleveland Gdns. Wor Pk —8D 42
Cleveland Pk. Stai —9N 7
Cleveland Rise. Mord —6J 43
Cleveland Rd. SW13 —5E 12
Cleveland Rd. Iswth —7G 10
Cleveland Rd. N Mald —3D 42
Cleveland Rd. Wor Pk —8D 42
Cleves Av. Eps —5G 61
Cleves Clo. Cobh —1J 77
Cleves Ct. Eps —8E 60
Cleves Ct. Wind —6C 4
Cleves Cres. New Ad —7M 65
Cleves Rd. Rich —4J 25
Cleves Way. Hamp —8N 23
Cleves Way. Sun —7G 22
Cleves Wood. Wey —1F 56
Clewborough Dri. Camb —9F 50
Clewer Av. Wind —5D 4
Clewer Ct. Rd. Wind —3E 4
Clewer Fields. Wind —4F 4
Clewer Hill Rd. Wind —5B 4
Clewer New Town. Wind —5D 4
Clewer Pk. Wind —3D 4
Clews La. Bisl —3D 72
Clifden Rd. Bren —2K 11
Clifden Rd. Twic —2F 24
Cliff End. Purl —8M 63
Cliffe Rise. G'ming —8F 132
Cliffe Rd. G'ming —9E 132
Cliffe Rd. S Croy —2A 64
Cliffe Wlk. Sutt —2A 62 (off Greyhound Rd.)
Clifford Av. SW14 —6A 12
Clifford Av. Wall —1G 62
Clifford Gro. Ashf —5B 22
Clifford Mnr. Rd. Guild —7A 114
Clifford Rd. SE25 —3D 46
Clifford Rd. Houn —6L 9
Clifford Rd. Rich —3K 25
Clifton Av. Felt —4K 23
Clifton Av. Sutt —7N 61
Clifton Clo. Add —8K 37
Clifton Clo. Cat —1A 104
Clifton Clo. Orp —2L 67
Clifton Clo. Wrec —7F 128
Clifton Ct. Stanw —9N 7
Clifton Gdns. W4 —1C 12
Clifton Gdns. Frim G —8D 70
Clifton Pde. Felt —5K 23
Clifton Pk. Av. SW20 —1H 43
Clifton Pl. Bans —2M 81
Clifton Rise. Wind —4A 4
Clifton Rd. SE25 —3B 46
Clifton Rd. SW19 —7J 27
Clifton Rd. Coul —2F 82
Clifton Rd. Craw —4G 183
Clifton Rd. Iswth —5E 10
Clifton Rd. King T —8M 25
Clifton Rd. Tedd —5E 24
Clifton Rd. Wall —2F 62
Clifton Rd. Wokgm —1A 30
Clifton's La. Reig —1J 121
Cliftonville. Dork —6H 119
Clifton Wlk. W6 —1G 13 (off King St.)
Clifton Way. H'row A —6C 8

Clifton Way—Coombe Hill Rd.

Clifton Way. *Wok* —4J **73**
Climping Rd. *Craw* —1N **181**
Cline Rd. *Guild* —5B **114**
Clinton Av. *E Mol* —3C **40**
Clinton Clo. *Knap* —5G **73**
Clinton Hill. *D'land* —2C **166**
Clinton Rd. *Lea* —1J **99**
Clintons Grn. *Brack* —9M **15**
Clippesby Clo. *Chess* —3M **59**
Clipstone Rd. *Houn* —6A **10**
Clitherow Ct. *Bren* —1J **11**
Clitherow Gdns. *Craw* —4C **182**
Clitherow Pas. *Bren* —1J **11**
Clitherow Rd. *Bren* —1H **11**
Cliveden Pl. *Shep* —5D **38**
Cliveden Rd. *SW19* —9L **27**
Clive Grn. *Brack* —4N **31**
(in two parts)
Clive Rd. *SE21* —4N **29**
Clive Rd. *SW19* —7C **28**
Clive Rd. *Alder* —3B **110**
Clive Rd. *Esh* —1B **58**
Clive Rd. *Felt* —9H **9**
Clive Rd. *Twic* —5G **24**
Clive Way. *Craw* —3G **182**
Clock Barn La. *Busb* —3J **153**
Clockhouse Clo. *SW19* —3H **27**
Clock Ho. Clo. *Byfl* —8A **56**
Clockhouse Ct. *Beck* —1H **47**
Clockhouse Ct. *Guild* —8M **93**
Clockhouse Ct. *Hasl* —2G **189**
Clockhouse Ind. Est., The. *Felt* —2C **22**
Clockhouse La. *Ashf & Felt* —5B **22**
Clockhouse La. *Brmly* —4B **134**
Clockhouse La. E. *Egh* —8D **20**
Clockhouse La. W. *Egh* —8C **20**
Clockhouse Mead. *Craw* —1D **70**
Clockhouse Pl. *SW15* —9K **13**
Clock Ho. Rd. *Beck* —2H **47**
Clockhouse Rd. *F'boro* —1N **89**
Clockhouse Roundabout. (Junct.) —2D **22**
Clockouse La. E. *Egh* —8D **20**
Clock Tower Rd. *Iswth* —6F **10**
Clodhouse Hill. *Wok* —9G **73**
Cloister Clo. *Tedd* —6H **25**
Cloister Gdns. *SE25* —5E **46**
Cloisters Mall. *King T* —1L **41**
Cloisters, The. *Frim* —5B **70**
Cloisters, The. *Wok* —8D **74**
Cloncurry St. *SW6* —5J **13**
Clonmel Rd. *SW6* —3L **13**
Clonmel Rd. *Tedd* —5D **24**
Clonmore St. *SW18* —2L **27**
Cloonmore Av. *Orp* —1N **67**
Close, The. *SE25* —5D **46**
Close, The. *Asc* —1H **33**
Close, The. *Beck* —3H **47**
Close, The. *Berr G* —3K **87**
Close, The. *Brack* —3A **32**
Close, The. *Cars* —5C **62**
Close, The. *Col T* —7K **49**
Close, The. *E Grin* —1N **185**
Close, The. *Farnh* —2J **129**
Close, The. *Frim* —6B **70**
Close, The. *G'ming* —8J **133**
Close, The. *Guild* —8N **113**
Close, The. *Horl* —1G **163**
Close, The. *Ifold* —5F **192**
Close, The. *Iswth* —5D **10**
Close, The. *Light* —6L **51**
Close, The. *Mitc* —3D **44**
Close, The. *N Mald* —1B **42**
Close, The. *Purl* —6M **63**
(Pampisford Rd.)
Close, The. *Purl* —6K **63**
(Russell Hill)
Close, The. *Reig* —4N **121**
Close, The. *Rich* —6A **12**
Close, The. *Str G* —7B **120**
Close, The. *Sutt* —6L **43**
Close, The. *Vir W* —4N **35**
Close, The. *W Byf* —9J **55**
Close, The. *Won* —4D **134**
Closeworth Rd. *F'boro* —5C **90**
Cloudesdale Rd. *SW17* —3F **28**
Clouston Clo. *Wall* —2J **63**
Clouston Rd. *F'boro* —9L **69**
Clovelly Av. *Warl* —6E **84**
Clovelly Dri. *Hind* —2A **170**
Clovelly Pk. *Hind* —2A **170**
Clovelly Rd. *Hind* —3A **170**
Clovelly Rd. *Houn* —5A **10**
Clover Clo. *Lind* —4B **168**
Clover Clo. *Wokgm* —1D **30**
Clover Ct. *Wok* —6N **73**
Clover Field. *Slin* —6L **195**
Cloverfields. *Horl* —7F **142**
Clover Hill. *Coul* —8F **82**
Cloverlands. *Craw* —1D **182**
Clover La. *Yat* —9A **48**
Clover Lea. *G'ming* —3H **133**
Clover Rd. *Guild* —2H **113**
Clovers Cotts. *H'ham* —8E **180**
Clovers End. *H'ham* —3N **197**
Clovers Way. *Fay* —1C **198**
Clover Wlk. *Eden* —9M **127**
Clover Way. *Small* —8N **143**
Clover Way. *Wall* —7E **44**
Clowser Clo. *Sutt* —2A **62**
Clubhouse Rd. *Alder* —8L **89**
Club La. *Crowt* —2J **49**
Club Row. *Pirb* —6A **72**
Clump Av. *Tad* —9B **100**
Clumps Rd. *Lwr Bo* —7K **129**
Clumps, The. *Ashf* —5E **22**
Clunbury Av. *S'hall* —1N **9**
Cluny M. *SW5* —1M **13**
Clyde Av. *S Croy* —2E **84**
Clyde Clo. *Red* —2E **122**
Clyde Rd. *Croy* —8C **46**
Clyde Rd. *Stai* —2M **21**
Clyde Rd. *Sutt* —2M **61**
Clyde Rd. *Wall* —3G **63**
Clydesdale Clo. *Iswth* —6F **10**
Clydesdale Gdns. *Rich* —7A **12**
Clymping Dene. *Felt* —1J **23**
Clyve Way. *Stai* —9G **21**
Coach Ho. Clo. *Frim* —3C **70**
Coach Ho. Gdns. *Fleet* —2B **88**
Coach Ho. La. *SW19* —5J **27**
Coach Ho. M. *Red* —4D **122**
Coach Ho. Yd. *SW18* —7N **13**
Coachlands Av. *Guild* —3J **113**
Coachman's Dri. *Craw* —7N **181**
Coach Rd. *Asc* —8J **17**
Coach Rd. *Brock* —4M **119**
Coach Rd. Horl —3F 162
(off Ring Rd. S.)
Coach Rd. *Ott* —3E **54**
Coaldale Wlk. *SE21* —1N **29**
Coalecroft Rd. *SW15* —7H **13**
Coast Hill. *Westc* —8N **117**
Coast Hill La. *Westc* —7A **118**
Coates Wlk. *Bren* —1L **11**
Coatham Pl. *Cranl* —7A **156**
Cobb Clo. *Dat* —4N **5**
Cobbets Ridge. *Farnh* —3A **130**
Cobbett Clo. *Craw* —1G **183**
Cobbett Rd. *Guild* —2J **113**
Cobbett Rd. *Twic* —2A **24**
Cobbetts Clo. *Norm* —7C **92**
Cobbetts Clo. *Wok* —4L **73**
Cobbetts Hill. *Wey* —3C **56**
Cobbett's La. *Yat* —1E **68**
Cobbetts Wlk. *Bisl* —2D **72**
Cobbetts Way. *Farnh* —5E **128**
Cobblers. *H'ham* —5L **195**
Cobblers Wlk. *Hamp & Tedd* —9C **24**
Cobbles Cres. *Craw* —2C **182**
Cobblestone Pl. *Croy* —7N **45**
Cobb's Rd. *Houn* —7N **9**
Cob Clo. *Craw D* —1F **184**
Cobden La. *Hasl* —1H **189**
Cobden Rd. *SE25* —4D **46**
Cobden Rd. *Orp* —1M **67**
Cobham Av. *N Mald* —4F **42**
Cobham Clo. *Wall* —3J **63**
Cobham Ct. *Mitc* —1B **44**
Cobham Ga. *Cobh* —1J **77**
Cobham Pk. Rd. *Cobh* —4J **77**
Cobham Rd. *Houn* —3K **9**
Cobham Rd. *King T* —1N **41**
Cobham Rd. *Stoke D & Fet* —5A **78**
Cobham Way. *Craw* —6F **162**
Cobham Way. *E Hor* —4F **96**
Cobnor Clo. *Craw* —5L **181**
Cobs Way. *New H* —6L **55**
Coburg Cres. *SW2* —2K **29**
Cob Wlk. *Craw* —3M **181**
Cochrane Pl. *W'sham* —2A **52**
Cochrane Rd. *SW19* —8L **27**
Cock-A-Dobby. *Sand* —6F **48**
Cock La. *Fet* —9C **78**
Cockpit Path. *Wokgm* —3B **30**
Cocks Cres. *N Mald* —3E **42**
Cocksett Av. *Orp* —3N **67**
Cockshot Hill. *Reig* —4N **121**
Cockshot Rd. *Reig* —4N **121**
Cock's La. *Warf* —3E **16**
Coda Cen., The. *SW6* —4K **13**
Codrington Ct. *Wok* —5J **73**
Cody Clo. *Wall* —4H **63**
Cody Rd. *F'boro* —2L **89**
Coe Av. *SE25* —5D **46**
Coe Clo. *Alder* —3M **109**
Cogman's La. *Out & Horl* —6A **144**
Cokenor Wood. *Wrec* —5E **128**
Cokers La. *SE21* —2N **29**
Colbarn Cres. *Guild* —9C **94**
Colbeck. *C Crook* —9C **88**
Colbeck M. *SW7* —1N **13**
Colborne Way. *Wor Pk* —9H **43**
Colbred Corner. *Fleet* —1D **88**
Colburn Av. *Cat* —2C **104**
Colburn Way. *Sutt* —9B **44**
Colby Rd. *W On T* —7H **39**
Colchester Vale. *F Row* —7G **187**
Colcokes Rd. *Bans* —3M **81**
Cold Blows. *Mitc* —2D **44**
Coldborough Rise. *Brack* —9L **15**
Coldharbour Clo. *Egh* —2E **36**
Coldharbour La. *Blet* —3C **124**
Coldharbour La. *Dork* —2E **138**
Coldharbour La. *Egh* —2E **36**
Cold Harbour La. *F'boro* —6K **69**
Coldharbour La. *Purl* —6L **63**
Coldharbour La. *W End* —7C **52**
Coldharbour La. *Wok* —2H **75**
Coldharbour Rd. *Croy* —2L **63**
Coldharbour Rd. *W Byf & Wok* —2H **75**
Coldharbour Way. *Croy* —2L **63**
Coldshott. *Oxt* —2C **126**
Coldstream Gdns. *SW18* —9L **13**
Colebrook. *Ott* —3F **54**
Colebrook Clo. *SW15* —1J **27**
Colebrooke Rise. *Brom* —1N **47**
Colebrooke Rd. *Red* —1C **122**
Colebrook Pl. *Ott* —4E **54**
Colebrook Rd. *SW16* —9J **29**
Cole Clo. *Craw* —8N **181**
Cole Ct. *Twic* —1G **24**
Coleford Bri. Rd. *Myt* —1B **90**
Coleford Clo. *Myt* —2D **90**
Coleford Paddocks. *Myt* —1D **90**
Coleford Rd. *SW18* —8N **13**
Cole Gdns. *Houn* —3H **9**
Coleherne Ct. *SW5* —1N **13**
Coleherne M. *SW10* —1N **13**
Coleherne Rd. *SW10* —1N **13**
Colehill Gdns. *SW6* —4K **13**
Colehill La. *SW6* —4K **13**
Colekitchen La. *Gom* —7E **116**
Coleman Clo. *SE25* —1C **46**
Coleman Rd. *Alder* —3B **110**
Colemans Hatch Rd. *Col H* —9N **187**
Colenorton Cres. *Eton W* —1B **4**
Cole Pk. Gdns. *Twic* —9G **10**
Cole Pk. Rd. *Twic* —9G **10**
Cole Pk. View. *Twic* —9G **11**
Coleridge Av. *Sutt* —1C **62**
Coleridge Av. *Yat* —1D **60**
Coleridge Clo. *Crowt* —3H **49**
Coleridge Clo. *H'ham* —2L **197**
Coleridge Cres. *Coln* —4G **6**
Coleridge Rd. *Ashf* —5N **21**
Coleridge Rd. *Croy* —6F **46**
Coleridge Way. *W Dray* —1N **7**
Cole Rd. *Twic* —9G **10**
Colesburg Rd. *Beck* —2J **47**
Colescroft Hill. *Purl* —2L **83**
Coleshill Rd. *Tedd* —7E **24**
Cole's La. *Dork* —4E **158**
Colesmead Rd. *Red* —9D **102**
Coleson Hill Rd. *Wrec* —6E **128**
Colet Gdns. *W14* —1J **13**
Colet Rd. *Craw* —6B **182**
Coleville Rd. *F'boro* —9L **69**
Coley Av. *Wok* —5C **74**
Colgate Clo. *Craw* —1N **181**
Colin Clo. *Croy* —9J **47**
Colin Clo. *W Wick* —1B **66**
Colinette Rd. *SW15* —7H **13**
Colin Rd. *Cat* —1D **104**
Coliston Pas. *SW18* —1M **27**
Coliston Rd. *SW18* —1M **27**
Collamore Av. *SW18* —2C **28**
Collards La. *Hasl* —2H **189**
College Av. *Egh* —7D **20**
College Av. *Eps* —1E **80**
College Clo. *Add* —9M **37**
College Clo. *Camb* —7B **50**
College Clo. *E Grin* —9B **166**
College Clo. *Ling* —7N **145**
College Clo. *Twic* —2D **24**
College Ct. W6 —1H 13
(off Queen Caroline St.)
College Cres. *Col T* —7K **49**
College Cres. *Red* —9E **102**
College Cres. *Wind* —5E **4**
College Fields Bus. Cen. *SW19* —9B **28**
College Gdns. *SW17* —3C **28**
College Gdns. *Farnh* —1G **128**
College Gdns. *N Mald* —4E **42**
College Hill. *G'ming* —9F **132**
College Hill. *Hasl* —2G **189**
College Hill Ter. *Hasl* —2G **189**
College La. *E Grin* —9B **166**
College La. *Wok* —6M **73**
College M. *SW18* —8N **13**
College Pl. *SW10* —3N **13**
College Ride. *Bag* —6E **50**
College Ride. *Camb* —8B **50**
College Rd. *SW19* —7B **28**
College Rd. *Ash V* —1E **110**
College Rd. *Brack* —3A **32**
College Rd. *Col T* —8K **49**
College Rd. *Craw* —3C **182**
College Rd. *Croy* —8A **46**
College Rd. *Eps* —1E **80**
College Rd. *Guild* —4N **113**
College Rd. *Iswth* —4F **10**
College Rd. *Wok* —3D **74**
College Roundabout. *King T* —2L **41**
College Wlk. *King T* —2L **41**
College Way. *Ashf* —5A **22**
Collendean La. *Horl* —7K **141**
Collens Field. *Pirb* —2C **92**
Collett's All. H'ham —6J 197
(off Carfax)
Colley La. *Reig* —2K **121**
Colley Mnr. Dri. *Reig* —2J **121**
Colley Way. *Reig* —9K **101**
Collier Clo. *Eps* —3N **59**
Collier Clo. *F'boro* —9J **69**
Collier Row. *Craw* —5B **182**
Colliers. *Cat* —3D **104**
Colliers Clo. *Wok* —4L **73**
Colliers Ct. *Croy* —1A **64**
Colliers Shaw. *Kes* —2F **66**
Colliers Water La. *T Hth* —4L **45**
Colliers Wood. (Junct.) —8B **28**
Collier Way. *Guild* —1F **114**
Collingdon. *Cranl* —9A **156**
Collingham Gdns. *SW5* —1N **13**
Collingham Pl. *SW5* —1N **13**
Collingham Rd. *SW5* —1N **13**
Collingsbourne. *Add* —1L **55**
Collingwood. *F'boro* —3C **90**
Collingwood Av. *Surb* —7B **42**
Collingwood Clo. *E Grin* —2B **186**
Collingwood Clo. *Horl* —7F **142**
Collingwood Clo. *H'ham* —4J **197**
Collingwood Clo. *Twic* —1A **24**
Collingwood Cres. *Guild* —2C **114**
Collingwood Grange Clo. *Camb* —7F **50**
Collingwood Pl. *W On T* —9H **39**
Collingwood Rise. *Camb* —8E **50**
Collingwood Rd. *Craw* —4H **183**
Collingwood Rd. *H'ham* —4J **197**
Collingwood Rd. *Mitc* —2C **44**
Collingwood Rd. *Sutt* —9M **43**
Collins Gdns. *Ash* —2F **110**
Collins Path. *Hamp* —7N **23**
Collins Rd. *Bew* —5K **181**
Collis All. *Twic* —2E **24**
Collyer Av. *Croy* —1J **63**
Collyer Rd. *Bedd* —1J **63**
Colman Clo. *Eps* —4H **81**
Colman Ho. *Red* —1D **122**
Colman's Hill. *Peasl* —4F **136**
Colman Way. *Red* —1C **122**
Colmer Rd. *SW16* —9J **29**
Colnbrook By-Pass. *Coln & W Dray* —2E **6**
Colnbrook Ct. *Coln* —4H **7**
Colndale Rd. *Coln* —5G **6**
Colnebridge Clo. *Stai* —5G **21**
Colne Ct. *Eps* —1B **60**
Colne Dri. *W On T* —9L **39**
Colne Pk. Cvn. Site. *W Dray* —1L **7**
Colne Reach. *Stai* —8H **7**
Colne Rd. *Twic* —2E **24**
Colne Wlk. *Craw* —5L **181**
Colne Way. *Ash* —3E **110**
Colne Way. *Stai* —3D **20**
Coln Trad. Est. *Coln* —4H **7**
Colonel's La. *Cher* —5J **37**
Colonial Av. *Twic* —8C **10**
Colonial Dri. *W4* —1B **12**
Colonial Rd. *Felt* —1F **22**
Colonsay Rd. *Craw* —6N **181**
Colson Rd. *Croy* —8B **46**
Colson Way. *SW16* —5G **29**
Colston Av. *Cars* —1C **62**
Colston Ct. Cars —1D 62
(off West St.)
Colston Rd. *SW14* —7B **12**
Coltash Rd. *Craw* —4E **182**
Coltsfoot Dri. *Guild* —9D **94**
Coltsfoot Dri. *H'ham* —3L **197**
Coltsfoot La. *Oxt* —2B **126**
Coltsfoot Rd. *Lind* —4B **168**
Columbia Av. *Wor Pk* —6E **42**
Columbia Cen., The. *Brack* —1N **31**
Columbia Sq. *SW14* —7B **12**
Columbine Av. *S Croy* —4M **63**
Columbus Dri. *F'boro* —1H **89**
Colville Gdns. *Light* —7N **51**
Colvin Rd. *T Hth* —4L **45**
Colwith Rd. *W6* —2H **13**
Colwood Gdns. *SW19* —8B **28**
Colworth Rd. *Croy* —7D **46**
Colwyn Clo. *SW16* —6G **28**
Colwyn Clo. *Craw* —5L **181**
Colwyn Clo. *Yat* —9B **48**
Colwyn Cres. *Houn* —4C **10**
Colyton Clo. *Wok* —5M **73**
Combe La. *Brmly* —6A **116**
Combe La. *C'fold* —4C **172**
Combe La. *F'boro* —8M **69**
Combe La. *G'ming* —9M **133**
Combemartin Rd. *SW18* —1K **27**
Combermere Clo. *Wind* —5E **4**
Combermere Rd. *Mord* —5N **43**
Combe Rd. *G'ming* —3H **133**
Comeragh Clo. *Wok* —7K **73**
Comeragh M. *W14* —1K **13**
Comeragh Rd. *W14* —1K **13**
Comet Rd. *Stai* —1M **21**
Comforts Farm Av. *Oxt* —2B **126**
Comfrey Clo. *F'boro* —9H **69**
Comfrey Clo. *Wokgm* —9D **14**
Commerce Rd. *Bren* —3J **11**
Commerce Way. *Croy* —8K **45**
Commerce Way. *Eden* —9L **127**
Commercial Rd. *Alder* —4A **110**
Commercial Rd. *Guild* —4N **113**
Commercial Rd. *Stai* —7J **21**
Commercial Way. *Wok* —4A **74**
Commodore Ct. *F'boro* —5A **90**
Common Clo. *Wok* —1N **73**
Commondale. *SW15* —6H **13**
Commonfield La. *SW17* —6C **28**
Commonfield Rd. *Bans* —1M **81**
Commonfields. *W End* —9C **52**
Common Ho. Rd. *Duns* —5B **174**
Common La. *Clay* —4G **58**
Common La. *Eton C* —1F **4**
Common La. *New H* —5L **55**
Common Rd. *SW13* —6G **12**
Common Rd. *Clay* —3G **58**
Common Rd. *Dor* —1A **4**
Common Rd. *Eton W* —1C **4**
Common Rd. *Red* —5D **122**
Common Rd. *Slou* —1C **6**
Commonside. *Bookh* —9A **78**
(in two parts)
Common Side. *Eps* —2N **79**
Commonside. *Kes* —1E **66**
Commonside Clo. *Coul* —7M **83**
Commonside Clo. *Sutt* —7N **61**
Commonside E. *Mitc* —2E **44**
Commonside W. *Mitc* —2D **44**
Common, The. *Asht* —3K **79**
Common, The. *Cranl* —6L **155**
Common, The. *Shaf* —1A **134**
(in two parts)
Common, The. *S'hall* —1L **9**
Common, The. *W Dray* —1L **7**
Common, The. *Won* —3D **134**
Commonwealth Rd. *Cat* —1D **104**
Community Clo. *Houn* —4J **9**
Compasses Mobile Home Pk. *Alf* —4H **175**
Compass Hill. *Rich* —9K **11**
Compassion Clo. *Bew* —4K **181**
Comper Clo. *Craw* —5K **181**
Comport Grn. *New Ad* —8A **66**
Compton Clo. *Brack* —5K **31**
Compton Clo. *C Crook* —8C **88**
Compton Clo. *Esh* —3D **58**
Compton Clo. *Sand* —6H **49**
Compton Ct. *Guild* —4B **114**
Compton Ct. *Sutt* —1A **62**
Compton Cres. *W4* —2B **12**
Compton Cres. *Chess* —2L **59**
Compton Gdns. Add —2K 55
(off Monks Cres.)
Compton Heights. *Guild* —6G **112**
Compton Rd. *SW19* —7L **27**
Compton Rd. *C Crook* —8C **88**
Compton Rd. *Croy* —7E **46**
Comptons Brow La. *H'ham* —5N **197**
Comptons Ct. *H'ham* —5M **197**
Comptons La. *H'ham* —4M **197**
Compton Way. *Farnh* —1M **129**
Comsaye Wlk. *Brack* —4A **32**
Conaways Clo. *Eps* —6F **60**
Concorde Bus. Pk. *Big H* —2F **86**
Concorde Clo. *Houn* —5B **10**
Conde Way. *Bord* —7A **168**
Condor Ct. *Guild* —5M **113**
Condor Rd. *Stai* —2L **37**
Conduit La. *Croy* —2D **64**
Conduit La. *Dat* —2A **6**
Conduit La. *S Croy & Croy* —2D **64**
Conduit, The. *Blet* —7A **104**
Coney Acre. *SE21* —2N **29**
Coneyberry. *Reig* —7A **122**
Coneybury. *Blet* —3B **124**
Coneybury Clo. *Warl* —6E **84**
Coney Clo. *Craw* —1N **181**
Coney Croft. *H'ham* —3A **198**
Coney Grange. *Warf* —7N **15**
Coneyhurst La. *Ewh* —3D **156**
Conford Dri. *Shalf* —1A **134**
Coniers Way. *Guild* —9D **94**
Conifer Clo. *C Crook* —8A **88**
Conifer Clo. *Orp* —1M **67**
Conifer Clo. *Reig* —1M **121**
Conifer Dri. *Camb* —9E **50**
Conifer Gdns. *SW16* —4K **29**
Conifer Gdns. *Sutt* —8N **43**
Conifer La. *Egh* —6E **20**
Conifer Pk. *Eps* —7D **60**
Conifers. *Wey* —1F **56**
Conifers Clo. *H'ham* —2A **198**
Conifers Clo. *Tedd* —8H **25**
Conifers, The. *Crowt* —9F **30**
Conifer Wlk. *Wind* —3A **4**
Coniger Rd. *SW6* —5M **13**
Coningsby. *Brack* —3A **32**
Coningsby Rd. *S Croy* —5N **63**
Conista Ct. *Wok* —3J **73**
Coniston Clo. *SW13* —3E **12**
Coniston Clo. *SW20* —5J **43**
Coniston Clo. *W4* —3B **12**
Coniston Clo. *Camb* —3G **71**
Coniston Clo. *F'boro* —2K **89**
Coniston Clo. *H'ham* —2A **198**
Coniston Clo. *If'd* —5J **181**
Coniston Ct. *Light* —6M **51**
Coniston Ct. *Wey* —3C **56**
Coniston Dri. *Farnh* —6F **108**
Coniston Gdns. *Sutt* —3B **62**
Coniston Rd. *Coul* —3G **82**
Coniston Rd. *Croy* —6D **46**
Coniston Rd. *Twic* —9B **10**
Coniston Rd. *Wok* —7D **74**
Coniston Way. *Chess* —9L **41**
Coniston Way. *C Crook* —8A **88**
Coniston Way. *Egh* —8D **20**
Coniston Way. *Reig* —2C **122**
Connaught Av. *SW14* —6B **12**
Connaught Av. *Ashf* —5N **21**
Connaught Av. *Houn* —7M **9**
Connaught Barracks. *Alder* —7B **90**
Connaught Clo. *Crowt* —4E **48**
Connaught Clo. *Sutt* —8B **44**
Connaught Clo. *Yat* —9A **48**
Connaught Cres. *Brkwd* —7C **72**
Connaught Dri. *Wey* —7B **56**
Connaught Gdns. *Craw* —1B **182**
Connaught Gdns. *Mord* —3A **44**
Connaught Rd. *Alder* —2A **110**
Connaught Rd. *Bag* —4G **51**
Connaught Rd. *Brkwd* —8C **72**
Connaught Rd. *Camb* —1D **70**
Connaught Rd. *Fleet* —5A **88**
Connaught Rd. *N Mald* —3D **42**
Connaught Rd. *Rich* —8M **11**
Connaught Rd. *Sutt* —8B **44**
Connaught Rd. *Tedd* —6D **24**
Connicut La. *Bookh* —6B **98**
Connolly Ct. *Vir W* —3A **36**
Connop Way. *Frim* —3D **70**
Conquest Rd. *Add* —2J **55**
Conrad Dri. *Wor Pk* —7H **43**
Consfield Av. *N Mald* —3F **42**
Consort Dri. *Camb* —8G **50**
Consort Ho. *Horl* —8E **142**
Consort M. *Iswth* —8D **10**
Consort Way. *Horl* —8E **142**
Consort Way E. *Horl* —9F **142**
Constable Ct. W4 —1A 12
(off Chaseley Dri.)
Constable Gdns. *Iswth* —8D **10**
Constable Rd. *Craw* —7D **182**
Constable Way. *Col T* —9K **49**
Constance Rd. *Croy* —6M **45**
Constance Rd. *Sutt* —1A **62**
Constance Rd. *Twic* —1B **24**
Constantius Ct. *C Crook* —9A **88**
Constitution Hill. *Wok* —6A **74**
Contessa Clo. *Orp* —2N **67**
Control Tower Rd. *Gat A* —4B **162**
Control Tower Rd. *H'row A* —6B **8**
Convent Gdns. *W5* —1J **11**
Convent Hill. *SE19* —7N **29**
Convent La. *Cobh* —7F **56**
Convent Lodge. *Ashf* —6C **22**
Convent Rd. *Ashf* —6B **22**
Convent Rd. *Wind* —5D **4**
Convent Way. *S'hall* —1K **9**
Conway Clo. *Frim* —5D **70**
Conway Dri. *Ashf* —8D **22**
Conway Dri. *F'boro* —1J **89**
Conway Dri. *Sutt* —3N **61**
Conway Gdns. *Mitc* —3J **45**
Conway Rd. *SW20* —9H **27**
Conway Rd. *Felt* —6L **23**
Conway Rd. *Houn* —1N **23**
Conway Rd. *H'row A* —6C **8**
Conway Wlk. *Hamp* —7N **23**
Conyers Clo. *W On T* —2L **57**
Conyer's Rd. *SW16* —6H **29**
Cook Cres. *H'ham* —6M **197**
Cooke Rise. *Warf* —7A **16**
Cookes La. *Sutt* —3K **61**
Cook Gro. *Eden* —2L **147**
Cookham Clo. *Sand* —6H **49**
Cookham Rd. *Brack* —1K **31**
Cook Rd. *Craw* —5C **182**
Cook Rd. *H'ham* —2K **197**
Cooks Hill. *Rud* —8A **176**
Cook's La. *H'ham* —3A **196**
Cooks Mead. *Rusp* —2C **180**
Cooks Meadow. *Rusp* —2C **180**
Coolarne Rise. *Camb* —9E **50**
Coolgardie Rd. *Ashf* —6D **22**
Coolham Ct. *Craw* —3L **181**
Coolhurst La. *H'ham* —7N **197**
Coombe Av. *Croy* —1B **64**
Coombe Bank. *King T* —9D **26**
Coombe Clo. *Craw* —9B **162**
Coombe Clo. *Frim* —6B **70**
Coombe Clo. *Houn* —7A **10**
Coombe Cres. *Hamp* —8N **23**
Coombe Dri. *Add* —3H **55**
Coombe Dri. *Fleet* —4D **88**
Coombe End. *King T* —8C **26**
Coombefield Clo. *N Mald* —4D **42**
Coombe Gdns. *SW20* —1F **42**
Coombe Gdns. *N Mald* —3E **42**
Coombe Hill Ct. *Wind* —7A **4**
Coombe Hill Glade. *King T* —8D **26**
Coombe Hill Rd. *E Grin* —3M **185**
Coombe Hill Rd. *King T* —8D **26**

Coombe Ho. Chase—Crayonne Clo.

Coombe Ho. Chase. N Mald —9C 26
Coombelands Bus. Pk. Add —3J 55
Coombelands La. Add —3J 55
Coombe La. SW20 —9E 26
Coombe La. Asc —3N 33
Coombe La. Croy —2E 64
Coombe La. King T —9A 26
Coombe La. W Vill —5G 56
Coombe La. Worp —7F 92
Coombe Lane. (Junct.) —9E 26
Coombe La. Flyover. King T —9E 26
Coombe La. W. King T —9A 26
Coombe Neville. King T —8C 26
Coombe Pk. King T —6B 26
Coombe Pine. Brack —5B 32
Coomber Ho. SW6 —6N 13
(off Wandsworth Bri. Rd.)
Coombe Ridings. King T —6B 26
Coombe Rise. King T —9B 26
Coombe Rd. W4 —1D 12
Coombe Rd. Croy —1A 64
Coombe Rd. Hamp —7N 23
Coombe Rd. King T —9N 25
Coombe Rd. N Mald —1D 42
Coombe Rd. Yat —8A 48
Coomber Way. Croy —6H 45
Coombes, The. Brmly —6C 134
Coombe, The. Bet —9C 100
Coombe View. C'fold —4D 172
Coombe Wlk. Sutt —9N 43
Coombe Way. Byfl —8A 56
Coombe Wood Hill. Purl —9N 63
Coombewood Rd. King T —6B 26
Coombfield. Eden —3L 147
Coomer M. SW6 —2L 13
Coomer Pl. SW6 —2L 13
Coomer Rd. SW6 —2L 13
Cooper Clo. Horl —8L 143
Cooper Cres. Cars —9D 44
Cooper Ho. Houn —6N 9
Cooper Rd. Croy —2L 63
Cooper Rd. Guild —5B 114
Cooper Rd. W'sham —3A 52
Cooper Row. Craw —6B 182
Coopers Clo. Stai —6G 21
Coopers Ct. Iswth —5F 10
(off Woodlands Rd.)
Coopers Hill Dri. Brkwd —7N 71
Coopers Hill La. Egh —4M 19
(in three parts)
Cooper's Hill Rd. Nutf —3L 123
Coopers Rise. G'ming —8E 132
Coopers Ter. Farnh —9H 109
Coopers Wood. Hand —5N 199
Coos La. Hand —9M 199
Cootes Av. H'ham —5G 196
Copelands Clo. Camb —2H 71
Copenhagen Wlk. Crowt —3G 49
Copenhagen Way. W On T —9J 39
Copleigh Dri. Tad —7K 81
Copley Clo. Red —1C 122
Copley Clo. Wok —6H 73
Copley Pk. SW16 —7K 29
Copley Way. Tad —7J 81
Copnall Way. H'ham —6J 197
Coppard Gdns. Chess —3J 59
Copped Hall Dri. Camb —9G 50
Copped Hall Way. Camb —9G 50
Copper Beech Clo. Wind —4A 4
Copper Beech Clo. Wok —8L 73
Copper Beeches Ct. Iswth —4D 10
Copperfield Av. Owl —5K 49
Copperfield Clo. S Croy —7N 63
Copperfield Ct. Lea —8G 79
Copperfield Pl. H'ham —4H 197
Copperfield Rise. Add —2H 55
Copperfields. Fet —9C 78
Copperfields. H'ham —8A 198
Copper Mill Dri. Iswth —5F 10
Copper Mill La. SW17 —5A 28
Coppermill Rd. Wray —9C 6
Coppice Clo. SW20 —2H 43
Coppice Clo. Farnh —6K 109
Coppice Clo. Guild —2G 113
Coppice Dri. SW15 —9G 12
Coppice Dri. Wray —1N 19
Coppice End. Wok —3G 74
Coppice Gdns. Crowt —2E 48
Coppice Gdns. Yat —1B 68
Coppice Grn. Brack —8L 15
(in two parts)
Coppice La. Reig —1L 121
Coppice Rd. H'ham —3N 197
Coppice, The. Ashf —7C 22
Coppice, The. Craw D —1E 184
Coppice Wlk. Craw —2E 182
Coppid Beech La. Wokgm —2F 30
Copping Clo. Croy —1B 64
Coppins, The. New Ad —3L 65
Coppsfield. W Mol —2A 40
Copse Av. Farnh —5K 109
Copse Av. W Wick —9L 47
Copse Clo. Camb —9E 50
Copse Clo. Chil —9E 114
Copse Clo. Craw D —1E 184
Copse Clo. E Grin —7C 166
Copse Clo. H'ham —2M 197
Copse Cres. Craw —2A 182
Copse Dri. Wokgm —1A 30
Copse Edge. Cranl —6A 156
Copse Edge. Elst —8G 131
Copse Edge Av. Eps —9E 60
Copse End. Camb —9D 50
Copse Glade. Surb —6K 41
Copse Hill. SW20 —9F 26
Copse Hill. Purl —9J 63
Copse Hill. Sutt —4N 61
Copse La. C Crook —8A 88
Copse La. Eve —7A 48
Copse La. Horl —7G 143
Copsem Dri. Esh —3B 58
Copsem La. Esh & Oxs —3C 58
Copsem Way. Esh —4C 58
Copsem Wood. Oxs —7C 58
Copse Rd. Cobh —9J 57
Copse Rd. Hasl —3B 188
Copse Rd. Red —5B 122
Copse Rd. Wok —5J 73
Copse Side. G'ming —3G 133
Copse, The. Cat —4D 104
Copse, The. F'boro —2J 89
Copse, The. Fet —1B 98
Copse, The. Rowl —7E 128
Copse, The. S Nut —5J 123
Copse View. S Croy —5G 65
Copse Way. Wrec —5E 128
Copsleigh Av. Red —1E 142
Copsleigh Clo. Salf —9E 122
Copsleigh Way. Red —9E 122
Copthall Gdns. Twic —2F 24
Copthall Way. New H —6H 55
Copt Hill La. Tad —7K 81
Copthorne Av. SW12 —1H 29
Copthorne Bank. Copt —7L 163
Copthorne Chase. Ashf —5A 22
Copthorne Clo. Shep —5D 38
Copthorne Comn. Rd. Copt —8L 163
Copthorne Ct. Lea —9G 79
Copthorne Dri. Light —6M 51
Copthorne Rise. S Croy —9A 64
Copthorne Rd. Copt & Felb —6E 164
Copthorne Rd. Craw —1H 183
Copthorne Rd. Lea —7H 79
Copthorne Way. Craw —8J 163
Copyhold Rd. E Grin —1N 185
Coram Ho. W4 —1D 12
(off Wood St.)
Corban Rd. Houn —6A 10
Corbet Clo. Wall —7E 44
Corbet Rd. Eps —6D 60
Corbett Clo. Croy —8N 65
Corbett Dri. Light —8K 51
Corbiere Ct. SW19 —7J 27
Corby Clo. Bew —6K 181
Corby Clo. Egh —7M 19
Corby Dri. Egh —7M 19
Cordelia Croft. Warf —9C 16
Cordelia Gdns. Ash V —4D 90
Cordelia Gdns. Stai —1N 21
Cordelia Rd. Stai —1N 21
Corderoy Pl. Cher —5H 37
Cordrey Gdns. Coul —2J 83
(in two parts)
Cordrey Ho. Add —8K 37
Cordwalles Rd. Camb —7D 50
Corelli Ct. SW5 —1M 13
(off W. Cromwell Rd.)
Corey Ho. Brack —1N 31
Corfe Clo. Asht —5J 79
Corfe Gdns. Frim —5D 70
Corfe Way. F'boro —4C 90
Coriander Clo. F'boro —1H 89
Coriander Cres. Guild —7K 93
Corinthian Way. Stanw —1M 21
Corkran Rd. Surb —6K 41
Corkscrew Hill. W Wick —8M 47
Cork Tree Ho. SE27 —6M 29
(off Lakeview Rd.)
Cormongers La. Nutf —1H 123
Cormorant Pl. Col T —8K 49
Cornbunting Clo. Col T —8J 49
Corn Croft. Warf —8B 16
Cornelia Clo. F'boro —2J 89
Corner Bungalows. G'ming —3E 132
Corner Fielde. SW2 —2K 29
Cornerside. Ashf —8D 22
Cornerstone Ho. Croy —6N 45
Corner, The. W Byf —9J 55
Corney Reach Way. W4 —2D 12
Corney Rd. W4 —2D 12
Cornfield Rd. Reig —4A 122
Cornfields. G'ming —3J 133
Cornfields. Yat —2A 68
Cornflower La. Croy —7G 47
Cornford Gro. SW12 —3F 28
Cornhill Clo. Add —8K 37
Cornish Ho. Bren —1M 11
Cornwall Av. Byfl —1A 76
Cornwall Av. Clay —4F 58
Cornwall Clo. Camb —8D 50
Cornwall Clo. Eton W —1B 4
Cornwall Clo. Warf —7D 16
Cornwall Gdns. SE25 —4C 46
Cornwall Gdns. E Grin —1B 186
Cornwall Gro. W4 —1D 12
Cornwallis Clo. Cat —9N 83
Cornwall Rd. Croy —8M 45
Cornwall Rd. Sutt —4L 61
Cornwall Rd. Twic —1G 25
Cornwall Way. Stai —7G 20
Cornwell Rd. Old Win —9K 5
Coronation Av. Wind —5K 5
Coronation Rd. Alder —5N 109
Coronation Rd. Asc —6L 33
Coronation Rd. E Grin —2A 186
Coronation Rd. Hayes —1G 9
Coronation Rd. Yat —8D 48
Coronation Sq. Wokgm —1C 30
Coronation Wlk. Twic —2A 24
Coronet Clo. Craw —2J 183
Coronet, The. Horl —1G 162
Corporate Dri. Felt —4J 23
Corporation Av. Houn —7M 9
Corrib Dri. Sutt —2C 62
Corrie Gdns. Vir W —6M 35
Corrie Rd. Add —1M 55
Corrie Rd. Wok —7D 74
Corrigan Av. Coul —2E 82
Corringway. C Crook —7C 88
Corry Rd. Hind —3A 170
Corsair Clo. Stai —1M 21
Corsair Rd. Stai —1N 21
Corscombe Clo. King T —6B 26
Corsehill St. SW16 —7G 28
Corsham Way. Crowt —2G 48
Corsletts Av. Broad H —5D 196
Corston Hollow. Red —4D 122
(off Woodlands Rd.)
Cortayne Ct. Twic —3E 24
Cortayne Rd. SW6 —5L 13
Cortis Rd. SW15 —9G 13
Cortis Ter. SW15 —9G 13
Corunna Dri. H'ham —6M 197
Cosdach Av. Wall —4H 63
Cosedge Cres. Croy —2L 63
Cosford Rd. Brook —6J 151
Costells Meadow. W'ham —4M 107
Coteford St. SW17 —5D 28
Cotelands. Croy —9B 46
Cotford Rd. T Hth —3N 45
Cotherstone. Eps —6C 60
Cotherstone Rd. SW2 —2K 29
Cotland Acres. Red —5B 122
Cotman Clo. SW15 —9J 13
Cotmandene. Dork —5H 119
Cotsford. Peas P —2N 199
Cotsford Av. N Mald —4B 42
Cotswold Clo. Craw —3N 181
Cotswold Clo. F'boro —7K 69
Cotswold Clo. Hin W —8F 40
Cotswold Clo. King T —7B 26
Cotswold Clo. Stai —6J 21
Cotswold Ct. Fleet —4A 88
Cotswold Ct. H'ham —6L 197
Cotswold Rd. Hamp —7A 24
Cotswold Rd. Sand —6E 48
Cotswold Rd. Sutt —6N 61
Cotswold St. SE27 —5M 29
Cotswold Way. Wor Pk —8H 43
Cottage Clo. H'ham —2A 198
Cottage Clo. Ott —3E 54
Cottage Farm Way. Egh —2E 36
Cottage Gdns. F'boro —1L 89
Cottage Gro. Surb —5K 41
Cottage Pl. Copt —7B 164
Cottage Rd. Eps —4C 60
Cottenham Dri. SW20 —8G 27
Cottenham Pde. SW20 —1G 43
Cottenham Pk. Rd. SW20 —9F 26
(in two parts)
Cottenham Pl. SW20 —8G 27
Cottenhams. Blind H —3H 145
Cotterell Clo. Brack —8N 15
Cotterill Rd. Surb —8L 41
Cottesbrooke Clo. Coln —4F 6
Cottesmore. Brack —6M 31
Cottimore Av. W On T —7J 39
Cottimore Cres. W On T —6J 39
Cottimore La. W On T —6J 39
Cottimore Ter. W On T —6J 39
Cottingham Av. H'ham —1K 197
Cottington Rd. Felt —5L 23
Cottongrass Clo. Croy —7G 46
Cotton Ho. SW2 —1J 29
Cotton Row. Holm M —3K 157
Cotton Wlk. Craw —8M 181
Cottrell Ct. C Crook —9A 88
Cottrell Flats. F'boro —5B 90
Cotts Wood Dri. Guild —7C 94
Couchmore Av. Esh —8E 40
Coulsdon Ct. Rd. Coul —3K 83
Coulsdon La. Coul —6E 82
Coulsdon Pl. Cat —9A 84
Coulsdon Rise. Coul —4J 83
Coulsdon Rd. Coul & Cat —2K 83
Coulthurst Ct. SW16 —8J 29
Council Cotts. Dork —6D 158
Council Cotts. W End —8C 52
Council Cotts. Wis —2M 75
Countisbury Gdns. Add —2K 55
Country Way. Hanw —7J 23
County La. Warf —7B 16
County Mall Shop. Cen. Craw —3C 182
County Oak La. Craw —8B 162
County Oak Retail Pk. Craw —8B 162
County Oak Way. Craw —8B 162
County Pde. Bren —3K 11
County Rd. T Hth —1M 45
Courland Rd. Add —9K 37
Course Rd. Asc —2L 33
Court Av. Coul —5L 83
Court Bushes Rd. Whyt —6D 84
Court Clo. E Grin —9B 166
Court Clo. Twic —4B 24
Court Clo. Wall —4H 63
Court Clo. Av. Twic —4B 24
Court Cres. Chess —3K 59
Court Cres. E Grin —9B 166
Court Downs Rd. Beck —1L 47
Court Dri. Croy —1K 63
Court Dri. Sutt —1C 62
Courtenay Av. Sutt —5M 61
Courtenay Dri. Beck —1N 47
Courtenay M. Wok —3C 74
Courtenay Rd. Farnh —5K 109
Courtenay Rd. Wok —3C 74
Courtenay Rd. Wor Pk —9H 43
Court Farm Av. Eps —2C 60
Court Farm Gdns. Eps —7B 60
Court Farm Rd. Warl —5D 84
Courtfield Gdns. SW5 —1N 13
Courtfield M. SW7 —1N 13
Courtfield Rise. W Wick —9N 47
Courtfield Rd. SW7 —1N 13
Courtfield Rd. Ashf —7C 22
Court Gdns. Camb —1B 70
Court Grn. Heights. Wok —7M 73
Court Haw. Bans —2C 82
Court Hill. Coul —5C 82
Court Hill. S Croy —8B 64
Courthope Rd. SW19 —6K 27
Courthope Vs. SW19 —8K 27
Court Ho. Mans. Eps —8C 60
Courtland Av. SW16 —8K 29
Courtlands. Rich —8N 11
Courtlands. W on T —6H 39
Courtlands Av. Esh —3N 57
Courtlands Av. Hamp —7N 23
Courtlands Av. Rich —4A 12
Courtlands Av. Slou —1N 5
Courtlands Clo. S Croy —6C 64
Courtlands Cres. Bans —3M 81
Courtlands Dri. Eps —3D 60
Courtlands Rd. Surb —6N 41
Court La. Eps —9B 60
Courtleas. Cobh —9A 58
Court Lodge Rd. Horl —7C 142
Courtmead Clo. SE24 —1N 29
Courtmoor Av. Fleet —6B 88
Courtney Cres. Cars —4D 62
Courtney Pl. Cobh —8N 57
Courtney Pl. Croy —9L 45
Courtney Rd. SW19 —8C 28
Courtney Rd. Croy —9L 45
Courtney Rd. H'row A —6B 8
Courtoak La. Red —5N 143
Court Rd. SE25 —1C 46
Court Rd. Alder —2M 109
Court Rd. Bans —3M 81
Court Rd. Cat —1A 104
Court Rd. God —9F 104
Court Rd. S'hall —1N 9
Courts Hill Rd. Hasl —2F 188
Courts Mt. Rd. Hasl —2F 188
Court, The. Guild —5M 113
Court, The. Warl —5H 85
Court Way. Twic —1F 24
Court Wood La. Croy —7J 65
Courtyard, The. Craw —4B 182
Courtyard, The. E Grin —9D 166
Courtyard, The. W'ham —5M 107
Courtyard, The. Wokgm —3B 30
Coutts Av. Chess —2L 59
Coval Gdns. SW14 —7A 12
Coval La. SW14 —7A 12
Coval Pas. SW14 —7B 12
Coval Rd. SW14 —7B 12
Coveham Cres. Cobh —9H 57
Coventry Hall. SW16 —6J 29
Coventry Rd. SE25 —3D 46
Coverack Clo. Croy —6H 47
Coverdale Gdns. Croy —9C 46
Cove Rd. F'boro —1L 89
Cove Rd. Fleet —1C 88
Covert Clo. Craw —2C 182
Covert La. Brack —3A 32
Covert Mead. Hand —9N 199
Coverton Rd. SW17 —6C 28
Coverts Clo. Farnh —8K 109
Coverts Rd. Clay —4F 58
Covert, The. Asc —6M 33
Covert, The. F'boro —6K 69
Coves Farm Wood. Brack —1J 31
Covey Clo. F'boro —6M 69
Covey, The. Worth —1J 183
Covington Gdns. SW16 —8M 29
Covington Way. SW16 —7K 29
(in two parts)
Cowdray Clo. Craw —4G 183
Cowdrey Rd. SW19 —6N 27
Cowfold Clo. Craw —6L 181
Cowick Rd. SW17 —5D 28
Cow La. G'ming —7G 133
Cowleaze Rd. King T —9L 25
Cowley Av. Cher —6H 37
Cowley Clo. S Croy —5F 64
Cowley Cres. W On T —1K 57
Cowley La. Cher —6H 37
Cowley Lodge. Ott —6H 37
Cowley Rd. SW14 —6D 12
Coworth Clo. Asc —4E 34
Coworth Pk. S'hill —3F 34
Coworth Rd. Asc —4D 34
Cowper Av. Sutt —1B 62
Cowper Clo. Cher —5H 37
Cowper Gdns. Wall —3G 63
Cowper Rd. SW19 —7A 28
Cowper Rd. King T —6M 25
Cowshot Cres. Brkwd —7A 72
Cowslip Clo. Lind —5B 168
Cowslip La. Hors —2L 73
Cowslip La. Mick —6G 99
Coxbridge Meadows. Farnh —2E 128
Coxcombe La. C'fold —5E 172
Coxcomb Wlk. Craw —5M 181
Coxdean. Eps —6H 81
Coxes Lock Mill. Add —2N 55
Cox Grn. Col T —9J 49
Cox Grn. Rd. H'ham —7C 176
Coxheath Rd. C Crook —7A 88
Cox Ho. W6 —2K 13
(off Field Rd.)
Cox Ho. H'ham —6H 197
Cox La. Chess —1M 59
Cox La. Eps —2A 60
Coxley Rise. Purl —9N 63
Coxmoor Clo. C Crook —8D 88
Coxs Av. Shep —2F 38
Coxwold Path. Chess —4L 59
Crabbet Pk. Craw —2K 183
Crabbet Rd. Craw —2F 182
Crabbs Croft Clo. Orp —2L 67
Crabhill La. S Nut —7K 123
Crabtree Clo. Bookh —4C 98
Crabtree Dri. Lea —2J 99
Crabtree Gdns. Head —4D 168
Crabtree La. SW6 —3H 13
(in two parts)
Crabtree La. Bookh —4C 98
Crabtree La. Churt —8M 149
Crabtree La. Head —4D 168
Crabtree La. H'ley —4B 100
Crabtree La. Westh —8F 98
Crabtree Office Village. Egh —1E 36
Crabtree Rd. Camb —4N 69
Crabtree Rd. Craw —2A 182
Crabtree Rd. Egh —1E 36
Crabtree Wlk. Croy —7D 46
Crabwood. Oxt —6A 106
Craddocks Av. Asht —4L 79
Craddocks Pde. Asht —4L 79
(in two parts)
Cradhurst Clo. Westc —6C 118
Cradle La. Bord —7B 148
Craigans. Craw —3M 181
Craigen Av. Croy —7E 46
Craigmore Tower. Wok —6A 74
(off Guildford Rd.)
Craignair Rd. SW2 —1L 29
Craignish Av. SW16 —1K 45
Craig Rd. Rich —5J 25
Craigwell Av. Felt —4H 23
Craigwell Clo. Stai —9G 21
Crail Clo. Wokgm —5A 30
Crakell Rd. Reig —4A 122
Crake Pl. Col T —7J 49
Cramhurst La. Witl —4B 152
Crammond Clo. W6 —2K 13
Cramond Ct. Felt —2F 22
Crampshaw La. Asht —6M 79
Cranberry Wlk. B'water —3L 69
Cranborne Av. S'hall —1A 10
Cranborne Av. Surb —9N 41
Cranborne Wlk. Craw —5D 182
Cranbourne Av. Wind —5C 4
Cranbourne Clo. SW16 —2J 45
Cranbourne Clo. Horl —6F 142
Cranbourne Cotts. Wind —4M 17
Cranbourne Hall Cvn. Site. Wink —2L 17
Cranbourne Hall Cotts. Wind —2M 17
Cranbrook Ct. Bren —2K 11
(off Somerset Rd.)
Cranbrook Ct. Fleet —2B 88
Cranbrook Dri. Esh —7C 40
Cranbrook Dri. Twic —2B 24
Cranbrook Rd. SW19 —8K 27
Cranbrook Rd. W4 —1D 12
Cranbrook Rd. Houn —7N 9
Cranbrook Rd. T Hth —1N 45
Cranbrook Ter. Cranl —7A 156
Cranbury Rd. SW6 —5N 13
Crane Av. Iswth —8G 10
Cranebrook. Twic —3C 24
Crane Ct. Col T —7J 49
Craneford Clo. Twic —1F 24
Craneford Way. Twic —1E 24
Crane Ho. Felt —4A 24
Crane Lodge Rd. Houn —2J 9
Crane Mead Ct. Twic —1F 24
Crane Pk. Rd. Twic —3B 24
Crane Rd. Twic —2E 24
Cranes Dri. Surb —3M 41
Cranes Pk. Surb —3L 41
Cranes Pk. Av. Surb —3L 41
Cranes Pk. Cres. Surb —3M 41
Craneswater. Hayes —3G 9
Craneswater Pk. S'hall —1N 9
Crane Way. Twic —1C 24
Cranfield Clo. SE27 —4N 29
Cranfield Ct. St J —5K 73
Cranfield Rd. E. Cars —5E 62
Cranfield Rd. W. Cars —5E 62
Cranford Av. C Crook —8A 88
Cranford Av. Stai —1N 21
Cranford Clo. SW20 —8G 26
Cranford Clo. Purl —9N 63
Cranford Clo. Stai —1N 21
Cranford Dri. Hayes —1G 8
Cranford La. Hayes —2E 8
Cranford La. H'row —4G 8
(in two parts)
Cranford La. Houn —3J 9
Cranford Pk. Dri. Yat —9C 48
Cranford Rise. Esh —2C 58
Cranleigh Clo. SE20 —1E 46
Cranleigh Clo. S Croy —8D 64
Cranleigh Ct. F'boro —1L 89
Cranleigh Ct. Rich —6N 11
Cranleigh Gdns. SE25 —2B 46
Cranleigh Gdns. King T —7M 25
Cranleigh Gdns. S Croy —8D 64
Cranleigh Gdns. Sutt —8N 43
Cranleigh Mead. Cranl —8A 156
Cranleigh Rd. SW19 —2M 43
Cranleigh Rd. Esh —7C 40
Cranleigh Rd. Ewh —6E 156
Cranleigh Rd. Felt —5G 22
Cranleigh Rd. Won —4D 134
Cranley Clo. Guild —3C 114
Cranley Gdns. Wall —4G 62
Cranley Pl. Knap —5G 72
Cranley Rd. Guild —3B 114
Cranley Rd. W On T —2G 56
Cranmer Clo. Mord —5J 43
Cranmer Clo. Warl —4H 85
Cranmer Clo. Wey —4B 56
Cranmer Farm Clo. Mitc —3D 44
Cranmer Gdns. Warl —4H 85
Cranmer Rd. Croy —9M 45
Cranmer Rd. Hamp —6B 24
Cranmer Rd. King T —6L 25
Cranmer Rd. Mitc —3D 44
Cranmer Ter. SW17 —6B 28
Cranmer Wlk. Craw —4G 183
Cranmore Av. Iswth —3C 10
Cranmore Clo. Alder —3K 109
Cranmore Cotts. W Hor —7C 96
Cranmore Gdns. Alder —3J 109
Cranmore La. Alder —4J 109
Cranmore La. W Hor —7C 96
(in two parts)
Cranmore Rd. Myt —1E 90
Cranston Clo. Houn —5M 9
Cranston Clo. Reig —4N 121
Cranston Rd. E Grin —8A 166
Cranston Way. Craw D —1F 184
Cranstoun Clo. Guild —8J 93
Cranwell Gro. Light —7K 51
Cranwell Gro. Shep —3A 38
Cranwell Rd. H'row A —5C 8
Craster Rd. SW2 —1K 29
Cravan Av. Felt —3H 23
Craven Clo. Lwr Bo —5H 129
Craven Gdns. SW19 —6M 27
Craven Rd. Croy —7E 46
Craven Rd. King T —9M 25
Craven Rd. M'bowr —4F 182
Cravens, The. Small —8L 143
Crawford Clo. Iswth —5E 10
Crawford Gdns. Camb —1N 69
Crawford Gdns. H'ham —4L 197
Crawfurd Way. E Grin —7B 166
Crawley Av. Craw —2N 181
Crawley Chase. Wink R —7F 16
Crawley Down Rd. Felb —7H 165
Crawley Dri. Camb —9D 50
Crawley Hill. Camb —1D 70
Crawley La. Craw —2G 182
Crawley Ridge. Camb —9D 50
Crawley Rd. Fay & Craw —1B 198
Crawley Rd. H'ham —4M 197
(in two parts)
Crawley S. W. By-Pass. Peas P —7K 181
Crawley Wood Clo. Camb —1D 70
Crawshaw Rd. Ott —3F 54
Crawters Clo. Craw —2D 182
Cray Av. Asht —3L 79
Crayke Hill. Chess —4L 59
Crayonne Clo. Sun —9F 22

Crealock St.—Dalton Av.

Crealock St. *SW18* —9N **13**
Creasys Dri. *Craw* —8M **181**
Credenhill St. *SW16* —7G **28**
Crediton Way. *Clay* —2G **58**
Credon Clo. *F'boro* —9L **69**
Creek Rd. *E Mol* —3E **40**
Creek, The. *Sun* —4H **39**
Cree's Meadow. *W'sham* —4N **51**
Crefeld Clo. *W6* —2K **13**
Cremorne Gdns. *Eps* —5C **60**
Crerar Clo. *F'boro* —2J **89**
Crescent Ct. *Horl* —1E **162**
Crescent Ct. *Surb* —4K **41**
Crescent Gdns. *SW19* —4M **27**
Crescent Gro. *Mitc* —4C **44**
Crescent La. *Ash V* —8F **90**
Crescent Rd. *SW20* —9J **27**
Crescent Rd. *Beck* —1L **47**
Crescent Rd. *Blet* —2N **123**
Crescent Rd. *Cat* —2D **104**
Crescent Rd. *E Grin* —9N **165**
Crescent Rd. *King T* —8N **25**
Crescent Rd. *Reig* —5M **121**
Crescent Rd. *Shep* —4D **38**
Crescent Rd. *Wokgm* —3B **30**
Crescent Stables. *SW15* —8K **13**
Crescent, The. *SW13* —5F **12**
Crescent, The. *SW19* —4M **27**
Crescent, The. *Ashf* —6A **22**
Crescent, The. *Beck* —1K **47**
Crescent, The. *Belm* —7M **61**
Crescent, The. *B'water* —2J **69**
Crescent, The. *Brack* —3A **32**
Crescent, The. *Cher* —2J **37**
Crescent, The. *Croy* —5A **46**
Crescent, The. *Egh* —7A **20**
Crescent, The. *Eps* —1N **79**
[illegible]
Crescent, The. *F'boro* —2A **90**
Crescent, The. *Farnh* —4J **109**
Crescent, The. *Felc* —2M **165**
Crescent, The. *Guild* —2K **113**
Crescent, The. *Hayes* —3E **8**
Crescent, The. *Horl* —2F **162**
(in two parts)
Crescent, The. *H'ham* —6G **196**
Crescent, The. *Lea* —9H **79**
Crescent, The. *N Mald* —1C **42**
Crescent, The. *Red* —6B **122**
Crescent, The. *Reig* —3N **121**
Crescent, The. *Shep* —6G **38**
Crescent, The. *Surb* —4L **41**
Crescent, The. *Sutt* —2B **62**
Crescent, The. *W Mol* —3A **40**
Crescent, The. *W Wick* —5N **47**
Crescent, The. *Wey* —9B **38**
Crescent, The. *Wold* —1K **105**
Crescent Way. *SW16* —7K **29**
Crescent Way. *Horl* —1E **162**
Crescent Way. *Orp* —2N **67**
Cresford Rd. *SW6* —4N **13**
*Cressage Ho. Bren —2L **11***
(off Ealing Rd.)
Cressall Clo. *Lea* —7H **79**
Cressal Mead. *Lea* —7H **79**
Cressex Clo. *Binf* —7H **15**
Cressida Chase. *Warf* —9C **16**
Cressingham Gdns. Est. *SW2* —1L **29**
Cressingham Gro. *Sutt* —1A **62**
Cresswell Gdns. *SW5* —1N **13**
Cresswell Pl. *SW10* —1N **13**
Cresswell Rd. *SE25* —3D **46**
Cresswell Rd. *Felt* —4M **23**
Cresswell Rd. *Twic* —9K **11**
Cresta Dri. *Wdhm* —6H **55**
Crest Hill. *Peasl* —2F **136**
Creston Av. *Knap* —3H **73**
Creston Way. *Wor Pk* —7J **43**
Crest Rd. *S Croy* —4E **64**
Crest, The. *Surb* —4N **41**
Crestway. *SW15* —9F **12**
Crestwood Way. *Houn* —8N **9**
Creswell Corner. *Knap* —4G **73**
Crewdson Rd. *Horl* —8F **142**
Crewe Ct. *Tad* —9H **81**
Crewe's Av. *Warl* —3F **84**
Crewe's Clo. *Warl* —4F **84**
Crewe's Farm La. *Warl* —4G **85**
Crewe's La. *Warl* —3F **84**
Crichton Av. *Wall* —2H **63**
Crichton Rd. *Cars* —4D **62**
Cricket Ct. *E Grin* —7A **166**
Cricketers Clo. *Chess* —1K **59**
Cricketers Clo. *Ockl* —6C **158**
Cricketers La. *Warf* —6E **16**
Cricketers La. *W'sham* —2A **52**
Cricketers Ter. *Cars* —9C **44**
Cricket Field Gro. *Crowt* —3J **49**
Cricket Field Rd. *H'ham* —7H **197**
Cricket Grn. *Hamb* —9F **152**
Cricket Grn. *Mitc* —2D **44**
Cricket Hill. *S Nut* —5K **123**
Cricket Hill. *Yat* —3D **68**
Cricket Hill La. *Yat* —3C **68**
Cricket La. *Lwr Bo* —5J **129**
Cricket Lea. *Lind* —4A **168**
Cricket Way. *Wey* —8F **38**
Cricklade Av. *SW2* —3J **29**
Crieff Ct. *Tedd* —8J **25**
Crieff Rd. *SW18* —1A **28**
Criffel Av. *SW2* —3H **29**
Crimea Rd. *Alder* —2N **109**
(in two parts)
Crimea Rd. *Deep* —6H **71**
Crimp Hill. *Old Win & Egh* —1J **19**
Cripley Rd. *F'boro* —8J **69**
Cripplecrutch Hill. *G'ming* —3C **190**
Cripps Ho. *Craw* —7N **181**
Crispen Rd. *Felt* —5M **23**
Crisp Gdns. *Binf* —8K **15**
Crispin Clo. *Asht* —4M **79**
Crispin Clo. *Croy* —8J **45**
Crispin Cres. *Croy* —9H **45**
Crisp Rd. *W6* —1H **13**
Cristowe Rd. *SW6* —5L **13**
Critchmere Hill. *Hasl* —1C **188**
Critchmere La. *Hasl* —2C **188**
Critchmere Vale. *Hasl* —2C **188**
Critten La. *Ran C* —3L **117**
Crocker Clo. *Asc* —9K **17**
Crockers La. *Ling* —7G **144**
Crockerton Rd. *SW17* —3D **28**
Crockery La. *E Clan* —7N **95**
Crockford Clo. *Add* —1L **55**
Crockford Pk. Rd. *Add* —2L **55**
Crockford Pl. *Binf* —8L **15**
Crockham Clo. *Craw* —5A **182**
Crocknorth Rd. *E Hor* —1G **117**
Crocus Clo. *Croy* —7G **47**
Croffets. *Tad* —8J **81**
Croft Av. *Dork* —3H **119**
Croft Av. *W Wick* —7M **47**
Croft Clo. *Hayes* —3D **8**
Croft Clo. [illegible]
Croft Ct. *Eden* —3L **117**
Crofters. *Old Win* —9K **5**
Crofters Clo. *Iswth* —8D **10**
Crofters Clo. *Sand* —7F **48**
Crofters Mead. *Croy* —5J **65**
Croft La. *Eden* —2L **147**
Croft La. *Yat* —8B **48**
Croftleigh Av. *Purl* —3M **83**
Crofton. *Asht* —5L **79**
Crofton Av. *W4* —3C **12**
Crofton Av. *W On T* —9K **39**
Crofton Clo. *Brack* —4C **32**
Crofton Clo. *Ott* —4E **54**
Crofton Rd. *Orp* —1J **67**
Crofton Ter. *Rich* —7M **11**
Croft Rd. *SW16* —9L **29**
Croft Rd. *SW19* —8A **28**
Croft Rd. *Alder* —4N **109**
Croft Rd. *G'ming* —7G **133**
Croft Rd. *Sutt* —2C **62**
Croft Rd. *W'ham* —4K **107**
Croft Rd. *Witl* —5B **152**
Croft Rd. *Wokgm* —7A **30**
Croft Rd. *Wold* —9K **85**
Crofts Clo. *C'fold* —4E **172**
Croftside, The. *SE25* —2D **46**
Crofts, The. *Shep* —3F **38**
Croft, The. *Brack* —8N **15**
Croft, The. *Craw* —3M **181**
Croft, The. *Eps* —1E **80**
Croft, The. *Houn* —3M **9**
Croft, The. *Wokgm* —3C **30**
Croft, The. *Yat* —8C **48**
Croft Way. *Frim* —4D **70**
Croft Way. *H'ham* —5G **196**
Croftway. *Rich* —4H **25**
Croham Clo. *S Croy* —4B **64**
Croham Mnr. Rd. *S Croy* —4B **64**
Croham Mt. *S Croy* —4B **64**
Croham Pk. Av. *S Croy* —2C **64**
Croham Rd. *S Croy* —2B **64**
Croham Valley Rd. *S Croy* —3D **64**
Croindene Rd. *SW16* —9J **29**
Cromar Ct. *Hors* —3M **73**
Cromer Rd. *SE25* —2E **46**
Cromer Rd. *SW17* —7E **28**
Cromer Rd. *H'row A* —5B **8**
Cromer Rd. W. *H'row A* —6B **8**
Cromer Vs. Rd. *SW18* —9L **13**
Cromford Clo. *Orp* —1N **67**
Cromford Rd. *SW18* —8M **13**
Cromford Way. *N Mald* —1C **42**
Crompton Fields. *Craw* —9C **162**
Crompton Way. *Craw* —9C **162**
Cromwell Av. *W6* —1G **12**
Cromwell Av. *N Mald* —4E **42**
Cromwell Clo. *W On T* —7J **39**
Cromwell Cres. *SW5* —1M **13**
Cromwell Gro. *Cat* —8N **83**
Cromwell Pl. *SW14* —6B **12**
Cromwell Pl. *Cranl* —9A **156**
Cromwell Pl. *E Grin* —2B **186**
Cromwell Rd. *SW19* —6M **27**
Cromwell Rd. *Asc* —3M **33**
Cromwell Rd. *Beck* —1H **47**
Cromwell Rd. *Camb* —8B **50**
Cromwell Rd. *Cat* —8N **83**
Cromwell Rd. *Croy* —6A **46**
Cromwell Rd. *Felt* —2J **23**
Cromwell Rd. *Houn* —7A **10**
Cromwell Rd. *King T* —9L **25**
Cromwell Rd. *Red* —3D **122**
Cromwell Rd. *Tedd* —7G **24**
Cromwell Rd. *W On T* —7J **39**
Cromwell Rd. *Wor Pk* —9C **42**
Cromwell St. *Houn* —7A **10**
Cromwell Wlk. *Red* —3D **122**
Cromwell Way. *F'boro* —7N **69**
Crondace Rd. *SW6* —4M **13**
Crondall Ct. *Camb* —2N **69**
Crondall End. *Yat* —8B **48**
Crondall La. *Farnh* —9B **108**
Crondall Rd. *Cron* —4A **128**
Cronks Hill. *Reig & Red* —5A **122**
Cronks Hill Clo. *Red* —5B **122**
Cronks Hill Rd. *Red* —5B **122**
Crooked Billet. *SW19* —7H **27**
Crooked Billet Roundabout. (Junct.) —5J **21**
Crookham Rd. *SW6* —4L **13**
Crookham Rd. *C Crook* —7A **88**
Crooksbury La. *Seale* —3C **130**
Crooksbury Rd. *Farnh* —9N **109**
Crosby Clo. *Felt* —4M **23**
Crosby Gdns. *Yat* —8A **48**
Crosby Hill Dri. *Camb* —8D **50**
Crosby Wlk. *SW2* —1L **29**
Crosby Way. *SW2* —1L **29**
Crosby Way. *Farnh* —2F **128**
Crossacres. *Wok* —2G **75**
Cross Deep. *Twic* —3F **24**
Cross Deep Gdns. *Twic* —3F **24**
Cross Fell. *Brack* —3M **31**
Crossfield Pl. *Wey* —4C **56**
Cross Gdns. *Frim G* —8D **70**
Cross Gates Clo. *Brack* —2D **32**
Cross Keys. *Craw* —3B [illegible]
[illegible]
Crossland Ho. *Vir W* —3A **36**
Crossland Rd. *Red* —3E **122**
Crossland Rd. *T Hth* —5M **45**
Crosslands. *Cher* —1G **55**
Crosslands Av. *S'hall* —1N **9**
Crosslands Rd. *Eps* —3C **60**
Cross La. *Frim G* —8D **70**
Cross La. *Ott* —3D **54**
Cross La. *Small* —2N **163**
Cross Lanes. *Guild* —3B **114**
Crossley Clo. *Big H* —2F **86**
Crossman Ct. *Craw* —8N **181**
Cross Oak. *Wind* —5D **4**
Cross Oak La. *Red* —4F **142**
Crosspath. *Craw* —2C **182**
Cross Rd. *SW19* —8M **27**
Cross Rd. *Asc* —7C **34**
Cross Rd. *Ash V* —1F **110**
Cross Rd. *Belm* —6M **61**
Cross Rd. *Croy* —7A **46**
Cross Rd. *Felt* —5M **23**
Cross Rd. *King T* —8M **25**
Cross Rd. *Purl* —9M **63**
Cross Rd. *Sutt* —2B **62**
Cross Rd. *Tad* —9H **81**
Cross Rd. *Wey* —9E **38**
Crossroads, The. *Eff* —6L **97**
Cross St. *SW13* —5D **12**
Cross St. *Alder* —2M **109**
Cross St. *F'boro* —5A **90**
Cross St. *Hamp* —6C **24**
Cross St. *Wokgm* —2B **30**
Crosswater La. *Churt* —6K **149**
Crossway. *SW20* —3H **43**
Crossway. *Brack* —1A **32**
Crossway. *W On T* —8J **39**
Crossways. *Alder* —3A **110**
Crossways. *Churt* —9K **149**
Crossways. *Craw* —2D **182**
Crossways. *Eff* —5L **97**
Crossways. *Egh* —7F **20**
Crossways. *S Croy* —4H **65**
Crossways. *Sun* —8G **23**
Crossways. *Sutt* —5B **62**
Crossways. *Tats* —7E **86**
Crossways Av. *E Grin* —9M **165**
Crossways Clo. *Churt* —9L **149**
Crossways Ct. *Craw* —2D **182**
Crossways La. *Reig* —6A **102**
(in three parts)
Crossways Rd. *Beck* —3K **47**
Crossways Rd. *Gray* —6A **170**
Crossways Rd. *Mitc* —2F **44**
Crossways, The. *Coul* —6L **83**
Crossways, The. *Guild* —5J **113**
Crossways, The. *Houn* —3N **9**
Crossways, The. *Red* —7G **102**
Crossways, The. *Surb* —7A **42**
Crosswell Clo. *Shep* —1D **38**
Crouchfield. *Dork* —8J **119**
Crouch Ho. Cotts. *Eden* —1K **147**
Crouch Ho. Rd. *Eden* —9J **127**
Crouch La. *Wink* —1J **17**
Crouch Oak La. *Add* —1L **55**
Crowberry Clo. *Craw* —7M **181**
Crowborough Clo. *Warl* —5H **85**
Crowborough Dri. *Warl* —5H **85**
Crowborough Rd. *SW17* —7E **28**
*Crowbourne Ct. Sutt —1N **61***
(off St Nicholas Way)
Crowhurst Clo. *Worth* —3J **183**
Crowhurst Keep. *Worth* —3J **183**
Crowhurst La. *Oxt & Crow* —7L **125**
Crowhurst Mead. *God* —8F **104**
Crowhurst Rd. *Ling* —3N **145**
Crowhurst Village Rd. *Crow* —1A **146**
Crowland Av. *Hayes* —1G **8**
Crowland Rd. *T Hth* —3A **46**
Crowland Wlk. *Mord* —5N **43**
Crowley Cres. *Croy* —2L **63**
*Crown All. H'ham —6J **197***
(off Carfax)
Crown Arc. *King T* —1K **41**
Crown Ash Hill. *W'ham* —1D **86**
Crown Ash La. *Warl & Big H* —3C **86**
Crownbourne Ct. *Sutt* —1N **61**
Crown Clo. *Coln* —3E **6**
Crown Clo. *W On T* —6K **39**
Crown Ct. *G'ming* —7H **133**
Crown Dale. *SE19* —7M **29**
Crown Dri. *Bad L* —7M **109**
Crown Gdns. *Fleet* —5C **88**
Crown Heights. *Guild* —6A **114**
Crown Hill. *Croy* —8N **45**
Crown La. *SW16* —6L **29**
Crown La. *Bad L* —7L **109**
Crown La. *Mord* —3M **43**
Crown La. *Vir W* —5N **35**
Crown La. Gdns. *SW16* —6L **29**
Crown Meadow. *Coln* —3D **6**
Crown M. *W6* —1F **12**
Crown Pde. *SE19* —7M **29**
Crown Pas. *King T* —1K **41**
[illegible]
Crown Pl. *Owl* —6K **49**
Crown Rise. *Cher* —7H **37**
Crown Rd. *Eden* —9M **127**
Crown Rd. *Mord* —3N **43**
Crown Rd. *N Mald* —9B **26**
Crown Rd. *Sutt* —1N **61**
Crown Rd. *Twic* —9H **11**
Crown Rd. *Vir W* —5M **35**
Crown Row. *Brack* —5B **32**
Crown Sq. *Wok* —4B **74**
Crown St. *Egh* —6C **20**
Crown Ter. *Rich* —7M **11**
Crown, The. *W'ham* —4M **107**
Crowntree Clo. *Iswth* —2F **10**
Crown Wlk. *G'ming* —7H **133**
Crown Yd. *Houn* —6C **10**
Crowther Av. *Bren* —1L **11**
Crowther Rd. *SE25* —3D **46**
Crowthorne Clo. *SW18* —1L **27**
Crowthorne Lodge. Brack
*(off Crowthorne Rd.) —3N **31***
Crowthorne Rd. *Brack* —4M **31**
Crowthorne Rd. *Crowt & Brack* —1J **49**
Crowthorne Rd. *Sand* —7F **48**
Crowthorne Rd. N. *Brack* —2N **31**
Croxall Ho. *W on T* —5K **39**
Croxden Wlk. *Mord* —5A **44**
Croxted Clo. *SE21* —1N **29**
Croxted M. *SE24* —1N **29**
Croxted Rd. *SE24 & SE21* —1N **29**
Croyde Av. *Hayes* —1F **8**
Croyde Clo. *F'boro* —8M **69**
Croydon Barn La. *Horne & God* —7C **144**
Croydon Flyover, The. *Croy* —9N **45**
Croydon Gro. *Croy* —7M **45**
Croydon La. *Bans* —1A **82**
Croydon La. S. *Bans* —1A **82**
Croydon Rd. *SE20* —1E **46**
Croydon Rd. *Beck* —3G **46**
Croydon Rd. *Cat* —1D **104**
Croydon Rd. *Kes* —1F **66**
Croydon Rd. *H'row A* —5C **8**
Croydon Rd. *Mitc & Bedd* —3E **44**
Croydon Rd. *Reig* —3N **121**
Croydon Rd. *Wall & Croy* —1F **62**
Croydon Rd. *W'ham* —1H **107**
Croydon Rd. *W Wick & Brom* —9N **47**
Croydon Rd. Ind. Est. *Beck* —3G **46**
Croylands Dri. *Surb* —6L **41**
Croysdale Av. *Sun* —2H **39**
Crozier Dri. *S Croy* —6E **64**
Cruch La. *Tap* —1C **16**
Cruikshank Lea. *Col T* —9K **49**
Crunden Rd. *S Croy* —4A **64**
Crundwell Ct. *Farnh* —9J **109**
Crusader Gdns. *Croy* —9B **46**
Crusoe Rd. *Mitc* —8D **28**
Crutchfield La. *Hkwd* —5M **141**
Crutchfield La. *W On T* —8J **39**
Crutchley Rd. *Wokgm* —1C **30**
Crystal Ter. *SE19* —7N **29**
Cubitt Ho. *SW4* —1G **29**
Cubitt St. *Croy* —2K **63**
Cubitt Way. *Knap* —5G **72**
Cuckfield Clo. *Craw* —6L **181**
Cuckmere Cres. *Craw* —4L **181**
Cuckoo La. *W End* —9A **52**
Cuckoo Pound. *Shep* —4F **38**
Cuckoo Vale. *W End* —9A **52**
Cudas Clo. *Eps* —1E **60**
Cuddington Av. *Wor Pk* —9E **42**
Cuddington Clo. *Tad* —7H **81**
Cuddington Ct. *Sutt* —5J **61**
Cuddington Glade. *Eps* —8N **59**
Cuddington Pk. Clo. *Bans* —9L **61**
Cuddington Way. *Sutt* —8J **61**
Cudham Clo. *Belm* —6M **61**
Cudham Dri. *New Ad* —6M **65**
Cudham La. N. *Cud & Orp* —1L **87**
Cudham La. S. *Cud* —2L **87**
Cudham Pk. Rd. *Cud* —6N **67**
Cudham Rd. *Orp* —7J **67**
Cudham Rd. *Tats* —6G **86**
Cudworth Cvn. Pk. *Newd* —2E **160**
Cudworth La. *Dork* —1B **160**
Culham Ho. *Brack* —3C **32**
Cullen Clo. *Yat* —1B **68**
Cullens M. *Alder* —3M **109**
Cullerne Clo. *Ewe* —6E **60**
Cullesden Rd. *Kenl* —2M **83**
Culmer Hill. *Worm* —8C **152**
Culmer La. *Wmly* —7C **152**
Culmington Rd. *S Croy* —5N **63**
Culsac Rd. *Surb* —8L **41**
Culvercroft. *Binf* —8K **15**
Culverden Rd. *SW12* —3G **28**
Culver Dri. *Oxt* —8A **106**
Culverhay. *Asht* —3L **79**
Culverhouse Gdns. *SW16* —4K **29**
Culverlands Cres. *Ash* —1D **110**
Culver Rd. *Owl* —6J **49**
Culvers Av. *Cars* —8D **44**
Culvers Retreat. *Cars* —8D **44**
Culvers Way. *Cars* —8D **44**
Culworth Ho. *Guild* —4A **114**
Cumberland Av. *Guild* —7K **93**
Cumberland Clo. *SW20* —8J **27**
Cumberland Clo. *Eps* —6D **60**
Cumberland Clo. *Twic* —9H **11**
Cumberland Dri. *Brack* —9B **16**
Cumberland Dri. *Chess* —9M **41**
Cumberland Dri. *Esh* —8G **40**
Cumberland Ho. *King T* —8A **26**
Cumberland Pl. *Sun* —3H **39**
Cumberland Rd. *SE25* —5E **46**
Cumberland Rd. *SW13* —4E **12**
Cumberland Rd. *Ashf* —4M **21**
Cumberland Rd. *Brom* —3N **47**
Cumberland Rd. *Camb* —1G **70**
Cumberland Rd. *Rich* —3N **11**
Cumberlands. *Kenl* —2A **84**
Cumberland St. *Stai* —6F **20**
Cumberlow Av. *SE25* —2C **46**
Cumbernaulds Gdns. *Sun* —6G **22**
Cumbernauld Wlk. *Bew* —7K **181**
Cumbrae Gdns. *Surb* —8K **41**
Cumbria Ct. *F'boro* —4C **90**
Cumnor Gdns. *Eps* —3F **60**
Cumnor Rise. *Kenl* —4N **83**
Cumnor Rd. *Sutt* —3A **62**
Cumnor Way. *Brack* —3C **32**
Cunliffe Clo. *H'ley* —2A **100**
Cunliffe Pde. *Eps* —1E **60**
Cunliffe Rd. *Eps* —1E **60**
Cunliffe St. *SW16* —7G **29**
Cunningham Av. *Guild* —2C **114**
Cunningham Clo. *W Wick* —8L **47**
Cunningham Rd. *Bans* —2B **82**
Cunnington Rd. *F'boro* —3C **90**
Cunworth Ct. *Brack* —5L **31**
Curfew Bell Rd. *Cher* —6H **37**
Curlew Clo. *S Croy* —7G **64**
Curlew Ct. *Surb* —9N **41**
Curlew Gdns. *Guild* —1F **114**
Curley Hill Rd. *Light* —8J **51**
Curling Clo. *Coul* —7K **83**
Curling Vale. *Guild* —5K **113**
Curl Way. *Wokgm* —3A **30**
Curly Bri. Clo. *F'boro* —6L **69**
Curnick's La. *SE27* —5N **29**
Curran Av. *Wall* —9E **44**
Currie Hill Clo. *SW19* —5L **27**
Curteys Wlk. *Craw* —6L **181**
Curtis Clo. *Camb* —8G **50**
Curtis Clo. *Head* —5A **168**
Curtis Ct. *C Crook* —8B **88**
Curtis Field Rd. *SW16* —5K **29**
Curtis Gdns. *Dork* —4G **118**
Curtis La. *Head* —3C **168**
Curtis Rd. *Dork* —4F **118**
Curtis Rd. *Eps* —1B **60**
Curtis Rd. *Houn* —1N **23**
Curtis's Cotts. *H'ham* —5M **179**
Curvan Clo. *Eps* —6E **60**
Curzon Av. *H'ham* —5H **197**
Curzon Clo. *Orp* —1M **67**
Curzon Clo. *Wey* —1B **56**
*Curzon Ct. SW6 —4N **13***
(off Maltings Pl.)
Curzon Dri. *C Crook* —8C **88**
Curzon Rd. *T Hth* —5L **45**
Curzon Rd. *Wey* —2B **56**
Cusack Clo. *Twic* —5F **24**
Cuthbert Gdns. *SE25* —2B **46**
Cuthbert Rd. *Ash V* —7F **90**
Cuthbert Rd. *Croy* —8M **45**
Cutthroat All. *Rich* —3J **25**
Cuttinglye La. *Craw D* —9D **164**
Cuttinglye Rd. *Craw D* —8E **164**
Cutting, The. *Red* —5D **122**
Cutts Rd. *Alder* —6B **90**
Cyclamen Clo. *Hamp* —7A **24**
Cyclamen Way. *Eps* —2B **60**
Cygnet Av. *Felt* —1K **23**
Cygnet Clo. *Wok* —3L **73**
Cygnet Ct. *Fleet* —2C **88**
Cygnets Clo. *Red* —1E **122**
Cygnets, The. *Felt* —5M **23**
Cypress Av. *Twic* —1C **24**
Cypress Clo. *Finch* —8A **30**
Cypress Dri. *Fleet* —4E **88**
Cypress Gro. *Ash V* —6D **90**
Cypress Ho. *Langl* —1D **6**
Cypress Rd. *SE25* —1B **46**
Cypress Rd. *Guild* —1M **113**
Cypress Wlk. *Egh* —7L **19**
Cypress Way. *Bans* —1J **81**
Cypress Way. *B'water* —1G **68**
Cypress Way. *Hind* —7B **170**
Cyprus Rd. *Deep* —6H **71**
*Cyprus Vs. Dork —5G **119***
(off Junction Rd.)

D

[illegible]
D'Abernon Clo. *Esh* —1A **58**
D'Abernon Dri. *Stoke D* —3M **77**
Dacre Rd. *Croy* —6J **45**
Dade Way. *S'hall* —1N **9**
Daffodil Clo. *Croy* —7G **47**
Daffodil Dri. *Bisl* —3D **72**
Daffodil Pl. *Hamp* —7A **24**
Dafforne Rd. *SW17* —4E **28**
Dagden Rd. *Shalf* —9A **114**
Dagley Farm Cvn. Pk. *Shalf* —9M **113**
Dagley La. *Guild* —8N **113**
Dagmar Rd. *SE25* —4B **46**
Dagmar Rd. *King T* —9M **25**
Dagmar Rd. *Wind* —5G **4**
Dagnall Pk. *SE25* —5A **46**
Dagnall Rd. *SE25* —4B **46**
Dagnan Rd. *SW12* —1F **28**
Dahlia Gdns. *Mitc* —3H **45**
Dahomey Rd. *SW16* —7G **28**
Daimler Way. *Wall* —4J **63**
Dairy Clo. *T Hth* —1N **45**
Dairyfields. *Craw* —4M **181**
Dairy La. *Crook C* —3J **127**
Dairyman's Wlk. *Guild* —7D **94**
Dairy Wlk. *SW19* —5K **27**
Daisy Clo. *Croy* —7G **47**
Daisy La. *SW6* —6M **13**
Dakin Clo. *M'bowr* —7G **183**
Dakins, The. *E Grin* —1A **186**
Dalby Rd. *SW18* —7N **13**
Dalcross. *Brack* —5C **32**
Dalcross Rd. *Houn* —5M **9**
Dale Av. *Houn* —6M **9**
Dalebury Rd. *SW17* —3D **28**
Dale Clo. *Add* —2K **55**
Dale Clo. *Asc* —4D **34**
Dale Clo. *H'ham* —3M **197**
Dale Clo. *Wrec* —4E **128**
Dale Gdns. *Sand* —7F **48**
Dalegarth Gdns. *Purl* —9A **64**
Daleham Av. *Egh* —7C **20**
Dale Lodge Rd. *Asc* —4D **34**
Dale Pk. Av. *Cars* —8D **44**
Dale Pk. Rd. *SE19* —9N **29**
Dale Rd. *F Row* —8H **187**
Dale Rd. *Purl* —8L **63**
Dale Rd. *Sun* —8G **22**
Dale Rd. *Sutt* —1L **61**
Dale Rd. *W On T* —6G **39**
Daleside Rd. *SW16* —6F **28**
Daleside Rd. *Eps* —3C **60**
Dale St. *W4* —1D **12**
Dale, The. *Kes* —1F **66**
Dale View. *Hasl* —3E **188**
Dale View. *H'ley* —1A **100**
Dale View. *Wok* —5L **73**
Dalewood Gdns. *Craw* —1D **182**
Dalewood Gdns. *Wor Pk* —8G **43**
Dalkeith Rd. *SE21* —2N **29**
Dallas Rd. *Sutt* —3K **61**
Dallaway Gdns. *E Grin* —9A **166**
Dalley Ct. *Sand* —8J **49**
Dalling Rd. *W6* —1G **12**
Dallington Clo. *W On T* —3K **57**
Dalmally Rd. *Croy* —6C **46**
Dalmeny Av. *SW16* —1L **45**
Dalmeny Cres. *Houn* —7D **10**
Dalmeny Rd. *Cars* —4E **62**
Dalmeny Rd. *Wor Pk* —9G **42**
Dalmore Av. *Clay* —3E **58**
Dalmore Rd. *SE21* —3N **29**
Dalston Clo. *Camb* —3H **71**
Dalton Av. *Mitc* —1C **44**

Dalton Clo.—Dixon Pl.

Dalton Clo. Craw —8N 181
Dalton Clo. Purl —8N 63
Dalton St. SE27 —3M 29
Damascene Wlk. SE21 —2F 26
Damask Clo. W End —9B 52
Damphurst La. Wott —1A 138
Dampier Wlk. Craw —8N 181
Danbrook Rd. SW16 —9J 29
Danbury M. Wall —1F 62
Danby Ct. Horl —6E 142
Dancer Rd. SW6 —4L 13
Dancer Rd. Rich —6N 11
Danebury. New Ad —3L 65
Danebury Av. SW15 —9D 12
(in two parts)
Danebury Wlk. Frim —6D 70
Dane Clo. Orp —2M 67
Dane Ct. Wok —2H 75
Danecourt Gdns. Croy —9C 46
Danehurst Ct. Eps —9E 60
Danehurst Cres. H'ham —6M 197
Danehurst St. SW6 —4K 13
Danemere St. SW15 —6H 13
Danemore La. S God —1G 145
Dane Rd. SW19 —9A 28
Dane Rd. Ashf —7D 22
Dane Rd. Warl —4G 84
Danesbury Rd. Felt —2J 23
Danesbury Wlk. Frim —6D 70
Danes Clo. Oxs —1C 78
Danescourt Cres. Sutt —8A 44
Danesfield Clo. W On T —9J 39
Danes Hill. Wok —5D 74
Daneshill Clo. Red —2C 122
Daneshill Dri. Oxs —1D 78
Danesrood. Guild —4B 114
Danes Way. Oxs —1D 78
Daneswood Clo. Wey —2C 56
Danetree Clo. Eps —4B 60
Danetree Rd. Eps —4B 60
Daniel Clo. SW17 —7C 28
Daniel Clo. Houn —1N 23
Daniell Way. Croy —7J 45
Daniels La. Warl —3J 85
Daniel Way. Bans —1N 81
Dan Leno Wlk. SW6 —3N 13
Danone Ct. Guild —3N 113
Danses Clo. Guild —1F 114
Danvers Dri. C Crook —1A 108
Danvers Way. Cat —1N 103
Da Palma Ct. SW6 —2M 13
(off Anselm Rd.)
Dapdune Ct. Guild —3M 113
Dapdune Rd. Guild —3N 113
Daphne Ct. Wor Pk —8D 42
Daphne Dri. C Crook —1A 108
Daphne St. SW18 —9N 13
Darby Clo. Cat —9N 83
Darby Cres. Sun —1K 39
Darby Gdns. Sun —1K 39
Darby Grn. La. B'water —1G 68
Darby Grn. Rd. B'water —1F 68
Darby Vale. Warf —7N 15
Darcy Av. Wall —1G 63
Darcy Clo. Coul —6M 83
D'Arcy Pl. Asht —4M 79
Darcy Rd. SW16 —1J 45
D'Arcy Rd. Asht —4M 79
Darcy Rd. Iswth —4G 11
D'Arcy Rd. Sutt —1J 61
Darell Rd. Rich —6N 11
Darenth Gdns. W'ham —4M 107
Darenth Way. Horl —6D 142
Dare's La. Ews —3A 108
Darfield Rd. Guild —9C 94
Darfur St. SW15 —6J 13
Dark Dale. Asc —4E 32
Dark La. P'ham —8M 111
Dark La. Shere —8A 116
Dark La. W'sham —3M 51
Darlan Rd. SW6 —3L 13
Darlaston Rd. SW19 —8J 27
Darley Clo. Add —2L 55
Darley Clo. Croy —5H 47
Darleydale. Craw —6A 182
Darleydale Clo. Owl —5J 49
Darley Dene Ct. Add —1L 55
Darley Dri. N Mald —1C 42
Darley Gdns. Mord —5A 44
Darlington Rd. SE27 —6M 29
Darmaine Clo. S Croy —4N 63
Darnley Pk. Wey —9B 38
Darracott Clo. Camb —7F 50
Darset Av. Fleet —3B 88
Dart Clo. Slou —2D 6
Dart Ct. E Grin —7C 166
Dartmouth Av. Sheer —1E 74
Dartmouth Clo. Brack —2C 32
Dartmouth Grn. Wok —1F 74
Dartmouth Path. Wok —1F 74
Dartmouth Pl. W4 —2D 12
Dartnell Av. W Byf —8K 55
Dartnell Clo. W Byf —8K 55
Dartnell Cres. W Byf —8K 55
Dartnell Pk. Rd. W Byf —8K 55
Dartnell Pl. W Byf —8K 55
Dartnell Rd. Croy —6C 46
Dart Rd. F'boro —8J 69
Darvel Clo. Wok —3K 73
Darvills La. Farnh —1J 129
Darvills La. Read —1E 14
Darwall Dri. Asc —1H 33
Darwin Clo. H'ham —4M 197
Darwin Clo. Orp —2M 67
Darwin Gro. Alder —1A 110
Darwin Rd. W5 —1J 11
Daryngton Dri. Guild —3D 114
Dashwood Clo. Brack —9B 16
Dashwood Clo. W Byf —8L 55
Dassett Rd. SE27 —6M 29
Datchet Pl. Dat —4L 5
Datchet Rd. Hort —6B 6
Datchet Rd. Old Win —7K 5
Datchet Rd. Slou —1J 5
Datchet Rd. Wind —3G 5
Dault Rd. SW18 —9N 13
Daux Hill. H'ham —1H 197
Davenant Rd. Croy —1M 63
Davenport Clo. Tedd —7G 25
Davenport Lodge. Houn —3M 9
Davenport Rd. Brack —9C 16
Daventry Clo. Coln —4H 7
Daventry Ct. Brack —9N 15
David Clo. Hayes —3F 8
David Clo. Horl —7F 142
David Rd. Coln —5H 7
Davidson Rd. Croy —6B 46
Davies Clo. Croy —5D 46
Davies Clo. G'ming —4G 133
Davis Clo. Craw —8M 181
Davis Gdns. Col T —8K 49
Davis Rd. Chess —1N 59
Davis Rd. Wey —6A 56
Davmor Ct. Bren —1J 11
Davos Clo. Wok —6A 74
Davy Clo. Wokgm —3B 30
Dawell Dri. Big H —4E 86
Dawes Av. Iswth —8G 10
Dawes Ct. Esh —2B 58
Dawes Rd. SW6 —3K 13
Dawley Ride. Coln —4G 6
Dawlish Av. SW18 —3N 27
Dawnay Clo. Asc —9K 17
Dawnay Gdns. SW18 —3B 28
Dawnay Rd. SW18 —3A 28
Dawnay Rd. Bookh —4B 98
Dawnay Rd. Camb —7N 49
Dawn Clo. Houn —6M 9
Dawney Hill. Pirb —8B 72
Dawneys Rd. Pirb —9B 72
Dawn Redwood Clo. Hort —6C 6
Dawn Rise. Copt —7L 163
Dawsmere Clo. Camb —1G 71
Dawson Clo. Wind —5D 4
Dawson Rd. Byfl —7M 55
Dawson Rd. King T —2M 41
Daybrook Rd. SW19 —1N 43
Day Ct. Cranl —8H 155
Daylesford Av. SW15 —7F 12
Daymerslea Ridge. Lea —8J 79
Days Acre. S Croy —6C 64
Daysbrook Rd. SW2 —2K 29
Dayseys Hill. Out —3L 143
Dayspring. Guild —8L 93
Deacon Clo. D'side —6J 77
Deacon Clo. Purl —5J 63
Deacon Clo. Wokgm —9B 14
Deacon Field. Guild —2K 113
Deacon Pl. Cat —1N 103
Deacon Rd. King T —9M 25
Deacons Ct. Twic —3F 24
Deacons Leas. Orp —1M 67
Deacons Wlk. Hamp —5A 24
Deadbrook La. Alder —1B 110
Deal Rd. SW17 —7E 28
Dealtry Rd. SW15 —7H 13
Dean Clo. Tad —2G 100
Dean Clo. Wind —6A 4
Dean Clo. Wok —3G 74
Deanery Pl. G'ming —7G 133
(off Church St.)
Deanery Rd. Crook C —2L 127
Deanery Rd. G'ming —6G 133
Deanfield Gdns. Croy —1A 64
Dean Gro. Wokgm —1B 30
Deanhill Ct. SW14 —7A 12
Deanhill Rd. SW14 —7A 12
Dean La. Red —1F 102
Deanoak La. Leigh —4H 141
Dean Pde. Camb —7D 50
Dean Rd. Croy —1A 64
Dean Rd. G'ming —5G 132
Dean Rd. Hamp —6A 24
Dean Rd. Houn —8B 10
Deans Clo. W4 —2A 12
Deans Clo. Croy —9C 46
Deans Clo. Tad —2G 100
Deans Ct. W'sham —4A 52
Deansfield. Cat —3C 104
Deansgate. Brack —6N 31
Deans La. W4 —2A 12
(off Deans Clo.)
Deans La. Nutf —2L 123
Dean's La. Tad —2G 101
Deans Rd. Red —8G 103
Deans Rd. Sutt —9N 43
Dean's Wlk. Coul —5L 83
Dean Wlk. Bookh —4B 98
Dearn Gdns. Mitc —2C 44
Deauville Ct. SW4 —1G 29
Debden Clo. King T —6K 25
Deborah Clo. Iswth —4E 10
De Brome Rd. Felt —2K 23
De Burgh Pk. Bans —2N 81
De Burgh Rd. SW19 —8A 28
Decimus Clo. T Hth —3A 46
Dedisham Clo. Craw —4E 182
Dedswell Dri. W Cla —7J 95
Dedworth Dri. Wind —4C 4
Dedworth Rd. Wind —5A 4
Deedman Clo. Ash —2E 110
Deepcut Bri. Rd. Deep —8G 70
Deepdale. SW19 —5J 27
Deepdale. Brack —3M 31
Deepdene. Hasl —2C 188
Deepdene. Lwr Bo —5J 129
Deepdene Av. Croy —9C 46
Deepdene Av. Dork —8J 119
Deepdene Av. Rd. Dork —3J 119
Deepdene Dri. Dork —4J 119
Deepdene Gdns. SW2 —1K 29
Deepdene Gdns. Dork —4J 119
Deepdene Pk. Rd. Dork —4J 119
Deepdene Roundabout. Dork —4J 119
Deepdene Vale. Dork —4J 119
Deepdene Wood. Dork —5K 119
Deepfield. Dat —3L 5
Deepfield Rd. Brack —1B 32
Deepfields. Horl —6D 142
Deepfield Way. Coul —3J 83
Deep Pool La. Hors —1L 73
Deepwell Clo. Iswth —4G 10
Deep Well Dri. Camb —1C 70
Deerbarn Rd. Guild —2L 113
Deerbrook Rd. SE24 —2M 29
Deerhurst Clo. Felt —5J 23
Deerhurst Cres. Hamp H —6C 24
Deerhurst Rd. SW16 —6K 29
Deerings Rd. Reig —3N 121
Deer Leap. Light —7L 51
Deerleap Rd. Westc —6B 118
Dee Rd. Rich —7M 11
Deer Pk. Clo. King T —8A 26
Deer Pk. Gdns. Mitc —3B 44
Deer Pk. Rd. SW19 —1N 43
Deer Rock Hill. Brack —5A 32
Deer Rock Rd. Camb —8D 50
Deers Farm Clo. Wis —3N 75
Deerswood Clo. Cat —2D 104
Deerswood Clo. Craw —2N 181
Deerswood Ct. Craw —2M 181
Deerswood Rd. Craw —3N 181
Deeside Rd. SW17 —4B 28
Dee Way. Eps —6D 60
Defiant Way. Wall —4J 63
Defoe Av. Rich —3N 11
Defoe Clo. SW17 —7C 28
De Havilland Dri. Wey —7N 55
De Havilland Rd. Houn —3K 9
De Havilland Rd. Wall —4J 63
De Havilland Way. Stai —9N 7
Delabole Rd. Red —7J 103
Delaford St. SW6 —3K 13
Delagarde Rd. W'ham —4L 107
Delamare Cres. Croy —5F 46
Delamere Rd. SW20 —9J 27
Delamere Rd. Reig —7N 121
Delaporte Clo. Eps —8D 60
De Lara Way. Wok —5N 73
De La Warr Rd. E Grin —9B 166
Delawyk Cres. SE24 —1N 29
Delcombe Av. Wor Pk —7H 43
Delderfield. Lea —8K 79
Delfont Clo. M'bowr —5H 183
Delia St. SW18 —1N 27
Delius Gdns. H'ham —4A 198
Dellbow Rd. Felt —8J 9
Dell Clo. Fet —1E 98
Dell Clo. Hasl —1E 188
Dell Clo. Mick —5J 99
Dell Clo. Wall —1H 63
Deller St. Binf —8L 15
Dell Gro. Frim —4D 70
Dell La. Eps —2F 60
Dell Rd. Eps —3F 60
Dell Rd. Finch —4A 48
Dell, The. Bren —2J 11
Dell, The. E Grin —9D 166
Dell, The. Farnh —5J 109
Dell, The. Felt —1J 23
Dell, The. Horl —7F 142
Dell, The. Reig —2M 121
Dell, The. Tad —8H 81
Dell, The. Wok —6M 73
Dell, The. Yat —1B 68
Dell Wlk. N Mald —1D 42
Delmey Clo. Croy —9C 46
Delorme St. W6 —2J 13
Delta Bungalows. Horl —1E 162
Delta Bus. Pk. SW18 —7N 13
(off Smugglers Way)
Delta Clo. Chob —6J 53
Delta Clo. Wor Pk —9E 42
Delta Dri. Horl —1E 162
Delta Ho. Horl —1E 162
(off Delta Dri.)
Delta Rd. Chob —6J 53
Delta Rd. Wok —3C 74
Delta Rd. Wor Pk —9D 42
Delta Way. Egh —9E 20
Delves. Tad —8J 81
Delville Clo. F'boro —2J 89
Delvino Rd. SW6 —4M 13
Demesne Rd. Wall —1H 63
De Montfort Pde. SW16 —4J 29
De Montfort Rd. SW16 —3J 29
De Morgan Rd. SW6 —6N 13
Dempster Clo. Surb —7J 41
Dempster Rd. SW18 —8N 13
Denbies Dri. Dork —1H 119
Denbigh Clo. Sutt —2L 61
Denbigh Gdns. Rich —8M 11
Denbigh Rd. Hasl —3H 189
Denbigh Rd. Houn —5B 10
Denby Rd. Cobh —8K 57
Denchers Plat. Craw —9B 162
Dencliffe. Ashf —6B 22
Den Clo. Beck —2N 47
Dene Av. Houn —6N 9
Dene Clo. Brack —8A 16
Dene Clo. Hasl —3G 188
Dene Clo. Horl —6C 142
Dene Clo. Lwr Bo —5K 129
Dene Clo. Wor Pk —8E 42
Denefield. Dork —7H 119
Denefield Dri. Kenl —2A 84
Dene Gdns. Th Dit —8G 40
Denehurst Gdns. Rich —7N 11
Denehurst Gdns. Twic —1D 24
Denehyrst Ct. Guild —4A 114
(off York Rd.)
Dene La. Lwr Bo —5J 129
Dene La. W. Lwr Bo —6K 129
Dene Pl. Wok —5M 73
Dene Rd. Asht —6M 79
Dene Rd. F'boro —2L 89
Dene Rd. Guild —4A 114
Dene St. Dork —5H 119
Dene St. Gdns. Dork —5H 119
Dene, The. Ab H —9J 117
Dene, The. Croy —1G 64
Dene, The. Sutt —7L 61
Dene, The. W Mol —4N 39
Dene Tye. Craw —2H 183
Dene Wlk. Lwr Bo —5J 129
Denfield. Dork —7H 119
Denham Cres. Mitc —3D 44
Denham Dri. Yat —1C 68
Denham Gro. Brack —5A 32
Denham Rd. Egh —5C 20
Denham Rd. Eps —8E 60
Denham Rd. Felt —1K 23
Denholm Gdns. Guild —9C 94
Denison Rd. SW19 —7B 28
Denison Rd. Felt —5G 23
Denleigh Gdns. Th Dit —5E 40
Denly Way. Light —6N 51
Denman Clo. Fleet —4D 88
Denman Dri. Ashf —7C 22
Denman Dri. Clay —2G 58
Denmans. Craw —2H 183
Denmark Av. SW19 —8K 27
Denmark Ct. Mord —5M 43
Denmark Gdns. Cars —9D 44
Denmark Path. SE25 —4E 46
Denmark Rd. SE25 —4D 46
Denmark Rd. SW19 —7J 27
Denmark Rd. Cars —9D 44
Denmark Rd. Guild —4A 114
Denmark Rd. King T —2L 41
Denmark Rd. Twic —4D 24
Denmark Sq. Alder —2B 110
Denmark St. Alder —2B 110
Denmark St. Wokgm —3B 30
Denmark Wlk. SE27 —5N 29
Denmead Ct. Brack —5C 32
Denmead Ho. SW15 —9E 12
(off Highcliffe Dri.)
Denmead Rd. Croy —7M 45
Denmore Ct. Wall —2F 62
Dennan Rd. Surb —7M 41
Dennard Way. Farn —1J 67
Denne Pde. H'ham —7J 197
Denne Rd. Craw —4B 182
Denne Rd. H'ham —7J 197
Dennett Rd. Croy —7L 45
Dennettsland Rd. Crook C —3L 127
Denning Av. Croy —1L 63
Denning Clo. Fleet —6A 88
Denning Clo. Hamp —6N 23
Denningtons, The. Wor Pk —8D 42
Dennis Clo. Ashf —8E 22
Dennis Clo. Red —1C 122
Dennis Ho. Sutt —1N 61
Dennison Gro. SW14 —6C 12
Dennis Pk. Cres. SW20 —9K 27
Dennis Reeve Clo. Mitc —9D 28
Dennis Rd. E Mol —3C 40
Dennistoun Clo. Camb —1B 70
Dennis Way. Guild —7A 94
Denny Rd. Slou —1B 6
Den Rd. Brom —2N 47
Denton Clo. Red —8E 122
Denton Gro. W On T —8M 39
Denton Rd. Twic —9K 11
Denton Rd. Wokgm —2B 30
Denton St. SW18 —9N 13
Denton Way. Frim —4B 70
Denton Way. St J —5J 73
Dents Gro. Tad —6L 101
Dents Rd. SW11 —1D 28
Denvale Wlk. Wok —5K 73
Denzil Rd. Guild —4L 113
Deodar Rd. SW15 —7K 13
Depot Rd. Craw —9B 162
Depot Rd. Eps —9D 60
Depot Rd. H'ham —6L 197
Depot Rd. Houn —6D 10
Derby Arms Rd. Eps —4E 80
Derby Clo. Eps —6G 81
Derby Est. Houn —7B 10
Derby Rd. SW14 —7A 12
Derby Rd. SW19 —8M 27
Derby Rd. Croy —7M 45
Derby Rd. Guild —3J 113
Derby Rd. Hasl —1F 188
Derby Rd. Houn —7B 10
Derby Rd. Surb —7N 41
Derby Rd. Sutt —3L 61
Derbyshire Grn. Warf —8D 16
Derby Stables Rd. Eps —4D 80
Derek Av. Eps —3N 59
Derek Av. Wall —1F 62
Derek Clo. Ewe —2A 60
Derek Horn Ct. Camb —9N 49
Deridene Clo. Stai —9N 7
Dering Pl. Croy —1N 63
Dering Rd. Croy —1N 63
Derinton Rd. SW17 —5D 28
Deronda Est. SW2 —2M 29
Deronda Rd. SE24 —2M 29
De Ros Pl. Egh —7C 20
Deroy Clo. Cars —3D 62
Derrick Av. S Croy —6N 63
Derrick Rd. Beck —2J 47
Derrydown. Wok —8M 73
Derry Rd. Croy —9J 45
Derry Rd. F'boro —6L 69
Derwent Av. SW15 —5D 26
Derwent Av. Ash V —9D 90
Derwent Clo. Add —2M 55
Derwent Clo. Clay —3E 58
Derwent Clo. Craw —4L 181
Derwent Clo. F'boro —1K 89
Derwent Clo. Farnh —6F 108
Derwent Clo. Felt —2G 22
Derwent Clo. H'ham —2A 198
Derwent Dri. Purl —9A 64
Derwent Ho. SE20 —1E 46
(off Derwent Rd.)
Derwent Lodge. Iswth —5D 10
Derwent Lodge. Wor Pk —8G 42
Derwent Rd. SE20 —1D 46
Derwent Rd. SW20 —4J 43
Derwent Rd. Egh —8C 20
Derwent Rd. Light —7M 51
Derwent Rd. Twic —9B 10
Derwent Wlk. Wall —4F 62
Desborough Clo. Shep —7B 38
Desborough Ho. W14 —2L 13
(off N. End Rd.)
Desford Ct. Ashf —3B 22
Desford Way. Ashf —3A 22
Detillens La. Oxt —7C 106
Detling Rd. Craw —8A 182
Dettingen Barracks. Deep —5H 71
Dettingen Rd. Deep —6J 71
Devana End. Cars —9D 44
Devas Rd. SW20 —9H 27
Devenish Clo. S'hill —5A 34
Devenish La. Asc —7A 34
Devenish Rd. Asc —5N 33
Devereux La. SW13 —3G 12
Devereux Rd. SW11 —1D 28
Devereux Rd. Wind —5G 4
Devey Clo. King T —8D 26
Devil's Highway, The. Crowt —2D 48
Devil's La. Egh & Stai —7E 20
De Vitre Grn. Wokgm —1E 30
Devitt Clo. Asht —3N 79
Devoil Clo. Guild —8D 94
Devoke Way. W On T —8L 39
Devon Av. Twic —2C 24
Devon Bank. Guild —6M 113
Devon Chase. Warf —7C 16
Devon Clo. Col T —8J 49
Devon Clo. Fleet —1C 88
Devon Clo. Kenl —3B 84
Devon Ct. Hamp —8A 24
Devon Cres. Red —3B 122
Devoncroft Gdns. Twic —1G 25
Devon Ho. Cat —2C 104
Devonhurst Pl. W4 —1C 12
Devon Rd. Red —8G 102
Devon Rd. Sutt —5K 61
Devon Rd. W On T —1K 57
Devonshire Av. Sutt —4A 62
Devonshire Av. Wok —1E 74
Devonshire Dri. Camb —8D 50
Devonshire Dri. Surb —7K 41
Devonshire Gdns. W4 —3B 12
Devonshire Ho. Sutt —4A 62
Devonshire M. W4 —1D 12
Devonshire Pas. W4 —1D 12
Devonshire Pl. W4 —1D 12
Devonshire Pl. Alder —3L 109
Devonshire Rd. SW19 —8C 28
Devonshire Rd. W4 —1D 12
Devonshire Rd. Cars —1E 62
Devonshire Rd. Croy —6A 46
Devonshire Rd. Felt —4M 23
Devonshire Rd. H'ham —6K 197
Devonshire Rd. Sutt —4A 62
Devonshire Rd. Wey —1B 56
Devonshire St. W4 —1D 12
Devonshire Way. Croy —8H 47
Devon Way. Chess —2J 59
Devon Way. Eps —2A 60
Devon Waye. Houn —3N 9
Dewar Clo. If'd —4K 181
Dewey St. SW17 —6D 28
Dewlands. God —9F 104
Dewlands Clo. Cranl —7N 155
Dewlands La. Cranl —7N 155
Dewlands Rd. God —9F 104
Dewsbury Ct. W4 —1B 12
Dewsbury Gdns. Wor Pk —9F 42
Dexter Dri. E Grin —1A 186
Dexter Way. Fleet —1C 88
Diamedes Av. Stai —1M 21
Diamond Ct. Red —2E 122
(off St Anne's Way)
Diamond Est. SW17 —4C 28
Diamond Hill. Camb —8C 50
Diamond Ridge. Camb —8B 50
Diana Cotts. Seale —8J 111
Diana Gdns. Surb —8M 41
Diana Ho. SW13 —4E 12
Dianthus Clo. Cher —6G 36
Dianthus Ct. Wok —5N 73
Dianthus Pl. Wink R —7F 16
Dibdene La. Sham G —7H 135
Dibdin Clo. Sutt —9M 43
Dibdin Rd. Sutt —9M 43
Diceland Rd. Bans —3L 81
Dickens Clo. E Grin —9M 165
Dickens Clo. Hayes —1F 8
Dickens Clo. Rich —3L 25
Dickens Ct. Wokgm —2A 30
Dickens Dri. Add —3H 55
Dickenson Rd. Felt —6L 23
Dickensons La. SE25 —4D 46
Dickensons Pl. SE25 —5D 46
Dickens Rd. Craw —6B 182
Dickens Way. Yat —1B 68
Dickerage La. N Mald —2B 42
Dickerage Rd. King T & N Mald —9B 26
Dickins Way. H'ham —8M 197
Dick Turpin Way. Felt —7G 9
Digby Mans. W6 —1G 13
(off Hammersmith Bri. Rd.)
Digby Pl. Croy —9C 46
Digby Way. Byfl —8A 56
Digdens Rise. Eps —2B 80
Dighton Rd. SW18 —8N 13
Dillon Cotts. Guild —7E 94
Dilston Rd. Lea —6G 79
Dilton Gdns. SW15 —2F 26
Dimes Pl. W6 —1G 13
Dingle Rd. Ashf —6C 22
Dingle, The. Craw —3N 181
Dingley La. SW16 —3H 29
Dingwall Av. Croy —8N 45
Dingwall Rd. SW18 —1A 28
Dingwall Rd. Cars —5D 62
Dingwall Rd. Croy —7A 46
Dinorben Av. Fleet —6A 88
Dinorben Beeches. Fleet —6A 88
Dinorben Clo. Fleet —6A 88
Dinsdale Clo. Wok —5C 74
Dinsdale Gdns. SE25 —4B 46
Dinsmore Rd. SW12 —1F 28
Dinton Rd. SW19 —7B 28
Dinton Rd. King T —8M 25
Dione Wlk. Bew —6K 181
Dippenhall Rd. Farnh —1B 128
Dirdene Clo. Eps —8E 60
Dirdene Gdns. Eps —8E 60
Dirdene Gro. Eps —8D 60
Dirtham La. Eff —6J 97
Dirty La. Ash W —3G 187
Disbrowe Rd. W6 —2K 13
Disraeli Ct. Coln —2D 6
Disraeli Gdns. SW15 —7L 13
Disraeli Rd. SW15 —7K 13
Distillery La. W6 —1H 13
Distillery Rd. W6 —1H 13
Distillery Wlk. Bren —2L 11
Ditches Grn. Cotts. Dork —8M 157
Ditches La. Coul & Cat —7J 83
Ditchling. Brack —6M 31
Ditchling Hill. Craw —6A 182
Ditton Clo. Th Dit —6G 40
Dittoncroft Clo. Croy —1B 64
Ditton Grange Clo. Surb —7K 41
Ditton Grange Dri. Surb —7K 41
Ditton Hill. Surb —7J 41
Ditton Hill Rd. Surb —7J 41
Ditton Lawn. Th Dit —7G 40
Ditton Pk. Rd. Slou —2A 6
Ditton Reach. Th Dit —5H 41
Ditton Rd. Dat —4N 5
Ditton Rd. Langl —1B 6
Ditton Rd. S'hall —1N 9
Ditton Rd. Surb —8K 41
Divis Way. SW15 —9G 13
(off Dover Pk. Dri.)
Dixon Dri. Wey —6A 56
Dixon Pl. W Wick —7L 47

Dixon Rd.—Duxberry Av.

Dixon Rd. *SE25* —2B **46**
Dobbins Pl. *If'd* —4J **181**
Doble Ct. *S Croy* —8D **64**
Dobson Rd. *Craw* —9B **162**
Dockenfield St. *Dock* —4C **148**
Dockett Eddy. *Cher* —7N **37**
Dockett Eddy La. *Shep* —7A **38**
Dock Rd. *Bren* —3K **11**
Dockwell Clo. *Felt* —7H **9**
Doctor Johnson Av. *SW17* —4F **28**
Doctors La. *Cat* —1L **103**
Dodbrooke Rd. *SE27* —4L **29**
Dodds Cres. *W Byf* —1K **75**
Dodd's La. *Wok* —1J **75**
Dodds Pk. *Brock* —5A **120**
Doel Clo. *SW19* —8A **28**
Dogflud Way. *Farnh* —9H **109**
Doghurst Av. *Hayes* —3C **8**
Doghurst Dri. *W Dray* —3C **8**
Doghurst La. *Coul* —7D **82**
Dogkennel Grn. *Ran C* —3L **117**
Dolby Rd. *SW6* —5L **13**
Dolleyshill Cvn. Pk. *Norm* —8K **91**
Dollis Clo. *M'bowr* —4G **182**
Dollis Dri. *Farnh* —9J **109**
Dolman Rd. *W4* —1C **12**
Dolphin Clo. *Hasl* —2C **188**
Dolphin Clo. *Surb* —4K **41**
Dolphin Ct. *Brack* —3A **32**
Dolphin Ct. *Stai* —4J **21**
Dolphin Ct. N. *Stai* —4J **21**
Dolphin Est. *Sun* —9F **22**
Dolphin Rd. *Sun* —9F **22**
Dolphin Rd. N. *Sun* —9F **22**
Dolphin Rd. S. *Sun* —9F **22**
Dolphin Rd. W. *Sun* —9F **22**
Dolphin [illegible] *W4* —[illegible] **13**
Dolphin St. *King T* —1L **41**
Doman Rd. *Camb* —2L **69**
Dome Hill. *Cat* —5B **104**
Dome Hill Peak. *Cat* —4B **104**
Dome, The. *Red* —2D **122**
Dome Way. *Red* —2D **122**
Dominica Ter. Frim G —6H 71
(off Cyprus Rd.)
Dominion Rd. *Croy* —6C **46**
Donald Rd. *Croy* —6K **45**
Donald Woods Gdns. *Surb* —8A **42**
Doncaster Wlk. *Craw* —5E **182**
Doncastle Rd. *Brack* —2K **31**
Doneraile St. *SW6* —5J **13**
Donkey La. *Ab C* —3L **137**
Donkey La. *Horl* —3H **163**
Donkey La. *W Dray* —1L **7**
Donnafields. *Bisl* —3D **72**
Donne Clo. *Craw* —1F **182**
Donne Ct. *SE24* —1N **29**
Donne Gdns. *Wok* —2G **74**
Donnelly Ct. SW6 —3K 13
(off Dawes Rd.)
Donne Pl. *Mitc* —3F **44**
Donnington Clo. *Camb* —2N **69**
Donnington Ct. *Craw* —6L **181**
Donnington Rd. *Wor Pk* —8F **42**
Donnybrook. *Brack* —6M **31**
Donnybrook Rd. *SW16* —8G **29**
Donovan Clo. *Eps* —6C **60**
Doods Pk. Rd. *Reig* —2A **122**
Doods Pl. *Reig* —2B **122**
Doods Rd. *Reig* —2A **122**
Doods Way. *Reig* —2B **122**
Doomsday Garden. *H'ham* —7N **197**
Doone Clo. *Tedd* —7G **24**
Doral Way. *Cars* —2D **62**
Doran Ct. *Red* —3B **122**
Doran Dri. *Red* —3B **122**
Doran Gdns. *Red* —3B **122**
Dora Rd. *SW19* —6M **27**
Dora's Grn. La. *Ews* —5C **108**
Dorcas Ct. *Camb* —3N **69**
Dorchester Ct. *Reig* —2B **122**
Dorchester Ct. *Stai* —5J **21**
Dorchester Ct. *Wok* —3C **74**
Dorchester Dri. *Felt* —9F **8**
Dorchester Gro. *W4* —1D **12**
Dorchester M. *N Mald* —3C **42**
Dorchester M. *Twic* —9J **11**
Dorchester Rd. *Mord* —6N **43**
Dorchester Rd. *Wey* —9C **38**
Dorchester Rd. *Wor Pk* —7H **43**
Doreen Clo. *F'boro* —7K **69**
Dore Gdns. *Mord* —6N **43**
Dorian Dri. *Asc* —9B **18**
Doria Rd. *SW6* —5L **13**
Doric Dri. *Tad* —7L **81**
Dorien Rd. *SW20* —1J **43**
Dorin Ct. *Warl* —7E **84**
Dorincourt. *Wok* —2G **74**
Doris Rd. *Ashf* —7E **22**
Dorking Bus. Pk. *Dork* —4G **118**
Dorking Clo. *Wor Pk* —8J **43**
Dorking Rd. *Bookh* —4B **98**
Dorking Rd. *Chil* —9G **115**
Dorking Rd. *Eps* —3N **79**
Dorking Rd. *Gom & Ab H* —8E **116**
Dorking Rd. *H'ham* —8G **178**
Dorking Rd. *Lea* —9H **79**
Dorking Rd. *Tad* —7D **100**
Dorking Vs. *Knap* —4G **72**
Dorlcote. *Witl* —5B **152**
Dorlcote Rd. *SW18* —1C **28**
Dorling Dri. *Eps* —8E **60**
Dorly Clo. *Shep* —4F **38**
Dormans. *Craw* —4M **181**
Dormans Av. *D'land* —9C **146**
Dormans Clo. *D'land* —2C **166**
Dormans Gdns. *Dor P* —4A **166**
Dormans High St. *Ling* —2C **166**
Dormans Pk. Rd. *Dor P* —4A **166**
Dormans Pk. Rd. *E Grin* —7N **165**
Dormans Rd. *D'land* —9C **146**
Dormans Sta. Rd. *Ling* —3B **166**
Dormay St. *SW18* —8N **13**
Dormer Clo. *Crowt* —2F **48**
Dormers Clo. *G'ming* —4G **133**
Dorncliffe Rd. *SW6* —5K **13**
Dorney Gro. *Wey* —8C **38**
Dorney Way. *Houn* —8M **9**
Dornford Gdns. *Coul* —6N **83**
Dornton Rd. *SW12* —3F **28**
Dornton Rd. *S Croy* —3A **64**
Dorothy Pettingell Ho. Sutt
(off Angel Hill) —9N 43
Dorrien Wlk. *SW16* —3H **29**
Dorrington Ct. *SE19* —1B **46**
Dorrit Cres. *Guild* —1H **113**
Dorset Av. *E Grin* —7M **165**
Dorset Av. *S'hall* —1A **10**
Dorset Ct. *Camb* —7D **50**
Dorset Ct. *Eps* —[illegible]
Dorset Dri. *Wok* —4D **74**
Dorset Gdns. *E Grin* —7M **165**
Dorset Gdns. *Mitc* —3K **45**
Dorset Rd. *SW19* —9M **27**
Dorset Rd. *Ashf* —4M **21**
Dorset Rd. *Ash V* —8F **90**
Dorset Rd. *Beck* —2G **46**
Dorset Rd. *Mitc* —1C **44**
Dorset Rd. *Sutt* —6M **61**
Dorset Rd. *Wind* —4F **4**
Dorset Sq. *Eps* —6C **60**
Dorset Vale. *Warf* —7C **16**
Dorset Way. *Byfl* —6M **55**
Dorset Way. *Twic* —2D **24**
Dorset Waye. *Houn* —3N **9**
Dorsten Pl. *Craw* —6L **181**
Dorsten Sq. *Craw* —6L **181**
Douai Clo. *F'boro* —1A **90**
Douai Gro. *Hamp* —9C **24**
Douglas Av. *N Mald* —3G **42**
Douglas Clo. *Guild* —6N **93**
Douglas Clo. *Wall* —3J **63**
Douglas Ct. *Big H* —4G **86**
Douglas Ct. *Cat* —9N **83**
Douglas Dri. *Croy* —9K **47**
Douglas Dri. *G'ming* —6J **133**
Douglas Gro. *Lwr Bo* —6H **129**
Douglas Ho. *Reig* —2M **121**
Douglas Ho. *Surb* —7M **41**
Douglas Houses. *Bookh* —2A **98**
Douglas Johnston Ho. SW6
(off Clem Attlee Ct.) —2L 13
Douglas La. *Wray* —8B **6**
Douglas Mans. *Houn* —6B **10**
Douglas Pl. *F'boro* —9M **69**
Douglas Rd. *Add* —9K **37**
Douglas Rd. *Esh* —8B **40**
Douglas Rd. *Houn* —6B **10**
Douglas Rd. *King T* —1A **42**
Douglas Rd. *Stai* —9M **7**
Douglas Rd. *Surb* —8M **41**
Douglas Robinson Ct. *SW16* —8J **29**
Douglas Sq. *Mord* —5M **43**
Doultons, The. *Stai* —7J **21**
Dounesforth Gdns. *SW18* —2N **27**
Dove Clo. *Craw* —1B **182**
Dove Clo. *S Croy* —7G **64**
Dove Cote Clo. *Wey* —9C **38**
Dovecote Gdns. *SW14* —6C **12**
Dovedale Clo. *Guild* —9C **94**
Dovedale Clo. *Owl* —5J **49**
Dovedale Cres. *Craw* —5N **181**
Dovedale Rise. *Mitc* —8D **28**
Dovehouse Grn. *Wey* —1E **56**
Dove M. *SW5* —1N **13**
Dover Ct. *Cranl* —7B **156**
Dovercourt Av. *T Hth* —4L **45**
Dovercourt La. *Sutt* —9A **44**
Doverfield Rd. *SW2* —1J **29**
Doverfield Rd. *Guild* —9C **94**
Dover Gdns. *Cars* —9D **44**
Dover Ho. Rd. *SW15* —7F **12**
Dover Pk. Dri. *SW15* —9G **12**
Dovers Grn. Rd. *Reig* —6N **121**
Doversmead. *Knap* —3H **73**
Doveton Rd. *S Croy* —2A **64**
Dowdeswell Clo. *SW15* —7D **12**
Dowding Ct. *Crowt* —1H **49**
Dowding Rd. *Big H* —2F **86**
Dower Av. *Wall* —5F **62**
Dower Pk. *Wind* —7B **4**
Dower Wlk. *Craw* —4M **181**
Dowes Ho. *SW16* —4J **29**
Dowlands La. *Small & Craw* —9A **144**
Dowlans Clo. *Bookh* —5A **98**
Dowlans Rd. *Bookh* —5B **98**
Dowman Clo. *SW19* —9N **27**
Downbury M. *SW18* —8M **13**
Downe Av. *Cud* —8L **67**
Downe Clo. *Horl* —6C **142**
Downer Meadow. *G'ming* —3H **133**
Downe Rd. *Cud* —9K **67**
Downe Rd. *Kes* —5F **66**
Downe Rd. *Mitc* —1D **44**
Downes Clo. *Twic* —9H **11**
Downe Ter. *Rich* —9L **11**
Downfield. *Wor Pk* —7E **42**
Down Hall Rd. *King T* —9K **25**
Downhurst Rd. *Ewh* —4F **156**
Downing Av. *Guild* —4J **113**
Downing St. *Farnh* —1G **129**
Downland Clo. *Eps* —5G **81**
Downland Ct. *Craw* —5A **182**
Downland Dri. *Craw* —5A **182**
Downland Gdns. *Eps* —5G **81**
Downland Pl. *Craw* —5A **182**
Downlands Clo. *Coul* —1F **82**
Downlands Rd. *Purl* —9J **63**
Downland Way. *Eps* —5G **81**
Down La. *Comp* —9E **112**
Downmill Rd. *Brack* —1L **31**
Down Pl. *W6* —1G **13**
Down Rd. *Guild* —3D **114**
Down Rd. *Tedd* —7H **25**
Downs Av. *Eps* —1D **80**
Downsbridge Rd. *Beck* —1N **17**
[illegible] Ct. [illegible] —9E **102**
Downs Ct. Rd. *Purl* —8M **63**
Downs Hill Rd. *Eps* —1D **80**
Downshire Way. *Brack* —1M **31**
(in two parts)
Downs Ho. Rd. *Eps* —5D **80**
Downside. *Brack* —2N **31**
Downside. *Cher* —7M **37**
Downside. *Eps* —1D **80**
Downside. *Hind* —2B **170**
Downside. *Sun* —9H **23**
Downside. *Twic* —4F **24**
Downside Bri. Rd. *Cobh* —1J **77**
Downside Clo. *SW19* —7A **28**
Downside Comn. Rd. *D'side* —5J **77**
Downside Ct. *Mers* —7G **102**
Downside Ind. Est. *Cher* —7H **37**
Downside Orchard. *Wok* —4C **74**
Downside Rd. *D'side* —3J **77**
Downside Rd. *Guild* —4D **114**
Downside Rd. *Sutt* —3B **62**
Downs La. *Lea* —1H **99**
Downs Link. *Chil* —8F **114**
Downs Lodge Ct. *Eps* —1D **80**
Downsman Ct. *Craw* —6B **182**
Downs Rd. *Beck* —1L **47**
Downs Rd. *Coul* —5H **83**
Downs Rd. *Eps* —1D **80**
(Epsom)
Downs Rd. *Eps* —7A **80**
(Langley Bottom)
Downs Rd. *Mick* —6J **99**
Downs Rd. *Purl* —7M **63**
Downs Rd. *Sutt* —6N **61**
Downs Rd. *T Hth* —9N **29**
Downs Side. *Sutt* —7L **61**
Downs, The. *SW20* —8J **27**
Downs, The. *Lea* —3H **99**
Down St. *W Mol* —4A **40**
Downs View. *Dork* —3K **119**
Downs View. *Iswth* —4F **10**
Downs View. *Tad* —8G **80**
Downsview Av. *Wok* —8B **74**
Downsview Clo. *D'side* —6J **77**
Downsview Ct. *Guild* —8M **93**
Downsview Gdns. *SE19* —8M **29**
Downsview Gdns. *Dork* —6H **119**
Downsview Rd. *SE19* —8N **29**
Downs View Rd. *Bookh* —5C **98**
Downsview Rd. *Head* —4H **169**
Downsview Rd. *H'ham* —2A **198**
Downs Way. *Bookh* —4C **98**
Downs Way. *Eps* —3E **80**
Downsway. *Guild* —3G **114**
Downsway. *Orp* —2N **67**
Downs Way. *Oxt* —5A **106**
Downsway. *S Croy* —7B **64**
Downs Way. *Tad* —8G **80**
Downsway. *Whyt* —3C **84**
Downs Way Clo. *Tad* —8F **80**
Downsway, The. *Sutt* —5A **62**
Downs Wood. *Eps* —4G **80**
Downswood. *Reig* —9B **102**
Downton Av. *SW2* —3J **29**
Downview Clo. *Hind* —3B **170**
Down Yhonda. *Elst* —8G **130**
Doyle Gdns. *Yat* —2B **68**
Doyle Rd. *SE25* —3D **46**
D'Oyly Carte Island. *Wey* —7C **38**
Draco Ga. *SW15* —6H **13**
Dragmire La. *Mitc* —3B **44**
Dragon La. *Wey* —7B **56**
Dragoon Ct. *Alder* —2K **109**
Drake Av. *Cat* —9N **83**
Drake Av. *Myt* —4E **90**
Drake Av. *Slou* —1N **5**
Drake Av. *Stai* —6H **21**
Drake Clo. *Brack* —4N **31**
Drake Clo. *H'ham* —2L **197**
Drakefield Rd. *SW17* —4E **28**
Drake Rd. *Chess* —2N **59**
Drake Rd. *Craw* —6C **182**
Drake Rd. *Croy* —6K **45**
Drake Rd. *Horl* —8C **142**
Drake Rd. *Mitc* —5E **44**
Drakes Clo. *Cranl* —7N **155**
Drake's Clo. *Esh* —1A **58**
Drakes Way. *Wok* —9N **73**
Drakewood Rd. *SW16* —8H **29**
Drax Av. *SW20* —8F **26**
Draxmont App. *SW19* —7K **27**
Draycot Rd. *Surb* —7N **41**
Draycott. *Brack* —4C **32**
Dray Ct. *Guild* —4L **113**
Dray Ct. *Wor Pk* —8F **42**
Drayhorse Dri. *Bag* —5J **51**
Draymans Way. *Iswth* —6F **10**
Drayton Clo. *Brack* —1B **32**
Drayton Clo. *Fet* —2E **98**
Drayton Clo. *Houn* —8N **9**
Drayton Gdns. *SW10* —1N **13**
Drayton Rd. *Croy* —8M **45**
Dresden Way. *Wey* —2D **56**
Drew Ho. *SW16* —4J **29**
Drewitts Ct. *W on T* —7G **39**
Drew Pl. *Cat* —1A **104**
Drewstead Rd. *SW16* —3H **29**
Drift Bridge (Junct.) [illegible] **81**
Drift La. *Stoke D* —4N **77**
Drift Rd. *E Hor* —2F **96**
Drift Rd. *Wink* —1L **17**
Drift, The. *Brom* —1F **66**
Drift Way. *Coln* —4E **6**
Driftway, The. *Bans* —2H **81**
Driftway, The. *Craw* —2B **182**
Driftway, The. *Lea* —1H **99**
(in two parts)
Driftway, The. *Mitc* —9E **28**
Driftwood Dri. *Kenl* —4N **83**
Drill Hall Rd. *Cher* —6J **37**
Drive Mans. SW6 —5K 13
(off Fulham Rd.)
Drive Mead. *Coul* —1J **83**
Drive Rd. *Coul* —7H **83**
Drivers Mead. *Ling* —8M **145**
Drive Spur. *Tad* —8N **81**
Drive, The. *SW16* —2K **45**
Drive, The. *SW20* —8H **27**
Drive, The. *Ashf* —8E **22**
Drive, The. *Bans* —3L **81**
Drive, The. *Beck* —1K **47**
Drive, The. *Cobh* —1M **77**
Drive, The. *Copt* —7N **163**
Drive, The. *Coul* —1J **83**
Drive, The. *Cranl* —8A **156**
Drive, The. *Dat* —4L **5**
Drive, The. *Eps* —3E **60**
Drive, The. *Esh* —7C **40**
Drive, The. *Felt* —1K **23**
Drive, The. *Fet* —9E **78**
Drive, The. *G'ming* —9J **133**
Drive, The. *Guild* —3J **113**
(Beech Gro.)
Drive, The. *Guild* —5K **113**
(Farnham Rd.)
Drive, The. *Guild* —7L **113**
(Sandy La.)
Drive, The. *Horl* —1F **162**
Drive, The. *H'ham* —2D **180**
Drive, The. *Houn & Iswth* —5D **10**
Drive, The. *Ifold* —5F **192**
Drive, The. *King T* —8B **26**
Drive, The. *Lea* —1M **99**
Drive, The. *Mord* —4B **44**
Drive, The. *Pep H & Lwr E* —7B **132**
(in two parts)
Drive, The. *Surb* —6L **41**
Drive, The. *Sutt* —7M **61**
Drive, The. *T Hth* —3A **46**
Drive, The. *Vir W* —4B **36**
Drive, The. *Wall* —5H **63**
Drive, The. *W Wick* —6N **47**
Drive, The. *Wok* —7L **73**
Drive, The. *Won* —5D **134**
Drive, The. *Wray* —8N **5**
Drodges Clo. *Brmly* —3B **134**
Droitwich Clo. *Brack* —2B **32**
Dromore Rd. *SW15* —9K **13**
Drove Rd. *Alb* —5N **115**
Drove Rd. *Guild* —5H **115**
Drovers End. *Fleet* —1D **88**
Drovers Rd. *S Croy* —2A **64**
Drovers Way. *Ash* —3G **111**
Drovers Way. *Brack* —2D **32**
Drovers Way. *Farnh* —6F **108**
Druce Wood. *Asc* —9J **17**
Druids Clo. *Asht* —7M **79**
Druids Way. *Brom* —3N **47**
Drumaline Ridge. *Wor Pk* —8D **42**
Drummond Cen. *Croy* —8N **45**
Drummond Clo. *Brack* —9D **16**
Drummond Gdns. *Eps* —7B **60**
Drummond Pl. *Croy* —8N **45**
Drummond Rd. *Croy* —8N **45**
Drummond Rd. *Guild* —3N **113**
Drummond Rd. *If'd* —4K **181**
Drungewick La. *Loxw* —9L **193**
Drury Clo. *M'bowr* —5H **183**
Drury Cres. *Croy* —8L **45**
Dryad St. *SW15* —6J **13**
Dry Arch Rd. *Asc* —5C **34**
Dryburgh Rd. *SW15* —6G **13**
Dryden. *Brack* —6M **31**
Dryden Mans. W14 —2K 13
(off Queen's Club Gdns.)
Dryden Rd. *SW19* —7A **28**
Dryden Rd. *F'boro* —8L **69**
Drynham Pk. *Wey* —9F **38**
Du Cane Ct. *SW12* —2E **28**
Ducavel Ho. *SW2* —2K **29**
Duchess of Kent Barracks. *Alder* —1N **109**
Ducklands. *Bord* —7A **168**
Ducks Wlk. *Twic* —8J **11**
Dudley Clo. *Add* —9L **37**
Dudley Ct. *C Crook* —8B **88**
Dudley Dri. *Mord* —7K **43**
Dudley Gro. *Eps* —1B **80**
Dudley Rd. *SW19* —7M **27**
Dudley Rd. *Ashf* —5A **22**
Dudley Rd. *Felt* —2D **22**
Dudley Rd. *King T* —2M **41**
Dudley Rd. *Rich* —5M **11**
Dudley Rd. *W On T* —5H **39**
Dudset La. *Houn* —4H **9**
Duffield Rd. *Tad* —[illegible]
Duffins Orchard. *Ott* —4E **54**
Dugdale Ho. Egh —6E 20
(off Pooley Grn. Rd.)
Duke Clo. *M'bowr* —7G **182**
Duke of Cambridge Clo. *Twic* —9D **10**
Duke of Connaught's Rd. *Alder* —6A **90**
(in two parts)
Duke of Cornwall Av. *Camb* —6B **50**
Duke of Edinburgh Rd. *Sutt* —8B **44**
Duke Rd. *W4* —1C **12**
Duke's Av. *W4* —1C **12**
Dukes Av. *Houn* —7M **9**
Dukes Av. *N Mald* —2E **42**
Dukes Av. *Rich & King T* —5J **25**
Dukes Clo. *Ashf* —5D **22**
Dukes Clo. *Cranl* —4B **156**
Dukes Clo. *Farnh* —6F **108**
Dukes Clo. *Hamp* —6N **23**
Dukes Ct. *Wok* —4B **74**
Dukes Covert. *Bag* —1J **51**
Dukes Grn. Av. *Felt* —8H **9**
Dukes Head Pas. *Hamp* —8C **24**
Dukes Hill. *Wold* —7H **85**
Dukeshill Rd. *Brack* —9N **15**
Dukes La. *Asc* —8D **18**
Dukes Pk. *Alder* —7B **90**
Duke's Ride. *Crowt* —3D **48**
Dukes Ride. *N Holm* —8K **119**
Duke's Rd. *Newd* —4B **160**
Dukes Rd. *W On T* —2L **57**
Duke's Ter. *Alder* —1N **109**
Duke St. *Rich* —7K **11**
Duke St. *Sutt* —1B **62**
Duke St. *Wind* —3F **4**
Duke St. *Wok* —4B **74**
Dukes Wlk. *Farnh* —6F **108**
Dukes Way. *W Wick* —9N **47**
Dukes Wood. *Crowt* —2G **49**
(in two parts)
Dulverton Rd. *S Croy* —6F **64**
Dumas Clo. *Yat* —1B **68**
Du Maurier Clo. *C Crook* —1A **108**
Dumbarton Ct. *SW2* —1J **29**
Dumbarton Rd. *SW2* —1J **29**
Dumbleton Clo. *King T* —9A **26**
Dumsey Eyot. *Cher* —6N **37**
Dumville Dri. *God* —9E **104**
Dunally Pk. *Shep* —6E **38**
Dunbar Av. *SW16* —1L **45**
Dunbar Av. *Beck* —3H **47**
Dunbar Ct. *W on T* —7K **39**
Dunbar Rd. *Frim* —7D **70**
Dunbar Rd. *N Mald* —3B **42**
Dunbar St. *SE27* —4N **29**
Dunboe Pl. *Shep* —6D **38**
Dunbridge Ho. SW15 —9E 12
(off Highcliffe Dri.)
Duncan Dri. *Guild* —2C **114**
Duncan Dri. *Wokgm* —3C **30**
Duncan Gdns. *Stai* —7J **21**
Duncannon Cres. *Wind* —6A **4**
Duncan Rd. *Rich* —7L **11**
Duncan Rd. *Tad* —6K **81**
Duncans Yd. *W'ham* —4M **107**
Duncombe Rd. *G'ming* —9G **133**
Duncroft. *Stai* —5G **20**
Duncroft. *Wind* —6C **4**
Duncroft Clo. *Reig* —2L **121**
Dunction Clo. *Craw* —1N **181**
Dundaff Clo. *Camb* —1E **70**
Dundas Clo. *Brack* —3N **31**
Dundas Gdns. *W Mol* —2B **40**
Dundee Rd. *SE25* —4E **46**
Dundela Gdns. *Wor Pk* —1G **61**
Dundonald Rd. *SW19* —8K **27**
Dundrey Cres. *Red* —7J **103**
Dunedin Dri. *Cat* —3B **104**
Dunelm Gro. *SE27* —4N **29**
Dunfee Way. *W Byf* —8N **55**
Dunfold Comn. *Duns* —5B **174**
Dunford Pl. *Binf* —8K **15**
Dungarvan Av. *SW15* —7F **12**
Dungates La. *Bkld* —2F **120**
Dungells Farm Clo. *Yat* —2C **68**
Dungells La. *Yat* —2B **68**
Dunheved Clo. *T Hth* —5L **45**
Dunheved Rd. N. *T Hth* —5L **45**
Dunheved Rd. S. *T Hth* —5L **45**
Dunheved Rd. W. *T Hth* —5L **45**
Dunkeld Rd. *SE25* —3A **46**
Dunkirk St. *SE27* —5N **29**
Dunleary Clo. *Houn* —1N **23**
Dunley Dri. *New Ad* —4L **65**
Dunlin Clo. *Red* —8C **122**
Dunlin Rise. *Guild* —1F **114**
Dunmail Dri. *Purl* —1B **84**
Dunmore. *Guild* —2G **113**
Dunmore Rd. *SW20* —9H **27**
Dunmow Clo. *Felt* —4M **23**
Dunmow Hill. *Fleet* —3B **88**
Dunnets. *Knap* —4H **73**
Dunnimans Rd. *Bans* —2L **81**
Dunning's Rd. *E Grin* —3A **186**
Dunnottar Clo. *Red* —5B **122**
Dunnymans Rd. *Bans* —2L **81**
Dunraven Av. *Red* —1F [illegible]
Dunsbury Clo. *Sutt* —9N **61**
Dunsdon Av. *Guild* —4L **113**
Dunsfold Aerodrome. *Duns* —4F **174**
Dunsfold Clo. *Craw* —4M **181**
Dunsfold Rise. *Coul* —9H **63**
Dunsfold Rd. *Alf* —5E **174**
Dunsfold Rd. *Loxh & Cranl* —1C **174**
Dunsfold Rd. *Plais* —2N **191**
Dunsfold Way. *New Ad* —5L **65**
Dunsford Way. *SW15* —9G **13**
Dunsmore Gdns. *Yat* —1A **68**
Dunsmore Rd. *W On T* —5J **39**
Dunstable Rd. *Rich* —7L **11**
Dunstable Rd. *W Mol* —3N **39**
Dunstall Pk. *F'boro* —7M **69**
Dunstall Rd. *SW20* —7G **27**
Dunstall Way. *W Mol* —2B **40**
Dunstan Rd. *Coul* —4H **83**
Dunster Av. *Mord* —7J **43**
Dunton Clo. *Surb* —7L **41**
Duntshill Rd. *SW18* —2N **27**
Dunvegan Clo. *W Mol* —3B **40**
Dunvegan Ho. *Red* —3D **122**
Dupont Rd. *SW20* —1J **43**
Duppas Av. *Croy* —1M **63**
Duppas Clo. *Shep* —4E **38**
Duppas Hill La. *Croy* —1M **63**
Duppas Hill Rd. *Croy* —1L **63**
Duppas Hill Ter. *Croy* —9M **45**
Duppas Rd. *Croy* —9L **45**
Durand Clo. *Cars* —7D **44**
Durban Rd. *SE27* —5N **29**
Durban Rd. *Beck* —1J **47**
Durbin Rd. *Chess* —1L **59**
Durfold Dri. *Reig* —3A **122**
Durfold Hill. *H'ham* —6H **179**
Durfold Rd. *H'ham* —1J **197**
Durfold Wood. *Plais* —2M **191**
Durford Cres. *SW15* —2G **26**
Durham Av. *Houn* —1N **9**
Durham Clo. *SW20* —1G **43**
Durham Clo. *Craw* —7C **182**
(in two parts)
Durham Clo. *Guild* —1J **113**
Durham Ct. *Tedd* —5D **24**
Durham Rd. *SW20* —9G **27**
Durham Rd. *Felt* —1K **23**
Durham Rd. *Owl* —5K **49**
Durham Wharf. *Bren* —3J **11**
Durkins Rd. *E Grin* —7N **165**
(in two parts)
Durleston Pk. Dri. *Bookh* —3C **98**
Durley Mead. *Brack* —4D **32**
Durlston Rd. *King T* —7L **25**
Durning Pl. *Asc* —2M **33**
Durnsford Av. *SW19* —3M **27**
Durnsford Av. *Fleet* —6B **88**
Durnsford Rd. *SW19* —3M **27**
Durnsford Way. *Cranl* —8A **156**
Durrant Way. *Orp* —2M **67**
Durrell Rd. *SW6* —5L **13**
Durrell Way. *Shep* —5E **38**
Durrington Av. *SW20* —8H **27**
Durrington Pk. Rd. *SW20* —9H **27**
Dutch Barn Clo. *Stai* —9M **7**
Dutchells Copse. *H'ham* —2L **197**
Dutch Elm Av. *Wind* —3J **5**
Dutch Gdns. *King T* —7A **26**
Dutch Yd. *SW18* —8M **13**
Duval Pl. *Bag* —4J **51**
Duxberry Av. *Felt* —4K **23**

Elmshaw Rd.—Falcourt Clo.

Elmshaw Rd. *SW15* —8F **12**
Elmshorn. *Eps* —3H **81**
Elmside. *Guild* —4K **113**
Elmside. *Milf* —1C **152**
Elmside. *New Ad* —3L **65**
Elmsleigh Cen., The. *Stai* —5H **21**
Elmsleigh Ct. *Sutt* —9N **43**
*Elmsleigh Ho. Twic —3D **24***
(off Staines Rd.)
Elmsleigh Rd. *F'boro* —1L **89**
Elmsleigh Rd. *Stai* —6H **21**
Elmsleigh Rd. *Twic* —3D **24**
Elmslie Clo. *Eps* —1B **80**
Elms Rd. *Alder* —3M **109**
Elms Rd. *Fleet* —4D **88**
Elms Rd. *Wokgm* —3A **30**
Elmstead Clo. *Eps* —2D **60**
Elmstead Gdns. *Wor Pk* —9F **42**
Elmstead Rd. *W Byf* —9J **55**
Elms, The. *SW13* —6E **12**
Elms, The. *B'water* —2J **69**
Elms, The. *Clay* —4F **58**
Elms, The. *Tong* —4D **110**
Elms, The. *Warf P* —7E **16**
Elmstone Rd. *SW6* —4M **13**
Elmsway. *Ashf* —6B **22**
Elmswood. *Bookh* —2N **97**
Elmsworth Av. *Houn* —5B **10**
Elm Tree Av. *Esh* —6D **40**
Elm Tree Clo. *Ashf* —6C **22**
Elm Tree Clo. *Byfl* —9N **55**
Elm Tree Clo. *Cher* —8G **37**
Elm Tree Clo. *Horl* —7E **142**
Elmtree Rd. *Tedd* —5E **24**
Elm View. *Ash* —1F **110**
Elm View Ho. *Hayes* —1F **8**
Elm Wlk. *SW20* —9H **10**
Elm Wlk. *Orp* —1H **67**
Elm Way. *Eps* —2C **60**
Elm Way. *Wor Pk* —9H **43**
Elmwood Av. *Felt* —3H **23**
Elmwood Clo. *Asht* —4K **79**
Elmwood Clo. *Eps* —4F **60**
Elmwood Clo. *Wall* —8F **44**
Elmwood Ct. *Asht* —4K **79**
Elmwood Dri. *Eps* —3F **60**
Elmwood Rd. *W4* —2B **12**
Elmwood Rd. *Croy* —6M **45**
Elmwood Rd. *Mitc* —2D **44**
Elmwood Rd. *Red* —8E **102**
Elmwood Rd. *Wok* —6G **73**
Elmworth Gro. *SE21* —3N **29**
Elphinstone Ct. *SW16* —7J **29**
Elsa Ct. *Beck* —1J **47**
Elsdon Rd. *Wok* —5K **73**
Elsenham St. *SW18* —2L **27**
Elsenwood Cres. *Camb* —8E **50**
Elsenwood Dri. *Camb* —8E **50**
Elsinore Av. *Stai* —2N **21**
Elsinore Way. *Rich* —6A **12**
Elsley Clo. *Frim G* —8D **70**
Elsrick Av. *Mord* —4M **43**
Elstan Way. *Croy* —6H **47**
Elstead Ct. *Sutt* —7K **43**
*Elstead Ho. SW2 —1K **29***
(off Redlands Way)
Elstead Rd. *Seale* —7E **110**
Elstead Rd. *Shack* —6N **131**
Elsted Clo. *Craw* —1N **181**
Elston Pl. *Alder* —4A **110**
Elston Rd. *Alder* —4A **110**
Elswick St. *SW6* —5N **13**
Elsworth Clo. *Felt* —2F **22**
Elsworthy. *Th Dit* —5E **40**
Elthiron Rd. *SW6* —4M **13**
Elthorne Ct. *Felt* —2K **23**
Elton Clo. *King T* —8J **25**
Elton Rd. *King T* —9M **25**
Elton Rd. *Purl* —8G **62**
Eltringham St. *SW18* —7N **13**
Elveden Clo. *Wok* —4K **75**
Elvedon Rd. *Cobh* —7J **57**
Elvetham Clo. *Fleet* —2B **88**
Elvetham Pl. *Fleet* —2A **88**
Elvetham Rd. *Fleet* —2A **88**
Elwell Clo. *Egh* —7C **20**
Elwill Way. *Beck* —3M **47**
Ely Clo. *SW20* —1E **42**
Ely Clo. *Craw* —7D **182**
Ely Clo. *Frim* —7E **70**
Ely Clo. *N Mald* —1E **42**
Ely Pl. *Guild* —1J **113**
Ely Rd. *Croy* —4A **46**
Ely Rd. *Houn* —6K **9**
Ely Rd. *H'row A* —5G **8**
*Elysium Pl. SW6 —5L **13***
(off Elysium St.)
Elysium St. *SW6* —5L **13**
Elystan Clo. *Wall* —4G **62**
Emanuel Dri. *Hamp* —6N **23**
Embankment. *SW15* —5J **13**
Embankment, The. *Twic* —2G **25**
Embankment, The. *Wray* —2M **19**
Embassy Ct. *Wall* —3F **62**
Ember Cen. *W on T* —8M **39**
Ember Clo. *Add* —2N **55**
Ember Ct. Rd. *Th Dit* —5E **40**
Ember Farm Av. *E Mol* —5D **40**
Ember Farm Way. *E Mol* —5D **40**
Ember Gdns. *Th Dit* —6E **40**
Ember La. *Esh & E Mol* —6D **40**
Emberwood. *Craw* —1A **182**
Embleton Rd. *Head* —3G **168**
Embleton Wlk. *Hamp* —6N **23**
Emden St. *SW6* —4N **13**
Emerald Ct. *Coul* —2H **83**
Emerson Ct. *Crowt* —2G **49**
Emerton Rd. *Fet* —8C **78**
Emery Down Clo. *Brack* —2E **32**
Emley Rd. *Add* —9J **37**
Emlyn La. *Lea* —9G **79**
Emlyn Rd. *Horl* —7C **142**
Emlyn Rd. *Red* —5E **122**
Emmanuel Clo. *Guild* —9K **93**
Emmanuel Rd. *SW12* —2G **28**
Emmets Nest. *Binf* —7H **15**
Emmets Pk. *Binf* —7H **15**
Emmetts Clo. *Wok* —4N **73**
Emms Pl. *King T* —1K **41**
Empire Vs. *Red* —4E **142**
Empress Av. *F'boro* —9N **69**
Empress Pl. *SW6* —1M **13**
Emsworth Clo. *M'bowr* —6G **183**
Emsworth Ct. *SW16* —4J **29**
Emsworth St. *SW2* —3K **29**
Ena Rd. *SW16* —2J **45**
Enborne Gdns. *Brack* —8B **16**
Endale Clo. *Cars* —8D **44**
Endeavour Way. *SW19* —5N **27**
Endeavour Way. *Croy* —6J **45**
Endlesham Rd. *SW12* —1E **28**
Endsleigh Clo. *S Croy* —6F **64**
Endsleigh Gdns. *Surb* —5J **41**
Endsleigh Gdns. *W On T* —2K **57**
Endsleigh Rd. *Red* —7G **102**
Ends Pl. *Warn* —9C **178**
End Way. *Surb* —6N **41**
Endymion Rd. *SW2* —1K **29**
Enfield Rd. *Ash V* —8F **90**
Enfield Rd. *Bren* —1K **11**
Enfield Rd. *Craw* —7N **181**
Enfield Rd. *H'row A* —5F **8**
Enfield Wlk. *Bren* —1K **11**
Engadine Clo. *Croy* —9C **46**
Engadine St. *SW18* —2M **27**
Engalee. *E Grin* —8M **165**
Englefield. *H'ham* —6E **196**
Englefield Clo. *Croy* —5N **45**
Englefield Clo. *Egh* —7M **19**
Englefield Rd. *Knap* —4G **72**
Engleheart Dri. *Felt* —9G **9**
Englehurst. *Egh* —7M **19**
Englemere Rd. *Brack* —8L **15**
Englesfield. *Camb* —1G **71**
Englewood Rd. *SW12* —1G **28**
Engliff La. *Wok* —3J **75**
English Gdns. *Wray* —8N **5**
Enmore Av. *SE25* —4D **46**
Enmore Gdns. *SW14* —8C **12**
Enmore Rd. *SE25* —4D **46**
Enmore Rd. *SW15* —7H **13**
Ennerdale. *Brack* —3M **31**
Ennerdale Clo. *Craw* —5N **181**
Ennerdale Clo. *Felt* —2G **22**
Ennerdale Clo. *Sutt* —1L **61**
Ennerdale Gro. *Farnh* —6F **108**
Ennerdale Rd. *Rich* —5M **11**
Ennismore Av. *W4* —1E **12**
Ennismore Av. *Guild* —3B **114**
Ennismore Gdns. *Th Dit* —5E **40**
Ennor Ct. *Sutt* —1H **61**
Ensign Clo. *Purl* —6L **63**
Ensign Clo. *Stai* —2M **21**
Ensign Way. *Stai* —2M **21**
Enterdent Cotts. *God* —2G **124**
Enterdent Rd. *God* —3F **124**
Enterdent, The. *God* —2G **124**
Enterprise Clo. *Croy* —7L **45**
Enterprise Est. *Guild* —8A **94**
Enterprise Ho. *H'ham* —7H **197**
Enterprise Ind. Est. *Ash V* —6D **90**
Enterprise Way. *SW18* —7M **13**
Enterprise Way. *Eden* —9K **127**
Enterprise Way. *Tedd* —7F **24**
Enton La. *Ent* —7E **152**
Envis Way. *Guild* —8F **92**
Epirus M. *SW6* —3M **13**
Epirus Rd. *SW6* —3L **13**
Epping Wlk. *Craw* —5D **182**
Epping Way. *Brack* —3D **32**
Epple Rd. *SW6* —4L **13**
Epsom Bus. Pk. *Eps* —7D **60**
Epsom Clo. *Camb* —7A **50**
Epsom Downs Metro Cen. *Tad* —7G **81**
Epsom Gap. *Lea* —2H **79**
Epsom La. N. *Eps & Tad* —5G **80**
Epsom La. S. *Tad* —8H **81**
Epsom Pl. *Cranl* —7A **156**
Epsom Rd. *Asht* —5M **79**
Epsom Rd. *Craw* —5E **182**
Epsom Rd. *Croy* —1L **63**
Epsom Rd. *Eps* —7E **60**
Epsom Rd. *Guild & E Clan* —4A **114**
Epsom Rd. *Lea* —8H **79**
Epsom Rd. *Sutt & Mord* —6L **43**
Epsom Rd. *W Hor* —8C **96**
Epsom Sq. *H'row A* —5G **8**
Epworth Rd. *Iswth* —3H **11**
Eresby Dri. *Beck* —7K **47**
Erfstadt Ct. *Wokgm* —3B **30**
Erica Clo. *W End* —9B **52**
Erica Ct. *Wok* —5N **73**
Erica Dri. *Wokgm* —3C **30**
Erica Gdns. *Croy* —9L **47**
Erica Way. *Copt* —7L **163**
Erica Way. *H'ham* —3K **197**
Ericcson Clo. *SW18* —8M **13**
Eridge Clo. *Craw* —3G **182**
Eriswell Cres. *W On T* —3F **56**
Eriswell Rd. *W On T* —2G **57**
Erkenwald Clo. *Cher* —5G **37**
Ermine Clo. *Houn* —5K **9**
Ermyn Clo. *Lea* —8K **79**
Ermyn Cotts. *Horl* —5D **144**
Ermyn Way. *Lea* —8K **79**
Erncroft Way. *Twic* —9F **10**
Ernest Av. *SE27* —5M **29**
Ernest Clo. *Beck* —4K **47**
Ernest Clo. *Lwr Bo* —5G **129**
Ernest Gdns. *W4* —2A **12**
Ernest Gro. *Beck* —4J **47**
Ernest Rd. *King T* —1A **42**
Ernest Sq. *King T* —1A **42**
Ernle Rd. *SW20* —8G **27**
Ernshaw Pl. *SW15* —8K **13**
Erpingham Rd. *SW15* —6H **13**
Erridge Rd. *SW19* —1M **43**
Errington Dri. *Wind* —4D **4**
Errol Gdns. *N Mald* —3F **42**
Erskine Clo. *Craw* —7K **181**
Erskine Clo. *Sutt* —9C **44**
Erskine Rd. *Sutt* —1B **62**
Esam Way. *SW16* —6L **29**
Escombe Dri. *Guild* —7L **93**
Escot Rd. *Sun* —8G **22**
Escott Pl. *Ott* —3E **54**
Esher Av. *Sutt* —9J **43**
Esher Av. *W On T* —6H **39**
Esher By-Pass. *Cobh & Esh* —9G **57**
Esher Clo. *Esh* —2B **58**
Esher Common. (Junct.) —6C **58**
Esher Cres. *H'row A* —5G **8**
Esher Gdns. *SW19* —3J **27**
Esher Grn. *Esh* —1B **58**
Esher Grn. Dri. *Esh* —1B **58**
Esher M. *Mitc* —2E **44**
Esher Pk. Av. *Esh* —1B **58**
Esher Pl. Av. *Esh* —1B **58**
Esher Rd. *Camb* —6E **50**
Esher Rd. *E Mol* —5D **40**
Esher Rd. *W On T* —2L **57**
Eskdale Gdns. *Purl* —1A **84**
Eskdale Way. *Camb* —2H **71**
Esmond St. *SW15* —7K **13**
Esparto St. *SW18* —1N **27**
Essame Clo. *Wokgm* —2C **30**
Essendene Clo. *Cat* —1B **104**
Essendene Rd. *Cat* —1B **104**
Essenden Rd. *S Croy* —4B **64**
Essex Av. *Iswth* —6E **10**
Essex Clo. *Add* —1L **55**
Essex Clo. *Frim* —7E **70**
Essex Clo. *Mord* —6J **43**
Essex Ct. *SW13* —5E **12**
Essex Dri. *Cranl* —8H **155**
Essex Pl. *W4* —1B **12**
Essex Pl. Sq. *W4* —1C **12**
Essex Rise. *Warf* —8D **16**
Essex Rd. *W4* —1C **12**
(in two parts)
Estate Cotts. *Mick* —5K **99**
Estcots Dri. *E Grin* —9B **166**
Estcourt Rd. *SE25* —5E **46**
Estcourt Rd. *SW6* —3L **13**
Estella Av. *N Mald* —3G **43**
Estoria Clo. *SW2* —1L **29**
Estreham Rd. *SW16* —7H **29**
Estridge Clo. *Houn* —7A **10**
Eswyn Rd. *SW17* —5D **28**
Etchworth Av. *Felt* —1G **22**
Eternit Wlk. *SW6* —4J **13**
Ethel Bailey Clo. *Eps* —8N **59**
Ethelbert Rd. *SW20* —9J **27**
Ethelbert St. *SW12* —2F **28**
Ethel Rd. *Ashf* —6N **21**
Etherley Hill. *Ockl* —3A **158**
Etherstone Grn. *SW16* —5L **29**
Etherstone Rd. *SW16* —5L **29**
Eton Av. *Houn* —2N **9**
Eton Av. *N Mald* —4C **42**
Eton Clo. *SW18* —1N **27**
Eton Clo. *Dat* —2K **5**
Eton Ct. *Eton* —3G **4**
Eton Ct. *Stai* —6H **21**
Eton Pl. *Farnh* —5G **108**
Eton Rd. *Dat* —1J **5**
Eton Rd. *Hayes* —3G **8**
Eton Sq. *Eton* —3G **4**
Eton St. *Rich* —8L **11**
Eton Wick Rd. *Eton W* —1B **4**
Etwell Pl. *Surb* —5M **41**
Eureka Rd. *King T* —1N **41**
Europa Pk. Rd. *Guild* —2M **113**
Eustace Cres. *Wokgm* —9C **14**
Eustace Rd. *SW6* —3M **13**
Eustace Rd. *Guild* —1F **114**
Euston Rd. *Croy* —7L **45**
Evans Clo. *Craw* —5H **183**
Evans Gro. *Felt* —3A **24**
Evans Ho. *Felt* —3A **24**
Evedon. *Brack* —6N **31**
Eveline Rd. *Mitc* —9D **28**
Evelyn Av. *Alder* —4N **109**
Evelyn Av. *T'sey* —2E **106**
Evelyn Clo. *Twic* —1B **24**
Evelyn Clo. *Wok* —7N **73**
Evelyn Cotts. *Dork* —3L **137**
Evelyn Cotts. *God* —6H **125**
Evelyn Cres. *Sun* —9G **22**
Evelyn Gdns. *God* —8F **104**
Evelyn Gdns. *Rich* —7L **11**
*Evelyn Mans. W14 —2K **13***
(off Queen's Club Gdns.)
Evelyn Rd. *SW19* —6N **27**
Evelyn Rd. *Ham* —4J **25**
Evelyn Rd. *Rich* —6L **11**
Evelyn Ter. *Rich* —6L **11**
Evelyn Wlk. *Craw* —6C **182**
Evelyn Way. *Stoke D* —3N **77**
Evelyn Way. *Sun* —9G **22**
Evelyn Way. *Wall* —1H **63**
Evelyn Wood's Rd. *Alder* —6A **90**
Evendon's Clo. *Wokgm* —5A **30**
Evendon's La. *Wokgm* —5A **30**
Evenlode Way. *Sand* —7H **49**
Evenwood Clo. *SW15* —8K **13**
Everall Av. *SW6* —5N **13**
Everall Pk. *Farnh* —1H **129**
Everard La. *Cat* —9E **84**
Everatt Clo. *SW18* —9L **13**
Everdon Rd. *SW13* —2F **12**
Everest Ct. *Wok* —3H **70**
Everest Rd. *Camb* —7B **50**
Everest Rd. *Crowt* —1G **49**
Everest Rd. *Stai* —1M **21**
Everglade. *Big H* —5F **86**
Evergreen Ct. *Stai* —1M **21**
Evergreen Oak Av. *Wind* —6K **5**
Evergreen Rd. *Frim* —4D **70**
Evergreen Way. *Stai* —1M **21**
Everington St. *W6* —2J **13**
Everlands Clo. *Wok* —5A **74**
Eve Rd. *Iswth* —7G **11**
Eve Rd. *Wok* —2D **74**
Eversfield Rd. *H'ham* —7L **197**
Eversfield Rd. *Reig* —3N **121**
Eversfield Rd. *Rich* —5M **11**
Eversley Cres. *Iswth* —4D **10**
Eversley Pk. *SW19* —7G **26**
Eversley Rd. *SE19* —8N **29**
Eversley Rd. *Surb* —3M **41**
Eversley Rd. *Yat* —8A **48**
Eversley Way. *Croy* —9K **47**
Eversley Way. *Egh* —1E **36**
Everton Rd. *Croy* —7D **46**
Evesham Clo. *Reig* —2L **121**
Evesham Clo. *Sutt* —4M **61**
Evesham Ct. *Rich* —9M **11**
Evesham Grn. *Mord* —5N **43**
Evesham Rd. *Mord* —5N **43**
Evesham Rd. *Reig* —2L **121**
Evesham Rd. N. *Reig* —2L **121**
Evesham Wlk. *Owl* —6J **49**
Ewald Rd. *SW6* —5L **13**
Ewelands. *Horl* —7G **142**
Ewell By-Pass. *Eps* —4F **60**
Ewell Ct. Av. *Ewe* —2D **60**
Ewell Downs Rd. *Eps* —7F **60**
Ewell Ho. Gro. *Eps* —6E **60**
Ewell Pk. Gdns. *Eps* —4F **60**
Ewell Pk. Way. *Eps* —3F **60**
Ewell Rd. *Dit H* —6H **41**
Ewell Rd. *Surb* —5L **41**
Ewell Rd. *Sutt* —4J **61**
Ewen Cres. *SW2* —2L **29**
Ewhurst Av. *S Croy* —5C **64**
Ewhurst Clo. *Craw* —3A **182**
Ewhurst Clo. *Sutt* —5H **61**
Ewhurst Rd. *Cranl* —7N **155**
Ewhurst Rd. *Craw* —3N **181**
Ewhurst Rd. *Peasl* —5E **136**
Ewins Clo. *Ash* —2E **110**
Ewood La. *Newd* —5M **139**
Ewshot La. *C Crook & Ews* —1A **108**
Excalibur Clo. *If'd* —3K **181**
Excelsior Clo. *King T* —1N **41**
Exchange Rd. *Asc* —4N **33**
Exchange Rd. *Craw* —3C **182**
Exeforde Av. *Ashf* —5B **22**
Exeter Clo. *Craw* —7C **182**
Exeter Gdns. *Yat* —8A **48**
*Exeter Ho. Felt —3M **23***
(off Watermill Way)
Exeter Pl. *Guild* —1J **113**
Exeter Rd. *Ash* —1E **110**
Exeter Rd. *Croy* —6B **46**
Exeter Rd. *Felt* —4N **23**
Exeter Rd. *H'row A* —6F **8**
Exeter Way. *H'row A* —5F **8**
Explorer Av. *Stai* —2N **21**
Eyebright Clo. *Croy* —7G **47**
Eyhurst Clo. *Kgswd* —1L **101**
Eyhurst Spur. *Tad* —2L **101**
Eyles Clo. *H'ham* —4H **197**
Eylewood Rd. *SE27* —6N **29**
Eyot Gdns. *W6* —1E **12**
Eyot Grn. *W4* —1E **12**
Eyston Dri. *Wey* —6B **56**

Fabian Rd. *SW6* —3L **13**
Facade, The. *Reig* —2M **121**
Factory La. *Croy* —7L **45**
Factory Sq. *SW16* —7J **29**
Fagg's Rd. *Felt* —7G **9**
Fairacre. *N Mald* —2D **42**
Fairacres. *SW15* —7F **12**
Fairacres. *Cobh* —8L **57**
Fair Acres. *Croy* —5J **65**
Fairacres. *Rowl* —7E **128**
Fairacres. *Tad* —8H **81**
Fairacres Ind. Est. *Wind* —5A **4**
Fairbairn Clo. *Purl* —9L **63**
Fairborne Way. *Guild* —9K **93**
Fairbourne. *Cobh* —9L **57**
Fairbourne Clo. *Wok* —5K **73**
Fairbourne La. *Cat* —9N **83**
Fairburn Ct. *SW15* —8K **13**
*Fairburn Ho. W14 —1L **13***
(off Ivatt Pl.)
Fairchildes Av. *New Ad* —8N **65**
Fairchildes Rd. *Warl* —1N **85**
Faircroft Ct. *Tedd* —7G **25**
Faircross. *Brack* —2N **31**
Fairdale Gdns. *SW15* —7G **13**
Fairdene Rd. *Coul* —5H **83**
Fairfax. *Brack* —9M **15**
Fairfax Av. *Eps* —6G **60**
Fairfax Av. *Red* —2C **122**
Fairfax Clo. *W On T* —7J **39**
Fairfax Rd. *F'boro* —7N **69**
Fairfax Rd. *Tedd* —7G **25**
Fairfax Rd. *Wok* —7D **74**
Fairfield App. *Wray* —9N **5**
Fairfield Av. *Dat* —3M **5**
Fairfield Av. *Horl* —9E **142**
Fairfield Av. *Stai* —5H **21**
Fairfield Av. *Twic* —2B **24**
Fairfield Clo. *Dat* —3N **5**
Fairfield Clo. *Dork* —3J **119**
Fairfield Clo. *Ewe* —2D **60**
Fairfield Clo. *Mitc* —8C **28**
Fairfield Cotts. *Bookh* —3B **98**
Fairfield Dri. *SW18* —8N **13**
Fairfield Dri. *Dork* —3H **119**
Fairfield Dri. *Frim* —3C **70**
Fairfield E. *King T* —1L **41**
Fairfield La. *W End* —8D **52**
Fairfield N. *King T* —1L **41**
Fairfield Pk. *Cobh* —1L **77**
Fairfield Path. *Croy* —9A **46**
Fairfield Pl. *King T* —2L **41**
Fairfield Rise. *Guild* —2J **113**
Fairfield Rd. *Beck* —1K **47**
Fairfield Rd. *Croy* —9A **46**
Fairfield Rd. *E Grin* —1B **186**
Fairfield Rd. *King T* —1L **41**
Fairfield Rd. *Lea* —8H **79**
Fairfield Rd. *Wray* —9N **5**
Fairfield S. *King T* —2L **41**
Fairfields Rd. *Houn* —6C **10**
Fairfield St. *SW18* —8N **13**
Fairfield, The. *Farnh* —1H **129**
(in two parts)
*Fairfield Wlk. Lea —8H **79***
(off Fairfield Rd.)
Fairfield Way. *Coul* —1H **83**
Fairfield Way. *Eps* —2D **60**
Fairfield W. *King T* —1L **41**
Fairford Av. *Croy* —4G **47**
Fairford Clo. *Croy* —4H **47**
Fairford Clo. *Reig* —1A **122**
Fairford Clo. *W Byf* —1H **75**
Fairford Ct. *Sutt* —4N **61**
Fairford Gdns. *Wor Pk* —9E **42**
Fairgreen Rd. *T Hth* —4M **45**
Fairground. *Cher* —7J **37**
Fairhaven. *Egh* —6B **20**
Fairhaven Av. *Croy* —5G **46**
Fairhaven Ct. *Egh* —6B **20**
Fairhaven Rd. *Red* —8E **102**
Fairholme. *Felt* —1E **22**
Fairholme Cres. *Asht* —4J **79**
Fairholme Gdns. *Farnh* —2H **129**
Fairholme Rd. *W14* —1K **13**
Fairholme Rd. *Ashf* —6N **21**
Fairholme Rd. *Croy* —6L **45**
Fairholme Rd. *Sutt* —3L **61**
Fairland Clo. *Fleet* —5C **88**
Fairlands Av. *Guild* —8F **92**
Fairlands Av. *Sutt* —8M **43**
Fairlands Av. *T Hth* —3K **45**
Fairlands Ct. *Guild* —8F **92**
Fairlands Rd. *Guild* —7F **92**
Fair La. *Coul* —3A **102**
Fairlawn. *Bookh* —2N **97**
Fairlawn. *Wey* —2F **56**
Fair Lawn Clo. *Clay* —3F **58**
Fairlawn Clo. *Felt* —5N **23**
Fairlawn Clo. *King T* —7B **26**
Fairlawn Cres. *E Grin* —8L **165**
Fairlawn Dri. *E Grin* —8L **165**
Fairlawn Dri. *Red* —5C **122**
Fairlawn Gro. *Bans* —9B **62**
Fairlawn Pk. *Wind* —7B **4**
Fairlawn Pk. *Wok* —1A **74**
Fairlawn Rd. *SW19* —8L **27**
Fairlawn Rd. *Bans* —7A **62**
(in three parts)
Fairlawns. *Add* —2K **55**
Fairlawns. *Guild* —3E **114**
Fairlawns. *Horl* —9F **142**
Fairlawns. *Sun* —2G **39**
Fairlawns. *Twic* —9J **11**
Fairlawns. *Wall* —2F **62**
Fairlawns. *Wdhm* —7H **55**
Fairlawns Clo. *Stai* —7K **21**
Fairlight Av. *Wind* —5G **4**
Fairlight Clo. *Wor Pk* —1H **61**
Fairlight Rd. *SW17* —5B **28**
Fairline Ct. *Beck* —1M **47**
Fairlop Wlk. *Cranl* —8H **155**
Fairmead. *Surb* —7A **42**
Fairmead. *Wok* —5M **73**
Fairmead Clo. *Col T* —8K **49**
Fairmead Clo. *Houn* —3L **9**
Fairmead Clo. *N Mald* —2C **42**
Fairmead Ct. *Rich* —5A **12**
Fairmead Rd. *Croy* —6K **45**
Fairmead Rd. *Eden* —7L **127**
Fairmeads. *Cobh* —9N **57**
Fairmile. *Fleet* —7A **88**
Fairmile Av. *SW16* —6H **29**
Fairmile Av. *Cobh* —9M **57**
Fairmile Ho. *Tedd* —5G **25**
Fairmile La. *Cobh* —8L **57**
Fairmile Pk. Copse. *Cobh* —9N **57**
Fairmile Pk. Rd. *Cobh* —9N **57**
Fairoak Clo. *Kenl* —2M **83**
Fairoak Clo. *Oxs* —8D **58**
Fairoak La. *Oxs & Chess* —8C **58**
Fairoaks Airport. *Chob* —6A **54**
Fairoaks Cvn. Pk. *Guild* —7D **92**
*Fairoaks Ct. Add —2K **55***
(off Lane Clo.)
Fairs Rd. *Lea* —6G **79**
Fairstone Ct. *Horl* —7F **142**
Fair St. *Houn* —6C **10**
Fairview. *Eps* —7H **61**
Fair View. *H'ham* —5G **197**
Fairview Av. *Wok* —5A **74**
Fairview Clo. *Wok* —5B **74**
Fairview Ct. *Ashf* —6B **22**
Fairview Ct. *Stai* —7J **21**
Fairview Dri. *Orp* —1M **67**
Fairview Dri. *Shep* —4A **38**
Fair View Gdns. *Farnh* —6J **109**
Fairview Ho. *SW2* —1K **29**
Fairview Ind. Est. *Oxt* —2C **126**
Fairview Pl. *SW2* —1K **29**
Fairview Rd. *SW16* —9K **29**
Fairview Rd. *Ash* —1F **110**
Fairview Rd. *Eps* —7E **60**
Fairview Rd. *Head* —4G **169**
Fairview Rd. *Sutt* —2C **62**
Fairview Rd. *Wokgm* —3B **30**
Fairwater Dri. *New H* —5M **55**
Fairway. *SW20* —2H **43**
Fairway. *Cars* —7A **62**
Fairway. *Cher* —7K **37**
Fairway. *Copt* —8M **163**
Fairway. *Guild* —3F **114**
Fairway. *If'd* —4J **181**
Fairway. *Vir W* —5M **35**
Fairway Clo. *Copt* —8L **163**
Fairway Clo. *Croy* —4H **47**
Fairway Clo. *Eps* —1B **60**
Fairway Clo. *Houn* —8K **9**
Fairway Clo. *Wok* —6L **73**
Fairway Gdns. *Beck* —5N **47**
Fairway Heights. *Camb* —9F **50**
Fairways. *Ashf* —7C **22**
Fairways. *Hind* —3N **169**
Fairways. *Iswth* —4E **10**
Fairways. *Kenl* —4N **83**
Fairways. *Tedd* —8K **25**
Fairway, The. *Camb* —3E **70**
Fairway, The. *F'boro* —5G **88**
Fairway, The. *Farnh* —5J **109**
Fairway, The. *G'ming* —9J **133**
Fairway, The. *Lea* —5G **79**
Fairway, The. *N Mald* —9C **26**
Fairway, The. *W Mol* —2B **40**
Fairway, The. *Wey* —7B **56**
Fairway, The. *Worp* —2F **92**
Fairwell La. *W Hor* —6C **96**
Fakenham Way. *Owl* —6J **49**
Falaise. *Egh* —6A **20**
Falaise Clo. *Alder* —2N **109**
Falcon Clo. *W4* —2B **12**
Falcon Clo. *Craw* —1B **182**
Falcon Clo. *Light* —7K **51**
Falcon Ct. *Frim* —5B **70**
Falcon Ct. *Wok* —9E **54**
Falcon Dri. *Stai* —9M **7**
Falconhurst. *Oxs* —2D **78**
Falcon Lodge. *H'ham* —8M **197**
Falcon Rd. *Guild* —4N **113**
Falcon Rd. *Hamp* —8N **23**
Falcons Clo. *Big H* —4F **86**
Falcon Way. *Felt* —8J **9**
Falcon Way. *Sun* —1F **38**
Falcon Way. *Yat* —9A **48**
Falconwood. *E Hor* —2G **96**
Falconwood. *Egh* —6A **20**
Falconwood Rd. *Croy* —5J **65**
Falcourt Clo. *Sutt* —2N **61**

Falkland Ct.—Fiske Ct.

Falkland Ct. F'boro —5C 90
Falkland Gdns. Dork —6G 119
Falkland Gro. Dork —6G 118
Falkland Pk. Av. SE25 —2B 46
Falkland Rd. Dork —6G 119
Falklands Dri. H'ham —4A 198
Falkner Ct. Farnh —1H 129
Falkner Rd. Farnh —1G 128
Falkners Clo. Fleet —1D 88
Fallow Deer Clo. H'ham —5A 198
Fallowfield. Fleet —1D 88
Fallowfield. Yat —8A 48
Fallowfield Way. Horl —7F 142
Fallsbrook Rd. SW16 —7F 28
Falmer Clo. Craw —5B 182
Falmouth Clo. Camb —2E 70
Falmouth Rd. W On T —1K 57
Falstaff M. Hamp —9C 24
Falstone. Wok —5L 73
Famet Av. Purl —9N 63
Famet Clo. Purl —9N 63
Famet Gdns. Kenl —9N 63
Famet Wlk. Purl —9N 63
Fanes Clo. Brack —9L 15
Fane St. W14 —2L 13
Fangrove Pk. Lyne —7D 36
Fanshawe Rd. Rich —5J 25
Fantail, The. (Junct.) —1H 67
Fanthorpe St. SW15 —6H 13
Faraday Av. E Grin —3B 186
Faraday Ct. Craw —8C 162
Faraday Rd. SW19 —7M 27
Faraday Rd. Craw —8D 162
Faraday Rd. F'boro —8A 70
Faraday Rd. W Mol —3A 40
Faraday Way. Croy —7K 45
Farcrosse Clo. Sand —7H 49
Farebrothers. Warn —9F 178
Fareham Dri. Yat —8A 48
Fareham Rd. Felt —1K 23
Farewell Pl. Mitc —9C 28
Farhalls Cres. H'ham —3M 197
Faringdon Clo. Sand —6H 49
Faringdon Dri. Brack —4B 32
Farington Acres. Wey —9E 38
Faris Barn Dri. Wdhm —8H 55
Faris La. Wdhm —7H 55
Farleigh Ct. Guild —3H 113
Farleigh Ct. Rd. Warl —1J 85
Farleigh Dean Cres. New Ad —7L 65
Farleigh Rd. New H —7J 55
Farleigh Rd. Warl —5G 85
Farleton Clo. Wey —3E 56
Farley Copse. Brack —9K 15
Farley Ct. F'boro —3B 90
Farleycroft. W'ham —4L 107
Farley Heath Rd. Sham G —7J 135
Farley La. W'ham —4K 107
Farley Nursery. W'ham —5L 107
Farley Pk. Oxt —8N 105
Farley Pl. SE25 —3D 46
Farley Rd. S Croy —4D 64
Farleys Clo. W Hor —4D 96
Farlington Pl. SW15 —1G 26
Farlow Rd. SW15 —6J 13
Farlton Rd. SW18 —1N 27
Farm Av. SW16 —5J 29
Farm Av. H'ham —5H 197
Farm Clo. Asc —4N 33
Farm Clo. Brack —9L 15
Farm Clo. Byfl —8N 55
Farm Clo. Coul —7D 82
Farm Clo. Craw —2E 182
Farm Clo. Crowt —9H 31
Farm Clo. E Grin —1D 186
Farm Clo. E Hor —6G 96
Farm Clo. Fet —2D 98
Farm Clo. Guild —9N 93
Farm Clo. Loxw —5J 193
Farm Clo. Lyne —5C 36
Farm Clo. Shep —6B 38
Farm Clo. Stai —6G 20
Farm Clo. Sutt —4B 62
Farm Clo. Wall —6G 63
Farm Clo. Warn —1F 196
Farm Clo. W Wick —1B 66
Farm Clo. Worp —7F 92
Farm Clo. Yat —1C 68
Farm Cotts. Wokgm —9A 14
Farm Ct. Frim —4D 70
Farmdale Rd. Cars —4C 62
Farm Dri. Croy —8J 47
Farm Dri. Fleet —1C 88
Farm Dri. Old Win —9L 5
Farm Dri. Purl —7H 63
Farmers Rd. Stai —6G 20
Farmfield Cotts. Horl —3N 161
Farmfield Dri. Horl —2N 161
Farm Fields. S Croy —7B 64
Farm Ho. Clo. Wok —2F 74
Farmhouse Rd. SW16 —8G 29
Farmington Av. Sutt —9B 44
Farm La. SW6 —2M 13
Farm La. Add —4J 55
Farm La. Asht & Eps —4N 79
Farm La. Croy —8J 47
Farm La. E Hor —6G 96
Farm La. Purl —6G 63
Farm La. Send —2E 94
Farm La. Clo. SW6 —3M 13 (off Farm La.)
Farmleigh Clo. Craw —1G 182
Farmleigh Gro. W On T —2G 56
Farm M. Mitc —1F 44
Farm Rd. Alder —1C 110
Farm Rd. Esh —7B 40
Farm Rd. Frim —4C 70
Farm Rd. Houn —2M 23
Farm Rd. Mord —4N 43
Farm Rd. Stai —7K 21
Farm Rd. Sutt —4B 62
Farm Rd. Warl —6H 85
Farm Rd. Wok —7D 74
Farmstead Dri. Eden —9L 127
Farmview. Cobh —3L 77
Farm View. Lwr K —5L 101
Farm View. Yat —1C 68
Farm Wlk. Ash —4G 111
Farm Wlk. Guild —5J 113
Farm Wlk. Horl —8D 142
Farm Way. Stai —9H 7
Farm Way. Wor Pk —9H 43
Farm Yd. Wind —3G 5
Farnan Rd. SW16 —6J 29
Farnborough Aerospace Pk. F'boro —5L 89
Farnborough Av. S Croy —5G 65
Farnborough Bus. Pk. F'boro —3M 89
Farnborough Comn. Orp —1H 67
Farnborough Cres. S Croy —5H 65
Farnborough Ga. F'boro —7A 70
Farnborough Hill. Orp —2M 67
Farnborough Rd. F'boro —5N 89
Farnborough Rd. Farnh & Alder —4J 109
Farnborough St. F'boro —8B 70
Farnborough Way. Orp —1L 67
Farncombe Hill. G'ming —4G 132
Farncombe St. G'ming —4H 133
Farnell M. SW5 —1N 13
Farnell Rd. Iswth —6D 10
Farnell Rd. Stai —4J 21
Farney Field. Peasl —2E 136
Farnham Bus. Cen. Farnh —9H 109
Farnham Bus. Pk. Farnh —2G 128
Farnham By-Pass. Farnh —3E 128
Farnham Clo. Brack —1B 32
Farnham Clo. Craw —9A 182
Farnham Ct. Sutt —3K 61
Farnham Gdns. SW20 —1G 42
Farnham La. Hasl —9E 170
Farnham Pk. Clo. Farnh —6G 108
Farnham Pk. Dri. Farnh —6G 109
Farnham Rd. Elst —6E 130
Farnham Rd. Ews —3A 108
Farnham Rd. Fleet —5E 88
Farnham Rd. Guild —6G 113
Farnham Rd. Holt P —1A 148
Farnham Trad. Est. Farnh —8L 109
Farnhurst La. Alf —4H 175
Farningham. Brack —5C 32
Farningham Ct. SW16 —8H 29
Farningham Cres. Cat —1D 104
Farningham Rd. Cat —1D 104
Farnley. Wok —4J 73
Farnley Rd. SE25 —3A 46
Farnwell M. Wey —9C 38
Farquhar Rd. SW19 —4M 27
Farquharson Rd. Croy —7N 45
Farrell Clo. Camb —3A 70
Farrer Ct. Twic —1K 25
Farrer's Pl. Croy —1G 64
Farrier Clo. Sun —2H 39
Farriers Clo. Eps —8D 60
Farriers, The. Brmly —6C 134
Farrier Wlk. SW10 —2N 13
Farthing Barn La. Orp —5J 67
Farthing Fields. Head —4D 168
Farthingham La. Ewh —4F 156
Farthings. Knap —3H 73
Farthings Hill. H'ham —5F 196
Farthings, The. King T —9N 25
Farthing St. Orp —4H 67
Fassett Rd. King T —3L 41
Fauconberg Ct. W4 —2B 12 (off Fauconberg Rd.)
Fauconberg Rd. W4 —2B 12
Faulkner Pl. Bag —3J 51
Faulkners Rd. W On T —2K 57
Favart Rd. SW6 —4M 13
Faversham Rd. Beck —1J 47
Faversham Rd. Mord —5N 43
Faversham Rd. Owl —6J 49
Fawcett Rd. Croy —9N 45
Fawcett Rd. Wind —4E 4
Fawcett St. SW10 —2N 13
Fawcus Clo. Clay —3E 58
Fawe Pk. Rd. SW15 —7L 13
Fawler Mead. Brack —3D 32
Fawley Clo. Cranl —8A 156
Fawns Mnr. Clo. Felt —2D 22
Fawns Mnr. Rd. Felt —2E 22
Fawsley Clo. Coln —3G 6
Fay Cotts. H'ham —5D 180
Faygate Bus. Cen. Fay —8E 180
Faygate La. H'ham —2D 180
Faygate La. S God —9H 125
Faygate Rd. SW2 —3K 29
Fayland Av. SW16 —6G 28
Fay Rd. H'ham —3J 197
Fearn Clo. E Hor —7F 96
Fearnley Cres. Hamp —6M 23
Featherbed La. Croy & Warl —4J 65
Feathers La. Wray —3C 20
Featherstone. Blind H —2G 145
Fee Farm Rd. Clay —4F 58
Felbridge Av. Craw —2H 183
Felbridge Cen., The. E Grin —7K 165
Felbridge Clo. SW16 —5L 29
Felbridge Clo. E Grin —7M 165
Felbridge Clo. Frim —4D 70
Felbridge Clo. Sutt —5N 61
Felbridge Ct. Felb —6K 165
Felbridge Ct. Hayes —2E 8
Felbridge Rd. E Grin —7G 165
Felcot Rd. Felb —7F 164
Felcott Clo. W On T —9K 39
Felcott Rd. W On T —9K 39
Felcourt La. E Grin —2M 165
Felcourt Rd. E Grin & Ling —3M 165
Felday Glade. Holm M —6J 137
Felday Houses. Holm M —4J 137
Felday Rd. Ab H —9G 116
Feldcmore Cotts. Dork —5K 137
Felden St. SW6 —4L 13
Felgate M. W6 —1G 12
Felix Dri. W Cla —6J 95
Felix La. Shep —5F 38
Felix Rd. W On T —5H 39
Felland Way. Reig —7B 122
Fellbrook. Rich —4H 25
Fellcott Way. H'ham —7F 196
Fellowes Rd. Cars —9C 44
Fellow Grn. W End —9C 52
Fellow Grn. Rd. W End —9C 52
Fellows Rd. F'boro —4B 90
Fell Rd. Croy —9N 45
Felmingham Rd. SE20 —1F 46
Felsberg Rd. SW2 —1J 29
Felsham Rd. SW15 —6H 13
Felstead Rd. Eps —7C 60
Feltham Av. E Mol —3E 40
Felthambrook Ind. Est. Felt —4J 23
Felthambrook Way. Felt —4J 23
Feltham Bus. Complex. Felt —3J 23
Feltham Hill Rd. Ashf —6B 22
Felthamhill Rd. Felt —5H 23
Feltham Rd. Ashf —6B 22
Feltham Rd. Mitc —1E 44
Feltham Rd. Red —8D 122
Feltham Wlk. Red —8D 122
Felwater Ct. E Grin —7L 165
Fenby Clo. H'ham —4A 198
Fenchurch Rd. M'bowr —5F 182
Fencote. Brack —5B 32
Fendall Rd. Eps —2B 60
Fender Ho. H'ham —6H 197
Fenelon Pl. W14 —1L 13
Fengates Rd. Red —3C 122
Fenhurst Clo. H'ham —7F 196
Fennel Clo. Croy —7G 47
Fennel Clo. F'boro —1G 89
Fennel Clo. Guild —9D 94
Fennel Cres. Craw —7N 181
Fennells Mead. Eps —5E 60
Fenn Ho. Iswth —4H 11
Fennscombe Ct. W End —9B 52
Fenns La. W End —9B 52
Fenns Way. Wok —2A 74
Fenn's Yd. Farnh —1G 128
Fenton Av. Stai —7L 21
Fenton Clo. Red —3E 122
Fenton Ho. Houn —2A 10
Fenton Rd. Red —3E 122
Fentum Rd. Guild —1K 113
Fenwick Clo. Wok —4L 73
Fenwick Pl. S Croy —4M 63
Ferbies. Fleet —7B 88
Ferguson Av. Surb —4M 41
Ferguson Clo. Brom —2N 47
Fermandy La. Craw D —9D 164
Fern Av. Mitc —3H 45
Fernbank Av. W On T —6M 39
Fernbank Cres. Asc —9H 17
Fernbank M. SW12 —1F 28
Fernbank Pl. Asc —9G 17
Fernbank Rd. Add —2J 55
Fernbank Rd. Asc —1H 33
Fernbrae Clo. Rowl —8G 128
Fern Clo. Crowt —9G 30
Fern Clo. Frim —3G 70
Fern Clo. Warl —5H 85
Fern Cotts. Dork —8F 116
Fern Ct. Ash —3D 110
Ferndale. Guild —1H 113
Ferndale Av. Cher —9G 36
Ferndale Av. Houn —6M 9
Ferndale Rd. SE25 —4E 46
Ferndale Rd. Ashf —6M 21
Ferndale Rd. Bans —3L 81
Ferndale Rd. C Crook —9A 88
Ferndale Rd. Wok —3B 74
Ferndale Way. Orp —2M 67
Fernden Heights. Hasl —6F 188
Fernden La. Hasl —5F 188
Ferndown. Craw —8H 163
Ferndown. Horl —6E 142
Ferndown Clo. Guild —4C 114
Ferndown Clo. Sutt —3B 62
Ferndown Ct. Guild —2M 113
Ferndown Gdns. Cobh —9K 57
Ferndown Gdns. F'boro —1K 89
Fern Dri. C Crook —7A 88
Fernery, The. Stai —6G 21
Ferney Ct. Byfl —7M 55
Ferney Meade Way. Iswth —5G 10
Ferney Rd. Byfl —8M 55
Fern Gro. Felt —1J 23
Fernham Rd. T Hth —2N 45
Fern Hill. Oxs —1D 78
Fernhill Clo. B'water —5L 69
Fernhill Clo. Brack —8L 15
Fernhill Clo. Craw D —9E 164
Fernhill Clo. Farnh —6G 109
Fernhill Clo. Wok —7M 73
Fernhill Dri. Farnh —6G 109
Fernhill Gdns. King T —6K 25
Fernhill La. B'water —5K 69
Fernhill La. Farnh —6G 109
Fernhill La. Wok —7M 73
Fernhill Pk. Wok —7M 73
Fern Hill Pl. Farn —2L 67
Fernhill Rd. B'water & Farn —4K 69
Fernhill Rd. Horl —3H 163
Fernhill Wlk. B'water —5L 69
Fernhurst Clo. Craw —1N 181
Fernhurst Rd. SW6 —4K 13
Fernhurst Rd. Ashf —5D 22
Fernhurst Rd. Croy —7E 46
Ferniehurst. Camb —2D 70
Fernihough Clo. Wey —6B 56
Fernlands Clo. Cher —9G 37
Fern La. Houn —1N 9
Fernlea. Bookh —2B 98
Fernlea Rd. SW12 —2F 28
Fernlea Rd. Mitc —1E 44
Fernleigh Clo. Croy —1L 63
Fernleigh Clo. W On T —9J 39
Fernleigh Rise. Deep —7G 70
Fernley Ho. G'ming —3J 133
Fern Rd. G'ming —5J 133
Ferns Clo. S Croy —6E 64
Fernshaw Rd. SW10 —2N 13
Fernside Av. Felt —5J 23
Fernside Rd. SW12 —2D 28
Ferns Mead. Farnh —2G 128
Ferns, The. Farnh —5H 109
Fernthorpe Rd. SW16 —7G 28
Fern Towers. Cat —3D 104
Fern Wlk. Ashf —6M 21
Fern Way. H'ham —3K 197
Fernwood. Croy —5H 65
Fernwood Av. SW16 —5H 29
Feroners Clo. Craw —5E 182
Feroners Ct. Craw —5E 182 (off Feroners Clo.)
Ferrard Clo. Asc —9H 17
Ferraro Clo. Houn —2A 10
Ferrers Av. Wall —1H 63
Ferrers Rd. SW16 —6H 29
Ferrier Ind. Est. SW18 —7N 13 (off Ferrier St.)
Ferrier St. SW18 —7N 13
Ferriers Way. Eps —5H 81
Ferring Clo. Craw —2N 181
Ferris Av. Croy —9J 47
Ferry Av. Stai —8G 21
Ferry La. SW13 —2E 12
Ferry La. Bren —2L 11
Ferry La. Cher —4J 37
Ferry La. Guild —7M 113
Ferry La. Lale —2L 37
Ferry La. Rich —2M 11
Ferry La. Shep —7B 38
Ferry La. Stai —3D 20
Ferrymoor. Rich —4H 25
Ferry Rd. SW13 —3F 12
Ferry Rd. Tedd —6H 25
Ferry Rd. Th Dit —5H 41
Ferry Rd. Twic —2H 25
Ferry Rd. W Mol —2A 40
Ferry Sq. Bren —3L 11
Ferry Sq. Shep —6C 38
Festing Rd. SW15 —6J 13
Festival Wlk. Cars —2D 62
Fetcham Comn. La. Fet —8B 78
Fetcham Pk. Dri. Fet —1E 98
Fettes Rd. Cranl —7B 156
Fiddicroft Av. Bans —1N 81
Field Clo. Chess —2J 59
Field Clo. Guild —1F 114
Field Clo. Hayes —3D 8
Field Clo. Houn —5J 9
Field Clo. S Croy —1E 84
Field Clo. W Mol —4B 40
Fieldcommon La. W On T —7M 39
Field Ct. SW19 —4M 27
Field Ct. Oxt —5A 106
Field Dri. Eden —9M 127
Field End. Coul —1H 83
Field End. Farnh —8L 109
Fieldend. H'ham —3A 198
Field End. Twic —5F 24
Field End. W End —9C 52
Fieldend Rd. SW16 —9G 29
Fielden Pl. Brack —1B 32
Fielders Grn. Guild —3C 114
Fieldfare Av. Yat —9A 48
Fieldgate La. Mitc —1C 44
Field Ho. Clo. Asc —7L 33
Fieldhouse Rd. SW12 —2G 29
Fieldhouse Vs. Bans —2C 82
Fieldhurst. Slou —1B 6
Fieldhurst Clo. Add —2K 55
Fielding Av. Twic —4C 24
Fielding Gdns. Crowt —3G 48
Fielding Ho. W4 —2D 12 (off Devonshire Rd.)
Fielding M. SW13 —2G 12 (off Castelnau Pl.)
Fielding Rd. Col T —9K 49
Fieldings, The. Horl —7G 142
Fieldings, The. Wok —3J 73
Field La. Bren —3J 11
Field La. Frim —5B 70
Field La. G'ming —4J 133
Field La. Tedd —6G 24
Field Pk. Brack —9B 16
Field Path. F'boro —5L 69
Field Pl. G'ming —4H 133
Field Pl. N Mald —5E 42
Field Pl. Cotts. H'ham —3D 196
Field Rd. W6 —1K 13
Field Rd. F'boro —5L 69
Field Rd. Felt —9J 9
Fieldsend Rd. Sutt —2K 61
Fieldside Clo. Orp —1L 67
Field Stores App. Alder —1A 110
Fieldview. SW18 —2B 28
Field View. Egh —6E 20
Field View. Felt —5E 22
Fieldview. Horl —7F 142
Field Wlk. Horl —8D 142 (off Court Lodge Rd.)
Field Wlk. Small —7N 143
Field Way. Alder —1C 110
Fieldway. Hasl —1G 189
Field Way. New Ad —4L 65
Field Way. Rip —3H 95
Field Way. Tong —5D 110
Fifehead Clo. Ashf —7N 21
Fife Rd. SW14 —8B 12
Fife Rd. King T —1L 41
Fife Way. Bookh —3A 98
Fifield La. Fren —9H 129
Fifth Cross Rd. Twic —3D 24
Figges Rd. Mitc —8E 28
Filbert Cres. Craw —3M 181
Filby Rd. Chess —3M 59
Filey Clo. Big H —6D 86
Filey Clo. Craw —5L 181
Filey Clo. Sutt —4A 62
Filmer Gro. G'ming —6H 133
Filmer Rd. SW6 —4K 13
Filmer Rd. Wind —5A 4
Finborough Rd. SW10 —1N 13
Finborough Rd. SW17 —7D 28
Fincham End Dri. Crowt —3E 48
Finchampstead Rd. Wokgm —8A 30
Finch Av. SE27 —5N 29
Finch Clo. Knap —4F 72
Finchdean Ho. SW15 —1E 26
Finch Dri. Felt —1L 23
Finches Rise. Guild —1E 114
Finch Rd. Guild —3N 113
Findhorn Clo. Col T —8J 49
Findings, The. F'boro —6K 69
Findlay Dri. Guild —8J 93
Findon Clo. SW18 —9M 13
Findon Ct. Add —2H 55
Findon Rd. Craw —1N 181
Findon Way. Broad H —5D 196
Finlay Gdns. Add —1L 55
Finlays Clo. Chess —2N 59
Finlay St. SW6 —4J 13
Finmere. Brack —6A 32
Finnart Clo. Wey —1D 56
Finnart Ho. Dri. Wey —1D 56
Finney Dri. W'sham —3A 52
Finsbury Clo. Craw —7A 182
Finstock Grn. Brack —3D 32
Fintry Pl. F'boro —7K 69
Fintry Wlk. F'boro —7K 69
Fiona Clo. Bookh —2A 98
Fir Acre Rd. Ash V —7D 90
Firbank Dri. Wok —6L 73
Firbank La. Wok —6L 73
Firbank Pl. Egh —7L 19
Fir Clo. Fleet —5A 88
Fir Clo. W On T —6H 39
Fircroft. Fleet —4A 88
Fircroft Clo. Wok —5B 74
Fircroft Ct. Wok —5B 74
Fircroft Rd. SW17 —3D 28
Fircroft Rd. Chess —1M 59
Fircroft Way. Eden —9L 127
Fir Dene. Orp —1J 67
Firdene. Surb —7B 42
Fir Dri. B'water —3J 69
Fireball Hill. Asc —6A 34
Fire Bell La. Surb —5L 41
Firefly Clo. Wall —4J 63
Fire Sta. M. Beck —1L 47
Fire Thorn Clo. Fleet —6B 88
Firfield Rd. Add —1J 55
Firfield Rd. Farnh —4F 128
Firfields. Wey —3C 56
Firglen Dri. Yat —8C 48
Fir Grange Av. Wey —2C 56
Fir Gro. N Mald —5E 42
Firgrove. Wok —6L 73
Firgrove Ct. F'boro —1N 89
Firgrove Ct. Farnh —2H 129
Firgrove Hill. Farnh —2H 129
Firgrove Pde. F'boro —1N 89
Firgrove Rd. F'boro —1N 89
Firlands. Brack —4A 32
Firlands. Horl —7F 142
Firlands. Wey —3F 56
Firlands Av. Camb —1B 70
Firle Clo. Craw —1C 182
Firle Ct. Eps —8E 60
Fir Rd. Felt —6L 23
Fir Rd. Sutt —7L 43
Firs Av. SW14 —7B 12
Firs Av. Brmly —5C 134
Firs Av. Wind —6C 4
Firsby Av. Croy —7G 47
Firs Clo. Cat —9A 84
Firs Clo. Clay —3E 58
Firs Clo. Dork —7G 119
Firs Clo. F'boro —3A 90
Firs Clo. Mitc —9F 28
Firs Dene Clo. Ott —3F 54
Firs Dri. Houn —3J 9
Firs La. Sham G —7F 134
Firs Rd. Kenl —2M 83
First Av. SW14 —6D 12
First Av. Eps —5D 60
First Av. W On T —5J 39
First Av. W Mol —3N 39
First Clo. W Mol —2C 40
First Cross Rd. Twic —3E 24
Firs, The. Bisl —3D 72
Firs, The. Brack —4D 32
Firs, The. Cat —9A 84 (off Milner App.)
Firs, The. Guild —7L 113
First Slip. Lea —5G 79
Firstway. SW20 —1H 43
Firsway. Guild —2J 113
Firswood Av. Eps —2E 60
Firth Gdns. SW6 —4K 13
Fir Tree All. Alder —2M 109 (off Victoria Rd.)
Fir Tree Av. Hasl —2B 188
Firtree Av. Mitc —1E 44
Firtree Clo. SW16 —6G 29
Fir Tree Clo. Asc —6L 33
Fir Tree Clo. Craw —9N 161
Fir Tree Clo. Eps —2H 81
Fir Tree Clo. Esh —2C 58
Firtree Clo. Ewe —1E 60
Fir Tree Clo. Lea —1J 99
Firtree Clo. Sand —6E 48
Firtree Gdns. Croy —1K 65
Fir Tree Gro. Cars —4D 62
Fir Tree Pl. Ashf —6B 22
Fir Tree Rd. Bans —1H 81
Fir Tree Rd. Eps —3G 80
Fir Tree Rd. Guild —9M 93
Fir Tree Rd. Houn —7M 9
Fir Tree Rd. Lea —1J 99
Fir Tree Wlk. Reig —3B 122
Fir Tree Way. Fleet —5C 88
Fir Wlk. Sutt —3J 61
Firway. Gray —4K 169
Firwood Clo. Wok —6H 73
Firwood Dri. Camb —1A 70
Firwood Rd. Vir W —5H 35
Fisher Clo. Craw —5C 182
Fisher Clo. Croy —7C 46
Fisher Clo. W On T —1J 57
Fisher Grn. Binf —7G 15
Fisher La. C'fold —1H 191
Fisherman Clo. Rich —5J 25
Fisherman's Pl. W4 —2E 12
Fishermen's Clo. Alder —8C 90
Fisher Rowe Clo. Brmly —5C 134
Fishers. Horl —7G 142
Fishers Ct. H'ham —4J 197
Fishers Dene. Clay —4G 58
Fisher's La. W4 —1C 12
Fisher St. C'fold & Petw —4C 190
Fishers Wood. Asc —7F 34
Fishponds Clo. Wokgm —4A 30
Fishponds Est. Wokgm —4A 30
Fishponds Rd. SW17 —5C 28
Fishponds Rd. Kes —2F 66
Fishponds Rd. Wokgm —4A 30
Fiske Ct. Yat —9D 48

Fitchet Clo.—Fulham High St.

Fitchet Clo. *Craw* —1N **181**
Fitzalan Ho. *Ewe* —6E **60**
Fitzalan Rd. *Clay* —4E **58**
Fitzalan Rd. *H'ham* —4N **197**
Fitzgeorge Av. *W14* —1K **13**
Fitzgeorge Av. *N Mald* —9C **26**
Fitzgerald Av. *SW14* —6D **12**
Fitzgerald Rd. *SW14* —6C **12**
Fitzgerald Rd. *Th Dit* —5G **40**
Fitzhugh Gro. *SW18* —1B **28**
Fitzjames Av. *W14* —1K **13**
Fitzjames Av. *Croy* —8D **46**
Fitzjohn Clo. *Guild* —9E **94**
Fitzrobert Pl. *Egh* —7C **20**
Fitzroy Cres. *W4* —3C **12**
Fitzwilliam Av. *Rich* —5M **11**
Fitzwilliam Ho. *Rich* —7K **11**
Fitzwygram Clo. *Hamp* —6C **24**
Fiveacre Clo. *T Hth* —5L **45**
Five Acres. *Craw* —1C **182**
Five Acres Clo. *Lind* —4A **168**
Five Elms Rd. *Brom* —1E **66**
Five Oaks. *Add* —3H **55**
Five Oaks Clo. *Wok* —6G **73**
Five Oaks Rd. *Slin* —9J **195**
Five Ways Bus. Cen. *Felt* —4J **23**
Fiveways Corner. (Junct.) —1L **63**
Flag Clo. *Croy* —7G **47**
Flambard Way. *G'ming* —7G **133**
Flamborough Clo. *Big H* —6D **86**
Flamsteed Heights. *Craw* —8N **181**
Flanchford Rd. *Reig* —9F **120**
Flanders Ct. *Egh* —6E **20**
Flanders Cres. *SW17* —8D **28**
Flanders Mans. *W4* —1E **12**
Flats, The. *B'water* —2G **69**
Flaxley Rd. *Mord* —6N **43**
Flaxman Ho. W4 —1D 12
(off Devonshire St.)
Flaxmore Pl. *Beck* —5N **47**
Fleece Rd. *Surb* —7J **41**
Fleet Bus. Pk. *C Crook* —9C **88**
Fleet Clo. *W Mol* —4N **39**
Fleet La. *W Mol* —5N **39**
Fleet Rd. *F'boro & Alder* —6F **88**
Fleet Rd. *Fleet & Farn* —2E **88**
(Cove Rd.)
Fleet Rd. *Fleet* —4A **88**
(Reading Rd. N.)
Fleetside. *W Mol* —4N **39**
Fleetway. *Egh* —2E **36**
Fleetwood Clo. *Chess* —4K **59**
Fleetwood Clo. *Croy* —9C **46**
Fleetwood Clo. *Tad* —7J **81**
Fleetwood Ct. *Stanw* —9N **7**
Fleetwood Ct. *W Byf* —9J **55**
Fleetwood Rd. *King T* —2A **42**
Fleetwood Sq. *King T* —2A **42**
Fleming Cen., The. *Craw* —8C **162**
Fleming Clo. *F'boro* —8B **70**
Fleming Ct. *Croy* —2L **63**
Fleming Mead. *Mitc* —8D **28**
Fleming Wlk. *E Grin* —3B **186**
Fleming Way. *Craw* —8C **162**
Fleming Way. *Isw th* —7F **10**
Fleming Way Ind. Cen. *Craw* —7D **162**
Flemish Fields. *Cher* —6J **37**
Fletcher Clo. *Craw* —5C **182**
Fletcher Clo. *Ott* —3G **54**
Fletcher Gdns. *Brack* —9J **15**
Fletcher Rd. *Ott* —3F **54**
Fletchers Clo. *H'ham* —7L **197**
Fleur Gates. *SW19* —1J **27**
Flexford Grn. *Brack* —5K **31**
Flexford Rd. *Norm* —4M **111**
Flexlands La. *W End* —6E **52**
Flint Clo. *Bans* —1N **81**
Flint Clo. *Bookh* —4C **98**
Flint Clo. *Grn St* —3N **67**
Flint Clo. *M'bowr* —6F **182**
Flint Clo. *Red* —2D **122**
Flintgrove. *Brack* —9B **16**
Flint Hill. *Dork* —7H **119**
Flint Hill Clo. *Dork* —8H **119**
Flintlock Clo. *Stai* —7J **7**
Flitwick Grange. *Milf* —1C **152**
Flock Mill Pl. *SW18* —2N **27**
Flood La. *Twic* —2G **25**
Flora Gdns. W6 —1G 12
(off Albion Gdns.)
Flora Gdns. *Croy* —7M **65**
Floral Ct. *Asht* —5J **79**
Floral Ho. Cher —7H 37
(off Fox La. S.)
Florence Av. *Mord* —4A **44**
Florence Av. *New H* —7J **55**
Florence Clo. *W On T* —6J **39**
Florence Clo. *Yat* —9B **48**
Florence Ct. *SW19* —7K **27**
Florence Gdns. *W4* —2B **12**
Florence Gdns. *Stai* —8K **21**
Florence Rd. *SW19* —7N **27**
Florence Rd. *Beck* —1H **47**
Florence Rd. *Col T* —8J **49**
Florence Rd. *Felt* —2J **23**
Florence Rd. *Fleet* —7C **88**
Florence Rd. *King T* —8M **25**
Florence Rd. *S Croy* —5A **64**
Florence Rd. *W On T* —6J **39**
Florence Ter. *SW15* —4D **26**
Florence Way. *SW12* —2D **28**
Florian Av. *Sutt* —1B **62**
Florian Rd. *SW15* —7K **13**
Florida Ct. *Stai* —5J **21**
Florida Rd. *Shalf* —9A **114**
Florida Rd. *T Hth* —9M **29**
Floss St. *SW15* —5H **13**
Flower Cres. *Ott* —3D **54**
Flower La. *God* —8G **105**
Flowersmead. *SW17* —3E **28**
Flower Wlk. *Guild* —6M **113**
Floyd's La. *Wok* —3J **75**
Flyers Way, The. *W'ham* —4M **107**
Folder's La. *Brack* —8A **16**
Foley M. *Clay* —3E **58**
Foley Rd. *Big H* —5F **86**
Foley Rd. *Clay* —4E **58**
Folkestone Ct. *Slou* —1C **6**
Follett Clo. *Old Win* —9L **5**
Folly Clo. *Fleet* —6B **88**
Follyfield Rd. *Bans* —1M **81**
Follyhatch La. *Ash* —1G **110**
Folly Hill. *Farnh* —6F **108**
Folly La. *Holmw* —4H **139**
Folly La. N. *Farnh* —5G **108**
Folly La. S. *Farnh* —6F **108**
Folly, The. *Light* —8M **51**
Fontaine Rd. *SW16* —8K **29**
Fontenoy Rd. *SW12* —3F **28**
Fonthill Clo. *SE20* —1D **46**
Fontley Way. *SW15* —1F **26**
Fontmell Clo. *Ashf* —6B **22**
Fontmell Pk. *Ashf* —6A **22**
Fontwell Rd. *Craw* —9E **162**
Footpath, The. *SW15* —8F **12**
Forbench Clo. *Rip* —9K **75**
Forbes Chase. *Col T* —8J **49**
Forbes Clo. *M'bowr* —7F **182**
Forbe's Ride. *Wind* —1L **17**
Force Grn. La. *W'ham* —2M **107**
Fordbridge Cvn. Pk. *Sun* —5G **38**
Fordbridge Clo. *Cher* —7K **37**
Fordbridge Rd. *Ashf* —7N **21**
Fordbridge Rd. *Sun* —5F **38**
Fordbridge Roundabout. (Junct.) —7N **21**
Ford Clo. *Ashf* —7N **21**
Ford Clo. *Shep* —3B **38**
Ford Clo. *T Hth* —4M **45**
Fordingbridge Clo. *H'ham* —7J **197**
Ford La. *Wrec* —5G **128**
Ford Mnr. Cotts. *Ling* —1D **166**
Ford Mnr. Rd. *D'land* —9D **146**
Ford Rd. *Ashf* —5A **22**
Ford Rd. *Bisl* —1B **72**
Ford Rd. *Cher* —7K **37**
Ford Rd. *Chob* —6F **52**
Ford Rd. *Wok* —7D **74**
Fordwater Rd. *Cher* —7K **37**
Fordwater Trad. Est. *Cher* —7L **37**
Fordwells Dri. *Brack* —3D **32**
Foreman Ct. *W6* —1H **13**
Foreman Ct. *Twic* —2F **24**
Foreman Pk. *Ash* —2F **110**
Foreman Rd. *Ash* —3F **110**
Forest Clo. *Asc* —2G **33**
Forest Clo. *Craw D* —1E **184**
Forest Clo. *E Hor* —3G **96**
Forest Clo. *H'ham* —4A **198**
Forest Clo. *Wok* —2F **74**
Forest Cres. *Asht* —3N **79**
Forestdale. *Hind* —6B **170**
Forestdale Cen., The. *Croy* —4J **65**
Forest Dean. *Fleet* —1D **88**
Forest Dene Ct. *Sutt* —3A **62**
Forest Dri. *Kes* —1G **66**
Forest Dri. *Kgswd* —8M **81**
Forest Dri. *Lwr Bo* —7H **129**
Forest Dri. *Sun* —8G **22**
Forest End. *Fleet* —7A **88**
Forest End. *Sand* —6E **48**
Forest End Rd. *Sand* —6E **48**
Forester Rd. *Craw* —5C **182**
Foresters Clo. *Wall* —4H **63**
Foresters Clo. *Wok* —5J **73**
Foresters Dri. *Wall* —4H **63**
Foresters Sq. *Brack* —2C **32**
Foresters Way. *Crowt* —9K **31**
Forestfield. *Craw* —6F **182**
Forestfield. *H'ham* —5N **197**
Forest Glade. *Rowl* —8C **128**
Forest Grange. *H'ham* —3C **198**
Forest Grn. *Brack* —9B **16**
Forest Hills. *Camb* —2N **69**
Forest La. *E Hor* —2G **97**
Forest La. *Lind* —3B **168**
Forest Oaks. *H'ham* —4A **198**
Forest Ridge. *Beck* —2K **47**
Forest Ridge. *Kes* —1G **67**
Forest Rd. *Crowt* —2H **49**
Forest Rd. *E Hor* —4G **96**
Forest Rd. *Eff J* —2G **97**
Forest Rd. *Felt* —3K **23**
Forest Rd. *F Row* —8K **187**
Forest Rd. *H'ham & Craw* —3A **198**
Forest Rd. *Rich* —3N **11**
Forest Rd. *Sutt* —7M **43**
Forest Rd. *Warf & Asc* —6C **16**
Forest Rd. *Wind* —2A **18**
(Cranbourne)
Forest Rd. *Wind* —5A **4**
(Windsor)
Forest Rd. *Wok* —2F **74**
Forest Rd. *Wokgm & Binf* —7A **14**
Forest Rd., The. *Ifold* —5D **192**
Forest Row Bus. Pk. *F Row* —6H **187**
Forest Side. *Wor Pk* —7E **42**
Forest View. *Craw* —6E **182**
Forest View Rd. *E Grin* —3A **186**
Forest Wlk. *Cranl* —8H **155**
Forest Way. *Asht* —4N **79**
Forest Way. *Warf P* —8D **16**
Forge Av. *Coul* —7L **83**
Forge Clo. *Broad H* —4D **196**
Forge Clo. *Farnh* —9J **109**
Forge Clo. *Hayes* —2E **8**
Forge Cotts. *H'ham* —4E **196**
Forge Croft. *Eden* —2L **147**
Forge Dri. *Clay* —4G **58**
Forge End. *Wok* —4A **74**
Forge Field. *Big H* —3F **86**
Forge La. *Alder* —7L **89**
Forge La. *Broad H* —4D **196**
Forge La. *Craw* —2E **182**
Forge La. *Felt* —6M **23**
Forge La. *Sun* —2H **39**
Forge La. *Sutt* —4K **61**
Forge Rd. *Craw* —2E **182**
Forge Ri. *Farnh* —9A **110**
Forge Steading. *Bans* —2N **81**
Forge, The. *Warn* —1E **196**
Forge Wood. *Craw* —7H **163**
Forge Wood Ind. Est. *Craw* —8F **162**
Forrest Gdns. *SW16* —2K **45**
Forster Rd. *SW2* —1J **29**
Forster Rd. *Beck* —2H **47**
Forsyte Cres. *SE19* —1B **46**
Forsythia Pl. *Guild* —1M **113**
Forsyth Path. *Wok* —9F **54**
Forsyth Rd. *Wok* —1E **74**
Fortescue Av. *Twic* —4C **24**
Fortescue Rd. *SW19* —8B **28**
Fortescue Rd. *Wey* —1A **56**
Forth Clo. *F'boro* —8J **69**
Forth Dri. *Coul* —3H **83**
Fort La. *Reig* —8N **101**
Fort Narrien. *Col T* —9K **49**
Fort Rd. *Guild* —6A **114**
Fort Rd. *Tad* —9A **100**
Fortrose Clo. *Col T* —8J **49**
Fortrose Gdns. *SW2* —2J **29**
Fortune Dri. *Cranl* —9N **155**
Forty Footpath. *SW14* —6B **12**
Forty Foot Rd. *Lea* —8J **79**
(in two parts)
Forum, The. *W Mol* —3B **40**
Forval Clo. *Mitc* —4D **44**
Foskett Rd. *SW6* —5L **13**
Foss Av. *Croy* —2L **63**
Fosseway. *Crowt* —2E **48**
Fosse Way. *W Byf* —9H **55**
Fossewood Dri. *Camb* —7B **50**
Foss Rd. *SW17* —5B **28**
Foster Av. *Wind* —6B **4**
Fosterdown. *God* —7E **104**
Foster Rd. *W4* —1C **12**
Fosters Gro. *W'sham* —1M **51**
Fosters La. *Knap* —4F **72**
Foster's Way. *SW18* —1N **27**
Foulser Rd. *SW17* —4D **28**
Foulsham Rd. *T Hth* —2A **46**
Founders Gdns. *SE19* —8N **29**
Foundry Clo. *H'ham* —4L **197**
Foundry Ct. *Cher* —6J **37**
Foundry La. *Hasl* —2E **188**
Foundry La. *H'ham* —5L **197**
Foundry La. *Hort* —6D **6**
Foundry M. *Cher* —6J **37**
Fountain Dri. *Cars* —4D **62**
Fountain Gdns. *Wind* —6G **5**
Fountain Rd. *SW17* —6B **28**
Fountain Rd. *Red* —5C **122**
Fountain Rd. *T Hth* —1N **45**
Fountain Roundabout. *N Mald* —3D **42**
Fountains Av. *Felt* —4N **23**
Fountains Clo. *Craw* —5M **181**
Fountains Clo. *Felt* —3N **23**
(in two parts)
Fountains Garth. *Brack* —2M **31**
Four Acres. *Cobh* —9M **57**
Four Acres. *Guild* —1E **114**
Fouracre View. *Big H* —4E **86**
Fouracre Way. *Alder* —3L **109**
Four Elms Rd. *Eden* —1L **147**
Fourfield Clo. *Eps* —9B **80**
Four Seasons Cres. *Sutt* —8L **43**
Four Sq. Ct. *Houn* —9A **10**
Fourth Cross Rd. *Twic* —3D **24**
Fourth Dri. *Coul* —3H **83**
Four Wents. *Cobh* —1K **77**
Fowler Clo. *M'bowr* —5G **182**
Fowler Rd. *F'boro* —2L **89**
Fowler Rd. *Mitc* —1E **44**
Fowlerscroft. *Comp* —1E **132**
Fowlers La. *Brack* —9N **15**
Fowlers Mead. *Chob* —5H **53**
Foxacre. *Cat* —9B **84**
Foxborough Clo. *Slou* —1C **6**
Foxborough Hill Rd. *Brmly* —4N **133**
Foxbourne Rd. *SW17* —3E **28**
Foxbridge La. *Plais* —8D **192**
Foxburrow Hill. *Brmly* —4N **133**
Foxburrows Av. *Guild* —3J **113**
Foxburrows Ct. *Guild* —2J **113**
Fox Clo. *Craw* —9N **161**
Fox Clo. *Wey* —2E **56**
Fox Clo. *Wok* —2F **74**
Foxcombe. *New Ad* —3L **65**
(in two parts)
Foxcombe Rd. *SW15* —2F **26**
Fox Corner. *Worp* —3E **92**
Foxcote. *Finch* —9A **30**
Fox Covert. *Fet* —2D **98**
Fox Covert. *Light* —7L **51**
Fox Covert Clo. *Asc* —4N **33**
Foxcroft. *C Crook* —8B **88**
Fox Dene. *G'ming* —9F **132**
Foxdown Clo. *Camb* —1A **70**
Fox Dri. *Yat* —8C **48**
Foxearth Clo. *Big H* —5G **87**
Foxearth Rd. *S Croy* —6E **64**
Foxearth Spur. *S Croy* —5F **64**
Foxenden Rd. *Guild* —3A **114**
Foxes Dale. *Brom* —2N **47**
Foxes Path. *Sut G* —4B **94**
Foxglove Av. *H'ham* —2L **197**
Foxglove Clo. *Stai* —2M **21**
Foxglove Clo. *Wink R* —7E **16**
Foxglove Gdns. *Guild* —1E **114**
Foxglove Gdns. *Purl* —7J **63**
Foxglove La. *Chess* —1N **59**
Foxglove Wlk. *Craw* —6N **181**
Foxglove Way. *Wall* —7F **44**
Fox Gro. *W On T* —6J **39**
Foxgrove Dri. *Wok* —2C **74**
Foxhanger Gdns. *Wok* —3C **74**
Foxheath. *Brack* —4C **32**
Fox Heath. *F'boro* —2H **89**
Fox Hill. *Kes* —2E **66**
Foxhill Cres. *Camb* —7F **50**
Fox Hills. *Wok* —4M **73**
Foxhills Clo. *Ott* —3D **54**
Fox Hills La. *Ash* —1G **110**
Foxhills Rd. *Ott* —1C **54**
Foxholes. *Rud* —9E **176**
Foxholes. *Wey* —2E **56**
Foxhurst Rd. *Ash V* —8E **90**
Foxlake Rd. *Byfl* —8A **56**
Fox La. *Bookh* —2M **97**
Fox La. *Cat* —8M **83**
Fox La. *Kes* —2D **66**
Fox La. *Ran C* —3B **118**
Fox La. N. *Cher* —7H **37**
Fox La. S. *Cher* —7H **37**
Foxleigh Chase. *H'ham* —4M **197**
Foxley Clo. *B'water* —1H **69**
Foxley Clo. *Red* —8E **122**
Foxley Ct. *Sutt* —4A **62**
Foxley Gdns. *Purl* —9M **63**
Foxley Hall. *Purl* —9L **63**
Foxley Hill Rd. *Purl* —8L **63**
Foxley La. *Binf* —7G **14**
Foxley La. *Purl* —7G **63**
Foxley Rd. *Kenl* —1M **83**
Foxley Rd. *T Hth* —3M **45**
Foxon Clo. *Cat* —8B **84**
Foxon La. *Cat* —8A **84**
Foxon La. Gdns. *Cat* —8B **84**
Fox Rd. *Brack* —3A **32**
Fox Rd. *Hasl* —2C **188**
Fox Rd. *Lwr Bo* —4H **129**
Fox's Path. *Mitc* —1C **44**
Foxton Gro. *Mitc* —1B **44**
Foxwarren. *Clay* —5F **58**
Fox Way. *Ews* —5C **108**
Foxwood. *Fleet* —2D **88**
Foxwood Clo. *Felt* —4J **23**
Fox Yd. *Farnh* —1G **128**
Foye La. *C Crook* —8C **88**
Frailey Clo. *Wok* —3D **74**
Frailey Hill. *Wok* —3D **74**
Framfield Clo. *Craw* —1M **181**
Framfield Rd. *Mitc* —8E **28**
Frampton Clo. *Sutt* —4M **61**
Frampton Rd. *Houn* —8M **9**
France Hill Dri. *Camb* —1A **70**
Frances Rd. *Wind* —6F **4**
Franche Ct. Rd. *SW17* —4A **28**
Francis Av. *Felt* —4H **23**
Francis Barber Clo. *SW16* —6K **29**
Franciscan Rd. *SW17* —6D **28**
Francis Chichester Clo. *Asc* —4M **33**
Francis Clo. *Eps* —1C **60**
Francis Clo. *Shep* —3B **38**
Francis Ct. *Guild* —1L **113**
Francis Edwards Way. *Craw* —7K **181**
Francis Gdns. *Warf* —7B **16**
Francis Gro. *SW19* —7L **27**
(in two parts)
Francis Rd. *Cat* —9A **84**
Francis Rd. *Croy* —6M **45**
Francis Rd. *Houn* —5L **9**
Francis Rd. *Wall* —3G **63**
Francis Way. *Camb* —2G **70**
Frank Beswick Ho. SW6 —2L 13
(off Clem Attlee Ct.)
Franklands Dri. *Add* —4H **55**
Franklin Clo. *SE27* —4M **29**
Franklin Clo. *King T* —2N **41**
Franklin Ct. Guild —3J 113
(off Derby Rd.)
Franklin Cres. *Mitc* —3G **44**
Franklin Rd. *M'bowr* —4G **183**
Franklin Sq. *W14* —1L **13**
Franklin Way. *Croy* —6J **45**
Franklyn Cres. *Wind* —6A **4**
Franklyn Rd. *G'ming* —8E **132**
Franklyn Rd. *W On T* —5J **39**
Franks Av. *N Mald* —3B **42**
Franksfield. *Peasl* —4F **136**
Frank Soskice Ho. SW6 —2L 13
(off Clem Attlee Ct.)
Franks Rd. *Guild* —9K **93**
Frank Towell Ct. *Felt* —1H **23**
Frantfield. *Eden* —2M **147**
Frant Rd. *T Hth* —4M **45**
Fraser Gdns. *Dork* —4G **118**
Fraser Ho. *Bren* —1M **11**
Fraser Mead. *Col T* —9K **49**
Fraser Rd. *Brack* —9N **15**
Fraser St. *W4* —1D **12**
Frederick Clo. *Sutt* —1L **61**
Frederick Gdns. *Sutt* —1L **61**
Frederick Pl. *Wokgm* —2A **30**
Frederick Rd. *Sutt* —2L **61**
Frederick Sanger Rd. *Sur R* —4G **113**
Frederick St. *Alder* —2M **109**
Freeborn Way. *Brack* —9C **16**
Freedown La. *Sutt* —9N **61**
Freehold Ind. Cen. *Houn* —8K **9**
Freelands Av. *S Croy* —5G **64**
Freelands Dri. *C Crook* —8A **88**
Freelands Rd. *Cobh* —1J **77**
Freeman Clo. *Shep* —3F **38**
Freeman Dri. *W Mol* —2N **39**
Freeman Rd. *Mord* —4B **44**
Freeman Rd. *Warn* —9F **178**
Freemantle Clo. *Bag* —3J **51**
Freemantle Rd. *Bag* —4K **51**
Freemasons Rd. *Croy* —7B **46**
Free Prae Rd. *Cher* —7J **37**
Freesia Clo. *Orp* —2N **67**
Freesia Dri. *Bisl* —3D **72**
French Apartments, The. *Purl* —8L **63**
Frenchaye. *Add* —2L **55**
Frenches Ct. *Red* —1E **122**
Frenches Rd. *Red* —1E **122**
Frenches, The. *Red* —1E **122**
French Gdns. *B'water* —2J **69**
French Gdns. *Cobh* —1K **77**
Frenchlands Hatch. *E Hor* —5F **96**
French La. *Witl* —6K **151**
Frenchmans Creek. *C Crook* —9A **88**
French St. *Sun* —1K **39**
French St. *W'ham* —6N **107**
French's Wells. *Wok* —4L **73**
Frensham. *Brack* —5B **32**
Frensham Av. *Fleet* —4D **88**
Frensham Clo. *Yat* —9A **48**
Frensham Dri. *SW15* —4E **26**
Frensham Dri. *New Ad* —4M **65**
Frensham Heights Rd. *Rowl* —9F **128**
Frensham La. *Churt* —8E **148**
Frensham La. *Lind & Head* —3B **168**
Frensham Rd. *Crowt* —1G **49**
Frensham Rd. *Farnh & Bourne* —4H **129**
Frensham Rd. *Kenl* —1M **83**
Frensham Vale. *Lwr Bo* —7G **129**
Frensham Way. *Eps* —3H **81**
Frere Av. *Fleet* —6A **88**
Freshborough Ct. *Guild* —4B **114**
Freshfield Bank. *F Row* —7G **187**
Freshfield Clo. *Craw* —4E **182**
Freshfields. *Croy* —7J **47**
Freshford St. *SW18* —4A **28**
Freshmount Gdns. *Eps* —7A **60**
Freshwater Clo. *SW17* —7E **28**
Freshwater Rd. *SW17* —7E **28**
Freshwood Clo. *Beck* —1L **47**
Freshwood Dri. *Yat* —2C **68**
Freshwood Way. *Wall* —5F **62**
Frewin Rd. *SW18* —2B **28**
Friar M. *SE27* —4M **29**
Friars Av. *SW15* —4E **26**
Friars Field. *Farnh* —9G **108**
Friar's Ga. *Guild* —5K **113**
Friars Keep. *Brack* —3N **31**
Friars La. *Rich* —8K **11**
Friars Orchard. *Fet* —8D **78**
Friars Rise. *Wok* —5C **74**
Friars Rd. *Vir W* —3N **35**
Friars Rookery. *Craw* —3D **182**
Friars Stile Pl. *Rich* —9L **11**
Friars Stile Rd. *Rich* —9L **11**
Friars Way. *Cher* —5H **37**
Friarswood. *Croy* —5H **65**
Friary Bri. *Guild* —5M **113**
Friary Ct. *Wok* —5J **73**
Friary Island. *Wray* —9M **5**
Friary Pas. *Guild* —5M **113**
Friary Rd. *Asc* —5L **33**
Friary Rd. *Wray* —1M **19**
Friary St. *Guild* —5N **113**
Friary, The. *Guild* —4M **113**
Friary, The. *Old Win* —9M **5**
Friary Way. *Craw* —4C **182**
Friday Rd. *Mitc* —8D **28**
Friday St. *Dork* —6D **158**
Friday St. *Rusp* —4L **179**
Friday St. *Warn* —1E **196**
Friday St. Rd. *Dork* —3M **137**
Friend Av. *Alder* —3B **110**
Friends Clo. *Craw* —9B **162**
Friendship Way *Brack* —2N **31**
Friends Rd. *Croy* —9A **46**
Friends Rd. *Purl* —8M **63**
Friends Wlk. *Stai* —6H **21**
Friesian Clo. *Fleet* —1C **88**
Frimley Av. *Wall* —2K **63**
Frimley Bus. Pk. *Frim* —6A **70**
Frimley By-Pass. *Frim* —6A **70**
Frimley Clo. *SW19* —3K **27**
Frimley Clo. *New Ad* —4M **65**
Frimley Cres. *New Ad* —4M **65**
Frimley Gdns. *Mitc* —2C **44**
Frimley Grn. Rd. *Frim* —6C **70**
Frimley Gro. Gdns. *Frim* —5B **70**
Frimley Hall Dri. *Camb* —9D **50**
Frimley High St. *Frim* —6A **70**
Frimley Rd. *Ash V* —4E **90**
Frimley Rd. *Camb & Frim* —1M **69**
Frimley Rd. *Chess* —2K **59**
Frinton Rd. *SW17* —7E **28**
Friston St. *SW6* —5N **13**
Friston Wlk. *Craw* —1M **181**
Fritham Clo. *N Mald* —5D **42**
Frith End Rd. *Bord* —4A **148**
Frith Hill Rd. *Frim* —5E **70**
Frith Hill Rd. *G'ming* —5G **133**
Frith Knowle. *W On T* —3J **57**
Frith Pk. *E Grin* —7A **166**
Frith Rd. *Croy* —8N **45**
Friths Dri. *Reig* —9N **101**
Frithwald Rd. *Cher* —6H **37**
Frobisher. *Brack* —6A **32**
Frobisher Clo. *Kenl* —4N **83**
Frobisher Cres. *Stai* —1N **21**
Frobisher Gdns. *Guild* —2C **114**
Frobisher Gdns. *Stai* —1N **21**
Frodsham Way. *Owl* —5K **49**
Froggetts La. *Wal W* —9K **157**
Frog Gro. La. *Wood S* —1C **112**
Frog Hall Dri. *Wokgm* —2D **30**
Froghole La. *Eden* —1M **127**
Frog La. *Brack* —2M **31**
Frog La. *Sut G* —3A **94**
Frogmore. *SW18* —8M **13**
Frogmore Border. *Wind* —6H **5**
Frogmore Clo. *Sutt* —9K **43**
Frogmore Ct. *B'water* —2H **69**
Frogmore Ct. *S'hall* —1N **9**
Frogmore Dri. *Wind* —4H **5**
Frogmore Gdns. *Sutt* —1K **61**
Frogmore Gro. *B'water* —2H **69**
Frogmore Pk. Dri. *B'water* —2H **69**
Frogmore Rd. *B'water* —1G **69**
Frome Clo. *F'boro* —8J **69**
Fromondes Rd. *Sutt* —2K **61**
Fromow Gdns. *W'sham* —3A **52**
Froxfield Down. *Brack* —4D **32**
Fruen Rd. *Felt* —1G **23**
Fry Clo. *Craw* —8N **181**
Fryern Wood. *Cat* —2N **103**
Frylands Ct. *New Ad* —7M **65**
Frymley View. *Wind* —4A **4**
Fry Rd. *Ashf* —5M **21**
Fry's Acre. *Ash* —1E **110**
Fry's La. *Yat* —8D **48**
Fryston Av. *Coul* —1F **82**
Fryston Av. *Croy* —8D **46**
Fuchsia Pl. *Brack* —1B **32**
Fuchsia Way. *W End* —9B **52**
Fugelmere Rd. *Fleet* —3D **88**
Fugelmere Wlk. *Fleet* —3D **88**
Fulbourne Clo. *Red* —1C **122**
Fulbrook Av. *New H* —7J **55**
Fulford Ho. *Eps* —4C **60**
Fulford Rd. *Cat* —8A **84**
Fulford Rd. *Eps* —4C **60**
Fulfords Hill. *H'ham* —9A **196**
Fulfords Rd. *H'ham* —9B **196**
Fulham B'way. *SW6* —3M **13**
Fulham Broadway. (Junct.) —3M **13**
Fulham Clo. *Craw* —7N **181**
Fulham High St. *SW6* —5K **13**

Fulham Pal. Rd.—Glendower Gdns.

Fulham Pal. Rd. W6 & SW6 —1H 13
Fulham Pk. Gdns. SW6 —5L 13
Fulham Pk. Rd. SW6 —5L 13
Fulham Rd. SW6 —5K 13
Fulham Rd. SW10 & SW3 —2N 13
Fullbrook La. Elst —6G 130
Fullbrooks Av. Wor Pk —7E 42
Fullers Av. Surb —8M 41
Fullers Hill. W'ham —4M 107
Fullers Rd. Rowl —7C 128
Fullers Vale. Head —4E 168
Fullers Way N. Surb —9M 41
Fullers Way S. Chess —1L 59
Fuller's Wood. Croy —1K 65
Fullers Wood La. S Nut —4G 123
Fullerton Clo. Byfl —1A 76
Fullerton Dri. Byfl —1N 75
Fullerton Rd. SW18 —8N 13
Fullerton Rd. Byfl —1N 75
Fullerton Rd. Cars —5C 62
Fullerton Rd. Croy —6C 46
Fullerton Way. Byfl —1N 75
Fuller Way. Hayes —1G 8
Fullmer Way. Wdhm —6H 55
Fulmar Clo. If'd —4J 181
Fulmar Ct. Surb —5M 41
Fulmar Dri. E Grin —7D 166
Fulmead St. SW6 —4N 13
Fulmer Clo. Hamp —6M 23
Fulstone Clo. Houn —7N 9
Fulvens. Peasl —2F 136
Fulwell Pk. Av. Twic —3B 24
Fulwell Rd. Tedd —5D 24
Fulwood Gdns. Twic —9F 10
Fulwood Wlk. SW19 —2K 27
Furlong Clo. Wall —7F 44
Furlong Rd. Westc —6C 118
Furlough, The. Wok —4C 74
Furmage St. SW18 —1N 27
Furnace Dri. Craw —5D 182
Furnace Farm Rd. Craw —5E 182
Furnace Farm Rd. Felb —7E 164
Furnace Pde. Craw —5E 182
Furnace Pl. Craw —5E 182
Furneaux Av. SE27 —6M 29
Furness. Wind —5A 4
Furness Pl. Wind —5A 4
Furness Rd. SW6 —5N 13
Furness Rd. Mord —5N 43
Furness Row. Wind —5A 4
Furness Sq. Wind —5A 4
Furness Wlk. Wind —5A 4
Furness Way. Wind —5A 4
Furniss Ct. Cranl —8H 155
Furnival Clo. Vir W —5N 35
Furrows Pl. Cat —1C 104
Furrows, The. W On T —8K 39
Furse Clo. Camb —2G 70
Furtherfield. Cranl —6N 155
Furtherfield Clo. Croy —5L 45
Further Vell-Mead. C Crook —9A 88
Furzebank. Asc —3A 34
Furze Clo. Ash V —5E 90
Furze Clo. Red —2D 122
Furzedown Dri. SW17 —6F 28
Furzedown Rd. SW17 —6F 28
Furzedown Rd. Sutt —7A 62
Furzefield. Craw —2N 181
Furze Field. Oxs —9D 58
Furzefield Chase. Dor P —4A 166
Furzefield Cres. Reig —5A 122
Furzefield Rd. E Grin —6N 165
Furzefield Rd. H'ham —3A 198
Furzefield Rd. Reig —5A 122
Furze Gro. Tad —8L 81
Furze Hill. Farnh —9B 110
Furze Hill. Kgswd —7L 81
Furze Hill. Purl —7J 63
Furze Hill. Red —2C 122
Furzehill Cotts. Pirb —9N 71
Furze Hill Cres. Crowt —3H 49
Furze Hill Rd. Head —5G 168
Furze La. E Grin —6L 165
Furze La. G'ming —3J 133
Furze La. Purl —7J 63
Furzemoors. Brack —4N 31
Furzen La. Rud & Dork —6H 177
Furze Rd. Add —3H 55
Furze Rd. Rud —9E 176
Furze Rd. T Hth —2N 45
Furze Vale Rd. Head —5G 169
Furze View. Slin —9J 195
Furzewood. Sun —9H 23
Fuzzens Wlk. Wind —5B 4
Fydler's Clo. Wink —7M 17
Fyfield Clo. B'water —1J 69
Fyfield Clo. Brom —3N 47

Gable Ct. Red —2E 122
(off St Anne's Mt.)
Gable End. F'boro —1N 89
Gables. Gray —6B 170
Gables Av. Ashf —6A 22
Gables Clo. Ash V —8E 90
Gables Clo. Dat —2K 5
Gables Clo. F'boro —1M 89
Gables Clo. Kingf —7B 74
(in two parts)
Gables Ct. Kingf —7B 74
Gables Rd. C Crook —9A 88
Gables, The. Bans —4L 81
Gables, The. Copt —7M 163
Gables, The. Horl —9E 142
Gables, The. H'ham —4K 197
Gables, The. Oxs —8C 58
Gabriel Clo. Felt —5M 23
Gabriel Dri. Camb —2F 70
Gabriel Rd. M'bowr —7G 183
Gadbridge La. Ewh —6F 156
Gadbrook Rd. Bet —9B 120
Gadd Clo. Wokgm —1E 30
Gadesden Rd. Eps —3B 60
(in two parts)
Gaffney Clo. Alder —6B 90
Gage Clo. Craw D —9F 164
Gage Ridge. F Row —7G 187
Gaggle Wood. Man H —9B 198
Gailys Rd. Wind —5A 4
Gainsborough. Brack —5A 32
Gainsborough Clo. Camb —8D 50
Gainsborough Clo. Esh —7E 40
Gainsborough Clo. F'boro —3B 90
Gainsborough Ct. W4 —1A 12
(off Chaseley Dri.)
Gainsborough Ct. Fleet —4B 88
Gainsborough Ct. W On T —1H 57
Gainsborough Dri. Asc —2H 33
Gainsborough Dri. S Croy —9D 64
Gainsborough Gdns. Iswth —8D 10
Gainsborough Rd. Craw —6D 182
Gainsborough Rd. Eps —6B 60
Gainsborough Rd. N Mald —6C 42
Gainsborough Rd. Rich —5M 11
Gaist Av. Cat —9E 84
Galahad Rd. If'd —3K 181
Galata Rd. SW13 —3F 12
Galba Ct. Bren —3K 11
Gale Clo. Hamp —7M 23
Gale Clo. Mitc —2B 44
Gale Cres. Bans —4M 81
Gale Dri. Light —6L 51
Galena Rd. W6 —1G 12
Galesbury Rd. SW18 —9N 13
Gales Clo. Guild —1F 114
Gales Dri. Craw —3D 182
Gales Pl. Craw —3E 182
Galgate Clo. SW19 —2K 27
Gallery Rd. Pirb —6A 72
Galleymead Rd. Coln —4H 7
Gallop, The. S Croy —4E 64
Gallop, The. Sutt —5B 62
Gallop, The. Wind —1F 18
Gallop, The. Yat —8C 48
Galloway Clo. Fleet —1D 88
Galloway Path. Croy —1A 64
Gallwey Rd. Alder —1N 109
Gally Hill Rd. C Crook —8A 88
Gallys Rd. Wind —5A 4
Galpin's Rd. T Hth —4J 45
Galsworthy Rd. Cher —6J 37
Galsworthy Rd. King T —9A 26
Galton Rd. Asc —5C 34
Galvani Way. Croy —7K 45
Galveston Rd. SW15 —8L 13
Galvins Clo. Guild —9K 93
Galway Rd. Yat —2B 68
Gambles La. Rip —2L 95
Gambole Rd. SW17 —5C 28
Gamlen Rd. SW15 —7J 13
Gander Grn. La. Sutt —8K 43
Gangers Hill. God & Wold —6H 105
Ganghill. Guild —1C 114
Ganymede Ct. Craw —6K 181
Gapemouth Rd. Pirb —9H 71
Gap Rd. SW19 —6M 27
Garbetts Way. Tong —6D 110
Garbrand Wlk. Eps —5E 60
Garden Av. Mitc —8F 28
Garden Clo. SW15 —1H 27
Garden Clo. Add —1M 55
Garden Clo. Ashf —7D 22
Garden Clo. Bans —2M 81
Garden Clo. E Grin —2B 186
Garden Clo. F'boro —2K 89
Garden Clo. Hamp —6N 23
Garden Clo. Lea —3J 99
Garden Clo. Sham G —7F 134
Garden Clo. Wall —2J 63
Garden Ct. Croy —9C 46
Garden Ct. Hamp —6N 23
Garden Ct. Rich —4M 11
Gardener Gro. Felt —3N 23
Gardeners Clo. Warn —9E 178
Gardeners Ct. H'ham —7K 197
Gardeners Grn. Rusp —3B 180
Gardener's Hill Rd. Wrec —6G 128
Gardeners Rd. Croy —7M 45
Gardeners Rd. Wink R —7E 16
Gardener's Wlk. Bookh —4B 98
Gardenfields. Tad —6K 81
Garden Ho. La. E Grin —2B 186
Gardenia Dri. W End —9C 52
Garden La. SW2 —2K 29
Garden Pl. H'ham —4J 197
Garden Rd. SE20 —1F 46
Garden Rd. Rich —6N 11
Garden Rd. W On T —5J 39
Gardens, The. Beck —1N 47
Gardens, The. Cobh —6D 76
Gardens, The. Esh —1A 58
Gardens, The. Felt —9E 8
Gardens, The. Pirb —9C 72
Gardens, The. Tong —5D 110
Garden Wlk. Beck —1J 47
Garden Wlk. Coul —1F 102
Garden Wlk. Craw —3A 182
Garden Wlk. H'ham —4J 197
Garden Wood Rd. E Grin —9L 165
Gardiner Ct. S Croy —3N 63
Gardner Ho. Felt —3N 23
Gardner La. Craw D —1D 184
Gardner Rd. Guild —3N 113
Garendon Gdns. Mord —6N 43
Garendon Rd. Mord —6N 43
Gareth Clo. Wor Pk —8J 43
Gareth Ct. SW16 —4H 29
Garfield Pl. Wind —5G 4
Garfield Rd. SW19 —6A 28
Garfield Rd. Add —2L 55
Garfield Rd. Camb —1A 70
Garfield Rd. Twic —2G 25
Garibaldi Rd. Red —4D 122
Garland Rd. E Grin —8N 165
Garlands Rd. Lea —8H 79
Garlands Rd. Red —4D 122
Garland Way. Cat —9A 84
Garlichill Rd. Eps —4G 81
Garnet Field. Yat —1A 68
Garnet Rd. T Hth —3N 45
Garrad's Rd. SW16 —4H 29
Garrard Rd. Bans —3M 81
Garratt Clo. Croy —1J 63
Garratt Ct. SW18 —1N 27
Garratt La. SW18 & SW17 —9N 13
Garratts La. Bans —3L 81
Garratt Ter. SW17 —5C 28
Garrett Clo. M'bowr —5G 183
Garrick Clo. Rich —8K 11
Garrick Clo. Stai —8J 21
Garrick Clo. W On T —1J 57
Garrick Cres. Croy —8B 46
Garrick Gdns. W Mol —2A 40
Garrick Ho. W4 —2D 12
Garrick Rd. Rich —5N 11
Garrick Wlk. Craw —6C 182
Garrick Way. Frim G —7C 70
Garrison La. Chess —4K 59
Garrones, The. Craw —2J 183
Garside Clo. Dork —7K 119
Garside Clo. Hamp —7B 24
Garson Clo. Esh —2N 57
Garson La. Wray —1N 19
Garson Rd. Esh —3N 57
Garson's La. Warf —2E 16
Garston Gdns. Kenl —2A 84
Garston La. Kenl —1A 84
Garstons, The. Bookh —3A 98
Garswood. Brack —5B 32
Garth Clo. W4 —1C 12
Garth Clo. Farnh —4F 128
Garth Clo. King T —6M 25
Garth Clo. Mord —6J 43
Garth Ct. W4 —2C 12
Garth Ct. Dork —7H 119
Garth Rd. W4 —1C 12
Garth Rd. King T —6M 25
Garth Rd. Mord —6H 43
Garth Rd. Ind. Est. Mord —7J 43
Garthside. Ham —6L 25
Garth Sq. Brack —8N 15
Garth, The. Ash —3D 110
Garth, The. Cobh —9M 57
Garth, The. F'boro —1B 90
Garth, The. Hamp —7B 24
Gartmoor Gdns. SW19 —2L 27
Garton Clo. If'd —4K 181
Garton Pl. SW18 —9N 13
Gascoigne Rd. New Ad —6M 65
Gascoigne Rd. Wey —9C 38
Gasden Copse. Witl —5A 152
Gasden Dri. Witl —4A 152
Gasden La. Witl —4A 152
Gaskarth Rd. SW12 —1F 28
Gaskyns Clo. Rud —1E 194
Gassiot Rd. SW17 —5D 28
Gassiot Way. Sutt —9B 44
Gasson Wood Rd. Craw —5K 181
Gastein Rd. W6 —2J 13
Gaston Bell Clo. Rich —6M 11
Gaston Bri. Rd. Shep —5E 38
Gaston Rd. Mitc —2E 44
Gaston Way. Shep —4E 38
Gate Cen., The. Bren —3G 11
Gateford Dri. H'ham —2M 197
Gatehouse Clo. King T —8B 26
Gates Clo. M'bowr —7G 182
Gatesden Rd. Fet —1C 98
Gates Grn. Rd. W Wick —1B 66
Gateside Rd. SW17 —4D 28
Gate St. Brmly —1C 154
Gateway. Wey —9C 38
Gateways. Guild —4D 114
Gateways Ct. Wall —2F 62
Gateway, The. Wok —1E 74
Gatfield Gro. Felt —3A 24
Gatfield Ho. Felt —3A 24
Gatley Av. Eps —2A 60
Gatley Dri. Guild —9B 94
Gatton Bottom. Reig —7B 102
Gatton Clo. Reig —9A 102
Gatton Clo. Sutt —5N 61
Gatton Pk. Bus. Cen. Red —7F 102
Gatton Pk. Ct. Reig —8D 102
Gatton Pk. Rd. Reig —1B 122
Gatton Rd. SW17 —5C 28
Gatton Rd. Reig —1A 122
Gatwick Bus. Pk. Gat A —6F 162
Gatwick Ga. Low H —5C 162
Gatwick Ga. Ind. Est. Low H —5C 162
Gatwick International Distribution Cen. Craw —6F 162
Gatwick Metro Cen. Horl —8F 142
Gatwick Rd. SW18 —1L 27
Gatwick Rd. Craw & Horl —9E 162
Gatwick Way. Horl —2D 162
Gauntlet Cres. Kenl —7A 84
Gauntlett Rd. Sutt —2B 62
Gavell Rd. Cobh —9H 57
Gaveston Clo. Byfl —9A 56
Gaveston Rd. Lea —7G 78
Gavina Clo. Mord —4C 44
Gayfere Rd. Eps —2F 60
Gayhouse La. Out —4A 144
Gayler Clo. Blet —2C 124
Gaynesford Rd. Cars —4D 62
Gay St. SW15 —6J 13
Gayton Clo. Asht —5L 79
Gayton Ct. Reig —2M 121
Gayville Rd. SW11 —1D 28
Gaywood Clo. SW2 —2K 29
Gaywood Rd. Asht —5M 79
Geary Clo. Small —1M 163
Geffers Ride. Asc —1J 33
Gemini Clo. Craw —5K 181
Genesis Bus. Cen. H'ham —5M 197
Genesis Bus. Pk. Wok —2E 74
Geneva Clo. Shep —1F 38
Geneva Rd. King T —3L 41
Geneva Rd. T Hth —4N 45
Genoa Av. SW15 —8H 13
Genoa Rd. SE20 —1F 46
Gentles La. Pass & Head —8F 168
Genyn Rd. Guild —4L 113
George Denyer Clo. Hasl —1G 189
George Eliot Clo. Witl —6C 152
George Gdns. Alder —5A 110
George Gro. Rd. SE20 —1D 46
Georgeham Rd. Owl —5J 49
George Horley Pl. Newd —1A 160
Georgelands. Rip —8K 75
George Lindgren Ho. SW6
(off Clem Attlee Ct.) —3L 13
George Pinton Ct. H'ham —5H 197
George Rd. Fleet —4C 88
George Rd. G'ming —4H 133
George Rd. Guild —3N 113
George Rd. King T —8A 26
George Rd. Milf —9C 132
George Rd. N Mald —3E 42
George Sq. SW19 —2M 43
George's Rd. Tats —7F 86
George's Sq. SW6 —2L 13
(off N. End Rd.)
Georges Ter. Cat —9A 84
George St. Croy —8N 45
George St. Houn —5N 9
George St. Pirb —8L 71
George St. Rich —8K 11
George St. S'hall —1M 9
George St. Stai —5H 21
George Wyver Clo. SW19 —1K 27
Georgian Clo. Camb —8C 50
Georgian Clo. Craw —4H 183
Georgian Clo. Stai —5K 21
Georgian Ct. SW16 —5J 29
Georgia Rd. N Mald —3B 42
Georgia Rd. T Hth —9M 29
Georgina Ct. Fleet —4B 88
Gerald Ct. H'ham —6L 197
Geraldine Rd. SW18 —8N 13
Geraldine Rd. W4 —2N 11
Geralds Gro. Bans —1J 81
Geranium Clo. Crowt —8G 30
Gerard Av. Houn —1A 24
Gerard Rd. SW13 —4E 12
Germander Dri. Bisl —2D 72
Gerrards Mead. Bans —3L 81
Gervis Ct. Houn —3C 10
Ghyll Cres. H'ham —8M 197
Giant Arches Rd. SE24 —1N 29
Gibbet La. Camb —7E 50
Gibbins La. Warf —6B 16
Gibbon Rd. King T —9L 25
Gibbons Clo. M'bowr —6G 183
Gibbons Clo. Sand —7H 49
Gibbon Wlk. SW15 —7F 12
Gibb's Acre. Pirb —1C 92
Gibbs Av. SE19 —6N 29
Gibbs Brook La. Oxt —5N 125
Gibbs Grn. W14 —1L 13
Gibbs Sq. SE19 —6N 29
Gibbs Way. Yat —2A 68
Giblets Way. H'ham —1L 197
Gibraltar Barracks. B'water —4D 68
Gibraltar Cres. Eps —6D 60
Gibson Clo. Chess —2J 59
Gibson Clo. Iswth —6E 10
Gibson Ct. Dat —1B 6
Gibson Ct. Hin W —9F 40
Gibson Ho. Sutt —1M 61
Gibson Pl. Stai —9L 7
Gibson Rd. Sutt —2N 61
Gibsons Hill. SW16 —8L 29
Gidd Hill. Coul —3E 82
Giffard Dri. F'boro —9L 69
Giffards Clo. E Grin —9B 166
Giffards Meadow. Farnh —2K 129
Giffard Way. Guild —9K 93
Giggshill Gdns. Th Dit —7G 40
Giggshill Rd. Th Dit —6G 40
Gilbert Clo. SW19 —9N 27
(off High Path)
Gilbert Rd. SW19 —8A 28
Gilbert Rd. Camb —5A 70
Gilbert St. Houn —6C 10
Gilbert Way. Croy —2K 45
Gilbey Rd. SW17 —5C 28
Gilders Rd. Chess —4M 59
Giles Travers Clo. Egh —2E 36
Gilham La. F Row —7G 187
Gilhams Av. Bans —8J 61
Gill Av. Guild —4H 113
Gillespie Ho. Vir W —3A 36
Gillett Ct. H'ham —4A 198
Gillette Corner. (Junct.) —3G 11
Gillett Rd. T Hth —3A 46
Gillham's La. Hasl —3A 188
Gilliam Gro. Purl —6L 63
Gillian Av. Alder —4A 110
Gillian Clo. Alder —4B 110
Gillian Pk. Rd. Sutt —7L 43
Gilliat Dri. Guild —1F 114
Gilligan Clo. H'ham —6H 197
Gilmais. Bookh —3C 98
Gilman Cres. Wind —6A 4
Gilmore Cres. Ashf —6B 22
Gilpin Av. SW14 —7C 12
Gilpin Clo. Mitc —1C 44
Gilpin Cres. Twic —1B 24
Gilpin Way. Hayes —3E 8
Gilsland Rd. T Hth —3A 46
Gilstead Rd. SW6 —5N 13
Gilston Rd. SW10 —1N 13
Gingers Clo. Cranl —8A 156
Ginhams Rd. Craw —3N 181
Gipsy La. SW15 —6G 12
Gipsy La. Brack —1B 32
Gipsy La. Wey —8C 38
Gipsy La. Wokgm —3B 30
Gipsy Rd. SE27 —5N 29
Gipsy Rd. Gdns. SE27 —5N 29
Girdwood Rd. SW18 —1K 27
Girling Way. Felt —6H 9
Gironde Rd. SW6 —3L 13
Girton Clo. Owl —6K 49
Girton Gdns. Croy —9K 47
Gisbourne Clo. Wall —9H 45
Givons Gro. Roundabout. Lea —2H 99
Glade Clo. Surb —8K 41
Glade Gdns. Croy —6H 47
Gladeside. Croy —5G 47
Gladeside Clo. Chess —4K 59
Gladeside Ct. Warl —7E 84
Glade Spur. Tad —8N 81
Glades, The. E Grin —9D 166
Glade, The. Asc —4N 33
Glade, The. Bucks H —1A 148
Glade, The. Coul —5M 83
Glade, The. Craw —4E 182
Glade, The. Croy —6H 47
Glade, The. Eps —3F 60
Glade, The. Farnh —5J 109
Glade, The. Fet —9B 78
Glade, The. H'ham —5N 197
Glade, The. Stai —8K 21
Glade, The. Sutt —5K 61
Glade, The. Tad —8N 81
Glade, The. W Byf —9G 54
Glade, The. W Wick —9L 47
Gladiator Way. F'boro —5M 89
Gladioli Clo. Hamp —7A 24
Gladsmuir Clo. W On T —8K 39
Gladstone Av. Felt —9H 9
Gladstone Av. Twic —1D 24
Gladstone Pl. E Mol —4E 40
Gladstone Rd. SW19 —8M 27
Gladstone Rd. Asht —5K 79
Gladstone Rd. Croy —6A 46
Gladstone Rd. H'ham —5K 197
Gladstone Rd. King T —2N 41
Gladstone Rd. Orp —2L 67
Gladstone Rd. Surb —8K 41
Gladwyn Rd. SW15 —6J 13
Glamis Clo. Frim —7D 70
Glamorgan Clo. Mitc —2J 45
Glamorgan Rd. King T —8J 25
Glanfield Rd. Beck —3J 47
Glanty, The. Egh —5E 20
Glanville Wlk. Craw —6M 181
Glasbrook Av. Twic —2N 23
Glasford St. SW17 —7D 28
Glassonby Wlk. Camb —1G 70
Glastonbury Rd. Mord —6M 43
Glayshers Hill. Head —3F 168
Glazbury Rd. W14 —1K 13
Glazebrook Clo. SE21 —3N 29
Glazebrook Rd. Tedd —8F 24
Glaziers La. Norm —1M 111
Gleave Clo. E Grin —8C 166
Glebe Av. Mitc —1C 44
Glebe Clo. W4 —1D 12
Glebe Clo. Bookh —4A 98
Glebe Clo. Craw —2C 182
Glebe Clo. Light —6N 51
Glebe Clo. S Croy —7C 64
Glebe Cotts. Felt —4A 24
Glebe Cotts. W Cla —1K 115
Glebe Ct. Fleet —4A 88
Glebe Ct. Guild —3B 114
Glebe Ct. Mitc —2D 44
Glebe Gdns. Byfl —1N 75
Glebe Gdns. N Mald —6D 42
Glebe Hyrst. S Croy —8C 64
Glebeland Rd. Camb —2L 69
Glebelands. Clay —5F 58
Glebelands Craw D —2D 184
Glebelands. Loxw —4H 193
Glebelands. W Mol —4B 40
Glebelands Gdns. Shep —5D 38
Glebelands Rd. Felt —2H 23
Glebelands Rd. Wokgm —1B 30
Glebe La. Ab C —3L 137
Glebe La. Tilf —5A 150
Glebe Path. Mitc —2D 44
Glebe Rd. SW13 —5F 12
Glebe Rd. Asht —5K 79
Glebe Rd. Cars —3D 62
Glebe Rd. Cranl —7M 155
Glebe Rd. Dork —5F 118
Glebe Rd. Egh —7E 20
Glebe Rd. F'boro —9L 69
Glebe Rd. Head —4D 168
Glebe Rd. Old Win —8L 5
Glebe Rd. Red —2F 102
Glebe Rd. Stai —6K 21
Glebe Rd. Sutt —5K 61
Glebe Rd. Warl —5H 85
Glebe Side. Twic —9F 10
Glebe Sq. Mitc —2D 44
Glebe St. W4 —1D 12
Glebe Ter. W4 —1D 12
Glebe, The. SW16 —5J 29
Glebe, The. B'water —2K 69
Glebe, The. Copt —7M 163
Glebe, The. Ewh —4F 156
Glebe, The. Felb —6K 165
Glebe, The. Horl —8D 142
Glebe, The. Leigh —1F 140
Glebe, The. Wor Pk —7E 42
Glebe Way. Felt —4A 24
Glebe Way. S Croy —8C 64
Glebe Way. W Wick —8M 47
Glebewood. Brack —4A 32
Gledhow Gdns. SW5 —1N 13
Gledhow Wood. Tad —8N 81
Gledstanes Rd. W14 —1K 13
Gleeson Dri. Orp —1N 67
Glegg Pl. SW15 —7J 13
Glen Albyn Rd. SW19 —3J 27
Glena Mt. Sutt —1A 62
Glen Av. Ashf —5B 22
Glenavon Clo. Clay —3G 58
Glenavon Ct. Wor Pk —8G 43
Glenavon Gdns. Yat —2C 68
Glenbuck Rd. Surb —5K 41
Glenburnie Rd. SW17 —4D 28
Glencairn Rd. SW16 —9J 29
Glen Clo. Hind —3A 170
Glen Clo. Shep —3B 38
Glen Clo. Tad —1K 101
Glencoe Clo. Frim —6E 70
Glencoe Rd. Wey —9B 38
Glen Ct. Add —2H 55
Glen Ct. St J —6K 73
Glen Ct. Flats. Hind —3A 170
Glendale Clo. H'ham —2N 197
Glendale Clo. Wok —5M 73
Glendale Dri. SW19 —6L 27
Glendale Dri. Guild —8D 94
Glendale M. Beck —1L 47
Glendale Rise. Kenl —2M 83
Glendarvon St. SW15 —6J 13
Glendene Av. E Hor —4F 96
Glendon Ho. Craw —4B 182
Glendower Gdns. SW14 —6C 12

Glendower Rd. *SW14* —6C **12**
Glendyne Clo. *E Grin* —1C **186**
Glendyne Way. *E Grin* —1C **186**
Gleneagle M. *SW16* —6H **29**
Gleneagle Rd. *SW16* —6H **29**
Gleneagles Clo. *Stai* —9M **7**
Gleneagles Ct. *Craw* —4B **182**
Gleneagles Dri. *F'boro* —2H **89**
Gleneagles Ho. *Brack* —5K **31**
Gleneldon M. *SW16* —5J **29**
Gleneldon Rd. *SW16* —5J **29**
Glenfield Clo. *Brock* —7A **120**
Glenfield Cotts. *Horl* —3J **161**
Glenfield Ho. *Brack* —3A **32**
Glenfield Rd. *SW12* —2G **29**
Glenfield Rd. *Ashf* —7C **22**
Glenfield Rd. *Bans* —2N **81**
Glenfield Rd. *Brock* —6A **120**
Glen Gdns. *Croy* —9L **45**
Glenheadon Clo. *Lea* —1K **99**
Glenheadon Rise. *Lea* —1K **99**
Glenhurst. *W'sham* —1L **51**
Glenhurst Clo. *B'water* —2K **69**
Glenhurst Rise. *SE19* —8N **29**
Glenhurst Rd. *Bren* —2J **11**
Gleninnes. *Col T* —6L **49**
Glenister Pk. Rd. *SW16* —8H **29**
Glenlea. *Gray* —8C **170**
Glenlea Hollow. *Gray* —9C **170**
Glenmill. *Hamp* —6N **23**
Glenmore Clo. *Add* —9K **37**
Glenmount Rd. *Myt* —3E **90**
Glenn Av. *Purl* —7M **63**
Glennie Rd. *SE27* —4L **29**
Glen Rd. *Chess* —1M **59**
Glen Rd. *Fleet* —5A **88**
Glen Rd. *Gray* —6B **170**
Glen Rd. *Hind* —3B **170**
Glen Rd. End. *Wall* —3F **62**
Glenrosa St. *SW6* —5N **13**
Glentanner Way. *SW17* —4B **28**
Glentham Gdns. *SW13* —2G **12**
Glentham Rd. *SW13* —2F **12**
Glen, The. *Add* —2H **55**
Glen, The. *Brom* —1N **47**
Glen, The. *Croy* —9G **47**
Glen, The. *Red* —5D **122**
Glen, The. *S'hall* —1N **9**
Glenthorne Av. *Croy* —7F **46**
Glenthorne Clo. *Sutt* —7M **43**
Glenthorne Gdns. *Sutt* —7M **43**
Glenthorne M. *W6* —1G **13**
Glenthorne Rd. *King T* —3M **41**
Glenthorpe Rd. *Mord* —4J **43**
Glentrammon Av. *Orp* —3N **67**
Glentrammon Clo. *Orp* —2N **67**
Glentrammon Gdns. *Orp* —3N **67**
Glentrammon Rd. *Orp* —3N **67**
Glenview Clo. *Craw* —1D **182**
Glenville Gdns. *Hind* —5D **170**
Glenville M. *SW18* —1N **27**
Glenville Rd. *King T* —9N **25**
Glen Vue. *E Grin* —9A **166**
Glen Wlk. *Iswth* —8D **10**
Glenwood. *Brack* —3B **32**
Glenwood. *Dork* —7J **119**
Glenwood Rd. *Eps* —3F **60**
Glenwood Rd. *Houn* —6D **10**
Glenwood Way. *Croy* —5G **47**
Gliddon Rd. *W14* —1K **13**
Globe Farm La. *B'water* —1G **68**
Glorney Mead. *Bad L* —6M **109**
Glory Mead. *Dork* —8J **119**
Glossop Rd. *S Croy* —5A **64**
Gloster Rd. *N Mald* —3D **42**
Gloster Rd. *Wok* —7C **74**
Gloucester Clo. *E Grin* —1C **186**
Gloucester Clo. *Frim G* —8C **70**
Gloucester Clo. *Th Dit* —7G **40**
Gloucester Ct. *Mitc* —4J **45**
Gloucester Ct. *Rich* —3N **11**
Gloucester Cres. *Stai* —7M **21**
Gloucester Dri. *Stai* —4E **20**
Gloucester Gdns. *Bag* —4J **51**
Gloucester Gdns. *Sutt* —8N **43**
Gloucester Ho. *Rich* —8N **11**
Gloucester Pl. *Wind* —5G **5**
Gloucester Rd. *Alder* —5A **110**
Gloucester Rd. *Bag* —4J **51**
Gloucester Rd. *Craw* —7C **182**
Gloucester Rd. *Croy* —6A **46**
Gloucester Rd. *Felt* —2K **23**
Gloucester Rd. *Guild* —1J **113**
Gloucester Rd. *Hamp* —8B **24**
Gloucester Rd. *Houn* —7M **9**
Gloucester Rd. *King T* —1N **41**
Gloucester Rd. *Red* —2D **122**
Gloucester Rd. *Rich* —3N **11**
Gloucester Rd. *Tedd* —6E **24**
Gloucester Rd. *Twic* —2C **24**
Gloucestershire Lea. *Warf* —8D **16**
Gloucester Sq. *Wok* —4A **74**
Gloucester Wlk. *Wok* —4A **74**
Glovers Field. *Hasl* —2D **188**
Glover's Rd. *Charl* —3J **161**
Glover's Rd. *Reig* —4N **121**
Gloxinia Wlk. *Hamp* —7A **24**
Glyn Clo. *SE25* —1B **46**
Glyn Clo. *Eps* —5F **60**
Glyn Ct. *SE27* —4L **29**
Glyndale Grange. *Sutt* —3N **61**
Glynde Ho. *Craw* —1C **182**
Glynde Pl. H'ham —7J 197
(off South St.)
Glyn Rd. *Wor Pk* —8J **43**
Glynswood. *Camb* —3D **70**
Glynswood. *Wrec* —7F **128**
Goater's All. SW6 —3L 13
(off Dawes Rd.)
Goaters Rd. *Asc* —1G **33**
Goat Ho. Bri. *SE25* —2D **46**
Goat Rd. *Mitc* —6E **44**
Goatsfield Rd. *Tats* —7E **86**
Goat Wharf. *Bren* —2L **11**
Godalming Av. *Wall* —2J **63**
Godalming Bus. Cen. *G'ming* —7J **133**
Godalming Rd. *Loxh* —7A **154**
Goddard Clo. *M'bowr* —6F **182**
Goddard Clo. *Shep* —2A **38**
Goddard Rd. *Beck* —3G **47**
Goddards La. *Camb* —3N **69**
Godfrey Av. *Twic* —1D **24**
Godfrey Way. *Houn* —1N **23**
Godley Rd. *SW18* —2B **28**
Godley Rd. *Byfl* —1A **76**
Godolphin Clo. *Sutt* —7L **61**
Godolphin Ct. *Craw* —5B **182**
Godolphin Rd. *Wey* —3E **56**
Godric Cres. *New Ad* —6N **65**
Godson Rd. *Croy* —9L **45**
Godstone By-Pass. *God* —7F **104**
Godstone Grn. *God* —9E **104**
Godstone Hill. *Cat & God* —5E **104**
Godstone Hill. *God* —8F **104**
Godstone Interchange. (Junct.) —7F **104**
Godstone Mt. *Purl* —8M **63**
Godstone Rd. *Blet* —2A **124**
Godstone Rd. *Cat* —2D **104**
Godstone Rd. *Ling* —6M **145**
Godstone Rd. *Oxt* —9K **105**
Godstone Rd. *Purl & Whyt* —8M **63**
Godstone Rd. *Sutt* —1A **62**
Godstone Rd. *Twic* —9H **11**
Godwin Clo. *Eps* —3B **60**
Goepel Ct. *Craw* —2E **182**
Goffs Clo. *Craw* —4A **182**
Goffs La. *Craw* —3N **181**
Goffs Pk. Rd. *Craw* —4A **182**
Goffs Rd. *Ashf* —7E **22**
Gogmore Farm Clo. *Cher* —6H **37**
Gogmore La. *Cher* —6J **37**
Goidel Clo. *Wall* —1H **63**
Goldcliff Clo. *Mord* —6M **43**
Goldcrest Clo. *Horl* —7C **142**
Goldcrest Clo. *Yat* —9A **48**
Goldcrest Way. *New Ad* —5N **65**
Goldcrest Way. *Purl* —6H **63**
Goldcup La. *Asc* —9H **17**
Golden Ct. *Rich* —8K **11**
Golden Orb Wood. *Binf* —9J **15**
Goldfinch Clo. *Alder* —4L **109**
Goldfinch Clo. *Craw* —1B **182**
Goldfinch Clo. *H'ham* —1J **197**
Goldfinch Gdns. *Guild* —2F **114**
Goldfinch Rd. *S Croy* —6G **65**
Goldfort Wlk. *Wok* —3H **73**
Goldhawk Rd. *W6 & W12* —1E **12**
Gold Hill. *Lwr Bo* —5H **129**
Golding Clo. *Chess* —3J **59**
Golding Clo. *M'bowr* —4G **182**
Golding La. *Man H* —9C **198**
Golding's Hill. *H'ham* —9C **198**
Goldings, The. *Wok* —3J **73**
Goldney Rd. *Camb* —2F **70**
Goldrings Rd. *Oxs* —9C **58**
Goldsmiths Clo. *Wok* —5M **73**
Goldsmith Way. *Crowt* —3G **48**
Goldstone Farm View. *Bookh* —5A **98**
Goldsworth Orchard. *Wok* —5K **73**
Goldsworth Pk. Cen., The. *Wok* —4K **73**
Goldsworth Pk. Trad. Est. *Wok* —3L **73**
Goldsworth Rd. *Wok* —5M **73**
Goldwell Rd. *T Hth* —3K **45**
Gole Rd. *Pirb* —8N **71**
Golf Clo. *T Hth* —9L **29**
Golf Clo. *Wok* —1G **75**
Golf Club Cotts. *S'dale* —7F **34**
Golf Club Dri. *King T* —8C **26**
Golf Club Rd. *Wey* —5C **56**
Golf Club Rd. *Wok* —7K **73**
Golf Dri. *Camb* —2D **70**
Golf Ho. Rd. *Oxt* —7E **106**
Golf Links Av. *Hind* —3N **169**
Golf Rd. *Kenl* —5A **84**
Golf Side. *Sutt* —7K **61**
Golf Side. *Twic* —4D **24**
Golfside Clo. *N Mald* —1D **42**
Goliath Clo. *Wall* —4J **63**
Gomer Gdns. *Tedd* —7G **24**
Gomer Pl. *Tedd* —7G **24**
Gomshall Av. *Wall* —2J **63**
Gomshall Gdns. *Kenl* —2B **84**
Gomshall La. *Shere* —8B **116**
Gomshall Rd. *Gom* —8C **116**
Gomshall Rd. *Sutt* —6H **61**
Gondreville Gdns. *C Crook* —9A **88**
Gong Hill. *Bourne* —8J **129**
Gong Hill Dri. *Bourne* —7J **129**
Gonston Clo. *SW19* —3K **27**
Gonville Rd. *T Hth* —4K **45**
Gonville St. *SW6* —6K **13**
Goodchild Rd. *Wokgm* —2C **30**
Goodden Cres. *F'boro* —2L **89**
Goodenough Clo. *Coul* —7L **83**
Goodenough Rd. *SW19* —8L **27**
Goodenough Way. *Coul* —7K **83**
Goodfellow Gdns. *King T* —6B **26**
Goodfellow Grn. *Brack* —5B **32**
Goodhart Way. *W Wick* —6N **47**
Goodhew Rd. *Croy* —5D **46**
Gooding Clo. *N Mald* —3B **42**
Goodings Grn. *Wokgm* —2E **30**
Goodley Stock Rd. *Crook C & W'ham* —9K **107**
Goodman Cres. *SW2* —3J **29**
Goodman Pl. *Stai* —5H **21**
Goodways Dri. *Brack* —1A **32**
Goodwin Clo. *Bew* —6L **181**
Goodwin Clo. *Mitc* —2B **44**
Goodwin Ct. *SW19* —8C **28**
Goodwin Gdns. *Croy* —3M **63**
Goodwin Rd. *Croy* —2M **63**
Goodwins Clo. *E Grin* —7N **165**
Goodwood Clo. *Camb* —7A **50**
Goodwood Clo. *Craw* —6F **183**
Goodwood Clo. *Mord* —3M **43**
Goodwood Pde. *Beck* —3H **47**
Goodwood Pl. *F'boro* —2C **90**
Goodwood Rd. *Red* —1D **122**
Goodwyns Pl. *Dork* —7H **119**
Goodwyns Rd. *Dork* —8J **119**
Goose Corner. *Warf* —6D **16**
Goose Grn. *D'side* —6J **77**
Goose Grn. *Gom* —8D **116**
Goose Grn. Clo. *H'ham* —3K **197**
Goose La. *Wok* —9L **73**
Goosepool. *Cher* —6H **37**
Goose Rye Rd. *Worp* —4G **93**
Goossens Clo. *Sutt* —2A **62**
Gordon Av. *SW14* —7D **12**
Gordon Av. *Camb* —2N **69**
Gordon Av. *C Crook* —7C **88**
Gordon Av. *N Mald* —1E **42**
Gordon Av. *S Croy* —6N **63**
Gordon Av. *Twic* —8G **11**
Gordon Clo. *Cher* —9G **37**
Gordon Clo. *Stai* —7K **21**
Gordon Ct. *Camb* —1A **70**
Gordon Ct. Red —5D 122
(off St John's Ter. Rd.)
Gordon Cres. *Camb* —2A **70**
Gordon Cres. *Croy* —7B **46**
Gordondale Rd. *SW19* —3M **27**
Gordon Dri. *Cher* —9G **37**
Gordon Dri. *Shep* —6E **38**
Gordon Henry Ho. *Eden* —2L **147**
Gordon Rd. *W4* —2A **12**
Gordon Rd. *Alder* —3M **109**
(in two parts)
Gordon Rd. *Ashf* —4N **21**
Gordon Rd. *Beck* —2J **47**
Gordon Rd. *Camb* —2A **70**
Gordon Rd. *Cars* —3D **62**
Gordon Rd. *Cat* —8A **84**
Gordon Rd. *Clay* —4E **58**
Gordon Rd. *Crowt* —4J **49**
Gordon Rd. *F'boro* —5B **90**
(in two parts)
Gordon Rd. *H'ham* —4K **197**
Gordon Rd. *Houn* —7C **10**
Gordon Rd. *King T* —9M **25**
Gordon Rd. *Red* —9E **102**
Gordon Rd. *Rich* —5M **11**
Gordon Rd. *Shep* —5E **38**
Gordon Rd. *S'hall* —1M **9**
Gordon Rd. *Stai* —5E **20**
Gordon Rd. *Surb* —6M **41**
Gordon Rd. *Wind* —5C **4**
Gordons Way. *Oxt* —6N **105**
Gordon Wlk. *Yat* —1D **68**
Gore Rd. *SW20* —1H **43**
Goring Rd. *Stai* —6F **20**
Goring's Mead. *H'ham* —7K **197**
Goring Sq. *Stai* —5G **21**
Gorling Clo. *If'd* —4K **181**
Gorrick Sq. *Wokgm* —5A **30**
Gorringe Pk. Av. *Mitc* —8D **28**
Gorringes Brook. *H'ham* —2K **197**
Gorse Bank. *Light* —8L **51**
Gorse Clo. *Copt* —8M **163**
Gorse Clo. *Craw* —9N **181**
Gorse Clo. *Tad* —7G **81**
Gorse Clo. *Wrec* —5F **128**
Gorse Cotts. *Fren* —1H **149**
Gorse Ct. *Guild* —1E **114**
Gorse Dri. *Small* —8N **143**
Gorse End. *H'ham* —3K **197**
Gorse Grn. *Cobh* —6H **77**
Gorse Hill La. *Vir W* —3N **35**
Gorse Hill Rd. *Vir W* —3N **35**
Gorselands. *Farnh* —5H **109**
Gorselands. *Yat* —2B **68**
Gorselands Clo. *Ash V* —8E **90**
Gorselands Clo. *Head* —5H **169**
Gorselands Clo. *W Byf* —7L **55**
Gorse La. *Chob* —4H **53**
Gorse La. *Wrec* —5G **128**
Gorse Path. *Wrec* —5F **128**
Gorse Pl. *Wink R* —8F **16**
Gorse Rise. *SW17* —6E **28**
Gorse Rd. *Croy* —1K **65**
Gorse Rd. *Frim* —4C **70**
Gorse Way. *Fleet* —6B **88**
Gorsewood Rd. *Wok* —6G **73**
Gorst Rd. *SW11* —1D **28**
Gort Clo. *Alder* —6C **90**
Gosberton Rd. *SW12* —2D **28**
Gosbury Hill. *Chess* —1L **59**
Gosden Clo. *Brmly* —3B **134**
Gosden Clo. *Craw* —4E **182**
Gosden Cotts. *Brmly* —4B **134**
Gosden Hill Rd. *Guild* —8E **94**
Gosden Rd. *W End* —9C **52**
Gosfield Rd. *Eps* —8C **60**
Goslar Way. *Wind* —5E **4**
Gosnell Clo. *Frim* —3H **71**
Gossops Dri. *Craw* —4L **181**
Gossops Grn. La. *Craw* —4M **181**
Gossops Pde. *Craw* —4L **181**
Gostling Rd. *Twic* —2A **24**
Goston Gdns. *T Hth* —2L **45**
Gostrode La. *C'fold* —8D **190**
Goswell Hill. *Wind* —4G **4**
Goswell Rd. *Wind* —4G **4**
Gothic Ct. *Hayes* —2E **8**
Gothic Rd. *Twic* —3D **24**
Goudhurst Clo. *Worth* —3J **183**
Goudhurst Keep. *Worth* —3J **183**
Gough Rd. *Fleet* —3A **88**
Gough's Barn La. *Brack* —1M **15**
(in two parts)
Gough's La. *Brack* —8B **16**
Gough's Meadow. *Sand* —8G **48**
Gould Ct. *Guild* —1F **114**
Goulding Gdns. *T Hth* —1N **45**
Gould Rd. *Felt* —1F **22**
Gould Rd. *Twic* —2E **24**
Government Ho. Rd. *Alder* —5M **89**
Government Rd. *Alder* —9B **90**
Governor's Rd. *Col T* —9L **49**
Govett Av. *Shep* —4D **38**
Govett Gro. *W'sham* —2A **52**
Gowan Av. *SW6* —4K **13**
Gower Clo. *SW4* —1G **28**
Gower Pk. *Col T* —8J **49**
Gower Rd. *Horl* —8C **142**
Gower Rd. *Iswth* —2F **10**
Gower Rd. *Wey* —3E **56**
Gower, The. *Egh* —2D **36**
Gowland Pl. *Beck* —1J **47**
Goy Mnr. Rd. *SW19* —7J **27**
Graburn Way. *E Mol* —2D **40**
Grace Bennett Clo. *F'boro* —7M **69**
Gracedale Rd. *SW16* —6F **28**
Gracefield Gdns. *SW16* —4J **29**
Grace Reynolds Wlk. *Camb* —9B **50**
Grace Rd. *Broadf* —8M **181**
Grace Rd. *Croy* —5N **45**
Gracious Pond Rd. *Chob* —4K **53**
Graemesdyke Av. *SW14* —6A **12**
Graffham Clo. *Craw* —1N **181**
Grafton Clo. *Houn* —2M **23**
Grafton Clo. *W Byf* —9H **55**
Grafton Clo. *Wor Pk* —9D **42**
Grafton Ct. *Felt* —2E **22**
Grafton Pk. Rd. *Wor Pk* —8D **42**
Grafton Rd. *Croy* —7L **45**
Grafton Rd. *N Mald* —2D **42**
Grafton Rd. *Wor Pk* —9C **42**
Grafton Way. *W Mol* —3N **39**
Graham Av. *Mitc* —9E **28**
Graham Clo. *Croy* —8K **47**
Graham Gdns. *Surb* —7L **41**
Graham Rd. *SW19* —8L **27**
Graham Rd. *Hamp* —5A **24**
Graham Rd. *Mitc* —9E **28**
Graham Rd. *Purl* —9L **63**
Graham Rd. *W'sham* —3N **51**
Grainger Rd. *Iswth* —5F **10**
Grampian Clo. *Hayes* —3E **8**
Grampian Rd. *Sand* —5F **48**
Grampian Way. *Slou* —1C **6**
Granada St. *SW17* —6C **28**
Granard Av. *SW15* —8G **13**
Granard Rd. *SW12* —1D **28**
Granary Clo. *Horl* —6E **142**
Granary Way. *H'ham* —7F **196**
Grand Av. *Camb* —9A **50**
Grand Av. *Surb* —4A **42**
Grand Dri. *SW20* —2H **43**
Granden Rd. *SW16* —1J **45**
Grandfield Ct. *W4* —2C **12**
Grandis Cotts. *Rip* —9K **75**
Grandison Rd. *Wor Pk* —8H **43**
Grand Pde. *Craw* —3B **182**
Grand Pde. M. *SW15* —8K **13**
Grandstand Rd. *Eps* —4E **80**
Grand View Av. *Big H* —4E **86**
Grange Av. *SE25* —1B **46**
Grange Av. *Crowt* —1G **48**
Grange Av. *Twic* —3E **24**
Grangecliffe Gdns. *SE25* —1B **46**
Grange Clo. *Blet* —2A **124**
Grange Clo. *Craw* —1E **182**
Grange Clo. *Eden* —2L **147**
Grange Clo. *G'ming* —6K **133**
Grange Clo. *Guild* —8L **93**
Grange Clo. *Houn* —2N **9**
Grange Clo. *Lea* —7K **79**
Grange Clo. *Mers* —6F **102**
Grange Clo. *Stai* —6J **21**
Grange Clo. *W'ham* —4L **107**
Grange Clo. *W Mol* —3B **40**
Grange Clo. *Wray* —9A **6**
Grange Ct. *Egh* —6B **20**
Grange Ct. *Mers* —6F **102**
Grange Ct. *Shep* —3B **38**
Grange Ct. *S God* —7H **125**
Grange Ct. *Stai* —6J **21**
Grange Ct. *Sutt* —4N **61**
Grange Ct. *W On T* —8H **39**
Grange Cres. *Craw D* —2E **184**
Grange Dri. *Mers* —6F **102**
Grange Dri. *Wok* —2A **74**
Grange End. *Small* —8L **143**
Grange Est. *C Crook* —8A **88**
Grange Farm Rd. *Ash* —1E **110**
Grangefields Rd. *Guild* —6N **93**
Grange Gdns. *SE25* —1D **40**
Grange Gdns. *Bans* —9N **61**
Grange Hill. *SE25* —1B **46**
Grange Lodge. *SW19* —7J **27**
Grange Lodge. *Wind* —3A **4**
Grange Mans. *Eps* —4E **60**
Grange Meadow. *Bans* —9N **61**
Grange Mt. *Lea* —7K **79**
Grange Pk. *Cranl* —7A **156**
Grange Pk. *Wok* —2A **74**
Grange Pk. Pl. *SW20* —8G **26**
Grange Pk. Rd. *T Hth* —3A **46**
Grange Pl. *Stai* —1L **37**
Granger Ho. *F'boro* —2L **89**
Grange Rd. *SE25 & SE19* —2A **46**
Grange Rd. *SW13* —4F **12**
Grange Rd. *W4* —1A **12**
Grange Rd. *Ash* —2F **110**
Grange Rd. *Brack* —9A **16**
Grange Rd. *Camb* —1C **70**
Grange Rd. *Cat* —3D **104**
Grange Rd. *Chess* —1L **59**
Grange Rd. *C Crook* —8A **88**
Grange Rd. *Craw D* —2D **184**
Grange Rd. *Egh* —6B **20**
(in two parts)
Grange Rd. *F'boro* —7N **69**
Grange Rd. *Guild* —7L **93**
Grange Rd. *King T* —2L **41**
Grange Rd. *Lea* —7K **79**
Grange Rd. *New H* —6J **55**
Grange Rd. *Pirb* —9N **71**
Grange Rd. *S Croy* —6N **63**
Grange Rd. *Sutt* —4M **61**
Grange Rd. *T Hth* —3A **46**
Grange Rd. *Tilf* —2N **149**
Grange Rd. *Tong* —7B **110**
Grange Rd. *W On T* —1M **57**
Grange Rd. *W Mol* —3B **40**
Grange Rd. *Wok* —1A **74**
Grange, The. *SW19* —7J **27**
Grange, The. *W4* —1A **12**
Grange, The. *Chob* —6H **53**
Grange, The. *Croy* —8J **47**
Grange, The. *Fren* —3J **149**
Grange, The. *Horl* —5F **142**
Grange, The. *Old Win* —8L **5**
Grange, The. *Vir W* —3A **36**
Grange, The. *W On T* —8J **39**
Grange, The. *Wor Pk* —1C **60**
Grange Vale. *Sutt* —4N **61**
Grangeway. *Small* —8L **143**
Grangewood Dri. *Sun* —8G **22**
Grangewood Ter. *SE25* —1A **46**
Gransden Clo. *Ewh* —5F **156**
Grantchester. King T —1N 41
(off St Peters Rd.)
Grant Clo. *Shep* —5C **38**
Grantham Clo. *Owl* —6K **49**
Grantham Rd. *W4* —3D **12**
Grantley Av. *Won* —5D **134**
Grantley Clo. *Shalf* —1A **134**
Grantley Ct. *Farnh* —5E **128**
Grantley Dri. *Fleet* —6A **88**
Grantley Gdns. *Guild* —2K **113**
Grantley Rd. *Guild* —2K **113**
Grantley Rd. *Houn* —5K **9**
Granton Rd. *SW16* —9G **29**
Grant Pl. *Croy* —7C **46**
Grant Rd. *Crowt* —4H **49**
Grant Rd. *Croy* —7C **46**
Grants La. *Oxt & Eden* —2E **126**
Grant Wlk. *Asc* —7B **34**
Grant Way. *Iswth* —2G **10**
Grantwood Clo. *Red* —8E **122**
Granville Av. *Felt* —3H **23**
Granville Av. *Houn* —8A **10**
Granville Clo. *Byfl* —9A **56**
Granville Clo. *Croy* —8B **46**
Granville Clo. *Wey* —3D **56**
Granville Gdns. *SW16* —8K **29**
Granville Pl. *SW6* —3N **13**
Granville Rd. *SW18* —1L **27**
Granville Rd. *SW19* —8M **27**
Granville Rd. *Hayes* —1G **9**
Granville Rd. *Oxt* —7B **106**
Granville Rd. *W'ham* —4L **107**
Granville Rd. *Wey* —4D **56**
Granville Rd. *Wok* —7B **74**
Granwood Ct. *Iswth* —4E **10**
Grasmere Av. *SW15* —5C **26**
Grasmere Av. *SW19* —2M **43**
Grasmere Av. *Houn* —9B **10**
Grasmere Clo. *Egh* —8D **20**
Grasmere Clo. *Felt* —2G **22**
Grasmere Clo. *Guild* —2D **114**
Grasmere Ct. *SW13* —2F **12**
Grasmere Ct. *Sutt* —3A **62**
Grasmere Gdns. *H'ham* —2A **198**
Grasmere Rd. *SE25* —4E **46**
Grasmere Rd. *SW16* —6K **29**
Grasmere Rd. *F'boro* —2K **89**
Grasmere Rd. *Farnh* —6F **108**
Grasmere Rd. *Light* —6M **51**
Grasmere Rd. *Purl* —7M **63**
Grasmere Way. *Byfl* —8A **56**
Grassfield Clo. *Coul* —6F **82**
Grasslands. *Small* —8L **143**
Grassmere. *Horl* —7G **142**
Grassmount. *Purl* —[illegible]
Grass Way. *Wall* —1G **62**
Gratton Dri. *Wind* —7B **4**
Grattons Dri. *Craw* —9G **162**
Grattons, The. *Slin* —5M **195**
Gravel Hill. *Croy* —3G **64**
Gravel Hill. *Lea* —8H **79**
Gravel Hill Rd. *Holt P* —7A **128**
(in two parts)
Gravelly Hill. *Cat* —6C **104**
Gravel Pitts Cotts. *Gom* —8D **116**
Gravel Pitts La. *Gom* —8D **116**
Gravel Rd. *C Crook* —7C **88**
Gravel Rd. *F'boro* —5B **90**
Gravel Rd. *Farnh* —5G **108**
Gravel Rd. *Twic* —2E **24**
Gravenel Gdns. SW17 —6C 28
(off Nutwell St.)
Graveney Rd. *SW17* —5C **28**
Graveney Rd. *M'bowr* —4G **182**
Gravetts La. *Guild* —8H **93**
Gravetye Clo. *Craw* —5E **182**
Gray Clo. *Add* —2K **55**
Grayham Cres. *N Mald* —3C **42**
Grayham Rd. *N Mald* —3C **42**
Graylands. *Wok* —3A **74**
Graylands Clo. *Wok* —3A **74**
Graylands Ct. *Guild* —4B **114**
Gray Pl. *Ott* —3F **54**
Grays Clo. *Hasl* —9J **171**
Grayscroft Rd. *SW16* —8H **29**
Grayshot Dri. *B'water* —1H **69**
Grayshott. *Gray* —6B **170**
Grayshott Laurels. *Lind* —4B **168**
Grayshott Rd. *Head* —3G **169**
Grays La. *Ashf* —5C **22**
Gray's La. *Asht* —6M **79**
Grays Rd. *G'ming* —4J **133**
Grays Rd. *W'ham* —8K **87**
Grays Wood. *Horl* —8G **143**
Grayswood Comn. *G'wood* —8K **171**
Grayswood Dri. *Myt* —4E **90**
Grayswood Gdns. *SW20* —1G **42**
Grayswood Rd. *Hasl* —1H **189**
Gt. Austins. *Farnh* —3J **129**
Gt. Austins Ho. *Farnh* —3K **129**
Gt. Benty. *W Dray* —1N **7**
Gt. Chertsey Rd. *W4* —5B **12**
Gt. Chertsey Rd. *Felt* —4N **23**
Gt. Church La. *W6* —1J **13**
Gt. Ellshams. *Bans* —3M **81**
Greatfield Clo. *F'boro* —6N **69**
Greatfield Rd. *F'boro* —6M **69**
Greatford Dri. *Guild* —3F **114**
Gt. George St. *G'ming* —7H **133**
Gt. Godwin Dri. *Guild* —1D **114**
Greatham Rd. *M'bowr* —6G **182**
Greatham Wlk. *SW15* —2F **26**
Gt. Hollands Rd. *Brack* —5K **31**
Gt. Hollands Sq. *Brack* —5L **31**
Gt. House Ct. *E Grin* —1B **186**
Greathurst End. *Bookh* —2N **97**
Greatlake Ct. Horl —7F 142
(off Tanyard La.)
Gt. Mead. *Eden* —9L **127**
Gt. Oaks Pk. *Guild* —8E **94**
Gt. Quarry. *Guild* —6N **113**
Gt. South W. Rd. *Felt & Houn* —1D **22**
Gt. Tattenhams. *Eps* —5G **81**
Gt. West Rd. *W4 & W6* —1E **12**
Gt. West Rd. *Bren* —3G **11**

Gt. West Rd.—Guinness Ct.

Gt. West Rd. Houn & Iswth —5L 9
Gt. West Rd. Trad. Est. Bren —2H 11
Gt. West Trad. Est. Bren —2H 11
Greatwood Clo. Ott —5E 54
Gt. Woodcote Dri. Purl —6H 63
Gt. Woodcote Pk. Purl —6H 63
Greaves Pl. SW17 —5C 28
Grebe Cres. H'ham —7N 197
Grebe Ter. King T —2L 41
Grecian Cres. SE19 —7M 29
Green Acre. Alder —3L 109
Green Acre. Knap —3H 73
Greenacre. Wind —5B 4
Greenacre Ct. Egh —7M 19
Greenacre Pl. Hack —8F 44
Greenacres. Bookh —2B 98
Greenacres. Bord —5A 168
Greenacres. Craw —4E 182
Green Acres. Croy —9C 46
Greenacres. H'ham —4J 197
Greenacres. Oxt —5A 106
Green Acres. Runf —1A 130
Greenacres Clo. Orp —1L 67
Green Bank Cotts. Dork —3M 157
Greenbank Way. Camb —4B 70
Greenbush La. Cranl —9A 156
Green Bus. Cen., The. Stai —5E 20
Green Clo. Brom —2N 47
Green Clo. Cars —8D 44
Green Clo. Felt —6M 23
Greencourt Av. Croy —8E 46
Greencourt Gdns. Croy —8E 46
Greencroft. F'boro —1N 89
Greencroft. Guild —3D 114
Green Croft. Wokgm —9D 14
Greencroft Rd. Houn —4N 9
Green Cross La. Churt —9M 149
Green Curve. Bans —1L 81
Green Dene. E Hor —4D 116
Green Dragon La. Bren —1L 11
Green Dri. Rip —1H 95
Green Dri. Slou —1A 6
(in two parts)
Green Dri. Wokgm —4D 30
Greene Fielde End. Stai —8M 21
Green End. Chess —1L 59
Green End. Yat —8C 48
Green Farm Clo. Orp —2N 67
Green Farm Rd. Bag —4K 51
Greenfield. Eden —2M 147
Greenfield. Farnh —4F 128
Greenfield Av. Surb —6A 42
Greenfield Link. Coul —2J 83
Greenfield Rd. Farnh —4E 128
Greenfield Rd. Slin —5L 195
Greenfield Rd. Sutt —1N 61
Greenfields Clo. Horl —6C 142
Greenfields Clo. H'ham —2N 197
Greenfields Pl. Bear G —7K 139
Greenfields Rd. Horl —6D 142
Greenfields Rd. H'ham —3N 197
Greenfields Way. H'ham —2N 197
Greenfield Way. Crowt —9F 30
Green Finch Clo. Crowt —1E 48
Greenfinch Way. H'ham —1K 197
Green Gdns. Orp —2L 67
Green Glades. C Crook —8A 88
Greenham Ho. Houn —6D 10
Greenham Wlk. Wok —5M 73
Greenham Wood. Brack —5A 32
Greenhanger. Churt —1M 169
Greenhaven. Yat —1A 68
Greenhayes Av. Bans —1M 81
Green Hayes Clo. Reig —3A 122
Greenhayes Gdns. Bans —2M 81
Green Hedge. Twic —9J 11
Green Hedges Av. E Grin —8N 165
Green Hedges Clo. E Grin —8N 165
Greenheys Pl. Wok —5B 74
Green Hill. Orp —8H 67
Greenhill. Sutt —8A 44
Greenhill Av. Cat —8E 84
Greenhill Clo. Camb —9G 51
Greenhill Clo. Farnh —4F 128
Greenhill Clo. G'ming —8G 132
Greenhill Gdns. Guild —1E 114
Green Hill La. Warl —4H 85
Green Hill Rd. Camb —9G 51
Greenhill Rd. Farnh —4J 129
Greenhills. Farnh —3K 129
Greenhill Way. Farnh —5F 128
Greenholme. Camb —1H 71
Greenhow. Brack —2M 31
Greenhurst La. Oxt —1B 126
Greenhurst Rd. SE27 —6L 29
Greenlake Ter. Stai —8J 21
Greenlands. Ott —9E 36
Greenlands Rd. Camb —5N 69
Greenlands Rd. Stai —5J 21
Greenlands Rd. Wey —9C 38
Green La. SW16 & T Hth —8K 29
Green La. Alf —5H 175
Green La. Asc —9B 18
Green La. Asht —4J 79
Green La. Bad L —6L 109
Green La. Bag —5K 51
Green La. Bear G —1H 159
Green La. B'water —2K 69
Green La. Blet —7B 104
Green La. Byfl —8A 56
Green La. Cat —9N 83
Green La. Cher & Add —8G 36
Green La. Chess —5K 59
Green La. Chob —6J 53
Green La. Churt —1L 169
Green La. Cobh —8M 57
Green La. Craw —1C 182
Green La. Craw D —6C 164
Green La. Crowt —9F 32
Green La. Dat —4L 5
Green La. Dock —4D 148
Green La. Egh —6D 20
(in two parts)
Green La. Farnh —3F 128
Green La. Felt —6M 23
Green La. Frogm —2G 69
Green La. G'ming —2H 133
Green La. Guild —3D 114
Green La. Hasl —4F 188
Green La. H'ham —5L 179
Green La. Houn —6J 9
Green La. Lea —8K 79
(in two parts)
Green La. Leigh —3D 140
Green La. Ling —8M 145
Green La. Milf —2B 152
Green La. Mord —6H 43
(Battersea Cemetery)
Green La. Mord —5M 43
(Morden)
Green La. Newd —2C 160
Green La. N Mald —4B 42
Green La. Ock —2C 96
Green La. Out —1J 143
Green La. Purl —7G 63
Green La. Red —1C 122
Green La. Reig —3L 121
Green La. Salf —8E 122
Green La. Sand —8H 49
Green La. Sham G —5H 135
Green La. Shep —5D 38
Green La. Ship B —3K 163
Green La. Sun —8G 22
Green La. Tad & Coul —4L 101
Green La. Thorpe & Stai —1E 36
Green La. Tilf —5B 130
Green La. Wal W —7M 157
Green La. W On T —3J 57
Green La. Warl —3H 85
Green La. W Cla —5J 95
Green La. W Mol —4B 40
Green La. Wind —5D 4
Green La. Wok —8L 73
Green La. Wokgm —6F 14
Green La. Wood S —1D 112
Green La. Wor Pk —7F 42
Green La. Worth —3H 183
(in two parts)
Green La. Yat —9A 48
Green La. Av. W On T —2K 57
Green La. Cvn. Pk. Red —1J 143
Green La. Clo. Byfl —8A 56
Green La. Clo. Camb —8A 50
Green La. Clo. Cher —8G 36
Green La. Cotts. Churt —9L 149
Green La. Cotts. Farnh —7L 109
Green La. E. Norm —4K 111
Green La. Gdns. T Hth —1N 45
Green Lanes. Eps —5D 60
(in two parts)
Green La. W. Alder —4J 111
Green La. W. W Hor —3B 96
Greenlaw Gdns. N Mald —6E 42
Green Leaf Av. Wall —1H 63
Greenleaf Clo. SW2 —1L 29
Greenleas. Frim —4C 70
Green Leas. Sun —7G 23
Green Leas Clo. Sun —7G 23
Greenleas Clo. Yat —8B 48
Greenlea Trad. Pk. SW19 —9B 28
Greenleaves Ct. Ashf —7C 22
Green Leys. C Crook —9A 88
Green Man La. Felt —7H 9
Green Mead. Esh —3N 57
Greenmead Clo. SE25 —4D 46
Greenmeads. Wok —9A 74
Greenoak Rise. Big H —5E 86
Greenoak Way. SW19 —5J 27
Greenock Rd. SW16 —9H 29
Greeno Cres. Shep —4B 38
Green Pde. Houn —8B 10
Green Pk. Stai —4G 20
Green Ride. Brack —6D 32
Green Rd. Egh —4B 36
Greensand Clo. Red —6H 103
Greensand Rd. Red —2E 122
Greenside. Crowt —2E 48
Greenside Clo. Guild —1E 114
Greenside Cotts. Rip —8L 75
Greenside Rd. Croy —6L 45
Greenside Wlk. Big H —5D 86
Greenslade Av. Asht —6A 80
Greens La. Dork —3A 160
Greens La. Man H —9C 198
Green's School La. F'boro —1M 89
Greenstead Gdns. SW15 —8G 12
Greenstede Av. E Grin —7B 166
Green St. Sun —9H 23
Green, The. SW19 —6J 27
Green, The. Ashf —6M 21
Green, The. Bad L —7M 109
Green, The. Bet —2F 120
Green, The. B'water —2H 69
Green, The. Brack —3N 31
Green, The. Bur H —6K 81
Green, The. Cars —1E 62
Green, The. C'fold —5F 172
Green, The. Clay —3F 58
Green, The. Copt —7M 163
Green, The. Craw —2A 182
Green, The. Croy —5J 65
Green, The. Dat —3L 5
Green, The. Duns —3B 174
Green, The. Elst —7H 131
Green, The. Eps —7F 60
Green, The. Ewh —6F 156
Green, The. Farnh —6H 109
Green, The. Felt —3J 23
Green, The. Fet —2D 98
Green, The. Frim G —8D 70
Green, The. God —1E 124
Green, The. Hers —2K 57
Green, The. Houn —2A 10
Green, The. Lav P —8D 190
Green, The. Mord —3K 43
Green, The. N Mald —2B 42
Green, The. Ockl —5D 158
Green, The. Orp —2K 67
Green, The. Rich —8K 11
Green, The. Rip —8L 75
Green, The. Seale —2C 130
Green, The. Sham G —7G 135
Green, The. Shep —3F 38
Green, The. Sutt —9N 43
Green, The. Twic —2E 24
Green, The. Warl —5G 84
Green, The. W'ham —4M 107
Green, The. W Vill —6F 56
Green, The. Wold —1K 105
Green, The. Wray —9A 6
Green, The. Yat —9A 48
Greenvale Rd. Knap —5G 73
Green View. Chess —4M 59
Green View. God —9E 104
Greenview Av. Beck —5H 47
Greenview Av. Croy —5H 47
Greenview Ct. Ashf —5A 22
Green Wlk. Craw —1C 182
Green Wlk. Hamp —7N 23
Green Wlk. S'hall —1A 10
Greenway. SW20 —3H 43
Green Way. Alder —1C 110
Greenway. Bookh —1B 98
Greenway. H'ham —5H 197
Green Way. Red —1C 122
Green Way. Sun —3H 39
Greenway. Tats —7E 86
Green Way. Wall —1G 62
Greenway Clo. W Byf —9J 55
Greenway Dri. Stai —9M 21
Greenway Gdns. Croy —9J 47
Greenways. Beck —2K 47
Greenways. Egh —6A 20
Greenways. Esh —1E 58
Greenways. Fleet —7A 88
Greenways. Sand —6G 49
Greenways. Tad —3G 100
Greenways Dri. Asc —7B 34
Greenways, The. Twic —9G 11
Greenways Wlk. Craw —8A 182
Greenway, The. Eps —2N 79
Greenway, The. Houn —7N 9
Greenway, The. Oxt —2D 126
Greenwell Clo. God —8E 104
Greenwich Clo. Craw —7A 182
Green Wood. Asc —9G 17
Greenwood Bus. Cen. Croy —6C 46
Greenwood Clo. Mord —3K 43
Greenwood Clo. Th Dit —7G 41
Greenwood Clo. Wdhm —7H 55
Greenwood Ct. Craw —8N 181
Greenwood Dri. Red —8E 122
Greenwood Gdns. Cat —3D 104
Greenwood La. Hamp —6B 24
Greenwood Pk. King T —8D 26
Greenwood Rd. Crowt —1F 48
Greenwood Rd. Croy —6M 45
Greenwood Rd. Iswth —6F 10
Greenwood Rd. Mitc —2H 45
Greenwood Rd. Pirb —8M 71
Greenwood Rd. Th Dit —7G 41
Greenwood Rd. Wok —7H 73
Greenwood, The. Guild —3C 114
Green Wrythe Cres. Cars —7C 44
Green Wrythe La. Cars —5B 44
Gregory Clo. M'bowr —7G 182
Gregory Dri. Old Win —9L 5
Gregsons La. Warn —9E 178
Grenaby Av. Croy —6A 46
Grenaby Rd. Croy —6A 46
Grenadier Rd. Ash V —9F 90
Grenadiers Way. F'boro —2H 89
Grena Gdns. Rich —7M 11
Grena Rd. Rich —7M 11
Grendon Clo. Horl —6D 142
Grenehurst Pk. Capel —6J 159
Grenfell Rd. Mitc —7D 28
Grennell Clo. Sutt —8B 44
Grennell Rd. Sutt —8A 44
Grenside Rd. Wey —9C 38
Grenville Clo. Cobh —9L 57
Grenville Clo. Surb —7B 42
Grenville Dri. C Crook —7A 88
Grenville Gdns. Frim G —8C 70
Grenville M. SW7 —1N 13
(off Harrington Gdns.)
Grenville M. Hamp —6B 24
Grenville Pl. Brack —1A 32
Grenville Rd. New Ad —5M 65
Grenville Rd. Shack —4A 132
Gresham Av. Warl —5H 85
Gresham Clo. Oxt —7B 106
Gresham Ind. Est. Alder —2C 110
Gresham Pl. Oxt —7B 106
Gresham Rd. SE25 —3D 46
Gresham Rd. Beck —1H 47
Gresham Rd. Hamp —7A 24
Gresham Rd. Houn —4C 10
Gresham Rd. Oxt —6B 106
Gresham Rd. Stai —6H 21
Gresham Wlk. Craw —6C 182
(in two parts)
Gresham Way. SW19 —4N 27
Gresham Way. Frim G —8C 70
Gressenhall Rd. SW18 —9L 13
Greswell St. SW6 —4J 13
Greta Bank. W Hor —4D 96
Greville Av. S Croy —6G 64
Greville Clo. Asht —6L 79
Greville Clo. Guild —3H 113
Greville Clo. Twic —1H 25
Greville Ct. Asht —5L 79
Greville Ct. Bookh —3B 98
Greville Pk. Av. Asht —5L 79
Greville Pk. Rd. Asht —5L 79
Greville Rd. Rich —9M 11
Grey Alders. Bans —1H 81
Greybury La. M Grn —9K 147
Greyfields Clo. Purl —9M 63
Greyfriars Dri. Asc —4M 33
Greyfriars Dri. Bisl —2D 72
Greyfriars Rd. Rip —2J 95
Greyhound Clo. Ash —3D 110
Greyhound La. SW16 —7H 29
Greyhound Mans. W6 —2K 13
(off Greyhound Rd.)
Greyhound Rd. W6 & W14 —2J 13
Greyhound Rd. Sutt —2A 62
Greyhound Slip. Worth —2H 183
Greyhound Ter. SW16 —9G 29
Greys Ct. Alder —2K 109
Greys Pk. Clo. Kes —2F 66
Greystead Pk. Wrec —6D 128
Greystoke Ct. Crowt —3F 48
Greystone Clo. S Croy —7F 64
Greystones Clo. Red —5B 122
Greystones Dri. Reig —1A 122
Greyswood St. SW16 —7F 28
Greythorne Rd. Wok —5K 73
Greywaters. Brmly —5C 134
Grice Av. Big H —9D 66
Grier Clo. If'd —4K 181
Grieve Clo. Tong —5C 110
Griffin Cen. Felt —8J 9
Griffin Ct. W4 —1E 12
Griffin Ct. Asht —6L 79
Griffin Ct. Bookh —4B 98
Griffin Ct. Bren —2L 11
Griffin M. Craw —5E 182
Griffin Way. Bookh —4A 98
Griffin Way. Sun —1H 39
Griffiths Clo. Wor Pk —8G 43
Griffiths Rd. SW19 —8M 27
Griffon Clo. F'boro —2J 89
Griggs Meadow. Duns —2B 174
Grimston Rd. SW6 —5L 13
Grimwade Av. Croy —9D 46
Grimwood Rd. Twic —1F 24
Grindall Clo. Croy —1M 63
Grindley Gdns. Croy —5C 46
Grindstone Cres. Knap —5E 72
Grinstead La. E Grin —8L 185
Grisedale Clo. Craw —5A 182
Grisedale Clo. Purl —1B 84
Grisedale Gdns. Purl —1B 84
Grobars Av. Wok —2M 73
Grogan Clo. Hamp —7N 23
Groombridge Clo. W On T —2J 57
Groombridge Way. H'ham —7F 196
Groom Cres. SW18 —1B 28
Groomfield Clo. SW17 —5E 28
Grooms, The. Worth —1H 183
Groom Wlk. Guild —9A 94
Grosse Way. SW15 —9G 13
Grosvenor Av. SW14 —6D 12
Grosvenor Av. Cars —3D 62
Grosvenor Av. Rich —8L 11
Grosvenor Ct. B'water —3J 69
Grosvenor Ct. Guild —9D 94
Grosvenor Gdns. SW14 —6D 12
Grosvenor Gdns. King T —7K 25
Grosvenor Gdns. Wall —4G 62
Grosvenor Hill. SW19 —7K 27
Grosvenor Ho. Guild —5B 114
Grosvenor Pl. Wey —9E 38
Grosvenor Pl. Wok —4B 74
(off Burleigh Gdns.)
Grosvenor Rd. SE25 —3D 46
Grosvenor Rd. W4 —1A 12
Grosvenor Rd. Alder —2M 109
Grosvenor Rd. Bren —2K 11
Grosvenor Rd. Chob —9G 53
Grosvenor Rd. E Grin —9N 165
Grosvenor Rd. Eps —6C 80
Grosvenor Rd. G'ming —8H 133
Grosvenor Rd. Houn —6N 9
Grosvenor Rd. Rich —8L 11
Grosvenor Rd. Stai —8J 21
Grosvenor Rd. Twic —2G 24
Grosvenor Rd. Wall —3F 62
Grosvenor Rd. W Wick —7L 47
Groton Rd. SW18 —3N 27
Grotto Rd. Twic —3F 24
Grotto Rd. Wey —9C 38
Grouse Rd. Colg & Craw —9E 198
Grove Av. Eps —9D 60
Grove Av. Sutt —3M 61
Grove Av. Twic —2F 24
Grove Bell Ind. Est. Wrec —4E 128
Grove Clo. Cranl —9A 156
Grove Clo. Felt —5M 23
Grove Clo. King T —3M 41
Grove Clo. Old Win —1L 19
Grove Clo. Wokgm —9D 30
Grove Corner. Bookh —4B 98
Grove Cotts. W4 —2D 12
Grove Ct. E Mol —4D 40
Grove Ct. Egh —6C 20
Grove Ct. Houn —7A 10
Grove Cres. Felt —5M 23
Grove Cres. King T —2L 41
Grove Cres. W On T —6J 39
Grove Cross Rd. Frim —5B 70
Grove End. Bag —3K 51
Grove End La. Esh —7D 40
Grove End Rd. Farnh —4G 128
Grove Farm Cvn. Site. Myt —4D 90
Grove Farm Ind. Est. Mitc —4D 44
Grovefields Av. Frim —5B 70
Grove Footpath. Surb —3L 41
Grove Gdns. Rich —9L 11
Grove Gdns. Tedd —5G 24
Grove Heath Ct. Rip —2L 95
Grove Heath N. Rip —9K 75
Grove Heath Rd. Rip —1K 95
Grovehill Rd. Red —3D 122
Grove Ho. Red —3D 122
(off Huntingdon Rd.)
Groveland Av. SW16 —8K 29
Groveland Rd. Beck —2J 47
Grovelands. Horl —9F 142
Grovelands. Lwr Bo —4K 129
Grovelands. W Mol —3A 40
Grovelands Rd. Purl —8J 63
Groveland Way. N Mald —4B 42
Grove La. Coul —9E 62
Grove La. King T —3L 41
Grove La. Wink R —6F 16
Groveley Rd. Sun —6G 22
Grove Pk. Bri. W4 —3B 12
Grove Pk. Gdns. W4 —3A 12
Grove Pk. M. W4 —3B 12
Grove Pk. Rd. W4 —3A 12
Grove Pk. Ter. W4 —3A 12
Grove Pl. Wey —2D 56
Grove Rd. SW13 —5E 12
Grove Rd. SW19 —8A 28
Grove Rd. Asht —5M 79
Grove Rd. Ash V —9E 90
Grove Rd. Bren —1J 11
Grove Rd. Camb —1D 70
Grove Rd. Cher —5H 37
Grove Rd. C Crook —8C 88
Grove Rd. Cranl —9A 156
Grove Rd. E Mol —3D 40
Grove Rd. Eps —9D 60
Grove Rd. G'ming —8F 132
Grove Rd. Guild —3E 114
Grove Rd. Hind —3N 169
Grove Rd. Horl —7C 142
Grove Rd. Houn —7A 10
Grove Rd. Iswth —4E 10
Grove Rd. Ling —6A 146
Grove Rd. Mitc —2E 44
Grove Rd. Oxt —2M 125
Grove Rd. Rich —9M 11
Grove Rd. Shep —5D 38
Grove Rd. Surb —4K 41
Grove Rd. Sutt —3M 61
Grove Rd. Tats —7E 86
Grove Rd. T Hth —3L 45
Grove Rd. Twic —4D 24
Grove Rd. Wind —5F 4
Grove Rd. Wok —3B 74
Grovers Farm Cotts. Wdhm —7G 55
Grovers Gdns. Hind —3B 170
Grove Shaw. Tad —2K 101
Groveside. Bookh —5A 98
Groveside Clo. Bookh —5A 98
Groveside Clo. Cars —8C 44
Grovestile Waye. Felt —1E 22
Grove Ter. Tedd —5G 24
Grove, The. Add —2K 55
Grove, The. Alder —3M 109
Grove, The. Asc —9G 17
Grove, The. Big H —5F 86
Grove, The. Cat —8N 83
Grove, The. Coul —1H 83
Grove, The. Craw —3A 182
Grove, The. Egh —6C 20
Grove, The. Eps —9D 60
(Epsom)
Grove, The. Eps —6E 60
(Ewell)
Grove, The. F'boro —4B 90
Grove, The. Frim —5B 70
Grove, The. Horl —9F 142
Grove, The. Iswth —4E 10
Grove, The. Tedd —5G 24
Grove, The. Twic —9H 11
Grove, The. W On T —6J 39
Grove, The. W Wick —8M 47
Grove, The. Wok —3B 74
Grove Way. Esh —6C 40
Grovewood. Rich —4N 11
Grove Wood Hill. Coul —1G 83
Grub St. Oxt —6E 106
Guardian Ct. Elst —8G 131
Guards Rd. Wind —5A 4
Guerdon Pl. Brack —6B 32
Guernsey Clo. Craw —7M 181
Guernsey Clo. Guild —7C 94
Guernsey Clo. Houn —3A 10
Guernsey Dri. Fleet —1C 88
Guernsey Farm Dri. Wok —2N 73
Guernsey Gro. SE24 —1N 29
Guildables La. Eden —4G 127
Guildcroft. Guild —3C 114
Guildersfield Rd. SW16 —8J 29
Guildford and Godalming By-Pass Rd. Milf & Guild —1B 152
Guildford Av. Felt —3G 23
Guildford Bus. Pk. Guild —2L 113
Guildford Ct. Guild —3K 113
Guildford Ind. Est. Guild —3K 113
Guildford La. Guild —6G 115
Guildford La. Wok —6A 74
Guildford Lodge Dri. E Hor —7G 96
Guildford Pk. Av. Guild —4L 113
Guildford Pk. Rd. Guild —4L 113
Guildford Rd. Alder —5B 110
Guildford Rd. Alf & H'ham —3J 175
Guildford Rd. Ash —1G 110
Guildford Rd. Bag —4J 51
(in two parts)
Guildford Rd. Cher —7D 54
Guildford Rd. Chob —9G 53
Guildford Rd. Croy —5A 46
Guildford Rd. Dork —8F 116
Guildford Rd. E Hor & Bookh —7G 96
Guildford Rd. Farnh —9J 109
(Farnham)
Guildford Rd. Farnh —8M 109
(Runfold)
Guildford Rd. Fet —3D 98
Guildford Rd. Fleet —5D 88
Guildford Rd. Frim G —8D 70
Guildford Rd. G'ming —4K 133
Guildford Rd. H'ham —1M 195
Guildford Rd. Light —6L 51
(in two parts)
Guildford Rd. Loxw —3H 193
Guildford Rd. Mayf —9N 73
Guildford Rd. Norm —1J 111
Guildford Rd. Pirb —1C 92
Guildford Rd. Sham G —6F 134
Guildford Rd. Westc —7B 118
Guildford Rd. W End —8B 52
Guildford Rd. Wok —6A 74
Guildford Rd. E. F'boro —4A 90
Guildford Rd. Trad. Est. Farnh —9K 109
Guildford Rd. W. F'boro —4A 90
Guildford St. Cher —7H 37
Guildford St. Stai —7J 21
Guildford Way. Wall —2J 63
Guildown Av. Guild —6L 113
Guildown Rd. Guild —6L 113
Guileshill La. Ock —1N 95
Guilford Av. Surb —4M 41
Guillemont Fields. F'boro —9J 69
Guillemot Path. If'd —4J 181
Guinevere Rd. If'd —3K 181
Guinness Ct. Craw —7A 182
Guinness Ct. Croy —8C 46
Guinness Ct. Wok —5J 73

Guinness Trust Bldgs.—Harvest Ct.

Guinness Trust Bldgs. W6
(off Fulham Pal. Rd.) —1J **13**
Guion Rd. *SW6* —5L **13**
Gull Clo. *Wall* —4J **63**
Gull's Rd. *Guild* —3M **111**
Gumbrells Clo. *Guild* —8F **92**
Gumleigh Rd. *W5* —1J **11**
Gumley Gdns. *Iswth* —6G **10**
Gunderson Corner. *Mitc*
—2D **44**
Gun Hill. *Alder* —1N **109**
Gunnell Clo. *Croy* —5C **46**
Gunnersbury Av. *W5 & W4*
—1N **11**
Gunnersbury Clo. *W4* —1A **12**
Gunnersbury M. *W4* —1A **12**
Gunners Rd. *SW18* —3B **28**
Gunning Clo. *Craw* —6M **181**
Gun Pit Rd. *Ling* —7N **145**
Gunter Gro. *SW10* —2N **13**
Gunters Mead. *Oxs* —7C **58**
Gunterstone Rd. *W14* —1K **13**
Gunton Rd. *SW17* —7E **28**
Gurdon's La. *Wmly* —9B **152**
Gurney Cres. *Croy* —7K **45**
Gurney Ho. *Hayes* —1F **8**
Gurney Rd. *Cars* —1E **62**
Gurney's Clo. *Red* —4D **122**
Guyatt Gdns. *Mitc* —1E **44**
Guy Rd. *Wall* —9H **45**
Gwalior Rd. *SW15* —6J **13**
Gwendolen Av. *SW15* —7J **13**
Gwendolen Clo. *SW15* —8J **13**
Gwendwr Rd. *W14* —1K **13**
Gwydor Rd. *Beck* —2G **47**
Gwyn Clo. *SW6* —3N **13**
Gwynne Av. *Croy* —6G **46**
Gwynne Clo. *W4* —2E **12**
Gwynne Clo. *Wind* —1D **4**
Gwynne Gdns. *E Grin* [illegible]M **100**
Gwynne Rd. *Cat* —1A **104**
Gwynne Vaughan Av. *Guild*
—8L **93**

Habershon Dri. *Frim* —4H **71**
Haccombe Rd. *SW19* —7A **28**
Hackbridge Grn. *Wall* —8E **44**
Hackbridge Pk. *Cars* —8D **44**
Hackbridge Pk. Gdns. *Cars*
—8D **44**
Hackbridge Rd. *Wall* —8E **44**
Hackenden Clo. *E Grin* —7A **166**
Hackenden La. *E Grin* —7A **166**
(in two parts)
Hacketts La. *Wok* —1H **75**
Hackhurst La. *Ab H* —8G **116**
Haddenhurst Ct. *Binf* —7H **15**
Haddon Clo. *N Mald* —4E **42**
Haddon Clo. *Wey* —9F **38**
Haddon Rd. *Sutt* —1N **61**
Hadfield Rd. *Stai* —9M **7**
Hadleigh Clo. *SW20* —1L **43**
Hadleigh Dri. *Sutt* —5M **61**
Hadleigh Gdns. *Frim G* —8C **70**
Hadley Gdns. *W4* —1C **12**
Hadley Gdns. *S'hall* —1N **9**
Hadley Pl. *Wey* —4B **56**
Hadley Rd. *Mitc* —3H **45**
Hadley Wood Rise. *Kenl*
—2M **83**
Hadmans Clo. *H'ham* —7J **197**
Hadrian Clo. *Stai* —2N **21**
Hadrian Clo. *Wall* —4J **63**
Hadrian Ct. *Sutt* —4N **61**
Hadrians. *Farnh* —8K **109**
Hadrian Way. *Stai* —1M **21**
Haggard Rd. *Twic* —1H **25**
Hagley Rd. *Fleet* —4A **88**
Haigh Cres. *Red* —5F **122**
Haig La. *C Crook* —8C **88**
Haig Pl. *Mord* —5M **43**
Haig Rd. *Alder* —3A **110**
Haig Rd. *Big H* —4G **86**
Haig Rd. *Col T* —9L **49**
Hailes Clo. *SW19* —7A **28**
Hailey Pl. *Cranl* —6A **156**
Hailsham Av. *SW2* —3K **29**
Hailsham Clo. *Owl* —6J **49**
Hailsham Clo. *Surb* —6K **41**
Hailsham Rd. *SW17* —7E **28**
Haines Ct. *Wey* —2E **56**
Haines Wlk. *Mord* —6N **43**
Haining Clo. *W4* —1N **11**
Haining Gdns. *Myt* —1E **90**
Hainthorpe Rd. *SE27* —4M **29**
Haldane Pl. *SW18* —2N **27**
Haldane Rd. *SW6* —3L **13**
Haldon Rd. *SW18* —9L **13**
Halebourne La. *W End* —4D **52**
Hale Clo. *Orp* —1L **67**
Hale End. *Brack* —3D **32**
Hale Ho. La. *Churt* —9L **149**
Hale Path. *SE27* —5M **29**
Hale Pit Rd. *Bookh* —4C **98**
Hale Pl. *Farnh* —7K **109**
Hale Reeds. *Farnh* —6J **109**
Hale Rd. *Farnh* —7J **109**
Hales Field. *Hasl* —2G **189**
Hales Oak. *Bookh* —4C **98**
Halesowen Rd. *Mord* —6N **43**
Hale St. *Stai* —5G **21**
Haleswood. *Cobh* —1J **77**
Hale Way. *Frim* —6B **70**
Halewood. *Brack* —5L **31**
Half Acre. *Bren* —2K **11**
Half Moon Cotts. *Rip* —8L **75**
Half Moon Hill. *Hasl* —2G **189**
Half Moon St. *Bag* —4J **51**
Halford Rd. *SW6* —2M **13**
Halford Rd. *Rich* —8L **11**
Halfpenny Clo. *Chil* —9F **114**
Halfpenny La. *Asc* —6E **34**
Halfpenny La. *Guild* —6E **114**
Halfway Grn. *W on T* —9J **39**
Halfway La. *G'ming* —7D **132**
Haliburton Rd. *Twic* —8G **11**
Halifax Clo. *Craw* —9J **163**
Halifax Clo. *F'boro* —2L **89**
Halimote Rd. *Alder* —3M **109**
Haling Down Pas. *Purl* —6M **63**
Haling Gro. *S Croy* —4N **63**
Haling Pk. Gdns. *S Croy* —3M **63**
Haling Pk. Rd. *S Croy* —2M **63**
Haling Rd. *S Croy* —3A **64**
Hallam Rd. *SW13* —6G **13**
Hallam Rd. *G'ming* —5J **133**
Halland Clo. *Craw* —2E **182**
Halland Ct. *Eden* —2L **147**
Hallane Ho. *SE27* —6N **29**
Hallbrooke Gdns. *Binf* —8K **15**
Hall Clo. *Camb* —9C **50**
Hall Clo. *G'ming* —4H **133**
Hall Ct. *Dat* —3L **5**
Hall Ct. *Tedd* —6F **24**
Hall Dene Clo. *Guild* —2E **114**
Halley Clo. *Craw* —8N **131**
Halley Dri. *Asc* —1H **33**
Halley's App. *Wok* —5K **73**
Halley's Ct. *Wok* —5K **73**
Halley's Wlk. *Add* —4L **55**
Hall Farm Cres. *Yat* —1C **68**
Hall Farm Dri. *Twic* —1D **24**
Hallgrove Bottom. *Bag* —2K **51**
Hall Gro. Farm Ind. Est. *Bag*
—2K **51**
Hall Hill. *Oxt* —9N **105**
Halliards, The. *W On T* —5H **39**
Halliford Clo. *Shep* —3E **38**
Halliford Rd. *Shep & Sun*
—4F **38**
Hallington Clo. *Wok* —4L **73**
Hall La. *Hayes* —3E **8**
Hall La. *Yat* —1B **68**
Hallmead Rd. *Sutt* —9N **43**
Hallowell Av. *Croy* —1J **63**
Hallowell Clo. *Mitc* —2E **44**
Hallowfield Way. *Mitc* —2B **44**
Hall Pl. *Wok* —3C **74**
Hall Pl. Dri. *Wey* —2F **56**
Hall Rd. *Brmly* —5B **134**
Hall Rd. *Iswth* —8D **10**
Hall Rd. *Wall* —5F **62**
Halls Farm Clo. *Knap* —4G **73**
Hallsland. *Craw D* —1F **184**
Hallsland Way. *Oxt* —1B **126**
Hall Way. *Purl* —9M **63**
Halnaker Wlk. *Craw* —6L **181**
Halsford Croft. *E Grin* —7L **165**
Halsford Grn. *E Grin* —7L **165**
Halsford La. *E Grin* —8L **165**
Halsford Pk. Rd. *E Grin*
—8M **165**
Halstead Clo. *Croy* —9N **45**
Halters End. *Gray* —6M **169**
Hamble Av. *B'water* —1J **69**
Hamble Clo. *Wok* —4K **73**
Hambleden Ct. *Brack* —3C **32**
Hambledon Gdns. *SE25* —2C **46**
Hambledon Hill. *Eps* —3B **80**
Hambledon Pl. *Bookh* —1A **98**
Hambledon Rd. *SW18* —1L **27**
Hambledon Rd. *Busb* —9J **133**
Hambledon Rd. *Cat* —1A **104**
Hambledon Rd. *Hamb* —7G **152**
Hambledon Vale. *Eps* —3B **80**
Hamblehyrst. *Beck* —1L **47**
Hamble St. *SW6* —6N **13**
Hambleton Clo. *Frim* —3F **70**
Hambleton Clo. *Wor Pk* —8H **43**
Hambleton Ct. *Craw* —5A **182**
Hambleton Hill. *Craw* —5A **182**
Hambleton Pk. *Hamb* —9E **152**
Hamble Wlk. *Wok* —5K **73**
Hambridge Way. *SW2* —1L **29**
Hambrook Rd. *SE25* —2E **46**
Hambro Rd. *SW16* —7H **29**
Ham Clo. *Rich* —4J **25**
(in two parts)
Ham Comn. *Rich* —4K **25**
Hamesmoor Rd. *Myt* —1C **90**
Hamesmoor Way. *Myt* —1D **90**
Ham Farm Rd. *Rich* —5K **25**
Hamfield Clo. *Oxt* —5M **105**
Ham Ga. Av. *Rich* —4K **25**
Hamhaugh Island. *Shep* —8B **38**
Hamilton Av. *Cobh* —9H **57**
Hamilton Av. *Surb* —8N **41**
Hamilton Av. *Sutt* —8K **43**
Hamilton Av. *Wok* —2G **75**
Hamilton Clo. *Bord* —5A **168**
Hamilton Clo. *Cher* —7H **37**
Hamilton Clo. *Eps* —8B **60**
Hamilton Clo. *Felt* —6G **22**
Hamilton Clo. *Guild* —7K **93**
Hamilton Clo. *Purl* —8M **63**
Hamilton Ct. *SW15* —6K **13**
Hamilton Ct. *Bookh* —3B **98**
Hamilton Cres. *Houn* —8B **10**
Hamilton Dri. *Asc* —6B **34**
Hamilton Dri. *Guild* —7K **93**
Hamilton Gordon Ct. *Guild*
—2M **113**
Hamilton Ho. *W4* —2D **12**
Hamilton M. *SW19* —9M **27**
Hamilton Pde. *Felt* —5H **23**
Hamilton Pl. *Alder* —3L **109**
Hamilton Pl. *Guild* —7K **93**
Hamilton Pl. *Sun* —8J **23**
Hamilton Rd. *SE27* —5N **29**
Hamilton Rd. *SW19* —8N **27**
Hamilton Rd. *Bren* —2K **11**
Hamilton Rd. *C Crook* —7C **88**
Hamilton Rd. *Felt* —5G **22**
Hamilton Rd. *H'ham* —5H **197**
Hamilton Rd. *T Hth* —2A **46**
Hamilton Rd. *Twic* —2E **24**
Hamilton Rd. M. *SW19* —8N **27**
Hamilton Way. *Wall* —5H **63**
Ham La. *Egh* —5L **19**
Ham La. *Elst* —7H **131**
Ham La. *Old Win* —8M **5**
Hamlash La. *Fren* —1H **149**
Hamlet Gdns. *W6* —1F **12**
Hamlet St. *Warf* —9C **16**
Hamm Ct. *Wey* —8A **38**
Hammerfield Dri. *Ab H* —1G **136**
Hammer Hill. *Hasl* —4A **188**
Hammer La. *Alf* —3M **175**
Hammer La. *Churt* [illegible]
Hammer La. *Churt & Gray*
—1K **169**
Hammer La. *Hasl* —2A **188**
Hammer Pond Cotts. *Witl*
—4K **151**
Hammerpond Rd. *H'ham*
—8N **197**
Hammersley Rd. *Alder* —6N **89**
Hammersmith Bri. *SW13 & W6*
—2G **13**
Hammersmith Bri. Rd. *W6*
(in two parts) —1G **13**
Hammersmith B'way. *W6*
—1H **13**
Hammersmith Broadway.
(Junct.) —1H **13**
(off Hammersmith B'way.)
Hammersmith Flyover. *W6*
—1H **13**
Hammersmith Flyover. (Junct.)
—1H **13**
Hammersmith Ind. Est. *W6*
—2H **13**
Hammersmith Rd. *W6 & W14*
—1J **13**
Hammersmith Ter. *W6* —1F **12**
Hammer Vale. *Hasl* —2A **188**
Hammerwood Rd. *Ash W*
—3F **186**
Hammer Yd. *Craw* —4B **182**
Hamm Moor La. *Add* —2N **55**
Hammond Av. *Mitc* —1F **44**
Hammond Clo. *Hamp* —9A **24**
Hammond Clo. *Wok* —2M **73**
Hammond Ct. *Brack* —9M **15**
Hammond Rd. *Wok* —2M **73**
Hammond Way. *Light* —6M **51**
Hamond Clo. *S Croy* —5M **63**
Hampden Av. *Beck* —1H **47**
Hampden Clo. *Craw* —9J **163**
Hampden Rd. *Beck* —1H **47**
Hampden Rd. *King T* —2N **41**
Hampers Ct. *H'ham* —6K **197**
Hamper's La. *H'ham* —6N **197**
Hampshire Clo. *Alder* —5B **110**
Hampshire Ct. *Add* —2L **55**
Hampshire Hog La. *W6* —1G **12**
Hampshire Rise. *Warf* —7D **16**
Hampshire Rd. *Camb* —7D **50**
Hampstead La. *Dork* —6F **118**
Hampstead Rd. *Dork* —6G **119**
Hampstead Wlk. *Craw* —7A **182**
Hampton Clo. *SW20* —8H **27**
Hampton Clo. *C Crook* —9B **88**
Hampton Court. (Junct.) —2E **40**
Hampton Ct. Av. *E Mol* —4D **40**
Hampton Ct. Bri. *E Mol* —3E **40**
Hampton Ct. Cres. *E Mol*
—2D **40**
Hampton Ct. Pde. *E Mol* —3E **40**
Hampton Ct. Rd. *E Mol & King T*
—1D **40**
Hampton Ct. Rd. *Hamp* —1C **40**
Hampton Ct. Way. *Th Dit & E Mol*
—8E **40**
Hampton Farm Ind. Est. *Felt*
—4M **23**
Hampton Gro. *Eps* —7E **60**
Hampton La. *Felt* —5M **23**
Hampton Rd. *Croy* —5N **45**
Hampton Rd. *Farnh* —6F **108**
Hampton Rd. *Hamp & Tedd*
—6D **24**
Hampton Rd. *Red* —8D **122**
Hampton Rd. *Twic* —4D **24**
Hampton Rd. *Wor Pk* —8G **42**
Hampton Rd. E. *Felt* —5N **23**
Hampton Rd. W. *Felt* —4M **23**
Hampton Way. *E Grin* —2B **186**
Ham Ridings. *Rich* —6M **25**
Hamsey Grn. Gdns. *Warl*
—3E **84**
Hamsey Way. *S Croy* —2E **84**
Ham Sq. *Rich* —3J **25**
Ham St. *Rich* —2H **25**
Ham, The. *Bren* —3J **11**
Ham View. *Croy* —5H **47**
Hanah Ct. *SW19* —8J **27**
Hanbury Dri. *Big H* —9D **66**
Hanbury Path. *Wok* —1F **74**
Hanbury Rd. *If'd* —4K **181**
Hanbury Way. *Camb* —3A **70**
Hancock Rd. *SE19* —7N **29**
Hancocks Mt. *Asc* —5A **34**
Hancombe Rd. *Sand* —6F **48**
Handcroft Rd. *Croy* —6M **45**
Handel Mans. *SW13* —3H **13**
Handford La. *Yat* —1C **68**
Handinhand La. *Tad* —8B **100**
Handside Clo. *Wor Pk* —7J **43**
Handsworth Ho. Craw —4B **182**
(off Brighton Rd.)
Hanford Clo. *SW18* —2M **27**
Hanford Row. *SW19* —7H **27**
Hangerfield Clo. *Yat* —1B **68**
Hanger Hill. *Wey* —3C **56**
Hanger, The. *Head* —3E **168**
Hangrove Hill. *Orp* —9K **67**
Hanley Clo. *Wind* —4A **4**
Hannah Clo. *Beck* [illegible] **17**
Hannah M. *Wall* [illegible]
Hannay Wlk. *SW16* —3H **29**
Hannell Rd. *SW6* —3K **13**
Hannen Rd. *SE27* —4M **29**
Hannibal Rd. *Stai* —1M **21**
Hannibal Way. *Croy* —2K **63**
Hanover Av. *Felt* —2H **23**
Hanover Clo. *Craw* —5D **182**
(in two parts)
Hanover Clo. *Egh* —7L **19**
Hanover Clo. *Frim* —5C **70**
Hanover Clo. *Red* —6G **102**
Hanover Clo. *Rich* —3N **11**
Hanover Clo. *Sutt* —1K **61**
Hanover Clo. *Wind* —4C **4**
Hanover Clo. *Yat* —8C **48**
Hanover Ct. *SW15* —7E **12**
Hanover Ct. *Dork* —5F **118**
Hanover Ct. *Guild* —1N **113**
Hanover Ct. *H'ham* —5M **197**
Hanover Ct. *Wok* —6N **73**
Hanover Dri. *Fleet* —1D **88**
Hanover Gdns. *Brack* —6L **31**
Hanover Gdns. *F'boro* —8K **69**
Hanover Rd. *SW19* —8A **28**
Hanover St. *Croy* —9M **45**
Hanover Ter. *Iswth* —4G **11**
Hanover Wlk. *Wey* —9F **38**
Hanover Way. *Wind* —5C **4**
Hansler Gro. *E Mol* —3D **40**
Hanson Clo. *SW12* —1F **28**
Hanson Clo. *SW14* —6B **12**
Hanson Clo. *Camb* —8F **50**
Hanson Clo. *Guild* —9B **94**
Hanworth Clo. *Brack* —5A **32**
Hanworth La. *Cher* —7H **37**
Hanworth Rd. *Brack* —7M **31**
Hanworth Rd. *Felt* —2J **23**
Hanworth Rd. *Hamp* —5N **23**
Hanworth Rd. *Houn* —2M **23**
Hanworth Rd. *Red* —8D **122**
Hanworth Rd. *Sun* —8H **23**
Hanworth Ter. *Houn* —7B **10**
Hanworth Trad. Est. *Cher*
—7H **37**
Hanworth Trad. Est. *Felt*
—4M **23**
Harberson Rd. *SW12* —2F **28**
Harbledown Rd. *SW6* —4M **13**
Harbledown Rd. *S Croy* —7D **64**
Harbord St. *SW6* —4J **13**
Harborough Rd. *SW16* —5K **29**
Harbour Av. *SW10* —4N **13**
Harbour Clo. *F'boro* —6M **69**
Harbourfield Rd. *Bans* —2N **81**
Harbridge Av. *SW15* —1E **26**
Harbury Rd. *Cars* —5C **62**
Harcourt. *Wray* —9A **6**
Harcourt Av. *Wall* —1F **62**
Harcourt Clo. *Egh* —7E **20**
Harcourt Clo. *Iswth* —6G **11**
Harcourt Cotts. *Guild* —8N **111**
Harcourt Field. *Wall* —1F **62**
Harcourt Lodge. *Wall* —1F **62**
Harcourt Rd. *SW19* —8M **27**
Harcourt Rd. *Brack* —5N **31**
Harcourt Rd. *Camb* —1N **69**
Harcourt Rd. *T Hth* —5K **45**
Harcourt Rd. *Wall* —1F **62**
Harcourt Rd. *Wind* —4B **4**
Harcourt Ter. *SW10* —1N **13**
Harcourt Way. *S God* —6H **125**
Hardcastle Clo. *Croy* —5D **46**
Hardcourts Clo. *W Wick* —9L **47**
Hardell Clo. *Egh* —6C **20**
Hardel Rise. *SW2* —2M **29**
Hardel Wlk. *SW2* —1L **29**
Hardham Clo. *Craw* —1M **181**
Harding Clo. *Croy* —9C **46**
Harding Rd. *Eps* —6D **80**
Harding's Clo. *King T* —9M **25**
Hardings Rd. *Dock* —2A **148**
Hardman Rd. *King T* —1L **41**
Hardwell Way. *Brack* —3C **32**
Hardwick Clo. *Oxs* —2C **78**
Hardwicke Av. *Houn* —4A **10**
Hardwicke Rd. *Reig* —2M **121**
Hardwicke Rd. *Rich* —5J **25**
Hardwick La. *Lyne* —6E **36**
Hardwick Rd. *Red* —5B **122**
Hardwicks Way. *SW18* —8M **13**
Hardy Av. *Yat* —2B **68**
Hardy Clo. *Craw* —2G **182**
Hardy Clo. *Horl* —8C **142**
Hardy Clo. *H'ham* —4H **197**
Hardy Clo. *N Holm* —9H **119**
Hardy Grn. *Crowt* —3G **48**
Hardy Ho. *SW4* —1G **29**
Hardy Rd. *SW19* —8N **27**
Hardys Clo. *E Mol* —3E **40**
Harebell Hill. *Cobh* —1L **77**
Harecroft. *Dork* —8J **119**
Harecroft. *Fet* —2B **98**
Harefield. *Esh* —9E **40**
Harefield Av. *Sutt* —5K **61**
Harefield Rd. *SW16* —8K **29**
Hare Hill. *Add* —3G **55**
Harehill Clo. *Wok* —2J **75**
Harelands Clo. *Wok* —4M **73**
Harelands La. *Wok* —4M **73**
Hare La. *Ling* [illegible]
Hare La. *Craw* —9N **161**
Hare La. *G'ming* —5J **133**
Hare La. *Ling* —7F **144**
Harendon. *Tad* —8H **81**
Hares Bank. *New Ad* —6N **65**
Harestone Dri. *Cat* —2C **104**
Harestone Hill. *Cat* —4C **104**
Harestone La. *Cat* —3B **104**
Harestone Valley Rd. *Cat*
—4B **104**
Hareward Rd. *Guild* —1E **114**
Harewood Clo. *Craw* —9E **162**
Harewood Clo. *Reig* —9A **102**
Harewood Gdns. *S Croy* —2E **84**
Harewood Rd. *SW19* —7C **28**
Harewood Rd. *Iswth* —3F **10**
Harewood Rd. *S Croy* —3B **64**
Harewood Ter. *S'hall* —1N **9**
Harfield Rd. *Sun* —1L **39**
Harkness Clo. *Eps* —3H **81**
Harland Av. *Croy* —9D **46**
Harland Clo. *SW19* —2N **43**
Harlands Gro. *Orp* —1K **67**
Harlech Gdns. *Houn* —2K **9**
Harlech Rd. *B'water* —2J **69**
Harlequin Av. *Bren* —2G **11**
Harlequin Cen. *S'hall* —1K **9**
Harlequin Clo. *Iswth* —8E **10**
Harlequin Rd. *Tedd* —8H **25**
Harley Gdns. *Orp* —1N **67**
Harlington Clo. *Hayes* —3D **8**
Harlington Rd. E. *Felt* —1J **23**
Harlington Rd. W. *Felt* —9J **9**
Harlington Way. *Fleet* —4A **88**
Harlow Ct. Reig —3B **122**
(off Wray Comn. Rd.)
Harman Pl. *Purl* —7M **63**
Harmans Dri. *E Grin* —9D **166**
Harmans Mead. *E Grin* —9D **166**
Harman's Water Rd. *Brack*
—4B **32**
Harmar Clo. *Wokgm* —2D **30**
Harmondsworth La. *W Dray*
—2N **7**
Harmondsworth Rd. *W Dray*
—1N **7**
Harmony Clo. *Bew* —5K **181**
Harmony Clo. *Wall* —5J **63**
Harms Gro. *Guild* —9E **94**
Harold Rd. *Sutt* —1B **62**
Harold Rd. *Worth* —3J **183**
Haroldslea. *Horl* —1H **163**
Haroldslea Clo. *Horl* —1G **163**
Haroldslea Dri. *Horl* —1G **162**
Harold Wilson Ho. SW6 —2L **13**
(off Clem Attlee Ct.)
Harpenden Rd. *SE27* —4M **29**
Harper Dri. *M'bowr* —7G **182**
Harper's Rd. *Ash* —1G **111**
Harpesford Av. *Vir W* —4L **35**
Harps Oak La. *Red* —3D **102**
Harpton Clo. *Yat* —8C **48**
Harpton Pde. *Yat* —8C **48**
Harpurs. *Tad* —9J **81**
Harrier Clo. *Cranl* —6N **155**
Harrier Ct. Craw —9H **163**
(off Wakehams Grn. Dri.)
Harrier Ho. King T —9L **25**
(off Sigrist Sq.)
Harriet Gdns. *Croy* —8D **46**
Harriet Tubman Clo. *SW2*
—1K **29**
Harrington Clo. *Croy* —8J **45**
Harrington Clo. *Leigh* —1F **140**
Harrington Clo. *Wind* —7C **4**
Harrington Gdns. *SW7* —1N **13**
Harrington Rd. *SE25* —3E **46**
Harriott's Clo. *Asht* —7J **79**
Harriott's La. *Asht* —6J **79**
Harris Clo. *Craw* —6N **181**
Harris Clo. *Houn* —4A **10**
Harrison Clo. *Reig* —4N **121**
Harrison Ct. *Shep* —4C **38**
Harrison Gdns. *G'ming* —7H **133**
Harrison Ho. *SW12* —1H **29**
Harrisons Rise. *Croy* —9M **45**
Harris Path. *Craw* —6N **181**
Harris Way. *Sun* —9F **22**
Harrogate Ct. *Slou* —1C **6**
Harrow Bottom Rd. *Vir W*
—5B **36**
Harrow Clo. *Add* —8K **37**
Harrow Clo. *Chess* —4K **59**
Harrow Clo. *Dork* —6G **119**
Harrow Clo. *Eden* —9L **127**
Harrowdene. *Cranl* —6N **155**
Harrowdene Gdns. *Tedd* —8G **25**
Harrow Gdns. *Warl* —2J **85**
Harrowgate Gdns. *Dork*
—7H **119**
Harrowlands Pk. *Dork* —6H **119**
Harrow La. *G'ming* —4H **133**
Harrow Pas. *King T* —1K **41**
Harrow Rd. *Cars* —3C **62**
Harrow Rd. *Felt* —2B **22**
Harrow Rd. *Warl* —2J **85**
Harrow Rd. E. *Dork* —7H **119**
Harrow Rd. W. *Dork* —6G **119**
Harrowsley Ct. *Horl* —7F **142**
Harrowsley Grn. La. *Horl*
[illegible] **143**
Harrow Way. *Shep* —1D **38**
Hart Cen., The. *Fleet* —4A **88**
Hart Clo. *Blet* —3B **124**
Hart Clo. *Brack* —8N **15**
Hart Clo. *F'boro* —6K **69**
Hart Dyke Clo. *Wokgm* —6A **30**
Harte Rd. *Houn* —5N **9**
Hartfield Cres. *SW19* —8L **27**
Hartfield Cres. *W Wick* —1C **66**
Hartfield Rd. *SW19* —8L **27**
Hartfield Rd. *Chess* —2K **59**
Hartfield Rd. *Eden* —5N **147**
Hartfield Rd. *F Row* —6H **187**
Hartfield Rd. *W Wick* —1C **66**
Hartford Rise. *Camb* —9B **50**
Hartford Rd. *Eps* —3A **60**
Hart Gdns. *Dork* —4H **119**
Hartham Clo. *Iswth* —4G **10**
Hartham Rd. *Iswth* —4F **10**
Harting Ct. *Craw* —6L **181**
Hartington Clo. *Farn* —2L **67**
Hartington Ct. *W4* —3A **12**
Hartington Pl. *Reig* —1M **121**
Hartington Rd. *W4* —3A **12**
Hartington Rd. *Twic* —1H **25**
Hartismere Rd. *SW6* —3L **13**
Hartland Clo. *New H* —6L **55**
Hartland Pl. *F'boro* —8M **69**
Hartland Rd. *Add* —4J **55**
Hartland Rd. *Hamp* —5B **24**
Hartland Rd. *Iswth* —6G **11**
Hartland Rd. *Mord* —6M **43**
Hartlands, The. *Houn* —2J **9**
Hartland Way. *Croy* —9H **47**
Hartland Way. *Mord* —6L **43**
Hartley Clo. *B'water* —1G **69**
Hartley Copse. *Old Win* —9K **5**
Hartley Down. *Purl* —2K **83**
Hartley Farm. *Purl* —2K **83**
Hartley Hill. *Purl* —2K **83**
Hartley Old Rd. *Purl* —2K **83**
Hartley Rd. *Croy* —6N **45**
Hartley Rd. *W'ham* —3M **107**
Hartley Way. *Purl* —2K **83**
Hartop Point. SW6 —3K **13**
(off Pellant Rd.)
Hart Rd. *Byfl* —9N **55**
Hart Rd. *Dork* —4H **119**
Hart Rd. *F'boro* —6M **89**
Harts Croft. *Croy* —5H **65**
Harts Gdns. *Guild* —9L **93**
Hartsgrove. *C'fold* —4E **172**
Hartshill. *Guild* —2G **113**
Hartshill Wlk. *Wok* —3L **73**
Hart's La. *S God* —5G **124**
Hartsleaf Clo. *Fleet* —5A **88**
Harts Leap Clo. *Sand* —6G **48**
Harts Leap Rd. *Sand* —7F **48**
Hartspiece Rd. *Red* —5E **122**
Hartswood. *N Holm* —8K **119**
Hartswood Av. *Reig* —7M **121**
Harts Yd. *Farnh* —1G **129**
Harts Yd. *G'ming* —7H **133**
Hart, The. *Farnh* —1G **128**
Harvard Hill. *W4* —2A **12**
Harvard La. *W4* —1B **12**
Harvard Rd. *W4* —1A **12**
Harvard Rd. *Iswth* —4E **10**
Harvard Rd. *Owl* —6K **49**
Harvest Bank Rd. *W Wick*
—1B **66**
Harvest Clo. *Yat* —2A **68**
Harvest Ct. *Esh* —8A **40**
Harvest Ct. *Shep* —3B **38**

Harvest Cres.—Helmsdale

Harvest Cres. Fleet —9C 68
Harvester Rd. Eps —6C 60
Harvesters. H'ham —3K 197
Harvesters Clo. Iswth —8D 10
Harvest Hill. E Grin —1A 186
Harvest Hill. G'ming —7G 132
Harvest La. Th Dit —5G 40
Harvest Ride. Brack —7M 15 (in two parts)
Harvest Rd. Egh —6N 19
Harvest Rd. Felt —5H 23
Harvest Rd. M'bowr —5G 183
Harvestside. Horl —7G 142
Harvey Clo. Craw —8M 181
Harvey Ho. Bren —1L 11
Harvey Rd. F'boro —9H 69
Harvey Rd. Guild —5A 114
Harvey Rd. Houn —1N 23
Harvey Rd. W On T —6H 39
Harwood Av. Mitc —2C 44
Harwood Gdns. Old Win —1L 19
Harwood Pk. Red —3E 142
Harwood Rd. SW6 —3M 13
Harwood Rd. H'ham —5L 197
Harwoods Clo. E Grin —2B 186
Harwoods La. E Grin —2B 186
Harwood Ter. SW6 —4N 13
Hascombe Cotts. Hasc —5M 153
Hascombe Ct. Craw —4M 181
Hascombe Ct. G'ming —6M 153
Hascombe Rd. Cranl —9E 154
Hascombe Rd. G'ming —1K 153
Haslam Av. Sutt —7K 43
Hasle Dri. Hasl —2F 188
Haslemere and Heathrow Est., The. Houn —5J 9
Haslemere Av. SW18 —3N 27
Haslemere Av. Houn —5K 9
Haslemere Av. Mitc —1B 44
Haslemere Clo. Frim —3G 70
Haslemere Clo. Hamp —6N 23
Haslemere Clo. Wall —2J 63
Haslemere Ind. Est. Hasl —1G 188
Haslemere Rd. Brook —4M 171
Haslemere Rd. Fern —7F 188
Haslemere Rd. T Hth —4M 45
Haslemere Rd. Wind —4D 4
Haslett Av. E. Craw —3C 182
Haslett Av. W. Craw —4B 182
Haslett Rd. Shep —1F 38
Hassocks Ct. Craw —6L 181
Hassocks Rd. SW16 —9H 29
Hassock Wood. Kes —1F 66
Haste Hill. Hasl —3H 189
Hastings Clo. Frim —7E 70
Hastings Ct. Tedd —6D 24
Hastings Dri. Surb —5J 41
Hastings Rd. Craw —3G 182
Hastings Rd. Croy —7C 46
Hastlemere Ind. Est. SW18 —3N 27
Hatch Clo. Add —9K 37
Hatch Clo. Alf —6J 175
Hatch End. F Row —7H 187
Hatch End. W'sham —3N 51
Hatches, The. Farnh —3F 128
Hatches, The. Frim G —8B 70
Hatchet La. Asc & Wind —7L 17
Hatchet La. Wink —4M 17
Hatchett Rd. Felt —2D 22
Hatchetts Dri. Hasl —2A 188
Hatch Gdns. Tad —7J 81
Hatchgate. Horl —9D 142
Hatchgate Copse. Brack —5K 31
Hatch Hill. Hasl —7F 188
Hatchlands. Capel —5J 159
Hatchlands. H'ham —1N 197
Hatchlands Rd. Red —3C 122
Hatch La. Coul —2E 82
Hatch La. Hasl —6F 188
Hatch La. Ock —7C 76 (in two parts)
Hatch La. Red —2K 143
Hatch La. W Dray —3M 7
Hatch La. Wind —6D 4
Hatch La. Wmly —1A 172
Hatch Pl. King T —6M 25
Hatch Ride. Crowt —9F 30
Hatch Rd. SW16 —1J 45
Hatfield Clo. Mitc —3B 44
Hatfield Clo. Sutt —5N 61
Hatfield Clo. W Byf —8K 55
Hatfield Gdns. F'boro —2C 90
Hatfield Mead. Mord —4M 43
Hatfield Rd. Asht —6M 79
Hatfield Wlk. Craw —6K 181
Hathaway Ct. Red —2E 122 (off St Anne's Rise)
Hathaway Rd. Croy —6M 45
Hatherleigh Clo. Chess —2K 59
Hatherleigh Clo. Mord —3M 43
Hatherley Rd. Rich —5M 11
Hatherop Rd. Hamp —8N 23
Hathersham Clo. Small —7L 143
Hathersham La. Small —4H 143
Hatherwood. Lea —8K 79
Hatherwood. Yat —1E 68
Hatton Ct. Wind —5F 4
Hatton Gdns. Mitc —4D 44
Hatton Grn. Felt —7H 9
Hatton Hill. W'sham —1M 51
Hatton Rd. Croy —7L 45
Hatton Rd. Felt —1D 22
Hatton Rd. S. Felt —7G 8
Havana Rd. SW19 —3M 27
Havelock Rd. SW19 —6A 28
Havelock Rd. Croy —8C 46
Havelock Rd. Wokgm —2A 30
Havelock St. Wokgm —2A 30
Havenbury Est. Dork —4G 118
Haven Clo. SW19 —4J 27
Haven Ct. Beck —1M 47
Haven Gdns. Craw D —9E 164
Havengate. H'ham —3M 197
Haven Rd. Ashf —5C 22
Haven Rd. Rud & Bil —2D 194
Haven, The. Rich —6N 11
Haven, The. Sun —8H 23
Haven Way. Farnh —8J 109
Haverfield Gdns. Rich —3N 11
Haverhill Rd. SW12 —2G 29
Havers Av. W On T —2L 57
Haversham Clo. Craw —3D 182
Haversham Clo. Twic —9K 11
Haversham Dri. Brack —5N 31
Havisham Pl. SW16 & SE19 —7M 29
Hawarden Clo. Craw D —1F 184
Hawarden Gro. SE24 —1N 29
Hawarden Rd. Cat —8N 83
Hawes La. W Wick —7M 47
Hawes Rd. Tad —7J 81
Hawker Clo. Wall —4J 63
Hawkesbourne Rd. H'ham —3M 197
Hawkesbury Rd. SW15 —8G 12
Hawkes Leap. W'sham —1M 51
Hawkesley Clo. Twic —5G 24
Hawkesmoor Rd. Craw —5K 181
Hawkes Rd. Felt —1H 23
Hawkes Rd. Mitc —9C 28
Hawkesworth Dri. Bag —6H 51
Hawkewood Rd. Sun —2H 39
Hawkfield Ct. Iswth —5E 10
Hawkhirst Rd. Kenl —2A 84
Hawkhurst. Cobh —1A 78
Hawkhurst Gdns. Chess —1L 59
Hawkhurst Rd. SW16 —9H 29
Hawkhurst Rd. Kenl —4B 84
Hawkhurst Wlk. Craw —5F 182
Hawkhurst Way. N Mald —4C 42
Hawkhurst Way. W Wick —8L 47
Hawkins Clo. Brack —1E 32
Hawkins Rd. Craw —6C 182
Hawkins Rd. Tedd —7H 25
Hawkins Way. Fleet —5D 88
Hawkins Way. Wokgm —2D 30
Hawk La. Brack —3B 32
Hawkley Gdns. SE27 —3M 29
Hawkridge Ct. Brack —3C 32
Hawksbrook La. Beck —5L 47
Hawkshaw Clo. SW2 —2J 29
Hawkshill Clo. Esh —3A 58
Hawks Hill Clo. Fet —1F 98
Hawkshill Pl. Esh —3A 58
Hawkshill Way. Esh —3N 57
Hawksmoore Dri. Dork —7J 139
Hawksmoor St. W6 —2J 13
Hawks Rd. King T —1M 41
Hawksview. Cobh —9N 57
Hawks Way. Stai —4H 21
Hawkswell Clo. Wok —4J 73
Hawkswell Wlk. Wok —4J 73
Hawkswood Av. Frim —4D 70
Hawkswood Ho. Brack —9K 15
Hawkwell. C Crook —9C 88
Hawkwood Dell. Bookh —4A 98
Hawkwood Rise. Bookh —4A 98
Hawley Clo. Hamp —7N 23
Hawley Ct. F'boro —6K 69
Hawley Grn. B'water —3K 69
Hawley La. F'boro —5M 69 (in two parts)
Hawley La. Ind. Est. F'boro —6N 69
Hawley Rd. B'water —2J 69
Hawley Way. Ashf —6B 22
Hawmead. Craw D —1F 184
Haworth Rd. M'bowr —4F 182
Haws La. Stai —9J 7
Hawth Av. Craw —5D 182
Hawth Clo. Craw —5C 182
Hawthorn Av. Big H —2F 86
Hawthorn Av. Rich —5L 11
Hawthorn Clo. Alder —4C 110
Hawthorn Clo. Bans —1K 81
Hawthorn Clo. Brack —9M 15
Hawthorn Clo. Craw —9A 162
Hawthorn Clo. Eden —1L 147
Hawthorn Clo. Hamp —6A 24
Hawthorn Clo. H'ham —4J 197
Hawthorn Clo. Houn —3J 9
Hawthorn Clo. Red —8E 122
Hawthorn Clo. Wok —7A 74
Hawthorn Cres. SW17 —6E 28
Hawthorn Cres. S Croy —7F 64
Hawthorn Dri. W Wick —1A 66
Hawthorne Av. Cars —4E 62
Hawthorne Av. Mitc —1B 44
Hawthorne Av. T Hth —9M 29
Hawthorne Av. Wink —3M 17
Hawthorne Clo. Sutt —8A 44
Hawthorne Ct. Stai —1M 21 (off Hawthorne Way)
Hawthorne Cres. B'water —2K 69
Hawthorne Dri. Wink —3M 17
Hawthorne Pl. Eps —8D 60
Hawthorne Rd. Stai —5E 20
Hawthorne Way. Guild —8D 94
Hawthorne Way. Stai —1M 21
Hawthorne Way. Wink —2M 17
Hawthorn Gro. SE20 —1E 46
Hawthorn Hatch. Bren —3H 11
Hawthorn La. Brack —1C 16
Hawthorn La. Rowl —8E 128
Hawthorn La. Wind —1B 16
Hawthorn Rd. Bren —3H 11
Hawthorn Rd. Frim —4D 70
Hawthorn Rd. G'ming —9E 132
Hawthorn Rd. Rip —2J 95
Hawthorn Rd. Sutt —3C 62
Hawthorn Rd. Wall —4F 62
Hawthorn Rd. Wok —7N 73
Hawthorns, The. Coln —4H 7
Hawthorns, The. Eps —4E 60
Hawthorns, The. Oxt —2C 126
Hawthorn Way. Bisl —3D 72
Hawthorn Way. New H —6L 55
Hawthorn Way. Red —4F 122
Hawthorn Way. Shep —3E 38
Hawtrey Rd. Wind —5F 4
Haxted Rd. Ling & Eden —5A 146
Haybarn Dri. H'ham —1L 197
Haycroft Clo. Coul —5M 83
Haycroft Rd. Surb —8K 41
Hayden Ct. New H —7K 55
Haydn Av. Purl —1L 83
Haydon Pk. Rd. SW19 —6M 27
Haydon Pl. Guild —4N 113
Haydons Rd. SW19 —6N 27
Hayes Barton. Wok —3F 74
Hayes Chase. W Wick —5N 47
Hayes Ct. SW2 —2J 29
Hayes Cres. Sutt —1J 61
Hayes Hill. Brom —7N 47
Hayes La. Beck —2M 47
Hayes La. Kenl —3M 83
Hayes La. Slin —8H 195
Hayes, The. Eps —6D 80
Hayes Wlk. Small —7L 143
Hayes Way. Beck —3M 47
Hayfields. Horl —7F 142
Haygarth Pl. SW19 —6J 27
Haygreen Clo. King T —7A 26
Haylett Gdns. King T —3K 41
Hayley Grn. Warf —6D 16
Hayling Av. Felt —4H 23
Hayling Ct. Craw —6A 182
Hayling Ct. Sutt —1H 61
Haymeads Dri. Esh —3C 58
Haymer Gdns. Wor Pk —9F 42
Hayne Rd. Beck —1J 47
Haynes Clo. Rip —9K 75
Haynes Clo. Slou —1B 6
Haynt Wlk. SW20 —2K 43
Hays Bri. Bus. Cen. S God —5F 144
Haysbridge Houses. God —4E 144
Hayse Hill. Wind —4A 4
Haysleigh Gdns. SE20 —1D 46
Hays Wlk. Sutt —6J 61
Haywain. Oxt —8N 105
Hayward Clo. SW19 —8N 27
Haywardens. Ling —6N 145
Hayward Gdns. SW15 —9H 13
Haywards. Craw —9H 163
Haywards Mead. Eton W —1C 4
Haywood. Brack —6A 32
Haywood Dri. Fleet —6B 88
Haywood Rise. Orp —2N 67
Hazel Av. F'boro —3L 89
Hazel Av. Guild —8M 93
Hazel Bank. SE25 —1B 46
Hazel Bank. Surb —7B 42
Hazelbank Ct. Cher —7L 37
Hazelbank Rd. Cher —7L 37
Hazelbourne Rd. SW12 —1F 28
Hazelbury Clo. SW19 —1M 43
Hazel Clo. Bren —3H 11
Hazel Clo. Craw —9A 162
Hazel Clo. Craw D —1F 184
Hazel Clo. Croy —6G 46
Hazel Clo. Egh —7L 19
Hazel Clo. Mitc —3H 45
Hazel Clo. Reig —5A 122
Hazel Clo. Twic —1C 24
Hazel Ct. Guild —8N 93
Hazel Dene. Add —2L 55
Hazeldene Ct. Kenl —2A 84
Hazel Dri. Rip —3H 95
Hazel Gro. Hind —7C 170
Hazel Gro. Stai —7K 21
Hazelhurst. Beck —1N 47
Hazelhurst. Horl —7G 143
Hazelhurst Clo. Guild —7D 94
Hazelhurst Cres. H'ham —7F 196
Hazelhurst Dri. Worth —3J 183
Hazelhurst Rd. SW17 —5A 28
Hazel La. Rich —3L 25
Hazell Hill. Brack —2A 32
Hazell Rd. Farnh —1E 128
Hazel Mead. Eps —6F 60
Hazelmere Clo. Felt —9F 8
Hazelmere Clo. Lea —6H 79
Hazelmere Ct. SW2 —2K 29
Hazel Pde. Fet —9C 78
Hazel Rd. Ash —5G 111
Hazel Rd. Myt —3E 90
Hazel Rd. Reig —5A 122
Hazel Rd. W Byf —1J 75
Hazel Wlk. N Holm —8J 119
Hazel Way. Coul —6D 82
Hazel Way. Craw D —1F 184
Hazel Way. Fet —9C 78
Hazelwick Av. Craw —1E 182
Hazelwick Ct. Craw —1E 182
Hazelwick Mill La. Craw (in two parts) —1E 182
Hazelwick Rd. Craw —2E 182
Hazelwood. Craw —3M 181
Hazelwood. Dork —6H 119
Hazelwood. Elst —7J 131
Hazelwood Av. Mord —3N 43
Hazelwood Clo. Craw D —1C 184
Hazelwood Cotts. G'ming —7G 132
Hazelwood Ct. Surb —5L 41
Hazelwood Gro. S Croy —9E 64
Hazelwood Heights. Oxt —9C 106
Hazelwood Houses. Short —2N 47
Hazelwood La. Binf —6L 15
Hazelwood La. Coul —5C 82
Hazelwood Rd. Cud —8M 67
Hazelwood Rd. Knap —5H 73
Hazelwood Rd. Oxt —1D 126
Hazlebury Rd. SW6 —5N 13
Hazledean Rd. Croy —8A 46
Hazledene Rd. W4 —2B 12
Hazlemere Gdns. Wor Pk —7F 42
Hazlewell Rd. SW15 —8H 13
Hazlitt Clo. Felt —5M 23
Hazon Way. Eps —8B 60
Headcorn Pl. T Hth —3K 45
Headcorn Rd. T Hth —3K 45
Headington Clo. Wokgm —9C 14
Headington Dri. Wokgm —9C 14
Headington Rd. SW18 —3A 28
Headlam Rd. SW4 —1H 29
Headland Way. Ling —7N 145
Headley Av. Wall —2K 63
Headley Clo. Craw —9H 163
Headley Clo. Eps —3N 59
Headley Comn. Rd. H'ley —4C 100
Headley Ct. Eden —1M 147
Headley Ct. H'ley —1A 100
Headley Dri. Eps —6H 81
Headley Dri. New Ad —4L 65
Headley Fields. Head —4D 168
Headley Gro. Tad —7G 81
Headley Heath App. Tad —8A 100
Headley Hill Rd. Head —4E 168
Headley La. Mick —7J 99
Headley La. Pass —8D 168
Headley Pk. Cotts. Head —9B 148
Headley Rd. Eps —5A 80
Headley Rd. Gray —5K 169
Headley Rd. Lea & Eps —9J 79
Headley Rd. Lind —4B 168
Headway Clo. Rich —5J 25
Headway, The. Eps —5E 60
Healy Dri. Orp —1N 67
Hearmon Clo. Yat —9D 48
Hearne Rd. W4 —2N 11
Hearn Vale. Head —2F 168
Hearnville Rd. SW12 —2E 28
Hearn Wlk. Brack —9C 16
Hearsey Gdns. B'water —9G 49 (in two parts)
Heathacre. Coln —4F 6
Heatham Pk. Twic —1F 24
Heathbridge. Wey —3B 56
Heathbridge App. Wey —3B 56
Heath Bus. Cen. Houn —7C 10
Heath Clo. Bans —1N 81
Heath Clo. Broad H —5E 196
Heath Clo. Farnh —5H 109
Heath Clo. Hayes —3E 8
Heath Clo. Hind —2A 170
Heath Clo. Stai —9L 7
Heath Clo. Vir W —3N 35
Heath Clo. Wokgm —4A 30
Heathcote. Tad —8J 81
Heathcote Clo. Ash V —1E 110 (off Church Path)
Heathcote Dri. E Grin —8L 165
Heathcote Rd. Ash —1F 110
Heathcote Rd. Camb —1B 70
Heathcote Rd. Eps —1C 80
Heathcote Rd. Twic —9H 11
Heath Cotts. Bourne —8J 129
Heath Ct. Bag —4J 51
Heath Ct. Broad H —5E 196
Heath Ct. Houn —7N 9
Heathcroft Av. Sun —8G 23
Heathdale Av. Houn —6M 9
Heathdene Rd. SW16 —8K 29
Heathdene Rd. Wall —4F 62
Heathdown Rd. Wok —2F 74
Heath Dri. SW20 —3H 43
Heath Dri. Brkwd —7D 72
Heath Dri. Send —9D 74
Heath Dri. Sutt —5A 62
Heath Dri. Tad —3F 100
Heather Clo. Alder —3K 109
Heather Clo. Ash V —8F 90
Heather Clo. Copt —8M 163
Heather Clo. Farnh —5E 128
Heather Clo. Guild —2L 113
Heather Clo. Hamp —9N 23
Heather Clo. H'ham —3K 197
Heather Clo. Iswth —8D 10
Heather Clo. New H —6K 55
Heather Clo. Tad —9K 81
Heather Clo. Wok —2M 73
Heather Cotts. Hind —1B 170
Heather Ct. Hind —5E 170
Heatherdale Clo. King T —8N 25
Heatherdale Rd. Camb —2A 70
Heatherdene. W Hor —3E 96
Heatherdene Av. Crowt —3D 48
Heatherdene Clo. Mitc —3B 44
Heather Dri. Asc —6E 34
Heather Dri. C Crook —8A 88
Heather Dri. Lind —4A 168
Heatherfields. New H —6K 55
Heather Gdns. F'boro —3J 89
Heather Gdns. Sutt —3M 61
Heatherlands. Horl —7F 142 (in two parts)
Heatherlands. Sun —7H 23
Heatherley Clo. Camb —1N 69
Heatherley Rd. Camb —1N 69
Heather Mead. Frim —4D 70
Heather Mead Ct. Frim —4D 70
Heathermount. Brack —3C 32
Heathermount Dri. Crowt —1E 48
Heathermount Gdns. Crowt —1E 48
Heather Pl. Esh —1B 58
Heather Ridge Arc. Camb —2G 71
Heatherset Clo. Esh —2C 58
Heatherset Gdns. SW16 —8K 29
Heatherside Dri. Vir W —5K 35
Heatherside Rd. Eps —4C 60
Heathersland. Dork —8J 119
Heathers, The. Stai —1A 22
Heathervale Cvn. Pk. New H —6L 55
Heathervale Rd. New H —6K 55
Heather View Cotts. Fren —1H 149
Heather Wlk. Brkwd —8A 72
Heather Wlk. Craw —6N 181
Heather Wlk. Small —8N 143
Heather Wlk. Twic —1A 24 (off Stephenson Rd.)
Heather Wlk. W Vill —6F 56
Heather Way. Chob —4H 53
Heatherway. Crowt —2F 48
Heatherway. Felb —3J 165
Heather Way. Hind —5D 170
Heather Way. S Croy —5G 65
Heathfield. Cobh —1A 78
Heathfield. Craw —9H 163 (in two parts)
Heathfield Av. SW18 —1B 28
Heathfield Av. Asc —4B 34
Heathfield Clo. G'ming —9H 133
Heathfield Clo. Kes —2E 66
Heathfield Clo. Wok —5C 74
Heathfield Ct. W4 —1C 12
Heathfield Ct. Fleet —6A 88
Heathfield Dri. Mitc —9C 28
Heathfield Dri. Red —8C 122
Heathfield Gdns. W4 —1B 12
Heathfield Gdns. Croy —1A 64
Heathfield N. Twic —1E 24
Heathfield Rd. SW18 —1A 28
Heathfield Rd. Chess —4M 59
Heathfield Rd. Croy —1A 64
Heathfield Rd. Kes —2E 66
Heathfield Rd. W On T —1M 57
Heathfield Rd. Wok —5C 74
Heathfields Ct. Houn —8M 9
Heathfield S. Twic —1F 24
Heathfield Sq. SW18 —1B 28
Heathfield Ter. W4 —1B 12
Heathfield Vale. S Croy —5G 65
Heath Gdns. Twic —2F 24
Heath Gro. Sun —8G 23
Heath Hill. Dock —7D 148
Heath Hill. Dork —5H 119
Heath Hill Rd. N. Crowt —2G 48
Heath Hill Rd. S. Crowt —2G 49
Heath Ho. Rd. Wok —9G 73
Heathhurst Rd. S Croy —5A 64
Heathlands. Brack —3M 31
Heathlands. Tad —9J 81
Heathlands Clo. Sun —1H 39
Heathlands Clo. Twic —3F 24
Heathlands Clo. Wok —1A 74
Heathlands Ct. Wokgm —8E 30
Heathlands Ct. Yat —2D 68
Heathlands Rd. Wokgm —5E 30
Heathland St. Alder —2M 109
Heathlands Way. Houn —8M 9
Heath La. Abry —1N 135
Heath La. Ews —6A 108
Heath La. Farnh —5H 109
Heath La. G'ming —9K 133
Heathmans Rd. SW6 —4L 13
Heath Mead. SW19 —4J 27
Heath Mill La. Worp —3E 92
Heathmoors. Brack —4A 32
Heathpark Dri. W'sham —3B 52
Heath Pl. Bag —4J 51
Heath Ride. Finch & Crowt —1A 48
Heath Ridge Grn. Cobh —9A 58
Heath Rise. SW15 —9J 13
Heath Rise. Camb —1B 70
Heath Rise. Rip —1K 95
Heath Rise. Vir W —3N 35
Heath Rise. Westc —7C 118
Heath Rd. Bag —4J 51
Heath Rd. Cat —1A 104
Heath Rd. Hasl —3B 188
Heath Rd. Houn —7B 10
Heath Rd. Oxs —8C 58
Heath Rd. T Hth —2N 45
Heath Rd. Twic —2F 24
Heath Rd. Wey —1B 56
Heath Rd. Wok —2B 74
Heathrow. Gom —8D 116
Heathrow Boulevd. W Dray —3A 8
Heathrow Causeway Cen. Houn —6H 9
Heathrow Clo. W Dray —4K 7
Heathrow International Trad. Est. Houn —6J 9
Heathrow Summit Cen. W Dray —3M 7
Heathside. Esh —9E 40
Heathside. Houn —1N 23
Heathside. Wey —2C 56
Heathside Clo. Esh —9E 40
Heathside Ct. Tad —1H 101
Heathside Cres. Wok —4B 74
Heathside Gdns. Wok —4C 74
Heathside La. Hind —3B 170
Heathside Pk. Rd. Wok —5B 74
Heathside Rd. Wok —5B 74
Heath, The. Cat —2A 104
Heath, The. P'ham —8A 112
Heathvale Bri. Rd. Ash V —7E 90
Heath View. E Hor —3G 97
Heathview Gdns. SW15 —1H 27
Heathview Rd. Milf —3B 152
Heathview Rd. T Hth —3L 45
Heathway. Asc —9J 17
Heathway. Camb —1B 70
Heathway. Cat —3N 103
Heathway. Croy —8J 47
Heathway. E Hor —2G 97
Heath Way. H'ham —3K 197
Heathway. S'hall —1L 9
Heathway Clo. Camb —1B 70
Heathwood Clo. Yat —8C 48
Heathyfields Rd. Farnh —6E 108
Heaton Rd. Mitc —8E 28
Hebbecastle Down. Warf —7A 16
Hebdon Rd. SW17 —4C 28
Heber Mans. W14 —2K 13 (off Queen's Club Gdns.)
Heckfield Pl. SW6 —3M 13
Heddon Clo. Iswth —7G 10
Heddon Wlk. F'boro —7M 69
Hedgecourt Pl. Felb —6H 165
Hedge Croft. Yat —9A 48
Hedgecroft Cotts. Rip —8K 75
Hedgehog La. Hasl —2F 188
Hedgerley Ct. Wok —4M 73
Hedger's Almshouses. Guild (off Wykeham Rd.) —2F 114
Hedgeside. Craw —8A 182
Hedgeway. Guild —5K 113
Hedingham Clo. Horl —7G 142
Hedley Rd. Twic —1A 24
Heenan Clo. Frim G —7C 70
Heidegger Cres. SW13 —3G 13
Heighton Gdns. Croy —2M 63
Heights Clo. SW20 —8G 27
Heights Clo. Bans —3K 81
Heights, The. Wey —6B 56
Helby Rd. SW4 —1H 29
Helder St. S Croy —3A 64
Heldmann Clo. Houn —7D 10
Helena Clo. Wall —4K 63
Helena Rd. Wind —5G 4
Helen Av. Felt —1J 23
Helen Clo. W Mol —3B 40
Helen Ct. F'boro —1N 89
Helford Wlk. Wok —5K 73
Helgiford Gdns. Sun —8F 22
Helicon Ho. Craw —4A 182
Helix Rd. SW2 —1K 29
Helme Clo. SW19 —6L 27
Helmsdale. Brack —4C 32

Helmsdale—Hill Crest

Helmsdale. *Wok* —5L **73**
Helmsdale Rd. *SW16* —9H **29**
Helson La. *Wind* —4E **4**
Helston Clo. *Frim* —7E **70**
Helston La. *Wind* —4E **4**
Helvellyn Clo. *Egh* —8D **20**
Hemingford Rd. *Sutt* —1H **61**
Hemlock Clo. *Tad* —1K **101**
Hemming Clo. *Hamp* —9A **24**
Hemmyng Corner. *Warf* —7A **16**
Hempshaw Av. *Bans* —3D **82**
Hemsby Rd. *Chess* —3M **59**
Hemsby Wlk. *Craw* —5F **182**
Hemsley Ct. *Guild* —9K **93**
Hemwood Rd. *Wind* —6A **4**
Henbane Ct. *Craw* —7N **181**
Henbit Clo. *Tad* —6G **81**
Henchley Dene. *Guild* —9F **94**
Henderson Av. *Guild* —8L **93**
Henderson Rd. *SW18* —1C **28**
Henderson Rd. *Big H* —8E **66**
Henderson Rd. *Craw* —8N **181**
Henderson Rd. *Croy* —5A **46**
Henderson Way. *H'ham* —8F **196**
Hendham Rd. *SW17* —3C **28**
Hendon Way. *Stai* —9M **7**
Hendrick Av. *SW12* —1D **28**
Hendy Sq. *Fleet* —4A **88**
Heneage Cres. *New Ad* —6M **65**
Henfield Rd. *SW19* —9L **27**
Henfold Cotts. *Dork* —9N **139**
Henfold Dri. *Bear G* —8K **139**
Henfold La. *Dork* —4L **139**
Hengelo Gdns. *Mitc* —3B **44**
Hengist Clo. *H'ham* —7G **197**
Hengist Way. *Brom* —3N **47**
Hengrove Cres. *Ashf* —4M **21**
Henhurst Cross La. *Cold* —[illegible]
Henhurst La. *Dork* —8G **138**
Henley Av. *Sutt* —9K **43**
Henley Bank. *Guild* —5K **113**
Henley Clo. *F'boro* —6K **69**
Henley Clo. *Iswth* —4F **10**
Henley Clo. *M'bowr* —5H **183**
Henley Ct. *Wok* —7D **74**
Henley Dri. *Frim G* —7C **70**
Henley Dri. *King T* —8E **26**
Henley Fort Bungalows. *Guild* —6K **113**
Henley Gdns. *Yat* —1C **68**
Henley Way. *Felt* —6L **23**
Henlow Pl. *Rich* —3K **25**
Henlys Roundabout. (Junct.) —5L **9**
Henrietta Ho. W6 —1H 13
(off Queen Caroline St.)
Henry Hatch Wlk. *Sutt* —4A **62**
Henry Jackson Rd. *SW15* —6J **13**
Henshaw Clo. *Craw* —5L **181**
Henslow Way. *Wok* —1F **74**
Henson Rd. *Craw* —2F **182**
Hensworth Rd. *Ashf* —6M **21**
Henty Clo. *Craw* —6K **181**
Henty Wlk. *SW15* —8G **12**
Hepple Clo. *Iswth* —5H **11**
Hepplestone Clo. *SW15* —9G **13**
Hepplewhite Clo. *Craw* —8N **181**
Hepworth Croft. *Col T* —9K **49**
Hepworth Rd. *SW16* —8J **29**
Hepworth Way. *W On T* —7G **39**
Heracles Clo. *Wall* —4J **63**
Herald Gdns. *Wall* —8F **44**
Herbert Clo. *Brack* —4N **31**
Herbert Cres. *Knap* —5H **73**
Herbert Gdns. *W4* —2A **12**
Herbert Morrison Ho. SW6
(off Clem Attlee Ct.) —2L 13
Herbert Rd. *SW19* —8L **27**
(in two parts)
Herbert Rd. *King T* —2M **41**
Herbs End. *F'boro* —9H **69**
Hereford Clo. *Craw* —7C **182**
Hereford Clo. *Eps* —9C **60**
Hereford Clo. *Guild* —1J **113**
Hereford Clo. *Stai* —9K **21**
Hereford Copse. *Wok* —6L **73**
Hereford Ct. *Sutt* —4M **61**
Hereford Gdns. *Twic* —2C **24**
Hereford La. *Farnh* —6G **109**
Hereford Mead. *Fleet* —1C **88**
Hereford Rd. *Felt* —2K **23**
Hereford Sq. *SW7* —1N **13**
Hereford Way. *Chess* —2J **59**
Hereward Av. *Purl* —7L **63**
Hereward Rd. *SW17* —5D **28**
Heriot Rd. *Cher* —6J **37**
Heritage Hill. *Kes* —2E **66**
Heritage Lawn. *Horl* —7G **142**
Herlwyn Gdns. *SW17* —5D **28**
Herm Clo. *Craw* —7M **181**
Herm Clo. *Iswth* —3C **10**
Hermes Clo. *Fleet* —4D **88**
Hermes Way. *Wall* —4H **63**
Hermitage Bri. Cotts. *Knap* —6G **72**
Hermitage Clo. *Clay* —3G **58**
Hermitage Clo. *F'boro* —4B **90**
Hermitage Clo. *Frim* —5D **70**
Hermitage Clo. *Shep* —3B **38**
Hermitage Dri. *Asc* —1J **33**
Hermitage Gdns. *SE19* —8N **29**
Hermitage Grn. *SW16* —9J **29**
Hermitage La. *SE25* —5D **46**
(in two parts)
Hermitage La. *SW16* —8K **29**
Hermitage La. *Croy & SE25* —6D **46**
Hermitage La. *E Grin* —1B **186**
Hermitage La. *Wind* —7D **4**
Hermitage Pde. *Asc* —2M **33**
Hermitage Path. *SW16* —9J **29**
Hermitage Rd. *SE19* —8N **29**
Hermitage Rd. *E Grin* —7N **165**
Hermitage Rd. *Kenl* —2N **83**
Hermitage Rd. *Wok* —7G **72**
Hermitage, The. *SW13* —4E **12**
Hermitage, The. *Felt* —4G **23**
Hermitage, The. *King T* —3K **41**
Hermitage, The. *Rich* —8L **11**
Hermitage Woods Cres. *Wok* —7G **73**
Hermitage Woods Est. *Knap* —6H **73**
Hermits Rd. *Craw* —2D **182**
Hermonger's La. *Rud* —7G **176**
Hernbrook Dri. *H'ham* —8L **197**
Herndon Clo. *Egh* —5C **20**
Herndon Rd. *SW18* —8N **13**
Herne Rd. *Surb* —8K **41**
Heron Clo. *Asc* —9H **17**
Heron Clo. *C Crook* —7D **88**
Heron Clo. *Craw* —1A **182**
Heron Clo. *Eden* —9L **127**
Heron Clo. *Guild* —9L **93**
Heron Clo. *Myt* —1D **90**
Heron Ct. *Eps* —1F **80**
Heron Dale. *Add* —2M **55**
Herondale. *Brack* —6A **32**
Herondale. *Hasl* —2C **188**
Herondale. *S Croy* —5G **65**
Herondale Av. *SW18* —2B **28**
Heronfield. *Egh* —7L **19**
Heron Pk. Pde. *SW19* —9L **27**
Heron Pl. *E Grin* —1B **186**
Heron Rd. *Croy* —8B **46**
Heron Rd. *Twic* —7G **11**
Heronry, The. *W On T* —3H **57**
Heronsbrook. *Asc* —1B **34**
Herons Clo. *Copt* —5D **164**
Herons Ct. *Light* —7N **51**
Herons Croft. *Wey* —3D **56**
Heron Shaw. *Cranl* —9N **155**
Herons Lea. *Copt* —5D **164**
Heron's Pl. *Iswth* —6H **11**
Heron Sq. *Rich* —8K **11**
Herons Way. *Brkwd* —8A **72**
Heron's Way. *Wokgm* —1D **30**
Herons Wood Ct. *Horl* —7F **142**
Herontye Dri. *E Grin* —1B **186**
Heron Wlk. *Wok* —1E **74**
Heron Way. *H'ham* —6N **197**
Heron Wood Rd. *Alder* —4B **110**
Herretts Gdns. *Alder* —3B **110**
Herrett St. *Alder* —4B **110**
Herrick Clo. *Craw* —1G **182**
Herrick Clo. *Frim* —3G **71**
Herrings La. *Cher* —5J **37**
Herrings La. *W'sham* —2A **52**
Herriot Ct. *Yat* —2B **68**
Herschel Grange. *Warf* —6B **16**
Herschel Wlk. *Craw* —8N **181**
Hersham By-Pass. *W on T* —2J **57**
Hersham Cen., The. *W on T* —2L **57**
Hersham Clo. *SW15* —1F **26**
Hersham Gdns. *W On T* —1K **57**
Hersham Pl. *W On T* —2L **57**
Hersham Rd. *W On T* —7H **39**
Hersham Trad. Est. *W on T* —8M **39**
Hertford Av. *SW14* —8C **12**
Hertford Sq. *Mitc* —3J **45**
Hertford Way. *Mitc* —3J **45**
Hesiers Hill. *Warl* —4A **86**
Hesiers Rd. *Warl* —3A **86**
Hesketh Clo. *Cranl* —7N **155**
Heslop Rd. *SW12* —2D **28**
Hesper M. *SW5* —1N **13**
Hessle Gro. *Eps* —7E **60**
Hestercombe Av. *SW6* —5K **13**
Hesterman Way. *Croy* —7K **45**
Hester Ter. *Rich* —6N **11**
Heston Av. *Houn* —2M **9**
Heston Cen., The. *Houn* —1K **9**
Heston Grange. *Houn* —2N **9**
Heston Grange La. *Houn* —2N **9**
Heston Ind. Cen. *Houn* —2K **9**
Heston Ind. Mall. *Houn* —3N **9**
Heston Rd. *Houn* —3A **10**
Heston Rd. *Red* —7D **122**
Heston Wlk. *Red* —7D **122**
Hetherington Rd. *Shep* —1D **38**
Hethersett Clo. *Reig* —9A **102**
Hever Rd. *Eden* —3M **147**
Hevers Av. *Horl* —7D **142**
Hevers Corner. *Horl* —7D **142**
Hewers Way. *Tad* —7G **81**
Hewitt Clo. *Croy* —9K **47**
Hewitts Ind. Est. *Cranl* —7K **155**
Hewlett Pl. *Bag* —4K **51**
Hexham Clo. *Owl* —5J **49**
Hexham Clo. *Worth* —3J **183**
Hexham Gdns. *Iswth* —3G **10**
Hexham Rd. *SE27* —3N **29**
Hexham Rd. *Mord* —7N **43**
Hextalls La. *Blet* —6A **104**
Heybridge Av. *SW16* —8J **29**
Heyford Av. *SW20* —2L **43**
Heyford Rd. *Mitc* —1C **44**
Heymede. *Lea* —1J **99**
Heythorpe Clo. *Knap* —4J **73**
Heythorp St. *SW18* —2L **27**
Heywood Ct. *G'ming* —4F **132**
Heywood Dri. *Bag* —5G **51**
Hibbert's All. *Wind* —4G **4**
Hibernia Gdns. *Houn* —7A **10**
Hibernia Rd. *Houn* —7A **10**
Hibiscus Gro. *Bord* —7A **168**
Hickey's Almshouses. *Rich* —7M **11**
Hickling Wlk. *Craw* —5F **182**
Hickmans Clo. *God* —1F **124**
Hicks La. *B'water* —1G **69**
Hidcote Clo. *Wok* —3D **74**
Hidcote Gdns. *SW20* —2G **42**
Higgs La. *Bag* —4H **51**
Highacre. *Dork* —8H **119**
Highams Hill. *Craw* —4L **181**
Highams Hill. *Warl* —8C **66**
Highams La. *Chob* —3D **52**
High Barn Rd. *Eff & Ran C* —7L **97**
Highbarrow Rd. *Croy* —7D **46**
High Beech. *Brack* —3D **32**
High Beech. *S Croy* —4B **64**
High Beeches. *Bans* —1H **81**
High Beeches. *Frim* —4B **70**
High Beeches Clo. *Purl* —6H **63**
Highbirch Clo. *H'ham* —3A **198**
High Broom Cres. *W Wick* —6L **47**
Highbury Av. *T Hth* —1L **45**
Highbury Clo. *N Mald* —3B **42**
Highbury Clo. *W Wick* —8L **47**
Highbury Cres. *Camb* —8E **50**
Highbury Gro. *Hasl* —9G **170**
Highbury Rd. *SW19* —6K **27**
High Cedar Dri. *SW20* —8H **27**
Highclere. *Asc* —4A **34**
Highclere. *Guild* —9C **94**
Highclere Clo. *Brack* —1C **32**
Highclere Clo. *Kenl* —2N **83**
Highclere Ct. *Knap* —4F **72**
Highclere Dri. *Camb* —8E **50**
Highclere Gdns. *Knap* —4F **72**
Highclere Rd. *Alder* —4B **110**
Highclere Rd. *Knap* —4F **72**
Highclere Rd. *N Mald* —2C **42**
Highcliffe Dri. *SW15* —9E **12**
High Coombe Pl. *King T* —8C **26**
High Copse. *Farnh* —6F **108**
Highcotts La. *Send* —3H **95**
(in two parts)
Highcroft. *Milf* —2B **152**
Highcroft. *Sham G* —7G **135**
Highcroft Ct. *Bookh* —1A **98**
Highcroft Dri. *Warn* —8F **176**
Highcross Way. *SW15* —2F **26**
Highdaun Dri. *SW16* —3K **45**
Highdown. *Fleet* —3B **88**
Highdown. *Wor Pk* —8D **42**
Highdown Ct. *Craw* —6F **182**
Highdown La. *Sutt* —7N **61**
Highdown Rd. *SW15* —9G **12**
Highdown Way. *H'ham* —2M **197**
High Dri. *N Mald* —9B **26**
High Dri. *Oxs* —1D **78**
High Dri. *Wold* —9K **85**
High Elms Rd. *Dow* —7J **67**
Higher Alham. *Brack* —6C **32**
Highercombe Rd. *Hasl* —9J **171**
Higher Dri. *Bans* —8J **61**
Higher Dri. *E Hor* —5F **96**
Higher Dri. *Purl* —9L **63**
Higher Grn. *Eps* —9F **60**
Highfield. *Bans* —4C **82**
Highfield. *Brack* —5L **31**
Highfield. *Felt* —2H **23**
Highfield. *Shalf* —2B **134**
Highfield Av. *Alder* —5M **109**
Highfield Clo. *Alder* —4N **109**
Highfield Clo. *Egh* —7M **19**
Highfield Clo. *F'boro* —1L **89**
Highfield Clo. *Farnh* —4G **128**
Highfield Clo. *Oxs* —7D **58**
Highfield Clo. *Surb* —7J **41**
Highfield Clo. *W Byf* —9J **55**
Highfield Clo. *Wokgm* —2B **30**
Highfield Cres. *Hind* —5D **170**
Highfield Dri. *Eps* —3E **60**
Highfield Dri. *W Wick* —8L **47**
Highfield Gdns. *Alder* —4M **109**
Highfield Ho. Craw —2B 182
(off Town Mead)
Highfield La. *P'ham* —9L **111**
Highfield La. *Thur* —9F **150**
Highfield Path. *F'boro* —1L **89**
Highfield Rd. *Big H* —4E **86**
Highfield Rd. *Cat* —9D **84**
Highfield Rd. *Cher* —7J **37**
Highfield Rd. *E Grin* —7N **165**
Highfield Rd. *F'boro* —1L **89**
Highfield Rd. *Felt* —3H **23**
Highfield Rd. *Iswth* —4F **10**
Highfield Rd. *Purl* —6K **63**
Highfield Rd. *Sun* —4G **38**
Highfield Rd. *Surb* —6B **42**
Highfield Rd. *Sutt* —2C **62**
Highfield Rd. *W On T* —7H **39**
Highfield Rd. *W Byf* —9J **55**
Highfield Rd. *Wind* —6C **4**
High Fields. *Asc* —4C **34**
Highfields. *Asht* —6K **79**
Highfields. *E Hor* —6G **96**
Highfields. *Fet* —2D **98**
Highfields. *F Row* —7H **187**
Highfields. *Sutt* —8M **43**
Highfields Rd. *Eden* —7L **127**
High Foleys. *Clay* —4H **59**
High Gdns. *Wok* —6L **73**
High Garth. *Esh* —3C **58**
Highgate Ct. *Craw* —7A **182**
Highgate La. *F'boro* —9A **70**
Highgate Rd. *F Row* —8G **187**
Highgate Works. *F Row* —8G **187**
Highgrove. *F'boro* —7N **69**
Highgrove Ct. *Sutt* —3M **61**
Highgrove Ho. *Guild* —1E **114**
Highgrove M. *Cars* —9D **44**
High Hill Rd. *Warl* —2M **85**
Highland Cotts. *Wall* —1G **62**
Highland Dri. *Fleet* —1D **88**
Highland Pk. *Felt* —5G **23**
Highland Rd. *Alder* —2B **110**
Highland Rd. *Bear G* —9J **100**
Highland Rd. *Camb* —7C **50**
Highland Rd. *Purl* —1L **83**
Highlands. *Asht* —6J **79**
Highlands Av. *H'ham* —6L **197**
Highlands Av. *Lea* —9J **79**
Highlands Clo. *Farnh* —4G **128**
Highlands Clo. *Houn* —4B **10**
Highlands Clo. *Lea* —9H **79**
Highlands Cres. *H'ham* —6L **197**
Highlands Heath. *SW15* —1H **27**
Highlands La. *Wok* —8A **74**
Highlands Pk. *Lea* —1K **99**
Highlands Rd. *Farnh* —5H **109**
Highlands Rd. *H'ham* —6L **197**
Highlands Rd. *Lea* —9H **79**
Highlands Rd. *Reig* —2B **122**
Highlands, The. *E Hor* —3F **96**
High La. *Hasl* —9G **170**
High La. *Warl* —5J **85**
High Loxley Rd. *Duns* —1C **174**
High Mead. Cars —7B 62
(off Pine Cres.)
High Mead. *W Wick* —8N **47**
High Meadow Clo. *Dork* —6H **119**
High Meadow Pl. *Cher* —5H **37**
High Oaks. *Craw* —5N **181**
High Pde., The. *SW16* —4J **29**
High Pk. Av. *E Hor* —4G **96**
(in two parts)
High Pk. Av. *Rich* —4N **11**
High Pk. Rd. *Farnh* —9G **109**
High Pk. Rd. *Rich* —4N **11**
High Path. *SW19* —9N **27**
High Path Rd. *Guild* —3E **114**
High Pewley. *Guild* —5A **114**
High Pine Clo. *Wey* —2D **56**
High Pines. *Warl* —6F **84**
High Pines Cvn. Site. *Brack* —4F **16**
High Pitfold. *Gray* —8B **170**
Highpoint. *Wey* —2B **56**
High Ridge. *G'ming* —9G **132**
Highridge Clo. *Eps* —1D **80**
Highridge La. *Bet* —9A **120**
High Rd. *Byfl* —8M **55**
High Rd. *Red & Coul* —5A **102**
High Standing. *Cat* —3N **103**
High St. Addlestone, *Add* —1K **55**
High St. Aldershot, *Alder* —2N **109**
High St. Ascot, *Asc* —2K **33**
High St. Bagshot, *Bag* —4J **51**
High St. Banstead, *Bans* —2M **81**
High St. Beckenham, *Beck* —1K **47**
High St. Bletchingley, *Blet* —2N **123**
High St. Bracknell, *Brack* —1N **31**
High St. Bramley, *Brmly* —5B **134**
High St. Brentford, *Bren* —3J **11**
High St. Camberley, *Camb* —9B **50**
High St. Carshalton, *Cars* —1E **62**
High St. Caterham, *Cat* —1B **104**
High St. Cheam, *Cheam* —3K **61**
High St. Chiddingfold, *C'fold* —8H **173**
High St. Chobham, *Chob* —7H **53**
High St. Claygate, *Clay* —3F **58**
High St. Cobham, *Cobh* —1J **77**
High St. Colliers Wood, *SW19* —8B **28**
High St. Colnbrook, *Coln* —3E **6**
High St. Cranford, *Cran* —4H **9**
High St. Cranleigh, *Cranl* —7L **155**
High St. Crawley, *Craw* —3B **182**
(in three parts)
High St. Crowthorne, *Crowt* —3H **49**
High St. Croydon, *Croy* —9N **45**
High St. Datchet, *Dat* —4L **5**
High St. Dorking, *Dork* —5H **119**
High St. Downe, *Dow* —7J **67**
High St. East Grinstead, *E Grin* —1B **186**
High St. East Molesey, *E Mol* —3A **40**
High St. Edenbridge, *Eden* —1L **147**
High St. Egham, *Egh* —6B **20**
High St. Epsom, *Eps* —9C **60**
High St. Esher, *Esh* —1B **58**
High St. Eton, *Eton* —2G **4**
High St. Ewell, *Ewe* —5E **60**
High St. Farnborough, *Farn* —2K **67**
High St. Farnborough, *F'boro* —5B **90**
High St. Feltham, *Felt* —4G **23**
High St. Godalming, *G'ming* —7G **133**
High St. Godstone, *God* —8E **104**
High St. Great Bookham, *Bookh* —3B **98**
High St. Green Street Green, *Grn St* —4N **67**
High St. Guildford, *Guild*
(in four parts) —5M **113**
High St. Hampton, *Hamp* —9C **24**
High St. Hampton Hill, *Hamp H* —7C **24**
High St. Hampton Wick, *Hamp W* —9J **25**
High St. Handcross, *Hand* —8N **199**
High St. Harlington, *Hayes* —2E **8**
High St. Harmondsworth, *Harm* —2M **7**
High St. Haslemere, *Hasl* —2H **189**
High St. Headley, *Head* —4D **168**
High St. Horley, *Horl* —8F **142**
High St. Horsell, *Hors* —2L **73**
High St. Hounslow, *Houn* —6B **10**
High St. Kingston upon Thames, *King T* —2K **41**
High St. Knaphill, *Knap* —4F **72**
High St. Langley, *Langl* —1B **6**
High St. Leatherhead, *Lea*
(in two parts) —9H **79**
High St. Limpsfield, *Limp* —6C **106**
High St. Lingfield, *Ling* —7N **145**
High St. Little Sandhurst, *Sand* —6E **48**
High St. Loxwood, *Loxw* —5H **193**
High St. Merstham, *Mers* —6F **102**
High St. New Malden, *N Mald* —3D **42**
High St. Nutfield, *Nutf* —2K **123**
High St. Old Woking, *Old Wok* —8C **74**
High St. Oxshott, *Oxs* —1D **78**
High St. Oxted, *Oxt* —8N **105**
High St. Purley, *Purl* —7L **63**
High St. Redhill, *Red* —3D **122**
High St. Reigate, *Reig* —3M **121**
High St. Ripley, *Rip* —8L **75**
High St. Rowledge, *Rowl* —8D **128**
High St. Rusper, *Rusp* —2B **180**
High St. Sandhurst, *Sand* —6E **48**
High St. Shepperton, *Shep* —5C **38**
High St. South Norwood, *SE25* —3C **46**
High St. Staines, *Stai* —5H **21**
High St. Stanwell, *Stanw* —9M **7**
High St. Sunningdale, *S'dale* —4D **34**
High St. Sunninghill, *S'hill* —4A **34**
High St. Sutton, *Sutt* —1N **61**
High St. Tadworth, *Tad* —1H **101**
High St. Teddington, *Tedd* —6F **24**
High St. Thames Ditton, *Th Dit* —5G **40**
High St. Thornton Heath, *T Hth* —3N **45**
High St. Walton-on-Thames, *W on T* —7H **39**
High St. West End, *W End* —8C **52**
High St. Westerham, *W'ham* —5L **107**
High St. West Wickham, *W Wick* —7L **47**
High St. Weybridge, *Wey* —1B **56**
High St. Whitton, *Whit* —1C **24**
High St. Wimbledon, *SW19* —6J **27**
High St. Windsor, *Wind* —4G **5**
High St. Woking, *Wok* —4B **74**
High St. Wraysbury, *Wray* —9A **6**
High St. M. *SW19* —6K **27**
High Thicket Rd. *Dock* —6C **148**
High Tree Clo. *Add* —2J **55**
High Trees. *SW2* —2L **29**
High Trees. *Croy* —7H **47**
High Trees Clo. *Cat* —9C **84**
High Trees Rd. *Reig* —4B **122**
Highview. *Cat* —2B **104**
High View. G'ming —7H 133
(off Flambards Way)
High View. *Gom* —8D **116**
Highview. *Knap* —4H **73**
High View. *Sutt* —7L **61**
Highview Av. *Wall* —2K **63**
High View Clo. *SE19* —1C **46**
High View Clo. *F'boro* —1M **89**
Highview Ct. Reig —3D 122
(off Wray Comn. Rd.)
Highview Cres. *Camb* —6D **50**
High View Lodge. *Alder* —2M **109**
Highview Path. *Bans* —2M **81**
High View Rd. *Dow* —6J **67**
High View Rd. *F'boro* —1M **89**
High View Rd. *Guild* —6G **113**
High View Rd. *Light* —7J **51**
Highway. *Crowt* —2F **48**
Highwayman's Ridge. *W'sham* —1M **51**
Highway, The. *Sutt* —5A **62**
Highwold. *Coul* —5E **82**
Highwood. *Short* —2N **47**
Highwood Clo. *Kenl* —4N **83**
Highwood Clo. *Yat* —2C **68**
Highwoods. *Cat* —3B **104**
Highwoods. *Lea* —8J **79**
Highworth. *H'ham* —7M **197**
Hilary Av. *Mitc* —2E **44**
Hilary Clo. *SW6* —3N **13**
Hilbert Rd. *Sutt* —9J **43**
Hilborough Way. *Orp* —2M **67**
Hilda Ct. *Surb* —6K **41**
Hilda Vale Clo. *Orp* —1K **67**
Hilda Vale Rd. *Orp* —1J **67**
Hildenlea Pl. *Brom* —1N **47**
Hildenley Clo. *Red* —6H **103**
Hildens, The. *Westc* —7B **118**
Hilder Gdns. *F'boro* —2B **90**
Hilders Clo. *Eden* —8K **127**
Hilders La. *Eden* —8H **127**
Hilders, The. *Asht* —4A **80**
Hildreth St. *SW12* —2F **28**
Hildyard Rd. *SW6* —2M **13**
Hilfield. *Yat* —1E **68**
Hilgay. *Guild* —3B **114**
Hilgay Clo. *Guild* —3B **114**
Hilland Rise. *Head* —5E **168**
Hillars Heath Rd. *Coul* —2J **83**
Hillary Clo. *E Grin* —7C **166**
Hillary Clo. *Farnh* —3G **128**
Hillary Cres. *W On T* —7K **39**
Hillary Dri. *Crowt* —1G **49**
Hillary Rd. *Farnh* —4G **128**
Hill Barn. *S Croy* —7B **64**
Hillberry. *Brack* —6A **32**
Hillborough Clo. *SW19* —8A **28**
Hillbourne Clo. *Hayes* —1H **9**
Hillbrook Gdns. *Wey* —4B **56**
Hillbrook Rise. *Farnh* —6G **108**
Hillbrook Rd. *SW17* —4D **28**
Hillbrow. *N Mald* —2E **42**
Hillbrow. *Reig* —3A **122**
Hillbrow Clo. *Wood S* —2E **112**
Hillbrow Ct. *God* —1F **124**
Hillbrow Rd. *Esh* —1C **58**
Hillbury Clo. *Warl* —5E **84**
Hillbury Gdns. *Warl* —5F **84**
Hillbury Rd. *SW17* —4F **28**
Hillbury Rd. *Whyt & Warl* —4D **84**
Hill Clo. *Purl* —9N **63**
Hill Clo. *Wok* —3N **73**
Hill Clo. *Won* —5D **134**
Hill Copse View. *Brack* —9C **16**
Hill Corner Farm Cvn. Pk. *F'boro* —7J **69**
Hillcote Av. *SW16* —8L **29**
Hill Ct. *G'ming* —4H **133**
Hill Ct. *Hasl* —2F **188**
Hill Cres. *Surb* —4M **41**
Hill Cres. *Wor Pk* —8H **43**
Hill Crest. *Dor P* —4A **166**

Hill Crest—Hookstile La.

Hill Crest. Elst —8H 131
(in two parts)
Hillcrest. Farnh —4J 109
Hillcrest. Fleet —2B 88
Hillcrest. Wey —1C 56
Hillcrest Av. Cher —9G 36
Hillcrest Cvn. Pk. Tad —9A 100
Hillcrest Clo. Beck —5J 47
Hillcrest Clo. Craw —3H 183
Hillcrest Clo. Eps —2E 80
Hillcrest Ct. Sutt —3B 62
Hill Crest Dri. Farnh —5E 128
Hillcrest Gdns. Esh —9F 40
Hillcrest Ho. Guild —1E 114
Hillcrest Pde. Coul —1F 82
Hillcrest Rd. Big H —3F 86
Hillcrest Rd. Camb —8F 50
Hillcrest Rd. Eden —8L 127
Hillcrest Rd. Guild —2J 113
Hillcrest Rd. Purl —6K 63
Hillcrest Rd. Whyt —4C 84
Hillcrest View. Beck —5J 47
Hillcroft Av. Purl —9G 63
Hillcroome Rd. Sutt —3B 62
Hillcross Av. Mord —5J 43
Hilldale Rd. Sutt —1L 61
Hilldeane Rd. Purl —5L 63
Hilldown Ct. SW16 —8J 29
Hilldown Rd. SW16 —8J 29
Hill Dri. SW16 —2K 45
Hillersdon Av. SW13 —5F 12
Hilley Field La. Fet —9C 78
Hill Farm Clo. Hasl —3D 188
Hill Farm La. Binf —4K 15
Hill Farm Rd. Binf —4K 15
Hillfield Av. Mord —5C 44
Hillfield Clo. Guild —1E 114
Hillfield Clo. Red —3E 122
Hillfield Cotts. H'ham —8B 196
Hillfield Ct. Esh —2B 58
Hill Field Rd. Hamp —8N 23
Hillfield Rd. Red —3E 122
Hillford Pl. Red —9E 122
Hillgarth. Hind —4B 170
Hillgate Pl. SW12 —1F 28
Hill Gro. Felt —3N 23
Hill Ho. Clo. Turn H —4D 184
Hill Ho. Dri. Reig —5N 121
Hill Ho. Dri. Wey —7B 56
Hillhouse La. Rud —8N 175
Hill Ho. Rd. SW16 —6K 29
Hillhurst Gdns. Cat —7B 84
Hilliary Dri. Crowt —1G 49
Hillier Gdns. Croy —2L 63
Hillier Ho. Guild —5L 113
Hillier Lodge. Tedd —6D 24
Hillier Pl. Chess —3J 59
Hillier Rd. SW11 —1D 28
Hillier Rd. Guild —3C 114
Hilliers La. Croy —9J 45
Hillingdale. Big H —5D 86
Hillingdale. Craw —8A 182
Hillingdon Av. Stai —2N 21
Hill La. Kgswd —8K 81
Hillmead. Craw —4L 181
Hill Mead. H'ham —5G 197
Hillmont Rd. Esh —9E 40
Hillmount. Wok —5A 74
(off Constitution Hill)
Hill Pk. Dri. Lea —6F 78
Hill Path. SW16 —6K 29
Hill Pl. Craw —5A 182
Hill Rise. Dork —3G 118
Hill Rise. Esh —8H 41
Hill Rise. Rich —8K 11
Hill Rise. Slou —2C 6
Hill Rise. W On T —6G 39
Hill Rd. Cars —3C 62
Hill Rd. Farnh —5J 109
Hill Rd. Fet —9B 78
Hill Rd. Gray —6A 170
Hill Rd. Hasl —2G 188
Hill Rd. Hind —3A 170
Hill Rd. Mitc —9F 28
Hill Rd. Purl —8K 63
Hill Rd. Sutt —2N 61
Hillsborough Pk. Camb —1G 70
Hills Farm La. H'ham —7F 196
Hillside. SW19 —7J 27
Hillside. Asc —4N 33
Hillside. Bans —2K 81
Hillside. Camb —8L 49
Hillside. Craw D —1E 184
Hillside. Esh —2B 58
Hillside. F Row —6H 187
Hillside. H'ham —6G 196
Hillside. Vir W —5M 35
Hillside. Wok —7N 73
Hillside Av. Purl —9M 63
Hillside Clo. Bans —3K 81
Hillside Clo. Brock —4N 119
Hillside Clo. Craw —5N 181
Hillside Clo. E Grin —7A 166
Hillside Clo. Head —3F 168
Hillside Clo. Knap —4G 72
Hillside Clo. Mord —3K 43
Hillside Ct. Guild —5A 114
Hillside Cres. Frim —7D 70
Hillside Dri. Binf —7H 15
Hillside Gdns. SW2 —3L 29
Hillside Gdns. Add —2H 55
Hillside Gdns. Brock —3N 119
Hillside Gdns. Wall —4G 63
Hillside La. Farnh —4J 109
Hillside Pk. S'dale —7C 34
Hillside Pas. SW16 —3K 29
Hillside Rd. SW2 —3K 29
Hillside Rd. Alder —4L 109
Hillside Rd. Asht —4M 79
Hillside Rd. Ash V —1F 110
Hillside Rd. Coul —5K 83
Hillside Rd. Croy —2M 63
Hillside Rd. Eps —6H 61
Hillside Rd. Farnh —5K 109
Hillside Rd. Fren —8H 129
Hillside Rd. Hasl —3D 188
Hillside Rd. Surb —3N 41
Hillside Rd. Sutt —4L 61
Hillside Rd. Tats —6G 87
Hillside Rd. Whyt —5D 84
Hillside Way. G'ming —4G 133
Hillsmead Way. S Croy —1D 84
Hills Pl. H'ham —6G 197
Hillspur Clo. Guild —2J 113
Hillspur Rd. Guild —2J 113
Hill St. Rich —8K 11
Hill, The. Cat —2C 104
Hill Top. Mord —5M 43
Hill Top. Sutt —6L 43
Hilltop Clo. Asc —1B 34
Hilltop Clo. Guild —8J 93
Hilltop Clo. Lea —1J 99
Hilltop La. Red & Cat —4L 103
Hilltop Rise. Bookh —4C 98
Hilltop Rd. Reig —5N 121
Hilltop Rd. Whyt —4B 84
Hilltop View. Yat —1A 68
Hilltop Wlk. Wold —7H 85
Hillview. SW20 —8G 27
Hill View. F Row —8H 187
Hillview. Whyt —5D 84
(off Slines Oak Rd.)
Hillview Clo. Purl —7M 63
Hill View Clo. Tad —8H 81
Hillview Clo. Wok —5B 74
Hill View Cres. Guild —1J 113
Hillview Dri. Red —4E 122
Hillview Gdns. Craw —9A 182
Hill View Rd. Clay —4G 59
Hill View Rd. Farnh —1E 128
Hillview Rd. Sutt —9A 44
Hill View Rd. Twic —9G 10
Hill View Rd. Wok —5B 74
Hillview Rd. Wray —9N 5
Hillworth. Beck —1L 47
Hillworth Rd. SW2 —1L 29
Hillybarn Rd. Craw —9H 161
Hilton Ct. Horl —7G 143
Hilton Way. S Croy —2E 84
Himley Rd. SW17 —6C 28
Hinchcliffe Clo. Wall —4K 63
Hinchley Clo. Esh —1F 58
Hinchley Dri. Esh —9F 40
Hinchley Way. Esh —9G 40
Hindell Clo. F'boro —6M 69
Hindhead Clo. Craw —5A 182
Hindhead Rd. Hasl & Hind —1C 188
Hindhead Way. Wall —2J 63
Hinkler Clo. Wall —4J 63
Hinstock Clo. F'boro —2M 89
Hinton Av. Houn —7L 9
Hinton Clo. Crowt —9G 31
Hinton Dri. Crowt —9G 31
Hinton Rd. Hurst —1A 14
Hinton Rd. Wall —3G 63
Hipley Ct. Guild —4C 114
Hipley St. Wok —7D 74
Hitchcock Clo. Shep —2A 38
Hitchings Way. Reig —7M 121
Hitherbury Clo. Guild —6M 113
Hitherfield Rd. SW16 —4K 29
Hitherhooks Hill. Binf —9K 15
Hithermoor Rd. Stai —9H 7
Hitherwood. Cranl —8N 155
Hitherwood Clo. Reig —1C 122
H. Jones Cres. Alder —1A 110
Hoadlands Cotts. Hand —6N 199
Hoadly Rd. SW16 —4H 29
Hobart Gdns. T Hth —2A 46
Hobart Pl. Rich —1M 25
Hobart Rd. Wor Pk —9G 42
Hobbes Wlk. SW15 —8G 12
Hobbs Clo. W Byf —9K 55
Hobbs Ind. Est. Newc —3H 165
Hobbs Rd. SE27 —5N 29
Hobbs Rd. Broadf —7M 181
Hobill Wlk. Surb —5M 41
Hocken Mead. Craw —1H 183
Hockering Est. Wok —5D 74
Hockering Gdns. Wok —5C 74
Hockering Rd. Wok —5C 74
Hockford Clo. Pirb —4E 92
Hodge La. Wink —6L 17
(in two parts)
Hodges Clo. Bag —6H 51
Hodgkin Clo. M'bowr —4G 182
Hodgson Gdns. Guild —9C 94
Hoe La. Hasc —6N 153
Hoe La. Peasl & Ab H —3F 136
Hogarth Av. Ashf —7D 22
Hogarth Bus. Pk. W4 —2D 12
Hogarth Clo. Col T —9K 49
Hogarth Ct. Houn —3M 9
Hogarth Cres. SW19 —9B 28
Hogarth Cres. Croy —6N 45
Hogarth Gdns. Houn —3A 10
Hogarth La. W4 —2D 12
Hogarth Pl. SW5 —1N 13
(off Hogarth Rd.)
Hogarth Rd. SW5 —1N 13
Hogarth Rd. Craw —6D 182
Hogarth Roundabout. (Junct.) —2D 12
Hogarth Ter. W4 —2D 12
Hogarth Way. Hamp —9C 24
Hogden Clo. Tad —3L 101
Hogden La. Ran C —9M 97
(in two parts)
Hoghatch La. Farnh —6F 108
Hogoak La. Wind —1E 16
Hog's Back. Comp & Guild —7A 112
Hog's Back. Putt —7K 111
Hog's Back. Seale —8B 110
Hogscross La. Coul —1D 102
Hog's Hill. Craw —6B 182
Hogshill La. Cobh —1J 77
Hogsmill Way. Eps —2B 60
Hogtrough La. God & Oxt —5K 105
Hogtrough La. Red —4G 123
Hogwood Rd. Ifold —5E 192
Holbeach M. SW12 —2F 28
Holbeche Clo. Yat —1A 68
Holbeck. Brack —5L 31
Holbein Rd. Craw —6D 182
Holbreck Pl. Wok —5B 74
Holbrook Clo. Farnh —4L 109
Holbrooke Pl. Rich —8K 11
Holbrook Meadow. Egh —7E 20
Holbrook School La. H'ham —1L 197
Holbrook Way. Alder —5N 109
Holcombe St. W6 —1G 13
Holcon Ct. Red —9E 102
Holden Brook La. Dork —7M 157
Holdernesse Clo. Iswth —4G 10
Holdernesse Rd. SW17 —4D 28
Holderness Way. SE27 —6M 29
Holder Rd. Alder —3C 110
Holder Rd. M'bowr —6F 182
Holdfast La. Hasl —9K 171
Holehill La. Dork —4A 118
Hole La. Eden —5H 127
Holford Rd. Guild —3E 114
Holland Av. SW20 —9E 26
Holland Av. Sutt —5M 61
Holland Clo. Farnh —3K 129
Holland Clo. Red —3D 122
Holland Cres. Oxt —2C 126
Holland Gdns. Egh —1H 37
Holland Gdns. Fleet —5B 88
Holland La. Oxt —2C 126
Holland Pines. Brack —6L 31
Holland Rd. SE25 —4D 46
Holland Rd. Oxt —2C 126
Hollands, The. Felt —5L 23
Hollands, The. Wok —5A 74
Hollands, The. Wor Pk —7E 42
Hollands Way. E Grin —6C 166
Hollands Way. Warn —9F 178
Holles Clo. Hamp —7A 24
Hollies Av. W Byf —9H 55
Hollies Clo. SW16 —7L 29
Hollies Clo. Twic —3F 24
Hollies Ct. Add —2L 55
Hollies, The. Add —2L 55
(off Crockford Pk. Rd.)
Hollies Way. SW12 —1E 28
Hollin Ct. Craw —9C 162
Hollingbourne Cres. Craw —9A 182
Hollingsworth Ct. Surb —6K 41
Hollingsworth Rd. Croy —3E 64
Hollington Cres. N Mald —5E 42
Hollingworth Way. W'ham —4M 107
Hollis Row. Red —5D 122
Hollis Wood Dri. Wrec —6D 128
Hollman Gdns. SW16 —7M 29
Holloway Clo. W Dray —1N 7
Holloway Dri. Vir W —3A 36
Holloway Hill. G'ming —7G 132
Holloway Hill. Lyne —9E 36
Holloway La. W Dray —2M 7
Holloway St. Houn —6B 10
Hollow Clo. Guild —4L 113
Hollow La. D'land & E Grin —1D 166
Hollow La. Head —3D 168
Hollow La. Vir W —2M 35
Hollow La. Wott —9L 117
Hollows, The. Bren —2M 11
Hollow, The. Craw —4L 181
Hollow, The. G'ming —7C 132
Hollow Way. Gray —5A 170
Holly Acre. Yat —1C 68
Holly Av. Frim —3F 70
Holly Av. New H —6J 55
Holly Av. W On T —7L 39
Hollybank. W End —9C 52
Hollybank Clo. Hamp —6A 24
Holly Bank Rd. W Byf —1J 75
Holly Bank Rd. Wok —8L 73
Hollybrook Pk. Bord —6A 168
Hollybush La. Alder —8C 90
Hollybush La. Fren —1H 149
Holly Bush La. Hamp —8N 23
Hollybush La. Rip —6M 75
Hollybush Ride. Finch —3B 48
Hollybush Ride. W'sham —9K 33
Hollybush Rd. Craw —2C 182
Hollybush Rd. King T —6L 25
Holly Clo. Alder —2A 110
Holly Clo. Craw —1E 182
Holly Clo. Egh —7L 19
Holly Clo. F'boro —1M 89
Holly Clo. Felt —6M 23
Holly Clo. Head —4H 169
Holly Clo. H'ham —3A 198
Holly Clo. Longc —9K 35
Holly Clo. Wall —4F 62
Holly Clo. Wok —6L 73
Hollycombe. Egh —5M 19
Holly Ct. Cher —7H 37
(off King St.)
Holly Ct. Sutt —4M 61
Holly Cres. Beck —4J 47
Holly Cres. Wind —5A 4
Hollycroft Clo. S Croy —2B 64
Hollycroft Clo. W Dray —2B 8
Hollycroft Gdns. W Dray —2B 8
Hollydale Dri. Brom —1H 67
Holly Dri. Old Win —8H 5
Holly Farm Rd. S'hall —1M 9
Hollyfield Rd. Surb —6M 41
Hollyfields Clo. Camb —1N 69
Holly Grn. Wey —1E 56
Hollygrove Clo. Houn —7N 9
Holly Hedge Clo. Frim —4C 70
Hollyhedge Rd. Cobh —1J 77
Holly Hedge Rd. Frim —4C 70
Holly Hill Dri. Bans —4M 81
Hollyhock Dri. Bisl —2D 72
Hollyhook Clo. Crowt —1F 48
Holly Ho. Brack —5N 31
Holly Ho. Iswth —2J 11
Holly La. Bans —3M 81
Holly La. G'ming —7F 132
Holly La. Worp —7F 92
Holly La. E. Bans —3N 81
Holly La. W. Bans —4N 81
Holly Lea. Guild —6N 93
Holly Lodge Mobile Home Pk. Tad —3K 101
Hollymead. Cars —9D 44
Hollymead Rd. Coul —5E 82
Hollymeoak Rd. Coul —6F 82
Hollymoor La. Eps —6C 60
Hollyridge. Hasl —2F 188
Holly Rd. W4 —1C 12
Holly Rd. Alder —2A 110
Holly Rd. F'boro —1L 89
Holly Rd. Hamp —7C 24
Holly Rd. Houn —7B 10
Holly Rd. Reig —5N 121
Holly Rd. Twic —2F 24
Holly Spring Cotts. Brack —8B 16
Holly Spring La. Brack —9A 16
Holly Tree Clo. SW19 —2J 27
Hollytree Gdns. Frim —6B 70
Holly Tree Rd. Cat —9B 84
Holly Wlk. Wind —5B 18
Hollywater Rd. Bord & Pass —8A 168
Holly Way. B'water —2J 69
Holly Way. Mitc —3H 45
Hollywood M. SW10 —2N 13
Hollywood Rd. SW10 —2N 13
Hollywoods. Croy —5J 65
Holman Clo. Craw —9N 181
Holman Ct. Ewe —5F 60
Holman Hunt Ho. W6 —1K 13
(off Field Rd.)
Holman Rd. Eps —2B 60
Holmbank Dri. Shep —3F 38
Holmbrook Clo. F'boro —1H 89
Holmbrook Gdns. F'boro —1H 89
Holmbury Av. Crowt —9F 30
Holmbury Clo. Craw —5A 182
Holmbury Ct. SW17 —4D 28
Holmbury Ct. S Croy —2B 64
Holmbury Dri. N Holm —8J 119
Holmbury Gro. Croy —4J 65
Holmbury Hill Rd. Dork —9J 137
Holmbury Keep. Horl —7G 142
(off Langshott La.)
Holmbury La. Dork —9L 137
Holmbury Rd. Dork & Ewh —9H 137
Holmbush Clo. H'ham —2K 197
Holmbush Potteries Ind. Est. Fay —8H 181
Holmbush Rd. SW15 —9K 13
Holm Clo. Wdhm —8G 55
Holm Ct. G'ming —4G 132
Holmcroft. Craw —4C 182
Holmcroft. Tad —3G 101
Holmdene Clo. Beck —1M 47
Holmead Rd. SW6 —3N 13
Holme Chase. Wey —3D 56
Holme Clo. Crowt —9F 30
Holmes Clo. Asc —5N 33
Holmesdale Av. SW14 —6A 12
Holmesdale Clo. SE25 —2C 46
Holmesdale Clo. Guild —2D 114
Holmesdale Rd. Croy & SE25 —4A 46
Holmesdale Rd. N Holm —9H 119
Holmesdale Rd. Reig —2M 121
Holmesdale Rd. Rich —4M 11
Holmesdale Rd. S Nut —5K 123
Holmesdale Rd. Tedd —7J 25
Holmesdale Ter. N Holm —9H 119
Holmesdale Vs. Dork —2H 139
Holmes Rd. SW19 —8A 28
Holmes Rd. Twic —3F 24
Holmethorpe Av. Red —9F 102
Holmethorpe Ind. Est. Red —9F 102
Holmewood Clo. Wokgm —6A 30
Holmewood Gdns. SW2 —1K 29
Holmewood Rd. SE25 —2B 46
Holmewood Rd. SW2 —1K 29
Holming End. H'ham —3A 198
Holmlea Rd. Dat —4M 5
Holmlea Wlk. Dat —4M 5
Holmoak Clo. SW15 —9L 13
Holmoaks Ho. Beck —1M 47
Holmside Rd. SW12 —1E 28
Holmsley Clo. N Mald —5E 42
Holmsley Ho. SW15 —1E 26
(off Tangley Gro.)
Holm Ter. Dork —8H 119
Holmwood Av. S Croy —9C 64
Holmwood Clo. Add —2J 55
Holmwood Clo. E Hor —6F 96
Holmwood Clo. Sutt —5J 61
Holmwood Gdns. Wall —3F 62
Holmwood Rd. Chess —2K 59
Holmwood Rd. Sutt —5H 61
Holmwood View Rd. Mid H —2H 139
Holne Chase. Mord —5L 43
Holroyd Clo. Clay —5F 58
Holroyd Rd. SW15 —7H 13
Holroyd Rd. Clay —5F 58
Holstein Av. Wey —1B 56
Holst Mans. SW13 —3H 13
Holsworthy Way. Chess —2J 59
Holt Clo. F'boro —6A 70
Holt La. Wokgm —1A 30
Holton Heath. Brack —3D 32
Holt Pound Cotts. Rowl —7B 128
Holt Pound La. Holt P —6B 128
Holt, The. Mord —3M 43
Holt, The. Wall —1G 62
Holtwood Rd. Oxs —9C 58
Holtye Av. E Grin —7B 166
Holtye Rd. E Grin —8B 166
Holtye Wlk. Craw —5E 182
Holwood Clo. W On T —8K 39
Holwood Pk. Av. Orp —1H 67
Holybourne Av. SW15 —1F 26
Holyoake Av. Wok —4M 73
Holyoake Cres. Wok —4M 73
Holyport Rd. SW6 —3J 13
Holyrood. E Grin —2C 186
Holyrood Pl. Broadf —7N 181
Holywell Clo. F'boro —7M 69
Holywell Clo. Stai —2N 21
Holywell Way. Stai —2N 21
Hombrook Dri. Brack —9K 15
Hombrook Ho. Brack —9K 15
Homebeech Ho. Wok —5A 74
(off Mt. Hermon Rd.)
Home Clo. Cars —8D 44
Home Clo. Craw —1G 183
Home Clo. Fet —8D 78
Home Clo. Vir W —5N 35
Home Ct. Felt —2H 23
Home Farm Clo. Bet —4D 120
Home Farm Clo. Eps —4J 81
Home Farm Clo. Esh —3B 58
Home Farm Clo. F'boro —8B 70
Home Farm Clo. Ott —4C 54
Home Farm Clo. Shep —3F 38
Home Farm Clo. Th Dit —6F 40
Home Farm Cotts. Pep H —6N 131
Home Farm Gdns. W On T —8K 39
Home Farm Rd. G'ming —9H 133
Homefield. Mord —3M 43
Homefield. Thur —7G 150
Homefield Av. W on T —1L 57
Homefield Clo. Horl —7F 142
Homefield Clo. Lea —8J 79
Homefield Clo. Wdhm —8G 55
Homefield Ct. SW16 —4J 29
Homefield Gdns. Mitc —1A 44
Homefield Gdns. Tad —7H 81
Homefield Pk. Sutt —3N 61
Homefield Rd. SW19 —7K 27
Homefield Rd. W4 —1E 12
Homefield Rd. Coul & Cat —6M 83
Homefield Rd. W On T —6M 39
Homefield Rd. Warl —6F 84
Homegreen Ho. Hasl —2E 188
Homeland Dri. Sutt —5N 61
Homelands. Lea —8J 79
Home Lea. Orp —2N 67
Homelea Clo. F'boro —6N 69
Homeleigh Cres. Ash V —5E 90
Home Meadow. Bans —3M 81
Homemead Rd. Croy —5H 45
Home Pk. Oxt —9C 106
Home Pk. Clo. Brmly —5B 134
Homepark Ho. Farnh —1H 129
Home Pk. Rd. SW19 —5L 27
Home Pk. Rd. Yat —9C 48
Home Pk. Wlk. King T —3K 41
Homer Rd. Croy —5G 47
Homersham Rd. King T —1N 41
Homers Rd. Wind —4A 4
Homesdale Rd. Cat —1A 104
Homestall. Guild —3G 113
Homestall Rd. Ash W —9G 166
Homestead. Cranl —6A 156
Homestead Gdns. Clay —2E 58
Homestead & Middle View Mobile Home Pk. Norm —9B 92
Homestead Rd. SW6 —3L 13
Homestead Rd. Cat —1A 104
Homestead Rd. Eden —7K 127
Homestead Rd. Stai —7K 21
Homestead Way. New Ad —7M 65
Homestream Ho. H'ham —7H 197
Homethorne Ho. Craw —4A 182
Home Vs. Alb —3L 135
Homewater Ho. Eps —9D 60
Homewaters Av. Sun —9G 23
Homewood. Cranl —7B 156
Homewood Clo. Hamp —7N 23
Homewoods. SW12 —1G 28
Homeworth Ho. Wok —5A 74
(off Mt. Hermon Rd.)
Hone Hill. Sand —7G 48
Hones Yd. Bus. Pk. Farnh —1J 129
Honeybrook Rd. SW12 —1G 28
Honeycrock Ct. Salf —1E 142
Honeycrock La. Red —1E 142
Honeydown Cotts. N'chap —8E 190
Honey Hill. Wokgm —6E 30
Honeyhill Rd. Brack —9M 15
Honey La. Rowh & Dork —6M 177
Honeypot La. Eden —8F 126
Honeypots Rd. Wok —9N 73
Honeysuckle Bottom. E Hor —3F 116
Honeysuckle Clo. Crowt —9F 30
Honeysuckle Clo. Horl —7G 143
Honeysuckle Clo. Yat —9A 48
Honeysuckle Gdns. Croy —6G 46
Honeysuckle La. Craw —9A 162
Honeysuckle La. Head —4G 168
Honeysuckle La. N Holm —8J 119
Honeysuckle Wlk. H'ham —3N 197
Honeywood La. Oke H —4M 177
Honeywood Rd. H'ham —4N 197
Honeywood Rd. Iswth —7G 11
Honeywood Wlk. Cars —1D 62
Honister Gdns. Fleet —3D 88
Honister Heights. Purl —1A 84
Honister Wlk. Camb —2H 71
Honnor Rd. Stai —8M 21
Hood Av. SW14 —8B 12
Hood Clo. Croy —7M 45
Hood Rd. SW20 —8E 26
Hooke Rd. E Hor —3G 97
Hookfield. Eps —9B 60
Hookfield M. Eps —9B 60
Hook Heath Av. Wok —6L 73
Hook Heath Gdns. Wok —8J 73
Hook Heath Rd. Wok —8J 73
Hook Hill. S Croy —6B 64
Hook Hill La. Wok —8L 73
Hook Hill Pk. Wok —8L 73
Hook Ho. La. Duns —3M 173
Hookhouse Rd. Duns —1N 173
Hook Junction. (Junct.) —9L 41
Hook La. Bisl —9N 51
Hook La. Shere —1B 136
Hookley Clo. Elst —8J 131
Hookley La. Elst —8J 131
Hook Mill La. Light —5A 52
Hook Rise Bus. Cen. Chess —9N 41
Hook Rise N. Surb —9L 41
Hook Rise S. Surb —9L 41
Hook Rise S. Ind. Pk. Surb —9M 41
Hook Rd. Chess & Surb —2K 59
Hook Rd. Eps —4B 60
Hookstile La. Farnh —2H 129

Hookstone La.—Ivydene Clo.

Hookstone La. *W End* —7C **52**
Hook St. *Alf* —8K **175**
Hookwood Corner. *Oxt* —6D **106**
Hooley La. *Red* —4D **122**
Hope Av. *Brack* —6C **32**
Hope Clo. *Sutt* —2A **62**
Hope Cotts. *Brack* —2A **32**
Hope Ct. *Craw* —8N **181**
Hope Fountain. *Camb* —2E **70**
Hope Grant's Rd. *Alder* —9M **89**
Hope La. *Farnh* —6G **108**
Hopeman Clo. *Col T* —8J **49**
Hopes Clo. *Houn* —2A **10**
Hope St. *Elst* —7H **131**
Hopfield. *Hors* —3A **74**
Hopfield Av. *Byfl* —8N **55**
Hop Garden. *C Crook* —9A **88**
Hopgarden Clo. *Eden* —9M **127**
Hophurst Clo. *Craw D* —1E **184**
Hophurst Dri. *Craw D* —1E **184**
Hophurst Hill. *Craw D* —8G **164**
Hophurst La. *Craw D* —9E **164**
Hopkins Ct. *Craw* —8N **181**
Hoppety, The. *Tad* —9J **81**
Hoppingwood Av. *N Mald* —2D **42**
Hopton Ct. Guild —3H 113
(off Chapelhouse Clo.)
Hopton Ct. Guild —3H 113
(off Park Barn Dri.)
Hopton Gdns. *N Mald* —5F **42**
Hopton Rd. *SW16* —6K **29**
Hopwood Clo. *SW17* —4A **28**
Horace Rd. *King T* —2M **41**
Horatio Av. *Warf* —9C **16**
Horatio Pl. *SW19* —9M **27**
Horatius Way. *Croy* —2K **63**
Hordern Ho. *H'ham* —7G **196**
Horder Rd. *SW6* —1K **10**
Horewood Rd. *Brack* —5N **31**
Horizon Ho. *Eps* —9D **60**
Horley Lodge La. *Red* —3D **142**
Horley Rd. *Charl* —4L **161**
Horley Rd. *Red* —5D **122**
Horley Row. *Horl* —7D **142**
Hormer Clo. *Owl* —6J **49**
Hornbeam Clo. *F'boro* —9H **69**
Hornbeam Clo. *H'ham* —7M **197**
Hornbeam Clo. *Owl* —6J **49**
Hornbeam Cres. *Bren* —3H **11**
Hornbeam Rd. *Guild* —9M **93**
Hornbeam Rd. *Reig* —6N **121**
Hornbeam Ter. *Cars* —7C **44**
Hornbeam Wlk. *Rich* —5M **25**
Hornbeam Wlk. *W Vill* —6F **56**
Hornbrook Copse. *H'ham* —8M **197**
Hornbrook Hill. *H'ham* —8M **197**
Hornby Av. *Brack* —6B **32**
Hornchurch Clo. *King T* —5K **25**
Hornchurch Hill. *Whyt* —5C **84**
Horndean Clo. *SW15* —2F **26**
Horndean Clo. *Craw* —8H **163**
Horndean Rd. *Brack* —5D **32**
Hornecourt Hill. *Horne* —4C **144**
Horner La. *Mitc* —1B **44**
Horne Rd. *Shep* —3B **38**
Hornes Field Ct. C Crook —9A 88
(off Brandon Rd.)
Horne Way. *SW15* —5H **13**
Hornhatch. *Chil* —9D **114**
Hornhatch Clo. *Chil* —9D **114**
(in two parts)
Hornhatch La. *Guild* —9C **114**
Horn Rd. *F'boro* —9K **69**
Hornshill La. *H'ham* —2A **194**
Horsa Clo. *Wall* —4J **63**
Horseblock Hollow. *Cranl* —3B **156**
Horsebrass Dri. *Bag* —5J **51**
Horsecroft. *Bans* —4L **81**
Horse Fair. *King T* —1K **41**
Horsegate Ride. *Asc* —5L **33**
(Coronation Rd.)
Horsegate Ride. *Asc* —4F **32**
(Swinley Rd.)
Horse & Groom Cvn. Site. *Brack* —3A **32**
Horse Hill. *Horl* —6M **141**
Horsell Birch. *Wok* —2L **73**
Horsell Comn. Rd. *Wok* —1M **73**
Horsell Ct. *Cher* —6K **37**
Horsell Moor. *Wok* —4N **73**
Horsell Pk. *Wok* —4A **74**
Horsell Pk. Clo. *Wok* —3N **73**
Horsell Rise. *Wok* —2N **73**
Horsell Rise Clo. *Wok* —2N **73**
Horsell Vale. *Wok* —3A **74**
Horsell Way. *Wok* —3M **73**
Horse Ride. *Cars* —6C **62**
Horseshoe Bend. *Gray* —6M **169**
Horseshoe Clo. *Camb* —7D **50**
Horseshoe Clo. *Craw* —2H **183**
Horseshoe Cres. *Bord* —6A **168**
Horseshoe Cres. *Camb* —7D **50**
Horse Shoe Grn. *Sutt* —8N **43**
Horseshoe La. *Ash V* —6E **90**
Horseshoe La. *Cranl* —6L **155**
Horseshoe La. E. *Guild* —2D **114**
Horseshoe La. W. *Guild* —2D **114**
Horseshoe, The. *Bans* —2M **81**
Horseshoe, The. *Coul* —9H **63**
Horseshoe, The. *G'ming* —8F **132**
Horsham Bus. Pk. *H'ham* —5J **179**
Horsham Northern By-Pass. *H'ham* —2H **197**
Horsham Rd. *Ab H* —2G **136**
Horsham Rd. *Brmly & Cranl* —1E **154**
Horsham Rd. *Capel* —1J **179**
Horsham Rd. *Cowf* —9H **195**
Horsham Rd. *Cranl & H'ham* —8N **155**
Horsham Rd. *Craw* —7K **181**
Horsham Rd. *Dork* —6G **119**
Horsham Rd. *Ewh & Wal W* —6F **156**
Horsham Rd. *Felt* —9D **8**
Horsham Rd. *F Grn* —5M **157**
Horsham Rd. *Hand* —9K **199**
Horsham Rd. *N Holm* —9H **119**
Horsham Rd. *Owl* —6J **49**
Horsham Rd. *Peas P* —2M **199**
Horsham Rd. *Rusp* —6N **179**
Horsham Rd. *Shalf & Brmly* —2A **134**
Horsley Clo. *Eps* —9C **60**
Horsley Dri. *King T* —6K **25**
Horsley Dri. *New Ad* —4M **65**
Horsley Rd. *D'side* —9H **77**
Horsnape Gdns. *Binf* —7G **15**
Horsneile La. *Brack* —8N **15**
Hortensia Rd. *SW10* —3N **13**
Horticultural Pl. *W4* —1C **12**
Horton Footpath. *Eps* —7B **60**
Horton Gdns. *Eps* —7B **60**
Horton Gdns. *Hort* —6B **6**
Horton Hill. *Eps* —7B **60**
Horton Ho. W6 —1K 13
(off Field Rd.)
Horton La. *Eps* —7N **59**
Horton Pl. *W'ham* —4M **107**
Horton Rd. *Coln* —6G **6**
Horton Rd. *Dat* —4M **5**
Horton Rd. *Hort* —5C **6**
Horton Rd. *Stai* —7H **7**
Hortons Way. *W'ham* —4M **107**
(in two parts)
Horton Trad. Est. *Hort* —6E **6**
Horton Way. *Croy* —4G **46**
Horvath Clo. *Wey* —1E **56**
Hosack Rd. *SW17* —3E **28**
Hosey Comn. La. *W'ham* —8N **107**
Hosey Comn. Rd. *Eden & W'ham* —2L **127**
Hosey Hill. *W'ham* —5N **107**
Hoskins Clo. *Hayes* —1G **8**
Hoskins Pl. *E Grin* —6C **166**
Hoskins Rd. *Oxt* —7A **106**
Hoskins Wlk. Oxt —7A 106
(off Station Rd. W.)
Hospital Bri. Rd. *Twic* —1B **24**
Hospital Bridge Roundabout. (Junct.) —3B **24**
Hospital Hill. *Alder* —1M **109**
Hospital Rd. *Alder* —1M **109**
Hospital Rd. *Houn* —6A **10**
Hostel Rd. *F'boro* —5N **89**
Hotham Clo. *W Mol* —2A **40**
Hotham Rd. *SW15* —6H **13**
Hotham Rd. *SW19* —8A **28**
Hotham Rd. M. *SW19* —8A **28**
Houblon Rd. *Rich* —8L **11**
Houghton Clo. *Hamp* —7M **23**
Houghton Rd. *M'bowr* —6G **182**
Houlder Cres. *Croy* —3M **63**
Houlton Ct. *Bag* —5J **51**
Hound Ho. Rd. *Shere* —1B **136**
Houndown La. *Thur* —6E **150**
Hounslow Av. *Houn* —8B **10**
Hounslow Bus. Pk. *Houn* —7A **10**
Hounslow Cen. *Houn* —6B **10**
Hounslow Gdns. *Houn* —8B **10**
Hounslow Rd. *Felt* —2J **23**
Hounslow Rd. *Hanw* —5L **23**
Hounslow Rd. *Twic* —9B **10**
Houseman Rd. *F'boro* —8L **69**
House Plat Ct. C Crook —9A 88
(off Annettes Croft)
Houston Pl. *Esh* —7D **40**
Houston Way. *Crowt* —2C **48**
Houstoun Ct. *Houn* —3N **9**
Hove Gdns. *Sutt* —7N **43**
Howard Av. *Eps* —6F **60**
Howard Clo. *Asht* —5M **79**
Howard Clo. *Fleet* —4D **88**
Howard Clo. *Hamp* —8C **24**
Howard Clo. *Lea* —1J **99**
Howard Clo. *Sun* —7G **22**
Howard Clo. *Tad* —3E **100**
Howard Clo. *W Hor* —3E **96**
Howard Cole Way. *Alder* —2K **109**
Howard Ct. *Reig* —3B **122**
Howard Dri. *F'boro* —1G **89**
Howard Gdns. *Guild* —2C **114**
Howard Ridge. *Guild* —8C **94**
Howard Rd. *SE25* —4D **46**
Howard Rd. *Ashf* —5M **21**
Howard Rd. *Bookh* —5B **98**
Howard Rd. *Coul* —2G **83**
Howard Rd. *Craw* —7K **181**
Howard Rd. *Dork* —5G **118**
Howard Rd. *Eff J* —1H **97**
Howard Rd. *H'ham* —4N **197**
Howard Rd. *Iswth* —6F **10**
Howard Rd. *N Mald* —2D **42**
Howard Rd. *N Holm* —9J **119**
Howard Rd. *Reig* —4N **121**
Howard Rd. *Surb* —5M **41**
Howard Rd. *Wokgm* —3B **30**
Howards Clo. *Wok* —7C **74**
Howards Crest Clo. *Beck* —1M **47**
Howards Ho. *Reig* —2N **121**
Howard's La. *SW15* —7G **13**
Howards La. *Add* —3H **55**
Howards Rd. *Wok* —7B **74**
Howard St. *Th Dit* —6H **41**
Howberry Rd. *T Hth* —9N **29**
Howden Ho. *Houn* —1M **23**
Howden Rd. *SE25* —1C **46**
Howe Dri. *Cat* —9A **84**
Howe La. *Binf* —1K **15**
Howell Clo. *Warf* —7A **16**
Howell Hill Clo. *Eps* —7H **61**
Howell Hill Gro. *Eps* —6H **61**
Howes Gdns. *C Crook* —7A **88**
Howgate Rd. *SW14* —6C **12**
Howland Ho. *SW16* —4J **29**
How La. *Coul* —4E **82**
Howley Rd. *Croy* —9M **45**
Howorth Ct. *Brack* —3C **32**
Howsman Rd. *SW13* —2F **12**
Howsan Ter. *Rich* —9L **11**
Hoylake Clo. *If'd* —4J **181**
Hoylake Gdns. *Mitc* —2G **45**
Hoyland Ho. *Craw* —3L **181**
Hoyle Cotts. *Dork* —1K **159**
Hoyle Rd. *SW17* —6C **28**
Hubbard Dri. *Chess* —3J **59**
Hubbard Rd. *SE27* —5N **29**
Hubberholme. *Brack* —2M **31**
Hubert Clo. SW19 —9A 28
(off Nelson Gro. Rd.)
Huddington Glade. *Yat* —1A **68**
Huddlestone Cres. *Red* —6H **103**
Hudson Ct. *Guild* —3J **113**
Hudson Gdns. *Grn St* —3N **67**
Hudson Rd. *Craw* —5C **182**
Hudson Rd. *Hayes* —2E **8**
Hudsons. *Tad* —8J **81**
Huggins Pl. *SW2* —2K **29**
Hugh Dalton Ho. SW6 —2L 13
(off Clem Attlee Ct.)
Hughenden Rd. *Wor Pk* —6F **42**
Hughes Rd. *Ashf* —7D **22**
Hughes Rd. *Wokgm* —1C **30**
Hughes Wlk. *Croy* —6N **45**
Hugh Gaitskell Ho. SW6 —2L 13
(off Clem Attlee Ct.)
Hugon Rd. *SW6* —6N **13**
Huguenot Pl. *SW18* —8N **13**
Hullbrook La. *Sham G* —7F **134**
Hullmead. *Sham G* —7G **134**
Hulton Clo. *Lea* —1J **99**
Hulverston Clo. *Sutt* —6N **61**
Humber Way. *Sand* —7J **49**
Humber Way. *Slou* —1C **6**
Humbolt Clo. *Guild* —3J **113**
Humbolt Rd. *W6* —2K **13**
Hummer Rd. *Egh* —5C **20**
Humphrey Clo. *Fet* —9C **78**
Humphrey Pk. *C Crook* —1A **108**
(in two parts)
Humphries Yd. *Brack* —3A **32**
Hungerford Clo. *Sand* —7H **49**
Hungerford Sq. *Wey* —1E **56**
Hungry Hill La. *Send* —4L **95**
Hunstanton Clo. *If'd* —4J **181**
Hunston Rd. *Mord* —7N **43**
Hunter Ho. *Craw* —6B **182**
Hunter Ho. King T —9L 25
(off Sigrist Sq.)
Hunter Rd. *SW20* —9H **27**
Hunter Rd. *Craw* —6B **182**
Hunter Rd. *F'boro* —2L **89**
Hunter Rd. *Guild* —4A **114**
Hunter Rd. *T Hth* —2A **46**
Hunters Chase. *S God* —6J **125**
Hunters Clo. *SW12* —2E **28**
Hunters Clo. *Eps* —9B **60**
Hunters Ct. *Rich* —8K **11**
Huntersfield Clo. *Reig* —9N **101**
Hunters Gro. *Orp* —1K **67**
Hunters M. *Wind* —4F **4**
Hunter's Rd. *Chess* —9L **41**
Hunter's Way. *Croy* —1B **64**
Hunting Clo. *Esh* —1A **58**
Huntingdon Clo. *Mitc* —2J **45**
Huntingdon Gdns. *W4* —3B **12**
Huntingdon Gdns. *Wor Pk* —9H **43**
Huntingdon Rd. *Red* —3D **122**
Huntingdon Rd. *Wok* —4J **73**
Huntingfield. *Croy* —4J **65**
Huntingfield Rd. *SW15* —7F **12**
Huntingfield Way. *Egh* —8F **20**
Huntingford Clo. *Hind* —2A **170**
Hunting Ga. Dri. *Chess* —4L **59**
Hunting Ga. M. *Sutt* —9N **43**
Hunting Ga. M. *Twic* —2E **24**
Huntley Way. *SW20* —1F **42**
Huntly Rd. *SE25* —3B **46**
Hunts Clo. *Guild* —2G **112**
Huntsgreen Ct. *Brack* —1A **32**
Hunts Hill Rd. *Guild* —8L **91**
Hunts La. *Camb* —3N **69**
Huntsmans Clo. *Felt* —5J **23**
Huntsmans Clo. *Fet* —2D **98**
Huntsmans Clo. *Warl* —6F **84**
Huntsmans Ct. Cat —8N 83
(off Coulsdon Rd.)
Huntsmans Meadow. *Asc* —9K **17**
Huntsmans M. *Myt* —2D **90**
Huntsmoor Rd. *Eps* —2C **60**
Huntspill St. *SW17* —4A **28**
Hurland La. *Head* —5E **168**
Hurlands Bus. Cen. *Farnh* —8L **109**
Hurlands Clo. *Farnh* —8L **109**
Hurlands La. *Duns* —8B **174**
Hurlands Pl. *Farnh* —8L **109**
Hurley Clo. *W On T* —8J **39**
Hurley Ct. *Brack* —3C **32**
Hurley Gdns. *Guild* —9C **94**
Hurlford. *Wok* —4K **73**
Hurlingham Bus. Pk. *SW6* —6M **13**
Hurlingham Ct. *SW6* —6L **13**
Hurlingham Gdns. *SW6* —6L **13**
Hurlingham Retail Pk. *SW6* —6N **13**
Hurlingham Rd. *SW6* —6L **10**
Hurlingham Sq. *SW6* —6M **13**
Hurlstone Rd. *SE25* —4B **46**
Hurn Ct. *Houn* —5L **9**
Hurn Ct. Rd. *Houn* —5L **9**
Hurnford Clo. *S Croy* —6B **64**
Huron Clo. *Grn St* —3N **67**
Huron Rd. *SW17* —3E **28**
Hurst-an-Clays. *E Grin* —1A **186**
Hurst Av. *H'ham* —5K **197**
Hurstbourne. *Clay* —3F **58**
Hurstbourne Ho. SW15 —9E 12
(off Tangley Gro.)
Hurst Clo. *Brack* —4M **31**
Hurst Clo. *Chess* —2N **59**
Hurst Clo. *Craw* —5L **181**
Hurst Clo. *H'ley* —2B **100**
Hurst Clo. *Wok* —7M **73**
Hurst Ct. *H'ham* —5K **197**
Hurstcourt Rd. *Sutt* —8N **43**
Hurst Croft. *Guild* —6A **114**
Hurstdene Av. *Stai* —7K **21**
Hurst Dri. *Tad* —1M **101**
Hurst Farm Clo. *Milf* —9C **132**
Hurst Farm Rd. *E Grin* —1N **185**
Hurstfield Rd. *W Mol* —2A **40**
Hurst Grn. Clo. *Oxt* —1C **126**
Hurst Grn. Rd. *Oxt* —1B **126**
Hurst Gro. *W On T* —7G **39**
Hurst Hill. *Rusp* —7N **179**
Hurst Hill Cotts. *Brmly* —6C **134**
Hurstlands. *Oxt* —1C **126**
Hurst La. *E Mol* —3C **40**
Hurst La. *Egh* —1C **36**
Hurst La. *H'ley* —2B **100**
Hurstleigh Clo. *Red* —1D **122**
Hurstleigh Dri. *Red* —1D **122**
Hurst Lodge. *Wey* —3E **56**
Hurstmere Clo. *Gray* —6B **170**
Hurst Rd. *Alder* —9A **90**
Hurst Rd. *Croy* —1A **64**
Hurst Rd. *E Mol* —2A **40**
Hurst Rd. *Eps* —7C **60**
Hurst Rd. *F'boro* —6N **69**
Hurst Rd. *H'ley & Tad* —1C **100**
Hurst Rd. *Horl* —7C **142**
Hurst Rd. *H'ham* —4J **197**
Hurst Rd. *W On T & W Mol* —4K **39**
Hurstview Grange. *S Croy* —4M **63**
Hurst View Rd. *S Croy* —4B **64**
Hurstway. *Pyr* —1G **75**
Hurst Way. *S Croy* —3B **64**
Hurstwood. *Asc* —5L **33**
Hurtbank Cotts. *Dork* —5K **137**
Hurtmore Chase. *Hurt* —4E **132**
Hurtmore Rd. *Hurt* —4C **132**
Hurtwood Rd. *W On T* —6N **39**
Huson Rd. *Warf* —7A **16**
Hussar Ct. *Alder* —2K **109**
Hussars Clo. *Houn* —6M **9**
Hutchingsons Rd. *New Ad* —7M **65**
Hutchins Way. *Horl* —6D **142**
Hutsons Clo. *Wokgm* —9C **14**
Hutton Clo. *W'sham* —4A **52**
Hutton Rd. *Ash V* —7E **90**
Huxley Clo. *G'ming* —4G **132**
Huxley Rd. *Sur R* —3G **113**
Hyacinth Clo. *Hamp* —7A **24**
Hyacinth Rd. *SW15* —2F **26**
Hyde Clo. *Ashf* —7F **22**
Hyde Dri. *Craw* —4K **181**
Hyde Heath Ct. *Craw* —1H **183**
Hyde La. *Churt & Thur* —9B **150**
Hyde La. *Ock* —7C **76**
Hyde Rd. *Rich* —8M **11**
Hyde Rd. *S Croy* —9B **64**
Hydestile Cotts. *Hyde* —5G **152**
Hyde Ter. *Ashf* —7F **22**
Hydethorpe Rd. *SW12* —2G **28**
Hyde Wlk. *Mord* —6M **43**
Hylands Clo. *Craw* —4E **182**
Hylands Clo. *Eps* —2B **80**
Hylands M. *Eps* —2B **80**
Hylands Rd. *Eps* —2B **80**
Hylle Clo. *Wind* —4B **4**
Hyperion Ct. *Bew* —5K **181**
Hyperion Ho. *SW2* —1K **29**
Hyperion Pl. *Eps* —5C **60**
Hyperion Wlk. *Horl* —1F **162**
Hyrstdene. *S Croy* —2M **63**
Hythe Clo. *Brack* —4C **32**
Hythe End Rd. *Wray* —3B **20**
Hythe Field Av. *Egh* —7F **20**
Hythe Pk. Rd. *Egh* —6E **20**
Hythe Rd. *Stai* —6F **20**
Hythe Rd. *T Hth* —1A **46**
Hythe, The. *Stai* —6G **21**

I.A.M. Rd. *F'boro* —5N **89**
Iberian Av. *Wall* —1H **63**
Iberian Way. *Camb* —9E **50**
Ibis La. *W4* —4B **12**
Ibsley Gdns. *SW15* —2F **26**
Icehouse Wood. *Oxt* —9A **106**
Icklesham Ho. *Craw* —6L **181**
Icklingham Ga. *Cobh* —8K **57**
Icklingham Rd. *Cobh* —8K **57**
Idlecombe Rd. *SW17* —7E **28**
Idmiston Rd. *SE27* —4N **29**
Idmiston Rd. *Wor Pk* —6E **42**
Idmiston Sq. *Wor Pk* —6E **42**
Ifield Av. *Craw* —9M **161**
Ifield Clo. *Red* —5C **122**
Ifield Dri. *Craw* —2L **181**
Ifield Grn. *If'd* —9M **161**
Ifield Rd. *SW10* —2N **13**
Ifield Rd. *Charl* —6K **161**
Ifield Rd. *Craw* —2N **181**
Ifield St. *If'd* —1L **181**
Ifield Wood. *If'd* —2H **181**
Ifold Bri. La. *Ifold* —4F **192**
Ifoldhurst. *Ifold* —6E **192**
Ifold Rd. *Red* —5E **122**
Ikona Ct. *Wey* —2D **56**
Ilex Clo. *Egh* —8L **19**
Ilex Clo. *Sun* —1K **39**
Ilex Clo. *Yat* —9A **48**
Ilex Ho. *Wdhm* —6J **55**
Ilex Way. *SW16* —6L **29**
Ilford Ct. *Cranl* —8H **155**
Illingworth. *Wind* —6B **4**
Illingworth Clo. *Mitc* —2B **44**
Illingworth Gro. *Brack* —9D **16**
Imadene Clo. *Lind* —5A **168**
Imadene Cres. *Lind* —5A **168**
Imber Clo. *Esh* —7D **40**
Imber Ct. Trad. Est. *E Mol* —5D **40**
Imber Cross. *Th Dit* —5F **40**
Imber Gro. *Esh* —6D **40**
Imberhorne Bus. Cen. *E Grin* —7L **165**
Imberhorne La. *E Grin* —7L **165**
Imberhorne Way. *E Grin* —7L **165**
Imber Pk. Rd. *Esh* —7D **40**
Imjin Clo. *Alder* —1N **109**
Impact Ct. *SE20* —1E **46**
Imperial Ct. *Wind* —6D **4**
Imperial Gdns. *Mitc* —2F **44**
Imperial Rd. *SW6* —4N **13**
Imperial Rd. *Felt* —1F **22**
Imperial Rd. *Wind* —6D **4**
Imperial Sq. *SW6* —4N **13**
Imperial Way. *Croy* —3K **63**
Ince Rd. *W On T* —3F **56**
Inchwood. *Brack* —7A **32**
Inchwood. *Croy* —1L **65**
Independant Bus. Pk., The. *E Grin* —7K **165**
Ingatestone Rd. *SE25* —3E **46**
Ingham Clo. *S Croy* —5G **64**
Ingham Rd. *S Croy* —5F **64**
Ingleboro Dri. *Purl* —9A **64**
Ingleby Way. *Wall* —5H **63**
Ingle Dell. *Camb* —2B **70**
Inglehurst. *New H* —6K **55**
Inglemere Rd. *Mitc* —8D **28**
Ingleside. *Coln* —4H **7**
Inglethorpe St. *SW6* —4J **13**
Ingleton. *Brack* —2M **31**
Ingleton Rd. *Cars* —5C **62**
Inglewood. *Cher* —9H **37**
Inglewood. *Croy* —5H **65**
Inglewood. *Wok* —5L **73**
Inglewood Av. *Camb* —2G **71**
Inglis Rd. *Croy* —7C **46**
Ingram Clo. *H'ham* —6G **197**
Ingram Rd. *T Hth* —9N **29**
Ingrams Clo. *W On T* —2K **57**
Ingress St. *W4* —1D **12**
Inholmes. *Craw* —3E **182**
Inholms La. *Dork* —9H **119**
Inkerman Rd. *Eton W* —1C **4**
Inkerman Rd. *Knap* —5H **73**
Inkerman Way. *Wok* —5H **73**
Inkpen La. *F Row* —8H **187**
Inman Rd. *SW18* —1A **28**
Inner Pk. Rd. *SW19* —2J **27**
Inner Quad., The. *Ash V* —8D **90**
Inner Ring E. *H'row A* —6C **8**
Inner Ring W. *H'row A* —6B **8**
Inner Staithe. *W4* —4B **12**
Innes Clo. *SW20* —1K **43**
Innes Gdns. *SW15* —9G **13**
Innes Rd. *H'ham* —4M **197**
Innings La. *Warf* —9C **16**
Innisfail Gdns. *Alder* —4L **109**
Innis Yd. *Croy* —9N **45**
Institute Rd. *Alder* —3B **110**
(Aldershot)
Institute Rd. *Alder* —6A **90**
(North Camp)
Institute Rd. *Westc* —6C **118**
Institute Wlk. *E Grin* —9A **166**
Instone Clo. *Wall* —4J **63**
Instow Gdns. *F'boro* —7M **69**
Interface Ho. Houn —6A 10
(off Staines Rd.)
International Av. *Houn* —1K **9**
Inval Hill. *Hasl* —9G **170**
Inveresk Gdns. *Wor Pk* —9E **42**
Inverness Rd. *Houn* —7N **9**
Inverness Rd. *Wor Pk* —7J **43**
Inverness Way. *Col T* —8J **49**
Invicta Clo. *Felt* —2G **22**
Invincible Rd. *Farnb* —3M **89**
Inwood Av. *Coul* —7L **83**
Inwood Av. *Houn* —6C **10**
Inwood Bus. Cen. *Houn* —7B **10**
Inwood Clo. *Croy* —8H **47**
Inwood Ct. *W on T* —8K **39**
Inwood Rd. *Houn* —7B **10**
Iona Clo. *Craw* —6N **181**
Ipswich Rd. *SW17* —7E **28**
Irene Rd. *SW6* —4M **13**
Irene Rd. *Stoke D* —1B **78**
Ireton Av. *W On T* —8F **38**
Irhome Cotts. *H'ham* —1M **179**
Iris Clo. *Croy* —7G **46**
Iris Clo. *Surb* —6M **41**
Iris Dri. *Bisl* —2D **72**
Iris Rd. *Bisl* —2D **72**
Iris Rd. *W Ewe* —2A **60**
Iron La. *Brmly* —6N **133**
Iron Mill Pl. *SW18* —9N **13**
Iron Mill Rd. *SW18* —9N **13**
Irons Bottom Rd. *Reig* —3L **141**
Irvine Dri. *F'boro* —6K **69**
Irvine Pl. *Vir W* —4A **36**
Irving Mans. W14 —2K 13
(off Queen's Club Gdns.)
Irving Wlk. *Craw* —6C **182**
Irwin Dri. *H'ham* —5G **196**
Irwin Rd. *Guild* —5K **113**
Isabella Ct. *Rich* —9M **11**
Isabella Dri. *Orp* —1L **67**
Isbells Dri. *Reig* —5N **121**
Isham Rd. *SW16* —1J **45**
Isis Clo. *SW15* —7H **13**
Isis Ct. *W4* —3A **12**
Isis St. *SW18* —3A **28**
Isis Way. *Sand* —7J **49**
Island Clo. *Stai* —5G **20**
Island Farm Av. *W Mol* —4N **39**
Island Farm Rd. *W Mol* —4N **39**
Island Rd. *Mitc* —8D **28**
Islandstone La. *Hurst* —3A **14**
Island, The. *Th Dit* —5G **40**
Island, The. *W Dray* —3L **7**
Island, The. *Wray* —4C **20**
Islay Gdns. *Houn* —8L **9**
Isleworth Bus. Complex. *Iswth* —5F **10**
Isleworth Promenade. *Twic* —7H **11**
Itchingfield Rd. *H'ham* —8A **196**
Itchingwood Comn. Rd. *Oxt* —2E **126**
Ivanhoe Clo. *Craw* —9B **162**
Ivanhoe Rd. *Houn* —6L **9**
Ivatt Pl. *W14* —1L **13**
Iveagh Clo. *Craw* —8A **182**
Iveagh Ct. *Beck* —2M **47**
Iveagh Ct. *Brack* —4B **32**
Iveagh Rd. *Guild* —4L **113**
Iveagh Rd. *Knap* —5J **73**
Ively Rd. *F'boro* —5F **88**
(in two parts)
Iverna Gdns. *Felt* —8E **8**
Ivers Way. *New Ad* —4L **65**
Ives Clo. *Yat* —8A **48**
Ivor Clo. *Guild* —4B **114**
Ivory Ct. *Felt* —3H **23**
Ivory Wlk. *Craw* —5K **181**
Ivybridge Clo. *Twic* —1G **24**
Ivy Clo. *Sun* —1K **39**
Ivydale Rd. *Cars* —8D **44**
Ivyday Gro. *SW16* —4K **29**
Ivydene. *Knap* —5E **72**
Ivydene. *W Mol* —4N **39**
Ivydene Clo. *Red* —8F **122**

Kilross Rd.—Lamberhurst Rd.

Kilross Rd. Felt —2E 22
Kilrue La. W On T —1G 57
Kilrush Ter. Wok —3C 74
Kilsha Rd. W On T —5K 39
Kimbell Gdns. SW6 —4K 13
Kimber Clo. Wind —6D 4
Kimber Ct. Guild —1F 114
Kimberely Rd. Beck —1G 47
Kimberley. Brack —7A 32
Kimberley. C Crook —9C 88
Kimberley Clo. Horl —8C 142
Kimberley Clo. Slou —1B 6
Kimberley Pl. Purl —7L 63
Kimberley Ride. Cobh —9B 58
Kimberley Rd. Beck —1G 47
Kimberley Rd. Craw —2F 182
Kimberley Rd. Croy —5M 45
Kimberley Wlk. W On T —6J 39
Kimber Rd. SW18 —1M 27
Kimbers La. Farnh —9J 109
Kimble Rd. SW19 —7B 28
Kimmeridge. Brack —5C 32
Kimpton Ind. Est. Sutt —8L 43
Kimpton Rd. Sutt —8L 43
Kinburn Dri. Egh —6A 20
Kindersley Clo. E Grin —7D 166
Kinfauns Rd. SW2 —3L 29
Kinglake Ct. Wok —5H 73
King Acre Ct. Stai —4G 20
King Charles Cres. Surb —6M 41
King Charles Ho. SW6 —3N 13 (off Wandon Rd.)
King Charles Rd. Surb —4M 41
King Charles Wlk. SW19 —2K 27
Kingcup Clo. Croy —6G 46
Kingcup Dri. Bisl —2D 72
King Edward Clo. H'ham —9D 196
King Edward Ct. Wind —4G 4
King Edward Dri. Chess —9L 41
King Edward Mans. SW6 (off Fulham Rd.) —3M 13
King Edward M. SW13 —4F 12
King Edward Rd. H'ham —9D 196
King Edward's Clo. Asc —9J 17
King Edward VII Av. Wind —3H 5
King Edwards Gro. Tedd —7H 25
King Edward's Rise. Asc —8J 17
King Edward's Rd. Asc —9J 17
Kingfield Clo. Wok —7B 74
Kingfield Dri. Wok —7B 74
Kingfield Gdns. Wok —7B 74
Kingfield Rd. Wok —7B 74
Kingfisher Clo. Bord —7A 168
Kingfisher Clo. C Crook —8B 88
Kingfisher Clo. Craw —9E 162
Kingfisher Clo. F'boro —8H 69
Kingfisher Clo. W On T —2M 57
Kingfisher Ct. SW19 —3J 27
Kingfisher Ct. Houn —8B 10
Kingfisher Ct. Wok —1E 74
Kingfisher Dri. Guild —1E 114
Kingfisher Dri. Red —9E 102
Kingfisher Dri. Rich —5H 25
Kingfisher Dri. Stai —5H 21
Kingfisher Dri. Yat —9A 48
Kingfisher Gdns. S Croy —7G 65
Kingfisher La. Turn H —4F 184
Kingfisher Rise. E Grin —1B 186
Kingfisher Wlk. Ash —2D 110
Kingfisher Way. Beck —4G 46
Kingfisher Way. H'ham —3J 197
King Gdns. Croy —2M 63
King George Av. E Grin —7M 165
King George Av. W On T —7L 39
King George Clo. Sun —6F 22
King George's Dri. New H —6J 55
King George VI Av. Big H —3F 86
King George VI Av. Mitc —3D 44
King George Sq. Rich —9M 11
King George's Trad. Est. Chess —1N 59
Kingham Clo. SW18 —1A 28
King Henry M. Orp —2N 67
King Henry's Dri. New Ad —5L 65
King Henry's Rd. King T —2A 42
King John's Clo. Stai —9M 5
Kinglake Ct. Wok —5H 73
Kingpost Pde. Guild —9D 94
Kings Acre. S Nut —6K 123
Kings Arbour. S'hall —1M 9
King's Arms All. Bren —2K 11
Kings Arms Way. Cher —7H 37
Kings Av. SW12 & SW4 —2H 29
Kings Av. Byfl —8M 55
King's Av. Cars —4C 62
Kings Av. Houn —4B 10
Kings Av. N Mald —3D 42
King's Av. Pirb —6A 72
Kings Av. Red —5C 122
King's Av. Sun —6G 23
Kings Av. Tong —4C 110
Kingsbridge Cotts. Wokgm —9C 30
Kingsbridge Rd. Mord —6J 43
Kingsbridge Rd. S'hall —1N 9
Kingsbridge Rd. W On T —6J 39
Kingsbrook. Lea —5G 79
Kingsbury Cres. Stai —5F 20
Kingsbury Dri. Old Win —1K 19
Kings Chase. E Mol —2C 40
Kingsclear Pk. Camb —2B 70
Kingsclere Clo. SW15 —1F 26
Kingscliffe Gdns. SW19 —2L 27
Kings Clo. Stai —7M 21
Kings Clo. Th Dit —5G 41
Kings Clo. W On T —7J 39
Kings Copse. E Grin —1B 186
Kingscote Hill. Craw —5N 181
Kingscote Rd. Croy —6E 46
Kingscote Rd. N Mald —2C 42
Kings Ct. W6 —1F 12
Kings Ct. Byfl —7M 55
King's Ct. H'ham —5L 197
King's Ct. Tad —9G 81
Kings Ct. Tong —4D 110
Kingscourt Rd. SW16 —4H 29
King's Cres. Camb —7A 50
Kingscroft. Fleet —5B 88
Kingscroft La. Brack —3D 16
Kingscroft Rd. Bans —2B 82
Kingscroft Rd. Lea —7H 79
Kings Cross La. S Nut —5H 123
Kingsdene. Tad —8G 80
Kingsdown Av. S Croy —6M 63
Kingsdowne Rd. Surb —6L 41
Kingsdown Rd. Eps —9F 60
Kingsdown Rd. Sutt —2K 61
King's Dri. Surb —6N 41
Kings Dri. Tedd —6D 24
Kings Dri. Th Dit —5H 41
Kings Dri., The. W On T —5G 57
Kings Farm Av. Rich —7N 11
Kingsfield. Abry —4N 135
Kingsfield. Wind —4A 4
Kingsford Av. Wall —4J 63
Kingsgate Rd. King T —9L 25
Kingsgrove Ind. Est. F'boro —2M 89
Kings Head La. Byfl —7M 55
Kingshill Av. Wor Pk —6F 42
Kings Keep. Fleet —7B 88
Kings Keep. King T —3L 41
King's Keep. Sand —6G 49
Kingsland. Newd —1N 159
Kings La. Egh —6A 20 (Egham)
Kings La. Egh —6K 19 (Englefield Green)
Kings La. Sutt —2B 62
Kings La. W'sham —2B 52
Kings La. Wrec —5E 128
Kingslawn Clo. SW15 —8G 13
Kingslea. H'ham —5L 197
Kingslea. Lea —7G 79
Kingsleigh Pl. Mitc —2D 44
Kingsley Av. Bans —2M 81
Kingsley Av. Camb —2A 70
Kingsley Av. Egh —7L 19
Kingsley Av. Houn —5C 10
Kingsley Av. Sutt —1B 62
Kingsley Clo. Crowt —4G 49
Kingsley Clo. Horl —6D 142
Kingsley Ct. Sutt —4N 61
Kingsley Ct. Wor Pk —8E 42 (off Avenue, The)
Kingsley Dri. Wor Pk —8E 42
Kingsley Gro. Reig —7N 121
Kingsley Rd. SW19 —6N 27
Kingsley Rd. Craw —6M 181
Kingsley Rd. Croy —7L 45
Kingsley Rd. F'boro —8L 69
Kingsley Rd. Horl —6D 142
Kingsley Rd. Houn —4B 10
Kingsley Rd. Orp —4N 67
Kingslyn Cres. SE19 —1B 46
Kings Mall. W6 —1H 13
Kingsmead. Big H —3F 86
Kingsmead. F'boro —1N 89
Kingsmead. Frim G —7C 70
Kings Mead. Rich —9M 11
Kings Mead. Small —8M 143
Kingsmead. S Nut —5J 123
Kingsmead. Wok —3C 74
Kingsmead Av. Mitc —2G 45
Kingsmead Av. Sun —1K 39
Kingsmead Av. Surb —8N 41
Kingsmead Av. Wor Pk —8G 42
Kingsmead Clo. Eps —4C 60
Kingsmead Clo. H'ham —2A 198
Kingsmead Clo. Tedd —7H 25
Kingsmeadow. King T —2A 42
Kings Mead Pk. Clay —4E 58
Kingsmead Pk. Cvn. Pk. Elst —9F 130
Kingsmead Pl. Broad H —5C 196
Kingsmead Rd. SW2 —3L 29
Kingsmead Rd. Broad H —5D 196
Kingsmead Shop. Cen. F'boro —2N 89
Kingsmere Clo. SW15 —6J 13
Kingsmere Rd. SW19 —3J 27
Kingsmere Rd. Brack —9L 15
Kings Mill La. Red —8G 122
Kingsnympton Pk. King T —7A 26
King's Paddock. Hamp —9C 24
Kings Pde. Fleet —4B 88
Kings Pas. King T —1K 41
King's Pl. W4 —1B 12
King's Ride. Asc —4G 32
King's Ride. Camb —6B 50
Kings Ride Ga. Rich —7N 11
Kingsridge. SW19 —3K 27
Kings Rd. SE25 —2D 46
King's Rd. SW6 & SW10 —3N 13
Kings Rd. SW14 —6C 12
Kings Rd. SW19 —7M 27
King's Rd. Alder —3K 109
King's Rd. Asc —4A 34
Kings Rd. Big H —3E 86
King's Rd. Cranl —8N 155
King's Rd. Crowt —3G 49
Kings Rd. Egh —5C 20
Kings Rd. Felt —2K 23
Kings Rd. Fleet —3B 88
King's Rd. G'ming —5J 133
King's Rd. Guild —3N 113
King's Rd. Hasl —3D 188
Kings Rd. Horl —8E 142
King's Rd. H'ham —5L 197
King's Rd. King T —9L 25
Kings Rd. Mitc —2E 44
Kings Rd. New H —6K 55
King's Rd. Orp —1N 67
Kings Rd. Rich —9M 11
Kings Rd. Rud —9E 176
Kings Rd. Shalf —1A 134
King's Rd. Surb —7L 41
King's Rd. Sutt —6M 61
King's Rd. Tedd —6D 24
Kings Rd. Twic —9H 11
Kings Rd. W On T —8J 39
King's Rd. W End —1D 72
King's Rd. Wind —7G 4
Kings Rd. Wok —3C 74
King's Shade Wlk. Eps —9C 60
Kingstable St. Eton —3G 4
Kings Ter. Fren —1J 149
King's Ter. Iswth —7G 11
Kingston Av. E Hor —4F 96
Kingston Av. Felt —9F 8
Kingston Av. Lea —8H 79
Kingston Av. Sutt —9K 43
Kingston Bri. King T —1K 41
Kingston Bus. Cen. Chess —9L 41
Kingston By-Pass. SW15 & SW20 —6D 26
Kingston By-Pass. Surb & N Mald —9K 41
Kingston By-Pass Rd. Esh & Surb —8E 40
Kingston Clo. Tedd —7H 25
Kingston Cres. Ashf —6L 21
Kingston Cres. Beck —1J 47
Kingston Gdns. Croy —9J 45
Kingston Hall Rd. King T —2K 41
Kingston Hill. King T —9N 25
Kingston Hill Pl. King T —5C 26
Kingston Ho. Est. Surb —5J 41
Kingston Ho. Gdns. Lea —8H 79
Kingston La. Tedd —6G 25
Kingston La. W Hor —5B 96
Kingston Rise. New H —6J 55
Kingston Rd. SW15 & SW19 —3F 26
Kingston Rd. SW20 & SW19 —1H 43
Kingston Rd. Camb —7E 50
Kingston Rd. Eps —5E 60
Kingston Rd. King T & N Mald —2A 42
Kingston Rd. Lea —8G 79 (in two parts)
Kingston Rd. Stai & Ashf —5J 21
Kingston Rd. Surb & Eps —8A 42
Kingston Rd. Tedd —6H 25
Kingstons Ind. Est. Alder —2C 110
Kingston Vale. SW15 —5C 26
King St. W6 —1F 12
King St. Cher —7J 37
King St. E Grin —9A 166
King St. Rich —8K 11
King St. Twic —2G 24
King St. Pde. Twic —2G 24 (off King St.)
King's Wlk. Col T —9L 49
King's Wlk. King T —9K 25
Kings Wlk. S Croy —1E 84
Kingsway. SW14 —6A 12
Kingsway. Alder —3K 109
Kingsway. B'water —1J 69
King's Way. Croy —2K 63
Kingsway. N Mald —4H 43
Kingsway. Stai —2M 21
Kingsway. W Wick —1A 66
Kingsway. Wok —5N 73
Kingsway Av. S Croy —5F 64
Kingsway Av. Wok —5N 73
Kingsway Bus. Pk. Hamp —9N 23
Kingsway Rd. Sutt —4K 61
Kingsway, The. Eps —6E 60
Kingswey Bus. Pk. Wok —1E 74
Kingswick Clo. Asc —3A 34
Kingswick Dri. Asc —3A 34
Kingswood Av. Brom —3N 47
Kingswood Av. Hamp —7B 24
Kingswood Av. Houn —5N 9
Kingswood Av. S Croy —2E 84
Kingswood Av. T Hth —4L 45
Kingswood Clo. Broadf —9A 182
Kingswood Clo. Egh —5N 19
Kingswood Clo. Guild —2E 114
Kingswood Clo. N Mald —5E 42
Kingswood Clo. Surb —6L 41
Kingswood Clo. Wey —4C 56
Kingswood Ct. Hors —3A 74
Kingswood Ct. Tad —2K 101
Kingswood Creek. Wray —8N 5
Kingswood Dri. Cars —7D 44
Kingswood Dri. Sutt —5N 61
Kingswood Firs. Gray —7A 170
Kingswood La. Hind —7A 170
Kingswood La. Warl —2F 84
Kingswood Rise. Egh —6N 19
Kingswood Rd. SW2 —1J 29
Kingswood Rd. SW19 —8L 27
Kingswood Rd. Brom —3N 47
Kingswood Rd. Tad —8G 81
Kingswood Way. S Croy —9F 64 (in two parts)
Kingswood Way. Wall —2J 63
Kingsworth Clo. Beck —4H 47
Kingsworthy Clo. King T —2M 41
Kings Yd. Asc —3J 33
Kingwood Rd. SW6 —4K 13
Kinloss Rd. Cars —6A 44
Kinnaird Av. W4 —3B 12
Kinnersley Wlk. Reig —8M 121
Kinnibrugh Dri. D'land —1C 166
Kinnoul Rd. W6 —2K 13
Kinross Av. Asc —4K 33
Kinross Av. Wor Pk —8F 42
Kinross Clo. Sun —6G 23
Kinross Ct. Asc —4K 33
Kinross Dri. Sun —6G 22
Kintyre Clo. SW16 —1K 45
Kintyre Ct. SW2 —1J 29
Kipings. Tad —8J 81
Kipling Clo. Craw —1G 182
Kipling Clo. Yat —2B 68
Kipling Ct. H'ham —4N 197
Kipling Ct. Wind —5E 4
Kipling Dri. SW19 —7B 28
Kipling Way. E Grin —9M 165
Kirby Clo. Eps —2E 60
Kirby Rd. Wok —4M 73
Kirby Way. W On T —5K 39
Kirdford Clo. Craw —1M 181
Kirkefields. Guild —9K 93
Kirkgate, The. Eps —9D 60
Kirkham Clo. Owl —5J 49
Kirk Knoll. Head —4E 168
Kirkland Av. Wok —3H 73
Kirkleas Rd. Surb —7L 41
Kirklees Rd. T Hth —4L 45
Kirkley Rd. SW19 —9M 27
Kirkly Clo. S Croy —5B 64
Kirk Rise. Sutt —9N 43
Kirkstall Gdns. SW2 —2J 29
Kirkstall Rd. SW2 —2H 29
Kirksted Rd. Mord —7N 43
Kirkstone Clo. Camb —2H 71
Kirrane Clo. N Mald —4E 42
Kirriemuir Gdns. Ash —1H 111
Kirton Clo. W4 —1C 12
Kitchener Rd. Alder —7B 90
Kitchener Rd. T Hth —2A 46
Kites Clo. Craw —3A 182
Kithurst Clo. Craw —5B 182
Kitley Gdns. SE19 —1C 46
Kitsmead. Copt —8L 163
Kitsmead La. Longc —7M 35
Kitson Rd. SW13 —4F 12
Kittiwake Clo. If'd —5J 181
Kittiwake Clo. S Croy —6H 65
Kitts La. Churt —9K 149
Klondyke Vs. Hasl —8L 171
Knapp Rd. Ashf —5A 22
Knapton M. SW17 —7E 28
Knaresborough Dri. SW18 —2N 27
Kneller Gdns. Iswth —9D 10
Kneller Rd. N Mald —6D 42
Kneller Rd. Twic —9C 10
Knepp Clo. Craw —3G 182
Knighton Clo. Craw —8H 163
Knighton Clo. S Croy —5M 63
Knighton Rd. Red —5E 122
Knightons La. Duns —5B 174
Knightsbridge Cres. Stai —7K 21
Knightsbridge Gro. Camb —8C 50
Knightsbridge Ho. Guild (off St Lukes Sq.) —4B 114
Knightsbridge Rd. Camb —8C 50
Knights Clo. Egh —7F 20
Knights Clo. Wind —4A 4
Knights Ct. King T —2L 41
Knights Hill. SE27 —6M 29
Knight's Hill Sq. SE27 —5M 29
Knight's Pk. King T —2L 41
Knights Rd. Farnh —5K 109
Knights Way. Camb —2G 70
Knightswood. Brack —7N 31
Knightswood. Wok —5J 73
Knightwood Clo. Reig —5M 121
Knightwood Cres. N Mald —5D 42
Knipp Hill. Cobh —9N 57
Knivet Rd. SW6 —2M 13
Knobfield. Ab H —3G 136
Knob Hill. Warn —9F 178
Knockholt Clo. Sutt —6N 61
Knockholt Main Rd. Knock —6N 87
Knole Clo. Croy —5F 46
Knole Clo. Worth —2H 183
Knole Gro. E Grin —7M 165
Knole Wood. Asc —7B 34
Knoll Clo. Fleet —3B 88
Knoll Ct. Fleet —2B 88
Knoll Farm Rd. Capel —7G 159
Knollmead. Surb —7B 42
Knoll Pk. Rd. Cher —7H 37
Knoll Quarry. G'ming —5H 133
Knoll Rd. SW18 —8N 13
Knoll Rd. Camb —9B 50
Knoll Rd. Dork —7G 119
Knoll Rd. Fleet —3B 88
Knoll Rd. G'ming —5G 133
Knoll Roundabout. Lea —8J 79
Knoll Roundabout. (Junct.) —8J 79
Knolls Clo. Wor Pk —9G 42
Knolls, The. Eps —3H 81
Knoll, The. Beck —1L 47
Knoll, The. Cher —7H 37
Knoll, The. Cobh —9A 58
Knoll, The. Lea —8J 79
Knoll Wlk. Camb —9B 50
Knoll Wood. G'ming —5G 133
Knollys Clo. SW16 —4L 29
Knollys Rd. SW16 —4L 29
Knollys Rd. Alder —1L 109
Knowle Clo. Copt —7N 163
Knowle Dri. Copt —7M 163
Knowle Gdns. W Byf —9H 55
Knowle Grn. Stai —6J 21
Knowle Gro. Vir W —6M 35
Knowle Gro. Clo. Vir W —6M 35
Knowle Hill. Vir W —6L 35
Knowle La. Cranl & Rudg —8M 155
Knowle Pk. Cobh —2M 77
Knowle Pk. Av. Stai —7K 21
Knowle Rd. Twic —2E 24
Knowles Av. Crowt —2E 48
Knowle, The. Tad —8H 81
Knowl Hill. Wok —6D 74
Knox Grn. Binf —6H 15
Knox Rd. Guild —7L 93
Kohat Ct. Alder —2L 109
Kohat Rd. SW19 —6N 27
Kohima Clo. Alder —1N 109
Koonowla Clo. Big H —2F 86
Kooringa. Warl —6E 84
Korda Clo. Shep —2A 38
Kramer M. SW5 —1M 13
Kreisel Wlk. Rich —2M 11
Kristina Ct. Sutt —4M 61 (off Overton Rd.)
Krooner Rd. Camb —3N 69
Kuala Gdns. SW16 —9K 29
Kyle Clo. Brack —2N 31
Kynaston Av. T Hth —4N 45
Kynaston Ct. Cat —3B 104
Kynaston Cres. T Hth —4N 45
Kynaston Rd. T Hth —4N 45
Kynnersley Clo. Cars —9D 44

Laburnum Av. Sutt —9C 44
Laburnum Clo. Alder —3M 109
Laburnum Clo. Guild —9M 93
Laburnum Ct. SE19 —1C 46
Laburnum Ct. Small —1N 163
Laburnum Cres. Sun —9J 23
Laburnum Gdns. C Crook —8C 88
Laburnum Gdns. Croy —7G 46
Laburnum Gro. Houn —7N 9
Laburnum Gro. N Mald —1C 42
Laburnum Gro. Slou —2D 6
Laburnum Ho. Brom —1N 47
Laburnum Pas. Alder —3M 109
Laburnum Pl. Egh —7L 19
Laburnum Rd. SW19 —8A 28
Laburnum Rd. Alder —3M 109
Laburnum Rd. Cher —7J 37
Laburnum Rd. Eps —9D 60
Laburnum Rd. Farnh —5K 109
Laburnum Rd. Hayes —1G 9
Laburnum Rd. Mitc —1E 44
Laburnum Rd. Wok —7N 73
Laburnums, The. B'water —1G 68
Laburnum Way. Stai —2A 22
Lacey Av. Coul —7L 83
Lacey Clo. Egh —8F 20
Lacey Dri. Coul —7M 83
Lacey Dri. Hamp —9N 23
Lacey Grn. Coul —7L 83
Lackford Rd. Coul —5D 82
Lackman's Hill. Brack —7N 15
Lacock Clo. SW19 —7A 28
Lacy Rd. SW15 —7J 13
Ladas Rd. SE27 —5N 29
Ladbroke Cotts. Red —2E 122 (off Ladbroke Rd.)
Ladbroke Ct. Red —1E 122
Ladbroke Gro. Red —2E 122
Ladbroke Hurst. D'land —1C 166
Ladbroke Rd. Eps —1C 80
Ladbroke Rd. Horl —6F 142
Ladbroke Rd. Red —2E 122
Ladbrook Rd. SE25 —3A 46
Ladderstile Ride. King T —6A 26
Ladybank. Brack —7N 31
Lady Booth Rd. King T —1L 41
Ladycroft Gdns. Orp —2L 67
Ladycroft Way. Orp —2L 67
Ladycross. Milf —2B 152
Ladyegate Clo. Dork —4K 119
Ladyegate Rd. Dork —5J 119
Ladygate Dri. Gray —6M 169
Ladygrove. Croy —5H 65
Ladygrove Dri. Guild —7C 94
Lady Hay. Wor Pk —8E 42
Lady Margaret Rd. Asc —7C 34
Lady Margaret Rd. Craw —2M 181
Lady Margaret Wlk. Craw —2M 181
Ladymead. Guild —2M 113
Ladymead Clo. M'bowr —6G 183
Ladymead Retail Pk. Guild —2M 113
Ladythorpe Clo. Add —1K 55
Ladywood Av. F'boro —1H 89
Ladywood Rd. Surb —8N 41
Laffan's Rd. Alder —7H 89
Lafone Av. Felt —3K 23
Lagham Pk. S God —6H 125
Lagham Rd. S God —7H 125
Laglands Clo. Reig —1A 122
Laings Av. Mitc —1D 44
Lainlock Pl. Houn —4B 10
Lainson St. SW18 —1M 27
Lairdale Clo. SE21 —2N 29
Laird Ct. Bag —6J 51
Laitwood Rd. SW12 —2F 28
Lake Clo. SW19 —6L 27
Lake Clo. Byfl —8M 55
Lake Dri. Bord —6A 168
Lake End Way. Crowt —3F 48
Lake Gdns. Rich —3H 25
Lake Gdns. Wall —9F 44
Lakehall Gdns. T Hth —4M 45
Lakehall Rd. T Hth —4M 45
Lakehurst Rd. Eps —2D 60
Lakeland Dri. Frim —5C 70
Lake La. Dock —4D 148
Lake La. Horl —6G 142
Lake Rd. SW19 —6L 27
Lake Rd. Croy —8J 47
Lake Rd. Deep —8E 70
Lake Rd. Dork —3C 158
Lake Rd. Vir W —3L 35
Laker Pl. SW15 —9L 13
Lakers Lea. Loxw —7H 193
Lakers Rise. Bans —3C 82
Lakes Clo. Chil —9D 114
Lakeside. Beck —2L 47
Lakeside. Brack —8A 16
Lakeside. Eps —3D 60
Lakeside. H'ham —3J 197
Lakeside. Red —1E 122
Lakeside. Wall —1F 62
Lakeside. Wey —8F 38
Lakeside. Wok —6H 73
Lakeside Clo. SE25 —1D 46
Lakeside Clo. Ash V —8D 90
Lakeside Clo. Wok —6H 73
Lakeside Ct. Fleet —2C 88
Lakeside Dri. Brom —1G 67
Lakeside Dri. Esh —3C 58
Lakeside Est. Coln —3H 7
Lakeside Grange. Wey —9D 38
Lakeside Rd. Ash V —9D 90
Lakeside Rd. Coln —3H 7
Lakeside Rd. F'boro —6M 89
Lakeside, The. B'water —2J 69
Lakes Rd. Kes —2E 66
Lakestreet Grn. Oxt —7F 106
Lake View. Dor P —5B 166
Lake View. N Holm —8J 119
Lake View Cvn. Site. Wink —2J 17
Lakeview Rd. SE27 —6L 29
Lake View Rd. Felb —7E 164
Laleham Clo. Stai —9K 21
Laleham Ct. Wok —3A 74
Laleham Rd. Shep —3A 38
Laleham Rd. Stai —6H 21
Lalor St. SW6 —5K 13
Lamberhurst Rd. SE27 —5L 29

Lamberhurst Wlk.—Lenten Clo.

Lamberhurst Wlk. Craw —4E 182
Lambert Av. Rich —6N 11
Lambert Clo. Big H —3F 86
Lambert Cotts. Blet —2B 124
Lambert Cres. B'water —2H 69
Lambert Lodge. Bren —1K 11
(off Layton Rd.)
Lambert Rd. Bans —1M 81
Lambert's Pl. Croy —7A 46
Lamberts Rd. Surb —4L 41
Lambeth Clo. Craw —7N 181
Lambeth Rd. Croy —7L 45
Lambeth Wlk. Craw —7N 181
Lambly Hill. Vir W —2A 36
Lamborne Clo. Sand —6F 48
Lambourn Clo. E Grin —7A 166
Lambourne Av. SW19 —5L 27
Lambourne Clo. Craw —5D 182
Lambourne Cres. Wok —9F 54
Lambourne Dri. Bag —5H 51
Lambourne Dri. Cobh —2L 77
Lambourne Gro. Brack —1C 32
Lambourne Way. Tong —5C 110
Lambourn Gro. King T —1A 42
Lamb Pas. Bren —2M 11
Lambrook Ter. SW6 —4K 13
Lambs Bus. Pk. S God —7E 124
Lambs Cres. H'ham —3M 197
Lambs Farm Clo. H'ham —3N 197
Lambs Farm Rd. H'ham —3M 197
Lambs Grn. Rusp —4E 180
Lambton Rd. SW20 —9H 27
Lambyn Croft. Horl —7G 143
Lammas Av. Mitc —1E 44
Lammas Clo. G'ming —5K 133
Lammas Clo. Stai —5G 20
Lammas Ct. Stai —3F 20
Lammas Ct. Wind —5F 4
Lammas Dri. Stai —5F 20
Lammas Hill. Esh —1B 58
Lammas La. Esh —2A 58
Lammas Mead. Binf —8K 15
Lammas Rd. G'ming —6K 133
Lammas Rd. Rich —5J 25
Lammermoor Rd. SW12 —1F 28
Lampard La. Churt —8J 149
Lampeter Clo. Wok —5A 74
Lampeter Sq. W6 —2K 13
Lampton Av. Houn —4B 10
Lampton Ct. Houn —4B 10
Lampton Ho. Clo. SW19 —5J 27
Lampton Pk. Rd. Houn —5B 10
Lampton Rd. Houn —5B 10
Lanark Clo. Frim —4C 70
Lanark Clo. H'ham —6L 197
Lancashire Hill. Warf —7D 16
Lancaster Av. SE27 —3M 29
Lancaster Av. SW19 —6J 27
Lancaster Av. Farnh —3H 129
Lancaster Av. Mitc —4J 45
Lancaster Clo. SE27 —3M 29
Lancaster Clo. Craw —9H 163
Lancaster Clo. Croy —8J 45
Lancaster Clo. Egh —6N 19
Lancaster Clo. King T —6K 25
Lancaster Clo. Stai —9N 7
Lancaster Clo. Wok —3C 74
Lancaster Cotts. Rich —9L 11
Lancaster Ct. SE27 —3M 29
Lancaster Ct. SW6 —3L 13
Lancaster Ct. Bans —1L 81
Lancaster Ct. Sutt —4M 61
(off Mulgrave Rd.)
Lancaster Ct. W on T —6H 39
Lancaster Dri. Camb —9B 50
Lancaster Dri. E Grin —7C 166
Lancaster Gdns. SW19 —6K 27
Lancaster Gdns. King T —6K 25
Lancaster Ho. Brack —4N 31
Lancaster Ho. Red —6C 122
Lancaster M. SW18 —8N 13
Lancaster M. Rich —9L 11
Lancaster Pk. Rich —8L 11
Lancaster Pl. SW19 —6J 27
Lancaster Pl. Houn —5L 9
Lancaster Pl. Twic —9G 11
Lancaster Rd. SE25 —1C 46
Lancaster Rd. SW19 —6J 27
Lancaster Way. F'boro —7A 70
Lancelot Clo. If'd —3K 181
Lancer Ct. Alder —2K 109
Lanchester Dri. Crowt —9H 31
Lancing Clo. Craw —1M 181
Lancing Ct. H'ham —4N 197
Lancing Rd. Croy —6K 45
Lancing Rd. Felt —3G 22
Landen Ct. Wokgm —4A 30
Landen Pk. Horl —6C 142
Landford Rd. SW15 —6H 13
Landgrove Rd. SW19 —6M 27
Landon Way. Ashf —7C 22
Landridge Rd. SW6 —5L 13
Landscape Rd. Warl —6E 84
Landsdowne Clo. Surb —8A 42
Landseer Clo. SW19 —9A 28
Landseer Clo. Col T —9K 49
Landseer Rd. N Mald —6C 42
Landseer Rd. Sutt —3M 61
Lane Clo. Add —2K 55
Lane End. SW15 —9J 13
Lane End. Eps —1A 80
Lane End. Hamb —1E 172
Lane End Dri. Knap —4F 72
Lanercost Clo. SW2 —3L 29
Lanercost Rd. SW2 —3L 29
Lanercost Rd. Craw —4A 182
Lane, The. Cher —2J 37
Lane, The. Plais —4E 192
Lane, The. Thur —6G 150
Lane, The. Vir W —2B 36
Laneway. SW15 —8G 12
Lanfrey Pl. W14 —1L 13
Langaller La. Fet —9B 78
Langborough Rd. Wokgm —3B 30
Langbourne Way. Clay —3G 58
Lang Clo. Fet —1B 98
Langcroft Clo. Cars —9D 44
Langdale Av. Mitc —2D 44
Langdale Clo. SW14 —7A 12
Langdale Clo. F'boro —1K 89
Langdale Clo. Wok —3M 73
Langdale Dri. Asc —1J 33
Langdale Pde. Mitc —2D 44
Langdale Rd. If'd —5J 181
Langdale Rd. T Hth —3L 45
Langdon Clo. Camb —2G 70
Langdon Pl. SW14 —6B 12
Langdon Rd. Mord —4A 44
Langdon Wlk. Mord —4A 44
Langford Rd. SW6 —5N 13
Langham Clo. G'ming —6J 133
Langham Ct. Farnh —4H 129
Langham Dene. Kenl —2M 83
Langham Gdns. Rich —5J 25
Langham Ho. Clo. Rich —5K 25
Langham Mans. SW5 —1N 13
(off Earl's Ct. Sq.)
Langham Pk. G'ming —6J 133
Langham Pl. W4 —2D 12
Langham Pl. Egh —6B 20
Langham Rd. SW20 —9H 27
Langham Rd. Tedd —6H 25
Langholm Clo. SW12 —1H 29
Langhurst Clo. H'ham —5K 179
Langhurstwood Rd. H'ham —8J 179
Langland Gdns. Croy —8J 47
Langlands Rise. Eps —9B 60
Langley Av. Surb —7K 41
Langley Av. Wor Pk —8J 43
Langley Broom. Slou —1B 6
Langley Clo. C Crook —9A 88
Langley Clo. Eps —6C 80
Langley Clo. Guild —2M 113
Langley Cres. Hayes —3G 9
Langley Dri. Camb —9C 50
Langley Dri. Craw —1A 182
Langley Gro. N Mald —1D 42
Langley La. Dork & Head —3A 100
Langley La. If'd —1M 181
Langley Oaks Av. S Croy —6D 64
Langley Pde. Craw —9A 162
Langley Pk. Rd. Sutt —2A 62
Langley Pl. Craw —9A 162
Langley Rd. SW19 —9L 27
Langley Rd. Beck —3H 47
Langley Rd. Iswth —5F 10
Langley Rd. S Croy —5G 64
Langley Rd. Stai —7H 21
Langley Rd. Surb —6L 41
Langley Roundabout. (Junct.) —2C 6
Langley Vale Rd. Eps —7B 80
Langley Wlk. Craw —9N 161
(in two parts)
Langley Wlk. Wok —6A 74
Langley Way. W Wick —7N 47
Langmans La. Wok —5L 73
Langmans Way. Wok —3H 73
Langmead St. SE27 —5N 29
Langport Ct. W on T —7K 39
Langridge Dri. E Grin —1A 186
Langridge Ho. H'ham —6H 197
Langridge M. Hamp —7N 23
Langroyd Rd. SW17 —3D 28
Langshott. Horl —6F 142
Langshott Clo. Wdhm —7G 55
Langshott La. Horl —8G 142
(in two parts)
Langside Av. SW15 —7F 12
Langsmead. Blind H —3H 145
Langstone Clo. M'bowr —6G 183
Langthorne Ho. Hayes —1F 8
Langthorne St. SW6 —3J 13
Langton Av. Eps —7E 60
Langton Clo. Add —9K 37
Langton Clo. Wok —4J 73
Langton Dri. Head —2F 168
Langton Pl. SW18 —2M 27
Langton Rd. W Mol —3C 40
Langton Way. Croy —1B 64
Langton Way. Egh —7E 20
Langwood Chase. Tedd —7J 25
Lanigan Dri. Houn —8B 10
Lankton Clo. Beck —1M 47
Lannoy Point. SW6 —3K 13
(off Pellant Rd.)
Lansbury Av. Felt —9J 9
Lansbury Rd. Craw —8N 181
Lansdell Rd. Mitc —1E 44
Lansdown. Guild —3C 114
Lansdown Clo. H'ham —2A 198
Lansdown Clo. W On T —7K 39
Lansdown Clo. Wok —6J 73
Lansdowne Clo. SW20 —8J 27
Lansdowne Clo. Twic —2F 24
Lansdowne Ct. Purl —6M 63
Lansdowne Ct. Wor Pk —8F 42
Lansdowne Hill. SE27 —4M 29
Lansdowne Rd. SW20 —8H 27
Lansdowne Rd. Alder —3M 109
Lansdowne Rd. Croy —8A 46
Lansdowne Rd. Eps —4B 60
Lansdowne Rd. Frim —6E 70
Lansdowne Rd. Houn —6B 10
Lansdowne Rd. Purl —8L 63
Lansdowne Rd. Stai —8K 21
Lansdowne Wood Clo. SE27 —4M 29
Lantern Clo. SW15 —7F 12
Lanyon Clo. H'ham —2N 197
Lanyon M. H'ham —2N 197
Lapwing Clo. H'ham —5M 197
Lapwing Clo. S Croy —6H 65
Lapwing Ct. Surb —9N 41
Lapwing Gro. Guild —1F 114
Lara Clo. Chess —4L 59
Larbert Rd. SW16 —8G 28
Larby Pl. Eps —6D 60
Larch Av. Asc —4B 34
Larch Av. Guild —1M 113
Larch Av. Wokgm —1A 30
Larch Clo. SW12 —3F 28
Larch Clo. Camb —7C 50
Larch Clo. Red —5A 122
Larch Clo. Tad —8A 82
Larch Clo. Warl —6H 85
Larch Cres. Eps —3A 60
Larch Dri. W4 —1N 11
Larch End. H'ham —5H 197
Larches Av. SW14 —7C 12
Larches, The. H'ham —2B 198
Larches, The. Warf P —8E 16
Larches, The. Wok —3A 74
Larches Way. B'water —1G 68
Larches Way. Craw D —1E 184
Larchfield Rd. Fleet —6B 88
Larch Ho. Brom —1N 47
Larch Rd. Head —3G 168
Larch Tree Way. Croy —9K 47
Larchvale Ct. Sutt —4N 61
Larch Way. F'boro —2H 89
Larchwood. Brack —4D 32
Larchwood Clo. Bans —2K 81
Larchwood Dri. Egh —7L 19
Larchwood Glade. Camb —8E 50
Larchwood Rd. Wok —7G 73
Larcombe Clo. Croy —1C 64
Larcombe Ct. Sutt —4N 61
(off Worcester Rd.)
Larges Bri. Dri. Brack —2A 32
Larges La. Brack —1A 32
Largewood Av. Surb —8N 41
Lark Av. Stai —4H 21
Larkfield. Cobh —9H 57
Larkfield. Ewh —6F 156
Larkfield Clo. Farnh —9E 108
Larkfield Ct. Small —8L 143
Larkfield Rd. Farnh —9E 108
Larkfield Rd. Rich —7L 11
Larkhall Clo. W On T —3K 57
Larkham Clo. Felt —4F 22
Larkin Clo. Coul —4K 83
Larkins Rd. Gat A —3B 162
Lark Rise. Craw —1A 182
Lark Rise. E Hor —9F 96
Lark Rise. Turn H —3F 184
Larksfield. Egh —8M 19
Larksfield. Horl —7F 142
Larkspur Clo. Alder —5M 109
Larkspur Way. Eps —2B 60
Larkspur Way. N Holm —8K 119
Larks Way. Knap —3F 72
Larkswood Clo. Sand —6F 48
Larkswood Dri. Crowt —2G 49
Lark Way. Cars —6C 44
Larnach Rd. W6 —2J 13
Larpent Av. SW15 —8H 13
Lascombe La. P'ham —8L 111
Lashmere. Copt —7A 164
Lashmere. Cranl —7J 155
Laski Ct. Craw —8N 181
Lasswade Ct. Cher —6G 37
Lasswade Rd. Cher —6H 37
Latchmere Clo. Rich —6L 25
Latchmere La. King T —7M 25
Latchmere Rd. King T —8L 25
Latchwood La. Lwr Bo —6J 129
Lateward Rd. Bren —2K 11
Latham Av. Frim —4C 70
Latham Clo. Big H —3E 86
Latham Clo. Twic —1G 24
Latham Ct. SW5 —1M 13
(off W. Cromwell Rd.)
Latham Rd. Twic —1F 24
Latham's Way. Croy —7K 45
Lathkill Ct. Beck —1J 47
Latimer. Brack —7N 31
Latimer Clo. Craw —9B 162
Latimer Clo. Wok —3D 74
Latimer Clo. Wor Pk —1G 61
Latimer Rd. SW19 —7N 27
Latimer Rd. Croy —9M 45
Latimer Rd. G'ming —7H 133
Latimer Rd. Tedd —6F 24
Latimer Rd. Wokgm —3A 30
Lattimer Pl. W4 —2D 12
Latton Clo. Esh —1B 58
Latton Clo. W On T —6M 39
Latymer Clo. Wey —1D 56
Latymer Ct. W6 —1J 13
Laud Dri. Craw —4H 183
Lauder Clo. Frim —4C 70
Lauderdale. F'boro —3J 89
Lauderdale Dri. Rich —4K 25
Laud St. Croy —9N 45
Laud Way. Wokgm —2D 30
Laughton Rd. H'ham —3M 197
Laundry Cotts. Craw —7L 181
Laundry La. Sand —9K 49
Laundry Rd. W6 —2K 13
Laundry Rd. Guild —4M 113
Laundry Way. Capel —5J 159
Lauradale. Brack —3M 31
Laurel Av. Egh —6L 19
Laurel Av. Twic —2F 24
Laurel Bank. Chob —7H 53
(off Bagshot Rd.)
Laurel Bank Gdns. SW6 —5L 13
Laurel Clo. SW17 —6C 28
Laurel Clo. Camb —2B 70
Laurel Clo. Coln —3G 6
Laurel Clo. Craw —6E 182
Laurel Clo. F'boro —2H 89
Laurel Ct. Brack —3D 32
(off Wayland Clo.)
Laurel Cres. Croy —9K 47
Laurel Cres. Wok —9E 54
Laurel Dene. E Grin —9B 166
Laureldene. Norm —3M 111
Laurel Dri. Oxt —9B 106
Laurel Gdns. Alder —5M 109
Laurel Gdns. Houn —7M 9
Laurel Gdns. New H —6K 55
Laurel Gro. Wrec —6E 128
Laurel Ho. Brom —1N 47
Laurel Mnr. Sutt —4A 62
Laurel Rd. SW13 —5F 12
Laurel Rd. SW20 —9G 26
Laurel Rd. Hamp —6D 24
Laurels, The. Bans —4L 81
Laurels, The. Cobh —2M 77
Laurels, The. Craw —9E 162
Laurels, The. Farnh —5L 109
Laurels, The. Fleet —4B 88
Laurels, The. Wey —9E 38
Laurel Wlk. H'ham —7M 197
Laurier Rd. Croy —6C 46
Lauriston Clo. Knap —4G 72
Lauriston Rd. SW19 —7J 27
Lauser Rd. Stai —1L 21
Laustan Clo. Guild —3E 114
Lavant Clo. Craw —4L 181
Lavender Av. Mitc —9C 28
Lavender Av. Wor Pk —9H 43
Lavender Clo. Cars —1F 62
Lavender Clo. Cat —3N 103
Lavender Clo. Coul —6G 82
Lavender Clo. Red —8F 122
Lavender Ct. Felt —9J 9
Lavender Ct. W Mol —2B 40
Lavender Gro. Mitc —9C 28
Lavender La. Rowl —7E 128
Lavender Pk. Rd. W Byf —8J 55
Lavender Rd. Cars —1E 62
Lavender Rd. Croy —5K 45
Lavender Rd. Eps —2A 60
Lavender Rd. Sutt —1B 62
Lavender Rd. Wok —3D 74
Lavender Vale. Wall —3H 63
Lavender Wlk. Mitc —2E 44
Lavender Way. Croy —5G 47
Lavengro Rd. SE27 —3N 29
Lavenham Rd. SW18 —3L 27
Laverstoke Gdns. SW15 —1E 26
Laverton M. SW5 —1N 13
Laverton Pl. SW5 —1N 13
Lavington Clo. Craw —2M 181
Lavington Rd. Croy —9K 45
Lawbrook La. Peasl —6D 136
Lawday Link. Farnh —5F 108
Lawday Pl. Farnh —5F 108
Lawday Pl. La. Farnh —5F 108
Lawdons Gdns. Croy —1M 63
Lawford Clo. Wall —5J 63
Lawford Cres. Yat —9C 48
Lawford Gdns. Kenl —3N 83
Lawford Rd. W4 —3B 12
Lawford's Hill Clo. Worp —2F 92
Lawford's Hill Rd. Worp —2F 92
Lawn Clo. Dat —3M 5
Lawn Clo. N Mald —1D 42
Lawn Cres. Rich —5N 11
Lawn Rd. Guild —6M 113
Lawnsmead Cotts. Won —4D 134
Lawns Rd. H'ham —6B 176
Lawns, The. SE19 —9N 29
Lawns, The. SW19 —6L 27
Lawns, The. Asc —2H 33
Lawns, The. Coln —4G 7
Lawns, The. F'boro —2K 89
Lawns, The. Milf —1C 152
Lawns, The. Sutt —4K 61
Lawn, The. S'hall —1A 10
Lawnwood Cotts. G'ming
(off Catteshall La.) —6K 133
Lawrence Av. N Mald —5C 42
Lawrence Clo. Guild —7D 94
Lawrence Clo. Wokgm —2C 30
Lawrence Ct. Wind —5F 4
Lawrence Cres. W'sham —3A 52
Lawrence Est. Houn —7K 9
Lawrence Gro. Binf —9J 15
Lawrence La. Bkld —1G 120
Lawrence Rd. SE25 —3C 46
Lawrence Rd. Fleet —5A 88
Lawrence Rd. Hamp —8N 23
Lawrence Rd. Houn —7K 9
Lawrence Rd. Rich —5J 25
Lawrence Rd. W Wick —1C 66
Lawrence Way. Camb —2L 69
Lawrence Weaver Clo. Mord —5M 43
Laws Clo. If'd —4K 181
Lawson Clo. SW19 —4J 27
Lawson Ct. Surb —6K 41
Lawson Hunt Bus. & Ind. Pk. H'ham —4D 196
Lawson Way. Asc —5E 34
Laws Ter. Alder —1A 110
Laxey Rd. Orp —3N 67
Laxton Gdns. Red —6H 103
Layard Rd. T Hth —1A 46
Layburn Cres. Slou —2D 6
Layhams Rd. W Wick & Kes —1A 66
Layton Ct. Bren —1K 11
Layton Ct. Wey —1C 56
Layton Cres. Croy —2L 63
Layton Rd. Bren —1K 11
Layton Rd. Houn —7B 10
Layton's La. Sun —1G 38
Lazenbys Est. Wal W —9L 157
Leach Gro. Lea —9J 79
Lea Clo. Ash —3E 110
Lea Clo. Bad L —6M 109
Lea Clo. Craw —4L 181
Lea Coach Rd. Thur —5L 151
Lea Ct. Farnh —5L 109
Leacroft. Asc —4D 34
Lea Croft. Crowt —1G 49
Leacroft. Stai —6J 21
Leacroft Av. SW12 —1D 28
Leacroft Clo. Kenl —3N 83
Leacroft Clo. Stai —5K 21
Leaf Clo. Th Dit —4E 40
Leafey La. Gray —3K 169
Leaf Gro. SE27 —6L 29
Leafield Clo. SW16 —7M 29
Leafield Clo. Wok —5L 73
Leafield Copse. Brack —3D 32
Leafield Rd. SW20 —2L 43
Leafield Rd. Sutt —8M 43
Leafy Gro. Kes —2E 66
Leafy Way. Croy —8C 46
Lea La. Fleet —6A 88
Leamington Av. Mord —3K 43
Leamington Av. Orp —1N 67
Leamington Clo. Houn —8C 10
Leamington Rd. S'hall —1L 9
Leamore St. W6 —1H 13
Leander Ct. Surb —6K 41
Leander Rd. SW2 —1K 29
Leander Rd. T Hth —3K 45
Leapale La. Guild —4N 113
Leapale Rd. Guild —4N 113
Lea Rd. Beck —1K 47
Lea Rd. Camb —4N 69
Lea Rd. S'hall —1M 9
Leas Clo. Chess —4M 59
Leaside. Bookh —1A 98
Leas La. Warl —5G 84
Lea's Rd. Guild —4M 113
Leas Rd. Warl —5G 84
Lea, The. Egh —8E 20
Lea, The. Fleet —6A 88
Leather Clo. Mitc —1E 44
Leatherhead By-Pass Rd. Lea —7H 79
Leatherhead Ind. Est. Lea —8G 78
Leatherhead Rd. Bookh & Oxs —4B 98
Leatherhead Rd. Chess —1H 79
Leatherhead Rd. Lea & Asht —8K 79
Leatherhead Rd. Oxs —1D 78
Leaveland Clo. Beck —3K 47
Leavesden Rd. Wey —2C 56
Leaves Grn. Brack —5B 32
Leaves Grn. Cres. Kes —7E 66
Leaves Grn. Rd. Kes —7F 66
Lea Way. Alder —1D 110
Leawood Rd. Fleet —6A 88
Leazes Av. Cat —2L 103
Leazes La. Cat —1L 103
Lebanon Av. Felt —6L 23
Lebanon Dri. Cobh —9A 58
Lebanon Gdns. SW18 —9M 13
Lebanon Gdns. Big H —4F 86
Lebanon Pk. Twic —1H 25
Lebanon Rd. SW18 —8M 13
Lebanon Rd. Croy —7B 46
Lechford Rd. Horl —9E 142
Leckford Rd. SW18 —3A 28
Leckhampton Pl. SW2 —1L 29
Leconfield Av. SW13 —6E 12
Ledbury Pl. Croy —1A 64
Ledbury Rd. Croy —1A 64
Ledbury Rd. Reig —2M 121
Ledger Clo. Guild —1D 114
Ledger Dri. Add —2H 55
Ledgers La. Warl —4L 85
Ledgers Rd. Warl —3K 85
Leechcroft Rd. Wall —9E 44
Leech La. Dork & Eps —4A 100
Leechpool La. H'ham —4N 197
Lee Ct. Alder —4A 110
Leegate Clo. Wok —3L 73
Lee Grn. La. Eps —2A 100
Lee Rd. SW19 —9N 27
Lee Rd. Alder —2K 109
Leeside. Rusp —3B 180
Leeson Gdns. Eton W —1B 4
Leeson Ho. Twic —1H 25
Lees, The. Croy —8J 47
Lee St. Horl —8C 142
Leeward Gdns. SW19 —6K 27
Leewood Way. Eff —5K 97
Legge Cres. Alder —3K 109
Leggyfield Ct. H'ham —3H 197
Legion Ct. Mord —5M 43
Legrace Av. Houn —5L 9
Legsheath La. E Grin —8M 185
Leicester. Brack —6C 32
Leicester Av. Mitc —3J 45
Leicester Clo. Wor Pk —1H 61
Leicester Rd. Croy —6B 46
Leigham Av. SW16 —4J 29
Leigham Clo. SW16 —4K 29
Leigham Ct. Rd. SW16 —3J 29
Leigham Dri. Iswth —3E 10
Leigham Vale. SW16 & SW2 —4K 29
Leigh Clo. Add —4H 55
Leigh Clo. N Mald —3C 42
Leigh Clo. Ind. Est. N Mald —3C 42
Leigh Corner. Cobh —2K 77
Leigh Ct. Clo. Cobh —1K 77
Leigh Cres. New Ad —4L 65
Leigh Hill Rd. Cobh —2K 77
Leighlands. Craw —1G 183
Leigh La. Farnh —3K 129
Leigh Orchard Clo. SW16 —4K 29
Leigh Pk. Dat —3M 5
Leigh Pl. Cobh —2K 77
Leigh Pl. Cotts. Reig —9F 120
Leigh Pl. La. God —1G 125
Leigh Pl. Rd. Reig —9F 120
Leigh Rd. Bet —9B 120
Leigh Rd. Cobh —1J 77
Leigh Rd. Houn —7D 10
Leigh Sq. Wind —5A 4
Leighton Gdns. Croy —7M 45
Leighton Gdns. S Croy —9E 64
Leighton St. Croy —7M 45
Leighton Way. Eps —1C 80
Leinster Av. SW14 —6B 12
Leipzig Rd. C Crook —1C 108
Leisure La. W Byf —8K 55
Leith Clo. Crowt —9F 30
Leithcote Gdns. SW16 —5K 29
Leithcote Path. SW16 —4K 29
Leith Gro. Bear G —7K 139
Leith Hill La. Dork —4M 137
Leith Lea. Bear G —7K 139
Leith Rd. Bear G —7J 139
Leith Rd. Eps —8D 60
Leith Towers. Sutt —4N 61
Leith Vale Cotts. Dork —7A 158
Leith View. N Holm —9J 119
Leith View Cotts. H'ham —3H 179
Leith View Rd. H'ham —3N 197
Lela Av. Houn —5K 9
Le Marchant Rd. Frim & Camb —3D 70
Le May Clo. Horl —7E 142
Lemington Gro. Brack —5N 31
Lemmington Way. H'ham —1M 197
Lemon's Farm Rd. Dork —5N 137
Lemuel St. SW18 —9N 13
Lendore Rd. Frim —6B 70
Lenelby Rd. Surb —7N 41
Leney Clo. Wokgm —9C 14
Len Freeman Pl. SW6 —3L 13
Lenham Rd. Sutt —1N 61
Lenham Rd. T Hth —1A 46
Lennard Rd. Croy —7N 45
Lennel Gdns. C Crook —7D 88
Lennox Ct. Red —2E 122
(off St Anne's Rise)
Lennox Gdns. Croy —1M 63
Lenten Clo. Peasl —2E 136

Lenton Rise—Logan Clo.

Lenton Rise. *Rich* —6L **11**
Leo Ct. *Bren* —3K **11**
Leominster Rd. *Mord* —5A **44**
Leominster Wlk. *Mord* —5A **44**
Leonard Av. *Mord* —4A **44**
Leonard Clo. *Frim* —6B **70**
Leonard Rd. *SW16* —9G **28**
Leonardslee Ct. *Craw* —6F **182**
Leopold Av. *SW19* —6L **27**
Leopold Av. *F'boro* —9N **69**
Leopold Rd. *SW19* —5L **27**
Leopold Rd. *Craw* —3A **182**
Leopold Ter. *SW19* —6M **27**
Le Personne Homes. Cat
(off Banstead Rd.) —9A **84**
Le Personne Rd. *Cat* —9A **84**
Leppington. *Brack* —6N **31**
Leret Way. *Lea* —8H **79**
Lesbourne Rd. *Reig* —4N **121**
Leslie Dunne Ho. *Wind* —5B **4**
Leslie Gdns. *Sutt* —4M **61**
Leslie Gro. *Croy* —7B **46**
Leslie Pk. Rd. *Croy* —7B **46**
Leslie Rd. *Chob* —6H **53**
Leslie Rd. *Dork* —3K **119**
Lessingham Av. *SW17* —5D **28**
Lessness Rd. *Mord* —5A **44**
Lestock Way. *Fleet* —4D **88**
Letchworth Av. *Felt* —1G **22**
Letchworth Ct. *Bew* —6K **181**
Letchworth St. *SW17* —5D **28**
Letcombe Sq. *Brack* —3C **32**
Letcomb Sq. *Brack* —3C **32**
Letterstone Rd. *SW6* —3L **13**
Lettice St. *SW6* —4L **13**
Levana Clo. *SW19* —2K **27**
Levehurst Ho. *SE27* —6N **29**
Leveret Clo. *New Ad* —7N **65**
Leveret La. *Craw* —1N **181**
Leverkusen Rd. *Brack* —2N **31**
Levern Dri. *Farnh* —6H **109**
Leverson St. *SW16* —7G **28**
Levett Rd. *Lea* —7H **79**
Levylsdene. *Guild* —3F **114**
Levylsdene Ct. *Guild* —3F **114**
Lewes Clo. *Craw* —3G **183**
Lewesdon Clo. *SW19* —2J **27**
Lewes Rd. *E Grin & F Row*
—1B **186**
Lewes Rd. *F Row* —9G **186**
Lewin Rd. *SW14* —6C **12**
Lewin Rd. *SW16* —7H **29**
Lewins Rd. *Eps* —1A **80**
Lewis Clo. *Add* —1L **55**
Lewisham Clo. *Craw* —7A **182**
Lewisham Way. *Owl* —6J **49**
Lewis Ho. *Brack* —5N **31**
Lewis Rd. *Mitc* —1B **44**
Lewis Rd. *Rich* —8K **11**
Lewis Rd. *Sutt* —1N **61**
Lexden Rd. *Mitc* —3H **45**
Lexington Ct. *Purl* —6N **63**
Lexton Gdns. *SW12* —2H **29**
Leyborne Pk. *Rich* —4N **11**
Leybourne Av. *Byfl* —9A **56**
Leybourne Clo. *Byfl* —9A **56**
Leybourne Clo. *Craw* —8A **182**
Leybourne Pk. *Rich* —4N **11**
Leyburn Gdns. *Croy* —8B **46**
Leycester Clo. *W'sham* —1M **51**
Leyfield. *Wor Pk* —7D **42**
Leylands La. *Stai* —7H **7**
(in two parts)
Ley Rd. *F'boro* —6M **69**
Ley Side. *Crowt* —2F **48**
Leys Rd. *Oxs* —8D **58**
Leys, The. *W On T* —1N **57**
Leyton Rd. *SW19* —8A **28**
Lezayre Rd. *Orp* —3N **67**
Liberty Av. *SW19* —9A **28**
Liberty Hall Rd. *Add* —2J **55**
Liberty La. *Add* —2J **55**
Liberty M. *SW12* —1F **28**
Liberty Rise. *Add* —3J **55**
Library Way. *Twic* —1C **24**
Lichfield Ct. *Rich* —7L **11**
Lichfield Gdns. *Rich* —7L **11**
Lichfield Rd. *Houn* —6K **9**
Lichfield Rd. *Rich* —4M **11**
Lichfields. *Brack* —1C **32**
Lichfield Ter. *Rich* —8L **11**
Lichfield Way. *S Croy* —6G **65**
Lickey Ho. W14 —2L **13**
(off N. End Rd.)
Lickfolds Rd. *Rowl* —9D **128**
Liddell. *Wind* —6A **4**
Liddell Pl. *Wind* —6A **4**
Liddell Sq. *Wind* —5A **4**
Liddell Way. *Asc* —4K **33**
Liddell Way. *Wind* —6A **4**
Liddington Hall Dri. *Guild*
—9H **93**
Liddington New Rd. *Guild*
—9H **93**
Lidiard Rd. *SW18* —3A **28**
Lidsey Clo. *M'bowr* —6G **183**
Lidstone Clo. *Wok* —4L **73**
Liffords Pl. *SW13* —5E **12**
Lifford St. *SW15* —7J **13**
Lightermans Wlk. *SW18*
—7M **13**
Lightwater By-Pass. *Light*
—5L **51**
Lightwater Meadow. *Light*
—7M **51**
Lightwater Rd. *Light* —7M **51**
Lightwood. *Brack* —5B **32**
Lilac Av. *Wok* —7N **73**
Lilac Clo. *Guild* —8M **93**
Lilac Ct. *Tedd* —5F **24**
Lilac Gdns. *Croy* —9K **47**
Lilian Rd. *SW16* —9G **28**
Lille Barracks. *Alder* —6B **90**
Lilleshall Rd. *Mord* —5B **44**
Lilley Ct. *Crowt* —3G **49**
Lilley Dri. *Kgswd* —9N **81**
Lillian Rd. *SW13* —2F **12**
Lillie Mans. SW6 —2K **13**
(off Lillie Rd.)
Lillie Rd. *SW6* —2J **13**
Lillie Rd. *Big H* —5F **86**
Lillie Yd. *SW6* —2M **13**
Lilliot's La. *Lea* —6G **79**
Lily Clo. *W14* —1J **13**
(in two parts)
Lilyfields Chase. *Ewh* —6F **156**
Lily Hill Dri. *Brack* —1C **32**
Lily Hill Rd. *Brack* —1C **32**
Lilyville Rd. *SW6* —4L **13**
Lime Av. *Asc* —5F **32**
Lime Av. *Camb* —9E **50**
Lime Av. *H'ham* —4N **197**
Lime Av. *Wind* —4J **5**
(Windsor)
Lime Av. *Wind* —4C **18**
(Windsor Great Park)
Limebush Clo. *New H* —5L **55**
Lime Clo. *Cars* —8D **44**
Lime Clo. [illegible] —7M **100**
Lime Clo. *Craw* —9A **162**
Lime Clo. *Reig* —6N **121**
Lime Clo. *W Cla* —6K **95**
Lime Ct. *Mitc* —1B **44**
Lime Cres. *Ash* —2F **110**
Lime Cres. *Sun* —1K **39**
Limecroft. *Yat* —1B **68**
Limecroft Clo. *Eps* —4C **60**
Limecroft Rd. *Knap* —4E **72**
Lime Gro. *Add* —1J **55**
Lime Gro. *Guild* —8L **93**
Lime Gro. *N Mald* —2C **42**
Lime Gro. *Twic* —9F **10**
Lime Gro. *Warl* —5H **85**
Lime Gro. *W Cla* —6J **95**
Lime Gro. *Wok* —8A **74**
Lime Meadow Av. *S Croy*
—9D **64**
Limerick Clo. *SW12* —1G **28**
Limerick Clo. *Brack* —9M **15**
Lime Rd. *Rich* —7M **11**
Limes Av. *SW13* —5E **12**
Limes Av. *Cars* —7D **44**
Limes Av. *Croy* —9L **45**
Limes Av. *Horl* —9F **142**
Limes Clo. *Ashf* —6B **22**
Limes Field Rd. *SW14* —6D **12**
Limes Gdns. *SW18* —9M **13**
Limes Pl. *Croy* —6A **46**
Limes Rd. *Beck* —1L **47**
Limes Rd. *Croy* —6A **46**
Limes Rd. *Egh* —6B **20**
Limes Rd. *F'boro* —9H **69**
Limes Rd. *Wey* —1B **56**
Limes Row. *Farn* —2K **67**
Limes, The. *SW18* —9M **13**
Limes, The. *Eden* —7A **44**
Limes, The. *Felb* —5K **165**
Limes, The. *Lea* —1H **99**
Limes, The. *W Mol* —3B **40**
Limes, The. *Wok* —2N **73**
Lime St. *Alder* —2L **109**
Lime Tree Av. *Esh & Th Dit*
—7E **40**
Limetree Clo. *SW2* —2K **29**
Lime Tree Clo. *Bookh* —2A **98**
Lime Tree Ct. *Asht* —5L **79**
Lime Tree Ct. *S Croy* —3N **63**
Lime Tree Gro. *Croy* —9J **47**
Lime Tree Pl. *Mitc* —9F **28**
Lime Tree Rd. *Houn* —4B **10**
Limetree Wlk. *SW17* —6E **28**
Lime Tree Wlk. *Vir W* —3A **36**
Lime Tree Wlk. *W Wick* —1B **66**
Lime Wlk. *Brack* —3A **32**
Lime Wlk. *Shere* —8A **116**
Limeway Ter. *Dork* —3G **118**
Limewood Clo. *Wok* —7G **73**
Lime Works Rd. *Mers* —4G **102**
Limpsfield Av. *SW19* —3J **27**
Limpsfield Av. *T Hth* —4K **45**
Limpsfield Rd. *S Croy & Warl*
—8D **64**
Linacre Dri. *H'ham* —7D **176**
Lince La. *Westc* —5D **118**
Linchfield Rd. *Dat* —4M **5**
Linchmere Pl. *Craw* —2M **181**
Linchmere Rd. *Hasl* —5A **188**
Lincoln Av. *SW19* —4J **27**
Lincoln Av. *Twic* —3C **24**
Lincoln Clo. *SE25* —5D **46**
Lincoln Clo. *Camb* —2F **70**
Lincoln Clo. *Craw* —6C **182**
Lincoln Clo. *Horl* —9E **142**
Lincoln Dri. *Wok* —2G **75**
Lincoln M. *SE21* —3N **29**
Lincoln Rd. *SE25* —2E **46**
Lincoln Rd. *Dork* —3J **119**
Lincoln Rd. *Felt* —4N **23**
Lincoln Rd. *Guild* —1J **113**
Lincoln Rd. *Mitc* —4J **45**
Lincoln Rd. *N Mald* —2B **42**
Lincoln Rd. *Wor Pk* —7G **42**
Lincolnshire Gdns. *Warf* —8C **16**
Lincolns Mead. *Ling* —8N **145**
Lincoln Wlk. *Eps* —6C **60**
(in two parts)
Lincoln Way. *Sun* —9F **22**
Lincombe Ct. *Add* —2K **55**
Lindale Clo. *Vir W* —3J **35**
Lindbergh Rd. *Wall* —4J **63**
Linden. *Brack* —4D **32**
Linden Av. *Coul* —3F **82**
Linden Av. *E Grin* —8M **165**
Linden Av. *Houn* —8B **10**
Linden Av. *T Hth* —3M **45**
Linden Clo. *Craw* —6E **182**
Linden Clo. *H'ham* —4L **197**
Linden Clo. *New H* —7J **55**
Linden Clo. *Tad* —7J **81**
Linden Clo. *Th Dit* —6F **40**
Linden Ct. *Camb* —8D **50**
Linden Ct. *Egh* —7L **19**
Linden Ct. *Lea* —8H **79**
Linden Cres. *King T* —1M **41**
Linden Dri. *Cat* —2N **103**
Linden Gdns. *W4* —1D **12**
Linden Gdns. *Lea* —8J **79**
Linden Gro. *N Mald* —2D **42**
Linden Gro. [illegible]
Linden Gro. *W On T* —8G **39**
Linden Gro. *Warl* —5H **85**
Lindenhill Rd. *Brack* —9L **15**
Linden Ho. *Hamp* —7B **24**
Linden Ho. *Langl* —1D **6**
Linden Lea. *Dork* —7J **119**
Linden Leas. *W Wick* —8N **47**
Linden Pit Path. *Lea* —8H **79**
(in two parts)
Linden Pl. *E Hor* —4F **96**
Linden Pl. *Eps* —8D **60**
Linden Pl. *Mitc* —3C **44**
Linden Pl. *Stai* —5J **21**
Linden Rd. *Guild* —3N **113**
Linden Rd. *Hamp* —8A **24**
Linden Rd. *Head* —4G **169**
Linden Rd. *Lea* —8H **79**
Linden Rd. *Wey* —5D **56**
Lindens Clo. *Eff* —6M **97**
Lindens, The. *W4* —4B **12**
Lindens, The. *Copt* —7M **163**
Lindens, The. *Farnh* —3J **129**
Lindens, The. *New Ad* —3M **65**
Linden Way. *Purl* —6G **63**
Linden Way. *Rip* —3H **95**
Linden Way. *Shep* —4D **38**
Linden Way. *Wok* —8B **74**
Lindfield Gdns. *Guild* —2B **114**
Lindfield Rd. *Croy* —5C **46**
Lindford Chase. *Lind* —4A **168**
Lindford Rd. *Bord* —3A **168**
Lindford Wey. *Lind* —4A **168**
Lindgren Wlk. *Craw* —8N **181**
Lindisfarne Rd. *SW20* —8F **26**
Lindley Ct. *King T* —9J **25**
Lindley Rd. *God* —8F **104**
Lindley Rd. *W On T* —9L **39**
Lindores Rd. *Cars* —7A **44**
Lind Rd. *Sutt* —2A **62**
Lindrop St. *SW6* —5N **13**
Lindsay Clo. *Chess* —4L **59**
Lindsay Clo. *Eps* —9B **60**
Lindsay Clo. *Stai* —8M **7**
Lindsay Dri. *Shep* —5E **38**
Lindsay Rd. *Hamp* —5B **24**
Lindsay Rd. *New H* —6J **55**
Lindsay Rd. *Wor Pk* —8G **43**
Lindsey Clo. *Mitc* —3J **45**
Lindsey Gdns. *Felt* —1E **22**
Lindum Clo. *Alder* —3M **109**
Lindum Dene. *Alder* —3M **109**
Lindum Rd. *Tedd* —8J **25**
Lindway. *SE27* —6M **29**
Linersh Dri. *Brmly* —5C **134**
Linersh Wood. *Brmly* —5C **134**
Linersh Wood Clo. *Brmly*
—6C **134**
Lines Rd. *Hurst* —5A **14**
Linfield Clo. *W On T* —2J **57**
Ling Cres. *Head* —3G **169**
Ling Dri. *Light* —8K **51**
Lingfield Av. *King T* —3L **41**
Lingfield Comn. Rd. *Ling*
—5M **145**
Lingfield Dri. *Worth* —2J **183**
Lingfield Gdns. *Coul* —6M **83**
Lingfield Rd. *SW19* —6J **27**
Lingfield Rd. *E Grin* —6N **165**
Lingfield Rd. *Eden* —3H **147**
Lingfield Rd. *Wor Pk* —9H **43**
Lingmala Gro. *C Crook* —8C **88**
Lings Coppice. *SE21* —3N **29**
Lingwell Rd. *SW17* —4C **28**
Lingwood. *Brack* —5A **32**
Lingwood Gdns. *Iswth* —3E **10**
Link Av. *Wok* —2F **74**
Linkfield. *W Mol* —2B **40**
Linkfield Corner. *Red* —3C **122**
Linkfield Gdns. *Red* —3C **122**
Linkfield La. *Red* —2C **122**
Linkfield Rd. *Iswth* —5F **10**
Linkfield St. *Red* —3C **122**
Link La. *Wall* —3H **63**
Link Rd. *Add* —1N **55**
Link Rd. *Dat* —4M **5**
Link Rd. *Felt* —1G **23**
Link Rd. *Wall* —7E **44**
Links Av. *Mord* —3M **43**
(in two parts)
Links Brow. *Fet* —2E **98**
Links Clo. *Asht* —4J **79**
Links Clo. *Ewh* —4F **156**
Linkscroft Av. *Ashf* —7C **22**
Links Gdns. *SW16* —8L **29**
Links Grn. Way. *Cobh* —1A **78**
Linkside. *N Mald* —1D **42**
Linkside E. *Hind* —2A **170**
Linkside N. *Hind* —2N **169**
Linkside S. *Hind* —3A **170**
Linkside W. *Hind* —2N **169**
Links Pl. *Asht* —4K **79**
Links Rd. *SW17* —7E **28**
Links Rd. *Ashf* —6N **21**
Links Rd. *Asht* —5J **79**
Links Rd. *Brmly* —4A **134**
Links Rd. *Eps* —9F **60**
Links Rd. *W Wick* —7M **47**
Links, The. *Asc* —1J **33**
Links, The. *W On T* —8H **39**
Links View Av. *Brock* —9N **119**
Links View Ct. *Hamp* —5D **24**
Links View Rd. *Croy* —9K **47**
Links View Rd. *Hamp* —6C **24**
Links Way. *Beck* —5K **47**
Links Way. *Bookh* —6M **97**
Links Way. *F'boro* —2H **89**
Link, The. *Craw* —2B **182**
(in two parts)
Link, The. *Tedd* —7F **24**
Link, The. *Yat* —9B **48**
Linkway. *SW20* —2G **43**
Linkway. *Camb* —2A **70**
Linkway. *Crowt* —2E **48**
Linkway. *Fleet* —7A **88**
Linkway. *Guild* —2J **113**
Linkway. *Rich* —3H **25**
Link Way. *Stai* —7K **21**
Linkway. *Wok* —4E **74**
Linkway Pde. *Fleet* —7A **88**
Linkway, The. *Sutt* —5A **62**
Linley Ct. *Sutt* —1A **62**
Linnell Rd. *Red* —4E **122**
Linnet Clo. *Craw* —4F **184**
Linnet Clo. *S Croy* —6G **65**
Linnet Gro. *Guild* —1F **114**
Linnet M. *SW12* —1E **28**
Linsford Bus. Pk. *Myt* —2D **90**
Linsford La. *Myt* —2D **90**
Linslade Clo. *Houn* —8M **9**
Linstead Rd. *F'boro* —6K **69**
Linstead Way. *SW18* —1K **27**
Linsted La. *Head* —2C **168**
Lintaine Clo. *W6* —2K **13**
Linton Clo. *Mitc* —6D **44**
Linton Glade. *Croy* —5H **65**
(in two parts)
Linton Gro. *SE27* —6M **29**
Lintons La. *Eps* —8D **60**
Lintott Ct. *Stanw* —9M **7**
Lintott Gdns. *H'ham* —5L **197**
Linver Rd. *SW6* —5M **13**
Lion Av. *Twic* —2F **24**
Lion Clo. *Hasl* —1D **188**
Lion Clo. *Shep* —2N **37**
Lionel Rd. *Bren* —1L **11**
(in two parts)
Lion Ga. Gdns. *Rich* —6M **11**
Liongate M. *E Mol* —2F **40**
Lion Grn. *Hasl* —2D **188**
Lion Grn. Rd. *Coul* —3H **83**
Lion & Lamb Way. *Farnh*
—1G **128**
Lion & Lamb Yd. *Farnh*
—1G **129**
Lion La. *Gray & Hasl* —8D **170**
Lion La. *Red* —2D **122**
Lion La. *Turn H* —5D **184**
Lion Mead. *Hasl* —2D **188**
Lion Pk. Av. *Chess* —1N **59**
Lion Retail Pk. *Wok* —3D **74**
Lion Rd. *Croy* —4N **45**
Lion Rd. *Twic* —2F **24**
Lion's La. *Alf* —3K **175**
Lion Way. *Bren* —3K **11**
Lion Way. *C Crook* —8C **88**
Lion Wharf Rd. *Iswth* —6H **11**
Lipcombe Cotts. *Alb* —3L **135**
Liphook Rd. *Hasl* —2C **188**
Liphook Rd. *Head & Pass*
—6D **168**
Liphook Rd. *Pass & Hasl*
—4A **188**
Liphook Rd. *Lind* —4A **168**
Liphook Rd. *W'hill* —9A **168**
Lipsham Clo. *Bans* —9B **62**
Lisbon Av. *Twic* —3C **24**
Liscombe. *Brack* —6N **31**
Liscombe Ho. *Brack* —6N **31**
Lisgar Ter. *W14* —1L **13**
Liskeard Dri. *F'boro* —8M **69**
Lismore. SW19 —6L **27**
(off Woodside)
Lismore Clo. *Iswth* —5G **10**
Lismore Cres. *Craw* —6N **181**
Lismore Rd. *S Croy* —3B **64**
Lismoyne Clo. *Fleet* —3A **88**
Lissoms Rd. *Coul* —5E **82**
Lister Av. *E Grin* —3A **186**
Lister Clo. *Mitc* —9C **28**
Listergate Ct. *SW15* —7H **13**
Lister Ho. *Hayes* —1F **8**
Litchfield Av. *Mord* —6L **43**
Litchfield Rd. *Sutt* —1A **62**
Litchfield Way. *Guild* —5J **113**
Lithgow's Rd. *H'row A* —7F **8**
Lit. Acre. *Beck* —2K **47**
Lit. Austins Rd. *Farnh* —3J **129**
Lit. Benty. *W Dray* —1M **7**
Lit. Birch Clo. *New H* —5M **55**
Lit. Boltons, The. *SW5 & SW10*
—1N **13**
Lit. Bookham St. *Bookh* —1N **97**
Lit. Borough. *Brock* —4N **119**
Littlebrook Clo. *Croy* —5G **47**
Lit. Browns La. *Eden* —8G **127**
Lit. Buntings. *Wind* —6C **4**
Lit. Collins. *Out* —4M **143**
Littlecombe Clo. *SW15* —9J **13**
Lit. Common La. *Blet* —1M **123**
Lit. Comptons. *H'ham* —6M **197**
Lit. Copse. *Fleet* —8A **88**
Lit. Copse. *Yat* —8C **48**
Littlecote Clo. *SW19* —1K **27**
Little Ct. *W Wick* —8N **47**
Lit. Crabtree. *Craw* —2A **182**
Lit. Cranmore La. *W Hor* —6C **96**
Lit. Croft. *Yat* —2C **68**
Littlecroft Rd. *Egh* —6B **20**
Littledale Clo. *Brack* —2C **32**
Lit. Dimocks. *SW12* —3F **28**
Lit. Elms. *Hayes* —3E **8**
Lit. Ferry Rd. *Twic* —2H **25**
Littlefield Clo. *Ash* —3E **110**
Littlefield Clo. *Guild* —8G **92**
Littlefield Clo. *King T* —1L **41**
Littlefield Gdns. *Ash* —3E **110**
Littlefield Way. *Guild* —8G **92**
Littleford La. *B'hth & Sham G*
—2G **135**
Lit. Fryth. *Finch* —1B **48**
Lit. Grebe. *H'ham* —3J **197**
Little Grn. *Rich* —7K **11**
Lit. Green La. *Cher* —9G **36**
Lit. Green La. *Farnh* —4F **128**
Lit. Green La. Farm Est. *Cher*
—1F **54**
Lit. Halliards. *W On T* —5H **39**
Lit. Haven La. *H'ham* —3M **197**
Littleheath La. *Cobh* —1A **78**
Lit. Heath Rd. *Chob* —5H **53**
Littleheath Rd. *S Croy* —4E **64**
Lit. Hide. *Guild* —1D **114**
Lit. Holland Bungalows. *Cat*
—1A **104**
Lit. Kiln. *G'ming* —3H **133**
Lit. King St. *E Grin* —9A **166**
Lit. London. *Abry* —1N **135**
Lit. London. *Witl* —5B **152**
Lit. London Hill. *H'ham* —7G **179**
Lit. Lullenden. *Ling* —6N **145**
Lit. Manor Gdns. *Cranl* —8N **155**
Lit. Mead. *Cranl* —8K **155**
Littlemead. *Esh* —1D **58**
Lit. Mead. *Wok* —3J **73**
Lit. Mead Ind. Est. *Cranl*
—7K **155**
Lit. Moor. *Sand* —6H **49**
Lit. Moreton Clo. *W Byf* —8K **55**
Lit. Orchard. *Wok* —1C **74**
Lit. Orchard. *Wdhm* —7J **55**
Lit. Orchard Way. *Shalf* —2A **134**
Lit. Paddock. *Camb* —7E **50**
Lit. Park Dri. *Felt* —3M **23**
Lit. Platt. *Guild* —2G **112**
Lit. Queen's Rd. *Tedd* —7F **24**
Lit. Ringdale. *Brack* —3C **32**
Lit. Roke Av. *Kenl* —1M **83**
Lit. Roke Rd. *Kenl* —1N **83**
Littlers Clo. *SW19* —1B **44**
Lit. St Leonard's. *SW14* —6B **12**
Little St. *Guild* —8L **93**
Lit. Sutton La. *Slou* —1E **6**
Lit. Thatch. *G'ming* —5J **133**
Lit. Thurbans Clo. *Farnh*
—5F **128**
Littleton La. *Guild* —8K **113**
Littleton La. *Reig* —5J **121**
Littleton La. *Shep* —6M **37**
Littleton Rd. *Ashf* —8D **22**
Littleton St. *SW18* —3A **28**
Lit. Tumners Ct. *G'ming*
—5H **133**
Lit. Vigo. *Yat* —2A **68**
Lit. Warkworth Ho. *Iswth*
—5H **11**
Lit. Warren Clo. *Guild* —5D **114**
Lit. Wellington St. *Alder*
—2M **109**
Littlewick Rd. *Knap* —3H **73**
Littlewood. *Cranl* —7A **156**
Lit. Woodcote Est. *Cars* —7E **62**
Lit. Woodcote La. *Cars & Purl*
—8F **62**
Lit. Woodlands. *Wind* —6C **4**
Lit. Wood St. *King T* —1K **41**
Littleworth Av. *Esh* —2D **58**
Littleworth Comn. Rd. *Esh*
—9D **40**
Littleworth La. *Esh* —1D **58**
Littleworth Pl. *Esh* —1D **58**
Littleworth Rd. *Esh* —2D **58**
Littleworth Rd. *Seale* —2C **130**
Liverpool Rd. *King T* —8N **25**
Liverpool Rd. *T Hth* —2N **45**
Livesey Clo. *King T* —2M **41**
Livingstone Mans. W14 —2K **13**
(off Queen's Club Gdns.)
Livingstone Rd. *Cat* —9A **84**
Livingstone Rd. *Craw* —5C **182**
Livingstone Rd. *H'ham* —7K **197**
Livingstone Rd. *Houn* —7C **10**
Livingstone Rd. *T Hth* —1A **46**
Llanaway Clo. *G'ming* —5J **133**
Llanaway Rd. *G'ming* —5J **133**
Llangar Gro. *Crowt* —2F **48**
Llanthony Rd. *Mord* —4B **44**
Llanvair Clo. *Asc* —5L **33**
Llanvair Dri. *Asc* —5K **33**
Lloyd Av. *SW16* —9J **29**
Lloyd Av. *Coul* —1E **82**
Lloyd Pk. Av. *Croy* —1C **64**
Lloyd Rd. *Wor Pk* —9J **43**
Lloyds Ct. *Craw* —9C **162**
Lloyds Way. *Beck* —4H **47**
Lobelia Rd. *Bisl* —2D **72**
Lochaline St. *W6* —2H **13**
Lochinvar St. *SW12* —1F **28**
Lochinver. *Brack* —6N **31**
Lock Clo. *Wdhm* —9G **55**
Locke King Clo. *Wey* —4B **56**
Locke King Rd. *Wey* —4B **56**
Lockesley Sq. *Surb* —5K **41**
Lockets Clo. *Wind* —4A **4**
Locke Way. *Wok* —4B **74**
Lockfield Dri. *Knap* —3H **73**
Lockfield Dri. *Wok* —4A **74**
Lockhart Rd. *Cobh* —9K **57**
Lockhurst Hatch La. *Alb*
—5N **135**
Lockie Pl. *SE25* —2D **46**
Lock Island. *Shep* —8B **38**
Lock La. *Wok* —3K **75**
Lock Path. *Dor* —2A **4**
Lock Rd. *Alder* —8B **90**
Lock Rd. *Guild* —9N **93**
Lock Rd. *Rich* —5J **25**
Locks La. *Mitc* —1E **44**
Locksley Dri. *Wok* —4J **73**
Locksmeade Rd. *Rich* —5J **25**
Locks Meadow. *D'land* —1C **166**
Locks Ride. *Asc* —8F **16**
Lockswood. *Brkwd* —7E **72**
Lockton Chase. *Asc* —2H **33**
Lockwood Clo. *F'boro* —6K **69**
Lockwood Clo. *H'ham* —3N **197**
Lockwood Ct. *Craw* —1D **182**
Lockwood Path. *Wok* —9G **54**
Lockwood Way. *Chess* —2N **59**
Loddon Clo. *Camb* —9E **50**
Loddon Rd. *F'boro* —8J **69**
Loddon Way. *Ash* —3E **110**
Loder Clo. *Wok* —9F **54**
Lodge Av. *SW14* —6D **12**
Lodge Av. *Croy* —9L **45**
Lodgebottom Rd. *Dork* —5N **99**
Lodge Clo. *Alder* —4M **109**
Lodge Clo. *Craw* —3A **182**
Lodge Clo. *E Grin* —9M **165**
Lodge Clo. *Egh* —6N **19**
Lodge Clo. *Eps* —6H **61**
Lodge Clo. *Fet* —9D **78**
Lodge Clo. *Iswth* —4H **11**
Lodge Clo. *N Holm* —9J **119**
Lodge Clo. *Stoke D* —3N **77**
Lodge Clo. *Wall* —7E **44**
Lodge Gdns. *Beck* —4J **47**
Lodge Gro. *Yat* —9E **48**
Lodge Hill. *Purl* —2L **83**
Lodge Hill Clo. *Lwr Bo* —5J **129**
Lodge Hill Rd. *Lwr Bo* —5J **129**
Lodge La. *Holmw* —4L **139**
Lodge La. *New Ad* —3K **65**
Lodge La. *Red* —3C **142**
Lodge La. *W'ham* —5L **107**
Lodge Pl. *Sutt* —2N **61**
Lodge Rd. *Croy* —5M **45**
Lodge Rd. *Fet* —9C **78**
Lodge Rd. *Wall* —2F **62**
Lodge Wlk. Horl —8D **142**
(off Thornton Pl.)
Lodge Way. *Ashf* —3N **21**
Lodge Way. *Shep* —1D **38**
Lodge Way. *Wind* —6B **4**
Lodkin Hill. *Hasc* —4N **153**
Lodsworth. *F'boro* —2J **89**
Loft Ho. Pl. *Chess* —3J **59**
Logan Clo. *Houn* —6N **9**

Logmore La. Dork —7B 118
Lois Dri. Shep —4C 38
Lollesworth La. W Hor —4D 96
Loman Rd. Myt —1E 90
Lomas Clo. Croy —4M 65
Lombard Bus. Pk. Croy —6K 45
Lombard Rd. SW19 —1N 43
Lombard Roundabout. (Junct.) —6K 45
Lombard St. Shack —5K 131
Lombardy Clo. Wok —4J 73
Lomond Gdns. S Croy —4H 65
Loncin Mead Av. New H —5L 55
London-Biggin Hill Airport. Big H —9F 66
London Fields Ho. Craw —8A 182
London-Gatwick Airport. Gat —4C 162
London-Heathrow Airport. H'row A —5N 7
London La. E Hor —9G 97
London La. Shere —7B 116
London Rd. SW16 & T Hth —9K 29
London Rd. Asc & S'hill —2M 33
London Rd. Bag —6F 50
London Rd. B'water —4A 68
London Rd. Brack & Asc —1B 32
London Rd. Cat —1A 104
London Rd. Craw —2B 182
London Rd. Croy —5M 45
London Rd. Dork —4H 119
London Rd. E Grin —7L 165
London Rd. Egh —1L 35
London Rd. Ewe & Sutt —5E 60
London Rd. Felt —4K 21
London Rd. F Row —5G 186
London Rd. Guild & Send —4A 114
London Rd. Hand —5N 199
London Rd. Hind —5D 170
London Rd. H'ham —6J 197
London Rd. Houn & Iswth —6C 10
London Rd. Iswth & Bren —5F 10
London Rd. King T —1L 41
London Rd. Mitc & SW17 —3C 44
London Rd. Mord —4M 43
London Rd. Red —2D 122
London Rd. Reig —3M 121
London Rd. Sand —1L 69
London Rd. Slou —1A 6
London Rd. Stai & Ashf —5J 21
London Rd. S'dale —7C 34
London Rd. Twic —8G 10
London Rd. Vir W —4H 35
London Rd. Wall & Mitc —1F 62
London Rd. W'ham —1L 107
London Rd. W'sham —1L 51
London Rd. Wokgm & Binf —2C 30
London Rd. N. Mers —4F 102
London Rd. S. Mers —8E 102
London Stile. W4 —1N 11
London St. Cher —6J 37
Loneacre. W'sham —3B 52
Lone Oak. Horl —1M 163
Lonesome La. Reig —7N 121
Lonesome Way. SW16 —9G 28
Longacre. Ash —2E 110
Long Acre. Craw D —1D 184
Longacre Pl. Cars —3E 62
Long Beech Dri. F'boro —2H 89
Longbourne Grn. G'ming —3H 133
Longbourne Way. Cher —5H 37
Longboyds. Cobh —2J 77
Long Bri. Farnh —1H 129
Longbridge Wlk. Horl —1D 162
Longbridge Way. Gat A —1D 162
Longchamp Clo. Horl —8G 143
Long Clo. Craw —3H 183
Long Comn. Sham G —8E 134
Long Copse Clo. Bookh —1B 98
Longcroft Av. Bans —1A 82
Long Cross Hill. Head —4D 168
Longcross Rd. Chob —9J 35
Longcross Rd. Longc —9K 35
Longdene Rd. Hasl —2F 188
Longdon Wood. Kes —1G 66
Longdown. Fleet —7A 88
Longdown Chase Cotts. Gray —6E 170
Longdown Clo. Lwr Bo —5H 129
Longdown La. N. Eps —1F 80
Longdown La. S. Eps —1F 80
Longdown Lodge. Sand —7G 48
Longdown Rd. Eps —1F 80
Longdown Rd. Guild —6D 114
Longdown Rd. Lwr Bo —6G 129
Longdown Rd. Sand —6F 48
Long Dyke. Guild —1D 114
Longfellow Clo. H'ham —1L 197
Longfellow Rd. Wor Pk —7F 42
Longfield Av. Wall —7E 44
Longfield Clo. F'boro —6M 69
Longfield Cres. Tad —7H 81
Longfield Dri. SW14 —8A 12
Longfield Dri. Mitc —9C 28
Longfield Rd. Ash —2E 110
Longfield Rd. Dork —6F 118
Longfield Rd. H'ham —8G 196
Longfield St. SW18 —1M 27
Longford Av. Felt —9F 8
Longford Av. Stai —2N 21
Longford Cir. W Dray —4K 7
Longford Clo. Camb —2B 70
Longford Clo. Hamp —5A 24
Longford Ct. Eps —1B 60
Longford Gdns. Sutt —9A 44
Longford Ho. Hamp —5A 24
Longford Rd. Twic —2A 24
Longford Wlk. SW2 —1L 29
Longford Way. Stai —2N 21
Long Garden M. Farnh —1G 129
(off Long Garden Wlk.)
Long Garden Pl. Farnh —1G 128
Long Garden Wlk. Farnh —1G 129
Long Garden Wlk. E. Farnh —9G 109
Long Garden Wlk. W. Farnh —9G 109
Long Garden Way. Farnh —1G 128
Long Gore. G'ming —2H 133
Long Gro. Rd. Eps —6A 60
Longheath Gdns. Croy —4F 46
Long Hedges. Houn —5A 10
Long Hill. Seale —2C 130
Long Hill. Wold —8G 85
Long Hill Rd. Asc —1E 32
Longhope Dri. Wrec —5F 128
Long Houses. Pirb —2A 92
Longhurst Rd. Craw —8M 181
Longhurst Rd. Croy —5E 46
Longhurst Rd. E Hor —7F 96
Longlands Av. Coul —1E 82
Longlands Way. Camb —1H 71
Long La. Croy —5F 46
Long La. Stai —3A 22
Long La. Wok —7E 14
Longleat Sq. F'boro —2C 90
Longleat Way. Felt —1E 22
Longley Rd. SW17 —7C 28
Longley Rd. Croy —6M 45
Longley Rd. Farnh —2J 129
Longley Trad. Est. Craw —4C 182
Long Lodge Dri. W On T —9K 39
Longmead. Fleet —7B 88
Longmead. Guild —3E 114
Longmead. Wind —4B 4
Longmead Bus. Cen. Eps —7C 60
Longmead Clo. Cat —9B 84
Longmead Ho. SE27 —6N 29
Longmeadow. Bookh —3N 97
Longmeadow. Frim —3D 70
Long Meadow Clo. W Wick —6M 47
Longmead Rd. SW17 —6D 28
Longmead Rd. Eps —7C 60
Longmead Rd. Th Dit —6E 40
Longmere Gdns. Tad —6H 81
Longmere Rd. Craw —1B 182
Long Mickle. Sand —6F 48
Longmoors. Brack —9K 15
Longmore Rd. W On T —1M 57
Longpoles Rd. Cranl —8A 156
Long Reach. Ock & W Hors —1B 96
Longridge Gro. Wok —1H 75
Longridge Rd. SW5 —1M 13
Long Rd., The. Rowl —8E 128
Longs Clo. Wok —3J 75
Longs Ct. Rich —7M 11
Long Shaw. Lea —7G 79
Longshot Ind. Est. Brack —1K 31
Longshot La. Brack —2K 31
(in two parts)
Longshott Ct. SW5 —1M 13
(off W. Cromwell Rd.)
Longside Clo. Egh —9E 20
Longstaff Cres. SW18 —1M 27
Longstaff Rd. SW18 —9M 13
Longstone Rd. SW17 —6F 28
Long's Way. Wokgm —1D 30
Longthornton Rd. SW16 —1G 45
Long Wlk. SW13 —5E 12
Long Wlk. Crock H —9K 107
Long Wlk. Eps —6H 81
Long Wlk. Farnh —9G 108
Long Wlk. Guild —8N 95
Long Wlk. N Mald —2B 42
Long Wlk. Send —7A 96
Long Wlk. W Byf —1L 75
Long Wlk., The. Wind —8G 5
Longwater Rd. Brack —5A 32
Long Ways. Stai —9G 21
Longwood Dri. SW15 —9F 12
Longwood Rd. Kenl —3A 84
Longwood View. Craw —6E 182
Longyard Ho. Horl —6F 142
Lonsdale Ct. Surb —6K 41
Lonsdale Gdns. T Hth —3K 45
Lonsdale M. Rich —4N 11
Lonsdale Rd. SE25 —3E 46
Lonsdale Rd. SW13 —4E 12
Lonsdale Rd. Dork —4H 119
Lonsdale Rd. Wey —4B 56
Loop Rd. Eps —3B 80
Loop Rd. Wok —7B 74
Loppets Rd. Craw —5D 182
Lorac Ct. Sutt —4M 61
Loraine Gdns. Asht —4L 79
Loraine Ho. Wall —1F 62
Loraine Rd. W4 —2A 12
Lord Chancellor Wlk. King T —9C 26
Lordell Pl. SW19 —7H 27
Lord Knyvett Clo. Stai —9M 7
Lord Napier Pl. W6 —1F 12
Lord Roberts M. SW6 —3N 13
Lordsbury Field. Wall —6G 63
Lords Clo. SE21 —3N 29
Lords Clo. Felt —3M 23
Lordsgrove Clo. Tad —7G 81
Lordshill Rd. Sham G —6E 134
Loretto Clo. Cranl —7A 156
Lorian Dri. Reig —2A 122
Loriners. Craw —6B 182
Loring Rd. Iswth —5F 10
Loring Rd. Wind —4C 4
Lorne Av. Croy —6G 47
Lorne Gdns. Croy —6G 47
Lorne Rd. Rich —8M 11
Lorne, The. Bookh —4A 98
Lorraine Rd. Camb —7D 50
Lory Ridge. Bag —3J 51
Loseberry Rd. Clay —2D 58
Loseley Rd. G'ming —3H 133
Losfield Rd. Wind —4B 4
Lothian Rd. Pirb —8L 71
Lothian Wood. Tad —9G 80
Lots Rd. SW10 —3N 13
Lotus Clo. SE21 —4N 29
Lotus Rd. Big H —5H 87
Loubet St. SW17 —7D 28
Loudwater Clo. Sun —3H 39
Loudwater Rd. Sun —3H 39
Loughborough. Brack —5C 32
Louisa Ct. Twic —3E 24
Louise Margaret Rd. Alder —1A 110
Louis Fields. Guild —8F 92
Louisville Rd. SW17 —4E 28
Lovat Wlk. Houn —3M 9
Lovedean Ct. Brack —5C 32
Lovejoy La. Wind —5A 4
Lovekyn Clo. King T —1L 41
Lovelace Clo. Eff J —1H 97
Lovelace Dri. Wok —3G 75
Lovelace Gdns. Surb —6K 41
Lovelace Gdns. W On T —2K 57
Lovelace Rd. SE21 —3N 29
Lovelace Rd. Brack —3K 31
Lovelace Rd. Surb —6J 41
Lovelands La. Chob —9F 52
Lovelands La. Tad —5N 101
Love La. SE25 —2E 46
(in two parts)
Love La. Ash —2F 110
Love La. Dork —6C 158
Love La. God —1F 124
Love La. Mitc —2C 44
(in two parts)
Love La. Mord —6M 43
Love La. Surb —8J 41
Love La. Sutt —3K 61
Love La. Tad —4E 100
Love La. Yat —9A 48
Loveletts. Craw —4M 181
Lovel La. Wink —5M 17
Lovell Path. If'd —4K 181
Lovell Rd. Rich —4J 25
Lovells Clo. Light —6M 51
Lovelock Clo. Kenl —4N 83
Lovel Rd. Wink —5K 17
Lovers La. Fren —3H 149
Lovers La. H'ham —9J 197
Lovett Dri. Cars —6A 44
Lovett Rd. Stai —5E 20
Lovibonds Av. Orp —1K 67
Lowbury. Brack —3C 32
Lowburys. Dork —8H 119
Lowdell's Clo. E Grin —6M 165
Lowdell's Dri. E Grin —6M 165
Lowdell's La. E Grin —6L 165
Lowe Clo. Craw —9N 181
Lwr. Addiscombe Rd. Croy —7B 46
Lwr. Barn Clo. H'ham —3M 197
Lwr. Barn Rd. Purl —8N 63
Lwr. Breache Rd. Ewh —6H 157
Lwr. Bridge Rd. Red —3D 122
Lwr. Broadmoor Rd. Crowt —3H 49
Lwr. Canes. Yat —9A 48
Lwr. Charles St. Camb —9A 50
Lwr. Church La. Farnh —1G 129
Lwr. Church Rd. Sand —6D 48
Lwr. Church St. Croy —8M 45
Lwr. Common S. SW15 —6G 13
Lwr. Coombe St. Croy —1N 63
Lwr. Court Rd. Eps —7B 60
Lwr. Dene. E Grin —9C 166
Lwr. Downs Rd. SW20 —9J 27
Lwr. Drayton Pl. Croy —8M 45
Lwr. Dunnymans. Bans —1L 81
Lwr. Eashing. G'ming —7C 132
Lwr. Edgeborough Rd. Guild —4B 114
Lwr. Farm Rd. Eff —2J 97
Lwr. Farnham Rd. Alder —5N 109
Lwr. Forecourt. Horl —3F 162
(off Ring Rd. S.)
Lwr. George St. Rich —8K 11
Lwr. Green Rd. Esh —8B 40
Lwr. Green W. Mitc —2C 44
Lwr. Grove Rd. Rich —9M 11
Lwr. Guildford Rd. Knap —4G 72
Lwr. Ham La. Elst —7J 131
Lwr. Hampton Rd. Sun —2K 39
Lwr. Ham Rd. King T —6K 25
Lwr. Hanger. Hasl —2A 188
Lwr. Hill Rd. Eps —8A 60
Lowerhouse La. Dork —7K 157
Lwr. House Rd. Witl —9K 151
Lwr. Mall. W6 —1G 12
Lwr. Manor Rd. G'ming —5H 133
Lwr. Manor Rd. Milf —1B 152
Lwr. Marsh La. King T —3M 41
Lwr. Mere. E Grin —1B 186
Lwr. Mill. Eps —4E 60
Lwr. Mill Field. Bag —5H 51
Lwr. Moor. Yat —1C 68
Lwr. Morden La. Mord —5H 43
Lwr. Mortlake Rd. Rich —7L 11
Lwr. Moushill La. Milf —1A 152
Lwr. Nelson St. Alder —2M 109
Lwr. Newport Rd. Alder —3B 110
Lwr. Northfield. Bans —1L 81
Lwr. Nursery. Asc —4D 34
Lwr. Park Rd. Coul —5C 82
Lwr. Peryers. E Hor —6F 96
Lwr. Pillory Downs. Cars —9F 62
Lwr. Pyrford Rd. Wok —3K 75
Lwr. Richmond Rd. SW15 —6G 12
Lwr. Richmond Rd. Rich & SW14 —6N 11
Lower Rd. Bookh & Fet —3A 98
Lower Rd. Eff —5L 97
Lower Rd. F Row —6H 187
Lower Rd. G'wood —7K 171
Lower Rd. Kenl —9M 63
Lower Rd. Red —5B 122
Lower Rd. Sutt —1A 62
Lwr. Sandfields. Send —2F 94
Lwr. Sawleywood. Bans —1L 81
Lwr. Shott. Bookh —4A 98
Lwr. South Pk. S God —9D 124
Lwr. South St. G'ming —7G 133
Lwr. South View. Farnh —9H 109
Lower Sq. F Row —6H 187
Lower Sq. Iswth —6H 11
Lower Sq., The. Sutt —2N 61
Lwr. Staithe. W4 —4B 12
Lower St. Hasl —2F 188
Lower St. Shere —8B 116
Lwr. Sunbury Rd. Hamp —1N 39
Lwr. Tanbridge Way. H'ham —6H 197
Lwr. Teddington Rd. King T —9K 25
Lwr. Village Rd. Asc —4M 33
Lwr. Weybourne La. Farnh —6L 109
Lwr. Wokingham Rd. Finch & Crowt —1C 48
Lwr. Wood Rd. Clay —3H 59
Lowestoft Wlk. Craw —5F 182
Loweswater Wlk. Camb —2H 71
Lowfield Clo. Light —7L 51
Lowfield Heath Ind. Est. Low H —5C 162
Lowfield Heath Rd. Charl —4L 161
Lowfield Rd. Slin —5L 195
Lowfield Way. Low H —5C 162
Lowicks Rd. Tilf —4N 149
Lowlands Dri. Stai —8M 7
Lowlands Rd. B'water —2H 69
Low La. Bad L —6N 109
Lowndes Bldgs. Farnh —9G 109
Lowry Clo. Col T —9J 49
Lowry Cres. Mitc —1C 44
Lowther Rd. SW13 —4E 12
Lowther Rd. King T —9M 25
Lowthorpe. St J —5K 73
Loxford Ct. Cranl —8H 155
Loxford Ho. Eps —8D 60
Loxford Rd. Cat —3C 104
Loxford Way. Cat —3C 104
Loxley Rd. SW18 —2B 28
Loxley Rd. Hamp —5N 23
Loxwood Av. C Crook —6A 88
Loxwood Clo. Felt —2E 22
Loxwood Rd. Alf —9H 175
Loxwood Rd. Plais —6B 192
Loxwood Rd. Rud —4N 193
Loxwood Wlk. Craw —1L 181
(in two parts)
Lucan Dri. Stai —8M 21
Lucas Clo. E Grin —9C 166
Lucas Clo. Yat —1C 68
Lucas Dri. Yat —1C 68
Lucas Field. Hasl —2D 188
Lucas Grn. Rd. W End —2A 72
Lucas Rd. Warn —9E 178
Lucerne Clo. Wok —6A 74
Lucerne Dri. M'bowr —6H 183
Lucerne Rd. T Hth —3N 45
Lucie Av. Ashf —7C 22
Lucien Rd. SW17 —5E 28
Lucien Rd. SW19 —3N 27
Lucilina Dri. Eden —3L 147
Luckley Path. Wokgm —2B 30
Luckley Rd. Wokgm —5A 30
Luckley Wood. Wokgm —5A 30
Luddington Av. Vir W —1B 36
Ludford Clo. Croy —9M 45
Ludlow. Brack —6N 31
Ludlow Clo. Frim —7E 70
Ludlow Rd. Felt —5H 23
Ludlow Rd. Guild —4L 113
Ludovick Wlk. SW15 —7E 12
Ludshott Gro. Head —4G 169
Luff Clo. Wind —6B 4
Luffs Meadow. N'chap —9D 190
Luke Rd. Alder —4K 109
Luke Rd. E. Alder —4K 109
Lullarook Clo. Big H —3E 86
Lulworth Av. Houn —4B 10
Lulworth Clo. Craw —6M 181
Lulworth Clo. F'boro —7M 69
Lulworth Cres. Mitc —1C 44
Lumley Ct. Horl —7E 142
Lumley Gdns. Sutt —2K 61
Lumley Ho. Horl —7E 142
Lumley Rd. Horl —7E 142
Lumley Rd. Sutt —2K 61
Lunar Clo. Big H —3F 86
Luna Rd. T Hth —2N 45
Lundy Clo. Craw —6A 182
Lundy Dri. Hayes —1F 8
Lunghurst Rd. Wold —7J 85
Lupin Clo. SW2 —3M 29
Lupin Clo. Bag —6G 51
Lupin Clo. Croy —7G 46
Lupin Clo. W Dray —1M 7
Lupin Ride. Crowt —9G 30
Lurgan Av. W6 —2J 13
Luscombe Ct. Short —1N 47
Lushington Dri. Cobh —1J 77
Lushington Ho. W on T —5K 39
Lusted Hall La. Tats —7D 86
Lusteds Clo. Dork —8J 119
Lutea Ho. Sutt —4A 62
(off Walnut M.)
Luther Rd. Tedd —6F 24
Lutterworth Clo. Brack —8A 16
Luttrell Av. SW15 —8G 13
Lutyens Clo. Craw —5K 181
Luxford Clo. H'ham —3M 197
Luxford's La. E Grin —4D 186
Luxted Rd. Orp —8J 67
Lyall Pl. Farnh —5G 108
Lychett Minster Clo. Brack —3D 32
Lych Ga. Clo. Sand —7E 48
Lych Ga. Ct. Eden —2L 147
Lych Way. Wok —3N 73
Lyconby Gdns. Croy —6H 47
Lydbury. Brack —2D 32
Lydden Gro. SW18 —1N 27
Lydden Rd. SW18 —1N 27
Lydele Clo. Wok —2B 74
Lydens La. Hever —6N 147
Lydford Clo. F'boro —7M 69
Lydford Clo. Frim —7E 70
Lydhurst Av. SW2 —3K 29
Lydney. Brack —6N 31
Lydney Clo. SW19 —3K 27
Lydon Ho. Craw —9B 162
Lye Copse Av. F'boro —6N 69
Lyefield La. F Grn —4K 157
Lyell Pl. E. Wind —6A 4
Lyell Pl. W. Wind —6A 4
(off Lyell)
Lyell Rd. Wind —6A 4
Lyell Wlk. E. Wind —6A 4
Lyell Wlk. W. Wind —6A 4
Lye, The. Tad —1H 101
Lyfield. Oxs —1B 78
Lyford Rd. SW18 —1B 28
Lygon Ho. SW6 —4K 13
(off Fulham Pal. Rd.)
Lyham Clo. SW2 —1J 29
Lyle Clo. Mitc —6E 44
Lymbourne Clo. Sutt —6M 61
Lymden Gdns. Reig —4N 121
Lyme Regis Rd. Bans —4L 81
Lymescote Gdns. Sutt —8M 43
Lyminge Gdns. SW18 —2C 28
Lymington Av. Yat —1A 68
Lymington Clo. SW16 —1H 45
Lymington Ct. Sutt —9N 43
Lymington Gdns. Eps —2E 60
Lynchborough Rd. Pass —9C 168
Lynchen Clo. Houn —4J 9
Lynchford La. F'boro —4C 90
Lynchford Rd. Ash V —5D 90
Lynchford Rd. F'boro —6N 89
(in two parts)
Lynch Rd. Farnh —1J 129
Lyncroft Gdns. Eps —5E 60
Lyncroft Gdns. Houn —8C 10
Lyndale. Th Dit —6E 40
Lyndale Ct. Red —9E 102
Lyndale Ct. W Byf —9J 55
Lyndale Dri. Fleet —4E 88
Lyndale Rd. Red —9E 102
Lynde Ho. W on T —5K 39
Lyndford Ter. Fleet —6A 88
Lyndhurst Av. SW16 —1H 45
Lyndhurst Av. Alder —6A 110
Lyndhurst Av. B'water —9H 49
Lyndhurst Av. Sun —2H 39
Lyndhurst Av. Surb —7A 42
Lyndhurst Av. Twic —2N 23
Lyndhurst Clo. Brack —2E 32
Lyndhurst Clo. Craw —4B 182
Lyndhurst Clo. Croy —9C 46
Lyndhurst Clo. Orp —1K 67
Lyndhurst Clo. Wok —2N 73
Lyndhurst Dri. N Mald —6D 42
Lyndhurst Farm Clo. Felb —6G 165
Lyndhurst Rd. Asc —3L 33
Lyndhurst Rd. Coul —3E 82
Lyndhurst Rd. Reig —6M 121
Lyndhurst Rd. T Hth —3L 45
Lyndhurst Vs. Red —9E 102
Lyndhurst Way. Cher —9G 36
Lyndhurst Way. Sutt —5M 61
Lyndon Av. Wall —9E 44
Lyndsey Clo. F'boro —1G 88
Lyndum Pl. Lind —4A 168
Lyndwood Dri. Old Win —9K 5
Lyne Clo. Vir W —5B 36
Lyne Crossing Rd. Lyne —5C 36
Lynegrove Av. Ashf —6D 22
Lyneham Rd. Crowt —2G 48
Lyne La. Lyne & Egh —5C 36
Lyne Rd. Vir W —5N 35
Lynmead Clo. Eden —8K 127
Lynmouth Av. Mord —5J 43
Lynmouth Gdns. Houn —4L 9
Lynn Clo. Ashf —6E 22
Lynn Ct. Whyt —5C 84
Lynne Clo. Orp —3N 67
Lynne Clo. S Croy —7F 64
Lynne Wlk. Esh —2C 58
Lynn Rd. SW12 —1F 28
Lynn Wlk. Reig —6N 121
Lynn Way. F'boro —7L 69
Lynscott Way. S Croy —5M 63
Lynsey Wlk. Bookh —4A 98
Lynstead Ct. Beck —1H 47
Lynsted Ct. Beck —1H 47
Lynton Clo. Chess —1L 59
Lynton Clo. E Grin —8C 166
Lynton Clo. Farnh —4F 128
Lynton Clo. Iswth —7F 10
Lynton Pk. Av. E Grin —8B 166
Lynton Rd. Croy —5L 45
Lynton Rd. N Mald —4C 42
Lynwick St. Rud —1C 194
Lynwood. Guild —4L 113
Lynwood Av. Coul —2F 82
Lynwood Av. Egh —7A 20
Lynwood Av. Eps —1E 80
Lynwood Chase. Brack —8A 16
Lynwood Clo. Lind —4B 168
Lynwood Clo. Wok —9F 54
Lynwood Ct. Eps —9E 60
Lynwood Ct. H'ham —5J 197
Lynwood Ct. King T —1A 42
Lynwood Cres. Asc —5B 34
Lynwood Dri. Myt —2E 90
Lynwood Dri. Wor Pk —8F 42
Lynwood Gdns. Croy —1K 63
Lynwood Rd. SW17 —4D 28
Lynwood Rd. Eps —1E 80
Lynwood Rd. Red —1E 122
Lynwood Rd. Th Dit —8F 40
Lynx Hill. E Hor —6G 96
Lyon Clo. M'bowr —7G 183
Lyon Ct. H'ham —6L 197
Lyon Oaks. Warf —7N 15
Lyon Rd. SW19 —9A 28
Lyon Rd. Crowt —1H 49
Lyon Rd. W On T —8M 39
Lyons Clo. Slin —5L 195
Lyons Ct. Dork —5H 119
Lyonsdene. Tad —5L 101
Lyons Dri. Guild —7K 93
Lyons Rd. Slin —5L 195
Lyon Way. Frim —5A 70
Lyric Clo. M'bowr —5H 183
Lyric Rd. SW13 —4E 12
Lysander Gdns. Surb —5M 41
Lysander Rd. Croy —3K 63
Lysias Rd. SW12 —1F 28
Lysia St. SW6 —3J 13
Lysons Av. Ash V —5D 90
Lyson's Rd. Alder —3M 109
Lysons Wlk. SW15 —7F 12
Lytchgate Clo. S Croy —4B 64
Lytcott Dri. W Mol —2N 39
Lytham. Brack —5K 31
Lytham Ct. S'hill —4N 33

Lythe Hill Pk. *Hasl* —3J **189**
Lytton Dri. *Craw* —2H **183**
Lytton Gdns. *Wall* —1H **63**
Lytton Gro. *SW15* —8J **13**
Lytton Rd. *Wok* —3D **74**
Lyveden Rd. *SW17* —7D **28**
Lywood Clo. *Tad* —9H **81**

Mabbotts. *Tad* —8J **81**
Mabel St. *Wok* —4N **73**
Maberley Rd. *Beck* —2G **47**
Mablethorpe Rd. *SW6* —3K **13**
Macadam Av. *Crowt* —9H **31**
McAlmont Ridge. *G'ming* —4G **132**
Macaulay Av. *Esh* —8F **40**
Macaulay Rd. *Cat* —9B **84**
Macbeth Ct. *Warf* —9C **16**
Macbeth St. *W6* —1G **13**
McCarthy Rd. *Felt* —6L **23**
Macclesfield Rd. *SE25* —4F **46**
Macdonald Rd. *Farnh* —5G **109**
Macdonald Rd. *Light* —8K **51**
McDonough Clo. *Chess* —1L **59**
Mace La. *Cud* —9M **67**
Macfarlane La. *Iswth* —2F **10**
McGrigor Barracks. *Alder* —1N **109**
McIndoe Rd. *E Grin* —7N **165**
McIntosh Clo. *Wall* —4J **63**
McIver Clo. *Felb* —6J **165**
McKay Clo. *Alder* —1A **110**
McKay Rd. *SW20* —8G **27**
McKay Trad. Est. *Coln* —5G **7**
Mackenzie Rd. *Beck* —1F **46**
McKernan Ct. *Sand* —7E **48**
Mackie Rd. *SW2* —1L **29**
Mackies Hill. *Peasl* —4F **136**
[illegible] —8A **122**
Maclaren M. *SW15* —7H **13**
Macleod Rd. *H'ham* —7L **197**
McNaughton Clo. *F'boro* —2H **89**
Macphail Clo. *Wokgm* —9D **14**
McRae La. *Mitc* —6D **44**
Macrae Rd. *Yat* —9B **48**
Madan Rd. *W'ham* —3M **107**
Madans Wlk. *Eps* —2C **80**
Maddison Clo. *Tedd* —7F **24**
Maddox La. *Bookh* —9M **77**
(in two parts)
Maddox Pk. *Bookh* —1M **97**
Madehurst Ct. *Craw* —6L **181**
Madeira Av. *H'ham* —6J **197**
Madeira Clo. *W Byf* —9J **55**
Madeira Cres. *W Byf* —9H **55**
Madeira Rd. *SW16* —6J **29**
Madeira Rd. *Mitc* —3D **44**
Madeira Rd. *W Byf* —9H **55**
Madeira Wlk. *Reig* —2B **122**
Madeira Wlk. *Wind* —4G **5**
Madeley Rd. *C Crook* —7C **88**
Madgehole La. *Sham G* —7J **135**
Madingley. *Brack* —7N **31**
Madox Brown End. *Col T* —8K **49**
Madrid Rd. *SW13* —4F **12**
Madrid Rd. *Guild* —4L **113**
Maesmaur Rd. *Tats* —8F **86**
Mafeking Av. *Bren* —2L **11**
Mafeking Rd. *Wray* —3D **20**
Magazine Pl. *Lea* —9H **79**
Magazine Rd. *Cat* —9M **83**
Magdala Rd. *Iswth* —6G **11**
Magdala Rd. *S Croy* —4A **64**
Magdalen Clo. *Byfl* —1N **75**
Magdalen Cres. *Byfl* —1N **75**
Magdalene Clo. *Craw* —9G **162**
Magdalene Rd. *Owl* —5L **49**
Magdalene Rd. *Shep* —3A **38**
Magdalen Rd. *SW18* —2A **28**
Magellan Ter. *Craw* —8E **162**
Magna Carta La. *Wray* —2N **19**
Magna Rd. *Egh* —7L **19**
Magnolia Clo. *King T* —7A **26**
Magnolia Clo. *Owl* —6J **49**
Magnolia Ct. *Horl* —8E **142**
Magnolia Ct. Sutt —4N ***61***
(off Grange Rd.)
Magnolia Ct. *Wall* —2F **62**
Magnolia Dri. *Big H* —3F **86**
Magnolia Pl. *Guild* —9M **93**
Magnolia Rd. *W4* —2A **12**
Magnolia St. *W Dray* —1M **7**
Magnolia Way. *Eps* —2B **60**
Magnolia Way. *Fleet* —6B **88**
Magnolia Way. *N Holm* —8K **119**
Magpie Clo. *Bord* —7A **168**
Magpie Clo. *Coul* —5G **83**
Magpie Clo. *Ews* —4C **108**
Magpie Grn. *Eden* —9L **127**
Magpie Wlk. *Craw* —1D **182**
Maguire Dri. *Frim* —3G **71**
Maguire Dri. *Rich* —5J **25**
Mahonia Clo. *W End* —9C **52**
Maida Rd. *Alder* —9N **89**
Maidenbower Dri. *M'bowr* —5F **182**
Maidenbower La. *Craw* —5F **182**
(in two parts)
Maidenbower Pl. *M'bowr* —5G **183**
Maidenbower Sq. *M'bowr* —5G **183**
Maidenhead Rd. *Binf* —3N **15**
Maidenhead Rd. *Wind* —3A **4**
Maidenhead Rd. *Wokgm* —6C **14**
Maiden La. *Craw* —1A **182**
Maiden's Grn. *Wink* —3F **16**
Maidenshaw Rd. *Eps* —8C **60**
Maids of Honour Row. *Rich* —8K **11**
Main Dri. *Brack* —8D **16**
Mainprize Rd. *Brack* —9C **16**
Main Rd. *Big H* —9E **66**
Main Rd. *Buck* —2F **120**
Main Rd. *Eden* —6K **127**
Main Rd. *Reig* —2H **121**
Main Rd. *Wind* —3A **4**
Mainstone Clo. *Deep* —7G **71**
Mainstone Cres. *Brkwd* —8A **72**
Mainstone Rd. *Bisl* —3C **72**
Main St. *Add* —9N **37**
Main St. *Felt* —6L **23**
Main St. *Yat* —8C **48**
Maisie Webster Clo. *Stai* —1L **21**
Maisonettes, The. *Sutt* —2L **61**
Maitland Clo. *Houn* —6N **9**
Maitland Clo. *W Byf* —9J **55**
Maitland Rd. *F'boro* —5N **89**
Maitlands Clo. *Tong* —6C **110**
Maize Croft. *Horl* —7G **142**
Maize La. *Warf* —7B **16**
Majestic Way. *Mitc* —1D **44**
Majors Farm Rd. *Dat* —3N **5**
Major's Hill. *Craw* —4N **183**
Makepiece Rd. *Brack* —8N **15**
[illegible] —8N **35**
Malan Clo. *Big H* —4G **87**
Malbrook Rd. *SW15* —7G **13**
Malcolm Dri. *Surb* —7K **41**
Malcolm Gdns. *Hkwd* —1B **162**
Malcolm Rd. *SE25* —5D **46**
Malcolm Rd. *SW19* —7K **27**
Malcolm Rd. *Coul* —2H **83**
Malden Av. *SE25* —2E **46**
Malden Ct. *N Mald* —2G **42**
Malden Grn. Av. *Wor Pk* —7E **42**
Malden Hill. *N Mald* —2E **42**
Malden Hill Gdns. *N Mald* —2E **42**
Malden Junction. (Junct.) —4E **42**
Malden Pk. *N Mald* —5E **42**
Malden Rd. *N Mald & Wor Pk* —4D **42**
Malden Rd. *Sutt* —1J **61**
Malden Way. *N Mald* —5D **42**
Maldon Ct. *Wall* —2G **62**
Maldon Rd. *Wall* —2F **62**
Malet Clo. *Egh* —7F **20**
Maley Av. *SE27* —3M **29**
Malham Clo. *M'bowr* —6G **183**
Malham Fell. *Brack* —3M **31**
Mallard Clo. *Ash* —1D **110**
Mallard Clo. *Hasl* —2C **188**
Mallard Clo. *Horl* —6E **142**
Mallard Clo. *H'ham* —3J **197**
Mallard Clo. *Red* —9E **102**
Mallard Clo. *Twic* —1A **24**
Mallard Pl. *E Grin* —1B **186**
Mallard Pl. *Twic* —4G **24**
Mallard Rd. *S Croy* —6G **65**
Mallards Reach. *Wey* —8E **38**
Mallards, The. *Frim* —4D **70**
Mallards, The. *Stai* —1K **37**
Mallards Way. *Light* —7L **51**
Mallard Wlk. *Beck* —4G **47**
Mallard Way. *Eden* —9L **127**
Mallard Way. *Wall* —5G **63**
Mallard Way. *Yat* —9A **48**
Malling Clo. *Croy* —5F **46**
Malling Gdns. *Mord* —5A **44**
Mallinson Rd. *Croy* —9H **45**
Mallow Clo. *Croy* —7G **46**
Mallow Clo. *H'ham* —2L **197**
Mallow Clo. *Lind* —4B **168**
Mallow Clo. *Tad* —7G **80**
Mallow Cres. *Guild* —9D **94**
Mallowdale Rd. *Brack* —6C **32**
Mall Rd. *W6* —1G **13**
Mall, The. *SW14* —8B **12**
Mall, The. *Bren* —2K **11**
Mall, The. *Croy* —8N **45**
Mall, The. *Surb* —5K **41**
Mall, The. *W on T* —2L **57**
Malmains Clo. *Beck* —3N **47**
Malmains Way. *Beck* —3M **47**
Malmesbury Rd. *Mord* —6A **44**
Malmstone Av. *Red* —6G **103**
Malta Barracks. *Alder* —8L **89**
Malta Rd. *Deep* —6J **71**
Maltby Rd. *Chess* —3N **59**
Malt Hill. *Egh* —6A **20**
Malt Hill. *Warf* —5C **16**
Malthouse Clo. *C Crook* —8A **88**
Malt Ho. Clo. *Old Win* —1L **19**
Malthouse Ct. *W End* —8C **52**
Malthouse Dri. *W4* —2D **12**
Malthouse Dri. *Felt* —6L **23**
Malthouse La. *Hamb* —9F **152**
Malthouse La. *Pirb & Worp* —1E **92**
Malthouse La. *W End* —9C **52**
Malthouse Mead. *Witl* —5C **152**
Malthouse Pas. SW13 —5E ***12***
(off Maltings Clo.)
Malthouse Rd. *Craw* —5B **182**
Malthouses, The. *Cranl* —7N **155**
Malt Ho., The. *Tilf* —8A **130**
Maltings. *W4* —1N **11**
Maltings Clo. *SW13* —5E **12**
Maltings Lodge. W4 —2D ***12***
(off Corney Reach Way)
Maltings Pl. *SW6* —4N **13**
Maltings, The. *Byfl* —9A **56**
Maltings, The. *Oxt* —9B **106**
Maltings, The. *Stai* —5G **20**
Malting Way. *Iswth* —6F **10**
Malus Clo. *Add* —4H **55**
Malus Dri. *Add* —4H **55**
Malva Clo. *SW18* —8N **13**
Malvern Clo. *SE20* —1D **46**
Malvern Clo. *Mitc* —2G **45**
Malvern Clo. *Ott* —3E **54**
Malvern Clo. *Surb* —7L **41**
Malvern Ct. *Coln* —2C **6**
Malvern Ct. *Eps* —1C **80**
Malvern Ct. *Sutt* —4M **61**
Malvern Dri. *Felt* —6L **23**
Malvern Rd. *Craw* —4A **182**
Malvern Rd. *F'boro* —7J **69**
Malvern Rd. *Hamp* —8A **24**
Malvern Rd. *Hayes* —3F **8**
Malvern Rd. *Surb* —8L **41**
Malvern Rd. *T Hth* —3L **45**
Malwood Rd. *SW12* —1F **28**
Malvern, The. [illegible]
[illegible] Rd. *W6* —[illegible] **13**
Manchester Rd. *T Hth* —2N **45**
Mandeville Clo. *SW20* —9K **27**
Mandeville Clo. *Guild* —9K **93**
Mandeville Ct. *Egh* —5C **20**
Mandeville Dri. *Surb* —7K **41**
Mandeville Rd. *Iswth* —5G **10**
Mandeville Rd. *Shep* —4B **38**
Mandora Rd. *Alder* —9N **89**
Mandrake Rd. *SW17* —3D **28**
Manfield Rd. *Ash* —2E **110**
Manfred Rd. *SW15* —8L **13**
Mangles Ct. *Guild* —4M **113**
Mangles Rd. *Guild* —1N **113**
Manitoba Gdns. *Grn St* —3N **67**
Manley Bri. Rd. *Rowl* —6D **128**
Mannamead. *Eps* —6D **80**
Mannamead Clo. *Eps* —6D **80**
Mann Clo. *Croy* —3N **45**
Manning Clo. *E Grin* —8N **165**
Manning Pl. *Rich* —9M **11**
Mannings Clo. *Craw* —9H **163**
Mannings Hill. *Cranl* —4M **155**
Manningtree Clo. *SW19* —2K **27**
Mann's Clo. *Iswth* —8F **10**
Manny Shinwell Ho. SW6
(off Clem Attlee Ct.) —2L ***13***
Manoel Rd. *Twic* —4C **24**
Manor Av. *Cat* —2B **104**
Manor Av. *Houn* —6L **9**
Manor Chase. *Wey* —2C **56**
Manor Circus. (Junct.) —6N **11**
Manor Clo. *Brack* —8M **15**
Manor Clo. *E Hor* —6F **96**
Manor Clo. *Hasl* —2C **188**
Manor Clo. *Horl* —8D **142**
Manor Clo. *Tong* —5D **110**
Manor Clo. *Warl* —4H **85**
Manor Clo. *Wok* —4H **75**
Manor Clo. *Wor Pk* —7D **42**
Manor Ct. *SW16* —4J **29**
Manor Ct. *W3* —1N **11**
Manor Ct. *C Crook* —9B **88**
Manor Ct. *Craw* —9D **162**
Manor Ct. *H'ham* —3N **197**
Manor Ct. *King T* —9N **25**
Manor Ct. *Twic* —3C **24**
Manor Ct. *W Mol* —3A **40**
Manor Ct. *W Wick* —7L **47**
Manor Ct. *Wey* —1C **56**
Manor Cres. *Brkwd* —7B **72**
Manor Cres. *Byfl* —9A **56**
Manor Cres. *Guild* —1L **113**
Manor Cres. *Hasl* —2C **188**
Manor Cres. *Surb* —5N **41**
Manorcrofts Rd. *Egh* —7C **20**
Manordene Clo. *Th Dit* —7G **40**
Manor Dri. *Eps* —3D **60**
Manor Dri. *Esh* —8F **40**
Manor Dri. *Felt* —6L **23**
Manor Dri. *Horl* —8D **142**
Manor Dri. *New H* —6J **55**
Manor Dri. *Sun* —1H **39**
Manor Dri. *Surb* —5M **41**
Manor Dri. N. *N Mald & Wor Pk* —6C **42**
Manor Dri., The. *Wor Pk* —7D **42**
Manor Farm. *Wanb* —6N **111**
Manor Farm Av. *Shep* —5C **38**
Manor Farm Bus. Cen. *Tong* —7D **110**
Manor Farm Clo. *Ash* —3D **110**
Manor Farm Clo. *Wind* —6C **4**
Manor Farm Clo. *Wor Pk* —7D **42**
Manor Farm Cotts. *Guild* —6N **111**
Manor Farm Ct. *Egh* —6C **20**
Manor Farm Est. *Byfl* —1A **76**
Manor Farm La. *Egh* —6C **20**
Manor Farm Rd. *SW16* —1L **45**
Manor Fields. *SW15* —9J **13**
Manorfields. *Craw* —7K **181**
Manor Fields. *H'ham* —4N **197**
Manor Fields. *Milf* —9B **132**
Manor Fields. *Seale* —7F **110**
Manor Gdns. *SW20* —1L **43**
Manor Gdns. *W4* —1D **12**
Manor Gdns. *Chil* —9E **114**
Manor Gdns. *Eff* —6L **97**
Manor Gdns. *G'ming* —4H **133**
Manor Gdns. *Guild* —1L **113**
Manor Gdns. *Hamp* —8B **24**
Manor Gdns. *Lwr Bo* —6J **129**
Manor Gdns. *Rich* —7M **11**
Manor Gdns. *S Croy* —3C **64**
Manor Gdns. *Sun* —9H **23**
Manorgate Rd. *King T* —9N **25**
Manor Grn. Rd. *Eps* —9A **60**
Manor Gro. *Beck* —1L **47**
Manor Gro. *Rich* —7N **11**
Manor Hill. *Bans* —2D **82**
Manor Ho. Ct. *Eps* —9B **60**
Manor Ho. Ct. *Shep* —6C **38**
Manor Ho. Dri. *Asc* —8L **17**
Manor Ho. Flats. *Tong* —6D **110**
Manor Ho. Gdns. *Eden* —2L **147**
Manorhouse La. *Bookh* —4M **97**
Manor Ho. La. *Dat* —3L **5**
Manor Ho. Way. [illegible]
Manor La. *Felt* —2H **23**
Manor La. *Hayes* —2E **8**
Manor La. *H'ham* —8A **198**
Manor La. *Sham G* —8G **134**
Manor La. *Sun* —1H **39**
Manor La. *Sutt* —2A **62**
Manor La. *Tad* —7M **101**
Manor Lea. *Hasl* —2C **188**
Manor Lea Clo. *Milf* —9B **132**
Manor Lea Rd. *Milf* —9B **132**
Manor Leaze. *Egh* —6D **20**
Manor Lodge. *Guild* —1L **113**
Manor Pk. *Rich* —7M **11**
Manor Pk. Clo. *W Wick* —7L **47**
Manor Pk. Dri. *Yat* —1C **68**
Manor Pk. Ind. Est. *Alder* —3A **110**
Manor Pk. Rd. *Sutt* —2A **62**
Manor Pk. Rd. *W Wick* —7L **47**
Manor Pl. *Felt* —2H **23**
Manor Pl. *Mitc* —2G **44**
Manor Pl. *Stai* —6K **21**
Manor Pl. *Sutt* —1N **61**
Manor Rd. *SE25* —3D **46**
Manor Rd. *SW20* —1L **43**
Manor Rd. *Alder* —4L **109**
Manor Rd. *Ashf* —6A **22**
Manor Rd. *Beck* —1L **47**
Manor Rd. *E Grin* —8M **165**
Manor Rd. *E Mol* —3D **40**
Manor Rd. *Eden* —2K **147**
Manor Rd. *F'boro* —2B **90**
Manor Rd. *Farnh* —8K **109**
Manor Rd. *Guild* —1L **113**
Manor Rd. *H'ham* —3N **197**
Manor Rd. *Mitc* —3G **44**
Manor Rd. *Red* —7G **102**
Manor Rd. *Reig* —1L **121**
Manor Rd. *Rich* —7N **11**
Manor Rd. *Rip* —1H **95**
Manor Rd. *Shur R* —1F **14**
Manor Rd. *Sutt* —4L **61**
Manor Rd. *Tats* —7G **86**
Manor Rd. *Tedd* —6G **25**
Manor Rd. *Tong & Ash* —5D **110**
Manor Rd. *Twic* —3C **24**
Manor Rd. *Wall* —1F **62**
Manor Rd. *W On T* —6G **39**
Manor Rd. *W Wick* —8L **47**
Manor Rd. *Wind* —5B **4**
Manor Rd. *Wok* —3M **73**
Manor Rd. *Wokgm* —6A **30**
Manor Rd. N. *Hin W & Th Dit* —9F **40**
Manor Rd. N. *Wall* —1F **62**
Manor Rd. S. *Esh* —1E **58**
Manor Royal. *Craw* —9C **162**
Mnr. Royal Est. *Craw* —8C **162**
Manor, The. *Milf* —1C **152**
Manor Vale. *Bren* —1J **11**
Manor Wlk. *Alder* —3N **109**
Manor Wlk. Horl —8D ***142***
(off Manor Dri.)
Manor Wlk. *Wey* —2C **56**
Manor Way. *Bag* —5J **51**
Manor Way. *Bans* —3D **82**
Manor Way. *Beck* —1K **47**
Manor Way. *Egh* —7B **20**
Manor Way. *Guild* —6H **113**
Manor Way. *Mitc* —2G **44**
Manor Way. *Oxs* —2C **78**
Manor Way. *Purl* —8J **63**
Manor Way. *S Croy* —3B **64**
Manor Way. *Wok* —8D **74**
Manor Way. *Wor Pk* —7D **42**
Manor Way, The. *Wall* —1F **62**
Manor Wood Rd. *Purl* —9J **63**
Mansard Beeches. *SW17* —6E **28**
Manse Clo. *Hayes* —2E **8**
Mansel Clo. *Guild* —7L **93**
Mansell Clo. *Wind* —4B **4**
Mansell Way. *Cat* —9A **84**
Mansel Rd. *SW19* —7K **27**
Mansfield Clo. *Asc* —9H **17**
Mansfield Cres. *Brack* —5N **31**
Mansfield Dri. *Red* —6H **103**
Mansfield Pk. *Cranl* —5K **155**
Mansfield Pl. *Asc* —1H **33**
Mansfield Rd. *Chess* —2J **59**
Mansfield Rd. *S Croy* —3A **64**
Manship Rd. *Mitc* —8E **28**
Mansions, The. *SW5* —1N **13**
Manson M. *SW7* —1N **13**
Manston Av. *S'hall* —1A **10**
Manston Clo. *SE20* —1F **46**
Manston Dri. *Brack* —5A **32**
Manston Gro. *King T* —6K **25**
Manston Rd. *Guild* —8C **94**
Mantilla Rd. *SW17* —5E **28**
Mantlet Clo. *SW16* —8G **29**
Manville Gdns. *SW17* —4F **28**
Manville Rd. *SW17* —3E **28**
Manygate La. *Shep* —6D **38**
Manygate Mobile Home Est.
(off Mitre Clo.) Shep —5E ***38***
Manygates. *SW12* —3F **28**
Maori Rd. *Guild* —3B **114**
Maple Clo. *Ash V* —6D **90**
Maple Clo. *B'water* —1H [illegible]
Maple Clo. *Craw* —4A **162**
Maple Clo. *Hamp* —7N **23**
Maple Clo. *H'ham* —3N **197**
Maple Clo. *Mitc* —9F **28**
Maple Clo. *Sand* —6E **48**
Maple Clo. *Whyt* —4C **84**
Maple Ct. *Brack* —3D **32**
Maple Ct. *Egh* —7L **19**
Maple Ct. *Hors* —3M **73**
Maple Ct. *N Mald* —2C **42**
Mapledale Av. *Croy* —8D **46**
Mapledrakes Clo. *Ewh* —5F **156**
Mapledrakes Rd. *Ewh* —5F **156**
Maple Dri. *Crowt* —9H **31**
Maple Dri. *E Grin* —9C **166**
Maple Dri. *Light* —7K **51**
Maple Dri. *Red* —9D **122**
Maple Gdns. *Stai* —3N **21**
Maple Gdns. *Yat* —1C **68**
Maplegreen. *Craw* —4A **182**
Maple Gro. *Bren* —3H **11**
Maple Gro. *Guild* —1N **113**
Maple Gro. *Wok* —8A **74**
Maple Gro. Bus. Cen. *Houn* —7K **9**
Maplehatch Clo. *G'ming* —9H **133**
Maplehurst. *Lea* —1D **98**
Maplehurst Clo. *King T* —3L **41**
Maple Ind. Est. *Felt* —4H **23**
Maple Leaf Clo. *Big H* —3F **86**
Maple Leaf Clo. *F'boro* —2L **89**
Maple Lodge. *Hasl* —4J **189**
Maple M. *SW16* —6K **29**
Maple Pl. *Bans* —1J **81**
Maple Rd. *SE20* —1E **46**
Maple Rd. *Asht* —6K **79**
Maple Rd. *Red* —7D **122**
Maple Rd. *Rip* —2J **95**
Maple Rd. *Surb* —5K **41**
Maple Rd. *Whyt* —4C **84**
Maplestead Rd. *SW2* —1K **29**
Maples, The. *Bans* —1N **81**
Maples, The. *Clay* —4G **59**
Maples, The. *Ott* —3E **54**
Maplethorpe Rd. *T Hth* —3M **45**
Mapleton Cres. *SW18* —9N **13**
Mapleton Rd. *SW18* —9M **13**
Mapleton Rd. *W'ham & Eden* —8N **107**
Maple Wlk. *Alder* —4B **110**
Maple Wlk. *Sutt* —6N **61**
Maple Way. *Coul* —8F **82**
Maple Way. *Felt* —4H **23**
Maple Way. *Head* —3G **169**
Marbeck Clo. *Wind* —4A **4**
Marble Hill Clo. *Twic* —1H **25**
Marble Hill Gdns. *Twic* —1H **25**
Marbles Way. *Tad* —6J **81**
Marbull Way. *Warf* —7N **15**
Marchbank Rd. *W14* —2L **13**
Marcheria Clo. *Brack* —5N **31**
Marches Rd. *H'ham* —5D **178**
Marches, The. *K'fold* —4H **179**
Marchmont Rd. *Rich* —8M **11**
Marchmont Rd. *Wall* —4G **62**
March Rd. *Twic* —1G **24**
March Rd. *Wey* —2B **56**
Marchside Clo. *Houn* —4L **9**
Marcuse Rd. *Cat* —1A **104**
Marcus St. *SW18* —9N **13**
Marcus Ter. *SW18* —9N **13**
Mardale. *Camb* —2G **71**
Mardell Rd. *Croy* —4G **46**
Marden Cres. *Croy* —5K **45**
Marden Rd. *Croy* —5K **45**
Mardens, The. *Craw* —2N **181**
Mare La. *Binf* —1K **15**
(in two parts)
Mare La. *Hasc* —6L **153**
Mareschal Rd. *Guild* —5M **113**
Mares Field. *Croy* —9B **46**
Maresfield Ho. Guild —2F ***114***
(off Merrow St.)
Mareshall Av. *Warf* —7N **15**
Mare St. *Hasc* —6N **153**
Mareth Clo. *Alder* —2N **109**
Marfleet Clo. *Cars* —8C **44**
Margaret Clo. *Stai* —7M **21**
Margaret Herbison Ho. SW6
(off Clem Attlee Ct.) —2L ***13***
Margaret Ingram Clo. *SW6* —3L **13**
Margaret Rd. *Guild* —4M **113**
Margaret Way. *Coul* —6M **83**
Margery Gro. *Tad* —7K **101**
Margery La. *Tad* —7L **101**
Margin Dri. *SW19* —6J **27**
Margravine Gdns. *W6* —1J **13**
Margravine Rd. *W6* —1J **13**
Marham Gdns. *SW18* —2C **28**
Marham Gdns. *Mord* —5A **44**
Marian Ct. *Sutt* —2N **61**
Marian Rd. *SW16* —9G **29**
Maria Theresa Clo. *N Mald* —4C **42**
Mariette Way. *Wall* —5J **63**
Marigold Clo. *Crowt* —9E **30**
Marigold Ct. *Guild* —9A **94**
Marigold Dri. *Bisl* —2D **72**
[illegible] Way. *Croy* —[illegible]
Marina Av. *N Mald* —4G **42**
Marina Clo. *Cher* —7L **37**
Marina Way. *Tedd* —8K **25**
Marinefield Rd. *SW6* —5N **13**
Mariner Gdns. *Rich* —4J **25**
Mariners Dri. *F'boro* —8A **70**
Marion Av. *Shep* —4C **38**
Marion Rd. *Craw* —5F **182**
Marion Rd. *T Hth* —4N **45**
Marius Pas. *SW17* —3E **28**
Marius Rd. *SW17* —3E **28**
Marjoram Clo. *F'boro* —1G **89**
Marjoram Clo. *Guild* —8K **93**
Marke Clo. *Kes* —1G **66**
Markedge La. *Coul & Red* —2D **102**
Markenfield Rd. *Guild* —3N **113**
Markenhorn. *G'ming* —4G **132**
Market Cen., The. *S'hall* —1J **9**
Marketfield Rd. *Red* —2D **122**
Marketfield Way. *Red* —3D **122**
Market Pde. *Felt* —4M **23**
Market Pl. *Brack* —1N **31**
Market Pl. *Bren* —3J **11**
Market Pl. *King T* —1K **41**
Market Pl. *Wokgm* —2B **30**
Market Rd. *Rich* —6N **11**
Market Sq. *H'ham* —7J **197**
Market Sq. *Stai* —5G **21**
Market Sq. *W'ham* —4M **107**
Market Sq. *Wok* —4A **74**
Market St. *Brack* —1N **31**
Market St. *Guild* —4N **113**
Market St. *Wind* —4G **5**
Market Ter. Bren —2L ***11***
(off Albany Rd.)
Market, The. *Sutt* —7A **44**
Market Way. *W'ham* —4M **107**
Markfield. *Croy* —6J **65**
(in two parts)
Markfield Rd. *Cat* —4E **104**
Markham Ct. *Camb* —9B **50**
Markham M. *Wokgm* —2B **30**
Markham Rd. *Capel* —5J **159**
Markhole Clo. *Hamp* —8N **23**
Mark Oak La. *Fet* —9A **78**
Marksbury Av. *Rich* —6N **11**
Marks Rd. *Warl* —5H **85**
Marks Rd. *Wokgm* —9A **14**
Marks St. *Reig* —3N **121**
Markville Gdns. *Cat* —3D **104**
Mark Way. *G'ming* —3E **132**
Markway. *Sun* —1K **39**
Markwick La. *Loxh* —6L **153**
Marlborough Clo. *SW19* —7C **28**
Marlborough Clo. *Craw* —7A **182**
Marlborough Clo. *Fleet* —5E **88**
Marlborough Clo. *H'ham* —3K **197**
Marlborough Clo. *W On T* —9L **39**
Marlborough Ct. *Dork* —5H **119**
Marlborough Ct. *Wokgm* —1C **30**
Marlborough Dri. *Wey* —9D **38**
Marlborough Gdns. *Surb* —6K **41**
Marlborough Hill. *Dork* —5H **119**
Marlborough Rise. *Camb* —9C **50**
Marlborough Rd. *SW19* —7C **28**
Marlborough Rd. *W4* —1B **12**
Marlborough Rd. *Ashf* —6M **21**
Marlborough Rd. *Dork* —5H **119**
Marlborough Rd. *Felt* —3L **23**

Marlborough Rd.—Merron Clo.

Marlborough Rd. Hamp —7A 24
Marlborough Rd. Iswth —4H 11
Marlborough Rd. Rich —9M 11
Marlborough Rd. Slou —1N 5
Marlborough Rd. S Croy —4N 63
Marlborough Rd. Sutt —9M 43
Marlborough Rd. Wok —3C 74
Marlborough View. F'boro —9H 69
Marld, The. Asht —5M 79
Marles La. Bil —7D 194
Marlet Corner. H'ham —1E 194
Marley Av. Hasl —5C 188
Marley Clo. Add —3H 55
Marley Coombe Rd. Hasl —3D 188
Marley Hanger. Hasl —5E 188
Marley La. Hasl —3C 188
Marley Rise. Dork —8G 119
Marlhurst. Eden —8K 127
Marlin Clo. Sun —7F 22
Marlingdene Clo. Hamp —7A 24
Marlings Clo. Whyt —4B 84
Marlins Clo. Sutt —2A 62
Marlow Clo. SE20 —2E 46
Marlow Ct. Craw —2B 182
Marlow Cres. Twic —9F 10
Marlow Dri. Sutt —8J 43
Marlowe Sq. Mitc —3G 44
Marlowe Way. Croy —8J 45
Marlow Rd. SE20 —2E 46
Marlpit Av. Coul —4J 83
Marlpit Clo. E Grin —7A 166
Marlpit Clo. Eden —8L 127
Marlpit La. Coul —3H 83
Marl Rd. SW18 —7N 13
Marlyns Clo. Guild —9C 94
Marlyns Dri. Guild —9C 94
Marmot Rd. Houn —6L 9
Marnell Way. Houn —6L 9
Marneys Clo. Eps —2N 79
Marnfield Cres. SW2 —2K 29
Marnham Pl. Add —1L 55
Marqueen Towers. SW16 —8J 29
Marrick Clo. SW15 —7F 12
Marriott Clo. Felt —9E 8
Marriott Lodge Clo. Add —1L 55
Marrowbrook Clo. F'boro —2M 89
Marrowbrook La. F'boro —3L 89
Marrowells. Wey —9G 38
Marryat Pl. SW19 —5K 27
Marryat Rd. SW19 —6J 27
Marryat Sq. SW6 —4K 13
Marshall Clo. SW18 —9N 13
Marshall Clo. F'boro —7L 69
Marshall Clo. Frim —4H 71
Marshall Clo. Houn —8N 9
Marshall Clo. S Croy —9D 64
Marshall Pl. New H —5L 55
Marshall Rd. Col T —8J 49
Marshall Rd. G'ming —6H 133
Marshall Rd. M'bowr —5G 182
Marshalls Clo. Eps —9B 60
Marshall's Rd. Sutt —1N 61
Marsham Ho. Brack —8N 15
Marsh Av. Eps —6D 60
Marsh Av. Mitc —1D 44
Marsh Clo. Bord —6A 168
Marsh Ct. Craw —8N 181
Marsh Farm Rd. Twic —2F 24
Marshfield. Dat —4M 5
Marsh Grn. Rd. M Grn —8G 147
Marshland Cotts. Dork —7B 160
Marsh La. Add —1K 55
Marshwood Rd. Light —7A 52
Marston. Eps —7B 60
Marston Av. Chess —3L 59
Marston Ct. W on T —7K 39
Marston Dri. F'boro —7N 69
Marston Dri. Warl —5H 85
Marston Rd. Farnh —1E 128
Marston Rd. Tedd —6H 25
Marston Rd. Wok —4L 73
Marston Way. SE19 —8M 29
Marston Way. Asc —1J 33
Martel Clo. Camb —8G 50
Martell Rd. SE21 —4N 29
Martin Clo. Craw —1B 182
Martin Clo. S Croy —7G 64
Martin Clo. Warl —3E 84
Martin Clo. Wind —4A 4
Martin Cres. Croy —7L 45
Martindale. SW14 —8B 12
Martindale Av. Camb —2G 71
Martindale Clo. Guild —1F 114
Martindale Rd. SW12 —1F 28
Martindale Rd. Houn —6M 9
Martindale Rd. Wok —5K 73
Martineau Clo. Esh —1D 58
Martineau Dri. Dork —7H 119
Martingale Clo. Sun —3H 39
Martingale Ct. Alder —2K 109
Martingales Clo. Rich —4K 25
Martin Gro. Mord —3M 43
Martin Rd. Guild —1K 113
Martins Clo. B'water —2J 69
Martins Clo. Guild —2E 114
Martins Clo. W Wick —8N 47
Martin's Dri. Wokgm —9A 14
Martin's La. Brack —2C 32
Martins Pk. F'boro —7J 69
Martins, The. Craw D —1F 184
Martins Wood. Milf —3B 152
Martinsyde. Wok —4E 74
Martin Way. SW20 & Mord —2K 43
Martin Way. Frim —5C 70
Martin Way. Wok —5K 73
Martlets Clo. H'ham —3J 197
Martlets, The. Craw —3C 182
Marts, The. Rud —1E 194
Martyns Pl. E Grin —1B 186
Martyr Rd. Guild —4N 113
Martyrs Av. Craw —9A 162
Martyr's La. Wok —8D 54
Marvell Clo. Craw —1G 182
Marville Rd. SW6 —3L 13
Marwell. W'ham —4K 107
Mary Adelaide Clo. SW15 —5D 26
Mary Drew Almshouses. Egh —7N 19
Maryhill Clo. Kenl —4N 83
Maryland Rd. T Hth —9M 29
Maryland Way. Sun —1H 39
Mary Macarthur Ho. W6 —2K 13
Mary Mead. Warf —7B 16
Mary Rd. Guild —4M 113
Mary Rose Clo. Hamp —9A 24
Mary's Ter. Twic —1G 24
Mary Vale. G'ming —9G 133
Marzena Ct. Houn —9C 10
Mascotte Rd. SW15 —7J 13
Masefield Ct. Surb —6K 41
Masefield Gdns. Crowt —4G 48
Masefield Rd. Craw —6K 181
Masefield Rd. Hamp —5N 23
Masefield Way. Stai —2A 22
Maskall Clo. SW2 —2L 29
Maskani Wlk. SW16 —8G 29
Maskell Rd. SW17 —4A 28
Maskell Way. F'boro —2H 89
Mason Clo. E Grin —8A 166
Mason Clo. Hamp —9A 24
Mason Clo. Yat —1D 68
Masonettes. Eps —6B 60 (off Sefton Rd.)
Masonic Hall Rd. Cher —5H 37
Mason Pl. Sand —7E 48
Mason Rd. Craw —5C 182
Mason Rd. F'boro —8K 69
Masons Av. Croy —9N 45
Mason's Bri. Rd. Red —8F 122
Masons Field. Man H —9B 198
Masons Paddock. Dork —3G 118
Masons Pl. Mitc —9D 28
Mason's Yd. SW19 —6J 27
Mason Way. Alder —5N 109
Massetts Rd. Horl —9D 142
Master Clo. Oxt —7A 106
Maswell Pk. Cres. Houn —8C 10
Maswell Pk. Rd. Houn —8B 10
Matham Rd. E Mol —4D 40
Matheson Rd. W14 —1L 13
Mathias Clo. Eps —9B 60
Mathisen Way. Coln —4G 7
Mathon Ct. Guild —3B 114
Matilda Clo. SE19 —8N 29
Matlock Cres. Sutt —1K 61
Matlock Gdns. Sutt —1K 61
Matlock Pl. Sutt —1K 61
Matlock Rd. Cat —8B 84
Matlock Way. N Mald —9C 26
Matthew Arnold Clo. Cobh —1H 77
Matthew Arnold Clo. Stai —7L 21
Matthew Ct. Mitc —4H 45
Matthew Rd. Alder —4K 109
Matthew Rd. Bans —4L 81
Matthews Chase. Binf —8L 15
Matthews Clo. F'boro —5C 90
Matthews Ct. Asc —3A 34
Matthews Dri. M'bowr —7F 182
Matthews Gdns. New Ad —7N 65
Matthewsgreen Rd. Wokgm —9A 14
Matthews La. Stai —5H 21
Matthews Rd. Camb —7A 50
Matthews St. Reig —7M 121
Matthews Way. Fleet —3A 88
Matthew Ter. Alder —2A 110
Matthey Pl. Craw —9H 163
Maudsley Ho. Bren —1L 11
Maultway Clo. Camb —7F 50
Maultway Cres. Camb —7F 50
Maultway N., The. Camb —6E 50
Maultway, The. Camb —7F 50
Maunsell Pk. Craw —3F 182
Maureen Ct. Beck —1F 46
Maurice Av. Cat —9A 84
Maurice Ct. Bren —3K 11
Mavins Rd. Farnh —3J 129
Mavis Av. Eps —2D 60
Mavis Clo. Eps —2D 60
Mawbey Rd. Ott —3F 54
Mawson Clo. SW20 —1K 43
Mawson La. W4 —2E 12
Maxine Clo. Sand —6G 48
Maxton Wlk. Craw —7N 181
Maxwell Clo. Croy —7J 45
Maxwell Dri. W Byf —7L 55
Maxwell Rd. SW6 —3N 13
Maxwell Rd. Ashf —7D 22
Maxwell Way. Craw —9E 162
Maybelle Clo. Bear G —8K 139
Mayberry Pl. Surb —6M 41
Maybourne Rise. Wok —2N 93
Maybrick Clo. Sand —6E 48
Maybury Clo. Frim —6B 70
Maybury Clo. Tad —6K 81
Maybury Est. Wok —3E 74
Maybury Hill. Wok —3D 74
Maybury Rd. Wok —4B 74
Maybury St. SW17 —6C 28
May Clo. Chess —3M 59
May Clo. G'ming —9E 132
May Clo. Head —5D 168
May Clo. Owl —7J 49
May Cres. Ash —3C 110
Maycross Av. Mord —3L 43
Mayday Rd. T Hth —5M 45
Mayell Clo. Lea —1J 99
Mayes Clo. M'bowr —4G 182
Mayes Clo. Warl —5G 85
Mayes La. Warn —7E 178
Mayfair Av. Twic —1C 24
Mayfair Av. Wor Pk —7F 42
Mayfair Clo. Surb —7L 41
Mayfield. Craw —3H 183
Mayfield. Ling —1C 166
Mayfield. Rowl —8E 128
Mayfield Av. W4 —1D 12
Mayfield Av. New H —6K 55
Mayfield Clo. SE20 —1E 46
Mayfield Clo. Ashf —7C 22
Mayfield Clo. New H —6L 55
Mayfield Clo. Red —9E 122
Mayfield Clo. Th Dit —7H 41
Mayfield Clo. W On T —1H 57
Mayfield Ct. Red —8D 122
Mayfield Cres. T Hth —3K 45
Mayfield Gdns. Stai —7H 21
Mayfield Gdns. W On T —1H 57
Mayfield Rd. SW19 —9L 27
Mayfield Rd. Camb —5N 69
Mayfield Rd. F'boro —7L 69
Mayfield Rd. S Croy —5A 64
Mayfield Rd. Sutt —3B 62
Mayfield Rd. T Hth —3K 45
Mayfield Rd. W On T —1H 57
Mayfield Rd. Wey —2A 56
Mayflower Clo. Craw —4H 183
Mayflower Dri. Yat —8A 48
Mayford Clo. SW12 —1D 28
Mayford Clo. Beck —2G 47
Mayford Clo. Wok —9N 73
Mayford Rd. SW12 —1D 28
Mayhurst Av. Wok —3E 74
Mayhurst Clo. Wok —3E 74
Mayhurst Cres. Wok —3E 74
Maynard Clo. SW6 —3N 13
Maynard Ct. Stai —5J 21
Maynooth Gdns. Cars —6D 44
Mayo Rd. Croy —4A 46
Mayo Rd. W On T —6G 39
Maypole Rd. Ash W —3G 186
Maypole Rd. E Grin —8N 165
May Rd. Twic —2E 24
Mayroyd Av. Surb —8N 41
Mays Clo. Wey —6A 56
Mays Croft. Brack —3M 31
Maysfield Rd. Send —1F 94
Mays Gro. Send —1F 94
Mays Hill Rd. Brom —1N 47
Mays Rd. Tedd —6D 24
May's Rd. Wokgm —2D 30
May St. W14 —1L 13
Maytree Clo. Guild —8M 93
Maytrees. Knap —4F 72
Maytree Wlk. SW2 —3L 29
Maywater Clo. S Croy —7A 64
Maywood Dri. Camb —8F 50
Maze Rd. Rich —3N 11
Meachen Ct. Wokgm —2B 30
Mead Av. Red —2E 142
Mead Clo. Cranl —8N 155
Mead Clo. Egh —7D 20
Mead Clo. Red —9E 102
Mead Ct. Egh —7E 20
Mead Ct. Knap —3H 73
Mead Cres. Bookh —3A 98
Mead Cres. Sutt —9C 44
Meade Clo. W4 —2N 11
Meade Ct. Bag —4K 51
Meade Ct. Tad —2F 100
Mead End. Asht —4M 79
Meades Clo. D'land —1D 166
Meades, The. D'land —1D 166
Meades, The. Wey —3D 56
Meadfoot Rd. SW16 —8G 28
Meadhurst Rd. Cher —7K 37
Meadlands Dri. Rich —3K 25
Mead La. Cher —6K 37
Mead La. Farnh —1G 128
Mead La. Cvn. Pk. Cher —7L 37
Meadow App. Copt —7L 163
Meadow Av. Croy —5G 47
Meadow Bank. E Hor —5G 96
Meadow Bank. Farnh —2G 128
Meadowbank. Surb —5M 41
Meadowbank Clo. SW6 —3H 13
Meadowbank Gdns. Houn —4J 9
Meadowbank Rd. Light —6N 51
Meadow Brook. Oxt —8M 105
Meadow Brook Clo. Coln —4H 7
Meadow Brook Ind. Cen. Craw —9E 162
Meadowbrook Rd. Dork —4G 119
Meadow Clo. SW20 —3H 43
Meadow Clo. Ash V —4D 90
Meadow Clo. B'water —2J 69
Meadow Clo. Copt —7L 163
Meadow Clo. Esh —9F 40
Meadow Clo. G'ming —4H 133
Meadow Clo. H'ham —3N 197
Meadow Clo. Houn —1A 24
Meadow Clo. Milf —1D 152
Meadow Clo. Old Win —8L 5
Meadow Clo. Purl —9H 63
Meadow Clo. Rich —2L 25
Meadow Clo. Sutt —8A 44
Meadow Clo. W On T —1N 57
Meadow Cotts. W End —8C 52
Meadow Ct. Eps —9B 60
Meadow Ct. F'boro —1L 89
Meadow Ct. Fleet —4A 88
Meadow Ct. Houn —9D 10
Meadow Ct. Stai —4G 20
Meadowcroft. W4 —1N 11 (off Brooks Rd.)
Meadowcroft Clo. Craw —4L 181
Meadowcroft Clo. E Grin —8M 165
Meadow Croft Clo. Horl —2G 162
Meadow Dri. Rip —1H 95
Meadow Farm La. H'ham —1M 197
Meadow Gdns. Stai —6F 20
Meadow Hill. N Mald —5D 42
Meadow Hill. Purl —1G 82
Meadow Ho. Guild —2F 114 (off Merrow St.)
Meadowlands. Cobh —9H 57
Meadowlands. Craw —3A 182
Meadowlands. Oxt —3C 126
Meadowlands. W Cla —8K 95
Meadowlands Cvn. Pk. Add —9N 37
Meadow La. Eden —8K 127
Meadow La. Eton —2E 4
Meadow La. Fet —9C 78
Meadow La. Stai —5H 21
Meadowlea Clo. Harm —2M 7
Meadow Pl. W4 —3D 12
Meadow Rise. Coul —9H 63
Meadow Rise. Knap —4F 72
Meadow Rd. SW19 —9A 28
Meadow Rd. Ashf —6E 22
Meadow Rd. Asht —4L 79
Meadow Rd. Brom —1N 47
Meadow Rd. Clay —3E 58
Meadow Rd. F'boro —7N 69
Meadow Rd. Felt —3M 23
Meadow Rd. Guild —8C 94
Meadow Rd. Sutt —1C 62
Meadow Rd. Vir W —4H 35
Meadow Rd. Wokgm —2A 30
Meadows End. Sun —9H 23
Meadowside. Bookh —1A 98
Meadowside. Horl —7F 142
Meadowside. Stai —6J 21
Meadowside. Twic —1K 25
Meadowside. W On T —8K 39
Meadowside Mobile Homes Pk. Ling —5M 145
Meadowside Rd. Sutt —5K 61
Meadows Leigh Clo. Wey —9D 38
Meadows, The. Ash —2F 110
Meadows, The. Camb —1K 69
Meadows, The. Churt —9L 149
Meadows, The. Guild —6M 113
Meadows, The. Warl —4G 85
Meadow Stile. Croy —9N 45
Meadow, The. Copt —7L 163
Meadow Vale. Hasl —2E 188
Meadow View. Bord —6A 168
Meadow View. Small —8N 143
Meadowview. Stai —8H 7
Meadowview Rd. Eps —5D 60
Meadow View Rd. T Hth —4M 45
Meadow Wlk. Eps —4E 60 (Ewell)
Meadow Wlk. Eps —3D 60 (West Ewell)
Meadow Wlk. Tad —2G 100
Meadow Wlk. Wall —9F 44
Meadow Wlk. Wokgm —2A 30
Meadow Way. Add —1K 55
Meadow Way. Alder —1D 110
Meadow Way. B'water —1H 69
Meadow Way. Bookh —1B 98
Meadow Way. Brack —8M 15
Meadow Way. Chess —2L 59
Meadow Way. Old Win —9L 5
Meadow Way. Orp —1J 67
Meadow Way. Reig —7N 121
Meadow Way. Rowl —8E 128
Meadow Way. Tad —4K 81
Meadow Way. W End —8C 52
Meadow Way. W Hor —3E 96
Meadow Way. Wokgm —3A 30
Meadow Waye. Houn —2M 9
Mead Path. SW17 —5A 28
Mead Pl. Croy —7N 45
Mead Rd. Cat —1C 104
Mead Rd. Cranl —7N 155
Mead Rd. Craw —2D 182
Mead Rd. Eden —4M 147
Mead Rd. Hind —5D 170
Mead Rd. Rich —4J 25
Mead Rd. W On T —1M 57
Meadrow. G'ming —6J 133
Meadside Clo. Beck —1H 47
Meads Rd. Guild —3D 114
Meads, The. E Grin —2A 186
Meads, The. Hasl —2D 188
Meads, The. Mord —4C 44
Meads, The. Sutt —9K 43
Mead, The. Asht —6L 79
Mead, The. Beck —1M 47
Mead, The. Dork —8J 119
Mead, The. F'boro —2N 89
Mead, The. Wall —3H 63
Mead, The. W Wick —7N 47
Meadvale. H'ham —6F 196
Meadvale Rd. Croy —6C 46
Mead Way. SW20 —3H 43
Meadway. Ashf —5B 22
Meadway. Beck —1M 47
Mead Way. Coul —5J 83
Mead Way. Croy —8H 47
Meadway. Eff —6M 97
Meadway. Eps —8B 60
Meadway. Esh —5B 58
Meadway. Frim —4D 70
Mead Way. Guild —7E 94
Meadway. Hasl —2D 188
Meadway. Oxs —1E 78
Meadway. Stai —8J 21
Meadway. Surb —7B 42
Meadway. Twic —2D 24
Meadway. Warl —3F 84
Meadway Clo. Stai —8H 21
Meadway Ct. Tedd —6J 25
Meadway Dri. Add —4L 55
Meadway Dri. Wok —3M 73
Meadway, The. Horl —8G 142
Meare Clo. Tad —1H 101
Meath Grn. Av. Horl —6D 142
Meath Grn. La. Horl —3C 142
Medawar Rd. Sur R —4G 113
Medcroft Gdns. SW14 —7B 12
Mede Clo. Wray —2N 19
Mede Ct. Stai —4G 20
Mede Field. Fet —2D 98
Medfield St. SW15 —1F 26
Medhurst Clo. Chob —5J 53
Medina Av. Esh —9E 40
Medlake Rd. Egh —7E 20
Medland Clo. Wall —7E 44
Medlar Clo. Craw —9A 162
Medlar Clo. Guild —1M 113
Medlar Dri. B'water —3L 69
Medmenham. Cars —7B 62 (off Pine Cres.)
Medonte Clo. Fleet —5C 88
Medora Rd. SW2 —1K 29
Medway. Turn H —4D 184
Medway Clo. Croy —5F 46
Medway Clo. F Row —7J 187
Medway Ct. H'ham —3A 198
Medway Dri. E Grin —3A 186
Medway Dri. F'boro —8K 69
Medway Dri. F Row —7J 187
Medway Rd. Craw —4L 181
Medway View. F Row —7J 187
Medwin Wlk. H'ham —6J 197
Medwin Way. H'ham —6J 197
Meek Rd. SW10 —3N 13
Melancholy Wlk. Rich —3J 25
Melbourne Clo. Wall —2G 62
Melbourne Rd. SW19 —9M 27
Melbourne Rd. Tedd —7J 25
Melbourne Rd. Wall —2F 62
Melbourne Way. H'ham —3M 197
Melbury Clo. Cher —6J 37
Melbury Clo. Clay —3H 59
Melbury Clo. W Byf —1J 75
Melbury Gdns. SW20 —9F 26
Meldon Clo. SW6 —4N 13
Meldone Clo. Surb —5A 42
Meldrum Clo. Oxt —1B 126
Melford Clo. Chess —2M 59
Melfort Av. T Hth —2M 45
Melfort Rd. T Hth —2M 45
Melina Ct. SW15 —6F 12
Melksham Clo. H'ham —7L 197
Melksham Clo. Owl —6J 49
Meller Clo. Croy —9J 45
Mellersh Clo. C Crook —9A 88
Mellersh Hill Rd. Won —4D 134
Mellison Rd. SW17 —6C 28
Mellor Clo. W On T —6N 39
Mellor Wlk. Wind —4G 4
Mellow Clo. Bans —1N 81
Mellows Rd. Wall —2H 63
Melody Rd. SW18 —8N 13
Melody Rd. Big H —5E 86
Melrose. Brack —7N 31
Melrose Av. SW16 —2L 45
Melrose Av. SW19 —3L 27
Melrose Av. F'boro —9H 69
Melrose Av. Mitc —8F 28
Melrose Av. Twic —1B 24
Melrose Cres. Orp —1M 67
Melrose Gdns. N Mald —2C 42
Melrose Gdns. W On T —2K 57
Melrose Rd. SW13 —5E 12
Melrose Rd. SW18 —9L 13
Melrose Rd. SW19 —9M 27
Melrose Rd. Big H —3E 86
Melrose Rd. Coul —2F 82
Melrose Rd. Wey —2B 56
Melrose Tudor. Wall —2J 63 (off Plough La.)
Melsa Rd. Mord —5A 44
Melton Ct. Sutt —4A 62
Melton Fields. Eps —5C 60
Melton Pl. Eps —5C 60
Melton Rd. Red —8G 102
Melville Av. SW20 —8F 26
Melville Av. Frim —5D 70
Melville Av. S Croy —2C 64
Melville Ct. Guild —6M 113
Melville Rd. SW13 —4F 12
Melvin Rd. SE20 —1F 46
Melvinshaw. Lea —8J 79
Membury Clo. Frim —7E 70
Membury Wlk. Brack —3C 32
Memorial Clo. Houn —2N 9
Mendip Clo. SW19 —3K 27
Mendip Clo. Hayes —3E 8
Mendip Clo. Slou —1C 6
Mendip Clo. Wor Pk —8H 43
Mendip Rd. Brack —4C 32
Mendip Rd. F'boro —7K 69
Mendip Wlk. Craw —3N 181
Mendora Rd. SW6 —3K 13
Menin Way. Farnh —2J 129
Menlo Gdns. SE19 —8N 29
Meon Clo. F'boro —8J 69
Meon Clo. Tad —9G 80
Meon Ct. Iswth —5E 10
Meopham Rd. Mitc —9G 28
Merantun Way. SW19 —9N 27
Mercer Clo. M'bowr —6G 182
Mercer Clo. Th Dit —6G 40
Mercer Rd. H'ham —9J 179
Mercia Wlk. Wok —4B 74
Mercier Rd. SW15 —8K 13
Mercury Cen. Felt —8H 9
Mercury Clo. Bord —6A 168
Mercury Clo. Craw —6K 181
Mercury Ho. Bren —2J 11 (off Glenhurst Rd.)
Mercury Rd. Bren —2J 11
Merebank. Bear G —7K 139
Merebank La. Croy —2K 63
Mere Clo. SW15 —1J 27
Meredyth Rd. SW13 —5F 12
Mere End. Croy —6G 47
Merefield Gdns. Tad —6J 81
Mere Rd. Shep —5C 38
Mere Rd. Tad —2G 101
Mere Rd. Wey —9E 38
Mereside Pl. Vir W —7K 35 (Knowle Hill)
Mereside Pl. Vir W —4N 35 (Virginia Water)
Merevale Cres. Mord —5A 44
Mereway Rd. Twic —2D 24
Mereworth Dri. Craw —1H 183
Meridian Ct. S'dale —7M 33
Meridian Gro. Horl —7G 143
Meridian Way. E Grin —7B 166
Merivale Rd. SW15 —7K 13
Merland Clo. Tad —7H 81
Merland Grn. Tad —7H 81
Merland Rise. Eps & Tad —6H 81
Merle Comn. Rd. Oxt —4C 126
Merle Way. Fern —9E 188
Merlewood. Brack —4B 32
Merlewood Clo. Cat —7A 84
Merlin Cen. Craw —8B 162
Merlin Clo. Croy —1B 64
Merlin Clo. If'd —3K 181
Merlin Clo. Mitc —2C 44
Merlin Clo. Slou —2D 6
Merlin Clove. Wink R —7F 16
Merlin Ct. Frim —5B 70
Merlin Ct. Wok —1E 74
Merling Clo. Chess —3K 59
Merlin Gro. Beck —3J 47
Merlins Clo. Farnh —2H 129
Merlin Way. E Grin —7C 166
Merlin Way. F'boro —2J 89
Merredene St. SW2 —1K 29
Merrilands Rd. Wor Pk —7H 43
Merrilyn Clo. Clay —3G 58
Merrington Rd. SW6 —2M 13
Merrit Gdns. Chess —3J 59
Merrivale Gdns. Wok —4M 73
Merron Clo. Yat —1B 68

Montrose Clo.—New England Hill

Montrose Clo. Fleet —5C 88
Montrose Clo. Frim —4C 70
Montrose Gdns. Mitc —1D 44
Montrose Gdns. Oxs —8D 58
Montrose Gdns. Sutt —8N 43
Montrose Rd. Felt —9E 8
Montrose Wlk. Wey —9C 38
Montrose Way. Dat —4N 5
Montrouge Cres. Eps —3H 81
Montserrat Rd. SW15 —7K 13
Monument Bri. Ind. Est. Wok —2C 74
Monument Bri. Ind. Est. E. Wok —2D 74
Monument Bri. Ind. Est. W. Wok —2C 74
Monument Grn. Wey —9C 38
Monument Hill. Wey —1C 56
Monument Rd. Wey —1C 56
Monument Rd. Wok —1C 74
Monument Way E. Wok —2D 74
Monument Way W. Wok —2C 74
Moon Hall Rd. Ewh —1D 156
Moons Hill. Fren —9G 129
Moons La. H'ham —7L 197
Moon's La. Ling —3F 166
Moor Clo. Owl —6K 49
Moorcroft Clo. Craw —2N 181
Moorcroft Rd. SW16 —4J 29
Moordale Av. Brack —9K 15
Moore Clo. SW14 —6B 12
Moore Clo. Add —2K 55
Moore Clo. C Crook —8B 88
Moore Clo. Mitc —1F 44
Moore Clo. Tong —4C 110
Moore Clo. Wall —4J 63
Moore Ct. H'ham —7G 196
Moore Gro. Cres. Egh —7B 20
Moore Pk. Rd. SW6 —3M 13
Moore Rd. SE19 —7N 29
Moore Rd. C Crook —8B 88
Moore Rd. Pirb —8M 71
Moores Grn. Wokgm —9D 14
Moores La. Eton W —1C 4
Moore's Rd. Dork —4H 119
Moore Way. Sutt —5M 61
Moorfield. Hasl —3D 188
Moorfield Cen., The. Guild —8N 93
Moorfield Rd. Chess —2L 59
Moorfield Rd. Guild —8N 93
Moorfields Clo. Stai —9G 20
Moorhayes Dri. Stai —2L 37
Moorhead Rd. H'ham —3A 198
Moorholme. Wok —6A 74
Moorhouse Rd. Oxt & W'ham —9H 107
Moorhurst La. Holmw —7G 138
Moorings, The. Felb —7K 165
Moorings, The. Hind —6C 170
Moorland Clo. Twic —1A 24
Moorland Rd. M'bowr —6G 183
Moorland Rd. W Dray —2L 7
Moorlands Clo. Fleet —5C 88
Moorlands Clo. Hind —5C 170
Moorlands Pl. Camb —1M 69
Moorlands Rd. Camb —2N 69
Moorlands, The. Wok —8B 74
Moor La. Brack —2H 31
Moor La. Chess —1L 59
Moor La. D'land & Eden —9D 146
Moor La. Stai —2F 20
Moor La. W Dray —2L 7
Moor La. Wok —9A 74
Moormead Cres. Stai —5H 21
Moormead Dri. Eps —2D 60
Moor Mead Rd. Twic —9G 11
Moor Pk. Horl —9F 142
(off Aurum Clo.)
Moor Pk. Cres. If'd —4J 181
Moor Pk. Gdns. King T —8D 26
Moor Pk. Ho. Brack —5K 31
Moor Pk. La. Farnh —9K 109
Moor Pk. Way. Farnh —1L 129
Moor Pl. E Grin —8N 165
Moor Pl. W'sham —2M 51
Moor Rd. F'boro —6M 69
Moor Rd. Frim —6D 70
Moor Rd. Hasl —3A 188
Moor Rd. Stai —9J 7
Moorside Clo. F'boro —5M 69
Moors La. Elst —8G 130
Moorsom Way. Coul —4H 83
Moors, The. Tong —5C 110
Moray Av. Col T —7J 49
(in two parts)
Morcote Clo. Shalf —1A 134
Mordaunt Dri. Wel C —4G 48
Morden Clo. Brack —3D 32
Morden Clo. Tad —7J 81
Morden Ct. Mord —3N 43
Morden Ct. Pde. Mord —3N 43
Morden Gdns. Mitc —3B 44
Morden Hall Rd. Mord —2N 43
Morden Rd. SW19 —9N 27
Morden Rd. Mord & Mitc —3A 44
Morden Way. Sutt —6M 43
More Circ. G'ming —4H 133
More Clo. W14 —1J 13
More Clo. Purl —7L 63
Morecombe Clo. Craw —5L 181
Morecoombe Clo. King T —8A 26
Moreland Av. Coln —3E 6
Moreland Clo. Coln —3E 6
More La. Esh —9B 40
Morella Clo. Vir W —3N 35
Morella Rd. SW12 —1D 28
More Rd. G'ming —4H 133
Moresby Av. Surb —6A 42
Moretaine Rd. Ashf —4M 21
Moreton Almshouses. W'ham —4M 107
Moreton Av. Iswth —4E 10
Moreton Clo. C Crook —9A 88
Moreton Clo. Churt —9K 149
Moreton Rd. S Croy —2A 64
Moreton Rd. Wor Pk —8F 42
Morgan Ct. Ashf —6C 22
Morgan Rd. Tedd —7E 24
Morie St. SW18 —8N 13
Moring Rd. SW17 —5E 28
Morland Av. Croy —7B 46
Morland Clo. Hamp —6N 23
Morland Clo. Mitc —2C 44
Morland Rd. Alder —5N 109
Morland Rd. Croy —7B 46
Morland Rd. Sutt —2A 62
Morley Clo. Yat —1A 68
Morley Rd. Farnh —2H 129
Morley Rd. S Croy —6C 64
Morley Rd. Sutt —7L 43
Morley Rd. Twic —9K 11
Morningside Rd. Wor Pk —8H 43
Mornington Av. W14 —1L 13
Mornington Clo. Big H —4F 86
Mornington Cres. Houn —4J 9
Mornington Rd. Ashf —6D 22
Mornington Wlk. Rich —5J 25
Morrell Av. H'ham —3M 197
Morris Clo. Croy —4H 47
Morris Gdns. SW18 —1M 27
Morrish Rd. SW2 —1J 29
Morrison Ct. Craw —8N 181
Morris Rd. F'boro —5B 90
Morris Rd. Iswth —6F 10
Morris Rd. S Nut —5J 123
Morston Clo. Tad —7G 81
Morten Clo. SW4 —1H 29
Morth Gdns. H'ham —7J 197
Mortimer Clo. SW16 —3H 29
Mortimer Cres. Wor Pk —9C 42
Mortimer Rd. Big H —8E 66
Mortimer Rd. Capel —4K 159
Mortimer Rd. Mitc —9D 28
Mortlake Clo. Croy —9J 45
Mortlake Dri. Mitc —9C 28
Mortlake High St. SW14 —6C 12
Mortlake Rd. Rich —3N 11
Mortlake Ter. Rich —3N 11
(off Mortlake Rd.)
Morton. Tad —8J 81
Morton Clo. Craw —9N 181
Morton Clo. Frim —7D 70
Morton Clo. Wok —2M 73
Morton Gdns. Wall —2G 62
Morton M. SW5 —1N 13
Morton Rd. E Grin —2A 186
Morton Rd. Mord —4B 44
Morton Rd. Wok —2N 73
Morval Clo. F'boro —1K 89
Morven Rd. SW17 —4D 28
Moselle Clo. F'boro —9J 69
Moselle Rd. Big H —5G 87
Mosford Clo. Horl —6D 142
Mospey Cres. Eps —2E 80
Mossfield. Cobh —9H 57
Moss Gdns. Felt —3H 23
Moss Gdns. S Croy —4G 64
Moss La. G'ming —7G 133
Mosslea Rd. Whyt —3C 84
Moss Pde. Cranl —7N 155
Mossville Gdns. Mord —2L 43
Moss Way. Houn —4L 9
Moston Clo. Hayes —1G 8
Mostyn Ho. Brack —8N 15
(off Merryhill Rd.)
Mostyn Rd. SW19 —9L 27
Mostyn Ter. Red —4E 122
Motspur Pk. N Mald —5E 42
Motts Hill La. Tad —1F 100
Mouchotte Clo. Big H —8D 66
Moulsham Copse La. Yat —8A 48
Moulsham Grn. Yat —8A 48
Moulsham La. Yat —8A 48
Moulton Av. Houn —5M 9
Mt. Angelus Rd. SW15 —1E 26
Mt. Ararat Rd. Rich —8L 11
Mt. Arlington. Short —1N 47
(off Park Hill Rd.)
Mount Av. Cat —2N 103
Mountbatten Clo. Craw —7A 182
Mountbatten Ct. Alder —2M 109
(off Birchett Rd.)
Mountbatten Gdns. Beck —3H 47
Mountbatten M. SW18 —1A 28
Mountbatten Rise. Sand —6E 48
Mountbatten Sq. Wind —4F 4
Mount Clo. Cars —5E 62
Mount Clo. Craw —2H 183
Mount Clo. Ewh —5F 156
Mount Clo. Fet —1E 98
Mount Clo. Kenl —3A 84
Mount Clo. Wok —8L 73
Mount Clo., The. Vir W —5N 35
Mountcombe Clo. Surb —6L 41
Mount Cotts. If'd —2H 181
Mount Ct. SW15 —6K 13
Mount Ct. Guild —5M 113
Mount Ct. W Wick —8N 47
Mount Dri., The. Reig —1B 122
Mountearl Gdns. SW16 —4K 29
Mt. Ephraim La. SW16 —4H 29
Mt. Ephraim Rd. SW16 —4H 29
Mt. Felix. W On T —6G 38
Mt. Hermon Clo. Wok —6N 73
Mt. Hermon Rd. Wok —6N 73
Mount Hill. Wink —3N 17
Mount La. Brack —2A 32
Mount La. Turn H —5D 184
Mt. Lee. Egh —6B 20
Mount M. Hamp —9B 24
Mt. Nod Rd. SW16 —4K 29
Mount Pk. Cars —4E 62
Mount Pk. Av. S Croy —5M 63
Mount Pl. Guild —5M 113
Mt. Pleasant. SE27 —5N 29
Mt. Pleasant. Big H —4F 86
Mt. Pleasant. Brack —2A 32
(in two parts)
Mt. Pleasant. Eff —6M 97
Mt. Pleasant. Eps —6E 60
Mt. Pleasant. Farnh —1F 128
Mt. Pleasant. Guild —5M 113
Mt. Pleasant. Sand —6F 48
Mt. Pleasant. W Hor —7C 96
Mt. Pleasant. Wey —9B 38
Mt. Pleasant. Wokgm —2A 30
Mt. Pleasant Clo. Light —6L 51
Mt. Pleasant Rd. Alder —2A 110
Mt. Pleasant Rd. Cat —1D 104
Mt. Pleasant Rd. Lind —4A 168
Mt. Pleasant Rd. Ling —7M 145
Mt. Pleasant Rd. N Mald —2B 42
Mount Rise. Red —5B 122
Mount Rd. SW19 —3M 27
Mount Rd. Chess —2M 59
Mount Rd. Chob —8L 53
Mount Rd. Cranl —8N 155
Mount Rd. Felt —4M 23
Mount Rd. Mitc —1B 44
Mount Rd. N Mald —2C 42
Mount Rd. Wok —8L 73
Mountsfield Clo. Stai —9J 7
Mounts Hill. Wink —3N 17
Mountside. Guild —5L 113
Mount St. Dork —5G 118
Mount, The. Coul —1F 82
Mount, The. Cranl —8N 155
Mount, The. Eps —6E 60
Mount, The. Esh —3A 58
Mount, The. Ewh —5F 156
Mount, The. Fet —2E 98
Mount, The. Fleet —3B 88
Mount, The. G'wood —8K 171
Mount, The. Guild —5M 113
Mount, The. Head —3F 168
Mount, The. If'd —9G 160
Mount, The. N Mald —2E 42
Mount, The. Tad —4L 101
Mount, The. Vir W —5N 35
Mount, The. Warl —6D 84
Mount, The. Wey —8F 38
Mount, The. Wok —5N 73
(off Elm Rd.)
Mount, The. Wok —6K 73
(St John's Hill Rd.)
Mount, The. Wor Pk —1G 61
Mount View. Alder —3M 109
Mountview Clo. Red —5C 122
Mountview Dri. Red —5C 122
Mt. View Rd. Clay —4H 59
Mount Vs. SE27 —4M 29
Mount Way. Cars —5E 62
Mount Wood. W Mol —2B 40
Mountwood Clo. S Croy —6E 64
Moushill La. Milf —2B 152
Mowat Corner. Wor Pk —8E 42
Mowat Ct. Wor Pk —8E 42
(off Avenue, The)
Mowatt Rd. Gray —7B 170
Mowbray Av. Byfl —9N 55
Mowbray Cres. Egh —6C 20
Mowbray Dri. Craw —5L 181
Mowbray Gdns. Dork —3H 119
Mowbray Rd. Rich —4J 25
Mower Clo. Wokgm —1E 30
Mower Pl. Cranl —6N 155
Moylan Rd. W6 —2K 13
Moyne Ct. Wok —5J 73
Moyne Rd. Craw —7A 182
Moys Clo. Croy —5J 45
Moyser Rd. SW16 —6F 28
Muchelney Rd. Mord —5A 44
Muckhatch La. Egh —2D 36
Muggeridge Clo. S Croy —2A 64
Muggeridges Hill. H'ham —1L 179
Muirdown Av. SW14 —7C 12
Muir Dri. SW18 —1C 28
Muirfield Clo. If'd —4J 181
Muirfield Ho. Brack —5K 31
Muirfield Rd. Wok —5K 73
Mulberries, The. Farnh —8L 109
Mulberry Av. Stai —2N 21
Mulberry Av. Wind —6J 5
Mulberry Bus. Pk. Wokgm —4A 30
Mulberry Clo. SW16 —5G 28
Mulberry Clo. Ash V —9E 90
Mulberry Clo. Crowt —3H 49
Mulberry Clo. H'ham —3J 197
Mulberry Clo. Owl —7J 49
Mulberry Clo. Wey —9C 38
Mulberry Clo. Wok —1A 74
Mulberry Ct. Brack —4C 32
Mulberry Ct. Guild —1F 114
Mulberry Ct. Surb —6K 41
Mulberry Ct. Twic —4F 24
Mulberry Ct. Wokgm —2B 30
Mulberry Cres. Bren —3H 11
Mulberry Dri. Slou —1A 6
Mulberry Ho. Brack —8N 15
Mulberry Ho. Short —1N 47
Mulberry La. Croy —7C 46
Mulberry M. Wall —3G 62
Mulberry Pl. W6 —1F 12
Mulberry Rd. Craw —9N 161
Mulberry Trees. Shep —6E 38
Mulgrave Ct. Sutt —3N 61
(off Mulgrave Rd.)
Mulgrave Rd. SW6 —2L 13
Mulgrave Rd. Croy —9A 46
Mulgrave Rd. Frim —4D 70
Mulgrave Rd. Sutt —4L 61
Mulgrave Way. Knap —5H 73
Mulholland Clo. Mitc —1F 44
Mullards Clo. Mitc —7D 44
Mullein Wlk. Craw —7M 181
Mullens Rd. Egh —6E 20
Muller Rd. SW4 —1H 29
Mullins Path. SW14 —6C 12
Mulroy Dri. Camb —9E 50
Multon Rd. SW18 —1B 28
Muncaster Clo. Ashf —5B 22
Muncaster Rd. Ashf —6C 22
Munday Ct. Binf —8K 15
Mundays Boro Rd. P'ham —8L 111
Munden St. W14 —1K 13
Mund St. W14 —1L 13
Munnings Dri. Col T —9J 49
Munnings Gdns. Iswth —8D 10
Munslow Gdns. Sutt —1B 62
Munstead Heath Rd. G'ming & Brmly —1K 153
Munstead Pk. G'ming —8M 133
Munstead View. Guild —7L 113
Munstead View Rd. Brmly —6N 133
Munster Av. Houn —8M 9
Munster Ct. SW6 —5L 13
Munster Ct. Tedd —7J 25
Munster Rd. SW6 —3K 13
Munster Rd. Tedd —7J 25
Murdoch Clo. Stai —6J 21
Murdoch Rd. Wokgm —3B 30
Murfett Clo. SW19 —3K 27
Murray Av. Houn —8B 10
Murray Ct. Asc —5N 33
Murray Ct. Craw —8M 181
Murray Ct. H'ham —4A 198
Murray Ct. Twic —3D 24
Murray Grn. Wok —1E 74
Murray Ho. Ott —3E 54
Murray Rd. SW19 —7J 27
Murray Rd. W5 —1J 11
Murray Rd. F'boro —2L 89
Murray Rd. Ott —3E 54
Murray Rd. Rich —3J 25
Murray Rd. Wokgm —2A 30
Murray's La. W Byf —1M 75
Murray Ter. W5 —1K 11
Murrellhill La. Binf —8H 15
Murrell Rd. Ash —1E 110
Murrells La. Camb —3N 69
Murrell's Wlk. Bookh —1A 98
Murreys Ct. Asht —5K 79
Murreys, The. Asht —6K 79
Murtmead La. Guild —9L 111
Musard Rd. W6 —2K 13
Muschamp Rd. Cars —8C 44
Museum Hill. Hasl —2H 189
Musgrave Av. E Grin —2A 186
Musgrave Cres. SW6 —3M 13
Musgrave Rd. Iswth —4F 10
Mushroom Castle. Brack —7F 16
Musquash Way. Houn —5K 9
Mustow Pl. SW6 —5L 13
Mutton Hill. Brack —9H 15
Mutton Hill. D'land —3C 166
Mutton Oaks. Binf —9J 15
Muybridge Rd. N Mald —1B 42
Myers Way. Frim —4H 71
Mylne Clo. W6 —1F 12
Mylne Sq. Wokgm —2C 30
Mylor Clo. Wok —1A 74
Mynn's Clo. Eps —1A 80
Mynthurst. Leigh —4G 141
Myrke, The. Dat —1J 5
Myrna Clo. SW19 —8C 28
Myrtle Av. Felt —8F 8
Myrtle Clo. Coln —4G 6
Myrtle Clo. Light —7M 51
Myrtle Dri. B'water —1K 69
Myrtle Gro. N Mald —1B 42
Myrtle Rd. Croy —9K 47
Myrtle Rd. Dork —4G 119
Myrtle Rd. Hamp —7C 24
Myrtle Rd. Houn —5C 10
Myrtle Rd. Sutt —2A 62
Mytchett Farm Cvn. Pk. Myt —3D 90
Mytchett Heath. Myt —3E 90
Mytchett Lake Rd. Myt —4E 90
Mytchett Pl. Rd. Myt & Ash V —2E 90
Mytchett Rd. Myt —1D 90
Myton Rd. SE21 —4N 29

Nadine Ct. Wall —5G 62
Nailsworth Cres. Red —7H 103
Nairn Clo. Frim —4C 70
Naldrett Clo. H'ham —4M 197
Naldretts La. H'ham —3E 194
Nallhead Rd. Felt —6K 23
Namba Roy Clo. SW16 —5K 29
Namton Dri. T Hth —3K 45
Napier Av. SW6 —6L 13
Napier Clo. Alder —6C 90
Napier Clo. Crowt —2H 49
Napier Ct. SW6 —6L 13
(off Ranelagh Gdns.)
Napier Ct. Cat —9B 84
Napier Dri. Camb —8E 50
Napier Gdns. Guild —2D 114
Napier La. Ash V —9E 90
Napier Rd. SE25 —3F 46
Napier Rd. Ashf —8E 22
Napier Rd. Crowt —3H 49
Napier Rd. Iswth —7G 11
Napier Rd. H'row A —4M 7
Napier Rd. S Croy —4A 64
Napier Wlk. Ashf —8E 22
Napier Way. Craw —9E 162
Napoleon Av. F'boro —8N 69
Napoleon Rd. Twic —1H 25
Napper Clo. Asc —1G 33
Napper Pl. Cranl —9N 155
Nappers Wood. Fern —9E 188
Narborough St. SW6 —5N 13
Narrow La. Warl —6E 84
Naseby. Brack —7N 31
Naseby Clo. Iswth —4E 10
Naseby Ct. W on T —8K 39
Nash Clo. F'boro —1L 89
Nash Dri. Red —1D 122
Nash Gdns. Asc —1J 33
Nash Gdns. Red —1D 122
Nashlands Cotts. Hand —6N 199
Nash La. Kes —4G 66
Nash Pk. Binf —7G 15
Nash Rd. Craw —6C 182
Nash Rd. Slou —1B 6
Nassau Rd. SW13 —4E 12
Nasturtium Dri. Bisl —2D 72
Natalie Clo. Felt —1E 22
Natalie M. Twic —4D 24
Natal Rd. SW16 —7H 29
Natal Rd. T Hth —2A 46
Neale Clo. E Grin —7L 165
Neale Ho. E Grin —8A 166
Neath Gdns. Mord —5A 44
Neb La. Oxt —9M 105
Needham Clo. Wind —4B 4
Needles Bank. God —9E 104
Needles Clo. H'ham —7H 197
Neil Clo. Ashf —6D 22
Neil Wates Cres. SW2 —2L 29
Nella Rd. W6 —2J 13
Nell Ball. Plais —6A 192
Nell Gwynne Av. Shep —5E 38
Nell Gwynne Clo. Asc —3A 34
Nello James Gdns. SE27 —5N 29
Nelson Clo. Big H —4G 87
Nelson Clo. Brack —9C 16
Nelson Clo. Croy —7M 45
Nelson Clo. Farnh —4J 109
Nelson Clo. Felt —2H 23
Nelson Clo. M'bowr —4G 183
Nelson Clo. W On T —7J 39
Nelson Ct. Cher —7J 37
Nelson Gdns. Guild —2C 114
Nelson Gdns. Houn —9A 10
Nelson Gro. Rd. SW19 —9A 28
Nelson Ind. Est. SW19 —9N 27
Nelson Rd. SW19 —8A 28
Nelson Rd. Ashf —6N 21
Nelson Rd. Cat —1A 104
Nelson Rd. Farnh —4J 109
Nelson Rd. H'ham —5H 197
Nelson Rd. Houn —9A 10
Nelson Rd. H'row A —4A 8
Nelson Rd. N Mald —4C 42
Nelson Rd. Twic —9A 10
Nelson Rd. Wind —6C 4
Nelson Rd. M. SW19 —8N 27
Nelson's La. Hurst —4A 14
Nelson St. Alder —2M 109
Nelson Way. Camb —2L 69
Nene Gdns. Felt —3N 23
Nene Rd. H'row A —4C 8
Nepean St. SW15 —9F 12
Neptune Clo. Bew —5K 181
Neptune Rd. Bord —7A 168
Neptune Rd. H'row A —4E 8
Nero Ct. Bren —3K 11
Nesbit Ct. Craw —6K 181
Netheravon Rd. N. W4 —1E 12
Netheravon Rd. S. W4 —1E 12
Netherby Pk. Wey —2F 56
Nethercote Av. Wok —4J 73
Netherfield Rd. SW17 —4E 28
Netherlands, The. Coul —6G 83
Netherleigh Pk. S Nut —6J 123
Nether Mt. Guild —5L 113
Nethern Ct. Rd. Wold —1K 105
Netherne La. Coul —1G 102
Netherton. Brack —3M 31
Netherton Gro. SW10 —2N 13
Netherton Rd. Twic —8G 11
Nether Vell-Mead. C Crook —9A 88
Netherwood. Craw —5N 181
Netley Clo. Craw —9A 182
Netley Clo. New Ad —4M 65
Netley Clo. Sutt —2J 61
Netley Dri. W On T —6N 39
Netley Gdns. Mord —6A 44
Netley Rd. Bren —2L 11
Netley Rd. H'row A —4E 8
Netley Rd. Mord —6A 44
Netley Rd. W. H'row A —4E 8
Netley St. F'boro —5N 89
Nettlecombe. Brack —5B 32
Nettlecombe Clo. Sutt —5N 61
Nettlefold Pl. SE27 —4M 29
Nettles Ter. Guild —3N 113
Nettleton Rd. H'row A —4C 8
Nettlewood Rd. SW16 —8H 29
Nevada Clo. F'boro —2J 89
Nevada Clo. N Mald —3B 42
Nevelle Clo. Binf —9J 15
Nevern Mans. SW5 —1M 13
(off Warwick Rd.)
Nevern Pl. SW5 —1M 13
Nevern Rd. SW5 —1M 13
Nevern Sq. SW5 —1M 13
Nevile Clo. Craw —6M 181
Neville Av. N Mald —9C 26
Neville Clo. Bans —1N 81
Neville Clo. Esh —3N 57
Neville Clo. Houn —5B 10
Neville Duke Rd. F'boro —6L 69
Neville Gill Clo. SW18 —9M 13
Neville Rd. Croy —6A 46
Neville Rd. King T —1N 41
Neville Rd. Rich —4J 25
Neville Wlk. Cars —6C 44
Nevis Rd. SW17 —3E 28
Newall Rd. H'row A —4D 8
Newark Clo. Guild —7D 94
Newark Clo. Rip —8J 75
Newark Cotts. Rip —8J 75
Newark Ct. W on T —7K 39
Newark La. Wok & Rip —5H 75
Newark Rd. Craw —1D 182
Newark Rd. S Croy —3A 64
New Barn La. Newd —9B 140
New Barn La. Ockl —7A 158
New Barn La. W'ham & Cud —5L 87
New Barn La. Whyt —3B 84
New Barns Av. Mitc —3H 45
New Battlebridge La. Red —8F 102
Newberry Cres. Wind —5A 4
New Berry La. W On T —2L 57
Newbolt Av. Sutt —2H 61
Newborough Grn. N Mald —3C 42
Newbridge Clo. Broad H —5C 196
Newbridge Ct. Cranl —7K 155
New B'way. Hamp —6D 24
Newbury Gdns. Eps —1E 60
Newbury Rd. H'row A —4A 8
New Causeway. Reig —6N 121
Newchapel Rd. Ling —1J 165
New Chapel Sq. Felt —2J 23
New Clo. SW19 —2A 44
New Clo. Felt —6M 23
New Colebrooke Ct. Cars —4E 62
(off Stanley Rd.)
Newcombe Gdns. SW16 —5J 29
Newcome Pl. Alder —5B 110
Newcome Rd. Farnh —6K 109
New Coppice. Wok —6H 73
New Cotts. Craw —5D 184
New Cotts. Pirb —9A 72
New Ct. Add —9L 37
New Cross Rd. Guild —1K 113
New Dawn Clo. F'boro —2J 89
Newdigate Rd. Bear G —9K 139
Newdigate Rd. Leigh —1D 140
Newdigate Rd. Rusp —1B 180
Newell Grn. Warf —6A 16
New England Hill. W End —8A 52

A-Z Surrey 245

Newenham Rd.—Nutcombe La.

Newenham Rd. *Bookh* —4A **98**
New Farthingdale. *D'land* —2D **166**
Newfield Av. *F'boro* —8K **69**
Newfield Clo. *Hamp* —9A **24**
Newfield Rd. *Ash V* —7E **90**
New Forest Ride. *Brack* —6C **32**
Newfoundland Rd. *Deep* —6H **71**
Newgate. *Croy* —7N **45**
Newgate Clo. *Felt* —4M **23**
Newhache. *D'land* —1C **166**
Newhall Gdns. *W On T* —8K **39**
Newhaven Cres. *Ashf* —6E **22**
Newhaven Rd. *SE25* —4A **46**
New Haw Rd. *Add* —2L **55**
New Heston Rd. *Houn* —3N **9**
New Horizons Ct. *Bren* —2J **11**
Newhouse Clo. *N Mald* —6D **42**
Newhouse Cotts. *Dork* —6B **160**
New Ho. Farm La. *Wood S* —2F **112**
New Ho. La. *Red* —2H **143**
Newhouse Wlk. *Mord* —6A **44**
Newhurst Gdns. *Warf* —6B **16**
New Inn La. *Guild* —8D **94**
New Kelvin Av. *Tedd* —7E **24**
New Kings Rd. *SW6* —5L **13**
Newlands. *Fleet* —7B **88**
Newlands Av. *Th Dit* —7E **40**
Newlands Av. *Wok* —8B **74**
Newlands Clo. *Horl* —6D **142**
Newlands Clo. *S'hall* —1M **9**
Newlands Clo. *W On T* —1M **57**
Newlands Clo. *Yat* —1C **68**
*Newlands Ct. Add —2K **55***
(off Addlestone Pk.)
*Newlands Ct. Cat —8N **83***
(off Coulsdon Rd.)
Newlands Cres. *E Grin* —8N **165**
Newlands Dri. *Ash V* —9F **90**
Newlands Dri. *Coln* —6G **7**
Newlands Est. *Witl* —5C **152**
Newlands Pk. *Copt* —7B **164**
Newlands Pl. *F Row* —6H **187**
Newlands Rd. *SW16* —1J **45**
Newlands Rd. *Camb* —5N **69**
Newlands Rd. *Craw* —4A **182**
Newlands Rd. *H'ham* —4J **197**
Newlands, The. *Wall* —4H **63**
Newlands Way. *Chess* —2J **59**
Newlands Wood. *New Ad* —5J **65**
New La. *Wok & Sut G* —9A **74**
New Lodge Dri. *Oxt* —6B **106**
Newman Clo. *M'bowr* —5G **182**
Newman Rd. *Croy* —7K **45**
Newman Rd. Ind. Est. *Croy* —6K **45**
Newmans Ct. *Farnh* —5F **108**
Newmans La. *Surb* —5K **41**
Newmarket Rd. *Craw* —5E **182**
New Meadow. *Asc* —9H **17**
New Mile Rd. *Asc* —1M **33**
New Mill Cotts. *Hasl* —2B **188**
Newminster Rd. *Mord* —5A **44**
New Moorhead Dri. *H'ham* —2B **198**
Newnes Path. *SW15* —7G **12**
Newnet Clo. *Cars* —7D **44**
Newnham Clo. *T Hth* —1N **45**
New N. Rd. *Reig* —6L **121**
New Pde. *Ashf* —5A **22**
New Pk. Rd. *SW2* —2H **29**
New Pk. Rd. *Ashf* —6D **22**
New Pk. Rd. *Cranl* —7N **155**
New Pl. *New Ad* —3K **65**
New Pond Rd. *Guild & G'ming* —1G **132**
New Poplars Ct. *Ash* —3E **110**
Newport Rd. *SW13* —4F **12**
Newport Rd. *Alder* —3A **110**
Newport Rd. *H'row A* —4B **8**
New Rd. *Alb* —8M **115**
New Rd. *Asc* —8J **17**
New Rd. *Bag & W'sham* —4K **51**
New Rd. *Bedf* —9E **8**
New Rd. *B'water* —2K **69**
New Rd. *Brack* —1B **32**
New Rd. *Bren* —2K **11**
New Rd. *Cher* —6H **37**
New Rd. *Chil* —1D **134**
New Rd. *C Crook* —7C **88**
New Rd. *Crowt* —2H **49**
New Rd. *Dat* —4N **5**
New Rd. *Dork* —6K **119**
New Rd. *E Clan* —9N **95**
New Rd. *Esh* —9C **40**
New Rd. *Felt* —2J **23**
New Rd. *F Grn* —4M **157**
New Rd. *Gom* —8D **116**
New Rd. *Hanw* —6M **23**
New Rd. *Hasl* —3D **188**
New Rd. *Hayes* —3D **8**
New Rd. *Houn* —7B **10**
New Rd. *Hyde* —5J **153**
New Rd. *King T* —8N **25**
New Rd. *Limp* —8D **106**
New Rd. *Milf* —2B **152**
New Rd. *Mitc* —7D **44**
New Rd. *Oxs* —7F **58**
New Rd. *Rich* —5J **25**
New Rd. *Sand* —7F **48**
New Rd. *Shep* —2B **38**
New Rd. *Small* —8M **143**
New Rd. *Stai* —6E **20**
New Rd. *Tad* —1H **101**
New Rd. *Tand* —5K **125**
New Rd. *Tong* —6D **110**
New Rd. *W Mol* —3A **40**
New Rd. *Wey* —2D **56**
New Rd. *Won* —3D **134**
New Rd. *Worm* —1D **172**
New Rd. Hill. *Kes & Orp* —5G **67**
Newry Rd. *Twic* —8G **11**
Newsham Rd. *Wok* —4J **73**
New Sq. *Felt* —2D **22**
Newstead Clo. *G'ming* —5G **132**
Newstead Rise. *Cat* —4E **104**
Newstead Wlk. *Cars* —6M **43**
Newstead Way. *SW19* —5J **27**
New St. *Craw* —2E **182**
New St. *H'ham* —7K **197**
New St. *Stai* —5J **21**
New St. *W'ham* —5L **107**
Newton Av. *E Grin* —3B **186**
Newton Ct. *Old Win* —9K **5**
Newton La. *Old Win* —9L **5**
*Newton Mans. W14 —2K **13***
(off Queen's Club Gdns.)
Newton Rd. *SW19* —8K **27**
Newton Rd. *Craw* —8D **162**
Newton Rd. *F'boro* —8B **70**
Newton Rd. *Iswth* —5F **10**
Newton Rd. *H'row A* —4N **7**
Newton Rd. *Purl* —8G **63**
Newtonside Orchard. *Old Win* —9K **5**
Newton's Yd. *SW18* —8M **13**
Newton Way. *Tong* —5C **110**
Newton Wood Rd. *Asht* —9M **79**
New Town. *Copt* —7M **163**
Newtown Rd. *Sand* —7G **48**
New Way. *G'ming* —8F **132**
New Wickham La. *Egh* —8C **20**
New Wokingham Rd. *Wokgm & Crowt* —9F **30**
New Zealand Av. *W On T* —7G **38**
*Nicholas Ct. W4 —2D **12***
(off Corney Reach Way)
Nicholas Gdns. *Wok* —3H **75**
Nicholas Rd. *Croy* —1J **63**
Nicholes Rd. *Houn* —7A **10**
Nicholls. *Wind* —6A **4**
Nicholls Wlk. *Wind* —6A **4**
Nichols Clo. *Chess* —3J **59**
Nicholsfield. *Loxw* —4H **193**
*Nicholson M. Egh —6C **20***
(off Nicholson Wlk.)
Nicholson Rd. *Croy* —7C **46**
Nicholson Wlk. *Egh* —6C **20**
Nicola Clo. *S Croy* —3N **63**
Nicol Clo. *Twic* —9H **11**
Nicosia Rd. *SW18* —1C **28**
*Nicotiana Ct. C Crook —9A **88***
(off Rye Croft)
Nigel Playfair Av. *W6* —1G **12**
Nightingale Av. *W Hor* —2E **96**
Nightingale Clo. *W4* —2B **12**
Nightingale Clo. *Big H* —2E **86**
Nightingale Clo. *Bord* —7A **168**
Nightingale Clo. *Cars* —8E **44**
Nightingale Clo. *Cobh* —7L **57**
Nightingale Clo. *Craw* —1A **182**
Nightingale Clo. *E Grin* —2N **185**
Nightingale Clo. *F'boro* —8H **69**
*Nightingale Ct. SW6 —4N **13***
(off Maltings Pl.)
*Nightingale Ct. Red —2E **122***
(off St Anne's Mt.)
Nightingale Ct. *Wok* —5H **73**
Nightingale Cres. *Brack* —4A **32**
Nightingale Cres. *W Hor* —3D **96**
Nightingale Dri. *Eps* —3A **60**
Nightingale Dri. *Myt* —2E **90**
Nightingale Gdns. *Sand* —7G **48**
Nightingale Ho. *Eps* —8D **60**
Nightingale Ho. *Ott* —3F **54**
Nightingale Ind. Est. *H'ham* —5K **197**
Nightingale La. *SW12 & SW4* —1D **28**
Nightingale La. *Rich* —1L **25**
Nightingale La. *Turn H* —4F **184**
Nightingale Rd. *Ash* —1G **111**
Nightingale Rd. *Cars* —9D **44**
Nightingale Rd. *E Hor* —3G **96**
Nightingale Rd. *Esh* —2N **57**
Nightingale Rd. *G'ming* —6H **133**
Nightingale Rd. *Guild* —3N **113**
Nightingale Rd. *Hamp* —6A **24**
Nightingale Rd. *H'ham* —5K **197**
Nightingale Rd. *S Croy* —7G **64**
Nightingale Rd. *W On T* —6K **39**
Nightingale Rd. *W Mol* —4B **40**
Nightingales. *Cranl* —9N **155**
Nightingales Clo. *H'ham* —6M **197**
Nightingale Sq. *SW12* —1E **28**
Nightingales, The. *Stai* —2A **22**
Nightingale Way. *Blet* —3B **124**
Nightjar Clo. *Ews* —4C **108**
Nikols Wlk. *SW18* —7N **13**
Nimbus Rd. *Eps* —6C **60**
*Nimrod Ct. Craw —9H **163***
(off Wakehams Grn. Dri.)
Nimrod Rd. *SW16* —7F **28**
Nineacres Way. *Coul* —3J **83**
Nine Elms Clo. *Felt* —2G **23**
Ninehams Clo. *Cat* —7A **84**
Ninehams Gdns. *Cat* —7A **84**
Ninehams Rd. *Cat* —8A **84**
Ninehams Rd. *Tats* —8E **86**
Nine Mile Ride. *Asc* —6J **33**
Nine Mile Ride. *Crowt & Brack* (in two parts) —7L **31**
Nine Mile Ride. *Wokgm* —1A **48**
Nineteenth Rd. *Mitc* —3J **45**
Ninfield Ct. *Craw* —7L **181**
Ninhams Wood. *Orp* —1J **67**
Niton Rd. *Rich* —6N **11**
Niton St. *SW6* —3J **13**
Niven Clo. *M'bowr* —4H **183**
Niven Ct. *S'hill* —3A **34**
Noahs Ct. *Turn H* —5D **184**
Nobel Dri. *Hayes* —4E **8**
Noble Corner. *Houn* —4A **10**
Noble Ct. *Mitc* —1B **44**
Nobles Way. *Egh* —7A **20**
Noel Ct. *Houn* —6N **9**
Noke Dri. *Red* —2E **122**
Nonsuch Ct. Av. *Eps* —6G **60**
Nonsuch Trad. Est. *Eps* —7D **60**
Nonsuch Wlk. *Sutt* —6H **61** (in two parts)
Noons Corner Rd. *Dork* —3N **137**
Norbiton Av. *King T* —9N **25**
Norbiton Comn. Rd. *King T* —2A **42**
Norbury Av. *SW16 & T Hth* —9K **29**
Norbury Av. *Houn* —7D **10**
Norbury Clo. *SW16* —9L **29**
Norbury Ct. Rd. *SW16* —2J **45**
Norbury Cres. *SW16* —9K **29**
Norbury Cross. *SW16* —2J **45**
Norbury Hill. *SW16* —8L **29**
Norbury Rise. *SW16* —2J **45**
Norbury Rd. *Reig* —3L **121**
Norbury Rd. *T Hth* —1N **45**
Norbury Trad. Est. *SW16* —1K **45**
Norbury Way. *Bookh* —3C **98**
Norcutt Rd. *Twic* —2E **24**
Norfolk Av. *S Croy* —6C **64**
Norfolk Chase. *Warf* —8D **16**
Norfolk Clo. *Craw* —7K **181**
Norfolk Clo. *Horl* —9E **142**
Norfolk Clo. *Twic* —9H **11**
Norfolk Ct. *Dork* —9K **119**
Norfolk Ct. *H'ham* —3A **198**
Norfolk Farm Clo. *Wok* —3F **74**
Norfolk Farm Rd. *Wok* —2F **74**
Norfolk Gdns. *Houn* —8N **9**
Norfolk Ho. Rd. *SW16* —4H **29**
Norfolk La. *Mid H* —2H **139**
Norfolk Rd. *SW19* —8C **28**
Norfolk Rd. *Clay* —2E **58**
Norfolk Rd. *Dork* —5G **119**
Norfolk Rd. *Felt* —2K **23**
Norfolk Rd. *Holmw* —5J **139**
Norfolk Rd. *H'ham* —6K **197**
Norfolk Rd. *T Hth* —2N **45**
Norfolk Ter. *W6* —1K **13**
Norfolk Ter. *H'ham* —6K **197**
Norgrove St. *SW12* —1E **28**
Norheads La. *Warl & Big H* —6C **86**
Norhyrst Av. *SE25* —2C **46**
Nork Gdns. *Bans* —1K **81**
Nork Rise. *Bans* —3J **81**
Nork Way. *Bans* —3H **81**
Norlands La. *Egh* —2G **36**
Norley La. *Sham G* —6D **134**
Norley Vale. *SW15* —2F **26**
Norman Av. *Eps* —8E **60**
Norman Av. *Felt* —3M **23**
Norman Av. *S Croy* —6N **63**
Norman Av. *Twic* —1J **25**
Normanby Clo. *SW15* —8L **13**
Norman Clo. *Bord* —7A **168**
Norman Colyer Ct. *Eps* —6C **60**
Norman Ct. *Eden* —1K **147**
Norman Ct. *Farnh* —2H **129**
Norman Cres. *Houn* —3L **9**
*Normand Gdns. W14 —2K **13***
(off Greyhound Rd.)
Normand M. *W14* —2K **13**
Normand Rd. *W14* —2L **13**
Normandy. *H'ham* —7J **197**
Normandy Barracks. *Alder* —9M **89**
Normandy Clo. *E Grin* —1B **186**
Normandy Clo. *M'bowr* —5F **182**
Normandy Gdns. *H'ham* —7J **197**
Normandy Wlk. *Egh* —6E **20**
Norman Hay Trad. Est., The. *W Dray* —3A **8**
Norman Ho. *Felt* —3N **23**
Normanhurst. *Ashf* —6B **22**
Normanhurst Clo. *Craw* —3D **182**
Normanhurst Dri. *Twic* —8G **11**
Normanhurst Rd. *SW2* —3K **29**
Normanhurst Rd. *W On T* —8L **39**
Norman Keep. *Warf* —9D **16**
Norman La. *Eden* —4G **147**
Norman Rd. *SW19* —8A **28**
Norman Rd. *Ashf* —7E **22**
Norman Rd. *Sutt* —2M **61**
Norman Rd. *T Hth* —4M **45**
Normansfield Av. *Tedd* —8J **25**
Normans Rd. *Small & Red* —6N **143**
Normanton Av. *SW19* —3M **27**
Normanton Rd. *S Croy* —3B **64**
Normington Clo. *SW16* —6L **29**
Norney. *Shack* —5B **132**
Norrels Dri. *E Hor* —4G **96**
Norrels Ride. *E Hor* —3G **97**
Norreys Av. *Wokgm* —2C **30**
Norris Hill Rd. *Fleet* —5D **88**
Norroy Rd. *SW15* —7J **13**
Norstead Pl. *SW15* —3F **26**
North Acre. *Bans* —3L **81**
Northampton Clo. *Brack* —2C **32**
Northampton Rd. *Croy* —8D **46**
Northanger Rd. *SW16* —7J **29**
North Ash. *H'ham* —4J **197**
North Av. *Cars* —4E **62**
North Av. *Farnh* —5J **109**
North Av. *Rich* —4N **11**
North Av. *W Vill* —5F **56**
Northborough Rd. *SW16* —2H **45**
Northbourne. *G'ming* —3J **133**
N. Breache Rd. *Ewh* —4H **197**
Northbrook Copse. *Brack* —5D **32**
Northbrook Rd. *Alder* —4N **109**
Northbrook Rd. *Croy* —4A **46**
Northcliffe Clo. *Wor Pk* —9D **42**
North Clo. *Alder* —3C **110**
North Clo. *Craw* —2D **182**
North Clo. *F'boro* —6M **69**
North Clo. *Felt* —9E **8**
North Clo. *Mord* —3K **43**
North Clo. *N Holm* —9J **119**
North Clo. *Wind* —4C **4**
North Comn. *Wey* —1D **56**
Northcote. *Add* —1M **55**
Northcote. *Oxs* —1C **78**
Northcote Av. *Iswth* —8G **10**
Northcote Av. *Surb* —6A **42**
Northcote Clo. *W Hor* —3D **96**
Northcote Cres. *W Hor* —3D **96**
Northcote La. *Sham G* —5F **134**
Northcote Rd. *Ash V* —6D **90**
Northcote Rd. *Croy* —5A **46**
Northcote Rd. *F'boro* —8L **69**
Northcote Rd. *N Mald* —2B **42**
Northcote Rd. *Twic* —8G **11**
Northcote Rd. *W Hor* —3D **96**
Northcott. *Brack* —7M **31**
North Ct. *G'ming* —4E **132**
Northcroft Clo. *Egh* —6L **19**
Northcroft Gdns. *Egh* —6L **19**
Northcroft Rd. *Egh* —6L **19**
Northcroft Rd. *Eps* —4C **60**
Northcroft Vs. *Egh* —6L **19**
Northdale Ct. *SE25* —2C **46**
North Dene. *Houn* —4B **10**
North Down. *S Croy* —7B **64**
Northdown Clo. *H'ham* —4M **197**
Northdown La. *Guild* —6A **114**
Northdown Rd. *Sutt* —6M **61**
Northdown Rd. *Wold* —2K **105**
Northdowns. *Cranl* —9N **155**
N. Downs Cres. *New Ad* —5L **65**
N. Downs Rd. *New Ad* —5L **65**
Northdown Ter. *E Grin* —7N **165**
North Dri. *SW16* —5G **28**
North Dri. *Brkwd* —8N **71**
North Dri. *Houn* —5C **10**
North Dri. *Orp* —1N **67**
North Dri. *Vir W* —4H **35**
North End. *Croy* —8N **45**
North End. *E Grin* —7L **165**
N. End Cres. *W14* —1L **13**
*N. End Ho. W14 —1K **13***
(off Fitzjames Av.)
N. End La. *Asc* —6E **34**
N. End La. *Orp* —7J **67**
*N. End Pde. W14 —1K **13***
(off N. End Rd.)
N. End Rd. *W14 & SW6* —1K **13**
Northernhay Wlk. *Mord* —3K **43**
Northern Perimeter Rd. *H'row A* —4C **8**
Northern Perimeter Rd. W. *H'row A* —4N **7**
Northey Av. *Sutt* —6J **61**
N. Eyot Gdns. *W6* —1E **12**
N. Farm Rd. *F'boro* —6L **69**
N. Feltham Trad. Est. *Felt* —8J **9**
Northfield. *Light* —7M **51**
Northfield. *Shalf* —2A **134**
Northfield. *Witl* —6C **152**
Northfield Clo. *Alder* —3B **110**
Northfield Clo. *C Crook* —8D **88**
Northfield Ct. *Stai* —9K **21**
Northfield Cres. *Sutt* —1K **61**
Northfield Pl. *Wey* —4C **56**
Northfield Rd. *C Crook* —7C **88**
Northfield Rd. *Cobh* —9H **57**
Northfield Rd. *Houn* —2L **9**
Northfield Rd. *Stai* —9K **21**
Northfields. *SW18* —7M **13**
Northfields. *Asht* —5L **79**
Northfields. *Eps* —7D **60**
Northfields Prospect Bus. Cen. *SW18* —7M **13**
N. Fryerne. *Yat* —7C **48**
North Gdns. *SW19* —8B **28**
Northgate Av. *Craw* —3C **182**
Northgate Dri. *Camb* —8E **50**
Northgate Pl. *Craw* —2C **182**
Northgate Rd. *Craw* —3B **182**
N. Gate Rd. *F'boro* —3A **90**
North Grn. *Brack* —9B **16**
North Gro. *Cher* —5H **37**
N. Hatton Rd. *H'row A* —4E **8**
N. Heath Clo. *H'ham* —3K **197**
N. Heath Est. *H'ham* —2K **197**
N. Heath La. *H'ham* —4K **197**
N. Holmes Clo. *H'ham* —3A **198**
N. Hyde La. *S'hall & Houn* —1L **9**
Northington Clo. *Brack* —5D **32**
Northlands Av. *Orp* —1N **67**
Northlands Bungalows. *Dork* —1A **160**
Northlands Cotts. *H'ham* —5D **178**
Northlands Rd. *H'ham* —1L **197**
Northlands Rd. *Warn* —6D **178**
North La. *Alder* —1B **110**
North La. *Tedd* —7F **24**
N. Lodge Clo. *SW15* —8J **13**
N. Lodge Dri. *Asc* —1G **33**
North Mall. *Fleet* —4A **88**
North Mall. *Stai* —5H **21**
North Mead. *Craw* —1C **182**
Northmead. *F'boro* —1N **89**
North Mead. *Red* —9D **102**
N. Moors. *Sly I* —8A **94**
N. Munstead La. *G'ming* —1K **153**
Northolt Rd. *H'row A* —4M **7**
North Pde. *Chess* —2M **59**
North Pde. *H'ham* —4J **197**
N. Park La. *God* —9D **104**
N. Perimeter Rd. *Horl* —3B **162**
North Pl. *SW18* —8M **13**
North Pl. *Mitc* —8D **28**
North Pl. *Tedd* —7F **24**
N. Pole La. *Kes* —3B **66**
North Rd. *SW19* —7A **28**
North Rd. *Alder* —6B **90**
North Rd. *Asc* —9F **16**
North Rd. *Ash V* —9D **90**
North Rd. *Bren* —2L **11**
North Rd. *Craw* —1E **182**
North Rd. *Felt* —9E **8**
North Rd. *Guild* —9L **93**
North Rd. *Reig* —6L **121**
North Rd. *Rich* —6N **11**
North Rd. *Surb* —5K **41**
North Rd. *W On T* —2K **57**
North Rd. *W Wick* —7L **47**
North Rd. *Wok* —3C **74**
Northrop Rd. *H'row A* —4F **8**
N. Side. *Tong* —5D **110**
Northspur Rd. *Sutt* —9M **43**
N. Station App. *S Nut* —5K **123**
Northstead Rd. *SW2* —3L **29**
North St. *Cars* —9D **44**
North St. *Dork* —5G **119**
North St. *Egh* —6B **20**
North St. *G'ming* —4H **133**
North St. *Guild* —4N **113**
North St. *H'ham* —6K **197**
North St. *Iswth* —6G **11**
North St. *Lea* —8G **79**
North St. *Red* —2D **122**
North St. *Turn H* —5D **184**
North St. *Wink* —5K **17**
North Ter. *Wind* —3H **5**
Northtown Trad. Est. *Ald* —3C **110**
Northumberland Av. *Iswth* —4F **10**
Northumberland Clo. *Stanw* —9N **7**
Northumberland Clo. *Warf* —8D **16**
Northumberland Cres. *Felt* —9F **8**
Northumberland Gdns. *Iswth* —3G **11**
Northumberland Gdns. *Mitc* —4H **45**
Northumberland Pl. *Rich* —9K **11**
Northumberland Row. *Twic* —2E **24**
N. Verbena Gdns. *W6* —1F **12**
North View. *SW19* —6H **27**
North View. *Binf* —2H **31**
N. View Cres. *Eps* —4H **81**
North Wlk. *New Ad* —3L **65** (in two parts)
Northway. *G'ming* —4E **132**
Northway. *Guild* —1K **113**
Northway. *Mord* —3K **43**
Northway. *Wall* —1G **63**
Northway Rd. *Croy* —5C **46**
Northweald La. *King T* —6K **25**
N. Weylands Ind. Est. *W On T* —8M **39**
Northwick Sq. *H'row A* —4D **8**
Northwood Av. *Knap* —5G **73**
Northwood Av. *Purl* —9L **63**
N. Wood Ct. *SE25* —2D **46**
Northwood Pk. *Craw* —8E **162**
Northwood Rd. *Cars* —3E **62**
Northwood Rd. *H'row A* —4M **7**
Northwood Rd. *T Hth* —1M **45**
N. Worple Way. *SW14* —6C **12**
Norton Av. *Surb* —6A **42**
Norton Clo. *Worp* —5G **93**
Norton Gdns. *SW16* —1J **45**
Norton La. *D'side* —6G **77**
Norton Pk. *Asc* —4N **33**
Norton Rd. *Camb* —2G **71**
Norton Rd. *Wokgm* —3B **30**
Norwich Av. *Camb* —3C **70**
Norwich Rd. *Craw* —5E **182**
Norwich Rd. *T Hth* —2N **45**
Norwood Clo. *Eff* —6M **97**
Norwood Clo. *S'hall* —1A **10**
Norwood Clo. *Twic* —3D **24**
Norwood Cres. *H'row A* —4D **8**
Norwood Farm La. *Cobh* —7H **57**
Norwood Grn. Rd. *S'hall* —1A **10**
Norwood High St. *SE27* —4M **29**
Norwood Hill. *Horl* —9H **141**
Norwood Hill Rd. *Charl* —8K **141**
Norwood Pk. Rd. *SE27* —6N **29**
Norwood Rd. *SE24* —2M **29**
Norwood Rd. *SE27* —3M **29**
Norwood Rd. *Eff* —6M **97**
Norwood Rd. *S'hall* —1N **9**
Norwood Ter. *S'hall* —1B **10**
Noss Clo. *Sutt* —2C **62**
Notley End. *Egh* —8M **19**
Notson Rd. *SE25* —3E **46**
Nottingham Clo. *Wok* —5J **73**
*Nottingham Ct. Wok —5J **73***
(off Nottingham Clo.)
Nottingham Rd. *SW17* —2D **28**
Nottingham Rd. *Iswth* —5F **10**
Nottingham Rd. *S Croy* —1N **63**
Nova M. *Sutt* —7K **43**
Nova Rd. *Croy* —6M **45**
Novello St. *SW6* —4M **13**
Nowell Rd. *SW13* —2F **12**
Nower Rd. *Dork* —5G **118**
Nower, The. *Chev* —6N **87**
Nowhurst Bus. Pk. *Broad H* —2A **196**
Nowhurst La. *Broad H* —3A **196**
Noyna Rd. *SW17* —4D **28**
Nuffield Dri. *Owl* —6L **49**
Nugee Ct. *Crowt* —2G **49**
Nugent Rd. *SE25* —2C **46**
Nugent Rd. *Sur R* —3G **112**
Numa Ct. *Bren* —3K **11**
Nunappleton Way. *Oxt* —1C **126**
Nuneaton. *Brack* —5C **32**
Nuns Wlk. *Ran C* —8B **98**
Nuns Wlk. *Vir W* —4N **35**
Nuptown La. *Nup* —2D **16**
Nursery Av. *Croy* —8G **46**
Nursery Clo. *SW15* —7J **13**
Nursery Clo. *Capel* —4J **159**
Nursery Clo. *Croy* —8G **46**
Nursery Clo. *Eps* —6D **60**
Nursery Clo. *Felt* —1J **23** (in two parts)
Nursery Clo. *Fleet* —5E **88**
Nursery Clo. *Frim G* —7D **70**
Nursery Clo. *Tad* —3G **100**
Nursery Clo. *Wok* —3M **73**
Nursery Clo. *Wdhm* —6H **55**
Nursery Gdns. *Chil* —9D **114**
Nursery Gdns. *Stai* —7K **21**
Nursery Gdns. *Sun* —1G **39**
Nursery Hill. *Sham G* —6F **134**
Nurserylands. *Craw* —3M **181**
Nursery La. *Asc* —9J **17**
Nursery La. *Hkwd* —9B **142**
Nursery Rd. *SW19* —1N **43** (Merton)
Nursery Rd. *SW19* —8K **27** (Wimbledon)
Nursery Rd. *G'ming* —4J **133**
Nursery Rd. *Knap* —4G **73**
Nursery Rd. *Sun* —1F **38**
Nursery Rd. *Sutt* —1A **62**
Nursery Rd. *Tad* —3F **100**
Nursery Rd. *T Hth* —3A **46**
Nursery Way. *Oxt* —7A **106**
Nursery Way. *Wray* —9N **5**
Nutbourne. *Farnh* —5L **109**
Nutbourne Cotts. *Hamb* —2H **173**
*Nutbourne Ct. H'ham —3K **197***
(off Woodstock Clo.)
Nutcombe La. *Dork* —5F **118**

Nutcombe La.—Old Swan Yd.

Nutcombe La. Hind —9C 170
Nutcroft Gro. Fet —8E 78
Nutfield Clo. Cars —9C 44
Nutfield Marsh Rd. Nutf —9H 103
Nutfield Rd. Coul —3E 82
Nutfield Rd. Mers —7G 102
Nutfield Rd. Red —3F 122
Nutfield Rd. T Hth —3M 45
Nuthatch Clo. Ews —5C 108
Nuthatch Clo. Stai —2A 22
Nuthatch Gdns. Reig —7A 122
Nuthatch Way. H'ham —1K 197
Nuthatch Way. Turn H —4F 184
Nuthurst. Brack —4C 32
Nuthurst Av. SW2 —3K 29
Nuthurst Av. Cranl —7N 155
Nuthurst Clo. Craw —2M 181
Nutley. Brack —7M 31
Nutley Clo. Yat —1C 68
Nutley Ct. Reig —3L 121
Nutley Gro. Reig —3M 121
Nutley La. Reig —2L 121
Nutmeg Ct. F'boro —9H 69
Nutshell La. Farnh —6H 109
Nutty La. Shep —2D 38
Nutwell St. SW17 —6C 28
Nutwood. G'ming —5G 133 (off Frith Hill Rd.)
Nutwood Av. Brock —4B 120
Nutwood Clo. Brock —4B 120
Nye Bevan Ho. SW6 —3L 13 (off Clem Attlee Est.)
Nyefield Pk. Tad —4F 100
Nylands Av. Rich —4N 11
Nymans Clo. H'ham —1N 197
Nymans Ct. Craw —6F 182
Nymans Gdns. SW20 —2G 42

Oakapple Clo. Craw —8N 181
Oakapple Clo. S Croy —1E 84
Oak Av. Croy —8K 47
Oak Av. Egh —8E 20
Oak Av. Hamp —6M 23
Oak Av. Houn —3L 9
Oak Av. Owl —6J 49
Oakbank. Fet —1D 98
Oak Bank. New Ad —3M 65
Oakbank. Wok —6A 74
Oakbank Av. W On T —6N 39
Oakbury Rd. SW6 —5N 13
Oak Clo. C'fold —5D 172
Oak Clo. Copt —7L 163
Oak Clo. G'ming —3H 133
Oak Clo. Sutt —8A 44
Oakcombe Clo. N Mald —9D 26
Oak Corner. Bear G —7J 139
Oak Cottage Clo. Wood S —2F 112
Oak Cotts. Hand —5N 199
Oak Cotts. Hasl —2C 188
Oak Ct. Craw —8B 162
Oak Ct. F'boro —4C 90
Oak Ct. Farnh —2G 129
Oak Croft. E Grin —1C 186
Oakcroft Bus. Cen. Chess —1M 59
Oakcroft Clo. W Byf —1H 75
Oakcroft Rd. Chess —1M 59
Oakcroft Rd. W Byf —1H 75
Oakcroft Vs. Chess —1M 59
Oakdale. Brack —5B 32
Oakdale La. Crook C —2L 127
Oakdale Rd. SW16 —6J 29
Oakdale Rd. Eps —5C 60
Oakdale Rd. Wey —9B 38
Oakdale Way. Mitc —6E 44
Oak Dell. Craw —2G 183
Oakdene. Asc —5C 34
Oakdene. Chob —6J 53
Oakdene. Tad —7K 81
Oakdene Av. Th Dit —7G 40
Oakdene Clo. Bookh —5C 98
Oakdene Clo. Brock —5B 120
Oakdene Ct. W On T —9J 39
Oakdene Dri. Surb —6B 42
Oakdene M. Sutt —7L 43
Oakdene Pde. Cobh —1J 77
Oakdene Rd. Bookh —2N 97
Oakdene Rd. Brock —5A 120
Oakdene Rd. Cobh —1J 77
Oakdene Rd. G'ming —8G 133
Oakdene Rd. Peas —2M 133
Oakdene Rd. Red —3D 122
Oake Ct. SW15 —8K 13
Oaken Coppice. Asht —6N 79
Oaken Copse. C Crook —9C 88
Oaken Copse Cres. F'boro —7N 69
Oak End. Bear G —8J 139
Oaken Dri. Clay —3F 58
Oak End Way. Wdhm —8G 55
Oakengates. Brack —7M 31
Oaken La. Clay —1E 58
Oakenshaw Clo. Surb —6L 41
Oak Farm Clo. B'water —1H 69
Oakfield. Plais —6A 192
Oakfield. Wok —4H 73
Oakfield Clo. N Mald —4E 42
Oakfield Clo. Wey —1D 56
Oakfield Cotts. Hasl —7M 189
Oakfield Ct. Horl —8E 142 (off Consort Way)
Oakfield Dri. Reig —1N 121
Oakfield Gdns. Beck —4L 47
Oakfield Gdns. Cars —7C 44
Oakfield Glade. Wey —1D 56
Oakfield La. Kes —1E 66
Oakfield Rd. SW19 —4J 27
Oakfield Rd. Ashf —6C 22
Oakfield Rd. Asht —4K 79
Oakfield Rd. B'water —2K 69
Oakfield Rd. Cobh —1J 77
Oakfield Rd. Croy —7N 45
Oakfield Rd. Eden —7K 127
Oakfields. Camb —1N 69
Oakfields. Guild —1J 113
Oakfields. Wal W —1L 177
Oakfields. W On T —7H 39
Oakfields. W Byf —1K 75
Oakfields. Worth —1H 183
Oakfield St. SW10 —2N 13
Oakfield Way. E Grin —7B 166
Oak Gdns. Croy —8K 47
Oak Glade. Eps —8N 59
Oak Grange Rd. W Cla —7K 95
Oak Gro. Cranl —9A 156
Oak Gro. Loxw —4J 193
Oak Gro. Sun —8J 23
Oak Gro. W Wick —7M 47
Oak Gro. Cres. Col T —9K 49
Oak Gro. Rd. SE20 —1F 46
Oakhall Dri. Sun —6G 22
Oakhaven. Craw —5B 182
Oak Hill. Burp —7E 94
Oakhill. Clay —3G 59
Oak Hill. Eps —3C 80
Oakhill. Surb —6L 41
Oak Hill. Wood S —1E 112
Oakhill Clo. Asht —5J 79
Oakhill Cotts. Dork —1N 177
Oakhill Ct. SW19 —8J 27
Oakhill Cres. Surb —6L 41
Oakhill Dri. Surb —6L 41
Oakhill Gdns. Wey —8F 38
Oakhill Gro. Surb —5L 41
Oakhill Path. Surb —5L 41
Oakhill Pl. SW15 —8M 13
Oakhill Rd. SW15 —8L 13
Oakhill Rd. SW16 —9K 29
Oakhill Rd. Add —3H 55
Oakhill Rd. Asht —5J 79
Oakhill Rd. Beck —1M 47
Oakhill Rd. Head —4G 169
Oakhill Rd. H'ham —6L 197
Oakhill Rd. Reig —4N 121
Oakhill Rd. Surb —5L 41
Oakhill Rd. Sutt —9N 43
Oakhurst. Chob —5H 53
Oakhurst. Gray —6B 170
Oakhurst Clo. Tedd —6E 24
Oakhurst Gdns. E Grin —8M 165
Oakhurst La. Loxw —2G 193
Oakhurst Rise. Cars —6C 62
Oakhurst Rd. Bil —9B 194
Oakhurst Rd. Eps —3B 60
Oakington Av. Hayes —1E 8
Oakington Dri. Sun —1K 39
Oakland Av. Farnh —5K 109
Oakland Ct. Add —9K 37
Oaklands. Fet —2D 98
Oaklands. Hasl —1G 188
Oaklands. Horl —8G 143
Oaklands. H'ham —6L 197
Oaklands. Kenl —1N 83
Oaklands. S God —7H 125
Oaklands. Yat —9C 48
Oaklands Av. Esh —7D 40
Oaklands Av. Iswth —2F 10
Oaklands Av. T Hth —3L 45
Oaklands Av. W Wick —9L 47
Oaklands Bus. Pk. Wokgm —5A 30
Oaklands Clo. Asc —8K 17
Oaklands Clo. Chess —1J 59
Oaklands Clo. Shalf —2A 134
Oaklands Dri. Asc —8K 17
Oaklands Dri. Red —5F 122
Oaklands Dri. Twic —1C 24
Oaklands Dri. Wokgm —3A 30
Oaklands Est. SW4 —1G 29
Oaklands Gdns. Kenl —1N 83
Oaklands La. Big H —9D 66
Oaklands La. Crowt —9F 30
Oaklands Pk. Wokgm —4A 30
Oaklands Rd. SW14 —6C 12
Oaklands Way. Tad —9H 81
Oaklands Way. Wall —4H 63
Oakland Way. Eps —3D 60
Oak La. Broad H —5E 196
Oak La. Dork —3H 139
Oak La. Egh —4M 19
Oak La. Iswth —7E 10
Oak La. Twic —1G 25
Oak La. Wind —4D 4
Oak La. Wok —3E 74
Oaklawn Rd. Lea —5E 78
Oaklea. Ash V —8E 90
Oak Leaf Clo. Eps —8B 60
Oak Leaf Ct. Asc —9H 17
Oaklea Pas. King T —2K 41
Oakleigh. God —8F 104
Oakleigh Av. Surb —7N 41
Oakleigh Flats. Eps —1D 80
Oakleigh Gdns. Orp —1N 67
Oakleigh Rd. H'ham —4M 197
Oakleigh Way. Mitc —9F 28
Oakleigh Way. Surb —7N 41
Oakley Av. Croy —1K 63
Oakley Clo. Add —1M 55
Oakley Clo. E Grin —2D 186
Oakley Clo. Iswth —4D 10
Oakley Ct. Red —2E 122 (off St Anne's Rise)
Oakley Dell. Guild —1E 114
Oakley Dri. Brom —1G 66
Oakley Dri. Fleet —5B 88
Oakley Gdns. Bans —2N 81
Oakley Ho. G'ming —3H 133
Oakley M. Wind —5B 4
Oakley Rd. SE25 —4E 46
Oakley Rd. Brom —1G 66
Oakley Rd. Camb —2N 69
Oakley Rd. Warl —5D 84
Oakley Wlk. W6 —2J 13
Oak Lodge. Crowt —2H 49
Oak Lodge. Hasl —4J 189
Oak Lodge Clo. W On T —2K 57
Oaklodge Dri. Red —2E 142
Oak Lodge Dri. W Wick —6L 47
Oak Lodge La. W'ham —3M 107
Oak Mead. G'ming —3G 133
Oakmead Grn. Eps —2B 80
Oakmead Pl. Mitc —9C 28
Oakmead Rd. SW12 —2E 28
Oakmead Rd. Croy —5H 45
Oakmede Pl. Binf —7H 15
Oak Pk. W Byf —9G 55
Oak Pk. Gdns. SW19 —2J 27
Oak Pl. SW18 —8N 13
Oak Ridge. Dork —8H 119
Oakridge. W End —9C 52
Oak Rd. Cat —9B 84
Oak Rd. Cobh —2L 77
Oak Rd. Craw —4A 182
Oak Rd. F'boro —2A 90
Oak Rd. Lea —5G 78
Oak Rd. N Mald —1C 42
Oak Rd. Reig —2N 121
Oak Rd. W'ham —3M 107
Oak Row. SW16 —1G 44
Oaks Av. Felt —3M 23
Oaks Av. Wor Pk —9G 43
Oaks Cvn. Pk., The. Dork —1K 159
Oaks Clo. H'ham —2A 198
Oaks Clo. Lea —8G 79
Oakshade Rd. Oxs —1C 78
Oakshaw. Oxt —5N 105
Oakshaw Rd. SW18 —1N 27
Oakside Ct. Horl —7G 143
Oakside La. Horl —7G 143
Oaks La. Croy —9F 46
Oaks La. Mid H —3H 139
Oaks Rd. Croy —2E 64
Oaks Rd. Kenl —1M 83
Oaks Rd. Reig —2B 122
Oaks Rd. Stai —9M 7
Oaks Rd. Wok —4A 74
Oaks, The. Brack —1B 32
Oaks, The. C'fold —5E 172
Oaks, The. Dork —8H 119
Oaks, The. E Grin —1C 186
Oaks, The. Eps —1D 80
Oaks, The. F'boro —2J 89
Oaks, The. Mord —3K 43
Oaks, The. Stai —5H 21
Oaks, The. W Byf —1K 75
Oaks, The. Yat —1C 68
Oaks Track. Cars & Wall —7D 62
Oaks Way. Cars —4D 62
Oaks Way. Eps —6G 80
Oaks Way. Kenl —1N 83
Oaksway. Surb —7K 41
Oak Tree Clo. Alder —4C 110
Oak Tree Clo. Ash V —4D 90
Oak Tree Clo. Burp —7E 94
Oak Tree Clo. Head —5E 168
Oak Tree Clo. Jac —6N 93
Oak Tree Clo. Knap —5E 72
Oak Tree Clo. Vir W —5N 35
Oak Tree Dri. Egh —6M 19
Oak Tree Dri. Guild —8M 93
Oak Tree La. Hasl —2B 188
Oak Tree M. Brack —2B 32
Oak Tree Rd. Knap —5E 72
Oak Tree Rd. Milf —1B 152
Oaktrees. Ash —3D 110
Oaktrees. Farnh —6G 109
Oaktrees Ct. Ash —3D 110 (off Oaktrees)
Oak Tree View. Farnh —6K 109
Oaktree Way. H'ham —4M 197
Oaktree Way. Sand —6F 48
Oak View. Eden —1K 147
Oakview Bus. Pk. Wmly —1C 172
Oakview Gro. Croy —7H 47
Oak Wlk. H'ham —8E 180
Oak Way. SW20 —3H 43
Oakway. Alder —4C 110
Oak Way. Asht —3N 79
Oakway. Brom —1N 47
Oak Way. Craw —1C 182
Oak Way. Croy —5G 47
Oak Way. Felt —2F 22
Oak Way. Man H —9B 198
Oak Way. Reig —4B 122
Oakway. Wok —6H 73
Oakway Dri. Frim —5C 70
Oakwood. C Crook —9B 88
Oakwood. Guild —7K 93
Oakwood. Wall —5F 62
Oakwood Av. Beck —1M 47
Oakwood Av. Mitc —1B 44
Oakwood Av. Purl —8M 63
Oakwood Clo. E Hor —5F 96
Oakwood Clo. Red —3E 122
Oakwood Clo. S Nut —5K 123
Oakwood Ct. Bisl —3D 72
Oakwood Dri. E Hor —5F 96
Oakwood Gdns. Knap —5D 72
Oakwood Gdns. Sutt —8M 43
Oakwood Ind. Pk. Craw —9E 162
Oakwood Pk. F Row —7H 187
Oakwood Pl. Croy —5L 45
Oakwood Rd. SW20 —9F 26
Oakwood Rd. Brack —1C 32
Oakwood Rd. Croy —5L 45
Oakwood Rd. Horl —7E 142
Oakwood Rd. Mers —7L 103
Oakwood Rd. Vir W —4M 35
Oakwood Rd. W'sham —3B 52
Oakwood Rd. Wok —6H 73
Oarborough. Brack —3C 32
Oareborough. Brack —3C 32
Oarsman Pl. E Mol —3E 40
Oast Ho. Clo. Wray —1A 20
Oast Ho. Cres. Farnh —6H 109
Oast Ho. Dri. Fleet —1D 88
Oast Ho. La. Farnh —7J 109
Oast La. Alder —5N 109
Oast Lodge. W4 —3D 12 (off Corney Reach Way)
Oast Rd. Oxt —9B 106
Oates Clo. Brom —2N 47
Oates Wlk. Craw —6D 182
Oatfield Rd. Tad —7G 80
Oatlands. Craw —4M 181
Oatlands. Horl —7G 142
Oatlands Av. Wey —2E 56
Oatlands Chase. Wey —9F 38
Oatlands Clo. Wey —1D 56
Oatlands Dri. Wey —1D 56
Oatlands Grn. Wey —9E 38
Oatlands Mere. Wey —9E 38
Oatlands Rd. Tad —6K 81
Oban Rd. SE25 —3A 46
Obelisk Way. Camb —9A 50
Oberon Way. Craw —6K 181
Oberon Way. Shep —2N 37
Oberursel Way. Alder —2L 109
Observatory Rd. SW14 —7B 12
Observatory Wlk. Red —3D 122
Occam Rd. Sur R —3G 112
Occupation Rd. Eps —4C 60
Ocean Ho. Brack —1N 31
Ockenden Clo. Wok —5B 74
Ockenden Gdns. Wok —5B 74
Ockenden Rd. Wok —5B 74
Ockfields. Milf —1C 152
Ockford Ct. G'ming —7G 132
Ockford Dri. G'ming —8F 132
Ockford Ridge. G'ming —8E 132
Ockford Rd. G'ming —8F 132
Ockham Dri. W Hor —2E 96
Ockham La. Ock & Cob —8B 76
Ockham Rd. N. Ock & W Hors —7N 75
Ockham Rd. S. E Hor —4F 96
Ockley Ct. Guild —7D 94
Ockley Ct. Sutt —1A 62
Ockley Rd. SW16 —5J 29
Ockley Rd. Croy —6K 45
Ockley Rd. Ewh —4F 156
Ockleys Mead. God —7F 104
O'Connor Rd. Alder —6C 90
Octagon Rd. W Vill —5F 56
Octavia. Brack —7M 31
Octavia Clo. Mitc —4C 44
Octavia Rd. Iswth —6E 10
Octavia Way. Stai —7J 21
Odard Rd. W Mol —3A 40
Odiham Rd. Farnh —5E 108
Ogden Ho. Felt —4M 23
Oglethorpe Ct. G'ming —7G 133 (off High St. Godalming,)
Oil Mill La. W6 —1F 12
Okeburn Rd. SW17 —6E 28
Okehurst Rd. Bil —9B 194
Okingham Clo. Owl —5J 49
Oldacre. W End —8C 52
Old Acre. Wok —1J 75
Oldacre M. SW12 —1F 28
Old Av. W Byf —9G 54
Old Av. Wey —4D 56
Old Av. Clo. W Byf —9G 54
Old Bakery M. Alb —8K 115
Old Barn Clo. Sutt —4K 61
Old Barn Cotts. H'ham —2J 179
Old Barn Dri. Capel —4K 159
Old Barn La. Churt —8N 149
Old Barn La. Kenl —3C 84
Old Barn Rd. Eps —4B 80
Old Barn View. G'ming —9F 132
Old Bisley Rd. Frim —3F 70
Old Bracknell Clo. Brack —2N 31
Old Bracknell La. E. Brack —2N 31
Old Bracknell La. W. Brack —2M 31
Old Brickfield Rd. Alder —5N 109
Old Bri. St. Hamp W —1K 41
Old Brighton Rd. Peas P (in two parts) —3N 199
Old Brighton Rd. S. Low H —6C 162
Old Brompton Rd. SW5 & SW7 —1M 13
Oldbury. Brack —2L 31
Oldbury Clo. Cher —6G 36
Oldbury Clo. Frim —6D 70
Old Bury Hill Ho. Dork —7E 118
Oldbury Rd. Cher —6G 37
Old Chapel La. Ash —2E 110
Old Charlton Rd. Shep —4D 38
Old Char Wharf. Dork —4F 118
Old Chertsey Rd. Chob —6L 53
Old Chestnut Av. Clar P —3A 58
Old Chu. La. Farnh —4J 129
Old Chu. Path. Esh —1C 58
Old Claygate La. Clay —2G 58
Old Coach Rd. Cher —4F 36
Old Comn. Rd. Cobh —9J 57
Old Compton La. Farnh —1K 129
Old Convent. E Grin —8A 166
Oldcorne Hollow. Yat —1A 68
Old Cote Dri. Houn —2A 10
Old Ct. Asht —6L 79
Old Ct. Rd. Guild —4K 113
Old Cove Rd. Fleet —2C 88
Old Crawley Rd. Fay —2B 198
Old Cross Tree Way. Ash —4G 111
Old Dean Rd. Camb —8B 50
Old Deer Pk. Gdns. Rich —6L 11
Old Denne Gdns. H'ham —7J 197
Old Devonshire Rd. SW12 —1F 28
Old Dock Clo. Rich —2N 11
Old Dorking Rd. H'ham —2H 197
Olde Farm Dri. B'water —9G 48
Old Elstead Rd. Milf —9B 132
Olden La. Purl —8L 63
Old Epsom Rd. Guild —9M 95
Old Esher Clo. W On T —2L 57
Old Esher Rd. W On T —2L 57
Old Farleigh Rd. S Croy & Warl —6F 64
Old Farm Clo. Houn —7N 9
Old Farm Dri. Brack —8A 16
Old Farm Ho. Dri. Oxs —2D 78
Old Farm Pas. Hamp —9C 24
Old Farm Rd. Guild —9N 93
Old Farm Rd. Hamp —7N 23
Old Farnham La. Farnh —2A 128 (Dippenhall)
Old Farnham La. Farnh —3H 129 (Farnham)
Old Ferry Dri. Wray —9N 5
Oldfield Clo. Horl —1D 162
Oldfield Gdns. Asht —5K 79
Oldfield Ho. W4 —1D 12 (off Devonshire Rd.)
Oldfield Rd. SW19 —7K 27
Oldfield Rd. Hamp —9N 23
Oldfield Rd. Horl —9D 142
Oldfields Rd. Sutt —9L 43
Oldfields Trad. Est. Sutt —9M 43
Oldfieldwood. Wok —4D 74
Old Forge Ct. Shalf —9B 114
Old Forge Cres. Shep —5C 38
Old Forge, The. H'ham —5L 195
Old Fox Clo. Cat —8M 83
Old Frensham Rd. Lwr Bo —5J 129
Old Glebe. Fern —9F 188
Old Grn. La. Camb —8A 50
Old Guildford Rd. Frim G —9F 70
Old Guildford Rd. H'ham —4D 196
Old Guildford Rd. Pirb —2H 91
Old Harrow La. W'ham —6L 87
Old Haslemere Rd. Hasl —3G 189
Old Heath Way. Farnh —5H 109
Old Hill. Orp —3M 67
Old Hill. Wok —7N 73
Old Hill Est. Wok —7N 73
Old Holbrook. H'ham —9L 179
Old Hollow. Worth —3K 183
Old Horsham Rd. Craw —5N 181
Old Hospital Clo. SW17 —2D 28
Old Ho. Clo. SW19 —6K 27
Old Ho. Clo. Eps —6E 60
Old Ho. Gdns. Twic —9J 11
Oldhouse La. Bisl —1D 72
Oldhouse La. W'sham & Light —4M 51
Old Kiln Clo. Churt —8L 149
Old Kiln La. Brock —4B 120
Old Kiln La. Churt —7L 149
Old Kingston Rd. Wor Pk —9B 42
Old Lands Hill. Brack —9B 16
Old La. Alder —1C 110 (Deadbrook La.)
Old La. Alder —5M 109 (Weybourne Rd.)
Old La. Cobh —4C 76
Old La. Dock —6C 148
Old La. Oxt —8B 106
Old La. Tats —7F 86
Old La. Gdns. Cobh —9H 77
Old Lodge Clo. G'ming —8E 132
Old Lodge La. Purl —9K 63
Old Lodge Pl. Twic —9H 11
Old London Rd. E Hor —4H 97
Old London Rd. Eps —5F 80
Old London Rd. Mick —5J 99
Old Malden La. Wor Pk —8D 42
Old Malt Way. Wok —4N 73
Old Mnr. Clo. Craw —1M 181
Old Mnr. Ct. Craw —1M 181
Old Mnr. Dri. Iswth —9C 10
Old Mnr. Ho. M. Shep —2B 38
Old Mnr. La. Chil —9E 114
Old Mnr. Yd. SW5 —1N 13
Old Martyrs. Craw —9B 162
Old Merrow St. Guild —9F 94
Old Mill La. Red —6F 102
Old Millmeads. H'ham —3J 197
Old Museum Ct. Hasl —2H 189
Old Nursery Pl. Ashf —6C 22
Old Oak Av. Coul —6C 82
Old Orchard. Byfl —8A 56
Old Orchard. Sun —1K 39
Old Orchards. M'bowr —3J 183
Old Orchard, The. Farnh —4E 128
Old Overthorpe. Horl —1M 163
Old Pal. La. Rich —8J 11
Old Pal. Rd. Croy —9M 45
Old Pal. Rd. Guild —4K 113
Old Pal. Rd. Wey —9C 38
Old Pal. Ter. Rich —8K 11
Old Pal. Yd. Rich —8J 11
Old Pk. Av. SW12 —1E 28
Old Pk. Clo. Farnh —6F 108
Old Pk. La. Farnh —5E 108 (in two parts)
Old Pk. M. Houn —3N 9
Old Parvis Rd. W Byf —8L 55
Old Pasture Rd. Frim —3D 70
Old Pharmacy Ct. Crowt —3G 49
Old Pond Clo. Camb —5A 70
Old Portsmouth Rd. Camb —1E 70
Old Portsmouth Rd. G'ming & Peas —3L 133
Old Portsmouth Rd. Thur —6H 151
Old Post Cotts. H'ham —5D 196
Old Pottery Clo. Reig —5N 121
Old Pound Clo. Iswth —5G 10
Old Pound Cotts. If'd —2J 181
Old Priory La. Warf —7B 16
Old Pump Ho. Clo. Fleet —3C 88
Old Quarry, The. Hasl —4D 188
Old Rectory Clo. Brmly —5B 134
Old Rectory Clo. Tad —2F 100
Old Rectory Dri. Ash —2F 110
Old Rectory Gdns. F'boro —1B 90
Old Rectory Gdns. G'ming —9J 133
Old Rectory La. E Hor —4F 96
Old Redstone Dri. Red —4E 122
Old Reigate Rd. Bet —3A 120
Old Reigate Rd. Dork —3L 119
Oldridge Rd. SW12 —1E 28
Old Rd. Add —4H 55
Old Rd. Bkld —3D 120
Old Rd. E Grin —9B 166
Old Row Ct. Wokgm —2B 30
Old St Mary's. W Hor —7C 96
Old Sawmill La. Crowt —1H 49
Old School Clo. SW19 —1M 43
Old School Clo. Ash —1E 110 (in two parts)
Old School Clo. Beck —1H 47
Old School Clo. Fleet —4B 88
Old School Ct. Wray —1A 20
Old School Ho. Eden —2L 147
Old School La. Brock —6A 120
Old School La. Yat —9B 48
Old School M. Wey —1E 56
Old School Pl. Ling —7N 145
Old School Pl. Wok —8A 74
Old Schools La. Eps —5E 60
Old School Sq. Th Dit —5F 40
Old School Ter. Sutt —4J 61
Old Slade La. Iver —1H 7
Old Sta. App. Lea —8G 78
Old Sta. Clo. Craw D —2E 184
Old Sta. Gdns. Tedd —7G 24 (off Victoria Rd.)
Old Sta. Way. G'ming —5H 133
Oldstead. Brack —4B 32
Old Swan Wharf. SW11 —4N 13
Old Swan Yd. Cars —1D 62

Old Tilburstow Rd.—Park Clo.

Old Tilburstow Rd. *God* —3F **124**
Old Town. *Croy* —9M **45**
Old Tye Av. *Big H* —3G **87**
Old Welmore. *Yat* —1D **68**
Old Westhall Clo. *Warl* —6F **84**
Old Wickhurst La. *Broad H* —7D **196**
Old Windsor Lock. *Old Win* —8M **5**
Old Wokingham Rd. *Wokgm & Crowt* —6G **31**
Old Woking Rd. *W Byf* —9H **55**
Old Woking Rd. *Wok* —6D **74**
Oldwood Chase. *F'boro* —2G **89**
Old York Rd. *SW18* —8N **13**
Oleander Clo. *Crowt* —9E **30**
Oleander Clo. *Orp* —2M **67**
Oliver Av. *SE25* —2C **46**
Oliver Clo. *W4* —2A **12**
Oliver Clo. *Add* —1K **55**
Oliver Gro. *SE25* —3C **46**
Olive Rd. *SW19* —8A **28**
Oliver Rd. *Asc* —3L **33**
Oliver Rd. *H'ham* —7G **197**
Oliver Rd. *N Mald* —1B **42**
Oliver Rd. *Sutt* —1B **62**
Olivette St. *SW15* —6J **13**
Olivia Ct. *Wokgm* —2A **30**
Olivier Rd. *M'bowr* —4H **183**
Ollerton. *Brack* —7M **31**
Olley Clo. *Wall* —4J **63**
Olveston Wlk. *Cars* —5B **44**
Olyffe Dri. *Beck* —1M **47**
(in two parts)
O'Mahoney Ct. *SW17* —4A **28**
Omega Rd. *Wok* —2C **74**
Omega Way. *Egh* —9E **20**
One Tree Hill Rd. *Guild* —4D **114**
Ongar Clo. *Add* —3H **55**
Ongar Hill. *Add* —3J **55**
Ongar Pde. *Add* —3J **55**
Ongar Pl. *Add* —3J **55**
Ongar Rd. *SW6* —2M **13**
Ongar Rd. *Add* —2J **55**
Onslow Av. *Rich* —8L **11**
Onslow Av. *Sutt* —6L **61**
Onslow Clo. *Th Dit* —7E **40**
Onslow Clo. *Wok* —4C **74**
Onslow Cres. *Wok* —4C **74**
Onslow Dri. *Asc* —8L **17**
Onslow Gdns. *S Croy* —8D **64**
Onslow Gdns. *Th Dit* —7E **40**
Onslow Gdns. *Wall* —3G **62**
Onslow M. *Cher* —5J **37**
Onslow Rd. *Asc* —6E **34**
Onslow Rd. *Croy* —6L **45**
Onslow Rd. *Guild* —3N **113**
Onslow Rd. *N Mald* —3F **42**
Onslow Rd. *Rich* —8L **11**
Onslow Rd. *W On T* —1G **57**
Onslow St. *Guild* —4M **113**
Onslow Way. *Th Dit* —7E **40**
Onslow Way. *Wok* —2H **75**
Ontario Clo. *Small* —9L **143**
Openfield. *Head* —4D **168**
Openview. *SW18* —2A **28**
Opladen Way. *Brack* —4A **32**
Opossum Way. *Houn* —6K **9**
Opus Pk. *Sly I* —8N **93**
Oracle Cen. *Brack* —1A **32**
Orange Ct. La. *Orp* —5J **67**
Orbain Rd. *SW6* —3K **13**
Orchard Av. *Ashf* —7D **22**
Orchard Av. *Croy* —7H **47**
Orchard Av. *Felt* —8E **8**
Orchard Av. *Houn* —3M **9**
Orchard Av. *Mitc* —7E **44**
Orchard Av. *N Mald* —2D **42**
Orchard Av. *Th Dit* —7G **41**
Orchard Av. *Wind* —4D **4**
Orchard Av. *Wdhm* —7H **55**
Orchard Bus. Cen. *Red* —3E **142**
Orchard Cvn. Site, The. *Tad* —8A **100**
Orchard Clo. *SW20* —3H **43**
Orchard Clo. *Ashf* —7D **22**
Orchard Clo. *Ash V* —8E **90**
Orchard Clo. *Bad L* —6N **109**
Orchard Clo. *Bans* —1N **81**
Orchard Clo. *B'water* —5L **69**
Orchard Clo. *E Hor* —2G **97**
Orchard Clo. *Eden* —1K **147**
Orchard Clo. *Egh* —5D **20**
Orchard Clo. *Fet* —9D **78**
Orchard Clo. *Guild* —3D **114**
Orchard Clo. *Hasl* —3D **188**
Orchard Clo. *Horl* —7D **142**
Orchard Clo. *Lea* —4F **78**
Orchard Clo. *Norm* —3M **111**
Orchard Clo. *Surb* —7H **41**
Orchard Clo. *W On T* —6J **39**
Orchard Clo. *W End* —9A **52**
Orchard Clo. *W Ewe* —3A **60**
Orchard Clo. *Wok* —3D **74**
Orchard Clo. *Wokgm* —2C **30**
Orchard Cotts. *Chil* —9G **114**
Orchard Cotts. *Horl* —3L **161**
Orchard Ct. *Brack* —1A **32**
Orchard Ct. *Iswth* —3D **10**
Orchard Ct. *Ling* —8N **145**
Orchard Ct. *Twic* —3D **24**
Orchard Ct. *W Dray* —3L **7**
Orchard Ct. *Wor Pk* —7F **42**
*Orchard Dene. W Byf —9J **55***
(off Madeira Rd.)
Orchard Dri. *Asht* —7K **79**
Orchard Dri. *Eden* —1K **147**
Orchard Dri. *Shep* —2F **38**
Orchard Dri. *Wok* —2A **74**
Orchard End. *Cat* —9B **84**
Orchard End. *Fet* —2C **98**
Orchard End. *Rowl* —8E **128**
Orchard End. *Wey* —8F **38**
Orchard Farm Cvn. Site. *Red* —3K **143**
Orchard Field Rd. *G'ming* —4J **133**
Orchard Gdns. *Alder* —4A **110**
Orchard Gdns. *Chess* —1L **59**
Orchard Gdns. *Cranl* —8A **156**
Orchard Gdns. *Eff* —6M **97**
Orchard Gdns. *Eps* —1B **80**
Orchard Gdns. *Sutt* —2M **61**
Orchard Ga. *Esh* —7D **40**
Orchard Ga. *Sand* —7G **49**
Orchard Gro. *Croy* —6H **47**
Orchard Hill. *Cars* —2D **62**
Orchard Hill. *Rud* —1D **194**
Orchard Hill. *W'sham* —4A **52**
*Orchard Ho. Guild —2F **114***
(off Merrow St.)
Orchard Ho. *Tong* —5D **110**
Orchard La. *SW20* —9G **27**
Orchard La. *E Mol* —5D **40**
Orchard Lea Clo. *Wok* —2G **75**
Orchard Leigh. *Lea* —9H **79**
Orchard Mains. *Wok* —6M **73**
Orchard Pl. *Wokgm* —2B **30**
Orchard Rise. *Croy* —7H **47**
Orchard Rise. *King T* —9B **26**
Orchard Rise. *Rich* —8A **12**
Orchard Rd. *Bad L* —6M **109**
Orchard Rd. *Bren* —2J **11**
Orchard Rd. *Burp* —8D **94**
Orchard Rd. *Chess* —1L **59**
Orchard Rd. *Dork* —6H **119**
Orchard Rd. *Farn* —2K **67**
Orchard Rd. *F'boro* —1M **89**
Orchard Rd. *Hamp* —8N **23**
Orchard Rd. *H'ham* —7L **197**
Orchard Rd. *Houn* —8N **9**
Orchard Rd. *King T* —1L **41**
Orchard Rd. *Mitc* —7E **44**
Orchard Rd. *Old Win* —9L **5**
Orchard Rd. *Onsl* —5J **113**
Orchard Rd. *Reig* —3N **121**
Orchard Rd. *Rich* —6N **11**
Orchard Rd. *Shalf* —9A **114**
Orchard Rd. *Shere* —8B **116**
Orchard Rd. *Small* —8N **143**
Orchard Rd. *S Croy* —1E **84**
Orchard Rd. *Sun* —8H **23**
Orchard Rd. *Sutt* —2M **61**
Orchard Rd. *Twic* —9G **11**
Orchards Clo. *W Byf* —1J **75**
*Orchard Sq. W14 —1L **13***
(off Sun Rd.)
Orchards, The. *Broad H* —3M **197**
Orchards, The. *If'd* —4J **181**
Orchard St. *Craw* —3B **182**
Orchard, The. *Bans* —2M **81**
Orchard, The. *Eps* —4E **60**
(Meadow Wlk.)
Orchard, The. *Eps* —6E **60**
(Tayles Hill)
Orchard, The. *Horl* —8E **142**
Orchard, The. *H'ham* —5D **196**
Orchard, The. *Houn* —5C **10**
Orchard, The. *Light* —7M **51**
Orchard, The. *N Holm* —9J **119**
Orchard, The. *Vir W* —4A **36**
Orchard, The. *Wey* —1C **56**
Orchard, The. *Wok* —9A **74**
Orchard Way. *Add* —2K **55**
Orchard Way. *Alder* —4A **110**
Orchard Way. *Ashf* —3A **22**
Orchard Way. *Camb* —4N **69**
Orchard Way. *Croy & Beck* —6H **47**
Orchard Way. *Dork* —6H **119**
Orchard Way. *E Grin* —9A **166**
Orchard Way. *Esh* —3C **58**
Orchard Way. *Guild* —3M **111**
Orchard Way. *Oxt* —2C **126**
Orchard Way. *Reig* —6N **121**
Orchard Way. *Send* —3E **94**
Orchard Way. *Sutt* —1B **62**
Orchard Way. *Tad* —4L **101**
Orchid Ct. *Egh* —5D **20**
Orchid Dri. *Bisl* —2D **72**
Orchid Mead. *Bans* —1N **81**
Orde Clo. *Craw* —9H **163**
Ordnance Clo. *Felt* —3H **23**
Ordnance Rd. *Alder* —2N **109**
Oregano Way. *Guild* —7K **93**
Oregon Clo. *N Mald* —3B **42**
Orestan La. *Eff* —5J **97**
Orewell Gdns. *Reig* —5N **121**
Orford Ct. *SE27* —3M **29**
Orford Gdns. *Twic* —3F **24**
Organ Crossroads. (Junct.) —4F **60**
Oriel Clo. *Craw* —9G **162**
Oriel Clo. *Mitc* —3H **45**
Oriel Ct. *Croy* —7A **46**
Oriel Hill. *Camb* —2B **70**
Oriental Clo. *Wok* —4B **74**
Oriental Rd. *Asc* —3A **34**
Oriental Rd. *Wok* —4B **74**
Orion. *Brack* —7M **31**
Orion Cen., The. *Croy* —9J **45**
Orion Ct. *Bew* —5J **181**
Orlando Gdns. *Eps* —6C **60**
Orleans Clo. *Esh* —8D **40**
Orleans Ct. *Twic* —1H **25**
Orleans Rd. *Twic* —1H **25**
Orltons La. *Rusp* —8E **160**
Ormathwaites Corner. *Warf* —8C **16**
Ormeley Rd. *SW12* —2F **28**
Orme Rd. *King T* —1A **42**
Ormerod Gdns. *Mitc* —1E **44**
Ormesby Wlk. *Craw* —5F **182**
Ormond Av. *Hamp* —9B **24**
Ormond Av. *Rich* —8K **11**
Ormond Cres. *Hamp* —9B **24**
Ormond Dri. *Hamp* —8B **24**
Ormonde Av. *Eps* —6C **60**
Ormonde Rd. *SW14* —6B **12**
Ormonde Rd. *G'ming* —5H **133**
Ormonde Rd. *Wok* —3M **73**
Ormonde Rd. *Wokgm* —3A **30**
Ormond Rd. *Rich* —8K **11**
Ormsby. *Sutt* —4N **61**
Ormside Way. *Red* —9F **102**
Orpin Rd. *Red* —8F **102**
Orpwood Clo. *Hamp* —7N **23**
Orwell Clo. [illegible]
Orwell Clo. *Wind* —6G **4**
Osborne Av. *Stai* —2A **22**
Osborne Clo. *Beck* —3H **47**
Osborne Clo. *Felt* —6L **23**
Osborne Clo. *Frim* —6D **70**
Osborne Ct. *Craw* —7N **181**
Osborne Ct. *F'boro* —5A **90**
Osborne Ct. *Wind* —5F **4**
Osborne Dri. *Fleet* —6C **88**
Osborne Dri. *Light* —7L **51**
Osborne Gdns. *T Hth* —1N **45**
Osborne La. *Warf* —6A **16**
Osborne M. *Wind* —5F **4**
Osborne Pl. *Sutt* —2B **62**
Osborne Rd. *Egh* —7B **20**
Osborne Rd. *F'boro* —5A **90**
Osborne Rd. *Houn* —6N **9**
Osborne Rd. *King T* —8L **25**
Osborne Rd. *Red* —9E **102**
Osborne Rd. *T Hth* —1N **45**
Osborne Rd. *W On T* —7H **39**
Osborne Rd. *Wind* —5F **4**
Osborne Rd. *Wokgm* —2B **30**
*Osborne Ter. SW17 —6E **28***
(off Church La.)
Osborn Rd. *Farnh* —8J **109**
Osbourne Ho. *Twic* —3C **24**
Osgood Av. *Orp* —2N **67**
Osgood Gdns. *Orp* —2N **67**
Osier M. *W4* —2D **12**
Osier Pl. *Egh* —7E **20**
Osiers Rd. *SW18* —7M **13**
Osier Way. *Bans* —1K **81**
Osier Way. *Mitc* —4D **44**
Osman's Clo. *Brack* —8F **16**
Osmond Gdns. *Wall* —2G **62**
Osmunda Bank. *Dor P* —4A **166**
Osmund Clo. *Worth* —3J **183**
Osnaburgh Hill. *Camb* —1N **69**
Osney Clo. *Craw* —4A **182**
Osney Wlk. *Cars* —5B **44**
Osprey Clo. *Fet* —9C **78**
Osprey Gdns. *S Croy* —6G **65**
Ostade Rd. *SW2* —1K **29**
Osterley Av. *Iswth* —3D **10**
Osterley Clo. *Wokgm* —3E **30**
Osterley Ct. *Iswth* —4D **10**
Osterley Cres. *Iswth* —4E **10**
Osterley Gdns. *T Hth* —1N **45**
Osterley La. *S'hall & Iswth* —1A **10**
*Osterley Lodge. Iswth —3E **10***
(off Church Rd.)
Osterley Rd. *Iswth* —3E **10**
Oswald Clo. *Fet* —9C **78**
Oswald Clo. *Warf* —7B **16**
Oswald Rd. *Fet* —9C **78**
Osward. *Croy* —6J **65**
(in three parts)
Osward Rd. *SW17* —3D **28**
Otford Clo. *Craw* —9A **182**
Othello Gro. *Warf* —9C **16**
Otho Ct. *Bren* —3K **11**
Otterbourne Rd. *Croy* —8N **45**
Otterburn Gdns. *Iswth* —3G **10**
Otterburn St. *SW17* —7D **28**
Otter Clo. *Crowt* —9F **30**
Otter Clo. *Ott* —3D **54**
Otterden Clo. *Orp* —1N **67**
Ottermead La. *Ott* —3E **54**
Otter Meadow. *Lea* —6F **78**
Ottershaw Pk. *Ott* —4C **54**
Ottway's Av. *Asht* —6K **79**
Ottways La. *Asht* —7K **79**
Otway Clo. *Craw* —5L **181**
Oulton Wlk. *Craw* —5F **182**
Ouseley Rd. *SW12* —2D **28**
Ouseley Rd. *Old Win* —1M **19**
Ousley Rd. *Wray* —1M **19**
Outdowns. *Eff* —8J **97**
Outram Pl. *Wey* —2D **56**
Outram Rd. *Croy* —8C **46**
*Outwood Ho. SW2 —1K **29***
(off Deepdene Gdns.)
Outwood La. *Blet* —2A **124**
Outwood La. *Tad & Coul* —9N **81**
Oval Rd. *Croy* —8A **46**
Oval, The. *Bans* —1M **81**
Oval, The. *G'ming* —4J **133**
Oval, The. *Guild* —4K **113**
Oval, The. *Wood S* —2E **112**
Overbrook. *G'ming* —6K **133**
Overbrook. *W Hor* —7C **96**
Overbury Av. *Beck* —2L **47**
Overbury Cres. *New Ad* —6M **65**
Overdale. *Asht* —3L **79**
Overdale. *Blet* —2N **123**
Overdale. *Dork* —4K **119**
Overdale Av. *N Mald* —1C **42**
Overdale Rise. *Frim* —3C **70**
Overdene Dri. *Craw* —3M **181**
Overford Clo. *Cranl* —8N **155**
Overford Dri. *Cranl* —8N **155**
Overhill. *Warl* —6F **84**
Overhill Rd. *Purl* —5L **63**
Overhill Way. *Beck* —4N **47**
Overlord Clo. *Camb* —7A **50**
Overstand Clo. *Beck* —4K **47**
Overstone Gdns. *Croy* —6J **47**
Overthorpe Clo. *Knap* —4H **73**
Overton Clo. *Alder* —6A **110**
Overton Clo. *Iswth* —4F **10**
Overton Ct. *Sutt* —4M **61**
*Overton Ho. SW15 —1E **26***
(off Tangley Gro.)
Overton Rd. *Sutt* —3M **61**
Overton Shaw. *E Grin* —6A **166**
Overtons Yd. *Croy* —9N **45**
Oveton Way. *Bookh* —4B **98**
Ovington Ct. *Wok* —3J **73**
Owen Clo. *Croy* —5A **46**
Owen Ho. *Felt* —1H **23**
Owen Ho. *Twic* —1H **25**
*Owen Mans. W14 —2K **13***
(off Queen's Club Gdns.)
Owen Pl. *Lea* —9H **79**
Owen Rd. *G'ming* —5J **133**
Owen Rd. *W'sham* —2A **52**
Owlbeech Ct. *H'ham* —4A **198**
Owlbeech Pl. *H'ham* —4A **198**
Owlbeech Way. *H'ham* —4A **198**
Owl Clo. *S Croy* —6G **65**
Owletts. *Craw* —2H **183**
Owlscastle Clo. *H'ham* —3K **197**
Owlsmoor Rd. *Owl* —7J **49**
Ownstead Gdns. *S Croy* —7C **64**
Ownsted Hill. *New Ad* —6M **65**
Oxberry Av. *SW6* —5K **13**
Oxdowne Clo. *Stoke D* —1B **78**
Oxenden Ct. *Tong* —4C **110**
Oxenden Rd. *Tong* —4C **110**
Oxenhope. *Brack* —3M **31**
Oxfield. *Eden* —9M **127**
Oxford Av. *SW20* —1K **43**
Oxford Av. *Hayes* —3G **8**
Oxford Av. *Houn* —1A **10**
Oxford Clo. *Ashf* —8D **22**
Oxford Clo. *Mitc* —2G **44**
Oxford Ct. *W4* —1A **12**
Oxford Ct. *Felt* —5L **23**
Oxford Cres. *N Mald* —5C **42**
Oxford Gdns. *W4* —1N **11**
Oxford Rd. *SW15* —7K **13**
Oxford Rd. *Cars* —3C **62**
Oxford Rd. *Craw* —7C **182**
Oxford Rd. *F'boro* —4A **90**
Oxford Rd. *Guild* —5N **113**
Oxford Rd. *H'ham* —6K **197**
Oxford Rd. *Owl* —5K **49**
Oxford Rd. *Red* —2C **122**
Oxford Rd. *Tedd* —6D **24**
Oxford Rd. *Wall* —2G **62**
Oxford Rd. *Wokgm* —2A **30**
Oxford Rd. N. *W4* —1A **12**
Oxford Rd. S. *W4* —1N **11**
Oxford Ter. *Guild* —5N **113**
Oxford Way. *Felt* —5L **23**
Ox La. *Eps* —5F **60**
Oxleigh Clo. *N Mald* —4D **42**
Oxlip Clo. *Croy* —7G **46**
Oxshott Rise. *Cobh* —9L **57**
Oxshott Rd. *Lea* —3E **78**
Oxshott Way. *Cobh* —2M **77**
Oxted Clo. *Mitc* —2B **44**
Oxted Grn. *Milf* —3B **152**
Oxted Rd. *God* —8F **104**
Oxtoby Way. *SW16* —9H **29**
Oyster La. *Byfl* —6M **55**

Pachesham Dri. *Oxs* —3F **78**
Pachesham Pk. *Lea* —3G **78**
Pacific Clo. *Felt* —2G **23**
Packer Clo. *E Grin* —7C **166**
Packway. *Farnh* —4K **129**
Padbrook. *Oxt* —7C **106**
Padbrook Clo. *Oxt* —7C **106**
Padbury Clo. *Felt* —2E **22**
Paddock Cvn. Site, The. *Vir W* —5A **36**
Paddock Clo. *Bear G* —7K **139**
Paddock Clo. *Camb* —9E **50**
Paddock Clo. *Farn* —1K **67**
Paddock Clo. *Hamb* —9F **152**
Paddock Clo. *Oxt* —9B **106**
Paddock Clo. *Wor Pk* —7D **42**
Paddock Gdns. *E Grin* —2A **186**
Paddock Gro. *Bear G* —7K **139**
*Paddock Ho. Guild —2F **114***
(off Merrow St.)
Paddockhurst Rd. *Craw* —4M **181**
Paddockhurst Rd. *Turn H* —9K **183**
Paddocks Clo. *Asht* —5L **79**
Paddocks Clo. *Cobh* —1K **77**
Paddocks Mead. *Wok* —3H **73**
Paddocks Rd. *Guild* —8C **94**
Paddocks, The. *Bookh* —4B **98**
Paddocks, The. *New Ad* —2K **65**
Paddocks, The. *New H* —6K **55**
Paddocks, The. *Norm* —3N **111**
Paddocks, The. *Wey* —9F **38**
Paddocks Way. *Asht* —5L **79**
Paddocks Way. *Cher* —7K **37**
Paddock, The. *Brack* —2A **32**
Paddock, The. *Cranl* —7M **155**
Paddock, The. *Craw* —2H **183**
Paddock, The. *Crowt* —1F **48**
Paddock, The. *Dat* —[illegible] **4**
Paddock, The. *Ewh* —6F **156**
Paddock, The. *G'ming* —9J **133**
Paddock, The. *Guild* —2F **114**
Paddock, The. *Hasl* —9E **170**
Paddock, The. *Head* —4D **168**
Paddock, The. *Light* —7M **51**
Paddock, The. *Westc* —6B **118**
Paddock, The. *W'ham* —4L **107**
Paddock, The. *Wink* —2M **17**
Paddock Wlk. *Warl* —6E **84**
Paddock Way. *Eps* —7H **61**
Paddock Way. *G'wood* —7L **171**
Paddock Way. *Oxt* —9B **106**
Paddock Way. *Wok* —1D **74**
Padstow Wlk. *Craw* —5K **181**
Padstow Wlk. *Felt* —2G **22**
Padwick Rd. *H'ham* —6N **197**
Pageant Wlk. *Croy* —9B **46**
Page Clo. *Hamp* —7M **23**
Page Ct. *H'ham* —7K **197**
Page Cres. *Croy* —2M **63**
Page Croft. *Add* —8K **37**
Pagehurst Rd. *Croy* —6E **46**
Page Rd. *Felt* —9E **8**
Page's Croft. *Wokgm* —3C **30**
Pages Yd. *W4* —2D **12**
Paget Av. *Sutt* —9B **44**
Paget Clo. *Camb* —8F **50**
Paget Clo. *Hamp* —5D **24**
Paget Clo. *H'ham* —8L **197**
Paget La. *Iswth* —6D **10**
Paget Pl. *King T* —7B **26**
Paget Pl. *Th Dit* —7G **40**
Pagewood Clo. *M'bowr* —5H **183**
Pagoda Av. *Rich* —6M **11**
Pagoda Vista. *Rich* —5M **11**
Paice Grn. *Wokgm* —1C **30**
Pain's Clo. *Mitc* —1F **44**
Pains Hill. *Oxt* —1E **126**
Painshill. (Junct.) —9G **56**
Paisley Rd. *Cars* —7B **44**
Pakenham Clo. *SW12* —2E **28**
Pakenham Rd. *Brack* —6B **32**
Palace Dri. *Wey* —9C **38**
Palace Grn. *Croy* —4J **65**
Palace M. *SW6* —3L **13**
Palace Rd. *SW2* —2K **29**
Palace Rd. *E Mol* —2D **40**
Palace Rd. *King T* —3K **41**
Palace Rd. *W'ham* —8J **87**
Palace View. *Croy* —1J **65**
Palace Way. *Wey* —9C **38**
Palestine Gro. *SW19* —9B **28**
Palestra Ho. *Craw* —3A **182**
Palewell Comn. Dri. *SW14* —8C **12**
Palewell Pk. *SW14* —8C **12**
Palgrave Ho. *Twic* —1C **24**
Pallant Way. *Orp* —1J **67**
Pallingham Dri. *M'bowr* —6G **182**
Palliser Rd. *W14* —1K **13**
Palmer Av. *Sutt* —1H **61**
Palmer Clo. *Horl* —6D **142**
Palmer Clo. *Houn* —4A **10**
Palmer Clo. *Red* —4E **122**
Palmer Clo. *W Wick* —8N **47**
Palmer Clo. *Wokgm* —8F **30**
Palmer Ct. *Wokgm* —2B **30**
Palmer Cres. *King T* —2L **41**
Palmer Cres. *Ott* —3F **54**
Palmer Rd. *M'bowr* —6G **182**
Palmer School Rd. *Wokgm* —2B **30**
Palmersfield Rd. *Bans* —1M **81**
Palmers Gro. *W Mol* —3A **40**
Palmers Lodge. *Guild* —4K **113**
Palmers Pas. *SW14* —6B **12**
Palmers Rd. *SW14* —6B **12**
Palmers Rd. *SW16* —1K **45**
Palmerston Clo. *F'boro* —2J **89**
Palmerston Clo. *Wok* —1C **74**
Palmerston Ct. *Surb* —6K **41**
Palmerston Gro. *SW19* —8M **27**
*Palmerston Mans. W14 —2K **13***
(off Queen's Club Gdns.)
Palmerston Rd. *SW14* —7B **12**
Palmerston Rd. *SW19* —8M **27**
Palmerston Rd. *Cars* —1D **62**
Palmerston Rd. *Croy* —4A **46**
Palmerston Rd. *Orp* —2L **67**
Palmerston Rd. *Sutt* —2A **62**
Palmerston Rd. *Twic* —9F **10**
Palmer St. *Ling* —7N **145**
Palm Gro. *Guild* —8M **93**
Pampisford Rd. *Purl & S Croy* —7L **63**
Pam's Way. *Eps* —2C **60**
Pankhurst Clo. *Iswth* —6F **10**
Pankhurst Ct. *Craw* —8N **181**
Pankhurst Dri. *Brack* —4B **32**
Pankhurst Rd. *W On T* —6K **39**
Panmuir Rd. *SW20* —9G **27**
Pannell Clo. *E Grin* —1N **185**
Pannells. *Lwr Bo* —6J **129**
Pannells Clo. *Cher* —7H **37**
Pannells Ct. *Guild* —4N **113**
Pan's Gdns. *Camb* —2D **70**
Pantile Rd. *Wey* —1E **56**
Pantiles Clo. *Wok* —4F **73**
Papercourt La. *Rip* —8H **75**
Paper M. *Dork* —4H **119**
Papermill Clo. *Cars* —1E **62**
Papworth Way. *SW2* —1L **29**
Parade Ct. *E Hor* —4F **96**
Parade M. *SE27* —3M **29**
Parade Rd. *Frim G* —6H **71**
Parade, The. *Ash V* —9E **90**
*Parade, The. Cars —2D **62***
(off Beynon Rd.)
Parade, The. *Clay* —3E **58**
Parade, The. *Craw* —2C **182**
Parade, The. *Croy* —5J **45**
Parade, The. *E Grin* —7L **165**
Parade, The. *Eps* —9C **60**
(in two parts)
Parade, The. *Frim* —6B **70**
Parade, The. *Hamp* —6D **24**
Parade, The. *Red* —4E **122**
Parade, The. *Stai* —6F **20**
Parade, The. *Sun* —8G **23**
Parade, The. *Tad* —6K **81**
Parade, The. *Vir W* —5N **35**
Parade, The. *Wind* —4A **4**
Parade, The. *Wor Pk* —1E **60**
Parade, The. *Yat* —1D **68**
Paradise Rd. *Rich* —8K **11**
Paragon Cotts. *Guild* —9M **95**
Paragon Gro. *Surb* —5M **41**
Paragon Pl. *Surb* —5M **41**
Parbury Rise. *Chess* —3L **59**
Parchmore Rd. *T Hth* —1M **45**
Parchmore Way. *T Hth* —1M **45**
Pares Clo. *Wok* —3N **73**
Parfitts Clo. *Farnh* —1F **128**
Parfour Dri. *Kenl* —3N **83**
Parfrey St. *W6* —2H **13**
Parham Rd. *Craw* —2L **181**
Parish Clo. *Ash* —3F **110**
Parish Clo. *Farnh* —6F **108**
Parish Ct. *Surb* —5L **41**
Parish Ho. *Craw* —4B **182**
Parish La. *Peas P* —1N **199**
(in two parts)
Parish Rd. *F'boro* —5A **90**
Park Av. *SW14* —7C **12**
Park Av. *Camb* —2A **70**
Park Av. *Cars* —3E **62**
Park Av. *Cat* —2B **104**
Park Av. *Eden* —1K **147**
Park Av. *Egh* —7E **20**
Park Av. *Houn* —9B **10**
Park Av. *Mitc* —8F **28**
Park Av. *Pep H* —6N **131**
Park Av. *Red* —2D **142**
Park Av. *Shep* —2F **38**
Park Av. *Stai* —7H **21**
Park Av. *W Wick* —8M **47**
Park Av. *Wokgm* —3A **30**
(in two parts)
Park Av. *Wray* —8N **5**
Park Av. E. *Eps* —3F **60**
Park Av. M. *Mitc* —8F **28**
Park Av. W. *Eps* —3F **60**
Park Barn Dri. *Guild* —1H **113**
Park Barn E. *Guild* —2J **113**
Park Chase. *G'ming* —9H **133**
Park Chase. *Guild* —3A **114**
Park Clo. *W4* —1C **12**
Park Clo. *Cars* —3D **62**
Park Clo. *Esh* —3B **58**
Park Clo. *Fet* —2D **98**
Park Clo. *G'wood* —8L **171**

Park Clo.—Percival Rd.

Park Clo. Hamp —9C 24
Park Clo. Houn —8C 10
Park Clo. King T —9N 25
Park Clo. New H —6K 55
Park Clo. Str G —8A 120
Park Clo. W On T —8G 38
Park Clo. Wind —5G 5
Park Copse. Dork —5K 119
Park Corner. Wind —6B 4
Park Corner Dri. E Hor —6F 96
Park Cotts. Dork —2L 157
Park Ct. Farnh —9J 109
Park Ct. King T —9J 25
Park Ct. N Mald —3C 42
Park Ct. Wok —5B 74
Park Cres. Asc —5C 34
Park Cres. F Row —7J 187
Park Cres. Twic —2D 24
Parkdale Cres. Wor Pk —9C 42
Park Dri. SW14 —8C 12
Park Dri. Asc —5C 34
Park Dri. Asht —5N 79
Park Dri. Brmly —5B 134
Park Dri. Cranl —6A 156
Park Dri. Wey —2C 56
Park Dri. Wok —5B 74
Parker Clo. Craw —5H 183
Parke Rd. SW13 —4F 12
Parke Rd. Sun —3H 39
Parker Rd. Croy —1N 63
Parker's Clo. Asht —6L 79
Parkers Ct. Bag —4J 51
Parker's Hill. Asht —6L 79
Parker's La. Asht —6L 79
Parkers La. Maid G —4F 16
Park Farm Clo. H'ham —1K 197
Park Farm Ind. Est. Camb —5A 70
Park Farm Rd. H'ham —1L 197
Park Farm Rd. King T —8L 25
Parkfield. G'ming —9H 133
Parkfield. H'ham —5J 197
Parkfield. Iswth —4E 10
Parkfield Av. SW14 —7D 12
Parkfield Av. Felt —4H 23
Parkfield Clo. Craw —3L 181
Parkfield Cres. Felt —4H 23
Parkfield Pde. Felt —4H 23
Parkfield Rd. Felt —4H 23
Parkfields. SW15 —7H 13
Parkfields. Croy —7J 47
Parkfields. Oxs —7D 58
Parkfields Av. SW20 —9G 26
Parkfields Clo. Cars —1E 62
Parkfields Rd. King T —6M 25
Park Gdns. King T —6M 25
Park Ga. Clo. King T —7A 26
Park Ga. Cotts. Cranl —7K 155
Park Ga. Ct. Wok —5A 74
Parkgate Gdns. SW14 —8C 12
Parkgate Rd. Newd —9A 140
Parkgate Rd. Reig —4N 121
Parkgate Rd. Wall —2E 62
Park Grn. Bookh —2A 98
Park Hall Rd. SE21 —4N 29
Park Hall Rd. Reig —1M 121
Park Hall Trad. Est. SE21 —4N 29
Park Hill. Cars —3C 62
Park Hill. C Crook —8A 88
Park Hill. Rich —9M 11
Parkhill Clo. B'water —2J 69
Park Hill Clo. Cars —2C 62
Park Hill Ct. SW17 —4D 28
Park Hill Rise. Croy —8B 46
Parkhill Rd. B'water —2J 69
Park Hill Rd. Brom —1N 47
Park Hill Rd. Croy —1B 64
Parkhill Rd. Eps —7E 60
Park Hill Rd. Wall —4F 62
Park Horsley. E Hor —7H 97
Park Ho. Dri. Reig —5L 121
Park Ho. Gdns. Twic —8J 11
Parkhurst. Eps —6B 60
Parkhurst Fields. Churt —9L 149
Parkhurst Gro. Horl —7D 142
Parkhurst Rd. Guild —2K 113
Parkhurst Rd. Horl —7C 142
Parkhurst Rd. Sutt —1B 62
Parkland Av. Slou —1N 5
Parkland Dri. Brack —9C 16
Parkland Gdns. SW19 —2J 27
Parkland Gro. Ashf —4B 22
Parkland Gro. Farnh —4L 109
Parkland Rd. Ashf —5B 22
Parklands. Add —2L 55
Parklands. Bookh —1A 98
Parklands. Oxt —9A 106
Parklands. Red —1E 122
Parklands. Surb —4M 41
Parklands Clo. SW14 —8B 12
Parklands Clo. Cher —9E 36
Parklands Cotts. Alb —1A 136
Parklands Ct. Houn —5L 9
Parklands Pde. Houn —5L 9
Parklands Pl. Guild —3D 114
Parklands Rd. SW16 —6F 28
Parklands Way. Wor Pk —8D 42
Park La. Asht —5M 79
Park La. Ash W —3F 186
Park La. Binf —8K 15
Park La. Brook —1G 170
Park La. Camb —1A 70
Park La. Cars & Wall —1E 62
Park La. Churt —9G 149
Park La. Coul —8H 83
Park La. Croy —9A 46
Park La. Dork —4F 158
Park La. Guild —9F 94
Park La. Houn —3H 9
Park La. Reig —5K 121
Park La. Rich —7K 11
Park La. Sutt —3K 61
Park La. Tedd —7F 24
Park La. Wink —2M 17
Park La. E. Reig —6L 121
Parklawn Av. Eps —9A 60
Park Lawn Av. Horl —6D 142
Park Lawn Rd. Wey —1D 56
Parkleigh Rd. SW19 —1N 43
Park Ley Rd. Wold —7G 85
Parkleys. Rich —5K 25
Park Mnr. Sutt —4A 62
(off Christchurch Pk.)
Parkmead. SW15 —9G 12
Parkmead. Cranl —6A 156
Park M. SE24 —1N 29
Park M. Stanw —1A 22
Parkpale La. Bet —8N 119
Park Pl. C Crook —8A 88
Park Pl. Hamp H —7C 24
Park Pl. H'ham —7J 197
Park Pl. Wok —5B 74
(off Hill View Rd.)
Park Ride. Wind —1A 18
Park Rise. H'ham —4H 197
Park Rise. Lea —8H 79
Park Rise Clo. Lea —8H 79
Park Rd. SE25 —3B 46
Park Rd. SW19 —7B 28
Park Rd. W4 —3B 12
Park Rd. Abry —9N 115
Park Rd. Alder —4N 109
Park Rd. Ashf —6C 22
Park Rd. Asht —5L 79
Park Rd. Bans —2N 81
Park Rd. Brack —1B 32
Park Rd. Camb —3N 69
Park Rd. Cat —1B 104
Park Rd. Dor P —4A 166
Park Rd. E Grin —9N 165
Park Rd. E Mol —3C 40
Park Rd. Egh —5C 20
Park Rd. Esh —1B 58
Park Rd. F'boro —4C 90
Park Rd. Farnh —8J 109
Park Rd. Fay —8E 180
Park Rd. Felt —5L 23
Park Rd. F Row —7H 187
Park Rd. G'ming —9H 133
Park Rd. Guild —3N 113
Park Rd. Hack —8F 44
Park Rd. Hamp H —5B 24
Park Rd. Hamp W —9J 25
Park Rd. Hand —9N 199
Park Rd. Hasl —3G 188
Park Rd. Houn —8B 10
Park Rd. Iswth —4H 11
Park Rd. Kenl —2N 83
Park Rd. King T —6M 25
Park Rd. Ling —9A 126
Park Rd. N Mald —3C 42
Park Rd. Oxt —6B 106
Park Rd. Red —1D 122
Park Rd. Rich —9M 11
Park Rd. Sand —8H 49
Park Rd. Shep —7B 38
Park Rd. Slin —5L 195
Park Rd. Small —1N 163
Park Rd. Stai —9K 7
Park Rd. Sun —8J 23
Park Rd. Surb —4M 41
Park Rd. Sutt —3K 61
Park Rd. Tedd —7F 24
Park Rd. Twic —9J 11
Park Rd. Wall —2F 62
Park Rd. Warl —1A 86
Park Rd. Wok —4B 74
Park Rd. Wokgm —2A 30
Park Rd. Ho. King T —8N 25
Park Rd. Ind. Est. Swan —2F 40
Park Rd. N. W4 —1C 12
Park Row. Farnh —9G 109
Parkshot. Rich —7K 11
Parkside. SW19 —4J 27
Parkside. Craw —3C 182
Parkside. E Grin —9M 165
Parkside. Farnh —6H 109
Parkside. Hamp —6D 24
Park Side. New H —7K 55
Parkside. Sutt —3K 61
Parkside Av. SW19 —6J 27
Parkside Clo. E Hor —3G 96
Parkside Cotts. Guild —1J 115
Parkside Ct. Wey —1B 56
Parkside Cres. Surb —5B 42
Parkside Gdns. SW19 —5J 27
Parkside Gdns. Coul —4F 82
Parkside M. H'ham —5K 197
Parkside Pl. E Hor —3G 96
Parkside Rd. Asc —4D 34
Parkside Rd. Houn —8B 10
Park Sq. Esh —1B 58
Park Sq. Wink —2M 17
Parkstead Rd. SW15 —8F 12
Parkstone Dri. Camb —2A 70
Park St. Bag —4J 51
Park St. Camb —9A 50
Park St. Coln —4F 6
Park St. Croy —8N 45
Park St. Guild —5M 113
Park St. H'ham —6K 197
Park St. Slin —5K 195
Park St. Tedd —7E 24
Park St. Wind —4G 5
Parkstreet La. Slin —5J 195
Park Ter. Wor Pk —7F 42
Park Ter. E. H'ham —7K 197
Park Ter. W. H'ham —7K 197
Park, The. Bookh —2A 98
Park, The. Cars —3D 62
Park, The. Dork —7G 118
Parkthorne Rd. SW12 —1H 29
Park View. Add —2L 55
Park View. Bag —4H 51
Park View. Bookh —3A 98
Park View. Horl —8E 142
Park View. N Mald —2E 42
Park View Clo. Eden —1K 147
Park View Ct. SE20 —1E 46
Parkview Ct. SW18 —8M 13
Park View Ct. Wok —6B 74
Parkview Dri. Mitc —1B 44
Park View Rd. Croy —7D 46
Park View Rd. Red —1E 142
Park View Rd. Wold —9H 85
Park View Vale. Guild —1E 114
Parkville Rd. SW6 —3L 13
Park Wlk. Asht —6M 79
Parkway. SW20 —3J 43
Park Way. Bookh —1A 98
Parkway. Camb —3A 70
Park Way. Craw —2F 182
Parkway. Crowt —2F 48
Parkway. Dork —4G 119
Park Way. Felt —1J 23
Parkway. Guild —2N 114
Parkway. Horl —8E 142
Park Way. H'ham —6J 197
Parkway. New Ad —5L 65
Park Way. W Mol —2B 40
Park Way. Wey —1E 56
Parkway, The. Houn & S'hall —1H 9
Parkway Trad. Est. Houn —2K 9
Parkwood Av. Esh —7C 40
Park Wood Clo. Bans —2J 81
Parkwood Gro. Sun —2H 39
Parkwood Rd. SW19 —6L 27
Park Wood Rd. Bans —2J 81
Parkwood Rd. Iswth —4F 10
Parkwood Rd. Nutf —2J 123
Parkwood Rd. Tats —8G 87
Park Wood View. Bans —3J 81
Park Works Rd. Red —2J 123
Parley Dri. St J —4M 73
Parliamentary Rd. Pirb —8L 71
Parliament M. SW14 —5B 12
Parnell Clo. M'bowr —5H 183
Parnell Gdns. Wey —7B 56
Parnham Av. Light —7A 52
Parr Av. Eps —5G 61
Parr Clo. Lea —7F 78
Parr Ct. Felt —5K 23
Parrington Ho. SW4 —1H 29
Parris Croft. Dork —8J 119
Parrish Ct. Hasl —1G 189
Parrock La. Cole H —8M 187
Parrs Clo. S Croy —5A 64
Parrs Pl. Hamp —8A 24
Parry Clo. Eps —4G 60
Parry Clo. H'ham —4B 198
Parry Dri. Wey —6B 56
Parry Grn. S. Slou —1C 6
Parry Rd. SE25 —2B 46
Parsley Gdns. Croy —7G 46
Parsonage Bus. Pk. H'ham —4L 197
Parsonage Clo. Warl —3H 85
Parsonage Clo. Westc —7C 118
Parsonage La. Westc —6C 118
Parsonage La. Wind —4D 4
Parsonage Rd. Cranl —7M 155
Parsonage Rd. Egh —6N 19
Parsonage Rd. H'ham —4K 197
Parsonage Sq. Dork —5G 118
(off Station Rd.)
Parsonage Way. Frim —5C 70
Parsonage Way. H'ham —4L 197
Parsons Clo. C Crook —8A 88
Parsons Clo. Hasl —9G 171
Parsons Clo. Horl —7C 142
Parsons Cotts. Ash —1G 111
Parsons Field. Sand —7G 49
Parsonsfield Clo. Bans —2J 81
Parsonsfield Rd. Bans —3J 81
Parson's Grn. SW6 —4M 13
Parsons Grn. Guild —1N 113
Parsons Grn. Hasl —9G 171
Parsons Grn. Ct. Guild —9N 93
Parson's Grn. La. SW6 —4M 13
Parsons La. Hind —3A 170
Parsons Mead. Croy —7M 45
Parsons Mead. E Mol —2C 40
Parson's Ride. Brack —6D 32
Parson's Wlk. H'ham —8M 196
Parthenia Rd. SW6 —4M 13
Parthia Clo. Tad —6G 81
Parthings La. H'ham —9E 196
Partridge Av. Yat —9A 48
Partridge Clo. Ews —4C 108
Partridge Clo. Frim —5C 70
Partridge Knoll. Purl —9M 63
Partridge La. Newd & H'ham —7C 140
Partridge Mead. Bans —3H 81
Partridge Pl. Turn H —3F 184
Partridge Rd. Hamp —7N 23
Partridge Way. Guild —1F 114
Parvis Rd. W Byf —9K 55
Paschal Rd. Camb —7D 50
Passage, The. Rich —8L 11
Passfield Enterprise Cen. Pass —9C 168
Passfield Rd. Pass —9D 168
Passfields. W14 —1L 13
(off May St.)
Passingham Ho. Houn —2A 10
Pastens Rd. Oxt —9E 106
Pasture, The. Craw —3G 182
Pasture Wood Rd. Dork —6K 137
Patching Clo. Craw —2L 181
Patchings. H'ham —5M 197
Paterson Rd. Ashf —6M 21
Pates Mnr. Dri. Felt —1E 22
Pathfield. C'fold —5E 172
Pathfield Clo. C'fold —5E 172
Pathfield Clo. Rud —1E 194
Pathfield Rd. SW16 —7H 29
Pathfield Rd. Rud —1E 194
Pathfields. Shere —8B 116
Pathfields Clo. Hasl —1H 189
Pathfinders, The. F'boro —2H 89
Path Link. Craw —2C 182
Path, The. SW19 —9N 27
Pathway, The. Binf —6H 15
Pathway, The. Send —3H 95
Patmore La. W On T —3G 56
Patricia Gdns. Sutt —7M 61
Patrick Gdns. Warf —8C 16
Patrington Clo. Craw —6M 181
Patten All. Rich —8K 11
Patten Ash Dri. Wokgm —1D 30
Patten Av. Yat —1B 68
Patten Rd. SW18 —1C 28
Patterdale Clo. Craw —5N 181
Patterson Clo. Frim —3G 71
Paul Av. Egh —9E 20
Paul Clo. Alder —4K 109
Paul Gdns. Croy —9C 46
Pauline Cres. Twic —2C 24
Pauls Mead. Ling —6A 146
Paul's Pl. Asht —6A 80
Paved Ct. Rich —8K 11
Pavement Sq. Croy —7D 46
Pavement, The. Craw —3C 182
Pavement, The. Iswth —6G 11
(off South St.)
Pavilion Gdns. Stai —8K 21
Pavilion La. Alder —2K 109
Pavilion Rd. Alder —3K 109
Pavilions End, The. Camb —3B 70
Pavilion, The. Reig —1C 122
Pavilion Way. E Grin —1A 186
Paviours. Farnh —9G 109
Pawley Clo. Tong —5D 110
Pawsons Rd. Croy —5N 45
Pax Clo. Bew —5K 181
Paxton Clo. Rich —5M 11
Paxton Clo. W On T —6K 39
Paxton Gdns. Wok —8G 54
Paxton Rd. W4 —2D 12
Payley Dri. Wokgm —9D 14
Payne Clo. Craw —1H 183
Paynesfield Av. SW14 —6C 12
Paynesfield Rd. Tats —8E 86
Paynes Wlk. W6 —2K 13
Peabody Clo. Croy —7F 46
Peabody Est. SE24 —1N 29
Peabody Est. SW6 —2M 13
(off Lillie Rd.)
Peabody Est. W6 —1H 13
Peabody Hill. SE21 —2M 29
Peabody Rd. F'boro —4B 90
Peace Clo. SE25 —3B 46
Peacemaker Clo. Bew —5K 181
Peaches Clo. Sutt —4K 61
Peach St. Wokgm —2B 30
Peach Tree Clo. F'boro —7M 69
Peacock Av. Felt —2E 22
Peacock Cotts. Brack —3H 31
Peacock Gdns. S Croy —6H 65
Peacock La. Wokgm & Brack —4G 31
Peacocks Shop. Cen., The. Wok —4A 74
Peacock Ter. Red —2D 122
Peacock Wlk. Craw —6M 181
Peacock Wlk. Dork —6G 119
Peakfield. Fren —3H 149
Peak Rd. Guild —9K 93
Peaks Hill. Purl —6H 63
Peaks Hill Rise. Purl —6J 63
Peall Rd. Croy —5K 45
Peall Rd. Ind. Est. Croy —5K 45
Pear Av. Shep —2F 38
Pearce Clo. Mitc —1E 44
Pearce Rd. W Mol —2B 40
Pearl Ct. Wok —3H 73
Pearmain Clo. Shep —4C 38
Pearscroft Ct. SW6 —4N 13
Pearscroft Rd. SW6 —4N 13
Pearson Rd. Craw —3F 182
Pears Rd. Houn —6C 10
Peartree Av. SW17 —4A 28
Pear Tree Av. Fleet —3A 88
Pear Tree Clo. Add —2J 55
Pear Tree Clo. Chess —2N 59
Pear Tree Clo. Lind —5A 168
Peartree Clo. Mitc —1C 44
Peartree Clo. S Croy —1E 84
Peartree Grn. Duns —2N 173
Pear Tree Hill. Salf —3E 142
Pear Tree La. Rowl —8E 128
Pear Tree Rd. Add —2J 55
Pear Tree Rd. Ashf —6D 22
Pear Tree Rd. Lind —5A 168
Peary Clo. H'ham —2K 197
Peascod Pl. Wind —4G 4
Peascod St. Wind —4F 4
Pease Pottage Hill. Craw —8A 182
Peaslake La. Peasl —5E 136
Peaslake Rd. Ewh —2E 156
Peat Comn. Elst —9G 131
Peat Cotts. Elst —9G 131
Peatmoor Clo. Fleet —3A 88
Peatmore Av. Wok —3J 75
Peatmore Clo. Wok —3J 75
Peatmore Dri. Brkwd —8N 71
Pebble Clo. Tad —7D 100
Pebble Hill Rd. Bet —7D 100
Pebble La. Lea & Eps —2M 99
Pebworth Ct. Red —1E 122
Peddlars Gro. Yat —9D 48
Peeble Hill. W Hor —2D 116
Peek Cres. SW19 —6J 27
Peeks Brook La. Horl —4J 163
Peel Av. Frim —7E 70
Peel Cen. Ind. Est. Eps —7E 60
Peel Cen., The. Brack —1M 31
Peel Clo. Wind —6E 4
Peel Ct. F'boro —5A 90
Peel Rd. Orp —2L 67
Pegasus Av. Alder —1C 110
Pegasus Clo. Hasl —3B 188
Pegasus Ct. Bew —5K 181
Pegasus Ct. Fleet —3A 88
Pegasus Ct. King T —2K 41
Pegasus Rd. F'boro —7L 69
Pegasus Way. E Grin —7D 166
Peggotty Pl. Owl —5K 49
Pegg Rd. Houn —3L 9
Pegwell Clo. Craw —5L 181
Peket Clo. Stai —9G 21
Peldon Ct. Rich —8M 11
Peldon Pas. Rich —7M 11
Pelham Ct. Craw —7N 181
Pelham Ct. H'ham —6H 197
Pelham Dri. Craw —7M 181
Pelham Ho. W14 —1L 13
(off Mornington Av.)
Pelham Pl. Craw —7N 181
Pelham Rd. SW19 —8M 27
Pelham Rd. Beck —1F 46
Pelham's Clo. Esh —1A 58
Pelham's Wlk. Esh —9A 40
Pelham Way. Bookh —4C 98
Pellant Rd. SW6 —3K 13
Pelling Hill. Old Win —1L 19
Pelton Av. Sutt —6N 61
Pemberley Chase. W Ewe —2A 60
Pemberley Clo. W Ewe —2A 60
Pemberton Pl. Esh —9C 40
Pemberton Rd. E Mol —3C 40
Pembley Grn. Copt —7B 164
Pembridge Av. Twic —2N 23
Pembridge Pl. SW18 —8M 13
Pembroke. Brack —6L 31
Pembroke Av. Surb —4A 42
Pembroke Av. W On T —1L 57
Pembroke B'way. Camb —1A 70
Pembroke Clo. Asc —4A 34
Pembroke Clo. Bans —4N 81
Pembroke Gdns. Wok —5C 74
Pembroke M. Asc —4A 34
Pembroke Pde. Yat —9D 48
Pembroke Pl. Iswth —5E 10
Pembroke Rd. SE25 —3B 46
Pembroke Rd. Craw —9G 163
Pembroke Rd. Mitc —1E 44
Pembroke Rd. Wok —5C 74
Pembroke Vs. Rich —7K 11
Pembury Av. Wor Pk —7F 42
Pembury Clo. Coul —1E 82
Pembury Ct. Hayes —2E 8
Pembury Pl. Alder —3A 110
Pembury Rd. SE25 —3D 46
Pemdevon Rd. Croy —6L 45
Pemerich Clo. Hayes —1G 8
Penates. Esh —1D 58
Penbury Rd. S'hall —1N 9
Pendarves Rd. SW20 —9H 27
Pendell Av. Hayes —3G 8
Pendell Rd. Blet —9M 103
Pendennis Clo. W Byf —1J 75
Pendennis Rd. SW16 —5J 29
Penderel Rd. Houn —8A 10
Pendine Pl. Brack —4N 31
Pendlebury. Brack —6M 31
Pendle Rd. SW16 —7F 28
Pendleton Clo. Red —4D 122
Pendleton Rd. Reig & Red —6A 122
Pendragon Way. Camb —2H 71
Pendry's La. Binf —1M 15
Penfold Clo. Croy —9L 45
Penfold Croft. Farnh —8L 109
(in two parts)
Penfold Rd. M'bowr —7F 182
Penge Rd. SE25 & SE20 —2D 46
Pengilly Rd. Farnh —2G 128
Penhurst. Wok —1B 74
Peninsular Clo. Felt —9E 8
Penistone Rd. SW16 —8J 29
Penlee Clo. Eden —1L 147
Pennards, The. Sun —2K 39
Penn Clo. Craw —9B 162
Penn Ct. Craw —3L 181
Pennefathers Rd. Alder —1L 109
Penner Clo. SW19 —3K 27
Pennine Clo. Craw —3N 181
Pennine Way. F'boro —7J 69
Pennine Way. Hayes —3E 8
Pennings Av. Guild —1J 113
Pennington Dri. Wey —9F 38
Penn Rd. Dat —4N 5
Penns Wood. F'boro —4B 90
Pennycroft. Croy —5H 65
Penny Dri. Wood S —2E 112
Pennyfield. Cobh —9H 57
Penny Hill Cvn. Pk. B'water —4B 68
Penny La. Shep —6F 38
Pennymead Dri. E Hor —5G 96
Pennymead Rise. E Hor —5G 96
Penny M. SW12 —1F 28
Pennypot La. Chob —9E 52
Penny Royal. Wall —3H 63
Penrhyn Clo. Alder —3N 109
Penrhyn Cres. SW14 —7B 12
Penrhyn Gdns. King T —3K 41
Penrhyn Rd. King T —3L 41
Penrith Clo. SW15 —8K 13
Penrith Clo. Beck —1L 47
Penrith Clo. Reig —2C 122
Penrith Pl. SE27 —3M 29
Penrith Rd. N Mald —3C 42
Penrith Rd. T Hth —1N 45
Penrith St. SW16 —7G 28
Penrose Ct. Egh —7M 19
Penrose Rd. Fet —9C 78
Pensfold La. H'ham —3F 194
Pensford Av. Rich —5N 11
Pensford Clo. Crowt —9G 30
Penshurst Clo. Craw —2H 183
Penshurst Rise. Frim —6D 70
Penshurst Rd. T Hth —4M 45
Penshurst Way. Sutt —5M 61
Pentelow Gdns. Felt —9H 9
Pentland Av. Shep —4B 38
Pentland Gdns. SW18 —9N 13
Pentland Pl. F'boro —7K 69
Pentlands Clo. Mitc —2F 44
Pentland St. SW18 —9N 13
Pentlow St. SW15 —6H 13
Pentney Rd. SW12 —2G 28
Pentney Rd. SW19 —9K 27
Penton Av. Stai —8H 21
Penton Hall. Stai —9J 21
Penton Hall Dri. Stai —9J 21
Penton Hook Rd. Stai —8J 21
Penton Pk. Cher —2K 37
Penton Pk. (Cvn. Site). Cher —2K 37
Penton Rd. Stai —8H 21
Pentreath Av. Guild —4J 113
Penwerris Av. Iswth —3C 10
Penwerris Ct. Houn —3C 10
Penwith Dri. Hasl —4B 188
Penwith Rd. SW18 —3M 27
Penwith Wlk. Wok —6N 73
Penwood End. Wok —8L 73
Penwood Gdns. Brack —5J 31
Penwood Ho. SW15 —9E 12
Penwortham Rd. SW16 —7F 28
Penwortham Rd. S Croy —6A 64
Pen-y-Bos Track. Hasl —7K 189
Penywern Rd. SW5 —1M 13
Peperham Ho. Hasl —1G 189
Peperham Rd. Hasl —9G 171
Peperharow La. Shack —5N 131
Peperharow Rd. G'ming —5E 132
Peppard Rd. M'bowr —6H 183
Pepperbox La. Brmly —5F 154
Pepper Clo. Cat —3B 104
Peppermint Clo. Croy —6J 45
Pepys Clo. Asht —4N 79
Pepys Clo. Slou —2D 6
Pepys Rd. SW20 —8H 27
Percheron Clo. Iswth —6F 10
Percheron Dri. Knap —6E 72
Percival Rd. SW14 —7B 12

Percival Rd.—Postford Farm Cotts.

Percival Rd. *Felt* —3G **22**
Percival Way. *Eps* —1C **60**
Percy Av. *Ashf* —6B **22**
Percy Bryant Rd. *Sun* —8F **22**
Percy Gdns. *Iswth* —6G **11**
Percy Gdns. *Wor Pk* —7D **42**
Percy Pl. *Dat* —4L **5**
Percy Rd. *SE20* —1G **46**
Percy Rd. *SE25* —4D **46**
Percy Rd. *Guild* —1L **113**
Percy Rd. *Hamp* —8A **24**
Percy Rd. *H'ham* —5H **197**
Percy Rd. *Iswth* —7G **11**
Percy Rd. *Mitc* —6E **44**
Percy Rd. *Twic* —2B **24**
Percy Way. *Twic* —2C **24**
Peregrine Clo. *Brack* —4N **31**
Peregrine Clo. *Cranl* —6N **155**
Peregrine Ct. *SW16* —5K **29**
Peregrine Gdns. *Croy* —8H **47**
Peregrine Rd. *Sun* —1G **38**
Peregrine Way. *SW19* —8H **27**
Perham Rd. *W14* —1K **13**
Perifield. *SE21* —2N **29**
Perimeter Rd. E. *Gat A* —3F **162**
Perimeter Rd. N. *Gat A* —2B **162**
Perimeter Rd. S. *Gat A* —5A **162**
Periwinkle Clo. *Lind* —4B **168**
Perkins Ct. *Ashf* —6A **22**
Perkins Way. *Wokgm* —3A **30**
*Perkstead Ct. Craw —6M **181***
(off Waddington Clo.)
*Perleybrooke La. Wok —4K **73***
(off Bampton Way)
Perowne St. *Alder* —2L **109**
Perran Rd. *SW2* —2M **29**
Perran Wlk. *Bren* —1L **11**
Perrin Clo. *Ashf* —6A **22**
Perrin Ct. *Wok* —2D **74**
Perring Av. *F'boro* —[illegible]
Perrior Rd. *G'ming* —4H **133**
Perry Av. *E Grin* —7A **166**
Perry Clo. *G'ming* —6K **133**
Perrycroft. *Wind* —6B **4**
Perryfield Rd. *Craw* —4A **182**
Perryfield Way. *Rich* —4H **25**
Perry Hill. *Worp* —5H **93**
Perryhill Dri. *Sand* —6E **48**
Perry How. *Wor Pk* —7E **42**
Perrylands. *Charl* —3L **161**
Perrylands La. *Horl* —9K **143**
Perrymead St. *SW6* —4M **13**
Perryn Ct. *Twic* —1G **24**
Perry Oaks. *Brack* —1C **32**
Perry Oaks Dri. *W Dray & Houn* —5K **7**
Perry Way. *Brack* —1C **32**
Perry Way. *Head* —5E **168**
Perry Way. *Light* —8K **51**
Perrywood Bus. Pk. *Red* —2F **142**
Perseverance Cotts. *Rip* —8L **75**
Perseverance Pl. *Rich* —7L **11**
Persevernce Pl. *Rich* —7L **11**
Persfield Clo. *Eps* —6E **60**
Persfield M. *Eps* —6E **60**
Pershore Gro. *Cars* —5B **44**
Perth Clo. *SW20* —1F **42**
Perth Clo. *Craw* —9B **162**
Perth Rd. *Beck* —1M **47**
Perth Way. *H'ham* —4M **197**
Petauel Rd. *Tedd* —6E **24**
Peter Av. *Oxt* —7N **105**
Peterborough M. *SW6* —5M **13**
Peterborough Rd. *SW6* —5M **13**
Peterborough Rd. *Cars* —5C **44**
Peterborough Rd. *Craw* —7C **182**
Peterborough Rd. *Guild* —1J **113**
Peterborough Vs. *SW6* —4N **13**
Peterhead M. *Langl* —1C **6**
Peterhouse Clo. *Owl* —5L **49**
Peterhouse Pde. *Craw* —9G **162**
Peterlee Wlk. *Bew* —7K **181**
Petersfield Av. *Stai* —6L **21**
Petersfield Cres. *Coul* —2J **83**
Petersfield Rise. *SW15* —2G **26**
Petersfield Rd. *Stai* —6L **21**
Petersham Av. *Byfl* —8N **55**
Petersham Clo. *Byfl* —8N **55**
Petersham Clo. *Rich* —3K **25**
Petersham Clo. *Sutt* —2M **61**
Petersham Rd. *Rich* —9K **11**
*Petersham Ter. Mitc —9J **45***
(off Richmond Grn.)
Petersmead Clo. *Tad* —1H **101**
Peterstow Clo. *SW19* —3K **27**
Peterswood. *Capel* —5J **159**
Peterwood Pk. *Croy* —8K **45**
Peterwood Way. *Croy* —8K **45**
Petley Rd. *W6* —2J **13**
Petridge Rd. *Red* —8D **122**
Petters Rd. *Asht* —3M **79**
Pettiward Clo. *SW15* —7H **13**
Petts La. *Shep* —3B **38**
Petworth Clo. *Coul* —6G **82**
Petworth Clo. *Frim* —6D **70**
Petworth Ct. *Craw* —6L **181**
Petworth Ct. *Hasl* —2H **189**
Petworth Dri. *H'ham* —1M **197**
Petworth Gdns. *SW20* —2G **42**
Petworth Rd. *Hasl* —2H **189**
Petworth Rd. *Milf* —3C **152**
Pevensey Clo. *Craw* —4G **182**
Pevensey Clo. *Iswth* —3C **10**
Pevensey Rd. *SW17* —5B **28**
Pevensey Rd. *Felt* —2M **23**
Pevensey Way. *Frim* —6E **70**
Peverel Rd. *If'd* —4K **181**
Peveril Dri. *Tedd* —6D **24**
Pewley Bank. *Guild* —5A **114**
Pewley Hill. *Guild* —5N **113**
Pewley Point. *Guild* —5A **114**
Pewley Way. *Guild* —5A **114**
Pewsey Vale. *Brack* —4D **32**
Peyton's Cotts. *Red* —1J **123**
Pharaoh Clo. *Mitc* —6D **44**
Pharaoh's Island. *Shep* —8A **38**
Pheasant Clo. *Purl* —9M **63**
Phelps Way. *Hayes* —1G **9**
Philanthropic Rd. *Red* —4E **122**
Philbeach Gdns. *SW5* —1M **13**
Philip Gdns. *Croy* —8J **47**
Philip Rd. *Stai* —7M **21**
Philips Clo. *Cars* —7E **44**
Phillip Copse. *Brack* —6B **32**
Phillips Clo. *G'ming* —9G **132**
Phillips Clo. *Head* —4E **168**
Phillips Clo. *M'bowr* —8F **182**
Phillips Clo. *Tong* —4C **110**
Phillips Cres. *Head* —4E **168**
Phillips Hatch. *Won* —3E **134**
Phillip's Quad. *Wok* —5A **74**
Philpot La. *Chob* —9L **53**
Philpot Sq. *SW6* —6N **13**
Phipp Point. *W Mol* —2B **40**
Phipp's Bri. Rd. *SW19 & Mitc* —1A **44**
Phoenix Bus. Pk. *Brack* —1H **31**
Phoenix Clo. *W Wick* —8N **47**
Phoenix Ct. *Alder* —3M **109**
Phoenix Ct. *Guild* —5N **113**
Phoenix Ct. *Houn* —8L **9**
Phoenix Ct. *S Croy* —2C **64**
Phoenix Dri. *Kes* —1F **66**
Phoenix Ho. *Sutt* —1N **61**
Phoenix La. *Ash W* —3G **186**
Phoenix Trad. Pk. *Bren* —1K **11**
Phoenix Way. *Houn* —2L **9**
Phyllis Av. *N Mald* —4G **42**
Picards, The. *Guild* —7M **113**
Pickering. *Brack* —3M **31**
Pickering Gdns. *Croy* —5C **46**
Picket Post Clo. *Brack* —2D **32**
Pickets St. *SW12* —1F **28**
Picketts Hill. *Head* —9A **148**
Pickett's La. *Horl* —4H **163**
Picketts La. *Red* —2G **142**
Pickford St. *Alder* —2N **109**
Pickhurst La. *W Wick & Brom* —4N **47**
Pickhurst Rise. *W Wick* —7N **47**
Pickhurst Rd. *C'fold* —6F **172**
Pickins Piece. *Hort* —5C **6**
Pickwick Clo. *Houn* —8M **9**
Picquets Way. *Bans* —4L **81**
Picton Clo. *Camb* —8F **50**
Picts Hill. *H'ham* —9G **197**
Pierrefonde's Av. *F'boro* —9M **69**
Pier Rd. *Felt* —8J **9**
Pierson Rd. *Wind* —4A **4**
Pier Ter. *SW18* —7N **13**
Pigbush La. *Loxw* —1H **193**
Pigeon Ho. La. *Coul* —3A **102**
Pigeonhouse La. *Wink* —4H **17**
Pigeon La. *Hamp* —5A **24**
Piggott Ct. *H'ham* —7K **197**
Pigott Rd. *Wokgm* —9C **14**
Pig Pound Wlk. *Hand* —6N **199**
Pike Clo. *Alder* —2A **110**
*Pikemans Ct. SW5 —1M **13***
(off W. Cromwell Rd.)
Pikes Hill. *Eps* —9D **60**
Pikes La. *Crow* —2A **146**
Pilgrim Clo. *Mord* —6N **43**
Pilgrim Ct. *Milf* —2C **152**
Pilgrim Hill. *SE27* —5N **29**
Pilgrims Clo. *Farnh* —3F **128**
Pilgrim's Clo. *Shere* —8B **116**
Pilgrims Clo. *Westh* —9G **99**
Pilgrims' La. *Cat* —4K **103**
Pilgrims La. *T'sey & W'ham* —2E **106**
Pilgrims Pl. *Reig* —1M **121**
Pilgrims View. *Ash* —4G **111**
Pilgrims Way. *Bisl* —3D **72**
Pilgrims Way. *Guild* —7N **113**
Pilgrim's Way. *Reig* —1L **121**
Pilgrim's Way. *Shere* —8B **116**
Pilgrims Way. *S Croy* —2C **64**
Pilgrims Way. *W'ham & Sund* —1J **107**
Pilgrims Way. *Westh* —9H **99**
Pilgrims Way Cotts. *Bet* —2B **120**
Pilsden Clo. *SW19* —2J **27**
Pilton Est., The. *Croy* —8M **45**
Pimms Clo. *Guild* —8C **94**
Pinckards. *C'fold* —4D **172**
Pincott La. *W Hor* —7C **96**
Pincott Rd. *SW19* —8A **28**
Pine Av. *Camb* —2B **70**
Pine Av. *W Wick* —7L **47**
Pine Bank. *Hind* —5C **170**
Pine Clo. *Ash V* —7E **90**
Pine Clo. *Craw* —9A **162**
Pine Clo. *Kenl* —4A **84**
Pine Clo. *New H* —7K **55**
Pine Clo. *Sand* —8K **49**
Pine Clo. *Wok* —3M **73**
Pine Coombe. *Croy* —1G **65**
Pinecote Dri. *Asc* —6C **34**
Pine Ct. *Alder* —2M **109**
Pine Ct. *Brack* —3C **32**
Pine Cres. *Cars* —7B **62**
Pinecrest Gdns. *Orp* —1K **67**
Pine Croft Rd. *Wokgm* —6A **30**
Pine Dean. *Bookh* —3B **98**
Pine Dri. *B'water* —3K **69**
*Pinefields. Add —1K **55***
(off Church Rd.)
Pinefields Clo. *Crowt* —2G **48**
Pine Gdns. *Horl* —9E **142**
Pine Gdns. *Surb* —5N **41**
Pine Glade. *Orp* —1H **67**
Pine Gro. *SW19* —6L **27**
Pine Gro. *C Crook* —8C **88**
Pine Gro. *E Grin* —7L **165**
Pine Gro. *Eden* —1K **147**
Pine Gro. *Lwr Bo* —5K **129**
Pine Gro. *Wey* —2C **56**
Pine Gro. *W'sham* —3A **52**
Pine Gro. M. *Wey* —2D **56**
Pine Hill. *Eps* —2C **80**
Pinehill Rise. *Sand* —7H **49**
Pinehill Rd. *Crowt* —3G **49**
Pinehurst. *H'ham* —4J **197**
Pinehurst. *S'hill* —4A **34**
Pinehurst Av. *F'boro* —9L **69**
Pinehurst Clo. *Tad* —9M **81**
Pinehurst Cotts. *F'boro* —3N **89**
Pinel Clo. *Vir W* —3A **36**
Pine Mt. Rd. *Camb* —2B **70**
Pine Pl. *Bans* —1J **81**
Pine Ridge. *Cars* —5E **62**
Pine Ridge Dri. *Lwr Bo* —6G **129**
Pine Rd. *Wok* —7M **73**
Pine Shaw. *Craw* —2H **183**
Pines Rd. *Fleet* —3A **88**
Pines, The. *SE19* —8M **29**
Pines, The. *Coul* —5F **82**
Pines, The. *Dork* —6H **119**
Pines, The. *H'ham* —3B **198**
Pines, The. *Purl* —9N **63**
Pines, The. *Sun* —2H **39**
Pines, The. *Wok* —1B **74**
Pines Trad. Est., The. *Guild* —1H **113**
Pine Tree Clo. *Houn* —4J **9**
Pine Tree Hill. *Wok* —3F **74**
Pine Trees Bus. Pk. *Stai* —6G **20**
Pinetrees Clo. *Copt* —7M **163**
Pine View. *Head* —3H **169**
Pine View Clo. *Bad L* —7M **109**
Pine View Clo. *Chil* —9H **115**
Pine View Clo. *Hasl* —9G **170**
Pine Wlk. *Bans* —4D **82**
Pine Wlk. *Bookh* —3B **98**
Pine Wlk. *Cars* —6B **62**
Pine Wlk. *Cat* —9B **84**
Pine Wlk. *Cobh* —1L **77**
Pine Wlk. *E Hor* —6G **97**
Pine Wlk. *Surb* —5N **41**
Pine Wlk. E. *Cars* —7B **62**
Pine Wlk. W. *Cars* —6B **62**
Pine Way. *Egh* —7L **19**
Pine Way Clo. *E Grin* —2A **186**
Pine Wood. *Sun* —9H **23**
Pinewood Av. *Crowt* —1H **49**
Pinewood Av. *New H* —5L **55**
Pinewood Cvn. Pk. *Wokgm* —8H **31**
Pinewood Clo. *Broad H* —5D **196**
Pinewood Clo. *Croy* —9H **47**
Pinewood Clo. *Sand* —7E **48**
Pinewood Clo. *Wok* —2C **74**
Pinewood Ct. *Add* —1L **55**
Pinewood Ct. *Fleet* —3B **88**
Pinewood Cres. *F'boro* —9H **69**
Pinewood Dri. *Orp* —2N **67**
Pinewood Dri. *Stai* —6J **21**
Pinewood Gdns. *Bag* —4G **50**
Pinewood Gro. *New H* —6K **55**
Pinewood Hill. *Fleet* —3B **88**
Pinewood M. *Stai* —9M **7**
Pinewood Pk. *F'boro* —7H **69**
Pinewood Pk. *New H* —7K **55**
Pinewood Pl. *Eps* —1C **60**
Pinewood Rd. *Ash* —1H **111**
Pinewood Rd. *Felt* —4J **23**
Pinewood Rd. *Vir W* —3K **35**
Pinfold Rd. *SW16* —5J **29**
Pinglestone Clo. *W Dray* —3N **7**
Pinkcoat Clo. *Felt* —4J **23**
Pinkerton Pl. *SW16* —5H **29**
Pinkham Mans. *W4* —1N **11**
Pinkhurst La. *Slin* —6A **196**
Pioneer Pl. *Croy* —5K **65**
Pioneers Ind. Pk. *Croy* —7J **45**
Piper Rd. *King T* —2N **41**
Pipers Clo. *Cobh* —2L **77**
Pipers Croft. *C Crook* —9B **88**
Pipers End. *Slin* —5M **195**
Piper's End. *Vir W* —2N **35**
Piper's Gdns. *Croy* —6H **47**
Pipers Hatch. *F'boro* —1N **89**
Pipers La. *N'chap* —9D **190**
Pipewell Rd. *Cars* —5C **44**
Pippbrook Gdns. *Dork* —4H **119**
Pippin Clo. *Croy* —7J **47**
Pippins Ct. *Ashf* —7C **22**
Pipson La. *Yat* —1C **68**
Pipsons Clo. *Yat* —9C **48**
Piquet Rd. *SE20* —1F **46**
Pirbright Cres. *New Ad* —3M **65**
Pirbright Grn. *Pirb* —1C **92**
Pirbright Rd. *SW18* —2L **27**
Pirbright Rd. *F'boro* —2A **90**
Pirbright Rd. *Norm* —1J **111**
Pirbright Rd. *Wok* —6A **92**
Pirbright Ter. *Pirb* —1C **92**
*Piries Pl. H'ham —6J **197***
(off East St.)
Pisley Farm Rd. *Ockl* —6N **157**
Pitcairn Rd. *Mitc* —8D **28**
Pitchfont La. *Oxt* —2B **106**
Pitch Pl. *Binf* —6J **15**
Pit Farm Rd. *Guild* —3C **114**
Pitfold Av. *Hasl* —2B **188**
Pitfold Clo. *Hasl* —2C **188**
Pitlake. *Croy* —8M **45**
Pitland St. *Dork* —6K **137**
Pit La. *Eden* —8L **127**
Pitson Clo. *Add* —1M **55**
Pitt Cres. *SW19* —5N **27**
Pitt Pl. *Eps* —1D **80**
Pitt Rd. *Eps* —1D **80**
Pitt Rd. *Orp* —1L **67**
[illegible]
Pitts Clo. *Binf* —7J **15**
Pittville Gdns. *SE25* —2D **46**
Pitt Way. *F'boro* —9L **69**
Pitwood Grn. *Tad* —7H **81**
Pitwood Pk. Ind. Est. *Tad* —7G **81**
Pixham End. *Dork* —2J **119**
Pixham La. *Dork* —2J **119**
Pixholme Gro. *Dork* —3J **119**
Pixton Way. *Croy* —5H **65**
Place Ct. *Alder* —5A **110**
Place Farm Rd. *Blet* —8A **104**
Placehouse La. *Coul* —6K **83**
Plain Ride. *Wind* —2N **17**
Plaistow Rd. *Duns* —1M **191**
Plaistow Rd. *Kird* —8D **192**
Plaistow Rd. *Loxw* —6D **192**
Plaistow St. *Ling* —7N **145**
Plane Ho. *Short* —1N **47**
Planes, The. *Cher* —6L **37**
Plane Tree Cres. *Felt* —4J **23**
Plantagenet Clo. *Wor Pk* —1C **60**
Plantagenet Pk. *Warf* —9D **16**
Plantain Cres. *Craw* —7M **181**
Plantation La. *Warl* —6H **85**
Plantation Row. *Camb* —1N **69**
Plateau, The. *Warf P* —8E **16**
Plat, The. *Eden* —2M **147**
Plat, The. *H'ham* —5G **196**
Platt Meadow. *Guild* —9F **94**
Platt, The. *SW15* —6J **13**
Platt, The. *D'land* —1C **166**
Plaws Hill. *Peasl* —5E **136**
Playden Clo. *Craw* —6M **181**
*Playfair Mans. W14 —2K **13***
(off Queen's Club Gdns.)
Playfair St. *W6* —1H **13**
Playground Clo. *Beck* —1G **47**
Pleasance Rd. *SW15* —8G **12**
Pleasance, The. *SW15* —7G **12**
Pleasant Gro. *Croy* —9J **47**
Pleasant Pl. *W On T* —3K **57**
Pleasant View Pl. *Orp* —2K **67**
Pleasure Pit Rd. *Asht* —5A **80**
Plesman Way. *Wall* —5J **63**
Plevna Rd. *Hamp* —9B **24**
Plough Clo. *If'd* —1L **181**
Plough Ind. Est. *Lea* —7G **79**
Ploughlands. *Brack* —9L **15**
Plough La. *SW19 & SW17* —6N **27**
Plough La. *D'side* —4H **77**
Plough La. *Ewh* —6G **156**
Plough La. *H'ham* —3L **197**
Plough La. *Purl* —5K **63**
Plough La. *Wall* —1J **63**
Plough La. *Wokgm* —1E **30**
Plough La. Clo. *Wall* —2J **63**
Ploughmans End. *Iswth* —8D **10**
Plough Rd. *D'land* —9C **146**
Plough Rd. *Eps* —5C **60**
Plough Rd. *Small* —8M **143**
Plough Rd. *Yat* —8D **48**
Plough Wlk. *Eden* —9L **127**
Plover Clo. *Craw* —1A **182**
Plover Clo. *Eden* —9L **127**
Plover Clo. *Stai* —4H **21**
Plovers Rise. *Brkwd* —7B **72**
Plovers Rd. *H'ham* —5M **197**
Plum Clo. *Felt* —2H **23**
Plum Garth. *Bren* —1K **11**
Plummer La. *Mitc* —1D **44**
Plummer Rd. *SW4* —1H **29**
Plumpton Way. *Cars* —9C **44**
Plumtree Clo. *Wall* —4H **63**
Pocket Clo. *Binf* —1J **31**
Pockford Rd. *C'fold* —5F **172**
Pococks La. *Eton* —1H **5**
Podmore Rd. *SW18* —7N **13**
Poels Ct. *E Grin* —8A **166**
Pointers Cotts. *Rich* —3J **25**
Pointers Hill. *Westc* —7C **118**
Pointers Rd. *Cobh* —3D **76**
Pointers, The. *Asht* —7L **79**
Point Pleasant. *SW18* —7M **13**
Polden Clo. *F'boro* —7K **69**
Polecat Hill. *Gray* —8D **170**
Polecat Valley. *Hind* —8D **170**
Polesden Gdns. *SW20* —1G **42**
Polesden La. *Send* —1H **95**
Polesden Rd. *Bookh* —7B **98**
Polesden View. *Bookh* —5B **98**
Poles La. *Low H* —6A **162**
Polesteeple Hill. *Big H* —4F **86**
Police Sta. Rd. *W On T* —3K **57**
Polkerris Way. *C Crook* —9C **88**
Pollard Clo. *Old Win* —8L **5**
Pollard Gro. *Camb* —2G **71**
Pollard Rd. *Mord* —4B **44**
Pollard Rd. *Wok* —3D **74**
Pollardrow Av. *Brack* —9L **15**
(in two parts)
Pollards. *Craw* —4M **181**
Pollards Cres. *SW16* —2J **45**
Pollards Dri. *H'ham* —5L **197**
Pollards Hill E. *SW16* —2K **45**
Pollards Hill N. *SW16* —2J **45**
Pollards Hill S. *SW16* —2J **45**
Pollards Hill W. *SW16* —2K **45**
Pollards Oak Cres. *Oxt* —1C **126**
Pollards Oak Rd. *Oxt* —1C **126**
Pollards Wood Hill. *Oxt* —8D **106**
Pollards Wood Rd. *SW16* —2J **45**
Pollards Wood Rd. *Oxt* —9D **106**
Pollocks Path. *Gray* —7B **170**
Polmear Clo. *C Crook* —9C **88**
Polsted La. *Comp* —1F **132**
Poltimore Rd. *Guild* —5K **113**
Polworth Rd. *SW16* —6J **29**
Polyanthus Way. *Crowt* —8G **30**
Polygon Bus. Cen. *Coln* —5H **7**
Pond Clo. *Loxw* —4H **193**
Pond Clo. *W On T* —3G **57**
(in two parts)
Pond Copse La. *Loxw* —3H **193**
Pond Cottage La. *W Wick* —7K **47**
Pond Croft. *Yat* —9D **48**
Pond Farm Clo. *Tad* —2G **100**
Pondfield Ho. *SE27* —6N **29**
Pondfield Rd. *G'ming* —4J **133**
Pondfield Rd. *Kenl* —3M **83**
Pondfield Rd. *Rud* —9E **176**
Pond Head La. *Dork* —5L **157**
Pond Hill Gdns. *Sutt* —3K **61**
Pond La. *Fren* —6H **149**
Pond La. *Peasl* —4D **136**
Pond Meadow. *Guild* —3H **113**
Pond Moor Rd. *Brack* —4N **31**
Pond Piece. *Oxs* —9B **58**
Pond Pl. *Asht* —4L **79**
Pond Rd. *Egh* —7E **20**
Pond Rd. *Head* —5F **168**
Pond Rd. *Wok* —7K **73**
Pondside Clo. *Hayes* —2E **8**
Ponds La. *Shere* —2N **135**
Ponds, The. *Wey* —3F **56**
Pondtail Clo. *Fleet* —5D **88**
Pondtail Clo. *H'ham* —2K **197**
Pondtail Copse. *H'ham* —2K **197**
Pondtail Gdns. *Fleet* —5D **88**
Pondtail Rd. *Fleet* —5D **88**
Pondtail Rd. *H'ham* —3J **197**
Pond View Clo. *Fleet* —3C **88**
Pond Way. *E Grin* —9D **166**
Pond Way. *Tedd* —7J **25**
Pond Wood Rd. *Craw* —1E **182**
Ponside Clo. *Hayes* —2E **8**
Ponsonby Rd. *SW15* —1G **26**
Pony Chase. *Cobh* —9N **57**
Pook Hill. *C'fold* —5B **172**
Pool Clo. *W Mol* —4N **39**
Poole Ct. *Houn* —5M **9**
Poole Ct. Rd. *Houn* —5M **9**
Pool End Clo. *Shep* —4B **38**
Poole Rd. *Eps* —3C **60**
Poole Rd. *Wok* —5A **74**
Pooles Cotts. *Rich* —3K **25**
Pooles La. *SW10* —3N **13**
Pooley Av. *Egh* —6D **20**
Pooley Grn. Clo. *Egh* —6E **20**
Pooley Grn. Rd. *Egh* —6D **20**
Poolmans Rd. *Wind* —6A **4**
Pool Rd. *Alder* —5A **110**
Pool Rd. *W Mol* —4N **39**
Pootings Rd. *Crock H* —4M **127**
Pope Clo. *SW19* —7B **28**
Pope Clo. *Felt* —2G **22**
Popes Av. *Twic* —3E **24**
Popes Clo. *Coln* —3D **6**
Popes Ct. *Twic* —3E **24**
Popes Gro. *Croy* —9J **47**
Popes Gro. *Twic* —3F **24**
Popes La. *Oxt* —3A **126**
Popes Mead. *Hasl* —1G **189**
Popeswood Rd. *Binf* —8J **15**
Popham Clo. *Brack* —4D **32**
Popham Clo. *Felt* —4N **23**
Popham Gdns. *Rich* —6N **11**
*Popinjays Row. Cheam —2J **61***
(off Netley Clo.)
Poplar Av. *Lea* —9H **79**
Poplar Av. *Mitc* —9D **28**
Poplar Av. *W'sham* —1L **51**
Poplar Clo. *Coln* —4G **7**
Poplar Clo. *Craw* —9A **162**
Poplar Clo. *F'boro* —9H **69**
Poplar Clo. *Myt* —2E **90**
Poplar Cotts. *Guild* —9H **93**
Poplar Ct. *SW19* —6M **27**
Poplar Cres. *Eps* —3B **60**
Poplar Dri. *Bans* —1J **81**
Poplar Farm Clo. *Eps* —3B **60**
Poplar Gdns. *N Mald* —1C **42**
Poplar Gro. *N Mald* —1C **42**
Poplar Gro. *Wok* —6A **74**
Poplar Ho. *Langl* —1B **6**
Poplar Rd. *SW19* —1M **43**
Poplar Rd. *Ashf* —6D **22**
Poplar Rd. *Lea* —9H **79**
Poplar Rd. *Shalf* —1A **134**
Poplar Rd. *Sutt* —7L **43**
Poplar Rd. S. *SW19* —2M **43**
Poplars, The. *Asc* —4L **33**
Poplars, The. *H'ham* —5L **197**
*Poplar Vs. Frim G —8D **70***
(off Beech Rd.)
Poplar Wlk. *Cat* —1B **104**
Poplar Wlk. *Croy* —7N **45**
Poplar Wlk. *Farnh* —5J **109**
Poplar Way. *Felt* —4H **23**
Poppy Clo. *Wall* —7E **44**
Poppyhills Rd. *Camb* —7D **50**
Poppy La. *Croy* —6F **46**
Poppy Pl. *Wokgm* —2A **30**
Porchester. *Asc* —3L **33**
Porchester Rd. *King T* —1A **42**
Porchfield Clo. *Sutt* —6N **61**
Porridge Pot All. *Guild* —5N **113**
Portal Clo. *SE27* —4L **29**
Portesbery Hill Dri. *Camb* —9C **50**
Portesbery Rd. *Camb* —9B **50**
Portia Gro. *Warf* —9C **16**
Portinscale Rd. *SW15* —8K **13**
Portland Av. *N Mald* —6E **42**
*Portland Bus. Cen. Dat —4L **5***
(off Manor Ho. La.)
Portland Cres. *Felt* —5E **22**
Portland Dri. *C Crook* —9A **88**
Portland Dri. *Red* —7H **103**
Portland Ho. *Mers* —7G **103**
*Portland Pl. SE25 —3D **46***
(off Portland Rd.)
Portland Pl. *Eps* —8D **60**
Portland Rd. *SE25* —3D **46**
Portland Rd. *Ashf* —4N **21**
Portland Rd. *Dork* —4G **119**
Portland Rd. *E Grin* —1A **186**
Portland Rd. *King T* —2L **41**
Portland Rd. *Mitc* —1C **44**
Portland Ter. *Rich* —7K **11**
Portley La. *Cat* —8B **84**
Portley Wood Rd. *Whyt* —7C **84**
Portman Av. *SW14* —6C **12**
Portman Clo. *Brack* —9M **15**
Portman Rd. *King T* —1M **41**
Portmore Pk. Rd. *Wey* —1A **56**
Portmore Quays. *Wey* —1A **56**
Portmore Way. *Wey* —9B **38**
Portnall Dri. *Vir W* —5H **35**
Portnall Rise. *Vir W* —4J **35**
Portnall Rd. *Vir W* —4J **35**
Portnalls Clo. *Coul* —3F **82**
Portnalls Rise. *Coul* —3G **82**
Portnalls Rd. *Coul* —5F **82**
Portsmouth Av. *Th Dit* —6G **40**
Portsmouth Rd. *SW15* —1G **27**
Portsmouth Rd. *Cobh & Esh* —4C **76**
Portsmouth Rd. *Esh* —3A **58**
Portsmouth Rd. *Frim & Camb* —5B **70**
Portsmouth Rd. *G'ming* —1E **152**
Portsmouth Rd. *Guild* —7M **113**
Portsmouth Rd. *Hind* —9M **169**
Portsmouth Rd. *King T* —3K **41**
Portsmouth Rd. *Rip* —3H **95**
Portsmouth Rd. *Th Dit & Surb* —8E **40**
Portsmouth Rd. *Thur & Milf* —9G **150**
Portswood Pl. *SW15* —9E **12**
Portugal Gdns. *Twic* —3C **24**
Portugal Rd. *Wok* —3B **74**
Port Way. *Bisl* —3D **72**
Portway. *Eps* —5F **60**
Portway Cres. *Eps* —5F **60**
Postford Farm Cotts. *Alb* —1J **135**

250 A-Z Surrey

Postford Mill Cotts.—Queen's Promenade

Postford Mill Cotts. Chil —7H 115
Post Horn Clo. F Row —8K 187
Post Horn La. F Row —8J 187
Post Ho. La. Bookh —3A 98
Post La. Twic —2D 24
Postmill Clo. Croy —9F 46
Post Office All. Hamp —1B 40
Post Office Row. Oxt —9G 107
Potley Hill Rd. Yat —9E 48
Potter Clo. Mitc —1F 44
Potteries La. Myt —2D 90
Potteries, The. F'boro —8J 69
Potterne Clo. SW19 —1J 27
Potters Clo. Croy —7H 47
Potters Clo. Milf —9C 132
Potters Cres. Ash —1F 110
Potter's Croft. H'ham —6L 197
Pottersfield. Craw —2B 182
Potters Ga. Farnh —1F 128
Potters Gro. N Mald —3B 42
Potter's Hill Hamb —5F 152
Potters Ind. Pk. C Crook —8D 88
Potter's La. SW16 —7H 29
Potters La. Send —1D 94
Potters Rd. SW6 —5N 13
Potters Way. Reig —7A 122
Pottery Ct. Wrec —5E 128
Pottery La. Wrec —5E 128
Pottery Rd. Bren —2L 11
Poulcott. Wray —9A 6
Poulett Gdns. Twic —2G 24
Poulters Wood. Kes —2F 66
Poulton Av. Sutt —9B 44
Pound Clo. G'ming —7H 133
Pound Clo. Head —4E 168
Pound Clo. Loxw —3H 193
Pound Clo. Surb —7J 41
Pound Ct. Asht —5M 79
Pound Ct. Wood S —2E 112
Pound Cres. Fet —8D 78
Pound Farm La. Ash —2H 111
Pound Field. Guild —2N 113
Poundfield Ct. Wok —8E 74
Poundfield Gdns. Wok —7E 74 (in two parts)
Poundfield La. Plais —4D 192
Poundfield Rd. Wok —7E 74
Pound Hill. Wood S —2E 112
Pound Hill Pde. Craw —2G 183
Pound Hill Pl. Craw —3G 183
Pound La. Eps —8B 60
Pound La. G'ming —7H 133
Pound La. Hurst —4A 14
Pound La. W'sham —3N 51
Pound La. Wood S —2E 112
Pound Pl. Shalf —9B 114
Pound Pl. Clo. Shalf —9B 114
Pound Rd. Alder —3A 110
Pound Rd. Bans —4M 81
Pound Rd. Cher —6K 37
Pound St. Cars —2D 62
Povey Cross Rd. Horl —1B 162
Powderham Ct. Knap —5G 72
Powder Mill La. Twic —2N 23
Powell Clo. Chess —3K 59
Powell Clo. Guild —5J 113
Powell Clo. Horl —7C 142
Powell Clo. Wall —4J 63
Powells Clo. Dork —8J 119
Powell's Wlk. W4 —2D 12
Power Rd. W4 —1N 11
Powers Ct. Twic —1K 25
Pownall Gdns. Houn —7B 10
Pownall Rd. Houn —7B 10
Poyle Clo. Coln —5G 6
Poyle Gdns. Brack —9B 16
Poyle Ho. Guild —2F 114 (off Merrow St.)
Poyle Ind. Est. Coln —6H 7
Poyle Rd. Coln —6G 6
Poyle Rd. Guild —5A 114
Poyle Rd. Tong —5D 110
Poyle Technical Cen. Coln —5G 7
Poyle Ter. Guild —5N 113
Poyle Trad. Est. Coln —6G 7
Poynders Ct. SW4 —1G 29
Poynders Gdns. SW4 —1G 29
Poynders Rd. SW4 —1G 29
Poynes Rd. Horl —6C 142
Poynings Rd. If'd —4J 181
Prae, The. Wok —5H 75
Prairie Clo. Add —9K 37
Prairie Rd. Add —9K 37
Pratts La. W On T —1L 57
Pratts Pas. King T —1L 41
Prebend Gdns. W6 & W4 —1E 12
Prebend Mans. W4 —1E 12 (off Chiswick High Rd.)
Precincts, The. Mord —5M 43
Precinct, The. Cranl —6N 155
Precinct, The. Egh —6C 20
Precinct, The. W Mol —2B 40
Premier Pde. Horl —8E 142 (off High St. Horley,)
Premier Pl. SW15 —7K 13
Prentice Clo. F'boro —6N 69
Prentice Ct. SW19 —6L 27
Prentis Rd. SW16 —5H 29
Presburg Rd. N Mald —4D 42
Presbury Ct. St J —5K 73
Prescott. Brack —6L 31
Prescott Clo. SW16 —8J 29
Prescott Rd. Coln —5G 6
Presentation M. SW2 —2K 29
Preshaw Cres. Mitc —2C 44
Prestbury Cres. Bans —3D 82
Preston Clo. Twic —4E 24
Preston Ct. W on T —7K 39
Preston Dri. Eps —3D 60
Preston Gro. Asht —4J 79
Preston La. Tad —8G 81
Preston Pl. Rich —8L 11
Preston Rd. SE19 —7M 29
Preston Rd. SW20 —8E 26
Preston Rd. Shep —4B 38
Prestwick Clo. If'd —4J 181
Prestwick Clo. S'hall —1M 9
Prestwick La. G'wood & C'fold —7L 171
Prestwood Clo. Craw —9N 161
Prestwood Gdns. Croy —6N 45
Prestwood La. If'd —9H 161
Prestwood La. Rusp & Craw —9F 160
Pretoria Rd. SW16 —7F 28
Pretoria Rd. Cher —7H 37
Pretty La. Coul —8F 82
Prey Heath Clo. Wok —2M 93
Prey Heath Rd. Wok —2L 93
Price Clo. SW17 —4D 28
Price Rd. Croy —2M 63
Prices La. Reig —6M 121
Price Way. Hamp —7M 23
Priddy's Yd. Croy —8N 45
Prides Crossing. Asc —8L 17
Pridham Rd. T Hth —3A 46
Priest Av. Wokgm —3E 30
Priestcroft Clo. Craw —3M 181
Priest Hill. Egh & Old Win —4M 19
Priest Hill. Oxt —7D 106
Priest La. W End —9N 51
Priestley Gdns. Wok —7C 74
Priestley Rd. Mitc —1E 44
Priestley Rd. Sur R —4G 112
Priestley Way. Craw —7E 162
Priest's Bri. SW14 & SW15 —6D 12
Priestwood Av. Brack —9L 15
Priestwood Ct. Rd. Brack —9M 15
Priestwood Sq. Brack —9M 15
Priestwood Ter. Brack —9M 15
Primrose Av. Horl —1F 162
Primrose Clo. Craw —6N 181
Primrose Clo. Mitc —6F 44
Primrose Copse. H'ham —1L 197
Primrose Ct. SW12 —1H 29
Primrose Ct. Ash —2E 110
Primrose Dri. Bisl —2D 72
Primrose Gdns. F'boro —2K 89
Primrose La. Croy —7F 46
Primrose La. F Row —8J 187
Primrose Ridge. G'ming —9E 132
Primrose Rd. W On T —2K 57
Primrose Wlk. Brack —4A 32
Primrose Wlk. Eps —4E 60
Primrose Wlk. Fleet —3A 88
Primrose Wlk. Yat —9A 48
Primrose Way. Brmly —6N 133
Primrose Way. Sand —6G 49
Primula Rd. Bord —6A 168
Prince Albert Dri. Asc —3H 33
Prince Albert Sq. Red —8E 122
Prince Albert's Wlk. Wind —4K 5
Prince Andrew Way. Asc —1H 33
Prince Charles Cres. F'boro —6N 69
Prince Charles Way. Wall —9F 44
Prince Consort Cotts. Wind —5G 4
Prince Consort Dri. Asc —3H 33
Prince Consort's Dri. Wind —9C 4
Prince Dri. Sand —6F 48
Prince George's Av. SW20 —1H 43
Prince Georges Rd. SW19 —9B 28
Prince of Wales Ct. Alder —2L 109 (off Queen Elizabeth Dri.)
Prince of Wales Rd. Out —2L 143
Prince of Wales Rd. Sutt —8B 44
Prince of Wales Ter. W4 —1D 12
Prince of Wales Wlk. Camb —9A 50
Prince Regent Rd. Houn —6C 10
Prince Rd. SE25 —4B 46
Prince's Av. Alder —8N 89
Princes Av. Cars —4D 62
Prince's Av. G'ming —4F 132
Princes Av. S Croy —2E 84
Princes Av. Surb —7N 41
Princes Clo. Eton W —1C 4
Princes Clo. S Croy —2E 84
Prince's Clo. Tedd —5D 24
Prince's Dri. Oxs —8E 58
Princes Mead Shop. Cen. F'boro —1N 89
Princes Rd. SW14 —6C 12
Prince's Rd. SW19 —7M 27
Princes Rd. Ashf —6A 22
Princes Rd. Egh —7B 20
Princes Rd. Felt —3G 22
Princes Rd. Kew —4M 11
Princes Rd. King T —8N 25
Prince's Rd. Red —5D 122
Princes Rd. Rich —8M 11
Prince's Rd. Tedd —5D 24
Princes Rd. Wey —2C 56
Princess Anne Rd. Rud —1E 194
Princess Av. Wind —6E 4
Princess Gdns. Wok —3D 74
Princess Ho. Red —2E 122
Princess Margaret Rd. Rud —1E 194
Princess Marys Rd. Add —1L 55
Princess Pde. Orp —1J 67
Princess Rd. Craw —3A 182
Princess Rd. Croy —5N 45
Princess Rd. Wok —3D 74
Princess Sq. Brack —1N 31
Princes St. Rich —7L 11
Princes St. Sutt —1B 62
Princess Way. Camb —9A 50
Princess Way. Red —2E 122
Princes Way. SW19 —1J 27
Princes Way. Alder —2M 109
Princes Way. Bag —6J 51
Princes Way. Croy —2K 63
Princes Way. W Wick —1B 66
Princeton Ct. SW15 —6J 13
Princeton M. King T —9N 25
Pringle Gdns. SW16 —5G 28
Pringle Gdns. Purl —6K 63
Prior Av. Sutt —4C 62
Prior Croft Clo. Camb —2E 70
Prior End. Camb —1E 70
Prioress Rd. SE27 —4M 29
Prior Rd. Camb —1E 70
Priors Clo. F'boro —6M 69
Priors Ct. Ash —3C 110
Priors Ct. St J —5K 73
Prior's Croft. Wok —7C 74
Priorsfield Rd. Comp & Hurt —9C 112
Priors Hatch La. Hurt —2C 132
Priors Keep. Fleet —5C 88
Prior's La. B'water —1F 68
Priors Mead. Bookh —3C 98
Priors Rd. Wind —6A 4
Priors, The. Asht —6K 79
Priors Wlk. Craw —3D 182
Priorswood. Comp —1C 132
Priors Wood. Crowt —3C 48
Priorswood. Hasl —2D 188
Priory Av. Sutt —1J 61
Priory Clo. SW19 —9N 27
Priory Clo. Asc —6D 34
Priory Clo. Beck —2H 47
Priory Clo. Dork —7G 119
Priory Clo. Hamp —9N 23
Priory Clo. Horl —7D 142
Priory Clo. Sun —8H 23
Priory Clo. W On T —9H 39
Priory Clo. Wok —9F 54
Priory Ct. Camb —1L 69
Priory Ct. Eps —5E 60
Priory Ct. Guild —7M 113
Priory Ct. Houn —6B 10
Priory Ct. Sutt —1K 61
Priory Cres. SE19 —8N 29
Priory Cres. Sutt —1J 61
Priory Dri. Reig —5M 121
Priory Gdns. SE25 —3C 46
Priory Gdns. SW13 —6E 12
Priory Gdns. Ashf —6E 22
Priory Gdns. Hamp —8N 23
Priory Grn. Stai —6K 21
Priory La. SW15 —9D 12
Priory La. Brack —8A 16
Priory La. Fren —2K 149
Priory La. Rich —3N 11
Priory La. W Mol —3B 40
Priory M. Stai —6K 21
Priory Pk. Fleet —4A 88
Priory Pl. W On T —9H 39
Priory Rd. SW19 —8B 28
Priory Rd. Chav D —9F 16
Priory Rd. Chess —9L 41
Priory Rd. Croy —6L 45
Priory Rd. F Row —9D 186
Priory Rd. Hamp —8N 23
Priory Rd. Houn —8C 10
Priory Rd. Reig —5M 121
Priory Rd. Rich —2N 11
Priory Rd. S'dale —6D 34
Priory Rd. Sutt —1J 61
Priory St. F'boro —1B 90
Priory Ter. Sun —8H 23
Priory, The. Croy —1L 63
Priory, The. God —1E 124
Priory, The. Lea —9H 79
Priory Wlk. Brack —3D 32
Priory Way. Dat —3L 5
Priory Way. W Dray —2N 7
Privet Rd. Lind —4B 168
Probyn Rd. SW2 —3M 29
Proctor Clo. M'bowr —5G 183
Proctor Clo. Mitc —9E 28
Proctor Gdns. Bookh —3B 98
Proctors Clo. Felt —2H 23
Proctors Rd. Wokgm —2E 30
Proffits Cotts. Tad —9J 81
Profumo Rd. W On T —2L 57
Progress Bus. Pk., The. Croy —8K 45
Progress Way. Croy —8K 45
Promenade App. Rd. W4 —3D 12
Promenade de Verdun. Purl —7H 63
Promenade, The. W4 —4D 12
Prospect Av. F'boro —8N 69
Prospect Clo. Houn —5N 9
Prospect Cotts. SW18 —7M 13
Prospect Cres. Twic —9C 10
Prospect Hill. Head —2D 168
Prospect La. Egh —6K 19
Prospect Pl. W4 —1C 12
Prospect Pl. Craw —3A 182
Prospect Pl. Egh —6A 20
Prospect Pl. Eps —8D 60
Prospect Pl. Stai —6H 21
Prospect Quay. SW18 —7M 13 (off Point Pleasant)
Prospect Rd. Ash V —8E 90
Prospect Rd. F'boro —1M 89
Prospect Rd. Rowl —8D 128
Prospect Rd. Surb —5J 41
Prossers. Tad —8J 81
Prothero Rd. SW6 —3K 13
Providence La. Hayes —3E 8
Providence Pl. Eps —8D 60
Providence Pl. W Byf —1J 75
Prune Hill. Egh —8N 19
Prunus Clo. W End —9B 52
Puckshill. Knap —4G 73
Puckshott Way. Hasl —9H 171
Puddenhole Cotts. Bet —2N 119
Pudding La. Horl —3K 161
Puddledock La. Eden —2N 127
Puffin Clo. Beck —4G 46
Puffin Rd. If'd —4J 181
Pulborough Rd. SW18 —1L 27
Pulborough Way. Houn —7K 9
Pullman Gdns. SW15 —9H 13
Pullman La. G'ming —9F 132
Pulton Pl. SW6 —3M 13
Pump All. Bren —3K 11
Pumping Sta. Rd. W4 —3D 12
Pump La. Asc —9B 18
Pump Pail N. Croy —9N 45
Pump Pail S. Croy —9N 45
Punchbowl La. Dork —4K 119
Punch Copse Rd. Craw —2D 182
Punnetts Ct. Craw —7L 181
Purbeck Av. N Mald —5E 42
Purbeck Clo. Red —6H 103
Purbeck Ct. Guild —3H 113
Purbeck Dri. Wok —1B 74
Purberry Gro. Eps —6E 60
Purbrook Ct. Brack —5C 32
Purcell Clo. Kenl —1N 83
Purcell Cres. SW6 —3K 13
Purcell Rd. Craw —6L 181
Purcell Rd. Crowt —9G 30
Purcell's Clo. Asht —5M 79
Purdey Ct. Wor Pk —7F 42
Purley Bury Av. Purl —7N 63
Purley Bury Clo. Purl —7N 63
Purley Clo. M'bowr —6H 183
Purley Cross. (Junct.) —7L 63
Purley Downs Rd. Purl & S Croy —6N 63
Purley Hill. Purl —8M 63
Purley Knoll. Purl —7K 63
Purley Oaks Rd. S Croy —5A 64
Purley Pde. Purl —7L 63
Purley Pk. Rd. Purl —6M 63
Purley Rise. Purl —8K 63
Purley Rd. Purl —7L 63
Purley Rd. S Croy —4A 64
Purley Vale. Purl —9M 63
Purley View Ter. S Croy —5A 64 (off Sanderstead Rd.)
Purley Way. Croy & Purl —6K 45
Purley Way. Frim —6C 70
Purley Way Cen., The. Croy —8L 45
Purley Way Corner. Croy —6K 45
Purley Way Cres. Croy —6K 45
Purmerend Clo. F'boro —9H 69
Purser Ho. SW2 —1L 29 (off Tulse Hill)
Pursers Cross Rd. SW6 —4L 13
Pursers La. Peasl —2E 136
Purslane. Wokgm —3C 30
Purton Rd. H'ham —4H 197
Putney Bri. SW15 & SW6 —6K 13
Putney Bri. App. SW6 —6K 13
Putney Bri. Rd. SW15 & SW18 —7K 13
Putney Comn. SW15 —6H 13
Putney Exchange Shop. Cen. SW15 —7J 13
Putney Heath. SW15 —1G 26
Putney Heath La. SW15 —9J 13
Putney High St. SW15 —7J 13
Putney Hill. SW15 —1J 27 (in two parts)
Putney Pk. Av. SW15 —7F 12
Putney Pk. La. SW15 —7G 12
Puttenham Heath Rd. Guild —8A 112
Puttenham Hill. P'ham —7N 111
Puttenham La. Shack —2N 131
Puttenham Rd. Seale —8F 110
Puttock Clo. Hasl —3B 188
Pyecombe Ct. Craw —6L 181
Pyegrove Chase. Brack —6C 32
Pye Rd. Cat —1A 104
Pyestock Cres. F'boro —1H 89
Pylbrook Rd. Sutt —9M 43
Pyle Hill. Wok —2N 93
Pylon Way. Croy —7J 45
Pymers Mead. SE21 —2N 29
Pyne Rd. Surb —7N 41
Pyramid Ho. Houn —6M 9
Pyrcroft La. Wey —2C 56
Pyrcroft Rd. Cher —6G 37
Pyrford Comn. Rd. Wok —3F 74
Pyrford Ct. Wok —4H 75
Pyrford Heath. Wok —3H 75
Pyrford Rd. W Byf & Wok —9J 55
Pyrford Wood Est. Wok —3E 74
Pyrford Woods Clo. Wok —2H 75
Pyrford Woods Rd. Wok —2G 75
Pyrland Rd. Rich —9M 11
Pyrmont Gro. SE27 —4M 29
Pyrmont Rd. W4 —2N 11
Pytchley Cres. SE19 —7N 29

Quadrangle, The. Guild —4K 113
Quadrant Ct. Brack —2C 32
Quadrant Rd. Rich —7K 11
Quadrant Rd. T Hth —3M 45
Quadrant, The. SW20 —9K 27
Quadrant, The. Ash V —9E 90
Quadrant, The. Rich —7L 11
Quadrant, The. Sutt —3A 62
Quadrant, The. Wey —1B 56
Quadrant Way. Wey —1B 56
Quail Clo. H'ham —1K 197
Quail Gdns. S Croy —6H 65
Quakers La. Iswth —3F 10
Quakers Way. Guild —8F 92
Qualitas. Brack —7L 31
Quality St. Red —6F 102
Quantock Clo. Craw —3N 181
Quantock Clo. Hayes —3E 8
Quantock Clo. Slou —1C 8
Quantock Dri. Wor Pk —8H 43
Quarrendon St. SW6 —5M 13
Quarries, The. Man H —9C 198
Quarr Rd. Cars —5C 44
Quarry Bank. Light —7L 51
Quarry Clo. H'ham —2M 197
Quarry Clo. Oxt —8A 106
Quarry Cotts. Reig —9N 101
Quarry Hill. G'ming —8E 132
Quarry Hill Pk. Reig —9A 102
Quarry La. Yat —1D 68
Quarry Pk. Rd. Sutt —3L 61
Quarry Path. Oxt —9A 106
Quarry Rise. E Grin —7C 166
Quarry Rise. Sutt —3L 61
Quarry Rd. God —6F 104
Quarry Rd. Hurt —4D 132
Quarry Rd. Oxt —8A 106
Quarry St. Guild —5N 113
Quarry, The. Bet —1C 120
Quarterbrass Farm Rd. H'ham —1K 197
Quartermaine Av. Wok —9B 74
Quarter Mile Rd. G'ming —9H 133
Quarters Rd. F'boro —3N 89
Quebec Av. W'ham —4M 107
Quebec Clo. Small —8L 143
Quebec Cotts. W'ham —5M 107
Quebec Gdns. B'water —2J 69
Quebec Sq. W'ham —4M 107
Queen Adelaide's Ride. Wind —9A 4
Queen Alexandra's Ct. SW19 —6L 27
Queen Anne Dri. Clay —4E 58
Queen Anne's Clo. Twic —4D 24
Queen Anne's Gdns. Lea —8H 79
Queen Anne's Gdns. Mitc —2D 44
Queen Anne's Ride. Asc & Wind —7D 18
Queen Anne's Rd. Wind —7F 4
Queen Anne's Ter. Lea —8H 79
Queen Ann's Ct. Wind —4F 4
Queen Caroline St. W6 —1H 13
Queen Charlotte St. Wind —4G 5
Queendale Ct. Wok —3J 73
Queen Eleanor's Rd. Guild —4J 113
Queen Elizabeth Barracks. C Crook —9B 88
Queen Elizabeth Dri. Alder —2L 109
Queen Elizabeth Gdns. Mord —3M 43
Queen Elizabeth Ho. SW12 —1E 28
Queen Elizabeth Rd. Camb —6B 50
Queen Elizabeth Rd. King T —1M 41
Queen Elizabeth Rd. Rud —1E 194
Queen Elizabeth's Dri. New Ad —5N 65
Queen Elizabeth's Gdns. New Ad —6N 65
Queen Elizabeth's Wlk. Wall —1H 63
Queen Elizabeth's Wlk. Wind —5H 5
Queen Elizabeth Wlk. SW13 —4F 12
Queen Elizabeth Way. Wok —6B 74
Queenhill Rd. S Croy —6E 64
Queenhythe Rd. Guild —6N 93
Queen Mary Av. Camb —1M 69
Queen Mary Av. Mord —4J 43
Queen Mary Clo. Fleet —2A 88
Queen Mary Clo. Surb —9A 42
Queen Mary Clo. Wok —3E 74
Queen Mary Rd. SE19 —7M 29
Queen Mary Rd. Shep —1D 38
Queen Mary's Av. Cars —4D 62
Queen Mary's Dri. New H —6H 55
Queens Acre. Sutt —4K 61
Queens Acre. Wind —7G 4
Queen's Av. Alder —1M 109
Queen's Av. Byfl —8M 55
Queens Av. Felt —5J 23
Queensbridge Pk. Iswth —8E 10
Queensbury Ho. Rich —8K 11
Queensbury Pl. B'water —3H 69
Queen's Clo. Asc —8J 17
Queens Clo. Bisl —3D 72
Queen's Clo. Esh —1B 58
Queens Clo. F'boro —5N 89
Queen's Clo. Old Win —8K 5
Queens Clo. Tad —2F 100
Queens Clo. Wall —2F 62
Queen's Club Gdns. W14 —2K 13
Queen's Ct. Eden —2M 147
Queen's Ct. F'boro —5A 90
Queen's Ct. Horl —8E 142
Queens Ct. Red —2E 122 (off St Anne's Way)
Queens Ct. Rich —9M 11
Queens Ct. Wey —3F 56
Queens Ct. Wok —5B 74
Queens Ct. Ride. Cobh —9H 57
Queen's Cres. Dork —6G 119
Queen's Cres. Rich —8M 11
Queen's Dri. G'ming —4E 132
Queens Dri. Guild —9K 93
Queen's Dri. Oxs —7C 58
Queen's Dri. Surb —6N 41
Queen's Dri. Th Dit —5G 41
Queensfield Ct. Sutt —1H 61
Queens Gdns. Houn —4M 9
Queensgate. Cobh —8L 57
Queen's Ga. Horl —3E 162
Queens Ga. Gdns. SW15 —7G 13
Queens Hill Rise. Asc —2N 33
Queens Ho. Tedd —7F 24
Queens Keep. Twic —9J 11
Queensland Av. SW19 —9N 27
Queens La. Ashf —5A 22
Queens La. Farnh —5H 109
Queen's Mead. C'fold —5E 172
Queensmead. Dat —4L 5
Queensmead. F'boro —1N 89
Queensmead. Oxs —7C 58
Queensmead Av. Eps —6G 61
Queensmere Clo. SW19 —3J 27
Queensmere Ct. SW13 —2E 12
Queensmere Rd. SW19 —3J 27
Queensmill Rd. SW6 —3J 13
Queen's Pde. Path. Alder —7N 89
Queen's Pk. Gdns. Felt —4G 23
Queen's Pk. Rd. Cat —1B 104
Queens Pine. Brack —5C 32
Queens Pl. Asc —2L 33
Queens Pl. Mord —3M 43
Queen's Promenade. King T —3K 41

Queens Reach. E Mol —3E **40**
Queens Reach. King T —1K **41**
Queens Ride. SW13 & SW15
—6F **12**
Queens Rise. Rich —9M **11**
Queen's Rd. SW14 —6C **12**
Queen's Rd. SW19 —7L **27**
Queen's Rd. Alder —3L **109**
Queens Rd. Asc —4A **34**
Queens Rd. Beck —1H **47**
Queens Rd. Bisl —7B **72**
Queens Rd. Camb —2N **69**
Queen's Rd. Croy —5M **45**
Queens Rd. Dat —3L **5**
Queen's Rd. E Grin —1A **186**
Queen's Rd. Egh —6B **20**
Queen's Rd. Eton W —1C **4**
Queen's Rd. F'boro —2B **90**
Queen's Rd. Farnh —6H **109**
Queen's Rd. Felt —2J **23**
Queen's Rd. Fleet —6B **88**
Queen's Rd. Guild —3N **113**
Queen's Rd. Hamp —6B **24**
Queen's Rd. Horl —8E **142**
Queen's Rd. Houn —6B **10**
Queen's Rd. King T —8N **25**
Queen's Rd. Knap —5F **72**
Queens Rd. Mitc —3J **45**
Queens Rd. Mord —3M **43**
Queens Rd. N Mald —3E **42**
Queen's Rd. Rich —1M **25**
Queen's Rd. Sutt —6N **61**
Queen's Rd. Tedd —7F **24**
Queens Rd. Th Dit —4F **40**
Queens Rd. Twic —2G **24**
Queen's Rd. Wall —2F **62**
Queen's Rd. Wey & W on T
—2D **56**
Queen's Rd. Wind —5F **4**
~~Queen's Sq. Craw —3C 100~~
Queens Ter. Iswth —1G **11**
Queen St. Alder —2B **110**
Queen St. Cher —7J **37**
Queen St. Croy —1N **63**
Queen St. G'ming —7H **133**
Queen St. Gom —8D **116**
Queen St. H'ham —7K **197**
Queensville Rd. SW12 —1H **29**
Queen's Wlk. Ashf —5M **21**
Queens Wlk. E Grin —9A **166**
Queensway. Brack —9K **15**
Queensway. Cranl —8A **156**
Queensway. Craw —3C **182**
Queensway. Croy —2K **63**
Queensway. E Grin —1A **186**
Queens Way. Felt —5K **23**
Queensway. Frim G —7E **70**
Queensway. H'ham —7J **197**
Queen's Way. Pirb —6A **72**
Queensway. Red —2D **122**
Queensway. Sun —1J **39**
Queensway. W On T —1K **57**
Queensway S. W On T —2K **57**
Queens Wharf. W6 —1H **13**
Queenswood Av. Hamp —7B **24**
Queenswood Av. Houn —5N **9**
Queenswood Av. T Hth —4L **45**
Queenswood Av. Wall —1H **63**
Queenswood Rd. Wok —6G **73**
Queen Victoria. (Junct.) —9H **43**
Queen Victoria St. F'boro
—9N **69**
Queen Victoria Rd. Pirb —6A **72**
Queen Victoria's Wlk. Col T
—9L **49**
Queen Victoria Wlk. Wind —4H **5**
Quell La. Hasl —9L **189**
Quelmans Head Ride. Wind
—3A **18**
Quelm La. Brack —7N **15**
Quennell Clo. Asht —6M **79**
Quennells Hill. Wrec —5D **128**
Quentins Dri. Berr G —3K **87**
Quentin Way. Vir W —3L **35**
Querrin St. SW6 —5N **13**
Questen M. Craw —1H **183**
Quetta Pk. C Crook —2C **108**
Quick Rd. W4 —1D **12**
Quicks Rd. SW19 —8N **27**
Quiet Clo. Add —1J **55**
Quiet Nook. Brom —1F **66**
Quill La. SW15 —7J **13**
Quillot, The. W On T —2G **56**
Quince Clo. Asc —3N **33**
Quince Dri. Bisl —2E **72**
Quincy Rd. Egh —6C **20**
Quinney's. F'boro —4A **90**
Quintilis. Brack —7L **31**
(in two parts)
Quinton Av. SW20 —9L **27**
Quinton Clo. Beck —2M **47**
Quinton Clo. Houn —3J **9**
Quinton Clo. Wall —1F **62**
Quinton Rd. Th Dit —7G **41**
Quinton St. SW18 —3A **28**
Quintrell Clo. Wok —4L **73**

Rabbit La. W On T —4H **57**
Rabies Heath Rd. Blet —2B **124**

Raby Rd. N Mald —3C **42**
Raccoon Way. Houn —5K **9**
Racecourse Rd. Ling —8A **146**
Rachael's Lake View. Warf
—8D **16**
Rackfield. Hasl —1B **188**
Rackham Clo. Craw —5B **182**
Rackham M. SW16 —7G **29**
Rack's Ct. Guild —5N **113**
Rackstraw Rd. Sand —6H **49**
Racquets Ct. Hill. G'ming
—5F **132**
Racton Rd. SW6 —2M **13**
Radbourne Rd. SW12 —1G **29**
Radbroke. Lea —9J **79**
Radcliffe Clo. Frim —7D **70**
Radcliffe Gdns. Cars —4C **62**
Radcliffe M. Hamp —6C **24**
Radcliffe Rd. Croy —8C **46**
Radcliffe Sq. SW15 —9J **13**
Radcliffe Way. Brack —9K **15**
Radford Clo. Farnh —7K **109**
Radford Rd. Tin G —6F **162**
Radipole Rd. SW6 —4L **13**
Radius Pk. Felt —7G **9**
Rad La. Peasl —2E **136**
Radley Clo. Felt —2G **23**
Radnor Clo. Mitc —3J **45**
Radnor Ct. Red —3C **122**
Radnor Gdns. Twic —3F **24**
Radnor La. Holm M —4H **137**
(Horsham Rd.)
Radnor La. Holm M —9H **137**
(Three Mile Rd.)
Radnor Rd. Brack —2D **32**
Radnor Rd. Peasl —5E **136**
Radnor Rd. Twic —2F **24**
Radnor Rd. Wey —9B **38**
~~Radnor Ter. Wey —9B 38~~
~~Radnor Wlk. Croy —3H 47~~
Radnor Way. Slou —1A **6**
Radolphs. Tad —9J **81**
Radstock Way. Red —6H **103**
Radstone Ct. Wok —5B **74**
Raeburn Clo. King T —8K **25**
Raeburn Ct. Wok —6K **73**
Raeburn Gro. St J —6K **73**
Raeburn Rd. Wok —6K **73**
Raeburn Way. Col T —9J **49**
Rafborough Footpath. F'boro
—2M **89**
Rag Hill Clo. Tats —8G **86**
Rag Hill Rd. Tats —8F **86**
Raglan Clo. Alder —3A **110**
Raglan Clo. Frim —6E **70**
Raglan Clo. Houn —8N **9**
Raglan Clo. Reig —1B **122**
Raglan Ct. S Croy —2M **63**
Raglan Precinct. Cat —9B **84**
Raglan Rd. Knap —5H **73**
Raglan Rd. Reig —9N **101**
Raikes Hollow. Ab H —2J **137**
Raikes La. Ab H —2J **137**
Railey Rd. Craw —2C **182**
Railpit La. Warl —2A **86**
Railshead Rd. Iswth —7H **11**
Rails La. Pirb —3N **91**
Railton Rd. Guild —8L **93**
Railway App. Cher —6H **37**
Railway App. E Grin —9A **166**
Railway App. Twic —1G **24**
Railway App. Wall —2F **62**
Railway Cotts. SW19 —5N **27**
Railway Cotts. Bag —3J **51**
Railway Cotts. Twic —9A **10**
Railway Pas. Tedd —7G **24**
Railway Pl. SW19 —7L **27**
Railway Rd. Tedd —5E **24**
Railway Side. SW13 —6E **12**
Railway Ter. Coul —2H **83**
(off Station App.)
Railway Ter. Felt —2H **23**
Railway Ter. Stai —6F **20**
Railway Ter. W'ham —3M **107**
Rainbow Ct. Wok —3H **73**
Rainville Rd. W6 —2H **13**
Rake La. Milf —1C **152**
Rakers Ridge. H'ham —3K **197**
Raleigh Av. Wall —1H **63**
Raleigh Ct. Craw —7E **162**
Raleigh Ct. Stai —5J **21**
Raleigh Ct. Wall —3F **62**
Raleigh Dri. Clay —2D **58**
Raleigh Dri. Small —8L **143**
Raleigh Dri. Surb —7B **42**
Raleigh Gdns. Mitc —2D **44**
(in two parts)
Raleigh Rd. Felt —4G **23**
Raleigh Rd. Rich —6M **11**
Raleigh Rd. S'hall —1M **9**
Raleigh Wlk. Craw —5C **182**
Raleigh Way. Felt —6K **23**
Raleigh Way. Frim —3D **70**
Ralliwood Rd. Asht —6N **79**
Ralph Perring Ct. Beck —3K **47**
Ralph's Ride. Brack —2C **32**
(in two parts)
Rama Clo. SW16 —8J **29**
Rambler Clo. SW16 —5G **28**
Ramblers Way. Craw —9N **181**

Rame Clo. SW17 —6E **28**
Ramillies Clo. Alder —6C **90**
Ramillies Rd. Alder —6A **90**
Ramin Ct. Guild —9M **93**
Ramornie Clo. W On T —1N **57**
Ram Pas. King T —1K **41**
Ramsay Clo. Camb —8F **50**
Ramsay Ct. Craw —8N **181**
Ramsay Rd. W'sham —2B **52**
Ramsbury Clo. Brack —5K **31**
Ramsdale Rd. SW17 —6E **28**
Ramsden Rd. SW12 —1E **28**
Ramsden Rd. G'ming —8G **133**
Ramsey Clo. Horl —8D **142**
Ramsey Clo. H'ham —3K **197**
Ramsey Pl. Cat —9N **83**
Ramsey Rd. T Hth —5K **45**
Ramslade Cotts. Brack —2A **32**
Ramslade Rd. Brack —3B **32**
Rams La. Duns —7C **174**
Ramster Cotts. C'fold —1C **190**
Ramuswood Av. Orp —2N **67**
Ranald Ct. Asc —7L **17**
Rances La. Wokgm —3D **30**
Randal Cres. Reig —5M **121**
Randall Clo. Slou —1B **6**
Randall Farm La. Lea —6G **79**
Randall Mead. Binf —7G **15**
Randall Schofield Ct. Craw
—2E **182**
Randalls Cres. Lea —7G **78**
Randalls Pk. Av. Lea —7G **78**
Randalls Pk. Dri. Lea —8G **78**
Randalls Research Pk. Lea
—7M **47**
Randalls Rd. Lea —6E **78**
Randalls Way. Lea —8G **78**
~~Randell Clo. B'water —5K 69~~
~~Randell Ho. Hawl —5K 69~~
Randle Rd. Rich —5J **25**
Rawchester Clo. SW18 —2L **27**
Rawdon Rise. Camb —1D **70**
Rawlins Clo. S Croy —4J **65**
Rawlinson Rd. Camb —9M **49**
Rawnsley Av. Mitc —4B **44**
Raworth Clo. M'bowr —5G **182**
Rawsthorne Ct. Houn —7N **9**
Raybell Ct. Iswth —5G **10**
Ray Clo. Chess —3J **59**
Ray Clo. Ling —6M **145**
Ray La. Ling —4M **145**
Rayleigh Av. Tedd —7E **24**
Rayleigh Ct. King T —1N **41**
Rayleigh Rise. S Croy —3B **64**
Rayleigh Rd. SW19 —9L **27**
Raymead Av. T Hth —4L **45**
Raymead Clo. Fet —9E **78**
Raymead Way. Fet —9E **78**
Raymond Clo. Coln —4G **7**
Raymond Ct. Sutt —3N **61**
Raymond Cres. Guild —4J **113**
Raymond Rd. SW19 —7K **27**
Raymond Rd. Beck —3H **47**
Raymond Way. Clay —3G **59**
Raynald Ho. SW16 —4J **29**
Rayners Clo. Coln —3E **6**
Rayners Rd. SW15 —8K **13**
Raynes Pk. Bri. SW20 —1H **43**
Ray Rd. W Mol —4B **40**
Ray's Av. Wind —3C **4**
Rays Rd. W Wick —6M **47**
Raywood Clo. Hayes —3D **8**
Readens, The. Bans —3C **82**
Reading Arch Rd. Red —3D **122**
Reading Rd. F'boro —4A **90**
Reading Rd. Sutt —2A **62**
Reading Rd. Wokgm —1A **30**
Reading Rd. Yat —8A **48**
Reading Rd. S. Fleet —5A **88**
Read Rd. Asht —4K **79**
Reads Rest La. Tad —7M **81**
Reapers Clo. H'ham —3K **197**
Reapers Way. Iswth —8D **10**
Rebecca Clo. C Crook —1A **108**
Rebecca Pl. Add —4H **55**
Reckitt Rd. W4 —1D **12**
Recovery St. SW17 —6C **28**
Recreation Rd. Guild —3N **113**
Recreation Rd. Rowl —6D **128**
Recreation Way. Mitc —2J **45**
Rectory Clo. SW20 —2H **43**
Rectory Clo. Asht —6M **79**
Rectory Clo. Brack —3A **32**
Rectory Clo. Byfl —9N **55**
Rectory Clo. Ewh —5F **156**
Rectory Clo. G'ming —9J **133**
Rectory Clo. Guild —1F **114**
Rectory Clo. Ockl —7C **120**
Rectory Clo. Sand —7E **48**
Rectory Clo. Shep —2B **38**
Rectory Clo. Surb —7J **41**
Rectory Clo. Wind —4D **4**
Rectory Clo. Wokgm —2B **30**
Rectory Ct. Felt —5K **23**
Rectory Ct. Wall —1G **63**
Rectory Flats. Craw —1L **181**
Rectory Garden. Cranl —7M **155**
Rectory Grn. Beck —1J **47**
Rectory Gro. Croy —8M **45**
Rectory Gro. Hamp —5N **23**

Ravensbury Rd. SW18 —3N **27**
Ravensbury Ter. SW18 —3N **27**
Ravenscar Clo. Surb —8M **41**
Ravens Clo. Knap —3F **72**
Ravens Clo. Red —2D **122**
Ravenscourt. Sun —9G **23**
Ravenscourt Av. W6 —1F **12**
Ravenscourt Pk. W6 —1F **12**
Ravenscourt Pl. W6 —1G **12**
Ravenscourt Rd. W6 —1G **12**
Ravenscroft Clo. Ash —1G **111**
Ravenscroft Ct. H'ham —5J **197**
Ravenscroft Rd. Beck —1H **46**
Ravenscroft Rd. Wey —7D **56**
Ravensdale Cotts. Bram C
—9A **170**
Ravensdale Ho. Stai —7K **21**
Ravensdale Rd. Asc —4L **33**
Ravensdale Rd. Houn —6M **9**
Ravensfield Gdns. Eps —2D **60**
Ravenshead Clo. S Croy —7F **64**
Ravenslea Rd. SW12 —1D **28**
Ravensmede Way. W4 —1E **12**
Ravenstone Rd. Camb —1H **71**
Ravenstone St. SW12 —2E **28**
Ravens Wold. Kenl —2N **83**
Ravenswood Av. Crowt —2D **48**
Ravenswood Av. Surb —8M **41**
Ravenswood Av. W Wick
—7M **47**
Ravenswood Clo. Cobh —2L **77**
Ravenswood Ct. King T —7A **26**
Ravenswood Cres. W Wick
Ravenswood Cres. W Wick
—7M **47**
Ravenswood Dri. Camb —1E **70**
Ravenswood Gdns. Iswth
—4E **10**
~~Ravenswood Rd. SW12 —1E 28~~
Ravenswood Rd. Croy —9M **45**

Rectory La. SW17 —7E **28**
Rectory La. Alder —6M **79**
Rectory La. Bans —2D **82**
Rectory La. Bookh —4N **97**
Rectory La. Bram —9K **169**
Rectory La. Brack —4N **31**
Rectory La. Bras —1G **106**
Rectory La. Bkld —9E **100**
Rectory La. Byfl —1N **75**
Rectory La. Charl —3J **161**
Rectory La. If'd —1L **181**
Rectory La. Shere —8B **116**
Rectory La. Surb —7H **41**
Rectory La. Wall —1G **63**
Rectory La. W'sham —3N **51**
Rectory Orchard. SW19 —5K **27**
Rectory Pk. S Croy —9B **64**
Rectory Rd. SW13 —5F **12**
Rectory Rd. Beck —1K **47**
Rectory Rd. Coul —3A **102**
Rectory Rd. F'boro —1A **90**
Rectory Rd. Houn —5K **9**
Rectory Rd. Kes —4F **66**
Rectory Rd. Sutt —9M **43**
Rectory Row. Brack —3N **31**
Red Admiral St. H'ham —3L **197**
Redan Gdns. Alder —2A **110**
Redan Hill Est. Alder —2A **110**
Redan Rd. Alder —2A **110**
Redbarn Clo. Purl —7M **63**
Redcliffe Clo. SW5 —1N **13**
Redcliffe Gdns. SW5 & SW10
—1N **13**
Redcliffe M. SW10 —1N **13**
Redcliffe Pl. SW10 —2N **13**
Redcliffe Rd. SW10 —1N **13**
Redcliffe Sq. SW10 —1N **13**
Redclose Av. Mord —4M **43**
Red Cotts. Hasl —7J **171**
Redcourt. Croy —9B **46**
Redcourt. Wok —2F **74**
Redcrest Gdns. Camb —1D **70**
Redcroft Wlk. Cranl —8N **155**
Red Deer Clo. H'ham —4A **198**
Reddings. If'd —5K **181**
Reddings, The. H'ham —5M **197**
Reddington Clo. S Croy —5A **64**
Reddington Dri. Slou —1B **6**
Redding Way. Knap —6E **72**
Redditch. Brack —6B **32**
Redditch Clo. Craw —7K **181**
Reddown Rd. Coul —5H **83**
Rede Ct. F'boro —4A **90**
Rede Ct. Wey —9C **38**
(off Old Pal. Rd.)
Redehall Rd. Small —9M **143**
Redenham Ho. SW15 —1F **26**
(off Tangley Gro.)
Redesdale Gdns. Iswth —3G **10**
Redfern Av. Houn —1A **24**
Redfield La. SW5 —1M **13**
Redfields Ind. Est. C Crook
—2A **108**
Redfields La. C Crook —2A **108**
Redford Av. Coul —2F **82**
Redford Av. H'ham —4H **197**
Redford Av. T Hth —3K **45**
Redford Av. Wall —3J **63**
Redford Clo. Felt —4F **22**
Redford Rd. Wind —4A **4**
Redgarth Ct. E Grin —7L **165**
Redgate Ter. SW15 —9J **13**
Redgrave Clo. Croy —5C **46**
Redgrave Ct. Ash —2D **110**
Redgrave Dri. Craw —4H **183**
Redgrave Rd. SW15 —6J **13**
Redhall Ct. Cat —1A **104**
Redhearn Fields. Churt —8K **149**
Redhearn Grn. Churt —8K **149**
Redhill Ct. SW2 —3L **29**
Redhill Ho. Red —2D **122**
Redhill Rd. Cobh —9C **56**
Red Ho. La. Elst —8G **131**
Red Ho. La. W On T —8H **39**
Redhouse Rd. Croy —5H **45**
Redhouse Rd. Tats —8E **86**
Redkiln Clo. H'ham —5M **197**
Redkiln Way. H'ham —4M **197**
Redlake La. Wokgm —6E **30**
Redland Gdns. W Mol —3N **39**
Redlands. Coul —3J **83**
Redlands. Tedd —7G **25**
Redlands Cotts. Dork —2H **139**
Redlands La. Ews —5A **108**
Redlands, The. Beck —1L **47**
Redlands Way. SW2 —1K **29**
Red La. Clay —3G **58**
Red La. Dork —1L **139**
Red La. Head —2G **168**
Red La. Oxt —3D **126**
Redleaves Av. Ashf —7C **22**
Redlees Clo. Iswth —7G **10**
Redlin Ct. Red —1D **122**
Red Lion Bus. Pk. Surb —9M **41**
Red Lion La. Chob —5H **53**
Red Lion La. Farnh —2G **129**
Red Lion Rd. Chob —5H **53**
Red Lion Rd. Surb —8M **41**
Red Lion Sq. SW18 —8M **13**

Red Lion St. Rich —8K **11**
Red Lodge. W Wick —7M **47**
Red Lodge Rd. W Wick —7M **47**
Redmayne Clo. Camb —2G **71**
Red River Ct. H'ham —3H **197**
Red Rd. Light —9H **51**
Red Rd. Tad —1A **120**
Red Rose. Binf —6H **15**
Red Rover. (Junct.) —7F **12**
Redruth Ho. Sutt —4N **61**
Redshank Ct. If'd —4J **181**
(off Stoneycroft Wlk.)
Redstart Clo. New Ad —6N **65**
Redstone Hill. Red —3E **122**
Redstone Hollow. Red —4E **122**
Redstone Mnr. Red —3E **122**
Redstone Pk. Red —3E **122**
Redstone Rd. Red —4E **122**
Redvers Buller Rd. Alder
—6A **90**
Redvers Rd. Brack —4N **31**
Redvers Rd. Warl —5G **84**
Redway Dri. Twic —1C **24**
Redwing Av. G'ming —3G **133**
Redwing Clo. H'ham —5M **197**
Redwing Clo. S Croy —7G **64**
Redwing Rise. Guild —1F **114**
Redwood. Egh —1G **37**
Redwood Clo. Craw —1C **182**
Redwood Clo. Kenl —1N **83**
Redwood Ct. Surb —6K **41**
Redwood Dri. Asc —6E **34**
Redwood Dri. Camb —2H **71**
Redwood Est. Houn —2J **9**
Redwood Gro. Chil —9E **114**
Redwood Mnr. Hasl —1G **188**
Redwood Mt. Reig —9M **101**
~~Redwoods. SW15 —2F 26~~
~~Redwoods Way. S Croy~~
—8C **88**
Redwood Wlk. Surb —7K **41**
Reed Av. Orp —1N **67**
Reed Clo. Alder —8B **90**
Reedham Dri. Purl —9K **63**
Reedham Pk. Av. Purl —3L **83**
Reed Pl. W Byf —9G **54**
Reedsfield Rd. Ashf —5C **22**
Reed's Hill. Brack —4N **31**
Reeds Rd., The. Bourne
—8L **129**
Rees Gdns. Croy —5C **46**
Reeve Ct. Guild —8K **93**
Reeve Rd. Reig —7A **122**
Reeves Corner. Croy —8M **45**
Reeves Path. Hayes —1G **8**
Reeves Rd. Alder —3A **110**
Reeves Way. Wokgm —4A **30**
Regal Cres. Wall —9F **44**
Regal Dri. E Grin —9B **166**
Regalfield Clo. Guild —8J **93**
Regal Pl. SW6 —3N **13**
(off Maxwell Rd.)
Regan Clo. Guild —7L **93**
Regatta Ho. Tedd —5G **25**
Regency Clo. Hamp —6N **23**
Regency Ct. Sutt —1N **61**
Regency Ct. Tedd —7H **25**
Regency Dri. W Byf —9H **55**
Regency Gdns. W On T —7K **39**
Regency M. Iswth —8E **10**
Regency Wlk. Croy —5H **47**
Regency Wlk. Rich —8L **11**
(off Grosvenor Av.)
Regent Clo. Fleet —5B **88**
Regent Clo. Houn —4J **9**
Regent Clo. New H —5M **55**
Regent Clo. Red —6G **102**
Regent Ct. Bag —5K **51**
Regent Ct. Guild —1L **113**
Regent Cres. Red —1D **122**
Regent Ho. Eps —7D **60**
Regent Ho. Red —2D **122**
Regent Pl. SW19 —6A **28**
Regent Pl. Croy —7C **46**
Regent Rd. Surb —4M **41**
Regent St. W4 —1N **11**
Regent St. Fleet —5B **88**
Regents Clo. Craw —7A **182**
Regents Clo. S Croy —3B **64**
Regents Clo. Whyt —5B **84**
Regents Dri. Kes —2F **66**
Regents Pl. Sand —7H **49**
Regent St. W4 —1N **11**
Regina Rd. SE25 —2D **46**
Regina Rd. S'hall —1M **9**
Reid Av. Cat —8A **84**
Reid Clo. Coul —3F **82**
Reidonhill Cotts. Knap —5E **72**
Reigate Av. Sutt —7M **43**
Reigate Clo. Craw —9H **163**
Reigate Hill. Reig —2M **121**
Reigate Hill Interchange. (Junct.)
—7N **101**
Reigate Rd. Bet —2N **119**
Reigate Rd. Dork —4J **119**
Reigate Rd. Eps & Tad —6F **60**
Reigate Rd. Lea —1J **99**

Reigate Rd.—Roman Ride

Reigate Rd. Leigh & Hook —1N 141
Reigate Rd. Reig & Red —3N 121
Reigate Way. Wall —2J 63
Reindorp Clo. Guild —4K 113
Relko Ct. Eps —7C 60
Relko Gdns. Sutt —2B 62
Rembrandt Way. W On T —8J 39
Rendle Clo. Croy —4C 46
Renfree Way. Shep —6B 38
Renfrew Ct. Houn —5M 9
Renfrew Rd. Houn —5M 9
Renfrew Rd. King T —8A 26
Renmans, The. Asht —3M 79
Renmuir St. SW17 —7D 28
Rennels Way. Iswth —5E 10
Rennie Clo. Ashf —4M 21
Rennie Ter. Red —4E 122
Renown Clo. Croy —7M 45
Replingham Rd. SW18 —2L 27
Reporton Rd. SW6 —3K 13
Repton Av. Hayes —1E 8
Repton Clo. Cars —2C 62
Restavon Cvn. Site. Berr G —3K 87
Restmor Way. Wall —8E 44
Restormel Clo. Houn —8A 10
Restwell Av. Cranl —4K 155
Retreat Rd. Rich —8K 11
Retreat, The. SW14 —6D 12
Retreat, The. Egh —6N 19
Retreat, The. Fleet —7A 88
Retreat, The. Surb —5M 41
Retreat, The. T Hth —3A 46
Retreat, The. Wor Pk —9G 43
Reubens Ct. W4 —1A 12 (off Chaseley Dri.)
Revell Clo. Fet —9B 78
Revell Dri. Fet —9B 78
Revell Rd. King T —1A 42
Revell Rd. Sutt —3L 61
Revelstoke Av. F'boro —8N 69
Revelstoke Rd. SW18 —3L 27
Revesby Clo. W End —9A 52
Revesby Rd. Cars —5C 44
Rewell St. SW6 —3N 13
Rewley Rd. Cars —5B 44
Rex Av. Ashf —7B 22
Rex Ct. Hasl —2D 188
Reynard Clo. H'ham —3A 198
Reynard Mills Trad. Est. Bren —1J 11
Reynolds Av. Chess —4L 59
Reynolds Clo. SW19 —9B 28
Reynolds Clo. Cars —7D 44
Reynolds Grn. Col T —9J 49
Reynolds Pl. Craw —2A 182
Reynolds Pl. Rich —9M 11
Reynolds Rd. Craw —2A 182
Reynolds Rd. N Mald —6C 42
Reynolds Way. Croy —1B 64
Rheingold Way. Wall —5J 63
Rhine Banks. F'boro —9J 69
Rhine Barracks. Alder —1M 109
Rhodes Clo. Egh —6E 20
Rhodes Ct. Egh —6E 20 (off Pooley Grn. Clo.)
Rhodesia Ter. Frim G —6H 71
Rhodesmoor Ho. Ct. Mord —5M 43
Rhodes Way. Craw —6D 182
Rhododendron Clo. Asc —8J 17
Rhododendron Ride. Egh —7J 19
Rhododendron Rd. Frim —6E 70
Rhododendron Wlk. Asc —8J 17
Rhodrons Av. Chess —2L 59
Rialto Rd. Mitc —1E 44
Ribble Pl. F'boro —8K 69
Ribblesdale. Dork —7H 119
Ribblesdale Rd. SW16 —7F 28
Ricardo Ct. Brmly —6B 134
Ricardo Rd. Old Win —9L 5
Ricards Rd. SW19 —6L 27
Ricebridge La. Reig —6G 120
Rices Corner. Won —2C 134
Rices Hill. E Grin —9B 166
Richard Clo. Fleet —6A 88
Richards Clo. Ash V —8E 90
Richards Clo. Hayes —2E 8
Richards Field. Eps —5C 60
Richard Sharples Ct. Sutt —4A 62
Richardson Ct. Craw —8N 181
Richards Rd. Stoke D —1B 78
Richbell Clo. Asht —5K 79
Richborough Ct. Craw —3A 182
Richland Av. Coul —1E 82
Richlands Av. Eps —1F 60
Rich La. SW5 —1N 13
Richmond Av. SW20 —9K 27
Richmond Av. Felt —9F 8
Richmond Bri. Twic & Rich —9K 11
Richmond Circus. (Junct.) —7L 11
Richmond Clo. Big H —6D 86
Richmond Clo. Eps —1D 80
Richmond Clo. F'boro —2J 89
Richmond Clo. Fet —2C 98
Richmond Clo. Fleet —7A 88
Richmond Clo. Frim —5D 70
Richmond Ct. Craw —4C 182
Richmond Cres. Stai —6H 21
Richmond Dri. Shep —5E 38
Richmond Grn. Croy —9J 45
Richmond Gro. Surb —5M 41
Richmond Hill. Rich —9L 11
Richmond Hill Ct. Rich —9L 11
Richmond Ho. Sand —8K 49
Richmond Mans. Twic —9K 11
Richmond M. Tedd —6F 24
Richmond Pde. Twic —9J 11 (off Richmond Rd.)
Richmond Pk. Rd. SW14 —8B 12
Richmond Pk. Rd. King T —8L 25
Richmond Rd. SW20 —9G 26
Richmond Rd. Col T —7K 49
Richmond Rd. Coul —2F 82
Richmond Rd. Croy —9J 45
Richmond Rd. G'ming —5H 133
Richmond Rd. H'ham —4J 197
Richmond Rd. Iswth —6G 11
Richmond Rd. King T —6K 25
Richmond Rd. Stai —6H 21
Richmond Rd. T Hth —2M 45
Richmond Rd. Twic —1H 25
Richmond Way. E Grin —1B 186
Richmond Way. Fet —1B 98 (in two parts)
Richmondwood. Asc —7E 34
Rickard Clo. SW2 —2L 29
Rickards Clo. Surb —7L 41
Ricketts Hill Rd. Tats —5F 86
Rickett St. SW6 —2M 13
Rickfield. Craw —4M 181
Rickford. Worp —3F 92
Rickford Hill. Worp —4G 93
Rickman Clo. Brack —5A 32
Rickman Ct. Add —9K 37
Rickman Cres. Add —9K 37
Rickman Hill. Coul —4F 82
Rickman Hill Rd. Coul —5F 82
Rickmans La. Plais —6B 192
Ricksons La. W Hor —5C 96
Rickwood. Horl —7F 142
Rickwood Cvn. Pk. Bear G —1K 159
Rickyard. Guild —3G 113
Riddings, The. Cat —3C 104
Riddlesdown Av. Purl —8N 63
Riddlesdown Rd. Purl —6N 63
Ride La. Alb —4M 135
Riders Way. God —9F 104
Ride, The. Bren —1J 11
Ride, The. Ifold —6F 192
Ride Way. Cranl —9C 136
Rideway Clo. Camb —2N 69
Ridge Clo. Str G —7A 120
Ridge Clo. Wok —8L 73
Ridge Ct. Warl —5D 84
Ridgegate Clo. Reig —1B 122
Ridge Grn. S Nut —6J 123
Ridge Grn. Clo. S Nut —6J 123
Ridgehurst Dri. H'ham —7F 196
Ridgelands. Fet —2D 98
Ridge Langley. S Croy —5D 64
Ridgemead Rd. Egh —4K 19
Ridgemoor Clo. Hind —4C 170
Ridgemount. Guild —4L 113
Ridgemount. Wey —8F 38
Ridgemount Av. Coul —4F 82
Ridgemount Av. Croy —7G 47
Ridgemount Est. Frim G —7G 70
Ridge Mt. Rd. Asc —7D 34
Ridgemount Way. Red —5B 122
Ridge Pk. Purl —6H 63
Ridge Rise. Add —2H 55
Ridge Rd. Mitc —8F 28
Ridge Rd. Sutt —7K 43
Ridgeside. Craw —3D 182
Ridges, The. Guild —8M 113
Ridge, The. Coul —1J 83
Ridge, The. Eps —5B 80
Ridge, The. Fet —2D 98
Ridge, The. Purl —6H 63
Ridge, The. Rud —9E 176
Ridge, The. Surb —4N 41
Ridge, The. Twic —1D 24
Ridge, The. Wok —4D 74
Ridge, The. Wold & Warl —3M 105
Ridgeway. E Grin —2A 186
Ridge Way. Eden —8L 127
Ridgeway. Eps —8B 60
Ridge Way. Felt —4M 23
Ridgeway. Hors —2N 73
Ridgeway. Rich —9L 11
Ridgeway Clo. Cranl —7B 156
Ridgeway Clo. Dork —7G 118
Ridgeway Clo. Light —7L 51
Ridgeway Clo. Oxs —1C 78
Ridgeway Clo. Wok —3N 73
Ridgeway Ct. Red —4D 122
Ridgeway Cres. Orp —1N 67
Ridgeway Dri. Dork —8G 119
Ridgeway Gdns. Wok —2N 73
Ridgeway Ho. Horl —1E 162 (off Crescent, The)
Ridgeway Pde. C Crook —8B 88
Ridgeway Rd. Dork —7G 118
Ridgeway Rd. Iswth —3E 10
Ridgeway Rd. Red —3D 122
Ridgeway Rd. N. Iswth —3E 10
Ridgeway, The. Brack —2A 32
Ridgeway, The. Brkwd —7D 72
Ridgeway, The. Cranl —7B 156
Ridgeway, The. Croy —9K 45
Ridgeway, The. Fet —2E 98
Ridgeway, The. Guild —4C 114
Ridgeway, The. Horl —1F 162
Ridgeway, The. H'ham —4H 197
Ridgeway, The. Light —6M 51
Ridgeway, The. Oxs —1C 78
Ridge Way, The. S Croy —6B 64
Ridgeway, The. W On T —7G 38
Ridgewood Dri. Frim —3H 71
Ridgley Rd. C'fold —5D 172
Ridgmount Rd. SW18 —8N 13
Ridgway. SW19 —8H 27
Ridgway. Pyr —2J 75
Ridgway Ct. SW19 —7J 27
Ridgway Gdns. SW19 —8J 27
Ridgway Hill Rd. Farnh —3H 129
Ridgway Pl. SW19 —7K 27
Ridgway Rd. Farnh —4H 129
Ridgway Rd. Pyr —2H 75
Ridgway, The. Sutt —3B 62
Riding Ct. Rd. Dat —3M 5
Riding Hill. S Croy —9D 64
Ridings La. Ock —1C 96
Ridings, The. Add —3G 55
Ridings, The. Asht —4K 79
Ridings, The. Big H —4G 86
Ridings, The. Cobh —8A 58
Ridings, The. E Hor —3G 96
Ridings, The. Eps —2E 80
Ridings, The. Ewe —5E 60
Ridings, The. Frim —3F 70
Ridings, The. Reig —1B 122
Ridings, The. Rip —1J 95
Ridings, The. Sun —9H 23
Ridings, The. Surb —4N 41
Ridings, The. Tad —7L 81
Ridings, The. Worth —2J 183
Riding, The. Cranl —6N 155
Riding, The. Wok —1D 74
Ridlands Gro. Oxt —8G 106
Ridlands La. Oxt —8F 106
Ridlands Rise. Oxt —8G 106
Ridley Clo. Fleet —6A 88
Ridley Ct. SW16 —7J 29
Ridley Ct. Craw —9H 163
Ridley Rd. SW19 —8N 27
Ridley Rd. Warl —5F 84
Ridsdale Rd. Wok —4L 73
Riesco Dri. Croy —3F 64
Rifle Butts All. Eps —1E 80
Rifle Way. F'boro —2H 89
Rigault Rd. SW6 —5K 13
Rigby Clo. Croy —9L 45
Riggindale Rd. SW16 —6H 29
Rillside. Craw —6E 182
Rill Wlk. E Grin —9D 166
Rimbault Clo. Alder —6B 90
Rimmer Clo. Craw —9N 181
Rinaldo Rd. SW12 —1F 28
Ringford Rd. SW18 —8L 13
Ringley Av. Horl —8E 142
Ringley Oak. H'ham —4M 197
Ringley Pk. Av. Reig —4B 122
Ringley Pk. Rd. Reig —3A 122
Ringley Rd. H'ham —4L 197
Ringmead. Brack —4K 31
Ringmer Av. SW6 —4K 13
Ringmore Dri. Guild —9E 94
Ringmore Rd. W On T —9K 39
Ring Rd. N. Horl —2F 162
Ring Rd. S. Horl —3G 162
Ringstead Rd. Sutt —1B 62
Ring, The. Brack —1A 32
Ringway. S'hall —1L 9
Ringwood. Brack —6L 31
Ringwood Av. Croy —6J 45
Ringwood Av. Red —9D 102
Ringwood Clo. Asc —3M 33
Ringwood Clo. Craw —5C 182
Ringwood Gdns. SW15 —2F 26
Ringwood Lodge. Red —9E 102
Ringwood Rd. B'water —9H 49
Ringwood Rd. F'boro —7A 70
Ringwood Way. Hamp —5A 24
Ripley Av. Egh —7N 19
Ripley By-Pass. Rip —1L 95
Ripley Clo. New Ad —3M 65
Ripley Ct. Mitc —1B 44
Ripley Gdns. SW14 —6C 12
Ripley Gdns. Sutt —1A 62
Ripley La. Rip & W Hors —1N 95
Ripley Rd. Hamp —8A 24
Ripley Rd. Send —4L 95
Ripon Clo. Camb —3H 71
Ripon Clo. Guild —1J 113
Ripon Gdns. Chess —2K 59
Ripplesmere. Brack —3B 32
Ripplesmore Clo. Sand —7G 48
Ripston Rd. Ashf —6E 22
Risborough Dri. Wor Pk —6F 42
Rise Rd. Asc —4B 34
Rise, The. Craw —3H 183
Rise, The. Crowt —2E 48
Rise, The. E Grin —1B 186
Rise, The. E Hor —4F 96
Rise, The. Eps —6E 60
Rise, The. S Croy —5F 64
Rise, The. S'dale —5B 34
Rise, The. Tad —7H 81
Rise, The. Wokgm —1A 30
Ritchie Clo. M'bowr —7G 182
Ritchie Rd. Croy —5E 46
Ritherdon Rd. SW17 —3E 28
River Av. Th Dit —6G 41
River Bank. E Mol —2E 40
Riverbank. Stai —7H 21
River Bank. Th Dit —4F 40
Riverbank. Westc —5B 118
River Bank. W Mol —2A 40
Riverbank, The. Wind —3E 4
Riverbank Way. Bren —2J 11
River Ct. Wok —1E 74
Rivercourt Rd. W6 —1G 12
River Crane Way. Felt —3N 23
Riverdale. Wrec —4D 128
Riverdale Dri. SW18 —2N 27
Riverdale Dri. Wok —8B 74
Riverdale Gdns. Twic —9J 11
Riverdale Rd. Felt —5M 23
Riverdale Rd. Twic —9J 11
Riverdene Ind. Est. W On T —2L 57
Riverfield Rd. Stai —7H 21
River Gdns. Cars —8E 44
River Gdns. Felt —8J 9
River Gdns. Bus. Cen. Felt —8J 9
River Gro. Pk. Beck —1J 47
Riverhead Dri. Sutt —6M 61
River Hill. Cobh —2J 77
Riverhill. Wor Pk —8C 42
Riverholme Dri. Eps —5C 60
River Island Clo. Fet —7D 78
River La. Farnh —4D 128
River La. Fet —8D 78
River La. Rich —2K 25
River La. Stoke D —3M 77
Rivermead. Byfl —9A 56
River Mead. H'ham —7H 197
River Mead. If'd —9M 161
Rivermead. King T —4K 41
Rivermead Clo. Add —4L 55
Rivermead Clo. Tedd —6H 25
Rivermead Ct. SW6 —6L 13
Rivermead Rd. Camb —4N 69
River Meads Av. Twic —4A 24
Rivermede. Bord —5A 168
River Mt. W On T —6G 38
Rivermount Gdns. Guild —6M 113
Rivernook Clo. W On T —4K 39
River Pk. Av. Stai —5F 20
River Reach. Tedd —6J 25
River Rd. Stai —9H 21
River Rd. Wind —3A 4
River Rd. Yat —7A 48
River Row Cotts. Farnh —4E 128
Rivers Clo. F'boro —4C 90
Riversdale Rd. Th Dit —4G 40
Riversdell Clo. Cher —6H 37
Riverside. Dork —3K 119
Riverside. Eden —2L 147
Riverside. Egh —4C 20
Riverside. F Row —6G 187
Riverside. Guild —1N 113
Riverside. Horl —1E 162
Riverside. H'ham —6G 196
Riverside. Rich —8K 11
Riverside. Shep —6F 38
Riverside. Stai —6H 21
Riverside. Sun —1L 39
Riverside. Twic —2H 25
Riverside. Wray —1M 19
Riverside Av. E Mol —4D 40
Riverside Av. Light —6N 51
Riverside Av. Rich —4L 11
Riverside Bus. Cen. SW18 —2N 27
Riverside Bus. Cen. Guild —3M 113
Riverside Bus. Cen. Iswth —7H 11
Riverside Bus. Pk. Farnh —9J 109
Riverside Clo. Brkwd —7C 72
Riverside Clo. F'boro —9L 69
Riverside Clo. King T —3K 41
Riverside Clo. Stai —9H 21
Riverside Clo. Wall —9F 44
Riverside Ct. Eden —3M 147
Riverside Ct. Farnh —9H 109
Riverside Ct. Felt —9F 8
Riverside Ct. Fet —9G 78
Riverside Ct. Iswth —5F 10 (off Woodlands Rd.)
Riverside Dri. W4 —3C 12
Riverside Dri. Brmly —4C 134
Riverside Dri. Esh —1A 58
Riverside Dri. Mitc —4C 44
Riverside Dri. Rich —3H 25
Riverside Dri. Stai —6G 21 (Chertsey La.)
Riverside Dri. Stai —8H 21 (Wheatsheaf La.)
Riverside Gdns. W6 —1G 13
Riverside Gdns. Wok —8D 74
Riverside Ind. Pk. Farnh —9H 109
Riverside M. Croy —9J 45
Riverside Pk. Add —2N 55
Riverside Pk. Camb —3M 69
Riverside Pk. Coln —5G 6
Riverside Pk. Farnh —9J 109
Riverside Pl. Stai —9M 7
Riverside Rd. SW17 —5N 27
Riverside Rd. Stai —8H 21
Riverside Rd. Stanw —8M 7
Riverside Rd. W On T —1M 57
Riverside, The. E Mol —2D 40
Riverside Wlk. SW6 —6K 13
Riverside Wlk. W4 —2E 12
Riverside Wlk. G'ming —6G 133
Riverside Wlk. Iswth —6E 10
Riverside Wlk. King T —2K 41
Riverside Wlk. W Wick —7L 47
Riverside Wlk. Wind —3G 5
Riverside Way. Camb —3M 69
River St. Wind —3G 4
River Ter. W6 —1H 13
River View. Add —2L 55
Riverview. Guild —3M 113
Riverview Gdns. SW13 —2G 13
Riverview Gdns. Cobh —9H 57
River View Gdns. Twic —3F 24
Riverview Gro. W4 —2A 12
Riverview Rd. W4 —3A 12
Riverview Rd. Eps —1B 60
River Wlk. W6 —3H 13
River Wlk. W On T —5H 39
River Way. Eps —2C 60
Riverway. Stai —9K 21
River Way. Twic —3B 24
Riverway Est. Guild —3L 133
Riverwood Ct. Guild —1M 113
Rivett Drake Rd. Guild —8K 93
Rivey Clo. W Byf —1H 75
Road Ho. Est. Old Wok —7C 74
Roakes Av. Add —8K 37
Roasthill La. Eton W —2A 4
Robert Clo. W On T —2J 57
Robert Owen Ho. SW6 —4J 13
Robertsbridge Rd. Cars —7A 44
Roberts Clo. Stai —9L 7
Roberts Clo. Sutt —4J 61
Robertson Ct. Wok —5H 73
Robertson Way. Ash —3D 110
Roberts Rd. Alder —3A 110
Roberts Rd. Camb —9M 49
Robert St. Croy —9N 45
Roberts Way. Egh —8M 19
Robert Way. H'ham —1M 197
Robert Way. Myt —2D 90
Robin Clo. Add —2M 55
Robin Clo. Ash V —7E 90
Robin Clo. Craw —1A 182
Robin Clo. E Grin —8B 166
Robin Clo. Hamp —6M 23
Robin Gdns. Red —1E 122
Robin Gro. Bren —2J 11
Robin Hill. G'ming —4G 133
Robin Hill Dri. Camb —3E 70
Robin Hood. (Junct.) —4D 26
Robin Hood Clo. F'boro —7M 69
Robinhood Clo. Mitc —3G 45
Robin Hood Clo. Wok —5J 73
Robin Hood Cres. Knap —4H 73
Robin Hood La. SW15 —5D 26
Robinhood La. Mitc —2G 45
Robin Hood La. Sutt —2M 61
Robin Hood La. Warn —3E 196
Robin Hood La. Wok & Sut G —2B 94
Robin Hood Rd. SW19 & SW15 —6F 26
Robin Hood Rd. Knap —4G 73
Robin Hood Way. SW15 & SW20 —4D 26
Robin Hood Works. Knap —4H 73 (off Robin Hood Rd.)
Robin La. Sand —7G 49
Robin Row. Turn H —4F 184
Robin's Bow. Camb —2N 69
Robin's Ct. Beck —1N 47
Robins Dale. Knap —4F 72
Robins Gro. W Wick —1C 66
Robins Gro. Cres. Yat —9A 48
Robinson Rd. SW17 & SW19 —7C 28
Robinson Rd. Craw —4B 182
Robinson Way. Bord —7A 168
Robinsway. W On T —1K 57
Robinswood Ct. H'ham —4M 197
Robin Way. Guild —8L 93
Robin Way. Stai —4H 21
Robin Willis Way. Old Win —9K 5
Robinwood Pl. SW15 —5C 26
Robson Rd. SE27 —4M 29
Roby Dri. Brack —6B 32
Robyns Way. Eden —3M 147
Roche Rd. SW16 —9K 29
Rochester Av. Felt —3G 23
Rochester Clo. SW16 —8J 29
Rochester Gdns. Cat —9B 84
Rochester Gdns. Croy —9B 46
Rochester Gro. Fleet —5B 88
Rochester Pde. Felt —3H 23
Rochester Rd. Cars —1D 62
Rochester Rd. Stai —7F 20
Rochester Wlk. Reig —8M 121
Roche Wlk. Cars —5B 44
Rochford Way. Croy —5J 45
Rock Av. SW14 —6C 12
Rockdale Dri. Gray —6B 170
Rockery, The. F'boro —2J 89
Rockfield Clo. Oxt —9B 106
Rockfield Rd. Oxt —8B 106
Rockfield Way. Col T —7J 49
Rock Gdns. Alder —3L 109
Rockhampton Clo. SE27 —5L 29
Rockhampton Rd. SE27 —5L 29
Rockhampton Rd. S Croy —3B 64
Rock Hill. Hamb —8G 152
Rockingham Clo. SW15 —7E 12
Rockland Rd. SW15 —7K 13
Rock La. Wrec —6F 128
Rockshaw Rd. Red —5G 103
Rocks La. SW13 —4F 12
Rocky La. Mers —6D 102
Rocque Ho. SW6 —3L 13 (off Estcourt Rd.)
Rodborough Hill Cotts. Witl —3N 151
Roden Gdns. Croy —5B 46
Rodenhurst Rd. SW4 —1G 29
Rodgate La. Hasl —3A 190
Rodgers Ho. SW4 —1H 29 (off Clapham Pk. Est.)
Roding Clo. Cranl —8H 155
Rodmel Ct. F'boro —4C 90
Rodmill La. SW2 —1J 29
Rodney Clo. Croy —7M 45
Rodney Clo. N Mald —4D 42
Rodney Clo. W On T —7K 39
Rodney Gdns. W Wick —1C 66
Rodney Grn. W On T —8K 39
Rodney Pl. SW19 —9A 28
Rodney Rd. Mitc —2C 44
Rodney Rd. N Mald —4D 42
Rodney Rd. Twic —9A 10
Rodney Rd. W On T —8K 39
Rodney Way. Coln —4G 7
Rodney Way. Guild —2C 114
Rodona Rd. Wey —7E 56
Rodway Rd. SW15 —1F 26
Rodwell Ct. Add —1L 55
Roebuck Clo. Asht —7L 79
Roebuck Clo. Felt —5J 23
Roebuck Clo. H'ham —4A 198
Roebuck Clo. Reig —3M 121
Roebuck Est. Binf —8H 15
Roebuck Rd. Chess —2N 59
Roedean Cres. SW15 —9D 12
Roedeer Copse. Hasl —2C 188
Roehampton Clo. SW15 —7F 12
Roehampton Ga. SW15 —9D 12
Roehampton High St. SW15 —1F 26
Roehampton La. SW15 —7F 12
Roehampton Lane. (Junct.) —2G 27
Roehampton Vale. SW15 —4E 26
Roe Way. Wall —3J 63
Roffe's La. Cat —2A 104
Roffey Clo. Horl —8D 142
Roffey Clo. Purl —3M 83
Roffey's Clo. Copt —6L 163
Roffords. Wok —4L 73
Roffye Ct. H'ham —4N 197
Rogers Clo. Cat —9E 84
Rogers Clo. Coul —5M 83
Roger Simmons Ct. Bookh —2N 97
Rogers La. Warl —5J 85
Rogers Mead. God —1E 124
Rogers Rd. SW17 —5B 28
Rokeby Clo. Brack —9B 16
Rokeby Ct. Wok —4J 73
Rokeby Pl. SW20 —8G 27
Roke Clo. Kenl —1N 83
Roke Clo. Witl —5B 152
Roke La. Witl —6N 151
Roke Lodge Rd. Kenl —9M 63
Roke Rd. Kenl —2N 83
Rokers La. Shack —4A 132
Rokes Pl. Yat —9A 48
Roland Way. Wor Pk —8E 42
Rolinsden Way. Kes —2F 66
Rollesby Rd. Chess —3N 59
Rolleston Rd. S Croy —4A 64
Rollit Cres. Houn —8A 10
Rolston Ho. Hasl —2D 188
Romana Ct. Stai —5J 21
Romanby Ct. Red —4D 122
Roman Clo. Felt —8K 9
Romanfield Rd. SW2 —1K 29
Romanhurst Av. Brom —3N 47
Romanhurst Gdns. Brom —3N 47
Roman Ind. Est. Croy —6B 46
Roman Ride. Crowt —2C 48

Roman Rd. *Dork* —7G **119**
Roman Rd. *M Grn* —6M **147**
Romans Bus. Pk. *Farnh*
    —9J **109**
Romans Way. *Wok* —2J **75**
Roman Way. *Croy* —8M **45**
Roman Way. *Farnh* —8K **109**
Roman Way. *Warf* —9D **16**
Romany Gdns. *Sutt* —6M **43**
Romany Rd. *Knap* —2F **72**
Roma Read Clo. *SW15* —1G **26**
Romayne Clo. *F'boro* —9M **69**
Romberg Rd. *SW17* —4E **28**
Romeo Hill. *Warf* —9D **16**
Romeyn Rd. *SW16* —4H **29**
Romily Ct. *SW6* —5K **13**
Rommany Rd. *SE27* —5N **29**
  (in two parts)
Romney Clo. *Ashf* —6D **22**
Romney Clo. *Chess* —1L **59**
Romney Ho. *Brack* —3C **32**
Romney Lock Rd. *Wind* —3G **5**
Romney Rd. *N Mald* —5C **42**
Romola Rd. *SE24* —2M **29**
Romsey Clo. *Alder* —6A **110**
Romsey Clo. *B'water* —9H **49**
Romsey Clo. *Orp* —1K **67**
Romulus Ct. *Bren* —3K **11**
Rona Clo. *Craw* —6N **181**
Ronald Clo. *Beck* —4J **47**
Ronelean Rd. *Surb* —9M **41**
Ronneby Clo. *Wey* —9F **38**
Roof of the World Cvn. Pk. *Tad*
    —9A **100**
Rookeries Clo. *Felt* —4K **23**
Rookery Clo. *Fet* —2E **98**
Rookery Dri. *Westc* —7A **118**
Rookery Hill. *Asht* —5N **79**
Rookery Hill. *Out* —4L **143**
Rookery La. *Small* —6L **143**
Rookery Rd. *Croy* —6K **65**
Rookery Rd. *Stai* —6K **21**
Rookery, The. *Westc* —7A **118**
Rookery Way. *Tad* —5L **101**
Rook La. *Cat* —3K **103**
Rookley Clo. *Sun* —5N **61**
Rooks Hill. *Brmly* —9E **134**
Rooksmead Rd. *Sun* —1H **39**
Rookstone Rd. *SW17* —6D **28**
Rookswood. *Brack* —8N **15**
Rook Way. *H'ham* —2M **197**
Rookwood Av. *N Mald* —3F **42**
Rookwood Av. *Owl* —5K **49**
Rookwood Av. *Wall* —1H **63**
Rookwood Clo. *Mers* —7F **102**
Rookwood Ct. *Guild* —6M **113**
Rookwood Pk. *H'ham* —5E **196**
Roosthole Hill. *H'ham* —8C **198**
Roothill Rd. *Bet* —1N **139**
Ropeland Way. *H'ham* —1L **197**
Ropers Wlk. *SW2* —1L **29**
Roper Way. *Mitc* —1E **44**
Rope Wlk. *Sun* —2K **39**
Rorkes Drift. *Myt* —1D **90**
Rosa Av. *Ashf* —5B **22**
Rosalind Franklin Clo. *Sur R*
    —4H **113**
Rosaline Rd. *SW6* —3K **13**
Rosamund Clo. *S Croy* —1A **64**
Rosamund Rd. *Craw* —5F **182**
Rosamun St. *S'hall* —1M **9**
Rosary Clo. *Houn* —5M **9**
Rosary Gdns. *SW7* —1N **13**
Rosary Gdns. *Ashf* —5C **22**
Rosary Gdns. *Yat* —9C **48**
Rosaville Rd. *SW6* —3L **13**
Roseacre. *Oxt* —3C **126**
Roseacre Clo. *Shep* —4B **38**
Roseacre Gdns. *Chil* —9H **115**
Rose Av. *Mitc* —9D **28**
Rose Av. *Mord* —4A **44**
Rosebank. *Eps* —1B **80**
Rosebank Clo. *Tedd* —7G **25**
Rosebank Cotts. *Reig* —5N **121**
Rose Bank Cotts. *Wok* —9A **74**
Rosebay. *Wokgm* —9D **14**
Roseberry Av. *N Mald* —1E **42**
Roseberry Av. *T Hth* —1N **45**
Roseberry Gdns. *Orp* —1N **67**
Rosebery Av. *Eps* —1D **80**
Rosebery Cres. *Wok* —7B **74**
Rosebery Gdns. *Sutt* —1N **61**
Rosebery Rd. *SW2* —1J **29**
Rosebery Rd. *Eps* —6C **80**
Rosebery Rd. *Houn* —8C **10**
Rosebery Rd. *King T* —1A **42**
Rosebery Rd. *Sutt* —3L **61**
Rosebery Sq. *King T* —1A **42**
Rosebine Av. *Twic* —1D **24**
Rosebriar Clo. *Wok* —3J **75**
Rosebriars. *Cat* —7B **84**
Rosebriars. *Esh* —2C **58**
  (in two parts)
Rosebury Dri. *Bisl* —2D **72**
Rosebury Rd. *SW6* —5N **13**
Rosebushes. *Eps* —3H **81**
Rose Cotts. *Fay* —9H **181**
Rose Cotts. *F Row* —6G **187**
Rose Cotts. *Rusp* —2M **179**
Rose Cotts. *Worm* —8D **152**

Rose Ct. *Wokgm* —2B **30**
Rosecourt Rd. *Croy* —5K **45**
Rosecroft Clo. *Big H* —5H **87**
Rosecroft Gdns. *Twic* —2D **24**
Rose & Crown Pas. *Iswth*
    —4G **11**
Rosedale. *Alder* —2A **110**
Rosedale. *Asht* —5J **79**
Rosedale. *Binf* —6H **15**
Rosedale. *Cat* —1B **104**
Rosedale Clo. *Craw* —5M **181**
Rosedale Gdns. *Brack* —4M **31**
Rosedale Rd. *Eps* —2F **60**
Rosedale Rd. *Rich* —7L **11**
Rosedene Av. *SW16* —4K **29**
Rosedene Av. *Croy* —6J **45**
Rosedene Av. *Mord* —4M **43**
Rosedene Gdns. *Fleet* —3A **88**
Rosedene La. *Col T* —9J **49**
Rosedew Rd. *W6* —2J **13**
Rose End. *Wor Pk* —7J **43**
Rosefield Clo. *Cars* —2C **62**
Rosefield Gdns. *Ott* —3F **54**
Rosefield Rd. *Stai* —5J **21**
Rose Gdns. *F'boro* —2K **89**
Rose Gdns. *Felt* —3H **23**
Rose Gdns. *Stai* —1M **21**
Rose Gdns. *Wokgm* —2B **30**
Rosehatch Rd. *Houn* —8N **9**
Rose Hill. *Binf* —6H **15**
Rosehill. *Clay* —3G **58**
Rose Hill. *Dork* —5H **119**
Rosehill. *Hamp* —9A **24**
Rosehill. *Sutt* —8N **43**
Rose Hill Arch M. *Dork* —5H **119**
Rosehill Av. *Sutt* —7A **44**
Rosehill Av. *Wok* —3M **73**
Rosehill Ct. *Mord* —6A **44**
  (off St Helier Av.)
Rosehill Ct. Pde. *Mord* —6A **44**
  (off St Helier Av.)
Rosehill Farm Meadow. *Bans*
    —2N **81**
Rosehill Gdns. *Sutt* —8N **43**
Rose Hill Pk. W. *Sutt* —7A **44**
Rosehill Rd. *SW18* —9N **13**
Rosehill Rd. *Big H* —4E **86**
Rose Hill Roundabout. (Junct.)
    —6A **44**
Rose La. *Rip* —8L **75**
Roseleigh Clo. *Twic* —9K **11**
Rosemary Av. *Ash V* —5E **90**
Rosemary Av. *Houn* —5L **9**
Rosemary Av. *W Mol* —2A **40**
Rosemary Clo. *Croy* —5J **45**
Rosemary Clo. *F'boro* —1J **89**
Rosemary Clo. *Oxt* —2C **126**
Rosemary Ct. *Hasl* —1G **188**
Rosemary Ct. *Horl* —7C **142**
Rosemary Cres. *Guild* —8J **93**
Rosemary Gdns. *SW14* —6B **12**
Rosemary Gdns. *B'water*
    —1H **69**
Rosemary Gdns. *Chess* —1L **59**
Rosemary La. *SW14* —6B **12**
Rosemary La. *Alf* —9E **174**
Rosemary La. *B'water* —1H **69**
Rosemary La. *Charl* —3K **161**
  (in two parts)
Rosemary La. *Egh* —2D **36**
Rosemary La. *Horl* —9F **142**
Rosemary La. *Rowl* —7D **128**
Rosemead. *Cher* —6K **37**
Rosemead Av. *Felt* —3G **22**
Rosemead Av. *Mitc* —2G **45**
Rosemead Clo. *Red* —5B **122**
Rosemont Rd. *N Mald* —2B **42**
Rosemont Rd. *Rich* —9L **11**
Rosemount Av. *W Byf* —9J **55**
Rosendale Rd. *SE21* —4N **29**
Rosendale Rd. *SE24 & SE21*
    —1N **29**
Roseneath Dri. *C'fold* —5E **172**
Rose Pk. Cvn. Site. *Wdhm*
    —5G **54**
Rosery, The. *Croy* —5G **46**
Rosery, The. *Egh* —5A **36**
Rose's Cotts. *Dork* —5G **119**
  (off West St.)
Roses La. *Wind* —5A **4**
Rose St. *Wokgm* —2B **30**
Rosethorn Clo. *SW12* —1H **29**
Rosetrees. *Guild* —4C **114**
Rose View. *Add* —2L **55**
Roseville Av. *Houn* —8A **10**
Roseville Rd. *Hayes* —1H **9**
Rosevine Rd. *SW20* —9H **27**
Rose Wlk. *Fleet* —3A **88**
Rose Wlk. *Purl* —7H **63**
Rose Wlk. *Surb* —4A **42**
Rose Wlk. *W Wick* —8M **47**
Rosewarne Clo. *Wok* —5K **73**
Rosewood. *Surb* —6A **42**
Rosewood. *Th Dit* —8G **40**
Rosewood. *Wok* —6C **74**
Rosewood Dri. *Shep* —4A **38**
Rosewood Gro. *Sutt* —8A **44**
Rosewood Rd. *Lind* —4B **168**
Rosewood Way. *W End* —9B **52**
Roshni Ho. *SW17* —7C **28**

Rowan Ho. *Hay* —1N **47**
Rowan Rd. *SW16* —1G **45**
Rowan Rd. *W6* —1J **13**
Rowan Rd. *Bren* —3H **11**
Rowan Rd. *W Dray* —1M **7**
Rowans Clo. *F'boro* —5K **69**
Rowanside Clo. *Head* —5H **169**
Rowans, The. *Hind* —7B **170**
Rowans, The. *Sun* —6G **23**
Rowans, The. *Wok* —5A **74**
Rowan Ter. *W6* —1J **13**
  (off Rowan Rd.)
Rowan Wlk. *Brom* —1H **67**
Rowan Wlk. *Craw D* —1F **184**
Rowan Way. *H'ham* —3B **198**
Rowbarns Way. *E Hor* —8G **97**
Rowberry Clo. *SW6* —3H **13**
Rowbury. *G'ming* —3K **133**
Rowcroft Clo. *Ash V* —7E **90**
Rowden Rd. *Beck* —1H **47**
Rowden Rd. *Eps* —1A **60**
Rowdown Cres. *New Ad* —5N **65**
Rowe La. *Pirb* —2D **92**
Rowfant Clo. *Worth* —3J **183**
Rowfant Rd. *SW17* —2E **28**
Rowfield. *Eden* —9M **127**
Row Hill. *Add* —3H **55**
Rowhill Av. *Alder* —3L **109**
Rowhill Cres. *Alder* —4L **109**
Rowhills. *Farnh* —4J **109**
Rowhills Clo. *Farnh* —4L **109**
Rowhook Hill. *H'ham* —8N **177**
Rowhook Rd. *H'ham* —8N **177**
Rowhurst Av. *Add* —3K **55**
Rowhurst Av. *Lea* —4F **78**
Rowland Clo. *Copt* —5B **164**
Rowland Clo. *Wind* —6A **4**
Rowland Hill Almshouses. *Ashf*
  (off Feltham Hill Rd.) —6C **22**
Rowland Rd. *Cranl* —7M **155**
Rowlands Rd. *H'ham* —2N **197**
Rowland Way. *SW19* —9N **27**
Rowland Way. *Ashf* —8D **22**
Row La. *Alb* —6N **135**
Rowley Clo. *Brack* —2C **32**
Rowley Clo. *Pyr* —3K **75**
Rowley Ct. *Cat* —9A **84**
Rowley Edge. *Cranl* —4J **155**
Rowls Rd. *King T* —2M **41**
Rowly Dri. *Cranl* —5J **155**
Rowntree Rd. *Twic* —2E **24**
Rowplatt La. *Felb* —6H **165**
Row, The. *Cranl* —4J **155**
Rowtown. *Add* —4H **55**
Roxborough Av. *Iswth* —3F **10**
Roxburgh Clo. *Camb* —2G **71**
Roxburgh Rd. *SE27* —6M **29**
Roxby Pl. *SW6* —2M **13**
Roxeth Ct. *Ashf* —6B **22**
Roxford Clo. *Shep* —4F **38**
Roxton Gdns. *Croy* —2K **65**
Royal Aerospace Establishment.
    F'boro —3N **89**
Royal Aerospace Establishment
  Rd. *F'boro* —4N **89**
Royal Av. *Wor Pk* —8D **42**
Royal Cir. *SE27* —4L **29**
Royal Clo. *Wor Pk* —8D **42**
Royal Dri. *Eps* —5G **80**
Royale Clo. *Alder* —4A **110**
Royal Free Ct. *Wind* —4G **4**
Royal Horticultural Society Cotts.
  Wis —3N **75**
Royal M. *Wind C* —4G **5**
Royal Oak Clo. *Yat* —9D **48**
Royal Oak Hill. *Knock* —5N **87**
Royal Oak Rd. *Wok* —5M **73**
Royal Orchard Clo. *SW18*
    —1K **27**
Royal Pde. *SW6* —3K **13**
Royal Pde. *Hind* —5D **170**
Royal Pde. *Rich* —4N **11**
Royal Rd. *Tedd* —6D **24**
Royal Victoria Gdns. *S Asc*
    —3L **33**
Royal Victoria Patriotic Building.
  SW18 —1B **28**
Royal Wlk. *Wall* —8F **44**
Royce Rd. *Craw* —7E **162**
Roycroft Clo. *SW2* —2L **29**
Roydon Ct. *W on T* —1J **57**
Roy Gro. *Hamp* —7B **24**
Roymount Ct. *Twic* —4E **24**
Royston Av. *Byfl* —8N **55**
Royston Av. *Sutt* —9B **44**
Royston Av. *Wall* —1H **63**
Royston Cen., The. *Ash V*
    —5D **90**
Royston Clo. *Craw* —8E **162**
Royston Clo. *Houn* —4J **9**
Royston Clo. *W On T* —7H **39**
Royston Ct. *SE24* —1N **29**
Royston Ct. *Hin W* —8F **40**
Royston Ct. *Rich* —4M **11**
Royston Gdns. *Wokgm* —1A **48**
Royston Rd. *SE20* —1G **47**
Royston Rd. *Byfl* —8N **55**
Royston Rd. *Rich* —8L **11**
Roystons, The. *Surb* —4A **42**
Rozeldene. *Hind* —6C **170**
Rubus Clo. *W End* —9B **52**

Ruckmans La. *Oke H* —3A **178**
Rudd Hall Rise. *Camb* —3B **70**
Ruddlesway. *Wind* —4A **4**
  (in three parts)
Ruden Way. *Eps* —3G **80**
Rudge Rise. *Add* —2H **55**
Rudgwick Keep. *Horl* —7G **142**
  (off Langshott La.)
Rudgwick Rd. *Craw* —2L **181**
Rudloe Rd. *SW12* —1G **28**
Rudsworth Clo. *Coln* —3F **6**
Ruffetts Clo. *S Croy* —4E **64**
Ruffetts, The. *S Croy* —4E **64**
Ruffetts Way. *Tad* —5K **81**
Rufford Clo. *Fleet* —7B **88**
Rufwood. *Craw D* —1D **184**
Rugby Clo. *Owl* —6K **49**
Rugby La. *Sutt* —5J **61**
Rugby Rd. *Twic* —8E **10**
Ruggles-Brise Rd. *Ashf* —6M **21**
Rugosa Rd. *W End* —9B **52**
Ruislip St. *SW17* —5D **28**
Rumbold Rd. *SW6* —3N **13**
Rumsey Clo. *Hamp* —7N **23**
Runcorn Clo. *Bew* —7K **181**
Runes Clo. *Mitc* —3B **44**
Runfold St George. *Bad L*
    —7N **109**
Runnemede Rd. *Egh* —5C **20**
Running Horse Yd. *Bren* —2L **11**
Runnymede. *SW19* —9B **28**
Runnymede Clo. *Twic* —9B **10**
Runnymede Ct. *SW15* —2F **26**
Runnymede Ct. *Egh* —5C **20**
Runnymede Ct. *F'boro* —7M **69**
Runnymede Cres. *SW16*
    —9H **29**
Runnymede Gdns. *Twic* —9B **10**
Runnymede Ho. *Cher* —6J **37**
Runnymede Rd. *Twic* —9B **10**
Runsooke Ct. *Craw* —6M **181**
Runtley Wood La. *Sut G* —3B **94**
Runwick La. *Farnh* —3A **128**
Rupert Ct. *W Mol* —3A **40**
  (off St Peters Rd.)
Rupert Rd. *Guild* —4M **113**
Rural Way. *SW16* —8F **28**
Rural Way. *Red* —3E **122**
Ruscoe Dri. *Wok* —4C **74**
Ruscombe Gdns. *Dat* —2K **5**
Ruscombe Way. *Felt* —1G **22**
Rusham Ct. *Egh* —7C **20**
Rusham Pk. Av. *Egh* —7B **20**
Rusham Rd. *SW12* —1D **28**
Rusham Rd. *Egh* —7B **20**
Rushams Rd. *H'ham* —6H **197**
Rushbury Ct. *Hamp* —9A **24**
Rushcroft. *G'ming* —3K **133**
Rushdene Wlk. *Big H* —4F **86**
Rushden Way. *Farnh* —5J **109**
Rushen Wlk. *Cars* —7B **44**
Rushett Clo. *Th Dit* —7H **41**
Rushett Dri. *Dork* —8H **119**
Rushett La. *Chess & Eps* —7J **59**
Rushett Rd. *Th Dit* —6H **41**
Rushetts Pl. *Craw* —9A **162**
Rushetts Rd. *Craw* —9N **161**
Rushetts Rd. *Reig* —7A **122**
Rushey Clo. *N Mald* —3C **42**
Rushfords. *Ling* —6A **146**
Rushley Clo. *Kes* —1F **66**
Rushmead. *Rich* —4H **25**
Rushmead Clo. *Croy* —1C **64**
Rushmere Ct. *Wor Pk* —8F **42**
Rushmere Pl. *Egh* —6A **20**
Rushmon Gdns. *W On T* —8J **39**
Rushmon Pl. *Cheam* —3A **61**
Rushmoor Clo. *Fleet* —6B **88**
Rushmoor Clo. *Guild* —9J **93**
Rushmoor Clo. *F'boro* —5A **90**
Rushmoor Rd. *Alder* —8J **89**
Rusholme Rd. *SW15* —9J **13**
Rush, The. *SW19* —1L **43**
  (off Kingston Rd.)
Rushton Av. *S God* —7F **124**
Rushworth Rd. *Reig* —2M **121**
Rushy Meadow La. *Cars* —9C **44**
Ruskin Av. *Felt* —9G **9**
Ruskin Av. *Rich* —3N **11**
Ruskin Clo. *Craw* —9G **163**
Ruskin Dri. *Wor Pk* —8G **43**
Ruskin Mans. *W14* —2K **13**
  (off Queen's Club Gdns.)
Ruskin Rd. *Cars* —2D **62**
Ruskin Rd. *Croy* —8M **45**
Ruskin Rd. *Iswth* —6F **10**
Ruskin Rd. *Stai* —7H **21**
Ruskin Way. *SW19* —9B **28**
Rusper Ct. Cotts. *H'ham*
    —3D **180**
Rusper Rd. *Capel* —6J **159**
Rusper Rd. *H'ham* —4M **197**
Rusper Rd. *Newd & H'ham*
    —2A **160**
Rusper Rd. *Rusp & Crawl*
    —2F **180**
Ruspers Keep. *If'd* —2L **181**
Russell Clo. *W4* —2E **12**

Russell Clo. *Beck* —2M **47**
Russell Clo. *Brack* —5B **32**
Russell Clo. *Tad* —3F **100**
Russell Clo. *Wok* —2M **73**
Russell Ct. *SW16* —6K **29**
Russell Ct. *B'water* —1J **69**
Russell Ct. *Guild* —9M **93**
Russell Ct. *Hind* —5D **170**
Russell Ct. *Lea* —9H **79**
Russell Ct. *S Croy* —6L **63**
Russell Ct. Wall —2G 63
  (off Ross Rd.)
Russell Dri. *Stai* —9M **7**
Russell Gdns. *Rich* —3J **25**
Russell Gdns. *W Dray* —1B **8**
Russell Grn. Clo. *Purl* —6L **63**
Russell Hill. *Purl* —6K **63**
Russell Hill Pl. *Purl* —7L **63**
Russell Hill Rd. *Purl* —7L **63**
Russell Kerr Clo. *W4* —3B **12**
Russell Rd. *SW19* —8M **27**
Russell Rd. *Mitc* —2C **44**
Russell Rd. *Shep* —6D **38**
Russell Rd. *Twic* —9F **10**
Russell Rd. *W On T* —5H **39**
Russell Rd. *Wok* —2M **73**
Russells. *Tad* —9J **81**
Russells Cres. *Horl* —9E **142**
Russell's Footpath. *SW16*
    —6J **29**
Russell St. *Wind* —4G **4**
Russell Wlk. *Rich* —9M **11**
Russell Way. *Craw* —4E **182**
Russell Way. *Sutt* —2N **61**
Russell Yd. *SW15* —7K **13**
Russet Av. *Shep* —2F **38**
Russet Clo. *Horl* —8G **143**
Russet Clo. *Stai* —9M **7**
Russet Clo. *Tong* —5C **110**
Russet Dri. *Croy* —7H **47**
Russet Gdns. *Camb* —3B **70**
Russet Glade. *Alder* —4J **109**
Russett Clo. *H'ham* —5N **197**
Russetts Clo. *Wok* —2B **74**
Russetts Dri. *Fleet* —5B **88**
Russet Way. *N Holm* —8K **119**
Russ Hill. *Charl* —5F **160**
Russ Hill Rd. *Charl* —4J **161**
Russington Rd. *Shep* —5E **38**
Russley Grn. *Wokgm* —7A **30**
Rustall Clo. *Croy* —4F **46**
Rustic Av. *SW16* —8F **28**
Rustic Glen. *C Crook* —8A **88**
Rustington Wlk. *Mord* —6L **43**
Ruston Av. *Surb* —6A **42**
Ruston Clo. *M'bowr* —6G **182**
Ruston Way. *Asc* —1J **33**
Rutford Rd. *SW16* —6J **29**
Ruth Clo. *F'boro* —9H **69**
Ruthen Clo. *Eps* —1A **80**
Rutherford Clo. *Sutt* —3B **62**
Rutherford Clo. *Wind* —4C **4**
Rutherford Way. *Craw* —7E **162**
Rutherwick Clo. *Horl* —8D **142**
Rutherwick Rise. *Coul* —4J **83**
Rutherwick Tower. *Horl*
    —8D **142**
Rutherwyke Clo. *Eps* —3F **60**
Rutherwyke Rd. *Cher* —6G **36**
Rutland Clo. *SW14* —6A **12**
Rutland Clo. *SW19* —8C **28**
Rutland Clo. *Alder* —1M **109**
Rutland Clo. *Asht* —4L **79**
Rutland Clo. *Chess* —3M **59**
Rutland Clo. *Eps* —6C **60**
Rutland Clo. *Red* —2D **122**
Rutland Dri. *Mord* —5L **43**
Rutland Dri. *Rich* —2L **25**
Rutland Gdns. *Croy* —1B **64**
Rutland Gro. *W6* —1G **13**
Rutland Rd. *SW19* —8C **28**
Rutland Rd. *Hayes* —1E **8**
Rutland Rd. *Twic* —3D **24**
Rutland Ter. *Alder* —1M **109**
Rutlish Rd. *SW19* —9M **27**
Rutson Rd. *Byfl* —1N **76**
Rutter Gdns. *Mitc* —3A **44**
Rutton Hill Rd. *G'ming* —2H **171**
Ruvigny Gdns. *SW15* —6J **13**
Ruxbury Rd. *Cher* —5E **36**
Ruxley Clo. *Eps* —2A **60**
Ruxley Ct. *Wor Pk* —2B **60**
Ruxley Cres. *Clay* —3H **59**
Ruxley La. *Eps* —3A **60**
Ruxley M. *Eps* —2A **60**
Ruxley Ridge. *Clay* —4G **58**
Ruxley Towers. *Clay* —4G **59**
Ryan Ct. *SW16* —8J **29**
Ryan Dri. *Bren* —2G **11**
Ryan Mt. *Sand* —7F **48**
Ryarsh Cres. *Orp* —1N **67**
Rycroft. *Wind* —6C **4**
Rydal Clo. *Camb* —1H **71**
Rydal Clo. *F'boro* —2J **89**
Rydal Clo. *If'd* —5J **181**
Rydal Clo. *Purl* —9A **64**
Rydal Dri. *C Crook* —8A **88**
Rydal Gdns. *SW15* —6D **26**
Rydal Gdns. *Houn* —9B **10**

Rydal Pl.—St Peter's Gdns.

Rydal Pl. Light —7M 51
Rydal Rd. SW16 —5H 29
Rydal Way. Egh —8D 20
Ryde Clo. Rip —8L 75
Ryde Ct. Alder —3A 110
Ryde Gdns. Yat —9A 48
Ryde Heron. Knap —4H 73
Ryde Lands. Cranl —6A 156
Rydens Av. W On T —8J 39
Rydens Clo. W on T —8K 39
Rydens Gro. W On T —1L 57
Rydens Pk. W On T —8L 39
Rydens Rd. W On T —9J 39
Rydens Way. Wok —7C 74
Ryde Pl. Twic —9K 11
Ryders Way. H'ham —1M 197
Rydes Av. Guild —9J 93
Rydes Clo. Wok —7E 74
Ryde's Hill Cres. Guild —8J 93
Ryde's Hill Rd. Guild —1J 113
Ryde, The. Stai —9K 21
Ryde Vale Rd. SW12 —3G 28
Rydings. Wind —6C 4
Rydon's La. Coul —7N 83
Rydon's Wood Clo. Coul —7N 83
Rye Ash. Craw —2E 182
(in two parts)
Ryebeck Rd. C Crook —8B 88
Ryebridge Clo. Lea —5G 79
Ryebrook. Lea —7G 79
Ryebrook Rd. Lea —5G 79
Rye Clo. Brack —8B 16
Rye Clo. F'boro —8K 69
Rye Clo. Fleet —9D 68
Rye Clo. Guild —1H 113
Rye Croft. C Crook —9A 88
Ryecroft Av. Twic —1B 24
Ryecroft Dri. H'ham —5G 196
Ryecroft Gdns. B'water —2K 69
Ryecroft Lodge. SW16 —7M 29
Ryecroft Rd. SW16 —7L 29
Ryecroft St. SW6 —4N 13
Ryefield Path. SW15 —2F 26
Ryefield Rd. SE19 —7N 29
Rye Gro. Light —4C 52
Ryehurst La. Binf —5K 15
Ryeland Clo. Fleet —1D 88
Ryelands. Craw —4M 181
Ryelands. Horl —7G 142
Ryelands Clo. Cat —8B 84
Ryelands Ct. Lea —5G 79
Ryelands Pl. Wey —9F 38
Ryelaw Rd. C Crook —8B 88
Ryemead La. Wink —4G 17
Ryersh La. Capel —3H 159
Rye Wlk. SW15 —8J 13
Ryfold Rd. SW19 —4M 27
Ryland Clo. Felt —5G 23
Rylandes Rd. S Croy —5E 64
Ryle Rd. Farnh —3G 128
Rylston Rd. SW6 —2L 13
Rymer Rd. Croy —6B 46
Rysted La. W'ham —4L 107
Ryst Wood Rd. F Row —7K 187
Rythe Ct. Th Dit —6G 41
Rythe Rd. Clay —2D 58
Rythe, The. Esh —6B 58
Ryves Av. Yat —1A 68

Sabah Ct. Ashf —5B 22
Sable Clo. Houn —6K 9
Sabre Ct. Alder —2K 109
Sachel Ct. Dri. Alf —7H 175
Sachel Ct. M. Alf —7G 174
Sachel Ct. Rd. Duns —6F 174
Sachel Hill La. Duns —7F 174
Sackville Clo. E Grin —7M 165
Sackville Cotts. Red —2A 124
Sackville Ct. E Grin —1B 186
Sackville Gdns. E Grin —7M 165
(in two parts)
Sackville Ho. SW16 —4J 29
Sackville La. E Grin —7L 165
Sackville Rd. Sutt —4M 61
Saddleback Rd. Camb —7C 50
Saddleback Way. Fleet —1C 88
Saddlebrook Pk. Sun —8F 22
Saddler Row. Craw —6B 182
Saddlers Clo. Guild —2F 114
Saddlers M. Hamp W —1J 41
Saddlers Scarp. Gray —5M 169
Saddlers Way. Eps —6C 80
Saddlewood. Camb —2A 70
Sadler Clo. Mitc —1D 44
Sadlers Ride. W Mol —2B 40
Sadlers Way. Hasl —1H 189
Saffron Clo. Craw —6M 181
Saffron Clo. Croy —5J 45
Saffron Clo. Dat —4L 5
Saffron Ct. F'boro —1H 89
Saffron Ct. Felt —1D 22
Saffron Platt. Guild —8K 93
Saffron Rd. Brack —3N 31
Saffron Way. Surb —7K 41
Sage Wlk. Warf —8B 16
Sahara Clo. Farn —2M 67
Sailors La. Thur —8D 150
Sainfoin Rd. SW17 —3E 28
St Agatha's Dri. King T —7M 25
St Agatha's Gro. Cars —7D 44
St Agnes Rd. E Grin —8A 166
St Albans Av. Felt —6L 23
St Albans Av. Wey —9B 38
St Alban's Clo. Wind —4G 5
St Albans Clo. Wood S —2E 112
St Alban's Gdns. Tedd —6G 25
St Alban's Gro. Cars —6C 44
St Alban's Rd. King T —7L 25
St Alban's Rd. Reig —1M 121
St Alban's Rd. Sutt —1L 61
St Alban's St. Wind —4G 5
St Alban's Ter. W6 —2K 13
St Andrews. Brack —5K 31
St Andrews. Horl —9F 142
(off Aurum Clo.)
St Andrew's Av. Wind —5C 4
St Andrew's Clo. Crowt —1E 48
St Andrew's Clo. Iswth —4E 10
St Andrew's Clo. Old Win —9K 5
St Andrews Clo. Reig —4N 121
St Andrew's Clo. Shep —3E 38
St Andrews Clo. Wok —4M 73
St Andrews Clo. Wray —9A 6
St Andrew's Ct. SW18 —3A 28
St Andrews Ct. Sutt —9C 44
St Andrew's Cres. Wind —5C 4
St Andrews Gdns. Cobh —9K 57
St Andrews Ho. Reig —3M 121
St Andrews Mans. W14 —2K 13
(off St Andrews Rd.)
St Andrew's Rd. W14 —2K 13
St Andrew's Rd. Cars —9C 44
St Andrew's Rd. Coul —3E 82
St Andrew's Rd. Croy —1N 63
St Andrews Rd. If'd —4J 181
St Andrew's Rd. Surb —5K 41
St Andrew's Sq. Surb —5K 41
St Andrew's Wlk. Cobh —2J 77
St Andrew's Way. Frim —7D 70
St Andrews Way. Oxt —9G 107
St Anne's Av. Stai —1M 21
St Anne's Ct. W Wick —1A 66
St Anne's Dri. Red —2E 122
St Annes Dri. Wokgm —2F 30
St Annes Glade. Bag —4H 51
St Anne's Mt. Red —2E 122
St Anne's Pas. SW13 —6D 12
St Anne's Rise. Red —2E 122
St Annes Rd. Craw —9G 163
St Anne's Rd. G'ming —6K 133
St Anne's Way. Red —2E 122
St Ann's Clo. Cher —5H 37
St Ann's Cres. SW18 —9N 13
St Ann's Hill. SW18 —8N 13
St Ann's Hill Rd. Cher —5F 36
St Ann's Pk. Rd. SW18 —9N 13
St Ann's Rd. SW13 —5E 12
St Ann's Rd. Cher —5G 36
(in three parts)
St Anns Way. Berr G —3K 87
St Ann's Way. S Croy —3M 63
St Anthony's Clo. SW17 —3C 28
St Anthonys Clo. Brack —9M 15
St Anthony's Way. Felt —7G 9
St Arvan's Clo. Croy —9B 46
St Aubin Clo. Craw —7L 181
St Aubyn's Av. SW19 —6L 27
St Aubyn's Av. Houn —8A 10
St Aubyn's Clo. Orp —1N 67
St Augustine's Av. S Croy —3N 63
St Augustine's Clo. Alder —3B 110
St Austins. Gray —6B 170
St Barnabas Clo. Beck —1M 47
St Barnabas Ct. Craw —2G 182
St Barnabas Gdns. W Mol —4A 40
St Barnabas Rd. Mitc —8E 28
St Barnabas Rd. Sutt —2B 62
St Bartholomews Ct. Guild —5B 114
St Benedict's Clo. SW17 —6E 28
St Benedicts Clo. Alder —3M 109
St Benet's Clo. SW17 —3C 28
St Benet's Gro. Cars —6A 44
St Bernards. Croy —9B 46
St Bernard's Clo. SE27 —5N 29
St Brelades Clo. Dork —7G 119
St Brelades Rd. Craw —7L 181
St Catherines. Wey —9C 38
St Catherines. Wok —6M 73
St Catherine's Clo. SW17 —3C 28
St Catherine's Ct. Brmly —4B 134
St Catherines Ct. Felt —2H 23
St Catherines Ct. Stai —5J 21
St Catherine's Cross. Blet —3B 124
St Catherine's Dri. Guild —7L 113
St Catherine's Hill. Guild —7M 113
St Catherines Pk. Guild —5B 114
St Catherines Rd. Craw —9G 163
St Catherines Rd. Frim —5D 70
St Chads Clo. Surb —6J 41
St Charles Pl. Wey —2B 56
St Christopher's. Ling —7N 145
St Christopher's Clo. Hasl —2E 188
St Christopher's Clo. H'ham —4J 197
St Christopher's Clo. Iswth —4E 10
St Christophers Gdns. Asc —9H 17
St Christopher's Gdns. T Hth —2L 45
St Christopher's Grn. Hasl —2E 188
St Christopher's M. Wall —2G 62
St Christopher's Pl. F'boro —2L 89
St Christopher's Rd. F'boro —2M 89
St Christopher's Rd. Hasl —2E 188
St Clair Clo. Oxt —8M 105
St Clair Clo. Reig —3A 122
St Clair Dri. Wor Pk —9G 42
St Claire Cotts. Ling —1D 166
St Clair's Rd. Croy —8B 46
St Clare Bus. Pk. Hamp —7C 24
St Clement Rd. Craw —7L 181
St Clement's Ct. F'boro —7N 69
St Clements Mans. SW6 —2J 13
(off Lillie Rd.)
St Cloud Rd. SE27 —5N 29
St Crispins Way. Ott —5E 54
St Cross Rd. Farnh —9H 109
St Cross Rd. Frim G —7E 70
St Cuthberts Clo. Egh —6N 19
St Cyprian's St. SW17 —5D 28
St David's. Coul —4K 83
St David's Clo. F'boro —6L 69
St David's Clo. Farnh —5K 109
St David's Clo. Reig —2A 122
St David's Clo. W Wick —6L 47
St David's Dri. Egh —8M 19
St Denis Rd. SE27 —5N 29
St Denys Clo. Knap —5F 72
St Dionis Rd. SW6 —5L 13
St Dunstan's. (Junct.) —3L 61
St Dunstan's Clo. Hayes —1G 9
St Dunstan's Hill. Sutt —2K 61
St Dunstan's La. Beck —5M 47
St Dunstan's Rd. SE25 —3C 46
St Dunstan's Rd. W6 —1J 13
St Dunstan's Rd. Felt —4G 23
St Dunstan's Rd. Houn —5K 9
(in two parts)
St Edith Clo. Eps —1B 80
St Edmund Clo. Craw —9B 162
St Edmund's Clo. SW17 —3C 28
St Edmund's La. Twic —1B 24
St Edmund's Steps. G'ming —7G 133
St Edward's Clo. E Grin —9M 165
St Edward's Clo. New Ad —7N 65
St Elizabeth Dri. Eps —1B 80
St Faith's Rd. SE21 —2M 29
St Francis Gdns. Copt —6N 163
St Francis Wlk. Bew —5K 181
St George's Av. Wey —3C 56
St Georges Bus. Pk. Wey —5B 56
St George's Clo. Bad L —6N 109
St Georges Clo. Horl —8F 142
St George's Clo. Wey —2D 56
St Georges Clo. Wind —4B 4
St George's Ct. SW15 —7L 13
St Georges Ct. Add —1L 55
St George's Ct. Craw —2B 182
St Georges Ct. E Grin —7M 165
St Georges Ct. Owl —5K 49
St George's Gdns. Eps —1E 80
St George's Gdns. H'ham —4L 197
St George's Gdns. Surb —8A 42
St George's Gro. SW17 —4B 28
St George's Hill. Red —2H 143
St George's Ind. Est. Camb —3N 69
St George's Ind. Est. King T —6K 25
St George's La. Asc —2M 33
St George's M. Farnh —9G 109
(off Bear La.)
St George's Pl. Twic —2G 25
St George's Rd. SW19 —7L 27
(in two parts)
St George's Rd. Add —1L 55
St George's Rd. Alder —3N 109
St George's Rd. Bad L —6N 109
(in two parts)
St George's Rd. Beck —1L 47
St George's Rd. Camb —9B 50
St George's Rd. Farnh —2J 129
St George's Rd. Felt —5L 23
St George's Rd. King T —8N 25
St George's Rd. Mitc —2F 44
St George's Rd. Red —2H 143
St Georges Rd. Rich —6M 11
St George's Rd. Twic —8H 11
St George's Rd. Wall —2F 62
St George's Rd. Wey —3E 56
St George's Rd. E. Alder —3N 109
St George's Sq. N Mald —2D 42
St George's Wlk. Croy —9N 45
St George's Yd. Farnh —1G 129
(off Castle St.)
St Giles Clo. Orp —2M 67
St Gothard Rd. SE27 —5N 29
St Helens. Th Dit —6F 40
St Helen's Cres. SW16 —9K 29
St Helens Cres. Sand —7G 48
St Helen's Rd. SW16 —9K 29
St Helier Av. Mord —6A 44
St Helier Clo. Craw —7M 181
St Helier Clo. Wokgm —5A 30
St Helier's Av. Houn —8A 10
St Hilda's Av. Ashf —6N 21
St Hilda's Clo. SW17 —3C 28
St Hilda's Clo. Craw —9G 163
St Hilda's Clo. Horl —8F 142
St Hilda's Clo. Knap —4G 73
St Hilda's Rd. SW13 —2G 12
Saint Hill Grn. E Grin —5M 185
Saint Hill Rd. E Grin —3L 185
St Hughes Clo. SW17 —3C 28
St Hughs Clo. Craw —9G 163
St Ives. Craw —2G 182
St James Av. Beck —2H 47
St James Av. Eps —7E 60
St James' Av. Farnh —9J 109
St James Av. Sutt —2M 61
St James Clo. Eps —1D 80
St James Clo. N Mald —4E 42
St James Clo. Wok —5K 73
St James Ct. Asht —4K 79
St James' Ct. Farnh —9H 109
St James M. Wey —1C 56
St James Rd. Cars —9C 44
St James Rd. E Grin —9N 165
St James Rd. Fleet —5A 88
St James' Rd. King T —1K 41
St James Rd. Mitc —8E 28
St James Rd. Purl —9M 63
St James Rd. Sutt —2M 61
St James's Av. Beck —2H 47
St James's Av. Hamp —6C 24
St James's Clo. SW17 —3D 28
St James's Cotts. Rich —8K 11
St James's Ct. King T —2L 41
St James's Dri. SW17 & SW12 —2D 28
St James's Pk. Croy —6N 45
St James's Pl. Cranl —7L 155
St James's Rd. Croy —6M 45
St James's Rd. Hamp —6B 24
St James's Rd. Surb —5K 41
St James St. W6 —1H 13
St James Ter. SW12 —2E 28
St James' Ter. Farnh —9H 109
St James Wlk. Craw —8A 182
St Joan Clo. Craw —9B 162
St John Clo. H'ham —7L 197
St John's. N Holm —9J 119
St John's. Red —5C 122
St John's Av. SW15 —8J 13
St John's Av. Eps —8F 60
St John's Av. Lea —8H 79
St Johns Chu. Rd. Dork —8N 117
St John's Clo. SW6 —3M 13
St John's Clo. E Grin —8A 166
St John's Clo. Guild —4K 113
St John's Clo. Lea —7J 79
St John's Ct. W6 —1G 13
(off Glenthorne Rd.)
St John's Ct. Brkwd —7C 72
St John's Ct. Egh —6C 20
St John's Ct. F'boro —9J 69
St John's Ct. Iswth —5F 10
St Johns Ct. S God —7J 125
St John's Ct. St J —6K 73
St John's Ct. Westc —6C 118
(off St John's Rd.)
St John's Cres. Broad H —5E 196
St Johns Dri. SW18 —2N 27
St John's Dri. W On T —7K 39
St John's Dri. Wind —5D 4
St John's Gro. SW13 —5E 12
St John's Gro. Rich —7L 11
St John's Hill. Coul —4L 83
(in two parts)
St John's Hill. Purl —3L 83
St John's Hill Rd. Wok —6K 73
St John's Lye. Wok —6J 73
St John's Meadow. Blind H —3G 145
St John's M. Wok —6K 73
St John's Pas. SW19 —7K 27
St Johns Rise. Berr G —3K 87
St John's Rise. Wok —6L 73
St John's Rd. SW19 —8K 27
St John's Rd. Asc —8H 17
St John's Rd. Cars —9C 44
St John's Rd. Craw —3A 182
St John's Rd. Croy —9M 45
St John's Rd. E Grin —8A 166
St John's Rd. E Mol —3D 40
St John's Rd. F'boro —9K 69
St John's Rd. Farnh —3G 129
St John's Rd. Felt —5M 23
St John's Rd. Guild —4J 113
St John's Rd. Iswth —5E 10
St John's Rd. King T —1J 41
St John's Rd. Lea —8J 79
St John's Rd. N Mald —2B 42
St John's Rd. Red —5D 122
St John's Rd. Rich —7L 11
St John's Rd. Sand —8G 49
St John's Rd. Sutt —8N 43
St John's Rd. Westc —6C 118
St John's Rd. Wind —5D 4
St John's Rd. Wok —5K 73
St John's St. G'ming —5J 133
St John's Ter. Rd. Red —5D 122
St Joseph's Rd. Alder —3M 109
St Jude's Clo. Egh —6M 19
St Jude's Rd. Egh —5M 19
St Julian's Clo. SW16 —5L 29
St Julian's Farm Rd. SE27 —5L 29
St Katherines Rd. Cat —3D 104
St Lawrence Bus. Cen. Twic —3J 23
St Lawrence Ct. Chob —7H 53
St Lawrence Ho. Chob —7H 53
(off Bagshot Rd.)
St Lawrence's Way. Reig —3M 121
St Lawrence Way. Cat —1N 103
St Leonard's Av. Wind —5F 4
St Leonard's Dri. Craw —5E 182
St Leonard's Gdns. Houn —4M 9
St Leonard's Hill. Wind —7A 4
St Leonards Pk. E Grin —9N 165
St Leonard's Rise. Orp —1N 67
St Leonard's Rd. SW14 —6A 12
St Leonard's Rd. Clay —3F 58
St Leonard's Rd. Croy —9M 45
St Leonard's Rd. Eps —6H 81
St Leonard's Rd. H'ham —8L 197
St Leonard's Rd. Surb —4K 41
St Leonard's Rd. Th Dit —5G 40
St Leonard's Rd. Wind —6D 4
(Windsor)
St Leonard's Rd. Wind —9A 4
(Windsor Safari Park)
St Leonards Sq. Surb —4K 41
St Leonard's Wlk. SW16 —8K 29
St Louis Rd. SE27 —5N 29
St Luke's Clo. SE25 —5E 46
St Luke's Pas. King T —9M 25
St Luke's Rd. Old Win —9K 5
St Luke's Rd. Whyt —5C 84
St Lukes Sq. Guild —4B 114
St Margaret Dri. Eps —1B 80
St Margaret's. Guild —3B 114
St Margaret's Av. Ashf —6C 22
St Margarets Av. Berr G —3K 87
St Margaret's Av. Dor P —4B 166
St Margaret's Av. Sutt —9K 43
St Margarets Bus. Cen. Twic —9H 11
St Margarets Cotts. Fern —9F 188
St Margaret's Cres. SW15 —8G 13
St Margaret's Dri. Twic —8H 11
St Margaret's Gro. Twic —9G 11
St Margaret's Rd. Coul —8F 82
St Margaret's Rd. E Grin —7B 166
St Margarets Rd. Iswth & Twic —7H 11
St Mark's Clo. F'boro —4A 90
St Mark's Gro. SW10 —2N 13
St Mark's Hill. Surb —5L 41
St Mark's La. H'ham —2K 197
St Mark's Pl. SW19 —7L 27
St Marks Pl. Farnh —5G 109
St Marks Pl. Wind —5F 4
St Mark's Rd. SE25 —3D 46
St Mark's Rd. Binf —8H 15
St Mark's Rd. Eps —5H 81
St Marks Rd. Mitc —1D 44
St Mark's Rd. Tedd —8H 25
St Marks Rd. Wind —5F 4
St Martha's Av. Wok —8B 74
St Marthas Ct. Chil —9D 114
St Martin's Av. Eps —1D 80
St Martins Clo. E Hor —7F 96
St Martins Clo. Eps —9D 60
St Martin's Ct. Ashf —6L 21
St Martin's Ct. E Hor —7F 96
St Martin's Dri. W On T —9K 39
St Martins Est. SW2 —2L 29
St Martins M. Dork —5G 119
St Martins M. Pyr —3J 75
St Martin's Wlk. Dork —4H 119
St Martins Way. SW17 —4A 28
St Mary Av. Wall —9F 44
St Marys. Wey —9E 38
St Mary's Av. Brom —2N 47
St Mary's Av. S'hall —1B 10
St Mary's Av. Stai —1M 21
St Mary's Av. Tedd —7F 24
St Mary's Clo. Chess —4M 59
St Mary's Clo. Eps —4E 60
St Mary's Clo. Fet —1D 98
St Mary's Clo. Oxt —7A 106
St Mary's Clo. Sand —7H 49
St Mary's Clo. Stai —1M 21
St Mary's Clo. Sun —3H 39
St Mary's Ct. Wall —1G 62
St Mary's Cres. Iswth —3D 10
St Mary's Cres. Stai —1M 21
St Mary's Dri. Craw —1F 182
St Mary's Dri. Felt —1D 22
St Marys Garden. Worp —6H 93
St Mary's Gdns. Bag —4J 51
St Mary's Gdns. H'ham —7J 197
St Mary's Grn. Big H —5E 86
St Mary's Gro. SW13 —6G 12
St Mary's Gro. W4 —2A 12
St Mary's Gro. Big H —5E 86
St Mary's Gro. Rich —7M 11
St Mary's Hill. Asc —5N 33
St Mary's La. Wink —4H 17
St Marys M. Rich —3J 25
St Marys Mill. C'fold —6E 172
St Mary's Rd. SE25 —2B 46
St Mary's Rd. SW19 —6K 27
St Mary's Rd. Asc —6M 33
St Mary's Rd. Ash V —8E 90
St Mary's Rd. Camb —9A 50
St Mary's Rd. Dit H —6J 41
St Mary's Rd. E Mol —4D 40
St Mary's Rd. Lea —9H 79
St Mary's Rd. Reig —4N 121
St Mary's Rd. S Croy —6A 64
St Mary's Rd. Surb —5K 41
St Mary's Rd. Wey —1E 56
St Mary's Rd. Wok —4M 73
St Mary's Rd. Wor Pk —8D 42
St Mary's Wlk. Blet —2A 124
St Mary's Wlk. H'ham —7J 197
St Matthew's Av. Surb —7L 41
St Matthew's Pl. Cat —1A 104
St Matthew's Rd. Red —2D 122
St Maur Rd. SW6 —4L 13
St Michael's Av. Guild —7F 92
St Michaels Clo. Fleet —5C 88
St Michael's Clo. W On T —8K 39
St Michael's Clo. Wor Pk —8E 42
St Michael's Ct. Wey —2D 56
(off Princes Rd.)
St Michael's Rd. Alder —3N 109
St Michaels Rd. Ashf —6B 22
St Michael's Rd. Camb —1N 69
St Michael's Rd. Cat —9A 84
St Michael's Rd. Croy —7N 45
St Michaels Rd. E Grin —8A 166
St Michael's Rd. F'boro —8N 69
St Michael's Rd. Sand —7E 48
St Michael's Rd. Wall —3G 62
St Michael's Rd. Wok —1F 74
St Mildred's Rd. Guild —2B 114
St Monica's Rd. Tad —8L 81
St Nazaire Clo. Egh —6F 20
St Nicholas Av. Bookh —3B 98
St Nicholas Cen. Sutt —2N 61
St Nicholas Clo. Fleet —4A 88
St Nicholas Ct. Craw —2G 182
St Nicholas Cres. Pyr —3J 75
St Nicholas Dri. Shep —6B 38
St Nicholas Glebe. SW17 —7E 28
St Nicholas Hill. Lea —9H 79
St Nicholas Rd. Sutt —2N 61
St Nicholas Rd. Th Dit —5F 40
St Nicholas Way. Sutt —1N 61
St Nicolas Av. Cranl —7N 155
St Nicolas Clo. Cranl —7N 155
St Normans Way. Eps —6F 60
St Olaf's Rd. SW6 —3K 13
St Olaves Clo. Stai —8H 21
St Olaves Wlk. SW16 —1G 45
St Omer Barracks. Alder —8B 90
St Omer Ridge. Guild —4C 114
St Omer Rd. Guild —4C 114
St Oswald's Rd. SW16 —9M 29
St Paul's Clo. Add —2J 55
St Paul's Clo. Ashf —6D 22
St Paul's Clo. Cars —7C 44
St Paul's Clo. Chess —1K 59
St Paul's Clo. Hayes —1E 8
St Paul's Clo. Houn —5M 9
St Paul's Ct. Houn —6M 9
St Paul's Ga. Wokgm —1A 30
St Paul's Rd. Bren —2K 11
St Paul's Rd. Rich —6M 11
St Paul's Rd. Stai —6F 20
St Paul's Rd. T Hth —2N 45
St Paul's Rd. Wok —4C 74
St Paul's Rd. E. Dork —5H 119
St Paul's Rd. W. Dork —6G 119
St Paul's Studios. W14 —1K 13
(off Talgarth Rd.)
St Paul's Wlk. King T —8N 25
St Peters Av. Berr G —3K 87
St Peter's Clo. SW17 —3C 28
St Peter's Clo. Old Win —8K 5
St Peter's Clo. Stai —7H 21
St Peter's Clo. Wok —7E 74
St Peters Ct. W Mol —3A 40
St Peter's Gdns. SE27 —4L 29

St Peters Gdns.—Settrington Rd.

St Peters Gdns. *Wrec* —5E **128**
St Peter's Gdns. *Yat* —9C **48**
St Peter's Gro. *W6* —1F **12**
St Peters Mead. *Ash* —2F **110**
St Peters Pk. *Alder* —4K **109**
St Peter's Rd. *W6* —1F **12**
St Peter's Rd. *Craw* —3A **182**
St Peter's Rd. *Croy* —1A **64**
St Peter's Rd. *King T* —1N **41**
St Peter's Rd. *Twic* —8H **11**
St Peter's Rd. *W Mol* —3A **40**
St Peter's Rd. *Wok* —7D **74**
St Peter's Sq. *W6* —1E **12**
St Peter's St. *S Croy* —2A **64**
St Peter's Ter. *SW6* —3L **13**
St Peter's Vs. *W6* —1F **12**
St Peter's Way. *Cher & Add* —1F **54**
St Peter's Way. *Frim* —7D **70**
St Peter's Way. *Hayes* —1E **8**
St Peter's Wharf. *W4* —1F **12**
St Philip's Av. *Wor Pk* —8G **42**
St Philips Ct. *Fleet* —4B **88**
St Phillips Rd. *Surb* —5K **41**
St Pier's La. *Ling & Eden* —8B **146**
St Pinnock Av. *Stai* —9J **21**
St Sampson Rd. *Craw* —7L **181**
St Saviour's College. *SE27* —5N **29**
St Saviours Pl. *Guild* —3M **113**
St Saviour's Rd. *Croy* —5N **45**
Saints Clo. *SE27* —5M **29**
St Sebastian's Clo. *Wokgm* —9D **30**
St Simon's Av. *SW15* —8H **13**
St Stephen Clo. *Craw* —9B **162**
St Stephen's Av. *Asht* —3L **79**
St Stephens Clo. *Hasl* —2D **188**
[illegible]
St Stephen's Gdns. *SW15* —8L **13**
St Stephen's Gdns. *Twic* —9J **11**
St Stephen's Pas. *Twic* —9J **11**
St Stephen's Rd. *Houn* —9A **10**
St Stephen's Wlk. *SW7* —1N **13**
St Stevens Clo. *Hasl* —1G **188**
St Swithun's Clo. *E Grin* —9B **166**
St Theresa Clo. *Eps* —1B **80**
St Theresa's Rd. *Felt* —7G **9**
St Thomas Clo. *Surb* —7M **41**
St Thomas Clo. *Wok* —4M **73**
St Thomas Rd. *W4* —2B **12**
St Thomas's Dri. *Guild* —9N **95**
St Thomas's M. *Guild* —5B **114**
St Thomas's Way. *SW6* —3L **13**
St Thomas Wlk. *Coln* —3F **6**
St Vincent Clo. *SE27* —6M **29**
St Vincent Clo. *Craw* —4H **183**
St Vincent Rd. *Twic* —9C **10**
St Vincent Rd. *W On T* —9J **39**
St Winifreds. *Kenl* —2N **83**
St Winifred's Rd. *Big H* —5H **87**
St Winifred's Rd. *Tedd* —7H **25**
Salamanca. *Crowt* —2D **48**
Salamanca Pk. *Alder* —1L **109**
Salamander Clo. *King T* —6J **25**
Salamander Quay. *King T* —9K **25**
Salbrook Rd. *Salf* —2E **142**
Salcombe Dri. *Mord* —7J **43**
Salcombe Rd. *Ashf* —5N **21**
Salcot Cres. *New Ad* —6M **65**
Salcott Rd. *Croy* —9J **45**
Sale Garden Cotts. *Wokgm* —3B **30**
Salehurst Rd. *Worth* —3J **183**
Salem Pl. *Croy* —9N **45**
Salerno Clo. *Alder* —1M **109**
Sales Ct. *Alder* —3L **109**
Salesian View. *F'boro* —5C **90**
Salford Rd. *SW2* —2H **29**
Salfords Ind. Est. *Red* —3E **142**
Salfords Way. *Red* —2E **142**
Salisbury Av. *Sutt* —3L **61**
Salisbury Clo. *Wokgm* —6A **30**
Salisbury Clo. *Wor Pk* —9E **42**
Salisbury Ct. *Cars* —2D **62**
Salisbury Gdns. *SW19* —8K **27**
Salisbury Gro. *Myt* —1D **90**
Salisbury M. *SW6* —3L **13**
Salisbury Pas. SW6 —3L 13 (off Dawes Rd.)
Salisbury Pl. *W Byf* —7L **55**
Salisbury Rd. *SE25* —5D **46**
Salisbury Rd. *SW19* —8K **27**
Salisbury Rd. *Ash* —1E **110**
Salisbury Rd. *Bans* —1N **81**
Salisbury Rd. *B'water* —2H **69**
Salisbury Rd. *Cars* —3D **62**
Salisbury Rd. *Craw* —7C **182** (in two parts)
Salisbury Rd. *F'boro* —1A **90**
Salisbury Rd. *Felt* —2K **23**
Salisbury Rd. *God* —9F **104**
Salisbury Rd. *H'ham* —8G **196**
Salisbury Rd. *Houn* —6K **9**
Salisbury Rd. *H'row A* —8D **8**
Salisbury Rd. *N Mald* —2C **42**
Salisbury Rd. *Rich* —7L **11**
Salisbury Rd. *Wok* —6A **74**
Salisbury Rd. *Wor Pk* —1C **60**
Salisbury Ter. *Myt* —2E **90**
Salix Clo. *Sun* —8J **23**
Salliesfield. *Twic* —9D **10**
Salmons La. *Whyt* —7B **84**
Salmons La. W. *Cat* —7B **84**
Salmons Rd. *Chess* —3L **59**
Salmons Rd. *Eff* —7J **97**
Saltash Clo. *Sutt* —1L **61**
Saltbox Hill. *Big H* —9D **66**
Salt Box Rd. *Guild* —7J **93**
Saltdean Clo. *Craw* —6B **182**
Salterford Rd. *SW17* —7E **28**
Salterns Rd. *M'bowr* —6G **182**
Salter's Hill. *SE19* —6N **29**
Saltire Gdns. *Brack* —9M **15**
Salt La. *Hyde* —4G **153**
Saltram Rd. *F'boro* —3C **90**
Salvador. *SW17* —6D **28**
Salvation Pl. *Lea* —2G **98**
Salvia Ct. *Bisl* —3D **72**
Salvington Rd. *Craw* —6L **181**
Salvin Rd. *SW15* —6J **13**
Salwey Clo. *Brack* —5N **31**
Samaritan Clo. *Bew* —5K **181**
Samarkand Clo. *Camb* —2F **70**
Samels Ct. *W6* —1F **12**
Samian Pl. *Binf* —8K **15**
Samos Rd. *SE20* —1E **46**
Samphire Clo. *Craw* —6M **181**
Sampleoak La. *Chil* —9G **114**
Sampson Pk. *Binf* —9J **15**
Sampson's Almshouses. *Farnh* —2E **128**
Sampsons Ct. *Shep* —4D **38**
Samuel Johnson Clo. *SW16* —5K **29**
Samuel Lewis Trust Dwellings. [illegible]
Samuel Lewis Trust Dwellings. (off Lisgar Ter.) W14 —1L 13
San Carlos App. *Alder* —2A **110**
Sanctuary Rd. *H'row A* —9B **8**
Sanctuary, The. *Mord* —5M **43**
Sandal Rd. *N Mald* —4C **42**
Sandalwood. *Guild* —4L **113**
Sandalwood Av. *Cher* —9G **36**
Sandalwood Rd. *Felt* —4J **23**
Sandbanks. *Felt* —2F **22**
Sandbourne Av. *SW19* —1N **43**
Sandcross La. *Reig* —6L **121**
Sandell's Av. *Ashf* —5D **22**
Sandeman Way. *H'ham* —8L **197**
Sanders Clo. *Hamp* —6C **24**
Sandersfield Gdns. *Bans* —2M **81**
Sandersfield Rd. *Bans* —2N **81**
Sanderstead Clo. *SW12* —1G **28**
Sanderstead Ct. Av. *S Croy* —9D **64**
Sanderstead Hill. *S Croy* —7B **64**
Sanderstead Rd. *S Croy* —4A **64**
Sandes Pl. *Lea* —5G **79**
Sandfield Gdns. *T Hth* —2M **45**
Sandfield Rd. *T Hth* —2M **45**
Sandfields. *Send* —2F **94**
Sandfield Ter. *Guild* —4N **113**
Sandford Ct. *Alder* —3L **109**
Sandford Down. *Brack* —4D **32**
Sandford Rd. *Alder* —3L **109**
Sandford Rd. *Farnh* —5G **109**
Sandford St. *SW6* —3N **13**
Sandgate La. *SW18* —2C **28**
Sandhawes Hill. *E Grin* —6C **166**
Sandheath Rd. *Hind* —2A **170**
Sand Hill. *F'boro* —7N **69**
Sand Hill Ct. *F'boro* —7N **69**
Sandhill La. *Craw D* —2E **184**
Sandhills. *Wall* —1H **63**
Sandhills. *Wmly* —9A **152** (in two parts)
Sandhills Ct. *Vir W* —4A **36**
Sandhills La. *Vir W* —4A **36**
Sandhills Meadow. *Shep* —6D **38**
Sandhills Rd. *Reig* —4M **121**
Sandhurst Av. *Surb* —6A **42**
Sandhurst Clo. *S Croy* —5B **64**
Sandhurst-Crowthorne By-Pass. *Crowt* —9K **31**
Sandhurst-Crowthorne By-Pass. *Sand* —1K **69**
Sandhurst La. *B'water* —9G **48**
Sandhurst Rd. *Crowt* —4G **49**
Sandhurst Rd. *Finch* —8A **30**
Sandhurst Rd. *Yat* —8E **48**
Sandhurst Way. *S Croy* —4B **64**
Sandiford Rd. *Sutt* —8L **43**
Sandilands. *Croy* —8D **46**
Sandilands Rd. *SW6* —4N **13**
Sandlands Gro. *Tad* —1F **100**
Sandlands Rd. *Tad* —1F **100**
Sandon Clo. *Esh* —6D **40**
Sandown Av. *Esh* —2C **58**
Sandown Clo. *B'water* —1J **69**
Sandown Clo. *Houn* —4H **9**
Sandown Ct. Red —2C 122 (off Station Rd.)
Sandown Ct. *Sutt* —4N **61**
Sandown Cres. *Alder* —5N **109**
Sandown Dri. *Cars* —5E **62**
Sandown Dri. *Frim* —4B **70**
Sandown Ga. *Esh* —8D **40**
Sandown Ind. Pk. *Esh* —8A **40**
Sandown Lodge. *Eps* —1C **80**
Sandown Rd. *SE25* —4E **46**
Sandown Rd. *Coul* —3E **82**
Sandown Rd. *Esh* —1C **58**
Sandpiper Clo. *If'd* —5J **181**
Sandpiper Rd. *S Croy* —7G **64**
Sandpit Cotts. *Pirb* —9B **72**
Sandpit Hall Rd. *Chob* —8K **53**
Sandpit Heath. *Guild* —8G **92**
Sandpit La. *Knap* —2F **72**
Sandpit Rd. *Red* —4C **122**
Sandpit Site. *Wey* —6B **56**
Sandpits Rd. *Croy* —1G **64**
Sandpits Rd. *Rich* —3K **25**
Sandra Clo. *Houn* —8B **10**
Sandringham Av. *SW20* —9K **27**
Sandringham Clo. *SW19* —1J **27**
Sandringham Clo. *E Grin* —1C **186**
Sandringham Clo. *Wok* —3J **75**
Sandringham Ct. *Sutt* —5M **61**
Sandringham Dri. *Ashf* —5M **21**
Sandringham Gdns. *Houn* —4H **9**
Sandringham Pk. *Cobh* —8A **58**
Sandringham Rd. *Craw* —7N **181**
Sandringham Rd. *H'row A* —8N **7**
Sandringham Rd. *T Hth* —4N **45**
Sandringham Rd. *Wor Pk* —9F **42**
Sandringham Way. *Frim* —6D **70**
Sandrock. *Hasl* —2G **188**
[illegible]
Sandrock Pl. *Croy* —1G **64**
Sandrock Rd. *Westc* —7B **118**
Sandroyd Way. *Cobh* —9A **58**
Sands Clo. *Seale* —1B **130**
Sand's End La. *SW6* —4N **13**
Sands Rd. *Runf* —9A **110**
Sandy Bury. *Orp* —1M **67**
Sandy Clo. *Wok* —4E **74**
Sandycombe Rd. *Felt* —2H **23**
Sandycombe Rd. *Rich* —6M **11**
Sandycoombe Rd. *Twic* —9J **11**
Sandy Croft. *Eps* —6H **61**
Sandy Dri. *Cobh* —7A **58**
Sandy Dri. *Felt* —2F **22**
Sandy Hill Rd. *Farnh* —5F **108**
Sandy Hill Rd. *Wall* —5G **62**
Sandy Holt. *Cobh* —9N **57**
Sandy La. *Alb* —1L **135**
Sandy La. *Bet* —4D **120**
Sandy La. *Blet* —1M **123**
Sandy La. *Brack* —9A **16**
Sandy La. *Camb* —9C **50**
Sandy La. *Chob* —5H **53**
Sandy La. *C Crook* —9B **88**
Sandy La. *Cobh & Oxs* —8N **57**
Sandy La. *Craw D* —1C **184**
Sandy La. *E Grin* —9A **166**
Sandy La. *F'boro* —8H **69**
Sandy La. *G'ming* —5G **133**
Sandy La. *G'wood* —8J **171**
Sandy La. *Guild* —8K **113**
Sandy La. *Hasl* —1A **188**
Sandy La. *Kgswd* —2L **101**
Sandy La. *Limp* —5D **106**
Sandy La. *Mitc* —9E **28**
Sandy La. *Norm* —9B **92**
Sandy La. *N Asc* —9G **16**
Sandy La. *Nutf* —4H **123**
Sandy La. *Oxt* —7M **105**
Sandy La. *Pyr* —4J **75**
Sandy La. *Reig* —4G **120**
Sandy La. *Rich* —3J **25**
Sandy La. *Sand* —6E **48**
Sandy La. *Send* —1E **94**
Sandy La. *Shere* —8B **116**
Sandy La. *S'dale* —4D **34**
Sandy La. *Sutt* —4K **61**
Sandy La. *Tedd & King T* —8G **25**
Sandy La. *Tilf* —4M **149**
Sandy La. *Vir W* —3A **36**
Sandy La. *W On T* —5J **39**
Sandy La. *W'ham* —3M **107**
Sandy La. *Wok* —4D **74**
Sandy La. N. *Wall* —2H **63**
Sandy La. S. *Wall* —5G **62**
Sandy Ride. *S'hill* —3B **34**
Sandy Rd. *Add* —3J **55**
Sandy Way. *Cobh* —8A **58**
Sandy Way. *Croy* —9J **47**
Sandy Way. *W On T* —7G **38**
Sandy Way. *Wok* —4E **74**
San Feliu Ct. *E Grin* —8D **166**
Sanger Av. *Chess* —2L **59**
Sanger Dri. *Send* —1E **94**
Sangers Dri. *Horl* —8D **142**
Sangers Wlk. *Horl* —8D **142**
Sangley Rd. *SE25* —3B **46**
Sankey La. *Fleet* —1E **88**
Santina Clo. *Farnh* —4J **109**
Santos Rd. *SW18* —8M **13**
Sanway Clo. *Byfl* —1N **75**
Sanway Rd. *Byfl* —1N **75**
Saphora Clo. *Orp* —2M **67**
Sappho Ct. *Wok* —3H **73**
Sapte Clo. *Cranl* —7B **156**
Saracen Clo. *Croy* —5A **46**
Sarel Way. *Horl* —6F **142**
Sargent Clo. *Craw* —7D **182**
Sarjant Path. SW19 —3J 27 (off Blincoe Clo.)
Sark Clo. *Craw* —7M **181**
Sark Clo. *Houn* —3A **10**
Sarsby Dri. *Stai* —3C **20**
Sarsen Av. *Houn* —5A **10**
Sarsfeld Rd. *SW12* —2D **28**
Sarum. *Brack* —7L **31**
Sarum Cres. *Wokgm* —1C **30**
Sarum Grn. *Wey* —9F **38**
Satellite Bus. Village. *Craw* —8C **162**
Satis Ct. *Eps* —7E **60**
Saturn Clo. *Bew* —5K **181**
Saturn Croft. *Wink R* —7E **16**
Saunders Clo. *Craw* —2F **182**
Saunders Copse. *Wok* —9L **73**
Saunders La. *Wok* —9H **73**
Saunton Av. *Hayes* —3G **8**
Saunton Gdns. *F'boro* —8M **69**
Savernake Wlk. *Craw* —6D **182**
Savernake Way. *Brack* —5C **32**
Savile Clo. *N Mald* —4D **42**
Savile Gdns. *Croy* —8C **46**
Saville Cres. *Ashf* —7E **22**
Saville Gdns. *Camb* —1F **70**
Saville Gdns. *Croy* —8C **46**
Saville Rd. *Twic* —2F **24**
Savill Gdns. *SW20* —2F **42**
Savill Ho. *SW4* —1H **29**
Savin Lodge. Sutt —4A 62 (off [illegible])
Savona Clo. *SW19* —8J **27**
Savory Wlk. *Binf* —7G **15**
Savoy Av. *Hayes* —1F **8**
Savoy Gro. *B'water* —3J **69**
Sawkins Clo. *SW19* —3K **27**
Sawpit La. *Guild* —9N **95**
Sawtry Clo. *Cars* —6C **44**
Sawyers Clo. *Wind* —3B **4**
Sawyers Hill. *Rich* —1M **25**
Saxby Rd. *SW2* —1J **29**
Saxby's La. *Ling* —7N **145**
Saxley. *Horl* —7G **142**
Saxon Av. *Felt* —3M **23**
Saxonbury Av. *Sun* —2J **39**
Saxonbury Clo. *Mitc* —2B **44**
Saxonbury Gdns. *Surb* —7J **41**
Saxon Bus. Cen. *SW19* —1A **44**
Saxon Clo. *Surb* —5K **41**
Saxon Cres. *H'ham* —4H **197**
Saxon Croft. *Farnh* —2H **129**
Saxon Dri. *Warf* —9D **16**
Saxonfield Clo. *SW2* —2K **29**
Saxon Ho. *Felt* —3N **23**
Saxon Rd. *SE25* —4A **46**
Saxon Rd. *Ashf* —7E **22**
Saxon Rd. *W On T* —8L **39**
Saxon Rd. *Worth* —4J **183**
Saxons. *Tad* —8J **81**
Saxon Way. *Old Win* —9L **5**
Saxon Way. *Reig* —2L **121**
Saxon Way. *W Dray* —2L **7**
Saxony Way. *Yat* —2B **68**
Sayers Clo. *Fet* —1C **98**
Sayers Clo. *Frim G* —7C **70**
Sayers Clo. *H'ham* —6L **197**
Sayers, The. *E Grin* —9M **165**
Sayer's Wlk. *Rich* —1M **25**
Sayes Ct. *Add* —2L **55**
Sayes Ct. Farm Dri. *Add* —2K **55**
Scallows Clo. *Craw* —2E **182**
Scallows Rd. *Craw* —2E **182**
Scampton Rd. *H'row A* —9A **8**
Scania Wlk. *Wink R* —7F **16**
Scarborough Clo. *Big H* —5E **86**
Scarborough Clo. *Sutt* —7L **61**
Scarborough Rd. *H'row A* —9D **8**
Scarbrook Rd. *Croy* —9N **45**
Scarlet Oaks. *Camb* —3C **70**
Scarlett Clo. *Wok* —5J **73**
Scarlette Mnr. Way. *SW2* —1L **29**
Scarlett's Rd. *Alder* —1M **109**
Scarth Rd. *SW13* —6E **12**
Scawen Clo. *Cars* —1E **62**
Scholars Rd. *SW12* —2G **28**
School All. *Twic* —2G **25**
School Allotment Ride. *Wind* —1M **17**
School Clo. *Bisl* —2C **72**
School Clo. *Guild* —9N **93**
School Clo. *H'ham* —2N **197**
School Cotts. *Asc* —9H **17**
School Cotts. *Wok* —9M **73**
School Field. *Eden* —1L **147**
School Hill. *Crowt* —3J **49**
School Hill. *Red* —6G **102**
School Hill. *Sand* —6F **48**
School Hill. *Seale* —8F **110**
School Hill. *Warn* —9F **178**
School Hill. *Wrec* —4E **128**
School Ho. La. *Tedd* —8H **25**
School La. *Add* —2J **55**
School La. *Asc* —9J **17**
School La. *Ash W* —3F **186**
School La. *Bag* —5H **51**
School La. *Cat* —4C **104**
School La. *C'fold* —5E **172**
School La. *E Clan* —9N **95**
School La. *Egh* —6C **20**
School La. *Ews* —4C **108**
School La. *Fet* —9D **78**
School La. *F Row* —7H **187**
School La. *Guild* —9K **91**
School La. *King T* —9J **25**
School La. *Lwr Bo* —5J **129**
School La. *Mick* —5J **99**
School La. *Ock* —9C **76**
School La. *Pirb* —9B **72**
School La. *Putt* —8N **111**
School La. *Shack* —5B **132**
School La. *Shep* —5C **38**
School La. *Surb* —7N **41**
School La. *Tad* —3F **100**
School La. *Westc* —6D **118**
School La. *W Hor* —7C **96**
School La. *W'sham* —2A **52**
School La. *Yat* —9A **48**
School Pas. *King T* —1M **41**
School Rd. *Asc* —4A **34**
School Rd. *Ashf* —7C **22**
School Rd. *B'ham* —2C **30**
School Rd. *E Mol* —3D **40**
School Rd. *Gray* —6N **169**
School Rd. *Hamp* —7C **24**
School Rd. *Hasl* —3D **188**
School Rd. *Houn* —6C **10**
School Rd. *King T* —9J **25**
School Rd. *Rowl* —8D **128**
School Rd. *W on T* —2G **57**
School Rd. *W Dray* —2M **7**
School Rd. *W'sham* —1L **51**
School Rd. Av. *Hamp* —7C **24**
School Road Junction. (Junct.) —8C **22**
School Wlk. *Horl* —8C **142**
School Wlk. *Sun* —3G **38**
Schroder Ct. *Egh* —6L **19**
Schubert Rd. *SW15* —8L **13**
Scillonian Rd. *Guild* —4K **113**
Scilly Isles. (Junct.) —8E **40**
Scizdons Climb. *G'ming* —7J **133**
Scoles Cres. *SW2* —2L **29**
Scory Clo. *Craw* —6M **181**
Scotia Rd. *SW2* —2L **29**
Scotland Bri. *New H* —7J **55**
Scotland Bri. Rd. *New H* —7J **55**
Scotland Clo. *Ash V* —8E **90**
Scotland Farm Rd. *Ash V* —8E **90**
Scotland Hill. *Sand* —6F **48**
Scotland La. *Hasl* —3F **188**
Scotlands Clo. *Hasl* —3F **188**
Scotney Clo. *Farn* —1J **67**
Scots Clo. *Stanw* —2M **21**
Scotsdale Clo. *Sutt* —4K **61**
Scotshall La. *Warl* —2M **85**
Scott Clo. *SW16* —9K **29**
Scott Clo. *Eps* —2B **60**
Scott Clo. *Guild* —1K **113**
Scott Clo. *W Dray* —1A **8**
Scott Farm Clo. *Th Dit* —7H **41**
Scott Gdns. *Houn* —3L **9**
Scott Rd. *Craw* —6D **182**
Scotts Av. *Brom* —1N **47**
Scotts Av. *Sun* —8F **22**
Scott's Ct. *F'boro* —7N **69**
Scotts Dri. *Hamp* —8B **24**
Scotts Farm Rd. *Eps* —3B **60**
Scott's Gro. Clo. *Chob* —9G **52**
Scott's Gro. Rd. *Chob* —1E **72**
Scott's Hill. *Out* —5A **144**
Scott's La. *Brom* —2N **47**
Scotts La. *W on T* —1L **57**
Scotts Way. *Sun* —8F **22**
Scott Ter. *Brack* —9C **16**
Scott Trimmer Way. *Houn* —5M **9**
Scrutton Clo. *SW12* —1H **29**
Scutley La. *Light* —5B **52**
Scylla Cres. *H'row A* —9C **8**
Scylla Pl. *St J* —6K **73**
Scylla Rd. *H'row A* —9C **8**
Seabrook Dri. *W Wick* —8N **47**
Seaford Ct. *Wokgm* —2C **30**
Seaford Rd. *Craw* —8M **181**
Seaford Rd. *H'row A* —8M **7**
Seaford Rd. *Wokgm* —2C **30**
Seaforth Av. *N Mald* —4G **42**
Seaforth Gdns. *Eps* —1E **60**
Seagrave Lodge. SW6 —2M 13 (off Seagrave Rd.)
Seagrave Rd. *SW6* —2M **13**
Sealand Rd. *H'row A* —9B **8**
Seale Hill. *Reig* —5M **121**
Seale La. *P'ham* —8J **111**
Seale La. *Seale* —8B **110** (in two parts)
Seale Rd. *Seale & Elst* —3F **130**
Searchwood Rd. *Warl* —5E **84**
Searle Rd. *Farnh* —3H **129**
Searle's View. *H'ham* —3L **197**
Seaton Clo. *SW15* —2G **27**
Seaton Clo. *Twic* —9D **10**
Seaton Dri. *Ashf* —3N **21**
Seaton Rd. *Camb* —1N **69**
Seaton Rd. *Mitc* —1C **44**
Seaton Rd. *Twic* —9C **10**
Sebastopol Rd. *Alder* —2N **109**
Second Av. *SW14* —6D **12**
Second Av. *W On T* —5J **39**
Second Clo. *W Mol* —3C **40**
Second Cross Rd. *Twic* —3E **24**
Seddon Ct. *Craw* —8N **181**
Seddon Hill *Warf* —7N **15**
Seddon Rd. *Mord* —4B **44**
Sedgefield Clo. *Worth* —2J **183**
Sedgemoor. *F'boro* —7N **69**
Sedgewick Clo. *Craw* —3G **183**
Sedgwick La. *H'ham* —9M **197**
Sedleigh Rd. *SW18* —9L **13**
Sedlescombe Rd. *SW6* —2M **13**
Seebys Oak. *Col T* —9K **49**
Seely Rd. *SW17* —7E **28**
Seething Wells La. *Surb* —5J **41**
Sefton Clo. *W End* —9C **52**
Sefton Ct. *Houn* —4B **10**
Sefton Rd. *Croy* —7D **46**
Sefton Rd. *Eps* —6C **60**
Sefton St. *SW15* —6H **13**
Sefton Vs. *Dork* —9H **119**
Segrave Clo. *Wey* —4B **56**
Segsbury Gro. *Brack* —3C **32**
Sekhon Ter. *Felt* —4A **24**
Selborne Av. *Alder* —5N **109**
Selborne Clo. *B'water* —9H **49**
Selborne Gdns. *Farnh* —4F **128**
Selborne Rd. *Croy* —9B **46**
Selborne Rd. *N Mald* —1D **42**
Selbourne Av. *New H* —6K **55**
Selbourne Av. *Surb* —8M **41**
Selbourne Clo. *Craw* —8H **163**
Selbourne Clo. *New H* —6K **55**
Selbourne Rd. *Guild* —9C **94**
Selbourne Sq. *God* —8F **104**
Selby Clo. *Chess* —4L **59**
Selby Grn. *Cars* —6C **44**
Selby Rd. *SE20* —1D **46**
Selby Rd. *Ashf* —7D **22**
Selby Rd. *Cars* —6C **44**
Selbys. *Ling* —6A **146**
Selby Wlk. *Wok* —5L **73**
Selcroft Rd. *Purl* —8M **63**
Selham Clo. *Craw* —2M **181**
Selhurst Clo. *SW19* —2J **27**
Selhurst Clo. *Wok* —2B **74**
Selhurst New Rd. *SE25* —5B **46**
Selhurst Pl. *SE25* —5B **46**
Selhurst Rd. *SE25* —5B **46**
Selkirk Rd. *SW17* —5C **28**
Selkirk Rd. *Twic* —3C **24**
Sellar's Hill. *G'ming* —4G **132**
Sellincourt Rd. *SW17* —6C **28**
Selsdon Av. *S Croy* —3A **64**
Selsdon Clo. *Surb* —4L **41**
Selsdon Cres. *S Croy* —6F **64**
Selsdon Pk. Rd. *S Croy* —5G **65**
Selsdon Rd. *SE27* —4M **29**
Selsdon Rd. *New H* —7J **55**
Selsdon Rd. *S Croy* —2A **64**
Selsey Ct. *Craw* —7N **181**
Selsey Rd. *Craw* —7M **181**
Selsfield Rd. *Turn H & E Grin* —6D **184**
Seltops Clo. *Cranl* —8A **156**
Selwood Clo. *Stai* —9L **7**
Selwood Gdns. *Stai* —9L **7**
Selwood Rd. *Chess* —1K **59**
Selwood Rd. *Croy* —8E **46**
Selwood Rd. *Sutt* —7L **43**
Selwood Rd. *Wok* —7D **74**
Selwyn Av. *Rich* —6L **11**
Selwyn Clo. *Craw* —9G **163**
Selwyn Clo. *Houn* —7M **9**
Selwyn Clo. *Wind* —5B **4**
Selwyn Dri. *Yat* —9A **48**
Selwyn Rd. *N Mald* —4C **42**
Semaphore Rd. *Guild* —5A **114**
Semley Rd. *SW16* —1J **45**
Semper Clo. *Knap* —4H **73**
Sen Clo. *Brack* —7A **16**
Send Barns La. *Send* —2F **94**
Send Clo. *Send* —1E **94**
Send Hill. *Send* —3E **94**
Send Marsh Rd. *Send* —2F **94**
Sendmarsh Works. *Rip* —1H **95**
Send Pde. Clo. *Send* —1E **94**
Send Rd. *Send* —9D **74**
Seneca Rd. *T Hth* —3N **45**
Senga Rd. *Wall* —7E **44**
Senhouse Rd. *Sutt* —9J **43**
Sepen Meade. *C Crook* —9A **88**
Sequoia Pk. *Craw* —5B **182**
Sergeant Ind. Est. *SW18* —9N **13**
Serpentine Grn. *Red* —7H **103**
Serrin Way. *H'ham* —3L **197**
Servite Ho. Wor Pk —8E 42 (off Avenue, The.)
Servius Ct. *Bren* —3K **11**
Setley Way. *Brack* —2D **32**
Settrington Rd. *SW6* —5N **13**

Sett, The—Smeaton Rd.

Sett, The. Yat —1A 68
Seven Acres. Cars —8C 44
Seven Arches App. Wey —4A 56
Seven Hills Clo. W On T —5F 56
Seven Hills Rd. W On T & Cob —5F 56
Seven Hills Rd. S. Cobh —9F 56
Sevenoaks Clo. Sutt —6M 61
Sevenoaks Rd. Grn St & Hals —2N 67
Severn Clo. Sand —7H 49
Severn Cres. Slou —1D 6
Severn Dri. Esh —8G 41
Severn Dri. W On T —8L 39
Severn Rd. F'boro —8K 69
Severn Rd. M'bowr —4G 182
Seward Rd. Beck —1G 47
Sewell Av. Wokgm —9A 14
Sewer's Farm Rd. Dork —5N 137
Sewill Clo. Charl —3L 161
Seymour Av. Cat —1N 103
Seymour Av. Eps —5G 61
Seymour Av. Mord —6J 43
Seymour Clo. E Mol —4C 40
Seymour Ct. Crowt —3D 48
Seymour Ct. Fleet —3B 88
Seymour Dri. Camb —7F 50
Seymour Gdns. Felt —5K 23
Seymour Gdns. Surb —4M 41
Seymour Gdns. Twic —1H 25
Seymour Pl. SE25 —3E 46
Seymour Rd. SW18 —1L 27
Seymour Rd. SW19 —4J 27
Seymour Rd. Cars —2E 62
Seymour Rd. Craw —7M 181
Seymour Rd. E Mol —4C 40
Seymour Rd. G'ming —8E 132
Seymour Rd. Hamp —6C 24
Seymour Rd. Head —5H 169
Seymour Rd. King T —9K 25
Seymour Rd. Mitc —6E 44
Seymour Ter. SE20 —1E 46
Seymour Vs. SE20 —1E 46
Seymour Wlk. SW10 —2N 13
Seymour Way. Sun —8F 22
Shackleford Rd. Elst —7L 131
Shackleford Rd. Shack —4A 132
Shackleford Rd. Wok —7C 74
Shacklegate La. Tedd —5E 24
Shackleton Rd. Craw —6C 182
Shackleton Wlk. Guild —3H 113 (off Chapelhouse Clo.)
Shackstead La. G'ming —8F 132
Shadbolt Clo. Wor Pk —8E 42
Shadyhanger. G'ming —5H 133
Shady Nook. Farnh —6G 108
Shaef Way. Tedd —8G 25
Shaftesbury Av. Felt —9H 9
Shaftesbury Clo. Brack —4B 32
Shaftesbury Ct. SW6 —4N 13 (off Maltings Pl.)
Shaftesbury Ct. SW16 —4H 29
Shaftesbury Ct. F'boro —5A 90
Shaftesbury Ct. Wokgm —1C 30
Shaftesbury Cres. Stai —8M 21
Shaftesbury Mt. B'water —3J 69
Shaftesbury Rd. Beck —1J 47
Shaftesbury Rd. Bisl —3C 72
Shaftesbury Rd. Cars —6B 44
Shaftesbury Rd. M'bowr —5H 183
Shaftesbury Rd. Rich —6L 11
Shaftesbury Rd. Wok —4D 74
Shaftesbury Way. Twic —4D 24
Shakespeare Av. Felt —9H 9
Shakespeare Gdns. F'boro —9J 69
Shakespeare Rd. Add —1M 55
Shakespeare Way. Felt —5K 23
Shakespeare Way. Warf —9C 16
Shalbourne Rise. Camb —1C 70
Shalden Ho. SW15 —9E 12
Shalden Rd. Alder —4B 110
Shaldon Dri. Mord —4K 43
Shaldon Way. W On T —9K 39
Shale Grn. Red —7H 103
Shalesbrook La. F Row —8H 187
Shalford Clo. Orp —1L 67
Shalford Rd. Guild —6N 113
Shalstone Rd. SW14 —6A 12
Shalston Vs. Surb —5M 41
Shambles, The. Guild —5N 113
Shamrock Clo. Fet —8D 78
Shamrock Clo. Frim —6B 70
Shamrock Cotts. Guild —6L 93
Shamrock Rd. Croy —5K 45
Shandys Clo. H'ham —7G 196
Shanklin Ct. Alder —3A 110
Shannon Clo. S'hall —1L 9
Shannon Corner. (Junct.) —3F 42
Shannon Corner Retail Pk. N Mald —3F 42
Shanti Ct. SW18 —2M 27
Shap Cres. Cars —7D 44
Sharland Clo. T Hth —5L 45
Sharon Clo. Bookh —2A 98
Sharon Clo. Craw —6E 182
Sharon Clo. Eps —9B 60
Sharon Clo. Surb —7K 41
Sharon Rd. W4 —1C 12
Sharpthorne Clo. If'd —3L 181
Shaw Clo. Eps —7E 60
Shaw Clo. Ott —3E 54
Shaw Clo. S Croy —8C 64
Shaw Ct. Old Win —8K 5
Shaw Cres. S Croy —8C 64
Shaw Dri. W On T —6K 39
Shawfield Cotts. Ash —2D 110
Shawfield La. Ash —2D 110
Shawfield Rd. Ash —3D 110
Shawford Ct. SW15 —1F 26
Shawford Rd. Eps —3C 60
Shawley Cres. Eps —5H 81
Shawley Way. Eps —5G 81
Shaw Pk. Crowt —4G 49
Shaw Rd. Tats —7E 86
Shaws Path. King T —9J 25 (off High St. Hampton Wick,)
Shaws Rd. Craw —2D 182
Shaw Way. Wall —4J 63
Shaxton Cres. New Ad —5M 65
Shearing Dri. Cars —6A 44
Shears Ct. Sun —8G 23
Shears, The. (Junct.) —8F 22
Shearwater Ct. If'd —4J 181 (off Stoneycroft Wlk.)
Sheath's La. Oxs —9B 58
Sheen Comn. Dri. Rich —7N 11
Sheen Ct. Rd. Rich —7N 11
Sheendale Rd. Rich —7M 11
Sheen Ga. Gdns. SW14 —7B 12
Sheen La. SW14 —8B 12
Sheen Pk. Rich —7L 11
Sheen Rd. Rich —8L 11
Sheen Way. Wall —2K 63
Sheen Wood. SW14 —8B 12
Sheepbarn La. Warl —8B 66
Sheepcote Clo. Houn —3H 9
Sheepcote Rd. Eton W —1D 4
Sheepcote Rd. Wind —5B 4
Sheepfold Rd. Guild —9J 93
Sheephatch La. Tilf —6N 129
Sheep Ho. Farnh —3H 129
Sheephouse Grn. Ab H —9N 117
Sheephouse La. Ab C —7N 137
Sheephouse La. Wott —8N 117
Sheephouse Way. N Mald —7C 42
Sheeplands Av. Guild —1E 114
Sheep Wlk. Eps —8C 80
Sheep Wlk. Reig —9L 101
Sheep Wlk. Shep —6A 38
Sheepwalk La. E Hor & Ran C —3G 116
Sheep Wlk. M. SW19 —7J 27
Sheep Wlk., The. Wok —5G 74
Sheerwater Av. Wdhm —8G 55
Sheerwater Rd. Wok & Wdhm —8G 54
Sheet's Heath La. Brkwd —6D 72
Sheet St. Wind —5G 5
Sheet St. Rd. Wind —5A 18
Sheffield Clo. Craw —5F 182
Sheffield Clo. F'boro —1L 89
Sheffield Rd. H'row A —9D 8
Sheffield Way. H'row A —8E 8
Shefford Cres. Wokgm —9C 14
Sheldon Clo. Craw —4H 183
Sheldon Clo. Reig —4N 121
Sheldon Ct. Guild —4B 114
Sheldon St. Croy —9N 45
Sheldrick Clo. SW19 —1B 44
Shelley Av. Brack —1C 32
Shelley Clo. Bans —2J 81
Shelley Clo. Coul —4K 83
Shelley Clo. Craw —1G 182
Shelley Clo. Fleet —5B 88
Shelley Clo. Slou —1C 6
Shelley Ct. Camb —1A 70
Shelley Cres. Houn —4L 9
Shelley Dri. Broad H —5C 196
Shelley Rise. F'boro —8L 69
Shelley Rd. E Grin —9M 165
Shelley Rd. H'ham —5H 197
Shelleys Ct. H'ham —4N 197
Shelley Wlk. Yat —1B 68
Shelley Way. SW19 —7B 28
Shellfield Clo. Stai —8J 7
Shellwood Dri. N Holm —9J 119
Shellwood Rd. Leigh —1B 140
Shelson Av. Felt —4G 22
Shelton Av. Warl —4F 84
Shelton Clo. Guild —7K 93
Shelton Clo. Warl —4F 84
Shelton Rd. SW19 —9M 27
Shelvers Grn. Tad —8H 81
Shelvers Hill. Tad —8G 81
Shelvers Spur. Tad —8H 81
Shelvers Way. Tad —8H 81
Shenfield Clo. Coul —6G 82
Shenley Rd. Houn —4M 9
Shenstone Clo. Finch —8A 30
Shenstone Pk. S'hill —3B 34
Shepherd Clo. Craw —6C 182
Shepherd & Flock Roundabout. Farnh —9K 109
Shepherd's Bush Rd. W6 —1H 13
Shepherds Chase. Bag —5J 51
Shepherds Clo. Shep —5C 38
Shepherds Ct. Farnh —3H 129
Shepherdsgrove La. Hamm —5H 167
Shepherds Hill. Brack —9A 16
Shepherd's Hill. Cole H —8M 187
Shepherd's Hill. Guild —1K 113
Shepherd's Hill. Hasl —2G 188
Shepherd's Hill. Red —4G 102
Shepherd's La. Brack —8M 15
Shepherd's La. Guild —9J 93
Shepherds La. W'sham —2D 52
Shepherd's Wlk. Eps —7A 80
Shepherds Wlk. F'boro —7K 69
Shepherds Way. Crowt —3D 48
Shepherd's Way. Guild —7A 114
Shepherds Way. H'ham —3N 197
Shepherds Way. S Croy —4G 64
Shepherds Way. Tilf —7B 130
Shepiston La. Hayes —1C 8
Shepley Clo. Cars —9E 44
Shepley Dri. Asc —5F 34
Shepley End. Asc —4F 34
Sheppard Clo. King T —3L 41
Sheppard Ho. SW2 —2L 29
Shepperton Bus. Pk. Shep —4D 38
Shepperton Ct. Shep —5C 38
Shepperton Ct. Dri. Shep —4C 38
Shepperton Rd. Stai & Shep —2L 37
Sheppey Clo. Craw —6N 181
Sheraton Clo. B'water —2K 69
Sheraton Dri. Eps —9B 60
Sheraton Wlk. Craw —8N 181
Sherborne Av. S'hall —1A 10
Sherborne Clo. Coln —4G 7
Sherborne Clo. Eps —4H 81
Sherborne Ct. Guild —5M 113
Sherborne Cres. Cars —6C 44
Sherborne Gdns. Shep —6F 38
Sherborne La. Peasl & Holm M —1G 157
Sherborne Rd. Chess —2L 59
Sherborne Rd. F'boro —4B 90
Sherborne Rd. Felt —2E 22 (in two parts)
Sherborne Rd. Sutt —8M 43
Sherborne Wlk. Lea —8J 79
Sherbourne. Abry —8M 115
Sherbourne Cotts. Alb —7N 115
Sherbourne Ct. Sutt —3A 62
Sherbourne Dri. Asc —4G 35
Sherbourne Dri. Wind —7C 4
Sherbrooke Rd. SW6 —3K 13
Shere Av. Sutt —6H 61
Shere Clo. Chess —2K 59
Shere Clo. N Holm —9J 119
Shere La. Shere —8B 116
Shere Rd. Ewh —2E 156
Shere Rd. W Cla & Alb —4J 115
Shere Rd. W Hor —8D 96
Sherfield Gdns. SW15 —9E 12
Sheridan Ct. Houn —8M 9
Sheridan Dri. Reig —1N 121
Sheridan Pl. SW13 —6E 12
Sheridan Pl. E Grin —9M 165
Sheridan Pl. Hamp —9B 24
Sheridan Rd. SW19 —9L 27
Sheridan Rd. Frim —6B 70
Sheridan Rd. Rich —4J 25
Sheridans Rd. Bookh —4C 98
Sheridan Wlk. Cars —2D 62
Sheridan Way. Beck —1J 47
Sheringham Av. Felt —4H 23
Sheringham Av. Twic —2N 23
Sheringham Ct. Felt —4H 23 (off Sheringham Av.)
Sheringham Rd. SE20 —2F 46
Sherland Rd. Twic —2F 24
Shernden La. M Grn —6L 147
Sherring Clo. Brack —8A 16
Sherrydon. Cranl —6A 156
Sherwin Cres. F'boro —6N 69
Sherwood Av. SW16 —8H 29
Sherwood Clo. SW13 —6G 13
Sherwood Clo. Brack —1E 32
Sherwood Clo. Fet —1C 98
Sherwood Ct. Coln —1B 6
Sherwood Cres. Reig —7N 121
Sherwood Pk. Rd. Mitc —3G 44
Sherwood Pk. Rd. Sutt —2M 61
Sherwood Rd. SW19 —8L 27
Sherwood Rd. Coul —3G 82
Sherwood Rd. Croy —6E 46
Sherwood Rd. Hamp —6C 24
Sherwood Rd. Knap —4H 73
Sherwood Wlk. Craw —6D 182
Sherwood Way. W Wick —8M 47
Shetland Clo. Craw —2J 183
Shetland Clo. Guild —7D 94
Shetland Way. Fleet —1C 88
Shewens Rd. Wey —1E 56
Shey Copse. Wok —4E 74
Shield Dri. Bren —2G 11
Shield Rd. Ashf —5D 22
Shilburn Way. Wok —5K 73
Shildon Clo. Camb —3H 71
Shillinglee Rd. Plais —4K 191
Shimmings, The. Guild —2C 114
Shingle End. Bren —3J 11
Shinners Clo. SE25 —4D 46
Shinwell Wlk. Craw —8N 181
Ship All. W4 —2N 11
Ship All. F'boro —8A 70
Shipfield Clo. Tats —8E 86
Ship Hill. Tats —8E 86
Shipka Rd. SW12 —2F 28
Shiplake Ho. Brack —3D 32
Ship La. SW14 —6B 12
Ship La. F'boro —8A 70
Shipleybridge La. Ship B & Craw —5K 163
Shipley Rd. Craw —2M 181
Ship St. E Grin —1A 186
Ship Yd. Wey —9C 38
Shire Av. Fleet —1D 88
Shire Clo. Bag —5J 51
Shire Ct. Alder —2K 109
Shire Ct. Eps —4E 60
Shire Horse Way. Iswth —6F 10
Shire La. Kes & Orp —4H 67 (in two parts)
Shire La. Orp —2N 67
Shire M. Whit —9C 10
Shire Pde. Worth —2H 183 (off Ridings, The)
Shire Pl. SW18 —1N 27
Shire Pl. Bren —3J 11
Shire Pl. Craw —2H 183 (off Ridings, The)
Shires Clo. Asht —6K 79
Shires Ho. Byfl —9N 55
Shires, The. Ham —5L 25
Shires Way. Yat —8C 48
Shirley Av. Cheam —5L 61
Shirley Av. Coul —6M 83
Shirley Av. Croy —7F 46
Shirley Av. Red —8D 122
Shirley Av. Sutt —1B 62
Shirley Av. Wind —4C 4
Shirley Chu. Rd. Croy —9G 46
Shirley Clo. Craw —7J 181
Shirley Clo. Houn —8C 10
Shirley Ct. SW16 —8J 29
Shirley Cres. Beck —3H 47
Shirley Dri. Houn —8C 10
Shirley Heights. Wall —5G 62
Shirley Hills Rd. Croy —2F 64
Shirley Oaks Rd. Croy —7G 46
Shirley Pk. Rd. Croy —7E 46
Shirley Pl. Knap —4F 72
Shirley Rd. Croy —6E 46
Shirley Rd. Wall —5G 62
Shirley Way. Croy —9H 47
Shoe La. Alder —7M 89
Shophouse La. Abry —4M 135
Shoppe Hill. Duns —4A 174
Shop Rd. Wind —3A 4
Shops, The. Won —3D 134
Shord Hill. Kenl —3A 84
Shore Clo. Felt —1H 23
Shore Clo. Hamp —7M 23
Shore Gro. Felt —3A 24
Shoreham Clo. SW18 —8N 13
Shoreham Clo. Croy —4F 46
Shoreham Rd. M'bowr —6G 183
Shoreham Rd. E. H'row A —8N 7
Shoreham Rd. W. H'row A —8N 7
Shores Rd. Wok —1A 74
Shorland Oaks. Brack —7A 16
Shorrold's Rd. SW6 —3L 13
Shortacres. Nutf —2K 123
Short Clo. Craw —9B 162
Shortcroft Rd. Eps —4E 60
Shortdale Rd. Alder —6A 110
Shortfield Rd. Fren —1H 149
Short Gallop. Craw —2H 183
Shortheath Crest. Farnh —5E 128
Shortheath Rd. Farnh —5F 128
Short Hedges. Houn —4A 10
Shortlands. W6 —1J 13
Shortlands. Fren —1G 149
Shortlands. Hayes —2E 8
Shortlands Gro. Brom —2N 47
Shortlands Rd. Brom —2N 47
Shortlands Rd. King T —8M 25
Short La. Oxt —1D 126
Short La. Stai —1A 22
Short Rd. W4 —2D 12
Short Rd. H'row A —9N 7
Shortsfield Clo. H'ham —3J 197
Shorts Rd. Cars —1C 62
Short St. Alder —2M 109
Short Way. Twic —1C 24
Shortwood Av. Stai —4K 21
Shotfield. Wall —3F 62
Shotfield Av. SW14 —7D 12
Shott Clo. Sutt —2A 62
Shottendane Rd. SW6 —4M 13
Shottermill. H'ham —1N 197
Shottermill Pond. Hasl —3C 188
Shottermill Rd. Hasl —3C 188
Shovelstrode La. E Grin —1E 186
Shrewsbury Av. SW14 —7C 12
Shrewsbury Clo. Surb —8L 41
Shrewsbury Rd. Beck —2H 47
Shrewsbury Rd. Cars —6C 44
Shrewsbury Rd. H'row A —9D 8
Shrewsbury Rd. Red —3C 122
Shrewsbury Wlk. Iswth —6G 11
Shrewton Rd. SW17 —8D 28
Shrivenham Clo. Col T —7J 49
Shropshire Clo. Mitc —3J 45
Shropshire Gdns. Warf —8D 16
Shrubbery Rd. SW16 —5J 29
Shrubbery, The. F'boro —2J 89
Shrubbs Hill. Chob —5F 52
Shrubbs Hill La. Asc —5F 34
Shrubbs La. Rowl —7E 128
Shrubland Gro. Wor Pk —9H 43
Shrubland Rd. Bans —3L 81
Shrublands Av. Croy —9K 47
Shrublands Dri. Light —7M 51
Shurlock Dri. Orp —1L 67
Shute End. Wokgm —2A 30
Shuters Sq. W14 —1L 13
Sian Clo. C Crook —8C 88
Sibthorp Rd. Mitc —1D 44
Sibton Rd. Cars —6C 44
Sickle Rd. Hasl —3D 188
Sidbury Clo. Asc —4D 34
Sidbury St. SW6 —4K 13
Siddons Rd. Croy —9L 45
Sidings, The. Alder —1A 110
Sidings, The. Rud —1E 194
Sidings, The. Stai —5K 21
Sidlaws Rd. F'boro —7J 69
Sidmouth Av. Iswth —5E 10
Sidney Gdns. Bren —2K 11
Sidney Rd. SE25 —4D 46
Sidney Rd. Beck —1H 47
Sidney Rd. Stai —5J 21
Sidney Rd. Twic —9G 11
Sidney Rd. W On T —6H 39
Sidney Rd. Wind —6A 4
Sigrist Sq. King T —9L 25
Silbury Av. Mitc —9C 28
Silchester Dri. Craw —5N 181
Silkham Rd. Oxt —5N 105
Silkin Wlk. Craw —8N 181
Silkmoor La. W Hor —3B 96
Silo Clo. G'ming —3J 133
Silo Dri. G'ming —3J 133
Silo Rd. G'ming —3J 133
Silver Birch Clo. C Crook —8A 88
Silver Birch Clo. Wdhm —8G 55
Silver Birch Cotts. Churt —9B 150
Silver Birches Way. Elst —8J 131
Silver Birch Ho. Craw —8A 182
Silver Clo. Kgswd —2K 101
Silver Cres. W4 —1A 12
Silverdale. Fleet —7B 88
Silverdale Av. Oxs —1C 78
Silverdale Av. W On T —8G 38
Silverdale Clo. Brock —7A 120
Silverdale Clo. Sutt —1L 61
Silverdale Ct. Stai —5K 21
Silverdale Dri. Sun —1J 39
Silver Dri. Frim —3G 70
Silverglade Bus. Pk. Chess —8J 59
Silver Glades. Yat —2B 68
Silverhall St. Iswth —6G 11
Silver Hill. Col T —7K 49
Silver Jubilee Way. Houn —5J 9
Silverlands Clo. Ott —9F 36
Silver La. Purl —8H 63
Silver La. W Wick —8N 47
Silverlea Gdns. Horl —9G 142
Silverleigh Rd. T Hth —3K 45
Silvermere Ct. Purl —8L 63
Silver Pk. Clo. C Crook —7C 88
Silversmiths Way. Wok —5M 73
Silverstead La. W'ham —8M 87
Silverstone Clo. Red —1D 122
Silverton Rd. W6 —2J 13
Silver Tree Clo. W On T —9H 39
Silver Wing Ind. Est. Croy —3K 63
Silverwood. Cranl —4K 155
Silverwood Clo. Croy —5J 65
Silverwood Cotts. Shere —7A 116
Silverwood Dri. Camb —8E 50
Silvester Way. C Crook —9A 88
Silwood. Brack —7K 31
Silwood Clo. Asc —1A 34
Silwood Rd. Asc —3C 34
Simkin's Clo. Wink R —7F 16
Simmil Rd. Clay —2E 58
Simmonds Clo. Brack —9K 15
Simmond's Cotts. G'ming —7E 132
Simmondstone La. Churt —8J 149
Simmons Clo. Chess —3J 59
Simmons Clo. Slou —1C 6
Simmons Pl. Stai —6G 21
Simms Clo. Cars —8C 44
Simone Dri. Kenl —3N 83
Simons Clo. Ott —3E 54
Simons Wlk. Egh —8M 19
Simplemarsh Ct. Add —1K 55
Simplemarsh Rd. Add —1J 55
Simpson Rd. Houn —9N 9
Simpson Rd. Rich —5J 25
Simrose Ct. SW18 —8M 13
Sinclair Clo. M'bowr —5G 182
Sinclair Ct. Croy —8B 46
Sinclair Dri. Sutt —5N 61
Sincots Rd. Red —3D 122
Sine Clo. F'boro —6N 69
Single St. Berr G —2K 87
Singleton Clo. SW17 —8D 28
Singleton Clo. Croy —6N 45
Singleton Rd. Broad H —5D 196
Sinhurst Rd. Camb —2N 69
Sion Ct. Twic —2H 25
Sion Rd. Twic —2H 25
Sipson Clo. W Dray —2B 8
Sipson Dri. W Dray —1A 8
Sipson La. W Dray & Hay —2B 8
Sipson Way. W Dray —3B 8
Sir Cyril Black Way. SW19 —8M 27
Sirdar Rd. Mitc —7E 28
Sir Oswald Stoll Foundation, The. (off Fulham Rd.) SW6 —3N 13
Sir William Atkins Ho. Eps —1C 80
Sir William Powell's Almshouses. SW6 —5K 13
Siskin Clo. H'ham —3L 197
Sispara Gdns. SW18 —9L 13
Sissinghurst Clo. Craw —2H 183
Sissinghurst Rd. Croy —6D 46
Sistova Rd. SW12 —2F 28
Siward Rd. SW17 —4A 28
Six Bells Roundabout. Farnh —7K 109
Sixth Cross Rd. Twic —4C 24
Skeena Hill. SW18 —1K 27
Skelbrook St. SW18 —3A 28
Skelgill Rd. SW15 —7L 13
Skelmersdale Wlk. Bew —7K 181
Skelton Fields. Warf —8N 15
Skelwith Rd. W6 —2H 13
Skerne Rd. King T —9K 25
Skeynes Rd. Eden —2K 147
Skid Hill La. Warl —8B 66
Skiffington Clo. SW2 —2L 29
Skiff La. Wis G —9H 193
Skimmington Cotts. Reig —4J 121
Skimped Hill La. Brack —1M 31
Skinners La. Asht —5K 79
Skinners La. C'fold —4G 172
Skinner's La. Eden —9M 127
Skinners La. Houn —4B 10
Skipton Way. Horl —6F 142
Sky Bus. Cen. Egh —1E 36
Skylark View. H'ham —1K 197
Skyport Dri. Harm —3M 7
Skyway Trad. Est. Coln —6H 7
Slade Ct. Ott —3F 54
Slade Ho. Houn —9N 9
Slade La. Ash —9H 91
Slade Rd. Brkwd —7A 72
Slade Rd. Ott —3F 54
Slaidburn Grn. Brack —6C 32
Slapleys. Wok —7A 74
Slattery Rd. Felt —2K 23
Slaugham Ct. Craw —6L 181
Sledmere Ct. Felt —2F 22
Sleets Rd. Broad H —5E 196
Slim Clo. Alder —6C 90
Slim Rd. Camb —8N 49
Slines New Rd. Wold —7G 84
Slines Oak Rd. Warl & Wold —6K 85
Slinfold Wlk. Craw —3M 181 (in two parts)
Slip of Wood. Cranl —6N 155
Slipshatch Rd. Reig —7K 121
Slipshoe St. Reig —3L 121
Slip, The. W'ham —4L 107
Sloane Wlk. Croy —5J 47
Slocock Hill. St J —4M 73
Sloughbrook Clo. H'ham —2M 197
Slough La. Bkld —1F 120
Slough La. H'ley —3B 100
Slough Rd. Dat —1K 5
Slough Rd. Eton C & Slou —2G 4
Slyfield Ct. Guild —9A 94
Slyfield Grn. Guild —8A 94
Slyfield Ind. Est. Guild —8A 94
Smallberry Av. Iswth —5F 10
Smallfield Rd. Horl —8F 142
Smallfield Rd. Horne —8A 144
Smallholdings Rd. Eps —1H 81 (in two parts)
Smallmead. Horl —8F 142
Smalls Hill Rd. Leigh & Norw H —1G 140
Small's La. Craw —3B 182
Smalls Mead. Craw —3A 182
Smallwood Rd. SW17 —5B 28
Smart's Heath La. Wok —1K 93
Smart's Heath Rd. Wok —1J 93
Smeaton Clo. Chess —3K 59
Smeaton Rd. SW18 —1M 27

Smitham Bottom La.—Spurs Ct.

Smitham Bottom La. *Purl* —7G **63**
Smitham Downs Rd. *Purl* —9H **63**
Smithbarn. *H'ham* —5N **197**
Smithbarn Clo. *Horl* —7F **142**
Smithbrook Kilns. *Cranl* —7F **154**
Smith Clo. *Craw* —6B **182**
Smith Ct. *Sheer* —9F **54**
Smithers, The. *Brock* —5A **120**
Smithfield La. *Head* —8F **148**
Smith Hill. *Bren* —2L **11**
Smith Rd. *Reig* —6L **121**
Smiths La. *Crook C* —2L **127**
Smith's La. *Wind* —5B **4**
Smith Sq. *Brack* —1B **32**
Smith St. *Surb* —5M **41**
Smith's Yd. *SW18* —3A **28**
Smithwood Av. *Cranl* —3K **155**
Smithwood Clo. *SW19* —2K **27**
Smithwood Comn. *Cranl* —2J **155**
Smithy Clo. *Tad* —4L **101**
Smithy La. *Dock* —8C **148**
Smithy La. *Lwr K* —5L **101**
Smithy's Grn. *W'sham* —3A **52**
Smock Wlk. *Croy* —5N **45**
Smokejack Hill. *Dork* —2L **177**
Smoke La. *Reig* —5N **121**
Smolletts. *E Grin* —1M **185**
Smoothfield. *Houn* —7A **10**
Smugglers End. *Hand* —8N **199**
Smugglers La. *Dork* —2E **178**
Smugglers La. *H'ham* —3F **180**
Smugglers Way. *SW18* —7N **13**
Smugglers Way. *Seale* —3B **130**
Snag La. *Cud* —7M **67**
Snailslynch. *Farnh* —1J **129**
Snatts Hill. *Oxt* —7B **106**
Snelgar Rd. *Wok* —8A **74**
Snelgate Cotts. *Guild* —9M **95**
Snell Hatch. *Craw* —3N **181**
Snellings Rd. *W On T* —2K **57**
Snipe Rd. *Hasl* —7E **188**
Snodland Clo. *Orp* —6J **67**
Snowbury Rd. *SW6* —5N **13**
Snowden Clo. *Wind* —7A **4**
Snowdenham La. *Brmly* —6A **134**
Snowdenham Links Rd. *Brmly* —5N **133**
Snowdon Rd. *F'boro* —7K **69**
Snowdon Rd. *H'row A* —9D **8**
Snowdown Clo. *SE20* —1G **46**
Snowdrop Clo. *Craw* —7M **181**
Snowdrop Clo. *Hamp* —7A **24**
Snowdrop Wlk. Fleet —3A **88**
(off Stockton Av.)
Snowdrop Way. *Bisl* —4D **72**
Snowerhill Rd. *Bet* —5D **120**
Snow Hill. *Craw* —7C **164**
(in two parts)
Snow Hill La. *Copt* —5C **164**
Snows Paddock. *W'sham* —9M **33**
Snows Ride. *W'sham* —2M **51**
Snowy Fielder Waye. *Iswth* —5H **11**
Snoxhall Field. *Cranl* —8M **155**
Soames Wlk. *N Mald* —9D **26**
Soane Clo. *Craw* —5K **181**
Solartron Rd. *F'boro* —2N **89**
Soldiers Rise. *Finch* —9C **30**
Solecote. *Bookh* —3A **98**
Sole Farm Av. *Bookh* —3N **97**
Sole Farm Clo. *Bookh* —2N **97**
Sole Farm Rd. *Bookh* —3N **97**
Solent Rd. *H'row A* —9A **8**
Solna Av. *SW15* —8H **13**
Soloms Ct. Rd. *Bans* —4B **82**
Solway Clo. *Houn* —6A **42**
Solway Clo. *Houn* —6M **9**
Somer Ct. SW6 —2M **13**
(off Anselm Rd.)
Somerfield Clo. *Tad* —6K **81**
Somergate. *H'ham* —6F **196**
Somersbury La. *Ewh & Rudg* —8G **157**
Somers Clo. *Reig* —2M **121**
Somerset Av. *SW20* —1G **42**
Somerset Av. *Chess* —1K **59**
Somerset Clo. *Eps* —5C **60**
Somerset Clo. *N Mald* —5D **42**
Somerset Clo. *W On T* —2J **57**
Somerset Ct. *F'boro* —4A **90**
Somerset Gdns. *SW16* —2K **45**
Somerset Gdns. *Tedd* —6E **24**
Somerset Gro. *Warf* —8D **16**
Somerset Ho. *Red* —2D **122**
Somerset Lodge. *Bren* —2K **11**
Somerset Rd. *SW19* —4J **27**
Somerset Rd. *Bren* —2J **11**
Somerset Rd. *F'boro* —4A **90**
Somerset Rd. *King T* —1M **41**
Somerset Rd. *Red* —5B **122**
Somerset Rd. *Tedd* —6E **24**
Somerset Waye. *Houn* —2M **9**
Somers Pl. *SW2* —1K **29**
Somers Pl. *Reig* —2M **121**
Somers Rd. *SW2* —1K **29**
Somers Rd. *Reig* —2M **121**
Somerswey. *Shalf* —2A **134**
Somerton Av. *Rich* —6A **12**
Somerton Clo. *Purl* —3L **83**
Somerton's Clo. *Guild* —9K **93**
Somerville Ct. Red —2C **122**
(off Oxford Rd.)
Somerville Cres. *Yat* —9D **48**
Somerville Dri. *Craw* —9G **163**
Somerville Rd. *Cobh* —1A **78**
Somerville Rd. *Eton* —1F **4**
Sondes Farm. *Dork* —5F **118**
Sondes Pl. Dri. *Dork* —5F **118**
Sonia Gdns. *Houn* —3A **10**
Sonnet Wlk. *Big H* —5D **86**
Sonninge Clo. *Col T* —7J **49**
Sonning Gdns. *Hamp* —7M **23**
Sonning Rd. *SE25* —5D **46**
Sontan Ct. *Twic* —2D **24**
Soper Dri. *Cat* —1A **104**
Sopwith Av. *Chess* —2L **59**
Sopwith Clo. *Big H* —3F **86**
Sopwith Clo. *King T* —6M **25**
Sopwith Dri. *Brook P* —7N **55**
Sopwith Rd. *Houn* —3K **9**
Sopwith Way. *King T* —9L **25**
Sorbie Clo. *Wey* —3E **56**
Sorrel Bank. *Croy* —5H **65**
Sorrel Clo. *Craw* —7M **181**
Sorrel Clo. *F'boro* —9H **69**
Sorrel Clo. *Wokgm* —9D **14**
Sorrel Dri. *Light* —8K **51**
Sorrell Clo. *Eden* —9M **127**
Sorrell Rd. *H'ham* —3L **197**
Sorrento Rd. *Sutt* —9N **43**
Sotheron Rd. *SW6* —3N **13**
S. Albert Rd. *Reig* —2L **121**
Southall La. *Houn & S'hall* —2J **9**
Southam Ho. Add —2K **55**
(off Addlestone Pk.)
Southampton Clo. *B'water* —9H **49**
Southampton Gdns. *Mitc* —4J **45**
Southampton Rd. *H'row A* —9N **7**
Southampton St. *F'boro* —5N **89**
Southampton Way. *Stanw* —9N **7**
S. Atlantic Dri. *Alder* —1A **110**
South Av. *Cars* —4E **62**
South Av. *Egh* —7E **20**
South Av. *Farnh* —6J **109**
South Av. *Rich* —5N **11**
South Av. *Wey* —6B **56**
South Av. *W Vill* —6F **56**
South Bank. *Surb* —5L **41**
Southbank. *Th Dit* —6H **41**
South Bank. *W'ham* —4M **107**
S. Bank Ter. *Surb* —5L **41**
S. Black Lion La. *W6* —1F **12**
S. Bolton Gdns. *SW5* —1N **13**
S. Border, The. *Purl* —7H **63**
Southborough Clo. *Surb* —7K **41**
Southborough Rd. *Surb* —7L **41**
Southbridge Pl. *Croy* —1N **63**
Southbridge Rd. *Croy* —1N **63**
Southbrook. *Craw* —8A **182**
Southbrook Rd. *SW16* —9J **29**
Southby Dri. *Fleet* —4C **88**
South Clo. *Craw* —2D **182**
South Clo. *Mord* —5M **43**
South Clo. *Twic* —4A **24**
South Clo. *Wok* —3M **73**
South Clo. *Wokgm* —2B **30**
(Peach St.)
South Clo. *Wokgm* —4C **30**
(South Dri.)
South Clo. Grn. *Red* —7F **102**
Southcote. *Wok* —2N **73**
Southcote Av. *Felt* —3H **23**
Southcote Av. *Surb* —6A **42**
Southcote Dri. *Camb* —1E **70**
Southcote Rd. *SE25* —4E **46**
Southcote Rd. *Red* —7G **102**
Southcote Rd. *S Croy* —6B **64**
South Croft. *Egh* —6L **19**
Southcroft Av. *W Wick* —8M **47**
Southcroft Rd. *SW17 & SW16* —7E **28**
Southdean Gdns. *SW19* —3L **27**
Southdown Clo. *H'ham* —3N **197**
Southdown Dri. *SW20* —8J **27**
Southdown Rd. *SW20* —9J **27**
Southdown Rd. *Cars* —5E **62**
Southdown Rd. *W On T* —1M **57**
Southdown Rd. *Wold* —9J **85**
South Dri. *Bans* —9C **62**
South Dri. *Brkwd* —8N **71**
South Dri. *Coul* —2H **83**
South Dri. *Dork* —5J **119**
South Dri. *Orp* —2N **67**
South Dri. *Sutt* —6K **61**
South Dri. *Vir W* —7K **35**
South Dri. *Wokgm* —3B **30**
S. Ealing Rd. *W5* —1K **11**
S. Eden Pk. Rd. *Beck* —5L **47**
South End. *Bookh* —4B **98**
South End. *Croy* —1N **63**
Southerland Clo. *Wey* —1D **56**
Southern Av. *SE25* —2C **46**
Southern Av. *Felt* —2H **23**
Southern Av. *Red* —1E **142**
Southern Cotts. *Stai* —8J **7**
Southern Perimeter Rd. *H'row A* —8K **7**
Southern Rd. *Camb* —9A **50**
Southerns La. *Coul* —3A **102**
Southern Way. *F'boro* —2J **89**
Southern Way. *Farnh* —2H **129**
Southey Ct. *Bookh* —2B **98**
Southey Rd. *SW19* —8M **27**
S. Farm La. *Bag & Light* —5L **51**
Southfield Gdns. *Twic* —5F **24**
Southfield Pl. *Wey* —4C **56**
Southfields. *E Mol* —5E **40**
Southfields Av. *Ashf* —7C **22**
Southfields Ct. *Sutt* —8M **43**
Southfields M. *SW18* —9M **13**
Southfields Pas. *SW18* —9M **13**
Southfields Rd. *SW18* —9M **13**
Southfields Rd. *Wold* —9L **85**
Southfleet Rd. *Orp* —1N **67**
South Gdns. *SW19* —8B **28**
Southgate Av. *Craw* —6B **182**
Southgate Av. *Felt* —5E **22**
Southgate Dri. *Craw* —5B **182**
Southgate Pde. *Craw* —5B **182**
Southgate Rd. *Craw* —5B **182**
South Gro. *Cher* —5H **37**
South Gro. *Fleet* —1D **88**
South Gro. *H'ham* —7K **197**
South Hill. *G'ming* —7H **133**
South Hill. *Guild* —5N **113**
S. Hill Rd. *Brack* —5M **31**
S. Hill Rd. *Brom* —2N **47**
S. Holmes Rd. *H'ham* —4A **198**
Southlands. *E Grin* —2A **186**
Southlands Av. *Horl* —7E **142**
Southlands Av. *Orp* —1M **67**
Southlands Clo. *Ash* —3F **110**
Southlands Clo. *Coul* —4[illegible] [illegible]
Southlands Clo. *Wokgm* —3C **30**
Southlands Dri. *SW19* —3J **27**
Southlands La. *Oxt* —3L **125**
Southlands Rd. *Ash* —3E **110**
Southlands Rd. *Wokgm* —4C **30**
Southland Way. *Houn* —8D **10**
South La. *Ash* —3F **110**
South La. *King T* —2K **41**
South La. *N Mald* —3C **42**
South La. W. *N Mald* —3C **42**
Southlea Rd. *Dat & Old Win* —4L **5**
S. Lodge. *Twic* —1C **24**
S. Lodge Av. *Mitc* —3J **45**
S. Lodge Rd. *W on T* —5H **57**
Southly Clo. *Sutt* —9M **43**
S. Lynn Cres. *Brack* —4N **31**
South Mall. *Fleet* —4A **88**
South Mall. *Stai* —5H **21**
South Mead. *Eps* —4E **60**
South Mead. *Red* —9D **102**
S. Meadow. *Crowt* —4J **49**
S. Meadow La. *Eton* —2F **4**
Southmead Rd. *SW19* —2K **27**
Southmead Rd. *Alder* —4N **109**
Southmont Rd. *Esh* —8E **40**
S. Munstead La. *G'ming* —3L **153**
S. Norwood Hill. *SE19 & SE25* —1B **46**
S. Oak Rd. *SW16* —5K **29**
South Pde. *Horl* —7D **142**
South Pde. *Red* —6G **102**
South Pde. *Wall* —3G **62**
South Pk. Gro. *N Mald* —3B **42**
South Pk. Hill Rd. *S Croy* —2A **64**
South Pk. La. *Blet* —5D **124**
South Pk. M. *SW6* —6N **13**
South Pk. Rd. *SW19* —7M **27**
S. Path. *Wind* —4F **4**
S. Pier Rd. *Horl* —3F **162**
South Pl. *Surb* —6M **41**
S. Ridge. *Wey* —6C **56**
Southridge Pl. *SW20* —8J **27**
S. Rise. *Cars* —5C **62**
South Rd. *SW19* —7A **28**
South Rd. *Ash V* —9E **90**
South Rd. *Bisl* —3C **72**
South Rd. *Crowt* —4K **49**
South Rd. *Egh* —7M **19**
South Rd. *Felt* —6L **23**
South Rd. *Guild* —1L **113**
South Rd. *Hamp* —7M **23**
South Rd. *Reig* —4N **121**
South Rd. *St G* —5C **56**
South Rd. *Twic* —4D **24**
South Rd. *Wey* —2D **56**
South Rd. *Wok* —2M **73**
South Rd. *Wokgm* —6J **31**
Southsea Rd. *King T* —3L **41**
South Side. *Cher* —2J **37**
South Side. *Tong* —5D **110**
Southside Comn. *SW19* —7H **27**
S. Station App. *S Nut* —5J **123**
South St. *Dork* —6G **119**
South St. *Eps* —9C **60**
South St. *F'boro* —4C **90**
South St. *Farnh* —1H **129**
South St. *G'ming* —7G **133**
South St. *H'ham* —7J **197**
South St. *Iswth* —6G **11**
South St. *Stai* —6H **21**
South Ter. *Dork* —6H **119**
South Ter. *Surb* —5L **41**
South View. *Brack* —2J **31**
Southview. *Fren* —1J **149**
Southview Clo. *SW17* —6E **28**
Southview Clo. *Copt* —7B **164**
S. View Ct. *SE19* —8N **29**
S. View Ct. *Wok* —5A **74**
Southview Gdns. *Wall* —4G **63**
S. View Rd. *Asht* —6K **79**
S. View Rd. *Head* —4G **168**
Southview Rd. *Warl* —6D **84**
Southview Rd. *Wold* —2L **105**
Southviews. *S Croy* —5G **65**
Southville Clo. *Eps* —5C **60**
Southville Clo. *Felt* —2F **22**
Southville Cres. *Felt* —2F **22**
Southville Rd. *Felt* —2F **22**
Southville Rd. *Th Dit* —6H **41**
South Wlk. *Alder* —2B **110**
South Wlk. *Reig* —3N **121**
South Wlk. *W Wick* —9N **47**
Southwark Clo. *Craw* —7N **181**
Southwark Clo. *Yat* —9B **48**
Southway. *SW20* —3H **43**
Southway. *Camb* —2N **69**
South Way. *Cars* —6B **62**
South Way. *Croy* —9H **47**
Southway. *Guild* —3H **113**
Southway. *Wall* —1G **63**
Southway Ct. *Guild* —3H **113**
Southwell Cotts. *Horl* —3K **161**
Southwell Pk. Rd. *Camb* —1N **69**
Southwell Rd. *Croy* —5L **45**
S. Western Rd. *Twic* —9G **11**
Southwick. *Bag* —6J **51**
Southwick Clo. *E Grin* —9N **165**
Southwick Ct. *Brack* —9C **32**
Southwold. *Brack* —7K **31**
Southwood. *Wokgm* —4C **30**
Southwood Av. *Coul* —2G **83**
Southwood Av. *King T* —9B **26**
Southwood Av. *Knap* —5G **73**
Southwood Av. *Ott* —4E **54**
Southwood Bus. Cen. *F'boro* —1J **89**
Southwood Chase. *Cranl* —9A **156**
Southwood Clo. *Wor Pk* —7J **43**
Southwood Cres. *Swd P* —1J **89**
Southwood Dri. *Surb* —6B **42**
Southwood Gdns. *Esh* —9G **40**
Southwood La. *F'boro* —2J **89**
Southwood La. *Fleet* —2E **88**
Southwood Rd. *F'boro* —2J **89**
Southwood Village Cen. *F'boro* —2J **89**
S. Worple Av. *SW14* —6D **12**
S. Worple Way. *SW14* —6C **12**
Sovereign Clo. *Purl* —6K **63**
Sovereign Ct. *Asc* —6E **34**
Sovereign Ct. *Houn* —6A **10**
Sovereign Ct. *W Mol* —3N **39**
Sovereign Dri. *Camb* —8F **50**
Soyer Ct. *Wok* —5H **73**
Space Waye. *Felt* —8H **9**
Spa Clo. *SE19* —1B **46**
Spa Ct. *SW16* —5K **29**
Spa Dri. *Eps* —1N **79**
Spa Hill. *SE19* —9N **29**
Spalding Rd. *SW17* —6F **28**
Sparks Clo. *Hamp* —7M **23**
Sparrow Clo. *Hamp* —7M **23**
Sparrow Farm Dri. *Felt* —1K **23**
Sparrow Farm Rd. *Eps* —1F **60**
Sparrowhawk Clo. *Ews* —5C **108**
Sparrow Row. *W End* —3E **52**
Sparrows Mead. *Red* —9E **102**
Sparvell Rd. *Knap* —6E **72**
Sparvell Way. *Camb* —9A **50**
Spats La. *Head* —1E **168**
Speakers Ct. *Croy* —7A **46**
Spear M. *SW5* —1M **13**
Speart La. *Houn* —3M **9**
Speedwell Clo. *Eden* —9M **127**
Speedwell Clo. *Guild* —9E **94**
Speedwell Way. *H'ham* —3L **197**
Speer Rd. *Th Dit* —5F **40**
Speirs Clo. *N Mald* —5E **42**
Speke Rd. *T Hth* —1A **46**
Spelthorne Gro. *Sun* —8G **22**
Spelthorne La. *Ashf* —9D **22**
Spence Av. *Byfl* —1A **76**
Spencer Clo. *C Crook* —8D **88**
Spencer Clo. *Eps* —6D **80**
Spencer Clo. *Frim G* —8C **70**
Spencer Clo. *Wok* —9F **54**
Spencer Ct. *Farn* —2L **67**
Spencer Gdns. *SW14* —8B **12**
Spencer Gdns. *Egh* —6N **19**
Spencer Hill. *SW19* —7K **27**
Spencer M. *W6* —2K **13**
Spencer Pk. *E Mol* —4C **40**
Spencer Pl. *Croy* —6A **46**
Spencer Rd. *SW20* —9G **27**
Spencer Rd. *W4* —3B **12**
Spencer Rd. *Brack* —9L **15**
Spencer Rd. *Cat* —8A **84**
Spencer Rd. *Cobh* —2J **77**
Spencer Rd. *E Mol* —3C **40**
Spencer Rd. *Iswth* —4C **10**
Spencer Rd. *Mitc* —2E **44**
Spencer Rd. *Mit J* —6E **44**
Spencer Rd. *S Croy* —2B **64**
Spencer Rd. *Twic* —4E **24**
Spencers La. *Horl* —1L **161**
Spencers Pl. *H'ham* —4H **197**
Spencers Rd. *Craw* —4A **182**
(in two parts)
Spencer's Rd. *H'ham* —5H **197**
Spencer Wlk. *SW15* —7J **13**
Spencer Way. *Red* —8E **122**
Spenser Av. *Wey* —4B **56**
Spenser M. *SE21* —3N **29**
Spiceall. *Comp* —1E **132**
Spicer Clo. *W On T* —5K **39**
Spicers Field. *Oxs* —9D **58**
Spice's Yd. *Croy* —1N **63**
Spiers Way. *Horl* —1F **162**
Spindle Way. *Craw* —4D **182**
Spindlewood Gdns. *Croy* —1B **64**
Spindlewoods. *Tad* —9G **81**
Spinis. *Brack* —7L **31**
Spinner Grn. *Brack* —4N **31**
Spinners Wlk. *Wind* —4F **4**
Spinney Clo. *Cobh* —7A **58**
Spinney Clo. *Craw D* —1F **184**
Spinney Clo. *H'ham* —2A **198**
Spinney Clo. *N Mald* —4D **42**
Spinney Clo. *Wor Pk* —8E **42**
Spinney Croft. *Oxs* —2D **78**
Spinney Dri. *Felt* —1D **22**
Spinney Hill. *Add* —2G **55**
Spinney La. *Wink* —2M **17**
Spinney Oak. *Ott* —3F **54**
Spinney, The. *SW13* —2G **12**
Spinney, The. *SW16* —4G **29**
Spinney, The. *Asc* —4B **34**
Spinney, The. *Bookh* —2B **98**
Spinney, The. *Camb* —9G **51**
Spinney, The. *Craw* —5N **181**
Spinney, The. *Eps* —9D **60**
(Epsom)
Spinney, The. *Eps* —6G **81**
(Tattenham Corner)
Spinney, The. *Hasl* —9G **171**
Spinney, The. *Horl* —6E **142**
Spinney, The. *Oxs* —8C **58**
Spinney, The. *Purl* —7M **63**
Spinney, The. *Send* —5L **95**
Spinney, The. *Shot* —3A **188**
Spinney, The. *Sun* —9H **23**
Spinney, The. *Sutt* —1H **61**
Spinney, The. *Yat* —8C **48**
Spinney Way. *Cud* —7M **67**
Spinning Wlk., The. *Shere* —8B **116**
Spinningwheel La. *Binf* —1H **15**
Spital Heath. *Dork* —4J **119**
Spitfire Est., The. *Houn* —1K **9**
Spitfire Rd. *H'row A* —9D **8**
Spitfire Way. *Houn* —1K **9**
Splash, The. *Binf* —7N **15**
Spode La. *Cowd* —1N **167**
Spoil La. *Tong* —5D **110**
Spokane Clo. *Alder* —4L **109**
Spook Hill. *N Holm* —1H **139**
Spooner Ho. *Houn* —2A **10**
Spooners Rd. *H'ham* —4N **197**
Spooner Wlk. *Wall* —2J **63**
Spout Hill. *Croy* —2K **65**
Spout La. *Crook C* —3L **127**
Spout La. *Stai* —7J **7**
Spout La. N. *Stai* —7K **7**
Spratts All. *Ott* —3G **54**
Spratts La. *Ott* —3G **54**
Spray La. *Twic* —9E **10**
Spread Eagle Wlk. *Eps* —9C **60**
Spreighton Rd. *W Mol* —3B **40**
Spring Av. *Egh* —7A **20**
Springbok Cotts. *Alf* —7G **174**
Springbok Est. *Alf* —7F **174**
(in two parts)
Spring Bottom La. *Blet* —5L **103**
Springbourne Ct. *Beck* —1M **47**
(in two parts)
Spring Clo. *G'ming* —3H **133**
Spring Clo. La. *Sutt* —3K **61**
Spring Copse. *Copt* —7N **163**
Spring Copse. *E Grin* —7B **166**
Springcopse Rd. *Reig* —5A **122**
Spring Corner. *Felt* —4H **23**
Spring Cotts. *Dork* —6J **139**
Spring Cotts. *Surb* —4K **41**
Spring Ct. *Eps* —5E **60**
Spring Ct. *Guild* —8L **93**
Springcross Av. *B'water* —3J **69**
Springfarm Rd. *Hasl* —3C **188**
Springfield. *E Grin* —6N **165**
Springfield. *Elst* —7H **131**
Springfield. *Light* —7A **52**
Springfield. *Oxt* —8N **105**
Springfield Av. *SW20* —2L **43**
Springfield Av. *Hamp* —7B **24**
Springfield Clo. *Knap* —5H **73**
Springfield Clo. *Wind* —5E **4**
Springfield Ct. *Craw* —4B **182**
Springfield Ct. *H'ham* —6J **197**
Springfield Ct. *Wall* —2F **62**
Springfield Cres. *H'ham* —6H **197**
Springfield Dri. *Lea* —7E **78**
Springfield Gdns. *W Wick* —8L **47**
Springfield Gro. *Sun* —9H **23**
Springfield La. *Colg* —5F **198**
Springfield La. *Fleet* —4A **88**
Springfield La. *Wey* —1C **56**
Springfield Meadows. *Wey* —1C **56**
Springfield Pk. Rd. *H'ham* —6H **197**
Springfield Pl. *N Mald* —3B **42**
Springfield Rd. *SW19* —6L **27**
Springfield Rd. *Ashf* —6A **22**
Springfield Rd. *Ash V* —8E **90**
Springfield Rd. *Binf* —1H **31**
Springfield Rd. *Camb* —1E **70**
Springfield Rd. *Craw* —4A **182**
Springfield Rd. *Eden* —2K **147**
Springfield Rd. *Eps* —6H **61**
Springfield Rd. *Guild* —3A **114**
Springfield Rd. *H'ham* —6H **197**
(in two parts)
Springfield Rd. *King T* —2L **41**
Springfield Rd. *Slou* —3D **6**
Springfield Rd. *Tedd* —6G **24**
Springfield Rd. *T Hth* —9N **29**
Springfield Rd. *Twic* —2A **24**
Springfield Rd. *Wall* —2F **62**
Springfield Rd. *Westc* —6B **118**
Springfield Rd. *Wind* —5E **4**
Springfields Clo. *Cher* —7K **37**
Springfield Way. *Elst* —8J **131**
Springflower Cotts. *Guild* —9F **92**
Spring Gdns. *Asc* —3M **33**
Spring Gdns. *Big H* —5F **86**
Spring Gdns. *Camb* —1E **70**
Spring Gdns. *Copt* —7N **163**
Spring Gdns. *Dork* —5G **118**
Spring Gdns. *F'boro* —7M **69**
Spring Gdns. *H'ham* —5J **197**
Spring Gdns. *N Asc* —8J **17**
Spring Gdns. *Wall* —2G **62**
Spring Gdns. *W Mol* —4B **40**
Spring Gro. *W4* —1N **11**
Spring Gro. *Fet* —1B **98**
Spring Gro. *G'ming* —3H **133**
Spring Gro. *Hamp* —9B **24**
Spring Gro. *Mitc* —9E **28**
Spring Gro. Cres. *Houn* —4C **10**
Spring Gro. Rd. *Houn & Iswth* —4B **10**
Spring Gro. Rd. *Rich* —8M **11**
Springhaven. *Elst* —8J **131**
Springhaven Clo. *Guild* —3C **114**
Springhill. *Elst* —8J **131**
Springhill Ct. *Brack* —3N **31**
Springholm Clo. *Big H* —5E **86**
Springhurst Clo. *Croy* —1J **65**
Springlakes Ind. Est. *Alder* —1C **110**
Spring La. *SE25* —5E **46**
Spring La. *Farnh* —5F **108**
Spring La. *Oxt* —9N **105**
Spring La. *Slin* —5K **195**
Spring La. W. *Farnh* —6F **108**
Springmead Ct. *Sand* —6K **49**
Spring Meadow. *Brack* —9B **16**
Spring Meadow. *F Row* —8H **187**
Spring M. *Eps* —5E **60**
Spring Pk. Av. *Croy* —8G **47**
Springpark Dri. *Beck* —2M **47**
Spring Pk. Rd. *Croy* —8G **47**
Spring Plat. *Craw* —3G **183**
Spring Plat Ct. *Craw* —3G **183**
Spring Rise. *Egh* —7A **20**
Spring Rd. *Felt* —4G **23**
Springside Ct. *Guild* —2M **113**
Spring St. *Eps* —5E **60**
Spring Ter. *Rich* —8L **11**
Springvale Av. *Bren* —1L **11**
Spring Wlk. *Horl* —8D **142**
Spring Way. *E Grin* —6C **166**
Springwell Clo. *SW16* —5K **29**
Springwell Ct. *Houn* —5L **9**
Springwell Rd. *SW16* —5L **29**
Springwell Rd. *Bear G* —8K **139**
Springwell Rd. *Houn* —4L **9**
Springwood. *Milf* —1D **152**
Springwood Ct. *S Croy* —1B **64**
Spring Woods. *Fleet* —6A **88**
Spring Woods. *Sand* —6H **49**
Spring Woods. *Vir W* —3L **35**
Sprint Ind. Est. *Byfl* —7M **55**
Sprucedale Gdns. *Croy* —1G **65**
Sprucedale Gdns. *Wall* —5J **63**
Spruce Dri. *Light* —8L **51**
Spruce Rd. *Big H* —3F **86**
Spruce Way. *Fleet* —4E **88**
Spurfield. *W Mol* —2B **40**
Spurgeon Av. *SE19* —9N **29**
Spurgeon Clo. *Craw* —2A **182**
Spurgeon Rd. *SE19* —9N **29**
Spur Rd. *Felt* —7J **9**
Spur Rd. *Iswth* —3G **11**
Spurs Ct. *Alder* —2K **109**

Stoneyfields—Sylvan Rd.

Stoneyfields. Farnh —2K 129
Stoneylands Ct. Egh —6B 20
Stoneylands Rd. Egh —6B 20
Stoney Rd. Brack —9M 15
Stonny Croft. Asht —4M 79
Stonor Rd. W14 —1L 13
Stonyfield. Eden —9M 127
Stony Hill. W End —4N 57
Stookes Way. Yat —2A 68
Stoop Ct. W Byf —8K 55
Stopham Rd. M'bowr —6G 182
Stormont Way. Chess —2J 59
Storrington Ct. Craw —2M 181
Storrington Rd. Croy —7C 46
Stoughton Av. Sutt —2J 61
Stoughton Clo. SW15 —2F 26
Stoughton Rd. Guild —9K 93
Stour Clo. Kes —1E 66
Stourhead Clo. SW19 —1J 27
Stourhead Clo. F'boro —1B 90
Stourhead Gdns. SW20 —2F 42
Stourton Av. Felt —5N 23
Stovell Rd. Wind —3E 4
Stovolds Hill. Cranl —1E 174
Stovold's Way. Alder —4L 109
Stowell Av. New Ad —6N 65
Stowting Rd. Orp —1N 67
Strachan Pl. SW19 —7H 27
Strachey Ct. Craw —8N 181
Stradella Rd. SE24 —1N 29
Strafford Rd. Houn —6N 9
Strafford Rd. Twic —1G 25
Straight Mile, The. Shur R & Wokgm —1C 14
Straight Rd. Old Win —8K 5
Stran Clo. Cat —1N 103
Strand Clo. Eps —6C 80
Strand Clo. M'bowr —5H 183
Strand on the Grn. W4 —2N 11
Strand School App. W4 —2N 11
Stranraer Rd. H'row A —9N 7
Stranraer Way. Stanw —9N 7
Stratfield. Brack —7K 31
Stratford Ct. Farnh —3H 129
Stratford Ct. N Mald —3C 42
Stratford Gro. SW15 —7J 13
Stratford Rd. Ash V —5D 90
Stratford Rd. H'row A —9C 8
Stratford Rd. S'hall —1M 9
Stratford Rd. T Hth —3L 45
Strathan Clo. SW18 —9L 13
Strathavon Clo. Cranl —3K 155
Strathbrook Rd. SW16 —8K 29
Strathcona Av. Bookh —6M 97
Strathdale. SW16 —6K 29
Strathdon Dri. SW17 —4B 28
Strathearn Av. Hayes —3G 9
Strathearn Av. Twic —2B 24
Strathearn Rd. SW19 —6M 27
Strathearn Rd. Sutt —2M 61
Strathmore Clo. Cat —8B 84
Strathmore Ct. Camb —9B 50
Strathmore Rd. SW19 —4M 27
Strathmore Rd. Croy —6A 46
Strathmore Rd. If'd —9M 161
Strathmore Rd. Tedd —5E 24
Strathville Rd. SW18 —3M 27
Strathyre Av. SW16 —2L 45
Stratton Av. Wall —5H 63
Stratton Clo. SW19 —1M 43
Stratton Clo. Houn —4A 10
Stratton Clo. W On T —7K 39
Stratton Ct. Guild —1K 113
Stratton Rd. SW19 —1M 43
Stratton Rd. Sun —1G 38
Stratton Ter. W'ham —5L 107
Stratton Wlk. F'boro —7M 69
Strawberry Clo. Brkwd —8A 72
Strawberry Fields. Bisl —3D 72
Strawberry Hill. Twic —4F 24
Strawberry Hill. Warf —7C 16
Strawberry Hill Clo. Twic —4F 24
Strawberry Hill Rd. Twic —4F 24
Strawberry La. Cars —9E 44
Strawberry Rise. Bisl —2D 72
Strawberry Vale. Twic —4G 24
Stream Clo. Byfl —8M 55
Stream Cotts. Frim —5B 70
(off Grove Cross Rd.)
Stream Farm Clo. Lwr Bo —4J 129
Stream Pk. E Grin —7K 165
Streamside. Fleet —5B 88
Stream Valley Rd. Lwr Bo —5H 129
Streatfield. Eden —2M 147
Streatham Clo. SW16 —3J 29
Streatham Comn. N. SW16 —6J 29
Streatham Comn. S. SW16 —7J 29
Streatham Ct. SW16 —4J 29
Streatham High Rd. SW16 —5J 29
Streatham Hill. SW2 —3J 29
Streatham Pl. SW2 —1J 29
Streatham Rd. Mitc & SW16 —9E 28
Streatham Vale. SW16 —9G 29
Streathbourne Rd. SW17 —3E 28
Streeters Clo. G'ming —5K 133
Streeters La. Wall —9H 45
Streetfield Rd. Slin —5L 195
Street Hill. Craw —4J 183
Streets Heath. W End —8C 52
(in two parts)
Street, The. Alb —8L 115
Street, The. Asht —5M 79
Street, The. Bet —3D 120
Street, The. Capel —3K 159
Street, The. Charl —3K 161
Street, The. E Clan —9N 95
Street, The. Eff —6L 97
Street, The. Ewh —4F 156
Street, The. Fet —1D 98
Street, The. Fren —3H 149
Street, The. Guild —1E 132
Street, The. Hasc —7A 154
Street, The. H'ham —5L 195
Street, The. Plais —6A 192
Street, The. Putt —8N 111
Street, The. Shack —4N 131
Street, The. Shalf —9A 114
Street, The. Shur R —1F 14
Street, The. Thur —6G 150
Street, The. Tilf —7B 130
Street, The. Tong —7D 110
Street, The. W Cla —7J 95
Street, The. W Hor —7C 96
Street, The. Won —4D 134
Street, The. Wrec —4E 128
Stretton Rd. Croy —6B 46
Stretton Rd. Rich —3J 25
Strickland Clo. If'd —4K 181
Strickland Row. SW18 —1B 28
Strickland Way. Orp —1N 67
Stringer's Av. Guild —6N 93
Stringhams Copse. Rip —2J 95
Strode Rd. SW6 —3K 13
Strode's College La. Egh —6B 20
Strode's Cres. Stai —6L 21
Strode St. Egh —5C 20
Strood La. Asc —7N 17
Strood La. Warn —1B 196
Stroud Clo. Wind —6A 4
Stroud Comn. Sham G —8H 135
Stroud Cres. SW15 —4F 26
Stroude Rd. Egh & Vir W —7C 20
Stroudes Clo. Wor Pk —6D 42
Stroud Grn. Gdns. Croy —6F 46
Stroud Grn. Way. Croy —6E 46
Stroud La. Sham G —9J 135
Stroudley Clo. M'bowr —4F 182
Stroud Rd. SE25 —5D 46
Stroud Rd. SW19 —4M 27
Stroudwater Pk. Wey —3C 56
Stroud Way. Ashf —7C 22
Struan Gdns. Wok —2A 74
Strudgate Clo. Craw —5F 182
Strudwicks Field. Cranl —6A 156
Stuart Av. W On T —7J 39
Stuart Clo. Craw —4H 183
Stuart Clo. F'boro —9M 69
Stuart Clo. Wind —5C 4
Stuart Ct. G'ming —7H 133
Stuart Ct. Red —2E 122
(off St Anne's Rise)
Stuart Cres. Croy —9J 47
Stuart Cres. Reig —6M 121
Stuart Gro. Tedd —6E 24
Stuart Pl. Mitc —9D 28
Stuart Rd. SW19 —4M 27
Stuart Rd. Reig —6M 121
Stuart Rd. Rich —3H 25
Stuart Rd. T Hth —3N 45
Stuart Rd. Warl —7E 84
Stuart Way. E Grin —2B 186
Stuart Way. Stai —7K 21
Stuart Way. Vir W —3K 35
Stuart Way. Wind —5B 4
Stubbs Ct. W4 —1A 12
(off Chaseley Dri.)
Stubbs Folly. Col T —8J 49
Stubbs Hill. Binf —5K 15
Stubbs La. Lwr K —6L 101
Stubbs Moor Rd. F'boro —9L 69
Stubbs Way. SW19 —9B 28
Stubfield. H'ham —5G 196
Stubpond La. Newc & E Grin —2F 164
Stubs Clo. Dork —7J 119
Stubs Hill. Dork —7J 119
Stucley Rd. Houn —3C 10
Studdridge St. SW6 —5M 13
Studios Rd. Shep —2A 38
Studland Rd. Byfl —9A 56
Studland Rd. King T —7L 25
Studland St. W6 —1G 12
Stumblets. Craw —2G 183
Stumps La. Whyt —4B 84
Sturdee Clo. Frim —5C 70
Sturges Rd. Wokgm —3B 30
Sturt Av. Hasl —3D 188
Sturt Ct. Guild —1D 114
Sturt Meadow Cotts. Hasl —3D 188
Sturt Rd. Farnh —5G 109
Sturt Rd. Frim G —9D 70
Sturt Rd. Hasl —2D 188
Sturt's La. Tad —5E 100
Stychens Clo. Blet —2N 123
Stychens La. Blet —9N 103
Styles End. Bookh —5B 98
Styles Way. Beck —3M 47
Styventon Pl. Cher —6H 37
Subrosa Cvn. Site. Red —8F 102
Succombs Hill. Warl —7E 84
Succombs Pl. Warl —6E 84
Sudbrooke Rd. SW12 —1D 28
Sudbrook Gdns. Rich —4L 25
Sudbrook La. Rich —2L 25
Sudbury Gdns. Croy —1B 64
Sudlow Rd. SW18 —8M 13
Suffield Clo. S Croy —8G 64
Suffield La. Elst & Putt —4H 131
Suffield Rd. SE20 —1F 46
Suffolk Clo. Bag —5J 51
Suffolk Clo. Horl —9E 142
Suffolk Combe. Warf —8D 16
Suffolk Dri. Guild —7D 94
Suffolk Rd. SE25 —3C 46
Suffolk Rd. SW13 —3E 12
Suffolk Rd. Wor Pk —8E 42
Sugden Rd. Th Dit —7H 41
Sulina Rd. SW2 —1J 29
Sulivan Ct. SW6 —5M 13
Sulivan Enterprise Cen. SW6 —6M 13
Sulivan Rd. SW6 —6M 13
Sullington Hill. Craw —5B 182
Sullington Mead. Broad H —5E 196
Sullivan Clo. F'boro —1N 89
Sullivan Clo. W Mol —2B 40
Sullivan Dri. Craw —6K 181
Sullivan Rd. Camb —1M 69
Sullivans Reach. W On T —6G 39
Sultan St. Beck —1G 47
Summer Av. E Mol —4F 40
Summerene Clo. SW16 —8G 29
Summerfield. Asht —6K 79
Summerfield Clo. Add —2H 55
Summerfield La. Fren —9F 128
Summerfield La. Surb —8K 41
Summerfield Pl. Ott —3F 54
Summer Gdns. Camb —1G 71
Summer Gdns. E Mol —4E 40
Summerhayes Clo. Wok —1A 74
Summerhays. Cobh —9L 57
Summerhill. G'ming —5G 132
Summerhill Clo. Orp —1N 67
Summerhill Way. Mitc —9E 28
Summerhouse Av. Houn —4M 9
Summerhouse Clo. G'ming —7G 133
Summerhouse Ct. Gray —6B 170
Summerhouse La. W Dray —2M 7
Summerhouse Rd. G'ming —8G 133
Summerlands. Cranl —6N 155
Summerlands Lodge. Orp —1J 67
Summerlay Clo. Tad —7K 81
Summerleigh. Wey —3E 56
(off Gower Rd.)
Summerley St. SW18 —3N 27
Summerly Av. Reig —2M 121
Summer Rd. E Mol & Th Dit —4E 40
Summersbury Dri. Shalf —2A 134
Summersby Clo. G'ming —4J 133
Summers Clo. Sutt —4M 61
Summers Clo. Wey —7B 56
Summers La. Hurt —3D 132
Summer's Rd. G'ming —4J 133
Summerstown. SW17 —4A 28
Summersvere Clo. Craw —9E 162
Summerswood Clo. Kenl —3A 84
Summer Trees. Sun —9J 23
Summerville Gdns. Sutt —3L 61
Summerwood Rd. Iswth —8F 10
Summit Av. Fleet & Farnh —1G 88
Summit Bus. Pk. Sun —8H 23
Summit Pl. Wey —4B 56
Sumner Clo. Fet —2D 98
Sumner Clo. Orp —1L 67
Sumner Ct. Farnh —9H 109
Sumner Gdns. Croy —7M 45
Sumner Pl. Add —2J 55
Sumner Rd. Croy —7L 45
Sumner Rd. Farnh —9H 109
Sumner Rd. S. Croy —7L 45
Sun All. Rich —7L 11
Sun Brow. Hasl —3D 188
Sunbury Av. SW14 —7C 12
Sunbury Ct. Eton —2G 4
Sunbury Ct. Island. Sun —2L 39
Sunbury Ct. M. Sun —1L 39
Sunbury Ct. Rd. Sun —1K 39
Sunbury Cres. Felt —5G 23
Sunbury Cross. (Junct.) —8H 23
Sunbury Cross Shop. Cen. Sun —8G 23
Sunbury La. W On T —5H 39
Sunburylock Ait. W On T —3J 39
Sunbury Rd. Eton —2G 4
Sunbury Rd. Felt —4G 23
Sunbury Rd. Sutt —9K 43
Sunbury Way. Felt —6K 23
Sun Clo. Eton —2G 4
Sundale Av. S Croy —6F 64
Sunderland Ct. Stanw —9N 7
Sunderland Rd. H'row A —9N 7
Sundew Clo. Craw —7M 181
Sundew Clo. Light —7A 52
Sundew Clo. Wokgm —9D 14
Sundial Av. SE25 —2C 46
Sundials Cvn. Site. Hkwd —9B 142
Sundon Cres. Vir W —4L 35
Sundown Av. S Croy —7C 64
Sundown Rd. Ashf —6D 22
Sundridge Pl. Croy —7D 46
Sundridge Rd. Croy —6C 46
Sundridge Rd. Wok —6C 74
Sun Hill. Wok —8K 73
Sun Inn Rd. Duns —4B 174
Sunkist Way. Wall —5J 63
Sunlight Clo. SW19 —7A 28
Sunmead Clo. Fet —9F 78
Sunmead Rd. Sun —1H 39
Sunna Gdns. Sun —1J 39
Sunning Av. Asc —6B 34
Sunningdale Av. Felt —3M 23
Sunningdale Clo. Surb —8L 41
Sunningdale Ct. Craw —5B 182
Sunningdale Ct. Houn —9D 10
(off Whitton Dene)
Sunningdale Rd. Sutt —1L 61
Sunninghill Clo. Asc —3A 34
Sunninghill Ct. Asc —3A 34
Sunninghill Rd. Asc —9C 18
Sunninghill Rd. S'hill —4A 34
Sunninghill Rd. W'sham —9L 33
Sunninghill Rd. Wind & Asc —6A 18
Sunningvale Av. Big H —2E 86
Sunningvale Clo. Big H —2F 86
Sunny Av. Craw D —1D 184
Sunny Bank. SE25 —2D 46
Sunnybank. Eps —3B 80
Sunnybank. Warl —4H 85
Sunnybank Rd. F'boro —8J 69
Sunnybank Vs. Red —1C 124
Sunnycroft Rd. SE25 —3D 46
Sunnycroft Rd. Houn —5B 10
Sunnydell La. Wrec —5F 128
Sunnydene Rd. Purl —9M 63
Sunny Down. Witl —5B 152
Sunny Hill. Witl —5B 152
Sunnyhill Clo. Craw D —1D 184
Sunnyhill Rd. SW16 —5J 29
Sunny Hill Rd. Alder —2J 109
Sunnyhurst Clo. Sutt —9M 43
Sunnymead. Craw —3B 182
Sunnymead. Craw D —1E 184
Sunnymead Av. Mitc —2H 45
Sunnymead Rd. SW15 —8G 12
Sunnymede Av. Cars —7B 62
Sunnymede Av. Eps —5D 60
Sunny Nook Gdns. S Croy —3A 64
Sunny Rise. Cat —2A 104
Sunnyside. SW19 —7K 27
Sunnyside. Eden —9K 127
Sunnyside. Fleet —3A 88
Sunnyside. W On T —4K 39
Sunnyside Cotts. Dork —6K 137
Sunnyside Pas. SW19 —7K 27
Sunnyside Rd. Head —5H 169
Sunnyside Rd. Tedd —5D 24
Sunny View Clo. Alder —3A 110
Sunoak Rd. H'ham —6B 198
Sun Pas. Wind —4G 4
Sunray Av. Surb —8A 42
Sun Ray Est. Sand —7F 48
Sunrise Clo. Felt —4N 23
Sun Rd. W14 —1L 13
Sunset Gdns. SE25 —1C 46
Sunshine Way. Mitc —1D 44
Sunstone Gro. Red —7J 103
Sunvale Av. Hasl —2B 188
Sunvale Clo. Hasl —2B 188
Superior Dri. Grn St —3N 67
Surbiton Ct. Surb —5J 41
Surbiton Cres. King T —3L 41
Surbiton Hall Clo. King T —3L 41
Surbiton Hill Pk. Surb —4M 41
Surbiton Hill Rd. Surb —4L 41
Surbiton Pde. Surb —5L 41
Surbiton Rd. Camb —6E 50
Surbiton Rd. King T —3K 41
Surly Hall Wlk. Wind —4C 4
Surrenden Rise. Craw —9A 182
Surrey Av. Camb —2M 69
Surrey Ct. Guild —3L 113
Surrey Ct. Warf —8D 16
Surrey Cres. W4 —1N 11
Surrey Gdns. Eff J —9H 77
Surrey Gro. Sutt —9B 44
Surrey Hills Residential Pk. Tad —8B 100
Surrey Rd. W Wick —7L 47
Surrey St. Croy —9N 45
Surridge Ct. Bag —5J 51
Surridge Gdns. SE19 —7N 29
Sussex Av. Iswth —6E 10
Sussex Clo. Knap —5F 72
Sussex Clo. N Mald —3D 42
Sussex Clo. Reig —4B 122
Sussex Clo. Twic —9H 11
Sussex Ct. Add —2L 55
Sussex Ct. Knap —4F 72
Sussex Gdns. Chess —3K 59
Sussex Gdns. Fleet —1C 88
Sussex Lodge. H'ham —4J 197
Sussex Mnr. Bus. Pk. Craw —8E 162
Sussex Pl. W6 —1H 13
Sussex Pl. Knap —5F 72
Sussex Pl. N Mald —3D 42
Sussex Rd. Cars —4D 62
Sussex Rd. Knap —5F 72
Sussex Rd. Mitc —4J 45
Sussex Rd. N Mald —3D 42
Sussex Rd. S Croy —3A 64
Sussex Rd. W Wick —7L 47
Sutherland Av. Big H —4F 86
Sutherland Av. Jac —6A 94
Sutherland Av. Sun —1G 39
Sutherland Chase. Asc —1H 33
Sutherland Dri. SW19 —9B 28
Sutherland Dri. Burp —9B 94
Sutherland Gdns. SW14 —6D 12
Sutherland Gdns. Sun —1G 39
Sutherland Gdns. Wor Pk —7G 42
Sutherland Gro. SW18 —9K 13
Sutherland Gro. Tedd —6E 24
Sutherland Rd. W4 —2D 12
Sutherland Rd. Croy —6L 45
Sutton Arc. Sutt —2N 61
Sutton Av. Wok —6H 73
Sutton Clo. Beck —1J 47
Sutton Comn. Rd. Sutt —6L 43
Sutton Ct. W4 —2B 12
Sutton Ct. Sutt —3A 62
Sutton Ct. Rd. W4 —3B 12
Sutton Ct. Rd. Sutt —3A 62
Sutton Dene. Houn —4B 10
Sutton Gdns. SE25 —4C 46
Sutton Gdns. Croy —4C 46
Sutton Gdns. Red —7H 103
Sutton Grn. Rd. Guild —4A 94
Sutton Gro. Sutt —1B 62
Sutton Hall Rd. Houn —3A 10
Sutton La. Dork —3J 137
Sutton La. Houn —6N 9
Sutton La. Slou —2D 6
Sutton La. Sutt & Bans —7N 61
Sutton La. N. W4 —1B 12
Sutton La. S. W4 —2B 12
Sutton Pk. Rd. Sutt —3N 61
Sutton Pl. Ab H —3G 136
Sutton Pl. Slou —2D 6
Sutton Rd. Camb —6E 50
Sutton Rd. Houn —4A 10
Sutton Sq. Houn —4N 9
Sutton Way. Houn —4N 9
Swabey Rd. Slou —1C 6
Swaby Rd. SW18 —2A 28
Swaffield Rd. SW18 —1N 27
Swain Clo. SW16 —7F 28
Swain Rd. T Hth —4N 45
Swains Rd. SW17 —8D 28
Swaledale. Brack —4M 31
Swaledale Clo. Craw —6A 182
Swaledale Gdns. Fleet —1C 88
Swale Rd. F'boro —8K 69
Swallow Clo. Milf —3B 152
Swallow Clo. Stai —5H 21
Swallow Clo. Yat —9A 48
Swallowdale. S Croy —5G 65
Swallow Field. D'land —1C 166
Swallowfield. Egh —7L 19
Swallowfields. Horl —8F 142
Swallow Gdns. SW16 —6H 29
Swallow La. Mid H —2H 139
Swallow Pk. Cvn. Site Surb —9N 41
Swallow Rise. Knap —4F 72
Swallow Rd. Craw —1A 182
Swallow St. Turn H —4F 184
Swallowtail Rd. H'ham —2L 197
Swanage Rd. SW18 —1A 28
Swan Barn Rd. Hasl —2H 189
Swan Cen., The. SW17 —4A 28
Swan Cen., The. Lea —8H 79
Swan Clo. Croy —6B 46
Swan Clo. Felt —5M 23
Swancote Grn. Brack —4N 31
Swan Ct. Guild —1N 113
Swan Ct. Iswth —6H 11
(off Swan St.)
Swan Ct. Lea —9H 79
Swandon Way. SW18 —8N 13
Swan La. Charl —3L 161
Swan La. Eden —8L 127
Swan La. Guild —4N 113
Swan La. Sand —8G 48
Swan Mill Gdns. Dork —3J 119
Swann Ct. Iswth —6G 11
(off South St.)
Swanns Meadow. Bookh —4A 98
Swann Way. Broad H —5E 196
Swan Pl. SW13 —5E 12
Swan Ridge. Eden —8M 127
Swan Rd. Felt —6M 23
Swanscombe Rd. W4 —1D 12
Swansea Rd. H'row A —9D 8
Swans Ghyll. F Row —6G 187
Swan Sq. H'ham —6J 197
Swan St. Iswth —6H 11
Swansway, The. Wey —9B 38
Swan Ter. Wind —3E 4
Swan, The. (Junct.) —8M 47
Swanton Gdns. SW19 —2J 27
Swan Wlk. H'ham —6J 197
Swan Wlk. Shep —6F 38
Swanwick Clo. SW15 —1E 26
Swanworth La. Mick —6G 99
Swaynesland Rd. Eden —3H 127
Swayne's La. Guild —3G 114
Swaythling Ho. SW15 —9E 12
(off Tunworth Cres.)
Sweeps Ditch Clo. Stai —9J 21
Sweeps La. Egh —6B 20
Sweetbriar. Crowt —9F 30
Sweet Briar La. Eps —1C 80
Sweet La. Peasl —3F 136
Sweetwater Clo. Sham G —7F 134
Sweetwater La. Sham G —7F 134
Sweetwater La. Witl —7D 152
Sweetwell Rd. Brack —1K 31
Swievelands Rd. Big H —6D 86
Swift Ct. Sutt —4N 61
Swift La. Bag —4K 51
Swift La. Craw —1A 182
Swift Rd. Farnh —5H 109
Swift Rd. Felt —5L 23
Swift's Clo. Farnh —2N 129
Swift St. SW6 —1L 13
Swinburne Cres. Croy —5F 46
Swinburne Rd. SW15 —7F 12
Swindon Rd. H'ham —4H 197
Swindon Rd. H'row A —8D 8
Swinfield Clo. Felt —4M 23
Swingate Rd. Farnh —3J 129
Swinley Rd. Asc —2G 32
Swinley Rd. Bag —1H 51
Swires Shaw. Kes —1F 66
Swiss Clo. Wrec —7F 128
Swissland Hill. Dor P —4A 166
Switchback La. Rowl —8F 128
Swithin Chase. Warf —8C 16
Swyncombe Av. W5 —1H 11
Sycamore Av. H'ham —2B 198
Sycamore Clo. Cars —1D 62
Sycamore Clo. Craw —9A 162
Sycamore Clo. Felt —4H 23
Sycamore Clo. Fet —1F 98
Sycamore Clo. Frim —5C 70
Sycamore Clo. Sand —7G 48
Sycamore Cotts. Camb —3N 69
(off Frimley Rd.)
Sycamore Ct. G'ming —3J 133
Sycamore Ct. Houn —7M 9
Sycamore Ct. N Mald —2D 42
Sycamore Ct. Wind —6F 4
Sycamore Cres. C Crook —7A 88
Sycamore Dri. Ash V —6E 90
Sycamore Dri. E Grin —9C 166
Sycamore Dri. Frim —4C 70
Sycamore Dri. Wrec —5F 128
Sycamore Gdns. Mitc —1B 44
Sycamore Gro. N Mald —2C 42
Sycamore Ho. Brom —1N 47
Sycamore Rise. Bans —1J 81
Sycamore Rise. Brack —2B 32
Sycamore Rd. SW19 —7H 27
Sycamore Rd. F'boro —3A 90
Sycamore Rd. Guild —3N 113
Sycamores, The. B'water —1G 68
Sycamores, The. F'boro —2B 90
Sycamore Wlk. Egh —7L 19
Sycamore Wlk. Reig —6A 122
Sycamore Way. Tedd —7J 25
Sycamore Way. T Hth —4L 45
Sydcote. SE21 —2N 29
Sydenham Pl. SE27 —4M 29
Sydenham Rd. Croy —7N 45
Sydenham Rd. Guild —5N 113
Sydney Av. Purl —8K 63
Sydney Clo. Crowt —9H 31
Sydney Cres. Ashf —7C 22
Sydney Pl. Guild —4B 114
Sydney Rd. SW20 —1J 43
Sydney Rd. Felt —2H 23
Sydney Rd. Guild —4B 114
Sydney Rd. Rich —7L 11
Sydney Rd. Sutt —1M 61
Sydney Rd. Tedd —6F 24
Sykes Dri. Stai —6K 21
Sylvan Clo. Oxt —7D 106
Sylvan Clo. S Croy —6E 64
Sylvan Clo. Wok —4D 74
Sylvan Est. SE19 —1C 46
Sylvan Gdns. Surb —6K 41
Sylvan Ridge. Sand —6F 48
Sylvan Rd. Craw —5E 182
Sylvanus. Brack —6L 31
Sylvan Rd. SE19 —1C 46

260 A-Z Surrey

Sylvan Way—Tilgate Dri.

Sylvan Way. C Crook —8A 88
Sylvan Way. Red —4E 122
Sylvan Way. W Wick —1A 66
Sylvaways Clo. Cranl —7B 156
Sylverdale Rd. Croy —9M 45
Sylverdale Rd. Purl —9M 63
Sylverns Ct. Warf —8B 16
Sylvestrus Clo. King T —9N 25
Symondson M. Binf —5H 15
Syon Ga. Way. Bren —3G 11
Syon La. Iswth —2E 10
Syon Pk. Gdns. Iswth —3F 10
Syon Pl. F'boro —1B 90
Syrett M. Cobh —1J 77
Sythwood. Wok —3L 73
Szabo Cres. Norm —3M 111

Tabarin Way. Eps —3H 81
Tabor Ct. Sutt —3K 61
Tabor Gdns. Sutt —4L 61
Tabor Gro. SW19 —8K 27
Tachbrook Rd. Felt —1G 23
Tadmor Clo. Sun —3G 39
Tadorne Rd. Tad —8H 81
Tadpole La. Ews —3C 108
Tadworth Av. N Mald —4E 42
Tadworth Clo. Tad —9J 81
Tadworth Ct. Tad —8J 81
Tadworth St. Tad —1H 101
Taffy's Row. Mitc —2C 44
Tait Rd. Croy —6B 46
Talavera Pk. Alder —1M 109
Talbot Clo. Myt —1E 90
Talbot Clo. Reig —4N 121
Talbot La. H'ham —7J 197
Talbot Pl. Bag —4J 51
Talbot Pl. Dat —4M 5
Talbot Rd. Ashf —6N 21
Talbot Rd. Cars —2E 62
Talbot Rd. Farnh —3G 128
Talbot Rd. Iswth —7G 11
Talbot Rd. Ling —8N 145
Talbot Rd. T Hth —3A 46
Talbot Rd. Twic —2E 24
Talcott Path. SW2 —2L 29
Taleworth Clo. Asht —7K 79
Taleworth Pk. Asht —7K 79
Taleworth Rd. Asht —6K 79
Talgarth Dri. F'boro —3B 90
Talgarth Mans. W14 —1K 13 (off Talgarth Rd.)
Talgarth Rd. W6 & W14 —1J 13
Talisman Clo. Crowt —2C 48
Talisman Way. Eps —3H 81
Tallis Clo. Craw —6L 181
Tall Pines. Eps —7E 60
Tall Trees. SW16 —3K 45
Tall Trees. Coln —4F 6
Tally Rd. Oxt —9G 107
Talma Gdns. Twic —9E 10
Talman Clo. If'd —4K 181
Tamar Clo. M'bowr —4G 182
Tamarind Clo. Guild —7K 93
Tamarind Ct. Egh —6B 20
Tamarisk Rise. Wokgm —1B 30
Tamar Way. Slou —1D 6
Tamerton Sq. Wok —5A 74
Tamesis Gdns. Wor Pk —8D 42
Tamian Ind. Est. Houn —7K 9
Tamian Way. Houn —7K 9
Tamworth. Brack —6B 32
Tamworth Dri. Fleet —1C 88
Tamworth La. Mitc —1F 44
Tamworth Pk. Mitc —2F 44
Tamworth Pl. Croy —8N 45
Tamworth Rd. Croy —8M 45
Tamworth St. SW6 —2M 13
Tamworth Vs. Mitc —3G 44
Tanbridge Pk. H'ham —7G 197
Tanbridge Pl. H'ham —7H 197
Tanbridge Retail Pk. H'ham —7H 197
Tandridge Gdns. S Croy —9C 64
Tandridge Hill La. God —6J 105
Tandridge La. Oxt & Ling —1K 125
Tandridge Rd. Warl —6G 84
Tanfield Ct. H'ham —6H 197
Tanfield Rd. Croy —1N 63
Tangier Ct. Alder —2K 109
Tangier Ct. Eton —2G 5
Tangier La. Eton —2G 4
Tangier Rd. Guild —4C 114
Tangier Rd. Rich —7N 11
Tangier Way. Tad —4K 81
Tangier Wood. Tad —5K 81
Tangle Oak. Felb —6H 165
Tanglewood. Finch —9A 30
Tanglewood Clo. Croy —9F 46
Tanglewood Clo. Longc —9L 35
Tanglewood Clo. Wok —3F 74
Tanglewood Ride. W End —8A 52
Tanglewood Way. Felt —4J 23
Tangley Dri. Wokgm —4A 30
Tangley Gro. SW15 —9E 12
Tangley La. Guild —8J 93
Tangley Pk. Rd. Hamp —6N 23
Tanglyn Av. Shep —4B 38
Tangmere Gro. King T —6K 25
Tangmere Rd. Craw —3L 181
Tanhouse La. Wokgm —3A 30
Tanhouse Rd. Oxt —1N 125
Tanhurst Ho. SW2 —1J 29 (off Redlands Way)
Tanhurst La. Holm M —1M 157
Tankerton Rd. Surb —8M 41
Tankerton Ter. Croy —5K 45
Tankerville Rd. SW16 —8H 29
Tank Rd. Sand —1L 69
Tanners Clo. W On T —5J 39
Tanners Ct. Brock —4A 120
Tanners Dean. Lea —9J 79
Tannersfield. Shalf —2A 134
Tanner's Hill. Bet —4A 120
Tanners La. Hasl —1G 188
Tanners Mead. Eden —2L 147
Tanners Meadow. Brock —7A 120
Tanners Yd. Bag —4J 51
Tannery Clo. Beck —3G 46
Tannery Clo. Slin —5L 195
Tannery La. Brmly —3A 134
Tannery La. Send —1F 94
Tannery, The. Red —3D 122
Tansy Clo. Guild —1E 114
Tantallon Rd. SW12 —2E 28
Tanyard Av. E Grin —1C 186
Tanyard Clo. H'ham —7L 197
Tanyard Clo. M'bowr —6G 182
Tanyard Way. Horl —6F 142
Tanya Rise. Cat —8B 84
Tapestry Clo. Sutt —4N 61
Tapners Rd. Bet & Reig —8E 120
Tara Ct. Beck —1L 47
Tarbat Clo. Sand —7J 49
Target Clo. Felt —9F 8
Target Hill. Warf —8B 16
Tarham Clo. Horl —6C 142
Tarmac Way. W Dray —3K 7
Tarnbrook Way. Brack —6C 32
Tarn Clo. F'boro —3K 89
Tarn Rd. Hind —6B 170
Tarragon Clo. Brack —8B 16
Tarragon Clo. F'boro —1H 89
Tarragon Ct. Guild —8K 93
Tarragon Dri. Guild —8K 93
Tarrant Grn. Warf —8A 16
Tarrington Clo. SW16 —4H 29
Tartar Hill. Cobh —9K 57
Tartar Rd. Cobh —9K 57
Tasker Clo. Hayes —3D 8
Tasman Ct. Sun —8F 22
Tasso Rd. W6 —2K 13
Tasso Yd. W6 —2K 13 (off Tasso Rd.)
Tatchbury Ho. SW15 —9E 12 (off Tunworth Cres.)
Tate Clo. Lea —1J 99
Tate Rd. Sutt —2M 61
Tate's Way. Rud —1E 194
Tatham Ct. Craw —8N 181
Tatsfield La. Tats —8H 87
Tattenham Corner Rd. Eps —4E 80
Tattenham Cres. Eps —5G 80
Tattenham Gro. Eps —5G 80
Tattenham Way. Tad —5J 81
Tattersall Clo. Wokgm —3D 30
Taunton Av. SW20 —1G 42
Taunton Av. Cat —1C 104
Taunton Av. Houn —5C 10
Taunton Clo. Craw —3J 183
Taunton Clo. Sutt —7M 43
Taunton La. Coul —6L 83
Tavern Clo. Cars —6C 44
Tavistock Clo. Stai —8M 21
Tavistock Cres. Mitc —3J 45
Tavistock Gdns. F'boro —7N 69
Tavistock Ga. Croy —7A 46
Tavistock Gro. Croy —6A 46
Tavistock Ho. Croy —7A 46
Tavistock Rd. Cars —7B 44
Tavistock Rd. Croy —7A 46
Tavistock Rd. Fleet —4A 88
Tavistock Wlk. Cars —7B 44
Tawfield. Brack —6K 31
Tawny Clo. Felt —4H 23
Tawny Croft. Sand —7K 49
Tayben Av. Twic —9E 10
Tay Clo. F'boro —8K 69
Tayles Hill. Eps —6E 60
Taylor Av. Rich —5A 12
Taylor Clo. Hamp —6C 24
Taylor Clo. Houn —4C 10
Taylor Clo. Orp —1N 67
Taylor Ct. SE20 —1F 46 (off Elmers End Rd.)
Taylor Rd. Asht —4K 79
Taylor Rd. Mitc —8C 28
Taylor Rd. Wall —2F 62
Taylor's Bushes Ride. Wind —3N 17
Taylors Clo. Lind —4A 168
Taylors Ct. Felt —3H 23
Taylors Cres. Cranl —7A 156
Taylors La. Lind —4A 168
Taylor Wlk. Craw —3A 182
Taymans Track. Hand —8L 199
Taynton Dri. Red —7H 103
Teal Clo. H'ham —3J 197
Teal Clo. S Croy —7G 64
Tealing Dri. Eps —1C 60
Teasel Clo. Craw —6N 181
Teasel Clo. Croy —7G 46
Teazlewood Pk. Lea —4G 78
Tebbit Clo. Brack —1B 32
Teck Clo. Iswth —5G 11
Tedder Clo. Chess —2J 59
Tedder Rd. S Croy —4F 64
Teddington Bus. Pk. Tedd —7F 24 (off Station Rd.)
Teddington Clo. Eps —6C 60
Teddington Pk. Tedd —6F 24
Teddington Pk. Rd. Tedd —5F 24
Tedham La. God —3E 144
Tees Clo. F'boro —8K 69
Teesdale. Craw —6A 182
Teesdale Av. Iswth —4G 11
Teesdale Gdns. SE25 —1B 46
Teesdale Gdns. Iswth —4G 11
Teevan Clo. Croy —6D 46
Teevan Rd. Croy —7D 46
Tegg's La. Wok —3H 75
Tekels Av. Camb —1B 70
Tekels Pk. Camb —1C 70
Tekels Way. Camb —3C 70
Telconia Clo. Head —5H 169
Telegraph La. Clay —2F 58
Telegraph Pas. SW2 —1J 29
Telegraph Rd. SW15 —1G 27
Telegraph Track. Cars —7E 62
Telephone Pl. SW6 —2L 13
Telferscot Rd. SW12 —2H 29
Telford Av. SW2 —2H 29
Telford Av. Crowt —9H 31
Telford Ct. Guild —3B 114
Telford Dri. W On T —6K 39
Telford Pl. Craw —4C 102
Telford Rd. Twic —1A 24
Telham Ct. Craw —6L 181
Tellisford. Esh —1B 58
Temperley Rd. SW12 —1E 28
Tempest Ho. King T —9L 25 (off Sigrist Sq.)
Tempest Rd. Egh —7E 20
Templar Clo. Sand —7F 48
Templar Pl. Hamp —8A 24
Templars Ct. Eden —9L 127
Temple Av. Croy —8J 47
Temple Bar Rd. Wok —6J 73
Temple Clo. Craw —4H 183
Temple Clo. Eps —8C 60
Templecombe M. Wok —3D 74
Templecombe Way. Mord —4K 43
Temple Ct. Eps —8C 60
Templecroft. Ashf —7E 22
Templedene Av. Stai —8K 21
Templefield Clo. Add —3K 55
Temple Gdns. Stai —9H 21
Temple La. Capel —4L 159
Templeman Clo. Purl —3M 83
Templemere. Wey —9E 38
Temple Rd. Big H —4F 86
Temple Rd. Croy —1A 64
Temple Rd. Eps —8C 60
Temple Rd. Houn —7C 10
Temple Rd. Rich —5M 11
Temple Rd. Wind —5F 4
Temple's Clo. Farnh —2A 130
Temple Sheen. SW14 —8B 12
Temple Sheen Rd. SW14 —7A 12
Templeton Clo. SE19 —1A 46
Templeton Pl. SW5 —1M 13
Temple Way. Brack —8K 15
Temple Way. Sutt —9B 44
Temple Wood Dri. Red —9D 102
Ten Acre. St J —5K 73
Ten Acre La. Egh —1E 36
Ten Acres. Fet —2D 98
Ten Acres Clo. Fet —2D 98
Ten Acre Wlk. Rowl —7E 128
Tenbury Ct. SW12 —2H 29
Tenby Dri. Asc —4A 34
Tenby Rd. Frim —6E 70
Tenchley's La. Oxt —9F 106
Tenham Av. SW2 —3H 29
Tennis Ct. La. E Mol —2F 40
Tennison Clo. Coul —7M 83
Tennison Rd. SE25 —3C 46
Tennyson Av. N Mald —4G 43
Tennyson Av. Twic —2F 24
Tennyson Clo. Craw —1F 182
Tennyson Clo. Felt —9G 9
Tennyson Clo. H'ham —2L 197
Tennyson Ct. SW6 —4N 13 (off Maltings Pl.)
Tennyson Mans. W14 —2K 13 (off Queen's Club Gdns.)
Tennyson Rise. E Grin —9M 165
Tennyson Rd. SW19 —7A 28
Tennyson Rd. Add —1N 55
Tennyson Rd. Ashf —6N 21
Tennyson Rd. Houn —5C 10
Tennyson's La. Hasl —4J 189
Tentelow La. S'hall —1A 10
Tenterden Gdns. Croy —6D 46
Tenterden Rd. Croy —6D 46
Teresa Vale. Warf —7C 16
Tern Rd. If'd —4J 181
Terrace Gdns. SW13 —5E 12
Terrace La. Rich —9L 11
Terrace Rd. W On T —6H 39
Terrace Rd. N. Binf —6H 15
Terrace Rd. S. Binf —7H 15
Terrace, The. SW13 —5D 12
Terrace, The. Add —2N 55
Terrace, The. Asc —4A 34
Terrace, The. Camb —1M 69
Terrace, The. Crowt —2K 49
Terrace, The. Dork —6J 119
Terrace, The. Wokgm —2A 30
Terra Cotta Rd. S God —7F 124
Terrapin Rd. SW17 —4F 28
Terry Rd. Craw —8N 181
Tesimond Dri. Yat —9A 48
Testard Rd. Guild —5M 113
Testers Clo. Oxt —9D 106
Testwood Rd. Wind —4A 4
Tetcott Rd. SW10 —3N 13 (in two parts)
Teviot Clo. Guild —9K 93
Tewkesbury Clo. Byfl —7M 55
Tewkesbury Rd. Cars —7B 44
Textile Est. Yat —8C 48
Teynham Ct. Beck —2M 47
Thackeray Clo. SW19 —8J 27
Thackeray Clo. Iswth —5G 11
Thackeray Lodge. Felt —9E 8
Thames Av. Cher —2J 37
Thames Av. Wind —3G 4
Thames Bank. SW14 —5B 12
Thames Clo. Cher —6K 37
Thames Clo. F'boro —8K 69
Thames Clo. Hamp —1B 40
Thames Cres. W4 —3D 12
Thamesfield Ct. Shep —6D 38
Thamesfield M. Shep —6D 30
Thames Ga. Stai —1K 37
Thamesgate Clo. Rich —5H 25
Thameside. Tedd —8K 25
Thameside. W Mol —2B 40
Thameside Cen. Bren —2M 11
Thames Lock. Sun —2J 39
Thames Lock. Wey —8B 38
Thames Mead. W On T —5H 39
Thames Mead. Wind —4B 4
Thames Meadow. Shep —7E 38
Thames Meadow. W Mol —1A 40
Thames Pl. SW15 —6J 13 (in two parts)
Thamespoint. Tedd —8K 25
Thames Rd. W4 —2N 11
Thames Rd. Rich —2N 11
Thames Rd. Wind —3A 4
Thames Side. King T —9K 25
Thames Side. Stai —1K 37
Thames Side. Wind —3G 4
Thames St. Hamp —9B 24
Thames St. King T —1K 41
Thames St. Stai —6H 21
Thames St. Sun —3J 39
Thames St. W On T —6G 39
Thames St. Wey —8C 38
Thames St. Wind —4G 4
Thames Vale Clo. Houn —5A 10
Thamesview Houses. W on T —5H 39
Thames Village. W4 —4B 12
Thanescroft Gdns. Croy —9B 46
Thanet Dri. Kes —1F 66
Thanet Pl. Croy —1N 63
Tharp Rd. Wall —2H 63
Thatcher Clo. Craw —6B 182
Thatchers Clo. Horl —6F 142
Thatchers Clo. H'ham —4L 197
Thatchers La. Worp —5G 93
Thatchers Way. Iswth —8D 10
Thaxted Pl. SW20 —8J 27
Thaxton Rd. W14 —2L 13
Thayers Farm Rd. Beck —1H 47
Theal Clo. Col T —7J 49
Theatre Ct. Eps —9C 60
Thelma Gro. Tedd —7G 24
Thelton Av. Broad H —5D 196
Theobald Rd. Croy —8M 45
Theobalds Way. Frim —3G 71
Thepps Clo. S Nut —6K 123
Therapia La. Croy —6H 45 (in two parts)
Theresa Rd. W6 —1F 12
Theresa's Wlk. S Croy —6A 64
Thetford Rd. Ashf —5N 21
Thetford Rd. N Mald —5C 42
Thetford Wlk. Craw —7K 181
Thetis Ter. Rich —2N 11
Theydon Clo. Craw —5E 182
Thibet Rd. Sand —7H 49
Thicket Cres. Sutt —1A 62
Thicket Rd. Sutt —1A 62
Thickthorne La. Stai —8L 21
Third Clo. W Mol —3C 40
Third Cross Rd. Twic —3D 24
Thirlmere Clo. Egh —8D 20
Thirlmere Clo. F'boro —1K 89
Thirlmere Cres. C Crook —8A 88
Thirlmere Rd. SW16 —5H 29
Thirlmere Rd. If'd —5J 181
Thirlmere Wlk. Camb —2H 71
Thirsk Rd. SE25 —3A 46
Thirsk Rd. Mitc —8E 28
Thistlecroft Rd. W On T —1K 57
Thistledene. Th Dit —5E 40
Thistledene. W Byf —9H 55
Thistle Way. Small —8N 143
Thistlewood Cres. New Ad —8N 65
Thistleworth Clo. Iswth —3D 10
Thistleworth Marina. Iswth —7H 11 (off Railshead Rd.)
Thistley La. Cranl —6N 155
Thomas Av. Cat —8N 83
Thomas Dri. Warf —8C 16
Thomas Ho. Sutt —4N 61
Thomas Moore Ho. Reig —3A 122
Thomas Pk. King T —7B 26
Thomas Turner Path. T Hth —2N 45 (off George St.)
Thomas Wall Clo. Sutt —2N 61
Thompson Av. Rich —6N 11
Thompson Clo. Slou —1B 6
Thompson's Clo. Pirb —1A 92
Thompson's La. Chob —5G 53
Thomson Ct. Craw —8N 181
Thomson Cres. Croy —7L 45
Thorburn Chase. Col T —9K 49
Thorburn Way. SW19 —9B 28
Thorkhill Gdns. Th Dit —7G 41
Thorkhill Rd. Th Dit —7G 41
Thorley Clo. W Byf —1J 75
Thorley Gdns. Wok —2J 75
Thornash Clo. Wok —2M 73
Thornash Rd. Wok —2M 73
Thornash Way. Wok —2M 73
Thorn Bank. Guild —5K 113
Thornbank Clo. Stai —8J 7
Thornbury Av. Iswth —3D 10
Thornbury Clo. Crowt —2G 48
Thornbury Ct. Iswth —3E 10
Thornbury Rd. SW2 —1J 29
Thornbury Rd. Iswth —3D 10
Thorncliffe Rd. SW2 —1J 29
Thorncliffe Rd. S'hall —1N 9
Thorn Clo. Wokgm —9F 30
Thorn Clo. Wrec —7E 128
Thorncombe St. Brmly —1A 154
Thorncroft. Egh —8M 19
Thorncroft Clo. Coul —6L 83
Thorncroft Dri. Lea —1H 99
Thorncroft Rd. Sutt —1N 61
Thorndean St. SW18 —3A 28
Thorndike Clo. SW10 —3N 13
Thorndon Gdns. Eps —2D 60
Thorndown La. W'sham —4A 52
Thorndyke Clo. Craw —4H 183
Thorne Clo. Ashf —8D 22
Thorne Ho. Clay —4H 59
Thorneloe Gdns. Croy —2L 63
Thorne Pas. SW13 —5D 12
Thornes Clo. Beck —2M 47
Thorne St. SW13 —6D 12
Thorneycroft Clo. W On T —5K 39
Thorney Hedge Rd. W4 —1A 12
Thornfield Grn. B'water —3L 69
Thornfield Rd. Bans —4M 81
Thornhill. Brack —3C 32
Thornhill. Craw —5N 181
Thornhill Av. Surb —8L 41
Thornhill Ho. W4 —1D 12 (off Wood St.)
Thornhill Rd. Alder —9B 90
Thornhill Rd. Croy —6N 45
Thornhill Rd. Surb —8L 41
Thornhill Way. Shep —4B 38
Thornlaw Rd. SE27 —5L 29
Thornleas Pl. E Hor —4F 96
Thorn Rd. Wrec —6E 128
Thornsett Pl. SE20 —1E 46
Thornsett Rd. SE20 —1E 46
Thornsett Rd. SW18 —2N 27
Thornsett Ter. SE20 —1E 46 (off Croydon Rd.)
Thornton Av. SW2 —2H 29
Thornton Av. W4 —1D 12
Thornton Av. Croy —5K 45
Thornton Clo. Guild —9K 93
Thornton Clo. Horl —8C 142
Thornton Cres. Coul —6L 83
Thornton Dene. Beck —1K 47
Thornton Gdns. SW12 —2H 29
Thornton Heath Pond. (Junct.) —4L 45
Thornton Hill. SW19 —8K 27
Thornton Pl. Horl —8C 142
Thornton Rd. SW12 —1H 29
Thornton Rd. SW14 —7C 12
Thornton Rd. SW19 —7J 27
Thornton Rd. Cars —7B 44
Thornton Rd. Croy & T Hth —6K 45
Thornton Rd. E. SW19 —7J 27
Thornton Row. T Hth —4L 45
Thornton Wlk. Horl —8D 142
Thornville Gro. Mitc —1B 44
Thornycroft Ho. W4 —1D 12 (off Fraser St.)
Thornyhurst Rd. Myt —1E 90
Thorold Clo. S Croy —6G 65
Thorold Rd. Farnh —9H 109
Thoroughfare, The. Tad —2F 100
Thorp Clo. Binf —6H 15
Thorpe By-Pass. Egh —1D 36
Thorpe Clo. New Ad —7M 65
Thorpe Clo. Wokgm —5A 30
Thorpe Lea Rd. Egh —7D 20
Thorpe Rd. Cher —4F 36
Thorpe Rd. King T —8L 25
Thorpe Rd. Stai —7F 20
Thorpe's Clo. Guild —9K 93
Thorpeside Clo. Stai —1G 37
Thorsden Clo. Wok —5A 74
Thorsden Ct. Wok —5A 74
Thrale Rd. SW16 —6G 28
Three Acres. H'ham —7G 197
Three Arches Pk. Red —7D 122
Three Arch Rd. Red —7D 122
Three Bridges Rd. Craw —3D 182
Three Gates. Guild —2E 114
Three Gates La. Hasl —1H 189
Three Mile Rd. Dork —9H 137
Three Pears Rd. Guild —3G 114
Threestile Rd. H'ham —8F 178
Three Stiles Rd. Farnh —9E 108
Threshers Corner. Fleet —1D 88
Threshfield. Brack —4M 31
Thrift La. Cud —4N 87
Thrift Vale. Guild —9F 94
Thrigby Rd. Chess —3M 59
Throgmorton Rd. Yat —1A 68
Throwley Rd. Sutt —2N 61
Throwley Way. Sutt —1N 61
Thrupp Clo. Mitc —1F 44
Thrupp Ho. Guild —2F 114 (off Merrow St.)
Thrupp's Av. W On T —2L 57
Thrupp's La. W On T —2L 57
Thundery Hill. Seale —8D 110
Thurbans Rd. Farnh —4F 128
Thurbarns Hill. Dork —1L 159
Thurlby Rd. SE27 —5L 29
Thurleigh Av. SW12 —1E 28
Thurleigh Rd. SW12 —1D 28
Thurleston Av. Mord —4K 43
Thurlestone Clo. Shep —5D 38
Thurlestone Pde. Shep —5D 38 (off High St. Shepperton,)
Thurlestone Rd. SE27 —4L 29
Thurlow Hill. SE21 —2N 29
Thurlow Ho. SW16 —4J 29
Thurlow Pk. Rd. SE21 —3M 29
Thurlow Wlk. Cranl —9N 155
Thurlton Ct. Wok —3A 74
Thurnby Ct. Twic —4E 24
Thurne Way. Rud —1E 194
Thurnham Way. Tad —7H 81
Thursby Rd. Wok —5K 73
Thursley Cres. New Ad —4N 65
Thursley Gdns. SW19 —3J 27
Thursley Ho. SW2 —1K 29 (off Holmewood Gdns.)
Thursley Rd. Churt & Elst —7A 150
Thursley Rd. Elst —4F 150
Thurso St. SW17 —5B 28
Thurstan Rd. SW20 —8G 26
Thurston Ho. Fleet —4A 88
Thyer Clo. Orp —1L 67
Thyme Ct. F'boro —9H 69
Thyme Ct. Guild —9D 94
Tibbet's Clo. SW19 —2J 27
Tibbet's Corner. (Junct.) —1J 27
Tibbet's Ride. SW15 —1J 27
Ticehurst Clo. Worth —3J 183
Tichborne Clo. B'water —1J 69
Tichborne Clo. Frim —3D 70
Tichborne Pl. Alder —4B 110
Tichmarsh. Eps —7B 60
Tickleback Row. Warf —3N 15
Tidenham Gdns. Croy —9B 46
Tideswell Rd. SW15 —7H 13
Tideswell Rd. Croy —9K 47
Tideway Clo. Rich —5H 25
Tidwells Lea. Warf —9C 16
Tierney Ct. Croy —8C 46
Tierney Rd. SW2 —2J 29
Tilburstow Hill Rd. God —1F 124
Tildesley Rd. SW15 —9H 13
Tile Barn Clo. F'boro —9M 69
Tile Farm Rd. Orp —1M 67
Tilehouse Rd. Guild —7A 114
Tilehurst La. Binf —6H 15
Tilehurst La. Dork —6L 119
Tilehurst Rd. SW18 —2B 28
Tilehurst Rd. Sutt —2K 61
Tiler's Wlk. Reig —7A 122
Tiler's Way. Reig —7A 122
Tilford Av. New Ad —5M 65
Tilford Gdns. SW19 —2J 27
Tilford Ho. SW2 —1K 29 (off Holmewood Gdns.)
Tilford Rd. Farnh & Tilf —2J 129
Tilford Rd. Hind —4D 170
Tilgate Comn. Blet —2N 123
Tilgate Dri. Craw —7B 182 (Brighton Rd.)

Tilgate Dri.—Tye La.

Tilgate Dri. *Craw* —4E **182**
(Water Lea)
Tilgate Forest (Forest Ga.) Bus. Cen. *Craw* —8B **182**
Tilgate Forest Row. *Peas P* —3N **199**
Tilgate Mans. *Craw* —8D **182**
Tilgate Pde. *Craw* —6C **182**
Tilgate Pl. *Craw* —6C **182**
Tilgate Way. *Craw* —6C **182**
Tilletts La. *Warn* —9E **178**
Tilley La. *H'ley* —9B **80**
Tillingbourne Rd. *Shalf* —9A **114**
Tillingdown Hill. *Cat* —9D **84**
Tillingdown La. *Cat* —2E **104**
(in two parts)
Tillotson Clo. *Craw* —4H **183**
Tilson Gdns. *SW2* —1J **29**
Tilson Ho. *SW2* —1J **29**
Tilstone Av. *Eton W* —1B **4**
Tilstone Clo. *Eton W* —1B **4**
Tilt Clo. *Cobh* —3M **77**
Tilthams Corner Rd. *G'ming* —3L **133**
Tilthams Grn. *G'ming* —3L **133**
Tilt Meadow. *Cobh* —3M **77**
Tilton St. *SW6* —2K **13**
Tilt Rd. *Cobh* —2K **77**
Tiltview. *Cobh* —2K **77**
Tiltwood Dri. *Craw D* —9F **164**
Timber Bank. *Frim G* —8E **70**
Timber Clo. *Bookh* —5C **98**
Timber Clo. *Farnh* —1G **128**
Timber Clo. *Wok* —1H **75**
Timber Ct. *H'ham* —5J **197**
Timbercroft. *Eps* —1D **60**
Timberham Way. *Horl* —2C **162**
Timberhill. *Asht* —6L **79**
Timber Hill Rd. *Cat* —2D **104**
Timberlands. *Craw* —8N **181**
Timber La. *Cat* —2D **104**
Timberley Pl. *Crowt* —3D **48**
Timberling Gdns. *S Croy* —5A **64**
Timbermill Ct. *Hasl* —2D **188**
Timberslip Dri. *Wall* —5H **63**
Timbers, The. *Man H* —9B **198**
Timbertop Rd. *Big H* —5E **86**
Times Sq. *Sutt* —2N **61**
Timline Grn. *Brack* —1D **32**
Timperley Ct. *Red* —1C **122**
Timperley Gdns. *Red* —1C **122**
Timsbury Wlk. *SW15* —2F **26**
Timsway. *Stai* —6H **21**
Tindal Clo. *Yat* —9C **48**
Tindale Clo. *S Croy* —7A **64**
Tinderbox All. *SW14* —6C **12**
Tinefields. *Tad* —6K **81**
Tinkers La. *S'dale* —5E **34**
Tinkers La. *Wind* —5A **4**
Tinsey Clo. *Egh* —6C **20**
Tinsley Grn. *Craw* —6F **162**
Tinsley La. *Craw* —8E **162**
Tinsley La. N. *Craw* —7F **162**
Tinsley La. S. *Craw* —1E **182**
Tintagel Clo. *Eps* —1E **80**
Tintagel Ct. *H'ham* —7K **197**
Tintagel Dri. *Frim* —5D **70**
Tintagel Rd. *Finch* —8A **30**
Tintagel Way. *Wok* —3C **74**
Tintells La. *W Hor* —6C **96**
Tintern Clo. *SW15* —8K **13**
Tintern Clo. *SW19* —7A **28**
Tintern Rd. *Cars* —7B **44**
Tintern Rd. *Craw* —5M **181**
Tippits Mead. *Brack* —9J **15**
Tippitts Mead. *Brack* —9K **15**
Tipton Dri. *Croy* —1B **64**
Tiree Clo. *Rich* —2K **25**
Tiree Path. *Craw* —6N **181**
Tirlemont Rd. *S Croy* —4N **63**
Tirrell Rd. *Croy* —5N **45**
Tisbury Rd. *SW16* —1J **45**
Tismans Comn. *Rud* —2A **194**
Titchfield Rd. *Cars* —7B **44**
Titchfield Wlk. *Cars* —6B **44**
Titchwell Rd. *SW18* —2B **28**
Tite Hill. *Egh* —6N **19**
Tithe Barn Clo. *King T* —9M **25**
Tithebarns La. *Send* —4J **95**
Tithe Clo. *Vir W* —5N **35**
Tithe Clo. *W On T* —5J **39**
Tithe La. *Wray* —9C **6**
Tithe Meadows. *Vir W* —5M **35**
Tithe Orchard. *Felb* —6H **165**
Tithepit Shaw La. *Warl* —4E **84**
Titlarks Hill Rd. *S'dale* —8E **34**
Titmus Dri. *Craw* —6D **182**
Titness Pk. *S'hill* —2D **34**
Titsey Hill. *T'sey* —1C **106**
Titsey Rd. *Oxt* —3D **106**
Tiverton Rd. *Houn* —5C **10**
Tiverton Rd. *T Hth* —4L **45**
Tiverton Way. *Chess* —2K **59**
Tiverton Way. *Frim* —5D **70**
Tivoli Rd. *SE27* —6N **29**
Tivoli Rd. *Houn* —7M **9**
Toad La. *B'water* —2K **69**
Toad La. *Houn* —7N **9**
Toat Hill. *H'ham* —8N **195**
Toby Way. *Surb* —8A **42**
Tocker Gdns. *Warf* —7N **15**
Tockington Ct. *Yat* —9C **48**
Todds Clo. *Horl* —6C **142**
Toftwood Clo. *Craw* —4G **183**
Token Yd. *SW15* —7K **13**
Toland Sq. *SW15* —8F **12**
Toll Bar Ct. *Sutt* —5N **61**
Tolldene Clo. *Knap* —4H **73**
Tollers La. *Coul* —5K **83**
Toll Gdns. *Brack* —2D **32**
Tollgate Av. *Red* —8D **122**
Tollgate Hill. *Craw* —9A **182**
Tollgate Rd. *Dork* —8H **119**
Tollhouse La. *Wall* —5G **62**
Tolpuddle Way. *Yat* —1E **68**
Tolson Rd. *Iswth* —6G **10**
Tolvaddon Clo. *Wok* —4K **73**
Tolverne Rd. *SW20* —9H **27**
Tolworth Clo. *Surb* —7A **42**
Tolworth Junction. (Junct.) —8A **42**
Tolworth Pk. Rd. *Surb* —8M **41**
Tolworth Rise N. *Surb* —7A **42**
Tolworth Rise S. *Surb* —7A **42**
Tolworth Rd. *Surb* —8L **41**
Tolworth Tower. *Surb* —8A **42**
Tomlin Clo. *Eps* —7C **60**
Tomlin Ct. *Eps* —7C **60**
Tomlins All. *Twic* —2G **24**
Tomlins Av. *Frim* —4D **70**
Tomlinscote Way. *Frim* —4E **70**
Tomlinson Clo. *W4* —1A **12**
Tomlinson Dri. *Finch* —9A **30**
Tompset's Bank. *F Row* —9H **187**
Tomtits La. *F Row* —8G **187**
*Tom Williams Ho. SW6 —2L **13***
(off Clem Attlee Ct.)
Tonbridge Clo. *Bans* —1D **82**
Tonbridge Rd. *W Mol* —3N **39**
Tonfield Rd. *Sutt* —7L **43**
Tonge Clo. *Beck* —4K **47**
Tonge Vs. *Beck* —4K **47**
Tongham Meadows. *Tong* —5D **110**
Tongham Rd. *Alder* —4B **110**
Tongham Rd. *Farnh* —8A **110**
Tonsley Hill. *SW18* —8N **13**
Tonsley Pl. *SW18* —8N **13**
Tonsley Rd. *SW18* —8N **13**
Tonsley St. *SW18* —8N **13**
Tonstall Rd. *Eps* —6C **60**
Tonstall Rd. *Mitc* —1E **44**
Tony Law Ho. *SE20* —1E **46**
Tooting Bec Gdns. *SW16* —5H **29**
(in two parts)
Tooting Bec Rd. *SW17 & SW16* —4E **28**
Tooting B'way. *SW17* —6C **28**
Tooting Gro. *SW17* —6C **28**
Tooting High St. *SW17* —6C **28**
Tooting Mkt. *SW17* —5D **28**
Tootswood Rd. *Brom* —4N **47**
Topcliffe Dri. *Farn* —1M **67**
Top Common. *Warf* —8B **16**
Topiary Sq. *Rich* —6M **11**
Topiary, The. *Asht* —7L **79**
Topiary, The. *F'boro* —2K **89**
Toplady Pl. *Farnh* —5H **109**
Top Pk. *Beck* —4N **47**
Topsham Rd. *SW17* —4D **28**
Torin Ct. *Egh* —6M **19**
Torland Dri. *Oxs* —9D **58**
Tor La. *Wey* —7E **56**
Tormead Clo. *Sutt* —3M **61**
Tormead Rd. *Guild* —3B **114**
Toronto Dri. *Small* —9L **143**
Torrens Clo. *Guild* —9K **93**
Torre Wlk. *Cars* —7C **44**
Torridge Rd. *Slou* —2D **6**
Torridge Rd. *T Hth* —4M **45**
Torridon Clo. *Wok* —4L **73**
Torrington Clo. *Clay* —3E **58**
Torrington Clo. *Lind* —4B **168**
Torrington Rd. *Clay* —3E **58**
Torrington Sq. *Croy* —6A **46**
Torrington Way. *Mord* —5M **43**
Tor Rd. *Farnh* —1E **128**
Torwood La. *Whyt* —7C **84**
Torwood Rd. *SW15* —8F **12**
Totale Rise. *Warf* —7N **15**
Totford La. *Seale* —9J **111**
Tot Hill. *H'ley* —4B **100**
Totland Clo. *F'boro* —8M **69**
Tottenham Rd. *G'ming* —5H **133**
Tottenham Wlk. *Owl* —6J **49**
Totterdown St. *SW17* —5D **28**
Totton Rd. *T Hth* —2L **45**
Tournai Clo. *Alder* —6C **90**
Tournay Rd. *SW6* —3L **13**
Tovil Clo. *SE20* —1E **46**
Tower Clo. *E Grin* —8A **166**
Tower Clo. *Hind* —5C **170**
Tower Clo. *Horl* —8D **142**
Tower Clo. *H'ham* —8G **196**
Tower Clo. *Wok* —4N **73**
Tower Ct. *E Grin* —8A **166**
Tower Gdns. *Clay* —4G **59**
Tower Gro. *Wey* —8F **38**
Tower Hill. *Dork* —7H **119**
Tower Hill. *F'boro* —2M **89**
Towerhill. *Gom* —9D **116**
Tower Hill. *H'ham* —9F **196**
Towerhill La. *Gom* —8D **116**
Towerhill Rise. *Gom* —9D **116**
Tower Hill Rd. *Dork* —7H **119**
Tower Ride. *Wind* —4B **18**
Tower Rise. *Rich* —6L **11**
Tower Rd. *Hind* —5C **170**
Tower Rd. *H'ham* —9E **180**
Tower Rd. *Tad* —1H **101**
Tower Rd. *Twic* —4F **24**
Towers Dri. *Crowt* —3G **48**
Towers Pl. *Rich* —8L **11**
Towers, The. *Kenl* —2N **83**
Towers Wlk. *Wey* —3C **56**
Tower View. *Croy* —6H **47**
Tower Yd. *Rich* —8M **11**
Towfield Ct. *Felt* —3N **23**
Towfield Rd. *Felt* —3N **23**
Town Barn Rd. *Craw* —3A **182**
Townend. *Cat* —9B **84**
Townend Clo. *Cat* —9B **84**
Town End Clo. *G'ming* —7H **133**
Town End St. *G'ming* —7H **133**
Town Farm Way. *Stanw* —1M **21**
Townfield Ct. *Dork* —6G **119**
Townfield Rd. *Dork* —6G **119**
Town Field Way. *Iswth* —5G **11**
Towngate. *Cobh* —2M **77**
Town Hall Av. *W4* —1C **12**
Town Hill. *Ling* —7N **145**
Town La. *Stanw* —9M **7**
(in two parts)
Town Mead. *Blet* —2A **124**
Town Mead. *Craw* —2B **182**
Townmead Bus. Cen. *SW6* —6N **13**
Town Meadow. *Bren* —2K **11**
Town Meadow Rd. *Bren* —3K **11**
Townmead Rd. *SW6* —6N **13**
Townmead Rd. *Rich* —3A **12**
Townsend Clo. *Brack* —4C **32**
Townsend La. *Wok* —8D **74**
Townsend Rd. *Ashf* —6N **21**
Townshend Rd. *Rich* —7M **11**
Townshend Ter. *Rich* —7M **11**
Townshott Clo. *Bookh* —4A **98**
Townside Pl. *Camb* —9B **50**
Townslow La. *Wis* —3L **75**
Town Sq. *Brack* —1A **32**
*Town Sq. Iswth —6H **11***
(off Swan St.)
Town Sq. *Wok* —4A **74**
Town Tree Rd. *Ashf* —6B **22**
Town Wharf. *Iswth* —6H **11**
Towpath. *Shep* —7A **38**
Towpath. *W On T* —4H **39**
Towpath Way. *Croy* —5C **46**
Towton Rd. *SE27* —3N **29**
Toynbee Rd. *SW20* —9K **27**
Tozer Wlk. *Wind* —6A **4**
Tracery, The. *Bans* —2N **81**
Tracious Clo. *Wok* —3L **73**
Tracious La. *St J* —3L **73**
Trafalgar Av. *Wor Pk* —7J **43**
Trafalgar Ct. *Farnh* —2G **129**
Trafalgar Dri. *W On T* —9J **39**
Trafalgar Rd. *SW19* —8N **27**
Trafalgar Rd. *H'ham* —4J **197**
Trafalgar Rd. *Twic* —3D **24**
Trafalgar Way. *Camb* —2L **69**
Trafalgar Way. *Croy* —8L **45**
Trafford Rd. *Frim* —6B **70**
Trafford Rd. *T Hth* —4K **45**
Tramway Path. *Mitc* —3C **44**
(in two parts)
Tranmere Ct. *Sutt* —4A **62**
Tranmere Rd. *SW18* —3A **28**
Tranmere Rd. *Twic* —1B **24**
Tranquil Dale. *Bkld* —1E **120**
Transport Av. *Bren* —1G **11**
Trap La. *Ockl* —8N **157**
Traps La. *N Mald* —9D **26**
Trashermead. *Dork* —7J **119**
Travellers Way. *Houn* —5K **9**
Travis La. *Sand* —8H **49**
Treadcroft Dri. *H'ham* —3L **197**
Treadwell Rd. *Eps* —3D **80**
Treaty Cen. *Houn* —6B **10**
Trebor Av. *Farnh* —2J **129**
Trebovir Rd. *SW5* —1M **13**
Tredenham Clo. *F'boro* —5A **90**
Tredwell Rd. *SE27* —5M **29**
Treebourne Rd. *Big H* —5E **86**
Treebys Av. *Guild* —6N **93**
Tree Clo. *Rich* —2K **25**
Treelands. *N Holm* —8J **119**
Treemount Ct. *Eps* —9D **60**
Treen Av. *SW13* —6E **12**
Treeside Dri. *Farnh* —5K **109**
Tree Tops. *S God* —6H **125**
Treetops. *Whyt* —5D **84**
Tree Tops Av. *Camb* —7E **50**
Tree Tops Cvn. Pk. *Alb* —6N **135**
Treeview. *Craw* —8A **182**
*Treeview Ct. Reig —3B **122***
(off Wray Comn. Rd.)
Tree Way. *Reig* —9N **101**
Trefoil Clo. *H'ham* —3L **197**
Trefoil Clo. *Wokgm* —1D **30**
Trefoil Cres. *Craw* —7M **181**
Trefusis Ct. *Houn* —4J **9**
Tregaron Gdns. *N Mald* —3D **42**
Tregarthen Pl. *Lea* —8J **79**
Tregarth Pl. *Wok* —4J **73**
Tregolls Dri. *F'boro* —2A **90**
Tregunter Rd. *SW10* —2N **13**
Trehaven Pde. *Reig* —6N **121**
Treherne Ct. *SW17* —5E **28**
Trehern Rd. *SW14* —6C **12**
Trelawn Clo. *Ott* —2E **54**
Trelawne Dri. *Cranl* —8N **155**
Trelawney Av. *Slou* —1B **6**
Trelawney Gro. *Wey* —3B **56**
Treloar Gdns. *SE19* —7N **29**
Tremaine Rd. *SE20* —1E **46**
Trematon Pl. *Tedd* —8J **25**
Tremayne Wlk. *Camb* —2G **70**
Trenance. *Wok* —4K **73**
Trenchard Clo. *W On T* —2K **57**
Trenchard Ct. *Mord* —5M **43**
Trenear Clo. *H'ham* —6L **197**
Trenham Dri. *Warl* —3F **84**
Trenholme Ct. *Cat* —9D **84**
Trent Clo. *Craw* —5L **181**
Trent Clo. *F'boro* —8K **69**
Trentham Cres. *Wok* —8C **74**
Trentham Rd. *Red* —5E **122**
Trentham St. *SW18* —2M **27**
Trenton Clo. *Frim* —4E **70**
Trent Rd. *Slou* —2D **6**
Trent Way. *Wor Pk* —9H **43**
Treport St. *SW18* —1N **27**
Tresham Cres. *Yat* —9A **48**
Tresillian Way. *Wok* —3K **73**
Tressider Ho. *SW4* —1H **29**
Tresta Wlk. *Wok* —3K **73**
Trevanion Rd. *W14* —1K **13**
Trevanne Plat. *Craw* —2H **183**
Trevelyan. *Brack* —6K **31**
Trevelyan Rd. *SW17* —6C **28**
Treveleux Hill. *Oxt* —9H **107**
Treville St. *SW15* —1G **26**
Trevithick Clo. *Felt* —2G **23**
*Trevone Ct. SW2 —1J **29***
(off Doverfield Rd.)
Trevor Clo. *Iswth* —8F **10**
Trevor Rd. *SW19* —8K **27**
Trevose Av. *W Byf* —1H **75**
Trewaren Ct. *Craw* —3N **181**
Trewenna Dri. *Chess* —2K **59**
Trewince Rd. *SW20* —9H **27**
Trewint St. *SW18* —3A **28**
Treyford Clo. *Craw* —3L **181**
Triangle, The. *King T* —1B **42**
Triangle, The. *Wok* —5M **73**
Trickett Ho. *Sutt* —5N **61**
Trident Ind. Est. *Coln* —6G **6**
Trigg's Clo. *Wok* —6N **73**
Trigg's La. *Wok* —6M **73**
Trigo Ct. *Eps* —7C **60**
Trig St. *Dork* —1L **159**
Trimmers Clo. *Farnh* —5G **109**
Trimmers Field. *Farnh* —2K **129**
Trimmers Wood. *Hind* —3C **170**
Trimmer Wlk. *Bren* —2L **11**
Trindledown. *Brack* —7M **15**
Trindles Rd. *S Nut* —5K **123**
Tring Ct. *Twic* —5G **24**
Tringham Clo. *Ott* —2E **54**
Tringham Cotts. *W End* —8C **52**
Trinity. *Owl* —5K **49**
Trinity Chu. Pas. *SW13* —2G **13**
Trinity Chu. Rd. *SW13* —2G **13**
Trinity Chyd. *Guild* —5N **113**
Trinity Clo. *Craw* —1G **183**
Trinity Clo. *Houn* —7M **9**
Trinity Clo. *S Croy* —5B **64**
Trinity Clo. *Stai* —9L **7**
Trinity Cotts. *Rich* —6M **11**
Trinity Ct. *SE25* —5B **46**
Trinity Ct. *Croy* —8N **45**
Trinity Cres. *SW17* —3D **28**
Trinity Cres. *Asc* —4D **34**
Trinity Fields. *Farnh* —6F **108**
Trinity Hill. *Farnh* —6F **108**
Trinity M. *SE20* —1E **46**
Trinity Pl. *Wind* —5F **4**
Trinity Rise. *SW2* —2L **29**
Trinity Rd. *SW18 & SW17* —7N **13**
Trinity Rd. *SW19* —7M **27**
Trinity Rd. *Knap* —5E **72**
Trinity Rd. *Rich* —6M **11**
Tritton Av. *Croy* —1J **63**
Tritton Rd. *SE21* —4N **29**
Trittons. *Tad* —8J **81**
Triumph Clo. *Hayes* —4D **8**
Trodd's La. *Guild* —2F **114**
Trojan Way. *Croy* —9K **45**
Troon Clo. *If'd* —4J **181**
Troon Ct. *Brack* —5K **31**
Troon Ct. *S'hill* —4N **33**
Trotsworth Av. *Vir W* —3A **36**
Trotsworth Ct. *Vir W* —3N **35**
Trotton Clo. *M'bowr* —6G **182**
Trotts La. *W'ham* —5L **107**
Trotwood Clo. *Owl* —5K **49**
Troutbeck Wlk. *Camb* —3H **71**
Trout Rd. *Hasl* —2C **188**
Trouville Rd. *SW4* —1G **29**
Trowers Way. *Red* —9F **102**
Trowlock Av. *Tedd* —7J **25**
Trowlock Way. *Tedd* —7K **25**
Troy La. *Eden* —8H **127**
Truggers. *Hand* —8N **199**
Trumble Gdns. *T Hth* —3M **45**
Trumbull Rd. *Brack* —8M **15**
Trumpets Hill Rd. *Reig* —4G **120**
Trumpsgreen Av. *Vir W* —5N **35**
Trumpsgreen Clo. *Vir W* —4A **36**
Trumpsgreen Rd. *Vir W* —7M **35**
Trumps Mill La. *Vir W* —5B **36**
Trundle Mead. *H'ham* —3J **197**
Trunk Rd. *F'boro* —1H **89**
Trunley Heath Rd. *Brmly* —4M **133**
Truslove Rd. *SE27* —6L **29**
Truss Hill Rd. *Asc* —4N **33**
Trust Wlk. *SE21* —2M **29**
Trystings Clo. *Clay* —3G **59**
Tubbenden Dri. *Orp* —1M **67**
Tubbenden La. *Orp* —1M **67**
Tubbenden La. S. *Orp* —2M **67**
Tucker Rd. *Ott* —3F **54**
Tuckers Corner. *Cranl* —7K **155**
Tuckers Dri. *Cranl* —7K **155**
Tuckey Gro. *Rip* —1H **95**
Tucklow Wlk. *SW15* —1E **26**
Tudor Av. *Hamp* —8A **24**
Tudor Av. *Wor Pk* —9G **42**
Tudor Circ. *G'ming* —4H **133**
Tudor Clo. *SW2* —1K **29**
Tudor Clo. *Ashf* —5N **21**
Tudor Clo. *Bans* —2K **81**
Tudor Clo. *Bookh* —2A **98**
(in two parts)
Tudor Clo. *Chess* —2L **59**
Tudor Clo. *Cobh* —9N **57**
Tudor Clo. *Coul* —5L **83**
Tudor Clo. *Craw* —4H **183**
Tudor Clo. *E Grin* —1B **186**
Tudor Clo. *Eps* —8E **60**
Tudor Clo. *Gray* —7B **170**
Tudor Clo. *Hamp* —6C **24**
Tudor Clo. *Small* —8M **143**
Tudor Clo. *S Croy* —2E **84**
Tudor Clo. *Sutt* —3K **61**
Tudor Clo. *Wall* —4G **63**
Tudor Clo. *Wok* —4C **74**
Tudor Clo. *Wokgm* —3E **30**
Tudor Ct. *Ash* —3D **110**
Tudor Ct. *Big H* —4G **86**
Tudor Ct. *Felt* —5K **23**
*Tudor Ct. Red —2E **122***
(off St Anne's Rise)
Tudor Ct. *Stanw* —9N **7**
Tudor Ct. *Tedd* —7F **24**
Tudor Dri. *King T* —6K **25**
Tudor Dri. *Mord* —5J **43**
Tudor Dri. *W on T* —7L **39**
Tudor Dri. *Yat* —2E **68**
Tudor Gdns. *SW13* —6D **12**
Tudor Gdns. *Twic* —2F **24**
Tudor Gdns. *W Wick* —9M **47**
Tudor Ho. *Brack* —4N **31**
Tudor La. *Old Win* —1M **19**
Tudor Pl. *Mitc* —8C **28**
Tudor Rd. *SE25* —4E **46**
Tudor Rd. *Ashf* —7E **22**
Tudor Rd. *Beck* —2M **47**
Tudor Rd. *G'ming* —4H **133**
Tudor Rd. *Hamp* —8A **24**
Tudor Rd. *Houn* —7D **10**
Tudor Rd. *King T* —8N **25**
Tudors, The. *Reig* —9A **102**
Tudor Wlk. *Lea* —7F **78**
Tudor Wlk. *Wey* —9C **38**
Tudor Way. *C Crook* —9B **88**
Tudor Way. *Wind* —4B **4**
Tuesley Corner. *G'ming* —8G **132**
Tuesley La. *G'ming* —8G **133**
Tufton Gdns. *W Mol* —1B **40**
Tugela Rd. *Croy* —5A **46**
Tuggles Plat. *Warn* —1E **196**
Tugmutton Clo. *Orp* —1K **67**
Tulip Clo. *Croy* —7G **46**
Tulip Clo. *Hamp* —7N **23**
Tulip Ct. *H'ham* —4J **197**
Tulip Tree Ct. *Belm* —7M **61**
Tullett Rd. *M'bowr* —7F **182**
Tulls La. *Stand* —7C **168**
Tull St. *Mitc* —6D **44**
Tulse Clo. *Beck* —2M **47**
Tulse Hill. *SW2* —1L **29**
Tulse Hill Est. *SW2* —1L **29**
Tulse Ho. *SW2* —1L **29**
Tulsemere Rd. *SE27* —3N **29**
Tulyar Clo. *Tad* —7G **81**
Tumber St. *H'ley* —3B **100**
Tumblewood Rd. *Bans* —3K **81**
Tumbling Bay. *W On T* —5H **39**
Tummons Gdns. *SE25* —1B **46**
Tunbridge La. *Bram* —8F **168**
Tunley Rd. *SW17* —2E **28**
Tunnel Rd. *Reig* —3M **121**
Tunnmeade. *If'd* —4K **181**
Tunsgate. *Guild* —5N **113**
*Tunsgate Sq. Guild —5N **113***
(off Tunsgate)
Tunstall Clo. *Orp* —1N **67**
Tunstall Rd. *Croy* —7B **46**
Tunstall Wlk. *Bren* —2L **11**
Tunworth Cres. *SW15* —9E **12**
Tuppers Ct. *Abry* —8L **115**
Tupwood La. *Cat* —3D **104**
Tupwood Scrubs Rd. *Cat* —6D **104**
Turf Hill Rd. *Camb* —7D **50**
Turfhouse La. *Chob* —5H **53**
Turle Rd. *SW16* —1J **45**
Turnberry. *Brack* —5K **31**
Turner Av. *Mitc* —9D **28**
Turner Av. *Twic* —4C **24**
Turner Clo. *Guild* —9B **94**
Turner Ct. *E Grin* —7C **166**
Turner Ho. *Dork* —7J **139**
Turner Pl. *Col T* —9J **49**
Turner Rd. *Big H* —8E **66**
Turner Rd. *N Mald* —6C **42**
Turners Clo. *Stai* —6K **21**
Turners Hill Pk. *Turn H* —4G **184**
Turners Hill Rd. *Craw D & Turn H* —7C **164**
Turners Hill Rd. *E Grin* —4J **185**
Turners Hill Rd. *P Hill & Worth* —3H **183**
Turners La. *W On T* —3J **57**
Turners Mead. *C'fold* —6F **172**
Turners Meadow Way. *Beck* —1J **47**
Turner's Way. *Croy* —8L **45**
Turner Wlk. *Craw* —6D **182**
Turneville Rd. *W14* —2L **13**
Turney Rd. *SE21* —1N **29**
Turnham Clo. *Guild* —7M **113**
Turnham Grn. Ter. *W4* —1D **12**
Turnham Grn. Ter. M. *W4* —1D **12**
Turnoak Av. *Wok* —7A **74**
Turnoak La. *Wok* —7A **74**
Turnoak Pk. *Wind* —7B **4**
Turnpike La. *Sutt* —8A **62**
Turnpike Link. *Croy* —8B **46**
Turnpike Pl. *Craw* —1B **182**
Turnpike Rd. *Brack* —1J **31**
Turnpike Way *Iswth* —4G **10**
Turnstone Clo. *S Croy* —6H **65**
Turnstone End. *Yat* —9A **48**
Turnvill Clo. *Light* —6L **51**
Turpin Rd. *Felt* —9G **9**
Turpins Rise. *W'sham* —1M **51**
Turpin Way. *Wall* —4F **62**
Turtledove Av. *Turn H* —4F **184**
Turtle Rd. *SW16* —1J **45**
Tuscam Way. *Camb* —2L **69**
Tuscany Gdns. *Craw* —9C **162**
Tuscany Way. *Yat* —2B **68**
Tushmore Av. *Craw* —9C **162**
Tushmore Ct. *Craw* —1C **182**
Tushmore Cres. *Craw* —9C **162**
Tushmore La. *Craw* —1C **182**
Tushmore Roundabout. *Craw* —1B **182**
Tussock Clo. *Craw* —5M **181**
Tuxford Clo. *M'bowr* —5G **182**
Tweed Clo. *F'boro* —8K **69**
Tweeddale Rd. *Cars* —7B **44**
Tweed La. *If'd* —9L **161**
Tweed La. *Str G* —7A **120**
Tweed Rd. *Slou* —2D **6**
Tweedsmuir Clo. *F'boro* —2J **89**
Twelve Acre Clo. *Bookh* —2N **97**
Twelve Acre Cres. *F'boro* —9J **69**
Tweseldown Rd. *C Crook* —9C **88**
Twickenham Bri. *Twic & Rich* —8J **11**
Twickenham Clo. *Croy* —9K **45**
Twickenham Rd. *Felt* —4N **23**
Twickenham Rd. *Iswth* —8G **10**
Twickenham Rd. *Rich* —7J **11**
Twickenham Rd. *Tedd* —5G **25**
Twickenham Trad. Est. *Twic* —9F **10**
Twilley St. *SW18* —1N **27**
Twin Bridges Bus. Pk. *S Croy* —3A **64**
Twining Av. *Twic* —4C **24**
Twinoaks. *Cobh* —9A **58**
Twisell Thorne. *C Crook* —9A **88**
Twitten La. *Felb* —6H **165**
Twitten, The. *Craw* —3A **182**
Two Mile Ash Rd. *Bar G* —9F **196**
Two Rivers Shop. Cen. *Stai* —5G **21**
Twycross Rd. *G'ming* —4G **132**
Twycross Rd. *Wokgm* —1D **30**
Twyford La. *Wrec* —5G **128**
Twyford Rd. *Binf* —9A **14**
Twyford Rd. *Cars* —7B **44**
Twyford Rd. *Wokgm* —9A **14**
Twyhurst Ct. *E Grin* —7N **165**
Twyne Clo. *Craw* —5L **181**
Twyner Clo. *Horl* —7H **143**
Twynham Rd. *Camb* —1A **70**
Tybenham Rd. *SW19* —2M **43**
Tychbourne Dri. *Guild* —9E **94**
Tydcombe Rd. *Warl* —6F **84**
Tye La. *Orp* —2L **67**
Tye La. *Tad* —5D **100**

Waddon Marsh Way—Weald Dri.

Waddon Marsh Way. Croy —7K 45
Waddon New Rd. Croy —9M 45
Waddon Pk. Av. Croy —1L 63
Waddon Rd. Croy —9L 45
Waddon Way. Croy —3L 63
Wades La. Tedd —6G 24
Wadham. Owl —6L 49
Wadham Clo. Craw —9G 162
Wadham Clo. Shep —6D 38
Wadham Rd. SW15 —7K 13
Wadhurst Clo. SE20 —1E 46
Wadlands Brook Rd. E Grin —5N 165
Wagbullock Rise. Brack —5A 32
Wagg Clo. E Grin —9C 166
Waggon Clo. Guild —2H 113
Waggoners Hollow. Bag —5J 51
Waggoners Roundabout. (Junct.) —4J 9
Waggoners Way. Gray —5M 169
Waggoners Wells Rd. Gray —6M 169
Wagon Yd. Farnh —1G 129
Wagtail Clo. H'ham —1M 197
Wagtail Gdns. S Croy —6G 65
Waight's Ct. King T —9L 25
Wain End. H'ham —3K 197
Wainford Clo. SW19 —1J 27
Wainhouse Clo. Eden —9M 127
Wainwright Gro. Iswth —7D 10
Wainwrights. Craw —6B 182
Wakefield Clo. Byfl —8N 55
Wakefield Rd. Rich —8K 11
Wakefords Copse. C Crook —1C 108
Wakefords Pk. C Crook —1C 108
Wakehams Grn. Dri. Craw —9H 163
Wakehurst Dri. Craw —6B 182
Wakehurst M. H'ham —1F 196
Wakehurst Path. Wok —1E 74
Wakely Clo. Big H —5E 86
Walburton Rd. Purl —9G 63
Walbury. Brack —3C 32
Waldby Ct. Craw —6M 181
Waldeck Gro. SE27 —4M 29
Waldeck Rd. SW14 —6B 12
Waldeck Rd. W4 —2N 11
Waldegrave Av. Tedd —6F 24
Waldegrave Gdns. Twic —3F 24
Waldegrave Pk. Twic —5F 24
Waldegrave Rd. Twic & Tedd —5F 24
Waldegrove. Croy —1C 64
Waldemar Av. SW6 —4K 13
Waldemar Rd. SW19 —6M 27
Walden Cotts. Norm —1L 111
Walden Gdns. T Hth —2K 45
Waldens Pk. Rd. Wok —3M 73
Waldens Rd. Wok —4N 73
Waldo Pl. Mitc —8C 28
Waldorf Clo. S Croy —5M 63
Waldorf Heights. B'water —3J 69
Waldron Gdns. Brom —2N 47
Waldron Hill. Brack —9D 16
Waldronhyrst. S Croy —1M 63
Waldron Rd. SW18 —4A 28
Waldron's Path. S Croy —1N 63
Waldrons, The. Croy —1M 63
Waldrons, The. Oxt —9B 106
Waldy Rise. Cranl —6N 155
Wales Av. Cars —2C 62
Walesbeech. Craw —4E 182
Waleton Acres. Wall —3H 63
Waleys La. Dork —9E 158
Walford Rd. N Holm —9J 119
Walham Grn. Ct. SW6 —3N 13 (off Waterford Rd.)
Walham Gro. SW6 —3M 13
Walham Rise. SW19 —7K 27
Walham Yd. SW6 —3M 13
Walker Clo. Felt —1G 22
Walker Clo. Hamp —7N 23
Walker Rd. M'bowr —5F 182
Walkerscroft Mead. SE21 —2N 29
Walkers Pl. SW15 —7K 13
Walker's Ridge. Camb —2C 70
Walkfield Dri. Eps —4G 81
Walking Bottom. Peasl —5D 136
Walk, The. Eton W —1D 4
Walk, The. Sun —8G 22
Walk, The. Tand —2K 125
Wallace Clo. Guild —9F 92
Wallace Clo. Shep —3E 38
Wallace Cres. Cars —2D 62
Wallace Fields. Eps —9F 60
Wallace Wlk. Add —1L 55
Wallage La. Craw —3N 183
Wallbrook Bus. Cen. Houn —6J 9
Wallcroft Clo. Binf —8L 15
Walldown Rd. W'hill —8A 168
Walled Garden, The. Bet —4C 120
Walled Garden, The. Loxw —1H 193
Walled Garden, The. Tad —9J 81
Waller Ga. Reig —2M 121
Waller La. Cat —1C 104
Waller Rd. Alder —4A 110
Wallgrave Rd. SW5 —1N 13
Wall Hill Rd. Ash W & F Row —4G 186
Wallingford Clo. Brack —3C 32
Wallington Corner. Wall —1F 62 (off Manor Rd. N.)
Wallington Ct. Wall —3F 62 (off Stanley Pk. Rd.)
Wallington Green. (Junct.) —1F 62
Wallington Rd. Camb —6E 50
Wallington Sq. Wall —3F 62
Wallis Ct. Craw —8D 162
Wallis's Cotts. SW2 —1J 29
Wallis Way. H'ham —4N 197
Walliswood Grn. Rd. Dork —1L 177
Wallner Way. Wokgm —3D 30
Wallorton Gdns. SW14 —7C 12
Walmer Clo. Crowt —2H 49
Walmer Clo. Farn —1M 67
Walmer Clo. Frim —7E 70
Walnut Clo. Alder —4M 109
Walnut Clo. Cars —2D 62
Walnut Clo. Eps —2E 80
Walnut Clo. Yat —2C 68
Walnut Dri. Tad —2K 101
Walnut Fields. Eps —5E 60
Walnut Gro. Bans —2J 81
Walnut La. Craw —9N 161
Walnut M. Sutt —4A 62
Walnuts, The. H'ham —4J 197
Walnut Tree Av. Mitc —2C 44
Walnut Tree Clo. SW13 —4E 12
Walnut Tree Clo. Bans —8K 61
Walnut Tree Clo. Guild —3M 113
Walnut Tree Clo. Shep —2D 38
Walnut Tree Cotts. SW19 —6K 27
Walnut Tree Gdns. G'ming —4H 133
Walnut Tree La. Byfl —8M 55
Walnut Tree Pk. Guild —3M 113
Walnut Tree Rd. Bren —2L 11
Walnut Tree Rd. Houn —2N 9
Walnut Tree Rd. Shep —1D 38
Walpole Av. Coul —6D 82
Walpole Av. Rich —5M 11
Walpole Ct. Twic —3E 24
Walpole Cres. Tedd —6F 24
Walpole Gdns. W4 —1B 12
Walpole Gdns. Twic —3E 24
Walpole Pk. Wey —4B 56
Walpole Pl. Tedd —6F 24
Walpole Rd. SW19 —7B 28
Walpole Rd. Croy —8A 46
Walpole Rd. Old Win —1L 19
Walpole Rd. Surb —6L 41
Walpole Rd. Tedd —6F 24
Walpole Rd. Twic —3E 24
Walsham Rd. Felt —1J 23
Walsh Av. Warf —8C 16
Walsh Cres. New Ad —8A 66
Walsingham Gdns. Eps —1D 60
Walsingham Rd. Mitc —4D 44
Walsingham Rd. New Ad —6M 65
Walstead Ho. Craw —4B 182
Walters Mead. Asht —4L 79
Walters Rd. SE25 —3B 46
Walter St. King T —9L 25
Waltham Av. Guild —8L 93
Waltham Clo. Owl —6J 49
Waltham Rd. Cars —6B 44
Waltham Rd. Cat —9E 84
Walton Av. N Mald —3E 42
Walton Av. Sutt —9L 43
Walton Bri. Shep & W on T —6F 38
Walton Bri. Rd. Shep —6F 38
Walton Clo. Fleet —5A 88
Walton Ct. Wok —2C 74
Walton Dri. Asc —9K 17
Walton Dri. H'ham —4A 198
Walton Gdns. Felt —5G 22
Walton Grn. New Ad —5L 65
Walton Heath. Craw —1H 183
Walton La. Shep —6E 38
Walton La. Wey & W on T —8C 38
Walton Pk. W On T —8L 39
Walton Pk. La. W On T —8L 39
Walton Rd. E Mol —3C 40
Walton Rd. Eps —8B 80 (Epsom)
Walton Rd. Eps —5E 80 (Epsom Downs)
Walton Rd. W on T & W Mol —4K 39
Walton Rd. Wok —3B 74
Walton St. Tad —2F 100
Walton Ter. Wok —2D 74
Walton Way. Mitc —3G 44
Wanborough Dri. SW15 —2G 26
Wanborough Hill. Guild —6N 111
Wanborough La. Cranl —6B 156
Wandle Bank. SW19 —7A 28
Wandle Bank. Croy —9J 45
Wandle Clo. Ash —3E 110
Wandle Clo. M'bowr —4G 182
Wandle Ct. Croy —9J 45
Wandle Ct. Eps —1B 60
Wandle Ct. Gdns. Croy —9J 45
Wandle Pk. Trad. Est., The. Croy —7L 45
Wandle Rd. SW17 —3C 28
Wandle Rd. Bedd —9J 45
Wandle Rd. Croy —9N 45
Wandle Rd. Mord —3A 44
Wandle Rd. Wall —9F 44
Wandle Side. Croy —9K 45
Wandle Side. Wall —9F 44
Wandle Way. SW18 —2N 27
Wandle Way. Mitc —4D 44
Wandon Rd. SW6 —3N 13
Wandsworth Bri. SW6 & SW18 —6N 13
Wandsworth Bri. Rd. SW6 —4N 13
Wandsworth Enterprise Cen. SW18 —7N 13
Wandsworth Gyratory. (Junct.) —8N 13
Wandsworth High St. SW18 —8M 13
Wandsworth Plain. SW18 —8N 13
Wanmer Ct. Reig —2M 121
Wansdown Pl. SW6 —3N 13
Wansdyke Clo. Frim —6D 70
Wansford Grn. Wok —4J 73
Wanstraw Gro. Brack —6C 32
Wantage Clo. Brack —4C 32
Wantage Clo. M'bowr —6G 182
Wantage Rd. Col T —7J 49
Waplings, The. Tad —2G 100
Wapses Roundabout. (Junct.) —7E 84
Wapshott Rd. Stai —7G 20
Warbank Clo. New Ad —6A 66
Warbank Cres. New Ad —6A 66
Warbank La. King T —8E 26
Warbler's Grn. Cobh —1N 77
Warbleton Ho. Craw —6L 181
Warboys App. King T —7A 26
Warboys Rd. King T —7A 26
Warburton Clo. E Grin —9C 166
Warburton Rd. Twic —2B 24
Warbury La. Knap —2F 72
War Coppice Rd. Cat —5A 104
Ward Clo. S Croy —3B 64
Ward Clo. Wokgm —9C 14
Wardens Field Clo. Grn St —3N 67
Ward La. Warl —3F 84
Wardle Clo. Bag —4J 51
Wardley St. SW18 —1N 27
Wardo Av. SW6 —4K 13
Ward Rd. SW19 —9A 28
Ward Royal Est. Wind —4F 4
Ward's Pl. Egh —7E 20
Wards Stone Clo. Brack —6C 32
Wards Stone Pk. Brack —6C 32
Ward St. Guild —4N 113
Ware Ct. Sutt —1L 61
Wareham Clo. Houn —7B 10
Wareham Rd. Brack —3D 32
Warenne Ct. Reig —2L 121
Warenne Rd. Fet —9C 78
Warfield Rd. Brack —7A 16
Warfield Rd. Felt —1F 22
Warfield Rd. Hamp —9B 24
Warfield St. Brack —6A 16
Wargrove Dri. Col T —7J 49
Warham Rd. S Croy —2M 63
Waring St. SE27 —5N 29
Warkworth Gdns. Iswth —3G 10
Warlingham Rd. T Hth —3M 45
Warltersville Way. Horl —1G 162
Warminster Gdns. SE25 —1D 46
Warminster Rd. SE25 —1C 46
Warminster Sq. SE25 —1D 46
Warminster Way. Mitc —9F 28
Warner Av. Sutt —8K 43
Warner Clo. Hamp —6N 23
Warner Clo. Hayes —3E 8
Warner Clo. M'bowr —7G 182
Warner Pde. Hayes —3E 8
Warners La. Abry —1N 135
Warners La. Rich —5K 25
Warnford Ho. SW15 —9D 12 (off Tunworth Cres.)
Warnham Ct. Rd. Cars —4D 62
Warnham Ho. SW2 —1K 29 (off Up. Tulse Hill)
Warnham Mnr. Warn —1C 196
Warnham Rd. Broad H —4D 196
Warnham Rd. Craw —5E 182
Warnham Rd. H'ham —3H 197
Warramill Rd. G'ming —6K 133
Warren Av. Orp —2N 67
Warren Av. Rich —7A 12
Warren Av. S Croy —4G 64
Warren Av. Sutt —6L 61
Warren Clo. SE21 —1N 29
Warren Clo. Esh —1B 58
Warren Clo. Felb —7H 165
Warren Clo. Fleet —6C 88
Warren Clo. Sand —7F 48
Warren Ct. Croy —7B 46
Warren Ct. Wey —2B 56
Warren Cutting. King T —8C 26
Warren Down. Brack —9K 15
Warren Dri. Craw —1M 181
Warren Dri. Kgswd —9L 81
Warren Dri. N. Surb —7A 42
Warren Dri. S. Surb —7B 42
Warreners La. Wey —4E 56
Warren Footpath. Twic —2J 25
Warren Hill. Eps —3C 80
Warren Home Farm. Wok —6K 75
Warren Ho. Rd. Wokgm —7C 14
Warrenhyrst. Guild —4C 114
Warren La. Alb —8L 115
Warren La. Oxs —7C 58
Warren La. Oxt —3C 126
Warren La. Wok —5J 75
Warren Lodge Dri. Kgswd —2K 101
Warren Mead. Bans —2H 81
Warrenne Heights. Red —5B 122
Warrenne Rd. Brock —5B 120
Warrenne Way. Reig —3M 121
Warren Pk. King T —7B 26
Warren Pk. Thur —5K 151
Warren Pk. Warl —5G 85
Warren Pk. Cvn. Site. Tad —9B 100
Warren Pk. Rd. Sutt —3C 62
Warren Rise. Frim —4C 70
Warren Rise. N Mald —9C 26
Warren Rd. SW19 —7C 28
Warren Rd. Ashf —8F 22
Warren Rd. Bans —1H 81
Warren Rd. Chels —2N 67
Warren Rd. Croy —7C 46
Warren Rd. G'ming —4H 133
Warren Rd. Guild —4B 114
Warren Rd. King T —7B 26
Warren Rd. New H —6J 55
Warren Rd. Purl —8M 63
Warren Rd. Reig —2N 121
Warren Rd. Twic —9C 10
Warren Row. Asc —1H 33
Warren, The. Alder —3L 109
Warren, The. Asht —7M 79
Warren, The. Brack —3E 32
Warren, The. Cars —6C 62
Warren, The. E Hor —8G 96
Warren, The. Farnh —4K 109
Warren, The. Houn —3N 9
Warren, The. Oxs —8C 58
Warren, The. Tad —1K 101
Warren, The. Wor Pk —9C 42
Warren Way. Wey —2D 56
Warrington Clo. Bew —7K 181
Warrington M. Alder —4K 109
Warrington Rd. Croy —9M 45
Warrington Rd. Rich —8K 11
Warrington Spur. Old Win —1L 19
Warsop Trad. Est. Eden —3M 147
Warwick. Brack —5C 32
Warwick Av. Egh —9E 20
Warwick Av. Stai —7L 21
Warwick Clo. SW15 —1E 26
Warwick Clo. Alder —4A 110
Warwick Clo. Camb —3F 70
Warwick Clo. Hamp —8C 24
Warwick Clo. Holmw —4K 139
Warwick Deeping. Ott —2E 54
Warwick Dri. SW15 —6G 12
Warwick Gdns. Asht —4J 79
Warwick Gdns. Th Dit —4F 40
Warwick Gdns. T Hth —2L 45
Warwick Gro. Surb —6M 41
Warwick La. Wok —6K 73
Warwick Lodge. Twic —4B 24
Warwick Pl. Th Dit —5G 40
Warwick Quad. Red —2E 122 (off London Rd.)
Warwick Rd. SE20 —2E 46
Warwick Rd. W14 & SW5 —1L 13
Warwick Rd. Ashf —6N 21
Warwick Rd. Ash V —5E 90
Warwick Rd. Coul —1G 83
Warwick Rd. Holmw —4J 139
Warwick Rd. Houn —6J 9
Warwick Rd. King T —9J 25
Warwick Rd. N Mald —2B 42
Warwick Rd. Red —2D 122
Warwick Rd. Sutt —1A 62
Warwick Rd. Th Dit —4F 40
Warwick Rd. T Hth —2L 45
Warwick Rd. Twic —2E 24
Warwick's Bench. Guild —5N 113
Warwick's Bench La. Guild —6B 114
Warwick's Bench Rd. Guild —6A 114
Warwick Vs. Egh —9E 20
Warwick Wold Rd. Red —7L 103
Wasdale Clo. Owl —5J 49
Washford Clo. Bord —5A 168
Washford La. Lind —4A 168
Washington Clo. Reig —1M 121
Washington Dri. Wind —6B 4
Washington Rd. SW13 —3F 12
Washington Rd. King T —1N 41
Washington Rd. Wor Pk —8G 42
Washpond La. Warl —5M 85
Wasp Grn. La. Out —3N 143
Wassand Clo. Craw —3E 182
Watchetts Dri. Camb —4A 70
Watchetts Lake Clo. Camb —3B 70
Watchetts Rd. Camb —2N 69
Watchfield Ct. W4 —1B 12
Watchmoor Pk. Camb —3M 69
Watchmoor Rd. Camb —2M 69
Watcombe Cotts. Rich —2N 11
Watcombe Pl. SE25 —3E 46
Watcombe Rd. SE25 —4E 46
Watercress Way. Wok —4L 73
Waterden Clo. Guild —4B 114
Waterden Rd. Guild —4A 114
Waterer Gdns. Tad —5J 81
Waterer Rise. Wall —3H 63
Waterers Rise. Knap —4G 72
Waterfall Clo. Vir W —2K 35
Waterfall Cotts. SW19 —7B 28
Waterfall Rd. SW19 —7B 28
Waterfall Ter. SW17 —7C 28
Waterfield. Tad —6G 81
Waterfield Clo. H'ham —5L 197
Waterfield Dri. Warl —6F 84
Waterfield Gdns. SE25 —3B 46
Waterfield Gdns. Bew —5K 181
Waterfield Grn. Tad —7H 81
Waterfields. Lea —6H 79
Waterford Clo. Cobh —7M 57
Waterford Rd. SW6 —3N 13
Waterford Way. Wokgm —2B 30
Watergardens, The. King T —7B 26
Waterham Rd. Brack —5N 31
Waterhouse Clo. W6 —1J 13
Waterhouse La. Blet —1C 124
Waterhouse La. Kenl —6N 83
Waterhouse La. Kgswd —8K 81
Waterhouse Mead. Col T —8J 49
Waterlakes. Eden —3L 147
Waterlands La. H'ham —9M 177
Water La. Ab H —3J 137
Water La. Bisl —5E 52
Water La. Bookh —3L 97 (in two parts)
Water La. Cobh —2M 77
Water La. Eden —4F 146
Water La. Ent —7D 152
Water La. F'boro —7M 69
Water La. Farnh —8K 109
Water La. Guild —6K 115
Water La. King T —9K 25
Water La. Red —8M 103
Water La. Rich —8K 11
Water La. S God —7G 124
Water La. T'sey —4C 106
Water La. Twic —2G 25
Water La. W'ham —5M 107
Water Lea. Craw —4E 182
Waterloo Clo. Camb —8F 50
Waterloo Clo. Felt —2G 23
Waterloo Clo. Wokgm —3D 30
Waterloo Cres. Wokgm —3D 30
Waterloo Pl. Crowt —3G 49
Waterloo Pl. Rich —2N 11 (Kew)
Waterloo Pl. Rich —7L 11 (Richmond)
Waterloo Rd. Alder —3A 110
Waterloo Rd. Crowt —3F 48
Waterloo Rd. Eps —8C 60
Waterloo Rd. Sutt —2B 62
Waterloo Rd. Wokgm —3D 30
Waterlow Rd. Reig —4A 122
Waterman Clo. Bord —7A 168
Watermans Bus. Pk. Stai —5F 20
Watermans Clo. King T —8L 25
Watermans Ct. Bren —2L 11
Waterman St. SW15 —6J 13
Watermead. Felt —2F 22
Watermead. Tad —8G 81
Watermead. Wok —3J 73
Watermead La. Cars —6D 44
Watermeadow La. SW6 —5N 13
Watermill Clo. Rich —4J 25
Water Mill Ho. Felt —3A 24
Watermill Way. SW19 —9B 28
Watermill Way. Felt —3N 23
Waterperry La. Chob —6J 53
Water Rede. C Crook —1A 108
Waters Dri. Stai —4H 21
Watersedge. Eps —1B 60
Waterside. Beck —1J 47
Waterside. E Grin —9D 166
Waterside. Horl —6E 142
Waterside Clo. Bew —5K 181
Waterside Clo. Bord —5A 168
Waterside Clo. G'ming —6K 133
Waterside Clo. Surb —8L 41
Waterside Ct. Fleet —2C 88
Waterside Dri. W On T —4H 39
Waterside La. G'ming —8F 132
Waterside Meadows. Guild —1M 113
Waterside M. Fleet —2C 88
Waterside Pk. Ind. Est. Brack —1K 31
Waterside Rd. Guild —9N 93
Waterside Trad. Est. Add —1N 55
Waterside Way. SW17 —5A 28
Waterside Way. Wok —5L 73
Waterslade. Red —2D 122
Watersmeet Clo. Guild —7C 94
Waters Pl. SW15 —5H 13
Watersplash Clo. King T —2L 41
Watersplash La. Asc —9A 18
Watersplash La. Hayes —1H 9 (in two parts)
Watersplash La. Warf —7N 15
Watersplash Rd. Shep —3B 38
Waters Rd. King T —1A 42
Waters Sq. King T —2A 42
Water Tower Hill. Croy —1A 64
Water View. Horl —8H 143
Waterway Rd. Fet —9G 78
Waterworks Cotts. F Row —6H 187
Waterworks Dri. F Row —5H 187
Waterworks Yd. Croy —9N 45
Watery La. SW20 —1L 43
Watery La. Chob —6G 52
Watery La. C Crook —1A 108
Watery La. Hayes —1F 8
Watery La. Lyne —6F 36
Wates Way. Mitc —5D 44
Watford Clo. Guild —3B 114
Wathen Rd. Dork —4H 119
Watlings Clo. Croy —5H 47
Watney Rd. SW14 —6B 12
Watney's Rd. Mitc —4H 45
Watson Av. Sutt —8K 43
Watson Clo. SW19 —7C 28
Watson Clo. M'bowr —6G 182
Watson Ho. Reig —2M 121
Watson Rd. Westc —6C 118
Wattendon Rd. Kenl —3M 83
Watts Clo. Tad —9J 81
Watts Farm Pde. Chob —6J 53 (off Barnmead)
Watt's La. Tad —9J 81
Watts La. Tedd —6G 24
Watt's Mead. Tad —9J 81
Watts Rd. F'boro —9L 69
Watts Rd. Th Dit —6G 40
Wavendene Av. Egh —8D 20
Wavendon Av. W4 —1C 12
Waveney Wlk. Craw —5F 182
Waverleigh Rd. Cranl —9N 155
Waverley. Brack —4K 31
Waverley Av. Fleet —2A 88
Waverley Av. Kenl —3B 84
Waverley Av. Surb —5A 42
Waverley Av. Sutt —8N 43
Waverley Av. Twic —2N 23
Waverley Clo. Camb —2D 70
Waverley Clo. Farnh —1J 129
Waverley Clo. Hayes —1E 8
Waverley Clo. W Mol —4A 40
Waverley Cotts. Farnh —3B 130
Waverley Ct. H'ham —6H 197
Waverley Ct. Wok —5A 74
Waverley Dri. Ash V —7E 90
Waverley Dri. Camb —1D 70
Waverley Dri. Cher —9F 36
Waverley Dri. Vir W —2K 35
Waverley Gdns. Ash V —7E 90
Waverley La. Farnh —1J 129
Waverley Pl. Lea —9H 79
Waverley Rd. SE25 —3E 46
Waverley Rd. Bag —4J 51
Waverley Rd. Eps —2G 60
Waverley Rd. F'boro —2B 90
Waverley Rd. Stoke D & Oxs —1B 78
Waverley Rd. Wey —2B 56
Waverley Way. Cars —3C 62
Waverton Rd. SW18 —1A 28
Wavertree Ct. SW2 —2J 29
Wavertree Rd. SW2 —2K 29
Waye Av. Houn —4H 9
Wayland Clo. Brack —3D 32
Waylands. Wray —9A 6
Waylands Mead. Beck —1L 47
Waylett Pl. SE27 —4M 29
Wayman Rd. F'boro —6K 69
Wayne Clo. Orp —1N 67
Wayneflete Tower Av. Esh —9A 40
Waynflete Av. Croy —9M 45
Waynflete La. Farnh —1E 128
Waynflete St. SW18 —3A 28
Ways End. Camb —2C 70
Wayside. SW14 —8B 12
Wayside. If'd —5K 181
Wayside. New Ad —3L 65
Wayside Cotts. Churt —7J 149
Wayside Cotts. Dork —5K 137
Wayside Ct. Twic —9J 11
Wayside Ct. Wok —3H 73
Wayside Dri. Eden —9M 127
Way, The. Reig —2B 122
Weald Clo. H'ham —8L 197
Weald Clo. Shaf —9A 114
Weald Dri. Craw —4E 182

Wealdon Ct. Guild —3J 113
Wealdstone Rd. Sutt —8L 43
Weald, The. E Grin —6B 166
Weald Way. Cat —6B 104
Weald Way. Reig —7A 122
Weare St. Dork —2C 178
Weasdale Ct. Wok —3J 73
Weatherall Clo. Add —2K 55
Weatherhill Clo. Horl —8K 143
Weatherhill Rd. Small —8K 143
Weaver Clo. If'd —4K 181
Weavers Clo. Iswth —7E 10
Weavers Gdns. Farnh —4E 128
Weavers Ter. SW6 —2M 13 (off Micklethwaite Rd.)
Weavers Yd. Farnh —1G 129
Weaver Wlk. SE27 —5N 29
Webb Clo. Bag —6J 51
Webb Clo. Binf —8K 15
Webb Clo. Craw —8N 181
Webb Ct. Wokgm —9D 14
Webb Ho. Felt —4M 23
Webb Rd. Witl —3N 151
Webster Clo. Oxs —1B 78
Websters Clo. Wok —7L 73
Weddell Rd. Craw —6D 182
Wedgwoods. Tats —8E 86
Wedgwood Way. SE19 —8N 29
Weighton M. SE20 —1E 46
Weighton Rd. SE20 —1E 46
Weihurst Ct. Sutt —2C 62
Weihurst Gdns. Sutt —2B 62
Weimar St. SW15 —6K 13
Weir Av. F'boro —2M 89
Weirbrook. Craw —6E 182
Weir Clo. F'boro —2M 89
Weir Pl. Stai —9G 21
Weir Rd. SW12 —2G 28
Weir Rd. SW19 —4N 27
Weir Rd. Cher —6K 37
Weir Rd. W On T —5H 39
Weiss Rd. SW15 —6J 13
Welbeck. Brack —4K 31
Welbeck Clo. Eps —4F 60
Welbeck Clo. F'boro —2L 89
Welbeck Clo. N Mald —4E 42
Welbeck Rd. Sutt & Cars —8B 44
Welbeck Wlk. Cars —7C 44
Welcomes Rd. Kenl —4A 84
Welcome Ter. Whyt —3C 84
Weldon Clo. C Crook —8C 88
Weldon Dri. W Mol —3N 39
Weldon Way. Red —7H 103
Welford Pl. SW19 —5K 27
Welham Rd. SW17 & SW16 —6E 28
Welhouse Rd. Cars —7C 44
Welland Clo. Slou —2D 6
Wellbrook Rd. Orp —1J 67
Wellburn Clo. Sand —8G 49
Well Clo. SW16 —5K 29
Well Clo. Camb —2N 69
Well Clo. Wok —4M 73
Weller Clo. Worth —4H 183
Weller Dri. Camb —3A 70
Weller Pl. Orp —7J 67
Wellers Clo. W'ham —5L 107
Wellers Ct. Shere —8B 116
Weller's La. Brack —3A 16
Wellesford Clo. Bans —4L 81
Wellesley Clo. Ash V —6D 90
Wellesley Clo. Bag —4G 51
Wellesley Ct. Sutt —7K 43
Wellesley Ct. Rd. Croy —8A 46
Wellesley Cres. Twic —3E 24
Wellesley Dri. Crowt —2D 48
Wellesley Garden. Farnh —5H 109
Wellesley Ga. Alder —3N 109
Wellesley Gro. Croy —8A 46
Wellesley Lodge. Sutt —4N 61 (off Worcester Rd.)
Wellesley Pde. Twic —4F 24
Wellesley Rd. W4 —1N 11
Wellesley Rd. Alder —1J 109
Wellesley Rd. Ash V —7D 90 (in two parts)
Wellesley Rd. Croy —7N 45
Wellesley Rd. F'boro —5J 89
Wellesley Rd. Sutt —3A 62
Wellesley Rd. Tilf —4N 149
Wellesley Rd. Twic —4D 24
Welley Av. Wray —7A 6
Welley Rd. Wray & Hort —9A 6
Well Farm Rd. Warl —6D 84
Wellfield. E Grin —2E 186
Wellfield Rd. SW16 —5J 29
Wellfield Wlk. SW16 —6K 29
Wellhouse Rd. Beck —3K 47
Wellhouse Rd. Bet —7B 120
Wellington Av. Alder —2K 109
Wellington Av. Fleet —3C 88
Wellington Av. Houn —8A 10
Wellington Av. Vir W —4L 35
Wellington Av. Wor Pk —9H 43
Wellington Bus. Pk. Crowt —3D 48
Wellington Cen., The. Alder —2M 109
Wellington Clo. Craw —9J 163
Wellington Clo. Sand —7H 49
Wellington Clo. W On T —7G 39
Wellington Cotts. E Hor —8F 96
Wellington Ct. SW6 —4N 13 (off Maltings Pl.)
Wellington Ct. Hamp —6D 24
Wellington Ct. Stanw —1N 21
Wellington Cres. N Mald —2B 42
Wellington Dri. Brack —4B 32
Wellington Dri. Purl —5K 63
Wellington Gdns. Alder —3L 109
Wellington Gdns. Twic —5D 24
Wellingtonia Av. Camb —1H 71
Wellingtonia Av. Crowt —3A 48
Wellingtonia Ho. Add —2J 55
Wellingtonia Roundabout. Crowt —3D 48
Wellingtonias. Warf P —8E 16
Wellingtonia Way. Eden —1L 147
Wellington La. Farnh —5J 109
Wellington Pl. Cobh —8A 58
Wellington Rd. SW19 —3M 27
Wellington Rd. Ashf —6N 21
Wellington Rd. Cat —9N 83
Wellington Rd. Crowt —3H 49
Wellington Rd. Croy —6M 45
Wellington Rd. Felt —8F 8
Wellington Rd. Hamp & Twic —6D 24
Wellington Rd. H'ham —6K 197
Wellington Rd. Sand —7G 48
Wellington Rd. Wokgm —2A 30
Wellington Rd. N. Houn —6N 9
Wellington Rd. S. Houn —7N 9
Wellington St. Alder —2M 109
Wellington Ter. Knap —5H 73
Wellington Ter. Sand —7H 49
Wellington Town Rd. E Grin —8N 165
Wellington Way. Horl —6D 142
Wellington Way. Wey —6A 56
Well La. SW14 —8B 12
Well La. Hasl —2H 189
Well La. Wok —4M 73
Well La. Wmly —1A 172
Wellow Wlk. Cars —7B 44
Wellpath. Wok —4M 73
Wells Clo. Bookh —2C 98
Wells Clo. H'ham —6F 196
Wells Clo. Red —8F 102
Wells Clo. Wind —4D 4
Wells Cotts. Farnh —4F 128
Wells Ho. Eps —1N 79
Wellside Gdns. SW14 —7B 12
Wells La. Asc —3M 33
Wells La. Norm —9N 91
Wells Lea. E Grin —7N 165
Wells Meadow. E Grin —7N 165
Wells Pl. Ind. Est. Mers —7F 102
Wells Rd. Craw —7C 182
Wells Rd. Eps —1N 79
Wells Rd. Guild —9E 94
Well Way. Eps —2N 79
Wellwood Clo. Coul —1J 83
Wellwood Clo. H'ham —4A 198
Wellwynds Rd. Cranl —8N 155
Welsingham Lodge. SW13 —4F 12
Weltje Rd. W6 —1F 12
Welwyn Av. Felt —9G 8
Welwyn Clo. Bew —7K 181
Wembley Rd. Hamp —9A 24
Wembury Pk. Newc —1H 165
Wendela Clo. Wok —5B 74
Wendley Dri. New H —6H 55
Wendling Rd. Sutt —7B 44
Wendover Dri. Frim —3G 70
Wendover Dri. N Mald —5E 42
Wendover Pl. Stai —6F 20
Wendover Rd. Stai —6E 20
Wendron Clo. Wok —5K 73
Wend, The. Coul —1H 83
Wendy Cres. Guild —1K 113
Wenlock Clo. Craw —5M 181
Wenlock Edge. Dork —7J 119
Wensleydale. Craw —6A 182
Wensleydale Dri. Camb —1H 71
Wensleydale Gdns. Hamp —8B 24
Wensleydale Pas. Hamp —8A 24
Wensleydale Rd. Hamp —8A 24
Wensley Dri. Fleet —2B 88
Wentworth Av. Asc —1G 33
Wentworth Clo. Ashf —5C 22
Wentworth Clo. Ash V —6E 90
Wentworth Clo. Crowt —1E 48
Wentworth Clo. Farnh —6L 109
Wentworth Clo. Mord —6M 43
Wentworth Clo. Orp —2N 67
Wentworth Clo. Rip —8K 75
Wentworth Clo. Surb —8K 41
Wentworth Clo. Yat —1C 68
Wentworth Ct. W6 —2K 13 (off Laundry Rd.)
Wentworth Ct. Twic —4E 24
Wentworth Cres. Ash V —7E 90 (in two parts)
Wentworth Dri. Craw —2H 183
Wentworth Dri. Vir W —3J 35
Wentworth Ho. Add —1K 55
Wentworth Rd. Croy —6L 45
Wentworth Rd. S'hall —1K 9
Wentworth Way. Asc —1G 33
Wentworth Way. S Croy —1D 84
Werndee Rd. SE25 —3D 46
Werter Rd. SW15 —7K 13
Wesco Ct. Wok —3C 74
Wescott Rd. Wokgm —2C 30
Wesley Av. Houn —5M 9
Wesley Clo. Craw —6K 181
Wesley Clo. Horl —6E 142
Wesley Clo. Reig —4L 121
Wesley Dri. Egh —7C 20
Wesley Pl. Wink —3M 17
Wessels. Tad —8J 81
Wessex Av. SW19 —2M 43
Wessex Clo. King T —9A 26
Wessex Ct. Beck —1H 47
Wessex Ct. Stanw —9N 7
Wessex Pl. Farnh —2H 129
Wessex Rd. H'row A —7L 7
W. Acres. Esh —4N 57
West Av. Craw —1E 182
West Av. Farnh —6J 109
West Av. Red —9E 122
West Av. Wall —2J 63
West Av. W Vill —5F 56
West Bank. Dork —6F 118
Westbank Rd. Hamp —7C 24
W. Barnes La. N Mald & SW20 —4G 42
Westbourne Av. Sutt —8K 43
Westbourne Ho. Houn —2A 10
Westbourne Rd. Col T —8K 49
Westbourne Rd. Croy —5C 46
Westbourne Rd. Felt —4G 22
Westbourne Rd. Stai —8K 21
Westbrook. F Row —6G 187
Westbrook Av. Hamp —8N 23
Westbrook Gdns. Brack —9B 16
Westbrook Hill. Elst —7F 130
Westbrook Rd. G'ming —6F 132
Westbrook Rd. Houn —3N 9
Westbrook Rd. Stai —6H 21
Westbrook Rd. T Hth —9N 29
Westbury Av. Clay —3F 58
Westbury Av. Fleet —5E 88
Westbury Clo. Crowt —1G 48
Westbury Clo. Fleet —5D 88
Westbury Clo. Shep —5C 38
Westbury Clo. Whyt —5C 84
Westbury Gdns. Farnh —8K 109
Westbury Gdns. Fleet —5E 88
Westbury Pl. Bren —2K 11
Westbury Rd. SE20 —1G 46
Westbury Rd. Beck —2H 47
Westbury Rd. Croy —5A 46
Westbury Rd. Felt —2L 23
Westbury Rd. N Mald —3C 42
Westbury Ter. W'ham —5L 107
Westcar La. W On T —3J 57
W. Chiltington La. H'ham —9M 195
West Clo. Ashf —5N 21
West Clo. Farnh —5J 109
West Clo. Fern —9F 188
West Clo. Hamp —7M 23
Westcombe Av. Croy —6J 45
Westcombe Clo. Brack —6C 32
West Comn. Rd. Hay & Kes —1D 66
Westcoombe Av. SW20 —9E 26
Westcote Rd. SW16 —6G 29
Westcott Clo. Craw —9A 182
Westcott Clo. New Ad —5L 65
Westcott Keep. Horl —7G 142 (off Langshott La.)
Westcott Rd. Dork —6E 118
Westcott Rd. Wokgm —2C 30
Westcotts Grn. Warf —7B 16
Westcott St. Westc —6B 118
Westcott Way. Sutt —6H 61
West Ct. Houn —3C 10
West Cres. Wind —4C 4
Westcroft Gdns. Mord —3L 43
Westcroft Rd. Cars & Wall —1E 62
Westcroft Sq. W6 —1F 12
W. Cromwell Rd. W14 & SW5 —1L 13
W. Cross Cen. Bren —2G 11
W. Cross Way. Bren —2H 11
W. Dean Clo. SW18 —9N 13
West Dene. Sutt —3K 61
Westdene Meadows. Cranl —7J 155
W. Dene Way. Wey —9F 38
West Down. Bookh —5B 98
West Dri. SW16 —5G 28
West Dri. Asc & Vir W —4G 34 (in two parts)
West Dri. Cars —6B 62
West Dri. Sutt —5J 61
West Dri. Tad —5J 81
W. End Gdns. Esh —2N 57
W. End Gro. Farnh —1F 128
W. End La. Esh —4N 57
W. End La. Fren —1D 148
W. End La. Hasl —9A 172
W. End La. Hayes —3D 8
W. End La. Warf —7N 15
W. End Rd. Warf —6N 15
Westerdale Dri. Frim —3F 70
Westerfolds Clo. Wok —4E 74
Westerham Clo. Add —3L 55
Westerham Clo. Sutt —6M 61
Westerham Hill. W'ham —8K 87
Westerham Rd. Kes —4F 66
Westerham Rd. Oxt —7B 106
Westermain. New H —6L 55
Western Av. Cher —2J 37
Western Av. Egh —2D 36
Western Cen., The. Brack —1L 31
Western Clo. Cher —2J 37
Western Dri. Shep —5E 38
Western International Mkt. S'hall —1J 9
Western La. SW12 —1E 28
Western Pde. Reig —6N 121
Western Perimeter Rd. W Dray & H'row A —6K 7
Western Pl. Dork —5G 119
Western Rd. SW19 & Mitc —9B 28
Western Rd. Alder —3K 109
Western Rd. Brack —9K 15
Western Rd. S'hall —1K 9
Western Rd. Sutt —2M 61
Western Ter. W6 —1F 12 (off Chiswick Mall)
W. Farm Av. Asht —5J 79
W. Farm Clo. Asht —6J 79
W. Farm Dri. Asht —6K 79
West Field. Asht —5M 79
Westfield. Dork —3G 136
Westfield. Reig —9N 101
Westfield Av. S Croy —9A 64
Westfield Av. Wok —8A 74
Westfield Clo. SW10 —3N 13
Westfield Clo. Sutt —1L 61
Westfield Comn. Wok —9A 74
Westfield Ct. Fleet —4B 88
Westfield Dri. Bookh —9B 78
Westfield Gro. Wok —7A 74
Westfield Ho. SW18 —2N 27
Westfield La. Wrec —5D 128
Westfield Pde. New H —6M 55
Westfield Rd. Beck —1J 47
Westfield Rd. Camb —4N 69
Westfield Rd. Craw —3N 181
Westfield Rd. Croy —8M 45
Westfield Rd. Mitc —1D 44
Westfield Rd. Sly I —8A 94
Westfield Rd. Surb —4K 41
Westfield Rd. Sutt —1L 61
Westfield Rd. W On T —6M 39
Westfield Rd. Wok —9N 73
Westfields. SW13 —6E 12
Westfields. Witl —5C 152
Westfields Av. SW13 —6D 12
Westfield Sq. Wok —9A 74
Westfield Way. Wok —9A 74
W. Flexford La. Wanb —3N 111
W. Fryerne. Yat —7C 48
West Gdns. SW17 —7C 28
West Gdns. Eps —6D 60
Westgate Clo. Eps —2C 80
Westgate Rd. SE25 —3E 46
Westgate Rd. Beck —1M 47
Westgate Ter. SW10 —1N 13
W. Glade. F'boro —1J 89
West Grn. Yat —8A 48
West Grn. Dri. Craw —2A 182
West Gro. W On T —2J 57
Westhall Pk. Warl —6F 84
W. Hall Rd. Rich —4A 12
Westhall Rd. Warl —5D 84
Westhatch La. Brack —5N 15
Westhay Gdns. SW14 —8A 12
W. Heath. Pirb —1A 92
W. Heath Rd. F'boro —1L 89
West Hill. SW15 & SW18 —1J 27
West Hill. Dor P —4A 166
West Hill. E Grin —1N 185
West Hill. Elst —8G 131
West Hill. Eps —9A 60
West Hill. Orp —8H 67
West Hill. Oxt —8N 105
West Hill. S Croy —6B 64
W. Hill Av. Eps —9A 60
W. Hill Bank. Oxt —8N 105
W. Hill Clo. Brkwd —7E 72
W. Hill Clo. Elst —8G 131
W. Hill Ct. Eps —9B 60 (off Court La.)
W. Hill Rd. SW18 —9L 13
W. Hill Rd. Wok —6N 73
W. Hoathly Rd. E Grin —4N 185
Westhorpe Rd. SW15 —6H 13
West Ho. Clo. SW19 —2K 27
Westhumble St. Westh —9H 99
W. Kensington Ct. W14 —1L 13 (off Edith Vs.)
W. Kensington Mans. W14 (off Beaumont Cres.) —1L 13
Westland Clo. Stai —9N 7
Westland Ct. F'boro —1J 89
Westlands. H'ham —5L 197
Westlands Ct. Eps —2B 80
Westlands Ter. SW12 —1G 28
Westlands Way. Oxt —5N 105
West La. Ab H —8L 117
West La. E Grin —1N 185
Westleas. Horl —6C 142
Westlees Clo. N Holm —8K 119
W. Leigh. E Grin —2A 186
Westleigh Av. SW15 —8G 13
Westleigh Av. Coul —3F 82
Westmacott Dri. Felt —2G 22
Westmead. SW15 —9G 12
West Mead. Eps —3D 60
Westmead. F'boro —2N 89
Westmead. Wind —6E 4
Westmead. Wok —4L 73
Westmead Corner. Cars —1C 62
Westmead Dri. Red —2E 142
Westmead Rd. Sutt —1B 62
W. Meads. Guild —4J 113
Westminster Av. T Hth —1M 45
Westminster Clo. Felt —2H 23
Westminster Clo. Fleet —3B 88
Westminster Clo. Tedd —6G 24
Westminster Ct. Wok —8C 74
Westminster Rd. Craw —4G 182
Westminster Rd. Sutt —8B 44
Westmont Rd. Esh —8E 40
Westmore Grn. Tats —7E 86
Westmoreland Dri. Sutt —4N 61
Westmoreland Rd. SW13 —4E 12
Westmoreland Rd. Brom —4N 47
Westmore Rd. Tats —8E 86
Westmorland Clo. Eps —6D 60
Westmorland Clo. Twic —9H 11
Westmorland Ct. Surb —6K 41
Westmorland Dri. Camb —3F 70
Westmorland Dri. Warf —8D 16
Westmorland Sq. Mitc —4J 45 (off Westmorland Way)
Westmorland Way. Mitc —4H 45
West Mt. Guild —5M 113 (in two parts)
Weston Av. Add —1K 55
Weston Av. Th Dit —6E 40
Weston Av. W Mol —3M 39
Weston Clo. Coul —7K 83
Weston Clo. G'ming —5H 133
Weston Ct. G'ming —5H 133
Weston Farm Cotts. Abry —8K 115
Westonfields. Abry —8L 115
Weston Gdns. Iswth —4E 10
Weston Gdns. Wok —3G 75
Weston Grn. Th Dit —7E 40 (in two parts)
Weston Grn. Rd. Esh & Th Dit —7D 40 (in two parts)
Weston Gro. Bag —5K 51
Weston Lea. Ock —3E 96
Weston Pk. King T —1L 41
Weston Pk. Th Dit —7E 40
Weston Pk. Clo. Th Dit —7E 40
Weston Rd. Eps —7D 60
Weston Rd. Guild —2K 113
Weston Rd. Th Dit —7E 40
Westons Clo. H'ham —1K 197
Weston Way. Wok —3G 75
Weston Yd. Abry —8L 115
Westover Clo. Sutt —5N 61
Westover Rd. SW18 —1A 28
Westover Rd. Fleet —4C 88
West Pal. Gdns. Wey —9C 38
West Pde. H'ham —4J 197
West Pk. Av. Rich —4A 12
West Pk. Clo. Houn —2N 9
West Pk. Rd. Copt —6C 164
West Pk. Rd. Eps —8M 59
West Pk. Rd. Hand —9N 199
West Pk. Rd. Newc —4D 164
West Pk. Rd. Rich —4N 11
West Pl. SW19 —6H 27
West Ramp. H'row A —4B 8
West Ring. Tong —5D 110
West Rd. Camb —1B 70
West Rd. Chess —8J 59
West Rd. F'boro —7N 69
West Rd. Felt —9E 8
West Rd. Guild —4A 114
West Rd. King T —9B 26
West Rd. Reig —4N 121
West Rd. Wey —5C 56
West Rd. Wokgm —6H 31
Westrow. SW15 —9H 13
W. Sheen Vale. Rich —7M 11
W. Side Comn. SW19 —6H 27
Westside Ct. W End —9B 52
West St. Bren —2J 11
West St. Cars —9D 44
West St. Craw —4B 182
West St. Croy —1N 63
West St. Dork —5G 119
West St. D'land —1C 166
West St. E Grin —1A 186
West St. Eps —9B 60
West St. Ewe —6D 60
West St. Farnh —2E 128
West St. Hasl —1G 189
West St. H'ham —6J 197
West St. Reig —3K 121
West St. Sutt —2N 61
West St. Wok —4B 74
West St. La. Cars —1D 62
W. Temple Sheen. SW14 —8A 12
West View. Felt —1D 22
W. View Av. Whyt —5C 84
Westview Clo. Red —5C 122
W. View Cotts. Dork —2A 160
W. View Gdns. E Grin —1A 186
W. View Rd. Head —5H 169
W. View Rd. Warl —6E 84
Westville Rd. Th Dit —7G 41
Westward Ho. Guild —1B 114
Westwates Clo. Brack —9B 16
Westway. SW20 —3G 43
West Way. Cars —6B 62
Westway. Cat —9A 84
Westway. Copt —7L 163
West Way. Craw —2E 182
West Way. Croy —8H 47
Westway. Guild —1J 113
Westway. Horl —3F 162
West Way. Houn —4N 9
West Way. Shep —5E 38
West Way. Slin —5L 195
West Way. W Wick —5N 47
Westway. Worm —1C 172
Westway Clo. SW20 —2G 43
W. Way Gdns. Croy —8G 47
Westway Gdns. Red —9E 102
Westways. Eden —1L 147
Westways. Eps —1E 60
Westways. W'ham —4L 107
Westwell M. SW16 —7J 29
Westwell Rd. SW16 —7J 29
Westwell Rd. App. SW16 —7J 29
Westwick Gdns. Houn —5J 9
Westwood Av. SE19 —9N 29
Westwood Av. Wdhm —8H 55
Westwood Clo. Esh —9D 40
Westwood Ct. Guild —2J 113
Westwood Gdns. SW13 —6E 12
Westwood La. Guild —1L 111
Westwood Rd. SW13 —6E 12
Westwood Rd. Coul —5H 83
Westwood Rd. W'sham —8B 34
Wetherby Gdns. SW5 —1N 13
Wetherby Gdns. F'boro —5A 90
Wetherby Mans. SW5 —1N 13 (off Earl's Ct. Sq.)
Wetherby M. SW5 —1N 13
Wetherby Pl. SW7 —1N 13
Wetherby Way. Chess —4L 59
Wettern Clo. S Croy —6B 64
Wetton Pl. Egh —6B 20
Wexfenne Gdns. Wok —3K 75
Wexford Rd. SW12 —1D 28
Wey Av. Cher —2J 37
Weybank. Wis —3N 75
Weybank Clo. Farnh —1H 129
Weybarton. Byfl —9A 56
Weybourne Pl. S Croy —6A 64
Weybourne Rd. Farnh & Alder —7K 109
Weybourne St. SW18 —3A 28
Weybridge Bus. Pk. Add —1N 55
Weybridge Mead. Yat —8D 48
Weybridge Pk. Wey —2B 56
Weybridge Rd. Add —1N 55
Weybridge Rd. T Hth —3L 45
Weybridge Trad. Est. Add —1N 55
Weybrook Dri. Guild —7D 94
Wey Clo. Ash —3E 110
Wey Clo. Camb —1N 69
Wey Clo. W Byf —9K 55
Weycombe Rd. Hasl —1G 189
Wey Ct. Eps —1B 60
Wey Ct. G'ming —5K 133
Wey Ct. New H —5M 55
Wey Ct. Clo. G'ming —5J 133
Weycrofts. Brack —8L 15
Weydon Farm La. Farnh —2G 128
Weydon Hill Clo. Farnh —3G 129
Weydon Hill Rd. Farnh —3G 129
Weydon La. Farnh —4E 128
Weydon Mill La. Farnh —2G 128
Weydown Clo. SW19 —2K 27
Weydown Clo. Guild —7K 93
Weydown Cotts. Hasl —8G 171
Weydown Ind. Est. Hasl —1G 188
Weydown La. Guild —7K 93
Weydown Rd. Hasl —2F 188
Wey Hill. Hasl —2E 188
Weylands Clo. W On T —7N 39
Weylands Pk. Wey —3E 56
Weylea Av. Guild —9C 94
Wey Mnr. Rd. New H —5M 55
Weymead Clo. Cher —7L 37
Wey Meadows. Add —2N 55
Weymede. Byfl —8A 56
Weymouth Ct. Sutt —4M 61
Wey Rd. G'ming —6K 133
Wey Rd. Wey —9A 38
Weyside. Farnh —1H 129
Weyside Clo. Byfl —8A 56
Weyside Gdns. Guild —1M 113
Weyside Rd. Guild —1L 113

Weysprings—Windlesham Ct.

Weysprings. *Hasl* —2E **188**
Weystone Rd. *Add* —1A **56**
Wey View Ct. *Guild* —4M **113**
Weywood Clo. *Farnh* —5L **109**
Weywood La. *Farnh* —5K **109**
Whaley Rd. *Wokgm* —9C **14**
Wharfedale Gdns. *T Hth* —3K **45**
Wharfedale St. *SW10* —1N **13**
Wharfenden Way. *Frim G* —8D **70**
Wharf La. *Rip* —5M **75**
Wharf La. *Send* —1E **94**
Wharf La. *Twic* —2G **24**
Wharf Rd. *Ash V* —9E **90**
Wharf Rd. *Frim G* —8D **70**
Wharf Rd. *Guild* —3M **113**
Wharf Rd. *Wray* —1M **19**
Wharf St. *G'ming* —7H **133**
Wharf, The. *G'ming* —7H **133**
Wharf Way. *Frim G* —8E **70**
Wharncliffe Gdns. *SE25* —1B **46**
Wharncliffe Rd. *SE25* —1B **46**
Whateley Rd. *Guild* —8L **93**
Whatley Av. *SW20* —2J **43**
Whatley Grn. *Brack* —5N **31**
Whatmore Clo. *Stai* —9J **7**
Wheatash Rd. *Add* —8K **37**
Wheatbutts, The. *Eton W* —1C **4**
Wheatfield Way. *Horl* —7F **142**
Wheatfield Way. *King T* —1L **41**
Wheathill Rd. *SE20* —1E **46**
Wheat Knoll. *Kenl* —3N **83**
Wheatlands. *Houn* —2A **10**
Wheatlands Rd. *SW17* —4E **28**
Wheatley. *Brack* —4K **31**
Wheatley Ho. SW15 —1F **26**
(off Tangley Gro.)
Wheatley Rd. *Iswth* —6F **10**
Wheatsheaf Clo. *H'ham* —2L **197**
Wheatsheaf Clo. *Ott* —3F **54**
Wheatsheaf Clo. *Wok* —3A **74**
Wheatsheaf La. *SW6* —3H **13**
Wheatsheaf La. *Stai* —8H **21**
Wheatsheaf Ter. *SW6* —3L **13**
Wheatstone Clo. *Craw* —7F **162**
Wheatstone Clo. *Mitc* —9C **28**
Wheeler Av. *Oxt* —7N **105**
Wheeler La. *Witl* —4B **152**
Wheeler Rd. *M'bowr* —5F **182**
Wheelers La. *Brock* —5A **120**
Wheelers La. *Eps* —1A **80**
Wheelers La. *Small* —9L **143**
Wheelerstreet. *Witl* —4C **152**
Wheelers Way. *Felb* —7H **165**
Wheelwrights La. *Gray* —5M **169**
Wheelwrights Pl. *Coln* —3E **6**
Whelan Way. *Wall* —9H **45**
Wherwell Rd. *Guild* —5M **113**
Whetstone Rd. *F'boro* —1H **89**
Whimbrel Clo. *S Croy* —7A **64**
Whinfell Clo. *SW16* —6H **29**
Whin Holt. *Fleet* —7B **88**
Whins Clo. *Camb* —2N **69**
Whins Dri. *Camb* —2N **69**
Whipley Clo. *Guild* —7D **94**
Whistler Clo. *Craw* —6D **182**
Whistler Gro. *Col T* —9J **49**
Whistley Clo. *Brack* —2C **32**
Whitby Clo. *Big H* —6D **86**
Whitby Clo. *F'boro* —4C **90**
Whitby Gdns. *Sutt* —8B **44**
Whitby Rd. *Sutt* —8B **44**
Whitchurch Clo. *Alder* —6B **110**
White Acres Rd. *Myt* —1D **90**
Whitebeam Dri. *Reig* —6N **121**
Whitebeam Gdns. *F'boro* —2H **89**
White Beam Way. *Tad* —8F **80**
White Beech La. *C'fold* —4K **173**
Whiteberry Rd. *Dork* —3B **138**
Whitebines. *Farnh* —1J **129**
White Bri. Av. *Mitc* —2B **44**
Whitebridge Clo. *Felt* —9G **8**
Whitebushes. *Red* —8E **122**
White City. *Crowt* —2J **49**
(in two parts)
White Cottage Clo. *Farnh* —6J **109**
Whitecroft. *Horl* —7F **142**
Whitecroft Clo. *Beck* —3N **47**
Whitecroft Way. *Beck* —4M **47**
White Down La. *Dork* —4K **117**
Whitefield Av. *Purl* —3L **83**
Whitefield Clo. *SW15* —9K **13**
Whitegates. *Whyt* —6D **84**
Whitegates. *Wok* —7B **74**
Whitegate Way. *Tad* —7G **81**
Whitehall Cres. *Chess* —2K **59**
Whitehall Dri. *If'd* —3K **181**
Whitehall Farm La. *Vir W* —2A **36**
Whitehall Gdns. *W4* —2A **12**
Whitehall La. *Egh* —8B **20**
Whitehall La. *S Pk* —7L **121**
Whitehall La. *Wray* —9C **6**
Whitehall Pk. Rd. *W4* —2A **12**
Whitehall Pl. *Wall* —1F **62**
Whitehall Rd. *T Hth* —4L **45**
White Hart Clo. *Hayes* —2E **8**
White Hart Ct. *H'ham* —4J **197**
White Hart Ct. *Rip* —8L **75**
White Hart Ind. Est. *B'water* —2K **69**
White Hart La. *SW13* —5D **12**
White Hart La. *Wood S* —2D **112**
White Hart Meadows. *Rip* —8L **75**
White Hart Row. *Cher* —6J **37**
Whitehead Clo. *SW18* —1A **28**
White Heron M. *Tedd* —7F **24**
White Hill. *Chips* —1C **102**
White Hill. *S Croy* —6A **64**
White Hill. *W'sham* —1M **51**
Whitehill Clo. *Camb* —8B **50**
Whitehill La. *Blet* —5A **104**
Whitehill La. *Cobh* —1D **96**
Whitehill Pl. *Vir W* —4A **36**
Whitehill Rd. *Stand* —8A **168**
Whitehorn Gdns. *Croy* —8E **46**
White Horse Dri. *Eps* —1B **80**
Whitehorse La. *SE25* —3A **46**
White Horse La. *Rip* —8L **75**
Whitehorse Rd. *Croy & T Hth* —6N **45**
Whitehorse Rd. *H'ham* —2A **198**
White Horse Rd. *Wind* —6A **4**
White Ho. SW4 —1H **29**
(off Clapham Pk. Est.)
White House. *Add* —1L **55**
White Ho. Dri. *Guild* —3D **114**
White Ho. Gdns. *Yat* —8B **48**
White Ho. La. *Guild* —7N **93**
White Ho. Wlk. *Farnh* —5J **109**
Whiteknights. *Cars* —7B **62**
White Knights Rd. *Wey* —4D **56**
White Knobs Way. *Cat* —3D **104**
Whitelands Dri. *Asc* —9H **17**
White La. *Ash & Tong* —3G **110**
White La. *Guild* —5E **114**
White La. *Oxt* —1D **106**
Whiteley. *Wind* —3B **4**
Whiteley's Cotts. *W14* —1L **13**
Whiteley's Way. *Felt* —4A **24**
White Lilies Island. *Wind* —3D **4**
White Lion Ct. *Iswth* —6H **11**
White Lion Wlk. *Guild* —4N **113**
White Lion Way. *Yat* —8C **48**
White Lodge. *SE19* —8M **29**
White Lodge Clo. *Sutt* —4A **62**
Whitelodge Gdns. *Red* —2E **142**
Whitely Hill. *Worth* —8K **183**
Whitemore Rd. *Guild* —8N **93**
White Oak Dri. *Beck* —1M **47**
Whiteoaks. *Bans* —9N **61**
Whitepost Hill. *Red* —3C **122**
(in two parts)
White Post La. *Wrec* —7F **128**
White Rd. *Bet & Tad* —2N **119**
White Rd. *Col T* —9L **49**
White Rose La. *Lwr Bo* —4H **129**
White Rose La. *Wok* —5B **74**
Whites La. *Dat* —2L **5**
Whites Rd. *F'boro* —4C **90**
Whitestile Rd. *Bren* —1J **11**
Whiteswan M. *W4* —1D **12**
Whitethorn Av. *Coul* —2E **82**
Whitethorn Clo. *Ash* —3F **110**
Whitethorn Cotts. *Cranl* —5K **155**
Whitethorn Gdns. *Croy* —8E **46**
Whitewalls. Craw —3L **181**
(off Rusper Rd.)
White Way. *Bookh* —4B **98**
Whitewood Cotts. *Tats* —7E **86**
Whitewood La. *S God* —5D **144**
Whitfield Clo. *Guild* —9K **93**
Whitfield Clo. *Hasl* —8G **171**
Whitfield Rd. *Hasl* —9G **171**
Whitford Gdns. *Mitc* —2D **44**
Whitgift Av. *S Croy* —2N **63**
Whitgift Cen. *Croy* —8N **45**
Whitgift Sq. *Croy* —8N **45**
Whitgift St. *Croy* —9N **45**
Whitgift Wlk. *Craw* —6B **182**
Whither Dale. *Horl* —7C **142**
Whitland Rd. *Cars* —7B **44**
Whitlet Clo. *Farnh* —2G **128**
Whitley Clo. *Stai* —9N **7**
Whitley Rd. *Yat* —2C **68**
Whitlock Dri. *SW19* —2K **27**
Whitmead Clo. *S Croy* —3B **64**
Whitmead La. *Tilf* —7B **130**
Whitmoor La. *Guild* —4N **93**
Whitmoor Rd. *Bag* —4K **51**
Whitmoor Vale. *Gray* —2K **169**
Whitmoor Vale Rd. *Hind* —2L **169**
Whitmore Clo. *Owl* —7J **49**
Whitmore Grn. *Farnh* —6K **109**
Whitmore La. *Asc* —4D **34**
Whitmore Rd. *Beck* —2J **47**
Whitmores Clo. *Eps* —2B **80**
Whitmore Way *Horl* —7C **142**
Whitnell Way. *SW15* —8H **13**
Whitstable Clo. *Beck* —1J **47**
Whittaker Av. *Rich* —8K **11**
Whittaker Ct. *Asht* —4K **79**
Whittaker Pl. Rich —8K **11**
(off Whittaker Av.)
Whittaker Rd. *Sutt* —9L **43**
Whittingham Ct. *W4* —3D **12**
Whittingstall Rd. *SW6* —4L **13**
Whittington Rd. *Craw* —6B **182**
Whittlebury Clo. *Cars* —4D **62**
Whittle Clo. *Sand* —6F **48**
Whittle Cres. *F'boro* —7L **69**
Whittle Rd. *Houn* —3K **9**
Whittle Way. *Craw* —6E **162**
Whitton Dene. *Houn & Iswth* —8C **10**
Whitton Mnr. Rd. *Iswth* —9C **10**
Whitton Rd. *Brack* —2D **32**
Whitton Rd. *Houn* —7B **10**
Whitton Rd. *Twic* —9E **10**
Whitton Waye. *Houn* —9A **10**
Whitworth Rd. *SE25* —2B **46**
Whitworth Rd. *Craw* —8B **162**
Whopshott Av. *Wok* —3M **73**
Whopshott Clo. *Wok* —3M **73**
Whopshott Dri. *Wok* —3M **73**
Whynstones Rd. *Asc* —5L **33**
Whyteacre. *Whyt* —7E **84**
Whyte Av. *Alder* —4B **110**
Whytebeam View. *Whyt* —5C **84**
Whytecliffe Rd. N. *Purl* —7M **63**
Whytecliffe Rd. S. *Purl* —7L **63**
Whytecroft. *Houn* —3L **9**
Whyteleafe Bus. Village. *Whyt* —4C **84**
Whyteleafe Hill. *Whyt* —7B **84**
(in two parts)
Whyteleafe Rd. *Cat* —7B **84**
Wicket Hill. *Wrec* —5F **128**
Wickets, The. *Ashf* —5N **21**
Wicket, The. *Croy* —2K **65**
Wickham Av. *Croy* —8H **47**
Wickham Av. *Sutt* —2H **61**
Wickham Chase. *W Wick* —7N **47**
Wickham Clo. *Bag* —1J **51**
Wickham Clo. *C Crook* —7A **88**
Wickham Clo. *Horl* —7D **142**
Wickham Clo. *N Mald* —5E **42**
Wickham Ct. *C Crook* —7A **88**
Wickham Ct. Rd. *W Wick* —8M **47**
Wickham Cres. *W Wick* —8M **47**
Wickham La. *Egh* —8C **20**
Wickham Pl. *C Crook* —7A **88**
Wickham Rd. *Beck* —1L **47**
Wickham Rd. *Camb* —7C **50**
Wickham Rd. *C Crook* —7A **88**
Wickham Rd. *Croy* —8G **46**
Wickham Vale. *Brack* —5K **31**
Wickham Way. *Beck* —3M **47**
Wickhurst Gdns. *Broad H* —5E **196**
Wickland Ct. *Craw* —6B **182**
Wick La. *Egh* —7J **19**
Wick Rd. *Egh* —9K **19**
Wick Rd. *Tedd* —8H **25**
Wick's Grn. *Binf* —5G **15**
Wicks La. *Shur R* —1D **14**
Wicksteed Ho. *Bren* —1M **11**
Wide Way. *Mitc* —2H **45**
Widgeon Way. *H'ham* —3J **197**
Widmer Ct. *Houn* —5M **9**
Wient, The. *Coln* —3E **6**
Wiggett Gro. *Binf* —7H **15**
Wiggie La. *Red* —1E **122**
Wiggins Yd. *G'ming* —7H **133**
Wigley Rd. *Felt* —3L **23**
Wigmore La. *Dork* —1J **159**
Wigmore Rd. *Cars* —8B **44**
Wigmore Wlk. *Cars* —8B **44**
Wilberforce Clo. *Craw* —9A **182**
Wilberforce Way. *SW19* —7J **27**
Wilberforce Way. *Brack* —4B **32**
Wilbury Av. *Sutt* —6L **61**
Wilbury Rd. *Wok* —4N **73**
Wilcot Clo. *Bisl* —3D **72**
Wilcot Gdns. *Bisl* —3D **72**
Wilcox Gdns. *Shep* —2N **37**
Wilcox Rd. *Sutt* —1N **61**
Wilcox Rd. *Tedd* —5D **24**
Wildacre Clo. *Ifold* —5F **192**
Wild Acres. *W Byf* —7L **55**
Wildbank Ct. *Wok* —5B **74**
Wildcroft Dri. *N Holm* —8K **119**
Wildcroft Dri. *Wokgm* —7A **30**
Wildcroft Mnr. *SW15* —1H **27**
Wildcroft Rd. *SW15* —1H **27**
Wildcroft Wood. *Witl* —4A **152**
Wilde Pl. *SW18* —1B **28**
Wilderness Ct. *Guild* —5J **113**
Wilderness Rise. *Dor P* —5C **166**
Wilderness Rd. *Frim* —4C **70**
Wilderness Rd. *Guild* —5J **113**
Wilderness Rd. *Oxt* —8N **105**
Wilderness, The. *E Mol* —4C **40**
Wilderness, The. *Hamp* —5B **24**
Wilders Clo. *Brack* —8M **15**
Wilders Clo. *Frim* —3C **70**
Wilders Clo. *Wok* —5M **73**
Wilderwick Rd. *Ling & E Grin* —3C **166**
Wildfield Clo. *Wood S* —2E **112**
Wildgoose Dri. *H'ham* —5F **196**
Wildridings Rd. *Brack* —3M **31**
Wildridings Sq. *Brack* —3M **31**
Wild Wood. *H'ham* —5F **196**
Wildwood Clo. *Cranl* —9A **156**
Wildwood Clo. *E Hor* —3G **96**
Wildwood Clo. *Wok* —2H **75**
Wildwood Ct. *Kenl* —2A **84**
Wildwood Gdns. *Yat* —2B **68**
Wildwood La. *Cranl* —4J **175**
Wilfred Owen Clo. *SW19* —7A **28**
Wilfred St. *Wok* —5N **73**
Wilhelmina Av. *Coul* —6G **83**
Wilkins Clo. *Hayes* —1G **9**
Wilkins Clo. *Mitc* —9C **28**
Wilkinson Ct. *SW17* —5B **28**
Wilkinson Ct. *Craw* —8N **181**
Wilks Gdns. *Croy* —7H **47**
Willats Clo. *Cher* —5H **37**
Willcocks Clo. *Chess* —9L **41**
Willett Pl. *T Hth* —4L **45**
Willett Rd. *T Hth* —4L **45**
Willey Broom La. *Cat* —3L **103**
Willey Farm La. *Cat* —4N **103**
Willey La. *Cat* —3A **104**
William Banfield Ho. SW6
(off Munster Rd.) —5L **13**
William Clo. SW6 —3K **13**
(off Dawes Rd.)
William Ellis Clo. *Old Win* —8K **5**
William Evelyn Ct. *Wott* —8N **117**
William Farthing Clo. *Alder* —2M **109**
William Gdns. *SW15* —8G **13**
William Hitchcock Ho. *F'boro* —6N **69**
William Morris Ho. W6 —2J **13**
(off Margravine Rd.)
William Morris Way. *SW6* —6N **13**
William Morris Way. *Craw* —9N **181**
William Rd. *SW19* —8K **27**
William Rd. *Cat* —9A **104**
William Rd. *Guild* —3M **113**
William Rd. *Sutt* —2A **62**
William Russell Ct. *Wok* —5H **73**
Williams Clo. *Add* —2K **55**
Williams Clo. *Ewh* —5F **156**
William Sim Wood. *Wink R* —7F **16**
William's La. *SW14* —6B **12**
Williams La. *Mord* —4A **44**
Williamson Clo. *G'wood* —8K **171**
Williams Rd. *S'hall* —1M **9**
Williams Ter. *Croy* —3L **63**
William St. *Cars* —9C **44**
William St. *Wind* —4G **4**
William's Wlk. *Guild* —8L **93**
Williams Way. *Craw* —3F **182**
Williams Way. *Fleet* —4D **88**
Willian Pl. *Hind* —3C **170**
Willingham Way. *King T* —2N **41**
Willington Clo. *Camb* —9N **49**
Willis Av. *Sutt* —3C **62**
Willis Clo. *Eps* —1A **80**
Willis Ct. *T Hth* —5L **45**
Willis Rd. *Croy* —6N **45**
Will Miles Ct. *SW19* —8A **28**
Willmore End. *SW19* —9N **27**
Willoughby Av. *Croy* —1K **63**
Willoughby Rd. *Brack* —2L **31**
Willoughby Rd. *King T* —9M **25**
Willoughby Rd. *Twic* —8J **11**
Willoughbys, The. *SW14* —6D **12**
Willow Av. *SW13* —5E **12**
Willow Bank. *SW6* —6K **13**
Willowbank. *Coul* —1J **83**
Willow Bank. *Rich* —4H **25**
Willow Bank. *Wok* —9B **74**
Willowbank Gdns. *Tad* —9G **81**
Willow Brean. *Horl* —6C **142**
Willowbrook. *Eton* —1G **4**
Willowbrook Rd. *Stai* —3N **21**
Willow Bus. Cen., The. *Mitc* —5D **44**
Willow Clo. *Bear G* —7J **139**
Willow Clo. *Bord* —6A **168**
Willow Clo. *Bren* —2J **11**
Willow Clo. *Coln* —3E **6**
Willow Clo. *Craw* —1C **182**
Willow Clo. *E Grin* —7N **165**
Willow Clo. *Myt* —1C **90**
Willow Clo. *Wdhm* —7H **55**
Willow Corner. *Charl* —3L **161**
Willow Cotts. *Hanw* —4M **23**
Willow Cotts. *Rich* —2N **11**
Willow Ct. W4 —3D **12**
(off Corney Reach Way)
Willow Ct. *Ash V* —6E **90**
Willow Ct. Frim —5B **70**
(off Grove Cross Rd.)
Willow Ct. *Horl* —6F **142**
Willow Ct. *Tad* —1G **101**
Willow Cres. *F'boro* —7N **69**
Willowdene Clo. *Twic* —1C **24**
Willow Dri. *Brack* —9A **16**
Willow Dri. *Norm* —3N **111**
Willow Dri. *Rip* —2J **95**
Willow End. *Surb* —7L **41**
Willow Farm La. *SW15* —6G **13**
Willowfield. *Craw* —4A **182**
Willowford. *Yat* —9C **48**
Willow Gdns. *Houn* —4A **10**
Willow Glade. *Reig* —6N **121**
Willow Grn. *N Holm* —9H **119**
Willow Grn. *W End* —9C **52**
Willowhayne Dri. *W On T* —6J **39**
Willowhayne Gdns. *Wor Pk* —9H **43**
Willowherb Clo. *Wokgm* —1D **30**
Willow Ho. *Brom* —1N **47**
Willow La. *B'water* —2J **69**
Willow La. *Guild* —2C **114**
Willow La. *Mitc* —4D **44**
Willow Lodge. *SW6* —4H **13**
Willow Mead. *Dork* —4G **119**
Willow Mead. *E Grin* —1B **186**
Willowmead. *Stai* —9K **21**
Willow Mead. *Witl* —5B **152**
Willowmead Clo. *Wok* —3K **73**
Willowmere. *Esh* —1C **58**
Willow M. *Witl* —5C **152**
Willow Mt. *Croy* —9B **46**
Willow Pk. *Ash* —2D **110**
Willow Pl. *Eton* —2F **4**
Willow Ridge. *Turn H* —6D **184**
Willow Rd. *Coln* —5G **7**
Willow Rd. *G'ming* —3J **133**
Willow Rd. *H'ham* —3A **198**
Willow Rd. *N Mald* —3B **42**
Willow Rd. *Red* —6A **122**
Willow Rd. *Wall* —4F **62**
Willow Rd. *W End* —9C **52**
Willows Av. *Mord* —4N **43**
Willows End. *Sand* —7G **48**
Willows Lodge. *Wind* —3A **4**
Willows Mobile Home Pk., The. *Guild* —9A **92**
Willows Path. *Eps* —1A **80**
Willows Riverside Pk. *Wind* —3A **4**
Willows, The. *Brack* —3D **32**
Willows, The. *Byfl* —9N **55**
Willows, The. *C'fold* —5D **172**
Willows, The. *Clay* —3E **58**
Willows, The. *Guild* —1F **114**
Willows, The. *H'ham* —3K **197**
Willows, The. *Light* —6A **52**
Willows, The. *Red* —4D **122**
Willows, The. *Wey* —9B **38**
Willows, The. *Wind* —3A **4**
Willow Tree Clo. *SW18* —2N **27**
Willowtree Way. *T Hth* —9L **29**
Willow Vale. *Fet* —1B **98**
(in two parts)
Willow View. *SW19* —9B **28**
Willow Wlk. *Cher* —6J **37**
Willow Wlk. *Egh* —6M **19**
Willow Wlk. *Orp* —1K **67**
Willow Wlk. *Red* —5F **122**
Willow Wlk. *Shere* —8B **116**
Willow Wlk. *Sutt* —9L **43**
Willow Way. *Alder* —4C **110**
Willow Way. *Eps* —3C **60**
Willow Way. *Farnh* —6J **109**
Willow Way. *God* —1E **124**
Willow Way. *Guild* —8L **93**
Willow Way. *Sand* —6E **48**
Willow Way. *Sun* —3H **39**
Willow Way. *Twic* —3B **24**
Willow Way. *W Byf* —7L **55**
Willow Way. *Wok* —8A **74**
Willow Wood Cres. *SE25* —5B **46**
Wills Cres. *Houn* —9B **10**
Willson Rd. *Egh* —6L **19**
Wilmar Gdns. *W Wick* —7L **47**
Wilmer Clo. *King T* —6M **25**
Wilmer Cres. *King T* —6M **25**
Wilmerhatch La. *Eps* —5A **80**
Wilmington Av. *W4* —3C **12**
Wilmington Clo. *Craw* —8A **182**
Wilmington Ct. *SW16* —8J **29**
Wilmot Clo. *Binf* —7H **15**
Wilmot Cotts. *Bans* —2N **81**
Wilmot Rd. *Cars* —2D **62**
Wilmot Rd. *Purl* —8L **63**
Wilmots Clo. *Reig* —2A **122**
Wilmot's La. *Horne* —4A **144**
Wilmot Way. *Bans* —1M **81**
Wilmot Way. *Camb* —3D **70**
Wilna Rd. *SW18* —1A **28**
Wilson Av. *Mitc* —8C **28**
Wilson Clo. *M'bowr* —6H **183**
Wilson Clo. *S Croy* —2A **64**
Wilson Clo. *W Dray* —2M **7**
Wilson Dri. *Ott* —2D **54**
Wilson M. *SW15* —8F **12**
Wilson Rd. *Alder* —3B **110**
Wilson Rd. *Chess* —3M **59**
Wilson Rd. *F'boro* —2L **89**
Wilsons. *Tad* —8J **81**
Wilson's Rd. *W6* —1J **13**
Wilsons Rd. *Head* —4G **169**
Wilson Wlk. W4 —1E **12**
(off Prebend Gdns.)
Wilson Way. *H'ham* —3K **197**
Wilson Way. *Wok* —3N **73**
Wilstrode Av. *Binf* —7L **15**
Wilton Av. *W4* —1D **12**
Wilton Clo. *W Dray* —2M **7**
Wilton Ct. *F'boro* —2B **90**
Wilton Cres. *SW19* —8L **27**
Wilton Cres. *Wind* —7A **4**
Wilton Gdns. *W On T* —7L **39**
Wilton Gdns. *W Mol* —2A **40**
Wilton Gro. *SW19* —8L **27**
Wilton Gro. *N Mald* —5E **42**
Wilton Pde. *Felt* —3J **23**
Wilton Pl. *New H* —5M **55**
Wilton Rd. *SW19* —8C **28**
Wilton Rd. *Camb* —3N **69**
Wilton Rd. *Houn* —6L **9**
Wilton Rd. *Red* —4D **122**
Wilton Row. *SW6* —3K **13**
Wiltshire Av. *Crowt* —1G **48**
Wiltshire Dri. *Wokgm* —1C **30**
Wiltshire Gdns. *Twic* —2C **24**
Wiltshire Gro. *Warf* —7D **16**
Wiltshire Rd. *T Hth* —2L **45**
Wiltshire Rd. *Wokgm* —9B **14**
Wilverley Cres. *N Mald* —5D **42**
Wilwood Rd. *Brack* —9K **15**
Wimbart Rd. *SW2* —1K **29**
Wimbledon Bri. *SW19* —7L **27**
Wimbledon Clo. *Camb* —6D **50**
Wimbledon Hill Rd. *SW19* —7K **27**
Wimbledon Pk. Rd. *SW19 & SW18* —3K **27**
Wimbledon Pk. Side. *SW19* —4J **27**
Wimbledon Rd. *SW17* —5A **28**
Wimbledon Rd. *Camb* —6D **50**
Wimbledon Stadium Bus. Cen. *SW17* —4N **27**
Wimblehurst Ct. *H'ham* —4K **197**
Wimblehurst Rd. *H'ham* —4J **197**
Wimborne Av. *Red* —8D **122**
Wimborne Av. *S'hall* —1A **10**
Wimborne Clo. *Eps* —9D **60**
Wimborne Clo. *Wor Pk* —7H **43**
Wimborne Way. *Beck* —2G **47**
Wimbourne Ct. *SW12* —4G **28**
Wimland Hill. *H'ham* —7C **180**
Wimland Rd. *H'ham* —4A **180**
Wimlands La. *Fay* —7C **180**
Wimpole Clo. *King T* —1M **41**
Wimshurst Clo. *Croy* —7J **45**
Wincanton Rd. *SW18* —1L **27**
Winch Clo. *Binf* —6H **15**
Winchcombe Clo. *Fleet* —5B **88**
Winchcombe Rd. *Cars* —6B **44**
Winchelsea Clo. *SW15* —8J **13**
Winchelsey Rise. *S Croy* —3C **64**
Winchendon Rd. *SW6* —4L **13**
Winchendon Rd. *Tedd* —5D **24**
Winchester Av. *Houn* —2N **9**
Winchester Clo. *Coln* —4G **7**
Winchester Clo. *Esh* —1A **58**
Winchester Clo. *King T* —8A **26**
Winchester Rd. *Ash* —1E **110**
Winchester Rd. *Craw* —7C **182**
Winchester Rd. *Felt* —4N **23**
Winchester Rd. *Hayes* —3F **8**
Winchester Rd. *Tilf* —3N **149**
Winchester Rd. *Twic* —9H **11**
Winchester Rd. *W On T* —7H **39**
Winchester St. *F'boro* —5A **90**
Winchester Way. *B'water* —9H **49**
Winches, The. *Colg* —2H **199**
Winchet Wlk. *Croy* —5F **46**
Winchfield Ho. *SW15* —9E **12**
Winchgrove Rd. *Brack* —8M **15**
Winchilsea Cres. *W Mol* —1C **40**
Winchstone Clo. *Shep* —3A **38**
Windall Clo. *SE19* —1D **46**
Windborough Rd. *Cars* —4E **62**
Windermere Av. *SW19* —2N **43**
Windermere Clo. *Egh* —8C **20**
Windermere Clo. *F'boro* —2K **89**
Windermere Clo. *Felt* —2G **22**
Windermere Clo. *Stai* —2N **21**
Windermere Ct. *SW13* —2E **12**
Windermere Ct. *Kenl* —2M **83**
Windermere Rd. *SW15* —5D **26**
Windermere Rd. *SW16* —9G **29**
Windermere Rd. *Coul* —2J **83**
Windermere Rd. *Croy* —7C **46**
Windermere Rd. *Light* —6M **51**
Windermere Rd. *W Wick* —8N **47**
Windermere Wlk. *Camb* —1H **71**
Windermere Way. *Farnh* —6F **108**
Windermere Way. *Reig* —2C **122**
Windfield. *Lea* —8H **79**
Windgates. *Guild* —9E **94**
Windham Av. *New Ad* —6N **65**
Windham Rd. *Rich* —6M **11**
Windings, The. *S Croy* —7C **64**
Winding Wood Dri. *Camb* —2F **70**
Windlebrook Grn. *Brack* —9M **15**
Windle Clo. *W'sham* —3A **52**
Windlesham Ct. *W'sham* —9N **33**

Windlesham Ct. Dri.—Woodside

Windlesham Ct. Dri. W'sham —1N 51
Windlesham Gro. SW19 —2J 27
Windlesham Rd. Brack —9L 15
Windlesham Rd. Chob —4D 52
Windlesham Rd. W End —7B 52
Windmill Av. Eps —7E 60
Windmill Bus. Village. Sun —9F 22
Windmill Clo. Cat —8N 83
Windmill Clo. Eps —8E 60
Windmill Clo. Horl —8F 142
Windmill Clo. H'ham —4N 197
Windmill Clo. Sun —8F 22
Windmill Clo. Surb —7J 41
Windmill Clo. Wind —5E 4
Windmill Ct. Craw —1B 182
Windmill Dri. Head —3G 168
Windmill Dri. Kes —1E 66
Windmill Dri. Lea —1J 99
Windmill Dri. Reig —1B 122
Windmill End. Eps —8E 60
Windmill Field. W'sham —3N 51
Windmill Gro. Croy —5N 45
Windmill Hill. Alder —3A 110
Windmill La. Ash W —2E 186
Windmill La. E Grin —7N 165
Windmill La. Eps —8E 60
Windmill La. Surb —5H 41
Windmill M. W4 —1D 12
Windmill Pas. W4 —1D 12
Windmill Platt. Hand —8N 199
Windmill Rise. King T —8A 26
Windmill Rd. SW18 —1B 28
Windmill Rd. SW19 —5G 27
Windmill Rd. W4 —1D 12
Windmill Rd. W5 & Bren —1J 11
Windmill Rd. Alder —3A 110
Windmill Rd. Brack —9L 15
Windmill Rd. Croy —6N 45
Windmill Rd. Hamp —6B 24
Windmill Rd. Mitc —4G 44
Windmill Rd. Sun —1F 38
Windmill Rd. W. Sun —1F 38
Windmill Ter. Shep —6F 38
Windmill Way. Reig —1B 122
Windrum Clo. H'ham —8F 196
Windrush Clo. W4 —4B 12
Windrush Clo. Brmly —5B 134
Windrush Clo. Craw —5L 181
Windrush Heights. Sand —7F 48
Windsor Av. SW19 —9A 28
Windsor Av. N Mald —4B 42
Windsor Av. Sutt —9K 43
Windsor Av. W Mol —2A 40
Windsor Castle. Wind —4H 5
Windsor Clo. SE27 —5N 29
Windsor Clo. Bren —2H 11
Windsor Clo. Craw —7A 182
Windsor Clo. Guild —5J 113
Windsor Ct. Alder —2L 109 (off Queen Elizabeth Dri.)
Windsor Ct. Brack —3A 32
Windsor Ct. Chob —5H 53
Windsor Ct. Fleet —4B 88
Windsor Ct. H'ham —5M 197
Windsor Ct. Sun —8H 23
Windsor Ct. Whyt —5C 84
Windsor Ct. Rd. Chob —5H 53
Windsor Cres. Farnh —6G 108
Windsor Dri. Ashf —5M 21
Windsor & Eton Relief Rd. Wind —4E 4
Windsor Forest Ct. Asc —9H 17
Windsor Gdns. Ash —3D 110
Windsor Gdns. Croy —9J 45
Windsor Gro. SE27 —5N 29
Windsor M. SW18 —1A 28 (off Wilna Rd.)
Windsor Pk. Rd. Hayes —3G 8
Windsor Pl. Cher —5J 37
Windsor Pl. E Grin —1C 186
Windsor Ride. Brack & Asc —5D 32
Windsor Ride. Camb & Crowt —7M 49
Windsor Rd. Asc & Wind —2J 33
Windsor Rd. Chob —1F 52
Windsor Rd. Dat —3K 5
Windsor Rd. F'boro —4B 90
Windsor Rd. Houn —5K 9
Windsor Rd. King T —8L 25
Windsor Rd. Lind —4A 168
Windsor Rd. Old Win & Egh —2M 19
Windsor Rd. Rich —5M 11
Windsor Rd. Sun —7H 23
Windsor Rd. Tedd —6D 24
Windsor Rd. T Hth —1M 45
Windsor Rd. Wor Pk —8F 42
Windsor Rd. Wind —4A 4
Windsor Rd. Wray —9A 6
Windsor St. Cher —5J 37
Windsor Wlk. Lind —4A 168
Windsor Wlk. W On T —7L 39
Windsor Wlk. Wey —2C 56
Windsor Way. Alder —2N 109
Windsor Way. Frim —6D 70
Windsor Way. Wok —3E 74
Winds Ridge. Send —3E 94
Windycroft Clo. Purl —9H 63
Windyridge. Craw —4M 181
Windy Ridge Clo. SW19 —6J 27
Windy Wood. G'ming —8F 133
Winern Glebe. Byfl —9M 55
Winery La. King T —2M 41
Wines Clo. Farnh —6G 109
Winfield Gro. Newd —1A 160
Winfrith Rd. SW18 —1A 28
Wingate Ct. Alder —2L 109
Wingate Cres. Croy —5J 45
Wingfield Clo. New H —6K 55
Wingfield Gdns. Frim —3H 71
Wingfield Rd. King T —7M 25
Wingford Rd. SW2 —1J 29
Wingrave Rd. W6 —2H 13
Wings Clo. Farnh —6H 109
Wings Clo. Sutt —1M 61
Wings Rd. Farnh —6G 109
Winifred Rd. SW19 —9M 27
Winifred Rd. Coul —3E 82
Winifred Rd. Hamp —5A 24
Winkfield Clo. Wokgm —5A 30
Winkfield La. Wink —2G 17
Winkfield Rd. Asc —7L 17
Winkfield Rd. Wind —2N 17
Winkfield Row. Brack —5E 16
Winkfield St. Wink —3F 16
Winkworth Pl. Bans —1L 81
Winkworth Rd. Bans —1L 81
Winnards. St J —5L 73
Winnington Way. Wok —5L 73
Winnipeg Dri. Grn St —3N 67
Winscombe. Brack —4K 31
Winslow Rd. W6 —2H 13
Winslow Way. Felt —4M 23
Winslow Way. W On T —9K 39
Winstanley Clo. Cobh —1J 77
Winstanley Wlk. Cobh —1J 77 (off Winstanley Clo.)
Winston Clo. Frim G —8D 70
Winston Dri. Stoke D —3M 77
Winston Wlk. Lwr Bo —5H 129
Winston Way. Old Wok —7D 74
Winterborne Av. Orp —1M 67
Winterbourne. H'ham —1M 197
Winterbourne Av. Orp —1M 67
Winterbourne Ct. Brack —1B 32
Winterbourne Gro. Wey —3D 56
Winterbourne Rd. T Hth —3L 45
Winterbourne Wlk. Frim —6D 70
Winter Box Wlk. Rich —8M 11
Winterbrook Rd. SE24 —1N 29
Winterdown Gdns. Esh —3N 57
Winterdown Rd. Esh —3N 57
Winterfold. Craw —6E 182
Winterfold Clo. SW19 —3K 27
Winterfold Cotts. Alb —7N 135
Winterhill Way. Guild —8D 94
Winterpit Clo. Man H —9C 198
Wintersells Ind. Est. Byfl —6N 55
Wintersells Rd. Byfl —6M 55
Winters Rd. Th Dit —6H 41
Winterton Ct. SE20 —1D 46
Winterton Ct. H'ham —6K 197
Winthorpe Rd. SW15 —7K 13
Winton Cres. Yat —1C 68
Winton Rd. Alder —3M 109
Winton Rd. Farnh —9J 109
Winton Rd. Orp —1K 67
Winton Way. SW16 —6L 29
Wire Cut. Fren —1J 149
Wireless Rd. Big A —2F 86
Wire Mill La. Newc —2H 165
Wisbeach Rd. Croy —4A 46
Wisborough Ct. Craw —6L 181
Wisborough Rd. S Croy —5C 64
Wisdom Ct. Iswth —6G 11 (off South St.)
Wise La. W Dray —1M 7
Wiseton Rd. SW17 —2C 28
Wishanger La. Churt —8G 148
Wishbone Way. Wok —3J 73
Wishford Ct. Asht —5M 79
Wishmoor Clo. Camb —7C 50
Wishmoor Rd. Camb —7C 50
Wisley Ct. Red —2D 122 (off Clarendon Rd.)
Wisley Gdns. F'boro —2J 89
Wisley Interchange. (Junct.) —3D 76
Wisley La. Wis —3L 75
Wistaria La. Yat —1B 68
Wiston Ct. Craw —6L 181
Wiston Ct. H'ham —3K 197 (off Woodstock Clo.)
Witham Rd. SE20 —2F 46
Witham Rd. Iswth —4D 10
Witherby Clo. Croy —1B 64
Witherby Clo. S Croy —2B 64
Withers Clo. Chess —3J 59
Witherslack Clo. Head —5H 169
Withey Clo. Wind —4B 4
Witheygate Av. Stai —7K 21
Withey Meadows. Hkwd —1C 162
Withies La. Comp —1F 132
Withies, The. Knap —4H 73
Withies, The. Lea —7H 79
Withybed Corner. Tad —1G 101
Withy Clo. Light —6N 51
Withycombe Rd. SW19 —1J 27
Withypitts. Turn H —6D 184
Withypitts E. Turn H —6D 184
Witley Cres. New Ad —3M 65
Witley Ho. SW2 —1K 29
Wittenham Rd. Brack —9D 16
Wittering Clo. King T —6K 25
Wittmead Rd. Myt —1D 90
Wivenhoe Ct. Houn —7N 9
Wix Hill. W Hor —8C 96
Woburn Av. F'boro —1B 90
Woburn Av. Purl —7L 63
Woburn Clo. SW19 —7A 28
Woburn Clo. Frim —5E 70
Woburn Hill. Add —8L 37
Woburn Rd. Cars —7C 44
Woburn Rd. Craw —5M 181
Woburn Rd. Croy —7N 45
Wodeland Av. Guild —5L 113
Woffington Clo. King T —9J 25
Woking Bus. Pk. Wok —2D 74
Woking Clo. SW15 —7E 12
Wokingham Rd. Brack —9K 15
Wokingham Rd. Crowt & Sand —3D 48
Wokingham Rd. Hurst —3A 14
Woking Rd. Guild —6M 93 (in five parts)
Wold Clo. Craw —5L 181
Woldhurstlea Clo. Craw —5M 181
Woldingham Rd. Wold —7E 84
Wolds Dri. Orp —1J 67
Wold, The. Wold —9K 85
Wolfe Cotts. W'ham —5M 107
Wolfe Rd. Alder —3A 110
Wolfington Rd. SE27 —5M 29
Wolf La. Wind —6A 4
Wolf's Hill. Oxt —9C 106
Wolfson Rehabilitation Cen., The. SW20 —8F 26
Wolf's Rd. Oxt —8D 106
Wolf's Row. Oxt —8D 106
Wolf's Wood. Oxt —1C 126
Wolseley Av. SW19 —3M 27
Wolseley Gdns. W4 —2A 12
Wolseley Rd. Alder —3M 109
Wolseley Rd. G'ming —5H 133
Wolseley Rd. Mitc —6E 44
Wolsey Av. Th Dit —4F 40
Wolsey Clo. SW20 —8G 26
Wolsey Clo. Houn —7C 10
Wolsey Clo. King T —9A 26
Wolsey Clo. Wor Pk —1F 60
Wolsey Cres. Mord —6K 43
Wolsey Cres. New Ad —5M 65
Wolsey Dri. King T —6L 25
Wolsey Dri. W On T —7L 39
Wolsey Gro. Esh —1B 58
Wolsey M. Orp —2N 67
Wolsey Pl. Shop. Cen. Wok —4A 74
Wolsey Rd. Ashf —5N 21
Wolsey Rd. E Mol —3D 40
Wolsey Rd. Esh —1B 58
Wolsey Rd. Hamp —7B 24
Wolsey Rd. Sun —8G 23
Wolsey Spring. King T —8B 26
Wolsey Wlk. Wok —4A 74
Wolsey Way. Chess —2N 59
Wolstonbury Clo. Craw —5A 182
Wolvens La. Dork —9A 118
Wolverton Av. King T —9N 25
Wolverton Clo. Horl —1D 162
Wolverton Gdns. W6 —1J 13
Wolverton Gdns. Horl —9D 142
Wolves Hill. Dork —6J 159
Wondesford Dale. Binf —5H 15
Wonersh Comn. Rd. Won —2D 134
Wonersh Way. Sutt —5J 61
Wonford Clo. King T —9D 26
Wonford Clo. Tad —4F 100
Wonham La. Bet —4D 120
Wonham Way. Gom —8E 116
Wontford Rd. Purl —2L 83
Wontner Rd. SW17 —3D 28
Woodberry Clo. C'fold —4D 172
Woodberry Clo. Sun —7H 23
Woodbine Clo. Sand —8H 49
Woodbine Clo. Twic —3D 24
Woodbine La. Wor Pk —9H 43
Woodbines Av. King T —2K 41
Woodborough Rd. SW15 —7G 12
Woodbourne. Farnh —5K 109
Woodbourne Av. SW16 —4H 29
Woodbourne Clo. SW16 —4J 29
Woodbourne Clo. Yat —9C 48
Woodbourne Dri. Clay —3F 58
Woodbourne Gdns. Wall —4F 62
Woodbridge Av. Lea —5G 79
Woodbridge Bus. Pk. Guild —2M 113
Woodbridge Corner. Lea —5G 78
Woodbridge Ct. H'ham —3N 197
Woodbridge Dri. Camb —8B 50
Woodbridge Gro. Lea —5G 79
Woodbridge Hill. Guild —2L 113
Woodbridge Hill Gdns. Guild —2K 113
Woodbridge Meadows. Guild —2M 113
Woodbridge Rd. B'water —1G 69
Woodbridge Rd. Guild —2M 113
Woodbury Av. E Grin —1D 186
Woodbury Clo. Big H —5H 87
Woodbury Clo. Croy —8C 46
Woodbury Clo. E Grin —1D 186
Woodbury Dri. Sutt —6A 62
Woodbury Rd. W'ham —5H 87
Woodbury St. SW17 —6C 28
Woodby Dri. Asc —6C 34
Wood Clo. Red —3E 142
Wood Clo. Wind —7F 4
Woodcock Dri. Chob —4F 52
Woodcock Hill. Felb —4J 165
Woodcock La. Chob —4E 52
Woodcote. Cranl —6K 155
Woodcote. G'ming —5G 133 (off Frith Hill Rd.)
Woodcote. Guild —7L 113
Woodcote. Horl —7F 142
Woodcote Av. T Hth —3M 45
Woodcote Av. Wall —5F 62
Woodcote Clo. Eps —1C 80
Woodcote Clo. King T —6M 25
Woodcote Ct. Sutt —3M 61
Woodcote Dri. Purl —6H 63
Woodcote End. Eps —2C 80
Woodcote Grn. Wall —5G 62
Woodcote Grn. Rd. Eps —2B 80
Woodcote Gro. Cars —8F 62
Woodcote Gro. Rd. Coul —2H 83
Woodcote Ho. Eps —2C 80
Woodcote Hurst. Eps —3B 80
Woodcote La. Purl —7H 63
Woodcote M. Wall —3F 62
Woodcote Pk. Av. Purl —8G 63
Woodcote Pk. Rd. Eps —3B 80
Woodcote Pl. SE27 —6M 29
Woodcote Rd. Eps —1C 80
Woodcote Rd. F Row —7G 187 (in two parts)
Woodcote Rd. Wall & Purl —3F 62
Woodcote Side. Eps —2A 80
Woodcote Ter. Alder —4B 110
Woodcote Valley Rd. Purl —9H 63
Woodcot Gdns. F'boro —1J 89
Woodcourt. Craw —8A 182
Wood Crest. Sutt —4A 62 (off Christchurch Pk.)
Woodcrest Rd. Purl —9J 63
Woodcrest Wlk. Reig —1C 122
Woodcroft Rd. If'd —5J 181
Woodcroft Rd. T Hth —4M 45
Woodcut Rd. Wrec —5E 128
Woodend. SE19 —7N 29
Wood End. Crowt —3E 48
Woodend. Esh —8C 40
Wood End. F'boro —2B 90
Wood End. H'ham —3B 198
Woodend. Lea —3J 99
Woodend. Sutt —8A 44
Woodend Clo. Asc —9J 17
Woodend Clo. Craw —1E 182
Wood End Clo. Pyr —3H 75
Woodend Clo. Wok —6K 73
Woodend Dri. Asc —4M 33
Woodend Pk. Cobh —2L 77
Woodend Ride. Asc & Wind —8M 17
Woodend Rd. Deep —7G 71
Woodend, The. Wall —5F 62
Woodenhill. Brack —6K 31
Wooderson Clo. SE25 —3B 46
Woodfield. Asht —4K 79
Woodfield Av. SW16 —4H 29
Woodfield Av. Cars —3E 62
Woodfield Clo. SE19 —8N 29
Woodfield Clo. Asht —4K 79
Woodfield Clo. Coul —6G 82
Woodfield Clo. Craw —2C 182
Woodfield Clo. Red —1C 122
Woodfield Gdns. N Mald —4E 42
Woodfield Gro. SW16 —4H 29
Woodfield Hill. Coul —6F 82
Woodfield La. SW16 —4H 29
Woodfield La. Asht —4L 79
Woodfield Rd. Asht —4K 79
Woodfield Rd. Craw —2C 182
Woodfield Rd. Houn —5J 9
Woodfield Rd. Rud —1E 194
Woodfield Rd. Th Dit —8F 40
Woodfields, The. S Croy —7C 64
Woodfield Way. Red —1C 122
Woodforde Ct. Hayes —1E 8
Woodford Grn. Brack —3D 32
Woodgate. Fleet —2D 88
Woodgate Av. Chess —2K 59
Woodgate Dri. SW16 —8H 29
Woodgates Clo. H'ham —5M 197
Woodgavil. Bans —3L 81
Woodger Clo. Guild —1E 114
Woodhall La. Asc —8B 34
Woodham La. Wok & New Haw —9D 54
Woodham Pk. Rd. Wdhm —5H 55
Woodham Pk. Way. Wdhm —7H 55
Woodham Rise. Wok —2C 74
Woodham Rd. Wok —2A 74
Woodham Waye. Wok —1D 74
Woodhatch Rd. Reig & Red —6A 122
Woodhatch Spinney. Coul —3J 83
Woodhaw. Egh —5D 20
Woodhayes Rd. SW19 —8H 27
Woodhill. Send —4F 94
Woodhill La. Sham G —7G 135
Woodhouse La. Holm M —3H 137
Woodhouse St. Binf —9K 15
Woodhurst La. Oxt —8A 106
Woodhurstlea Clo. Craw —5M 181
Woodhurst Pk. Oxt —8A 106
Woodhyrst Gdns. Kenl —2M 83
Woodies Clo. Brack —8H 15
Wooding Gro. Craw —8N 181
Woodland Av. Cranl —7A 156
Woodland Av. Wind —7C 4
Woodland Clo. E Hor —5G 97
Woodland Clo. Eps —3D 60
Woodland Clo. H'ham —4A 198
Woodland Clo. Wey —1E 56
Woodland Ct. Eps —8E 60
Woodland Ct. Oxt —6N 105
Woodland Cres. Brack —8A 16
Woodland Dri. Craw D —1E 184
Woodland Dri. Dork —5G 159
Woodland Dri. E Hor —5G 96
Woodland Dri. Eden —9L 127
Woodland Dri. Wrec —5G 128
Woodland Gdns. Iswth —6E 10
Woodland Gdns. S Croy —7F 64
Woodland Gro. Wey —1E 56
Woodland La. Colg —6G 198
Woodland Rise. C Crook —8A 88
Woodland Rise. Oxt —8A 106
Woodland Rd. T Hth —3L 45
Woodlands. SW20 —3H 43
Woodlands. Add —9N 37
Woodlands. Asht —5M 79
Woodlands. Craw —1H 183
Woodlands. Fleet —3A 88
Woodlands. Horl —7G 143
Woodlands. Wok —5A 74
Woodlands. Yat —3C 68
Woodlands Av. Farnh —5L 109
Woodlands Av. N Mald —9B 26
Woodlands Av. Red —4D 122
Woodlands Av. W Byf —9H 55
Woodlands Av. Wor Pk —8E 42
Woodlands Cvn. Pk. Ash —3D 110
Woodlands Clo. Asc —5K 33
Woodlands Clo. Ash V —8E 90
Woodlands Clo. B'water —5K 69
Woodlands Clo. Clay —4F 58
Woodlands Clo. Cranl —8A 156
Woodlands Clo. Craw D —2E 184
Woodlands Clo. Ott —6D 54
Woodlands Cotts. Dork —7B 160
Woodlands Ct. Owl —6L 49
Woodlands Ct. St J —5K 73
Woodlands Ct. Wok —6A 74
Woodlands Dri. S God —7H 125
Woodlands Dri. Sun —1K 39
Woodlands Est. Knap —5G 73
Woodlands Ga. SW15 —8L 13
Woodlands Gro. Coul —4F 82
Woodlands Gro. Iswth —5E 10
Woodlands Ho. Sheer —1E 74
Woodlands La. Hasl —1D 188
Woodlands La. Stoke D —4A 78
Woodlands La. W'sham —3A 52
Woodlands Pde. Ashf —7D 22
Woodlands Pk. Add —2H 55
Woodlands Pk. Guild —2D 114
Woodlands Pk. Tad —9A 100
Woodlands Ride. Asc —5K 33
Woodlands Rd. SW13 —6E 12
Woodlands Rd. Bookh —6N 97
Woodlands Rd. Camb —1N 69
Woodlands Rd. E Grin —6C 166
Woodlands Rd. Eps —2N 79
Woodlands Rd. F'boro —8J 69
Woodlands Rd. Guild —8N 93
Woodlands Rd. Hamb —9G 152
Woodlands Rd. Iswth —6D 10
Woodlands Rd. Lea —4D 78
Woodlands Rd. Red —5D 122
Woodlands Rd. Surb —6K 41
Woodlands Rd. Vir W —3M 35
Woodlands Rd. W Byf —1H 75
Woodlands Rd. E. Vir W —3M 35
Woodlands Rd. W. Vir W —3M 35
Woodlands, The. SE19 —8N 29
Woodlands, The. Esh —7C 40
Woodlands, The. Iswth —5F 10
Woodlands, The. Small —8M 143
Woodlands, The. Wall —5F 62
Woodlands View. Dork —2H 139
Woodlands Wlk. B'water —5K 69
Woodlands Way. SW15 —8L 13
Woodlands Way. Asht —3N 79
Woodland View. G'ming —2H 133
Woodland Way. Cat —6B 104
Woodland Way. Croy —7H 47
Woodland Way. H'ham —4A 198
Woodland Way. Kgswd —9K 81
Woodland Way. Mitc —8E 28
Woodland Way. Mord —3L 43
Woodland Way. Purl —9L 63
Woodland Way. Surb —8A 42
Woodland Way. W Wick —1L 65
Woodland Way. Wey —2E 56
Wood La. Binf —7J 15
Wood La. Brack —7J 15
Wood La. Cat —2A 104
Wood La. F'boro —2M 89
Wood La. Fleet —4D 88
Wood La. Iswth —2E 10
Wood La. Knap —5G 72
Wood La. Seale —8F 110
Wood La. Tad —4L 81
Wood La. Wey —5D 56
Woodlawn Clo. SW15 —8L 13
Woodlawn Cres. Twic —3B 24
Woodlawn Dri. Felt —3L 23
Woodlawn Gro. Wok —2B 74
Woodlawn Rd. SW6 —3J 13
Woodlawns. Eps —4C 60
Wood Lea Cotts. H'ham —1N 195
Woodlee Clo. Vir W —1M 35
Wood Leigh. Fleet —5B 88
Woodleigh Gdns. SW16 —4J 29
Woodley Clo. SW17 —8D 28
Woodley Ho. G'ming —3H 133
Woodley La. Cars —9C 44
Woodlodge. Asht —4L 79
Wood Lodge La. W Wick —9M 47
Woodmancote Gdns. W Byf —9J 55
Woodmancott Clo. Brack —5D 32
Woodman Ct. Fleet —5A 88
Woodmancourt. G'ming —3F 132
Woodman Rd. Coul —2G 83
Woodmans Hill. Craw —8A 182
Woodmansterne La. Bans —2N 81
Woodmansterne La. Cars & Wall —8D 62
Woodmansterne Rd. SW16 —8G 29
Woodmansterne Rd. Cars —8D 62
Woodmansterne Rd. Coul —2G 83
Woodmansterne St. Bans —2C 82
Woodmere. Brack —3C 32
Woodmere Av. Croy —6F 46
Woodmere Clo. Croy —6G 47
Woodmere Gdns. Croy —6G 46
Woodmere Way. Beck —4N 47
Woodnook Rd. SW16 —6F 28
Woodpecker Clo. Cobh —8M 57
Woodpecker Clo. Eden —9M 127
Woodpecker Clo. Ews —4C 108
Woodpecker La. Newd —9B 140
Woodpecker Mt. Croy —5H 65
Woodpeckers. Milf —3B 152
Woodpecker Way. Turn H —4F 184
Woodpecker Way. Wok —2N 93
Woodplace Clo. Coul —6G 83
Woodplace La. Coul —5G 83
Woodridge Clo. Brack —2A 32
Wood Riding. Wok —2G 75
Woodridings. Wey —3B 56
Wood Rise. Guild —1H 113
Wood Rd. Big H —5E 86
Wood Rd. Camb —5N 69
Wood Rd. Farnh —5H 109
Wood Rd. G'ming —4J 133
Wood Rd. Hind —3B 170
Wood Rd. Shep —3B 38
Woodroffe Benton Ho. Craw —3L 181 (off Rusper Rd.)
Woodrough Copse. Brmly —6C 134
Woodrow Dri. Wokgm —2D 30
Woodroyd Av. Horl —9D 142
Woodroyd Gdns. Horl —1D 162
Woodruff Av. Guild —9C 94
Woods Hill Clo. Ash W —3F 186
Woods Hill La. Ash W —3F 186
Woodshore Clo. Vir W —5L 35
Woodside. SW19 —7L 27
Woodside. B'water —4H 69

Woodside—Zion Rd.

Woodside. Camb —8L 49
Woodside. F'boro —7N 69
Woodside. Fet —9B 78
Woodside. H'ham —4A 198
Woodside. Tad —6L 101
Woodside. W on T —7H 39
Woodside. W Hor —4D 96
Woodside Av. SE25 —5E 46
Woodside Av. Esh —6E 40
Woodside Av. W On T —1J 57
Woodside Clo. Cat —2B 104
Woodside Clo. C'fold —5E 172
Woodside Clo. Knap —4G 73
Woodside Clo. Surb —6B 42
Woodside Cotts. Elst —8G 131
Woodside Ct. Rd. Croy —6D 46
Woodside Cres. Small —8L 143
Woodside Grn. SE25 —5D 46 (in two parts)
Woodside La. Wink —6N 17
Woodside Pk. SE25 —5E 46
Woodside Pk. Est. G'ming —7J 133
Woodside Rd. SE25 —5E 46
Woodside Rd. Bear G —8K 139
Woodside Rd. C'fold —4C 172
Woodside Rd. Cobh —9A 58
Woodside Rd. Craw —1D 182
Woodside Rd. F'boro —6L 89
Woodside Rd. Farnh —5K 109
Woodside Rd. Guild —2J 113
Woodside Rd. King T —8L 25
Woodside Rd. N Mald —1C 42
Woodside Rd. Purl —9H 63
Woodside Rd. Sutt —9A 44
Woodside Rd. Wink —6M 17
Woodside Way. Croy —5F 46
Woodside Way. Mitc —9F 28
Woodside Way. Red —4E 122
Woodside Way. [illegible]
Woodside Way. Vir W —2L 35
Woodsome Lodge. Wey —3D 56
Woodspring Rd. SW19 —3K 27
Woodstock. E Grin —8M 165
Woodstock. W Cla —6K 95
Woodstock Av. Iswth —8G 10
Woodstock Av. Slou —1N 5
Woodstock Av. Sutt —6L 43
Woodstock Clo. Cranl —9A 156
Woodstock Clo. H'ham —3K 197
Woodstock Clo. Wok —3A 74
Woodstock Ct. Eps —8C 60
Woodstock Gro. G'ming —4H 133
Woodstock La. N. Surb —8J 41
Woodstock La. S. Clay & Chess —3H 59
Woodstock Rise. Sutt —6L 43
Woodstock Rd. Cars —2E 62
Woodstock Rd. Coul —3F 82
Woodstock Rd. Croy —9A 46
Woodstocks. F'boro —8A 70
Woodstock, The. (Junct.) —6L 43
Woodstock Way. Mitc —9F 28
Woodstone Av. Eps —2F 60
Wood St. W4 —1D 12
Wood St. Ash V —7E 90
Wood St. E Grin —9N 165
Wood St. King T —1K 41
Wood St. Mitc —6E 44
Wood St. Red —7G 103
Wood St. Grn. Wood S —1D 112
Woodsway. Oxs —1E 78
Woodthorpe Rd. SW15 —7G 13
Woodthorpe Rd. Ashf —7M 21
Woodvale Av. SE25 —2C 46
Woodvale Wlk. SE27 —6N 29
Woodview. Chess —7J 59
Woodview Clo. SW15 —5C 26
Woodview Clo. S Croy —1E 84
Woodville Clo. B'water —1G 68
Woodville Clo. Tedd —5G 24
Woodville Ct. SE19 —1C 46
Woodville Gdns. Surb —6K 41
Woodville Pl. Cat —8N 83
Woodville Rd. Mord —3M 43
Woodville Rd. Rich —4H 25
Woodville Rd. T Hth —3N 45
Woodvill Rd. Lea —7H 79
Woodward Clo. Clay —3F 58
Woodwards. Craw —8N 181
Woodward's Footpath. Twic —9D 10
Wood Way. Camb —1N 69
Woodway. Guild —2D 114
Woodyers Clo. Won —4D 134
Woolacombe Way. Hayes —1F 8
Wooland Ct. C Crook —9A 88 (off Brandon Rd.)
Woolborough Clo. Craw —2C 182
Woolborough La. Craw —9D 162
Woolborough La. Out —3K 143
Woolborough Rd. Craw —2C 182
Woolford Clo. Brack —8G 16
Woolfords La. Thur —3E 150
Woolhampton Way. Brack —4B 32
Woollards Rd. Ash V —9F 90
Woolmead Rd. Farnh —9H 109
Woolmead, The. Farnh —9H 109
Woolmead Wlk. Farnh —9H 109 (off Woolmead Rd.)
Woolmer Hill Rd. Hasl —9A 170
Woolmer La. Bram —8F 168
Woolmer View. Gray —6B 170
Woolneigh St. SW6 —6N 13
Wool Rd. SW20 —[illegible]
Woolsack Ct. Guild —3L 113
Woolsack Way. G'ming —7J 133
Wootton Clo. Eps —3E 80
Worbeck Rd. SE20 —1E 46
Worcester Clo. Croy —8K 47
Worcester Clo. F'boro —7N 69
Worcester Clo. Mitc —2F 44
Worcester Ct. W on T —7K 39
Worcester Ct. Wor Pk —9D 42
Worcester Dri. Ashf —6C 22
Worcester Gdns. Wor Pk —9D 42
Worcester Pk. Rd. Wor Pk —9C 42
Worcester Rd. SW19 —6L 27
Worcester Rd. Craw —7C 182
Worcester Rd. Guild —1J 113
Worcester Rd. Reig —2M 121
Worcester Rd. Sutt —4M 61
Worcestershire Lea. Warf —8D 16
Wordsworth. Brack —4K 31
Wordsworth Av. Kenl —2A 84
Wordsworth Av. Yat —1A 68
Wordsworth Clo. Craw —1F 182
Wordsworth Dri. Sutt —1H 61
Wordsworth Mead. Red —1E 122
Wordsworth Pl. H'ham —1L 197
Wordsworth Rise. E Grin —9M 165
Wordsworth Rd. Add —1M 55
Wordsworth Rd. Hamp —5N 23
Wordsworth Rd. Wall —3G 63
Wordsworth Way. W Dray —1N 7
World's End. Cobh —1H 77
Worlds End Hill. Brack —5D 32
Worlds End La. Orp —3N 67
Worlidge St. W6 —1H 13
Wormley La. Hamb —9E 152
Worple Av. SW19 —8J 27
Worple Av. Iswth —8G 10
Worple Av. Stai —7K 21
Worple Rd. SW20 & SW19 —1H 43
Worple Rd. Eps —2C 80
Worple Rd. Iswth —7G 10
Worple Rd. Lea —9H 79
Worple Rd. Stai —7K 21
Worple Rd. M. SW19 —7L 27
Worplesdon Hill. Wok —9F 72
Worplesdon Rd. Guild —7J 93
Worple St. SW14 —6C 12
Worple, The. Wray —9B 6
Worple Way. Rich —8L 11
Worslade Rd. SW17 —5B 28
Worsley Rd. Frim —6C 70
Worsted Grn. Red —7G 103
Worsted La. E Grin —1D 186
Worth Clo. Orp —1N 67
Worth Ct. Craw —8M 183
Worthfield Clo. Eps —4C 60
Worthing Rd. H'ham —9G 197
Worthing Rd. Houn —2N 9
Worthington Clo. Mitc —2F 44
Worthington Rd. Surb —7M 41
Worth Pk. Av. Craw —2F 182
Worth Rd. Craw —2G 182
Worth Way. Worth —4J 183
Wortley Rd. Croy —6L 45
Worton Ct. Iswth —7E 10
Worton Gdns. Iswth —5D 10
Worton Hall Ind. Est. Iswth —7E 10
Worton Rd. Iswth —7E 10
Worton Way. Houn & Iswth —5D 10
Wotton Dri. Dork —9L 117
Wotton Way. Sutt —6H 61
Wrabness Way. Stai —9K 21
Wrangthorn Wlk. Croy —1L 63
Wray Clo. Ash W —3F 186
Wray Comn. Rd. Reig —2A 122
Wrayfield Av. Reig —2A 122
Wrayfield Pl. Reig —2N 121
Wrayfield Rd. Sutt —9J 43
Wraylands Dri. Reig —1B 122
Wray La. Reig —8A 102
Waymill Ct. Reig —3B 122
Wray Mill Pk. Reig —1C 122
Wray Pk. Rd. Reig —2N 121
Wray Rd. Sutt —5L 61
Wraysbury Clo. Houn —8M 9
Wraysbury Rd. Stai —3D 20
Wrecclesham Hill. Wrec —6C 128
Wrecclesham Rd. Farnh —4E 128
Wrekin, The. F'boro —4C 90
Wren Clo. H'ham —1K 197
Wren Clo. S Croy —5G 65
Wren Clo. Yat —9A 48
Wren Ct. Ash —1F 110
Wren Ct. Craw —6C 182
Wren Cres. Add —2M 55
Wren's Av. Ashf —5D 22
Wrens Hill. Oxs —2C 78
Wren St. Turn H —4F 184
Wren Way. F'boro —7L 69
Wright. Wind —6A 4
Wright Clo. M'bowr —7F 182
Wright Gdns. Shep —4B 38
Wright Rd. Houn —3K 9
Wrights All. SW19 —7H 27
Wright Sq. Wind —6A 4
Wrights Rd. SE25 —2B 46
Wrights Row. Wall —1F 62
Wrights Wlk. SW14 —6C 12
Wright Way. Wind —6A 4
Wriotsley Way. Add —3J 55
Wrotham Hill. Duns —6A 174
Wroughton Rd. SW11 —1D 28
Wroxham. Brack —4L 31
Wroxham Wlk. Craw —5F 182
Wrythe Grn. Cars —9D 44
Wrythe Grn. Rd. Cars —9D 44
Wrythe La. Cars —7A 44
Wulwyn Ct. Crowt —2E 48
Wulwyn Side. Crowt —2E 48
Wyatt Clo. Felt —2K 23
Wyatt Dri. SW13 —2G 13
Wyatt Pk. Rd. SW2 —3J 29
Wyatt Rd. Stai —6J 21
Wyatt Rd. Wind —6A 4
Wyatt's Almshouses. G'ming —5K 133 (off Wyatt's Clo.)
Wyatt's Clo. G'ming —5K 133
Wyche Gro. S Croy —4N 63
Wych Elm Pas. King T —8M 25
Wych Elm Rise. Guild —6A 114
Wychelm Rd. Light —7N 51
Wych Hill. Wok —6M 73
Wych Hill La. Wok —6N 73
Wych Hill Pk. Wok —6N 73
Wych Hill Rise. Wok —6M 73
Wych Hill Way. Wok —7N 73
Wychwood Av. Brack —3D 32
Wychwood Av. T Hth —2N 45
Wychwood Clo. Ash —2D 110
Wychwood Clo. Sun —7H 23
Wychwood Pl. Camb —6F 50
Wycliffe Ct. Craw —6K 181
Wycliffe Rd. SW19 —7N 27
Wycombe Pl. SW18 —9N 13
Wydehurst Rd. Croy —6D 46
Wydell Clo. Mord —5J 43
Wydenhurst Rd. Croy —6D 46
Wyecliffe Gdns. Red —8G 103
Wye Clo. Ashf —5C 22
Wye Clo. Craw —9A 182
Wyeths M. Eps —9E 60
Wyeth's Rd. Eps —9E 60
Wyfold Rd. SW6 —3K 13
Wyke Av. Ash —1H 111
Wyke Bldgs. Ash —1H 111
Wyke Clo. Iswth —2F 10
Wyke Cross. Guild —1L 111
Wykeham Clo. W Dray —1B 8
Wykeham Rd. Farnh —9H 109
Wykeham Rd. Guild —2F 114
Wykehurst La. Ewh —4D 156
Wyke La. Ash —1H 111
Wyke Rd. SW20 —1H 43
Wylam. Brack —4L 31
Wylands Rd. Slou —1C 6
Wymering Ct. F'boro —2B 90
Wymond St. SW15 —6H 13
Wynash Gdns. Cars —2C 62
Wyncombe Av. W5 —1H 11
Wyncote Way. S Croy —5G 64
Wyndham Av. Cobh —9H 57
Wyndham Clo. Sutt —4M 61
Wyndham Clo. Yat —8C 48
Wyndham Cres. Cranl —7J 155
Wyndham Cres. Houn —9A 10
Wyndham Rd. King T —8M 25
Wyndham Rd. Wok —5L 73
Wyndham St. Alder —3A 110
Wynfields. Myt —2D 90
Wynlea Clo. Craw D —1D 184
Wynne Gdns. C Crook —8C 88
Wynnstow Pk. Oxt —9B 106
Wynsham Way. W'sham —2M 51
Wynton Gdns. SE25 —4C 46
Wynton Gro. W On T —9H 39
Wyphurst Rd. Cranl —6N 155
Wyre Gro. Hayes —1H 9
Wyresdale. Brack —6C 32
Wysemead. Horl —7G 143
Wythemede. Binf —7G 15
Wyvern Clo. Brack —3N 31
Wyvern Est. N Mald —3F 42
Wyvern Pk.Ind. Est. Peas —2L 133
Wyvern Pl. Add —1K 55
Wyvern Rd. Purl —6M 63

Xylon Ho. Wor Pk —8G 42

Yaffle Rd. Wey —6D 56
Yale Clo. Houn —8N 9
Yale Clo. Owl —5L 49
Yarborough Rd. SW19 —9B 28
Yarbridge Clo. Sutt —6N 61
Yardley. Brack —4L 31
Yardley Clo. Reig —1N 121
Yardley Ct. Sutt —1H 61
Yard Mead. Egh —4C 20
Yarm Clo. Lea —1J 99
Yarm Ct. Rd. Lea —1J 99
Yarmouth Clo. Craw —5E 182
Yarm Way. Lea —1K 99
Yarnold Clo. Wokgm —1E 30
Yarrow Clo. H'ham —3L 197
Yarrowfield. Wok —1N 93
Yateley Cen. Yat —9B 48
Yateley Ct. S Croy —1N 83
Yateley Rd. Sand —7E 48
Yatesbury Clo. Farnh —4E 128
Yattendon Rd. Horl —8F 142
Yaverland Dri. Bag —5H 51
Yeats Clo. Red —6A 122
Yeend Clo. W Mol —3A 40
Yeldham Rd. W6 —1J 13
Yellowcress Dri. Bisl —3D 72
Yelverton Lodge. Twic —1J 25
Yenston Clo. Mord —5M 43
Yeoman Clo. SE27 —4M 29
Yeoman Ct. Houn —3N 9
Yeomanry Clo. Eps —[illegible]
Yeomans Clo. F'boro —9M 69
Yeomans Clo. Tong —4D 110
Yeomans M. Iswth —9D 10
Yeomans Pl. Head —4D 168
Yeomans Way. Camb —1C 70
Yeoman Way. Red —8F 122
Yeoveney Clo. Stai —3F 20
Yeovil Clo. F'boro —4B 90
Yeovil Rd. F'boro —4C 90
Yeovil Rd. Sand —6J 49
Yeovilton Pl. King T —6K 25
Yetminster Rd. F'boro —4B 90
Yewbank Clo. Kenl —2A 84
Yewdells Clo. Bet —2F 120
Yewens. C'fold —4E 172
Yewlands Clo. Bans —2A 82
Yewlands Wlk. If'd —5J 181
Yew La. E Grin —7L 165
Yew Pl. Wey —1G 56
Yews, The. Ashf —4C 22
Yew Tree Bottom Rd. Eps —3G 81
Yew Tree Clo. Coul —6D 82
Yew Tree Clo. F'boro —2H 89
Yew Tree Clo. Horl —7E 142
Yew Tree Clo. Wor Pk —7D 42
Yew Tree Cotts. Craw —5N 199
Yew Tree Cotts. H'ham —8B 196
Yew Tree Ct. Horl —6E 142
Yew Tree Ct. Sutt —4A 62 (off Walnut M.)
Yew Tree Dri. Cat —3C 104
Yew Tree Dri. Guild —8M 93
Yew Tree Gdns. Eps —2B 80
Yewtree La. Ran C —9A 98
Yew Tree La. Reig —9N 101
Yew Tree Lodge. SW16 —5G 28
Yewtree Rd. Beck —2J 47
Yew Tree Rd. Charl —3K 161
Yew Tree Rd. Dork —3G 119
Yew Tree Rd. Witl —4A 152
Yew Trees. Egh —2E 36
Yew Trees. Shep —3A 38
Yew Tree Wlk. Eff —5L 97
Yew Tree Wlk. Frim —5D 70
Yew Tree Wlk. Houn —8N 9
Yew Tree Wlk. Purl —6N 63
Yew Tree Way. Croy —6H 65
Yew Wlk. E Hor —1F 116
Yockley Clo. Camb —2H 71
Yolland Clo. Farnh —5H 109
York Av. SW14 —8B 12
York Av. E Grin —1B 186
York Av. Wind —5E 4
York Clo. Byfl —8N 55
York Clo. H'ham —5M 197
York Clo. Mord —3N 43
York Cres. Alder —3L 109
Yorke Gdns. Reig —2M 121
Yorke Ga. Cat —9A 84
Yorke Rd. Reig —2M 121
York Gdns. W On T —8L 39
York Hill. SE27 —4M 29
York Ho. Brack —9L 15
York La. Ter. Camb —1N 69 (off York La.)
York Mans. SW5 —1N 13 (off Earl's Ct. Rd.)
York Pde. Bren —1K 11
York Rd. SW18 & SW11 —7N 13
York Rd. SW19 —7A 28
York Rd. Alder —3L 109
York Rd. Ash —1E 110
York Rd. Big H —6D 86
York Rd. Binf —6J 15
York Rd. Bren —1K 11
York Rd. Byfl —8M 55
York Rd. Camb —8B 50
York Rd. Craw —7C 182
York Rd. Croy —6L 45
York Rd. F'boro —1A 90
York Rd. Farnh —3H 129
York Rd. Guild —4N 113
York Rd. Houn —6B 10
York Rd. King T —8M 25
York Rd. Rich —8M 11
York Rd. S Croy —6G 64
York Rd. Sutt —3M 61
York Rd. Tedd —5E 24
York Rd. Wey —2D 56
York Rd. Wind —5E 4
York Rd. Wok —6N 73
Yorkshire Pl. Warf —8D 16
Yorkshire Rd. Mitc —4J 45
York St. Mitc —6E 44
York St. Twic —2G 25
York Ter. La. Camb —1M 69
Yorktown Rd. Sand & Col T —7F 48
York Way. Chess —4L 59
York Way. Felt —4N 23 (in two parts)
York Way. Sand —7G 48
Youlden Clo. Camb —1E 70
Youlden Dri. Camb —1E 70
Youngs Dri. Ash —2D 110
Young St. Fet —3E 98
Youngstroat La. Wok —6A 54
Yukon Rd. SW12 —1F 28

Zealand Av. W Dray —3M 7
Zennor Rd. SW12 —2G 28
Zermatt Rd. T Hth —3N 45
Zig Zag Rd. Dork & Tad —8J 99
Zig Zag Rd. Kenl —3N 83
Zinnia Dri. Bisl —3D 72
Zion Pl. T Hth —3A 46
Zion Rd. T Hth —3A 46

PLACES OF INTEREST
covered by this atlas
with their map square reference

HOSPITALS, HEALTH CENTRES and HOSPICES
covered by this atlas
with their map square reference

N.B. Where Hospitals and Health Centres are not named on the map, the reference
given is for the road in which they are situated.

ABRAHAM COWLEY UNIT —9F **36**
Holloway Hill, Lyne, Chertsey,
Surrey. KT16 0AE
Tel: (01932) 872010

Addlestone Health Centre —1L **55**
45 Station Rd., Addlestone,
Surrey. KT15 2BH
Tel: (01932) 840123

Aldershot Health Centre —2L **109**
Wellington Av., Aldershot,
Hants. GU13 9BJ
Tel: (01252) 24577

ASHFORD HOSPITAL —3N **21**
London Rd., Ashford,
Middx. TW15 3AA
Tel: (01784) 884488

ASHTEAD HOSPITAL —6L **79**
The Warren, Ashtead,
Surrey. KT21 2SB
Tel: (01372) 276161

Ash Vale Health Centre —0E **90**
Wharf Rd. Ash Vale,
Aldershot, Hants.
GU12 5BA
Tel: (01252) 317551

ATKINSON MORLEY'S HOSPITAL —8G **26**
31 Copse Hill, Wimbledon,
London. SW20 0NE
Tel: (0181) 946 7711

Balham Health Centre —3F **28**
120 Bedford Hill, Balham,
London. SW12 9HP
Tel: (0181) 700 0600

BARNES HOSPITAL —6D **12**
South Worple Way,
London. SW14 8SU
Tel: (0181) 878 4981

BECKENHAM HOSPITAL —1J **47**
379 Croydon Rd., Beckenham,
Kent. BR3 3QL
Tel: (0181) 289 6600

BEECHLAWN DAY HOSPITAL —1G **29**
Belthorn Cres., Weir Rd.,
London. SW12 0NS
Tel: (0181) 675 3415

BETHLEM ROYAL HOSPITAL, THE —6K **47**
Monks Orchard Rd.,
Eden Park, Beckenham,
Kent. BR3 3BX
Tel: (0181) 777 6611

Bourne Hall Health Centre —5E **60**
Chessington Rd., Ewell,
Surrey. KT17 1TG
Tel: (0181) 394 1301

Brentford Health Centre —2J **11**
Boston Manor Rd., Brentford,
Middx. TW8 8DR
Tel: (0181) 321 3800

BRITISH HOME & HOSPITAL FOR INCURABLES
—6M **29**
Crown La., Streatham,
London. SW16 3JB
Tel: (0181) 670 8261

Broadfield Health Centre —7N **181**
Coachman's Dri., Broadfield,
Crawley, West Sussex.
RH11 9YZ
Tel: (01293) 531951

BROADMOOR HOSPITAL —3J **49**
Crowthorne, Berks. RG45 7EG
Tel: (01344) 773111

Brocklebank Health Centre —1N **27**
249 Garratt La., Wandsworth,
London. SW18 4DU
Tel: (0181) 870 1341

Camberley Health Centre —3N **69**
159 Frimley Rd., Camberley,
Surrey. GU15 2QA
Tel: (01276) 20101

CAMBRIDGE MILITARY HOSPITAL —1N **109**
Hospital Rd., Aldershot, Hants. GU11 2AN
Tel: (01252) 350434

CANE HILL FORENSIC MENTAL HEALTH UNIT
—4G **82**
Brighton Rd., Coulsdon,
Surrey. CR3 3YL
Tel: (01737) 556300

CARSHALTON WAR MEMORIAL HOSPITAL
—3D **62**
The Park, Carshalton,
Surrey. SM5 3DB
Tel: (0181) 647 5534

CASSEL HOSPITAL, THE —5K **25**
1 Ham Comn., Richmond,
Surrey. TW10 7JF
Tel: (0181) 940 8181

CATERHAM DENE HOSPITAL —1I, **104**
Church Rd., Caterham-on-the-Hill,
Surrey. CR3 5RA
Tel: (01883) 349324

CHARING CROSS HOSPITAL —2J **13**
Fulham Palace Rd.,
London. W6 8RF
Tel: (0181) 383 0000

CHELSEA & WESTMINSTER HOSPITAL
—2N **13**
369 Fulham Rd., Chelsea,
London. SW10 9NH
Tel: (0181) 746 8000

CHILDREN'S TRUST, THE —8J **81**
Tadworth St., Tadworth,
Surrey. KT20 5RU
Tel: (01737) 357171

Chiswick Health Centre —1C **12**
Fishers La., Chiswick,
London. W4 1RX
Tel: (0181) 995 8051

CHURCH HILL HOUSE HOSPITAL —5M **31**
Crowthorne Rd., Bracknell,
Berkshire. RG12 7EP
Tel: (01344) 422722

CLARE PARK BUPA HOSPITAL —8A **108**
Crondall La., Crondall,
Farnham, Surrey. GU10 5XX
Tel: (01252) 850216

CLAYPONDS HOSPITAL —1L **11**
Sterling Pl., South Ealing,
London. W5 4RN
Tel: (0181) 560 4013

COBHAM HOSPITAL —9J **57**
Portsmouth Rd., Cobham,
Surrey. KT11 1HT
Tel: (01932) 867231

COTTAGE DAY HOSPITAL —4C **28**
Springfield University Hospital,
61 Glenburnie Rd.,
London. SW17 7DJ
Tel: (0181) 682 6514

Cranleigh Health Centre —7M **155**
High St., Cranleigh,
Surrey. GU6 8AE
Tel: (01483) 273951

CRANLEIGH VILLAGE HOSPITAL —8M **155**
High St., Cranleigh,
Surrey. GU6 8AE
Tel: (01483) 782000

Crawley Down Health Centre —1E **184**
Bowers Pl., Crawley,
West Sussex. RH10 4HY
Tel: (01342) 713031

CRAWLEY HOSPITAL —3A **182**
West Grn. Dri.,
West Green, Crawley,
West Sussex. RH11 7DH
Tel: (01293) 600300

DORKING HOSPITAL —6H **119**
Horsham Rd., Dorking,
Surrey. RH4 2AA
Tel: (01737) 768511

EAST SURREY HOSPITAL —7E **122**
Canada Av., Redhill,
Surrey. RH1 5RH
Tel: (01737) 768511

EDENBRIDGE & DISTRICT WAR MEMORIAL
HOSPITAL —4L **147**
Mill Hill, Edenbridge.
Kent. TN8 5DA
Tel: (01732) 863164

ELLESMERE DAY HOSPITAL —2F **56**
Queens Rd., Walton-on-Thames,
Surrey. KT12 5AA
Tel: (01932) 241481

Englefield Green Health Centre —0M **19**
Bond St., Englefield Green,
Egham, Surrey. TW20 0PF
Tel: (01784) 437671

EPSOM & EWELL COTTAGE HOSPITAL —7L **59**
Horton La., Epsom,
Surrey. KT18 8PB
Tel: (01372) 734734

EPSOM GENERAL HOSPITAL —2B **80**
Dorking Rd., Epsom,
Surrey. KT18 7EG
Tel: (01372) 735735

Family Health Centre —7K **37**
Stepgates, Chertsey,
Surrey. KT16 8HZ
Tel: (01932) 565655

FARNBOROUGH HOSPITAL —1J **67**
Farnborough Comn.,
Locksbottom, Orpington,
Kent. BR6 8ND
Tel: (01689) 814000

FARNHAM GENERAL HOSPITAL —9K **109**
Hale Rd., Farnham,
Surrey. GU9 9QL
Tel: (01252) 726666

Farnham Health Centre —1H **129**
Brightwells Rd., East St.,
Farnham, Surrey. GU9 7SA
Tel: (01252) 724044

FARNHAM ROAD HOSPITAL —5L **113**
Farnham Rd., Guildford,
Surrey. GU2 5JN
Tel: (01483) 573852

FLEET COMMUNITY HOSPITAL —3A **88**
Church Rd., Fleet, Aldershot,
Hants. GU13 8LD
Tel: (01252) 613117

FRIMLEY PARK HOSPITAL —4B **70**
Portsmouth Rd., Camberley,
Surrey. GU16 5UJ
Tel: (01276) 604604

GATWICK PARK BUPA HOSPITAL —9C **142**
Povey Cross Rd., Horley,
Surrey. RH6 0BB
Tel: (01293) 785511

Goldsworth Park Health Centre —4K **73**
Denton Way, Woking,
Surrey. GU21 3LQ
Tel: (01483) 728201

Great Hollands Health Centre —5L **31**
Great Hollands Sq., Bracknell,
Berks. RG12 8WY
Tel: (01344) 54338

Grove Community Health Centre, The —6C **20**
Church Rd., The Grove,
Egham, Surrey. TW20 9QL
Tel: (01784) 477677

Hampton Community Health Centre —7N **23**
Tangley Park Rd., Hampton Nurserylands,
Hampton, Middx. TW12 3YH
Tel: (0181) 979 1726

HASLEMERE & DISTRICT HOSPITAL —1H **189**
Church La., Haslemere,
Surrey. GU27 2BJ
Tel: (01482) 653881

Haslemere Health Centre —1H **189**
Church La., Haslemere,
Surrey. GU27 2BQ
Tel: (01428) 653881

HEATHERWOOD HOSPITAL —2K **33**
London Rd., Ascot,
Berks. SL5 8AA
Tel: (01344) 23333

HENDERSON HOSPITAL —5N **61**
Homeland Dri., Sutton,
Surrey. SM2 5LY
Tel: (0181) 661 1611

Heston Health Centre —3M **9**
Cranford La., Heston,
Middx. TW5 9ER
Tel: (0181) 570 5891

HOLY CROSS HOSPITAL —1C **188**
Hindhead Rd., Haslemere,
Surrey. GU27 1NQ
Tel: (01428) 643311

HOMEWOOD RESOURCE CENTRE —9E **36**
Bournewood House,
Guildford Rd., Chertsey,
Surrey. KT16 0QA
Tel: (01932) 872010

Hook Health Centre —1L **59**
1 Gosbury Hill, Hook,
Surrey. KT9 1BT
Tel: (0181) 397 5737

Horley Health Centre —8E **142**
Kings Rd., Horley,
Surrey. RH6 7AQ
Tel: (01293) 772681

HORSHAM HOSPITAL —5J **197**
Hurst Rd., Horsham,
West Sussex. RH12 2DR
Tel: (01403) 227000

HORTON HOSPITAL —7A **60**
Long Gro. Rd., Epsom,
Surrey. KT19 8PZ
Tel: (01372) 729696

HRH PRINCESS CHRISTIAN'S HOSPITAL
—4F **4**
12 Clarence Rd., Windsor,
Berks. SL4 5AG
Tel: (01753) 853121

KING EDWARD VII HOSPITAL —6F **4**
St Leonard's Rd., Windsor,
Berks. SL4 3DP
Tel: (01753) 860441

KINGSTON HOSPITAL —9A **26**
Galsworthy Rd.,
Kingston-upon-Thames,
Surrey. KT2 7QB
Tel: (0181) 546 7711

Langley Health Centre —1C **6**
Common Rd., Langley,
Slough, Berks. SL3 8LE
Tel: (01753) 544288

LEATHERHEAD HOSPITAL —9J **79**
Poplar Rd., Leatherhead,
Surrey. KT22 8SD
Tel: (01372) 384300

Lewin Road Community Mental Health Centre
—7H **29**
55-57 Lewin Rd.,
London. SW16 6JZ
Tel: (0181) 664 6406

Lifecare Trust —1A **104**
Coulsdon Rd., Caterham,
Surrey. CR3 5YA
Tel: (01883) 346411

Manor Drive Health Centre —7F **42**
3 The Manor Dri., Worcester Park,
Surrey. KT4 7LG
Tel: (0181) 337 0246

MANOR HOSPITAL, THE —7N **59**
Christ Church Rd., Epsom,
Surrey. KT19 8NL
Tel: (01372) 202020

Manor House Health Centre, The —3H **23**
Manor La., Feltham,
Middx. TW13 4JQ
Tel: (0181) 321 3757

Marie Curie Centre —3C **104**
Caterham Harestone Dri., Caterham,
Surrey. CR3 6YQ
Tel: (01883) 342226

Maswell Park Health Centre —8C **10**
Hounslow Av., Hounslow,
Middx. TW3 2DY
Tel: (0181) 898 2321

MAYDAY UNIVERSITY HOSPITAL —5M **45**
Mayday Rd., Thornton Heath,
Surrey. CR7 7YE
Tel: (0181) 401 3000

MEDICAL RECEPTION STATION HOSPITAL
—7M **49**
The Royal Military Academy,
Egerton Rd., Camberley,
Surrey. GU15 4PH
Tel: (01276) 63344

Merstham Health Centre —7G **103**
Bletchingley Rd., Merstham,
Surrey. RH1 3PN
Tel: (01737) 642684

MILFORD HOSPITAL —2F **152**
Tuesley La., Godalming,
Surrey. GU7 1UF
Tel: (01483) 414411

MOLESEY HOSPITAL —4A **40**
Approach Rd., High St.,
West Molesey,
Surrey. KT7 0LU
Tel: (0181) 941 4481

Mollison Drive Health Centre —4J **63**
Mollison Dri., Wallington,
Surrey. SM6 9HF
Tel: (0181) 773 2820

MOUNT ALVERNIA HOSPITAL —5A **114**
Harvey Rd., Guildford,
Surrey. GU1 3LX
Tel: (01483) 570122

NELSON HOSPITAL —1L **43**
Kingston Rd., Merton,
London. SW20 8DB
Tel: (0181) 296 2000

NEW VICTORIA HOSPITAL —9D **26**
184 Coombe La. W.,
Kingston-upon-Thames,
Surrey. KT2 7EG
Tel: (0181) 949 9000

Norbury Health Centre —2K **45**
2b Pollards Hill N., Norbury,
London. SW16 4NL
Tel: (0181) 679 1700

NORMANSFIELD HOSPITAL —8J **25**
Kingston Rd., Teddington,
Middx. TW11 9JH
Tel: (0181) 977 7583

NORTH DOWNS IBH HOSPITAL —3D **104**
46 Tupwood La., Caterham,
Surrey. CR3 6DP
Tel: (01883) 348981

Oakhill Health Centre —5L **41**
Oakhill Rd., Surbiton,
Surrey. KT6 6EN
Tel: (0181) 390 6755

ORCHARD HILL —6D **62**
Fountain Dri., Carshalton,
Surrey. SM5 4NR
Tel: (0181) 770 8000

OXTED & LIMPSFIELD HOSPITAL —6N **105**
Eastlands Way, Oxted,
Surrey. RH8 0LR
Tel: (01883) 714344

Oxted Health Centre —7B **106**
Gresham Rd., Oxted,
Surrey. RH8 0BQ
Tel: (01883) 712238

PARKLANDS DAY HOSPITAL —8L **59**
West Park Hospital,
Horton La., Epsom,
Surrey. KT19 8PB
Tel: (01372) 202020

PARKSIDE HOSPITAL —4J **27**
53 Parkside, Wimbledon,
London. SW19 5NX
Tel: (0181) 971 8000

Parkway Health Centre —6M **65**
Parkway, New Addington,
Surrey. CR0 0JA
Tel: (01689) 842554

Parson's Green Health Centre —4M **13**
5-7 Parson's Grn.,
London. SW6 4UL
Tel: (0181) 846 6767

Phyllis Tuckwell Memorial Hospice —2K **129**
Waverley La., Farnham,
Surrey. GU9 8BL
Tel: (01252) 725814

Princess Alice Hospice —2A **58**
West End La., Esher,
Surrey. KT10 8NA
Tel: (01372) 468811

PRINCESS MARGARET HOSPITAL —5G **4**
Osborne Rd., Windsor,
Berks. SL4 3SJ
Tel: (01753) 868292

PRIORY HOSPITAL —7E **12**
Priory La., Roehampton,
London. SW15 5JJ
Tel: (0181) 876 8261

PURLEY HOSPITAL —7L **63**
Brighton Rd., Purley,
Surrey. CR8 2YL
Tel: (0181) 401 3232

PUTNEY HOSPITAL —6H **13**
Commondale,
Lower Richmond Rd.,
Putney, London. SW15 1HW
Tel: (0181) 789 6633

QUEEN ELIZABETH HOUSE —6M **19**
Torin Ct., Bond St.,
Englefield Green, Egham,
Surrey. TW20 0PJ
Tel: (01784) 471452

QUEEN MARY'S HOSPITAL FOR CHILDREN
—7A **44**
Wrythe La., Carshalton,
Surrey. SM5 1AA
Tel: (0181) 296 2000

QUEEN MARY'S UNIVERSITY HOSPITAL
—9F **12**
Roehampton La., Roehampton,
London. SW15 5PN
Tel: (0181) 789 6611

QUEENS HOSPITAL —5N **45**
66a Queens Rd., Croydon,
Surrey. CR9 2PQ
Tel: (0181) 401 3000

QUEEN VICTORIA HOSPITAL —7B **166**
Holtye Rd., East Grinstead,
West Sussex. RH19 3DZ
Tel: (01342) 410210

Rathmell Drive Health Centre —1H **29**
9A Rathmell Dri.,
London. SW4 8JG
Tel: (0181) 674 7400

RICHMOND HEALTHCARE HAMLET —6L **11**
Kew Foot Rd., Richmond,
Surrey. TW9 2TE
Tel: (0181) 940 3331

Robin Hood Lane Health Centre —2N **61**
Camden Rd., Sutton,
Surrey. SM1 2RJ
Tel: (0181) 643 8611

Rosslyn Clinic —9J **11**
15 Rosslyn Rd.,
East Twickenham,
Middx. TW1 2AR
Tel: (0181) 891 3173

ROYAL HOSPITAL FOR NEURO-DISABILITY
—9K **13**
West Hill, Putney,
London. SW15 3SW
Tel: (0181) 780 4500

ROYAL MARSDEN HOSPITAL (SUTTON), THE
—6A **22**
Downs Rd., Sutton,
Surrey. SM2 5PT
Tel: (0181) 642 6011

ROYAL SURREY COUNTY HOSPITAL, THE
—3H **113**
Egerton Rd., Guildford,
Surrey. GU2 5XX
Tel: (01483) 571122

RUNNYMEDE HOSPITAL —9F **36**
Guildford Rd., Ottershaw,
Chertsey, Surrey. KT16 0RQ
Tel: (01932) 872007

ST ANTHONY'S HOSPITAL —8J **43**
London Rd., North Cheam,
Surrey. SM3 9DW
Tel: (0181) 337 6691

St Catherine's Hospice —5B **182**
Malthouse Rd., Crawley,
West Sussex. RH10 6BH
Tel: (01293) 547333

ST EBBA'S —5B **60**
Hook Rd., Epsom,
Surrey. KT19 8QJ
Tel: (01372) 202020

ST GEORGE'S HOSPITAL —6B **28**
Blackshaw Rd., Tooting,
London. SW17 0QT
Tel: (0181) 672 1255

ST HELIER HOSPITAL —7A **44**
Wrythe La., Carshalton,
Surrey. SM5 1AA
Tel: (0181) 296 2000

St John's Health Centre —1G **25**
Oak La., Twickenham,
Middx. TW1 3PH
Tel: (0181) 891 3101

St John's Health Centre —6J **73**
Hermitage Rd.,
St Johns, Woking,
Surrey. GU21 1TD
Tel: (01483) 764871

ST JOHN'S HOUSE HOSPITAL —1G **25**
Strafford Rd.,
London. SW1 3HQ
Tel: (0181) 744 9943

ST PETER'S HOSPITAL —9F **36**
Guildford Rd.,
Ottershaw, Chertsey,
Surrey. KT16 0PZ
Tel: (01932) 872000

St Raphael's Hospice —7J **43**
London Rd., North Cheam,
Surrey. SM3 9DX
Tel: (0181) 337 7475

Sheen Lane Health Centre —6B **12**
Sheen La., London. SW14 8LP
Tel: (0181) 878 7561

Shepperton Health Centre —4C **38**
Laleham Rd., Shepperton,
Middx. TW17 8EJ
Tel: (01932) 713200

SHIRLEY OAKS HOSPITAL —6F **46**
Poppy La., Shirley Oaks,
Croydon, Surrey. CR9 8AB
Tel: (0181) 655 2255

Shotfield Health Centre —3F **62**
Shotfield, Wallington,
Surrey. SM6 0HY
Tel: (0181) 647 0031

Skimped Hill Health Centre —1N **31**
Skimped Hill La., Bracknell,
Berks., RG12 1LH
Tel: (01344) 485333

SLOANE HOSPITAL, THE —1N **47**
125-133 Albemarle Rd., Beckenham,
Kent. BR3 5HS
Tel: (0181) 466 6911

SPRINGFIELD UNIVERSITY HOSPITAL
—4C **28**
61 Glenburnie Rd.,
London. SW17 7DJ
Tel: (0181) 672 9911

Springvale Community Mental Health Centre
—8A **166**
72-74 Moat Rd., East Grinstead,
West Sussex. RH19 3LH
Tel: (01342) 326928

Staines Health Centre —6H **21**
Knowle Grn., Staines,
Middx. TW18 1XD
Tel: (01784) 883666

Stanwell Health Centre —1M **21**
Hadrian Way, Stanwell,
Middx. TW19 7HT
Tel: (01784) 246281

Sunbury Health Centre —1H **39**
Green St., Sunbury-on-Thames,
Middx. TW16 6RH
Tel: (01932) 787861

SURBITON HOSPITAL —5L **41**
Ewell Rd., Surbiton,
Surrey. KT6 6EZ
Tel: (0181) 399 7111

SUTTON HOSPITAL —6N **61**
Cotswold Rd., Sutton,
Surrey. SM2 5NF
Tel: (0181) 644 4343

Tattenham Health Centre —5G **81**
Tattenham Cres., Burgh Heath,
Surrey. KT18 5NU
Tel: (01737) 361031

TEDDINGTON MEMORIAL HOSPITAL
—7E **24**
Hampton Rd., Teddington,
Middx. TW11 0JL
Tel: (0181) 977 2212

Thames Valley Hospice —6D **4**
Pine Lodge,
Hatch La., Windsor,
Berks. SL4 3RW
Tel: (01753) 842121

Thornton Heath Health Centre —3A **46**
61a Gillett Rd., Thornton Heath,
Surrey. CR7 8RL
Tel: (0181) 684 2424

TOLWORTH HOSPITAL —8N **41**
Red Lion Rd., Surbiton,
Surrey. KT6 7QU
Tel: (0181) 390 0102

Tudor Lodge Health Centre —2J **27**
8c Victoria Dri., Wimbledon Park,
London. SW19 6AE
Tel: (0181) 788 1525

UNSTED PARK REHABILITATION HOSPITAL
—6M **133**
Munstead Heath Rd., Godalming,
Surrey. GU7 1UW
Tel: (01483) 892061

WALTON COMMUNITY HOSPITAL —8J **39**
Rodney Rd., Walton-on-Thames,
Surrey. KT12 3LD
Tel: (01932) 220060

Walton Health Centre —8J **39**
Rodney Rd.,
Walton-on-Thames,
Surrey. KT12 3LB
Tel: (01932) 228999

WARLINGHAM PARK HOSPITAL —2K **85**
Warlingham, Surrey. CR6 9YR
Tel: (01883) 622101

West Byfleet Health Centre —9J **55**
Madeira Rd., West Byfleet,
Surrey. KT14 6DH
Tel: (01932) 340411

Hospitals, Health Centres & Hospices

WEST MIDDLESEX UNIVERSITY HOSPITAL
—5G **11**
Twickenham Rd., Isleworth,
Middx. TW7 6AF
Tel: (0181) 560 2121

WEST PARK HOSPITAL —8L **59**
Horton La., Epsom, Surrey. KT19 8PB
Tel: (01372) 202020

WEYBRIDGE COMMUNITY HOSPITAL —1B **56**
Church St., Weybridge,
Surrey. KT13 8DY
Tel: (01932) 852931

Weybridge Health Centre —1B **56**
Minorca Rd., Weybridge,
Surrey. KT13 8DU
Tel: (01932) 853366

WOKING COMMUNITY HOSPITAL —5B **74**
Heathside Rd., Woking,
Surrey. GU22 7HS
Tel: (01483) 715911

WOKINGHAM HOSPITAL —2A **30**
41 Barkham Rd., Wokingham,
Berks. RG41 2RE
Tel: (01189) 495000

WOKING NUFFIELD HOSPITAL —1A **74**
Shores Rd., Woking,
Surrey. GU21 4BY
Tel: (01483) 763511

Woodside Health Centre —4D **46**
3 Enmore Rd., South Norwood,
London. SE25 5NT
Tel: (0181) 656 0213

World's End Health Centre —3N **13**
529 King's Rd.,
London. SW10 0UD
Tel: (0181) 846 6333

Yateley Health Centre —9C **48**
Oaklands, Reading Rd., Camberley,
Surrey. GU17 5TL
Tel: (01252) 878992